CONTENTS

PART 5: GENRE

PART 6: AUTHORSHIP AND CINEMA

THE CINEMA BOOK

2ND EDITION

Edited by
Pam Cook
and
Mieke Bernink

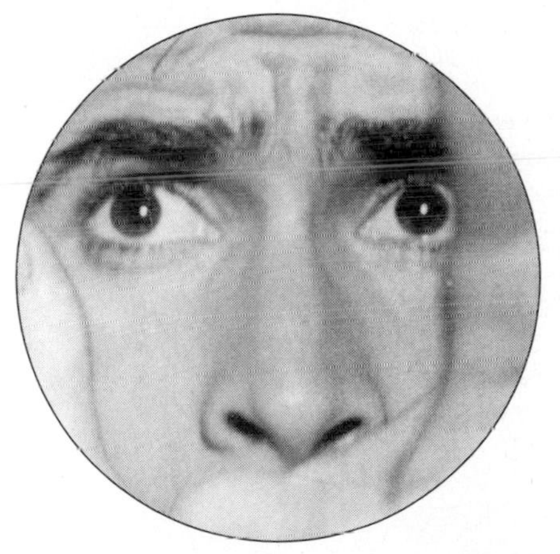

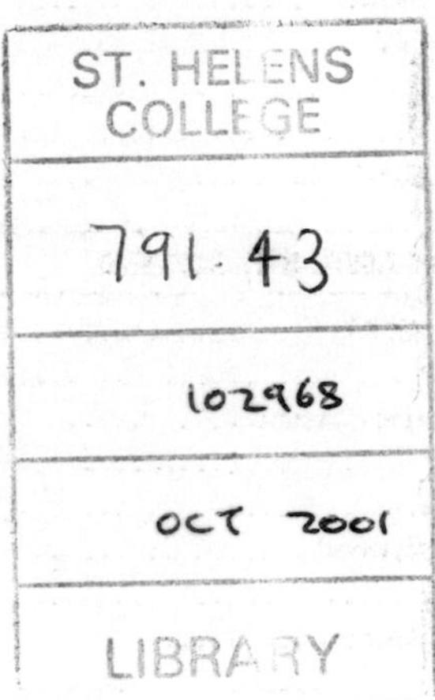

Second Edition published in 1999 by the
British Film Institute
21 Stephen St, London W1P 2LN

The British Film Institute is the UK national agency with responsibility for encouraging the arts of film and television and conserving them in the national interest.

First Edition published 1985

Reprinted 2000, 2001

Cover design: Ketchup
Cover images: (front) Anthony Perkins in *Psycho* (Alfred Hitchcock, 1960); (back) *Titanic* (James Cameron, 1998), Monica Vitti in *L'avventura* (Michelangelo Antonioni, 1960), Jack Nicholson in *Chinatown* (Roman Polanski, 1974), Theda Bara in *Salome* (J. Gordon Edwards, 1918)

Set in Minion and ScalaSans by Fakenham Photosetting Limited, Fakenham, Norfolk
Printed in Great Britain by St Edmundsbury Press, Bury St Edmunds

British Library Cataloguing-in-Publication Data
A catalogue record for this book is available from the British Library
ISBN 0-85170-729-7 hbk
ISBN 0-85170-726-2 pbk

PART 7: THEORETICAL FRAMEWORKS

GREY BOXES

PART 1: CLASSIC HOLLYWOOD CINEMA

PART 2: TECHNOLOGY

PART 3: NATIONAL CINEMAS AND FILM MOVEMENTS

PART 4: ALTERNATIVES TO CLASSIC HOLLYWOOD

PART 5: GENRE

PART 6: AUTHORSHIP AND CINEMA

PART 7: THEORETICAL FRAMEWORKS

INTRODUCTION TO THE SECOND EDITION

Film History itself has a history. In her introduction to *The Cinema Book* nearly fifteen years ago, Pam Cook explained how the form and content of the first edition reflected the development in Britain of Film Studies as a discipline from the mid-sixties to the late seventies, and she explained the key role played in this development by the film extract collection at the BFI. The remarkable development of audiovisual technology in the last two decades explains how one important element in the first edition, with its five main parts reflecting five major directions of research and teaching in eighties' Britain, based on the BFI extract catalogue as primary source material, has been superseded by the far wider range of accessible primary material now available to teachers, students and the general reader. The reference base provided by the extract catalogue printed as a long appendix to the first edition is replaced by an area of the new BFI website (http://www.bfi.org.uk/cinemabook) launched in conjunction with this new *Cinema Book*.

It would be foolish to guess, in 1999, just how far accelerating technological change will overtake the traditional printed form of *The Cinema Book* itself as the BFI's prime resource for Film Studies, fifteen years hence. But it is safe to insist, with Pam Cook, that each printed edition constitutes 'a valuable historical document' charting the field of Film History and Film Studies at a key point in its continuing development, and that, following on from its predecessor, the present edition will provide an essential, balanced yet pluralistic introduction to the discipline as a whole for another generation of readers and viewers.

The common motivation of first and second editions explains most of their similarities and differences. The new edition maintains the system of comprehensive overviews of the main directions in contemporary Film Studies by leading authorities, writing from diverse but complementary perspectives; it employs the same system of cross-reference within and between parts of the book, and places the same emphasis on linking theoretical discussion to the concrete analysis of specific films through the apparatus of 'grey boxes' that illustrate the argument throughout the written texts.

One key difference, already noted, lies in the wider range of reference in this second edition, freed from constraints imposed by the BFI extract collection, and updated to reflect the wealth of new materials and methods produced by filmmakers in the last fifteen years. Bibliographical references have also been expanded to reflect the growing breadth and great development of Film History and Film Theory in the eighties and nineties, with selective lists of material for deeper exploration at the close of each section, and a systematic bibliography of the whole discipline at the close of the book.

Pam Cook situated the Film Studies surveyed in the first edition within the broader cultural dynamic of production and consumption of films and film theory. An ever-growing international exchange between historians and theorists means that the second edition, though still rooted in the British institutional dynamic which produced the first, presents a widening culture of debate and research, reflected in a more international range of contributors and perspectives in this new edition. And if one succumbs, for a moment, to the perennial temptation for film historians to impose simplified schematic models – perhaps borrowed from film itself, with its different expository resources – one might say it reflects a shift toward a new phase in Film History and Film Theory in the eighties and nineties whose mythic origin might retrospectively be dated to a now legendary international conference of film historians and archivists held at the British coastal town of Brighton in 1978, towards the close of the seminal period charted by Pam Cook in the first edition.

The shift corresponds to a systematic questioning of the 'classic narrative' of Film History, with its 'great moments' from the Lumières' first screening onward, charting an apparently inevitable 'progress' towards the establishment of the Classic Hollywood system of film production, film narrative and so on: a sort of simplified Hollywood narrative of the history of film, with its great watershed between 'pre-Griffith' and 'post-Griffith', and a limited cast of great producers, directors, actors, technicians and so on, largely isolated from the complex sociological, aesthetic and material dynamic in which Classic Hollywood was just one possible – and temporary – configuration. Having learned to set the Lumières, Griffith and others within a long and often diffuse development with its multiple dimensions, prehistories and parallel paths, convergences and divergences, dead-ends and forgotten byways, it is of course highly ironic to present the history of Film Studies in terms of great moments – 'pre-Brighton' and 'post Brighton' – and the presence in this new edition of *The Cinema Book* of much material from the first edition demonstrates the broad underlying continuity of Film Studies from its birth as a formal discipline in the mid sixties to the close of the twentieth century. But let me take this notional shift, whose wider context is well portrayed in the first edition of *The Cinema Book*, as an initial narrative scheme to outline the new form and content of the second edition. The success of Hollywood demonstrates the organising power of simple narrative schemes, and the book itself provides various models for embedding such schemes in complex contexts.

The new *Cinema Book* opens with a 'revisionist' history of Classic Hollywood and the rise of 'classic narrative', expanded and updated from the opening part of the first edition ('Classic Hollywood Cinema'). The new second part embeds this story within the technological dynamic of the twentieth century as a whole, not only explaining from a new perspective the astonishing rise of the most powerful medium of the century, but reflecting the vast amount of research in this once neglected area over the last twenty years, and assessing the place of cinema at the dawn of the digital age ('Technology'). The third part maps the diverse lines of 'non-Hollywood' European traditions from their common roots in the new technology of the Moving Image at the close of the nineteenth century, through to the New Cinemas of post-war Europe with their twin roots in earlier national traditions and the worldwide breakdown of 'classic' narrative models after the Second World War ('National Cinema and Film Movements').

The broad historical map provided by these three complementary surveys leads into a more comprehensive overview of the dominant medium of the twentieth century: an 'alternative' history, freed from the long ascendancy of 'the Hollywood model' in production, distribution, reception and analysis ('Alternatives to Classic Hollywood'). From this broader perspective on twentieth-century cinema as a (very diverse) whole, it becomes possible to resituate the classic 'generic' models, first developed in relation to Classic Hollywood, within a wider analytic frame, which also casts new light on Hollywood itself ('Genre'). The next section moves deeper into more abstract models of analysis initially developed in association with post-war French New Cinema, redefining itself through a new understanding of 'Classic Hollywood' and the film director as the 'author' of his (or occasionally – and controversially – her) films ('Authorship'). Continuing and concluding this sequential account – only one scheme of reading, one path through the book, questionably privileged by the 'old' medium of print – the last part attempts to survey complementary and often competing theoretical perspectives on film as a more or less coherent field of debate ('Theoretical Frameworks'). It moves from the genesis of Film Studies as a formal discipline within the French culture of the fifties and sixties that produced the filmmaker-critics of the Nouvelle Vague, through to the energetic international dialogue at the dawn of a new millennium, to which we hope this new Cinema Book will provide a useful and much-needed introduction.

I write 'we', and in my formal role as editor and presenter of this remake of a classic, I am extremely conscious of the great debts accumulated in the long production process. The first and greatest debt is, of course, to Pam Cook and those who preceded her in the establishment of the BFI education programme that engendered the first Cinema Book in 1985. Like my predecessor, I am also very conscious of the debts owed to a succession of managing editors at the BFI (Paul Willemen, Ed Buscombe, Rob White and Andrew Lockett) and their teams (Roma Gibson, Liz Heasman and Tom Cabot, among many others). The debt to named contributors is to some extent obvious – without their texts the book would not exist; but I would like here to thank them all for their great energy and patience throughout a complicated international project, and I hope none will be offended if I single out from their large number Richard Abel, John Thompson and Steve Neale.

Mieke Bernink,
Amsterdam, August 1999

INTRODUCTION TO THE FIRST EDITION

This is a book about cinema – the different ways in which it has been described, defined and discussed in film theory and criticism, and the implications of those discussions for film education. It is also a valuable historical document, tracing the shifts in debates over a particular period roughly, from the mid-60s to the late 70s – in which Film Studies underwent a radical transformation in response to general social and cultural changes. The introduction of theories of ideology influenced by structuralism and psychoanalysis, for example, which still appears shrouded in mystery to many, is here placed in its historical context in order to make it more accessible. The collision of these new ideas with more traditional ways of approaching cinema (through authorship and genre for instance), is addressed from a perspective which is both critical of the wholesale incorporation of difficult, often obscure theories, and sympathetic to the enlivening effects of theory on a mainly empiricist film culture. The central premise of the book is that cinema is kept alive not just through systems of production, distribution and exhibition, but also through the circulation of debates which provide the cultural context in which it can flourish.

The Cinema Book is itself part of the process of debate, and is intended to provoke discussion. Each of the five main sections – History, Genre, Authorship, History of Narrative and Narrative and Structuralism – is separately authored by writers who argue from their different perspectives on film theory and criticism. Each section stands on its own, but a system of cross references indicates where the reader might look to find certain questions discussed differently, or elaborated upon, in other sections.

Something needs to be said about the development of the project, which has taken over five years to complete, and was itself transformed in that time. *The Cinema Book* began life as a catalogue of the film study extract material held by the British Film Institute Film and Video Library, selected over the years by the BFI Education Department to facilitate the teaching of film. The existing Extract Catalogue was in the form of an unwieldy set of duplicated documents dating back to the inception of the extract collection in the early 60s. The intention was to update these documents, expanding on the teaching categories which had informed extract selection, and showing how extracts could be used in the context of these categories. It soon became clear that this would entail the larger task of charting the history of the arguments covered in each category. Rather than a catalogue of extracts, the book became an account of the Education Department's involvement in the shifting terrain of Film Studies over a certain period. Nevertheless, the shape of the final product has to a great extent been determined by the extract collection, which is geared mainly towards Hollywood cinema and inevitably reflects the changes in selection criteria during that period. Certain discussion areas could only be updated within the limits of the collection. This is particularly obvious in the History section, where gaps in the collection meant that some important historical developments could not adequately be covered; and in the Authorship section, where the work of certain directors is dealt with specifically in terms of the films available in extract form. In the latter case, the emphasis is on showing how the work of the director in question has figured in authorship debates, rather than providing an auteurist chronology. In general, the presentation of film education debates in the book reflects the dynamic process of historical change and does not pretend to offer a definitive or prescriptive guide to Film Studies.

This precept has informed the book's structure, which is intended to be open to many different kinds of reader. Those wishing to concentrate on specific aspects of cinema history may confine themselves to one or two sections or sub-sections, while the reader with more general interests can range freely backwards and forwards across all sections. Teachers wishing to use the extract collection in their classes will find a complete list of available extract material at the back of the book. This includes plot synopses of each film title and incorporates italicised descriptions of the contents of each extract. In the body of the book at the end of the discussion sections are tinted boxes containing selected extracts which may be useful in illustrating discussion points, and for those who prefer to use the original teaching categories to guide them, these are reprinted, in updated form, after Extract Information. In addition, an index is provided for those who need to find information in a hurry.

It is hoped that the book will provide a useful and stimulating resource for teachers, students and the growing numbers of film enthusiasts with an interest in cinema history and film theory. *The Cinema Book* makes its appearance during British Film Year, and during a transition period for British cinema generally. A history of debates in British film culture could not be more timely.

Pam Cook,
May 1985

THE EDITORS

Pam Cook is Professor of European Film and Media at the University of Southampton. Her most recent book is *Gainsborough Pictures* (1997) and she is currently working on a study of Powell and Pressburger's *I Know Where I'm Going!* in the BFI Film Classics series.

Mieke Bernink, from 1991 editor of the Dutch magazine *Skrien*, has written and edited many texts on cinema and contemporary audiovisual culture.

CONTRIBUTORS AND ADVISORS

Richard Abel is Center for Humanities Director and Professor of English at Drake University, where he teaches cinema, media and cultural studies. His latest books include *The Cine Goes to Town: French Cinema, 1896-1914* (1996) and *The Red Rooster Scare or Making Cinema American, 1900-1910* (1998).

Michael Allen has previously worked for Rank Video and taught Film and Television Studies at several universities. He has developed a number of multimedia programs for use in studying moving image culture and is author of *Family Secrets: The Films of D. W. Griffith* (1999).

Guy Barefoot teaches Film Studies at the Department of Visual Culture and Media at Middlesex University.

Edward Buscombe was Head of Publishing at the British Film Institute. He is now a freelance writer and teacher, currently at Southampton Institute.

Alison Butler teaches Film Studies in the Department of Film and Drama at the University of Reading.

Elizabeth Cowie teaches at the University of Kent at Canterbury. Her publications include *Representing the Woman: Cinema and Psychoanalysis* (1997) and articles on documentary and fiction, *film noir* and contemporary psychoanalytic theory and its contribution to film theory.

James Donald is Professor of Media and Head of the School of Media and Information at Curtin University of Technology, Western Australia and is author of *Sentimental Education: Schooling, Popular Culture and the Regulation of Liberty* (1992) and *Imagining the Modern City* (forthcoming). Among the books he has edited are *Fantasy and the Cinema* (1989) and *Close Up, 1927-1933: Cinema and Modernism* (1998). He has been editor of 'Screen Education' and 'New Formations'.

Antony Easthope is Professor of English and Cultural Studies at Manchester Metropolitan University. His publications include *What a Man's Gotta Do: The Masculine Myth in Popular Culture* (1992) and an edition of essays *Contemporary Film Theory* (1994).

Leslie Felperin is a critic, broadcaster and Deputy Editor of *Sight and Sound.*

Kathe Geist is the author of many articles on Japanese Cinema. She lives and works in Brookline, Massuchessets.

Christine Gledhill is Head of Media and Cultural Studies, Staffordshire University and the editor of *Home Is Where the Heart Is: Studies in Melodrama and the Woman's Film* (1987) . She has written widely on feminist film and melodrama and is currently working on a study of British Cinema of the 1920s.

Michael Grant is Senior Lecturer in Film Studies at the University of Kent. His book *Dead Ringers* was published by Flicks Books in 1997. He has also published a number of articles on horror cinema.

Leighton Grist is a Lecturer in Film and Media Studies at King Alfred's College, Winchester. He has published on classical and post-classical Hollywood, including essays in *The Movie Book of Film Noir* (1992) and *The Movie Book of the Western* (1996).

Shelia Johnston wrote her PhD (University College London, 1979) on Rainer Werner Fassbinder and the concept of the 'Autor' in the Federal Republic of Germany. She is now a journalist based in London.

Frank Krutnik is the author of *In a Lonely Street: Film Noir, Genre and Masculinity*, *Popular Film and Television Comedy* (with Steve Neale, 1991) and *Inventing Jerry Lewis* (forthcoming). He has lectured at universities in England, Scotland, the US and Spain. He currently teaches at Roehampton Institute London.

Toby Miller works in the Department of Cinema Studies, New York University and is the author of *The Well-Tempered Self* (1993), *The Avengers* (1997) and *Technologies of Truth* (1998). He is editor of the journals *Television and New Media* and *Social Text.*

Nöel King teaches in the Faculty of Humanities at the University of Technology, Sydney, Australia.

Julia Knight is Senior Lecturer in the Media Arts Department at The University of Luton. She is author of *Women and the New German Cinema* (1992) and editor of *Diverse Practices: A Critical Reader on British Video Art* (1996).

Annette Kuhn is Reader and Director of Cinema Studies in the Institute for Cultural Research, Lancaster University. Her recent publications include *Family Secrets: Acts of Memory and Imagination* (1995) and *Screen Histories: A Screen Reader* co-edited with Jacky Stacey (1998)

Andy Medhurst teaches media studies at the University of Sussex and has published widely on issues of popular film and television.

Steve Neale is Research Professor in Film, Media and Communication, Sheffield Hallam University. He is author of *Genre* (1980), co-author of *Popular Film and Television Comedy* (1990) and co-editor of *Contemporary Hollywood Cinema* (1998).

Richard Neupert is Associate Professor of Cinema Studies at the University of Georgia. He is author of *The End: Narration and Closure in the Cinema* (1995) and is currently writing *The French New Wave: History and Narration.*

Geoffrey Nowell-Smith is Senior Lecturer in Film Studies at Sheffield Hallam University and is the author of *L'avventura* (1997) in the BFI Film Classics series and editor of *The Oxford History of World Cinema* (1996) and *Hollywood and Europe: Economics, Culture, National Identity, 1945-1995* (with Stephen Ricci, 1998).

Julian Petley lectures in Media and Communications Studies at Brunel University. His most recent publication is *Ill Effects: the Media Violence Debate* (1997) and he co-edited with Alan Burton the first volume of the *Journal of Popular British Cinema.*

Ashish Rajadhyaksha is a Senior Fellow at the Centre for the Study of Culture and Society, Bangalore and the co-author of *The Encyclopaedia of Indian Cinema: 2nd Edition* (1999).

Jane Root works in television at the BBC where she is Head of the Independent Commissioning Group.

Anneke Smelik is Senior Lecturer in Film Studies at the University of Nijmegen, Netherlands. She published *And the Mirror Cracked: Feminist Cinema and Film Theory* (1998) and co-edited *Women's Studies and Culture: A Feminist Introduction* (1995).

Murray Smith is a lecturer in film studies at the University of Kent at Canterbury and the author of *Engaging Characters: Fiction, Emotion and the Cinema* (1995) and co-editor *of Film Theory and Philosophy* (1997) and *Contemporary Hollywood Cinema* (1998).

Pamela Robertson Wojick is Assistant Professor of Film at the University of Notre Dame, Indiana. She is the author of *Guilty Pleasures: Feminist Camp from Mae West to Madonna* (1996) and co-author of the forthcoming anthology *Soundtrack Available: Essays on Film and Popular Music.*

Thomas Schatz is Professor and Chair of the Department of Radio, Television and Film at the University of Texas at Austin. He has published widely in film and media studies, with articles appearing in *Film Comment, Premiere, The Nation, The New York Times* and *The Los Angeles Times*. He has written four books on American film including ,*The Genius of the System: Hollywood Film-making in the Studio Era* (1996) and most recently *Boom and Bust: American Cinema in the 1940's* (forthcoming).

Robert Stam is Professor of Cinema Studies at New York University. Among his books are *Tropical Multiculturalism*; *Unthinking Eurocentricism* (with Ella Shoat, 1997); *Subversive Pleasures* (1992); *Brazilian Cinema* (with Randal Johnson, 1995); and *Reflexivity in Film and Literature* (1992).

John Thompson is Senior Lecturer at London College of Music and Media at Thames Valley University. He is currently engaged on a study of the thought of Andre Bazin and is the author of 'Vanishing' Worlds: Film Adaptation and the Mystery of the Original' in *Pulping Fictions* (edited by Deborah Cartmell et al, 1996) and 'A Film of Thought' in *David Lloyd George: The Movie Mystery* (David Berry and Simon Horrocks (eds), 1998).

Rob White has written about psychoanalysis for the *Oxford Literary Review* and *Angelekai: Journal of the Theoretical Humanities*. His D Phil thesis was entitled *Freud's Memory: Textuality, Art and the Problem of Mourning*. He edits the BFI Film and Modern Classics series.

ATTRIBUTIONS

KEY:
EARLY CINEMA = A-head Section
Science Fiction = B-head Sub-section
HINDI CINEMA = Grey box

PART ONE: CLASSIC HOLLYWOOD CINEMA INTRODUCTION, THE RISE OF THE AMERICAN FILM INDUSTRY, Annette Kuhn revised by Richard Abel; *AMERICAN FILM INDUSTRY,* Annette Kuhn; THE STUDIOS, **Introduction**, Annette Kuhn revised by Thomas Schatz; **Paramount**, *PARAMOUNT,* **Metro-Goldwyn Mayer**, METRO-GOLDWYN MAYER, Thomas Schatz; Warner Brothers, WARNER BROTHERS, **Columbia Pictures** *COLUMBIA PICTURES,* **20th Century–Fox**, *20th CENTURY–FOX;* **RKO**, *RKO*; **Universal**, *UNIVERSAL,* Annette Kuhn; STARS, *STARS,* James Donald; **Classic Hollywood Narrative**, *CLASSIC HOLLYWOOD NARRATIVE,* Annette Kuhn.

PART TWO: TECHNOLOGY Michael Allen; SOUND, Michael Allen and Annette Kuhn

PART THREE: NATIONAL CINEMAS AND FILM MOVEMENTS GERMAN EXPRESSIONISM AND NEW GERMAN CINEMA, Annette Kuhn revised by Julia Knight; *GERMAN EXPRESSIONISM AND KAMMERSPIEL FILM,* Annette Kuhn; NEW GERMAN CINEMA, *NEW GERMAN CINEMA,* Julia Knight; SOVIET CINEMA, *SOVIET CINEMA,* Annette Kuhn; ITALIAN NEO-REALISM, Geoffrey Nowell-Smith; *ITALIAN NEO-REALISM* (*Paisa, La terra terma, Umberto D, La strada*), Shelia Johnston; THE FRENCH NOUVELLE VAGUE, THE BRITISH FILM INDUSTRY, Annette Kuhn

PART FOUR: ALTERNATIVES TO CLASSIC HOLLYWOOD EARLY CINEMA, *EARLY CINEMA,* Richard Abel; NEW HOLLYWOOD, *NEW HOLLYWOOD,* Nöel King; ART CINEMA, *ART CINEMA,* Julian Petley; EAST ASIAN CINEMA, *EAST ASIAN CINEMA,* Kathe Geist; AVANT-GARDE AND COUNTER CINEMA, *AVANT-GARDE AND COUNTER CINEMA*, Alison Butler; THIRD WORLD AND POSTCOLONIAL CINEMA, *THIRD WORLD AND POSTCOLONIAL CINEMA,* Robert Stam; HINDI CINEMA, *HINDI CINEMA,* Ashish Rajadhyaksha.

PART FIVE: GENRE (**Edited by Steve Neale**); HISTORY OF GENRE CRITICISM, Christine Gledhill; **Genre Theory Since the early 1980s**, Steve Neale; THE WESTERN, Christine Gledhill; Westerns in the 1980s and 1990s, Edward Buscombe; *THE WESTERN,* Christine Gledhill, (*The Unforgiven* Ed Buscombe); MELODRAMA, Christine Gledhill; **Recent Work on Melodrama and the Women's Film**, Steve Neale; *MELODRAMA,* Christine Gledhill; (*Broken Blossoms, Way Down East,* Michael Allen), (*Gaslight,* Guy Barefoot); CONTEMPORARY CRIME, **The Detective Film**, Steve Neale; **The Gangster Film**, Christine Gledhill; **The Suspense Thriller**, Steve Neale; *CRIME,* Christine Gledhill (*Homicide,* Murray Smith), (*Mean Streets,* Leighton Grist); FILM NOIR, Jane Root; **Noir and Neo-Noir Recent Developments**, Steve Neale; *FILM NOIR,* Jane Root, (*Chinatown,* Steve Neale); SCIENCE FICTION AND HORROR, **Science Fiction**, Steve Neale; **Horror**, Christine Gledhill, revised with additional material by Michael Grant; *SCIENCE FICTION AND HORROR* (*Star Wars, Alien,* Steve Neale), (*Frankenstein, Psycho, The Thing, Dead Ringers,* Michael Grant); THE MUSICAL, Steve Neale, *THE MUSICAL* (*Singin' in the Rain, Meet me in St. Louis,* Steve Neale); (*Gold Diggers of 1933, Top Hat, Sweet Charity, On a Clear Day You Can See Forever,* Andy Medhurst); *TEENPICS,* Steve Neale; *TEENPICS,* Leslie Felperin; COMEDY, Steve Neale; *COMEDY,* Frank Krutnik; ACTION-ADVENTURE, Steve Neale.

PART SIX: AUTHORSHIP AND CINEMA Pam Cook; **Auteurism in the 1990s**, Nöel King and Toby Miller.

PART SEVEN: THEORETICAL FRAMEWORKS LOOKING AT FILM, Richard Neupert; *LOOKING AT FILM,* Richard Neupert; STRUCTURALISM AND ITS AFTERMATHS, John Thompson (Editorial Advisor: Antony Easthope); *STRUCTURALISM AND ITS AFTERMATHS* (*Adieu Phillipine, Tout va Bien, Kiss Me Deadly, To Have and Have Not, The Magnificent Ambersons, The Little Foxes, The Best Years of Their Lives,* Shelia Johnston); PSYCHOANALYSIS, *PSYCHOANALYSIS,* Rob White; FEMINIST FILM THEORY, Anneke Smelik; *FEMINIST FILM THEORY,* Anneke Smelik; SPECTATORSHIP AND AUDIENCE RESEARCH, *SPECTATORSHIP AND AUDIENCE RESEARCH,* Pamela Robertson Wojick.

PART 1

CLASSIC HOLLYWOOD CINEMA

Girl Shy (1924)

INTRODUCTION

In 1891 Thomas Edison took out patents on two new processes, the Kinetograph and the Kinetoscope. In spite of such precautions, however, Edison underestimated the economic potential of these inventions and failed either to secure foreign rights or effectively to exploit the domestic market. In 1893, a Kinetoscope Company was set up independent of Edison to retail 'Kinetographic' material and coin-operated Kinetoscope machines, both of which Edison agreed to manufacture for a price. In the same year, Edison opened what was perhaps the first purpose-built production studio, at a cost of some $700, a sum that was soon recovered by charging $200 for every Kinetoscope sold.

The first films to flicker inside the Kinetoscopes featured such exotica as boxers, ballerinas and bears, ran only a fragment of a single reel (about 50 feet, less than a minute on average), and were watched by individual customers. In 1894, the first Kinetoscope parlour opened in New York's Broadway, and a new company – the Kinetoscope Exhibition Company (KEC) – was set up to exploit an exclusive contract with Edison to exhibit his films. Realising that greater profits could be made if more than one customer could watch a film at any one time, the KEC introduced a projection process, the Panoptikon. Other companies employing similar processes also began to appear in the mid-1890s. Among the earliest of these were Mutoscope in America and the Lumière Brothers in France. In 1896 Lumière's Cinématographe and Mutoscope's American Biograph were both exhibited in New York, and the machines – rather than the material which passed through them – were clearly the main attraction. Indeed, Edison and his competitors made most of their money in these early years not from their films, which were sold outright, but from the cinematographic equipment for which they held the patents. The films themselves functioned in fact as little more than inducements to customers considering either the purchase of Kinetoscopes or the hire of an exhibition service which could provide a projecting apparatus and operator on a regular basis.

Exhibition services like Biograph, Vitagraph, Kinodrome, and even Edison's Kinetograph (each with its own different apparatus) enabled vaudeville theatres to use a single reel of motion pictures as top-of-the bill novelties or as popular 'chasers' at the beginning and end of an advertised programme. As exhibition outlets began to multiply, first through the expansion of 'cheap' or family vaudeville and then through the conversion of storefront spaces (including penny arcades) into nick-

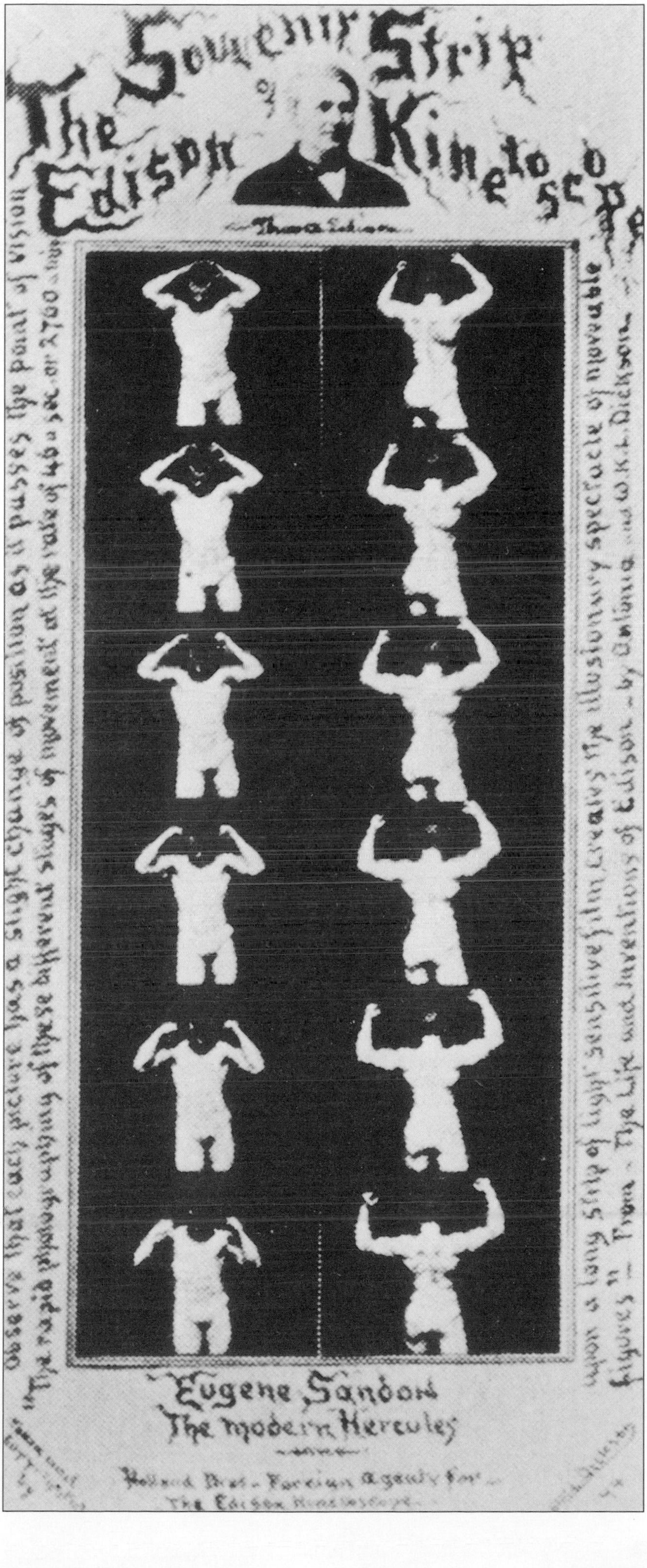

Single reel 'exotica'

A Country Girl's Seminary Life and Experience – Edison's New York Studio

elodeons, the demand grew for more and more new films. Initially, the French magician Georges Méliès, working out of a studio in Paris, proved a crucial supplier, especially with titles such as *A Trip to the Moon* (1902) and *Fairyland* (1903).

It was another French company, Pathé-Frères, however, that most exploited this expanding market. By 1905, Pathé was moving into film production on a mass-scale (across the full spectrum of genres) and was setting up a worldwide network of sales agencies for its films. It operated three studios (two with double stages) on the outskirts of Paris and employed more than a thousand workers in a cluster of laboratories (for developing, perforating, printing, splicing and colouring film stock). By the fall of 1906, Pathé was releasing six new film titles per week, printing 100,000 feet of positive film stock per day, and had advance orders for a minimum of seventy-five copies of each title shipped to the US. Within another year or so, the company's weekly list of titles had nearly doubled; its daily production of positive film footage had reached 230,000 feet; and it was selling on average 200 prints of each new title on the American market. This production and distribution capacity (which easily matched that of the combined American companies) arguably made the nickelodeon 'revolution' possible, and Pathé's 'red rooster' films consistently amounted to from one-third to one-half of all films circulating on the American market from 1905 to 1908 (see Early cinema, p. 93).

Pathé's prominence as a film supplier opened a gap between production and exhibition, and the need for some sort of liaison was exploited by 'film exchanges' which bought, or later leased, films and then sold, or later rented, them to exhibitors. Sales and rentals were set not in accordance with studio expenditure or cinema returns, of course, but simply in proportion to purchase price, cinema size and/or film footage. By 1905, the standard length of a film was between 250 and 400 feet (4–6 mins), although longer films of between 800 and 1,000 feet (13–16 mins) were becoming increasingly common. At first, Pathé was able to sell its titles at a single low rate, undercutting Edison's effort to impose different prices for different 'categories' of films. As exhibition expanded, selling and rental arrangements became complicated, and by 1907 there were more than 125 film exchanges, each with its own idiosyncratic pricing practices, serving the seven or eight thousand nickelodeons in operation. In order to gain some control over these chaotic conditions (and increase their profits), certain distributors like Fred Aiken in Chicago consolidated rental exchange businesses on a large scale; certain exhibitors like Carl Laemmle in Chicago and William Fox in New York invested heavily in rental businesses; and still others began to build up chains of cinemas (by 1910, for example, Marcus Loew's Theatrical Enterprises was reaching well beyond its base in New York). These distributors and exhibitors would soon form the nucleus of the independent sector.

The most blatant attempt to control the expanding cinema industry, however, came from Edison who had long sought to create a monopoly through the exercise of his company's patent rights. In late 1907, a new court decision favouring Edison led to the formation of the Film Service Association which linked most of the country's rental exhanges with a majority of film manufacturers (excepting Biograph), all of whom agreed to pay licence fees to Edison. One objective of this agreement was to channel the industry's profits to the manufacturers; perhaps more important, however, it set limits on Pathé's operations. Ever wary of Edison's patent rights in the US, and unable to make the huge investment needed to establish its own viable rental exchange (it had just opened a factory for printing positive film stock in New Jersey), Pathé reluctantly agreed to Edison's terms. As the trade press became caught up in a national hysteria over 'Americanization' and increasingly described Pathé films as 'foreign' to American tastes, the French company realised that its days of dominating the American market were numbered. By late 1908, it accepted the transformation of the Film Service Association into the Motion Picture Patents Company (MPPC, also known as the 'Trust') which now linked Biograph and George Kleine (the distributor for Gaumont and Eclipse) with Pathé, Vitagraph, Lubin, Essanay, Selig, Kalem, and Méliès, as Edison licensees. As a consequence, Pathé began to shift film production to subsidiaries (not only in France but Italy, Russia, and the US), redirect film distribution to central and eastern Europe, and concentrate its investment in manufacturing cameras, projectors, and negative film stock.

In 1910 the Trust had extended its technological monopoly into the field of distribution with the formation of the General Film Company, an MPPC subsidiary: ironically this example of vertical integration was similar to the model Pathé had already established, by 1908, in France and several adjacent countries (see The studios, p. 11). The General Film Company proceeded to buy up film exchanges at such a rate that by the following year only one of the former exchanges remained independent. With this single exception, General Film became the sole film distributor in the US. By this time profits in the film industry were already enormous: in 1910, American cinemas were attracting 26 million people a week. However, this very success effectively discouraged most MPPC members from experimenting with new modes of production, distribution or exhibition, which contributed to the MPPC's ultimate downfall.

Perhaps the most prolific, and certainly the most profitable of the American production companies in the MPPC at this period, was Vitagraph. Organised in 1897 with capital of $1,000, by 1912, Vitagraph had accumulated a gross income of $6 million. At that time the company had a staff of 400 actors, actresses, executives and technicians, and was producing about 300 films a year. Vitagraph's success probably was due to its early developments of systematic production methods, its decision to set up an aggressive sales office in Europe (with a printing factory in Paris), and its recognition that the Trust's technological monopoly was hardly sufficient guarantee of long-term economic survival. Consequently, the company began to invest in longer films and familiar faces, pioneering the production of films of two reels or more in length (30 min.) and assembling an impressive array of popular contract performers, among them the 'Vitagraph Girl', Florence Turner, Maurice Costello, and John Bunny. Unlike multiple-reel European titles then being screened as complete films (in France, Italy and Denmark), Vitagraph's *Uncle Tom's Cabin* (1910), *A Tale of Two Cities* (1911), and *Vanity Fair* (1911) were released one reel at a time through the General Film Company.

The MPPC's attempt to gain a monopoly over film production and distribution was undercut by the formation of independent companies like Laemmle's Independent Moving Picture Company (IMP), the New York Motion Picture Company (Thoman Ince), Aiken's Mutual Film Company, and the Fox Film Corporation. It also was challenged by the construction of or the renovation of existing theatres into large cinemas that could offer longer programmes (hence longer films). Moreover, in 1912 the MPPC was brought to court on antitrust charges, and by 1915 the General Film Company had been dissolved. Two years later the Trust itself was finally outlawed by the Supreme Court. The abolition of the MPPC was not, however, a case of independent companies defeating a monopoly, nor was it merely a matter of Congress and the court system enforcing 'free enterprise'. Rather, one kind of vertical integration within the industry simply replaced another. More than anything, the Trust failed to exploit the cinematic potential of longer films (whose initial advances came in Europe) and star performers. Thus, while General Film remained committed to releasing films in 1,000-foot reels, the independents were beginning to take advantage of additional selling points or 'production values', including roadshow releases of 'foreign imports', as Adolph Zukor did with *Queen Elizabeth* (1912), starring Sarah Bernhardt. In this context, box office attractions assumed paramount importance.

THE RISE OF THE AMERICAN FILM INDUSTRY

BOX-OFFICE ATTRACTIONS

In 1910 Carl Laemmle lured the famous 'Biograph Girl' to his Independent Moving Picture Company and took the hitherto unprecedented step of revealing her real name, Florence Lawrence, to her fans. In 1914 William Fox, who had entered film production two years before with the formation of a studio-subsidiary, Box Office Attractions, went one better by tempting director Frank Powell away from Biograph. Powell fabricated a new star persona for his first Fox film: the star was Theda Bara and the film was *A Fool There Was* (1915). Fox needed box-office attractions in order to outmanoeuvre the MPPC, and the combination of a mysteriously exotic star and a melodramatic plot provided exactly the publicity Fox had required. Indeed, Fox himself was largely responsible for that publicity: the very name Theda Bara was a suggestive anagram of 'Arab Death', and rumours were leaked to the press of Bara's 'parents' being a French artist and his Arabian mistress, and of her childhood spent under the shadow of the Sphinx, while stories were circulated of the star's smoking in public and burning incense in private and even of conducting interviews with reporters in her boudoir.

By this time, more and more licensee producers were going independent in order to exploit the flexibility of 'feature-length' films, and more and more licensee exhibitors were building or converting special film theatres. One of the directors at Biograph, for example, whose 1911 two-reeler *Enoch Arden* was released by the studio in two parts, and whose four-reel film of the following year, *Judith of Bethulia*, Biograph refused to release at all, left the Trust to work for an independent production company, Reliance-Majestic. There he began work on an ambitious adaptation of Thomas Dixon's bestseller, *The Clansman*. That director was D. W. Griffith, and the film was *The Birth of a Nation* (1915).

The original budget for *The Birth of a Nation* was $40,000, but Griffith was allowed to expand the project to twelve reels and an estimated total cost of $110,000. To protect his investment in the film, Harry Aitken – President of Majestic's parent company – formed the Epoch Producing Corporation and decided to exploit the film's extravagant length and budget by releasing it as an unprecedented cinematic event. Prints were hand-tinted, and orchestral accompaniment commissioned and composed to synchronise with the on-screen action. Wherever the film was exhibited, white-robed horsemen were employed to gallop up and down the nearest streets and publicise every screening. Seat prices in New York, where the film was premièred, were increased from the usual 10–25 cents to an astounding two dollars. Following its premiere, *The Birth of a Nation* was 'roadshowed' across the major American cities in the larger first-run theatres. Finally the film was released to independent distributors, and broke box-office records wherever it played. Louis B. Mayer, for instance, who operated a string of theatres in New England, made more than $50,000 from the film and with this bought Aitken's old Culver City Studio, which was later used by MGM (see MGM, p. 16). Estimates of the film's total earnings are notoriously unreliable, varying from 5 to 50 million dollars, but it seems certain that by 1916 a million tickets had been sold in New York alone. The film was first approved and then condemned by the National Board of Censorship; this,

Theda Bara – Fox's box-office attraction

while barely affecting the number of screenings permitted, certainly increased the considerable publicity generated around the film. Griffith invested the bulk of *The Birth of a Nation*'s profits in his next project, *Intolerance* (1916), and, of a budget estimated at $1.9 million, Griffith advanced almost a million himself. The film was considerably less successful than its predecessor, however, and it virtually bankrupted Griffith. To finance the film Griffith had formed the Wark Producing Corporation and the investors behind this endeavour included a number of Wall Street financiers. In seeking artistic independence from the Trust studios, Griffith instead walked into the hands of the economic empires of Morgan and Rockefeller, whose domination of the industry would be cemented ten years later with the coming of sound.

As roadshow releases and regional releases began to compete for domestic distribution and exhibitor earnings, the economic necessity of a national network of distribution became increasingly apparent. In 1914 the first such network, Paramount Pictures Corporation, was set up: it released 104 films a year to its members' circuits. To supply this amount of product Adolph Zukor and Jesse Lasky merged their production units to form Famous Players–Lasky and, to ensure that the films they produced and distributed were all actually exhibited, Famous Players–Lasky introduced the policy of 'block booking' whereby exhibitors wishing to screen a particular film would be forced to book, unseen, an entire package which included that film. Famous Players–Lasky assembled a roster of 'stars' including Mary Pickford, Douglas Fairbanks, Gloria Swanson, Fatty Arbuckle, William S. Hart, Norma and Constance Talmadge as well as 'name' directors like Cecil B. DeMille, Griffith and Mack Sennett. With the collapse of competition from the European film industry during the First World War, Paramount escalated its annual output to 220 films for almost 5,000 cinemas. To counter Paramount's increasing stranglehold over exhibition, 27 of America's largest first-run cinemas combined in 1917 to form their own 'independent' distribution network, the First National Exhibitors Circuit (FNEC). During the following year, the FNEC lured Charlie Chaplin away from Mutual and Mary Pickford away from Paramount with offers of million-dollar contracts, and themselves entered into film production.

Chaplin's early film career highlights a period of 'struggle for control' in American cinema, a struggle in which stars became important economic assets. At Keystone, Chaplin was artistically and economically restricted, and he subsequently moved to Essanay and a salary of $1,250 a week, where he produced fifteen films, most of them two-reelers. In 1915, the year in which the General Film Company was dissolved, Essanay expanded Chaplin's two-reel *Burlesque on Carmen* to four reels. The collapse of the Trust itself immediately elevated the economic value of the stars as box-office attractions, and Chaplin left Essanay for Mutual and a weekly salary of $10,000. At Mutual, Chaplin perfected the persona of the tramp which he had developed at Essanay, and made a further twelve films including *The Vagabond*, *The Pawnshop* and *Easy Street* – before leaving for First National with an eight-film million-dollar contract. Like Essanay before it, Mutual soon collapsed without Chaplin, who was at this time probably the biggest box-office draw in the United States.

THE ORIGINS OF THE STUDIO SYSTEM

By 1921 First National was linked to some 3,500 film theatres in the United States, and in 1922 added a production studio to its already extensive distribution and exhibition holdings. Recognising the threat to Paramount's profits, Zukor began by buying up cinemas himself, and by the end of 1926 had acquired a controlling interest in more than a thousand theatres. As Paramount expanded from production through distribution to exhibition, First National responded by increasing its investment in

The struggle for artistic control – Charlie Chaplin in *The Pawnbroker*

production and distribution; the industry was becoming characterised by vertical integration (see The studios, p. 11), dominated by Carl Laemmle's Universal, William Fox's Fox Film Corporation, Zukor's Paramount, the exhibitors First National and, in 1924, a fifth group, Metro-Goldwyn-Mayer – which combined Marcus Loew's cinema chain, Metro's film exchanges and the production units of Goldwyn and Mayer. As inter-company competition became increasingly fierce, film publicity and production values became crucially important in attracting both independent exhibitors and audiences to studio-specific productions. Thus while most of the packages of films distributed by these companies were of similar budgets and scales, each studio also produced occasional 'specials', often for roadshow release, and boasting huge investments, large crews and costs and impressive sets and settings. These included *The Covered Wagon* (Paramount/Famous Players–Lasky, 1923), *The Lost World* (First National, 1925), *Foolish Wives* (Universal, 1922), and *Sunrise* (Fox, 1927).

All four of these films exploited special effects and/or elaborate sets and settings and were released as exceptional cinematic events. *The Lost World*, for example, was one of the first full-length features to use animated models, *The Covered Wagon* was the first epic western, *Foolish Wives* was a fourteen-reel blockbuster, while *Sunrise* employed the largest single set since *Intolerance*, covering an area of a mile long and half a mile across. *The Covered Wagon* cost $350,000 and netted $1.5 million. *Foolish Wives* cost $1,400,000 and almost broke Universal. *Sunrise* cost even more. The emphasis of these specials was on literary sources – *The Covered Wagon* for instance, was adapted from a popular novel by Emerson Hough, *The Lost World* based on a Conan Doyle story, *Sunrise* on Sudermann. These were all films based on stories already familiar to the general public which, in addition, featured the studio's biggest stars and highest paid directors.

Meanwhile companies with less capital found it increasingly difficult to compete with the vertically integrated majors. United Artists, for instance, which had been founded in 1919 by four of the industry's best paid employees – Pickford, Fairbanks, Chaplin and Griffith – was only a distributor, lacking either studios or cinemas of its own and rising to major status only in the 1950s in the wake of antitrust judgments. Universal, with limited capital and only a small number of cinemas, was also frustrated in its efforts to expand. Similarly, Warner Bros., a minor but prosperous production company, found itself with neither distribution nor exhibition outlets, and so decided in 1925 to acquire the ailing Vitagraph with its national network of film exchanges.

THE COMING OF SOUND AND THE STUDIO SYSTEM IN THE 1930s

In 1926 Warner Bros., in combination with Western Electric, a subsidiary of the American Telephone and Telegraph Co. (AT&T), founded the Vitaphone Corporation to make sound films and market sound equipment, and in October 1927 Warners released *The Jazz Singer*. Capitalising on the success of the 'first talkie', Warners acquired and equipped for sound the First National exhibition circuit. AT&T's corporate rival RCA swiftly responded by setting up its own sound subsidiary, RKO. By 1930, then, the film industry was an oligopoly in which five vertically integrated companies, that is, five companies with holdings in production, distribution and exhibition, dominated the American market: Warner Bros., Loews–MGM, Fox, Paramount and RKO. Three smaller companies or 'minors' – United Artists, Universal and Columbia – lacking exhibition outlets of their own, had to rely on the independent cinemas.

Of the 23,000 theatres operating in 1930 the majors controlled only 3,000 but these accounted for almost three-quarters of the annual box-office takings in the US. The majors produced only 50 per cent of the total output of the industry, but this figure represented 80 per cent of the A-films exhibited in the first-run theatres. And while the 'flagship' cinemas of each chain boasted blockbusters like *King Kong* (1933) the second-run cinemas thrived on less ambitious genre pictures like those of Warners and Universal. The coming of sound postponed for a while the effects of the Depression on the film industry, but eventually a combination of reduced receipts and increasing overheads hit the industry hard. In 1931 Warner Bros. lost $8 million, Fox $3 million and RKO $5.5 million. In 1933 Paramount went into bankruptcy with a $21 million deficit, while RKO and Universal were forced into receivership. Even MGM, the only major company not to go into debt, saw its profits plunge from $10 million in 1930 to $1.3 million three years later. Audience attendance, which had been estimated in 1929 at more than 80 million a week, fell to less than 60 million in 1932. The common stock value of the majors fell from a high of $960 million in 1930 to $140 million in 1934. To meet the crisis, President Roosevelt's New Deal administration passed a National Industrial Recovery Act (NIRA), encouraging 'fair competition' in the film industry as in other industries. A Code of Fair Competition for the Motion Picture Industry was ratified as law in 1933, and antitrust cases against the oligopoly were suspended in return for the signing of minimum wage and maximum-hour agreements and the right to collective bargaining for employees. One of the consequences of the Depression for exhibition practices was the development of the 'double bill', developed as an 'added attraction' during the Depression, and allowed by the Code as fair competition. In 1935 the Supreme Court revoked NIRA but by then the industry was too firmly reorganised to be adversely affected.

CENSORSHIP

As early as 1895 an innocuous short, *Dolorita in the Passion Dance*, was removed from an Atlantic City Kinetoscope to appease local authorities. Two years later another film, *Orange Blossoms*, was closed by court order in New York as 'offensive to public decency'. As the number of nickelodeons multiplied, a variety of pressure groups, including churches, reform groups, police and press, began attempting to exert influence on the new medium of cinema. These pressures were institutionalised in the formation of state censorship boards with the objective of outflanking possible extra-industrial 'interference' in the content of films. The Motion Picture Patents Company combined in 1909 with a self-appointed social research organisation to form the first National Board of Censorship (NBC).

The NBC, subsequently renamed the National Board of Review, employed rather erratic censorship principles in relation to the films it reviewed. *The Birth of a Nation* (1915), for instance, was initially approved by the Board, only to have that approval revoked when the film met with criticism from liberal newspapers and anti-racist organisations. The MPPC, which was responsible for the production of almost two-thirds of the films made in the US, agreed to submit all its films to the Board for pre-release inspection, but the independent States' Rights system entitled individual states to impose their own censorship. In 1915 the production company of *The Birth of a Nation* took the Ohio State censor to the Supreme Court for alleged infringement of constitutionally guaranteed free speech. However, the Supreme Court dismissed the case, on the grounds that motion pictures were a 'business pure and simple' and thus not entitled to First Amendment protection.

With the collapse of the Trust and the emergence of the vertically integrated companies in the early 1920s, the need for a new national industry-appointed censorship board became increasingly pressing. In 1921 the National Association of the Motion Picture Industry (NAMPI), a consortium of representatives of the major companies, adopted a 13-point code to serve as a yardstick for the production and exhibition of films. NAMPI's code proscribed certain kinds of subject matter – illicit love, nakedness, undue violence, vulgarity and so on – but lacked the means effectively to enforce its proscriptions. A series of scandals during the next two or three years – involving Mary Pickford in an apparently fraudulent divorce testimony, Fatty Arbuckle in a rape and murder trial, and director William Desmond Taylor in a murder case – provided the excuse the industry needed: in 1922 Will Hays, President Harding's Postmaster General, was invited by the majors to head the Motion Pictures Producers and Distributors of America (MPPDA).

Since state censorship boards were becoming increasingly influential, Hays launched a fierce campaign under a 'free speech' banner aimed at defeating demands for film censorship legislation. At the same time, to offset press criticism and opposition from educational and religious organisations, the majors began to increase the output of films for 'women and children', and film-makers like Erich von Stroheim found themselves at the mercy of censors both in the studio and at the Hays office. Stroheim complained bitterly about interference on *Foolish Wives*: 'My ears have rung with their united cry: "It is not fit for children!" Children! Children! God, I did not make that picture for children.' After several unsatisfactory years in which the MPPDA published lists of 'Don'ts' and 'Be Carefuls', Hays together with Martin Quigley (publisher of the trade paper *Motion Picture Herald*) introduced a revised Production Code, which was adopted by the industry in 1930 and under whose terms every film made by members of the MPPDA would be censored by a Studio Relations Committee both in script and pre-release film form.

Griffith's *The Birth of a Nation* ... 'business pure and simple'

While the majors tended, at least at first, to accommodate the Code, independent productions occasionally went beyond its provisions. One such production was Howard Hughes's *Scarface* (1932), directed by Howard Hawks, which was alleged to contain scenes of hitherto unprecedented violence. On its submission to the Hays office dozens of cuts were demanded and, knowing that without Hays's approval most theatres would refuse to screen the film, Hughes compromised and agreed to several of them. Hays then granted the film a licence, but several local censorship boards still refused to allow *Scarface* to be shown. Hughes sued these censors and as a result of the publicity that the case (which Hughes in fact won) received, the film was a huge box-office success. These events were instrumental in ensuring that the Hays office rather than the local or national legislatures became the arbiter of American film content: it was to remain so for more than two decades.

For some time the studios tended to conform to the stipulations of the Production Code, but falling attendances at film theatres during 1932 and 1933 led to the deployment of more 'daring' material, and the very adverse publicity such films received increased their box-office earnings. Mae West was a frequent target of moral crusades, and indeed after *She Done Him Wrong* (1933) West became a symbol of everything the Code condemned. Meanwhile, however, Paramount grossed $2 million during the first three months of the film's release. The Catholic Church mobilised its forces, threatened the majors with mass picketing of Paramount's theatres, and formed the Legion of Decency. In 1934, under pressure from the Legion, the MPPDA abolished the Studio Relations Committee and replaced it with the more powerful Production Code Administration (PCA). By the end of the year, the impact of the Production Code on the American cinema had become apparent. The PCA followed production from the script stage through to the final editing. 'The new regulatory structure made a changed woman of Mae West ... the title of her latest film *It Ain't No Sin* was transformed to *Belle of the Nineties* and her scintillating repartee and sexual independence were toned down considerably' (Stanley, 1978, p. 196).

In 1935, partly in order to placate the PCA, a number of studios began a cycle of 'prestige' literary adaptations, which included Warner Bros.'s *A Midsummer Night's Dream* (1935), Fox's *The Informer* (1935), and Goldwyn's *Stella Dallas* (1937). According to *Fortune*:

> It is generally conceded by leaders in the industry that productions like *A Midsummer Night's Dream* ... would have been unthinkable even ten years ago, and that Hays's national publicity

Mae West in *It Ain't No Sin* censored to *Belle of the Nineties*

> grapevine, reaching several millions of the 'best people' who attend movies infrequently has been the chief factor in making them possible. ('The Hays Office', in Balio, 1976, p. 311)

But while prestigious Oscar-winning films like *A Midsummer Night's Dream* and *The Informer* were being made, the studios were also engaged in producing film series and genres that could accommodate the Code and be 'fit for children'. Partly as a result of such pressure, Warner Bros. revised their gangster films to explicitly condemn gangsterism: in 1935 emphasis moved from the gangsters themselves to the G-men (FBI agents) who gallantly battled against them. Once the Code's provisions had entered cinematic currency, in fact, they informed both the style and the content of the genres themselves.

For more than two decades the PCA was responsible for reviewing some 95 per cent of the films exhibited in the US. Indeed, as long as the industry remained vertically integrated, the power of the PCA remained virtually unchallenged. Finally, however, in 1952 the Supreme Court extended the protection of the First Amendment to the film industry. The case in point centred on Roberto Rossellini's *The Miracle* (1948),

Baby Doll – condemned by the Legion of Decency

which had been deemed 'blasphemous' by the Legion of Decency. While Howard Hughes continued to offend the censors with his exploitation of Jane Russell in 3D for RKO, United Artists released a string of independent productions with 'controversial' and hitherto unpermitted subject matter. The link between the Catholic Church and the movie industry had remained intact as long as profits were high, but antitrust legislation, the rise of television, and the growth of the art cinema and drive-in circuits fuelled Hollywood's hostility toward restraints, which were no longer economically viable.

The film which best illustrated – and indeed also influenced – these changes is Elia Kazan's *Baby Doll* (1956). The film received PCA approval, despite its portrayal of an unconsummated marriage between a child-wife and a middle-aged, sexually frustrated man. The Legion of Decency promptly condemned the film's 'carnal suggestiveness' as morally repellent both in theme and treatment, and Catholic cinemagoers were instructed to forego the film and picket the theatres in which it was shown (see Elia Kazan, p. 272).

Such action may have reduced the film's potential audience, but it also prompted an outcry from other religious bodies and civil liberties groups against the Church's encroachment on individual freedoms. Late in 1956 the Production Code was revised, and in the following year the Legion of Decency expanded its film classification system. Finally in 1968 a National Motion Picture Rating System was introduced, and the PCA was replaced by the Code and Rating Administration, which operates a system based on labelling films as suitable for specific audiences.

Selected Reading

Robert C. Allen, 'William Fox presents *Sunrise*', *Quarterly Review of Film Studies* 2(3), August 1977.

Tino Balio (ed.), *The American Film Industry*, Madison, University of Wisconsin Press, 1976.

Geoffrey Nowell-Smith (ed.), 'Silent cinema 1895–1930', Part I of *The Oxford History of World Cinema*, Oxford, Oxford University Press, 1996.

Robert Stanley, *The Celluloid Empire: A History of the American Movie Industry*, New York, Hastings House, 1978.

THE STUDIOS

INTRODUCTION

The high point, economically and stylistically, of Hollywood cinema is usually seen in the years in which the 'studio system' flourished, when the film industry prospered as an oligopoly: when, in other words, the production of films was dominated almost entirely by a small number of vertically integrated companies – companies with controlling interests in the distribution and exhibition, as well as in the production, of films. The full consolidation of the system can be dated from around 1930, but its roots lie in the 'assembly line' methods of film-making introduced by producers like Ince and Sennett as early as 1913–15, in the first attempts at vertical integration by Paramount, First National and others in 1915, and in the opening that year at Hollywood of Universal City, the first full-blown motion-picture 'factory' for the mass-production and mass-marketing of the new product. When the stock market crash of October 1929 coupled with the new financial demands on the studios of the coming of sound drove a number of production companies to the wall, the way was open for a few 'majors' – companies which for various reasons managed to weather the economic vicissitudes of the time – to establish their joint control of the industry. The end of their dominance is often dated (by Gomery, 1986, and others) very precisely to 3 May 1948, when an antitrust suit filed in 1938 against the majors and the large unaffiliated theatre chains who colluded with them was finally decided, outlawing vertical integration, block booking and blind bidding. But this event, like the crash of 1929, marks only one key point in a long-term process. The majors' oligopoly was increasingly threatened before 1948 by the rapid growth in the 1940s of 'independent' production largely driven by war-related income-tax laws that encouraged top talent (like stars and producer–directors) to go freelance.

The studios fought the 1948 decision in the courts for nearly two years, with Paramount being the first to comply by divesting its theatre chain at midnight on 31 December 1949, and MGM the last, maintaining control of its theatres until 1957. The widening of the market with the rise of television in the 1950s was an additional challenge to the integrated studio system, but the 'red scare' – the vetting of creative and technical personnel by the House Un-American Activities Committee (HUAC) – though often linked to the decline of the studios, actually hit TV production harder than film.

Of the eight companies that dominated the Hollywood film industry in the 1930s and 1940s, the 'Big Five' – Warner Bros., RKO, 20th Century-Fox, Paramount and MGM – were completely vertically integrated: they owned distribution companies and chains of film theatres as well as the means to produce films. The 'Little Three' – Universal, Columbia and United Artists – were not vertically integrated, but are usually included among the majors because their films had access to the first-run theatres owned by the Big Five. During the period of mature oligopoly, the eight majors jointly owned only about a sixth of all theatres in the US, but these included most (around 80 per cent) of the first-run theatres, which generated between 50 per cent and 75 per cent of the industry's revenues – and the control of first-run exhibition gave the studios effective control over the flow of product through the entire market.

The study of the economic organisation of the film industry may be justified on a variety of grounds, ranging from an interest in its various modes of production, to a concern with the relationships between particular forms of organisation of film production, distribution and exhibition, and the films which were, on the face of it at least, the reasons for the industry's existence. If films are to be approached this way, however, some thought has to be given to the nature of the relation-

The Pickwick Papers (USA 1912 *p.c* – Vitagraph; *d* – Larry Trimble; st b/w)

A Fool There Was (USA 1915 *p.c* – Fox Film Corporation; *d* – Frank Powell; st b/w)

The Birth of a Nation (USA 1915 *p.c* – Epoch Producing Corp/Reliance-Majestic; *d* – D. W. Griffith; st b/w)

Intolerance (USA 1916 *p.c* – Wark Producing Corp; *d* – D. W. Griffith; st b/w)

Charlie Chaplin's Burlesque on 'Carmen' (USA 1916 *p.c* – Essanay; *d* – Charles Chaplin; st b/w)

The Pawnshop (USA 1916)/**The Vagabond** (USA 1916)/**Easy Street** (USA 1917 *p.c* – Mutual; *d* – Charles Chaplin; st b/w)

Hearts of the World (USA 1918 *p.c* – Griffith Inc; *d* – D. W. Griffith; st b/w)

Foolish Wives (USA 1921 *p.c* – Universal; *d* – Erich von Stroheim; st b/w)

The Covered Wagon (USA 1923 *p.c* – Paramount/Famous Players–Lasky; *d* – James Cruze; st b/w)

The Lost World (USA 1924 *p.c* – First National; *d* – Harry Hoyt; st b/w)

Sunrise (USA 1927 *p.c* Fox Film Corporation; *d* – F. W. Murnau; st b/w)

The Jazz Singer (USA 1927 *p.c* – Warner Bros.; *d* – Alan Crosland; st + sd b/w)

King Kong (USA 1933 *p.c* – RKO; *d* – Ernest B. Schoedsack/Merian C. Cooper; sd b/w)

Scarface (USA 1932 *p.c* Hughes Production; *d* – Howard Hawks; sd b/w)

I'm No Angel (USA 1934)/**Belle of the Nineties** (USA 1935 *p.c* – Paramount; *d* – Wesley Ruggles/Leo McCarey; sd b/w)

A Midsummer Night's Dream (USA 1935 *p.c* – Warner Bros.; *d* – Max Reinhardt/William Dieterle; sd b/w)

G-Men (USA 1935 *p.c* – Warner Bros.; *d* – William Keighley; sd b/w)

The Informer (USA 1935 *p.c* – RKO; *d* – John Ford; sd b/w)

Stella Dallas (USA 1937 *p.c* – Goldwyn Productions; *d.* – King Vidor; sd b/w)

Baby Doll (USA 1956 *p.c* – Newtown/Elia Kazan; *d* – Elia Kazan; sd b/w)

ship between film texts and their immediate contexts. As Mae Huettig argues, there is a connection between the form taken by a film and the mechanics of the business, even if the connection is somewhat obscure ('The motion picture industry today', in Balio, 1976). How is this expressed in the Hollywood studio system as a particular form of economic organisation of film production?

How far, that is to say, did the economic organisation and the production relations (the ways in which the work involved in making films was organised) characteristic of studios determine the character of their products, the films themselves? On the side of economic organisation, the nature and provenance of capital investment in the film industry between 1930 and 1948, and also vertical integration, can be seen to have important consequences. The enormous investment required to equip studios and film theatres for sound, in combination with the effects of the general recession in the US economy in the late 1920s and early 1930s, led the industry to seek outside financial backing, usually from Eastern banking groups. During the early 1930s, all the major companies in fact underwent extensive financial reorganisation, which eventually led to the domination of some of the studios by these outside sources of finance. One of the consequences of this was to reinforce the majors' dependence on vertical integration, for their assets – the collateral against which they obtained financial backing – were chiefly in the form of real-estate: by the mid-1940s, about two-thirds of the majors' total capital was invested in film theatres. It has in fact been suggested that in this context the production of films by the majors was no more than a means towards the primary objective of maintaining the property value of film theatres.

In this situation, the balance of power in determining the nature of the product lay largely on the side of the 'front office' – the industry's businessmen, rather than its creative personnel. The demand was for films that would secure financial return from exhibition. A 'good picture' in these terms was one which had access to first-run theatres, and hence combined production values with a certain degree of predictability. The emphasis was clearly not on the side of experimentation in film form and content.

The relations of film production characteristic of the studio system may also be examined in the light of the industry's overall economic organisation. As part of the reorganisations which took place in the major companies in the early 1930s, the studios began to organise production increasingly on an 'assembly line' basis. The main features of this form of organisation of production are highly developed divisions of labour and hierarchies of authority and control, and detailed breakdown of tasks: the industrial model for this form of organisation is, of course, the mass production of commodities pioneered by Henry Ford's car plants. Since the studio system was geared increasingly to the production of a constant flow of films to supply film theatres, there was an impetus towards organising film production along mass production lines. This resulted in a high degree of demarcation of skills, and a breakdown of the overall production process into small parts dealt with by different groups of workers. This development is evident also in the increased tendency for workers to be employed directly by the studios and kept on studio payrolls: a characteristic not only of technicians, but also of creative personnel, as the 'contract system' for actors indicates. All this was undoubtedly instrumental in the unionisation of the film industry which took place around the mid-1930s, a trend which probably itself served to consolidate the effects on the industry of the division of labour and the breakdown of tasks.

The Public Enemy – simple sets and low-key lighting

The overall trend of these developments in the economic organisation and production relations of the Hollywood film industry was clearly in the direction of standardisation of the product, film. And indeed, during the period of the studio system's ascendancy, at least two forms of product standardisation may be observed. First of all, the 1930s and 1940s are commonly regarded as the golden years of the classic Hollywood text: of films, that is, marked by a highly specific type of narrative structure combined with a circumscribed range of cinematic expressions of narrative (see The Classic Hollywood narrative, p. 39). Secondly, during this period, film genres – such as the gangster film, the western and the musical – were developed and refined into what is now regarded as their classic form: genre films, which are of course a means of securing standardisation, may be regarded as guarantors of a reliable return of investment (see What is genre criticism?, p. 137).

Contrasting with this convergence toward a 'standard product' in the industry as a whole, however, was a divergence produced by the conscious need for each studio to develop an identifiable 'house style' that would differentiate its films from those of rivals, and a similar tension between standardisation and differentiation within each studio: each film had to be different, to some extent at least, to attract the paying public. These factors combined to produce the classic star–genre cycles periodically adapted to new talent that typify studio production, with in-house technical and creative personnel often forming fixed production units to maintain continuity, keep the cycle 'turning'. And the tensions were expressed in various struggles between creative personnel – directors in particular – and the front office, the business side of the industry, as well as in conflicts and disputes over the content, editing and marketing of individual films. If 'the production of films, essentially fluid and experimental as a process, is harnessed to a form of organisation which can rarely afford to be speculative . . .' (Huettig, in Balio, 1976, p. 238), we find an industry articulated by the evolving tensions and conflicts that dominated both the Hollywood studio system in its maturity as an oligopoly and the products of that system.

Selected Reading

John Belton, *American Cinema/American Culture*, New York, McGraw-Hill, 1994.

David Bordwell, Janet Staiger and Kristin Thompson, *The Classical Hollywood Cinema: Film Style and Mode of Production to 1960*, New York, Columbia University Press, 1985.

Douglas Gomery, *The Hollywood Studio System*, London, Macmillan, 1986.

Thomas Schatz, *The Genius of the System: Hollywood Film-making in the Studio Era*, New York, Pantheon, 1988.

PARAMOUNT PICTURES

Introduction

The history of Paramount Pictures coincided with and in many ways defined Hollywood's classical era. Created in 1916, Paramount established the prototype of the vertically integrated motion picture company, rapidly expanding under Adolph Zukor during the 1920s into an industry colossus. Paramount foundered in the early Depression era but then rebounded in the late 1930s under Barney Balaban, and far outpaced the other majors in the 1940s – only to be cut down at its peak in 1948 by the Supreme Court's epochal Paramount Decree.

Despite its autocratic corporate management under Zukor and then Balaban, Paramount's film-making operations lacked the kind of executive leadership provided by Louis B. Mayer at MGM, Jack Warner at Warner Bros., or Darryl Zanuck at 20th Century–Fox. In fact Paramount's uneven and inconsistent production management rendered it more of a 'director's studio' than any of the other majors – or rather a producer–director's studio, given its penchant for film-making 'hyphenates'. The key figure here was Cecil B. DeMille, whose epic spectacles, from the silent version of *The Ten Commandments* in 1923 to its widescreen remake in 1956, were Paramount's signature products.

Paramount also formulated successful cycles for a remarkable range of stars, including a number of European imports as well as recruits from other American entertainment fields such as radio, vaudeville, and musical recording. This wide-ranging star stable indicated two important aspects of Paramount's market strategy and house style: first, the international quality and appeal of many of its films, especially in the 1920s and 1930s; and second, its continual efforts to expand and diversify its media-related interests. Paramount was in fact the first studio to establish not only a national but a global distribution system. It also was heavily involved in a range of 'ancillary' media interests, particularly radio and television.

Thus Paramount was among the more complex and paradoxical of Hollywood's major studios during the classical era. On the one hand, it was the most aggressive company of the majors in its efforts to dominate (if not completely control) the industry. Zukor was widely considered the most ruthless chief executive in the motion-picture business, and Balaban's mentality proved to be equally market-driven. But on the other hand, Paramount's top talent enjoyed far more authority over the actual film-making process than their peers at the other major studios. Indeed, film-makers like DeMille, Josef von Sternberg, Ernst Lubitsch, Preston Sturges, and Billy Wilder were the chief architects of Paramount's 'house style'.

Paramount and the studio system

From its formation in a production–distribution merger in 1916 to the final consolidation of its exhibition interests a decade later, Paramount provided a veritable blueprint for vertical integration. In the process, it created a motion-picture behemoth which other companies had no choice but to challenge and to emulate if they were to survive.

The initial merger involved three principal entities. Two were production companies: Adolph Zukor's Famous Players Film Company, a New York-based production firm created in 1912 which successfully developed feature-length films and a star-driven market strategy; and the Jesse L. Lasky Feature Play Co., co-founded by Lasky, Samuel Goldfish (later Goldwyn), and Cecil B. DeMille in 1913, which scored with its first picture, *The Squaw Man* (1914), and quickly emerged as a Hollywood-based producer of top features. The third was Paramount Pictures, a nationwide distribution company created by W. W. Hodkinson in 1914 to handle the release of Famous Players' and Lasky's films.

With the demise of the Patents Trust and the explosive growth of the motion-picture industry in the mid-teens, Zukor engineered the merger of Famous Players and Lasky (as well as a number of smaller producers) in 1916, which then merged with Paramount to create the first fully integrated production–distribution company with a nationwide marketing and sales system. Fierce in-fighting for control saw Zukor force Hodkinson and Goldfish out and then assume the presidency, with Lasky and DeMille overseeing the film-making operations of Famous Players–Lasky – Lasky as vice president in charge of production, and DeMille as 'director general' while continuing to produce and direct his own films.

With the Famous Players facility in New York and scattered production operations in and around L.A., Famous Players–Lasky was scarcely a centralised 'studio'. It was, rather, a far-flung film-making enterprise which turned out a staggering number of features – over 100 a year in the late teens and early 1920s – in Zukor's aggressive effort to corner the motion-picture market. This effort was facilitated by a block-booking policy, which involved the packaging of second-rate product along with top features. Zukor ensured the appeal of those top features by signing leading stars like Mary Pickford, Douglas Fairbanks, Fatty Arbuckle, and William S. Hart to lucrative contracts.

In direct response to Paramount's rapid expansion, a number of first-run exhibitors joined forces in 1917 to create First National Exhibitors Circuit, a nationwide distribution company which promptly moved into production, signing a number of top stars like Charlie Chaplin and Mary Pickford to unprecedented contracts. These stars saw their salaries soar – Pickford's 1912 Famous Players salary of $500 per week, for example, hit $10,000 after the merger and then reached $350,000 per picture for First National. Despite these escalating salaries, the stars were still dependent on, in turn, Paramount and First National. Thus another crucial response to vertical integration was the 1919 formation of United Artists by Pickford, Chaplin, Fairbanks, and D. W. Griffith – a veritable declaration of independence from the burgeoning studio system.

Zukor, meanwhile, responded to First National's challenge by moving more aggressively into exhibition in 1919–20. His build-up of Paramount's theatre chain culminated in the 1925 merger with the Chicago-based Balaban and Katz chain, giving Paramount 1,200 theatres. Zukor also expanded international operations, setting up a worldwide distribution system and investing in production and exhibition overseas, particularly in Europe. Paramount owned considerable stock in the UFA studios in Germany, for instance, and was involved in a range of distribution and co-production deals, and in the recruitment of top German stars, directors, and other film-making talent as well.

While Paramount was a model of vertical integration by 1925, its production operations remained dispersed and somewhat ill-coordinated. After the Balaban and Katz merger, however, Zukor and Lasky began to develop a more coherent production operation, based primarily in Hollywood. In 1926 Paramount moved into a larger and better-equipped Hollywood studio which became its film-making headquarters, with B. P. Schulberg installed as head of West Coast production (under Lasky). This set-up proved very successful, and after sound conversion in 1928–9, Paramount began to function as a more centralised 'Hollywood studio'.

Paramount rode the 'talkie boom' of 1929–30 to new heights, with its 1930 profits hitting a record high of $18.4 million (versus $10.3 million for Fox, $9.9 million for MGM, $7.1 for Warner Bros. and $3.4 for RKO). But the Depression devastated Paramount in late 1931, due largely to the company's massive theatre holdings with their debilitating mortgage payments. Paramount lost $21 million in 1932 (another industry record), and declared bankruptcy a year later. Zukor was stripped of his power but stayed on as board chairman, while Lasky, Schulberg, Selznick, and other top executives left or were fired. Theatre czar Sam Katz was named chief executive, thanks largely to his close ties with Chicago and New York financiers who guided the company out of bankruptcy. A succession of studio heads from 1932 to 1936 included Lubitsch, remarkably enough, but there was no real stability in either the home office nor the studio until Barney Balaban (Katz's former partner) was appointed president in 1936. Balaban installed another 'theatre man', Y. Frank Freeman, as studio head in 1938, initiating an executive partnership which would continue for two decades.

Spectacular style. DeMille's 'prototype' for Paramount, *The Ten Commandments*

Authorship and house style

Early on, given its far-flung production operations and rapid expansion, Paramount evinced little stylistic consistency or coherence, although there were harbingers of later trends. DeMille's bedroom farces and 'modern' comedies, particularly those starring Gloria Swanson (*Male and Female*, 1919; *The Affairs of Anatol*, 1921), anticipated the sophisticated comedies of later years. And the films of Italian-born Rudolph Valentino (*The Sheik*, 1921; *Blood and Sand*, 1922) and imported German star Pola Negri (*The Cheat*, 1923; *Forbidden Paradise*, 1924) anticipated the more exotic 'Continental' films of the sound era. In 1923, Paramount also produced two historical epics, *The Covered Wagon* and DeMille's *The Ten Commandments*, which were prototypes of its trademark spectacles of the next three decades.

The mid-1920s consolidation of management and production cost Paramount several top stars and film-makers, who bridled at the prospect of greater constraints over their careers. In 1925/26, Valentino, Swanson, and William S. Hart bolted for United Artists, while co-founder DeMille left to set up his own production unit at MGM. Lasky and Schulberg signed a number of new stars, including Clara Bow, Harold Lloyd, Emile Jannings, Gary Cooper, Claudette Colbert, Frederic March, and Maurice Chevalier. They recruited several new directors as well – notably Ernst Lubitsch, Josef von Sternberg, and Rouben Mamoulian, all of whom had film-making experience in Europe and were signed in 1927.

Ironically enough, in the light of DeMille's departure, these film-makers enjoyed considerable autonomy under the new regime, attaining producer–director status under the 'unit production' system developed by Schulberg and his executive assistant David Selznick. Moreover, Paramount's house style coalesced under this system and this group of film-makers. As Joel Finler has aptly noted, 'It was under the Schulberg–Lasky regime that Paramount first developed the unique style associated with the studio during its peak creative years, ... [which] must be credited, primarily, to their many outstanding directors' (Finler, 1988, p. 162).

Paramount's production units were geared to specific star–genre cycles – von Sternberg's quasi-expressionistic Dietrich vehicles (*Morocco*, 1930; *Shanghai Express*, 1932; *Blonde Venus*, 1932), for instance, and Lubitsch's stylised musical operettas with Jeanette MacDonald (*The Love Parade*, 1929; *Monte Carlo*, 1930; *One Hour With You*, 1932). The units generally included key individuals besides the director and star; screenwriter Jules Furthman and cameraman Lee Garmes on the Dietrich films, for example. The production design on all of the Sternberg and Lubitsch films from 1927 to 1932 was done by Hans Dreier, who came to Paramount from UFA in 1923 and would serve as supervising art director for some three decades at Paramount. Indeed, Dreier along with film-makers like von Sternberg, Lubitsch, and Mamoulian (*Applause*, 1929; *City Streets*, 1931; and *Dr Jekyll and Mr Hyde*, 1931), fashioned a distinctly 'European' style in films designed with both the Continental and American markets in mind.

This European dimension to Paramount's emergent house style was countered in two significant areas. One was the studio's remarkable comedy output, featuring established vaudeville and radio stars like W. C. Fields, the Marx Brothers, Bing Crosby, George Burns and Gracie Allen, Jack Oakie and the inimitable Mae West. Several staff directors specialised in film comedy, most notably Leo McCarey (*Duck Soup*, 1933; *Belle of the Nineties*, 1935; *Ruggles of Red Gap*, 1935). A second factor involved the 1932 return of Cecil B. DeMille, who thereafter concentrated on his signature spectacles, alternating between epic Americana and biblical sagas, hitting his stride in the mid-1930s with *The Crusades* (1935) and *The Plainsman* (1936).

By the late 1930s, significantly, DeMille's films began to focus exclusively on American subjects while Paramount's European emphasis steadily waned. This signalled an important shift in studio style, and was related to the impending war in Europe, which wiped out the Continental market in the late 1930s, and also a severe cost-cutting campaign under Balaban. Balaban curtailed Paramount's more exotic and costly fare (apart from the DeMille epics), working the domestic market with an output of contemporary drama, light comedy and women's pictures. This meant wholesale changes in the roster of stars and film-makers in the late 1930s and 1940s. Among the new stars to emerge were Ray Milland, Bob Hope, Fred MacMurray, Dorothy Lamour, Paulette Goddard, Alan Ladd, Veronica Lake, William Holden, and Barbara Stanwyck. Paramount's leading film-makers of the era included producer–director Mitchell Leisen (*Easy Living*, 1937; *Midnight*,

Specialising in comedy – the Marx brothers in *Duck Soup*

1939; *Arise My Love*, 1940; among others), and two staff writers who graduated to hyphenate writer–director status in the 1940s: Preston Sturges (*The Lady Eve*, 1941; *Sullivan's Travels*, 1941; *Hail the Conquering Hero*, 1943; *The Miracle at Morgans Creek*, 1943, among others), and Billy Wilder (*Double Indemnity*, 1944; *The Lost Weekend*, 1945; *Sunset Boulevard*, 1950, among others).

While Sturges's irreverent black humour and Wilder's *noir* thrillers displayed the darker side of Paramount's style in the 1940s, the studio lightened things up in other areas, especially in its Bob Hope and Bing Crosby vehicles. The two completely dominated the 1940s box office, teaming with Dorothy Lamour in a cycle of hit 'road pictures' (e.g. *Road to Singapore*, 1940; *Road to Zanzibar*, 1941), and enjoying enormous success as solo stars as well – Hope in a cycle of cowardly-hero comedies, and Crosby in light musicals. The latter included *Going My Way* (1944), a curious blend of sentimental comedy, piety, and song (with Crosby and Barry Fitzgerald as priests in a struggling New York parish), produced and directed by Leo McCarey. The film clearly struck a cord with wartime Americans, sweeping the Oscars (including best picture, best actor and best director) and returning over $6 million in domestic rentals.

The war boom, the Paramount Decree and the television era

Under Balaban, Paramount also increased its efforts to diversify, particularly with regard to the emerging video and television technologies. As mentioned earlier, Paramount had long pursued various broadcast-related interests – dating back to its 1928 investment in the newly formed CBS radio network. The trend continued under Balaban, with many of its biggest stars moving freely between movies and radio in the late 1930s and 1940s. Even DeMille was involved, hosting (and directing) the 'Lux Radio Theater' from 1936 to 1945. Far more significant was Paramount's heavy investment in television in the 1930s and 1940s, notably a partnership with DuMont, a video technology pioneer, and its purchase of television stations in Chicago and Los Angeles. The DuMont relationship involved not only home transmission and television sets but also theatre television; Balaban, in other words, hoped to equip Paramount's theatres with video projection systems.

The Second World War stalled these television-related efforts, although with the surging 'war economy', Balaban was scarcely

The Sheik (USA 1921 *p.c* – Famous Players–Lasky; *d* George Melford; st b/w)

Among Paramount's biggest silent era hits, this story of an upright English heiress who falls in love with a desert chieftain secured Valentino's stardom.

The Covered Wagon (USA 1923 *p.c* – Famous Players–Lasky; *d* – James Cruze; st b/w)

The first of Paramount's grand historical epics and a trend-setting western saga, the film is more notable for its lavish production values than for its writing or performances.

The Love Parade (USA 1929 *p.c* – Paramount; *d* – Ernst Lubitsch; sd b/w)

Jeanette MacDonald's screen début and her initial teaming with Maurice Chevalier in the first of Lubitsch's musical operettas. A fantasy-romance and sophisticated comedy of manners about the European aristocracy. The famed 'Lubitsch touch' is very much in evidence.

Morocco (USA 1930 *p.c* – Paramount; *d* – Josef von Sternberg; sd b/w)

The first Sternberg–Dietrich collaboration in Hollywood and a stunning follow-up to their 1930 German masterpiece, *The Blue Angel*. A stylish, innovative melodrama, the film features Dietrich as a man-eating cabaret singer who finally finds true love with a foreign legionnaire (Gary Cooper).

Duck Soup (USA 1933 *p.c* – Paramount; *d* – Leo McCarey; sd b/w)

The fifth and arguably the best of the Marx Brothers' comic–chaotic romps for Paramount, with Groucho as Rufus T. Firefly, prime minister of Fredonia, waging war on neighbouring Sylvania. Harpo, Chico and Zeppo co-star in what is now widely considered a satiric masterpiece, although the film was a commercial and critical disappointment on initial release.

She Done Him Wrong (USA 1933 *p.c* – Paramount; *d* – Lowell Sherman; sd b/w)

Mae West's reprise of her stage role as Gay Nineties saloon-keeper Diamond Lil, who falls for the undercover cop (Cary Grant) out to arrest her. West, who co-scripted the film from her own Broadway hit, is in top form in this witty, sexy spoof.

The Plainsman (USA 1936 *p.c* – Paramount; *d* – Cecil B. DeMille; sd b/w)

The American west in epic DeMille fashion, with Gary Cooper's Wild Bill Hickcock taking up with Calamity Jane (Jean Arthur) and various other romanticised historical figures. The film was among the more successful A-class westerns of the decade, and an early sign of DeMille's wartime focus on American subjects.

Road to Singapore (USA 1940 *p.c* – Paramount; *d* – Victor Schertziner; sd b/w)

The first of the Bob Hope–Bing Crosby–Dorothy Lamour road series, with Hope and Crosby as two rich playboys on the run and in love with the same saronged beauty. While lacking the inspired lunacy of their later outings, this was a huge and unexpected hit for Paramount.

Hail the Conquering Hero (USA 1944 *p.c* – Paramount; *d* – Preston Sturges; sd b/w)

The satiric and irreverent Preston Sturges (who produced, directed and scripted) at his best, poking fun at the wartime home front and the sacred verities of heroism, motherhood and small-town life. Eddie Bracken stars as an army reject (due to hay fever) who is passed off as a war hero by a group of well-meaning Marines. A masterpiece of verbal and visual comedy.

The Lost Weekend (USA 1945 *p.c* – Paramount; *d* – Billy Wilder; sd b/w)

Searing, relentlessly downbeat drama (co-scripted by Wilder and producer Charles Brackett) about an alcoholic writer's two-day binge. Pioneering postwar 'social-problem film' starring Ray Milland, who won an Academy Award for his performance, with Oscars for best picture, best script and best director as well.

Rear Window (USA 1954 *p.c* – Paramount; *d* – Alfred Hitchcock; sd col)

One of several taut, stylish romantic thrillers produced and directed by Hitchcock in an elaborate financing-and-distribution deal with Paramount (put together by his agent Lew Wasserman). James Stewart stars as a photographer confined to a wheelchair who tries to convince his society girlfriend (Grace Kelly) that he may have witnessed a murder.

The Ten Commandments (USA 1956 *p.c* – Paramount; *d* – Cecil B. DeMille; sd col)

DeMille's last film, consummate biblical epic, and by far the biggest hit in Paramount's history at the time. Charlton Heston as Moses challenges Egypt's might (embodied in Yul Brynner's pharoah) and leads the Jews from slavery. DeMille and 1950s Hollywood at either their best or their worst, depending on one's viewpoint and penchant for sentiment and spectacle.

concerned. During the war, Paramount returned to the kind of industry domination it had enjoyed two decades earlier, thanks largely to its massive theatre chain and a war-induced market boom. While Paramount's theatres had been a drag on its finances during the Depression, now they were a source of huge profits. At the war boom's peak in 1946, Paramount earned record profits of nearly $40 million, roughly twice those of its major competitors.

The war boom ended all too quickly in 1947/48, however, due to various social and economic factors – suburban migration, the baby boom, the rise of commercial television, and so on. Equally devastating was the Supreme Court's 1948 Paramount Decree, an antitrust ruling which forced Paramount (the first studio named in the suit) and the other majors to divest their all-important theatre chains and to severely curtail the sales policies which had enabled them to control the industry for decades. Moreover, the antitrust ruling enabled the FCC (Federal Communications Commission) to bar the Hollywood studios from active involvement in the television industry – a blow which was especially serious to Paramount.

Paramount handled dis-integration by splitting into separate production-distribution and exhibition firms: Paramount Pictures and United Paramount Theaters (UPT). Both entities continued to pursue television – UPT by investing in the ABC-television network, and Paramount Pictures by syndicating its classic films and producing television series. Paramount's movie-related fortunes turned primarily on DeMille's epics. *Samson and Delilah* (1949) earned $9 million in domestic rentals and sparked the biblical blockbuster trend of the 1950s. DeMille followed it with his last two films and the biggest hits in Paramount's history: *The Greatest Show on Earth* (1952), which returned $12.8 million, and *The Ten Commandments* (1956), which earned an astounding $34.2 million.

The studio began to fade badly in the early 1960s, however, due to the ongoing erosion of the movie-going audience and a succession of costly flops. That led to Balaban's retirement and the 1966 sale of Paramount to Gulf & Western – the first of many studio buyouts by huge conglomerates, and a crucial step in the transition from the Old Hollywood to the New. Paramount would survive and indeed would flourish in the New Hollywood of the 1980s and 1990s (see New Hollywood, p. 000). And its resurgence, interestingly enough, has been due not only to its merger with another industry behemoth, Viacom, but also to its continued reliance on film-making hyphenates, epic-scale blockbusters, cross-over stars, global marketing and media diversification – all features of studio success in the classical era.

Selected Reading

Leslie Halliwell, *Mountain of Dreams: The Golden Years at Paramount*, New York, Stonehill, 1976.

Thomas Schatz, *The Genius of the System: Hollywood Film-making in the Studio Era*, New York, Pantheon, 1998.

METRO-GOLDWYN-MAYER

Introduction

A relative late-comer to the ranks of Hollywood's integrated major studios, MGM rose rapidly to industry leadership during the late 1920s and then went on to dominate the industry throughout the 1930s and into the 1940s. With superb resources, top film-making talent, and 'all the stars in the heavens', MGM specialised in A-class star vehicles for the first-run movie market. But despite its wealth of film-making talent, production at MGM was controlled by its studio executives and producers. Its films tended to project a sanguine (if not saccharine) world-view – well indicated by its penchant for historical romances, lavish musicals and family fare. Still, MGM's films appealed to critics and the Academy as well as moviegoers, as the studio managed to factory-produce what Hollywood defined as 'quality' for some three decades.

Film historians scarcely endorse that view, however, as MGM accounts for remarkably few canonised film classics or anointed *auteurs* – with the exception of its stunning cycle of postwar musicals (notably *An American in Paris*, 1951; *Singin' in the Rain*, 1951). But even here, aptly enough, the driving creative force was star-choreographer Gene Kelly, and the ultimate *auteur* was producer Arthur Freed. Thus MGM, perhaps the most accomplished of classical Hollywood studios, represents a significant challenge to an *auteur*-based theory of film history or criticism (see Part 6).

The emergence of MGM

Metro-Goldwyn-Mayer was created via merger in 1924 by Loew's, Inc., following the lead of other motion-picture powers in its quest for vertical integration. Created by Marcus Loew some two decades earlier, Loew's chief asset was its first-class theatre chain, centred in the New York area, which it augmented in 1920 with the purchase of Metro Pictures, a nationwide film distribution company with a modest production facility in Los Angeles. With this solid basis in exhibition and distribution, Loew's completed its expansion in 1924 with two acquisitions: Goldwyn Pictures, an integrated company whose chief strength was its massive production facility in Culver City; and Louis B. Mayer Productions, a small company geared to first-run pictures whose chief asset was the management team of Mayer and his young production chief, Irving Thalberg (then aged twenty-five).

Metro-Goldwyn was run out of New York by Nicholas Schenck, the chief executive of Loew's, Inc., while the Culver City studio and all production operations were closely controlled by Mayer and Thalberg, who, along with studio attorney Robert Rubin, were known as the 'Mayer Group'. The importance of the Mayer Group was underscored by the merger agreement giving them 20 per cent of Loew's production-related profits (an exceptional arrangement in Hollywood at the time), and also by the addition of 'Mayer' to the official studio title in 1925.

Metro-Goldwyn-Mayer made an immediate impression via two huge 1925 hits, *Ben-Hur* and *The Big Parade*. But the real keys to its rapid industry rise were, first, its astute studio management team and efficient production operations; second, its well-stocked 'star stable' and savvy manipulation of the star system; and third, the effective coordination of production and marketing operations, keyed to a steady output of A-class star vehicles designed for the 'major metropolitan' market (and Loew's theatre holdings). While the merger gave MGM top stars like Lon Chaney, Lillian Gish, and Marion Davies, Mayer and Thalberg quickly cultivated a stable of home-grown stars including John Gilbert, Norma Shearer, Joan Crawford and Greta Garbo. MGM also signed New York stage stars Marie Dressler and John and Lionel Barrymore, enhancing the prestige value of its pictures while also appealing to Loew's predominant New York-based clientele.

Early on, Mayer and Thalberg developed a dual strategy of lavish spectacles and more modest star vehicles, with the latter frequently centred on romantic co-starring teams. After the unknown John Gilbert burst to stardom in the downbeat First World War epic, *The Big Parade*, for instance, MGM quickly developed him as a romantic lead and enjoyed tremendous success teaming him with Swedish import Greta Garbo in *Flesh and the Devil* (1926), *Love* (1927), and *A Woman of Affairs* (1928). MGM's move to sound was punctuated by a huge 1929 musical hit, *Broadway Melody* ('All Talking! All Singing! All Dancing!') and also by *Anna Christie* ('Garbo Talks!') in 1930. Complementing these upbeat hits were more sombre 'prestige dramas' like King Vidor's *The Crowd* (1927), Victor Sjöström's *The Wind* (1928, starring Lillian Gish), and *Min and Bill* (1930), the waterfront fable which launched Marie Dressler and Wallace Beery to top stardom.

By decade's end MGM was vying successfully with established industry giants Fox and Paramount, and the newly-emerged 'major' Warner Bros. In 1929/30, at the height of the 'talkie boom' and before the Depression hit Hollywood, Metro's combined profits were $25.8 million, versus $33.9 million for Paramount, $19.8 million for Fox and $21.6 million for Warners. Interestingly enough, however, MGM did not parlay this success into expanded theatre holdings, as did its major competitors. (Paramount and Fox built their chains to over 1,000 theatres in the late 1920s, and Warners to 600, while Loew's remained at about 150.) Loew's decision to maintain a limited chain of first- and second-run houses proved fortuitous for two reasons: first, the cost of sound conversion was much lower; second and more importantly, Loew's was not saddled with the enormous mortgage commitments which devastated its chief competitors in the early 1930s.

MGM in the 1930s

MGM's Depression-era success and domination of the movie industry was simply staggering, fuelled not only by the consistent quality of its films but also by the economic travails of its rivals. Three of the Big Five (Paramount, Fox, and RKO) suffered financial collapse in the early 1930s, while Warner Bros. had to siphon off one-quarter of its assets to stay afloat. Loew's/MGM, meanwhile, turned a profit every year of the 1930s and saw its assets actually increase. From 1931 to 1940, the combined net profits of Hollywood's Big Eight studios totalled $128.2 million; MGM's profits alone were $93.2 million, nearly three quarters of the industry total.

Equally impressive was the consistent quality of its films and the industry recognition they routinely garnered. During the 1930s, MGM accounted for over 30 per cent of the Academy nominees for best picture (27 out of 87 pictures, including four winners), and over 30 per cent of both the best actor and best actress nominees as well (with six male and five female Oscar winners). During the first ten years of the Motion Picture Herald's Exhibitors Poll of top ten box-office stars (1932–41), an astounding 47 per cent were under contract to MGM – with MGM's Clark Gable the only Hollywood star to be named in all ten years.

The consummate example of MGM's house style in the early Depression era was *Grand Hotel*, an all-star drama of star-crossed lovers (including Garbo, John Barrymore, Joan Crawford, Lionel Barrymore and Wallace Beery) which won the Oscar for best picture in 1932. Produced at a cost of $700,000, over twice the industry average, the film returned $2.3 million in North America alone. It emphasised glamour, grace, and beauty in its polished settings and in its civilised characters – all of whom are doomed or desperate, but suffer life's misfortunes with style. Indeed, the film in many ways is about the triumph of style, expressed not only by its characters but by cinematographer William Daniels, editor Blanche Sewell, recording engineer Douglas Shearer, art director Cedric Gibbons and costume designer Adrian. Each was singled out in the opening credits of *Grand Hotel* (along with director Edmund Goulding and playwright William Drake), and they were, in fact, the key artisans of MGM's house style.

The chief architect of that style was Irving Thalberg. In the 1920s and early 1930s, MGM exemplified the 'central producer system' which dominated Hollywood at the time. While Louis Mayer handled studio operations and contract negotiations, Thalberg and his half-dozen 'supervisors' (among them Harry Rapf, Hunt Stromberg, Bernie Hyman) oversaw actual film-making. Thalberg refused to be mentioned in MGM's film credits, but his importance to the studio was well known. 'For the past five years,' wrote *Fortune* in a 1932 article, 'M-G-M has made the best and most successful motion pictures in the United States'. That success was directly attributed to Thalberg: 'He is what Hollywood means by M-G-M, . . . he is now called a genius more often than anyone else in Hollywood.' MGM's success was due to 'Mr. Thalberg's heavy but sagacious spending,' noted *Fortune*, which ensured 'the glamour of M-G-M personalities' and the 'general finish and glossiness which characterizes M-G-M pictures' (Balio, 1985, pp. 312, 318).

There were other key components to Thalberg's management and market strategy as well. He was vitally concerned about 'story values', as evidenced not only by his active role in story and script conferences, which was legendary, but also his penchant for assigning up to a dozen staff writers to a film. Thalberg also was a major proponent of using preview screenings to decide whether a picture required rewrites, retakes, and re-editing. This rarely involved the original writer(s) or director, and thus evinced an ethos of 'teamwork' at MGM. Significantly, Metro's writers and directors rarely complained about the practice, as they were very well paid (by industry standards) and were deftly handled by Thalberg.

Another key factor was Thalberg's penchant for 'romance' in the form of love stories or male-oriented adventure – or preferably both, as in co-starring ventures like *Red Dust* (1932) and *China Seas* (1935) with Gable and Jean Harlow. A more nebulous but equally important factor was Thalberg's impeccable and oft-noted 'taste', which was evident not only in his inclination for the occasional highbrow prestige picture, but also in his ability to render frankly erotic stories and situations (as in the Gable–Harlow films just mentioned) palatable to Hollywood's Production Code Administration and to mainstream audiences.

While many of these qualities remained essential to MGM's house style into the 1940s, Thalberg's control of production actually ended in the mid-1930s. His ill health and an internal power struggle at Loew's/MGM (spurred by the growing resentment of Thalberg's authority and increased profit share by both Mayer and Schenck) led to a shake-up in studio management. In 1932/33, Metro began shifting to a 'unit-producer' system, with a few top executive producers – principally Thalberg, David Selznick and Hunt Stromberg – supervising high-end features, while Harry Rapf and several others produced the studio's second-rank films. (Up to 50 per cent of the other majors' pictures during the 1930s were recognisably B-movies; however, Mayer prohibited the use of the term 'B-movie' on the MGM lot, and few if any of its pictures would have qualified.)

Under the new management set-up, both Thalberg and Selznick concentrated on high-cost prestige pictures, mainly costume dramas. Many of these were very successful both commercially and critically – Thalberg's *Mutiny on the Bounty* (1935), *Romeo and Juliet* and *Camille* (both 1936), for instance, and Selznick's *David Copperfield* (1935), *Anna Karenina* and *A Tale of Two Cities* (both 1935). Stromberg, meanwhile, proved especially adept at creating successful star–genre cycles – as in the succession of Jeanette MacDonald–Nelson Eddy operettas (for instance *Naughty Marietta*, 1935 and *Rose-Marie*, 1936), and in the 'Thin Man' films with William Powell and Myrna Loy. MGM's success continued under this new regime, but the studio was severely shaken in 1936 by two events. One was Selznick's departure to create his own company, Selznick International Pictures, which would join forces with MGM in 1939 for the most successful film in Hollywood's history, *Gone With the Wind*. The other was Thalberg's sudden, untimely death (at age 37), which marked the end of an era for MGM.

The Mayer regime: star–genre cycles and steady decline

After Selznick's departure and Thalberg's death, Mayer took charge of film-making operations, establishing a management-by-committee system which oversaw production for the next decade. While still very much a producer's studio, MGM's management ranks steadily swelled with executives who had little or no film-making experience. A few production executives like Dore Schary and Joe Mankiewicz did come up through the writers' ranks, and its top active producer, Mervyn LeRoy, had been a producer–director at Warner Bros. LeRoy's first project for MGM was *The Wizard of Oz* (1939), an ambitious, innovative, and costly film which was scarcely typical of the studio's – or of LeRoy's subsequent films. MGM took a decidedly conservative turn under Mayer, its films becoming ever more predictable and formulaic.

One indication of this conservative turn was MGM's reliance on upbeat film series with strong 'entertainment values' – best exemplified by the Hardy Family films, which the studio cranked out like clockwork, and which made Mickey Rooney (as Andy Hardy) the top box-office star in America from 1938 to 1940. Spurred by the series' huge success,

The Wizard of Oz – MGM's most expensive film of the decade

Mayer developed other child stars as well, notably Margaret O'Brien (*Journey for Margaret*, 1942) and Elizabeth Taylor (*Lassie Come Home*, 1943). Mayer also favoured more wholesome depictions of love, marriage, and motherhood, as seen in the rapid wartime rise of Greer Garson and her usual co-star, Walter Pidgeon (*Mrs Miniver*, 1942; *Madame Curie*, 1943; *Mrs Parkington*, 1944).

Garson and Pidgeon were among several co-starring teams which embodied Mayer's idealised vision of on-screen coupling – a far cry, indeed, from the hard-drinking, wise-cracking Nick and Nora Charles of *The Thin Man* a decade earlier. As Rooney outgrew his Andy Hardy role, he teamed with Judy Garland in a successful cycle of painfully wholesome post-adolescent show-musicals (including *Babes in Arms*, 1939; *Strike Up the Band*, 1940; *Babes on Broadway*, 1941). A more interesting couple, Katharine Hepburn and Spencer Tracy emerged in *Woman of the Year* (1941), although not until their fourth outing in *Adam's Rib* (1949) did they recapture the spark of that first teaming.

While these and other MGM films did exceptional business, the studio's glory days clearly were waning in the 1940s. Indeed, due to the general fall-off in terms of product quality, along with the booming movie marketplace during the war which favoured the studios with larger theatre chains (a reversal of market conditions in the 1930s), the once-invincible MGM was quickly surpassed by its chief competitors. In 1946, at the peak of the 'war boom', MGM's profits totalled $18 million, less than one-half of Paramount's ($39 million), and well behind both Fox ($22 million) and Warners ($19.4 million). Its critical cachet was fading as well; Oscar nominations were increasingly rare, and the MGM style was looking downright anachronistic in the postwar era of *film noir* and social-problem dramas.

One bright spot was Metro's postwar musicals output, which included fully one-quarter of its release schedule and roughly one-half of Hollywood's overall musical output during the postwar decade. Several MGM producers specialised in musicals, but the individual most responsible for its 'musical golden age' was Arthur Freed. Freed's breakthrough came in 1944 with *Meet Me in St Louis*, a Technicolor musical starring Garland and directed by Vincente Minnelli. The success of that film enabled Freed to assemble his own production unit, which emphasised dance as well as music and relied on the talents of choreographers like Gene Kelly and Stanley Donen. Kelly and Donen co-directed *On the Town* in 1949, confirming the currency and vitality of the Freed unit's 'dance musicals', and paving the way for such classics as *An American in Paris* (Minnelli, 1951), *Singin' in the Rain* (Donen–Kelly, 1951), *The Band Wagon* (Minnelli, 1953), *It's Always Fair Weather* (Donen–Kelly, 1955) and *Gigi* (Minnelli, 1958).

While the Freed unit musicals marked a sustained peak in terms of quality film-making, they were symptomatic of Metro's lavish (and thus costly) production operations. This meant narrower profit margins as changing social and economic conditions, along with the emergence of television, eroded Hollywood's audience base. Dore Schary was installed as MGM production chief in 1948 with the express goal of reducing costs, which proved impossible given the studio's entrenched production operations. In fact, MGM held out longer than any of the majors after the 1948 Paramount Decree (demanding theatre divorcement), trying in vain through legal appeals and other means to sustain the studio system in terms of both factory-based production and vertical integration.

By the mid-1950s MGM grudgingly recognised the realities of the changing media marketplace. The studio steadily shifted its film-making operations toward 'telefilm' (that is, television series) production, sold off its vault of old films to television syndicators, and in a particularly telling move, made arrangements with CBS in 1956 for a colour broadcast of *The Wizard of Oz* on prime-time

The Big Parade (USA 1925 *p.c* – MGM; *d* – King Vidor; st b/w)

The first major critical and commercial hit to be produced by the newly formed company. This First World War anti-war saga established Vidor as MGM's leading director, and also made John Gilbert an overnight star.

Broadway Melody (USA 1928 *p.c* – MGM; *d* – Harry Beaumont; sd b/w with col. sequences)

Hollywood's first 'all-talking, all-singing' musical, and MGM's first Academy Award for best picture. MGM also produced a 'series' of Broadway Melody musicals in the late 1930s.

Anna Christie (USA 1929 *p.c* – MGM; *d* – Clarence Brown; sd b/w)

Garbo's first talkie and a breakthrough for Marie Dressler, who was an even bigger box-office star than Garbo in the early 1930s. Based on Eugene O'Neill's play about a waterfront prostitute who falls in love with a sailor, this well exemplified MGM's stylised 'realism' during Thalberg's regime.

Grand Hotel (USA 1932 *p.c* – MGM; *d* – Edmund Goulding; sd b/w)

A trend-setting portmanteau drama with an all-star cast (Greta Garbo, John and Lionel Barrymore, Joan Crawford, Wallace Beery, Jean Hersholt), this film gave MGM its second Oscar for best picture.

Mutiny on the Bounty (USA 1935 *p.c* – MGM; *d* – Frank Lloyd; sd b/w)

MGM's biggest critical and commercial hit of 1935, this adaptation of the Nordhoff and Hall novel co-starred Clark Gable (as Fletcher Christian) and Charles Laughton (as Captain Bligh). An impressive production on all counts, the film won another best-picture Oscar for MGM.

The fourth in MGM's successful Hardy family series – *Love Finds Andy Hardy*

Love Finds Andy Hardy (USA 1938 *p.c* – MGM; *d* – George B. Seitz; sd b/w)

The fourth in MGM's hugely successful Hardy Family series, which was itself a scaled-down spin-off of MGM's 1935 adaptation of O'Neill's *Ah, Wilderness*. This instalment brought Judy Garland into the mix, setting up MGM's subsequent series of Rooney–Garland musicals.

The Wizard of Oz (USA 1939 *p.c* – MGM; *d* – Victor Fleming; sd col.)

Timeless fantasy–musical based on Frank L. Baum's children's classic, and MGM's most expensive and ambitious film of the decade. The film solidified Judy Garland's star status and earned over $3 million, but actually lost money on its initial release.

Mrs Miniver (USA 1942 *p.c* – MGM; *d* – William Wyler; sd b/w)

Huge hit not only commercially and critically, but also as a pro-British morale booster and pre-war propaganda in the US. The story of an English housewife and her upright husband established Greer Garson and Walter Pidgeon as MGM's ideal wartime couple, and brought the studio another best-picture Oscar.

Battleground (USA 1949 *p.c* – MGM; *d* – William Wellman; sd b/w)

A pet project of new production chief Dore Schary, this downbeat ensemble piece about the Battle of the Bulge was a surprise hit and helped break the post-war taboo against war pictures.

An American in Paris (USA 1951 *p.c* – MGM; *d* – Vincente Minnelli; sd col.)

Arguably the best of the Freed unit's innovative dance musicals and the peak of MGM's postwar 'musical golden age'. Deftly blending Minnelli's visual sophistication and Gene Kelly's enormous talents as both choreographer and performer, the film brought MGM yet another Academy Award for best picture and Arthur Freed the Irving Thalberg Award for distinguished production.

television. As much as any single event in the 1950s, that signalled the end of MGM's – and Hollywood's – classical era, and the beginning of a very different period in film history.

Selected Reading

Joel W. Finler, *The Hollywood Story*, New York, Crown Publishers, 1988.

Douglas Gomery, *The Hollywood Studio System*, New York, St. Martin's Press, 1986.

WARNER BROS.

Introduction

Warner Bros. is probably best known as the studio that introduced sound to cinema. Warners, which started in the 1920s as a small family-owned film production company, in 1925 signed an agreement with Western Electric to develop a sound system. The famous talking picture *The Jazz Singer* was released in 1927, and in 1928 the company further consolidated its position by acquiring the First National film theatre circuit, a large studio in Burbank, and several prominent stars. In the same year, Warners made a net profit of more than $17 million, a record high for the film industry at that time. The momentum of this success carried the company through the following year, but by 1931 the effects of the Depression began to make themselves felt: between 1931 and 1934, the company's losses were of the order of $13 million. Warners' response to the crisis set it apart from the other major studios, and was an important factor in its economic recovery during the later 1930s.

The rationalisations made at Warner Bros. during the early 1930s involved the adoption of 'assembly line' film production methods, rigid adherence to production schedules and low budgets. During his time as head of production at Warners (between 1931 and 1933), Darryl F. Zanuck assumed much of the immediate responsibility for implementing the new regime. Throughout the 1930s, the studio was able to maintain a regular annual output of about sixty films, and unlike most of the majors managed to survive the Depression without losing managerial and financial control to Wall Street.

Warners and 'studio style'

As Edward Buscombe has pointed out, 'studio style' is a term which occasionally crops up in film criticism, but in a loose way. While, for example, MGM went in for large-budget costume drama and later, musicals, and Paramount had a taste for raciness and decadence (Buscombe, 1974, p. 52), the products of Warner Bros. are commonly held as embodying studio style in a particularly marked way, combining certain genres (the gangster movies, the backstage musical, and later romantic adventure films) with a characteristic visual style (low-key lighting, simple sets), and a kind of populism in key with the studio's rather downmarket image (see Genre, p.176).

The Roaring Twenties – Warner's gangster genre

But how is the identification of a particular style or set of styles within a studio to be explained? What, in other words, is the relationship between the 'house' and the 'style'? On the one hand, the fact that Warner Bros. films are so often remembered exactly as Warner Bros. films rather than, say, as films by their individual directors may be explained in terms of the tendency inherent in the studio's institutional structure to subordinate individuals to the organisation. But the ways in which production was organised may well, in turn, be considered in relation to the economic restrictions impinging on the studio:

> Sets at Warners were customarily bare and workmanlike . . . The scale of a film could be judged by its budget, and in 1932 the average production cost per feature at Warners was estimated at $200,000, lowest of the majors except for Columbia ($175,000): MGM by comparison, averaged $450,000. (Campbell, 1971, p. 2)

These economic conditions, it may further be suggested, had certain aesthetic or stylistic consequences. They can certainly explain the relative simplicity of the settings of many Warner Bros. films – of the action melodramas and gangster films in particular and the low-key lighting which did much to conceal the cheapness of the sets, as well as the repetitions from film to film of financially successful formulae. (*The Public Enemy*, 1931, for example, was made in only sixteen days at a cost of $151,000.) It has also been argued that something less easily observable than economic restrictions may also have been instrumental in its populism during the 1930s – its use of working-class characters in films, and also the concern with social problems of the day. The notion of studio style, then, may incorporate an ideological as well as an economic component.

The Public Enemy (USA 1931 *p.c* – Warner Bros.; *d* – William Wellman; sd b/w)

The title sequence brings together a number of gangster stereotypes, recalling for Warners' audience the range of images of the city criminals the cinema was accumulating. Warners was not simply exploiting a genre for its sensational (in this case violent) potential but was also committed to situating that crime socially. Thus it could be argued that the prologue to the film, 'To honestly depict . . . rather than glorify' is not only a gesture to the demands for moral self-censorship by the Hays Code, it is also a statement of Warners' 'social conscience' ideology. This is exemplified in the way the film looks to socio-economic factors as the source of crime, and views the gangsters' rise to success as a result of the introduction of Prohibition.

Little Caesar (USA 1930 *p.c* – Warner Bros.; *d* – Mervyn Leroy; sd b/w)

The film deals with the relationship of the Italian immigrant community to the growth of organised large-scale racketeering in the Chicago underworld. In the context of Warners' populist ideology, the ending of the film in which one of the gangsters is eliminated by the gang when he tries to 'go straight', confirms the film's fatalistic view of the relationship between social deprivation and crime.

G-Men (USA 1935 *p.c* – Warner Bros.; *d* – William Keighley; sd b/w)

Warner Bros' response, partly, to pressure from the Hays Code was the revamping of the gangster genre in the mid-1930s. The central character was no longer the social outcast, the gangster, but the G-Man, the federal agent. The G-Men films retained many of the features of the earlier gangster-centred ones, but the iconography of the genre changed from an emphasis on the tools of the gangsters' trade to the procedure of police detection.

Racket Busters (USA 1938 *p.c* – Warner Bros.; *d* – Lloyd Bacon; sd b/w)

In *Racket Busters*, as in *G-Men*, the focus is on the police rather than the racketeers. Also as in *G-Men* and *Each Dawn I Die*, authenticity is created by the use of newspaper headlines, a documentary touch reinforced by the occasional documentary-style sequence. A characteristic Warners scene is the confrontation between the mobsters and the private enterprise truck drivers. It could be argued that the early populist sentiments of Warners were being gradually transformed into a moral crusade against crime, and that consequently the original commitment of the studio to situate crimes in a social context had been dropped.

I Am a Fugitive from a Chain Gang (USA 1932 *p.c* – Warner Bros.; *d* – Mervyn Leroy; sd b/w)

A hard-hitting film about a returned soldier who is wrongfully imprisoned for a hold-up. Warners' social-realist aesthetic is visible in its observation of Depression America and its effect on the people. The documentary influence is apparent in the montage (reminiscent of 'March of Time' newsreels) of maps and trains, and later, of the prisoners' picks and calendar pages. In the jail the horn sounds the same as that of the factory at the beginning of the film; an 'expressive' use of sound characteristics of Warners' early sound films. However, it could also be argued that the focus is presented in individualistic terms in that they are shown to be the result of accidental circumstances rather than political or economic factors.

Gold Diggers of 1933 (USA 1933 *p.c* – Warner Bros.; *d* – Mervyn Leroy; sd b/w)

Gold Diggers of 1933 is an interesting combination of the backstage musical and social realist form. The 'Remember My

Warners and genre

The genre for which Warner Bros. is perhaps most famous is the gangster film (see The gangster film, p. 173). In 1931, Darryl F. Zanuck announced a series of films whose subject matter would be drawn from newspaper stories. This is the inspiration behind both *Little Caesar* (1930) and *The Public Enemy* (1931), and the commercial success of these films determined studio policy throughout the rest of the decade. Gangster films, it was clear, made money.

From the box-office success of the 'exposé' films emerged a style of 'critical social realism'. Campbell (1971) argues that the success of these films is attributable to the fact that Depression disillusion made Warners' predominantly working-class audiences receptive to attacks on the established power structure of American society. But it seems equally likely that audiences were attracted by the action and violence in these films. Indeed, after the institution of the Production Code Administration (see Censorship, p. 7) some of Warners' more violent films were subjected to criticism from within the industry, and pressure was put on the studio to concentrate more on the enforcement of the law and less on the deeds of criminals. Warner Bros.' response was to produce a cycle of films in which the central characters are federal agents rather than gangsters: these included *G-Men* (1935) and *Racket Busters* (1938).

They Drive By Night – Warner's socio-political conscience

The social conscience of Warner Bros.

Within its economic and ideological conditions of operation, Warner Bros.' studio policy has often been equated with a particular politics – that of President Roosevelt's Democratic New Deal. Indeed, one Warners' advertisement of 1933 made this association quite explicit: 'Watch this industry turn over a New Leaf . . . In the New Year . . . With our New President . . . And this New Deal . . . New Leaders . . . New Styles . . . New Stars . . .' (quoted in Campbell, 1971, p. 34).

It has sometimes been suggested that the

Forgotten Man' number – a reference to First World War soldiers – is an unusual example of direct social comment in a musical and at the time was considered to be in poor taste. The numbers were staged by the great Busby Berkeley.

Sergeant York (USA 1941 *p.c* – Warner Bros.; *d* – Howard Hawks; sd b/w)

Made shortly before Pearl Harbor, *Sergeant, York* tells the 'true' story of a man who became a national hero after his war service in 1917. The real York was offered a considerable sum to sell his story to Jesse L. Lasky of Famous Players–Lasky at the end of the war, but only agreed in 1940 to an adaptation on condition that he could supervise the production in every detail.

'Of all the films of the period *Sergeant York* (July 1941) deals most directly with the problems of the country on the eve of the new war . . . To dispel any uncertainty concerning the film's message, Warners quoted York in their advertising: "By our victory in the last war, we won a lease on liberty, not a deed to it. Now after 23 years, Adolf Hitler tells us that lease is expiring and, after the manner of all leases, we have the privilege of renewing it or letting it go by default." *Sergeant York*'s popularity (it was the top-grossing film of 1941) suggests that it dealt with questions which deeply concern the country.' (Campbell, 1972, p. 29.)

The Roaring Twenties (USA 1939 *p.c* – Warner Bros.; *d* – Raoul Walsh; sd b/w)

The Roaring Twenties, like other Warners' gangster films, makes an implicit connection between social deprivation and crime, with Cagney's taxi-driver hero returning from the war to find his job gone and attempting to set up his own business as a taxi operator. This is, argues Buscombe, an example of the small-scale entrepreneurial capitalism which remains the ideal of most Warners' films of the period (Buscombe, 1974, p. 56). The film takes a documentary, sociological approach to the creation of the gangsters and their lifestyle, characteristic of Warners' 1930s gangster films.: e.g. the tommy-gun as an invention of the First World War; the set-piece montage of gang warfare; the conflict between the gangster-by-default, for whom gangsterdom is the only available means of business, over the function of violence in their operations; the heroine, whose classy femininity is the object of the gangster hero's sexual desire and social aspirations and who, as a consequence, is unobtainable, unlike the faithful gangster's moll; the role of the lawyer, who for social reasons or personal weakness gets involved with the mob but ultimately crosses the gang leader by virtue of his superior knowledge of how the system works; the gangster's lifelong and faithful friend who goes down with him in his fall.

They Drive by Night (USA 1940 *p.c* – Warner Bros.; *d* – Raoul Walsh; sd b/w)

An example of Warner Bros' crime/thriller melodrama with elements of social comment. Warners' relative financial independence from East Coast financiers perhaps made it easier for the studio to make films which, within the capitalist film industry and by the standards of other Hollywood products, were fairly radical in terms of subject matter. The film's socio-political concern is demonstrated by the Fabrini brothers who are shown as victims of capitalist exploitation from various directions. The independent truckers operating within this economic context co-operate to protect each other from the exploiters. Ultimately, the dominant ideology is re-established and any radicalism recuperated, in that Joe Fabrini's problems are solved on an individual basis by his take-over of a trucking business. The *film noir* style is evident throughout, particularly in the *femme fatale* stereotype, played by Ida Lupino (see *Film noir*, p. 184).

studio's embrace of a relatively radical political stance is directly related to its financial and managerial independence from outside bodies. While Warners had been forced to borrow from the banks in order to expand into exhibition and invest in sound, by 1933 the three surviving Warner brothers still owned 70 per cent of the preferred stock in their company. Consequently during the 1930s Warner Bros., along with Columbia and Universal, was not subject to direct interference from Wall Street (Buscombe, 1974, p. 53).

Within the framework of the overall capitalist economy and the specific industrial enterprise of cinema, Warner Bros. as a studio was relatively independent of the Rockefeller/Morgan banking empires and was able in the short term to produce whatever films both it and its audiences wanted. Buscombe concludes that this economic independence is not unconnected with the fact that Warner Bros. made a number of pictures which were notably to the left of other Hollywood products (Buscombe, 1974, p. 53). Certainly a considerable number of early 1930s Warner Bros. productions were explicit about their endorsement of Roosevelt and the New Deal; indeed, several of the studio's films in that period even borrowed the National Recovery Administration's Eagle insignia for their credits and employed it in the choreography of its musicals (e.g. *Footlight Parade*, 1933). Buscombe points out, for instance:

> The famous 'Forgotten Man' sequence of *Gold Diggers of 1933* (1933) derives from Roosevelt's use of the phrase in one of his speeches . . . Pictures like *I Am a Fugitive from a Chain Gang*, *Black Legion*, *Heroes for Sale*, *Black Fury*, *A Modern Hero*, *20,000 Years in Sing Sing*, *They Won't Forget*, and *Confessions of a Nazi Spy* to mention only the best known, all testify to the vaguely and uncertainly radical yearnings which the studio shared with the New Deal. (Buscombe, 1974, p. 54)

Warners' social conscience may also be seen at work in the studio's productions of the Second World War; indeed, Buscombe has argued that Warner Bros. was the first Hollywood studio to throw its whole weight behind government policy on the war. In place of Warners' earlier social criticism (which had to be dropped for the duration to maintain morale) came a crudely patriotic affirmation of the American way of life and an attack on pacifism, isolationism and, of course, Nazism (e.g. *Sergeant York*, 1941).

Warners and authorship

In 1944, Warner Bros. released *To Have and Have Not*, a film which may be read as a typical example of a Warners' wartime film with its implicit anti-isolation argument. But at the same time, it was directed by one of the studio's contract directors, Howard Hawks, who subsequently came to be regarded as an important *auteur* in his own right (see Howard Hawks. p. 295). Interestingly enough, in the light of the tendency for the concept of studio style to dominate in discussions of Warner Bros. films, Robin Wood has attempted to sort out the various contributing strands of the film, which he describes as 'a Hollywood genre movie (species: "adventures in exotic location") clearly conceived (by the studio at least) as a starring vehicle for Bogart, adapted from a novel by Hemingway, scripted by William Faulkner and Jules Furthman, and specifically indebted to at least two previous movies (*Morocco* and *Casablanca*) and perhaps a third (*Across the Pacific*) . . .' (Wood, 1973).

While Wood isolates the studio as itself a 'contributor', he is wary of crediting it with more than a minor role. Thus while acknowledging, for example, that the lighting in *To Have and Have Not* is easily identifiable as Warners' style, Wood adds that the overall style is also 'the perfect visual expression of the essential Hawksian view'. At the same time, however, he argues that the film is marked not only by its studio provenance but also by its kinship with a certain genre: *film noir*. If this is the case, then *To Have and Have Not* encapsulates some of the tensions between authorship and studio style.

Similar problems arise when the work of another of Warners' contract directors, Raoul Walsh, is looked at in terms of authorship (see The evacuation of the author: Raoul Walsh, p. 292). Given the way in which production was organised at Warner Bros., once Walsh became a contract director he was obliged to work with contract crews and casts within the studio hierarchy, on projects that could capitalise both on recent financially successful formulae and also on the inclination and aptitudes of the rest of the contract staff. Discussing *The Roaring Twenties* and *They Drive by Night* Buscombe suggests:

> These films are typical of the studio for which they were made; to such an extent that one must call into question the simple notion of Walsh as an *auteur* who directed the style and content of his pictures. Firstly, in working for Warner Bros., Walsh was obliged to use the stars which the studio had under contract. So, *The Roaring Twenties* had Bogart and Cagney, *They Drive by Night* Bogart and George Raft . . . One can't say exactly that Walsh was forced to make gangster pictures because he had to use these stars, for they weren't the only ones available on the Warner lot. But stars and genre were, particularly at Warners, mutually reinforcing. Because the studio had Bogart, Cagney and the rest under contract they made a lot of gangster pictures; and because they made a lot of gangster pictures they had stars like this under contract. (Buscombe, 1974, p. 59)

Apart from the determining effects on Walsh's work of stars and genres, however, the character of the films' production units may also be of some importance. Thus the 'social content' of *The Roaring Twenties* (1939) and *They Drive by Night* (1940) might have something to do with the sociology of the studio's personnel:

> Mark Hellinger, who produced *The Roaring Twenties*, was a Broadway reporter in the 20s and 30s, covering New York crime stories. Jerry Wald, who helped write *The Roaring Twenties* and *They Drive by Night*, came from Brooklyn and worked with Walter Winchell on *The Graphic* in New York. Robert Rossen, who co-wrote *The Roaring Twenties*, came from the East Side in New York, where his early experiences turned him to the left politically. (Buscombe, 1974, p. 60)

Selected Reading

Edward Buscombe, 'Walsh and Warner Bros', in Phil Hardy (ed.), *Raoul Walsh*, Edinburgh Film Festival, 1974.

Nick Roddick, *A New Deal in Entertainment: Warner Brothers in the 1930s*, London, BFI, 1983.

COLUMBIA PICTURES

Introduction: Columbia's populism

Columbia, one of the 'Little Three' majors, began in 1920 as a Poverty Row company, CBC, named after the initials of its three founders, Harry Cohn, Joe Brandt and Jack Cohn. In 1924, the company was renamed Columbia Pictures, and by the end of the decade had acquired a production studio of its own and was already operating a national distribution network. In 1932 Joe Brandt was bought out by the Cohn brothers and his place on the voting trust taken by Attilio Giannini, an unorthodox banker who was also a supporter of President Roosevelt's New Deal, anathema to the Wall Street establishment. Harry Cohn replaced Brandt as president of the company – becoming the only movie mogul to be simultaneously president, production head and principal shareholder of a studio. In his role as production head, Cohn instituted the hitherto unknown practice of shooting film scenes out of sequence to ensure maximum economy, and in general, the company operated under rigid cost controls.

Throughout the 1930s, Columbia, like United Artists and Universal, supplied the cinemas owned by the 'Big Five' (MGM, Fox, Warner Bros., RKO and Paramount) with low-budget supporting features for double bills, with running times of only seventy minutes or so, few – if any – stars, and little or no prestigious production values. Around 70 per cent of Columbia's annual output of fifty to sixty pictures were in fact in this B-category. Columbia's continued solvency during the early 1930s, when so many other studios went bankrupt, is partly to be explained by the fact that the company was not itself encumbered by empty film theatres, while at the same time it enjoyed access to cinemas owned by the larger majors.

Columbia, like Warner Bros., is often regarded as an exponent of New Deal-type populism, evidenced in particular in the films of the studio's sole *auteur*, Frank Capra. Columbia's populism is perhaps explicable partly in terms of the company's history – its Poverty Row origins and its backing by the maverick banker Giannini – and by the fact that exactly half of the Hollywood Ten were actually employed at Columbia during the 1930s (Buscombe, 1975, p. 78; the Hollywood Ten was a group of radical directors and screenwriters who were imprisoned in the early 1950s for alleged communist subversion of the industry). Although it is clearly impossible to determine whether or not there was any deliberate policy of favouritism at Columbia towards the New Deal or left causes, it is perhaps significant that screenwriter Garson Kanin and actress Judy Holliday, both of whom worked at Columbia in the 1940s, were listed as 'subversives' in 'Red Channels', a compilation of 'radical names' by supporters in the film industry of the House Un-American Activities Committee. Indeed, *Born Yesterday* (1950), based on a play by Kanin and starring Holliday was extensively picketed on its release by the association of Catholic War Veterans (Cogley, in Balio, 1976). Although it seems unlikely that there was a concerted communist effort at the studio, its economic structure and encouragement of 'freelancers' might well have facilitated the employment of radicals where the more careful vetting of employees by studios with large numbers of long-term contracts might not.

Capra and populism

Although the bulk of Columbia's productions during the 1930s were low-budget B-features, the studio occasionally invested in more expensive films. One such was the comedy *It Happened One Night* (1934), directed by Frank Capra. This film was enormously successful, won Columbia its first Oscars, and led the company to supplement its B-feature productions with more prestigious films. After *It Happened One Night*, Capra signed a six-film contract with Columbia at $100,000 per film plus 25 per cent of profits, and was given increasingly larger production budgets. In 1936 Capra directed *Mr Deeds Goes to Town*, which examines the unacceptable face of capitalism (in the form of anti-New Dealers) and portrays its hero as a charitable tycoon, lending out his wealth to dispossessed farmers to give them a fresh start.

Capra – Columbia's *auteur* – at work with the cast of *You Can't Take it With You*

The success of Capra's films has been such that the director and the company are often equated, which has tended in fact to reduce studies of the studio to studies of Capra as an *auteur*. It may be argued, however, that Capra's films and the populism which characterises them might be related not simply to Capra's personal 'vision' or to the director being 'in touch' with America, but also to the economic and ideological structures of Columbia itself (see Early structuralist film analysis: Frank Capra, p. 285).

Stars at Columbia

> Though Columbia had contract players of its own (for example Jack Holt, Ralph Bellamy or, in westerns, Buck Jones and Charles Starrett), they could not compare in box-office appeal with the stars of bigger studios. Columbia could not afford the budgets which bigger stars would have entailed. On the other hand it could never break into the big-time without them. Harry Cohn's solution to this vicious circle was to invite successful directors from other studios to make occasional pictures for Columbia, pictures which would have stars borrowed from other studios. Careful planning permitted short production schedules and kept costs down to what Columbia could afford . . . Thus a number of big-name directors came to work at Columbia during the later 1930s, often tempted by the offer of being allowed to produce their own films. (Buscombe, 1975, p. 80)

One of Columbia's 'more expensive productions', with 'bigger stars' and a 'big name producer–director' was Howard Hawks's *His Girl Friday* (1939) starring Cary Grant and Rosalind Russell with Ralph Bellamy in a supporting role. Grant, like Gable in *It Happened One Night* and Cooper in *Mr Deeds Goes to Town*, was a star from outside the studio. It was in fact a not uncommon practice in the industry to rent the stars of one studio to another. The lending studio generally received about 75 per cent more than the star's salary to compensate for its temporary loss. The borrowing studio enjoyed the advantage of the star's services without incurring the cost of a long-term contract. Perhaps something of the appeal of those Columbia films which combined its own contract players with outside stars was exactly the pleasure of seeing familiar faces in unfamiliar settings. Cary Grant, for instance, without the costume and décor with which he was associated at Paramount. Columbia's practice of bringing in outside stars (and also directors and writers) for large-budget productions would, of course, tend to militate against any deliberate or unitary political stance (for instance, on the New Deal) within the studio or its productions.

While most of Columbia's contract performers were character actors like Ralph Bellamy, the studio occasionally succeeded in signing up a little-known actor or actress before he or she became too expensive, 'grooming' him or her for stardom itself. By the end of the 1930s the policy of bringing in outside stars and directors and paying them percentages was proving an important part of Columbia's economic strategy, and certain stars (such as Cary Grant) returned to Columbia again and again. However, one thing the studio lacked in comparison with the other majors was a star it could claim to have created and developed for itself. By 1937, Columbia had only one female star under contract, Jean Arthur: but Arthur's resistance to publicity and her allegedly 'unglamorous' image encouraged Columbia to invest in another. Rita Hayworth, a little-known Fox employee, provided Columbia

Rita Hayworth . . . 'the fourth most valuable property in the business' . . . in *Gilda*

with its opportunity, and she was signed for a seven-year contract. She was at first restricted to Columbia's B-features, cast in a succession of cheap musicals and melodramas, but after 1941 played a number of singing and dancing roles opposite Fred Astaire, Gene Kelly and other borrowed stars. By the mid-1940s Hayworth was established, in Cohn's words, as 'the fourth most valuable property in the business' (quoted in Kobal, 1977, p. 198).

With the release of *Gilda* in 1946 Rita Hayworth became a household name: the film was a massive success at the box office, making $3 million for Columbia on its initial release. It may be argued that the combination of the Hayworth *femme fatale* and musical personas, and the combination of genres – the bleakness of *film noir* with the décor and choreography of the musical – permitted publicity for the film to be widely spread – from pin-ups in magazines to recordings of Hayworth's (albeit dubbed-over) songs on the radio.

Columbia and the decline of the studio system

The industry-wide recession that followed the antitrust legislation in 1946 was due not only to the dismantling of the vertically integrated structures of the 'Big Five', however, but also to the rise of television, the effects of the anti-communist scare within the film industry, and probably changing social trends in general. Columbia, not having been fully vertically integrated during the period of oligopoly (see The studios, p. 000), was in a relatively good position to survive the recession, since after divorcement they found the theatres more open to their product than before. But survival also depended on the studio's ability to differentiate its product from its rivals – who were no longer only the other studios, but television as well.

One of several strategies Columbia embarked upon in the face of fierce competition from television in the early 1950s was the adaptation of established successes, either from the bestsellers lists or from Broadway hits. *Born Yesterday* (1950) is an example of the latter policy, and Columbia paid a million dollars for the rights to Garson Kanin's play, as well as contracting Judy Holliday, its original star, to repeat her role as Billie Dawn. By this time, while the majors were being forced to reduce their assets, selling off theatres and making contract players, technicians and other employees redundant, Columbia had assembled a stable (albeit modest) of contract actors which could be economically drawn upon (as William Holden and Broderick

Mr Deeds Goes to Town (USA 1936 *p.c* – Columbia; *d* – Frank Capra; sd b/w)

Gary Cooper stars as Mr Deeds, a simple man from the backwoods who goes to New York after inheriting a fortune. The end of the film illustrates the way in which the narrative is resolved in favour of populism, validating Deeds as a hero whose qualities of innate goodness and common sense mark him off from 'the enemy': the patronising intellectuals who are isolated from the common people. Buscombe (1975) has suggested that this populism was characteristic of Columbia's output at this time. However, the ending seems to parody itself, raising the question of whether the apparent project of the film to validate populist ideology can be taken seriously (see Early structuralist film analysis: Frank Capra, p. 285).

The Big Heat (USA 1953 *p.c* – Columbia; *d* – Fritz Lang; sd b/w)

The film deals with the violence and sadism of a gang of racketeers, and their effect on a policeman who pursues the gang in a relentless quest to avenge his wife's death. The police series was a popular form on television at that time, and this was probably an attempt to capitalise on that success while providing something more sensational than TV could offer; hence the excessive brutality. It has been argued (Flinn, 1974) that *The Big Heat* owes more to studio style than to either *film noir* genre conventions or the authorship of Fritz Lang (see Fritz Lang, p. 241).

The Man from Laramie (USA 1955 *p.c* – Columbia; *d* – Anthony Mann; sd col. scope)

A revenge western starring James Stewart. During the 1950s cinema capitalised on its potential for spectacle as it began to lose its audiences to the new medium of television. The westerns, such as this one, offered the possibility of panoramic views in widescreen and colour, location shooting rather than studio sets, and sensationally violent content, none of which TV could match (see The western, p. 147).

Crawford were for *Born Yesterday*, relatively inexpensively to offset other expenditures such as, in this case, on the screenplay). *Born Yesterday* turned out to be the top box-office draw of the year for Columbia and earned the studio an estimated $4 million as well as winning Judy Holliday an Academy Award.

Columbia and television

While expensive adaptations of Broadway successes and bestsellers form obvious examples of the studio's attempts to sell its products, Columbia was also the first of the eight majors to enter television production. Unable to afford excursions into widescreen, or Cinerama, Columbia chose around 1950 to invest some of its still very limited resources in the formation of a television subsidiary, Screen Gems (the first of the majors to follow Columbia's lead, Warners Bros., did not act until 1955). Thus Columbia, more than any of its competitors, was able to produce films which both related to, and also to some extent differed from, contemporary trends in television drama. For instance, when *The Big Heat* (1953) was released, a police series, *Dragnet*, was at the top of the American television ratings: Columbia was quick to exploit the trend. The violence and eccentricity of the characters in *The Big Heat*, however, illustrate how Columbia combined its exploitation of trends in television with a differentiated content. This proved a particularly important strategy for Columbia in the wake of the relaxation of censorship in the film industry after 1951.

By the mid-50s, with television becoming increasingly popular and cinema attendance dropping, the need to differentiate cinema product from the filmed television episodes that Hollywood was itself beginning to pro duce had become increasingly urgent. Two 1955 Columbia releases reveal how the studio attempted to weather the crisis. Both films were made in Technicolor and CinemaScope – technologies obviously unavailable to small-screen, black-and-white television transmitters – and boasted the kind of production values that television could not hope to afford. In 1955, the first western television series made by one of the Hollywood majors – Warner Bros.' *Cheyenne* – appeared on the American networks. Screen Gems was not slow to follow suit, while Columbia's film division produced *The Man from Laramie*, one of their relatively rare A-feature westerns. The film's use not only of colour, widescreen and location cinematography, but also its violence, differentiated it successfully from its small-screen competitors.

Columbia 'rents' big-name stars – Cary Grant and Rosalind Russell in *His Girl Friday*

Selected Reading

Edward Buscombe, 'Notes on Columbia Pictures Corporation, 1926–41', *Screen* 16(3), autumn 1975.

John Cogley, 'The mass hearings', in Tino Balio (ed.), *The American Film Industry*, Madison, University of Wisconsin Press, 1976.

20TH CENTURY–FOX

Introduction: The Fox Film Corporation

The Fox Film Corporation, which was founded in 1914, took its first steps towards 'major' status in 1925 when William Fox, the owner of the company, embarked on an ambitious programme of expansion, investing in a sound process and acquiring chains of film theatres. In 1927 Fox controlled, very briefly, the production studios of Fox and MGM, Loew's and Fox's theatre chains, one third of First National and other assorted holdings. This ambitious industrial programme was paralleled by attempts to enhance the prestige of Fox productions and the company made a number of 'specials', often adapted from Broadway hits and bestsellers. Two such blockbusters, *7th Heaven* (1927) and *What Price Glory* (1926), both of them big-budget adaptations of plays, had been successful at the box office, and Fox needed further major successes of this kind in order to offset excessive outlays incurred from production budgets and acquisitions of real estate.

This is the context within which Murnau's *Sunrise* (1927) was produced. Indeed it has been argued that *Sunrise* should be seen exactly as,

> an integral part of one of the most carefully orchestrated and ambitious bids for power and prestige in the history of the American cinema, and in large measure *Sunrise*'s historical significance is to be found in its relation to other Fox films that were equally part of William Fox's truly grandiose scheme to control the movie industry. (Allen, 1977, p. 237)

The film cost more than $1.5 million to make and included one of the largest sets ever constructed in the history of the cinema, a section of a city, complete with elevated trains and streetcars, constructed over an area a mile long and half a mile wide on the Fox studio lot (Lipkin, 1977).

By the end of the 1920s, however, William Fox had dangerously overstretched the company with big-budget productions of this kind, as well as by his ambitions for expanding. In 1930 he was ousted from the board and in the following year the Fox Film Corporation made a loss of more than $5

My Sister Eileen (USA 1955 *p.c* – Columbia; *d* – Richard Quine; sd col.)

An example of cinema's exploitation of its potential for spectacle in its attempt to win back audiences from the new medium of television. The film's dance numbers indicate some of the ways in which choreographer Bob Fosse's distinctive style meshed with cinema's need to differentiate itself from TV's small screen.

The Lineup (USA 1958 *p.c* – Columbia; *d* – Don Siegel; sd b/w)

A Columbia film with origins more specifically in the small screen, *The Lineup* was a spin-off from a television series. Don Siegel, who had directed the pilot episode of the television version, was hired to direct the film, which was made in black-and-white with a cast of relative unknowns. In this case the difference between the source (the TV series) and the spin-off was that the former had focused on the police while the latter concentrated on the gangsters: television at this time would certainly have prohibited such a focus. Siegel's film exploits this relative licence accorded the cinema by including scenes of some violence (see Expressive esoterica: Don Siegel, p. 257).

Anatomy of a Murder (USA 1959 *p.c* – Columbia; *d* – Otto Preminger; sd b/w)

Anatomy of a Murder also exploits restrictions placed on the content of television programmes, dealing in this instance with the subject of rape with a certain amount of frankness. Preminger had already made a number of films independently (released through United Artists) and successfully outmanoeuvred the declining censorship powers of the Production Code Administration, even releasing some of them without the PCA seal of approval (see Censorship, p. 7). The director's record in this respect may well have attracted Columbia to this film, since it was the only studio never to register with the PCA. Preminger, moreover, had a reputation for bringing in films under budget (see Otto Preminger, p. 271).

million. In 1933 a combination of reduced receipts and increasing overheads forced Fox to place its theatres into receivership: in 1934 the company with two studios and a comprehensive national distribution network valued at $36 million had an annual earning power of only $1.8 million. Meanwhile Darryl F. Zanuck, former production head at Warner Bros. had set up a small independent unit without studio space of its own, 20th Century Pictures. In 1935 the Fox Film Corporation announced a merger with 20th Century: henceforth, with Zanuck as head of production, the company would be known as 20th Century–Fox.

The Littlest Rebel – 'black characters . . . geared towards southern "taste" '

20th Century–Fox and its stars

When Zanuck took over production at 20th Century–Fox, the studio possessed two highly valuable assets, Will Rogers and the 7-year-old Shirley Temple. Charles Eckert has suggested that Temple was an asset to the Fox studios in that they held a monopoly on her star image, and were able to use that monopoly to control the distributors' choice of films. According to Eckert, the enormous commercial success of Shirley Temple's films – including, for example, *The Littlest Rebel* (1935) – has to do, in part, with their expression of a New Deal 'ideology of charity' (Eckert, 1974).

Even more successful than Temple however, in 20th Century–Fox's first year at least, was Will Rogers. Darryl F. Zanuck himself regarded a Rogers vehicle *Thanks a Million* (1935) as the film that made 20th Century–Fox. By 1936, moreover, Zanuck was already expanding 20th Century–Fox's small stable of stars with performers like Tyrone Power and Sonja Henie. But Zanuck's small stable of talent could not compete with the likes of MGM or Warners and so he made his screenplays his stars. The studio's success during this period, then, is perhaps not attributable solely to the success of its players.

Politics and the studio

20th Century–Fox's increasing commercial success during the latter half of the 1930s is commonly attributed on the one hand to the appeal of certain stars contracted to the studio and on the other to the fact that its films expressed a characteristic and attractive political philosophy, which Charles Eckert characterises as 'opportunist':

> When one takes into account Fox's financial difficulties in 1934, its resurgence with Shirley Temple and its merger with Twentieth Century under the guidance of Rockefeller banking interests, one feels that the least that should be anticipated is a lackeying to the same interests that dominated Hoover and Roosevelt. (Eckert, 1974, p. 18)

In other words the 'line' taken up in 20th Century–Fox's productions of the later 1930s was basically pro-Republican. It has been suggested, for example, that the 1939 Fox production *Young Mr Lincoln* constitutes a Republican offensive against the New Deal (see *Cahiers du cinéma*'s 'John Ford', p. 301).

Fox's political 'opportunism' may not, however, be quite as straightforward as this argument would suggest. How, for example, is *The Grapes of Wrath* (1940) to be explained? The production of *The Grapes of Wrath* was made possible when in May 1939 Zanuck acquired the rights to Steinbeck's novel for an unprecedented $70,000 – the third largest amount ever paid for such rights in film history up to that time. In the 1938/39 financial year 20th Century–Fox was the third most successful studio in Hollywood (after MGM and Warners) and two of their 1938/39 releases reached the top ten box-office grossers list. This success prompted a decision by Fox executives to produce more A-pictures – including *The Grapes of Wrath* (see John Ford, p. 303).

Rebecca Pulliam argues that the film represents, in fact, not a Republican but a Roosevelt/Democratic/New Deal perspective and explains this with reference to Zanuck's experiences in the early 1930s at Warner Bros. As at Warners, Zanuck's primary interest and influence was on the screenplay.

> The screenplay for *The Grapes of Wrath* was contractually bound to preserve the theme of Steinbeck's book. Zanuck stated his impression of the book's theme as '. . . a stirring indictment of conditions which I think are a disgrace and ought to be remedied'. Left-wing groups feared that he had bought the book to shelve it and see that it was never filmed. The large California growers were strongly against its production and threatened Zanuck with legal suits. The studio believed that the film might never be released in California. (Pulliam, 1971, p. 3)

Zanuck hired a private investigating firm to authenticate the novel's assertions and, having satisfied himself, refused to be thwarted by the Hays Office: 'If they . . . interfere with this picture I'm going to take full-page ads in the papers and print our correspondence.' *The Grapes of Wrath* took seven weeks and cost $800,000. At its preview the first three rows of seats were reserved for executives of the Chase National Bank, the financial backer of 20th Century–Fox – and also, ironically, one of the institutions which controlled the land companies responsible for forcing the dispossessed farmers portrayed in *The Grapes of Wrath* from their land. Although the film did well commercially, it was not a massive box-office success. But it was perhaps more important to 20th Century–Fox that the company won from it the prestige and acclaim that had eluded it during the 1930s: *The Grapes of Wrath* won two Oscars. The film may therefore be regarded as marking the company's move from the economic security associated with earlier pro-Republican vehicles to the aesthetic prestige associated with its productions of the 1940s.

20th Century–Fox and the decline of the studio system

In the immediate postwar years 20th Century–Fox embarked on a series of 'serious', 'realistic' crime films employing semi-documentary devices and often including newsreel footage of the kind Fox had made famous with their *March of Time* newsreels (see Warner Bros., p. 19). *The House on 92nd Street* (1945), for instance, includes just such a sequence: the film was

Sunrise (USA 1927 *p.c* – Fox Film Corporation; *d* – F. W. Murnau; st b/w)

This production is noted for its use of location shooting and for bringing a European sensibility to a Hollywood film. A real village was constructed on a lake for the early scenes between husband and wife. The trolley-ride to the city, too, shows the trouble the studio went to, by using deep-focus and long takes to indicate continuity and authenticity, to present the scene as realistically as possible. The demands of realism make an interesting contrast with the 'expressionist' techniques characteristic of Murnau's style in his early films.

The Littlest Rebel (USA 1936 *p.c* – 20th Century–Fox; *d* – David Butler; sd b/w)

It has been argued that the Southern box-office was of paramount importance to Hollywood in the 1930s, and that the depiction of black characters had to be geared towards Southern 'taste' to ensure the film's success. Films, such as *The Littlest Rebel*, romanticise the South of the Civil War. They play up paternalistic notions of chivalry and gracious living, into which blacks are accommodated as loyal family retainers or Uncle Tom figures, or by offering comic relief. Shirley Temple's star persona (one of the studio's hottest properties at that time) meshes with this appeal to an audience of white liberals, and, indeed, detracts from the presentation of the racial issues of the Civil War by supporting nostalgic *ante bellum* myths of the South.

The Grapes of Wrath (USA 1940 *p.c* – 20th Century–Fox; *d* – John Ford; sd b/w)

Based on John Steinbeck's novel about the dust-bowl migration of the 1930s, the film is a fine example of Ford's treatment of populist ideology and the family. Displaying stunning black and white photography, Henry Fonda stars as Tom Joad who leads his family away from poverty to the promise of a new life in California. This film raises the question of the director's contribution to the ideological meaning of the film in relation to changes in studio policy during the 1930s and 1940s (see John Ford, p. 300).

Populist ideology and the family – Ford's *The Grapes of Wrath*

Cry of the City (USA 1948 *p.c* – 20th Century–Fox; *d* – Robert Siodmak; sd b/w)

Cry of the City is about a gangster on the run who is pursued by a policeman (Victor Mature). It combines a documentary style with the characteristics of *film noir* - a technique which was adopted by the studio in the 1940s when it began to produce bleak urban thrillers and to move to cheaper location shooting rather than studio shooting.

The Gunfighter (USA 1950 *p.c* – 20th Century–Fox, *d* – Henry King; sd b/w)

A western much admired by Robert Warshow for its combination of greater realism with traditional western themes. The film marks a change in the depiction of the Western hero in its story of a weary itinerant gunman (Gregory Peck), target for every small-time sharpshooter, and wanting to settle down.

Broken Arrow (USA 1950 *p.c* – 20th Century–Fox; *d* – Delmer Daves; sd col.)

As well as the stylistic and aesthetic changes brought about by Fox's move to economise during the 1950s, *Broken Arrow* indicates a shift in the conventions of the western genre towards a sympathetic understanding of the American Indian as operating within the codes of his own culture. This can be seen in the character of Cochise (Jeff Chandler) who befriends James Stewart's US army scout (see: The western, p. 147).

produced by Louis De Rochemont who had, in fact, launched and supervised the *March of Time* series. In 1948 20th Century–Fox followed the De Rochemont documentary style thrillers with *Cry of the City* which combined the latter's grittiness with the characteristics of the contemporary *film noir*. More important, perhaps, than either style or subject matter in these bleak urban thrillers was Fox's decisive move to location shooting which prepared the studio for the westerns, musicals and spectaculars which were to follow the antitrust decision, and the advent of competition from the small screen and 'live' studio drama.

In the wake of the 1948 antitrust decision, declining audiences, and increasing competition from television, Fox's first response was to reduce production budgets. In 1947 the average cost of a full-length Fox feature was about $2,400,000; by 1952 films were regularly being produced at less than half that amount, since location shooting actually proved cheaper than studio shooting. Both *Broken Arrow* (1950) and *The Gunfighter* (1950) illustrate such economies. They serve at the same time to illustrate the ways in which the end of vertical integration in the film industry affected not only the studios but also stars and genres, in that both films concern the activities of ageing western stereotypes – the 'veteran scout' and the 'retired gunfighter' (see The western, p. 147).

In 1952 Fox finally signed the Consent Decree agreeing to divorce its exhibition chain from its production/distribution apparatus in accordance with antitrust laws. The company could no longer guarantee the screening of its films simply by controlling first-run theatres. Moreover, by the early 1950s the celebrated 'social realism' of Fox's crime genre was hard to distinguish from innumerable television crime series such as *Dragnet*. The company's response was to employ bigger, brighter stars – like Marlon Brando (*Viva Zapata!*, 1952), Marilyn Monroe (*River of No Return*, 1954, and *The Seven Year Itch*, 1955), Jane Russell (*The Revolt of Mamie Stover*, 1956), Monroe and Russell together (*Gentlemen Prefer Blondes*, 1953), and specifically cinematic technologies – colour and CinemaScope (*Carmen Jones*, 1954), Technicolor and CinemaScope

(*River of No Return*, 1954). *The Seven Year Itch*, in fact, employs an explicit send-up of television in the 'dumb blonde' character of advertising model Marilyn Monroe, who makes her living by modelling for an advertising company in toothpaste commercials.

Selected Reading

Robert C. Allen, 'William Fox presents *Sunrise*', *Quarterly Review of Film Studies* 2(3), August 1977.

Rebecca Pulliam, 'The Grapes of Wrath', *The Velvet Light Trap* no. 2, August 1971.

Tony Thomas and Aubrey Solomon, *The Films of 20th Century–Fox: A Pictorial History*, Secaucus, NJ, Citadel Press, 1979.

RKO RADIO PICTURES

Introduction

RKO, a creation of the Rockefeller-backed Radio Corporation of America (RCA), was formed at the beginning of the era of sound in cinema. RCA had patented its own sound-on-film system – Photophone – in conjunction with its radio subsidiary NBC. In response to Warner Bros.' experiments with sound, RCA acquired its own theatre circuit, Keith-Albee-Orpheum, and a film production company, FBO. Together these groups formed the new company RKO Radio Pictures. The studio's earliest productions, were, predictably enough, dominated by dialogue-heavy comedies and musicals.

Although the company enjoyed modest financial success in its first few years of operation, the directors were not completely satisfied, and so in order to increase production capacity and distribution outlets, Pathé, with its 60-acre studio, was purchased, and in 1931 David O. Selznick immediately instituted 'unit production', a system whereby independent producers were contracted to make a specific number of films for RKO entirely free from studio supervision, with costs shared by the studio and the producer, and distribution guaranteed by RKO. Despite a series of administrative reorganisations and policy changes within the company in subsequent years, RKO's most famous pictures – including *King Kong* (1933) and *Citizen Kane* (1941) – were nearly all produced in this way.

Selznick was also partially responsible for the construction of the Radio City Music Hall, the world's largest motion-picture house. It was felt that exhibition at Radio City would secure solid New York openings for RKO films. But this strategy proved extremely expensive, and by the end of 1932 Selznick was gone and RKO had made a net loss in that year of more than $10 million. Selznick's replacement was Merian C. Cooper, who had been acting as Selznick's adviser on evaluating future projects. One of the first films they had agreed upon had been *King Kong* (1933). After much opposition from the studio's New York office, the film was made (at a cost of more than $650,000) and finally opened at Radio City and the Roxy. In four days it had grossed $89,931. It was the perfect film for RKO's Radio City Music Hall – for which it made a great deal of money and publicity. In 1930 RKO had announced its own inauguration as 'The Radio Titan' with full-page advertisements in the trade press, and *King Kong*, too, was launched with a massive wave of publicity.

The year of *King Kong*'s release, 1933, also saw the first teaming of Fred Astaire and Ginger Rogers in the film *Flying Down to Rio*. Almost immediately Astaire and Rogers became RKO's biggest stars of the decade. It is significant that as musical stars they were eminently exploitable on radio. In *The Gay Divorcee* (1934) and *Top Hat* (1935) the two stars epitomise the sophisticated musical comedy tradition that RKO had made its own, combining leisurely playboy and/or heiress plots with spectacular big white sets in art deco styles especially appropriate for the ornate decor of Radio City Music Hall and RKO's first-run theatres.

After 1937, when George Schaefer became production head at RKO, some of Selznick's ideas – including unit production – were revived. Schaefer claimed that he

The 6,200-seat Radio City Music Hall – the world's largest motion-picture house

intended to concentrate the studio's energy on the production of a few big features in the hope that they would prove to be big moneymakers as well. Thus prestige productions, often produced and directed by independents, were encouraged (for example *Bringing Up Baby*, 1938, directed by Howard Hawks), and RKO continued its musical comedy traditions with films like *Dance, Girl, Dance* (1940), also by an outside director, Dorothy Arzner (see p. 309; see also Howard Hawks, p. 295).

But the most famous production at RKO under Schaefer's supervision is undoubtedly *Citizen Kane* (1941). There can, perhaps, be no better test case of the importance of industrial determinants than *Citizen Kane*. Pauline Kael has devoted a book to the film, most of which is concerned with deciding between Orson Welles, the director, and Herman J. Mankiewicz, its screenwriter, as the film's *auteurs* (see Orson Welles, p. 250). Kael's starting point, however, is her insistence that *Citizen Kane* was not an ordinary assignment, and she goes on to argue:

> It is one of the few films ever made inside a major studio in the United States in freedom – not merely in freedom from interference but in freedom from the routine methods of experienced directors. George J. Schaefer, who, with the help of Nelson Rockefeller, had become president of RKO late in 1938, when it was struggling to avert bankruptcy, needed a miracle to save the company, and after the national uproar over Orson Welles's *The War of the Worlds* broadcast, Rockefeller apparently thought that Welles – the wonder boy – might come up with one, and urged Schaefer to get him. (Kael, 1971, pp. 1–2)

Shooting on the film officially began in July 1940 and was completed in October: a twelve-week shooting schedule and a budget of $700,000 were at this period extraordinarily low for RKO prestige productions. Before *Citizen Kane* opened, Schaefer was summoned to New York by Nicholas Schenck, the president of the board of Loew's Inc., the MGM parent company that controlled the distribution of MGM pictures, and offered $842,000 if he would destroy the negative and all the prints. The reason for the offer was the well-founded suspicion that Welles and Mankiewicz had modelled the characters of Kane and Susan Alexander on the publisher William Randolph Hearst and the actress Marion Davies. Kael quotes from the trade press of the time: 'The industry could ill afford to be made the object of counter-attack by the Hearst newspapers' (Kael, 1971, pp. 3–4). When Schaefer refused Mayer's offer, the Hearst press launched a tirade of front-page denunciations of RKO and its employees, while banning all publicity of RKO pictures. RKO's usual theatrical showcase – the Radio City Music Hall – retracted its offer to screen *Citizen Kane*, and other first-run cinemas proved equally reluctant. Eventually, Warner Bros. opened the film – Schaefer was by this time threatening to sue the majors on a charge of conspiracy – but it was too late and the film was rapidly withdrawn from circulation to be reissued only in the late 1950s on the art-cinema circuit.

Although Kael's analysis is of the authorial contributions of Welles and Mankiewicz, she does emphasise how different the whole feeling of *Kane* would be if it had been made at MGM instead of at RKO, and discusses the collaborative work that went into the film:

> Most big-studio movies were made in such a restrictive way that the crews were hostile and bored and the atmosphere was oppressive. The worst aspect of the factory system was that almost everyone worked beneath his capacity. Working on *Kane*, in an atmosphere of freedom, the designers and technicians came forth with ideas they'd been bottling up for years; they were all in on the creative process . . . *Citizen Kane* is not a great work that suddenly burst out of a young prodigy's head. It is a superb example of collaboration. (Kael, 1971, p. 62)

By 1942, with heavy losses, prestige again began to be seen as a less urgent priority than profits, and Charles Koerner was appointed under the slogan 'showmanship instead of genius'. Double features and low budgets became the new rule. After Koerner's death in 1946, Dore Schary was appointed his successor. Schary in his turn attempted to revive certain practices of the Selznick period, and once more RKO went upmarket, co-producing a number of films with independent production companies like Goldwyn (*The Best Years of Our Lives*, 1946), Liberty (*It's a Wonderful Life*, 1947), International Pictures (*The Stranger*, 1946), and John Ford's argosy (*Fort Apache*, 1948, *She Wore a Yellow Ribbon*, 1949 and *Wagon Master*, 1950).

In 1948 Howard Hughes acquired a controlling interest in RKO for just under $9 million, and within a matter of weeks Schary, together with 150 other RKO employees, had been sacked. In 1949 RKO signed a Consent Decree agreeing to divorce its exhibition arm from its production–distribution apparatus, in accordance with the Supreme Court's antitrust decision. In 1955 the company was sold to General Teleradio, a television production company; the RKO Hollywood studios had been acquired by Desilu in 1953.

RKO and studio style

Unlike MGM with its lavish family melodramas and musicals, or Warner Bros. with its gangster films, or Universal with its horror films, RKO is rarely associated with any specific style or genre: indeed, it is often suggested that RKO is an example of a studio without a style:

> One problem was that no movie mogul had ever attached himself to RKO's banner – as did Louis B. Mayer at MGM, Harry Cohn at Columbia, and Darryl F. Zanuck at 20th Century–Fox . . . RKO's ownership was for the most part anonymous – just like the movies it put out. Today a large audience remember the famous RKO productions, but few associate them with RKO. Its roster of stars are still household names – Katharine Hepburn, Ingrid Bergman, Fred Astaire, Robert Mitchum and Cary Grant – but in time there would be other studios with which they would become more closely identified. Even the famous films, *Citizen Kane*, the Fred Astaire musicals, *The Informer*, Val Lewton horror shows, *King Kong* and *Gunga Din* – give RKO no recognisable image: the range of styles was so large, so miscellaneous, and RKO's interest in sustaining any single style or genre (with the exception of the Astaire musicals) so short-lived, that the movies blur rather than blend together. (Merritt, 1973, pp. 7–8)

One of the reasons for RKO's lack of any identifiable 'brand image' may be not so much the fact that the company lacked its own 'moguls' as the very number of such men who attached themselves to the studio, reversing its production policies and stylistic commitments so often that no overall house style ever had the opportunity to become established.

RKO and genre: the *film noir* cycle

Although the number and diversity of the executive regimes at RKO obviously inhibited the development of an easily recognisable studio style, the studio nevertheless did sustain one genre over a period of several years during the middle and late 1940s: the 'low-key' *film noir* (see *Film noir*, p. 184). Ron Haver associates the development of this genre at RKO with the work there of writers Daniel Mainwaring, John Paxton and Charles Schnee, and directors Nicholas Ray, Jacques Tourneur and Edward Dmytryk (Haver, 1977).

At the same time, by 1944 Charles Koerner's emphasis on low-budget, atmospheric thrillers had almost entirely replaced George Schaefer's prestige pictures and musical comedies. RKO made $5 million net in 1944, and the *film noir* became a formula product for the studio until the end of the decade. These films featured players like Robert Mitchum and Robert Ryan, Jane Greer and Audrey Totter – all of them popular but none of them quite ranking with the stars of RKO's rival studios. In 1947, however, RKO's brief period of postwar profitability

King Kong – grossed $89,931 in four days

was punctured by losses of $1,800,000, but the studio's commitment to low-budget, low-key film-making continued.

As long as the popularity of the genre continued, losses could be attributed, at least in part, not to overspending but to declining audiences. The year 1946 was, after all, the peak box-office year in the history of the American film industry; at the end of the war it had to face competition from television and alternative leisure activities.

RKO's B-pictures

As well as the 'prestige' films produced under its various regimes, RKO also usually had a production programme of B-pictures – low-budget movies designed as second features on double bills. If the B-production units were economically restricted, they did have a degree of aesthetic and ideological independence from the front office that prestige pictures were often denied. An interesting case in point is provided by the films made under the aegis of Val Lewton, *Cat People* (1943) in particular. By 1942 it had become obvious that the Schaefer 'prestige' policy was not paying dividends at the box office. In 1940 the studio had lost almost half a million dollars and by 1942 had sunk $2 million in debt. The Atlas Corporation's Floyd B. Odlum bought shares from RCA and Rockefeller until he had acquired a controlling interest in RKO. Schaefer was fired and the more businesslike Ned Depinet replaced him as head of RKO. In 1942, Depinet's vice president in charge of production, Charles Koerner, set up a number of B-units at the studio, and Val Lewton was assigned to head one of them. Lewton's contract stipulated that he was to produce only horror films, that budgets were not to exceed $150,000, that shooting schedules were not to exceed three weeks and that running times were to average about seventy minutes. Within these limits, however, Lewton had relative freedom: he was able to select and contract a stable core of creative personnel, functioning as an independent production unit in much the same way as the units producing prestige pictures in the Selznick era. Editors (and later directors) Mark Robson and Robert Wise, scriptwriter DeWitt Bodeen, secretary Jessie Ponitz, cinematographer Nicholas Musuraca, art directors Albert D'Agostino and Walter Keller, and director Jacques Tourneur all worked together for several years in this way.

Budgetary restraint coupled with generic convention encouraged Lewton's unit to economise on labour and lighting costs by employing low-key effects. Furthermore, studio-wide set budgets, imposed by the War Production Board, limited expenditure on sets to $10,000 per picture, which meant that where possible existing sets were redressed rather than new sets being built. The unit's first production, *Cat People*, was completed in three weeks at a cost of $134,000, and on its initial release grossed more than $3 million, saving RKO from a second bankruptcy in a year of several big box-office disasters, which included *The Magnificent Ambersons.*

Selected Reading

Ron Haver, 'The mighty show machine', *American Film* 3(2), November 1977.

Russell Merritt, 'RKO Radio: the little studio that couldn't', *Marquee Theatre*, University of Wisconsin, Madison, 1972.

Budgetary restraint and low-key effects – Val Lewton's *Cat People*

King Kong (USA 1933 *p.c* – RKO Radio; *d* – Ernest B. Schoedsack/Merian C. Cooper; sd b/w)

A classic monster movie which at the time was considered remarkable for its trick photography. The climactic moment when King Kong wreaks havoc in New York, capturing Fay Wray and climbing the Empire State Building, provides a good example of the ambitious special effects on which the studio were banking to make the film a success.

Dance, Girl, Dance (USA 1940 *p.c* – RKO Radio; *d* – Dorothy Arzner; sd b/w)

An example of RKO's investment in the women's picture, that is, films featuring strong female protagonists, directed mainly at a female audience, offering a critical perspective on male values from a female point of view. Generally a despised or underrated genre, at least critically, the women's pictures of the 1930s and 1940s were nevertheless box-office successes, featuring popular stars, and obviously thought of as 'bankable' by the studios.

The Magnificent Ambersons (USA 1942 *p.c* – RKO Radio; *d* – Orson Welles; sd b/w)

Russell Merritt has usefully described the industrial atmosphere of this film's production and is cautious about privileging Welles's role as genius–victim as so many film histories have done. Instead, he situates it in a moment midway between the ousted 'prestige policy' and unit production system of Schaefer, and the economics and 'showmanship' of Koerner (Merritt, 1973, p. 18).

Arzner's *Dance Girl Dance* – an example of RKO's investment in the women's picture

UNIVERSAL

Introduction

Universal was a relatively minor studio, one of the 'Little Three' companies (the others being Columbia and United Artists) which lacked their own theatres and depended for exhibition outlets on the cinema circuits of the 'Big Five' (Warner Bros., RKO, Fox, Paramount and MGM), the vertically integrated majors. The company established itself in the 1920s under the ownership of Carl Laemmle and adapted its studio to sound production relatively early: by 1930, all of its releases were 'talkies'. However, by this time the recession which affected the entire film industry had forced Universal to re-examine its approach to film production. Laemmle decided to make fewer pictures, but 'of the highest excellence that the resources of Universal City could achieve' (quoted in Pendo, 1975, p. 155).

In 1930 Carl Laemmle jun. who had been put in charge of the studio by his father, began a series of horror films, which became Universal's speciality in the early 1930s, with the production of *Dracula* and *Frankenstein*. In the first few years of the decade, however, the effects of the Depression made themselves felt particularly keenly at Universal, the studio's output decreased substantially, and during an industry-wide strike the studio actually closed down for several months. In 1931 film budgets were cut, production schedules shortened and static 'dialogue' shooting emphasised at the expense of expressionist visual styles. In 1933, despite Laemmle sen.'s ambitions, the company entered a two-year period of receivership. The studio was re-established, after some administrative reorganisation, at the end of the decade.

However, by the mid-1940s Universal was once again in economic difficulties. The studio's financial welfare was resting somewhat precariously on Deanna Durbin and

Dracula – Universal's horror output

on Abbott and Costello; their pictures, while still profitable, were not doing as well as in the past (Eyles, 1978).

Universal's response to this situation was to attempt to attract major stars to the studio by giving them a percentage of the profits from their films, and simultaneously to increase budgets, thereby attracting a number of independent producers. The company also merged its distribution activities with the independent production company, International. This reorganisation was finalised in November 1946, when it was announced that all B film units would be shut down immediately, whether in production or not. From then on, all Universal films were to be prestige pictures and absolutely no B-cheap films would be produced. What would happen, however, to B-films – rather than units – already in production? While Universal was in no position, economically, simply to abandon B-films in production, low-budget films were redundant because, with the banning of block booking, they would henceforth have to be sold individually. *The Killers* (1946) and *Brute Force* (1947), therefore, are examples of B-project given 'prestige' treatment on very slim budgets in order to attract buyers.

Universal, studio style and genre

Universal's output of the early 1930s is identifiable primarily with a single genre, horror (see The horror film, p. 194), though they did make *All Quiet on the Western Front* (1930). A consideration of Universal films of the period thus calls for an examination of the intersection of genre and studio style within a set of industrial determinants. A variety of explanations have been put forward for Universal's specialisation in

The Magnificent Ambersons was 'slashed from two hours to eighty-eight minutes so that it would fit on a double bill' (Haver, 1977, p. 30) and Koerner replaced the absent Welles and the ousted Mercury Theatre units with 'second unit crews ... and then released it on a split bill with a Lupe Velez Mexican Spitfire comedy' (Merritt, 1973, p. 20). It is important to emphasise, however, that *The Magnificent Ambersons* was never, even under Schaefer, autonomous of economic and industrial determinants. It was based on Booth Tarkington's Pulitzer prize-winning novel, starred Tim Holt, a familiar RKO western performer, and was a melodrama about the decline of the aristocracy, reminiscent of the previous year's production of *The Little Foxes* (see: Orson Welles, p. 250; William Wyler, p. 250).

Cat People (USA 1942 *p.c* – RKO Radio; *d* – Jacques Tourneur; sd b/w)

'The wreck of *The Magnificent Ambersons* may have taken as one monument to the Koerner regime; but from its ashes rose another: the famous cycle of Val Lewton's *Cat People*, sometimes actually filmed on the abandoned *Ambersons* sets' (Merritt, 1973, p. 18).

The *Ambersons* staircase, in fact, was to become a central icon in *Cat People* – re-dressed sets were considerably cheaper than purpose-built ones. And the fact of having to re-dress and disguise such sets encouraged an attention to detail often absent from more expensive production. The 'bus' sequence is a useful illustration of an extremely (cost) effective and remarkably expressionist approach to concealing economies. The use of low-key lighting, low-angle camerawork, heightened sound effects and so on – animation, shadows in the swimming pool scene, silence in the walking scene – indicate the aesthetic potential in such economic imperatives. And the minute detail with which the Lewton unit were able to invest their films bears witness to the continuity and relative cohesiveness of the low-budget unit production system.

the horror genre. Stephen Pendo, for example, argues:

> Depression audiences wanted the escapist entertainment which horror provided . . . Universal's contribution was to assemble the best and most imaginative technicians – cameramen, directors, make-up artists, set designers and special effects men available. Many of them had graduated with horror from the classic German silent film school. (Pendo, 1975, p. 161)

Thus, it is implied, Universal's output would be predisposed, because of the contributions of some of the studio's personnel, to the Expressionism characteristic of the visual style of horror movies. In Universal's case, too, the existence of certain types of stars in the studio's stable – Boris Karloff and Bela Lugosi in particular – would serve to reinforce the existing tendency to concentrate on this genre. Lugosi, for example, had played horror roles on the stage and had also appeared in silent horror films for Universal. Moreover, once horror films were identified as Universal's genre, stars of this type would tend to be employed at the studio. Furthermore, as a minor studio which needed to establish a certain kind of 'product identification' in order to sell its films to the exhibition circuits controlled by the majors, Universal particularly needed to develop a generic area of its own.

The dominance of horror films in Universal's output of the early 1930s has also been explained in terms of the transition from silent to sound cinema – that the visual style of such films enabled the move to sound to take place as economically as possible. As far as individual films are concerned, *Dracula* (1931) illustrates this argument quite well. Production on the film was begun in 1930 as part of Universal's intended move into pictures 'of the highest excellence'. The desire to make such pictures involved attempting to recapture the visual qualities of silent cinema which were considered in some quarters to be under threat from sound cinema with its temporary immobilisation of the movie camera. In *Dracula* there is consequently a great deal of mobile framing and only a minimal use of sound. The film's relative 'silence' served to increase the chilling atmosphere. There is an emphasis too on 'night' and 'outdoor' sequences with tracking shots concentrating on actors and props rather than on sets.

In *Frankenstein* (1931) the camera is considerably less mobile than in *Dracula*, and there is far more dialogue. However, *Frankenstein* compensates for lack of camera movement with use of low angle shots and Expressionist sets. But at the same time, this film was intended to be the first of a series, and is consequently less of a prestigious production than *Dracula*: 'With an eye towards sequels, the finish was reshot so that Baron Frankenstein escaped a fiery death – a fortunate change . . . *Frankenstein* was an outstanding success. This convinced Universal even more that horror pictures should henceforth be an integral part of its production schedule' (Pendo, 1975, p. 157).

Universal in the 1950s and 1960s

After the 1948 antitrust decision (see The studios, p. 11) which put an end to the industry's monopolistic practices of block booking and blind selling, Universal could no longer be guaranteed exhibition of its films, and so returned to its earlier practice of providing an easily identifiable studio style and subject matter. After the late 1940s Universal's output was dominated by several genres: thrillers like *Brute Force* (1947), *The Killers* (1946) and *Touch of Evil* (1958); melodramas like *Letter from an Unknown Woman* (1948), *All That Heaven Allows* (1955) and *Written on the Wind* (1956), and westerns such as *Winchester 73* (1950), *Bend of the River* (1951) and *The Far Country* (1954). The combination of such specialisation with reduced receipts and competition from television had a dramatic effect on the quantity of Universal's annual output. In 1950, for instance, Universal only released two major productions, *Winchester 73* and *Harvey*, both of which featured James Stewart: the studio was able to present stars like Stewart because of its offering them a percentage of the profits from its films. Such stars were central to Universal's success at this time. One of the independent directors who worked at Universal during this period was Orson Welles, whose *Touch of Evil* was released in 1958. The film was shot in 1957 after Welles had been away from Hollywood for nearly ten years. According to Joseph McBride:

> Charlton Heston agreed to appear in a Universal police melodrama, thinking that Welles had been signed to direct it, when actually he had only been signed as an actor. The studio, undaunted by Welles's pariah status in Hollywood, then asked him to direct . . . he accepted with alacrity, and received no salary as writer or director. He never read the source novel, Whit Masterson's *Badge of Evil*, but found the studio's scenario 'ridiculous' and demanded the right to write his own . . . Nonplussed by the result, the studio called it *Touch of Evil* . . . and slipped it into release without a trade showing. (McBride, 1972, p. 131)

There are, however, conflicting accounts of how Welles came to direct *Touch of Evil*:

> Newsweek reported that Welles had been offered the film as a sop for a character role he had played previously at Universal. Charlton Heston has said he suggested Welles as director after reading the film's uncompromising script . . . but producer Albert Zugsmith . . . tells still another story. According to Zugsmith, Welles had come to Universal in the late 50s in need of money to pay tax debts . . . and Welles offered to direct the 'worst' script the producer had to offer – the Paul Monash adaptation of Whit Masterson's novel, *Badge of Evil*. (Naremore, 1978, p. 177)

What is possibly most interesting about the film in relation to its studio provenance, however, is the degree to which it has been seen to depart from the Universal norm of the period. Perhaps because Welles's films tend to offer themselves up immediately to an *auterist* analysis (Orson Welles, p. 250), the marks of the studio are either ignored, or seem particularly difficult to determine, in relation to *Touch of Evil*.

Dracula (USA 1931 *p.c* – Universal; *d* – Tod Browning; sd b/w)

Frankenstein (USA 1931 *p.c* – Universal; *d* – James Whale; sd b/w)

The Killers (USA 1946 *p.c* – Universal; *d* – Robert Siodmak; sd b/w)

Brute Force (USA 1947 *p.c* – Universal; *d* – Jules Dassin; sd b/w)

Letter from an Unknown Woman (USA 1948 *p.c* – Universal; *d* – Max Ophuls; sd b/w)

The Far Country (USA 1954 *p.c* – Universal; *d* – Anthony Mann; sd col.)

All That Heaven Allows (USA 1955 *p.c* – Universal; *d* – Douglas Sirk; sd col.)

Written on the Wind (USA 1956 *p.c* – Universal; *d* – Douglas Sirk; sd col.)

Touch of Evil (USA 1958 *p.c* – Universal–International; *d* – Orson Welles; sd b/w)

The Killers (USA 1964 *p.c* – Universal; *d* – Don Siegel; sd col.)

Spartacus (USA 1959–60 *p.c* – Universal; *d* – Stanley Kubrick; sd col. scope)

Touch of Evil – big stars attracted by percentage of profits

It may, however, be significant that in 1958 Universal recorded $2 million worth of losses, and that since the mid-1950s space in the Universal studio lot had been regularly rented out to television production companies. Furthermore, while *Touch of Evil* was being made, 'trade papers were filled with rumours of sweeping changes within the Universal hierarchy, including reports that the film division would fold altogether in order to save their second arm, Decca records' (Naremore, 1978, p. 176).

Perhaps it was industrial indecision which permitted the 'ridiculous' (Welles's word) project of *Touch of Evil*? But the presence in the film of Marlene Dietrich, Dennis Weaver, Zsa Zsa Gabor, Joseph Cotten, Akim Tamiroff, Mercedes McCambridge, Janet Leigh, Charlton Heston and Welles himself may also suggest that *Touch of Evil* is a final example of Universal's ability to attract big stars by offering them a percentage of the profits from its films. Henceforth almost all Universal features were to be made with an eye toward future television scheduling.

By 1959 when Universal sold its studio lot to MCA, its westerns and melodramas were being undercut by competition from television. The studio's new owners divided film production into expensive blockbusters (e.g. *Spartacus*, 1960) on the one hand and small (often made-for-television) movies such as *The Killers* (1964) on the other.

Selected Reading

Michael G. Fitzgerald, *Universal Pictures: A Panoramic History in Words, Pictures and Filmographies*, New Rochelle, NY, Arlington House, 1977.

Joseph McBride, *Orson Welles*, London, Secker & Warburg/BFI, 1972.

Stephen Pendo, 'Universal's golden age of horror', *Films in Review* 26(3), March 1975.

STARS

THE HOLLYWOOD STAR MACHINE

Although film studies only began to address the theoretical questions raised by stars in the 1970s, the fascination of film stars for both intellectual and popular audiences goes back a long way. A report on *The Film in National Life* by the Commission on Educational and Cultural Films in 1932 observed:

> A fellow of an Oxford college no longer feels an embarrassed explanation to be necessary when he is recognised leaving a cinema. A growing number of cultivated and unaffected people enjoy going to the pictures, and frequent not merely the performances of intellectual film societies, but also the local picture house, to see, for instance, Marlene Dietrich. (p. 10)

Apart from the pleasures of looking at a Dietrich, stars have also provided a useful point of reference for intellectuals' speculations around popular culture. Thus Simone de Beauvoir (1960) has used Brigitte Bardot as a scalpel with which to dissect the anxieties of French bourgeois masculinity in the 1950s, and Norman Mailer (1973) has worked over the image of Marilyn Monroe to bolster his mythologising of the American dream.

The broad range of more popular writing about stars can seem overwhelming – from histories by journalists like Alexander Walker, to gossip, hack hagiographies and salacious muckraking. Until the mid-1970s, though, there seemed to be little inclination by film theorists to engage with the topic (see Dyer, 1979), a sign, perhaps, of the gulf between theory and popular experience, but more significantly of the difficult problems posed for the academic study of film, at whatever level, by the phenomenon of stardom. The circulation, reception and cultural currency of stars cannot be explained convincingly by exclusively textual, sociological or economic forms of analysis. More expansive conceptions of the various 'machineries' of cinema seem a step in the right direction. But in the end, as figures which (like 'Robinson Crusoe', 'Mata Hari' or 'Margaret Thatcher') condense a number of ideological themes, stars have a currency which runs beyond the institution of cinema. They require an analysis capable of explaining the resilience of these images which we pay to have haunt our minds (see Nowell-Smith, 1977, p. 12) – an account which must attend to both industrial and psychic processes.

Work has developed in two main areas. One is the very diverse body of film analysis inspired by, and contributing to feminist and gay politics. To begin with, much of this work was concerned with the appropriation of certain stars (Katharine Hepburn, Bette Davis) as figures for positive identification, as in Molly Haskell's *From Reverence to Rape* (1974); alternatively, it offered a critical diagnosis of 'stereotypes of women' or, as in Joan Mellen's *Big Bad Wolves* (1978), of male Hollywood stars as images of American patriarchy. Richard Dyer's (1979) attempt to give a firmer theoretical grounding to such concerns provoked a lively debate in which his attempt to combine sociological and semiological approaches has been challenged by critics drawing on a psychoanalytically oriented feminist theory (see Cook, 1979/80; Gledhill, 1982).

The other approach has followed the renaissance of more theoretically informed historical writing on the cinema. This has emphasised, on the one hand, the material determinants of film production and distribution (the political economy of Hollywood, court actions and patents wars, real-estate deals and zoning agreements) and, on the other hand, the constitution of the codes of classic narrative film (see deCordova, 1982; Staiger, 1983). Such work allows stars to be analysed as marketing devices for selling films and simultaneously as organising presences in cinematic fictions (see Spectatorship and audience research, p. 366).

The Hollywood system

'Mass culture', according to Roland Barthes, 'is a machine for showing desire. Here is what must interest you, it says, as if it guessed that men are incapable of finding what to desire by themselves' (Barthes, quoted in Mazzocco, 1982). What is involved, Barthes suggests, is some investment by us, the punters, which involves not conscious choice but a repertoire of unconscious processes. The object in which we make that investment is always provided for us – some would say imposed on us – by the 'machine' of culture. This machine involves not just the bricks and mortar of Hollywood studios and chains of cinemas, but also certain cultural orientations and competences (shared languages, for example, and shared conceptions of time, personality and aesthetic value) and the psychic processes whereby we enter culture and negotiate shifting, insecure positions within it.

The implications of this argument are that, in investigating the phenomenon of stardom, we are not just dealing with a person or an image with particular characteristics (talent, beauty, glamour, charisma) but with a complex set of cultural processes. The interesting question is not so much, 'what is a star?' as, 'how do stars function – within the cinema industry, within film narratives, at the level of individual fantasy and desire?' In considering their production, circulation and reception, for example, John Ellis has suggested a preliminary definition of a star as 'a performer in a particular medium whose figure enters into subsidiary forms of circulation and then feeds back into future performances' (Ellis, 1982, p. 1). This indicates that, from the film industry's perspective, the purpose of disseminating star images so widely is to draw audiences back into the cinema. Anne Friedberg takes a similar approach, but indicates some of the complexities implied by terms like *performer*, *figure* and *circulation*. 'The film star is . . . a particular commoditised human, routed through a system of signs with exchange value' (Friedberg, 1982, p. 47). The concepts of commodities, signs and exchange value suggest a model in which a homology might be established between the circulation of the star image in a circuit of exchange value which produces profit (production, distribution, exhibition) and its circulation in a circuit of semiotic use value (performance, publicity and spectatorship) which produces pleasure. Just as a commodity is defined as having both exchange value (it can be bought and sold) and use value, so the two circuits of stardom are separable only analytically. For the profit to be realised, there must be at least a promise of pleasure. Enjoyment of the star has to be paid for.

This model, based on a conventional account of the elements of the cinema industry, can be fleshed out in a number of ways. It provides a useful peg on which to hang more detailed historical studies. It can be used to organise the empirical research produced within conflicting perspectives; and it can provide a reasonably accessible focus for some of the theoretical debates. Here are some possible lines of development.

'The Biograph Girl' (Florence Lawrence) – early movie star . . . and Marilyn Monroe – 'mythologising the American dream'

Production/performance

What does a star contribute to the production of a Hollywood movie? Talent, glamour, and charisma – 'that little bit extra' – might provide the terms for one answer, but they probably indicate what has to be explained rather than explain it. Richard Dyer has suggested a model that seems to offer a more useful starting point by indicating the sort of labour done by the star (Dyer, 1979, p. 18). To begin with, there is a person who constitutes the raw material to be transformed into an image or product – hence talent schools, dialogue coaches, beauticians, dazzling blond hair, nose jobs and, in Clark Gable's case, a new set of teeth. This product is both a form of capital, owned either by the studio or the individual, and also a form of raw material which, through further labour, is incorporated into another product, the film, which is sold in a market for a profit.

What distinguishes stars from other performers is that, apart from their input of labour (their acting), their 'image' gives them an additional value. This is important in two ways. On the one hand, it can be used to attract financial backing for a film and, on the other, it provides a signal for exhibitors and audiences that this will be a particular type of film. The two aspects are closely related. Investors will only back a film that seems likely to make a profit. Hence Hollywood's task within the cinema industry has been to provide high quality product that is both predictable enough and, at the same time, novel enough to attract and satisfy audiences. This economic function of stars was certainly recognised by 1927. In that year, the Wall Street stockbrokers Halsey, Stuart and Co. made clear that stars, despite their high salaries, were an integral part of the studios' investment strategy.

> In the 'star' your producer gets not only a 'production' value in the making of his picture, but a 'trademark' value, and an 'insurance' value, which are very real and very potent in guaranteeing the sale of the product to cash customers at a profit.
> ('The motion picture industry as a basis for bond financing', 1976, p. 179)

In the earliest years of Hollywood, producers saw things differently. When films were hired out by the foot and nickelodeon audiences still paid for the novel experience of seeing pictures that moved, players remained anonymous. Most histories suggest that stars were introduced as a marketing device by independent producers trying to challenge the monopolistic stranglehold of the Patents Trust, formed by the equipment manufacturers. Janet Staiger (1983) has cast some doubt on this account, suggesting closer links to developments within the theatre. But whatever the details, it is clear that stardom, along with narrative and the classic Hollywood style, became institutionalised during the second decade of the century. It would be interesting to explore the affinities in this period between the organisation of these narratives around the position of the spectator and the psychology of novelistic character, the development of the continuity style, and the role and presentation of the star on screen (see The classic narrative system, p. 40).

Stars can also provide a useful way into an understanding of Hollywood's shifting political economy. Interesting topics from this point of view might include the crisis provoked in the 1920s by the economic power of stars like Pickford, Fairbanks and Chaplin, especially when they formed United Artists (see Balio, 1976); the unionisation of Hollywood players, from freelance stars to extras, in the Screen Actors Guild set up in 1933 during Hollywood's economic blizzard (see Ross, 1941); the contracts and work patterns imposed on their stables of stars by the oligopolistic Big Five studios from the mid-1920s until the early 1940s; the collapse of that system under pressure from antitrust suits, independent studios and newly aggressive Hollywood agents; and the bargaining power of stars in the subsequent era of packages, deals and independent production companies (see Pirie, 1981; Maltby, 1982).

What such accounts of stars as labour cannot reveal is their specific contribution to a film in terms of performance – the

JAMES CAGNEY

The Public Enemy (USA 1931 *p.c* – Warner Bros.; *d* – William Wellman; sd b/w)

This was the film that made Cagney a star and the role which provided the model for the way in which he is generally remembered (though he was only a gangster in a quarter of his films). The film emphasises two 'Cagney' characteristics, his working-class background and toughness (seen in the representation of the stockyards, beer parlours, etc.) and his brusque, dismissive attitude towards women (the film includes a now notorious scene in which Cagney thrusts a grapefruit in Mae Clark's face). It also offers an early example of the Cagney persona's relationship with his mother, which was to become explicitly neurotic in later films (e.g. *White Heat*, 1949).

G-Men (USA 1935; *p.c* – Warner Bros.; *d* – William Keighley; sd b/w)

Although in this film Cagney is seen on the 'right' side of the law for a change, the emphasis is still on his East Side background, his competence and competitiveness (the shooting gallery), his nervousness and impatience (desire for a transfer to New York), his ease with men (the card game) and unease with women (the embarrassed meeting with Margaret/Kay McCord.) The orthodox explanation for Cagney's conversion from criminal to lawman is the pressure of Hays Code censorship, but Patrick McGilligan points out that Cagney had himself begun to change his persona two years earlier (McGilligan, 1975, p. 57).

Each Dawn I Die (USA 1939 *p.c* – Warner Bros.; *d* – William Keighley; sd b/w)

The good/bad Cagney persona is crucial to the plot of *Each Dawn I Die*, in which he plays a crusading journalist wrongly imprisoned after being framed for drunken driving. He epitomises the downtrodden 'little guy' who refuses to stay down. Patrick McGilligan has described this aspect of Cagney as follows: 'He was hard times and bad luck but spit-grin-and-fight-back' (McGilligan, 1975, p. 184).

The Roaring Twenties (USA 1939 *p.c* – Warner Bros.; *d* – Raoul Walsh; sd b/w)

This film illustrates the two 'types' of gangster generally represented in the genre: the gangster by default, for whom gangsterdom is the only available means of making a living – represented by Cagney – and the psychotic gangster – represented by Humphrey Bogart (in *The Public Enemy* Cagney had incorporated both these characteristics into a single persona). Ironically, this as to be Cagney's last gangster role for more than a decade; he returned to the genre in *White Heat* (1949) as a psychotic gangster. Meanwhile Bogart dominated the roles of good/bad anti-hero protagonists throughout the 40s. The alleged tendency for stars to embody social types is discussed by Richard Dyer (1979).

HUMPHREY BOGART

The Maltese Falcon (USA 1941 *p.c* – Warner Bros.; *d* – John Huston; sd b/w)

Edgar Morin in his study *The Stars* (1960), has attempted to isolate the stars' historic significance – and significations – by attending to specific roles and genres in specific periods. Bogart, for instance, he associates with *film noir*, a genre which, he argues, 'secularised' stardom and made stereotypes increasingly ambiguous. This was an era of good/bad protagonists of which Bogart is Morin's example:

> Humphrey Bogart in *The Maltese Falcon* (1941) incarnates the new synthesis which the crime film (*film noir*) is to spread over the whole American screen. The crime film suppresses the opposition of the odious ex-gangster and the good-policeman-arbiter of justice, proposing instead a new confused and confusing type ... half good, half bad ... (Morin, 1960, pp. 25–6)

Bogart's image embodies this shift: in the 1930s, in films like *Racket Busters* (1938) and *The Roaring Twenties* (1939) he was an archetypal gangster. In the 1940s he was cast as the private eye of *The Maltese Falcon* and *The Big Sleep* (1946) and as the American interventionist hero of *Casablanca* (1942) and *To Have and Have Not* (1944). Throughout these films Bogart provided a continuity of voice, gesture, movement, costume and even world-view: the cigarette, the pulled back lip, the gravelly voice, the trenchcoat, the sentimental sarcasm. His gestural repertoire was minimal but accumulated a maximum expressiveness on the level of generic conventions: the cupping of a cigarette, the lisp, the meditative tugging of an earlobe, the squint, the grimace, the tightening of the lower lip over the teeth. The specific attributes of Bogart's persona take on different meanings (within limits) across different films suggesting that star images consist of multiple contradictory elements which can be mobilised differently according to context (see Dyer, 1979). In *The Roaring Twenties*, for instance, Bogart's George is a violent, distrustful gangster characteristic of the roles the actor often assumed in gangster films in the 1930s. These same characteristics feed into the role of Sam Spade in *The Maltese Falcon* (see the sequence in which Bogart's Spade suddenly knocks Lorre/Cairo out and neither men trust each other for all their actions to the contrary). The film also employs the earlier Bogart persona's aggressive self-confidence and relish of violence – see, for instance, Bogart's gangland boss in *Racket Busters* dedicated to taking over the Truckers Association and impervious to the attempts of the Special Prosecutor to stop him.

The characteristic Bogart persona in *To Have and Have Not*

Racket Busters (USA 1938 *p.c* – Warner Bros.; *d* – Lloyd Bacon; sd b/w)

The Roaring Twenties (USA 1939 *p.c* – Warner Bros.; *d* – Raoul Walsh; sd b/w)

They Drive By Night (USA 1940 *p.c* – Warner Bros.; *d* – Raoul Walsh; sd b/w)

High Sierra (USA 1941 *p.c* – Warner Bros.; *d* – Raoul Walsh; sd b/w)

To Have and Have Not (USA 1944 *p.c* – Warner Bros.; *d* – Howard Hawks; sd b/w)

The Treasure of the Sierra Madre (USA 1948 *p.c* – Warner Bros.; *d* – John Huston; sd b/w)

MARLENE DIETRICH

The Scarlet Empress (USA 1934 *p.c* – Paramount; *d* – Josef von Sternberg; sd b/w)

Discussing approaches to star study which see the director–star relationship as complementary, Richard Dyer summarises different versions of the Dietrich–Sternberg duality. Marjorie Rosen sees the Dietrich–Sternberg films as the 'canonization' of Dietrich 'as the von Sternberg ideal'. Claire Johnston, on the other hand, regards them as proposing a denial of the female rather then promoting a male ideal of the feminine. Sternberg dresses Dietrich in masculine clothing, a masquerade which indicates the absence of man, and simultaneously negates and recuperates that absence so that the image of the woman becomes merely the trace of her exclusion and repression. Both these views correspond to Sternberg's own statement: 'In my films Marlene is not herself. Remember that, Marlene is not Marlene. I am Marlene' (quoted in Dyer, 1979, p. 179). Molly Haskell, however, has placed Dietrich in a category of women stars who successfully resist the stereotypes they are supposed to embody. Her resplendent beauty, or 'charisma', transcends her role as a projection of male dreams, an idea echoed by Tom Flinn (Haskell, 1974). Laura Mulvey (1975) attempts to theorise the Dietrich–Sternberg relationship as projecting the voyeuristic fantasies of the male director, seeing the star figure as a formal element in those fantasies. These arguments differ as to where responsibility for producing meaning lies – with director or star. On the one hand, Dietrich is seen as an empty vehicle for Sternberg's erotic formalism, and on the other, her star charisma transcends all attempts to objectify her. Dyer suggests that it might be productive to view the films in a more complex way as revealing the tensions and contradictions in the star–director relationship (Dyer, 1979, p. 180).

Bogart's off-screen image?

Marlene Dietrich – part of the Sternberg's *mise-en-scène* in *The Scarlet Empress*

Rancho Notorious (USA 1952 *p.c* – Fidelity Pictures/RKO; *d* – Fritz Lang; sd col.)

Touch of Evil (USA 1958 *p.c* – Universal/International; *d* – Orson Welles; sd b/w)

MARLON BRANDO

A Streetcar Named Desire (USA 1951 *p.c* – Group Productions; *d* – Elia Kazan; sd b/w)

Marlon Brando is associated with two traditions: the 'rebel hero' and Method acting, this can be seen in the trunk-searching scene described by James F. Scott thus:

> In *Streetcar* Brando evidently built the part around his sense of Stanley Kowalski's animal aggressiveness. Sometimes this is innocently canine, as when his incessant scratching of back and belly remind us of a dog going after fleas. But the Kowalski character is also destructive, as we are told in Brando's use of the mouth: he chews fruit with loud crunching noises, munches up potato chips with the same relentless jaw muscles, washes beer around in his mouth and then swallows it with physically noticeable gulps. These two Brando-generated metaphors come together in the scene where Kowalski rummages through Blanche's trunk, his clawlike hands burrowing furiously and throwing velveteen dresses and fake fur back over his shoulders with fierce determination. These apparently insubstantial bits of stage business prepare us for the climactic scene in which Kowalski, having worked havoc upon Blanche's wardrobe, at last destroys the woman herself, devouring her little illusions of Southern gentility. (Scott, 1975, p. 249)

The details Scott detects in Brando's performance are clearly those of Method acting, but their connotations are also those of the rebel – 'the surly proletarian who suspects every smell of middle-class decorum'. Indeed, the casting of this film with Method-trained Brando as the proletarian Kowalski and British repertory actress Vivien Leigh as Blanche DuBois reveals the class association of different schools of acting. Brando's performance suggests an authenticity which contrasts dramatically with the apparent artificiality of Leigh's DuBois, although both styles are in fact equally mannered. Richard Dyer has suggested that Method acting, for all its claims to authenticity, reveals a sexist ideological bias since the characteristics of disturbance and anguish on which it places such value are reserved for men, while women represent the repression of those values (Dyer, 1979, p. 161).

Last Tango in Paris (Italy/France 1972 *p.c* – P.E.A. Cinematografica (Rome)/Les Artistes Associés (Paris); *d* – Bernardo Bertolucci; sd col.)

E. Ann Kaplan has criticised this film on the grounds that its star, Brando, prohibits the film from achieving that criticism of its main characters which it attempts. Kaplan describes the film's intentions as a critique of two types of film styles – 1950s American and French New Wave – which she associates respectively with 'Hemingway-tough male dominance and anguish, and chic and "modern" irresponsibility and permissiveness', and which correspond to Brando's 'methodism' and Jean-Pierre Leaud's 'modernism'. Richard Dyer summarises Kaplan's argument:

> Brando – as image (the reverberations of *A Streetcar Named Desire* and *On the Waterfront* still remaining) and as performer (the compelling interiority of the Method) is so powerful that 'it was logical for people to take Brando's consciousness for the consciousness of the film'. Since Brando's view – a hatred of 'the false middle-class way of being' which is taken out on women – becomes identified as the truth about the character and the film, the seemingly anti-sexist intentions of the latter are overturned by the (very complexly) sexist attitudes of the former. (Dyer, 1979, p. 142)

Rebel hero and method actor, Brando made up for *On the Waterfront* ... and poised animal-like in *A Streetcar Named Desire*

Dyer points out that *Last Tango in Paris* represents a specific case in which the star persona can be seen as the ultimate source of truth about a character, and cautions that character is established in multiple ways.

Viva Zapata! (USA 1952 *p.c* – 20th Century–Fox; *d* – Elia Kazan; sd b/w)

On the Waterfront (USA 1954 *p.c* – Horizon; *d* – Elia Kazan; sd b/w)

The Godfather (USA 1971 *p.c* – Alfran Productions; *d* – Francis Ford Coppola; sd col.)

JANE FONDA

Walk on the Wild Side/Barbarella (USA 1962/France/Italy 1967 *p.c* – Famous Artists/Marianne Productions (Paris)/Dino De Laurentiis (Rome); *d* – Edward Dmytryk/Roger Vadim; sd b/w and col.)

Richard Dyer takes Jane Fonda as a test case for his approach to 'rebel' stereotypes and concludes with a cautious speculation that her rebelliousness does not lie in a simple rejection of dominant values, but might better be understood 'not only in the reconciliation of radicalism and feminism with Americanness and ordinariness but also in her ability to suggest (as a tomboy) redefinitions of sexuality while at the same time overtly reasserting heterosexuality' (Dyer, 1979, p. 98).

Dyer identifies *Walk on the Wild Side* as one of Fonda's films which illustrates how crudely her sex appeal was often constructed. 'She was often photographed in a manner that vulgarised rather than beautified her body. Her bottom, in particular, was focused on – in the early scenes' (Dyer, 1979, pp. 81–3). Despite this emphasis on sexuality, the 'tomboyism' that Dyer points to is central to *Walk on the Wild Side*. Indeed, Dyer notes that all her most successful roles up until *Klute* (1971), including *Cat Ballou* (1965) and *Barbarella* (1967) were basically tomboys.

The way in which Fonda's image reconciles apparently oppositional characteristics (described by Dyer above) is

Contradictions for Fonda's star image – sexual tomboy in *Walk on the Wide Side* and middle-class radical in *Tout va bien*

integral to *Barbarella*. For Dyer, an 'indelible Americanness has been an important element in her later career, which, with its French sex films and radical politics, has in substance been the antithesis of all-Americanness' (Dyer, 1979, p. 78). *Barbarella* is perhaps the most famous of those sex films. In spite of its exploitation of 'kinky' eroticism associated with European sex cinema, Fonda was seen by many critics as retaining her all-American morality nevertheless (Dyer, 1979, p. 87).

Klute (USA 1971 *p.c* – Warner Bros.; *d* – Alan J. Pakula; sd col. scope)

Having argued that Fonda's image is organised around elements of eroticism, radicalism, all-Americanism, 'tomboyism', etc., Dyer (1979) suggests that 'not till the time of *Klute* (1971) did the elements of the image come together in a certain dynamic tension' (p. 77). Thus, for instance, Fonda's earlier 'sexy' roles (in French erotic films, deep South melodramas and so on) are simultaneously invoked and inflected in feminist terms by her performance as a prostitute in *Klute*. Dyer points out, however, that

> What is not clear is whether the role does cut free from the exploitative quality of the earlier image, or whether the latter contributes to reducing the radical potential of the character . . . It depends how the audience member reads these films, what sort of interest in or knowledge of Fonda s/he has. (p. 84)

The tension between such elements in Fonda's films in general and *Klute* in particular is negotiated by her acting skills, and she won an Oscar for her performance. She has developed the naturalistic style characteristic of contemporary American cinema and in *Klute* employs many of its devices – interrupted speech, hesitation, mumbling, tics and other techniques that give an air of improvisation to the performance (Dyer, 1979, p. 89).

Tout va bien (France/Italy 1972 *p.c* – Anouchka Films/Vicco Films (Paris)/Empire Films (Rome); *d* – Jean-Pierre Gorin, Jean-Luc Godard; sd col.)

Dyer (1979) argues that Fonda's adoption of radical politics since the late 1960s raises sharp contradictions for her star image (p. 89). The political issues are obfuscated by the overriding presence of the extraordinary star persona, a point also made by Godard and Gorin in their film *Letter to Jane* (1974). This argument suggests that the star is a sign inevitably imbued with reactionary values, and this proposition is tested in *Tout va bien*, particularly in the scene where Susan (Fonda) and Jacques (Yves Montand), both middle-class radicals, are shown doing the same work as the strikers. Dyer argues that this exploration of class issues is absent from her American 'radical' films (e.g. *Julia*, 1977, *Coming Home*, 1978) and is only possible because the Godard–Gorin film is far removed from Fonda's actual situation and public (Dyer, 1979, p. 90).

particular way they 'represent' a particular character. One approach to this question considers the clusters of connotations already associated with a star and how these create resonances for the audience watching not just Lorelei Lee but also Marilyn Monroe, not just Wyatt Earp but also Henry Fonda. Richard Dyer discusses the relationship between character and star image, pointing out that star image or persona may either 'fit' the fictional character or work to produce a disjuncture which may have ideological significance (Dyer, 1979, p. 148). Thus the star image carries powerful cultural connotations which both exceed the fictional codes of character and identification and work to bind us into the fictional world of the film. John O. Thompson (1978) has suggested that one way of understanding how these cultural connotations work in relation to specific film performances is to borrow the commutation test from linguistics where it is used to see whether or not the substitution of one unit of sound for another produces a change in meaning. Thompson considers the difference that might result from substituting a particular facial detail and also asks what would happen if one star were to be replaced with another. What would happen if Lorelei Lee in *Gentlemen Prefer Blondes* were played not by Marilyn Monroe but by, say, Jayne Mansfield or Gloria Grahame, or Wyatt Earp in *My Darling Clementine* were played not by Fonda but by John Wayne or Gary Cooper? This would enable us to separate out connotations specific to the star from those specific to the fictional character, and helps to explain the elusive and relatively unanalysed notion of 'star presence' or 'charisma'. However, there remains an argument about whether the star figure can be seen as *mediating* pre-existing social meanings, as a sociological approach would have it, or whether it works, together with other cinematic codes, to *produce* apparently coherent meaning from unstable and contradictory material (see Cook, 1979/80). It has been argued that the erotic play of the 'look' around the female star figure in classic Hollywood cinema is an integral part of the narrative drive towards closure and the reinstatement of equilibrium (Mulvey, 1975).

This argument uses psychoanalytic concepts to address the question of the fantasy relationship between spectators and film and the role of the star in that relationship (see also Cook, 1982; Friedberg, 1982). Whether the emphasis is sociological, semiotic or psychoanalytic, though, the appeal of the star cannot be understood solely in the context of production and performance.

Distribution/publicity

Although less glamorous than Hollywood production and less familiar than cinema exhibition, distribution has always been at the heart of the organisation and profitability of the film industry. This is where the star's 'trademark' value and 'insurance' value come in: they embody the distributor's promise to the exhibitor of both the audience guaranteed by the familiar presence of the star and also the novelty appeal of a new vehicle.

But more important than this trade promotion, from our point of view, is the use of stars in advertising films to the public. As we have seen, John Ellis (1982) sees stars primarily as a marketing device, as an 'invitation to cinema'. This appeal is manufactured not solely by the industry's promotional and advertising machinery, but also more diffusely through fan magazines, through feature articles, news items and reviews in the press, and so forth. All these play upon the central paradoxes of stardom: that stars are both ordinary and glamorous, both like us and unlike us, both a person and a commodity, both real and mythical, both public and intimate. These dualities seem to work in two ways. They draw us into the cinema, where we can be in the presence of a more complete (moving, talking) image of the star, an idealised image. At the same time, that performance is never somehow enough and helps to fuel again our insatiable curiosity about what the star is 'really' like – hence the cycle of fandom, gossip and scandal. This view of stardom is also fostered by Hollywood's own representations of the phenomenon most notably, perhaps, in *A Star Is Born* (see Dyer, 1982).

Exhibition/spectatorship

Consumption of a star's performance in a film has two aspects: you pay your money and you watch your film. This spectatorship is by no means a passive activity: what it involves is the most complex and hotly disputed question in the whole study of stars. Nor is it the end point of the circulation of a star, although the production-distribution-consumption model may suggest that it is. Indeed, there would be a good case for starting not with the return on capital invested in film production, but with the unquantifiable returns on our emotional investments in these pleasurable images. The pleasure derived from those moments of erotic contemplation of the spectacular figure of the star constantly threatens to spill over, to exceed the bounds of narrative which work to regulate our desires (see Mulvey, 1975). Indeed, for some spectators this excess may well overturn the delicate balance between static image and narrative flow on which classic Hollywood cinema rests. The 'management', or containment of excess, successful or not, represents one of the ways in which Hollywood cinema attempts to hold spectators in place as consumers of its product, drawing them in with the promise of fulfilment of forbidden desires played out in the safety and secrecy of a darkened chamber. And it is widely supposed that these fantasies are awakened in ways that tend to sustain existing social definitions and relations of power.

How does this work when you or I sit watching a movie in the cinema? Here there is considerably less unanimity. There are different conceptions of the relationship between narrative and spectator. Do the structure of the narrative and presentation of bodies (especially women's bodies) on the screen implicitly address a 'masculine' spectator? If so, where does that leave the women in the audience? What is involved in identifying with a star? Can star images be read in 'subversive' ways by oppressed groups, and thus appropriated in their construction of social identities? Or is the star image simply one more cue guiding the cognitive activity of the spectator (see Clarke *et al.*, 1981 and 1982; Stacey, 1993). These are just some of the questions; the debates continue (see Stars and fans, p. 371).

Studying stars

One reason for including work on stars in courses of film study has been that, as an integral part of the machinery of Hollywood, they provide an accessible way into an analysis of its political economy, the organisation of the narratives it produces, and the relationship between the two. A more problematic, often troubling aspect of studying stars is our own fascination with them, which can prove disturbing of apparently objective academic analysis. We do not fully understand these pleasures. We may think them too embarrassingly banal for academic study. Equally, we may be reluctant to put them under the microscope for fear they may dissolve or reveal a darker side we had only dimly and uneasily perceived. Not surprisingly, these hesitations can provoke resistance to what are, in any case, undeniably difficult theoretical questions. So what may appear at first glance an attractively straightforward topic turns out to be anything but. Here we are studying the disregarded processes of popular culture and our own place within them with no pat academic routines to provide a compensating sense of balance. That is what can make a study of stars so compelling. That cultivated and unaffected Oxford don back in the '30s would no doubt have been able to chat lucidly about the merits of the film being shown at the intellectual film society. He may also have been able to give some account of Hollywood as a significant fact of modern economic life. He would probably have found it more difficult to give a persuasive analysis of his fascination with Dietrich.

Selected Reading

Pam Cook, 'Star signs', *Screen* 20(3/4), winter 1979/80.

Richard Dyer, *Stars*, new edition, London, BFI, 1998.

Christine Gledhill (ed.), *Stardom – Industry of Desire*, London, Routledge, 1991.

Jackie Stacey, *Star Gazing*, London, Routledge, 1993.

Janet Staiger, 'Seeing stars', *The Velvet Light Trap* no. 20, summer 1983.

CLASSIC HOLLYWOOD NARRATIVE

In spite of the fact that the history of cinema may be approached in a variety of ways, most accounts have been dominated by a concern with cinematographic technology or by an emphasis on individual *auteurs*. Such a focus on matters strictly external to the films themselves tends to deflect attention from specific questions concerning the nature and implications of variations and developments in the 'language' of cinema. However there are historical difficulties in the way of a proper study of film language. In particular, many early films have been lost, while those remaining in existence are rarely easily accessible for viewing. Nevertheless, work in this field is increasingly being undertaken. One of the most interesting aspects of this research is its concern to trace the process through which, by the 1930s and 1940s, a highly specific mode of cinematic representation had become dominant. In the 1930s, the cultural ascendancy of narrative cinema was complete, and a particular set of cinematic codes through which film narratives were constructed and articulated was already quite firmly in place. Noël Burch (1973) has called this set of codes the Institutional Mode of Representation (IMR). The IMR could be said to consist basically of conventions of *mise-en-scène*, framing, and in particular of editing, by means of which coherent narrative space and time are set up and fictional characters individuated in ways which both engage, and are imperceptible to, the spectator.

Crucial in this process is the organisation of shots in a film according to the rules of continuity editing. Perhaps the foremost effect of continuity editing is to efface the moment of transition between shots, with the result that spectators are caught up in the film to such an extent that disbelief is suspended, and they are swept along with the story, unaware of the artifice of the means of representation. It is commonly accepted that this 'zero point of cinematic style' enjoyed its apotheosis in the Hollywood cinema of the 1930s and 1940s, the era of the 'classic' narrative system (see Bordwell and Thompson, 1979).

But all-powerful though the IMR may seem even today, its dominance is in no way historically necessary. Like all representations, the IMR exists within a particular social and historical context, and in other circumstances modes of cinematic representation might well have developed differently. The dominance of the IMR may therefore be regarded as contingent – the outcome of struggles within the cinematic institution between different modes of representation. That there is indeed nothing inevitable or final about this dominance may be demonstrated simply by pointing to the existence of many other forms of cinema. For example, narrative films made in the early years of the medium, before the IMR was fully established, look very different from narrative films of the 'classic' era. Moreover, throughout the entire history of cinema alternative approaches to cinematic representation have coexisted alongside the Institutional Mode. Avant-garde and experimental cinema, 'art' cinema and various counter-cinemas and the nexus of modes of filmic address and reception in early cinema dubbed by Tom Gunning the 'cinema of attractions' all relativise the dominance of the IMR (see Elsaesser, 1990; Gunning, 1986).

THE CLASSIC NARRATIVE SYSTEM

By the early to middle 1930s, the modes of representation now held to be characteristic of 'classic' narrative cinema were more or less consolidated and had already attained a large degree of dominance, certainly in Hollywood, but also in varying degrees in film industries elsewhere. By this time, of course, sound cinema was also established. The era of classic cinema may be regarded as a period in which the cinematic image remained largely subservient to the requirements of a specific type of narrative structure. This structure is that of the classic, sometimes also called the 'realist', narrative which calls forth certain modes of narration which are then put into effect by a limited set of cinematic codes (see The classic realist text, p. 332).

The classic narrative structure

In the classic narrative, events in the story are organised around a basic structure of enigma and resolution. At the beginning of the story, an event may take place which disrupts a pre-existing equilibrium in the fictional world. It is then the task of the narrative to resolve that disruption and set up a new equilibrium (see Barthes, 1977). The classic narrative may thus be regarded as a process whereby problems are solved so that order may be restored to the world of the fiction. But the process of the narrative – everything that takes place between the initial disruption and the final resolution – is also subject to a certain ordering. Events in the story are typically organised in a relationship of cause and effect, so that there is a logic whereby each event of the narrative is linked with the next. The classic narrative proceeds step-by-step in a more-or-less linear fashion, towards an apparently inevitable resolution. The 'realist' aspects of the classic narrative are overlaid on this basic enigma–resolution structure, and typically operate on two levels: first, through the verisimilitude of the fictional world set up by the narrative and second through the inscription of human agency within the process of the narrative.

The world of the classic narrative is governed by verisimilitude, then, rather than by documentary-style realism. The narration ensures that a fictional world, understandable and believable to the recipient of the story, is set up. Verisimilitude may be a feature of the representation of either, or preferably both, the spatial location of events in the narrative and the temporal order in which they occur. Temporal and spatial coherence are in fact preconditions of the cause-effect logic of events in the classic narrative (see Burch, 1973). In classic narrative, moreover, events are propelled forward through the agency of fictional individuals or characters. Although this is true also of other types of narrative, the specificity of the classic narrative lies in the nature of the human agency it inscribes, and also in the function of such agency within the narrative as a whole. The central agents of classic narrative are typically represented as fully rounded individuals with certain traits of personality, motivations, desires and so on. The chain of events constituting the story is then governed by the motivations and actions of these characters. An important defining feature of the classic narrative is its constitution of a central character as a 'hero', through whose actions narrative resolution is finally brought about. These actions are rendered credible largely in terms of the kind of person the hero is represented to be.

Finally, classic narrative may be defined by the high degree of closure which typically marks its resolution. The ideal classic narrative is a story with a beginning, a middle and an end (in that order), in which every one of the questions raised in the course of the story is answered by the time the narration is complete (see Barthes, 1975).

Classic codes of narrative cinema

Narratives may be communicated through various modes of expression, that is, stories can be told through a variety of media. The classic narrative is perhaps most often considered in its literary form, as a certain type of novel. However, stories may also be transmitted by word of mouth, in live theatre, on the radio, and in comic strips. Film is simply one narrative medium among many but the distinguishing features of film are its mode of production and consumption, and the specifically cinematic codes by which film narratives are constructed. Cinematic codes constitute a distinct set of expressive resources which can be drawn on for, among other things, telling stories (see Applying Saussure: the early work of Christian Metz, p. 324).

The classic narrative system would appear to make certain basic demands of these resources. First, it demands that cinematic codes function to propel the narrative from its beginning through to its resolution, keeping the story moving along. Second, it is important that in the narration of fictional events the causal link between each event be clear. Third, the narration called for would encompass the construction of a location, a credible fictional world, for the events of the story. Finally, it should be capable of constructing the individuated characters pivotal to the classic narrative, and of establishing and sustaining their agency in the narrative process.

Perhaps the foremost of the specifically cinematic codes is that of editing. Although editing is simply the juxtaposition of individual shots, this juxtaposition can take place according to a variety of principles. Editing in classic cinema works in conjunction with the basic demands of the classic narrative structure in highly circumscribed ways. First, the individual shots are ordered according to the temporal sequence of events making up the story. In this way, editing functions both to move the story along and also, through the precise juxtapositions of shots, to constitute the causal logic of narrative events (see *Stagecoach*). The specificity of classic editing lies in its capability to set up a coherent and credible fictional space, and often also to orchestrate quite complex relationships of narrative space and time.

The principles of classical editing have been codified in a set of editing techniques whose objective is to maintain an appearance of 'continuity' of space and time in the finished film; all budding film-makers have to master the rules of continuity editing. Continuity editing establishes spatial and temporal relationships between shots in such a way as to permit the spectator to 'read' a film without any conscious effort, precisely because the editing is 'invisible'. Despite the fact that every new shot constitutes a potential spatial disruption, and each gap of years, months, days and even minutes between narrated events a potential temporal disjuncture, an appearance of continuity in narrative space and time can be set up (see *Mildred Pierce*). The function of continuity editing is to 'bridge' spatial and temporal ellipses in cinematic narration, through the operation of such conventions as match on action, consistency of screen direction, and the 30° rule (see Burch, 1973). Coherence of fictional space is ensured by adherence to the

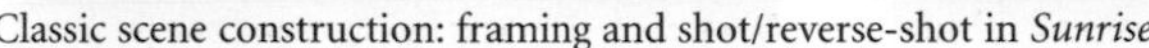

Classic scene construction: framing and shot/reverse-shot in *Sunrise*

180° rule, whereby 'the line' is never crossed in the editing of shots taken from different set-ups in a single location. Since the 180° rule, in particular, depends on the hypothesis that screen direction signified direction in three-dimensional space, the credibility of the fiction is maintained through a form of editing which signifies verisimilitude (see Bordwell and Thompson, 1979).

In the classic narrative system editing is governed by the requirements of verisimilitude, hence the characteristic pattern in any one film sequence of establishing shot, closer shots which direct the gaze of the spectator to elements of the action to be read as significant, followed by further long shots to re-establish spatial relations (see *His Girl Friday*). Since the classic narrative sets up fictional characters as primary agents of the story, it is not surprising that characters' bodies, or parts of their bodies, notably faces, figure so frequently in close shots. Close shots of this kind function also in relation to characterisation: personality traits are represented through costume, gesture, facial expression and speech (see *Klute*). At the same time, relationships between fictional protagonists are typically narrated through certain configurations of close shots, particularly those where an exchange of looks between characters is implied (see *Marnie*). Here, editing is organised on the principle of the eyeline match, according to the direction of characters' gaze. The eyeline match also governs point of view in the shot/reverse-shot figure, which in fact reached the peak of its exploitation during the 1940s, at the height of the classic era of cinema. This method of organising the looks of protagonists, through a combination of *mise-en-scène* and editing, is a crucial defining characteristic of classic narrative cinema (see Browne, 1975/76).

The conventions of classic editing constitute a particular mode of address to the spectator. In accepting a certain kind of verisimilitude in the spatial and temporal organisation of the film narrative the spectator becomes witness to a complete world, a world which seems even to exceed the bounds of the film frame. In looking at the faces of characters in close-up, and in identifying with characters in the text through taking on their implied point of view, the spectator identifies with the fictional world and its inhabitants, and so is drawn into the narration itself. Consequently, a resolution of the narrative in which all the ends are tied up is in certain ways pleasurable for the spectator.

Although classic narrative cinema moves towards the regulation of cinematic codes according to the requirements of a particular narrative structure, it is arguable that this objective can never be completely attained (see Guzzetti, 1975). Narrative and image in film are never entirely reducible to one another, if only because the demands of the classic narrative could in fact be met by a range of conventions of cinematic narration, of which the classic system is but one. Conventions, by their nature, are subject to change. Even if the classic narrative retains its dominance as a *structure*, its basic requirements could conceivably be met by *cinematic codes* different from those of classic cinema. And indeed, since the 1950s it appears that a rather wider range of cinematic codes has entered circulation in forms of cinema which still on the whole rely on a classic approach to narrative structure. This trend is exemplified by modes of narration characteristic of films on widescreen formats (see *River of No Return*) and by the recent development of a New Hollywood cinema (see *Klute*).

Selected Reading

Charles Barr, 'CinemaScope: before and after', in G. Mast and M. Cohen (eds), *Film Theory and Criticism*, New York, Oxford University Press, 1974.

David Bordwell and Kristin Thompson, *Film Art: An Introduction*, Reading, Mass., Addison-Wesley, 1979.

Noël Burch, *Theory of Film Practice*, London, Secker & Warburg, 1973.

His Girl Friday (USA 1939 *p.c* – Colombia; *d* – Howard Hawks; sd b/w)

In the opening sequence of the film the heroine Hildy and her fiancé Bruce arrive at the newspaper office where Hildy formerly worked. Hildy's ex-husband Walter, the editor, tries to persuade her to return to her old job. Shots 1 and 2 of the film function in the classic manner as establishing shots: a tracking shot moves through a busy and crowded newspaper office. A virtually invisible lap dissolve introduces shot 2, in which the space of the office is further delineated, here in a closer shot but again with mobile framing. Hildy and Bruce are introduced into this same shot as they leave the lift adjacent to the office entrance. Shot 3 is a medium two-shot of Bruce and Hildy, shots 4, 5 and 6 a shot/reverse-shot figure. The next five shots follow Hildy back through the office, re-establishing the space already introduced in shot 1, and show her entering Walter's room with a perfect match on action that moves her from one side of the door to another. This sequence demonstrates very clearly how the classic narrative system functions through cinematic codes to set up characterisation and organise a coherent narrative space (see Howard Hawks, p. 294).

Stagecoach (USA 1939 *p.c* – Walter Wanger Productions; *d* – John Ford; sd b/w)

A stagecoach carrying an assortment of characters voyages to Lordsburg with a mixed group of passengers. The final part of the journey includes a chase sequence in which the coach is attacked by American Indians. Since at this point in the narrative the character traits of the protagonists are already well established, the narration is free to focus more-or-less exclusively on action and suspense. Suspense is generated by the familiar device of crosscutting, which in this case initially functions to establish narrative space. In the first segment of the actual chase, shots of the stagecoach and the American Indians alternate, and it is only later that both groups are seen within one shot. Spectator identification with the passengers of the stage is sustained through two devices. The stage is placed first in the alternating sequence of shots in such a way that it is clear that it is the object of pursuit. Second, such point-of-view shots as are to be found in this sequence originate predominantly from the coach or its passengers rather than from the American Indians. The main burden of narration falls here on the editing, which functions almost entirely to keep the story and the action moving along. Moreover, the specific form of editing – crosscutting – also generates suspense and excitement, while sustaining the spectator's identification with the passengers of the stagecoach (see John Ford, p. 302).

Mildred Pierce (USA 1945 *p.c* – Warner Bros; *d* – Michael Curtiz; sd b/w)

Mildred Pierce is the story of a woman's rise to success and her betrayal by her daughter and husband. Mildred, at the beginning of her second flashback, talks about the success of her restaurant business. The flashback is marked as such by conventionalised framing and editing quite prevalent in films of the 1940s, and a mark of narratives involving complex temporal relations. A close-up of Mildred dissolves very slowly into a long shot of one of her restaurants, and Mildred's direct speech then becomes voice-over for the image as her face fades from the screen. The temporal ellipsis referred to in the voice-over ('In three years I built up five restaurants') is marked by a series of discontinuous shots punctuated by brief dissolves. In the classic narrative system the dissolve is a conventional signifier of passage of brief but indefinite time. The voice-over, which is sustained throughout the montage sequence, functions simultaneously to mark the sequence as subjective, told from Mildred's point of view, that is, and to bridge the substantial spatial and temporal ellipses dividing individual shots.

River of No Return (USA 1954 *p.c* – 20th Century–Fox; *d* – Otto Preminger; sd col. scope)

This film is in CinemaScope, a widescreen format which pulled the traditional screen ratio of 1: 1.33 out to 1: 2.35. The Scope image is thus relatively wide in relation to its height. In *River of No Return*, as in other Scope films, a transformation in the shape of the screen image seems to have motivated an approach to composition, editing and narration rather different from that characteristic of the classic narrative system. In particular, long takes – often involving mobile framing – predominate, and in dialogue sequences two- and three-shots are much more common than shot/reverse-shots (see Widescreen, p. 00).

These variations on the classic narrative system have been hailed as conferring a greater 'realism' (in the Bazinian sense) upon the cinematic image (see Barr, 1974). So, for example, in the scene in which Calder is seen conversing with the storekeeper, several different sets of actions are dealt with in one single long take. Calder moves over to the window, picks up a rifle for Mark and exchanges some words with the boy. He then looks out of the window, moves forward and is joined from off-screen by the storekeeper; both men look out onto the street. Here the space of the store is established not by the classic method of giving an establishing shot and subsequent shots which break down the space, but through 'composition in width' and mobile framing. The scene as a whole may serve as a demonstration of the potential which exists within the Institutional Mode of Representation for variation in the cinematic articulation of narratives which remain basically classical in structure.

Marnie (USA 1964 *p.c* – Geoffrey Stanley Inc./Universal International; *d* – Alfred Hitchcock; sd col.)

Tippi Hedren as Marnie plays a kleptomanic and sexually frigid woman who marries a rich man, Mark (Sean Connery) who attempts to 'cure' her. The scene in which Mark enters Marnie's room as she wakes up after a nightmare is constructed as a series of nine or ten alternating shot/reverse-shots. Since Marnie is not fully awake, however, and so does not see Mark, the shots of Mark are not strictly from her point of view, but those of Marnie are quite evidently from Mark's: as he moves closer to the bed, for example, the framing of the shots of Marnie contract from long shot to medium shot. In the next segment Marnie evades Mark's questions about her dream. Marnie's rival Lil passes by the bedroom door, looks into the next room and sees the book Mark has been reading: *The Sexual Aberrations of the Criminal Female.*

The extraordinarily high incidence of point-of-view shots in this scene is quite typical for a Hitchcock film. This is, of course, partly because the narratives of many of his films are actually organised around 'voyeuristic' situations. *Marnie* is no exception, and Mark's function as investigator of the enigma presented by Marnie is repeatedly condensed in the image by his gaze at her. Marnie is presented as a puzzle whose solution demands a close scrutiny, as she says to Mark: 'Stare – that's what you do' (See Mulvey, 1975).

Also in this scene optical point of view dominates the narration of a phase of an investigation. Classically, point of view functions to engage the spectator through identification with the look of a character. Here, however, identification is not simply with the character whose point of view dominates the sequence (Mark) but also, and perhaps more importantly, with the investigation which he is conducting. The solution to the enigma presented by Marnie is a necessary condition of narrative closure (see Alfred Hitchcock, p. 000).

Klute (USA 1971 *p.c* – Warner Bros.; *d* – Alan Pakula; sd col. scope)

Klute is often regarded as an example of New Hollywood cinema, a recent variant of the classic narrative system in which a certain openness or ambiguity is admitted into the cinematic narration (see Neale, 1976). *Klute* does in fact combine quite traditional elements of classic narrative cinema with a degree of openness which would certainly have been inadmissible in the classic era. The story takes off from the conventions of the classic 1940s *film noir*, in that it deals both with a mystery and the process of investigation which leads to the mystery's solution. The archetypal detective-hero is Klute, who falls in love with Bree, who herself becomes the object of the detective's enquiry.

In the first part of the film Bree is represented both as a puzzle to be solved and as an object of the gaze. Klute's face is seen in close-up, silent, bearing a penetrating look, while Bree on the other hand is twice represented as object of the gaze of an unknown, and implicitly threatening, intruder. Later, the ambiguity of the narrative is foregrounded in a scene involving Bree and her therapist, in which Bree expresses some cynicism about her relationship with Klute. This is followed by an idyllic and romantic sequence with Bree and Klute together. Because Bree's cynical therapeutic voice-over continues into this second sequence, a degree of contradiction between sound and image becomes evident.

PART 2

TECHNOLOGY

The Mask (1994)

INTRODUCTION

'The motion picture did not originate as art, but as a machine. They were invented. That is, the machinery that makes pictures, and that makes them motion pictures, was invented. Thus the term motion pictures means the device as well as the art' (A. R. Fulton, in Balio, 1976).

Cinema is one of the most technological of art forms. The result of an extraordinary confluence of disciplines in both science (chemistry, physics, engineering, optics) and the humanities (writing, painting, photography, drama), it began by explicitly foregrounding the apparatus. '[I]n the first moments of the history of cinema, it [was] the technology which [provided] the immediate interest: what [was] promoted or sold [was] the experience of the machine' (Heath in Heath and de Lauretis, 1980, p. 1). The machine was, effectively, inserted between the film and the viewer. Floor-standing Kinetoscopes or Mutoscopes which were hand-operated by patrons, or projectors which were visible to the crowd during filmshows, testify to that technological foundation of cinema. The subject of technology and film, therefore, is central to any consideration of the cinema as a cultural and historical phenomenon.

Traditional film histories ascribe most technological innovations in the cinema to a combination of individual genius and aesthetic predestination. Peter Wollen (in Heath and de Lauretis, 1980) summarises this view as seeing the history of film technology in terms of 'legendary moments' (Lumière's projector; the arrival of sound; the adoption of colour; the acceptance of widescreen). This teleological model positions technological advances as solutions to recognised aesthetic problems.

Brian Winston argues otherwise. For him, 'a technology moves from inchoate scientific knowledge (which itself is conditioned by society) to wide diffusion in society via a number of transactions' (Winston, 1996, p. 4). Therefore, within the social sphere, at a particular historical time, a certain scientific competence will exist, which creates the base potential for technological development. A transformation termed 'ideation' – the idea of the device – produces technological performances which are called prototypes. These prototypes can languish indefinitely, until external social forces produce the right circumstances to transform the prototype into invention – society must come to want or need the device. Winston terms this external social influence 'supervening social necessity'. When a new technology appears, it can promise substantial disruption to existing practices. That this potential is largely curbed, so that the technology can operate effectively in a prescribed area of usage, is termed by Winston the 'suppression of radical potential. As he argues, '[n]ew technologies are constrained and diffused only insofar as their potential for radical disruption is contained or suppressed'. Winston's theory makes society, rather than 'genius inventors', the driving force for technological development.

The development of any new film technology is, therefore, grounded in its socio-economic context. Central to this argument is that any innovation and development in film technology is market-led or, at least, is in a symbiotic relationship with the market. The audience must want what the technology can provide before it succeeds and becomes naturalised. This was the case with colour and widescreen, both of which could have been adopted by the industry in the late 1920s, but had to wait until the 1950s to have the correct social and economic conditions (including, prominently, the threat from black-and-white television) present for their acceptance. In this context, it is wrong to see technologies as self-animated. 'New technologies do not simply emerge, but by virtue of their development, the market promotes their use (sometimes to the point of insistence), creating needs which the new technologies serve to commercial advantage' (Wollen in Heath and de Lauretis, 1980). The same situation is being repeated with the emergence of multimedia and virtual reality:

> without agreement on what these systems are expected to do, there can be no mass market. This implies making an unsuspecting public familiar with a new device and persuading it not only of its merit, but of its ease of operation. In this respect, the introduction of multimedia products into the home is a 'technology driven' push, rather than a 'culturally led' pull. (Rickett in Heath and de Lauretis, 1980, pp. 80–1)

Part of this push occurs as a means of industrial self-regeneration. Commercial and industrial stasis, in anything other than the extreme short term, is perceived to be an undesirable state. Technological development should also, therefore, be seen as an important player in the game of product differentiation. Film companies invest in, and develop, new technologies partly in order to steal a march on their rivals and thereby improve (or maintain) their position of power within the industry. In this way, a differentiation–appropriation cycle is constructed, whereby companies differentiate themselves from one another by developing unique products, the features of which then become absorbed within the industry as standard practice. Such was the case of Warner Bros. championing sound technologies in the late 1920s, and Fox doing likewise for CinemaScope in the early 1950s. Integral to this trajectory is the opposition of short-term novelty to long-term industrial acceptance. 'Each new technological development – the advent of sound, colour, widescreen, and so on – can be seen, through a materialist scenario, to restore briefly the cinema's initial identity as a novelty, foregrounding the new technology in ways which disrupt the medium's carefully constructed, seamless surface of invisibility' (Belton, 1992, p. 14). This disruption continues, attracting audiences by its difference and 'newness', until its frequency and longevity normalise it within the industry and the culture. At this point, usually, a new novelty is required to rejuvenate the arena.

In addition to being offered 'externally' to audiences as novelties, new technologies are also introduced 'internally' within the industry in order to improve production efficiency. This can take two tracks: improving existing practices – effectively, doing what is already being done, but faster and better – and allowing new techniques to be developed. The latter are surprisingly few. '[T]he majority of technical developments in the film industry have been aimed at facilitating extant production practices rather than at changing the "look" or sound of commercial films' (Eidsvik, 1988 9). After the first few years of film, when most of the basic techniques had been developed, any new technology tended to improve existing techniques, rather than produce a radically new film-making tool. The latest example of this are the newly emergent digital technologies.

Each instance of technological innovation presents the industry with a number of options, variations upon the theme which the innovation generally represents. The choice of one option over another propels the trajectory promised by the innovation along a slightly different track. That is to say, significant new technologies tend to develop and/or appear during times of flux and uncertainty. Sometimes only one of these possibilities is adopted, sometimes several. An example of this would be the appearance of sound in the late 1920s, which prompted a significant debate regarding the type of sound that should be created to accompany the image track, before one option was determined upon (see Sound, p. 47). 'The road not taken is just as much a part of the cinema event as cinema itself' (Altman, 1992, p. 12).

One effect of this emphasis on specific areas of film technology is that it explicitly differentiates film from other media, such as stills photography, radio, or television. Certainly, this has been a common perspective on the history of film technology, with many commentators noting the differentiation–appropriation cycle as an important trajectory for the industry as a whole. Other writers, for example Altman (in Belton and Weis, 1985), argue otherwise, suggesting that different media have often been linked together in such ways that their identities partly blur. The adoption of any new technological development has inevitable consequences in a number of other areas within the industry. Peter Wollen describes, for example, the knock-on effect caused by the coming of sound, which necessitated changes in lighting methods (from noisy carbon to silent tungsten lamps), film stock (othochromatic was 'blind' to the red-biased tungsten lights, whereas panchromatic stock was not), and make-up (which had to be reformulated to look acceptable on panchromatic stock). No new technology either develops or becomes naturalised within the industry in isolation. It is always caught in a complex series of interrelations with other technologies. This issue of media identity takes on renewed importance when the new, computer-based, multimedia technologies are considered, in which several different media are combined in the one site.

While it might be argued that Hollywood internally generates the technological innovations it needs, the reality is that it either usually employs or, more often, simply takes advantage of, developments produced externally to itself, by 'outsiders'. 'Almost all the major technical innovations have been introduced by outsiders with the support of economic interests wishing to break into the industry . . .' (Wollen in Heath and de Lauretis, 1980, p. 19). This is certainly the case with the development of sound technology (by electronics, record and radio companies) and digital special effects (by computer specialists for advertising and industrial presentation).

Foremost amongst these alternative arenas has been that of warfare. Film has always been vital to the military for propaganda purposes. In the Second World War, some German platoons had their own film units, responsible for gathering and immediately processing information. The difficulties of filming in dangerous or physically uncomfortable locations have forced many developments in equipment design. From improvements in lighting stemming from research into the design of searchlights, through the development of lighter cameras for reconnaissance purposes, better lenses to allow filming from greater (safer) distances, to the simulation of complex wargame scenarios in virtual reality, the results of military research have always had a major input into technological development in the cinema. Many leading figures in the development of film technology began in the audio-visual sector of the military. For example, optics professor Henri Chretien's work during the First World War on the development of naval artillery telemetry helped to lay the foundations for what would become CinemaScope; André Coutant's work in developing a small film mechanism to control the telemetry of French guided missiles eventually led to the silent-running, hand-held Éclair camera; and the computer-controlled Dykstraflex camera used on the film *Star Wars* (1977) was initially developed for a pilot training system. The ever-increasing speed and complexity of modern warfare has prompted equivalent developments in film technologies simply in order to maintain the possibility of recording and representation. 'For the United States, it was becoming an urgent matter to have new information-gathering methods at its disposal. And so it was that Eastman–Kodak came up with its Mylar-based film and Dr Edwin Land of Hycon Corporation with the high-resolution camera – both of which laid the basis for regular aerial reconnaissance over the Soviet Union' (Virilio, 1989, p. 81).

Star Wars – industry and innovation

More abstractly, military technology has produced a shift from the visible and physical (face-to-face fighting in the trenches of the First World War) to the invisible and virtual (combatants represented by blips on radar screens, virtual reality (VR) simulations, 'smart' missiles directed onto targets via miniature television screens mounted on the missile itself). 'Eyesight and direct vision have gradually given way to optical or opto-electronic processes, to the most sophisticated forms of "telescopic sight"' (Virilio, 1989, p. 69). This making the real unreal, invisible, and virtual has had, and will have, a dramatic impact upon the development of media technologies both in the 1990s and into the first decades of the next century.

Developments in film technology have often been employed in the creation of illusion and magic. In the earliest years of cinema, for example, Georges Méliès used special cameras adapted to allow rewinding, to produce the multiple exposure image effects which make his films so strikingly fantastic. As often, however, the production of fantastic images has been in the service of the realist aesthetic, producing a filmic world which, although logically impossible, looks completely believable. Within these terms, the aesthetic of realism dominates the history of film technology. All major technological innovations contribute towards increasing the sense of experiencing 'real-life' when watching, and listening to, a film in the cinema. Each technical development is seen as helping to close the gap between the represented 'real-world' and its cinematic representation. Deep-focus photography, for example, in the way it presents all elements within the same frame, is seen to be an 'unmanipulated mode of cinematic representation'. Similarly, CinemaScope, it has been argued, increases the spectator's freedom to choose what to look at and when to look at it (Barr, 1974). We can find this argument repeated for each of the other major technological innovations: colour (more like 'real life' than black and white); stereo sound (we listen to the real world in stereo), and virtual reality (the represented world can actually be experientially entered and actively engaged with, via headsets and sensitised bodysuits). In the area of the modern special effects film, James Cameron, director of the *Terminator* movies, discussing the special effects used to produce the alien water creature in his film *The Abyss* (1989), has commented: '[The audience] understood intuitively what was magical about the scene. They were seeing something which was impossible, and yet looked completely photorealistic. It defied their power to explain how it was being done and

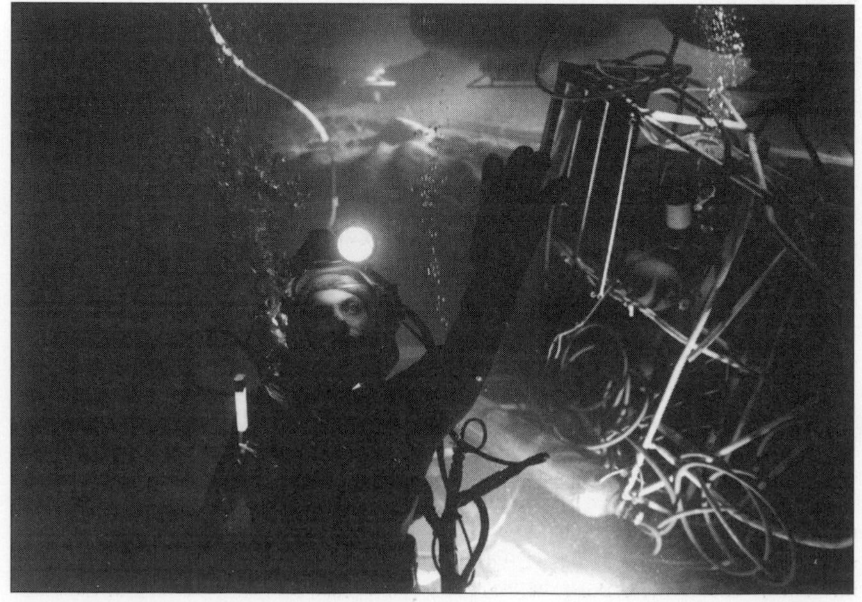
Cameron's *The Abyss* – 'photorealistic' effects

returned them to a childlike state of pure entertainment. The sufficiently advanced technology had become magic to them' (Cameron, 1992, p. 7).

It may, however, be argued to the contrary that technological transitions have often involved – initially at least – the adoption of apparently non-realist aesthetic strategies, until such time as the innovation in question has entered general cinematic currency. Edward Buscombe has suggested, for example, that both sound and colour were originally associated, in the American film industry, with that least realistic of genres, the musical (Buscombe, 1978). Indeed, rather than recognising an all-embracing trend towards realism in cinema, it seems that some kind of movement between product differentiation and the eventual appropriation of such differentiation by prevailing cinematic orthodoxy has been the model for much of cinema's aesthetic development.

The Jazz Singer – Warner Bros. proved the commercial viability of the sound movie

Selected Reading

Brian Winston, *Technologies of Seeing*, London, BFI, 1996.

Peter Wollen, 'Cinema and technology: a historical overview', in Stephen Heath and Teresa de Lauretis, *The Cinematic Apparatus*, London, Macmillan, 1980.

SOUND

The sound era of cinema is generally dated from the release of *The Jazz Singer* in 1927 – although this was neither the first sound feature nor the first 'talking' film. Attempts to give film a voice were being made from the very beginnings of cinema: Thomas Edison's main interest for encouraging his assistant W. K. L. Dickson to develop the Kinetograph was that he hoped it would complement the Edison Phonograph. In 1895 Edison introduced his Kinetophone – an adaptation of the Kinetoscope peep-hole machine with which films were viewed using a combination film-viewer and audio-playback machine (via headphones). The device was unsuccessful, due to a combination of technical problems and public disinterest (audiences were more than satisfied with the novelty of moving pictures, even if silent), although it resurfaced briefly, and again unsuccessfully, for a second time in 1913 in a screen-projected form. Gaumont also experimented with synchronised sound films over a number of years from 1901/2, with his Chronophone. Other, unsuccessful, disc-based systems were developed by George Pomerade in 1907, E. H. Armet between 1912 and 1918 and William Bristol, from 1917.

Probably the earliest and certainly the most common method of adding sound to silent films involved the placing of actors, musicians, and noise-making machines directly behind the screen. This practice was employed as late as 1915 in special road-show presentations of D. W. Griffith's *The Birth of a Nation*. Meanwhile, the most prestigious productions – which, in the 1920s, were those shown in the lavish movie palaces – had the benefit of orchestral accompaniment while even the smallest of cinemas, from the days of the nickelodeon until the advent of sound, employed improvising pianists. The unreliability of 'live' accompanists and developments in radio and electronic research together led to experimentation throughout the 1920s. More significant in the long term, however, was the development of photographing sound directly on to film, the first patent for such a process being issued as early as 1900.

The advent of sound in cinema provides an excellent illustration of the fact that technologies are not necessarily implemented as soon as they become available. The American Telephone and Telegraph Company (AT&T) and the Radio Corporation of America (RCA) both conducted experiments in sound cinema from the early years of the century, but executives in the film studios were unwilling to make changes in an already profitable industry. The major film companies were all listed on the stock exchange and in 1926 the total capital invested in the industry exceeded $1.5 billion. A move to sound would involve vast expenditure in re-equipping studios and theatres and retraining casts and crews all for a commodity for which there could hardly be said to be a demand. The film industry was thus not, for the most part, keen to move from silent to sound production.

At Warner Bros., however, the situation was somewhat different. Although by 1925 Warners had built up a relatively prosperous production company, the bulk of the audiences for their films was the clientele of small independent theatre circuits and neighbourhood film theatres, and it was becoming increasingly difficult to compete with the opulent picture palaces of the vertically integrated companies. If, however, they installed sound into their studios and theatres as a direct alternative to the pit orchestras of their rivals, they might be able to compete with them. Warners impressed investment banker Wadill Catchings of Wall Street's Goodman Sachs Company with their cost accounting and strict budgetary control, and the bank agreed to finance the company through a period of carefully planned expansion. Warners then appointed Catchings to their board of directors and purchased the ailing Vitagraph Corporation with its fifty film exchanges, a worldwide distribution system, and a Hollywood radio station equipped by Western Electric.

In April 1926, Warners and Western Electric co-founded the Vitaphone Corporation to make sound films and market sound equipment. In August of that year, Warners presented its first sound feature, *Don Juan*, together with a supporting programme of Vitaphone shorts, including recorded concerts and an address by Will Hays. At this point, the Fox Film Corporation decided to join the move to sound, and with the acquisition of their own sound system, began to produce sound newsreels under the Movietone banner. In October 1927, Warners followed its earlier success with the release of *The Jazz Singer*, although the film was more of a 'singing' than a 'talking' film, as the dialogue-only sections of the film were still conveyed via intertitles. By the following spring, all the majors were busily engaged in equipping studios for the transition to sound, and the Vitaphone system was rapidly revised. On both *Don Juan* and *The Jazz Singer* the 'soundtrack' had been recorded on discs whose playing time equalled the

The Jazz Singer (USA 1927 *p.c* – Warner Bros..; d – Alan Crosland; st + sd b/w)

The most notable aspect of the use of sound in *The Jazz Singer* is its incompleteness. Only the musical sequences and the dialogue which immediately surround them are carried by a recorded soundtrack. Elsewhere, dialogue-only sequences are conveyed by written intertitles which was the standard technique of the time. This mixture of styles creates a 'text' whereby the sound sequences, which would have already been considered novel at the time, become even more so by virtue of seeming to burst forth from the silence of the film. This 'textual violence' is echoed by the actors' performances which alternate between the overly gestural and expressive delivery of the opening and closing sequences, and the more restrained and improvisational style of the dramatic sections.

Indeed, the improvisational element of the film, partly generated by Jolson's status as a performer, is also a result of the demands of early sound production. The live recording of the sound on to disc at the same time as the scene was filmed meant that the performance had to continue even if the actors forgot their lines. There are moments in the dialogues between Jolson and his screen mother when one can sense that Jolson is keeping the 'banter' from stalling. The success of these improvised dialogues precisely depends on Jolson's talent for extemporisation; the pleasure is in seeing him 'pulling it off live', reinforced by hearing him doing so as well. It is very much Jolson's performance alone; the actress playing his mother contributes little at these moments except acquiescent giggles.

Sur les Toits de Paris (France 1930 *p.c* – Societe des Films Sonores Tobis; *d* – René Clair; sd b/w)

The Public Enemy (USA 1931 *p.c* – Warner Bros..; *d* – William Wellman; sd b/w)

The opening sequence to this film is a good illustration of the way in which the studio attempted to negotiate the transition to synchronised sound recording. The tracking shot which reveals the working-class Chicago streets has a dubbed soundtrack, while the conversation between two boys has synchronised sound, necessitating an immobile camera. Although we may experience the scene as continuous, the transition is marked by a cut which signals the difference between the two recording techniques.

The Deserter (USSR 1933 *p.c* – Mezhrabpom-Russ; *d* – Vsevolod Pudovkin; sd b/w)

Now Voyager (USA 1942 *p.c* – Warners; *d* – Irving Rapper; sd b/w)

Ben-Hur (USA 1959 *p.c* – MGM; *d* – William Wyler; sd col.)

West Side Story (USA 1961 *p.c* – Mirisch Pictures/Seven Arts; *d* – Robert Wise; sd col.)

Earthquake (USA 1974 *p.c* – Filmmakers Group/Universal Pictures; *d* – Mark Robson; sd col.)

Apocalypse Now (USA 1979 *p.c* – Omni Zoetrope; *d* – Francis Ford Coppola; sd col. scope)

Jurassic Park (USA 1993 *p.c.* – Amblin Entertainment; *d* – Steven Spielberg; sd col.)

Although critical and popular attention has concentrated on the visual special effects used to create the credibly moving dinosaurs in *Jurassic Park*, the soundtrack plays an equally important role, and won the film an Oscar for Best Sound in 1993. *Jurassic Park* was the first to feature Digital Theatre System (DTS) sound, in which the sound is recorded on to a digital compact disc and is then replayed on a CD-ROM machine that can read timecode.

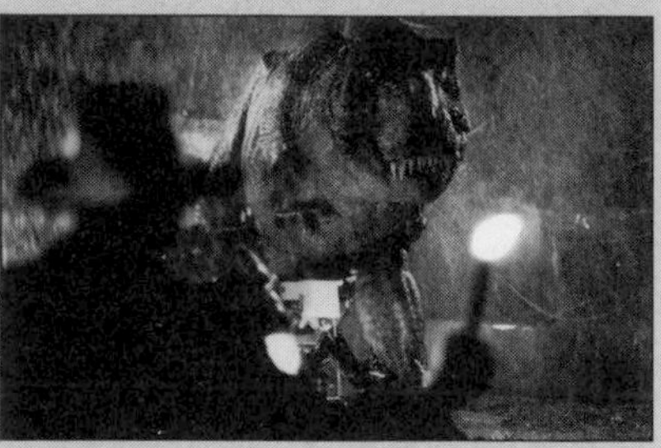

Complex sound in *Jurassic Park*

The CD quality sound is most apparent in the wide dynamic range found in *Jurassic Park*. The mining sequence near the beginning of the film, for example, displays a broad layering of sound, from industrial noises, metal hammers chipping away at rock, birds calling in the trees, and dialogue between characters. All levels of sound – from the quietest to the loudest – is equally 'present'.

In the scene in which the T-Rex attacks the truck containing two children, the soundtrack begins simply with the sound of pouring rain. This sparcity helps to build up suspense. The soundtrack is then broadened by the dull, resonant thud of the T-Rex's footsteps as they disturb the surface of a glass of water. The noises become increasingly layered as the fence wires begin to snap and its frame creaks under pressure from the dinosaur. When the dinosaur eventually attacks, the soundtrack reaches its fullest complexity: the roars of the T-Rex, the screams of the children, squelching mud, occasional snatches of dialogue, and the continual sound of pouring rain are clearly discernible from one another while simultaneously combining to form the dense body of sound which complements the visuals.

Heat (USA 1995 *p.c* – Forward pass Productions; *d* – Michael Mann; sd col.)

running time of one reel of film. Because the disc-synchronisation process was rather unreliable, it was soon replaced by sound recorded directly onto film. Douglas Gomery argues that this process is an example of an economic theory of technological innovation, which posits that production processes are introduced to increase profits in three systematic phases: invention, innovation and diffusion (Gomery, 1976).

By the end of 1930 Warner Bros. not only entirely controlled its former rival, First National, but had also boosted its own assets from $5m in 1925 to $230m. Western Electric had quickly secured contracts with all existing production companies, while AT&T's rival, RCA, responded in 1928 by creating a wholly-owned integrated company of its own, RKO, to exploit its Photophone sound system. On several occasions over the next decade, RKO threatened AT&T with antitrust action because of the latter's virtual monopoly over the sound market, but by 1943 some 60 per cent of all equipment in the industry was in fact being supplied by RKO. As has been expected, sound boosted production costs to an average $375,000 per film in 1930 as against less than $80,000 a decade earlier. The conversion to sound cost the industry an estimated $500m, and established alliances between production companies and Wall Street that were to last for many years.

The advent of sound briefly curtailed the possibilities of mobile framing only recently established in silent cinema. The new sound cameras were enclosed in soundproof booths which had to remain virtually immobile during shooting. Actors at first had to be grouped around concealed microphones. Consequently, for some time the use of close-ups was virtually abandoned as the camera was forced to keep a greater distance from the actors, and as shots became longer and cuts fewer.

Rick Altman notes that there was considerable debate in the early years of sound cinema on exactly what kind of sound should be developed to accompany the image track. This debate centred around the issue of 'sound space' – should film sound attempt to recreate the sonic landscape of real life, in which a wide number of audio elements (voices, objects, ambiance) were of equal importance, or adopt some other logic whereby certain elements were privileged over others? (Altman, 1992). In the first years of sound cinema, there was an attempt to control sound quality and balance during projection, but such systems, while theoretically producing a more realistic soundscape, were practically unfeasible, and were soon replaced by processes which controlled the sound during production. At first, multiple microphones picked up the various areas of sound which were then controlled by a mixing engineer. Central to this technique was the idea that sound level should match image size (loud for close-ups, quieter for long shots). This theory was soon found to be flawed, creating a disorienting cacophony of sound. A choice was made to use only one microphone, placed closer to the camera axis, and to maintain a constant audio level, irrespective of image framing distance. Favouring intelligibility over sonic complexity and authenticity, this process had its source in the similar sound strategies found in the dramatic theatre of the time. As such, it was dialogue-biased, and consequently narrative-biased. This process of decision-making is one instance where several options were reduced to one choice, which then became the industry standard.

Despite constant improvements in sound quality, especially at the prestige end of the market, the next decisive innovation in sound came only with the introduction, after the Second World War, of magnetic tape; a development aided by the allies capture of German technological innovations, which also included hand-held cameras and Agfacolor film stock. The great advantage of magnetic tape recording was that, unlike photographic sound which had to be chemically developed, it could be replayed immediately. The result was a greater flexibility, and greater security, in film production. 'However, every move forward has a tendency to mark a step back. Sound editors complained that, with the new-fangled magnetic sound, it was no longer possible to see the actual optical sound modulation on the track. This tended to make sound editing more difficult. (Today, with audio post-production work stations using digital sound, this facility is once again available)' (Aymes, 1990, p. 3).

Later, stereophonic sound accompanied the widescreen movies of the 1950s, although only after a power struggle between Fox and Paramount. Fox initially insisted that any theatre equipping itself for CinemaScope would also have to install stereo sound equipment. However, after resistance from theatres who could not afford installation costs, and threatening progress by Paramount who were developing an alternative widescreen system, Fox relented, and supplied their films with a variety of soundtracks. During the 1960s, Quadrophonic, Sensurround and Dolby sound were developed as a result of the acquisition of film companies by multiple-media conglomerates, who could draft technical expertise and innovations over from other sections of their media empires (most notably, the music industry).

In the early 1980s, a new sound system was developed that further redefined the experience of sound in the cinema auditorium: THX, a sound system developed by George Lucas and Tom Holman in the early 1980s, premièred as a demonstration trailer before Lucas's *The Return of the Jedi* in 1983. (The name is an amalgam of Lucas's first film – *THX1138* – and, slightly tortuously, an extrapolation of Tom Holman eXperiment). THX produces a 'stable sound, extremely well defined in high frequencies, powerful in volume, with superb dynamic contrasts, and also, despite its strength and the probably large theatre space, a sound that does not seem very reverberant at all. One finds in THX theatres the realisation of the modern ideal of a great "dry strength"' (Chion, 1994). The result is that, even in the largest of auditoriums, the spectator has the feeling of receiving a sound meant only for them: 'The big THX theatres no longer give us a collective sound in the old style: it's inflated personal stereo sound' (Chion, 1994). A rival system, DTS (Digital Theatre Systems) premièred in 1993 with the release of *Jurassic Park*. In a curious echo of Vitaphone's sound-on-disc, the soundtrack is provided on separate CDs, synchronised to the film via timecode. In the event of a technical fault on the CD player, the system automatically switches over to a traditional analogue soundtrack running alongside the filmstrip itself.

Digital technologies of the 1980s and 1990s, imported from the music industry, have further altered the status of film sound. Chion notes that the difference both Dolby and digital sound technologies have made to modern recording techniques is that more ambient noise can be included on the soundtrack. Early sound systems were not sophisticated enough to allow the adequate and equal separation of voice, noise and music. Voice was therefore priviledged, for reasons outlined earlier, and the other two components subordinated, with noise coming off worst. Modern systems allow complex layers of all three to co-exist on the same soundtrack. The result is a heightened realism, in which the film's world is more fully drawn. In some sense, therefore, we are returning to the soundscape model jettisoned in the earliest years of sound.

Although virtual reality's 'heightened realism' is often described in terms which privilege the visual over the aural, in fact, the role of sound in the virtual reality environment is a vital part of the toolkit for developers, being used to further distract the user's attention from the non-virtual world, and, thereby, solidify the technology's 'authority over the observer'. Digital reverb units such as the Quantec Room Simulator and the Roland Sound Space Processor, allow engineers both to simulate the sound of prescribed spaces (types of room, qualities of texture) and to localise sound within a 360° horizontal, and a limited vertical, location. The general aim is to produce a 3-D audio to match the 3-D visuals of the virtual reality environment, to dismantle the sense of audio as a 'surface' projected from stereo speakers, by creating, instead, the sensation that it is 'all around', and that it moves with the user as they change their physical position in space (see Jones, 1993).

Selected Reading

Rick Altman, *Sound Theory, Sound Practice*, New York, Routledge, 1992.

Michael Chion, *L'Audio Vision*, Paris, Editions Nathan, 1990; trans. *Audio-vision*, New York, Columbia University Press, 1994.

COLOUR

As with sound, colour was one of the aesthetic options available to film-makers from the earliest years of cinema and, as with sound, the technical problems involved in making colour films were sufficiently daunting to dissuade many practitioners from exploring its potentials for some time after its initial development. But unlike sound, which was adopted fairly quickly when social conditions made it an attractive option in the late 1920s, colour lay largely dormant for almost three decades before being fully accepted by the industry. This was due in large part to social and economic circumstances outside the control of the film industry itself.

The earliest films were hand coloured, frame by frame. As films increased in length, and the number of prints soared, hand colouring became increasingly less practicable. As a solution, Pathé Frères patented Pathecolor, a semi-automated device for stencilling prints according to simple colour correspondences, as one can see in *Ali Baba et ses Quarante Voleurs* (1902), for example, where the colour of Ali Baba's yellow and red costume maintains a fair registration with his body as he moves across the screen. (The modern method of colourising black-

and-white films via computer technology, in some ways repeats both the process and the 'block-colour' effect of hand colouring, albeit in a hi-tech way.) At the same time in America, less expensive tinting and toning processes converted black-and-white images to colour chemically. By the time of the transition to sound, this process was a long-standing tradition for the more prestigious productions. However, as soon as the sound-on-disc device was replaced by the recording of sound directly on film, the practice of tinting and toning was threatened because it became evident that the process affected the quality of the optical soundtrack (the dye used to stain the filmstrip also went over the soundtrack area, distorting the optical information). To combat the problem, Kodak immediately introduced a range of seventeen Sonochrome positive stocks whose soundtrack areas were not affected by the dyeing process. In spite of this, however, it was eventually decided that post-production conversion of black-and-white images to colour was less sensible than actually filming with colour stock.

The principle of colour photography had been introduced in the 1850s and demonstrated in 1861 by the Scottish physicist James Clerk Maxwell. The cinematic process that first successfully employed those principles – Kinemacolour – which had been patented in 1906 and first began to appear in public film shows in 1909, employed a standard Bioscope projector fitted with a shutter of red and green filters rotating at 32 frames per second, and was a considerable commercial success. Nevertheless such 'additive' colour processes had several drawbacks, and were soon superseded by other two-colour methods, such as Kodachrome (introduced for stills photography in 1913, and adopted for movies in 1916), a 'subtractive' process in which colour images were formed directly on the celluloid rather than indirectly on the screen. In the mid-1920s Technicolor developed a two-colour process, in which two filmstrips – one red-, and the other green-biased – were pasted together to produce a composite print, but the limited effects and the various technical limitations, including the double thickness of the filmstrip and the high light levels required during filming to obtain a bright enough final image, hardly justified their expense. In 1932 it was replaced by Technicolor's superior 'tri-pack' three-colour format, in which a beam-splitting mechanism simultaneously exposed a blue/red 'bi-pack' and a separate green-biased negative. Technicolor was able to capitalise on the coming of sound by offering a process that had no adverse effect on the optical soundtrack. By means of combining superior print quality with patent control, Technicolor continued to dominate the American colour movie market for three decades.

At first, the two-colour process proved insufficiently attractive to the majors to induce them to experiment with it, and so Technicolor began to produce shorts of its own and also to provide MGM and Warner Bros. with Technicolor supervisors when the two companies began their own series of colour shorts and introduced short colour sequences into primarily black-and-white films. Finally, in 1929, Warner Bros. released two 'all-colour, all talking' features – *On With the Show* and *Gold Diggers of Broadway*, the first results of a twenty-feature contract Jack Warner had signed

The Black Pirate (USA 1926 *p.c* – Elton Corporation; *d* – Albert Parker; st two-strip Technicolor)

The Adventures of Robin Hood (USA 1938 *p.c* – Warner Bros.; *d* – Michael Curtiz; sd col.)

Wizard of Oz (USA 1939 *p.c* – Loew's Incorporated/MGM; *d* – Victor Fleming; sd b/w and col.)

She Wore a Yellow Ribbon (USA, 1948 *p.c* – Argosy Pictures Corp.; *d* – John Ford; sd col.)

She Wore a Yellow Ribbon is, in many respects, a perfect film for the Technicolor process. Its subject matter – the attempts of a Union cavalry troop to maintain peace in American Indian territory – allows an art design which covers the range of primary colours, especially in the cavalry's uniforms (blue with yellow trouser stripes and epaulettes) the American flag (predominantly red) and the surrounding landscape (blue sky, ochre and red sand). More subtlely, the various pastel shades of the women's dresses, and the many different muted colours of the American Indian costumes, all display Technicolor's wider, more sensitively hued, palette range. The colour, generally, is soft, more so in the night scenes when colour definition is lost and takes on a murky brown quality.

In the scene where Sergeant Quincannon (Victor McLaglen) picks a fight with several soldiers in order to be sent to jail, the colour contrast between interior and exterior areas is emphasised by the constant movement between the two as the soldiers are thrown out of, and run back into, the bar. The basic uniforms, the more brightly coloured underclothes, and the strong sunlight outside, all confirm the ability of the Technicolor system to reproduce faithfully the required colour tones and hues, whether in direct or artificial light.

The Technicolor consultant for the film, Natalie Kalmus, acted as consultant for many of the most famous and significant Technicolor features, for example, *Mystery of the Wax Museum* (1933), *The Adventures of Robin Hood* (1938), *Wizard of Oz* (1939) and *Meet Me In St Louis* (1944).

Under Capricorn (USA 1949 *p.c* – Transatlantic Pictures; *d* – Alfred Hitchcock; sd col.)

Rancho Notorious (USA 1952 *p.c* – Fidelity Pictures/RKO Radio; *d* – Fritz Lang; sd col.)

Shane (USA 1952 *p.c* – Paramount; *d* – George Stevens; sd col.)

Gentlemen Prefer Blondes (USA 1953 *p.c* – 20th Century–Fox; *d* – Howard Hawks; sd col.)

Carmen Jones (USA 1954 *p.c* – 20th Century–Fox; *d* – Otto Preminger; sd col.)

Written on the Wind (USA 1956 *p.c* – Universal–International; *d* – Douglas Sirk; sd col.)

Sergeant Rutledge (USA 1960 *p.c* – John Ford/Warner Bros.; *d* – John Ford; sd col.)

Marnie (USA 1964 *p.c* – Geoffrey Stanley Inc/Universal–International; *d* – Alfred Hitchcock; sd col.)

The St Valentine's Day Massacre (USA 1967 *p.c* – Los Altos/20th Altos/20th Century–Fox; *d* – Roger Corman; sd col.)

Sweet Charity (USA 1968 *p.c* – Universal; *d* – Bob Fosse; sd col.)

Easy Rider (USA 1969 *p.c* – Pando Company; *d* – Dennis Hopper; sd col.)

Dirty Harry (USA 1971 *p.c* – Warner Bros./Malpaso; *d* – Donald Siegel; sd col.)

Klute (USA 1971 *p.c* – Warner Bros.; *d* – Alan J. Pakula; sd col. scope)

Shaft (USA 1971 *p.c* – MGM/ Shaft Productions; *d* – Gordon Parks; sd col.)

Two-Lane Blacktop (USA 1972 *p.c* – Universal/Michael Laughlin Enterprises; *d* – Monte Hellman; sd col.)

Blue Velvet (USA 1986 *p.c* – De Lauretiis Entertainment Group; *d* – David Lynch; sd col.)

with Technicolor. At the beginning of the new decade, when the industry began to feel the effects of the Depression, the majors, unable to withdraw from their commitment to sound, chose instead to reduce their interest in colour cinematography, and the musical – the genre with which colour had been most closely associated – was briefly considered to be 'box-office poison'. Undaunted, Technicolor invested a further $180,000 in their three-colour process, and instead of entering the market themselves, offered exclusive contracts to two independent production companies – Walt Disney and Pioneer Films. Disney acquired exclusive rights for colour cartoons and released a series of 'Silly Symphonies' which won critical acclaim, Academy Awards and massive box-office returns. Meanwhile Pioneer, after experimenting with three-colour shorts and sequences, released the first three-colour feature, *Becky Sharp*, in 1935. When Becky Sharp proved only a modest commercial success, Pioneer's executives joined forces with the independent producer David O. Selznick and, under the banner of Selznick International Pictures absorbed Pioneer's eight-feature contract with Technicolor. There followed a string of three-colour successes, including *The Garden of Allah* (1936), *A Star is Born* (1937) and *Gone with the Wind* (1939).

By the time the economic viability of Technicolor was established, the Second World War, the shrinking world market for films, and reduced budgets and production schedules curtailed the expansion of colour cinematography for some time. Into the 1950s, Technicolor improved their process to make the emulsions more sensitive; however, Eastman Color had replaced Technicolor as a negative source by 1953, because of the convenience of shooting a single negative in a smaller camera. From 1955, the name 'Technicolor' only referred to the laboratory process which produced three separately dyed negatives.

In 1935, Kodak offered Kodachrome as a new 'tri-pack' monopack for amateur use, but it took until 1943 for a professional version to appear, largely because the continued popular success of monochrome film made it an unattractive option for film-makers: in 1935 it was estimated that colour added approximately 30 per cent to production costs which then averaged about $300,000; in 1949 this figure had fallen to 10 per cent while the average costs of American A-features had risen to about $1 million. In 1948, *Variety* estimated that colour could add as much as 25 per cent to a feature film's financial return, but this was not sufficient to cover additional production costs. In 1940, only 4 per cent of American features were in colour. By 1951, this figure had risen to 51 per cent but in 1958 had fallen to 25 per cent as a result of shrinking budgets and the emergence of the black-and-white television market. By 1967, however, the television networks having turned to colour broadcasting, the percentage rose once more to 75 per cent, and in 1976, to 94 per cent.

Selected Reading

Stephen Neale, *Cinema and Technology: Image, Sound, Colour*, London, BFI/Macmillan, 1985.

Brian Winston, *Technologies of Seeing*, London, BFI Publishing, 1996.

DEEP-FOCUS

Deep-focus cinematography, in which objects in several planes of depth are kept in equally sharp focus, is commonly associated with certain Hollywood films of the 1940s. Patrick Ogle dates its emergence at around 1941, and argues that its development was influenced by a matrix of cinematic and non cinematic factors, such as the rise of photojournalism and social realist and documentary film movements during the 1930s, as well as the availability of new kinds of film stock, lighting equipment and lenses. According to this argument, cinematographers of this period were attempting to duplicate on film the perspective and foreground–background image size relationships seen in picture magazines. Since the normal focal length of a 35-mm still camera is (relatively speaking) half that of the 35-mm motion-picture camera, most still-camera pictures take in an angle of view twice as wide as that taken in by a movie camera filming the same event from the same distance. In order to reproduce the effects of still photographs, cinematographers had to use what, in motion-picture terms, were considered unusually wide-angle lenses (Ogle, 1977).

In the mid-1930s, improved arc lights which, because of noise and flicker problems, had been virtually abandoned in favour of incandescents better suited to panchromatic film stock and sound filming – were introduced specifically, at first, for Technicolor cinematography, which demanded high levels of lighting. In the latter half of the decade, however, faster film stocks became available, and while many cinematographers chose to underdevelop their footage in order to maintain the soft tones and low contrast levels they had been used to, a few opted for the possibilities of increased crispness and depth of field. In 1939, a new emulsion type was introduced which reproduced both sound and image more clearly and crisply than ever before, and, at the same time, new lens coatings were produced which resulted in improvements in light transmissions of more than 75 per cent under some conditions. This more efficient use of light led to better screen illumination, image contrast, and sharpness of focus for both colour and black-and-white cinematography.

Although this conjunction of powerful point source arc lights, fast film emulsions and crisp coated lenses were necessary preconditions for deep-focus cinematography, they were by no means sufficient. According to Ogle, for deep-focus to develop as it did, a number of essentially aesthetic choices and creative syntheses had to occur. The aesthetic in question is cinematic realism, which Ogle defines as 'a sense of presence' similar to that experienced by spectators in the theatre, in that the viewer is provided with 'visually acute high information imagery that he may scan according to his own desires without the interruptions of intercutting . . .' This argument echoes Bazin, for whom deep focus brought the spectator into a relation with the image closer to that which they enjoy with reality. For Ogle, deep-focus cine-

Deep-focus, complex characters – *La Règle du jeu*

matography as a recognised visual style first came to critical and public attention with the release of *Citizen Kane* (1941), though it had certainly been practised before (see Barr, 1974; Harpole, 1980). Although not obviously realistic in style, *Citizen Kane* manifested an unprecedented depth of field in the scene photographed, which led a contemporary reviewer to claim that it produced '. . . a picture closely approximating to what the eye sees. . . The result is realism in a new dimension: we forget we are looking at a picture, and feel the living, breathing presence of the characters' (*American Cinematographer*, May 1941, p. 222). For Toland, the aesthetic framework for the filming of *Citizen Kane* was always one of realism: 'Its keynote is realism . . . both Welles and I felt this, and felt that if it was possible, the picture should be brought to the screen in such a way that the audience would feel it was looking at reality, rather than merely at a movie' (quoted in Turner, 1982, pp. 1221–2).

But the development of a deep-focus aesthetic should not be seen solely in terms of Hollywood. European directors, most notably the French director Jean Renoir, were also instrumental in using it. Renoir's

La Grande Illusion (France 1938 *p.c* – Réalisations d'Art Cinématographique; *d* – Jean Renoir; sd b/w)

La Règle du jeu (France 1938 *p.c* – La Nouvelle Édition Française; *d* – Jean Renoir; sd b/w)

Renoir employs the deep-focus technique more frugally and more subtlely than Welles's flamboyant usage in *Citizen Kane.* Indeed, it becomes an integral part of his formal armoury of camera framings and movements, which Renoir uses to describe the complex relationships between his set of characters. This is evident in the scene in which Schumacher, the gamekeeper, descends to the kitchen to confront his partner, Lisette. She is entwined with Marceau, whom she is forced to hide in an adjoining room when Schumacher appears. Schumacher and Lisette meet in the foregound space, at the foot of the stairs, before moving to the kitchen table in the background. A reverse angle then frames them again in the foreground, while showing Marceau attempting to tip-toe away to the back of the room. Both foreground and background planes are kept in focus in both shots, thereby establishing and then confirming spatial relations, as well as creating the comic suspense of Marceau's attempted escape.

In a later scene, the airman, André Jurieux, arrives at the house. We see two of the leading women reacting to his appearence as the camera circles around behind them to show André in the doorway. As the scene progresses, other characters appear from an opposite doorway, and walk forward from the background to join the main group milling around just in front of the camera. Again, all spatial planes are kept in focus to create the sense of a group of equals. As the scene ends, however, the action focuses on the hostess, Christine, as she recounts the history of her friendship with André. She is framed in foreground, André behind her in mid-distance; he is in blurred focus until she moves backwards to join him, when the camera refocuses on them both. The focusing obviously relates to the idea of memory and inclusion which is the subject of the action.

Stagecoach (USA 1939 *p.c* – Walter Wanger Productions; *d* – John Ford; sd b/w)

Citizen Kane (USA 1941 *p.c* – RKO; *d* – Orson Welles; sd b/w)

The Little Foxes (USA 1941 *p.c* – Goldwyn; *d* – William Wyler; sd b/w)

The Magnificent Ambersons (USA 1942 *p.c* – RKO; *d* – Orson Welles; sd b/w)

The Best Years of our Lives (USA 1942 *p.c* – Goldwyn; *d* – William Wyler; sd b/w)

Six years after his pioneering deep-focus work on *Citizen Kane*, Gregg Toland acted as Cinematographer on William Wyler's *The Best Years of Our Lives.* The study of the postwar emotional and social problems of several returning veterans, the film won several Oscars in 1946, including Best Film, Best Director and Best Actor. But not Best Cinematography.

Wyler and Toland's use of deep-focus can be seen in the celebrated scene in which Frederic March tries to dissuade Dana Andrews from seeing his daughter. As Andrews enters the bar, clearly in focus, in deep background March, also in clear focus, sits with his back to the camera, in a booth in the near foreground. Andrews walks the length of the bar to join March. Their tense conversation is covered in two-shots and shot-reverse shot interchanges. The takes are generally quite long. When Andrews leaves March at the end of their conversation, he walks the length of the bar, again in full focus, and enters a phonebooth back in deep background. March then joins the disabled ex-sailor and Hoagy Carmichael at the piano as they show him a double-handed routine they have evolved. As they play, in one long continuous take, March alternately looks at them and glances backwards to watch Andrews as he makes his phone call. While the spectator's attention is theoretically able to freely roam the image, March's glances back and forth from background to foreground control the audience's gaze to some extent. Obviously, also, the deep-focus is used to keep all planes and areas of action equally clear, thereby increasing the scene's emotional tension.

The Best Years of Our Lives – deep-focus and realism

1939 film *La Règle du jeu*, for example, extensively employs deep-focus to establish and maintain the complex relationships between characters as they move around the house and gardens of the main location. In one particular scene, as Paul Schrader describes it:

> The long hallway scene. . . . With so many people, how do you shoot that kind of situation? You have your actors blocked like crazy and you keep leading them off and going with them and coming back with someone else . . . He has a group shot and instead of cutting in for a close-up, he moves people out, moves in to a two-shot, pans with one of the characters to bring you to something else. Very similar to the stuff Welles was doing. (Schrader, quoted in Smith, 1995)

Although Ogle disagrees that the human eye sees in deep-focus, he believes the sense of realism celebrated by the reviewer consists in deep-focus cinematography's tendency towards long-duration sequences, avoidance of cut-aways and reaction shots, the employment of a relatively static camera, and the use of unobtrusive editing – once again echoing Bazin. Avoiding an argument based on technological determinism, Ogle insists that deep-focus could never have emerged without the timely creative input of Gregg Toland, William Wyler, John Ford and Orson Welles, and indeed, without certain production conditions. He considers that *Citizen Kane*, for example, 'constituted a major coming together of technological practice with aesthetic choice in an environment highly conducive to creativity' (see p. 337).

Against Ogle's account, however, it has been argued (Williams, 1977) that neither technological practice nor aesthetic choice are independent of ideological and economic choices and practices, as Ogle's analysis suggests; moreover, realism is not simply an aesthetic but also an ideology, an 'ideology of the visible'. The importance of deep-focus cinematography for film criticism lies in its encapsulation of issues concerning economics and technology, aesthetics and ideology. An economic imperative might be detected, for instance, in the industry's need to mark a difference, a new kind of product; and part of the aesthetics of deep-focus may well have emerged from cinematographers' desire to assert their 'creative' status in the industry hierarchy.

Selected Reading

Patrick Ogle, 'Technological and aesthetic influence upon the development of deep-focus cinematography in the United States', in *Screen Reader* 1, London, SEFT, 1977.

Christopher Williams, 'The deep-focus questions: some comments on Patrick Ogle's Article', in *Screen* 13(1), 1977.

LIGHTING

In the 1890s, the major source of illumination for shooting film was sunlight. Sets were built and filmed on outdoor stages with muslin diffusers and various kinds of reflectors used to control the levels of brightness and shadow. The first film studio, Edison's Black Maria, built in 1893, had blackened walls and stages draped in black cloth. Its roof opened to adjust sunlight, and the whole building could be rotated to maximise daylight. Only occasionally did early films employ artificial lighting effects; all that was expected from lighting was that it facilitated the correct exposure of film-making. Thus the Cooper–Hewitt vapour lamps with which by 1905 several studios, including Biograph and Vitagraph, had equipped themselves, were initially used sparingly to supplement the diffused sunlight filtering through studio roofs. It was not until around 1910 – when the introduction of floor-standing floodlights permitted more distinct facial modelling and separation of actors from their backgrounds, as well as offering the possibility of simulating 'directed' lamp or window light with far greater precision than the diffused vapour lights that had preceded them – that the industry began to formulate an aesthetic of lighting, based both on economic and artistic considerations. Charles W. Handley (1954) has argued that the desire for product differentiation between the Motion Picture Patents

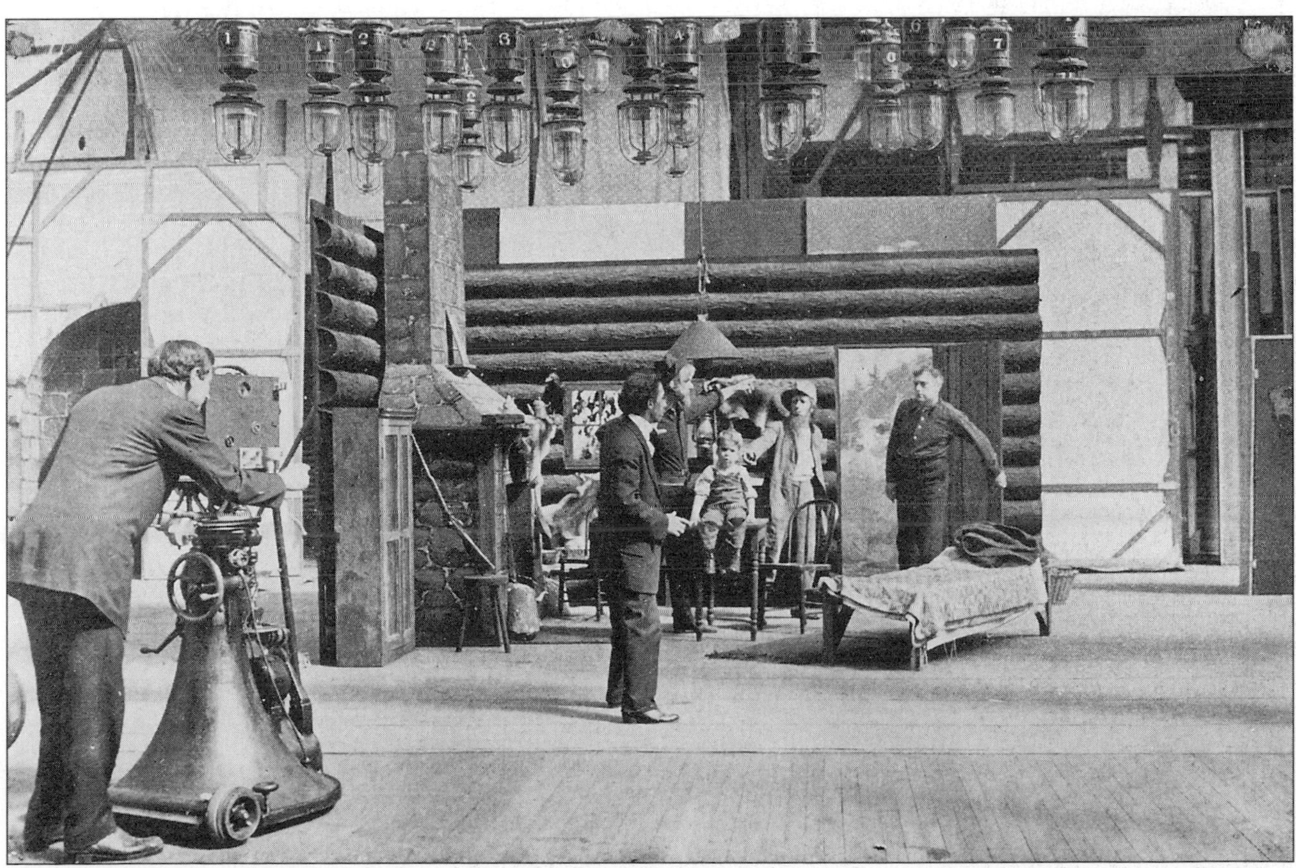

Lighting advances at Edison's New York Studio

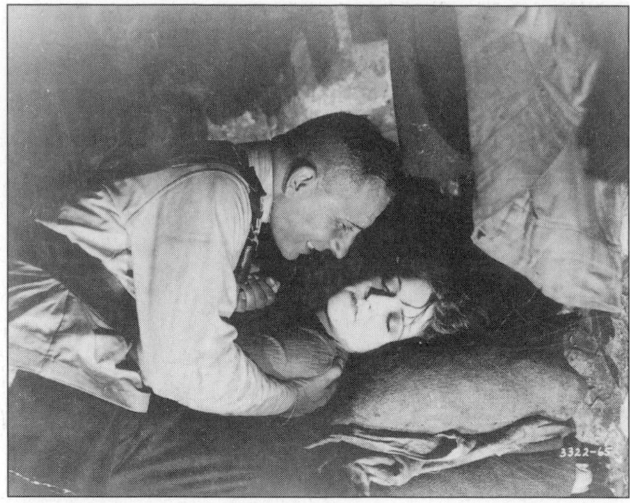

Elaborate and expressionistic lighting on the set of *Foolish Wives*

Company and rival independent producers was a major factor in lighting innovations during the 1910s. Baxter (1975) argues instead that industry consolidation and the move to expressive use of lighting effects were harnessed to the naturalistic aesthetic evident in American theatre of the time.

By 1915, therefore, lighting for illumination was gradually being replaced by lighting for dramatic effect, and Klieg spotlights were becoming normal in studio practice. And by 1918, the conventions of lighting (revelation and expression) which were to dominate Hollywood production up to the present day, and which were grounded in the realist aesthetic which demanded the avoidance of all artificial or abstract effects, were more or less established.

As the Klieg lights came into general use, so too did three-dimensional rather than painted sets, and sunlight was finally eliminated altogether from studios. The 1920s saw the gradual conventionalisation of the use of stronger and weaker arc floodlights functioning as key (hard, direct light), fill (soft, diffused light filling in the shadows cast by key lighting) and backlighting. The coming of sound, however, called forth a new range of technological demands, including the replacement of humming carbon lights by silent mazda tungsten incandescent lamps, and the consequent changes to the more light- and colour-sensitive film stocks noted earlier.

During the 1930s and 1940s, several technological developments significantly improved lighting processes. By 1931, improved carbon arcs were introduced to provide the high-key bright light required by, first, two-colour, and then, in the late 1930s, three-colour, Technicolor. Initially this caused technical problems related to the temperature of the bulbs, but by the end of the decade, the arrival of faster Technicolor film stock allowed a reduction in lighting power requirements for colour cinematography. During the 1930s, arc design improved, with the introduction of the Bardens arc (descended from French naval searchlights) and the Mole Richardson in 1935, all allowing greater control over a wide range of settings, from sharp spot to full flood. Further improvements lessened noise and lessened AC mains fluctuations to provide steadier output. War-developed lighting technology such as the Colortran, a relatively lightweight and mobile source which required fewer lighting units and involved a cruder use of fill lights, facilitated location filming. Until the late 1940s, studio lighting was either low key (for genres such as *film noir*) or high key (for genres such as the musical, as well as for deep-focus cinematography). But the codes of 'dramatic lighting' which had been established much earlier, and which demanded that lighting should be subordinated to aesthetic coherence, continued to dominate Hollywood production.

'The development of quartz-iodine (tungsten-halogen) lamps in the mid-1960s gave a much needed boost to designers of studio lighting equipment, providing them with a lamp of much smaller dimensions and greatly improved performance' (Earle-Knight, 1981). This, together with the advent of television causing studio redesigns to enable the same spaces to be used for both media, resulted in significant changes to lighting methods. Overhead lighting grids were installed, modified for film lighting (strengthened for the extra weight of film lighting units).

The technical development of studio lighting has, therefore, been governed throughout its history by a number of interlocking factors. Lights had to be of sufficient quality to ensure acceptable images; quiet enough not to interfere with sound recording; portable enough to cope with all types of location filming; and flexible enough to cope with changing production methods, most notably the merging of film and television studio production from the mid-1960s onwards. These technical considerations have always been in the service of film aesthetics, such as narrative and character development and the ideological intent.

Selected Reading

Peter Baxter, 'On the history and ideology of film lighting', in *Screen* 16(3), autumn, 1975.

T. Earle-Knight, 'Studio lighting 1930–1980', *The BKSTS Journal*, January 1981.

WIDESCREEN

During the first twenty years of cinema, the industry was engaged in a number of patent wars, one of which also determined the development of widescreen film formats. In August 1897 Thomas Edison was granted a patent for his 35-mm motion-picture camera, after his assistant, W. L. Dickson had already determined, five years earlier, the 35-mm standard for cinematic film-stock by simply splitting the readily available Eastman 70-mm stock down the middle to produce twice as much 35-mm stock, with a 4:3 (1.33:1) ratio (Belton, 1992, p.18). The Lumière Brothers adopted 35-mm film in 1896, while British film-makers used 35-mm stock supplied by the Blair Company. Having experimented before with film stock that produced both square and circular frame shapes, the 4:3 ratio was preferred by Dickson on both aesthetic and economic grounds. Aesthetically, the 4:3 ratio coped best with movement which was dominantly horizontal in nature. Economically, there was less wastage between frames.

In an attempt to circumvent Edison's patent stranglehold, rival film companies developed a variety of film formats. Biograph, for example, produced a 68-mm format, while Lumière worked in 75 mm. This variety was continued until the film industry became a mass-production phenomenon. '[T]he triumph of a single standard over the variety of standards, including wide-film formats was clearly a necessary stage in the evolution of a viable, technologically based industry which relies on mass production, mass distribution and mass consumption for its success' (Belton,

Lighting

Pippa Passes (USA 1909 *p.c.* – Biograph; *d* – D. W. Griffith; st b/w)

Foolish Wives (USA 1921 *p.c* – Universal; *d* – Erich von Stroheim; st b/w)

Sunrise (USA 1927 *p.c* – Fox Film Corporation; *d* – F. W. Murnau; st mu.sd b/w)

Dracula (USA 1931 *p.c* – Universal; *d* – Tod Browning; sd b/w)

The Scarlet Empress (USA 1934 *p.c* – Paramount; *d* – Joseph von Sternberg; sd b/w)

The Informer (USA 1935 *p.c* – RKO Radio; *d* – John Ford; sd b/w)

Citizen Kane (USA 1941 *p.c* – Mercury Productions/RKO; *d* – Orson Welles; sd b/w)

The Little Foxes (USA 1941 *p.c* – RKO/Goldwyn; *d* – William Wyler; sd b/w)

Double Indemnity (USA 1944 *p.c* – Paramount; *d* – Billy Wilder; sd b/w)

Rancho Notorious (USA 1952 *p.c* – Fidelity Pictures/RKO; *d* – Fritz Lang; sd col.)

Shane (USA 1952 *p.c* – Paramount; *d* – George Stevens; sd col.)

Written on the Wind (USA 1956 *p.c* – Universal–International; *d* – Douglas Sirk; sd col.)

Touch of Evil (USA 1958 *p.c* – Universal–International; *d* – Orson Welles; sd b/w)

Barry Lyndon (GB 1975 *p.c* – Hawk Films; *d* – Stanley Kubrick; sd col.)

Titanic (USA 1997 *p.c* – Fox/Paramount; *d* – James Cameron; sd col.)

1992). In the late 1920s, the adoption of optical sound caused a reconsideration of screen ratios, because the soundtrack demanded a significant portion of the available frame area. Considerable industry discussion, regarding alternative ratios which might accommodate sound more efficiently, took place in the last years of the 1920s. Eventually, the Academy of Motion Pictures Arts and Sciences reinstalled the 1.33:1 ratio, slightly enlarged to 1.37:1, to allow space for the soundtrack (but even with this amendment, the advent of sound had still reduced the frame area by 31 per cent).

Despite the standardisation of the 35-mm screen format, experimentation with wider formats continued. In the late silent period, a number of 'spectacular' wide-film processes developed, including Abel Gance's three-screen Polyvision and Paramount's Magnascope. The novelty value of each system quickly wore off, however, and the technical demands, including cumbersomely synchronising three cameras during filming, and three projectors during screening, were such that these particular systems never captured long-term industry attention. Experiments with wide-film formats were, however, initiated by other major studios. Fox developed the Grandeur 70-mm format, and persuaded MGM to adopt it. Warners, First National and United Artists chose 65 mm, while Paramount went with 56 mm. By early 1930, both RKO and Paramount had shifted to 65 mm. There was considerable expectation that one of these formats would soon be chosen as the

CinemaScope in *River of No Return*

The Robe (USA 1953; *p.c* – 20th Century–Fox; *d* – Henry Koster; sd col. scope)

Gentlemen Prefer Blondes (USA 1953; *p.c* – 20th Century–Fox; *d* – Howard Hawks; sd col. scope)

White Christmas (USA 1954; *p.c* – Paramount; *d* – Michael Curtiz; sd col. Vistavision)

River of No Return (USA 1954, *p.c* – 20th Century–Fox; *d* – Otto Preminger; sd col. scope)

In *River of No Return* CinemaScope ratio is used to set up a series of character tensions and spectator positions. An example of this is in the scene in which Harry lifts Kay from the raft. Kay drops her valise, which then drifts off downstream as the characters move away from the raft towards the cabin. The series of shots showing this action repeatedly frame the valise, either to one side of the wide frame, or in the distant background between two characters in the foreground. The director, Otto Preminger, has been widely ascribed as having a neutral style, lacking in any distinctive features. V. F. Perkins (1962) argues that 'The director presents the action clearly and leaves the interpretation to the spectator.' Whereas Bordwell (1985) sees the sequence 'emphasis[ing] the bundle in ways which manifest the classical aim of repeating narratively salient information, particularly through several channels. . . . It is common for a classical film to establish a locale in a neutral way and then return to this already-seen camera set-up when we are to notice a fresh element in the space. We thus identify the new information as significant against a background of familiarity'.

Perkins's interpretation operates within a realist framework, seeing the widescreen frame as open and unmediated, thus allowing sufficient space for actions to occur naturally, with the spectator empowered with the responsibility of scanning the information and determining the most important elements. Bordwell's reading occupies a more formalist position, suggesting that the space afforded by the wider ratio allows more information to be consciously presented to the spectator by the film-maker.

The Far Country (USA 1954 *p.c* – Universal–International; *d* – Anthony Mann; sd col. scope)

Rebel Without a Cause (USA 1955 *p.c.* – Warner Bros.; *d* – Nicholas Ray; sd col. scope)

Rebel Without a Cause was James Dean's second starring film. He fills the film, and its widescreen image, with a brooding, tortured presence. Dean's Method-acting techniques are well known, as is the resistance they engendered in his more traditional-acting colleagues. This resistance fed into the film itself, increasing the palpable tension between the characters in many of the scenes.

One such example is when Dean returns home after the fatal 'chicken-run', in which a teenager has died, to seek help and comfort from his parents. The widescreen ratio is used throughout the scene to complement and comment on the various stages of emotional manouevring performed by the characters. Initially Dean sits at the foot of the stairs; the first shot shows him to the right of frame, behind the stair railings, with his mother in centre frame, and his father to the extreme left of frame. Already the *mise-en-scène* reflects the family relations: trapped son, strong dominant mother, peripheralised father.

A cut frontally shows us the contained figure of Dean; his isolation emphasised by empty space on either side of him. He raises both arms to catch hold of the stair rail, filling the frame with an image of cruxifiction. His mother and father move into the frame to stand on either side of him. A long take, as he pleads with them to hear his account of his confused emotions, preserves the length and intensity of his performance, while its conflicting, overlapping dialogue makes apparent the characters' emotional distance from one another. As the argument develops, the characters shift position, with the mother now half-way up the stairs, Dean at the foot, and his father sitting behind him. A canted angle pushes the mother into the top left corner, and the father into the bottom left corner, of the frame. In contrast, the subsequent cut to a closer shot of just Dean and his mother shows them close together in centre frame, again with space on either side, their physical closeness echoing their emotional intensity. In this way, the arrangement of actors either across the width of, or crammed into the centre of, the widescreen frame provides a continuous commentary on the emotional integrity of the scene. (See Teenpics, p. 220.)

Land of the Pharaohs (USA 1955 *p.c* – Continental Company; *d* – Howard Hawks; sd col. scope)

High Society (USA 1956 *p.c* – MGM; *d* – Charles Walters; sd col. VistaVision)

The Girl Can't Help It (USA 1956 *p.c.* – 20th Century–Fox; *d* – Frank Tashlin; sd col. scope)

How the West Was Won (USA 1962 *p.c* – MGM; *d* – Henry Hathaway; sd col. Cinerama)

new industry standard. An industry-wide ban on experimentation was introduced by the SMPE (Society of Motion Picture Engineers) to block new formats being developed, and at the end of 1931, the SMPE proposed a 50 mm standard, but this was universally rejected. For a time, Fox's Grandeur format appeared to be the favourite, but changes in Fox's management structure, and the resultant company rationalisation, meant that the Grandeur process was abandoned on the eve of its potential success. As already noted, the industrial adoption of sound in the late 1920s was a further factor in the failure to standardise a wide-film format. Nor was there enough funding for research or theatre conversion. Also, audiences, entranced by the recent arrival of sound, simply did not demand the feature. As a result, as Belton notes, 'widescreen remained more of a novelty than a norm' (Belton, 1992, p. 51).

The Second World War and the subsequent postwar social and economic changes created conditions which were conducive to the adoption of widescreen cinema. People had become more active, favouring sports and action-based pastimes, all of which tempted them away from the cinema. Moreover, they had moved to the suburbs, further away from the centre of cities where cinemas tended to be concentrated. The advent of television provided the third substantial threat to the future of the film as a communal entertainment experience. 'To compete with other leisure-time amusements, the motion-picture experience was in need of redefinition. Movies had to become more participatory; the movie theatre had to become the equivalent of an amusement park. The advent of Cinerama launched this revolution' (Belton, 1992).

Cinerama was a three-camera/three-projector process, each filmstrip providing a third of the full image projected onto a curved screen and synchronised together with a soundtrack generator. Because of this technical complexity, however, it proved to have a number of inherent problems – it restricted shot variation, because certain close framings were impossible due to lens distortion, and it required very careful lighting and colour grading to ensure consistency across the three separate images which made up the composite widescreen image.

In spite of this, Cinerama was an industry sensation, attracting mass audiences to its literally overwhelming experience. It also provided yet another mechanism of ideology – early Cinerama documentaries were big hits by emphasising the grandeur, beauty and power of the American landscape.

Ultimately, however, CinemaScope provided the most industrially efficient format, by combining a widescreen image, together with its stereo soundtrack, on a single filmstrip. Just as Warner Bros.. had invested in sound in the late 1920s in an attempt to become an industry major, CinemaScope was developed by a 20th Century–Fox which was, as Belton argues, 'caught up in the turmoil of an industry-wide financial crisis and self-definition' (Belton, 1992, p. 113). For a short period (1952–4) a format war once again raged, this time between Fox's CinemaScope and Paramount's VistaVision, which employed a horizontal shooting and projection system in an attempt to increase image quality. Eventually, almost every major studio (primarily, United Artists, MGM, Warners, and Disney), who had all stood back nervously to watch the development of the competition between Fox and Paramount, joined Fox by agreeing to use CinemaScope. The one major sticking point – Fox's insistence on theatres being equipped with stereo sound to accompany the widescreen images – was solved when Fox relented and agreed to provide a variety of soundtrack formats for theatres to choose from. The adoption of CinemaScope did, however, have serious effects upon exhibition, with the highly capitalised theatre chains converting at great expense, but realising enormous profits as a result, while some of the smaller chains were forced out of business.

Another widescreen format, IMAX began life as a series of Expo attractions – 1967 in Montreal and 1970 in Osaka. Between those two dates, as Tana Wollen argues, 'a completely original film system had been developed in almost cottage industry conditions' (Wollen in Hayward and Wollen, 1993, p. 16). Originally, like Cinerama, IMAX consisted of several separate 70-mm images, synchronised together. This was achieved by developing a 70-mm frame which passed horizontally rather than vertically through the projector (cf. VistaVision, although VistaVision required non-standard projectors, whereas IMAX could be run on standard 70-mm projection equipment). The 49-mm × 70-mm frame gives three times the exposed surface area of conventional 70 mm. The IMAX sound system is free of the filmstrip itself, initially on 6-channel 35-mm magnetic film, and then on a system of CDs (again, like with the DTS sound system, a curious return to the sound-on-disc system of early sound film). The exhibition sites have dozens of loudspeakers positioned around the theatre space, 'mean[ing] the sound can be positioned as much as the visual image and, since the image extends beyond the audience's effective field of vision, sound cues can be deployed to move the viewer's focus onto action in different spaces on the screen' (Wollen in Hayward and Wollen, 1993, p. 18). The other huge-image film system – OMNIMAX – shoots its images using a fish-eye lens. The films are then projected onto hemispheric screens angled above and below rather then in front of the audience. This extends the image beyond the field of human vision, effectively immersing the audience in the image.

The image size of both IMAX and OMNIMAX inevitably influences the type of subjects chosen for their films. Like early CinemaScope, documentaries, especially concerning epic natural history, are favoured. Certain framings have to be carefully considered, because the audience is viewing the film image from a position lower than in conventional cinemas. Moreover, since screen size can be used to direct viewers' focus to different points of its surface, IMAX edits are paced at longer intervals to give the audience time to absorb both images and sounds. (cf. early widescreen formats and deep-focus). Narrative films are ill-suited to these huge-format systems. Close framings are impossible, which in turn, disables the emotional intensities built via shot/reverse-shot strategies in narrative films. Moreover, both IMAX and OMNIMAX theatres have to be custom built. While initially seeming a discouraging factor, certainly considering the historical resistance of the exhibition sector to building costs involved in previous innovations such as sound and widescreen, this phenomenon might actually suit modern social practices. IMAX screens are currently being installed in American shopping malls, to provide a one-hour entertainment/diversion/rest from the rigours of an all-day visit to this modern compendium consumer space. The acceptance of IMAX could therefore signal a significant change in contemporary viewing practices.

Selected Reading

John Belton, *Widescreen Cinema*, Cambridge, Mass., Harvard University Press, 1992.

Tana Wollen (ed), 'The bigger the better: from CinemaScope to Imax', in Philip Hayward and Tana Wollen, *Future Visions: New Technologies of the Screen*, London, BFI Publishing, 1993.

CAMERAS

One of the first recognised technical problems of cinema was how to take a sharp and moving image which could then be clearly replayed by a projector. The technical and scientific problems posed by this desire motivated a colony of scientists and engineers to continually push forward the bounds of design, resulting in a breathtaking profusion of cameras during the first decade of film. Many of these were, simply, minimal modifications of originals, made by unscrupulous operators eager to circumvent patent restrictions. The purpose of this 'plagarised modification' was partly to present a new and improved product to expectant audiences.

The production of acceptably stable images; that is to say, images which effaced themselves and allowed the audience to think it was experiencing unmediated reality, obviously positions film within the realist aesthetic. A parallel trajectory of early camera technology, however, was the desire to make the camera perform literally marvellous effects. For example, designing them to run in reverse allowed several special effects to be achieved, including reverse motion and multiple-exposure images perfected by 'fantastic' film-makers such as Méliès.

At any point in the history of film, a number of discrete camera designs have always coexisted, but the preference of one over the other has always been partly determined by demands in other areas of film technology. For example, with the coming of sound, the Mitchell camera gradually became an industry leader because its viewfinder-lens mechanism was easier to use within the soundproofed blimps covering the noisy camera. Later, the CinemaScope camera won out over the Cinerama camera because its design allowed the widescreen image to be squeezed onto a single filmstrip, as opposed to the three separate filmstrips required by Cinerama.

At other times, social and economic factors have created the circumstances in which new camera technologies have been developed. In 1938, on the eve of the Second World War, Munich camera manufacturers Arnold and Richter delivered the first 35-mm Arriflex camera. With a through-the-lens mirror-reflex viewfinder, a DC motor in its hand-grip, and three lenses on a rotating turret, the Arriflex became one of the standard camera designs over the next forty years (Postwar, a 16-mm version was built). Arriflex reflex cameras were used extensively by German newsreel cameramen during the Second World War. The war, with its need for reconnaissance photography, also initiated continued research into lightweight cameras which could be

Intolerance (USA 1916 *p.c* – Wark Producing Corp.; *d* – D W. Griffith; st b/w)

Gone With the Wind (USA 1939 *p.c* – Selznick International Pictures; *d* – Victor Fleming; sd col.)

How the West Was Won (USA 1962 *p.c* – MGM; *d* – Henry Hathaway; sd col.)

Don't Look Back (USA 1967 *p.c* – Leacock Pennebaker; *d* – D. A. Pennebaker; sd b/w)

High School (USA1968 *p.c* – Osti Film; *d* – Frederick Wiseman; sd b/w)

Halloween (USA 1978 *p.c* – Falcon International Pictures; *d* – John Carpenter; sd col.)

Das Boot (GER 1981 *p.c* – Bavaria Atelier; *d* – Wolfgang Petersen; sd

taken into inaccessible spaces. The Bell and Howell Eyemo and Palliard Bolex offered competition to the Arriflex. Of the two, the Bolex was the more user-friendly especially as, being spring-driven, it could be taken to places inaccessible to electrical or battery-driven cameras.

Walter Bach's 16-mm Auricon camera, which had a built-in optical sound system allowing both sound and picture to be recorded on the same stock, furnished a good-quality, stable-image quality which was extensively used in TV news. The German TV station Sudwestfunk-Fernsehen adapted the Auricon by replacing the optical sound mechanism with a magnetic recorder. 'Either way the Auricon remained a single system device. It had recorded image and sound on one strip of film (comopt); now it recorded them on a combined strip of film and tape (commag)' (Winston, 1996, p. 79). The problems of editing commag meant its usefulness was largely restricted to 'soundbite' use on TV news.

The documentary field provided another impetus to the development of 16-mm sound technology, this time in the direction of separate sound and image devices. A new generation of documentary film-makers appeared, who were intent upon not using what they saw as the staid, tripod-restricted techniques of established documentary makers. Foremost amongst these was Richard Leacock, who had found frustration in shooting Flaherty's last film *The Louisiana Story* (1948) because of the inability to move the camera while shooting sound sequences. He, and other film-makers around him, adapted Bach's Auricon by recasting the body in a lighter metal to make it more portable. This, together with the use of camera mounted lighting and/or faster stocks which could be used in lower-light conditions meant that the film-makers could get unobtrusively closer to events as they occured. 'All these factors contributed to create a grainy, hand-held, authentic-sound, go-anywhere style of film that was entirely new. Documentary had entered its direct-cinema phase' (Winston, 1996, p. 82).

In 1962, Andre Coutant marketed the Éclair – a silent-running, hand-held 16-mm camera in which the weight of the lens was balanced by a film magazine shaped to sit on the shoulder, and a motor which was mounted below the lens and forward of the magazine. The Éclair was designed to be a double system, with a separate sound recorder running in sync with the camera; the recorder was called the Perfectone. Camera and recorder were connected by a cable, and a synchronising pulse emitted from the camera was recorded on one track of the tape, while the sound was recorded on the second. The system – called the Éclair NPR – was introduced commercially in America in 1963. The Nagra was introduced in the same year, and has since become an industry standard. By the early 1960s, several sync systems – including the Pilot-Tone – appeared, which involved separate units in which the camera emitted a pulse from a crystal transmitter to the tape recorder. 'By the mid-60s the modern 16-mm synch sound outfit was in place – Nagra with crystal control and an NPR or Arri BL' (Winston, 1996, p. 86).

Selected Reading

Brian Winston, *Technologies of Seeing*, London, BFI, 1996.

ALTERNATIVE PRODUCTION FORMATS: 16 MM, 8 MM AND VIDEO

'From the moment 35 mm was established as *the* professional production format, the dominant Film Industry has either consciosly and unconsciously positioned alternative production media formats – 16 mm, 8 mm and video – as inferior, and as substandard' (Baddeley, 1981). The histories of these formats are interlocked in the movement which has seen all three in turn (first 16 mm, then 8 mm and finally video) assume the mantle of the medium for the amateur, 'home-movie', hobbyist. This movement is aesthetic, economic and social. Aesthetically, the film industry has partly identified its professional status by differentiating the quality of its 35-mm product from the 'inferior' results achievable on 16 mm. Socially and economically, manufacturers of equipment in all three formats have identified and targeted a home market for their product, and have been keen to maintain a clear and separate identity for it. Artists interested in using 16 mm, 8 mm or video explicitly *for* the particular aesthetic qualities of each, have always had to battle against this pejorative attitude.

Although in existence from the earliest days of cinema, as one of the plethora of available film formats, 16 mm was introduced in 1923, when the Eastman Kodak Company began to manufacture 16-mm film on a safety acetate base. From the very start, it was intended both as a distribution format (in situations where 35-mm prints were unusable) and, primarily, as a production format for the 'hobby' market of amateur home movies. During the 1930s, however, 16 mm began to be seen as a serious production format. This required a series of technical improvements in other areas: the replacement of orthochromic stock with panchromatic stock; the development of photoflood lighting and light meters to obtain satisfactory exposure; and the introduction of colour (16-mm Kodachrome appeared by the late 1930s). In the late 1940s, Disney decided to use 16 mm for its 'Wild Life Series' (the footage was later blown up to 35-mm Technicolor for projection), a decision which was important in persuading professionals that 16 mm was a viable format. In the early 1950s, printers with lens shutters allowed complex effects to be created from raw footage, rather than in-camera, and 'the way was open for the more robust and straightforward cameras such as the Arriflex, with its continuous through-the-lens viewing' (Baddeley, 1981). Also in the 1950s, more portable lighting was developed, and sound capabilities were improved with the introduction of the Leevers-Rich Synchropulse, which ran off a 12-volt car-type battery and recorded a sync pulse, generated from the camera onto one track of the magnetic tape. It is important to note that 16-mm technology has actually played an important part in the development of many professional production techniques: non-flammable film; single-strip colour; portable cameras and lighting; and miniaturised sound equipment.

Between 1947 and 1954 16-mm equipment lost ground, at least in terms of the 'home-movie' market, to the emergent 8-mm format. In 1964–5, Kodak brought out their improved Super 8 mm, with smaller sprocket holes allowing a 50 per cent larger frame size, magnetic sound stripe offering sync sound, and simplified controls. Together, these features were sufficient to establish Super 8 mm as the substandard gauge for amateur use. Camera equipment was marketed on its technical simplicity, marking it out as different from the more complex cameras used by the professional film industry. The public was persuaded that it was ever easier to capture life's unrepeatable moments with a minimum of fuss. Such a strategy is located within what Zimmerman has identified as the 'professionalisation of leisure' evident in society of the period, being part of the home-consumer push of the 1950s and 1960s which emphasised strategies of engagement with new-found leisure time, and the ideological foregrounding of the nuclear family (Zimmerman, 1988). By the mid-1980s, both 16 mm and 8 mm had, in their turn, been superseded as the amateur, 'home' format by the video camcorder. Video offers several advantages over the film formats for domestic use, primarily its instant replay capability, re-usability and technical simplicity.

A political role for all three alternative formats has also been in process, operating on the margins of both media production and society as a whole; out of control, organised around underground systems of exhibition and distribution. This use of the 'substandard' formats promised freedom of personal expression through ease-of-use and immediacy of results. Within this context it was seen as important that the formats were kept separate from the industry standard, as markers of difference. 'Avant-garde and serious film-makers began to use the narrow gauges in earnest during the late Fifties and early Sixties' (Hudson, 1995, p. 53) and '[p]ortable video technology became available in Britain in the late sixties and, as in North America, was immediately taken up by users whose interests could be described as counter-cultural' (Marshall, 1985, p. 66). It became an important medium for young artists of the 1960s, especially as they began working outside the commercial gallery structure, and also entered the education arena. This double movement had a distinct effect upon both production practices and aesthetics with an emphasis on self-reflexivity in an attempt to identify a definite video aesthetic in comparison with the other fine arts (Marshall, 1985). Into the 1970s, both Super 8 mm and video were taken up by both the women's and black movements, with their emphasis on works which give testimony to personal experience. Both formats were seen as ideal for this in their relative cheapness, ease of use and immediacy.

Selected Reading

Laura Hudson, 'Promiscuous 8', *Coil* no. 2, November 1995.

Stuart Marshall, 'Video: from art to independence: a short history of a new technology', *Screen* 26(2), March/April 1985.

EDITING

During the first years of cinema, films consisted only of single shots and, therefore, required no editing. However, sequences of such films, especially those relating to the same subject – the Spanish–American or Boer Wars, for example – were often edited together by projectionists to make up self-contained units which could be screened between the acts on a vaudeville programme.

Later in the early cinema and then in the classic Hollywood periods, film editing was performed by roomfuls of workers (mainly female), who hand-crafted each physical edit. Editing on the earliest narrative films was a matter of joining the separate shots (which were often shot sequentially) together, perhaps interspersed with explanatory titles. Later, when film syntax had expanded considerably, the editing process became correspondingly complex, and a team of editors would work from detailed production notes to create the finished edit.

The introduction of the KEM Universal editing table at the very end of the 1960s, offered a range of improvements in the editing process, and enabled, for the first time on a general scale, the editing to be performed by the film's director. It was a modular machine, allowing the basic table to be customised by a range of components to deal with all combinations of image and audio editing in all formats. By the early 1970s, a video version had been created, with three video cameras trained, via mirrors, onto the three monitoring screens. By rolling all three filmstrips, and electronically cutting between video images, practice edits could be rehearsed without any cutting of the actual film. Video-assisted film editing became more commonplace by the early 1980s. The main problem was that of frame incompatibility – film running at 24 frames per second, and video at 25 (PAL) or 30 (NTSC). A 3:2 pulldown process was developed, with most film frames having a direct equivalent on the video, but some video frames having partial information from two adjoining film frames. This caused considerable problems in matching film with video frame-by-frame for editing purposes.

During the 1980s, five companies entered the electronic editing market – the Montage Computer Corp., Lucasfilm Droid Works with its EditDroid system, the laserdisc-based Spectra Image/Laser Edit, B&H Touchvision, and Cinedco's Ediflex. Acceptance by the film industry was inconsistent at best. Three types of electronic editing developed: linear, random access and non-linear random access. Linear editing appeared in the early 1970s, with the CMX600 system, which used timecode identification of edit points. Edit decisions proceeded one at a time in linear fashion. It received limited acceptance at the time. Random access systems – the CMX6000 and Spectra Image/Laser Edit systems – utilise laserdisc or multiple copies of material. Laserdisc allows the editor to search to a specified point within a few seconds. The multiple copy system requires several machines to seek scenes from various places on the tapes simultaneously. With both systems, the 'edited' sequences had to be recorded onto master videotape for viewing. With non-linear random access systems – the Montage and Ediflex – the rushes have to be assembled in sequence and transferred onto ¾" video. The script is fed into the computer to create a detailed coding and logging file. With the Ediflex the keyboard is replaced with a light pen used on an operating screen, and the computer keeps track of how far into a scene the editor has cut and cues the next take to the same point. The precise timing of each edit point is logged and stored in the computer. When the final version has been approved, the assistant editor generates the edit decision list which will be used to perform the final video edit, or identify film frames for the film edit.

The 1990s has seen the development of the computer-based editing and image manipulation processes which have precipitated the large-budget, special-effects laden blockbuster feature film. In order to preserve the quality of the original negative in the transfer from celluloid to digital image, the huge amounts of data needing to be handled – several gigabytes per minute for full-colour, full frame images – require very powerful computers to run the programs. This has created a specialist market for digital and effects editing, such that dedicated third-party companies, who invest in the latest generation of machines, now handle much of the editing work on Hollywood productions. The field of editing is being blurred with that of special effects, as post-production work requires substantial reworking of the images on the raw footage itself at the same time as it is edited into the final work.

The advent of computer and digital editing technologies in the 1980s and 1990s has, therefore, threatened to change the relationship between time and the creative process in editing. The use of computers, the digitising of material, the replacing of film with laserdisc and/or videotape at some stages of the process in order to facilitate the creation of special effects, have all made the editing process paradoxically both quicker and more complex. Some practitioners disagree with this prognosis: 'No film editing system can match the electronic editing system's speed in making numerous versions of an edit, comparing different edits, reviewing coverage, and making changes. This speed translates into either a lower ultimate editorial cost, or the ability to go further in editorial perfection, or a combination of the two' (Wasko, 1994). Others take the opposite view, claiming that the systems may even be too fast, giving too little time for reflection on cuts, and too little lead-time into complex problem areas. The process, effectively, threatens to run out of control. As with any aspect of technical development, those using the technology need to adapt to its new capabilities. For better or worse, ever-increasing speed, instantaneous access, and radical manipulation are now part of the editing process. Procedures need to be developed to maximise the opportunities these offer.

Selected Reading

Barry Salt, 'Film style and technology: history and analysis', London, Starword, 1983.

Les Paul Robley, 'Digital offline video editing: expanding creative horizons', *American Cinematographer* 74(4–7), April–July 1993.

A modern digital editing suite at TVI, London

THE 'NEW' TECHNOLOGIES: INTERACTIVITY, MULTIMEDIA AND VIRTUAL REALITY

The impetus for the take-up and employment of 'new' technologies by the film industry has been five-fold: to provide tools for the creation of new and different images (special effects); to improve work efficiencies in production (for example, computer-controlled cinematography) and post-production (editing and special effects); to produce other types of entertainment product (video games, theme rides, virtual-reality experiences); and to develop new distribution channels (CD-Rom, satellite and cable). All five have been determined by the interrelationship of technical and economic criteria, the question being: is the technology capable of achieving the desired result and is it economical to make it do so?

The advent of the various 'new' technologies has required a confluence of several discreet technologies – film and television, computer hardware and software, telephony, engineering and robotics – over a period of several decades. Initial research and development, it is important to note, was conducted almost exclusively in non-entertainment arenas such as the military, science, business and training. Initial uses were therefore practical in emphasis – the improvement of cockpit control for pilots using multi-sensory headsets, or interactive laserdisc training drills for bank employees, for example. Only since the late 1970s and early 1980s has there been seen an adaptation of these 'extra-entertainment' applications, for a broad-based leisure use (initially in the form of videogames). This delay has partly been due to technical limitations (mostly in the area of computers powerful enough to produce acceptable images), and partly to do with film-industry resistance (prohibitive costs, and a general mistrust of new and unfamiliar techniques using untried technology originating from outside the film world). Only when the equipment began to prove itself capable of delivering the goods did the film industry begin using it.

The first use of digital and computer-based technologies within the film industry was in the area of special effects. Solman places it in 1976, with what he terms the 'Effects Renaissance' (Solman, 1992). At that stage, special effects were still model-based, and computers were used only, for example, to control camera trajectory. A little later, in the early 1980s, the first completely computer-generated special effects appeared. These were marked by a certain primitiveness. The software lacked the necessary subtlety, the hardware was very expensive, and very few people knew how to use it. As with so many other areas of film aesthetics, what was driving this effort was the desire to create new 'realities' which were wholly believable at the same time as wholly artificial. And, as with so many other areas of technological development in the film industry, such improvements were dependent upon research conducted by companies in other disciplines; in this case the computer industry. Although the film industry did experiment with computer effects in films of the late 1970s and early 1980s (for example *Alien* in 1979 and *Tron* in 1982), satisfactory computer-generated graphics had to wait until the late 1980s, by which time the computer industry had developed sufficiently powerful, flexible machines. Only then could the specialised applications be developed which were required to produce the desired cinematic special effects. These companies had developed their techniques in arenas separate to mainstream film-making – primarily advertising and computer/video games. Although in many ways financially cautious, advertising companies are, by nature, creatively adventurous. The drive towards the creation of new and arresting images is, indeed, their very *raison d'être*. As a result, the development of the techniques and the technologies necessary for creating believeable, high-tech, high resolution images using computers was developed in an arena absolutely focused upon the quality of those images.

The groundbreaking 'impact aesthetics' of *Terminator 2*

It perhaps comes as no surprise, therefore, that such overdetermination of the spectacularly artificial image became the staple of much of Hollywood's late 1980s and 1990s product. Baker calls this Impact Aesthetics – 'It is as if the quest for technological magic, exceeding the effects in previous movies, becomes the paramount concern . . . a preoccupation with the use of the new technologies for novel image effects' (Baker in Hayward and Wollen, 1993, p. 41). This manipulation of reality results in a new reality, an unreal reality (or hyper-reality). The resultant films become spectacles of technological possibility, experienced for their awesome effects as much as, if not more than, 'traditional' elements such as narrative, character development, and so on. In this sense, cinema seems to have succeeded in developing in the 1990s a distinctively different product which can compete favourably with the smaller, less overpoweringly impressive, audio-visual product offered by television.

INTERACTIVE ENTERTAINMENTS

In the mid-1990s, another significant development is evolving, which might influence more 'traditional' (two-hour, linear, narrative) film-making. Interactive movies are now being produced which offer the viewer/user the possibility of choosing from an image and sound database in order to construct a number of different routes through a film's narrative; in effect, to construct his or her own narrative. A variety of different scenarios are filmed, and all are put onto a CD-Rom disc. The user then begins the program, and, when prompted by suspensions in the program's flow, makes a decision regarding what should happen next. The program then selects and displays the footage which depicts that choice. Recent productions have included movie spin-offs, in which additional footage of actors and locations is shot at the same time as the film itself. Furthermore, original interactive movie productions (including the $6m *The Darkening*, featuring recognised stars, produced by videogames company Electronic Arts, and released in mid-1997) are beginning to appear. That such productions are 'published' on CD-Rom, to be viewed/ played on games consoles, rather than 'screened' in cinemas, indicates the shift in cultural practice represented by this new work. That most of these productions will be made by consortia, composed of the leaders in the film, video, communications and videogame markets, is an indication of the recognised potential (both creative and financial) for this type of product. By mid-1994, all major film studios had opened interactive divisions, exploring the potential that the new computer-based, digital technologies open up. Once again, technologies developed by 'outsiders' (videogames and computer companies) have been taken up and adapted by the film industry both as a means of regeneration, and of absorbing the threat of competition within itself.

The possibilities offered by the new tech nologies have brought with them a range of conceptual and philosophical questions which are only just beginning to be articulated and explored. Written material on the subject has largely been of a factual kind – descriptions of what the technology looks like and does – rather than abstract considerations of its implications. For film production itself, the new technologies promise potential efficiency gains, which in turn suggest changes in staffing levels and job descriptions. There is some fear in the industry that jobs will be cut because machines will be able to perform tasks quicker and easier, and also that the technologies are developing at such a speed and are becoming so specialised that there is a fear of practitioners becoming unable to keep pace with developments. Both fears are at least partly unfounded, but serve to demonstrate the nervousness which still surrounds the subject of the new technologies within the film industry of the late 1990s.

Theoretical thinking on the form and content of the product has organised itself around several key issues: narrative, linearity, temporality, subjectivity and activity. These issues are explored in order to differentiate the intentions and effects of the new technologies from previous, more traditional forms. Biocca and Levy (1995) differentiate 'presence', which refers to a natural perception of an environment, from 'telepresence' which refers to the mediated perception of an environment. Pennefather talks about the difference between 'participative' (video game or virtual reality) and 'contemplative' (traditional cinema) interactivity (Pennefather, 1994). Andrew Cameron describes the 'imperfective' (spectator inside the time being represented, as in virtual reality) compared to the 'perfective' (time completed and viewed from outside, as in traditional linear narrative) experience (Cameron, 1995). Weinbren modifies this by arguing that the particular narrative forms possible with the new technologies create a 'subjunctive' state – a 'what could have been otherwise' – as the narrative is pieced together during a session (Weinbren, 1995). For Cotton and Oliver, the 'window onto' of traditional pictorial media (painting, film, etc.) becomes the 'door into' of virtual reality, a means of intensifying the sense of actually being in the fictional experience, rather than watching it from 'outside' (Cotton and Oliver, 1993). Whatever the specific terminology used, the general agreement is that the new technologies are capable of producing a more active, more involved 'receiver', who is empowered by the program to make decisions determining the narrative structure, character make-up, time and space of the work.

The debate also concerns itself with the implications of this upon how future works will be conceived and structured – how this interactivity can be predicted and satisfied; whether it spells the end of traditional linear narrative; whether interactive multimedia narratives will actually prove satisfying as entertainment experiences.

'Much of cinema's power over us is our lack of power over it . . . It could be argued that the introduction of viewer impact on the representation is a destructive step for the cinema. The removal of the possibility of suspense is the removal of desire from the cinematic, and ultimately, the removal of the very fascination of the medium. To find interactive forms in which desire can be sustained will require the construction of a new cinematic grammar' (Weinbren, 1995, pp. 19–20).

To counter this, closure must be read in a more radical light, possibly by constructing a work around multiple diegetic narratives and temporalities, any of which can provide the necessary end to the fiction. It is these very potentials which makes Le Grice argue that the repetitive and non-linear form of interactive entertainments will position them within the avant-garde arena (Le Grice, 1995). This movement begs the question: what will be left occupying the mainstream against which the avant-garde fights its fight? Possibly, there will no longer be a recognised 'mainstream', but rather a number of alternative forms of equal legitimacy?

VIRTUAL REALITY

Virtual reality (VR) promises to offer its user/player/participant (the correct term is currently undetermined, indicating VR's multiple identity) the possibility of entering an artificial, computer-generated environment in which he or she can physically move around the space, interact with objects, characters and events, and influence the formation and progress of the narrative. Such a description immediately indicates what is new about virtual reality; namely its experiential intensity and its empowering of the user. Whether this potential is fulfilled remains to be seen.

'Government money helped develop VR technology. Government funding agencies like the National Science Foundation supported much work at university research centres such as the University of North Carolina and the Massachusetts Institute of Technology. Other agencies like the US Air Force, the Navy, and NASA were instrumental in building early versions of many components' (Biocca and Levy, 1995). Initial uses of VR have all been 'serious' in nature – providing individual training for medics, pilots or astronauts, as well as simulating large-scale military wargames which would have proved prohibitively complex and expensive to stage in reality. This complexity and expense was the reason the technology was initially perceived to have no entertainment value. Only in the 1990s has there been a move to introduce it into the entertainment and domestic arenas, largely due to radical improvements in personal computer (PC) power and cost, and on the back of the over-hyped consumer interest in the information superhighway. Virtual reality has become the buzzword for all future possibilities offered by digital communications. Current emphasis is on equipment rather than implications, although Negroponte (1995) argues that VR actually refers to the *experience*, and thereby to the perceptions of an individual, rather than to the machine.

VR also offers new forms of meaning: 'something new has been added with the arrival of VR, and the process of meaning construction and meaning reception will be subtly altered' (Biocca and Levy, 1995). In a way, in its attempt to create a virtual environment which, ideally, would be indistinguishable from 'real-life' itself, VR potentially represents the furthest movement yet made along the realist axis. The word 'potentially' is used here advisedly, because such a perfect representation is still a significant way off. That notwithstanding, the debate surrounding virtual reality, indeed its very name, positions it within the realist aesthetic. This realist agenda operates around several key terms. The *vividness* of the system is argued to be its ability to produce a sensorially rich mediated environment; its *interactivity* and *responsiveness* is the degree to, and speed by, which users of the medium can influence the form or content of the mediated environment, and thereby feel a part of that environment; its *sensory breadth* is the number of sensory dimensions (vision, sound, touch) working together to create the virtual environment; and its *sensory depth*, the resolution, or 'quality', within each of those dimensions. The sense of a believable reality is therefore created through sensory overload, by several channels of information reinforcing one another's depiction of 'reality'. So, for example, not only will a door be seen to be slammed shut, it will be heard to do so (in 3-D sound) and even felt to do so (via a dataglove which presses against parts of the user's hand).

At the same time as providing a surfeit of virtual information, the VR system simultaneously deprives the user of real-world sensory information, immersing users in the artifical environment via a head-mounted display which totally encloses the head, eyes and ears. Consequently, the only spatial, aural and relational cues possible come from the system itself. This sensory deprivation substitution process is essential to the ability of virtual reality to convince its user of the 'reality' of the virtual world. In a way, this can be seen as the latest stage of a process which has always been a part of cinema presentation, from the sound effects produced behind the screen of silent film shows, through 3-D and Sensurround, to modern-day THX sound and IMAX screens. The difference is that with any of the cinematic systems, the spectator remains in the real world while experiencing the effect; disbelief is suspended, but not totally denied. With virtual reality, if the system eventually becomes sophisticated enough, the 'enabling of belief' promises to be total.

Cost has also been a determining factor in the physical location of the new technologies at the consumer end of the entertainment business. Affordable multimedia PCs, equipped with CD-Rom drives and capable of handling digital sound and vision, have been heavily promoted in the domestic market since 1994, and have experienced an exponential sales growth since the mid-1990s. Consequently, interactive games, 'infotainment' and 'edutainment' products are becoming big business. Additionally, in the new, global communications community, where all information, whether textual, visual and aural, is digital, the same machine can be used to view entertainment as to collect information of many kinds, conduct business or order shopping. Audio-visual material, in binary digit form, can be beamed by satellite, sent down cable and fibre-optic lines, or read from CD-Rom. At the end of the 1980s, with movie-theatre attendance reaching the lowest level in a decade, many consumers were, through the use of VCRs and pay-per-view television, choosing to view movies in their homes rather than go to the theatre. 'This trend created a need for a new form of out-of-home entertainment that could not be replicated in the home. The fact that virtual reality was perceived as a sexy new medium that could not be replicated in the home made it a prime technology to replace or supplement the ailing movie theatre market' (Negroponte, 1995).

The anticipated projection for the entertainment exploitation of virtual reality, therefore, sees it occupying a multiplicity of public locations, including games arcades and shopping malls, before entering the home at the point when the technology has become sufficiently miniaturised and economical to create a domestic market. This trajectory echoes that of cinema as a whole which, for the first three-quarters of its life to date, was solely a public-space entertainment form, before beginning a move into the domestic space, via television and video.

Selected Reading

Philip Hayward and Tana Wollen (eds), *Future Visions: New Technologies of the Screen*, London, BFI Publishing, 1993.

Star Wars (USA 1977 *p.c* – Lucasfilm; *d* – George Lucas; sd col.)

Tron (USA 1982 *p.c* – Walt Disney; *d* – Steven Lisberger; sd col.)

The Abyss (USA 1989 *p.c* – GJP; *d* – James Cameron; sd col.)

Terminator 2: Judgment Day (USA 1991 *p.c* – Carolco Pictures; *d* – James Cameron; sd col.)

James Cameron's sequel to *The Terminator* (1984), is viewed as groundbreaking in terms of its digital special effects; in particular the sophistication and photorealistic quality of its images. In fact, a version of the effects, especially the morphing scenes, can be seen in Cameron's 1989 film, *The Abyss*. In *The Abyss* Cameron is noted for his use of the then untested computer-based effects technology to produce the fluid water creature which appears in the film's climax. *Terminator 2* continues and expands on this technical experimentation by staging extravagant stunts and by integrating the special effects to such an extent that they become virtually indistinguishable from the actors. An example of this is the scene in which the cyborg leaps into a helicopter cockpit and morphs from its cop persona back into its steel form. The motorcycle leap from building to helicopter required the post-production removal of the wires and supports used in the original stunt. Each frame of the scene was fed into a powerful computer, and the unwanted information was replaced with material copied from the surrounding area. Each completed image was then transferred back on to film. The level of software sophistication required for the morphing process can be seen in its ability to map the reflection of the human actor (the pilot) on to the surface of the steel cyborg.

For all the film-makers' intentions to integrate effects and 'live action' into a seamless whole, the impressiveness of the special effects is such that frequently they stand out from the narrative. The foregrounding (the publicity hype) of the effects results in the film being watched simultaneously for two reasons: first, as a narrative taking place in a fantastic, yet believable, world, involving credible characters, and second, as a sequence of spectacular effects. The most sophisticated special effects feature films depend on this tension between the two agendas.

Jurassic Park (USA 1993 *p.c* – Amblin Entertainment; *d* – Steven Spielberg; sd col.)

The Mask (USA 1994 *p.c* – Dark Horse Entertainment; *d* – Chuck Russell; sd col.)

The special effects in *The Mask*, created by Industrial Light & Magic, make use of some of the tools developed the previous year for *Jurassic Park*. Additional effects were supplied by Dream Quest Images. The visual details of the Mask character were modified to suit comic actor Jim Carrey's unique physical features. Carrey's distinctive comic physicality also determined the style and extent of the computer-generated (CG) effects: 'Jim Carrey is such a character, sometimes people think we're creating effects when we're not, but when he goes to his extreme, we just push that a bit further ... In this case, we transitioned from Jim's head to our CG head. We made him look cartoonish by exaggerating the size of his eyes and expressions, but we rendered those images realistically' (Magid, 1994, p. 54). The effects team used 3-D modelling software rather than what they regarded as 'clichéd morph technology' which operated only in 2-D. Over footage of Carrey, 3-D wire frames were built which were then filled out with surface detail to create the cartoonish version of the real-life original. So, for example, when the Mask spots a beautiful woman in a nightclub, and transforms into a lustful wolf, 'a CG wireframe had to be built over Carrey's features in the computer, animated over several frames into a wolf's head, then rendered with photorealistic textures, highlights and shadows to blend seamlessly into the scene' (Magid, 1994, p. 55). Similarly, to create the massive pounding heart which almost bursts out of his chest, Carrey's real shirt was mapped on to an animated CG wireframe of the heart which had been superimposed over footage of Carrey. The success of the effects is achieved through a combination of prosthetic make-up on Carrey's face, computer-generated images and the actor's exaggerated physical comedy.

Toy Story (USA 1995 *p.c* – Walt Disney; *d* – John Lassiter; sd col.)

Independence Day (USA 1996 *p.c* – 20th Century–Fox; *d* – Roland Emmerich; sd col.)

Titanic (USA 1997 *p.c* – 20th Century–Fox/Paramount; *d* – James Cameron; sd col.)

Titanic, costing a massive $250m. to make and release but recouping over $1bn. in box-office receipts, scooped eleven Oscars at the 1998 Academy Awards. A central attraction of the film was its special effects, especially the highly convincing sinking of the ship during the last half of the film. In fact, special effects are used from the beginning to create the 'reality' of the huge ship in port and on the open sea, and to populate it with over 2,000 passengers. James Cameron and his technical crew decided to shoot the ship 'for real'; that is, as if it existed and could be filmed by, for example, cameras flying past in helicopters. To achieve this, Cameron's Digital Domain effects house had to 'force into existence' (as visual effects supervisor Rob Legato describes it) the software programs and digital tools required to create computer-generated (CG) images of the *Titanic*. These tools can be seen in action in the spectacular single sweeping 'helicopter' shot which takes the spectator from characters standing on the bow of the ship up and over its four funnels and down its length, before twisting back to frame its stern as it

Shooting for real? James Cameron's *Titanic*

sails off into the distance. Only the two initial actors are real; the rest is computer generated, including the many tiny passengers seen walking the various decks.

But these seemingly entirely computer-generated images are used in combination with many scale- and full-sized models of sections of the *Titanic* (Cameron ended up building 90 per cent of the ship full sized). Indeed, almost every special effects shot or sequence in the film is a combination of actual model or actor(s) and CG imaging. Although it is Cameron's stated wish to make the first wholly computer-generated film (involving ostensibly 'human' figures, as opposed to the puppets of *Toy Story*), there is a long way to go before that happens. In the meantime, scale models and real actors will be an integral part of the 'special effects' film-making process.

PART 3

NATIONAL CINEMAS AND FILM MOVEMENTS

Alice in den Städten (1974)

GERMAN EXPRESSIONISM AND NEW GERMAN CINEMA

GERMAN EXPRESSIONISM

The term Expressionism (borrowed from painting and theatre and applied to a number of films made in Germany between about 1919 and 1930) refers to an extreme stylisation of *mise-en-scène* in which the formal organisation of the film is made very obvious. The stylistic features of German Expressionism are fairly specific and include chiaroscuro lighting, surrealistic settings and, frequently, a remarkable fluidity of mobile framing. The 'Gothic' appearance of these films is often accompanied by similar acting styles and macabre or 'low-life' subject matters. The overall effect is to create a self-contained fantasy world quite separate from everyday reality, a world imbued with angst and paranoia in the face of that which cannot be rationally explained. This 'other world' often functions as a criticism of bourgeois society, though not always.

Analyses of German Expressionism have tended to focus either on German Expressionism as a 'national' cinema – assuming that the films of a nation reflect its 'mentality' and do so better than other artistic media – or on German Expressionism as a label grouping together certain films by certain film-makers – emphasising the *auteur* rather than 'national character'. In both cases there is a tendency to ignore the industrial context in which these films were created. Historian Siegfried Kracauer, however, writing in 1974, does not. Although he is ultimately interested in German Expressionism as a national cinema, he starts off with a discussion of the German film industry:

> Since in those early days the conviction prevailed that foreign markets could only be conquered by artistic achievements, the German film industry was of course anxious to experiment in the field of aesthetically qualified entertainment. Art ensured export, and export meant Salvation. (Kracauer, 1974, p. 65)

Although the origins of German cinema can be traced back to the 1890s, the output of the German film industry before the First World War was relatively insignificant, and movie theatres showed mostly foreign imported films. The outbreak of war in 1914 resulted in the imposition of import restrictions, and in the absence of American, Italian, French or Danish competition, a number of German production companies were created to exploit the newly expanded domestic market. According to Kracauer, the number of such companies rose from 28 in 1913 to 245 in 1919. During this period of consolidation, the German government, increasingly aware of cinema's propaganda potential for supporting an unpopular war, founded Deulig (1916), an amalgamation of independents involved exclusively in the production of propaganda shorts, and Bufa (1917) an agency concerned with providing frontline troops with a steady supply of films and film theatres.

By the end of the war some industrialists were beginning to recognise the economic advantages of paying close attention to foreign audiences, and accordingly in December 1917 the Universum Film AG (Ufa) was set up to facilitate further unification of the film industry. One-third of Ufa's finance came from the state, and the rest from banking interests and big business. Almost at once Ufa became the major production company in Germany, attracting foreign film-makers (like Alfred Hitchcock) and embarking on co-productions with other countries which were to give it considerable control of the postwar international market.

The end of the war, the collapse of the November uprising and massive inflation all contributed to an export boom in the German film industry that began in 1919. Of 250-odd independent production companies in Germany that year, Decla-Bioscop was second only to Ufa in assets and output. Its chief executive was Erich Pommer, who was convinced that foreign markets could only be conquered by artistic achievements. Perhaps the earliest artistic success among Decla's output was *The Cabinet of Dr Caligari* (1919), which inaugurated a long series of entirely studio-made films. Kracauer suggests that this withdrawal into the studio was part of a general retreat into a shell, but it may also be explained in terms of rationalisation of the film industry in the immediate postwar period. *The Cabinet of Dr Caligari* is generally regarded as the film which first brought Expressionism to the German cinema. After the war, the German film industry had concentrated on spy and detective serials, sex exploitation films and historical epics in an attempt to control the domestic and foreign markets. *Caligari* started a stylistic movement, derived from avant-garde painting, theatre, literature and architecture, which for a few short years became Germany's internationally respected national cinema, successfully differentiated from, and competing with, those of other countries, particularly America.

In 1921, the year in which *The Cabinet of Dr Caligari* was finally premièred in New York (subsequently becoming an international success), Decla-Bioscop was absorbed by Ufa along with producer Erich Pommer. Two years later Pommer became overall head of Ufa film production. One of the last Decla-Bioscop films to be made before Ufa took over was *Der müde Tod* (*Destiny*, 1921). Shot in a nine-week period and involving three exotic settings – one Arabic, one Venetian and one Chinese – the film illustrated the kind of ingredients that German companies were inserting into their films in order to appeal to the international, and particularly the American, market.

During this period, there was a considerable amount of vertical integration in the German film industry, and Ufa continued to expand throughout the early 1920s, absorbing a number of smaller production companies as well as larger enterprises like Decla-Bioscop. *Dr Mabuse der Spieler* (1921), for instance, was a co-production of Ullstein-Uco Film and Decla-Bioscop, and released by Ufa. Despite its length of more than three hours, *Dr Mabuse der Spieler* was successful at the box office, perhaps because it was easy to market as a thriller. Its plot, concerning a gambler who makes a fortune on the stock exchange, can be related interestingly not only to the economic conditions of contemporary Germany but also to those of the film industry itself.

Another short-lived studio, Prana Film, supplied Ufa with its next bid for international success, *Nosferatu* (1921). In 1922, Ufa's capital stock was increased to 200 million marks, and the company was able to increase its dividend from 30 per cent to 700 per cent thanks mainly to a boom in its export business (inflation notwithstanding). What films like *Nosferatu* lacked in 'stars' was compensated for in their gothic subject matter and atmospheric visual style. By contrast, *Warning Shadows* (*Schatten*, 1923) exemplifies all the stylistic features of German Expressionism, but was unable to capitalise on them, apparently because the film only found a response among 'film aesthetes' and made no impression upon the general public.

Ufa continued to produce, through its subsidiary Decla-Bioscop, large-budget and ambitious films. *Die Nibelungen* (1923–4) for example, a two-part project, took a total of 31 weeks to shoot. But Ufa had overestimated the film's likely profitability. In 1924, with the settlement of German reparations under the Dawes plan, the mark was stabilised and Germany was reintroduced to the gold standard, leading American firms to invest in the German film industry. The export boom in the film industry collapsed almost as swiftly as it had started, and the market was once again flooded with imports. By the end of the year, 40 per cent of the films being shown in Germany were American. It is not surprising, in the light of the changed situation, that *Die Nibelungen* was a catastrophe at the box office. Ufa's *The Last Laugh* (*Der letzte Mann*, 1924) met

The Cabinet of Dr Caligari – 'brought Expressionism to the German cinema'

much the same fate as *Die Nibelungen*, although the film's director, F. W. Murnau, was invited to Fox in Hollywood on the strength of its critical success. The sorry fate of these two films in the context of renewed American influence signalled in fact the end of German Expressionism. Although Expressionist tendencies can be found in later German films, and its influence seen in Hollywood (particularly in horror films and *films noirs*), Expressionism as a national movement began to die out around 1924.

An industry in decline

From 1926 until 1930, income from German film exports fell to less than 50 per cent of total takings, and soon even Ufa was in difficulties. As Julian Petley has pointed out, enormously costly films aimed partly at an export art-house market clamouring for 'Expressionism' simply could not cover their production costs (Petley, 1979, p. 36). *Metropolis* provides a typical example; released in 1926, it was the most expensive German film to date: budgeted at 1,900,000 marks, production costs eventually exceeded 5 million marks.

> At one point the Ufa governing board had considered halting the production because of the enormous expense, but decided to complete the picture in the hope that its distribution abroad, particularly in the United States, would recoup the losses. *Metropolis* proved to be a financial failure and in April 1927, Ufa, which controlled 75 per cent of German film production, was reorganised by a new board of directors. (Ott, 1979, p. 30)

In producing such a failure Fritz Lang had employed some 800 actors, 30,000 extras and taken 310 days and 60 nights of filming. He was never permitted such an extravagant experiment again (Fritz Lang, p. 241).

In order to stabilise a dangerous economic situation, the major German film companies made a series of agreements, disadvantageous to themselves, with the large American companies. Ufa formed Parufamet with Paramount and MGM. The agreement was that Ufa would exhibit 20 of each of the American companies' releases in exchange for the distribution of a total of 10 Ufa films by MGM and Paramount, and a loan of 17 million marks. Other German companies made similar agreements: Terra with Universal, Rex with United Artists, Phoebus (like Ufa) with MGM.

> The Government responded to the flood of imports with a quota law which decreed that for every foreign film released in Germany, a German film should be produced, but this resulted merely in a flood of . . . cheap films often . . . made solely to acquire a quota certificate . . . Since the Americans wanted as many quota certificates as possible they even produced their own quota films in Germany. (Petley, 1979, p. 34)

The Parufamet deal and others like it offered the industry only temporary respite from receding receipts. These deals represented the culmination of American attempts to bring the German film industry to rely on American financial support and thus to weaken its strongest foreign competitor. In 1927, however, Alfred Hugenberg, a powerful industrialist and fervent nationalist, acquired Ufa, buying out all American interests in the company. Ufa's production programme was rapidly rationalised and fewer films were henceforth commissioned from independents. All but the best-funded of Ufa's rivals soon went under: as profits and production declined only the export end of the business was expanded. Aware as the German majors were of the dangers of financial, aesthetic and technological dependence upon America, they had little alternative but to endure it.

Sound cinema, it was hoped, would cut down foreign imports because of language difficulties, while still allowing German

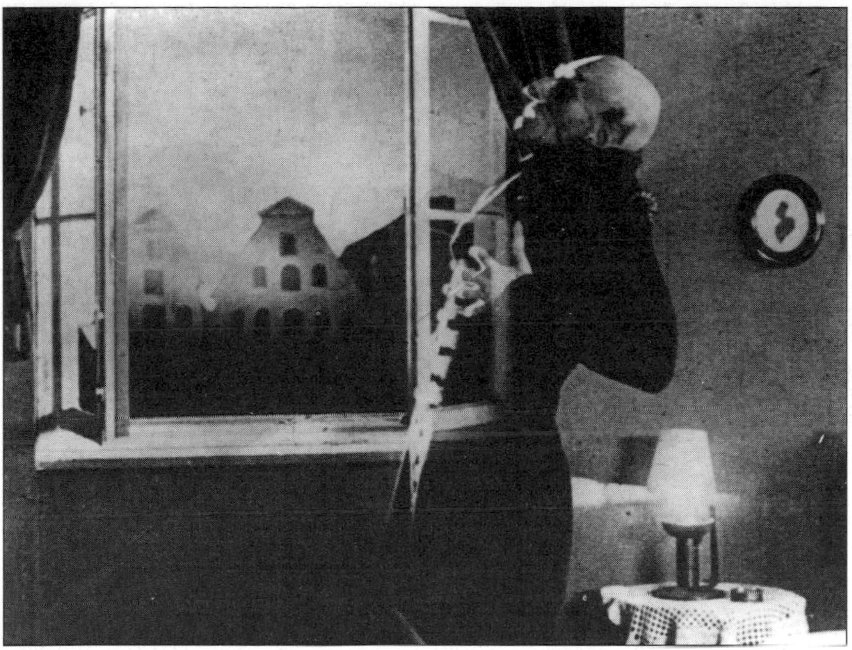

The gothic style – *Nosferatu*

exports to exploit the possibility of dual versions. German film companies had begun taking out patents on sound systems as early as 1924, and in 1929 an agreement was eventually signed to employ the Tobis-Klangfilm process. Some early German sound films, such as *The Blue Angel* (*Der blaue Engel*, 1930), *M* (1931) and *Kameradschaft* (1931) all enjoyed international success. *The Blue Angel* and *M*, produced in English and German versions, made world-famous stars of Marlene Dietrich and Peter Lorre, while *Kameradschaft*, made simultaneously in German and French to suit its subject matter, was popular across Europe. By 1933, however, when Fritz Lang's *M* was finally released in America by Paramount both Lang and Lorre were already in the US, as were Josef von Sternberg, director of *The Blue Angel*, and Dietrich.

It was not until the 1960s that any significant renewal of German film-making took place.

Selected Reading

Siegfried Kracauer, *From Caligari to Hitler: a psychological history of the German film*, Princeton N.J., Princeton University Press, 1974.

Julian Petley, *Capital and Culture: German cinema 1933–45*, London, BFI, 1979.

Thomas Elsaesser, 'Germany: The Weimar Years', in Nowell-Smith (ed.), *The Oxford History of World Cinema*, Oxford University Press, 1996.

Das Cabinet des Dr Caligari (The Cabinet of Dr Caligari) (Germany 1919 *p.c* – Decla-Bioscop; *d* – Robert Wiene; st b/w)

Der müde Tod (Destiny) (Germany 1921 *p.c* – Decla-Bioscop; *d* – Fritz Lang; st b/w)

Nosferatu, Eine Symphonie des Grauens (Nosferatu) (Germany 1921 *p.c* – Prana Film; *d* – Friedrich Wilhelm Murnau; st b/w)

Dr Mabuse der Spieler: I (Dr Mabuse the Gambler: I) (Germany 1922 *p.c* – Ullstein-Uco Film/Decla-Bioscop/Ufa; *d* – Fritz Lang; st b/w)

Dr Mabuse der Spieler: II (Dr Mabuse the Gambler: II)(Germany 1922 *p.c* – Ullstein-Uco Film/Decla-Bioscop/Ufa; *d* – Fritz Lang; st b/w)

Schatten (Warning Shadows) (Germany 1923 *p.c* – Pan Film/Dafu Film Verleih; *d* – Arthur Robison; st b/w)

Die Nibelungen: II – Kriemhilds Rache (Kriemhild's Revenge) (Germany 1924 *p.c* – Decla-Bioscop/Ufa; *d* – Fritz Lang; st b/w)

Der letzte Mann (The Last Laugh) (Germany 1924 *p.c* – Ufa; *d* – Friedrich Wilhelm Murnau; st b/w)

Metropolis (Germany 1925 *p.c* – Ufa; *d* – Fritz Lang; st b/w)

M (Germany 1931 *p.c* – Nero Films; *d* – Fritz Lang; st b/w)

Kameradschaft (Comradeship) (Germany 1931 *p.c* – Nero Films; *d* – G. W. Pabst; st b/w)

NEW GERMAN CINEMA

The term New German Cinema has been used to delineate a loose grouping of films made in West Germany over a period from the 1960s through to the early 1980s. Made by young film-makers who had been born around the time of the Second World War and grown up in a postwar divided Germany, these films have been noted for their contemporary relevance and formal experimentation and were regarded as heralding the most promising development in German cinema since German Expressionism.

Initially commentators tended to focus on the personalities of the film-makers, treating them as individual creative geniuses, and examining their films almost exclusively in terms of their directors' personal visions. This critical reception was largely the result of the deliberate promotion of the new films as an *Autorenkino* (cinema of authors) by the film-makers themselves. This notion of an *Autorenkino* was most clearly theorised by Alexander Kluge, who believed that film-makers should familiarise themselves with all aspects of production, thus becoming *Filmautoren* and having the potential to exercise a high degree of authorial control.

Due to the lobbying efforts of Kluge and others, combined with a political will at the time to see film acquire the status of 'Kultur', the concept of an *Autorenkino* informed the film subsidy agencies that the West German government began to set up in the mid-1960s. In order to ensure that film-makers retained as much artistic control over their work as possible, the funding agencies encouraged them to assume more than just a directorial role, and to become, for example, their own scriptwriter and/or producer as well and to take many of the artistic, casting and editing decisions.

Thus, when the films came out, it was very easy to attribute them solely to an individual author figure and neglect other factors that help to shape a national cinema or film movement. Given the sway being gained by *auteurist* film criticism in the 1960s and 1970s, New German Cinema attracted critical acclaim largely because it had been produced within a conceptual and institutional framework which actively encouraged critics to evaluate it as the product of gifted *auteurs*. As a result, the early major studies of the New German Cinema singled out a small number of (male) directors for particular attention – usually R. W. Fassbinder, Werner Herzog, Alexander Kluge, Volker Schlöndorff, Jean-Marie Straub, Hans-Jürgen Syberberg and Wim Wenders – while marginalising all other areas of work that equally formed part of the New German Cinema.

It is clear, though, that the key factor in the emergence of the New German Cinema was the handling of the West German film industry by the occupying powers after the

Second World War. In order to help to both 'de-Nazify' the country and to build up the western zones as a buffer to Soviet influence in eastern Europe, the western Allies flooded West Germany with Hollywood films. As no import quotas were imposed, American companies quickly achieved a position of economic dominance in Germany by the beginning of the 1950s. To help protect this market domination, the Allies dismantled the remnants of the centralised Nazi film industry and licensed only small independent production companies in its place.

Forced to remain small scale, the new West German film industry failed to attract substantial investment and films had to be produced relatively cheaply. Unable to compete with the expensive Hollywood spectacle, indigenous production became expressly orientated towards the home market, and during the 1950s the *Heimat* film genre with its depiction of simple country life was particularly popular. Although this popularity precipitated a brief boom for the industry in the mid-1950s, the films did not boast high production values and West German cinema soon acquired a reputation abroad for being drab, provincial and 'escapist'.

As early as the mid-1950s representatives from the industry and film-makers had started calling for government intervention. Criticism reached a peak in 1961 when the organisers of the Venice Film Festival rejected all West German entries and the Federal Film Prize given annually at home went unawarded. The following year a group of twenty-six young film-makers, writers and artists – spearheaded by Kluge – published the *Oberhausen Manifesto:*

> The collapse of the conventional German film finally removes the economic justification from a mentality which we reject. The new German film thereby has a chance of coming to life.
>
> In recent years German short films by young authors, directors and producers have received a large number of prizes at international festivals and have won international critical acclaim. These works and their success shows that the future of the German film lies with those who have demonstrated that they speak a new film language.
>
> In Germany, as in other countries, the short film has become a training ground and arena of experimentation for the feature film.
>
> We declare our right to create the new German feature film.
>
> This new film needs new freedoms. Freedom from the usual conventions of the industry. Freedom from the influence of commercial partners. Freedom from the tutelage of other groups with vested interests.
>
> We have concrete ideas about the production of the new German film with regard to its intellectual, formal and economic aspects. We are collectively prepared to take economic risks.
>
> The old film is dead. We believe in the new.

In its criticism of the 'old' German film, the Manifesto also presaged Kluge's notion of an *Autorenkino*. By stressing the need for freedom from economic and other vested interests, it effectively defined the new German film in opposition to industrial modes of production and demanded the freedom of expression normally associated with 'artistic' production. Kluge subsequently reinforced this opposition when he contrasted the new German film with the *Zutatenfilm* (recipe film): a typical industry product made up of ingredients such as stars, ideas, directors, technicians, scriptwriters and so on which the producer simply went out and purchased according to requirements. Such a comparison implied that the 'new' film would be more than just the sum of its parts, that the film-makers would bring something personal to their work.

Although the government responded to this mounting criticism as early as April 1962 by announcing plans to provide public funding for feature film production, three years passed before the first film subsidy agency – the Kuratorium junger deutscher Film (Board of Young German Film) – was set up. In the meantime Kluge and co-signatory Edgar Reitz started to develop the demands of the *Oberhausen Manifesto* into a coherent education programme at the Ulm Film Institute. A four-year course was set up with the express purpose of training a new generation of film-makers as *Filmautoren*. Rather than training as specialists in particular areas such as camera, scriptwriting, editing or direction – as is normally the case in the film industry – students received an all-round film-making education. Not only did a number of New German Cinema directors, including Ula Stöckl and Claudia von Alemann, study at Ulm during the 1960s, but when the Berlin Film and Television Academy opened in 1966 it followed Ulm's model.

Set up in 1965 with a brief to stimulate a renewal of the German film, the Kuratorium provided production loans for first-time feature film directors. Within two years, twenty-five films had been funded, including Alexander Kluge's *Yesterday Girl* (1966) which won several prizes. Several other films also attracted critical acclaim, especially Edgar Reitz's *Mealtimes* (1967), Peter Schamoni's *Schonzeit für Füchse/Closed Season for Foxes* (1966) and Volker Schlöndorff's *Young Törless* (1966). In contrast to the 'escapist' genre films of the 1950s, the new cinema drew on contemporary subject matter and included documentaries (for instance, Werner Herzog's *Land des Schweigens und der Dunkelheit/Land of Silence and Darkness*, 1971), formally experimental work (e.g. Jean-Marie Straub and Danièle Huillet's *Nicht versöhnt/Not Reconciled*, 1965) and episodic narratives (for example Kluge's *Yesterday Girl*) alongside more conventional feature films (such as Fassbinder's *Katzelmacher*, 1969). Thomas Elsaesser's description gives a good indication of the radical departure the first films represented:

> Young German films . . . often bore little reference explicitly or implicitly to national or international film culture. The early films of Syberberg or Herzog, for instance, were to a remarkable degree objects *sui generis*, outside any recognisable tradition of film-making either commercial or avant-garde. Kluge's essays on celluloid, and even Jean-Marie Straub's or Vlado Kristl's films seemed . . . inspired by what one might call 'cinephobia', a revulsion against the commercial film industry and its standard product, the fictional narrative film. (Elsaesser, 1989, p. 25)

Over the next twelve years a network of film subsidy agencies developed, providing five major sources of funding: the Kuratorium, the Film Promotion Board, Federal Film Awards, regional initiatives and television. After successive revisions the subsidy system offered a range of types of funding – for production, exhibition, distribution, and script and project development – aimed at promoting a national cinema that was both culturally motivated and economically viable. By the late 1970s an unprecedented half of all feature films being made were deemed to belong to the new cinema; and when Volker Schlöndorff's *The Tin Drum* (1979) won the American Oscar for the best foreign film in 1980, one British critic commented that the New German Cinema was 'one of the most remarkable, enduring, and promising developments in the cinema of the 1970s' (Sandford, 1980, p. 6). The funding agencies also facilitated an enormous range of work that would not otherwise have been possible. In the early 1970s the television channel WDR, for instance, produced the critically acclaimed *Arbeiterfilme* (worker films) made by a predominantly Berlin-based group of film-makers (including Christian Ziewer, Erika Runge, Ingo Kratisch, Marianne Lüdcke and Fassbinder) which focused on the lives and experiences of the contemporary German working classes. By the end of the decade the subsidy system had also enabled a number of women film-makers (including Helke Sander, Helma Sanders-Brahms, Ulrike Ottinger and Margarethe von Trotta) to make the difficult transition from documentaries and shorts into feature film produc-

Political cinema of the 1970s – *The Lost Honour of Katherina Blum*

tion which gave rise to a vibrant and critically acclaimed women's cinema.

But few of the films thus produced were box-office successes, a fact that elicited some criticism at home. In 1977, for instance, Eckart Schmidt declared: 'Filmmakers like Kluge, Herzog, Geissendörfer and Fassbinder, all of whom have collected subsidies more than once, and who despite such public funding are incapable of directing a success, should in future be barred from receiving subsidies' (quoted in Elsaesser, 1989, p. 37). The increasing fragmentation of the cinema audience (due to the dominance of television, the demise of the traditional family audience and the politicisation of the student movement in the late 1960s), combined with a lack of interest from commercial exhibitors, the dominance of American distributors and the absence of a film culture in Germany (outside Berlin, Hamburg and Munich), meant that the new German film found it difficult to win a national audience.

Over the years the film-makers themselves voiced criticism of the subsidy system. Although there was a desire to create a 'quality' national cinema, funding was often

Warum läuft Herr R. Amok? (Why Does Herr R. Run Amok?) (West Germany 1969 *p.c* – antitheater/Maran Munich; *d* – Rainer Werner Fassbinder/Michael Fengler; sd col.)

Eika Katappa (West Germany 1969 *p.c* – Werner Schroeter; *d* – Werner Schroeter; sd col. b/w)

Aguirre, der Zorn Gottes (Aguirre, Wrath of God) (West Germany 1972 *p.c* – Werner Herzog Filmproduktion Munich/HR; *d* – Werner Herzog; sd col.)

Alice in den Städten (Alice in the Cities) (West Germany 1974 *p.c* – Produktion 1 im Filmverlag der Autoren (Peter Geneé) Munich/WDR; *d* – Wim Wenders; sd b/w)

Die verlorene Ehre der Katherina Blum (The Lost Honour of Katherina Blum) (West Germany 1975 *p.c* – Paramount–Orion (Willi Benninger)/Bioskop Munich (Eberhard Junkersdorf)/WDR; *d* – Volker Schlöndorff/Margarethe von Trotta; sd col.)

Im Lauf der Zeit (Kings of the Road) (West Germany 1975 *p.c* – Wim Wenders Filmproduktion; *d* – Wim Wenders; sd b/w)

Der amerikanische Freund (The American Friend) (West Germany 1977 *p.c* – Road Movies Berlin/Wim Wenders Filmproduction Munich/WDR; *d* – Wim Wenders; sd col.)

Die allseitig reduzierte Persönlichkeit – Redupers (The All-round Reduced Personality – Redupers) (West Germany 1977 *p.c* – Basis Film Berlin/ZDF; *d* – Helke Sander; sd b/w)

Hitler – ein Film aus Deutschland (Hitler – A Film from Germany) (West Germany 1977 *p.c* – TMS (Hans Jürgen Syberberg)/ Solaris (Bernd Eichinger)/ WDR/INA Paris/ BBC; *d* – Hans Jürgen Syberberg; sd col.)

In einem Jahr mit 13 Monden (In a Year of 13 Moons) (West Germany 1978 p.c – Tango/Project/Filmverlag der Autoren; *d* – Rainer Werner Fassbinder; sd col.)

Deutschland im Herbst (Germany in Autumn) (West Germany 1978 *p.c* – Project Film Produktion/Filmverlag der Autoren/Hallelujah Film/Kairos Film Munich; *d* – Alf Brustellin, Rainer Werner Fassbinder, Alexander Kluge, Maximiliane Mainka, Edgar Reitz, Katja Ruppé, Hans Peter Cloos, Berhard Sinkel, Volker Schlöndorff; sd col.)

Bildnis einer Trinkerin (Ticket of No Return) (West Germany 1979 *p.c* – Autorenfilm; *d* – Ulrike Ottinger; sd col.)

Yesterday Girl (Abschied von gestern) (West Germany 1966 *p.c* – Kairos Film Munich/Independent Film Berlin; *d* – Alexander Kluge; sd b/w)

Alexander Kluge is viewed as one of the most vocal advocates of a new German cinema, and spearheaded the group of film-makers, writers and artists that drew up the *Oberhausen Manifesto* in 1962. Although he played a key role in developing the notion of an *Autorenkino*, he later criticised those film-makers who presented themselves as *auteurs*, and stressed the importance of the audience, arguing that 'the cinema is its spectators' (Corrigan, 1994, p. 90).

Yesterday Girl was one of the first films to be funded by the Kuratorium, and given its mixing of documentary, fiction and experimental film conventions, it can be viewed as an explicit endeavour to create the new cinema called for in the *Oberhausen Manifesto*. The filmic devices employed – such as the use of inter-titles to break up the narrative flow, voice-over commentary, direct address to camera, and at times a non-synchronous soundtrack – have also been described as 'Brechtian'. It has been compared with Godard's work, especially *Vivre sa vie* (*It's my Life*), 1962 and Kluge has acknowledged both Godard and Eisenstein as influences.

Yesterday Girl is based on the true story of a young Jewish woman, Anita G., who arrives in West Germany from the former GDR. According to Elsaesser (1989) the film can be read as an 'issue oriented' film about pregnancy, vagrancy, petty crime and social work, and hence represents a stark contrast to the 'escapism' of the 1950s *Heimat* films. But, in view of Anita's Jewishness and her East German background, it has also been read as being about the inseparability of past and present and the intertwining of individual and national history, a theme that frequently recurs in New German Cinema films in relation to the Nazi past. Throughout the film, Anita's presence serves as both a reminder of the Nazi persecution of the Jews and of the communist rejection of capitalism – thus linking questions of German history and the contemporary situation of postwar divided Germany.

Unwelcome questions – *Germany, Pale Mother*

Germany, Pale Mother (Deutschland bleiche Mutter) (West Germany 1979; *p.c* – Helma Sanders-Brahms/Literarisches Colloquium Berlin/WDR; *d* – Helma Sanders-Brahms; sd col.)

Germany, Pale Mother caused something of a controversy on its release for its handling of the recent German past. Mixing archive newsreel footage with the conventions of art-house realism, the predominantly narrative-based film looks back to Sanders-Brahm's own childhood, her experiences of growing up in the 1950s and the lives of her parents.

However, the film was also made at the time the American TV series *Holocaust* was broadcast on German television – an event which according to contemporary observers played a key role in precipitating a 'remembering' of the Nazi past that had been systematically repressed after the Second World War (see Kaes, 1989, p. 30). Although partly welcomed, this process of remembering also raised unwelcome questions of who should bear responsibility for the Nazi regime. At the end of the 1970s, West Germans became preoccupied with the past and with German identity, resulting in, as Anton Kaes puts it, attempts on the part of a number of New German Cinema directors and other cultural producers 'to rewrite German history, to fit the atrocities of the Hitler period into a tolerable master narrative'.

Although Sanders-Brahms had begun developing the idea of *Germany, Pale Mother* as early as 1976, it was widely 'read' as just such an attempt. The director has stressed she wanted to make a film which dealt with those people like her parents who may not have voted for Hitler, but did not protest, resist or emigrate either. However, for many, *Germany, Pale Mother* seemed to suggest that her parents – and, by implication, others like them – bore *no* responsibility for the Nazi atrocities, and that rather they were simply victims of historical circumstances.

The Marriage of Maria Braun (Die Ehe der Maria Braun)(West Germany 1978 *p.c* – Albatros (Michael Fengler)/Trio (Hans Eckelkamp)/WDR; *d* – Rainer Werner Fassbinder; sd col)

Fassbinder made over twenty full-length feature films and numerous television productions in just over ten years. Although he is one of the best-known New German Cinema directors, he was not part of the Oberhausen 'scene' and in fact worked initially in theatre. Whereas Elsaesser has characterised the early work of Syberberg, Herzog, Kluge and others as 'outside any recognisable tradition of film-making', much of Fassbinder's work self-consciously drew on the conventions of Hollywood genre films (Elsaesser, 1989). Although he dealt with specifically German subject matter, they have also been read as articulating a love–hate relationship with both Hollywood cinema in particular and American cultural imperialism generally.

Some of Fassbinder's early work, for instance, uses the gangster genre to explore the criminal underworld of Munich, such as *Love is Colder Than Death* (*Liebe is kälter als der Tod*, 1969) and *The American Soldier* (*Der amerikanische Soldat*, 1970). Subsequently he turned his attention to melodrama, influenced by the films of Douglas Sirk. In the latter stage of his career he made what he described as German Hollywood films, such as *The Marriage of Maria Braun* and *Lili Marleen* (1980).

The Marriage of Maria Braun focuses on a woman's struggle to survive in immediate postwar Germany when her husband, Hermann, goes to prison for a murder she commits. Although devoted to Hermann, Maria embarks on a long-term affair with her boss, Oswald, in order to be able to provide a home for Hermann when he is released.

According to Elsaesser, the film addresses the recurring themes identified as the main preoccupations of the New German Cinema: loneliness, homelessness, isolation, fear and failure. For Elsaesser, Oswald and Maria's relationship is based on the assumption that 'sharing loneliness is the best that two people can achieve'. But since the film focuses on Maria's struggle to survive and her love for Hermann, Kaes (1989) suggests that the film also offers a 'rewriting' of German history. Not only does it highlight the purely personal experiences of the individual at the cost of exploring the political realities of the post-Nazi era, but Maria is seen as bearing no responsibility for the situation in which she finds herself.

awarded with commercial priorities in mind. Consequently, the formal experimentation that characterised many of the early films gradually gave way during the 1970s to a cinema of narrative-based feature films (typified by Fassbinder's *The Marriage of Maria Braun*, 1978, and Wenders's *The American Friend*, 1977). Given that the cinema was completely dependent on public money, projects that addressed politically sensitive issues or were socially critical also either failed to find funding or had to adopt highly oblique approaches to their subject matter. Margarethe von Trotta's film *The German Sisters* (1981), for instance, alludes to the terrorist activity that swept across West Germany during the 1970s but does not overtly examine its causes.

By the mid-1980s a number of critics had pronounced the demise of the New German Cinema. This was partly because the directors most closely associated with it had moved abroad, and one of the cinema's most prolific directors, R. W. Fassbinder, had died in 1982. That year also saw the return to power of the CDU/CSU political union and the introduction of a more conservative approach to film policy which clearly favoured commercial projects over any form of artistic experimentation. At the same time, the cost of producing films rocketed during the 1980s, necessitating pan-European funding strategies since national funding initiatives alone were rarely adequate.

Nevertheless, it is possible to argue that as the 1980s progressed, the aim of promoting a culturally motivated and economically viable national cinema was realised. Kluge's notion of an *Autorenkino* may have been somewhat eroded in favour of commercialism, but films like Wolfgang Petersen's *The Boat* (1981), Doris Dörrie's *Men* (1985) and Percy Adlon's *Bagdad Café* (1987) were successful on both the art cinema and commercial circuits. Although not typical of what exemplified the New German Cinema – given their more conventional narrative structures and commercial orientation – neither were they lacking in cultural specificity.

And while some of the goals of the New German Cinema were thus realised in a different form, some of its more characteristic forms persisted beyond the demise of New German Cinema as an identifiable movement. Throughout the 1980s and 1990s a number of German film-makers, including Herbert Achternbusch (e.g. *Heilt Hitler*, 1986), Edgar Reitz (e.g. *Die zweite Heimat/Heimat 2*, 1992), Kluge (e.g. *Der Angriff der Gegenwart auf die übrige Zeit/The Blind Director*, 1986), Elfi Mikesch (e.g. *Marocain*, 1989), Werner Schroeter (e.g. *Malina*, 1991) and Monika Treut (e.g. *My Father is Coming*, 1991) have continued to produce innovative and challenging work of contemporary relevance. And as if in recognition of this work, the Berlin Film Festival maintained, at least until the mid-1990s, a 'New German Film' section in its International Forum of Young Film. Reitz's epic TV series, *Heimat* (1984) also demonstrated that such work could be commercially viable, when the series was sold to several major national TV networks.

As *auteurist* methodology began to be

superseded, in the 1980s, by other critical approaches to the study of film, a number of writers (e.g. Elsaesser, Kaes, Knight, Rentschler) began to critically reassess the New German Cinema. In the process they rescued a number of film-makers from critical oblivion – especially women directors such as Helke Sander and Helma Sanders-Brahms who fared particularly badly in the early *auteurist* studies. But just as importantly these writers explored more fully the social, political and economic factors that helped shape the new cinema: the postwar American legacy and US cultural imperialism; the development of the film subsidy system at the cost of political and artistic censorship; modes of production, distribution and exhibition; and concern with contemporary socio-political issues such as terrorism, the Nazi past and the women's movement. These studies demonstrate that the phenomenon of the New German Cinema, while informed by the notion of an *Autorenkino*, can only be fully understood as the product of a complex network of nationally and historically specific conditions.

Selected Reading

Timothy Corrigan, *New German Film: The Displaced Image*, Bloomington and Indianapolis, Indiana University Press, rev. edn, 1994.

Thomas Elsaesser, *New German Cinema: A History*, Basingstoke, Macmillan/BFI, 1989.

Anton Kaes, *From 'Hitler' to 'Heimat': The Return of History as Film*, Cambridge, Mass, Harvard University Press, 1989.

Julia Knight, *Women and the New German Cinema*, London and New York, Verso, 1992.

Eric Rentschler, *West German Film in the Course of Time*, Bedford Hills, NY, Redgrave, 1984.

SOVIET CINEMA

Until 1907 the only film companies operating in Russia were foreign, and the domestic market was dominated by the likes of the Lumière Brothers and Pathé. In 1907, however, the first Russian production company, Drankov, was set up in competition with foreign films and film companies which nevertheless continued to flourish in Russia until the outbreak of the First World War and the consequent collapse of the import boom. By 1917 there were more than twenty Russian film companies exploiting a steadily expanding home market, whose output consisted mainly of literary and dramatic adaptations, and costume spectaculars. This situation was suddenly and radically changed by the October Revolution. Veteran directors, actors and technicians emigrated as a period of violent transition totally disrupted normal conditions of production. The new Bolshevik government saw film as a vital tool in the revolutionary struggle, and immediately set about reconstructing the film industry to this end. On 9 November 1917, a centralised film subsection of the State Department of Education, Narkompros, was set up. This centralisation was resisted at first by the private sector, which boycotted the state-sanctioned films, and even went so far as to destroy precious raw film stock. Lack of supplies of equipment and new film stock made production very difficult for the emerging revolutionary cinema, but nevertheless, by the summer of 1918 the first agit-trains (mobile propaganda centres) left for the eastern front, specially equipped to disseminate political propaganda through films, plays and other media to the farthest corners of Russia.

The transition from entrepreneurial to state control of film production, distribution and exhibition proved a slow and difficult process, with postwar famine and continuing political and military conflict postponing the revival of the industry until the early to mid-1920s. By 1920 Soviet film production had dwindled to a trickle, but in 1921 when Lenin's New Economic Policy encouraged a cautious short-term return to limited private investment, releases rose from 11 in 1921 to 157 in 1924. The resumption of imports in the early 1920s following the restabilisation of the economy allowed profits to be ploughed back into domestic production, and, as film equipment and stock resurfaced, the several Soviet studios by then in existence began to expand to pre-Revolution proportions. In 1922, Goskino, the State Cinema Trust, was established as a central authority with a virtual monopoly over domestic film production, distribution and exhibition in Russia, although certain companies retained a degree of independence, and film industries in the more distant republics were allowed some autonomy from Moscow and Leningrad. Studios were set up in the various regions, such as VUFKU in the Ukraine, while others, Mezhrabpom-Russ for example, expanded in mergers with private industry. In 1923 a special propaganda production unit, Proletkino, was formed specifically for the production of political films in line with party ideology. Until 1924, films remained conventional in style, apparently untouched by the explosion of avant-garde experiment transforming the other arts in post-revolutionary Russia. Then in 1925, when the industry was allowed an increased aesthetic independence in the wake of a Politburo decision endorsing state non-intervention in matters of form and style in the arts, the new Soviet cinema entered its most exciting and formally adventurous period.

By the mid-1920s all the production units including Goskino (renamed Sovkino in 1925), Proletkino, Kultkino, Sevzapkino and Mezhrabpom-Russ, had begun to assemble their own personnel – directors, cinematographers, editors and so on, as well as performers. Vsevolod Pudovkin worked at Mezhrabpom, Sergei Eisenstein at Sovkino, Alexander Dovzhenko at VUFKU, for example. During this period, cinema came into productive collision with the energetic theoretical and artistic activity taking place in the other arts. The work of poet Vladimir Mayakovsky and theatre director Vsevolod Meyerhold, for example, profoundly influenced the early work of Eisenstein, whose avant-garde film experiments were accompanied by an impressive body of theoretical writings which are still influential today. In the wake of the 1925 Politburo decision, Eisenstein was commissioned by the Central Committee to produce a film commemorating the 1905 Revolution. This film, *Battleship Potemkin*, was premièred at Moscow's Bolshoi Theatre, an indication of its prestige. But despite a relatively positive critical response, the film's domestic release was relegated to Russia's second-run cinemas and

Soviet agit-prop train

its foreign sales delayed until pressure from influential writers, journalists and party officials induced Sovkino to send it to Berlin. Subsequently it was a huge international success, reflecting small credit on the conservative policies of the Soviet film industry at that time. *Battleship Potemkin*'s success heralded a series of ambitious and expensive productions. In 1926 Mezhrabpom-Russ released Pudovkin's *Mother*, another prestigious film which, like *Battleship Potemkin*, exceeded average budget allowances. By 1927 all the major production units were engaged in equally extravagant and prestigious projects in order to celebrate the tenth anniversary of the 1917 Revolution.

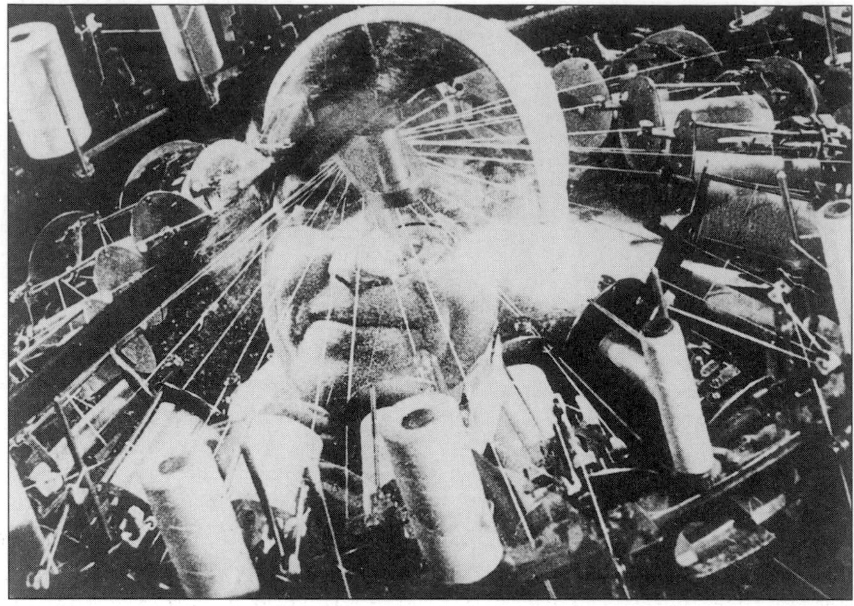

Formal extravagance in Vertov's *The Man with a Movie Camera*

THE JUBILEE FILMS

The impulse to produce the best, as well as the first, of the tenth-anniversary films resulted in a race involving Esfir Shub and Eisenstein at Sovkino and Pudovkin at Mezhrabpom-Russ. Pudovkin won with the release of *The End of St Petersburg*. Almost simultaneously, however, Sovkino completed two films recreating Russia's pre-revolutionary history entirely from archive footage – *The Great Road* and *The Fall of the Romanov Dynasty*. Both were directed by Shub, who had been trained as an editor at Sovkino. Production schedules and budgets were adjusted across the board for these Jubilee celebrations. At Sovkino, for example, Eisenstein and his collaborators were ordered away from production on *The General Line* to produce *October*.

The last of the Jubilee films, *October* was not in fact released until 1928. The delayed release was due in part to the film's reliance on recent Soviet history, which by the late 1920s was the subject of intense ideological scrutiny and rewriting in the wake of Trotsky's expulsion from the Party. In the event, *October* was extensively re-edited, and references to the role of Stalin's political opponents in the Revolution eliminated. The film was finally released in March 1928 to a hostile reception from the party leadership, who objected to its experimental style as 'formalist'. Simultaneously, the first All-Union Party Congress on Film Questions concluded that in future all fictional films should be accessible to the mass audience. The Congress ruled that film-makers should cease to employ formalist devices and seek instead to emphasise socialist content along strict party lines. This resolution has been seen as marking the beginnings of official sanction for a certain artistic method, that of socialist realism, which was to dominate Soviet cinema until after Stalin's death.

EMERGENCE OF SOCIALIST REALISM

In the words of the 1928 Congress resolution: 'the basic criterion for evaluating the art qualities of a film is the requirement that it be presented in a form which can be understood by the millions' (quoted in Katz, 1980, p. 1076). On completing *October* Eisenstein returned to the unfinished *The General Line* and decided to simplify his experimentations to a level more easily understood by a general audience, choosing objects like a bull, a tractor and a cream separator to symbolise the transition from primitive farming to mechanised modern agriculture, though he did not abandon his montage experiments. *The General Line* was symptomatic also of the transition to centralised control of film production: indeed, its title was changed to *The Old and the New* because the original title was criticised for implying that the film had received official sanction which, for all its extensive re-editing on Stalin's orders, it never actually achieved. *Earth* was similarly symptomatic: its controversial poetic lyricism was condemned as 'counter-revolutionary' and 'defeatist', though it managed to escape outright prohibition.

Other projects managed to sidestep, if not altogether escape, the aesthetic consequences of the directives of the 1928 Congress by producing or selling films at some geographical distance from the metropolitan centres of power in the Soviet Union. The Vertov Unit's experimental *Man with a Movie Camera* (1928) was produced at VUFKU in the Ukraine, for instance. Vertov had been sacked by Sovkino in early 1927 and ordered to leave Moscow, in some measure no doubt because his work was regarded as overly formalist. With his editor wife Elisaveta Svilova and cameraman brother, Mikhail Kaufman (Kino-Eye's Council of Three), Vertov made his way to the Ukraine. Between 1926 and 1928 VUFKU was engaged in an embargo on all Sovkino films, and employed the exiled Vertov on condition that his first project would be to complete the film *The Eleventh Year*, which was to have been Vertov's contribution to Sovkino's celebration of the tenth anniversary of the October Revolution. Once this film was finished Vertov embarked on *Man with a Movie Camera*, whose formal extravagance marks it off from others in the 1920s 'City' cycle of films, exemplified by Kaufman's *Moscow*, Ruttmann's *Berlin*, Cavalcanti's *Rien que les heures* and Vigo's *À propos de Nice*. Vertov continued his imaginative experiments after the advent of sound, but then gradually faded away after Stalin's consolidation of power.

Stalin's decrees under his first Five Year Plan led to increased production of documentaries in support of the Plan's industrial objectives, and in 1930 Sovkino was dissolved and replaced by Soyuzkino, an organisation directly supervised by the Politburo's Economic (rather than as previously, the Education) Department. Soyuzkino, under Stalin's appointee Boris Shumyatsky, was to function in close correspondence with Proletkino. It also officially adopted the resolution of the 1928 Congress in determining its aesthetic policy. After a brief transition period in which some interesting sound experiments emerged (e.g. Vertov's *Enthusiasm*, 1931), the coming of sound in 1930 combined with government-imposed restrictions on form and content encouraged an increasing realism of dialogue and character. Musicals and literary adaptations dominated the film industry's output, though there was also a spate of historical biopics celebrating the achievements of Lenin and Stalin. Eisenstein's first sound film *Alexander Nevsky* (1938) was made during this period, after a campaign by Shumyatsky to discredit and humiliate the director which involved hostile government interference in the production of *Bezhin Meadow*, and finally abandonment of the project. Only after a painful confession in which he was forced to renounce *Bezhin Meadow* was Eisenstein assigned the patriotic *Alexander Nevsky*, an important project intended to strengthen Russian national identity in the

The Battleship Potemkin (USSR 1925 *p.c* – Sovkino; *d* – Sergei M. Eisenstein; st b/w)

After the success of *The Strike* (1925), Eisenstein was commissioned by the appointed jubilee committee to direct a film to celebrate the abortive 1905 Revolution, which became *Battleship Potemkin*. Eisenstein took the Potemkin mutiny as the central metaphor for the Revolution.

Eisenstein worked closely with cameraman Tisse on the film and the famous 'Odessa steps sequence' required radical new filming techniques to put the director's ideas into practice (see Leyda, 1973, p. 195). The editing was planned in advance and the film was photographed accordingly. The principle behind the cutting was the editing together of disparate images to produce new ideas, which would emerge from the collision itself rather than the individual images (see Looking at film, p. 320). This idea has much in common with theories of counter-cinema (see Authorship and counter-cinema, p. 305) and with the linguistic theories which influenced much structuralist work on cinema (see Structuralism and its aftermaths, p. 323).

The 'Odessa steps sequence' is an example of Eisenstein's agitational cinema, using montage to build a tension which finally provokes a violent emotional response. It is also interesting as an attempt to make history itself the motivating force of the action, rather than individual men and women. If the Revolution speaks through the combination of images, however, the staging of events still clearly rests with Eisenstein. Later he would be heavily criticised for this manipulative approach to his material.

Mother (USSR 1926 *p.c* – Mezhrabpom-Russ; *d* – Vsevolod Pudovkin; st b/w)

The End of St Petersburg (USSR 1927 *p.c* – Mezhrabpom-Russ; *d* – Vsevolod Pudovkin; st b/w)

The Fall of the Romanov Dynasty (USSR 1927 *p.c* – Sovkino and the Museum of the Revolution; *d* – Esfir Shub; st b/w)

This film is an example of Shub's pioneering work in the development of reconstructed documentary. She put enormous energy into researching and collecting her material, often a difficult task given the poor condition and fragmentary nature of the newsreel clips. By editing the pieces together according to a system of juxtaposition of connecting images she was able to achieve effects of irony, absurdity and pathos which few of the pieces had intrinsically. Through this editing technique she gave Russia's history and its progress towards socialist reconstruction great emotional power.

Although her work was held up as an example of pure 'factography' (clearly by its very nature it could never aspire to the visual stylistic flourishes of Eisenstein, Vertov and others) there is a level of playful irony in the films which could be seen as characteristic of Shub's approach.

The Great Road (USSR 1928 *p.c* – Sovkino and The Museum of the Revolution; *d* – Esfir Shub; st b/w)

Symbols of transition – *The Old and the New*

October (USSR 1928 *p.c* – Sovkino; *d* – Sergei M. Eisenstein and Grigori Alexandrov; st b/w)

Man with a Movie Camera (USSR 1928 *p.c* – VUFKU; *d* – Dziga Vertov; st b/w)

New Babylon (USSR 1929 *p.c* – Leningrad Studio of Sovkino; *d* – Grigori Kozintsev and Leonid Trauberg; st b/w)

The General Line (The Old and the New) (USSR 1929 *p.c* – Sovkino; *d* – Sergei M. Eisenstein and Grigori Alexandrov; st b/w)

The Ghost that Never Returns (USSR 1929 *p.c* – Sovkino; *d* – Abram Room; st b/w)

Earth (USSR 1930 *p.c* – VUFKU; *d* – Alexander Dovzhenko; st b/w)

The end sequence of *Earth*, with the villagers and family mourning the young village chairman Vasili, offers a demonstration of 'poetic' modes of organising relations of space and time in narrative film. Thus it includes several instances of creative geography; for example, at one point the father of the dead boy is transported between shots from his son's deathbed to a hilltop, while the spatial transition is bridged by a match on action. Here the verisimilitude of fictional space is opened to question by a foregrounding of the cinematic language used to articulate spatial relations. But at the same time the device is an economical way of effecting a spatial transition required by the narrative.

Later, there is a sequence of three identical shots showing the father sitting at a table grieving. Each of these fairly lengthy shots is punctuated by a slow fade out and in. Whereas in creative geography, spatial coherence is broken, here it is the conventional articulation of narrative time which is infringed.

The Childhood of Maxim Gorky (USSR 1938 *p.c* – Children's Film Studio; *d* – Mark Donskoi; sd b/w)

Ivan the Terrible Part I (USSR 1944 *p.c* – Mosfilm; *d* – Sergei M. Eisenstein; sd b/w)

Ballad of a Soldier (USSR 1959 *p.c* – Mosfilm; *d* – Grigori Chukhrai; sd b/w)

face of the growing threat from Nazi Germany. In 1938 Shumyatsky was sacked, though there was no change in policy as a result. The administrative reshuffling in the film industry which followed, combined with the outbreak of the Second World War, led to a reduction in film output and a revival of the documentary. During the war, film industry personnel were evacuated from Moscow to remote parts of the USSR, and feature film production gave way to morale-boosting political propaganda in the form of documentary material gathered from the fronts. *Alexander Nevsky*, which had been made as implicit anti-Fascist propaganda, was withdrawn in 1939 in the wake of the German–Soviet Pact. In 1940 Eisenstein, having emerged from disgrace for his formalism in 1938, was appointed artistic head of Mosfilm, the revamped Soyuzkino, and in 1945 won the Stalin Prize for Part I of *Ivan the Terrible*. The following year Eisenstein began work on a sequel, but Part II met with none of the support that had greeted Part I, and its release was postponed for a decade. During the cold-war period Stalinist repression reached its highest level, repudiating the faintest hint of formalism as deviation from socialist realism, and several films were banned outright. It was only in 1956, three years after Stalin's death, that the effects of Khrushchev's denunciation of some aspects of Stalinism allowed a gradual withdrawal from the aesthetic orthodoxies of the cold-war years and a return to a more 'poetic' cinema. Chukhrai's *Ballad of a Soldier* (1959) is an illustration of this liberalisation. However, Khrushchev's enforced retirement in 1964 and the reintroduction of state controls in the film industry under the auspices of the Cinematography Commission of the USSR Council of Ministers resulted in another retreat to prestige literary adaptation and 'safe' historical reconstructions, until the late 1960s, when an international co-production programme resulted in a broadening of scope (e.g. Akira Kurosawa's *Dersu Uzala*, 1975).

Selected Reading

David Bordwell, *The Cinema of Eisenstein*, Cambridge, Mass., Harvard University Press, 1993.

Jay Leyda, *Kino: A History of the Russian and Soviet Film*, London, George Allen and Unwin, 1973.

Richard Taylor (ed.), *The Eisenstein Reader*, London, BFI, 1998.

Richard Taylor and Ian Christie (eds), *The Film Factory: Russian and Soviet Cinema in Documents 1896–1939*, London, Routledge, 1988.

ITALIAN NEO-REALISM

A national cinema, in the full sense of the term, is not just the national production registered in a particular country but a cinema which in some way signifies itself to its audiences as the cinema through which that country speaks. By this token the Italian neo-realism of the late 1940s and early 1950s was a quintessentially national cinema. Neo-realist films represented only a small proportion of box-office takings on the home market and their claim to signify on behalf of the nation was bitterly contested within Italy – not least by the Italian government itself. But the critical reputation acquired by neo-realism, in Italy and abroad, and the unequivocal way in which the films developed a national and popular subject matter meant that for many years 'Italian cinema' was synonymous with the neo-realist production of film-makers like Rossellini, De Sica and Visconti, while other forms of film-making in Italy, however commercially successful, were relegated to a secondary role.

Italian neo-realism was the product of the Second World War and the defeat of Italian and German Fascism. Ideologically it arose from the need, widely felt throughout Italy and most clearly articulated among intellectuals of the left, to break with the cultural heritage of Fascism and in particular with rhetorical artistic schemata which seemed to bear no relation to life as it was lived. Industrially, the conditions for the emergence of the neo-realist cinema were provided by the economic breakdown that followed the Allied invasion and the collapse of the Mussolini regime in 1943–5.

The Italian cinema had a long if not always distinguished history. Like many European national industries it had a flourishing period just before the First World War, before the Americans established their stranglehold on the world market. Of particular significance were the giant historical spectaculars (e.g. *Cabiria*, 1914) which reputedly impressed both Griffith and Eisenstein and which for many years functioned as a model, for some, of what the Italian cinema should once again become and, for others, of what it should avoid. The coming of Fascism in 1922 at first affected Italian cinema very little. But throughout the 1920s the industry was in economic and cultural decline, which the coming of sound at the end of the decade only aggravated. Having at first adopted more or less *laissez-faire* policies, the government took steps from about 1926 onwards to remedy the decline. The purpose of the intervention was not to create a distinctively 'Fascist' cinema, but simply an 'Italian' one, which would be economically and culturally self-sufficient. Though a number of patriotic and pro-Fascist features were produced, overt propaganda was confined mainly to the newsreels. After a brief period of experimenting with the 'art film', encouragement was given principally to the development of efficient studio production and out of this there emerged a steady stream of comedies and dramas which were designed to compete successfully, at least on the home market, with their Hollywood equivalents. To ensure that this would be possible, various protectionist measures were introduced, in the form first of quotas and then of import restrictions; these culminated in 1938 in a situation where the films from the 'major' Hollywood studios could not be seen in Italy at all, whereas those from the 'minors' could. In December 1941, with America's entry into the war, the importation of Hollywood films ceased entirely.

Although Fascism had a firm grip on economic and political life, its ability to secure popular consent was much less certain. Whereas in the 1920s, when the Fascists were struggling to consolidate their power, they did enjoy the active support of sections of the population; after 1930 when that power had been consolidated Fascist rule became something of an empty shell, receiving little more than a formal and grudging obeisance on the part of the population at large. Political opposition, crushed in 1926, began to revive in clandestine conditions from the mid-1930s onwards. Intellectually, opposition and the seeds of a national renewal began to develop within the ranks of the Fascist organisations themselves. When war came, this opposition was to transfer itself to the ranks of the Resistance. For the cinema, key centres of the oppositional culture out of which the neo-realist aesthetic was to develop were to be found in the government-sponsored film school, the Centro Sperimentale (founded 1935) and in the Cine-GUF or Fascist university film societies.

In July 1943, Allied troops invaded Sicily. Mussolini was deposed by an internal *coup*, rescued by a German commando unit and restored to nominal power as head of a puppet republic based in the northern resort town of Salò. One of the more bizarre acts of this puppet regime was an unsuccessful attempt to transfer the headquarters of the Italian film industry from Rome, where the grandiose film studios of Cinecittá had been opened in 1937, to the relative safety of Venice. When the Allies entered Rome in June 1944, they found the studios deserted but intact, and turned them into a refugee camp.

The final defeat of the German forces in Italy in April 1945 left the country liberated but also under Allied military occupation pending an official transition to civilian government. The Italian film industry was saddled with a control commission dominated by American trade representatives (in military uniform), whose main objective was the reopening of the Italian market to American

One of the first 'truly' neo-realist films – *Paisà*

films. Within the Italian industry a sharp divide emerged between the exhibitors, who made common cause with the Americans in their eagerness to fill the cinemas with the Hollywood films of which the public had been deprived during the war, and the producers (supported in this by the British on the commission), who wanted import restrictions at least for the time it would take to reconstruct the indigenous industry.

It was during this immediately postwar period, before the dismantled Italian film industry had been restructured in monopolistic form, that the neo-realist cinema was able to establish itself and to achieve a modest box-office success. This was also a period of political and social ferment, in which a radical cultural project such as that of neo-realism could enjoy a lot of political goodwill among the groupings that had emerged from the Resistance and in which a public could be found for an art which sought to reflect immediate reality in simple terms. Neo-realism survived so long as these conditions lasted; when they began to change what survived was no longer neo-realism.

Aesthetically the 'realism' of the neo-realist movement consisted principally of a commitment to the representation of human reality. This commitment could not and did not translate itself into any precise technical or stylistic prescriptions. In so far as there were prescriptions for a specifically realist practice, these tended to be dictated by (or rationalisations of) material conditions and were often contradictory and confused. Thus a preference for visual authenticity (coupled with the non-availability of studio space) led to a lot of scenes being shot on location, both indoors and outdoors, and also to the use of nonprofessional actors. But a necessary corollary of this was that sound almost always had to be dubbed or post-synchronised (which was standard Italian practice for imported films anyway), and the dubbing was generally done, not by the people whose faces appeared on the screen, but by professionals. Visual style and that of the soundtrack were thus regularly at odds with one another, with the former aspiring to a strong form of realism and the latter merely mimicking ordinary dramatic illusionism. If this contradiction were to be avoided – as, for example, in Visconti's *La terra trema* (1947), where the Sicilian fisherfolk speak their own lines in their native dialect – others would be generated. Thus in *La terra trema* the use of a dialect which most audiences would find incomprehensible breaks the dramatic illusion and imposes the need for a commentary; for commercial release on the home market the distributors in fact reverted to dubbing the film back into standard Italian. It is also noticeable that there is no consistency of camera and editing techniques in films of the neo-realist movement. The long-held deep-focus shot singled out by André Bazin as a distinguishing feature of neo-realism (as well as of the style of Wyler and Welles) is not in fact very common. The incidence of cut-aways and other elements of the editor's stock-in-trade is quite high, even in the films of Rossellini which Bazin found stylistically so exemplary. For *Germany Year Zero* (1947), Rossellini shot the dramatic action of the film in the studio in Italy, set against back-projected material filmed on location in Berlin.

Neo-realism in fact comprised a number of tendencies, which differed in their conception of realism as well as politically and in other ways. For a while these differences were masked, but with the break-up of the united anti-Fascist 'front' and a political realignment imposed by the cold war, the aesthetic differences also came to the fore. The disintegration of the movement in the early 1950s also coincided with the successful re-establishment of a commercial industry, supported by a centre-right Christian Democrat government, able to produce popular films in competition with the Americans. Although the political left continued for some years to promote the idea of a national cinema based on neo-realist ideals, the idea that this cinema was a homogeneous entity and that it was, or could be, the true and only 'national cinema' became increasingly hard to sustain. By the end of the 1950s neo-realism had effectively disappeared, giving way to a mixture of 'art' and 'genre' films, some of which (e.g. 'underworld' pictures) contained a certain neo-realist heritage.

The core of original neo-realism – most typically represented by the work in tandem of director Vittorio De Sica and scriptwriter Cesare Zavattini (e.g. *Bicycle Thieves*, 1948, and *Umberto D*, 1951) – was a strongly humanist and reformist impulse. In Zavattini's conception, the honest portrayal of ordinary life would be sufficient to create a bond between audience and film such that the protagonist would display his or her inherent humanity and the audience would grasp the nature of the circumstances which had to

The desperate search for the stolen bike – Zavattini/De Sica's *Bicycle Thieves*

change if that humanity was to display itself more fully. The preferred narrative mode was realist in the sense that fictional events were portrayed as if they were real and without the sort of dramatisation which would draw attention to their fictional character. Except in the immediately postwar period, when ordinary life was experienced in quite dramatic terms, the ordinariness and lack of drama of neo-realist films of this type gave them on the whole little appeal at the box office.

Flanking the humanists, on their left as it were, stood the Marxist tendency – represented for example by Luchino Visconti and Giuseppe De Santis. For the Marxists, a descriptive portrayal of ordinary life was not sufficient to convey a proper understanding of the circumstances to be struggled against. Increasingly the realism favoured by these film-makers came to be either contaminated by melodrama (rather splendidly in the case of De Santis's *Bitter Rice*, 1949) or reinterpreted in the light of Marxist aesthetic theory to become a 'critical realism' which was avowedly non-naturalistic. The high point of this tendency comes with Visconti's *Senso* (1954), which is a costume picture that offers a highly dramatised figuration of personal and class conflict in a nineteenth-century Risorgimento setting. The political–aesthetic justification for such a radical change from the style of *La terra trema* was to be found in the debate about realism going on in Marxist circles in Italy where the *Prison Notebooks* of Antonio Gramsci had recently been published and the ideas of Georg Lukács were also beginning to circulate. An equally important consideration, however, was the change in the structure of the industry and in audience expectations. As well as being 'realist' in the Lukácsian sense of producing a narration that captures historical truth, *Senso* (starring Farley Granger and Alida Valli) was designed as a high-class entertainment film with export as well as home-market potential.

While the majority of the neo-realists remained aligned with the political left, where they were to be joined by a second wave of Italian film-makers such as Francesco Rosi and Pier Paolo Pasolini, there also existed tendencies which were either non-aligned or specifically aligned with Christian Democracy. The anti-Fascist front, which had comprised all the democratic parties during and after the Resistance, broke up in 1947/48, leaving the Christian Democrats (the Catholic party) at the head of a centre-right government, with the Socialists and Communists in opposition on the left and monarchist and non-Fascist parties on the right. Of the major neo-realist film-makers, Roberto Rossellini was the only one to throw in his lot squarely with the Christian Democrats, but other Catholic film-makers such as Federico Fellini sheltered within the same politico-cultural space and there also developed a generically Catholic form of sub-neo-realism which produced dramas of guilt and redemption. Although melodramatic in conception, these films borrowed many of the trappings of neo-realism, particularly in the choice of humdrum settings and an emphasis (Catholic, however, rather than left-reformist) on the nobility of poverty.

The case of Rossellini deserves treatment on its own. During the early part of the war, Rossellini had made feature films about the war and service life which were government-backed though not excessively Fascistic in ideology. After the fall of Mussolini in 1943, he joined the anti-German Resistance and made the first Resistance feature, *Rome, Open City*, in 1945. *Rome, Open City* tells the story of a priest and a communist partisan which ends with the partisan being tortured to death while the priest is forced to look on, and the priest then being shot. While the film celebrates Catholic–communist unity in resistance to the Germans, its focus is spiritual rather than political and it is the priest rather than the partisan who is the real hero.

Rome, Open City was followed by two other films about war and its aftermath, *Paisà* (1946) and *Germany Year Zero* (1947), which belong within the neo-realist mainstream, even though their existential Catholic tone is untypical of the movement as a whole. But with the series of films that he embarked on with Ingrid Bergman beginning with *Stromboli* (1949), and even more with his film about St Francis (*Francesco, giullare di Di/Flowers of St Francis*, 1950), Rossellini distanced himself emphatically from the rest of neo-realism. Not only is the spirituality even more prominent, but the address of the films is toward European and American audiences, rather than toward Italy itself. As a commercial ploy this was not successful – none of the films was a great box-office success and *Stromboli* was mangled by RKO for American release. But the choice of direction is significant since it mirrors the political priorities of the Christian Democrat government which was committed both to the Atlantic alliance and to western European integration; it was also a deliberate repudiation of the 'national-popular' cultural strategy promoted by the Communists and supported by the rest of the left.

This political break with the rest of the neo-realist movement, however, did not mean that Rossellini should no longer be considered as a neo-realist in the aesthetic sense. Indeed the case has been made, most notably by André Bazin, that Rossellini was the truest neo-realist of all. For Bazin, neo-realism was an advance on conventional literary realism in that it was less constructed; thanks to the camera, film artists could represent immediate reality, filtering it through their consciousness, without having to impose an artificial purposive form on it. Bazin found this immediacy – an immediacy of things in themselves and an immediacy of the intervening consciousness – in Rossellini's films, far more than – for example – in the films of Visconti, which he judged realistic only in the conventional literary and theatrical sense. In a celebrated passage, defending Rossellini's *Journey to Italy* (1954) from its Lukácsian critics in Italy, Bazin wrote:

> With classical and with traditional realist art forms, I would say, the work of art is constructed like a house, of bricks or cut stone. There is no reason to question the usefulness of houses and their possible beauty, or the suitability of bricks for their construction, but it may be agreed that the reality of the brick lies less in its [physical] composition than in its shape and strength. One would not define it as a piece of clay and its mineral origin is irrelevant; what matters is the convenience of its volume. The brick is an element of the house, and this is already implicit in appearances themselves. Similarly with the cut stones that make a bridge. They fit perfectly to form an arch. But blocks of stone scattered in a ford are and remain stones; their reality as stone is not altered by the fact that, by jumping from one to another, I can use them to cross the stream. If they provisionally performed the task of a bridge, this is due to the fact that I have been able to complement the accident of their layout with my own inventiveness and to perform the motion which, without modifying their nature or appearance, has provisionally given these stones a sense and a use. (Bazin, Défense de Rossellini, 1962, p. 157)

Although the metaphor (as he himself admitted) is a bit stretched, Bazin here hits on a quality that other critics too have felt to be present in many of Rossellini's films from *Paisà* onwards, and especially in *Europe '51* (1951) and *Journey to Italy*. The films give evidence of an *ad hoc* construction in which bits of the external world which happen to be there, together with reactions solicited from the actors/characters from the events of the filming/scenario, are fused together in an apparently unpremeditated way. It is not only the director but the spectator too who is being asked to 'make sense' by hopping over the stepping stones. Although Rossellini's films have their own forms of contrivance, including a strong dramatic push towards a moment of spiritual illumination, and sometimes bend reality towards their purposes, it is also often the case that the film is bent to submit to elements of reality which stand outside, or in the way of, the film-makers' intentions and plans. Politically fairly conservative, Rossellini was in this respect artistically extremely radical, and has since come to be recognised as such.

Paisà (Italy 1946 *p.c* – Organisation Films International/Foreign Film Productions (USA); *d* – Roberto Rossellini; sd b/w)

Paisà, made by Rossellini in 1946 following the international acclaim of *Rome, Open City*, was among the first films to be labelled neo-realist. For Bazin (writing in 1948) it was one of the most significant events in the history of the cinema since 1940 – the other was *Citizen Kane*. Both films, he believed, marked a 'decisive progress towards realism', though by very different routes. *Citizen Kane* employed deep-focus and long takes in order to preserve continuity, but paradoxically had to sacrifice verisimilitude in other ways since the technical requirements of this shooting method virtually precluded the use of location shooting, natural light and non-professional actors. *Paisà* in contrast, incorporated all these features: unscripted dialogue, predominantly exterior settings and 'actors' recruited on the spot, as well as an unusual dramatic form. Instead of one self-contained narrative, the film consisted of six loosely-linked episodes, each set in a different part of Italy (moving from south to north with the Allied invasion) but sharing the common theme of the confrontation of people from different cultures thrown together by the fortunes of war.

In many respects *Paisà* therefore seems to respond to the demands of the non-realists (and of Bazin) for an unemphatic, contemplative style and a relaxed, open-ended narrative structure: the neo-realist movement was in part a reaction against the contrived and mannered melodramas and comedies, often called 'white telephone' films, popular during the Mussolini regime.

However, sequences such as the retrieval of the partisan's corpse and the parachute drop in the sixth and last episode depend heavily on suspense, reinforced in the former case by incidental music and extensive crosscutting between the groups of combatants. Though the events are, as Bazin points out, elliptically presented, they fall into a coherent pattern which hardly seems 'multiple and ambiguous'. Far from being undramatic or desultory the episode is orchestrated around a series of small climaxes that build up to a clearly signalled conclusion.

In spite of certain broad resemblances in their use of narrative conventions, Bazin's conclusion that Welles and Rossellini share similar world-views and the same aesthetic conception of 'realism' seems quite extraordinary. *Paisà*'s avoidance of star players, for instance, and its use of a *mise-en-scène* which focuses on the group rather than the individual, suggest an outlook and concerns that are very different from those of *The Magnificent Ambersons* or *Citizen Kane*. Bazin's claim suggests the weaknesses of his enduring belief that the form of a film is an invisible vehicle for, rather than itself constructing, a meaning (see Bazin, p. 337).

Vivere in pace (Live in Peace) (Italy 1946 *p.c* – Lux Pao; *d* – Luigi Zampa; sd b/w)

La terra trema (Italy 1947 *p.c* – Universalia; *d* – Luchino Visconti; sd b/w)

La terra trema went even further than *Paisà* in paring down all dramatic residue and is often seen as the consummation of the neo-realist aesthetic. Of note in this respect is the preoccupation with social issues from a radical perspective (like several other film-makers of the period Visconti was concerned to expose the problems of the impoverished south, in this case Sicily); a cast which consists entirely of non-professional performers (fishermen recruited from the village where the story is set); dialogue improvised by the players along lines suggested by Visconti; the virtual avoidance of sound effects and music that are not motivated within the narrative world of the film; an extremely low-key scenario with minimal drama and suspense.

In spite of its impeccably neo-realist approach and some images of remarkable beauty, *La terra trema* was a box-office disaster, and Bazin had to admit that the film which perhaps came the closest to his ideal ended up by thoroughly boring the public. He saw the reasons for this failure as lying partly in the exceptional length of the film (nearly three hours), but also, more crucially, in the total absence of drama, of 'emotional eloquence', which, he felt, was a 'wager which it might not be feasible to keep to, at least as far as the cinema is concerned' (see Bazin, p. 337).

Stromboli (Italy 1949 *p.c* – Be-Ro Film; *d* – Roberto Rossellini; sd b/w)

Umberto D (Italy 1951 *p.c* – Dear Films; *d* – Vittorio De Sica; sd b/w)

Umberto D reunited the team of Vittorio De Sica (director) and Cesare Zavattini (scriptwriter) who had previously worked together on *Sciuscià* and the highly successful *Bicycle Thieves*. According to Zavattini, who was perhaps the most celebrated propagandist and theorist of the neo-realist movement, the neo-realist approach to the cinema should renounce the relentless forward drive of the conventional narrative film in favour of a more leisurely pace which would savour every moment, however seemingly insignificant, for its own sake. Zavattini is often quoted as having wanted to make a film of a man to whom nothing happened. Yet his 'Thesis on Neo-Realism' indicates that he was aware of the risk of boredom involved in rejecting a strong narrative based on drama and suspense.

Umberto D clearly exploits the full melodramatic potential of a helpless old man and his dog. For example, the joyful (and extremely coincidental) reunion of Umberto and Flike his dog is underlined by incidental music, the chorus of barking which rises to a crescendo and a track in to Flike as he emerges from the van. The old man's acting performance at this point is also worth considering, bearing in mind the neo-realists' belief that using non-professionals would increase authenticity. The use of editing in the sequence in which the desperate Umberto encourages the dog to beg for money, suggests an affectionate understanding between man and dog (a practice condemned by Bazin in 'The virtues and limitations of montage').

The powerful impetus of these sequences, deriving from the mythical theme of the *quest* (see also *Bicycle Thieves*) casts doubts on Zavattini's declared aim to defy narrative conventions. The events in the film eventually lead to the man's despair and attempted suicide, so his life could not be said to be entirely devoid of incident! Bazin was aware that *Umberto D* deviated from the neo-realist model in a number of ways and his essays on De Sica have to argue long and hard in order to justify his approval of the aim behind the film. Though this work tried to give the impression of perfect spontaneity, it would, Bazin realised, be naïve to accept it at face value: in striving to achieve the illusion of chance, De Sica employed meticulous planning.

As in the case of Wyler, this contrived quality is explained away as a measure of expedience whose function is purely to sustain the drama (if the worker had found his bicycle in the middle of *Bicycle Thieves*, this would be the end of the film!). But it could be argued that these films' aura of inevitability blocks the neo-realist thrust towards penetrating social criticism, giving rise to a diffuse sentimentality and melodramatic fatalism.

La signora senza camelie (Italy 1952 *p.c* – Produzioni Domenico Forges Davanzati/ENIC; *d* – Michelangelo Antonioni; sd b/w)

La strada (Italy 1954 *p.c* – Ponti-De Laurentiis; *d* – Federico Fellini; sd b/w)

Though Fellini had been involved with the neo-realists, in particular as a scriptwriter

Fellini's *La Strada* – the circus comes to town

and assistant director for Rossellini, he began making his own films (1950) just before the financial disaster of *Umberto D*, which was widely held to signal the end of the movement. Partly for tactical reasons connected with their struggle against the economic and political developments which were stifling the new Italian cinema, Zavattini and his colleagues angrily condemned Fellini's work as betraying the ideals of neo-realism. Bazin's articles on these films were conceived as a riposte to their attacks and as an attempt to reintegrate Fellini within the movement.

Their dominant characteristic was seen as what Bazin called a *phenomenological* realism, by which he meant a *mise-en-scène* that observes and describes but without having recourse to explanation or interpretation. Phenomena do not function as the mediators of some higher meaning; instead, the relationship between meaning and appearance is reversed, so that appearance is constantly presented as a strange discovery, a 'quasi-documentary revelation'. Extended to the human figures, this approach breaks with the practice of affording privileged insight into their inner psychology. The peasant girl Gelsomina's unpredictable behaviour could be considered in this light (can it be 'explained' as feeble-mindedness?) and her clown make-up could perhaps be seen as a masking, distancing device.

The relatively traditional type of scenario used in Fellini's earlier films had, Bazin wrote, been discarded in *La strada* in favour of an amorphous series of chance events without any dramatic linkage; in his view, a revolution in narrative. Although this relaxed, contemplative *mise-en-scène* and meandering, almost picaresque plot structure appear compatible with Bazin's model of realism, it could be argued that these features lead precisely away from realism and towards Fellini's fascination with the inexplicable, bizarre and incongruous dimensions of experience. (See Bazin, p. 337.)

Once it had so visibly split, aesthetically and politically, there was no way that neo-realism was going to be reconstituted. The Italian cinema that followed the neo-realist phase of the late 1940s and early 1950s was very different in character. Neo-realist directors continued to make films, but with very few exceptions these films were not neo-realist. The revived commercial cinema which grew up alongside neo-realism was extremely eclectic. It had room for the occasional prestige production from Visconti or Fellini, but its staple was genre films. These genres included comedies and dramas of a type which had flourished under Fascism in the 30s and had been temporarily eclipsed in the immediately postwar years. They also included fantasy and costume pictures, generally low-budget, which engaged the talents of such masters of the genre as Riccardo Freda, Mario Bava and Vittorio Cottafavi. Along with the dramas of Raffaello Matarazzo and others, these became the Italian popular cinema, which lasted until the cinema ceased to be the major popular art. By comparison neo-realism must be rated a popular cinema that might have been.

Selected Reading

Morando Morandini, 'Italy from Fascism to neo-realism', in Geoffrey Nowell-Smith (ed.), *The Oxford History of World Cinema*, Oxford, Oxford University Press, 1996.

Geoffrey Nowell-Smith with James Hay and Gianni Volpi, *The Companion to Italian Cinema*, London, Cassell/BFI, 1996.

Christopher Wagstaff and Christopher Duggan, *Italy and the Cold War: Politics, Culture and Society*, Oxford, Berg, 1995.

THE FRENCH *NOUVELLE VAGUE*

The new wave (*nouvelle vague*) blossomed for a brief period in the history of French cinema – between 1959 and 1963 – when certain historical, technological and economic factors combined to enable some young film-makers to influence French cinema temporarily in diverse ways. Commentators on the new wave have tended to focus on the film-makers, ignoring the combination of factors which permitted them to work in the way they did. Roy Armes, for example, attributes the development of a new wave of film-making to the emergence of a new generation of critics-turned-film-makers. According to Armes, at the beginning of the 1950s:

> [T]he French cinema presented, on the surface at least, a rather depressing and moribund scene. No new director of the first rank had emerged . . . since 1949 and the veteran directors were showing their first signs of lassitude. Experiment was rare and the newcomers of the 40s were moving towards big-budget films and international co-productions . . . But beneath the surface things were stirring. Young critics under the guidance of André Bazin were laying the foundations of a new approach, particularly in *Cahiers du Cinéma*.' (Armes, 1970, p. 7)

Another critic, James Monaco, begins more cautiously with the term 'new wave' itself, admitting that, like most such critical labels, it resists easy definition. According to Monaco, the term was first used by Françoise Giroud in 1958 to refer to a 'youthful' spirit in contemporary cinema, but it swiftly became a synonym for the avant-garde in general. For Monaco himself, however, the term refers much more specifically to the work during a certain period of five film-makers – Truffaut, Godard, Chabrol, Rohmer and Rivette who shared a common film intellectual background influenced on the one hand by Henri Langlois, founder of the Cinémathèque Française, and on the other by André Bazin, co-founder of the film magazine *Cahiers du Cinéma*: 'Astruc sounded the call; Langlois provided the material; Bazin supplied the basic architectonics. In the pages of *Cahiers du Cinéma* in the 1950s, Truffaut, Godard, Chabrol, Rohmer and Rivette argued out a new theory of film' (Monaco, 1976, p. vii).

This theory hinged on two crucial propositions: the first was that of individual authorship in cinema, the *politique des auteurs* (see The *politique des auteurs*, p. 240); the second was that of cinematic genre, of creative conventions in film language. Although simple enough, these ideas seemed at the time perverse, and indeed they served a polemical function in the context of critical attitudes in currency at the time. The new wave directors have been considered as a unitary group, therefore, largely on the grounds of their common intellectual background. The five film-makers isolated by Monaco, for example, had all written for *Cahiers du Cinéma*, and even other directors associated with the new wave who had not been critics had usually learned about cinema as consumers rather than as producers: of all the major film-makers of the new wave, only Alexandre Astruc, Roger Vadim and Louis Malle had any previous experience in the film industry.

And Woman Was Created – a commercial success with Brigitte Bardot

Armes and Monaco are thus able to explain the new wave aesthetic in terms of film criticism, pointing to a critical response to French cinema of the 1940s – a cinema of classical virtues, literary scripts, smooth photography and elegant décor. These virtues had been repeatedly attacked by Truffaut, among others, in the pages of *Cahiers du Cinéma*. By contrast, the aesthetic of new wave cinema was improvisational (unscripted), and its photography and editing were far less mannered than those of its predecessors. The fragmented style of many new wave films thus came in part as a response to the cohesiveness of 'quality' French cinema. Apparent improvisations in camera technique (the long take, the freeze-frame), editing (the jump cut), dialogue, plot and performance were all deployed because cinema was seen for the first time not as a neutral form through which something else (literature or 'reality') could be transmitted, but as a specific aesthetic system, a language in itself.

Why was this aesthetic initiative undertaken when it was? One of the new wave directors, François Truffaut, has described how 'at the end of 1959 there was a kind of euphoric ease in production that would have been unthinkable a couple of years earlier' (interview with Truffaut, in Graham, 1968, p. 9). According to Raymond Durgnat:

> The invention of fast emulsions led to low budgets, minimum crews, location work and 'independent' finance. These new styles in aesthetics and production accompany new thematic perspectives . . . Commercially, the *raison d'être* of the New Wave was a renewal of tone and theme (the industry was already speaking of a '*crise des sujets*') and the cheapness of the films' budgets (Durgnat, 1963, pp. 3–4)

During the 1950s, the film industry in France had been very closed. However, when Roger Vadim's film *And Woman was Created* (1956) was a commercial success despite its low budget, the industry did open its doors for a while to low-budget productions, encouraging a climate of experimentation. The new wave constituted an attempt to make saleable films cheaply through reduced shooting schedules, the use of natural locations, day and night shooting out in the streets, and the employment of small units. The new wave may in fact be compared with Italian neo-realism in this respect, since both operated under similar material constraints. However, the influence of television is also apparent in new wave cinema in a way it could not be in neo-realism. 'A certain kind of reportage and "direct" camera (shooting with a handheld camera; an acting style closer to the interview than the theatre) came into fashion . . . ' (Siclier, 1961, p. 117).

One of the few writers who has dealt in any depth with the economic, ideological and political underpinnings of the new wave is Terry Lovell. She offers an outline of the characteristic qualities of new wave film-making:

> The lack of any social dimension is one of the most notable features of the typical new wave film. Its heroes are neither personally or socially integrated, and are dissociated from their social roles. These are, in any case, difficult or impossible to identify. They are marginal men, disaffected intellectuals, students and in one case (Rohmer's *The Sign of Leo*), a rather high-class tramp. Interest centres exclusively on immediate face-to-face relations. They have no family ties that are apparent, and on the whole, no political affiliations: action is for its own sake, having no further end, arbitrary and motiveless. There are no social antecedents of action, only emotional and volitional. There is no point of contact between the individual and society, nor are these anomic lives placed in any broader context within which they can be understood. The milieu of the individual exhausts the film's compass . . .
>
> . . . This stands in marked contrast to the naive realism of the films of the 1940s and 1950s. Stylistic and technical innovations are equally marked. In addition to new cadres of directors and actors, certain cameramen and other technical experts emerged, and were specifically associated with New Wave films. (Lovell, 1972, pp. 341–2)

Lovell goes on to describe a number of the social conditions underlying the existence of the new wave: the advent of Gaullism, peace in Algeria, the postwar economic miracle, and a crisis in the role of the French intellectual. However, she places greater emphasis on determinants relating more immediately to cinema and the film industry, including:

> The huge influx of American films upon the market immediately after the war, in the circumstances in which the American allies were also liberators. This influx may have something to do with the near-obsession with all things American and especially with American movies, which the New Wave evidenced so strongly in both its films and in its critical judgements. (Lovell, 1972, p. 343)

Les Quatre cents coups (The 400 Blows) (France 1959 *p.c* – Les Films du Carosse, SEDIF; *d* – François Truffaut; sd b/w)

'When I was shooting *Les Quatre cents coups* I was horrified to see that my budget – about £20,000 – had gone up to £25,000. I got into a panic, and felt I had involved myself in something that would not easily make a profit. But once it was finished the film more than paid for itself, what with the Cannes Film Festival and sales abroad. In the USA alone it was bought for £35,000' (interview with Truffaut, in Graham, 1968, p. 9).

In 1958 Truffaut was banned from the Cannes Film Festival for his violent denunciation of festivals and his uncompromising attitude to most of the films shown there. The following year *Les Quatre cents coups* was the official French entry at Cannes and Truffaut won the Best Director award. James Monaco has pointed out that the film's 'instant critical and commercial success not only afforded Truffaut considerable artistic independence right from the beginning of his career, but also made it much easier for other *Cahiers* critics turned film-makers to finance their own projects; at least a modicum of success for the new movement in film was assured' (Monaco, 1976, p. 13).

Influence of 'all things American' in *À bout de souffle*

À bout de souffle (Breathless) (France 1959 *p.c* – SNC; *d* – Jean-Luc Godard; sd b/w)

In early 1959 Jean-Luc Godard offered four scripts to film financier Georges de Beauregard, one of which was the screenplay of *À bout de souffle*. Beauregard accepted the script and on a very small budget (400,000 francs) Godard shot and edited the film between 17 August and 15 September. The film finally premièred in Paris on 16 March 1960 and was a considerable critical and small-scale commercial success. According to the Chronology in *Focus on Godard*, Beauregard eventually recouped more than 150 million francs on his investment (Brown, 1972). Although Godard directed, scripted and edited the film, it was based on an idea by François Truffaut, and Claude Chabrol was artistic supervisor – typical of the way in which the *Cahiers* group collaborated on their early films, an aesthetic factor but also an economic one. *À bout de souffle* is dedicated to Monogram Pictures, a Hollywood B- movie studio of the 1930s and 1940s, and, in James Monaco's words 'it is a film about film noirs' (Monaco, 1976, p. 120). In the sequence during the police pursuit of Michel's car, the shooting, and the poster of Humphrey Bogart all refer to the conventions of the American gangster film/thriller, but at the same time these references could have the function of easing the film into an international market. Jean Seberg, who plays Patricia, had recently starred in Preminger's *Saint Joan* and here plays an 'American in Paris' role which would also be familiar to the international audience.

Jean-Paul Belmondo's attempts to model himself on Bogart include wearing a hat and smoking a cigarette in the hard-boiled Hollywood mould. In an early scene, his silhouette in a shop window echoes images from low-budget *films noirs* of the 1940s. A little later we see Belmondo in front of a poster for *The Harder They Fall* stroking his lip Bogart-style. The construction of the narrative in this sequence is characteristically inconsequential, consisting of fragmented monuments from a petty criminal milieu – stealing a car, taking money from a girlfriend's purse, being pursued by two motor-cycle cops and, later, two plainclothes men. The dialogue is both perfunctory and perverse: 'It's nice in the country . . . I like France a lot' says Belmondo to the camera as he drives a stolen car through the provinces.

Adieu Philippine (France 1961–2 *p.c* – Unitec France/Alpha Productions/Rome-Paris Films/Euro-International Films; *d* – Jacques Rozier; sd b/w)

Director Jacques Rozier had already worked in television (and made several short films), which may help explain the laboured parody of television commercials to which a long episode is devoted. According to Roy Armes:

> The circumstances of production and distribution, which resulted in the film's waiting two years for release, have given it an undeserved reputation of an unacknowledged masterpiece. Rozier exceeded his budget and failed to meet completion dates, taking a year to complete the film, including five months spent recovering the film's improvised dialogue for post-synchronisation (Armes, 1970, p. 178–9).

For Armes the film's 'chief qualities are its youthful vitality, and the improvised *cinéma-verité* style of the language, characters and settings', while its weaknesses are largely those of construction: 'it is a disjointed and often somewhat incoherent telling of what is in essence a simple story . . . ' (p. 179). It was precisely these qualities of narrative disjuncture which attracted film theorist Christian Metz, who subjected *Adieu Philippine* to a syntagmatic analysis (see Applying Saussure: the early work of Christian Metz, p. 326).

Bande à part (France 1964 *p.c* – Anouchka Films/Orsay Films; *d* – Jean-Luc Godard; sd b/w)

Bande à part is a feature-length film shot in twenty-five days. Godard has described how such restraints can be creative:

> I always like to have a balance between the shooting of a film and its financing, between the budget and the subject . . . It's in that vein that I shot the film in twenty-five days. I always like to impose restraints on myself. I never agree with the conditions my producers set up, simply because these are never the right conditions with respect to the film's subject' (interview with Godard in Brown, 1972, pp. 41–2).

Godard's description of his mode of production echoes that of 1940s American films. To achieve the necessary 'balance' Godard set up his own production company, Anouchka Films. *Bande à part* is based on a *série noir* novel *Fool's Gold*, and is another example of Godard's critical interest in and capitalisation on the American cinema, specifically here the musical and gangster genres. A characteristic scene, for example, is the one in which the three characters – Arthur, Odile and Franz – are sitting in a cafe with little to say. Then they dance to a record on the juke box in a tribute to the non-narrative choreography of the Hollywood musical. Their dance – or rather the music for their dance – is repeatedly interrupted by a voice-over commentary on the characters: 'It is time to open another parenthesis and describe our characters' feelings.' Outside in the night-time streets of Paris we see Odile and Arthur drive past a *nouvelle vague* nightspot. There is another similarly self-conscious moment somewhat later in the film when they observe a boy with an unhappy expression on the metro and consider different 'readings' of that expression according to alternative fictional contexts – the package he is holding is either a teddy bear or a bomb.

Another significant feature of the industrial context of the new wave, according to Lovell, is the horizontal structure of the French film industry – in contrast with the vertical integration of the American industry – (see The studios, p. 11) – and the fact that state intervention in French film production is greater than in any other non-socialist country. She concludes however, that:

> such conditions, being relatively stable over time, cannot explain the emergence of the new wave. More proximate causes relate to the crisis in the industry in the 1950s. The history of the French film industry is a history of crises. After the war the Blum Byrnes agreement resulted in a flood of American films, with which a war-damaged indigenous industry could not compete. The 1949 Temporary Aid Law was ameliorative, but the situation remained precarious. Many well-established directors were unable to work, or did so at a much reduced rate. Clair, Autant Lara, Becker, Duvivier and Carné had each directed only one film between 1945–59. The opportunity structure for film personnel was extremely poor. This situation was exacerbated from the point of view of new entrants by the policy of using well-known actors and directors, in adaptations of literary works to prestige productions, aimed at the foreign market. (It is interesting that it was precisely these films with which the New Wave competed.) Union regulations were formidable, though loosely enforced.
>
> The crisis in the cinema traditionally and misleadingly associated with the advent of television came late in France, and can be dated almost precisely at 1957. At the same time, 'quality films' were waning in their success. The old formula was failing, and the result was a widespread openness to innovation. The success of Vadim's *And Woman was Created* let loose the flood. (Lovell, 1972, pp. 345–6)

Lovell concludes that in spite of the considerable critical, theoretical and aesthetic achievements of the French new wave:

> At the structural level, it resulted in little change. Controls were if anything tighter than they had been previously. Initial capital requirements, for instance, for a film were raised out of all proportion to increased costs, in order to deter ill-considered ventures. Union requirements were more strictly enforced. The net result was merely that a generation of filmmakers were able to force an entry into a moribund industry, without in any way changing its structure so as to make it any easier for future generations. (Lovell, 1972, pp. 346 – 7)

Although the French new wave is thought of as a national movement, it also had some distinctly international traits. It could be argued that its self-conscious references to Hollywood were an attempt to provide effective competition for the American films which threatened to invade French cinema screens, and at the same time made inroads into the American home market itself. Moreover, new wave films made explicit reference to other national and international film movements: Italian neorealism, for example, and European art cinema, which, although primarily deployed for aesthetic reasons, could help their insertion into other European markets. A number of new wave films were European co-productions: *Le Feu follet* was a French–Italian co-production, *La Guerre est finie* was French–Swedish, *Pierrot le fou* was French–Italian as was *Adieu Philippine*. The looseness of the plots of these films – as of other productions of this period – together with the often minimal and desultory dialogue, the fragmented scenes and shots, may perhaps have made them more easily understood by foreign audiences, who would also probably recognise the familiar Parisian and/or Mediterranean locations. It may even be argued that the geographical locations of new wave films correspond to a tourist's view of France in general and of Paris in particular – the café (*La Peau douce*, *À bout de souffle*, *Bande à part*, *Masculin/Féminin*), the airport (*Une Femme mariée*, *Bande à part*), Paris streets at night (*Les Quatre cents coups*, *La Peau douce*, *À bout de souffle*, *Une Femme mariée*, *Bande à part*, *Masculin/Féminin*, etc.), sun-drenched summer in the countryside (*Pierrot le fou*). And, of course, the new wave had its own easily recognisable 'stars' – Jean-Paul Belmondo in *À bout de souffle* and *Pierrot le fou*, Jeanne Moreau in *Jules et Jim*, Jean-Pierre Léaud in *Les Quatre cents coups* and *Masculin/Féminin* – whose international familiarity might ease the films' insertion into both domestic and foreign markets.

Paris streets in *Les Quatre cents coups*

Selected Reading

Peter Graham (ed.), *The New Wave: Critical Landmarks*, London, Secker & Warburg/BFI, 1968.

James Monaco, *The New Wave*, New York, Oxford University Press, 1976.

Ginette Vincendeau (ed.), *The Companion to French Cinema*, London, Cassell/BFI, 1996.

THE BRITISH FILM INDUSTRY

EALING STUDIOS

In 1929 a company called Associated Talking Pictures was set up to exploit the advent of cinematic sound in Britain. In 1931 the company built its own sound-equipped studio in Ealing and by 1936 some sixty films had been made there, about half of them by ATP, the rest by various independents. In the financial year 1937–8, however, extravagant overproduction took its toll, forcing several studios to close down. The government responded to the crisis with a revised quota system to protect and promote British films, but American production companies were quick to exploit loopholes in the quota legislation. MGM, for instance, set up a British studio at Borehamwood making films for Anglo-American audiences with American stars and creative staff, British technicians and facilities and 'transatlantic' subjects. The first of three such MGM productions of the period was *A Yank at Oxford*; on its release MGM's Borehamwood production head, Michael Balcon, whose hopes of making high-quality Anglo-American films for the world market had been frustrated, resigned, and by the end of the year replaced Basil Dean who had retired after running ATP since its inception. Ealing Studios Limited, which had previously been no more than a holding company for ATP's studio lot, became a production company and ATP was quietly phased out.

During the 1940s, Britain produced an annual average of forty feature films: of these Ealing studios provided about five. To maximise profits, Ealing and its rivals would obviously benefit from an arrangement with one of the three major cinema circuits – ABC, Odeon and Gaumont-British. By 1941 Odeon and Gaumont-British were both owned by J. Arthur Rank, who controlled 70 per cent of Britain's studio space as well as being the biggest single domestic distributor. In 1944 Rank signed an agreement with Ealing guaranteeing the screening, as top of the bill attractions, of all its features as well as providing 50 per cent of the company's finances. In 1952 Rank increased its financial interest to 75 per cent, but in 1955 the relationship came to an end, and the studios at Ealing were sold to the British Broadcasting Corporation (BBC). Television had been encroaching on cinema audiences for some years and the advent of commercial television proved a major setback to Rank and Ealing. Ealing struggled on as a production company, operating from MGM's Borehamwood premises until 1959.

This sketch of the history of Ealing Studios is taken from the work of two writers on the history of Ealing, Charles Barr (1977) and John Ellis (1975). While Barr concentrates on the atmosphere of the studio and the attitudes of its personnel, Ellis examines its economic and institutional structures. Barr begins his book by analysing an example of what he sees as the studio's characteristic product. This analysis explores the analogy between the world of the film and the world of Ealing. The film in question is *Cheer Boys Cheer* (1939), which concerns the competition between a small family brewery and a large impersonal beer factory. The two firms are called Greenleaf and Ironside and, Barr argues, these names and firms stand not only for England and Germany but also for Ealing and Rank/MGM. The relation between the stories told on the screen and the experiences of the studio itself is a central theme of Barr's book.

Barr establishes that Ealing, like Greenleaf, was 'a small production centre' with 'the air of a family business, set on the village green' (Barr, 1977, p. 6). Ealing, Barr suggests, exemplifies one of the two choices for the film industry in postwar Britain, the small business; the other, collaboration with the Americans, Barr sees as epitomised by Borehamwood.

In attempting to trace the relation between the stories told on the screen and the experience of the studio itself, Barr is aware of the problems of a simple 'reflection' thesis in which the films act as a mirror for England, or for the studio. And he admits that 'the celebration of the little man, of the small-scale enterprise, is a traditional theme not confined to Ealing or to England; one need only refer to Frank Capra's Hollywood comedies of the thirties' (Barr, 1977, p. 6). Clearly, an equation which simply revises the traditional slogan: 'film reflects society', to read: 'film reflects studio' is somewhat problematic. Nevertheless, attention to industrial determinations can throw considerable light on the aesthetics of a studio's products, and not only at a level of analogy or internal reference. John Ellis, in a 1975 article on Ealing has attempted to provide such economic and organisational data.

Ellis's emphasis is on the economics, technology and industrial organisation of Ealing. He establishes that the studio's average of five films per year were all A-features almost all with U-certificates, running some 80 or 90 minutes each and costing between £120,000 and £200,000 with the comedies averaging out at about £160,000. Each film would take about 8 to 10 weeks to shoot with an average of about two minutes screen time completed every day. Ealing had its own pre-production and post-production departments at the studio including scripting and advertising as well as having access (between 1944 and 1955) to Rank's laboratories. The studio employed about 400 people and Ellis cites figures which support Michael Balcon's contention that at Ealing 'the most important work is done before and after a film goes on the floor' (quoted in Ellis, 1975, p. 93). Under Balcon's leadership studio production was stabilised with a contract staff of about 50 who constituted Ealing's 'creative élite' of directors, producers, editors, scriptwriters and cinematographers, protected by a system of internal staff promotion and a regular 'round-table' discussion of present and future projects at which all 'creative' personnel could have a say. Director Alexander Mackendrick has since commented: 'We weren't paid much but we had the advantage of being very free' (interview in *Positif* no. 92, 1968), but the extent of that freedom seems to have depended to a considerable degree on the agreement of the staff's attitudes with those of Balcon, who had clear ideas about the boundaries within which the studio should work: 'Nothing would induce us to do anything against the public interest just for the sake of making money' (quoted in Ellis, 1975, p. 123). Ellis argues that the extremely tight production conditions had a number of effects, and describes Ealing's overall aesthetic as a combination of bland studio lighting, short takes and static camera shots, little or no reliance on 'atmospheric' music and an unusual emphasis on dialogue and performance – and thus on scripting and casting, both pre-production elements. Location sequences were kept to an economic minimum unless, of course, they cost less than sequences shot in the studio. Thus in *The Lavender Hill Mob* a scene originally scripted for Victoria Station was rewritten for Northolt Airport at 'a tenth of the price' (quoted in Ellis, 1975, p. 98).

With the signing of the 1944 Rank–Ealing agreement, the studio was able to step up its production schedule and resume its pre-war policy of assembling a stable roster of contract staff while mapping out a path along which the company could profitably travel in the years to come. Charles Barr identifies the period until 1943 with the war films, and the period after 1947/48 with 'Ealing comedies', arguing that the films produced in the interval between these periods 'cover a greater range than before or since' (Barr, 1977, p. 50). Following Ellis, it might be argued that industrial conditions determined such a variety. A film like *Dead of Night* (1945) explores the possibilities of a genre unfamiliar to Ealing and, as an anthology, allowed several apprentice talents to be tried out at less than feature length. But *Dead of Night* was an isolated experiment for Ealing. The studio consequently retreated to the cosy, familiar, rational, domestic world of the comedies. In Barr's terms 'Ealing became typed as the safe, respectable, "U"-certificate British cinema par excellence' (Barr, 1977, p. 58). Why did Ealing fail to follow up the experiment of *Dead of Night*, which was by no means a commercial disaster? One possible explanation is Balcon's admission in an interview than 'none of us would ever suggest any subject, whatever its box-office potential, if it were socially objectionable or doubtful. We want to achieve box-office success, of course, but we consider it our primary task to make pictures worthy of that name' (quoted in Barr, 1977, p. 58). Yet if this is true how did the 'horrific' *Dead of Night* ever slip through Ealing's self-censorship? Barr has argued that the supernatural nature of the film's subject sanctions its ideologically 'doubtful' content, while its episodic form functions to guarantee that those very elements remain at the level of suggestions.

If *Dead of Night* represents a closed avenue for Ealing, *The Lavender Hill Mob* (1951) and *The Man in the White Suit* (1951) are examples of the path the studio did choose to follow, that of comedy. The year 1951 was a pinnacle one for Ealing, as for the British film industry as a whole. Between 1942 and 1951 no one came in as a director from outside the studio, and a stable core of contract players and creative personnel transformed it into the cinematic equivalent of a repertory theatre company. In 1951 British censorship regulations were relaxed and the X-certificate was introduced. But in 1952 the Rank–Ealing agreement was revised, and only three years later terminated. Attendances at film theatres

Passport to Pimlico – the staff of Ealing studios working on location

were diminishing considerably, film production costs were spiralling and American companies were finding it easier than ever before to exploit the British market. Moreover, in 1952 the BBC finally achieved its ambition of national television transmission, and in the following year some two million TV sets were tuned in to watch the Coronation. The cinema circuits could compete only by offering feature-length Technicolor coverage of the same event some weeks later.

In this period of low receipts and increasing competition from both television and American cinema, other film companies responded by exploiting subjects unavailable to television (e.g. Hammer and the horror film), thus differentiating their products from those of the competition. Ealing, too, had either to change its production values radically or to cease production. In the end the company took the latter course.

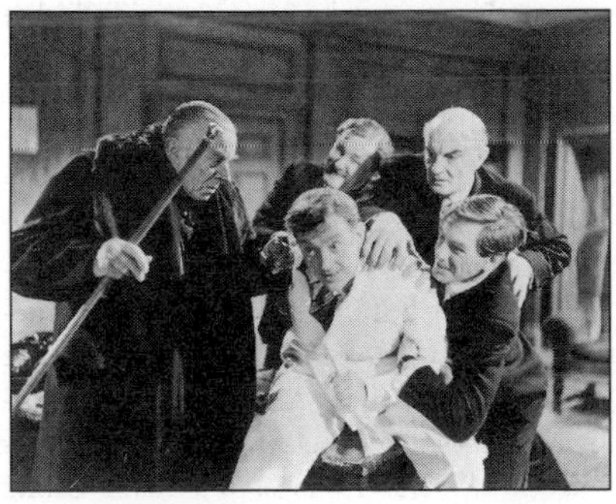

Made in Ealing's pinnacle year – *The Man in the White Suit*

Selected Reading

Charles Barr, *Ealing Studios*, London, Cameron and Taylcur/Newton Abbot, David and Charles, 1977; rev edn, London Studio Vista, 1992.

John Ellis, 'Made in Ealing', *Screen* 16(1), spring 1975.

HAMMER PRODUCTIONS

Hammer Productions Limited was first registered as a film company in 1934, but soon after disappeared for almost a decade. In the wake of a short-lived exhibition quota imposed by protectionist postwar legislation (the Dalton Duty, 1947–8), Hammer's controlling company, Exclusive Films was 'encouraged by the ABC cinema circuit to supply low-budget supporting features . . . [and] . . . this was the impetus for reforming Hammer' (Eyles, 1973, p. 22). Very rapidly it became company policy to produce films which could 'capitalise on subjects and characters that were pre-sold to the public either through radio and television or via myth and legend' (Pirie, 1973, p. 26). Adaptations of recent BBC radio programmes proved a particularly reliable and profitable source and a cycle of low-budget B-feature quota quickies was launched, featuring such familiar radio characters as Dick Barton, PC 9 and The Man in Black.

Between 1948 and 1950 Hammer moved its production base several times from one large country house to another. The decision to use country houses rather than studios was determined by cost factors, and it proved to be one of the company's most important policy decisions, for it gave the films a distinctive style and put them in the ideal position to recreate historical/mythical subjects. In 1951 Hammer finally settled at Bray in Berkshire, in a large building which housed the company until 1968. Also in 1951 Hammer negotiated an agreement with an independent American producer, Robert Lippert, which guaranteed a 20th Century-Fox release for their product in return, among other things, for Hammer's agreement to employ American stars in leading roles to ease their films into the US market. For almost four years Hammer produced B-films starring American actors such as Zachary Scott, Paul Henreid and Cesar Romero, with the result that American studios began to see the benefits of low-budget British production of supporting features. But when the Americans withdrew from this arrangement around 1954, Hammer, like the rest of the British film industry found themselves in a critical position:

> An industry observer might very well have written Hammer off . . . Bray Studios lay miserably empty for twelve months apart from a series of featurettes and one particularly dreary 'B' feature . . . If the 1954 films had failed or had had only a routine success it is not impossible that the whole course of British film history might have been very different. (Pirie, 1973, p. 27)

Characteristically, Hammer negotiated this crisis by changing their production policy as the structure of the industry and the expectations of the audiences changed. In the mid-1950s there were a number of such changes for the company to exploit. At the beginning of the decade there existed three main cinema circuits in Britain – Odeon, Gaumont-British and ABC. Rank owned both Odeon and Gaumont-British and had an agreement with Ealing. ABC, who already had a longstanding agreement with Hammer, may have decided that a degree of differentiation from Rank's Ealing comedy 'family audiences' policy was worth attempting (see Ealing studios, p. 83). Since the relaxation of British film censorship and the introduction of the X-certificate in 1951, Rank had only very rarely exhibited 'adults-only' films. Indeed, only one X was screened in Rank cinemas in 1956, and only fourteen in the entire decade. ABC, on the other hand, showed more than fifty Xs in the 1950s, many of which came from Hammer. The mid-1950s also saw an expansion in the black-and-white television industry, with each new TV licence 'costing' approximately 100 cinema attendances a year (Limbacher, n.d., p. 15). Hammer's decision to exploit colour and X-certificate material at this point set them on the road to success. The house at Bray provided the perfect location for the period of intensive production and expansion that followed. At Bray, Hammer became

> a production company utterly unlike anything that the British cinema had previously known. There is a very slight echo of Ealing in the structure that emerged, but perhaps the most obvious analogy is with one of the small Hollywood studios of the 1930s and 40s like Republic or Monogram; for almost overnight Hammer became a highly efficient factory for a vast series of exploitation pictures made on tight budgets with a repertory company of actors and a small, sometimes over-exposed series of locations surrounding their tiny Buckinghamshire estate. (Pirie, 1973, p. 42)

This set-up combined with a continuity of personnel at all levels throughout the company enabled Hammer to produce a distinctive and professional product at low cost. Anthony Hinds, a producer and prolific screenwriter at Hammer, has summarised the studio's aesthetic/economic policy with the slogan 'Put the money on the screen' (quoted in *Little Shoppe of Horrors* no. 4, p. 40). Certainly, in the 1960s, when Hammer's budgets averaged around £120,000 per film, £15,000 or even £20,000 would be spent on sets and décor, with additional amounts spent on lighting, Technicolor and occasionally widescreens. Scripts, on the other hand, were much less expensive, deriving as they did almost entirely from radio, television, theatre, published works, myth, legend and, of course, other films.

Hammer's move into the horror cycle for which they became famous was by no means simple, though it was certainly facilitated both by the economic and industrial conditions just described, and by the social climate of Britain in the 1950s (Pirie, 1980). The decision was helped by the peculiar attributes of the company's set-up at Bray:

> the studio was a partial anachronism, out of time and out of place. All the other small self-contained British studios run by production companies were in the process of closing down or selling out to television . . . But in a way, it was the very old fashioned nature of the production set-up at Bray which made it so ideal as a focal point for Hammer's recreation of its own horrific version of nineteenth-century Europe. Bray could present the past because it was the past. (Pirie, 1980, p. 13)

And, paradoxically, American financial interests in the British film industry also contributed to the success of Hammer's choice of the British Gothic novel tradition as a source of inspiration. Pirie has described how

> By the 1950s production in Hollywood had become so costly that Britain became a viable filmmaking centre for low-cost production. One of the advantages for American producers was that they could in this way spend some of the money earned from distribution in Britain which the Anglo-American Agreement of 1948 prohibited them from converting from pounds into dollars . . . (Pirie, 1980, p. 4)

According to this agreement, American companies could only take an annual amount of £17 million out of Britain. There were, however, ways round this prohibition, co-production of films or co-ownership of facilities among them. It was, for instance, the loan capital of the National Film Finance Corporation which paid for the production of *The Curse of Frankenstein* (1957) but the film was distributed by Warner Bros. Similarly, the Eady Levy, which returned a proportion of box-office takings to the production companies of the respective best-grossing British films, was so slack in defining nationality that American subsidiaries or partnerships could easily profit from it. The 'Britishness' of films set in the Victorian period and featuring a decadent aristocracy made Hammer an attractive investment for American companies and allowed the American film industry to secure an economic foothold in Britain. For a while Hammer profited enormously from this kind of arrangement, but the bubble was to burst when the Americans eventually pulled out, leaving the British film industry in a great many difficulties (see British social realism 1959–63, p. 88). But perhaps the most influential factor was the company's ability to capitalise on the situation when their luck broke with the success of *The Quatermass Xperiment*. In 1954, like Ealing ten years before, Hammer were being forced to experiment to find a new product and a new market. One 1954 production was the studio's first film in Technicolor, *Men of Sherwood Forest*. Another film, much more successful, was an experiment with a new genre – horror: *The Quatermass Xperiment* (1955) combined the then unfamiliar territory of horror with the science fiction elements which Hammer had already explored in films like *Spaceways* (1953). Moreover, the eccentric spelling of the word 'experiment' in the title capitalised upon the film's X-certificate while also functioning as ready-made publicity. Furthermore, it was an adaptation of an already very successful BBC serial, first broadcast in July and August of 1953. 'The film opened at the London Pavilion on Friday 26 August 1955 with Hammer's fortunes at their lowest ebb and immediately began breaking box office records both here and subsequently in America' (Pirie, 1973, p. 28).

After the unexpected success of *The Quatermass Xperiment*, Hammer commissioned another science fiction script as well as a Quatermass sequel. Pirie points to the relationship between the themes that Hammer (and in due course many other film companies) began to approach in 1956, and the political events in the country during those crucial twelve months (Pirie, 1973, p. 31). On the very day that the greatest British anxiety movie of all, *Quatermass II* (1957), followed *X – The Unknown* (1956) into production at Bray, a headline in *The Times* read 'Giant H-Bomb Dropped'. Both films received X-certificates in Britain and were distributed as adult entertainment: once again the title *X – The Unknown* simultaneously exploited and re-emphasised its certificate. In the same year, 1956, the Production Code of the Motion Picture Association of America was revised and relaxed, which widened the market for Hammer's product in the United States. Nevertheless, for Hammer to survive the demise of the double bill it was necessary for the studio to shake off their B-feature repu-

Taste the Blood of Dracula – marked the decline of Hammer Horror

tation and explore entirely new generic avenues in order to succeed in the American market. Hammer was thus encouraged to continue employing American actors in leading roles: Dean Jagger as the Professor in *X – The Unknown*, for example, and Brian Donlevy as Quatermass.

Pirie argues in *A Heritage of Horror* that it is easy to underestimate the aesthetic and economic risk Hammer were taking in 1956 when the decision was made to elevate horror to a privileged role in their production hierarchy. 'By the time *Quatermass II* finished filming in July 1956 Hammer had more or less finalised plans for a complete change in their output . . . No less than ten projects were abandoned in 1956' and in their place 'Hammer embarked on their most significant and ambitious venture so far, *The Curse of Frankenstein* which went into production at Bray on 19 November' (Pirie, 1973, p. 38), and enjoyed enormous international success.

'*Dracula* went into production at Bray about a year after the shooting of *The Curse of Frankenstein*, in November 1957 . . . While the *Frankenstein* film had been made on behalf of Warners, the new *Dracula* was sponsored by Universal, the same American studio which had fathered the whole horror movie tradition in Hollywood during the 1930s with Karloff and Lugosi . . . The final seal was set on Hammer's new status in the summer of 1958 when *Dracula* began to register its enormous success all over the world. Universal announced at this point that they would turn over to Hammer the remake rights of their entire library of horror movies' (Pirie, 1973, p. 43).

Sir James Carreras, then head of Hammer, has explained the studio's initial interest in the horror genre (rather than in sci-fi) as the result of a realisation that there had never been a *Frankenstein* or a *Dracula* in colour. Colour certainly differentiated Hammer's remakes from Universal's monochrome horror films, but this in itself was not enough. At this time, Universal's copyright expressly forbade imitation of the make-up and the neck bolts of the earlier *Frankenstein*, and for similar reasons on *Dracula* (1957) (retitled *Horror of Dracula* in the US to avoid confusion with the original) Hammer's sets were designed so as to be as unlike those in the American version as possible.

It has been estimated that between them *Dracula* and *The Curse of Frankenstein* grossed more than $4 million. That two such inexpensive films could be such a gigantic success was due in part to the interest of the American market. It also meant that sequels, spin-offs and so on were bound to follow. Eventually, having received the rights to remake Universal's entire horror library, and finally released from the copyright problems that had plagued the productions of *Dracula* and *Frankenstein*, Hammer embarked on a series of adaptations of Universal's 1930s tales of the supernatural. The proven success of previous entries in the series prompted Rank to reconsider its virtual embargo on Hammer horror films, and *The Mummy* (1959) was released in Britain not by ABC but by Rank's Odeon circuit. *The Mummy* reunited Peter Cushing and Christopher Lee for the first time since *Dracula* and proved a considerable success.

Another Rank release, *The Brides of Dracula* (1960), was Hammer's response to Christopher Lee's unwillingness to be typecast as Dracula, a role which he had played in 1957 but was not to repeat until 1965. Thus, according to Pirie, Hammer were forced into the position of having to find some way of making a *Dracula* movie without Dracula. The absence of Count Dracula encouraged Hammer to compensate by adding ingredients to the formula: the brides themselves, for instance, provided an increased sexual component. However, even before 1960 Hammer were obviously aware of the need to vary the formula of the vampire myth. Once an audience has grasped the basic elements of the vampire hunters' artillery – stake, crucifix, strong daylight, communion host – the plot could all too easily subside into a succession of shopping lists. So Hammer carefully elaborated the paraphernalia and in doing so were able to persuade the audiences of the late 1950s that this time evil might just triumph (see The horror film, p. 194).

In 1968, Hammer received the Queen's Award for industry for having brought in £1.5 million from America over three successive years. However, 1968 was probably the last year in which Hammer could be certain of obtaining American distribution for its films. *The Devil Rides Out* (1967) was in fact advertised under the name of Dennis Wheatley – upon whose novel it was based – rather than that of Hammer Productions. By this time American finance had more or less abandoned the British film industry to its fate.

> Hammer, who were still in an extremely good box-office position, found it at once necessary to fix up deals with British, as opposed to American companies, in order to secure regular finance. Distribution in America was still guaranteed, but in return the British companies who were themselves in trouble began to insist that Hammer use their own studio space rather than Bray, to make the films. Consequently, after much deliberation, Hammer were forced to sell Bray to a property company in 1968. (Pirie, 1973, pp. 47–8)

Having finally been forced by 1969 into vacating Bray, some of the company's confidence in the horror genre was lost with the studio. *Taste the Blood of Dracula* (1969) was advertised with the tongue-in-cheek slogan 'Drink A Pint of Blood A Day' and its deviation from formula requirements proved unpopular at the box office. Once again Hammer tried hard to differentiate their product from television: the film opens with Roy Kinnear, a familiar TV comedian, being confronted with the horrific Technicolor Count Dracula, an opening which illustrated the complicated rituals Hammer utilised to reinvest their Count Dracula character with life at the start of each film in the series. This was the fourth Hammer *Dracula* film and, at the end of the third, the Count had fallen hundreds of yards from the battlements of his own castle to be impaled on a sharp cross. The resurrection of the Count from absolute death to life is one of the key ingredients of the series. Indeed, one film, *Dracula Prince of Darkness* (1965) took almost half its length to effect the Count's reappearance.

Following the financial failure of *Taste the Blood of Dracula*, which had compensated for the absence of Peter Cushing with other box-office attractions such as violence and sexuality, Hammer were uncertain as to the future of the horror genre. At the end of the 1960s the company vacillated between EMI–Elstree and Rank–Pinewood, the exhibition circuits ABC and Odeon, and between straightforward horror and self-parody. With a change of management at Hammer in the early 1970s and encouragement from Warners, Hammer decided to bring the Dracula story up to date with films such as *Dracula AD 1972* and *The Satanic Rites of Dracula*. *The Satanic Rites of Dracula* (1973) reunited Cushing and Lee, injected a number of controversial contemporary issues – such as property speculation and political corruption – and included a characteristic Hammer scene, with Van Helsing being interviewed by a television reporter. All these elements were unable to generate an audience in the UK large enough to convince American distributors that the film was worth releasing in the US. In the same year American and British audiences were watching *The Exorcist*, beside which *Dracula* was all too ordinary. Once the American horror and sci-fi cycles were under way in the mid-1970s, films like *The Omen* (1976) and *Star Wars* (1977) were being produced in the same studios and with the same facilities that Hammer had employed. Meanwhile, Hammer returned to the source of their original success – the television spin-off. In 1972/73, for instance, Hammer released *Mutiny on the Buses*, *That's Your Funeral*, *Love Thy Neighbour* and *Nearest and Dearest*. None of these ever appeared on the American circuits. Since the late 1970s, Hammer's horror film production has virtually ceased, confining itself mainly to television series.

Selected Reading

Allen Eyles *et al.* (eds), *The House of Horror: The Complete Story of Hammer Films*, London, Lorrimer, 1973.

Peter Hutchings, *Hammer and Beyond*. Manchester, Manchester University Press, 1993.

David Pirie, *A Heritage of Horror: The English Gothic Cinema 1946–1972*, London, Gordon Fraser, 1973.

BRITISH SOCIAL REALISM: 1959–63

In 1969 Alan Lovell described the British cinema as an almost unknown quantity, pointing to the lack of a framework for discussion as partly responsible.

'There is no model for an examination of a particular cinema over a period of time. Or, to be more precise, there is not a model which doesn't dissolve into a discussion of particular artists with a few general remarks about the context they worked in' (Lovell, 1969, p. 1).

Lovell's complaint was echoed that same year by the influential critic Peter Wollen, who argued that 'the English cinema . . . is still utterly amorphous, unclassified, unperceived' (Wollen, 1969; 1972, p. 115), and set in motion a shift towards more thorough critical work on British cinema – work that would attempt to reconcile history and industrial conditions of production with aesthetics and would do so in interesting and productive ways. Barr's analysis of the history of the Ealing studios can be cited as a good example (see Ealing studios, p. 83), as can the feminist writing on the little-known 1940s Gainsborough melodramas.

In his 1969 paper, Lovell himself provided a tentative historical analysis to explain what he perceived as the aesthetic underdevelopment of British cinema: an 'art' cinema dominated by the Griersonian ethic of documentary in the service of propaganda; an entertainment cinema hamstrung by notions of 'good taste'; and a 'New Wave' of critics-turned-film-makers (the Free Cinema movement) forced by exclusion from the feature film industry to make documentaries. This analysis, which implies a judgement of the stultifying effects of a prevailing social realist aesthetic hostile to formal experiment, is shared by other critics. John Hill, for example, writing about the group of social realist films made around 1959–63 sees them in similar terms as emerging from the documentary prerogative in both commercial and non-commercial film-making, and 'the insulation of British culture from European modernism in the 1920s and 1930s at the very time that the "documentary spirit" was achieving its hegemony across the arts' (Hill, 1979, pp. 130–1). However, Hill points to the complex nature of the relationship between the aesthetic prejudices and procedures internalised by film-makers and film audiences alike and the final products, the films themselves. He argues that the British social realist movement related not only to an internalised aesthetic ideology but also to an external economy. Recognising that it constituted part of a particular response to the development of postwar British capitalism, Hill is careful also to specify both the social formation and historical context in which the movement developed, and the industrial and institutional foundations upon which it was built. But he emphasises that the movement, far from simply expressing social attitudes or a response to the economic climate, actively contributed to that response 'which was likewise refracted through the particular context and struggles of the British film industry and its cinematic conventions' (Hill, 1979, p. 129). During this period, British cinema was in the process of being redefined and reorganised. Hill discusses several aspects of this transformation, including the advent of commercial television, X-certificates, the disintegration of the American majors and the impetus towards independent production, and the role of the National Film Finance Corporation. A wish to turn the tide of cinema's decline led to a certain 'openness' to new ideas which permitted 'a possibility of innovation . . . subject to the demands of financial success' (Hill, 1979, p. 132). This combination of factors, then, enabled a group of socially committed directors to put into practice their aspirations, to produce a popular cinema which would reconnect with the traditional working class rather than provide escapist fantasies for its audience. The space given to those aspirations, however, lasted just as long as they proved to be commercially viable.

Alan Lovell provides another account of the short-lived success of the social realist movement. He argues that the *Sequence* film magazine critics who became independent Free Cinema film-makers in the 1950s (Linday Anderson and Karel Reisz for example), together with ex-theatre directors (such as Tony Richardson):

> were forced into documentary because of the basic situation of the British film industry at that time. The feature industry was difficult to enter because it was contracting under the pressure of television and changing leisure habits. The documentary industry was conversely expanding as a result of increased industrial sponsorship for films . . . And once this generation made the break into the feature industry it created feature films within the Social Documentary genre. (Lovell, 1969, p. 8)

Lovell concludes that once the 'Free Cinema aesthetic' had acquired the status of a genre, it could no longer license innovation. John Hill also suggests that the social realist movement may have destroyed itself through becoming 'conventional' and hence delegitimising its claims to realism. Lovell's epitaph on the British social realists – that because of the lack of a clear analysis of the situation in British cinema at the time they became prisoners of the very situation they had criticised – is echoed in Hill's suggestion that the critique of commerce implied in social realist cinema exemplified a liberal humanist culture that was itself in crisis. The financial failure of Anderson's *This Sporting Life* (1963) signalled more or less the end of the movement and a return to 'entertainment' films, which, Hill argues, tells us something of the limits of the challenge that had been made to the industry. The control apparently given to the directors was circumscribed by a system in which the real control rested with the Rank–ABC monopoly of distribution and exhibition, which gave them the right to define what was 'entertainment' and what was not (Hill, 1979, p. 132).

However, Hill and Lovell perhaps overemphasise the influence of the documentary/Free Cinema tradition on the aesthetics and ideology of social realist cinema. Another critic has attributed the social realist aesthetic to new developments in literature and theatre:

> If we look at the development of the newer style in features, we find the trailblazer is Jack Clayton's *Room at the Top*, based on a best-selling novel. It wasn't *Momma Don't Allow* that brought Tony Richardson into the directorial chair of *Look Back in Anger*; it was the fact that he had directed the play on the London stage. While the partisans of Free Cinema were directing stage plays and TV commercials, the new wave arose in response to the work of artists in other media. Far from originating a new documentary approach, the impulse came from the plays of John Osborne, Keith Waterhouse and Willis Hall, Wolf Mankowitz and Shelagh Delaney, novels by John Braine and Alan Sillitoe, Stan Barstow and David Storey, and a new generation of actors, like Albert Finney, Rita Tushingham, Rachel Roberts, Tom Courtenay, Richard Harris and Ronald Fraser. (Durgnat, 1970, p. 129)

According to this argument, the 'transparency' of the social realist aesthetic not only resided in cinema's alleged ability to reproduce reality unmediated but also in its apparent ability to transmit, without adversely transforming, literary texts. And most important to this aesthetic was a notion of 'quality' grounded in the established artistic status of British literature and theatre.

Whatever its origins, the brief flowering of British social realism testifies to Hill's argument that as a movement it must be seen in the context of the British film industry of the time, although he tends to underestimate the influence exerted on this situation by American capital. In 1959, according to Michael Balcon, 'you couldn't run a studio in the way Ealing was run – certainly not in this country, and perhaps nowhere in the world' (Balcon, 1959, p. 133). Balcon was speaking as the newly appointed chairman of Bryanston Films, a confederation of sixteen independent producers and production companies, financed by the producers themselves as well as by the distributors British Lion and by Lloyds Bank, Alliance Film Studios and Rank Laboratories, and releasing through British Lion. British Lion was modelled on the American Company, United Artists, and like United Artists lacked an exhibition circuit of its own. American financier Walter Reade's presence on the British Lion Board was part of a campaign to secure showings of British films in the United States, for without exhibition back-up they would be unlikely to make a profit in the domestic market. According to George Perry (1974) at this time 'up to 90 per cent of the films made in Britain derived their financing at least in some part from American sources' (p. 215). However, this financial interest was likely to be withdrawn as soon as production conditions in Hollywood improved, with disastrous effects for the British industry. When this eventually happened, British cinema in general, and the social realist movement in particular, were suddenly and radically affected.

One of the most important independent companies linked to Bryanston was Woodfall. Formed by playwright John Osborne and Tony Richardson, one of the co-founders of Free Cinema, the company was dedicated to British social realism. Bryanston Films themselves were financed by American moneymen like Walter Reade, the NFFC (National Film Finance Corporation) and theatrical impresarios like Harry Saltzman and Oscar Lewenstein. This theatrical connection was important to Woodfall: not only were Osborne, Richardson, Saltzman and Lewenstein all identified with it, but many of the company's screenplays and performances derived from Royal Court Theatre successes. In the early 1960s, however, Reade withdrew from British Lion, Harry Saltzman left Woodfall for the James Bond series and Bryanston began producing blockbusters for the American market. In 1963, British social realism, as a coherent movement, was abruptly brought to an end.

Selected Reading

Geoff Brown, 'Paradise found and lost: the course of British realism', in Robert Murphy, *The British Cinema Book*, London, BFI, 1997.

Raymond Durgnat, *A Mirror for England: British Movies from Austerity to Affluence*, London, Faber & Faber, 1970.

John Hill, *Sex, Class and Realism: British Cinema 1956–1963*, London, BFI, 1986.

Alan Lovell, *The British Cinema: The Unknown Cinema*, London, BFI Education, Seminar Paper, 1969.

Robert Murphy, *Sixties British Cinema*, London, BFI, 1992.

Dead of Night (UK 1945 *p.c* – Ealing Studios; *d* – Robert Hamer (*The Haunted Mirror*); sd b/w)

The Lavender Hill Mob (UK 1951 *p.c* – Ealing Studios; *d* – Charles Crichton; sd b/w)

The Man in the White Suit (UK 1951 *p.c* – Ealing Studios; *d* –Alexander Mackendrick; sd b/w)

The Quatermass Xperiment (UK 1955 *p.c* – Hammer; *d* – Val Guest; sd b/w)

X – The Unknown (UK 1956 *p.c* – Hammer; *d* – Leslie Norman; sd b/w)

Quatermass II (UK 1957 *p.c* – Hammer; *d* – Val Guest; sd b/w)

The Curse of Frankenstein (UK 1957 *p.c* – Hammer; *d* – Terence Fisher; sd col.)

Dracula (UK 1958 *p.c* – Hammer; *d* – Terence Fisher; sd col.)

The Hound of the Baskervilles (UK 1959 *p.c* – Hammer; *d* – Terence Fisher; sd col.)

The Mummy (UK 1959 *p.c* – Hammer; *d* – Terence Fisher; sd col.)

The Brides of Dracula (UK 1960 *p.c* – Hammer; *d* – Terence Fisher; sd col.)

The Damned (UK 1961 *p.c* – Hammer; *d* – Joseph Losey; sd b/w scope)

The Evil of Frankenstein (UK 1964 *p.c* – Hammer; *d* – Freddie Francis; sd col.)

Dracula, Prince of Darkness (UK 1965 *p.c* – Hammer; *d* –Terence Fisher; sd col. scope)

Fanatic (UK 1965 *p.c* – Hammer/Seven Arts; *d* – Silvio Narizzano; sd col.)

The Plague of the Zombies (UK 1966 *p.c* – Hammer; *d* – John Gilling; sd col.)

The Devil Rides Out (UK 1967 *p.c* – Hammer; *d* – Terence Fisher; sd col.)

Taste the Blood of Dracula (UK 1969 *p.c* – Hammer; *d* – Peter Sasdy; sd col.)

The Satanic Rites of Dracula (UK 1973 *p.c* – Hammer; *d* – Alan Gibson; sd col.)

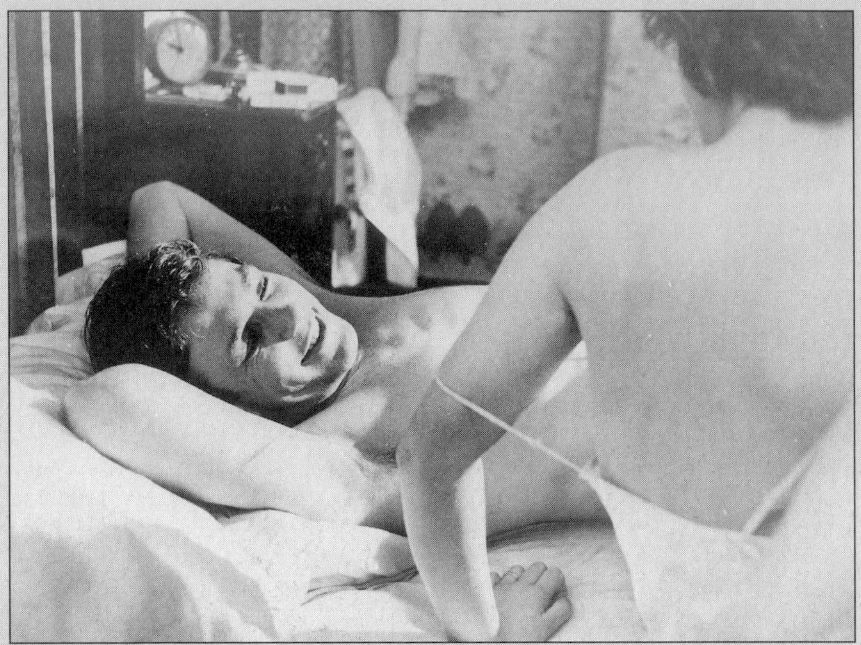

Finney and Roberts's *Saturday Night and Sunday Morning*

Room at the Top (UK 1958 *p.c* – Remus; *d* – Jack Clayton; sd b/w)

Both Alexander Walker and Raymond Durgnat suggest a direct relationship between British society of the late 1950s and films like *Room at the Top*. Thus, for Durgnat, 'hints of disquiet about the time of Suez (1956), led rapidly to *Room at the Top* (1958) and *Look Back in Anger* (1959). Their success established another, and continuing mood of uneasiness . . . ' (Durgnat, 1970, p. 13). Walker argues that working-class anti-hero Joe Lampton's envy in *Room at the Top* was the same feeling that swept the post war Labour government to power, and was immediately recognised by the audience that went to movies. However, Walker also points to the influence of box-office concerns and the attempt to attract international audiences, citing as evidence the casting of international star Simone Signoret and the use of the American rather than the English pronunciation of the word 'brassiere' (Walker, 1974, p. 46). In its desire to have this international appeal, Walker argues, the film plays down Joe's social origins and the class conflict in favour of the clash of generations and an emphasis on Joe's sexuality, and this is what won it its large audiences. John Hill had also noted that the social realist films' attitude to class was less a positive affirmation than a displacement of it to make way for the generalised category of the 'social problem' (Hill, 1979, p. 129).

In the case of *Room at the Top*, the combination of class, youth and sex with a best-selling literary source was an innovation in British cinema and proved to be enormously successful. The film took two of the 1959 Academy Awards (for Neil Paterson's screenplay and Simone Signoret's performance), made Laurence Harvey into an international star, and introduced Jack Clayton to full-length feature film-making.

Saturday Night and Sunday Morning (UK 1960 *p.c* – Woodfall; *d* – Karel Reisz; sd b/w)

Since 1960 several critics have attempted to explain the unexpected box-office success of *Saturday Night and Sunday Morning*. Albert Finney's performance as Arthur has often been cited as responsible. Harry Saltzman, the film's producer, has said 'People's identification with Finney, especially young people and working young people, was total. Of course it was well directed and acted, and a very well-written film, but it was this empathy people had for the character which was more responsible than anything else for the business it did' (Walker, 1974, p. 88), and director Karel Reisz agrees that 'in a metaphorical way Arthur embodied what was happening in England' (Walker, 1974, p. 85).

Woodfall and Bryanston made more than half a million pounds from the success of *Saturday Night and Sunday Morning*. But that success may have been due to more than the popular appeal of the Arthur Seaton character. Walker's argument is that its success resulted, at least to some extent, from the truculent tone which marked it as different from other films in the genre. This truculence is apparent in the 'workbench soliloquy' at the beginning of the film in which Arthur's attitudes are spoken in some detail: 'Don't let the bastards grind you down. That's one thing you learn. What I'm out for is a good time. All the rest is propaganda' (Walker, 1974, p. 83).

For its language and frank representation of sex and violence, the film received an 'X-certificate from the censor, and was even banned outright in one country. But despite the box-office value of such measures *Saturday Night and Sunday Morning* very nearly did not get the chance to do any business at all. According to Alexander Walker, the bookers refused to show it in their cinemas, and only the unexpected failure of a Warner Bros. film at their West End showcase cinema, plus the advantage to the cinema of at last playing a British film and gaining quota credit, allowed the film to open. The first week's business was so phenomenal as to cause an instantaneous turn-round in the popularity of the film-makers *vis-à-vis* the film industry (Walker, 1974, p. 88).

A Taste of Honey (UK 1961 *p.c* – Woodfall; *d* – Tony Richardson; sd b/w)

Soon after *Saturday Night and Sunday Morning* opened it was announced that Harry Saltzman was leaving Woodfall. Walker quotes Saltzman to the effect that the parting of the ways was over the filming of *A Taste of Honey*, which he felt was too provincial to appeal to an international market (Walker, 1974, p. 91).

Shelagh Delaney's play *A Taste of Honey* was acquired for adaptation at a price of £6,000, a project which Woodfall had been unable to get Bryanston to finance until the breakthrough of *Saturday Night and Sunday Morning*. The director, Tony Richardson, having just returned from a frustrating trip to America where he had directed Delaney's play on Broadway, determined that no sets would be built for *A Taste of Honey*, and that it would be entirely shot on location. His experience of directing *Sanctuary* for 20th Century–Fox in Hollywood had been less than happy. For *A Taste of Honey* the unit was entirely based in Fulham, with the top floor of a derelict house being used as the 'rooming house' and the rest as production offices for Woodfall. An unknown actress, Rita Tushingham, played the central role; Richardson rejected an offer from American financiers to back the film if Audrey Hepburn played the part.

PART 4

ALTERNATIVES TO CLASSIC HOLLYWOOD

Soleil Ô (1970)

EARLY CINEMA: AFTER BRIGHTON

Until recently, the history of cinema has been written according to a set of long-held and often peremptory assumptions about the significance or insignificance of its early years. Cinema's first twenty or thirty years were regarded simply as a preparatory period for what came later. From Terry Ramsaye (1926, 1964) and Lewis Jacobs (1939) to Jean Mitry (1968) and Noël Burch (1990), historians conceived this period in terms of infancy or immaturity as 'primitive' cinema. Built into this evolutionary account was the assumption that the best, most efficient model of narrative continuity was to be found in American cinema (whose 'father' was D. W. Griffith), in what Burch (1990) called, disparagingly, the Institutional Mode of Representation or what David Bordwell, Janet Staiger, and Kristin Thompson (1985) later proclaimed as the 'classic Hollywood cinema' (see Classic Hollywood narrative, p. 39). Early cinema was by this account merely the workshop in which classical conventions of editing, framing and narrative were gradually formed. Early films were the building blocks, unimportant in themselves, which underpinned the edifice of classic Hollywood cinema.

Our assumptions about early cinema, however, have changed radically since the early 1980s. The impetus for this change came from the 1978 Congress of the International Federation of Film Archives (FIAF), held in Brighton, which brought together archivists and academics for one full week to view and discuss hundreds of fiction films (from 1900 to 1906), many of them newly rediscovered and printed. This event turned out to be a revelation that spurred scores of researchers, in a collaborative endeavour soon called the Brighton Project, to begin rethinking and rewriting the history of early cinema. This rethinking and rewriting was supported by film archive restorations, many of them showcased at the annual Pordenone Silent Film Festival in Italy (launched in 1982), by the organisation of an international society devoted to the study of early cinema, Domitor (instituted in 1987), and by numerous conferences and workshops, some prompted by the centennial celebrations of cinema in 1995/6. All this work has led historians to reconceive early cinema in a number of ways. One has been to re-examine the first ten years or so of cinema's emergence worldwide, not only as an object of study for its own sake but in terms of a theoretical question: how to explain what Burch once aptly described as early cinema's 'distinctive otherness' in relation to what came later (Burch, 1986, p. 486). Another has been to modify and complicate the received account of the development of a narrative cinema, investigating the contribution of films produced in countries other than the United States, questioning the historical inevitability and dominance of the 'classic Hollywood' model, and granting equal value to various alternatives to that model. A third has even gone beyond the Brighton Project to reconceptualise early cinema by focusing on exhibition – with its changes over time and variations in different social contexts rather than on production and textual representation. Here, cinema is defined as a cultural practice whose 'meaning' depends, in large part, on its material conditions of reception.

A CINEMA OF ATTRACTIONS

One line of research on early cinema has continued, after Brighton, to redraw the historical map of the cinema's first decade. This research is exemplified in the term 'cinema of attractions', first coined by Tom Gunning (and André Gaudreault) in Gunning's 1986 article 'The Cinema of Attraction: Early Film, Its Spectator and the Avant-Garde'. Gunning's work assumes a principle of discontinuity at work in cinema history (early

The Great Train Robbery (USA 1903 *p.c* – Edison; *d* – Edwin S. Porter; st b/w)

This film is based on a 1896 stage play as well as accounts of actual train robberies in the Far West. Over the course of its 13 shots, an outlaw gang disables a telegraph operator, robs the passengers on a train, escapes a posse on horseback, only to be killed in a climactic gunfight. The film already departs from the usual practice of the 'cinema of attractions' in that it includes one virtual match on action and rudimentary crosscutting. Yet the robbery itself is narrated in a single 2-minute static shot which may have required an exhibitor's commentary to clarify the action. Exhibitors also could place the 'emblematic close-up' at either the beginning or the end to maximise its 'shock value', which came partly from 'duping' a notorious poster for Gold Dust cleaning powder. This film enjoyed a huge success in vaudeville houses in the US throughout 1904, and later was sometimes used on the opening programmes of new nickelodeons.

Facing up to the camera – *The Great Train Robbery*

A Policeman's Tour of the World (France 1906 *p.c* – Pathé; *d* – Charles Lepine; st b/w & col.)

A Policeman's Tour combines a half-dozen different kinds of film, as if condensing a single programme of diverse subjects into one. Its 27 shots mix the 'attractions' of *actualités*, trick films, and travelogues with the episodic narrative of a Paris policeman pursuing a banker-embezzler across the globe. More specifically, it includes a sequence of point-of-view shots (the thief tours the Suez Canal), a tableau (set in an opium den) in which multiple exposures create contrasting dreams for the two men, a Far West sequence (shot on location) in which the policeman rescues the thief from American Indians, and a close-up insert of a letter absolving the thief of guilt. This 'imperialist' adventure ends in an apotheosis tableau, with the two men (now financial partners) posing before the spectacle of a large stage-set globe surrounded by representatives of the world's peoples, over which they exert a benevolent control.

A Narrow Escape, or The Physician of the Caste (France 1908 *p.c* – Pathé; *d* – Albert Capellani; st b/w)

This film is based on André de Lorde's one-act Grand Guignol play, *Au Téléphone* (1902), in which *apaches* (a criminal gang) falsely send a doctor away on a distant house call so they can break into his home and threaten his family. Unlike the stage play, or Pathé's earlier *Terrible angoisse* (1906), this film invents a 'happy ending'. Composed of 29 shots, *A Narrow Escape* is remarkable as an early example of sustained alternation or parallel editing (a frequent feature of Pathé films between 1906 and 1908). It quickly establishes adjacent spaces inside and outside the doctor's home, then alternates two lines of action (the break-in and threat versus the doctor's journey and arrival at a 'castle'), and culminates in two cut-in medium close-ups of the doctor and his wife, in matching profile (a good example of an attraction 'motivated' for narrative purposes), linked tenuously by telephone at the climactic moment of greatest vulnerability.

Cross-cutting shots from *A Narrow Escape*

The Lonedale Operator (USA 1911 *p.c* – Biograph; *d* – D.W. Griffith; st b/w and col.)

Based on a script by Mack Sennett, this is a 'classic' example of Griffith's early suspense thrillers. The telegraph operator at a remote railway station falls ill, and his daughter (Blanche Sweet) has to defend the station against thieves as her fiancé races to the rescue in his locomotive. Composed of 97 shots, the film uses a multiple system of parallel editing which intercuts the locomotive engineer and his embattled sweetheart at the same time it shows her glimpsing the thieves outside, barricading herself in the telegraph office, and then outmanœvring them when they finally break in. Several cut-in medium shots accentuate the woman's anxiety as she realises her signals for help may have gone unheard, and one cut-in close-up reveals that the 'gun' she had used to hold off the thieves is actually a wrench: blue tinting in the earlier shots had kept it 'unreadable' to spectators as well.

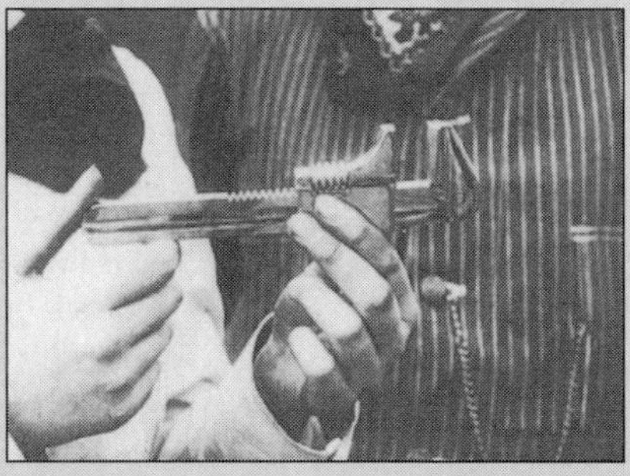

Narrative revelation through selective detail – *The Lonedale Operator*

The Greater Love (USA 1912 *p.c* – Vitagraph; *d* – Rollin Sturgeon; st col.)

This western is notable as an early example of 'classical' continuity editing, especially in its repeated shot/reverse-shots (in medium and long shot): first, to link a cowboy and his lover, then to break up his duel with a rival, and finally, to intercut the two gunfighters on horseback. Its tinting and toning are also suggestive: although changes in colour sometimes distinguish day from night and exterior from interior, they primarily function to mark off one segment of the narrative from another, concisely signalling shifts in the story's development, but also could serve as cues for a pianist to change the musical accompaniment.

In the Clutch of the Paris Apaches (France 1913 *p.c* – Gaumont; *d* – Léonce Perret; st b/w & col.)

A topical feature-length melodrama in which a little girl falls into the hands of an *apache* gang, but is rescued by a young shoemaker who reunites her with her father. This film includes a range of *mise-en-scène* and framing strategies characteristic of European cinema just before the First World War: 'deep staging' in both studio décors and natural landscapes (a good example would be the high-angle long shot from behind the father, in uniform, speaking from an apartment balcony to a cheering crowd below), moments of selective arc lighting, silhouetted figures in doors and windows, and 'pictorial' toning effects. It also displays Perret's own 'style' of continuity editing which often relied, not on shot/reverse-shot, but on 90° and 180° shifts in camera position. Finally, it is notable for sustaining narrative action across several 'breaks' between one film reel and another, taking advantage of the cinemas which could run multiple-reel films continuously (the Gaumont-Palace, for instance, began using two, alternating projectors in late 1911).

cinema's 'distinctive otherness'), which he extrapolates with reference to aspects of early cinema which do not directly contribute to the evolution of narrative cinema.

Early cinema involved an 'aesthetic of attractions' in which visual curiosity was aroused and satisfied by novelty, surprise, even shock. More specifically, it tended to show or display – as an 'attraction' – either the technical possibilities of the new medium (the moving camera in Biograph's *Brooklyn Bridge*, 1899) or the spectacle of human figures (from Veriscope's *Corbett & Fitzsimmons Fight*, 1897, to Edison's views of President McKinley's funeral, 1901), natural landscapes (Biograph's *Niagara Falls, Winter*, 1897), and elaborately constructed décors (Méliès's *Cinderella*, 1899). Moreover, early films generally were comprised of a single, autonomous tableau or a series of tableaux or 'scenes,' frontally framed and often static, as in photographs or on the theatre stage. The objective, in Gaudreault's words, was 'to present the totality of an action unfolding in an homogenous space' (Gaudreault, 1984 p. 322), whether in the single-take scene of robbing and killing in Edison's *The Great Train Robbery* (1903) or in a Méliès trick film such as *One-Man Orchestra* (1900), where multiple exposure and 'invisible editing' produce a host of magical disappearances, reappearances, and other transformations. In addition, the tableau's single, unified viewpoint assumed a camera relatively distant from what was being filmed, which turned human subjects primarily into performers of physical action rather than characters. Closer shots (as in Williamson's *The Big Swallow*, 1901) served as comic and/or trick 'attractions'. Finally, films were sold, in Thomas Elsaesser's words, as 'semi-finished products' that could be 'finished' in exhibition in different ways (Elsaesser, 1992). All kinds of practices – variable projection speeds, re-edited or reordered shots, colours applied to the filmstock, accompanying music and sound effects, lecturers offering explanations – promoted a wide range of textual variance.

Early cinema emerged within a network of mass cultural practices throughout Europe and North America, practices which partly determined its range of 'attractions'. Many of these cultural practices provided familiar subjects for early films: newspaper and magazine cartoons for Lumière's *L'Arroseur arrosé* (1895), magazine photographs for Méliès's *The Dreyfus Affair* (1899), wax-museum exhibits for Pathé's *Story of a Crime* (1901), *féerie* plays and even an amusement park ride for Méliès's *A Trip to the Moon* (1902), popular stage melodramas for Edison's *Uncle Tom's Cabin*

(1903) or *The Miller's Daughter* (1905), and penny press stories for Pathé's *Annie's Love Story* or *Indians and Cowboys* (both 1904). These kinds of material formed the basis of a dozen 'genres', and Pathé in particular took advantage of their marketability in a broad spectrum of exhibition venues, most of which provided a specific context for viewing. In a Boston-Keith vaudeville house (supplied by Vitagraph's projection service), for instance, one or two reels of film shared a programme with a dozen or more live acts (and not only as 'chasers' at the end). Week after week, the film 'performance' offered something different: a short playlet, a comic or magic act, a 'history lesson', a 'current event' or *fait divers*, scenic views of distant lands and peoples. On his lecture circuits, by contrast, Lyman Howe – one of America's most important travelling exhibitors and lecturers in the years up to 1910 – amalgamated dozens of disparate films into a clear narrative line which allowed all three of his touring companies for example, to arrange, in 1904, a different order of scenes from the Russo-Japanese War. At the same time, on one British fairground after another, the touring 'Bioscope' shows, having replaced the popular nineteenth-century 'ghost shows' (a condensed form of theatricals, conjuring tricks, and optical devices), disseminated throughout the countryside the latest news, *fait divers*, fads, comic turns and 'scientific wonders' of that year's season. It is little wonder, as Charles Musser concludes, that during this period it was exhibitors and not producers who exercised 'editorial control' over films and their mode of representation (1991, pp. 103–56).

THE EMERGENCE OF A NARRATIVE CINEMA

A second line of research has continued to focus on the emergence of narrative cinema but in terms of Burch's critique of the historical inevitability of its dominant form (Burch, 1990). However, historians have proposed different accounts of the relationship between early and late forms. Some, such as Barry Salt (1983, 1992) continue to accept a teleological model of cinema history, privileging the development of a 'classic Hollywood cinema'. Burch himself has advanced a binary model of film practice, positing a break or rupture between an industrialised Institutional Mode of Representation and an earlier, 'primitive' mode which he valorises because he sees it taken up later in 'avant-garde' films (Burch, 1986, 1990). Others, such as Gunning (1991), Kristin Thompson (1985), and Richard Abel (1994), have posited something like a tripartite model, with a transitional period more or less distinct from, yet sharing elements with, both the 'cinema of attractions' and the later narrative cinema. A good example of what might be a transitional form would be Pathé's *A Policeman's Tour of the World* (1906), which combines a story of theft and pursuit with several travelogue scenes (the ones on the Suez Canal include point-of-view-shot 'attractions'), a secondary story of attacking 'Redskins' in the Far West, an *actualité* (a political campaign in New York), and a stencil-coloured apotheosis ending in which thief and pursuer join hands as financial partners before a huge globe and massed group of colonial subjects.

Whatever the model, there is general agreement on the early stages of the transformation from one form to another. Initially, what was involved was a change in spatial coherence: the autonomous tableau gave way to a synthetic space constructed out of interrelated, discrete shots. Correlated with this was a change in temporality, with greater attention given to issues of succession, simultaneity and internally generated causality. Both of these changes contributed to a new form of contiguity and sequentiality clearly evident, for instance, in British chase films, from Hagger's *Desperate Poaching Affray* (1903) to Hepworth's *Rescued by Rover* (1905). In the latter film, a coherent narrative space is constructed by editing separate shots into sequences, matchcutting the action, as Rover seeks out a kidnapped baby and then guides the father back to the kidnappers' lair. As 'narrativisation' was extended to every level of film discourse, the 'attractions' that once served an aesthetics of display – for instance, pans, close shots (like the gun fired at the camera in *The Great Train Robbery* (1903)), point-of-view shots – were subordinated to narrative development as in films as diverse as Pathé's *The Life of a Convict* (1905) and Vitagraph's *The 100-to-1 Shot* (1906). Soon this system of narrative continuity included alternations between adjacent spaces (sometimes with reverse-angle cutting) and crosscut parallel lines of action, visible in Pathé films from *The Dog Smugglers* (1906) to *A Narrow Escape* (1908). The latter film, reworked in Griffith's *The Lonely Villa* (1909), crosscuts not only between as many as three separate locations but between close shots of the endangered wife and her rescuer-to-be-husband, joined by another technological instrument, the telephone (see p. 94). By 1908 or 1909, in many French and American films, everything having to do with *mise-en-scène*, framing, and editing was being 'remotivated', subordinated to a causal narrative chain dependent on such devices as repetition, delay, surprise, suspense and, above all, closure.

One consequence of these changes – and their chief motivation, Musser (1991a) and Elsaesser (1990) argue – was to wrest from the exhibitor control over the process of 'making meaning'. A different kind of 'film narrator' or position from which to narrate a story was being constructed, which positioned the audience differently, engaging the spectator (increasingly individualised) in 'stitching' together a synthetic spatial temporal whole and a sequential process of 'narrative knowledge'. No longer would a film's intelligibility as a story need to rely on prior knowledge and familiarity – as it did in Edison films from *Uncle Tom's Cabin* (1903) to *Kathleen Mavourneen* (1906) – or on an exhibitor's commentary. Consonant with this change was the increasing use of intertitles (which Pathé had pioneered in 1903). Instead intelligibility began to derive from what Gunning, in his analysis of Griffith's early Biograph films, calls an 'internalized lecturer', from the way a film such as *The Story of the Shirt* (1908) or *The Country Doctor* (1909) told its story, selecting and organising 'narratively important elements from a mass of contingent details', building up a hierarchy of knowledge or point of view concerning that material (1991, pp. 93–4). By the time of Griffith's *The Lonedale Operator* (1911), that selection could create a concise sense of character as well as a narrative revelation in such 'details' as the close shot of the heroine's anxious face (at the telegraph) and the close up of a wrench she has used like a revolver to keep the villains at bay (in earlier shots tinted blue in the release print). The use to which the 'internalized lecturer' was put did vary. Whereas Griffith films usually assumed a strongly 'moral voice' in their narration, some of Pathé's,

An early example of the construction of narrative by editing – *Rescued by Rover*

Figures in a setting of 'considerable depth' – Sjöström's *Ingeborg Holm*

such as *The Man with White Gloves* (1908) and *The Mill* (1909), Abel (1994) writes, adopted the 'ironic voice' of '*grand guignol*'. In the latter film, a miller kills his wife's lover, binds the body to a revolving blade of his windmill, and ties up the wife so she is forced to watch the spectacle; as he then drowns himself in a nearby pool, the surface of the water grows smooth, reflecting the upside-down image of the distant windmill.

The transition from a 'cinema of attractions' to a narrative cinema, however, probably did not occur at the same time, and in the same way, in every country. Rather than assume a degree of uneven development, privileging the 'classic Hollywood cinema', historians are exploring the possibility of distinct, parallel developments. The American cinema, with its emphasis on individuated characters, came to depend on 'close shots' of faces, especially those of female stars like Mary Pickford (e.g. in Biograph's *The New York Hat*, 1912), and a continuity system of eyeline matches and shot/reverse-shots – developing from Essanay's *The Loafer* (1911) or Vitagraph's *The Greater Love* (1912) through Reliance's *Detective Burton's Triumph* (1914). European cinemas, by contrast, advanced a different mode of representation characterised by 'deep staging' (see Kristin Thompson, 1995; John Fullerton, 1995; and Yuri Tsivian, 1995). Here, the emphasis was on the precise movement of one or more characters within a set or natural landscape of considerable depth, evident in such films as Perret's *In the Clutch of the Paris Apaches* (1913), Sjöström's *Ingeborg Holm* (1913) or Bauer's *Twilight of a Woman's Soul* (1913). As Tsivian suggests, geometrical patterns of actor positioning and movement (from a fixed viewpoint) might define, equally as well as any feature of the American system, a model of cinematic 'essence' or specificity in the 1910s. By the same token, Abel claims, French cinema developed an alternative model of continuity editing, perhaps most evident in Perret's films for Gaumont, from comic shorts like *Eugene in Love* (1911) to lengthy features like *The Tale of a Cabin Boy* (1914). Instead of eyeline matches and shot/reverse-shots, this system was characterised by relatively consistent 90° and 180° changes in camera position.

However crucial ideas like these may have become for understanding and analysing early cinema, many questions remain open to debate. Did the music and sound effects which accompanied film projections change in kind and function, for instance, in the transition from a cinema of attractions to a narrative cinema? Was the gradual standardisation of sound accompaniment, beginning around 1910, similar or different in the American and European cinemas? Similarly, did the processes used to colour positive film prints (tinting, toning, hand-painting, stencil-colouring), all of which Pathé initially exploited more than any other company and which so distinguished its films on the American market, change in kind and function in the transition to a narrative cinema? If most films were released in tinted prints by the end of the 1910s, did that tinting function differently in the American and European cinemas and, if so, how? Finally, in the shift from one standard release format (the single-reel film) to another (the feature-length film) by the mid-1910s, did significant differences develop in Europe or America? If, as Gunning has gone on to argue, neither 'cinema of attractions' nor 'narrative cinema' can be considered a monolithic category (Gunning, 1993), then all of silent cinema may be marked by a perpetually shifting negotiation between 'the desire to display' and 'the desire to tell a story', with the parameters of that negotiation changing from one historically specific moment or social space to another.

EXHIBITION AND RECEPTION

Several other lines of historical research, although ultimately deriving from the Brighton Project, have drawn attention away from the production of films and their textual features to reconceive early cinema by focusing on exhibition and reception. From this perspective, the cultural arena within which cinema circulated can be seen to have had national, regional, and even local variations, variations which pertained beyond the period of a 'cinema of attractions'. In France and Britain, for instance, early films were shown in two principal venues: fairground shows and urban music halls (both drew a mass audience from the lower and middle classes). Each of these venues presented relatively long programmes – two or more hours of short films, lantern slides, and live acts – although in both countries fairground shows soon featured films exclusively. The permanent urban cinemas that began to open throughout France, in 1907, generally adopted this long-programme format, and the larger, more prestigious cinemas soon competed directly with music halls and even theatres. In Paris, by early 1909, both the Omnia-Pathé and the Cirque d'hiver presented two daily programmes of a dozen or more Pathé films, with orchestral accompaniment and song interludes. In Britain, the fairground shows (also chiefly supplied by Pathé) developed into great shows with elaborate façades custom-built around massive organs. Only in 1909 did 'purpose-built' urban cinemas begin to appear in numbers, and these adopted, as the French did earlier, the two-tiered format of the music halls: full programmes for the middle classes in the more expensive galleries and boxes; continuous shows (allowing short visits) for the lower classes on the ground floor. For the French and British, 'going to the cinema' seems to have been class-specific (for the middle classes, it was a 'special occasion'); it also remained tied to a long cultural history of seasonal fairs, most especially in Britain.

The conditions of exhibition and reception were quite different in the United States. At first, films were presented primarily in vaudeville houses and, to a lesser extent, on lecture circuits and fairgrounds, usually as one act among many on a lengthy programme. By 1904 with the development of 'cheap' family vaudeville venues (some in summer amusement parks), films featured as one of four, five or six acts on a programme lasting no more than one hour. By 1906, with the rapid expansion of nickelodeons, programmes – several films, again usually supplied by Pathé, and illustrated songs, often totalling no more than 15 to 30 minutes – ran continuously from noon, or even earlier, to late at night.

The 'cheap' nickelodeons served different functions depending on their location. Those in shopping districts offered a mixed

The travelling cinema and the permanent cinema: The New Theatre Boston and the interior Omnia-Pathé, Paris, 1912

class of shoppers, office workers, and others (many of them women and children) comfortable places to 'spend time', especially the 'waiting time' between one activity and another so common to 'modern life'. As Kathy Peiss has shown, for single white-collar workers, nickelodeons became a significant 'woman's space' in the world of public, commercial amusements (Peiss, 1986). Those in working-class (often immigrant) residential areas, according to moral reformers and the trade press, even turned into neighbourhood 'social centres' where people could congregate. In response to the *Chicago Tribune*'s attack on nickelodeons, in April 1907, for instance, the Chicago Relief and Aid Society defended such residential cinemas, which catered chiefly to families, because they 'answer[ed] ... a real need of the community'. Even when larger cinemas began to appear in 1908, with programmes lasting 45 or 50 minutes, films still ran continuously so spectators could 'drop in' and walk out whenever they wanted. For Americans, then, 'going to the cinema' could be integrated into 'everyday life' (as a worker or consumer), providing a new source of autonomy and pleasure (for women), or a means of either renewing one's bonds with a community (for immigrants) or else rejecting them for a larger sense of social identity.

This kind of research, then, focuses critical attention on how different audiences and spectators experienced films, on what 'use value' the cinema had for them, and on how that experience and its significance may have changed over time. In short, the argument is that 'making meaning' in the cinema is determined by conditions of exhibition, by the range of 'reading positions' or 'interpretive strategies' available to particular audiences at particular historical moments (see Spectatorship and audience research, p. 366). Uricchio and Pearson (1993) take Vitagraph's *Julius Caesar* (1908) as an example of how specific social groups could 'read' a film text differently. In New York, 'business and leisure class viewers' probably responded to the film's scenes of spectacle, which imitated theatrical staging in a way which was familiar. Yet the city's slum tenement viewers may have been more responsive to its 'key phrase, key image approach to Shakespeare' which dominated the public school system as well as the recitals and 'bare stage' productions sponsored by the People's Institute and the Educational Alliance. Another Vitagraph 'quality' film, *Francesca da Rimini* (1908), may have promoted the value of an Italian heritage for some (especially immigrants), but it may also have confirmed anti-Italian feelings in others. Similarly, Pathé's *Christmas Eve Tragedy* (1908) would have been capable of eliciting contradictory reactions. *Variety*, for instance, deployed a moral reform discourse to condemn this and other *grand guignol* French films as so 'objectionable for children' as to justify censorship ('Film Reviews', 25 April 1908); yet for shoppers at Keith's 14th Street cinema, according to New York reporter Walter Eaton, the film was seen as a 'touching domestic tragedy', made all the more poignant by the sung ballad which followed, all about a forsaken maiden 'in a village by the sea' ('New Theatrical Problem: Age of Mechanical Amusement', *New York Sun*, 9 May 1908).

Such analyses invite further research on certain questions about early cinema. The basic one, of course, is: who actually went to the cinema, when, where, how often and for what reasons? Whatever materials one might investigate – government documents, company records, ads and articles in newspapers and magazines, moral reform movement surveys, oral interviews or memoirs, even the films themselves (as they construct possible reading positions) – research on this question has to unpack and explain the historical conditions for the specific interrelations of actual spectators and films. Given the emergence of a global capitalist economy, centred in Europe and North America, geared to growing levels of consumption and the production of consumers to support such an economy, what was the role of the nickelodeons, fairground shows and first permanent cinemas? To what degree did they occupy a 'relatively autonomous public sphere' distinct from 'the more comprehensive, less class-specific public sphere' of the later 'picture palaces' (Miriam Hansen, 1991, p. 63), and did they offer some kind of resistance to the emergence of modern consumer society (Burch, 1990)? In the United States, the huge numbers of immigrants, women and children (none of them full citizens) 'going to the show' weekly or even daily give such questions a particular twist. Within the context of a heightened nationalism, and heated debates over the 'process of assimilation' and the construction of an 'American' identity, how did the cinema serve to 'train' such people to take up that identity and become proper social subjects within an 'American' culture? What was the role, in that 'training', for instance, of the 'Indian and Western' films, which had become incredibly popular with urban audiences by 1909? In that westerns so quickly became the quintessential 'American subject', and distinctly different from Pathé's 'foreign film product', perhaps they not only formed the basis for what the trade weekly *Moving Picture World* would call 'an American school of moving picture drama' (20 November 1909), but represented the most visible sign of an 'Americanisation process' in early American cinema.

The study of early cinema has become a 'burning passion', to cite Paolo Cherchi Usai's apt metaphor. For some it has led, he writes, to 'going back to the origins of a truly inflammable, even explosive relationship between image and mind', that is, when 'cultivated with the rigour of the historian and the imagination of a spectator aware of reliving another's past in a beam of light projected onto a screen' (Usai, 1994, p. 7). But it also can lead to seeing a parallel between early or pre-classic cinema and our own post-classic cinema, condensing around modes of film consumption and spectatorship. Both historical moments, Hansen argues, 'mark a major transition in the development of the public sphere', and the potential for a critical, utopian public sphere (1993). To study early cinema, then, is to perceive that our own postmodern media culture may involve a similar opening-up of possibilities and to intervene on the side of promoting their development.

Selected Reading

Richard Abel, *The Ciné Goes to Town: French Cinema, 1896–1914*, Berkeley, University of California Press, 1994.

Eileen Bowser, *The Transformation of Cinema, 1907–1915*, New York, Scribner's, 1991.

Noël Burch, *Life to those Shadows*, Berkeley, University of California Press, 1990.

Paolo Cherchi Usai, *Burning Passions: An Introduction to the Study of Silent Cinema*, London, BFI, 1994.

Thomas Elsaesser (ed.), *Early Cinema: Space, Frame, Narrative*, London, BFI, 1990.

Tom Gunning, '"The cinema of attractions": early cinema, its spectator and the avant-garde', *Wide Angle* 8 (314), pp. 63–70, 1986.

Tom Gunning, 'Now you see it, now you don't: the temporality of the cinema of attractions', *The Velvet Light Trap* 32, 1993, pp. 3–12.

Miriam Hansen, *Babel & Babylon: Spectatorship in American Silent Film*, Cambridge, Harvard University Press, 1991.
Charles Musser, *Before the Nickleodeon: Edwin S. Porter and the Edison Manufacturing Company*, Berkeley: University of California Press, 1991.
Barry Salt, *Film Style and Technology: History and Analysis*, 1st edn 1983; rev. edn, London, Starword, 1992.
Kristin Thompson, 'From primitive to classical', in Bordwell *et al.*, *The Classical Hollywood Cinema*, London, RKP, 1985, pp. 157–73.

Five Easy Pieces – art cinema practices in a Hollywood film

NEW HOLLYWOOD

As Hollywood cinema moved through the 1960s into the 1970s it was shadowed by a series of film critical and film journalistic declarations of the emergence of a 'New Hollywood cinema', a 'Hollywood renaissance', and in apparent deference to this notion of 'New Hollywood', contemporary American film is starting to be described as 'New New Hollywood', 'New American Cinema' and 'Contemporary Hollywood' (see Madsen, 1975; Jacobs, 1977; Pye and Myles, 1979; Schatz, 1983; *Wide-Angle*, 1983; Lewis, 1995; Colker and Virrel, 1978; *GQ*, 1995). Consequently, any notion of a 'New Hollywood' is always a discursive construction in which different critical accounts seek to describe changes in Hollywood film-making from the 1960s onwards. And since 'New Hollywood' does not remain the same object across its different critical descriptions we need to be aware from the outset that although these acts of criticism target an agreed period of Hollywood film history they make different claims for what is significant about that period, producing thereby a series of competing accounts of 'the new' in relation to New Hollywood.

Although the 'New Hollywood' concept–label clearly has been a success in the sense that it is widely used, dispute surrounds what is 'new' about New Hollywood when compared with the way Old Hollywood ('classic Hollywood') went about its business. Some film scholars claim that the forms of post-1970s American film-making differ little from the practices that sustained classic Hollywood cinema. Such a viewpoint prompts David Bordwell and Janet Staiger to see in post-1960 Hollywood cinema 'the persistence of a mode of film practice' – by which they mean the classic Hollywood style (Bordwell and Staiger, 1985). Their view is supported by a number of other critics. Douglas Gomery claims that 'in terms of economic structure and power, little changed in the American film industry during the seventies' (Gomery, 1983, p. 52) and Robert B. Ray, in his survey of American cinema from 1930 to 1980, argued that the traditional forms of classic Hollywood cinema persisted into the moment of New Hollywood: 'Not surprisingly ... the majority of American movies of the 1970s were remarkably similar to those of the 1930s' (Ray, 1985, p. 68). Quite early in his book, *The New Hollywood*, Jim Hillier comments: 'in spite of all the changes that have taken place, Hollywood in the late 1980s and early 1990s does not look that different from the Hollywood of the previous forty years' (Hillier, 1992, p. 18).

A similar viewpoint can be found even within accounts whose brief it is to declare a moment of profound change. At the beginning of her book, *Hollywood Renaissance*, Diane Jacobs announces, 'the New Hollywood is not all that different from the Old' (Jacobs, 1977/1980, p. 2). Writing around the same time as Jacobs, William Paul argued that,

> contrary to all the trendy journalism about the 'New Hollywood' and the imagined rise of artistic freedom in American films, the 'New Hollywood' remains as crass and commercial as the old ... If anything, the New Hollywood has produced economic restrictions more severe and artistic options more limiting than anything in the bad old Hollywood. (Paul, 1977, p. 40)

So these different critical commentaries all agree that it is not clear whether the post-1960s period of American film-making constitutes a decisive break with classical traditions.

The highpoint of classic Hollywood cinema (see Part One) is usually thought of as occurring during the period from 1930 to 1945, when film-going was such a habitual national pastime that 'the movies attracted 83 cents of every US dollar spent on recreation' (Ray, 1985, p. 26). No one disputes that Hollywood cinema went through a series of substantial institutional changes after the 1948 Paramount Decree. Once the studios surrendered their theatres it was the end of the vertical integration that had characterised the 'mature' studio system. The impact of television, the decrease in the number of theatrical films produced, the arrival of the 'package' and the 'deal' to replace the studio-era 'assembly-line' production, the changing leisure interests of an American population that no longer saw movie-going as its principal entertainment–recreational pursuit, all led to a context in which the studios became financing, and distribution entities, film production became more 'one-off' and independent, and certain stars, directors and agents assumed a great deal of power. Pauline Kael has a succinct way of characterising this shift of power: 'To put it simply: A good script is a script to which Robert Redford will commit himself. A bad script is a script which Redford has turned down. A script that "needs work" is a script about which Redford has yet to make up his mind' (Kael, 1980, p. 16). Kael wrote this in 1980 after spending a year on leave from her *New Yorker* film column working for Warren Beatty in Hollywood. There she found that the real power in the new, conglomerate Hollywood rested with the advertising and marketing people 'who not only determine which movies get financed but which movies they are going to sell' (Godard and Kael, 1982, pp. 174–5).

Given the list of specific alterations to an existing industrial–institutional set-up, it might seem curious that so many discussions of post-1960s American cinema run a 'business as usual' line rather than proclaiming an economic–aesthetic revolution within, and reorganisation of, the American film industry (though the fact that, in the Reaganite mid-1980s, the studios were allowed to reacquire cinema theatres shows how quickly a landscape of difference can come to seem like a landscape of sameness). This apparent anomaly is explained by the fact, already indicated, that 'New Hollywood' does not remain the same object across its different critical descriptions. For example, three distinct moments are referred to by different critical discourses as constituting the moment of New Hollywood cinema and although these moments overlap, they are not identical. A further degree of uncertainty derives from the tendency for critical discussion to slide between assessing recent Hollywood film as a discrete textual artefact that is either 'better' or 'worse' than the artefact produced under the studio regime (let us sit upon the ground and tell

Five Easy Pieces (USA 1970 *p.c* – Columbia; *d* – Bob Rafelson; sd col.)

Shortly after the release of *Five Easy Pieces*, Stephen Farber praised the way in which the film had moved on from *Easy Rider* (1969) in its critiquing the quintessential American myth of 'the freedom of the open road . . . the journey away from civilisation as a regenerative experience containing the secret of life' (Farber, 1971, p. 128). The American literary tradition of Thoreau, Emerson, Twain, Whitman and Kerouac received a somewhat different rendering in Rafelson's film, which rejected the notion of drifting as a poetic adventure.

On one level, the Jack Nicholson (Robert/Bobby) 'character–function' works in a purely classical narrative fashion. The camera moves with him; he functions as the link between shots and sequences, ensuring narrative progression and continuity. He is also the means by which the film can move across its two cultural locales: the world of classical music in Puget Sound and the blue-collar world of oil rigs and bowling alleys into which Robert has ventured, becoming Bobby.

Robert/Bobby's family life operates within strict social–cultural codes. The low culture version of this is given in the celebrated restaurant scene involving the confrontation with the roadside diner waitress as Bobby attempts to order a sandwich. The waitress is shown to be a rule-bound literalist by the Nicholson character–function which, now working as 'Robert', is able to out-think/out-speak the waitress before smashing the glasses from the table. By contrast, in the cerebral space of the home, the character–function works as 'Bobby', asserting his physicality – 'taking' Catherine, fighting with Spicer. The main interest in this character–function lies in the way it is able to shatter the pretensions and decorum of each social context it encounters, simply by revealing its appropriate alternative side.

The 'character–function' in *Five Easy Pieces* at once activates the process of identification with a 'character' as a means of tying the viewer into the fiction, but is also a part of the unification procedures of the classic narrative text. The distinctiveness of the form of character given in the film derives from the extent to which it layers the tradition of character in classic Hollywood narrative with aspects more often found in art cinema (see Art cinema, p. 106).

The conclusion of *Five Easy Pieces* typifies the way art cinema practices have been mapped onto Hollywood practices throughout the film. The *mise-en-scène* obeys the rules of art cinema: the signs GULF–CAFE –MEN are prominent, a pole partitions the frame, and Bobby/Robert re-enters the totalised male world by emerging from the world of MEN to move into the truck whereas much of the imagery and dialogue in the manner of classic cinema 'rhymes' with earlier scenes thereby highlighting contrasts in narrative and character trajectories by means of visual or verbal echoes. This provides a final foregrounding of the two sets of film practices, art cinema and Hollywood, the intersection of which marks out the textual space of New Hollywood cinema.

Chinatown (USA 1974 *p.c* – Paramount; *d* – Roman Polanski; sd col.)

One classic narrative convention in *Chinatown* concerns the relation between narrative and knowledge, character and viewer. Narrative theorists enjoy taking examples from crime/detective fiction, because these genres inscribe explicitly certain general conditions and conventions of narrative. The detective's activities become a surrogate for the activity of reading/ viewing, involving the assessing and sorting of information in order to find a secure position from which to judge events. A typical hard-boiled plot begins with the hiring of a private eye; the person who does this usually has something to hide from the detective. The subsequent narrative is generated by the detective's activity: investigating and receiving mini-narratives (often untruthful, always incomplete). As the detective uncovers the 'true' story, we follow his movement, thereby gaining a narrative plenitude that replaces our initial position of not knowing. A further convention is that, since the detective is usually male, the client will be female and the knowledge the detective eventually gains will be inextricably bound up with knowledge of the woman: her past, her sexuality.

Given that *Chinatown* has incest at its centre we can expect the film to emphasise the narrative–knowledge–sexuality relation and there are many instances of the way in which the film plays against this particular convention while at the same time invoking it. The scenes involving Gittes and Noah Cross in conversations where Cross refers to 'the girl' and 'my daughter' (before the audience or Gittes are aware of the overlap of these apparently separate terms) offer one example, as does the scene of Gittes and an operative in a rowboat spying on what Gittes assumes is Mr Mulwray and his 'little girlfriend'. Gittes blows a kiss to his partner, a parodic play with sexual boundaries and identity (since the machoness of these two characters codes the allusion to gayness as comic). We later learn that Gittes was wrong (when he describes to Mrs Mulwray her husband's 'lover': 'she was pretty in a cheap sort of way') and this typifies the way the film plays against traditional modes of detection and distributions of narrative knowledge. Misprision is a strong theme in the film, often based on verbal slippage and overlap, as in the Chinese gardener's 'Bad for the glass/grass'; Applecore/Albacore and 'the girl/my daughter'.

Chinatown plays with two other classic narrative conventions. According to Bellour (1976), beginnings and endings of Hollywood films tend to rhyme with one another, thus providing a sense of closure and completion, and this macro-rhyming is also present at smaller levels of segments and sequences.

In *Chinatown*, Gittes is waiting in a car outside a house, Evelyn comes out, he confronts her and tells her (and us) that she has the missing child held hostage inside. As Evelyn starts to tell (half) a story ('she's my sister'), her head momentarily touches the car horn, at which moment she starts upright, recovers and the storyline resumes its strategy of narrative delay and deferral. At the end of the film Evelyn is killed and her head falls onto the car horn. In the

Playing with narrative conventions – *Chinatown*

narrative movement between these two 'rhyming' actions, much of the tragedy of *Chinatown* is played out. A different example is offered in Gittes's first visit to the Mulwray house. Such repetition of locale and action is what Bellour means when he says that the Hollywood film is always repeating itself (always with a slight difference) because it is always driving towards its completion. The interruption of Gittes's action (reaching for the spectacles) allows the Gittes/Evelyn Mulwray plotline (the formation of the couple) to overwhelm, for a while, the plotline concerning the mystery of Kathryn, until eventually the two plotlines intertwine (see *Film noir*, p. 191)

Pulp Fiction (USA 1994 *p.c* – Buena Vista/Miramax/A Band Apart/Jersey; *d* – Quentin Tarantino; sd col.)

Although initially Tarantino may have seemed to be the new David Lynch (see p. 310), delivering a cool, stylised *petit guignol* of slapstick and slaughter, his closest links are with the 'film-school-generation' and 'movie brats' of the 1970s with whom he shares a love of European cinema combined with mainstream American film.

Tarantino's name for his production company for *Pulp Fiction*, A Band Apart, is taken from the 1964 Godard film, *Band à part*. Apparently, Tarantino showed the dance sequence from this film to John Travolta and Uma Thurman as an example of how he wanted the 'twist' sequence to work in his movie. And the upbeat end of *Pulp Fiction*, in which a character killed earlier in the film jives out of a diner, shows that Tarantino has taken on board Godard's reply to George Franju's exasperated insistence that a film should have a beginning, a middle and an end: 'Yes, but not necessarily in that order.'

Much commentary on Tarantino regards the issue of screen violence. He cites approvingly Godard: 'there is no blood in *Pierrot le fou*, only the colour red.' Critical discussion of Tarantino's earlier film, *Reservoir Dogs* (1992), focused on violence partly because one of the characters bleeds on screen for almost the entire film, but more as a consequence of the scene in which one of the gangsters psycho-tortures a cop.

Tarantino's play with violence is in the cinematic 'blood tragedy/revenge' tradition of such films as Peckinpah's *Bring Me the Head of Alfredo Garcia* (1974), Coppola's *Godfather* trilogy and Tony Scott's *Revenge* (1989). His films mix 'realistic' violence with intertextual homage. He wants an audience to notice the way his films relate to a history of earlier film, fiction and television and thus he combines movie fictions with movie criticism by playfully referring to movie history and the mini-history contained in the presence of his stars. When Bruce Willis chooses an appropriate weapon to intervene in the anal rape sequence in *Pulp Fiction* (baseball bat, chainsaw, samurai sword), he's choosing – among movie-hero options – not *Walking Tall* (1973), not *Texas Chainsaw Massacre* (1974), but the samurai figure from Schrader's script for *The Yakuza* (1974).

Tarantino describes this process of playing with movie clichés (the boxer who throws the fight, the gangster employee who takes out the boss's girl but must not seduce her) as 'having these old chestnuts and going to the moon with them'. Because he believes audiences today are sophisticated to the point that they can predict which way a film is heading within the first five minutes, he uses this knowledge in order to take the movie and its viewer someplace else: 'I like to fuck up the breadcrumb trail.'

In the mid-1990s the Tarantino 'effect' was all-pervasive. The debate surrounding his cinematic practice replayed the critical description of the first two moments of New Hollywood. *Pulp Fiction* cost $6 million and made over $100 million in the US alone. Debate centred on whether Tarantino was the ultimate postmodern pastiche rip-off artist or something genuinely new. Whatever one's verdict, Tarantino has emerged as the latest in a long line of cinema guys and move brats.

sad stories of the deaths of studios) and/or trying to see the textual form of recent Hollywood as expressive of changed production circumstances that lead to a different kind of textual artefact.

THREE VERSIONS OF NEW HOLLYWOOD

For some critics 'New Hollywood' refers to a brief window of opportunity that existed from the late 1960s to the early 1970s, when an adventurous new cinema emerged, linking the traditions of classic Hollywood genre film-making with the stylistic innovations of European art cinema (Art cinema, p. 106). It was a period of productive uncertainty during which Hollywood became open to new blood and new ideas simply because no one knew for certain which direction to take. In 1970, so this story goes, sclerotic studios were on the brink of economic ruin after having made a string of costly flops (usually musicals attempting to cash in on the success of 1965's *The Sound of Music*) that showed how out of touch they were with a college-educated, ciné-literate, 'youth audience' who had been politicised by the era now immortalised/mythologised as 'the sixties'. This audience made hits of a cluster of so-called 'youth' or 'alternative' films of the late and early 1970s, all involving 'anti-heroes'. Films like *The Graduate* and *Bonnie and Clyde* (both 1967), and *Easy Rider*, *Butch Cassidy and the Sundance Kid*, *M*A*S*H* and *Midnight Cowboy* (all 1969) seemed to define a new period in American film-making. This moment of 'the new' is predicated on a new audience demographic making its aesthetic preferences felt by opting for a new kind of cinema, alliteratively described by Andrew Sarris as a cinema of 'alienation, anomie, anarchy and absurdism' (Sarris, 1978, p. 37). It was a period which saw Robert Altman, Mike Nichols and Arthur Penn gain directorial favour and Dustin Hoffman, Robert Redford and Jack Nicholson attain a stardom they still possess.

This account of 'the new' is followed quickly by the arrival of the 'movie brats', a film-school educated and/or film-critical generation who began making commercial American cinema with an *élan* that, for some, recalled the emergence of the 'French new wave' (see The French *nouvelle vague*, p. 80). The 1960s saw Martin Scorsese graduate from NYU film school (as Jim Jarmusch, Susan Seidelman and Spike Lee would later), Brian De Palma attend Columbia and Sarah Lawrence, while on the West coast Francis Coppola, John Milius, Paul Schrader and George Lucas graduated from UCLA and USC. They were all reading the 1960s American film criticism of Pauline Kael, Andrew Sarris and Manny Farber, absorbing the influence of *Cahiers du Cinéma*, and admiring the cinema of Fellini, Antonioni, Bergman, Bertolucci and Godard. Accordingly, some accounts (e.g. Bernardoni, 1991) see this moment as the explicit inscription within American film-making of the critical practice of *auteurism*, resulting in a self-consciously *auteurist* cinema.

Noel Carroll dubbed it a 'cinema of allusion', a cinema generated by references to other cinematic practices, most particularly, classic Hollywood cinema and European art cinema (Caroll, 1982). Carroll's view of New Hollywood's cinema of citation was anticipated to some extent by Stuart Byron's (1979) claim that John Ford's *The Searchers* (1956) was the ur-text of this New Hollywood, a cult movie with references to be found in Scorsese's *Taxi Driver* (1976), Lucas's *Star Wars* (1977), and Schrader's *Hardcore* (1978). Similarly, the three films that brought Peter Bogdanovich to prominence, *The Last Picture Show* (1971), *What's Up Doc?* (1972) and *Paper Moon* (1973) were loving tributes to the cinema of Howard

Hawks and John Ford (on whom he had made the AFI documentary, *Directed by John Ford*), and to lapsed classic Hollywood genres such as madcap/screwball comedy. Bogdanovich's attachment to the stylistic practices of classic Hollywood is evident from the way he would instruct his cinematographer by referring to the work of previous cinematographers ('I want you to James Wong Howe this shot'). This New Hollywood practice of cinematic citation continued into the 1980s with Schrader's 1982 remake of Tourneur's 1943 horror classic, *Cat People* and *American Gigolo*'s (1980) concluding homage to Bresson's *Pickpocket* (1959). Schrader cites Bertolucci's *Il Conformista* (1970) as 'a film I've stolen from repeatedly' and adds that the Nicolas Roeg/Douglas Cammell cult film *Performance* (1970) 'is a good one to check up on if you ever need something to steal' (Schrader in Jackson, 1990, pp. 210–11). Scorsese's *Raging Bull* (1980) alluded to Powell–Pressburger's *the Red Shoes* (1948) and Kazan's *On the Waterfront* (1954) and in 1992 Scorsese remade J. Lee Thompson's *Cape Fear* (1961).

Functioning alongside the movie brat film school and often overlapping with it was another film school. the Roger Corman exploitation world of AIP and New World Films. Corman's influence on the New Hollywood can scarcely be overestimated. From his time with AIP through to his establishing of New World Films, Corman provided opportunities for such directors as Scorsese, Coppola, Bogdanovich, Monte Hellman, James Cameron, John Sayles, Joe Dante, Jonathan Demme, Jonathan Kaplan, John Milius, Dennis Hopper, Ron Howard, Amy Jones and Stephanie Rothman; and for such actors as Nicholson, De Niro, Dern and Carradine. Carroll credits Corman with having established the 'two-tiered' film: 'Increasingly Corman's cinema came to be built with the notion of two audiences in mind – special grace notes for insiders, appoggiatura for the cognoscenti, and a soaring, action-charged melody for the rest' (Carroll, 1982, p. 74) and a link with the 'Old Hollywood' is apparent in the fact that both Carroll and Hillier note that Corman's workers likened themselves to the 'Hollywood professionals' of the studio era, specifically to Raoul Walsh (see Roger Corman, p. 258).

DISPUTING 'THE NEW'

When Bordwell and Staiger distance themselves from some of the critical enthusiasms attaching to descriptions of a New Hollywood, they do so by observing that the New Hollywood directors were neither more youthful nor more technologically competent than their classical predecessors (Bordwell and Staiger, 1985, pp. 372–3). Their account of the grafting of art cinema conventions onto classical traditions similarly underplays any tendency to proclaim a genuinely new aesthetic moment: 'In keeping with the definition of a non-Hollywood Hollywood, American films are imitating the look of European art films; Classical film style and codified genres swallow up art-film borrowings, taming the (already limited) disruptiveness of the art cinema' (Bordwell and Staiger, 1985, p. 375). They are also unpersuaded by the claims for a new narrative adventurousness, saying that 'most American commercial cinema has continued the classical tradition' and laconically observing that 'the New Hollywood can explore ambiguous narrational possibilities but those explorations remain within classical boundaries'(Bordwell and Staiger, 1985, p. 377).

This view can be set alongside Thomas Elsaesser's claim, made a decade earlier, that the emergence of a 'new liberal cinema' marked a shift away from the classic Hollywood fictional world in which the heroes were 'psychologically or morally motivated: they had a case to investigate, a name to clear, a woman (or man) to love, a goal to reach', towards cinematic fictions in which any notion of goal-orientation can only figure as nostalgic (Elsaesser, 1975, p. 14). According to Elsaesser, American cinema of the 1970s saw the model of the classic Hollywood film altered as an 'affirmative consequential model' was replaced by a more open-ended, looser-structured narrative (Elsaesser, 1975, p. 14). But Elsaesser was also careful to say that the New Hollywood cinema achieved its innovations by 'shifting and modifying traditional genres and themes, while never quite shedding their support' (Elsaesser, 1975, p. 18).

One of the films offered by Elsaesser (and by German director Wim Wenders) as evidence of a new kind of American cinema was Bob Rafelson's *Five Easy Pieces* (1970) (see p. 99), a product of the independent BBS production group, who had enjoyed great success the year before with Dennis Hopper's *Easy Rider*. David Thomson tells of the way BBS productions (Bert Schneider, Bob Rafelson, Steve Blauner) 'did a deal with Columbia for a series of low-budget features that would draw on new talent' (Thomson, 1993, p. 43). This resulted in *Five Easy Pieces, The Last Picture Show, Drive, He Said* (1970), *A Safe Place* (1971), and *The King of Marvin Gardens* (1972), the first two of which were hits.

Elsaesser's way of characterising this new, liberal cinema was to say that the shift from the goal-oriented protagonist of classic Hollywood to an unmotivated protagonist necessitated a departure from the classic narrative model. As a result, New Hollywood cinema displayed 'a kind of malaise already frequently alluded to in relation to the European cinema – the fading confidence in being able to tell a story' (Elsaesser, 1975, p. 13).

It might be more accurate to say that a film like *Five Easy Pieces*, Elsaesser's example, confidently enacts a 'fading confidence in being able to tell a story' since the story it tells invokes the enduring American myth of travelling on the open road, with the European art cinema aspect residing in the Nicholson character–function. This is the textual device which links the familiar Hollywood archetype of the hero/anti-hero as self-willed social outcast (from Huck Finn onwards) with elements of the existential protagonists of, say, an Antonioni film. Throughout *Five Easy Pieces*, Nicholson's character–function is able to cross two classes, two cultures: it functions as 'Bobby' in the world of trailers, oil rigs, bowling alleys, and as 'Robert' in the world of classical music and island homes in Puget Sound. The way Nicholson's character is presented throughout the film indicates the recruitment to traditional Hollywood film practices of a specific feature of art cinema: namely, the strategy of implying that a character will always retain an unknowable otherness, although this unknowable otherness will be the clear, unproblematic knowledge–effect of a viewer's familiarity with the conventions that organise art cinema texts. As one critic has said of Antonioni's films, they are baffling, but 'baffling in a highly intelligible way' (Lockhart, 1985, p. 77) or, as David Bordwell described a central reading protocol of art cinema, 'read for maximum ambiguity'.

For Noel Carroll, a shared practice of allusionistic interplay is a distinguishing feature of the work of New Hollywood filmmakers, as references to classic Hollywood films become 'a major expressive device ... to make comments on the fictional worlds of their films' (Carroll, 1982, p. 52). By 'allusion' Carroll means 'a mixed lot of practices including quotations, the memorialisation of past genres, homages, and the recreation of '"classic" scenes, shots, plot motifs, lines of dialogue, themes, gestures, and so forth from film history, especially as that history was crystallized and codifed in the sixties and early seventies' (Carroll, 1982, p. 52). Stephen Neale's description of *Raiders of the Lost Ark* (1981) as a film which 'uses an idea (the signs) of classic Hollywood in order to promote, integrate and display modern effects, techniques and production values' (Neale, 1982, p. 37) would support Carroll's view. (If we were to add television as another element in the intertextual–nostalgia–memorialisation process, Carroll's description would apply just as well to attempts in the 1990s to unify parent and child via a nostalgic cinematic recovery of television memory: witness such films as *The Fugitive, The Flintstones, The Addams Family, Addams Family Values, Maverick, The Brady Bunch, The Beverly Hillbillies, Mission Impossible, The Avengers* and *The Saint.* Whereas in the 1950s television programmes often came as spin-offs from theatrical films, in the 1980s and 1990s theatrical films plunder the television archives.)

Carroll also claims that this allusive cinematic compositional practice assumed a particular reading competence on the part of its ciné-literate audience: 'It is a rule of seventies film viewing ... that a similarity between a new film and an old film generally can count as a reference to the old film' (Carroll, 1982, p. 52). Consequently, there developed a two-tiered allusionistic genre film combining a strong generic, action, through-line deriving from classic Hollywood with some of the more recondite, abstract aspects of European art cinema: 'there was the genre film pure and simple, and there was also the art film in the genre film' (Carroll, 1982, p. 56). A similar perspective is apparent in Patricia Patterson and Manny Farber's review of *Taxi Driver* which saw the film as 'a tale of Two Cities: the old Hollywood and the new Paris of Bresson–Rivette–Godard' (Patterson and Farber, 1976, p. 30).

Roman Polanski's *Chinatown* (1974) is a film which has become one of the most famous and enduring instances of the New Hollywood cinema, melding the classic Hollywood genre film with the art film, chiefly by reworking some of the hard-boiled conventions of such classic Hollywood films as *The Maltese Falcon* (1941) and *The Big Sleep* (1946). Robert Towne's screenplay has been discussed in screenwriting manuals (Syd Field's *Screenplay*) and, together with *Shampoo* (1975) and *The Last Detail* (1973) (and his earlier script doctoring on *Bonnie and Clyde* and *The Godfather*), helped forge his reputation as the pre-eminent New Hollywood screenwriter (with William Goldman). The central convention that is challenged is the one which has the detective perform a narratorial retelling, rearrangement at the end of the film (e.g. Spade to Brigid at the end of *The Maltese Falcon*). This convention confirms the detective's role as the one who can see things as they really are, who can put together sight and sound, vision and aurality, through his investigative expertise. *Chinatown* plays with this trope when Gittes comes to visit Evelyn Mulwray's house for the first time. As he waits at the door, the soundtrack carries an enigmatic (because unsourced) squeaking sound. Gittes looks in the direction of the car parked in the driveway and soon a servant comes into view, shammying/cleaning the car. Sight and sound fall into place as we follow the look of Gittes. But as the film progresses the subversion of this convention becomes more apparent, through Gittes's inability to perform this traditional detective function. He consistently misperceives people and their relationships until eventually, in the infamous face-slapping scene, he is defeated by the fact of incest, as Evelyn tells him, 'She's my daughter and my sister! Understand? Or is it too tough for you?'

After the first two moments of the 'New Hollywood' (the brief period of studio uncertainty that allowed experimentation in the early 1970s – under the alibi of the pursuit of the youth audience – and the time of the 'movie brats') the next distinctive moment of 'New Hollywood' is one on which all critics agree: the period of Hollywood after 1975, after the release of Steven Spielberg's *Jaws*. As Thomas Schatz puts it: 'If any single film marked the arrival of the New Hollywood, it was *Jaws*, the Spielberg-directed thriller that recalibrated the profit potential of the Hollywood hit, and redefined its status as a marketable commodity and cultural phenomenon as well' (Schatz, 1993, p. 17).

Although this post-1975 period and its main financial successes are central to any notion of a 'New Hollywood' cinema, in some ways the period represents a relaunching of an early-to-mid-1950s Hollywood strategy that had stalled by 1970: namely, the production of a calculated blockbuster as a departure from classic Hollywood's reliance on routine A-class features to generate revenues. In an earlier book devoted to a study of the studio system, Schatz had remarked on an inglorious distinguishing feature of the New Hollywood: its concentration on the blockbuster. In the classic Hollywood studio system, 'ultimately both blockbuster and B movie were ancillary to first-run feature production, which had always been the studios' strong suit – and which the New Hollywood has proved utterly incapable of turning out with any quality or consistency' (Schatz, 1988, p. 492). The post-*Jaws* world, however, was one in which blockbuster films were conceived as 'multi-purpose entertainment machines that breed music videos and soundtrack albums, tv series and videocassettes, video games and theme park rides, novelizations and comic books' (Schatz, 1993, pp. 9–10).

The media hype surrounding the theatrical release of such a film (*Batman*, *Dick Tracy*, *Terminator 2*, *Hook*, *Who Framed Roger Rabbit?*, *Jurassic Park*), 'creates a cultural commodity that might be regenerated in any number of media forms' (Schatz, 1993, p. 29). Schatz completes his account of the New Hollywood by suggesting that it produces three different classes of movie – 'The calculated blockbuster designed with the multimedia marketplace and franchise status in mind, the mainstream A-class star vehicle with sleeper-hit potential, and the low-cost independent feature targeted for a specific market and with little chance of anything more than "cult film" status' (Schatz, 1993, p. 35) – but his account repeatedly emphasises the imposing commodity presence of the blockbuster.

Blockbuster merchandise for *Jaws*, a defining film of New Hollywood

'EVENT' CINEMA AND HIGH CONCEPT

The clarity of this third moment of change is conveyed by a brute commercial fact: the post-1975 blockbusters have proved the most profitable films of all time. 'Hollywood's ten top-grossing films have all been released since 1975. And even if one adjusts the figures to compensate for the dollar's reduced purchasing power – seven of the all-time blockbusters were still made between 1975 and 1985' (Hoberman, 1985, p. 58). In *A Cinema Without Walls*, Timothy Corrigan meditates on this changed situation by looking back on the conglomerate takeovers of the majors in the 1960s and 1970s, the later pressures from video and cable television and the way the status of the blockbuster has come to figure in the corporate thinking of New Hollywood:

> Far more than traditional epic successes or the occasional predecessor in film history, these contemporary blockbuster movies became the central imperative in an industry that sought the promise of massive profit from large financial investments; the acceptable return on these investments (anywhere from $20 million to $70 million) required, most significantly, that these films would attract not just a large market, but all the markets. (Corrigan, 1991, p. 12)

As has already been indicated, several critics felt this form of cinema was achieved at the expense of a more meditative, adult cinema that had been present in the first two moments of the New Hollywood. Pauline Kael felt that conglomerate control of the studios meant there was less chance for any unusual project to get financed, Andrew Sarris mused that 'the battle was lost when Hollywood realized in 1970 that there was still a huge middle-American audience for *Airport*' (Sarris, 1978, p. 37), and, in a much-quoted phrase, James Monaco said, 'Increasingly we are all going to see the same ten movies' (Monaco, 1979, p. 393). As David Denby bleakly put it: 'When the studios eliminate their down-side risk, most of the time they make the same dumb movie because they are eager to pull everyone in on opening day. They want the smash hit. They're not interested in modest profit' (Denby, 1986, p. 34). The phrase that came to characterise this emphasis in Hollywood's economic–aesthetic strategy was 'film event'. Hoberman explains, 'At the time of the release of *Earthquake*, Jennings Lang, its executive producer, wrote an article for *American Cinematographer* in which he proclaimed that a movie had to be an "event" in order to succeed in today's market' (Hoberman, 1985, p. 59).

Thomas Elsaesser termed classic Hollywood cinema a predominantly narrative and psychological cinema characterised by an inviolable transparency of storyline. It was a 'remarkably homogenous practice ... governed by a certain fundamental dramatic logic ... its prima facie concern is with telling a story, to analyse in fictional terms certain human situations and experiences. Its structural constraints are dramatic conflict and narrative progression' (Elsaesser, 1971, p. 6). To convey the aesthetic *realpolitik* that underlay such a form of cinema, Elsaesser relayed the anecdote of Louis B. Mayer, chief of MGM, saying that he judged a film by whether or not his bottom ached by the time the lights came up. Mayer 'thereby indicated that a good movie, one that he was putting his money on, should activate certain psychological processes – of identification, of emotive participation or imaginative projection' (Elsaesser, 1971, p. 6).

In more recent times a different litmus test of movie entertainment is to be found in the shift in bodily direction from Louis Mayer's (or Harry Cohn's) bottom to Steven Spielberg's hand. In a much quoted remark, Spielberg characterised a good film idea thus: 'If a person can tell me the idea in 25 words or less it's going to make a pretty good movie. I like ideas, especially movie ideas, that you can hold in your hand' (quoted in Hoberman, 1985, p. 36). Spielberg's remark has been cited as evidence of the impact of the notion of 'high concept' on contemporary American film-making. This is not surprising given that *Jaws*'s 'presold property and media-blitz saturation release pattern heralded the rise of marketing men and "high concept"' (Hoberman, 1985, p. 36). So Justin Wyatt would seem justified in claiming 'high concept' as 'one central development – and perhaps the central development within post-classical cinema, a style of film-making modeled by economic and institutional forces' (Wyatt, 1994, p. 8).

'High concept' refers to a mode of film-making predicated on two things: the successful pitching of a film at the pre-production stage and the successful saturation television advertising of it after it has been made. Economics and aesthetics are linked via a notion of 'front-loading' an audience by way of pre-sold marketability ('the look, the hook and the book' as Wyatt puts it) that is deemed attractive both to television and cinema advertising. Hence the regularity with which 'high concept' projects involve a hyped bestselling novel (a John Grisham thriller for example), a star and a star director, and a genre strongly identified with either or both. Wyatt's example of one of the earliest 'high concept' films is *Saturday Night Fever* (1977) with John Travolta, a project that linked television and cinema (via Travolta's television stardom), the music industry and popular cultural dance (via the Bee Gees soundtrack and nightclub disco). In contrast to this film, Bob Fosse's musical, *All that Jazz* (1979) did not march to the high concept tune, seeming to belong more to an earlier period when the art film snuggled inside the classic genre film.

It now seems clear that when *Jaws* opened at 464 cinemas and went on to become the biggest grossing film of all time (well, for two years, until George Lucas's *Star Wars* came along and topped it) we entered the era of high concept and summer hits. J. Hoberman described *Star Wars* as

> not just the highest-grossing film before *E.T.*, but arguably the quintessential Hollywood product. Drawing on the western and the war film, borrowing motifs from fantasies as varied as *The Wizard of Oz* and *Triumph of the Will*, George Lucas pioneered the genre pastiche ... *Star Wars* was the first and greatest cult blockbuster. (Hoberman, 1985, pp. 41–2)

He could have added that *Star Wars* and *Close Encounters of the Third Kind* (1977) also drew on the stylistic tradition contained in Sergio Leone's mid-1960s *Dollars* trilogy that brought Clint Eastwood to stardom. Textual pillaging aside, *Star Wars* cost $11 million and within three years had grossed over $500 million. Lucas has said that he felt the strongest analogy was with Disney films and no Disney film had grossed as much as his film needed to in order to see profit. However, Lucas felt that the sales of products associated with his film could see the generation of sufficient profit. From *Star Wars* on we encounter the process of merchandising the contemporary Hollywood blockbuster into so many franchisable 'pieces'.

But there are other ways in which the exceptional commercial success of *Star Wars*, *E.T.* (1982) and *Raiders of the Lost Ark* (1981), indicates a change from the first two moments of New Hollywood. If we set aside questions concerning saturation release and merchandising opportunities, the first two moments saw an *auteurist* cinema explore and stretch genres such as the western (*The Wild Bunch*), the gangster film (*The Godfather* and *The Godfather Part 2*) and the detective–*noir* film (*Chinatown*, *Night Moves*, *The Long Goodbye*). For some critics, this laudable moment of thoughtful metafilmic exploration was cast aside by the ascendancy of the late 1970s and 1980s films of Lucas and Spielberg, which marked a less philosophical, a more calculatedly naïve,

Retro-nostalgia and middle-class populism? *American Graffiti* – foreshadowing many blockbusters of the late 70s and 80s

relation to classical genres. In this lapsarian narrative, Lucas's *American Graffiti* (1973) would seem a transitional text. It was adventurous in so far as it took the then-unusual narrative step of basing its forty-five or so scenes around as many pop songs, achieving, through the labours of Walter Murch, an innovative sonic depth of field. But the film's great commercial success (made for less than $1 million and recouping $55 million) foreshadowed the mix of retro-nostalgia and middle-American populism that would be found in most of Lucas's and Spielberg's blockbuster films of the late 1970s and the 1980s. For Hoberman, the success of these films meant that, 'as the seventies wore on, it became apparent that the overarching impulse was less an attempt to revise genres than to revive them' (Hoberman, 1985, p. 38). Or, as Carroll said, 'After the experimentation of the early seventies, genres have once again become Hollywood's bread and butter' (Carroll, 1982, p. 56).

INTO THE NINETIES

In trying to determine what is at stake in the concept of the 'new' in post-1960s American cinema, in pondering how much the Hollywood cinematic institution set in place during the studio years has been transformed and to what extent the forms of classic Hollywood cinema have been modified or superseded, we now need to set those views which say, 'the more things change, the more they remain the same/meet the new boss, same as the old boss', alongside some clear evidence of change. Even if we accept that the textual cinematic form of the films we currently watch has strong similarities with the textual form of classic Hollywood cinema, it is also clear that our current modes of consuming these films, being in the world with them, are quite different from the situation that obtained into the 1960s. An earlier experience of film-going, one which was likely to involve a double bill at a neighbourhood cinema and/or a visit to a lavish, art-deco 'cinema palace', has been replaced by a newer world of malls and multiplexes (see Rosenbaum, 1980 and Paul, 1994). In the 1990s one is used to speaking of 'screens' rather than cinemas and if it used to be the case that 'the show started on the sidewalk', the show now starts with a barrage of television advertisements preparing cinema viewers for a multi-screen release of a 'blockbuster.' So *The Lion King* opened onto 2,552 screens. Which is simply to say that we live in a film-viewing world transformed by the delivery and reception of films like *Jaws* and *Star Wars*. No doubt there is a nice irony surrounding the fact that such grand social spaces as the 'picture palaces' were part of a cinematic institution less interested in gigantic hits than in a series of modestly profitable A-films, 'nice little earners', whereas by the 1990s we are likely to enter a diminished social space (cinemas, as exhibition locales, have became smaller) in order to watch a film that is aspiring to be a smash hit. For decades now more Americans have lived in the suburbs than in the city or the country and the shopping mall, brilliantly written about by Don DeLillo in his novel *White Noise* (1984), inevitably has become the diegetic site for Hollywood fictions as well as the social site of their consumption: witness *Bill and Ted's Excellent Adventure* (1989) and *Scenes from a Mall* (1991). Another instance of change can be seen in the extent to which films like *Jurassic Park* (1993) offer themselves as immersive kinaesthetic spectacles, linking three-act classic Hollywood screenplay structure to the sensations of a theme park ride. From this perspective the classic Hollywood tradition is relaunched in a changed media environment with the audience now conceived as a mall shopper, a freeway driver, or videogame player, placed at the centre of a mobile, kinetic word (see Technology, p. 44). And although contemporary critics are quick to insist that movies must now be understood as 'always and simultaneously text and commodity, intertext and product line' (Meehan, 1991, p. 62) debate centres on whether this constitutes a difference of kind or of degree from earlier film-making arrangements.

Reference can be made here to the economic story underlying contemporary industrial film-making: John Belton (1994) points out that a process begun in the mid-1970s with the arrival of the VCR and the proliferation of cable television had a major effect on the cinema of the 1980s and 1990s. The home video rental market which expanded so quickly in the mid-1980s had by 1992 reached a point where $11 billion dollars was generated from this area as opposed to $5 billion from theatrical release. Belton also claims that the viewing habits of television watching in the home (talking back to the screen, having conversations with fellow viewers) have come to infiltrate public film viewing with a 'back to the future' effect of making 1990s film viewers resemble the earliest film viewers, when a film screening was part of a mixed vaudeville entertainment programme (see Early cinema, p. 93).

If contemporary film viewing is being taken to resemble the film-viewing practices attached to the time of early cinema then perhaps we should not be surprised that so much debate concerns just how decisive a change is to be found in post-1960s Hollywood cinema. In 'The Cinema of Attractions' (1986), Tom Gunning says that 'recent spectacle cinema has re-affirmed its roots in stimulus and carnival rides, in what might be called the Spielberg–Lucas–Coppola cinema of effects'.

Hollywood cinema has always been a repetition machine, repeating, remaking and recycling earlier textual forms either from 'within' its own history or from European cinema. Some instances of Hollywood remaking European films include *Down and Out in Beverley Hills* remaking *Boudu Saved from Drowning*, *Sommersby* as a version of *The Return of Martin Guerre*, *The Vanishing* remaking *The Vanishing* and *Assassin* remaking *Nikita*. Remake/repetition from within the classic Hollywood system include *Speed*'s relation to *The Taking of Pelham 123* and Joel Schumaker's *Falling Down* as an off-centre remake of Frank Perry's late 1960s film, *The Swimmer*. The notion of repetition has always included the phenomenon of the sequel and within that gambit one now encounters the instance of the sequel within the remake (*Father of the Bride Part 2*, *Addams Family Values*).

By the 1990s the notion of remake or repetition included the 'director's cut' (the re-release of Ridley Scott's cut of *Blade Runner*) and even, in some cases (Sam Peckinpah's *Pat Garrett & Billy the Kid* and *The Wild Bunch*) the 'dead director's cut'. Hollywood also now plays a kind of cinematheque memorialising function when it re-releases films on their twentieth or twenty-fifth anniversary. Thus *Midnight Cowboy* and *Easy Rider* were delivered to a new audience as Hollywood generates a public memory of cinema history. The various releases of films on laser disc with trailers and production information also show the overlap between a cinephilic archivalising role and the pursuit and feeding of new markets.

The difficulty in deciding how much of an economic and aesthetic rupture is contained in the post-1960s period is conveyed by the fact that David Thomson can remember 1970s American cinema as 'the decade when movies mattered' (Thomson, 1993, pp. 43–7) while also seeing that decade of film production as one which ushered in 'a terrifying spiral . . . whereby fewer films were made, more of them cost more, and a fraction were profitable' (Thomson, 1981, p. 27).

For Thomson, Rafelson's *Five Easy Pieces* and *The King Of Marvin Gardens* (1972), Ashby's *The Last Detail* and Polanski's *Chinatown* (all with Nicholson) come to constitute a nostalgic moment in the history of post-1960s Hollywood cinema, representing a time when 'the movies mattered', in a way they have not since. The attitude that views this early 1970s moment as the aesthetic 'path not taken' shows how closely the three different moments of New Hollywood impinge on one another. Thomson laments the passing of that brief half-decade period of productive, innovative, uncertainty as the youth brigade took control and a countercultural cinema flourished. This paradisal, transformative, cultural moment is lost as mainstream genre film-making is re-established by the very young turks who supposedly were moving away from traditional forms of cinema towards more 'personal' films. In one of the paradoxes of the decade, the already existing practice of 'blockbuster cinema' is taken by the movie brats to new levels of profitability.

It is such a context that prompted David Denby, in 1986, to ask, 'Can the Movies be Saved?' At the centre of his account of American film-making is the familiar attack on conglomerate control: 'The movie business, perhaps American culture, has never recovered from that electric media weekend in June 1975 when *Jaws* opened all over the country and Hollywood realized a movie could gross nearly 48 million dollars in three days. Ever since, the only real prestige has come from having a runaway hit' (Denby, 1986, p. 30). For Denby, as for Kael (and, in many ways, Hoberman and Schatz), this moment marks a fall from the great virtue of the classical system, the fact that Hollywood then produced around 450 films a year, most of them modestly budgeted and safely profitable whereas by the 1990s around 200 films a year are released with 'a daunting increase in budgets . . . and [a] greater dependence for fiscal visibility on a very few pictures, helplessly expensive and necessarily generalised in their subjects and their demands on the public'.

> The economic disaster of 1970 produced a lot of official proclamations of change, but in the final analysis things didn't change very much . . . For all the successes of a few small films, it was finally the more predictable successes of big films and big stars that carried Hollywood bookkeeping back into the black . . . Now more than ever before, Hollywood is on the lookout for the 'pre-sold' project, the films that come with a formula for guaranteed success – films based on runaway best-sellers and hit plays, or films with stars who in themselves are so big that they generate their own publicity. (Paul, 1977, p. 62)

The gloom evinced here by Denby and Paul could only have increased as we move through the nineties. For a film to 'open' now (i.e. have the enormously profitable first three days) all the same urgencies, paranoias and uncertainties that supposedly destabilise film production continue in a context which has seen the cost of making and releasing the average Hollywood film move towards $50 million, with stars (Cruise, Gibson, Stallone, Schwarzenegger) paid $20 million for a single film and 'star' directors paid $10 million. Once again we hear of a 'crazy' escalation of production costs (Shapiro and King, 1996), one consequence of which presumably is that it becomes even more essential to have the 'high concept', the 'elements', in place to ensure that a film will 'open'.

In the late 1990s, however, some commentators saw the commercial success of low-budget, independent films like *Pulp Fiction* (1995) and *Four Weddings and a Funeral* (1995) as suggesting the possibility of a new era of the independent–major (Thompson, 1995). What does seem clear is that independence increasingly functions as a niche-marketing aspect of the production–distribution policies of the majors rather than being a pure artistic place, set apart from the majors. The fortunes of black film-making through the 1980s and 1990s seem appropriate to discuss in this context. Although a black film-making presence had existed since *The Birth of a Race* (1918), Emmett J. Scott's explicit critique–reply to Griffith's *The Birth of a Nation* controversy had always surrounded the extent of African-American involvement in actual film-making and the kinds of representations of black Americans that were to be found in Hollywood films. Just before the 1996 Academy Awards, Reverend Jesse Jackson protested against the paucity of black nominees and accused Hollywood of 'cultural distortion.' One of the major black stars of the 1990s, Denzell Washington, has said that he had no one of colour to look at as he was learning his craft because no black dramatic actors were stars. A strong comedic presence flowed from Richard Pryor in the 1970s and Eddie Murphy in the 1980s but only James Earl Jones, and then mainly as a stage actor, provided Washington with a role model. This situation is now partly redressed by virtue of such actors as Washington himself, Morgan Freeman, Lou Gossett jun., Laurence Fishburne and Samuel L. Jackson.

Spike Lee is probably the best known of the group of black directors who have come to prominence through the 1980s and into the 1990s. His *She's Gotta Have It* (1986) cost

Independence and niche marketing – Spike Lee's *Do the Right Thing*

Daughters of the Dust – a hard-won success

$175,000 and made $8 million while his later *Do the Right Thing* cost $6. 5 million and made $28 million. Following this, commercial success was had by Reginald and Warrington Hudlin with their 1989 hip-hop movie, *House Party* and Marvin Peebles's *New Jack City*; both films grossed more than $50 million.

Many of these film-makers pay homage to the work of black film-makers in the 1960s and 1970s as making possible their achievements. Spike Lee acknowledges the influence of Sidney Poitier, the pre-eminent black dramatic actor of the 1960s. Lee also cast Ossie Davis, director of *Cotton Comes to Harlem* (1970) in *Do the Right Thing* and *Jungle Fever* while Melvin Van Peebles, director of *Sweet Sweetback's Baaadassss Song* (1971) has a cameo in his son's *New Jack City* (1991). And in 1988 Keenan Wayan's *I'm Gonna Git You Sucka* pastiched the early 1970s cycle of blaxploitation films (*Shaft*, *Shaft's Big Score*, *Slaughter*, *Superfly*) allowing some of the original actors (Jim Brown, Isaac Hayes) to pastiche their earlier perfromances.

Hollywood's interest in black film-making seems another version of niche marketing: they remain interested so long as the films provide the successful economic returns that a number of them have achieved. It is salutary to remember that Warner refused to give Spike Lee a further $5 million he needed to complete *Malcolm X* (1992) and he eventually got the money from fellow black celebrities, Bill Cosby and Oprah Winfrey. And if the situation of black male film-makers is tenuous the position of black women film-makers is even more so. Julie Dash's *Daughters of the Dust* (1991) found an audience and made money but only did so by way of a dedicated group of people who contacted black churches, social organisations, television and radio stations and newspapers (Belton, 1994, p. 340).

The increasing critical and consumer attention paid in the 1990s to independent cinema confirms a certain ineffability in film-going. As Schatz said of *Jaws*, 'hype and promotion aside, *Jaws*' success ultimately centred on the appeal of the film itself: one enduring verity in the movie business is that, whatever the marketing efforts, only positive audience response and favorable word-of-mouth can propel a film to genuine hit status' (Schatz, 1983, p. 18). Although it is the unpredictable nature of viewers' cinematic uptakes that has seen 'independent cinema' take on its current importance there are, as ever, solid institutional supports working in tandem with the vagaries of the punters' tastes. Soderbergh's *sex, lies and videotape* (1990) won at Cannes in 1989 as did Tarantino's *Pulp Fiction* and Lucy Kaylin sees the following significance in this: 'what *Sex, Lies* had hinted at, *Pulp Fiction* confirmed – that small budget, *auteurish* films directed and produced without big-studio interference have the potential to be not only good business, but publicity-generating, star making, motion-picture events' (Kaylin, 1995). The coming to prominence across the 1980s and 1990s of film-makers such as Wayne Wang (*Chan is Missing*, *Dim Sum*, *Smoke*), Jim Jarmusch (*Stranger than Paradise*, *A Night on Earth*, *Dead Man*), Allison Anders (*Gas Food Lodging*), Carl Franklin (*One False Move*, *Devil in a Blue Dress*), the Coen brothers (*Blood Simple*, *Fargo*), Hal Hartley (*Trust*, *Simple Men*) and Greg Araki (*The Living End*) shows the economic–aesthetic strength of this sector. The great critical and popular attention attaching to the independent cinema of Quentin Tarantino in the 1990s shows how the practices described in the various discourses on New Hollywood persist in this newly fashionable independent sector. Tarantino himself links the two periods when he says, 'I think right now is the most exciting time in Hollywood since 1971. Because Hollywood is never more exciting than when you don't know' (quoted in Udovich, 'Tarantino and Juliette', 1996, p. 114).

Selected Reading

David Bordwell and Janet Staiger, 'Since 1960: the persistence of a mode of film practice', in Bordwell, K. Thompson and Staiger, *Classical Hollywood Cinema: Film Style and Mode of Production*, London, RKP, 1985, pp. 367–77.

John Belton, *American Cinema/American Culture*, New York, McGraw-Hill, 1994.

Noel Carroll, 'The future of allusion: Hollywood in the seventies (and beyond)', *October* 20, 1982, pp. 51–78.

Thomas Elsaesser, 'The pathos of failure: notes on the unmotivated hero', *Monogram* 6, 1975, pp. 13–19.

Jim Hillier, *The New Hollywood*, London, Studio Vista, 1992.

Jon Lewis, *Whom God Wishes to Destroy: Francis Coppola and the New Hollywood*, Durham and London, Duke University Press, 1995.

Realistic violence and intertextual homage – Quentin Tarantino's *Pulp Fiction*

Robert B. Ray, *A Certain Tendency of the Hollywood Cinema 1930–1980*, Princeton, NJ, Princeton University Press, 1985.

Thomas Schatz, 'The New Hollywood', in Jim Collins, Hilary Radner and Ava Preacher Collines (eds), *Film Theory Goes to the Movies*, New York, Routledge, 1993, pp. 8–36.

Justin Wyatt, *High Concept: Movies and Marketing in Hollywood*, Austin, University of Texas Press, 1994.

ART CINEMA

Serious anglophone discussion of art cinema, as such, dates back to the late 1970s, with the publication of David Bordwell's article 'The Art Cinema as a Mode of Film Practice' (1979), later substantially expanded into a chapter in his 1985 book *Narration in the Fiction Film* and Steve Neale's 'Art Cinema as Institution' (1981) in *Screen*. Typically, the term referred to films such as those of the French new wave, the New German Cinema, Bergman, Antonioni, Fellini, Kurosawa, Ray (Satyajit not Nicholas) and the like, but it was also employed retrospectively to denote such disparate cinematic phenomena as Italian neo-realism, German silent cinema, the Soviet classics, and the pre-war French cinema, from *films d'art* through surrealist works such as Germaine Dulac's *La Coquille et le clergyman* (1928), Buñuel's *Un Chien andalou* (1928) and *L'Âge d'or* (1930) to the *œuvres* of Cocteau, Renoir, Carné, Prévert and others (see Avant-garde and counter-cinema, p. 113).

Of course, debates about art cinema long pre-date the invention and widespread use of the term since the late 1970s. For example, no discussion of art cinema would be complete without mention of Alexandre Astruc's 1948 article 'The Birth of a New Avant-garde: La Caméra-stylo' or André Bazin's work on neo-realism, and on Rossellini in particular. Nor should it be forgotten that in the 1950s and 1960s *Cahiers du Cinéma* ranked Ozu, Mizoguchi, Bresson and Dreyer among its directorial pantheon. By the early sixties, however, there was a definite sense that a new kind of cinema was developing, though there was little agreement on what its characteristics actually were. Typical of the kind of discussions going on at the time was the critical forum 'Qu'est-ce que le cinéma moderne?' in *Cinéma 62*, January 1962. For example, René Gilson noted a 'de-dramatisation' which he associated with Antonioni, and Marcel Martin with Mizoguchi; Pierre Billard spoke of a cinema which took a more direct approach to reality, a fundamental realism which would displace conventional narrative habits; Michel Mardore perceived the development of a cinema of the shot as opposed to the narrative sequence of interlinked shots; and Martin saw a 'script-writer's cinema' being replaced by a 'film-maker's cinema'. There are distinct echoes here of *Cahiers*' rejection of the 'cinéma de qualité' in favour of a 'cinéma d'écriture', in which both film-makers and audiences would enjoy a degree of freedom not to be found in the classic Hollywood film. In other words, we were witnessing the development of 'pure cinema' or 'cinema cinema', or the 'cinema of poetry' which Pasolini would talk about in 1965. Another key text, in this respect, was Christian Metz's 1966 essay 'The Modern Cinema and Narrativity' (reprinted in Metz, 1974) which attempted to define the specificity of what at that time was being described as 'new cinema' or 'young cinema'. As Metz himself put it:

> everyone agrees in recognising the new cinema as defined by the fact that it has 'gone beyond' or 'rejected' or 'broken down' something; but the identity of that something – whether spectacle, narrative, theatre, 'syntax', inflexible signification, 'devices' of the script writer etc. – varies considerably from critic to critic. (Metz, 1974)

Nor was such discussion confined to France, although unsurprisingly it found its most elaborate and sophisticated expression there. In 1962 Parker Tyler's *Classics of the Foreign Film* appeared, followed by Penelope Houston's *The Contemporary Cinema* in 1963 and John Russell Taylor's *Cinema Eye, Cinema Ear* in 1964. By the mid-1960s the idea that the European film might legitimately be regarded as 'art' had become quite commonplace, witness the following quotation from the by-no-means-highbrow American critic Arthur Knights:

> Art is not manufactured by committees. Art comes from an individual who has something that he must express, and who works out what for him is the most forceful or affecting manner of expressing it. And this, specifically, is the quality that people respond to in European pictures – the reason why we hear so often that foreign films are 'more artistic' than our own. There is in them the urgency of individual expression, an independence of vision, the coherence of a single-minded statement. (Knights, quoted in Bordwell, 1985, p. 231)

ART CINEMA IN BRITAIN

In Britain, seeds of the art cinema idea can be perceived in the debate about the 'quality film' which took place between 1942 and 1948, and which has been brilliantly analysed by John Ellis in 'Art, Culture and Quality: Terms for a Cinema in the Forties and Seventies' (1978). This was a critical project designed to encourage the production and consumption of 'quality' films such as *Brief Encounter* (Lean, 1945), *Henry V* (Olivier, 1944), *Millions Like Us* (Launder and Gilliat, 1943), *Odd Man Out* (Reed, 1947), *Great Expectations* (Lean, 1946) and the like. It does need to be firmly stressed, however, that what was being proposed here, at first at least, was not 'art' (always a suspect notion in the only European country in which 'intellectual' is a dirty word) but, rather, what were seen as traditional British values of humanism, restraint, unobtrusive technique, documentary verisimilitude, organic unity and so on. The voices of the philistine, the xenophobe, the populist and the paternalist are never particularly hard to spot in this particular project, and here they are all at once in a passage from *Sight and Sound*, summer 1947:

> The arty boys have so far confined their activities to the productions of the French and Russian cinemas, with a faint bleat about cashing in on Shakespeare. The cinema may think itself fortunate that its name is not bandied back and forth with those of Sartre, Connolly, Lady Gregory and Dylan Thomas. But it may think itself unfortunate that no one, with the exception of Roger Manvell, has seen fit to publish a book about it for the mass of the public whose opinion, totalled, should be the criterion for good taste. (quoted in Ellis, 1978, pp. 19–20)

Sneering remarks about 'arty boys' nicely demonstrate just how alien was the notion of the 'quality film' to what would later be called art cinema. However, as the 'quality film' project foundered as a strategy for British production so the 'quality film' came to be increasingly redefined as the imported, predominantly European, product, and the concern with production became a concern with exhibition, namely the desire to promote specialist cinemas along the lines of the film society movement. As an article in the *Penguin Film Review* put it:

> The peculiar strategic importance of the specialised cinema resides in the fact that it is not simply a place where good films in foreign languages are

> shown, but that it is the ONLY channel through which creative and experimental work in the field of international film art is brought before the general public. It thereby performs a possibly slow, but certainly constant and cumulative work of improving public taste with regard to ALL films which come before it, and thus enables the commercial film producer to take for granted a rising level of public taste. (quoted in Ellis, 1978, p. 45)

By the early 1960s this kind of assessment had become deeply ingrained in British film culture; for the critics of the 'quality' press and those associated with *Sight and Sound* and the *Monthly Film Bulletin* it was virtually axiomatic that the highest form of cinematic artistry was to be found outside Hollywood (and Britain, of course) and usually, though not exclusively, in mainland Europe. This was one of the main reasons why part of the assault on the critical establishment by *Screen*, *Movie*, *Monogram*, *Framework* and other 'dissidents' in the early 1970s took the form of a polemic on behalf of popular Hollywood cinema. European cinema was by no means ignored entirely, although there certainly were those who regarded it as a bastion of 'high art' ideologies and therefore the 'enemy' to be fought; rather, it received more rigorous and theoretically informed treatment than it would have done in the pages of *Sight and Sound* and the 'serious' papers – take, for example, the ways in which *Screen* championed Ozu, Rossellini, Dreyer and Straub-Huillet among others.

It was not until the late 1970s, when the then Labour government in Britain began to take an unusual interest in both film and television production, that issues to do with art cinema began to seep into discussions about what a revitalised British film industry might look like. What needs to be made clear, however, is that nobody ever openly canvassed the creation of a specifically British 'art cinema'; put at its simplest, there was, on the one hand, the Association of Independent Producers (AIP) arguing for the state underwriting of what they called 'indigenous British films' and, on the other, the Independent Film-makers' Association (IFA) which wanted something far more radical: an 'alternative' British film industry organised around regional workshops producing work that was truly 'independent' in every sense of the word. That this conception was actively hostile to the notion of art cinema can be seen in the remark by Alan Fountain, then commissioning editor for Independent Film and Video at Channel 4, and a former leading light of the IFA, that:

> we suspect that the fantasy of the [BFI] Production Board is to create a cinema in Britain of a Fassbinder, Bertolucci or Truffaut. We never had such a cinema in Britain and *we* don't want such a cinema, we don't want this tacky glamour of the metropolitan EC bourgeoisie. We have a completely different cultural conception. (IFVA, 1984, p. 25)

As was said before and as is also cogently explained by John Ellis, the discourse of art cinema was brought into play in Britain in the late 1970s simply as an act of political calculation, as a means of trying to further the creation of an independent cinema: 'state finance "knows" the discourses of art cinema, recognises it as an object, so independent cinema has to exploit this space in order to produce itself as a recognisable practice for state funding' (Ellis, 1978, p. 16). The absence of what one might call a space of indigenous British art cinema is graphically described by Geoffrey Nowell-Smith in his discussion of Chris Petit's Wenders-like *Radio On* at the time of its release in 1979:

> Put quite simply, *Radio On* is a film without a cinema. It is a British film (co-production elements notwithstanding) inserted into the context of a non-existent British cinema. Its context could be something else – world cinema, independent cinema, road movies international – but in so far as a national context is concerned the vacuum is total. On an economic level there is no given market or circuit of distribution into which a feature of this kind can comfortably slot. On a cultural level, there is no set of co-ordinates laying out a profile of what 'British cinema' could actually mean in a period when very few identifiably British films are being produced – except, marginally, in the independent sector. And on the level of address, there is, consequently, no place to or from which a film can confidently speak, identifying its discourse in relation to either audience or content. (Nowell-Smith, 1979/80, p. 30)

ART CINEMA AS AN INSTITUTION

As the above discussion makes clear, debates about art cinema are almost always intimately bound up with debates about how to create indigenous cinemas and, therefore, with arguments against American cinematic imperialism and for state and/or private funding for home-grown production. As Steve Neale has put it: 'art is thus the space in which an indigenous cinema can develop and make its critical and economic mark' (Neale, 1981, p. 14). However difficult it may be to define art cinema in positive terms, that is, to say what it actually is, it is relatively easy to define it negatively as simply being 'not Hollywood' or even 'anti-Hollywood'. As Neale notes:

> Art films tend to be marked by a stress on visual style (an engagement of the look in terms of a marked individual point of view rather than in terms of institutionalised spectacle), by a suppression of action in the Hollywood sense, by a consequent stress on character rather than plot and by an interiorisation of dramatic conflict. A different textual weight is accorded the proairetic code, whose units are inscribed and articulated in a manner that tends to be distinct from that marking Hollywood films. A different hierarchy is established between action and actant. Different orders of motivation sustain the relations between the two . . . Art films are marked at a textual level by the inscription of features that function as marks of enunciation – and, hence, as signifiers of an authorial voice (and look). The precise nature of these features has varied historically and geographically, as it were, since it derives in part from another, simultaneous function that these features perform: that of differentiating the text or texts in question from the texts produced by Hollywood. Hence they change in accordance with which features of Hollywood films are perceived or conceived as dominant or as basically characteristic at any one point in time. (Neale, 1981, pp. 13–14)

In other words, the presence of art is defined at least partly as the absence of Hollywood.

It is also extremely important to note, however, that formal differences from Hollywood are complemented by all sorts of other kinds of difference. Art films may well be shown in different cinemas, distributed by different distributors, and written about in different spaces and by different writers, from Hollywood films. Nor should art cinema be described, as it still sometimes is, as being 'non-commercial'. Indeed, as the above reference to cinemas, distributors and critics suggests, it needs to be conceptualised as a particular and specific space within the commercial institution of cinema as a whole. With the growth in the 1960s and 1970s, in both Europe and the United States, of an informed audience of cinephiles eager for something more than Hollywood was then offering – something closer to literary and artistic modernism – there was a distinct market for art cinema for which it was, economically, worth catering. These were spectators who consciously sought out foreign films precisely because they were different from Hollywood films. Indeed, their foreign-ness was a quintessential part of that difference – people went to see French films at least partly for their 'French-ness', Swedish films for their 'Swedish-ness', and so on. Art films were (and are) quite consciously pro-

Subjective cinema – Bergman's *Wild Strawberries*

Unresolved narrative – *L'Avventura*

duced for international distribution and exhibition (including the all-important film festival circuit) as well as for home consumption. As Bordwell observes:

> formal process and economic demands merge: the tendency to play a cognitive game with the spectator, to modify and foreground the text's operations, matches the institution's need for the saleable differentiated product. The fullest flower of the art-cinema paradigm occurred at the moment that the combination of novelty and nationalism became the marketing device it has been ever since: the French New Wave, New Polish Cinema, New Hungarian Cinema, New German Cinema, New Australian Cinema . . . (Bordwell, 1979, 1985, p. 231)

It may be, then, that art cinema is best conceptualised not as a certain historical period of mainly European output, which reached its apogee in the 1960s, nor as a directional canon, nor as a set of distinctive subjects and styles, but, as Tom Ryall has suggested, as an institution in which certain films are 'assigned a position within the general film culture and are defined in terms of a particular mode of consumption'. As mentioned above, key components of this institution are film festivals, critical discourses and specialist distributors and exhibitors. As Ryall puts it:

> This institutional context is critical to the stabilisation of the genre and the films' separate status as cultural objects for a literate, self-conscious minority. It may be the case, in fact, that the fundamental unifying feature of the 'art' film genre is this special circulatory network that serves to confirm the distinction between its minority audience and the mass audience of the commercial mainstream cinema. (Ryall, 1981)

Art cinema as author's cinema – Fellini's *8½*

ART CINEMA'S FORMAL CHARACTERISTICS

The question of whether it is still possible to describe art cinema in formal terms does still need to be addressed, however, since it is important to understand what formal properties are being referred to when the term 'art cinema' is used in critical discourse. Bordwell's chapter on the subject in *Narration in the Fiction Film* (1985) remains the most extended attempt to analyse the formal nature of art cinema, so it is worth summarising in some detail.

Bordwell begins by distinguishing between classical and art cinema in terms of their different attitudes to, and ways of representing, reality:

> For the classical cinema, rooted in the popular novel, short-story and well-made drama of the late nineteenth century, 'reality' is assumed to be a tacit coherence among events, a consistency and clarity of individual identity. Realistic motivation corroborates the compositional motivation achieved through cause and effect. But art-cinema narration, taking its cue from literary modernism, questions such a definition of the real: the world's laws may not be knowable, personal psychology may be indeterminate. Here new aesthetic conventions claim to seize other 'realities': the aleatoric world of 'objective' reality and the fleeting states that characterize 'subjective' reality. (Bordwell, 1985, p. 206)

Lest the slightly awkward distinction between 'subjective' and 'objective' realities be thought to imply an essentialist epistemology, Bordwell hastily adds that: 'of course, the realism of the art cinema is no more "real" than that of the classical film; it is simply a different canon of realistic motivation, a new *vraisemblance*, justifying particular compositional options and effects' (Bordwell, 1985, p. 206).

For Bordwell, the 'objective realism' of the art cinema expresses itself in a number of ways. (In what follows, the filmic examples are not necessarily Bordwell's own.) In terms of subject matter, for example, the art film tends to deal with real contemporary problems such as 'alienation' or 'lack of communication' (Antonioni exemplifies *par excellence* this tendency, as does the Bergman of *The Silence*, 1963, and *Persona*, 1966). In more formal terms, the *mise-en-scène* in art cinema may emphasise verisimilitude of behaviour and of space: for instance the utilisation of reallocations and non-professional actors in neo-realist films. Long takes may be used, and even 'sequence-shots', in order (as in Jansco and late Rosselini), as Bazin put it, 'to do away with montage and to transfer to the screen the continuum of reality' (Bazin, 1967, vol. 1, p. 37). Similarly, 'the tight causality of classic Hollywood construction is replaced by a more tenuous linking of events', such as the highly ellipical narrative(s) in Rosselini's *Paisà* (1946), or the unexplained and ultimately unresolved disappearance of Anna in Antonioni's *L'Avventura* (1959). Often, chance and coincidence play a significant role in advancing the narrative; indeed, many narratives are of an episodic and decidedly picaresque nature, such as *La Strada* (1954) and *Alice in the Cities* (1974) (or, indeed, most of the early works of both Fellini and Wenders). These films have an open-ended approach to narrative causality

L'Avventura (Italy/France 1959 *p.c* – Cino del Duca/PCE/Lyre; *d* – Michelangelo Antonioni; sd b/w)

L'Avventura is the film with which Michelangelo Antonioni came to international prominence in 1960, although he had made his first feature, *Cronaca di un amore*, ten years previously. *L'Avventura* divided critics at the 1960 Cannes film festival, but now stands as one of the undoubted archetypes of 'art cinema'.

The film's plot is simple: Claudia, her friend Anna, and Anna's lover, Sandro, go on a cruise in the Mediterranean. Anna mysteriously disappears, and Claudia and Sandro go in search of her, becoming lovers in the process. And that is it really. However, Antonioni's originality lies precisely in his de-emphasis of the dramatic potential of film plot with its linear problem/resolution structure and its personal conflicts between fully 'psychologised' characters. Thus Anna's disappearance, the subsequent inquest, the mystery of her whereabouts – in short, the 'essential' elements of the story as a more conventional director would have conceived it – are more or less ignored, or rather, they become only as important as Claudia and Sandro feel they are, since the way in which the story is told deliberately limits the spectator's knowledge to what the characters know.

When *L'Avventura* was first released there was much talk of it being an 'existentialist' film in that it revolved around characters who seemed alienated and out of place in their environments. And indeed, in a statement distributed at the time of the film's Cannes première, Antonioni stated that people today live in a world without the moral tools necessary to match their technological skills: they are incapable of authentic relationships with each other or with their environment because they carry within them a fossilised value system quite out of step with modern times. As a result, they often attempt to find in sex or love an answer to their moral dilemma, but this too proves to be a blind alley offering neither solutions nor possibilities for self-fulfilment, let alone a substitute for outmoded values. The result is a kind of existential *ennui*, and it is this state that *L'Avventura* so perfectly captures.

However, Antonioni's genius lies not in his use of this particular theme (which was something of a commonplace in the culture of the postwar years) but in rendering it in such distinctive visual images. The visualisation of subjective states by representational means becomes, with Antonioni, a wholly distinctive stylistic approach. To this end the director exercises an absolute control over his compositions; every aspect of an individual shot is artistically organised for the fullest effect, just as if the director were a painter or a stills photographer: a shot or sequence by Antonioni is marked as surely as though his signature were affixed to the celluloid.

Quintessential art cinema – *L'Année dernière à Marienbad*

L'Année dernière à Marienbad (Last Year at Marienbad) (France/Italy 1961 *p.c* – Terrafilm/Precitel; *d* – Alain Resnais; sd b/w)

The very fact that it is almost impossible to describe the story of *L'Année dernière à Marienbad* marks it out as a quintessential work of art cinema. Set in a vast baroque hotel it revolves around a man, X, who attempts to entice a woman, A, away from a man, M, by persuading her that they had met there the previous year. Whether they actually did meet or not remains, however, a mystery.

The nature of the 'reality' of the events we see on screen is thus at the very heart of the film. As the film's writer Alain Robbe-Grillet has said: 'the whole film is the story of a *persuading*: it deals with a reality which the hero creates out of his own vision, out of his

and display a greater tolerance of narrative 'gaps' than do more classical forms. Here, as in real life, questions remain unanswered, ends are left loose and situations unresolved (see Antonioni's *La Notte*, 1960, Resnais's *L'Année dernière à Marienbad*, 1961 and Truffaut's *Les Quatre Cents Coups*, 1959).

Turning to the 'subjective realism' of the art cinema, Bordwell notes that the art film, like the classic narrative film, relies heavily on psychological causation. By comparison, however, its characters tend to lack clear-cut motives and goals: 'If the Hollywood protagonist speeds towards the target, the art-film protagonist is presented as sliding passively from one situation to another ... If the classical protagonist struggles, the drifting protagonist traces out an itinerary which surveys the film's social world' (Bordwell, 1985, p. 207).

The art film often tends towards the biographical or autobiographical format (Ray's *Apu* trilogy, Truffaut's Antoine Doinel series), but it is also interested in situating its subjects socially – hence, perhaps, a penchant for the 'slice-of-life chronicle' (Varda's *Cleo de 5 à 7*, 1962; or *Paris vu par* ... (this film was made in 1964 by six directors, among them Rohmer, Chabrol and Godard)). Narratives often revolve around characters who are undergoing some form of acute existential crisis (Fellini's *8½*, 1963, Bergman's *Wild Strawberries*, 1957), and this gives the films their peculiarly 'interior' quality, though, this being cinema, the characters' internal crises are rarely expressed through dialogue, or through dialogue alone. As Bordwell puts it:

> Even if a character remains unaware of or inarticulate about his or her mental state, the viewer must be prepared to notice how behaviour and setting can give the character away. The art cinema developed a range of *mise-en-scène* cues for expressing character mood: static postures, covert glances, smiles that fade, aimless walks, emotion-filled landscapes, and associated objects. (Bordwell, 1985, p. 208)

This is a highly subjective cinema, and one that uses the full range of subjectivity charted by Edward Branigan (1984). Dreams, memories and fantasies

own words. And if his persistence, his secret conviction, finally prevail, they do so among a labyrinth of false trains, variants, failures and repetitions' (Robbe-Grillet, 1961, p. 9). Or to put it a slightly different way, this is a film that is all plot and no story – it is impossible for the spectator to disentangle a causal, consistent, chronological story from the plot details with which we are presented.

L'Année dernière à Marienbad is full of ambiguities and contradictions; spatial, temporal and causal. The statue to which A and X frequently return seems constantly to shift location, A's room becomes progressively more cluttered with furniture, day and night appear to alternate within the same scene, an action may carry from one time and space to a different time and space, the narrator's voice-over account of events is often in conflict with the images shown. The entire structure of *Marienbad* is a play with logic, space and time which does not offer us a single, complete story as a prize for winning this 'game' (Bordwell and Thompson, 1993, p. 396). Or as Robbe-Grillet himself has said:

> it will be said that the spectator risks getting lost if he is not occasionally given the 'explanations' that permit him to locate each scene in its chronological place and at its level of objective reality. But we have decided to trust the spectator, to allow him . . . to come to terms with pure subjectivities. Two attitudes are then possible: either the spectator will try to reconstitute some 'Cartesian' scheme – the most linear, the most rational he can devise – and this spectator will certainly find the film difficult, if not incomprehensible; or else the spectator will let himself be carried along by the extraordinary images in front of him, by the actors' voices, by the soundtrack, by the music, by the rhythm of the cutting, by the passion of the characters . . . and to this spectator, the film will seem the 'easiest' he has ever seen. (Robbe-Grillet, 1961, pp. 12–13)

Alice in the Cities (Alice in den Städten)
West Germany 1974 *p.c* – Produktion 1 im Filmverlag der Autoren (Peter Geneé) Munich/WDR; *d* – Wim Wenders; sd b/w)

The New German Cinema emerged in the late 1960s but came to critical prominence in the mid-1970s, making it one of the later manifestations of art cinema (see New German Cinema, p. 69). Wim Wenders is one of the best-known directors associated with this movement, and his films are especially interesting for the way in which they explore the links between German and American culture in general, and cinema in particular.

Through the story of Philip Winter, a disillusioned young photojournalist who unwittingly becomes involved in a little girl's search for her family in the industrial heartland of northern Germany, Wenders forges a distinctly European version of the road movie and one of his most lyrical explorations of his favourite theme – the American 'colonisation' of the German subconscious. For although, on one level, *Alice in the Cities* is about the search for personal identity (a classic art cinema theme), on another it is concerned with German cultural identity in an age increasingly dominated by Americanised cultural forms. Moreover, it also takes in the difference between the 'mythical' America represented by the movies and music which Winter (like Wenders) loves, and the 'real' America which Winter (also like Wenders) finds disillusioning. This interplay between the 'real' and the 'mythic' finds its most richly resonant expression in Wenders's use of music: 'Under the Boardwalk' as Winter sits beneath a real boardwalk morosely rifling through his Polaroids, 'On the Road Again' on a cafe jukebox, and, above all, the Chuck Berry concert at Wuppertal, where 'Memphis Tennessee' echoes the story of *Alice* and Winter seems finally able to accept the contradictions of his background.

Alice is also a highly self-conscious film about the 'media landscape', and the American sections prefigure Baudrillard's *America* (London, Verso, 1988) by over ten years. Pictures and signs proliferate – cinema images pour forth from TVs in innumerable motel rooms. Philip gazes endlessly at his mounting stock of Polaroids in an increasingly vain attempt to decipher and make sense of the world around him, while Wenders's own images effect a remarkably haunting transformation of the commonplace and the everyday. In particular, the film's leisurely pace, its willingness simply to stop and look, is reminiscent of Ozu, whilst its oblique moments of haunting, idiosyncratic beauty recall John Ford. Regretting the changes in American cinema, Wenders once remarked that: 'I miss the friendliness, the care, the thoroughness, the confidence, the seriousness, the calmness, the humanity of the films of John Ford; I miss the faces that are never forced into anything, the landscapes that are never simply only backgrounds, the feelings that are never obtrusive or strange, the stories that, even when they are funny, never make fun.' Thus, by a curious process of cultural migration and stylistic transmogrification, the qualities of a 'classic' Hollywood *auteur* came to inform the work of one of the leading film-makers of the New German Cinema, just as they had influenced the French new wave a decade earlier, which shows that the differences between Hollywood and art cinema are by no means as fixed as sometimes supposed.

abound, and are transcribed by means of optical point-of-view shots, modulations of light, sound and colour, freeze-frames, slow motion and a host of other cinematic conventions for connoting the subjective.

A further important ingredient of the art cinema, according to Bordwell, is the presence of 'overt narrational commentary', which he defines as 'those moments in which the narrational act interrupts the transmission of fabula [story] information and highlights its own role' (Bordwell, 1985, p. 209). In other words, art cinema narration tends towards the self-conscious and self-reflexive. Even if the spectator is not made aware of the film-making process *à la* Godard, the very process of actively and consciously having to try to make sense of a difficult and opaque narrative structure tends to render overt the act of narration and the processes of narrative comprehension. With exposition often delayed or widely distributed, temporal order fractured and fragmented, the camera moving for reasons which are not obviously motivated by the action, and so on, the spectator no longer asks the kind of question associated with watching a classical narrative ('Will x do y?'); rather: 'the very construction of the narration becomes the object of spectator hypotheses: how is the story being told? why tell the story in this way?' (Bordwell, 1985, p. 210).

In such circumstances the voice of the author becomes both audible and visible, or is at least actively sought by the puzzled spectator. The art cinema is thus decidedly an author's cinema (see Author in art cinema, p. 236).

CONCLUSION

One of the problems in trying to define art cinema in formal terms is, of course, the fact that Hollywood has consistently 'borrowed' from it. As Bordwell himself notes, Hollywood not only 'took up' certain established art cinema directors such as Antonioni (*Blow-Up*, 1966, *Zabriskie Point*, 1969) and Truffaut (*Fahrenheit 451*, 1966) but, in the so-called 'New Hollywood' films of the 1960s and 1970s, adapted a large part of the art cinema stylistic repertoire to its own ends (see New Hollywood, p. 99).

Of course, such a process of assimilation, adoption and adaptation could suggest that perhaps art cinema was never so radically different from Hollywood cinema as some of its admirers maintained. This was certainly the position taken by the IFA and *Screen* in the above mentioned debate over independent cinema in Britain, and finds an echo in Steve Neale's statement that:

> In the division of labour it sustains (with the ideology of authorship reinforcing a distinction between intellectual and manual labour); in the practices of production, distribution and exhibition it entails (with the relations between distribution and exhibition on the one hand and production on the other taking the form of commodity circulation); and in the forms and relations of representation with which it is associated, Art Cinema has rarely disturbed or altered fundamentally the commodity-based struc tures, relations and practices of what it likes nevertheless to label the 'commercial' film industry. It has merely modified them slightly. Certainly, radically avant-garde and insistently political practices have been persistently relegated either to its margins or else to a different social and cinematic space altogether. (Neale, 1981, p. 37)

In conclusion, one needs to ask whether the art cinema as described by Bordwell is actually as unified a body of work as he seems to suggest. After all, to take a few examples from Bordwell (1985, pp. 230–1), there are as many differences as similarities between, say, Fellini's *Le Notti di Cabiria* (1956), Satayajit Ray's *Aparajito* (1956), *The Silence*, *Chytilova's Daisies* (1966), Resnais's *Hiroshima mon amour* (1959) and Kluge's *Artists at the Top of the Big Top: Disoriented* (1968). Furthermore, British readers may be surprised to find that his list includes Richardson's *The Loneliness of the Long-Distance Runner* (1962), Losey's *The Servant* (1963), *King and Country* (1964) and *Accident* (1967), Anderson's *This Sporting Life* (1963), Schlesinger's *Darling* (1965), and Lester's *How I Won the War* (1967), which they are unlikely to perceive as art films but merely as British films. This in turn relates to our earlier suggestion that one of the key characteristics of an art film may well be its 'foreign-ness'. It also strongly emphasises the point that art cinema needs to be understood not simply in formal, textual terms but also as a means of film consumption within its own particular institutional context, which will vary from country to country.

Selected Reading

David Bordwell, 'The art cinema as a mode of film practice', *Film Criticism* 4(1), 1979; expanded in *Narration in the Fiction Film*, London, Methuen, 1985.

John Ellis, 'Art, culture and quality: terms for a cinema in the forties and seventies', *Screen* 19(3), autumn 1978.

Steve Neale, 'Art cinema as institution', *Screen* 22(1), 1981.

Geoffrey Nowell-Smith, 'Art cinema', in G. Nowell-Smith (ed.), *The Oxford History of World Cinema*, Oxford, Oxford University Press, 1996, pp. 567–75.

EAST ASIAN CINEMA

A Japanese woodblock print from the early 1800s shows a baby reaching for a revolving lantern on which silhouetted foxes chase each other. Spinning the lantern would have enhanced their chase. When Lumière films and projectors reached East Asia in 1897, this region of paper lanterns and shadow puppetry was well prepared to understand the possibilities of projected light. The Chinese would name cinema 'dian ying', 'electric shadows'.

Over the years East Asian cinema, and Japanese cinema in particular, has attracted the attention of many film scholars. Since the late 1980s that attention has been focused on the question of representation in films from Japan, the People's Republic of China, Taiwan, Korea and Hong Kong. To the extent that representation in Asian cinema differs from that in the west, some scholars see in it similarities to modernist art cinema as we know it in the west, while others see in its particular aesthetics native characteristics with a long history in the art and culture of Asia (see Anderson and Hoekzema, 1977; Bordwell, 1988; Ehrlich and Desser, 1994; and Thompson, 1977).

Among its East Asian counterparts, the Japanese film industry has enjoyed a particularly strong and uninterrupted development since 1899. Because of Japan's political domination before 1945 and its subsequent economic hegemony in the region, Japanese cinema has had a substantial influence on East Asian cinema as a whole, although each region has developed a distinctive body of work.

DISINTEREST IN ILLUSIONISM

Early Japanese film audiences were so fascinated with the film projector and its crew that one early exhibitor set up his projector on the right side of the stage and the screen on the left (see Anderson and Richie, 1982, p. 26). This arrangement allowed the audience to watch the projector as well as the film and indicates that early Japanese audiences had less interest in the illusion of reality offered by the newly invented moving pictures than in understanding how the illusion was created. In the west such an interest is considered modernist, because modernism, which came about as a critical response to the classicism which characterised western art after the Renaissance, seeks to expose the illusion of reality that classical art takes such pains to create.

Chinese ink-brush painting, for instance, although based on nature, was never intended as an illusion but as a medium for meditation. Japanese painters, interested in surface decoration, played with the tensions between the surface and an illusion of depth centuries before it became a concern for modern artists in the west. Native theatrical traditions in Asia have always been highly stylised, giving little illusion of reality. In *bunraku* puppet theatre, for example, the puppet operators, though dressed in black and therefore inconspicuous, share the stage with the puppets.

Japanese of the Meiji period (1868–1912) were familiar with western art and theatre, but this did not lead them to seize on the illusionistic possibilities in cinema, as the example of the early Japanese exhibitor indicates. They saw no reason for a film to appear self-contained. Thus, all through the silent era, narrators, called *benshi*, stood alongside the screen and narrated the story. The film text of early Japanese silents was intentionally vague so that the *benshi* could make up the stories as they went along (see Hiroshi Komatsu, 1992).

As Japanese studios developed, they were organised around directors rather than producers and, copying traditional art practices, adopted a master/apprentice system in which assistant directors were assigned to learn their craft from established directors. Thus *auteurism*, a hallmark of the art film, was no hard-won privilege in Japan, as it frequently was in the west, but an accepted condition of film production.

MIZOGUCHI AND OZU

Among the first westerners to write seriously about Japanese cinema were the early *Cahiers du Cinéma* critics into whose *auteur* theory the Japanese fitted perfectly. They particularly admired the films of Kenji Mizoguchi. They praised his lyricism and adept *mise-en-scène*, and were quick to link his work to other Japanese arts and artists (e.g. *kabuki* theatre and woodblock artist Hokusai). Because of his preference for long takes and a moving camera, the *Cahiers* critics also compared him to Renoir, Welles and Wyler. Critic Noël Burch, however, disputes this similarity, noting that Mizoguchi's long takes differ from those of western directors in not being centred and rarely closing in on the actors, thus maintaining a 'non-anthropocentric' approach. Burch has suggested that Mizoguchi's long takes have the character of scroll paintings or *emakimono*, in which there is no fixed perspective (Burch, 1979).

Yasujiro Ozu, known for his contributions to a popular Japanese genre known as the 'home drama', also takes a 'non-

The aesthetics of space and narration – Ozu's *The End of Summer*

anthropocentric' approach in his films. According to David Bordwell (1988) and Kristin Thompson (1977), Ozu privileges space over narration in ways that include consistently using a 360° shooting space instead of the 180° space of classical cinema, foregrounding objects that are not correspondingly important in the narrative, and cutting away to shots and shot sequences that, while related to the narrative, are not motivated by it. According to Bordwell, Ozu's consistent foregrounding of space in preference to narrative sets him apart from other Japanese directors and places him in the ranks of 'parametric' film-makers like Bresson and Dreyer. Bordwell and Thompson thus see Ozu as essentially a modernist, arguing that since he was a devotee of American films, he must have been aware of the extent to which he was 'transgressing' classical film practices. Other writers, including Burch, see Ozu's film practice as rooted in traditional Japanese aesthetics and perceptions of space.

Classical *découpage* – the way in which Hollywood films are edited to put a story across – had, to a great extent, become the norm in Japan by the 1930s, and certainly Ozu knew he was flouting classical film practice. However, even as a young man, he was enthralled with the aesthetic term *mu*. *Mu* refers to the empty space in traditional painting and carries deeper Taoist and Buddhist philosophical connotations of 'void' or infinity. The transition spaces in Ozu's films, sometimes called 'empty shots', can equally be seen as expressions of *mu* rather than modernist thrusts against a classical norm.

Likewise Ozu frequently plays with the tension between surface and depth. Often this takes the form of placing an object or face close to the camera in a space that then plunges into depth. The long alleyways typical of old Japanese cities proved ideal for showing off extreme depth. In *The End of Summer* (1961), Ozu graphically matches three shots, the first two shallow, the last showing a long alley. At first all three shots look the same until one recognises the need to read much greater depth into the last one (see Geist, 1994).

Although most of Ozu's contemporaries were not as radical as he and operated within the ground rules of classical cinema, they too included 'empty shots' in their films (though not as frequently or as systematically as Ozu) and they too had a tendency to call attention to surface and emphasise the decorative through flashy transitions, unusual camera angles, mirror shots, and so on, consistent with the decorative tendencies in Japanese art.

Another striking feature of many East Asian films is the tendency to refer to seasons. Although at times little more than a cultural overlay, more often a deeper philosophical tendency can be seen to be at work. The notion of transience, for example – which is linked to the idea of seasons as measurements of the life cycle – is derived from Buddhism and fundamental to Japanese eschatology. Ozu's films abound in symbols of transience, passage, and passing time such as clocks, smoke, trains, bridges, and so on. And many of his later films, bearing seasonal references in their titles, involve marriage and death – pivotal points in the life cycle. Even Akira Kurosawa, famous for the western humanism in even his period and samurai films, makes integral use of cyclical, seasonal references. For example, *Seven Samurai* (1954), where a revolving mill wheel is a recurring motif, builds its story around the harvesting and planting of rice and includes a famous love scene that takes place among the spring blossoms.

Seasonal motifs – the rice fields of *The Seven Samurai*

REDISCOVERING TRADITIONAL CULTURE

Although much of what seems modern in Japanese cinema, that is, contrary to the rules of classical film-making, is rooted in traditional arts and philosophies, some of it may, as Bordwell (1995) argues, have come as a deliberate attempt on the part of the Japanese to recuperate and reaffirm their traditional culture in the 1930s and 1940s (and even more so in the 1950s after Japan's defeat in the Second World War). In Bordwell's view, the Japanising tendencies noticeable in films from the 1930s, for example, were conscious efforts by film-makers to reverse a trend towards westernisation that had all but overwhelmed traditional culture in the 1910s and 1920s. A similar tendency is apparent in Chinese cinema. Chinese cinema, having come even more under the influence of western norms than the Japanese because of the large European presence in Shanghai before the Second World War and because of the influence of Marxist dicta after 1946, frequently 'sinicised' its images to give them a Chinese flavour. Examples of this process include arranging scenes to look like classical painting, framing shots with branches of blossoms, or adopting symbols from classical poetry (see Berry and Farquhar, 1994).

Self-conscious movements in East Asian cinema such as the Japanese new wave of the 1960s and China's Fifth Generation films, made by young directors in the 1980s, fit western patterns of modernism less equivocally since they were intended as revisions of dominant cinema practice, not merely in the west but in their own countries as well. Nevertheless, the influence of indigenous culture is strong in both movements. While Japanese new wave films, like Yoshishige Yoshida's *Eros Plus Massacre* (1969), are allied to Japanese modernism, which developed its own identity in the course of the twentieth century, many of the new Chinese films, like Chen Kaige's *Yellow Earth* (1984), have deliberately incorporated traditional culture and turned it into a signifying practice.

Elsewhere East Asian cinemas have developed unique genres such as Chinese kung fu and swordfight films (a Hong Kong speciality). These are allied to Japanese swordfight or samurai films but employ a type of theatrics and acrobatics originally derived from Chinese opera. A new movement in Taiwanese cinema, which has gained international reknown since the 1980s, developed the conventions of melodrama and derives in part from the quiescent Japanese 'home drama'. Directors like Hou Hsiao-Hsien have adopted and developed a quiet, measured style, not unlike Ozu's, and have even turned it to political protest in films like *City of Sadness* (1988). His 1995 *Good Men, Good Women* includes a clip from Ozu's *Late Spring*, which suggests an acknowledgement of his debt to the Japanese director. In 1991 Hou produced *Raise the Red Lantern*, which, directed by PRC Fifth Generation film-maker Zhang Yimou, combines Hou's quiet, formal discipline with the monumentality and brilliant use of colour that characterises Zhang's and other Fifth Generation films.

The tendency in Asian films from the 1980s and early 1990s to explore and foreground, thematically as well as formally, specific aspects of Asian cultural identity, has given way in the late 1990s to an exploration of changing social patterns and the internationalisation that has accompanied Asia's fast-paced, globalised economy. Examples include Japanese director Masayiki Suo's comedic yet poignant melodrama *Shall We Dance* (1996) and veteran Taiwanese director Edward Yang's brilliant foray into the punk gangster genre, *Mahjong* (1996). While exploring themes of internationalisation, both films, nevertheless, exhibit a supreme confidence in the specifically Asian film-making traditions both directors have inherited and, in the case of Yang, helped to create.

Late Spring (Japan 1949 *p.c* – Shochiku/Ofuna, *d* – Yasujiro Ozu sd, b/w)

Late Spring, the earliest of Ozu's 'marriage films', concerns a widower's ultimately successful attempts to marry off his daughter. Ozu's use of unusual spatial devices, as described by Bordwell (1988) and Thompson (1977), can be seen throughout. For example, in one scene the father is asked by a friend in which direction the sea lies. The friend points behind himself, and the father replies, 'no', it is in the opposite direction, and points behind himself. The friend asks the direction of the shrine and points to his left. The father again says 'no', and points to his right. However, because Ozu crosses the 180° line as he cuts from the friend to the father, both men point in the same screen direction, adding to the confusion. Two more requests for directions have the same result. The sequence has no narrative significance and instead serves as a commentary on Ozu's use of a 360° shooting space and his puckish delight in confounding an audience with it.

The film contains more references to traditional Japanese art than any other Ozu film – and many of the 'empty shots' are concerned with this. Certain empty shots also make reference to passing time; and several others help elucidate the odd relationship between the daughter and her father's assistant, who is engaged to someone else. The famous 'vase sequence', in which cutaways to a vase link shots of the daughter smiling peacefully to images of her tearful face, has been the subject of much debate. Some critics see in the shot an emptiness allied to *mu* (void) which bridges the daughter's change of mood and suggests transcendence, while others see only Ozu's formal rigour and his penchant for foregrounding objects with little narrative significance.

Sisters of the Gion (Japan 1936 *p.c* – Dai-Ichi, *d* – Kenji Mizoguchi; sd b/w)

Sisters of the Gion follows the attempts of two sisters, both geisha, to survive in a male-dominated world. Whereas one sister is traditional, the other is modern and tries to use men in a practical, cold-blooded way. Mizoguchi demonstrates the hopelessness of the geisha world, and the film's theme – the plight of women – is a typical concern of the director's work.

Stylistically, the film incorporates Mizoguchi's long takes, moving camera and 'non-anthropomorphic' space. In many of his long takes, a fairly distant camera is maintained – at times a travelling camera dodges behind objects and partitions to maintain its distance. A scene in which the traditional sister finds she cannot pay a delivery boy transpires in long shot with nothing in the foreground except an empty table, a sign that her penniless patron is taking no responsibility for the lunch being delivered for his sake. A crucial subsequent scene in which the modern sister undertakes to get rid of the patron also takes place entirely in long shot. Characters are usually decentred. A travelling shot in

The plight of women – Mizoguchi's *Sisters of Gion*

which the two sisters visit a temple generally keeps them in the right third of the frame and leaves the left two-thirds empty. Much of the film is shot with high angles reminiscent of twelfth-century scroll painting. Bordwell has suggested that high angles such as these were an attempt to revive 'Japaneseness' in the 1930s.

Yellow Earth (China 1984 *p.c* – Guangxi studio; *d* – Chen Kaige; sd col.)

Yellow Earth is the flagship film of the Fifth Generation, China's first generation of directors to graduate from film school after the Cultural Revolution. The disruptions of the Cultural Revolution made their entry into the profession different from that of their predecessors. They were able to begin making films soon after graduation, and

The land and the people – *Yellow Earth*

many, like Chen Kaige, worked out of regional studios instead of Beijing. Since the Cultural Revolution had sent young people into the countryside to work with the peasants, film-makers in this generation had a knowledge and appreciation of the various regions of China and of the peasants who lived there.

The story concerns a young peasant girl in Shanbei Province in the 1950s who becomes enamoured of a Party cadre when he visits, on a mission from Mao's stronghold in Yan'an, to collect peasant songs. Forced into an arranged marriage, the girl tries vainly to escape by boat to Yan'an.

In making *Yellow Earth*, Chen and his cameraman Zhang Yimou decided to adapt a specific regional school of Chinese painting, Chang'an, to the film. They stressed the monumentality and high horizon of the loess plain above the Yellow River and the yellow colour of the region in keeping with the stylistics of the Chang'an school. Like Chinese landscape artists, they tried to convey their ideas – of the relationship between male and female principles (yin and yang), the relationship of the land to the people, and so on – through the images rather than through dialogue, which is scant in the film. The heroine, the Yellow River, and the yellow earth are linked visually and suggest stillness (yin) in contrast to the rousing songs and noisy festivals associated with the male characters (yang). The result is a visually striking, intriguing film, whose meaning is more suggestive than explicit.

Selected Reading

David Bordwell, *Ozu and the Poetics of Cinema*, Princeton, Princeton University Press, 1988.

David Bordwell, 'Visual style in Japanese cinema, 1925–1945', *Film History* 7(1), spring 1995, pp. 5–31.

Noël Burch, *To the Distant Observer: Form and Meaning in the Japanese Cinema*, Berkeley, University of California Press, 1979.

Linda Ehrlich and David Desser (eds), *Cinematic Landscapes: Observations on the Visual Arts and Cinema of China and Japan*, Austin, University of Texas Press, 1994.

Kathe Geist, 'Playing with space: Ozu and two-dimensional design in Japan', in Ehrlich and Desser, *Cinematic Landscapes*.

Hiroshi Komatsu, 'Some characteristics of Japanese cinema before World War I', in Nolletti and Desser, *Reframing Japanese Cinema*.

Arthur Nolletti and David Desser (eds), *Reforming Japanese Cinema: Authorship, Genre, History*, Bloomington, Indiana University Press, 1992.

AVANT-GARDE AND COUNTER-CINEMA

The term 'avant-garde' was introduced into French socialist theory from military terminology in the nineteenth century. By the end of the first decade of the twentieth century it had been widely adopted to designate art and literature which challenged institutionalised cultural forms.

The first avant-garde cinema emerged in Europe in the period 1914–30 from the ferment of modern art. To a generation of artists and writers registering the impact of modernity on every aspect of life from war to entertainment, film appealed as the medium most capable of rendering the striking new attributes of the machine age: shock and speed. Futurist artists including Giacomo Balla and Umberto Boccioni used techniques derived from photography and film to create dynamic effects in painting, and the 1916 manifesto *The Futurist Cinema* argued the case for a new kind of cinema:

> At first look the cinema, born only a few years ago, may seem to be Futurist already, lacking a past and free from traditions. Actually, by appearing in the guise of *theatre without words*, it has inherited all the most traditional sweepings of the literary theatre ... The cinema is an autonomous art. The cinema must therefore never copy the stage. The cinema, being essentially visual, must above all fulfil the evolution of painting, detach itself from reality, from photography, from the graceful and solemn. It must become anti-graceful, deforming, impressionistic, synthetic, dynamic, free-working. (cited in Hein, 'The Futurist Film', 1979, p. 19)

The desire to prise film from the grip of bourgeois and popular theatrical traditions came to typify much of the work of the European avant-garde. Coming mostly from backgrounds in the fine and plastic arts, which were revolutionised in the first two decades of the century by Futurism, Cubism and Dada, the earliest avant-garde film-makers sought to redefine film as a visual art (Hein, 1979; Lawder, 1975; Kuenzli, 1987). By the 1920s three distinct variants on this project had emerged: the development of a specifically cinematic aesthetic, associated with French Impressionism (Delluc and Epstein's *photogénie* and Dulac's *cinégraphie intégrale*); the use of film to extend the scope of painting, in pursuit of, in the words of one critic, 'kinetic solutions to pictorial problems' (Barbara Rose, cited by Wollen, 1975/1982, p. 97), seen in the works of Laszlo Moholy-Nagy, Man Ray and Marcel Duchamp; and the search for equivalences between the arts or for ways of combining them, particularly film and music, as in the work of German abstract animators Viking Eggeling's *Diagonal-Symphonie* and Hans Richter's *Rhythmus 21*, which developed from their joint experiments with 'rhythm in painting', and Walter Ruttmans' and Oskar Fischinger's 'optical music' (Russett and Starr, 1988).

Soviet avant-garde film, which evolved under the influence of Russian Futurism and Cubism in a revolutionary context, has either been discussed by some historians of experimental cinema as a related or parallel current to the French and German work (Curtis, 1971) or excluded because of its strong narrative element (Lawder, 1975). Phillip Drummond (1979) has commented that such discussions involve simplifications and exclusions and are the result of a monolithic opposition between mainstream and avant-garde which leads to a polemical drawing of the lines. A more nuanced view of the internal dynamics and tensions of the 1920s avant-garde has been possible since Peter Wollen remapped the terrain in his essay 'The Two Avant-Gardes', first published in 1975.

Wollen argues that the historical avant-garde actually comprised two quite separate tendencies: on the one hand, a group of film-makers closely associated with painting and committed to formal experiment, who were part of a trend, at its most radical, towards 'an art of pure signifiers detached from meaning as much as from reference' (Wollen, 1982, p. 95); on the other hand, a much smaller group around Eisenstein and Vertov whose concern with film form arose from an interest in cinema as a site for the mediation of social and political concerns. As Wollen puts it, 'What we find with the Soviet film-makers is a recognition that a new type of content, a new realm of signifieds, demands formal innovation, on the level of the signifier, for its expression' (Wollen, 1982, p. 98). By mapping the differences between the Soviet cinema of montage and western European practices contemporaneous with it onto the relationship between political and aesthetic modernism, Wollen's model suggests a more dynamic, heterogeneous history for the avant-garde.

SURREALISM

Surrealism is not mentioned in Wollen's essay, but nevertheless deserves to be discussed in the context of avant-garde film-making. Despite its closeness to Dadaism, surrealism cannot be assimilated to a painterly, formalist European avant-garde. The surrealists consolidated the Dadaists' contempt for bourgeois art by repudiating all avant-gardes and denouncing purist aesthetics. They positioned themselves as a counter-avant-garde, attacking Impressionist cinema, carrying on a campaign of abuse against Cocteau and praising popular films such as Feuillade's serials, Stroheim's melodramas and American crazy comedies. Playing on the codes of narrative cinema, in films such as *L'Étoile de mer* (1928), *Un Chien andalou* (1928) and *L'Âge d'or* (1930), the surrealists created a film world in which the chance collisions of Dada were bound by obsessional desire. Instead of the illogical, non-narrative and abstract strategies characteristic of Dada films, surrealist film-makers used conventional cinematography, optical realism and narrative to invite identification, in order to make the misappropriation and rupture of these techniques all the more shocking. Their use of narrative systems also enabled them to address social and ideological issues discursively, as in Buñuel's passionately anti-clerical documentary *Land Without Bread* (1932), where the grotesque incongruities of the film's surrealist aesthetic testify to the terrible existence of the impoverished mountain people. Summing up the importance of surrealism for the history of avant-garde film, Ian Christie has written:

> The impact of surrealism has been pervasive and, in many respects, progressive. The Surrealists effectively redefined the scope of avant-garde activity, giving it a political and a

> psychoanalytic dimension. Yet the immediate effect of the Surrealist counter avant-garde was a repression of modernist work in favour of neo-romantic, primitivist and eclectic activity. In the cinema, they sought to tap the 'unconscious' of popular cinema; but from *Un Chien andalou* onwards, surrealism began to construct its own model of avant-garde cinema, based upon procedures of subversion, rupture and the dysfunction of dominant narrative cinema ... In the final analysis, surrealism destroyed one conception of avant-garde activity and irrevocably altered the terms on which any future avant-garde would emerge. (Christie, 1979, p. 44).

The first flowering of avant-garde film ended with the politicial reconfiguration of Europe in the 1930s. In the Soviet Union the emergence of socialist realism eclipsed the experimentalism of the 1920s. Abstract and experimental art was banned in Germany by the Nazis and fell from favour in France under the influence of the Popular Front, which favoured the direct approach of realist forms.

THE POSTWAR AVANT-GARDE

The postwar resurgence of avant-garde cinema began in the US, fostered there by cultural and industrial conditions. The arrival of scores of refugee artists fleeing the totalitarian regimes of Europe in the 1930s and 1940s brought modernism to North America where it flourished in all the visual and performing arts. After the war, an increasing availability of 16-mm equipment made film production and exhibition more accessible to those outside the industry, thus encouraging the spread of film societies, film education and amateur film-making. This also created the context in which an underground film culture could develop around organisations such as Amos Vogel's avant-garde film society, Cinema 16, and the New York Film-Makers' Co-operative.

Personal film

Between the early 1940s and the mid-1960s, the North American film avant-garde took shape in 'a great burst of personal film-making' (Curtis, 1971, p. 49) which gave it its distinctive character. Across a diverse range of styles, encompassing the film poetry of Maya Deren, Kenneth Anger and Stan Brakhage, the film diaries of Jonas Mekas and self-portraits of Carolee Schneemann, and the 'trash' underground movies of Ron Rice, Jack Smith and the Kuchar brothers, the films of this period share a concern with the personal as subject matter and with the development of cinematic forms equivalent to first-person discourse. Even the abstract cinema of West Coast avant-garde film-makers such as Jordan Belson and James Whitney developed under the influence of a personal metaphysics.

The terms for discussion of these films and film-makers were set by P. Adams Sitney's *Visionary Film* (1974, 1979) which posits a Romantic tradition primarily concerned with the representation of states of

Un Chien andalou (France 1929 *p.c* – Luis Buñuel; *d* – Luis Buñuel, st b/w)

From its startling opening sequence, in which a man appears to slice through a woman's eyeball with a cut-throat razor, to the grotesque corpses of its closing scene, *Un Chien andalou* is a deliberate assault on the bourgeois artistic and social conventions of its time. Buñuel described it as 'a desperate and passionate appeal to murder'. The surrealists were interested in releasing the power of the unconscious through procedures which followed the logic of dreams. Dali and Buñuel used bizarre imagery and incongruous juxtapositions to recreate their own dreams, almost as in surrealist automatic writing. Although some of their

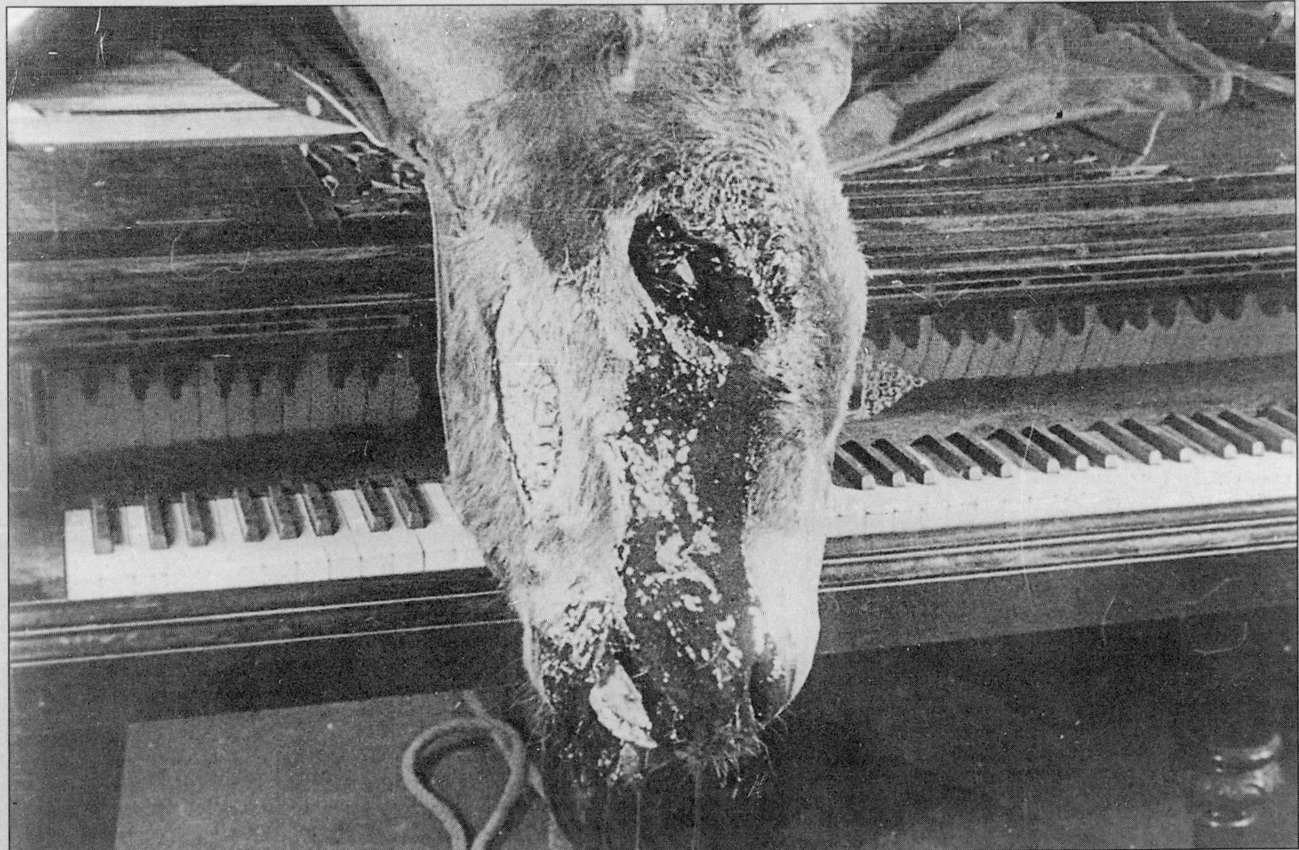

Releasing the power of the unconscious. The bizarre imagery of *Un Chien andalou*

images, such as the rotting donkeys on pianos and the severed hand, were staged before the camera, the most visceral sequences are those where editing is used to imitate the metonymic patterns of unconscious thought, such as the sequence of puns which cuts between a moth, a mouth, a smile which is wiped off a man's face, an outraged woman frantically applying lipstick, a beard of pubic hair and an armpit. In place of linear narrative and Hollywood continuity, the film uses graphic continuity, playing on similar shapes and patterns in contiguous shots (for example, in the series of images showing a hand full of ants, a hairy armpit and a sea urchin). At the same time, its skilful parody of Hollywood style is no doubt part of its enduring success.

The similarity of the film's signifying practices to the workings of the unconscious as described by Freud has invited much interpretation (for a variety of approaches see Drummond, 1977; Sandro, 1987; Williams, 1981). Buñuel famously insisted that nothing in the film has any symbolic value, although this is clearly not the case. He may have been warning against readings of the film which would assimilate it to Impressionism or Symbolism, thereby lessening the force of its deliberate offensiveness. The subversive aesthetic of surrealism has been claimed as a precursor for American underground film-makers such as Maya Deren and Kenneth Anger (Renan, 1968), but its direct appeal to the unconscious has also been appropriated by the advertising industry.

Vent d'est (France/Italy/West Germany 1970 *p.c* – Anouchka Films; *d* – the Dziga–Vertov Group; sd col.)

Vent d'est was inspired by an idea of the student leader Daniel Cohn-Bendit to make a left-wing western about a miners' strike. The Dziga–Vertov Group argued that it would be impossible to make a western that was genuinely left-wing because the genre would reproduce the relations and ideology of mainstream cinema. In the event, Cohn-Bendit fell out with the film-makers and does not appear in the film. Although elements of western imagery appear, the film is above all an essay on revolutionary film-making.

In the film's dense articulation of sound and image, written and spoken language tend to dominate. An intertitle which states 'Ce n'est pas une image juste, c'est juste une image' ('This is not a just image, it's just an image') indicates the mistrust of the photographic form. A sequence in which members of the film company discuss the possible inclusion of still images of Stalin is offered as a demonstration of the way

An essay on revolutionary film-making – *Vent d'est*

images can be mobilised by one side or the other in class struggle. Another sequence demystifies mainstream cinema by introducing 'a typical character in bourgeois cinema' who addresses the audience in an insulting way. The place of cinema in revolution is debated in a scene in which the Brazilian film-maker Glauber Rocha stands at a dusty crossroads and is approached by a pregnant woman with a movie camera who asks him the way to political cinema. Rocha points one way and then another, saying: 'That way is the cinema of aesthetic adventure and philosophical enquiry, while this way is the Third World cinema – a dangerous cinema, divine and marvellous, where the questions are practical ones like production, distribution, training 300 film-makers to make 600 films a year for Brazil alone, to supply one of the world's biggest markets.' The woman sets off down the path to Third World cinema, but is harassed by a red plastic ball which inexplicably gets in her way; she returns to the crossroads and takes the other path. The sequence dramatises the dilemma of the Dziga–Vertov Group as radical film-makers in the west, although whether the film solves it is another question. Glauber Rocha intensely disliked *Vent d'est*. Many spectators find it difficult and unpleasurable to watch, including Andrew Britton, who wrote: '*Vent d'est* is, quite simply, one of the most repressive films ever made' (Britton, 1976, p. 9).

Privilege (USA 1990 *p.c* – Zeitgeist Films; *d* – Yvonne Rainer; sd b/w + col.)

In *Privilege*, Rainer uses a fragmentary narrative form to juxtapose different ways of thinking about privilege and the lack of it. Women are interviewed for a documentary about menopause, putatively authored by 'Yvonne Washington', Rainer's African-American alter ego. One of the interviewees, a white woman named Jenny, tells the story of an occurrence in her youth, which is narrated in flashback. Jenny's neighbour, Brenda, a white lesbian, presses charges against Carlos, a Puerto Rican man, whom she finds naked in her room. Jenny perjures herself, saying she actually saw Carlos in Brenda's apartment. Jenny subsequently has an affair with the assistant district attorney. Rainer offers this anecdote as a model of privilege, demonstrating its distribution according to the culturally coded categories of race, gender and class.

The film addresses the question of privilege not only through its content but through its forms. Rainer claims that: 'Every character in the film can be seen as either having or not having privilege, depending on race, sex, class, age. If they didn't have it, I gave it *to* them' (MacDonald, 1992, p. 352). She accomplishes this by privileging certain characters' points of view at key junctures in the narrative. Digna, a Puerto Rican woman, moves invisibly, omnisciently through the film, commenting ironically on the action; Carlos speaks a text by Frantz Fanon, which in turn refracts on a text by Eldridge Cleaver spoken by an African-American 'double' who replaces Carlos in some of the shots in Brenda's apartment; Jenny appears as her middle-aged self in her flashback, exchanging the privilege of youth for the privilege of hindsight. Anti-illusionist devices including reverse shots of the film crew, direct address to camera and several appearances by Rainer in minor 'roles' serve as reminders of the privilege of the film-maker.

The film's prismatic structure of points of view, which are often irreconcilable with each other, represents Rainer's attempt to go beyond 'the limitations of feminist film theory' in order to address issues of race, age and sexuality (MacDonald, 1992, p. 346). Its coherence is not at the level of narrative or character identification but in the questions confronting the viewers about their own relationships with privilege. The dialogical form of *Privilege* opens it to a variety of readings, depending on the critic's view of the film's exposition of contradictions and assumptions in white liberal thinking. E. Ann Kaplan's sympathetic reading takes these problems as the subject matter of the film, offered as questions for the audience's consideration (Kaplan, 1997, pp. 273–80). Michelle Wallace argues that inequality is structured into the film's discursive strategies: 'The positions from which women of colour speak . . . are inferior to positions from which white women, white men, and men of color speak' (Wallace, 1991, p. 8). Patricia Mellencamp argues that the film is trapped in its own logic: 'Caught up in the tenets of heterosexual romance (perhaps unconsciously so), *Privilege* enacts what it attempts to critique' (Mellencamp, 1995, p. 184).

mind. According to Sitney: 'the preoccupations of the American avant-garde film-makers coincide with those of our post-Romantic poets and Abstract Expressionist painters. Behind them lies a potent tradition of Romantic poetics' (Sitney, 1979, p. ix). At the core of this tradition, Sitney perceives a common concern with the phenomenology of mind: 'the great unacknowledged aspiration of the American avant-garde film has been the cinematic reproduction of the human mind' (Sitney, 1979, p. 370). It should be noted that this assertion has been much criticised, not least for its vagueness with regard to the notion of 'mind' and its failure to address the role of language (Penley and Bergstrom, 1978).

Structural film

In the second half of the 1960s, an alternative to personal film emerged: structural film, defined by Sitney as 'a cinema of structure in which the shape of the whole film is predetermined and simplified' (Sitney, 1979, p. 369). Like minimalist painting or serial music, structural film foregrounds the materials and processes of film itself by substituting very explicit organising structures for the self-effacing structures of tradition (in the case of film, illusionist narrative systems). Through anti-illusionism and reflexivity, structural film attempts to approach the condition of 'pure film'. Such self-referentiality has been connected by more than one critic to the variant of modernism described by Clement Greenberg:

> It quickly emerged that the unique and proper area of competence of each art coincided with all that was unique to the nature of its medium ... Realistic, illusionist art had dissembled the medium, using art to conceal art. Modernism used art to call attention to art. (cited in James, 1989, pp. 239–40)

Many of the structural films are systematic investigations of a restricted number of filmic codes or aspects of film's material substrate: Michael Snow's *Wavelength* (1967) explores the potentialities of the fixed frame and the zoom; George Landow's *Film In Which There Appear Sprocket Holes, Edge Lettering, Dirt Particles, Etc.* (1966) investigates the relationship between the cinematic image and the filmstrip; Nam June Paik's *Zen for Film* (1964) makes projection its subject matter.

The movement's British offshoot, 'structural/materialism', travelled a '*via negativa* of unprecedented severity' (James, 1989, p. 278) to a position of anti-representationalism that was much more rigorous than that of its American counterpart. Peter Gidal (an American in London) argued that representational content should be eliminated as far as possible: 'The Structural/Materialist film must minimise the content in its overpowering, imagistically seductive sense, in an attempt to get through the miasmic area of "experience" and proceed with film as film' (Gidal, 1978, p. 2). Gidal's *Room Film 1973* (1973) has been described as 'almost relentless in its denial of tangible images' (Dusinberre, 1978, p. 109).

Where most critics see a clear break between personal film and structural film, Sitney argues that structural film renewed and intensified the visionary tradition out of which personal film developed: 'the structural film approaches the condition of meditation and evokes states of consciousness without mediation; that is, with the sole mediation of the camera' (Sitney, 1979, p. 370). According to Sitney, structural film's interrogation of the ontology of film acts as a springboard for an exploration of the nature of perception, thought and feeling. Other critics, including Annette Michelson (1974) and Peter Wollen (1982), articulate an opposing view of structural film, according to which its ontological investigation is an end in itself, the only meanings produced being concerned with the medium. As Wollen puts it: 'The frontier reached by this avant-garde has been an ever-narrowing preoccupation with pure film, with film "about" film, a dissolution of signification into objecthood or tautology' (Wollen, 1982, p. 97).

To some extent, national contexts illuminate the variations in avant-garde practice. In British structural film-making for instance, ontological inquiry was undertaken in a Marxist frame of reference rather than a phenomenological one: reflexive, anti-illusionist strategies were employed with the aim of breaking with ideology and demonstrating the materiality of filmic practice. There were also structural film-makers in Germany and Austria who were directly involved with movements such as Fluxus and Actionism, which, far from notions of ontological purity, emphasised aleatory methods of composition and mixed media.

Avant-garde versus modernism

Underlying the differences in avant-garde practice and interpretation that had emerged by the 1970s were profound differences in the assimilation of the legacy of the 1920s and the notion of avant-garde itself. Peter Wollen argues that modernism became divorced from the avant-garde when it was transplanted to the US and institutionalised in the New York art world, while the avant-garde, which centred on Paris, gained a new agenda from the events of May 1968 which led it away from modernist aesthetics (Wollen, 1981). (Paul Willemen makes a similar point more trenchantly, arguing that modernism and the avant-garde 'are, in fact, two simultaneous but antagonistic tendencies' (Willemen, 1994, p. 145).) Modernism, according to Wollen, is characterised by reflexivity, semiotic reduction, foregrounding of the signifier and suppression or suspension of the signified, whereas the avant-garde rejects purism and ontological speculation in favour of semiotic expansion and a heterogeneity of signifiers and signifieds. These two opposing tendencies are rooted in those of the historical avant-garde. One tendency reflects a preoccupation with the specificity of the signifier, holding the signified in suspense or striving to eliminate it. The other has tried to develop new types of relation between signifier and signified through the montage of heterogeneous elements (Wollen, 1981, p. 10).

Wollen sees structural film as a continuation of the first tendency, the modernist avant-garde of the 1920s, and the post-1968 work of, say, Godard and Straub-Huillet as a continuation of the second tendency, the avant-garde of Eisenstein and 1920s Soviet cinema. The potential of the first tendency, Wollen argues, is limited by the exhaustion of modernism, which, by the late twentieth century had been transposed into conceptualism and minimalism and played out in ever-decreasing circles of ontological purity. Although Wollen emphasises that these are only tendencies, pointing out for example that the American avant-garde is far more heterogeneous than most if its criticis have acknowledged, he nevertheless sees far more potential in the tradition of montage than in the tradition of ontological purity.

GODARD AND COUNTER-CINEMA

Unlike the American personal and structural film-makers, Jean-Luc Godard came into avant-garde film from a background in commercial art cinema (see Godard, p. 253) Between 1968 and 1971 Godard broke with the industry in order to work with Jean-Pierre Gorin and others in the Dziga–Vertov Group, a small cooperative set up to make political films. Writing on Godard in the early 1970s, Wollen introduced the term 'counter-cinema' as a precise description of Godard's negation of the values of mainstream cinema (in place of the term 'avant-garde' which implies being in advance of mainstream cinema in an indeterminate way).

Counter-cinema starts from the assertion that the illusionist conventions of mainstream cinema function to obscure the real conditions of its production. Ideology, by this analysis, is ingrained in mainstream film at the level of form and it is the task of radical cinema to break with that form as well as with its political contents. Central to the counter-cinema project is the attempt to involve an audience in political struggle by inviting active engagement rather than passive spectatorship. Counter-cinema therefore systematically challenges illusionism with strategies that subvert each of its major codes – disrupting linear causal relations, denying narrative closure, fracturing spatial and temporal verisimilitude, undermining identification and putting pleasure into question. In 'Godard and Counter-Cinema: *Vent d'est*' (1972, 1982), Wollen tabulates the seven deadly sins of 'Hollywood–Mosfilm' (in Godard's phrase) against the seven cardinal virtues of counter-cinema:

> Narrative transitivity/Narrative intransitivity
> Identification/Estrangement
> Transparency/Foregrounding
> Single diegesis/Multiple diegesis
> Closure/Aperture
> Pleasure/Unpleasure
> Fiction/Reality

Although a complex web of political and theoretical thought (Marx, Mao, Saussure, Lacan, Althusser) provides the intellectual background to Godard's counter-cinema strategies, the strategies themselves are more directly developed from the ideas of Brecht and Eisenstein.

From Brecht, Godard takes the idea of distanciation, embodied in devices which break the spectator's involvement and empathy and draw attention to the wider social context of the play or film. In *Vent d'est* (1969), for example, Godard estranges the viewer by introducing 'real people' into the fiction, by using the same voice for different characters and different voices for the same character, by directly addressing the camera and insulting the audience. The crucial difference between these strategies and the superficially similar reflexive ploys of Greenbergian modernism is that Godard tries to draw our attention not to the film and its specific ontology but to the socio-economic context in which the film is made and seen.

Eisenstein's notion of montage was developed by Godard into 'a concept of conflict, not between the content of images, but between different codes and between signifier and signified' (Wollen, 1982, p. 99). Godard disrupts the traditional organisation of mainstream cinema by splitting up and recombining cinematic codes which are distributed across the multiple channels that characterise film as a medium, and which illusionist conventions aim to unify: sound and image, time and space, character and actor. With the removal of the traditional hierarchy of filmic codes the text becomes polyphonic: discourses are juxtaposed, re-contextualised, and put into conflict and dialogue with each other. Thus in *Pravda* (1969) images are accompanied by a commentary, spoken by 'Vladimir Lenin' and 'Rosa Luxembourg', which alters their meanings. Interviews with Czech workers, students and peasants go untranslated (the commentary advises: 'If you don't know Czech you'd better learn it fast'). And images from a munitions factory are intercut with images of film production. The spectator's activity in reading the film consists of assembling the various sounds and images meaningfully and evaluating the relationships between the film's many discourses.

As much as counter-cinema is a political cinema, then, it is equally a problematisation of the relationships between cinema and politics. As Wollen puts it:

> The cinema cannot show the truth, or reveal it, because the truth is not out there in the real world, waiting to be photographed. What the cinema can do is produce meanings and meanings can only be plotted, not in relation to some abstract yardstick or criterion of truth, but in relation to other meanings. (Wollen, 1982, p. 91)

However, if counter-cinema's strengths derive from this kind of analysing, then so do its weaknesses. Wollen expresses quite strong reservations about some aspects of Godardian counter-cinema. Godard's refusal of pleasure is grounded in the notion that entertainment cinema is a drug which mollifies the masses into giving up their long-term (millenarian) dreams in favour of ephemeral (false, illusory, deceptive) fantasies. Wollen finds this logic questionable as well as puritanical. He argues that in placing the reality principle before the pleasure principle, Godard overlooks the adaptive nature of the former and the transformative potential of the latter: 'desire, and its representation in fantasy, far from being necessary enemies of revolutionary politics – and its cinematic auxiliary – are necessary conditions' (Wollen, 1982, p. 88). In addition, Godard's suspicion of fiction, which the post-1968 films equate with deception, ideology and mystification, results in a 'flattening out', as Wollen sees it, of the more complex philosophical questioning of appearance and reality, truth and lies that plays a part in his earlier films. Finally, Wollen points out that counter-cinema, by definition, cannot have an absolute existence in its own right, but can only exist as a negation of mainstream film, having been conceived as its antagonist. *Vent d'est* is therefore not revolutionary cinema, but a starting point for work on revolutionary cinema. Ultimately, Wollen and many others were disappointed by the outcome of Godard's 'adventures in the wilderness'. From the mid-1970s onwards Godard gradually reverted to the forms and concerns of art-cinema, leaving the pursuit of counter-cinema to others. As the revolutionary fervour of the late 1960s faded and the new politics of cultural and sexual identity emerged, a new constituency for counter-cinema took shape around feminism.

FEMINIST COUNTER-CINEMA

Feminist counter-cinema theory emerged in the 1970s in tandem with the critique of Hollywood developed by Claire Johnston and Laura Mulvey (see Feminism film theory, p. 354). Johnston and Mulvey argued for the creation of a feminist counter-cinema on the grounds that patriarchal ideology is thoroughly embedded in film technique and cinematic convention:

> If we accept that cinema involves the production of signs, the idea of non-intervention is pure mystification. The sign is always a product. What the camera in fact grasps is the 'natural' world of the dominant ideology. Women's cinema cannot afford such idealism; the 'truth' of our oppression cannot be 'captured' on celluloid with the 'innocence' of the camera: it has to be constructed/manufactured. New meanings have to be created by disrupting the fabric of male bourgeois cinema within the text of the film. (Johnston, 1974, p. 29)

Both Johnston and Mulvey argued that since the narrative conventions, iconographic traditions and identificatory structures of mainstream film were shaped by their development in a patriarchal society, a change in content alone would merely reproduce the bias in the system. Both also rejected the idea of an essential and timeless feminine aesthetic which simply awaited discovery or clarification ('a developed tradition winding through the overt history of cinema like an unseen thread', Mulvey, 1979, p. 7). Instead, they imagined a feminist aesthetic evolved through contestation of existing forms. However, where Mulvey argued for an avant-garde women's cinema ('feminist film practice has ... almost an objective alliance with the radical avant-garde', 1979, p. 4), Johnston, writing under the influence of *Cahiers du Cinéma*, argued for a women's cinema which would reconcile politics with entertainment. Thus Mulvey: 'Women, whose image has continually been stolen ... cannot view the decline of traditional film form with anything more than sentimental regret' (Mulvey, 1975, p. 18), and Johnston: 'In order to counter our objectification in the cinema our collective fantasies must be released: women's cinema must embody the working through of desire: such an objective demands the use of the entertainment film' (Johnston, 1974, p. 31).

Mulvey's radical position was in tune

Feminist form – the exemplary *Jeanne Dielman, 23 Quai du Commerce 1080 Bruxelles*

with its times and quickly achieved wide currency on the feminist film scene. In the year that Mulvey's 'Visual Pleasure and Narrative Cinema' was published, Chantal Akerman completed the film *Jeanne Dielman, 23 Quai du commerce 1080 Bruxelles* (1975) which was received by many feminist critics as the exemplar of Mulvey's 'passionate detachment'. Using a minimalist form comprising long takes, static camerawork and no analytic editing or reverse-shot, Akerman presents the daily existence of a widowed Belgian housewife whose routine chores include prostituting herself to support herself and her son. The three-and-a-half hour film observes the tiny lapses in control building up to Jeanne's loss of self-control with a client, whom she murders. Most of the film's action consists of domestic labour and it is the way that this is filmed that has led feminist critics to see it as a 'discourse of women's looks, through a woman's viewpoint' (Bergstrom, 1977, p. 118).

Mulvey's suspicion of narrative ('Sadism demands a story ...', 1975, p. 14) was also widely shared. Sally Potter's short film *Thriller* (1979), informed by 'Visual Pleasure and Narrative Cinema' and other feminist texts, interrogates and restructures traditional narrative. The film is a reworking of the opera *La Bohème* as a *film noir* investigation by the heroine into the causes of her own death (see *Film noir*, p. 184). It begins where the opera ends, with Mimi's death, and retells its story in the retrospective manner of a criminal investigation. Potter's *The Gold Diggers* (1984) is constructed as a 'semiotic shuffle' with the history of the cinema (Cook, 1984, p. 15) in which two women, Celeste and Ruby, seek answers to the riddle of their own existence as figures in a cinematic landscape. In both films traditional narrative is displaced by reflexive critique and intertextual reference. At the same time, Potter is clearly not an anti-narrative film-maker in the sense that Brakhage and Snow are. Her films enter into dialogue with existing narratives in order to generate new narrative possibilities centring on female subjectivity.

Return to narrative

Potter's early work is situated on the brink of the return to narrative which took place in alternative cinema from the late 1970s. A key figure in this development was Yvonne Rainer. Her films, often described as ironic melodramas, work 'with and against narrative', as Teresa de Lauretis puts it (1987, p. 108), using quotation, contradiction, commentary, interruption and multiple diegeses. Rainer's approach to narrative is pragmatic: 'For me the story is an empty frame on which to hang images and thoughts which need support. I feel no obligation to flesh out this armature with credible details of time and place' (Rainer, 1976, p. 89). Since she began making films in 1972 her work has increasingly moved toward narrative:

> From description of individual feminine experience floating free of social context and narrative hierarchy, to descriptions of individual feminine experience placed in radical juxtaposition against historical events, to explicitly feminist speculations about feminine experience, I have just formulated an evolution which in becoming more explicitly feminist seems to demand a more solid anchoring in narrative conventions. (Rainer, 1985, p. 8)

Interrogating traditional narrative – Sally Potter's *The Gold Diggers*

Rainer is one of many feminist film-makers who have discovered in narrative an indispensable 'strategy of coherence' (De Lauretis, 1987) for mapping differences and making meaning. This conditional rehabilitation of narrative has been accompanied by a growing concern with fantasy and subjectivity. Bette Gordon's *Variety* (1983), Valie Export's *Die Praxis der Liebe* (1985) and Sheila McLaughlin's *She Must be Seeing Things* (1987) all use fantasy, framed by investigative narratives, to explore the formal problems of desire and the look in women's – heterosexual and lesbian – representation (see Feminist film theory, p. 000). With these films, women's counter-cinema rejoins Johnston's 1974 position, although with the benefit of a period of radical negation behind it.

Inevitably this evolution has rendered some feminist films less noticeably avant-garde as their formal problematics are embedded within a narrative infrastructure. Teresa de Lauretis argues that formalist definitions of alternative film have been renderend obsolete with the dissolution of the rigid divide between avant-garde and mass culture. Instead, she suggests that women's cinema is 'guerrilla film', which she defines in the following terms:

> In sum, what I would call alternative films in women's cinema are those which engage the current problems, the real issues, the things actually at stake in feminist communities on a local scale, and which, although informed by a global perspective, do not assume or aim at a universal, multinational audience, but address a particular one in its specific history of struggles and emergence. (De Lauretis, 1990, p. 17)

This description borrows from the theory and practice of Third Cinema (see below), and might also be applied to New Queer Cinema. Between them, these engaged cinemas have redefined the scope and nature of alternative film. Thus the work of radical film-makers such as Trinh T. Minh-ha (see Feminist film theory, p. 364), Isaac Julien, John Greyson and Tracey Moffatt cuts accross traditional categories such as mainstream, art cinema and avant-garde in its effort to address historically specific audiences and engage with precisely located issues. At the same time, changing media technologies have created new fields for formal innovation, ranging from video art and music video to virtual reality and the Internet. After the purism of the 1960s and the formalism of the 1970s the combinatory, eclectic conception of avant-garde is again in the ascendancy under the influence of new politics and new media. To the extent that the current avant-garde has a common project, it is concerned with crossing boundaries between art forms, between traditions and between cultural and social identities.

Selected Reading

Claire Johnston, 'Women's cinema as counter-cinema', in Johnston (ed.), *Notes on Women's Cinema*, London, SEFT, 1974.

Laura Mulvey, 'Visual pleasure and narrative cinema', *Screen* 16(3), autumn 1975.

Yvonne Rainer, 'Yvonne Rainer: interview', *Camera Obscura* no. 1, 1976.

A. L. Rees, *A History of Experimental Film and Video*, London, BFI, 1999.

Peter Wollen, 'Godard and counter-cinema: *Vent d'est*' (1972), 'The two avant-gardes' (1975), '"Ontology" and "materialism" in film' (1976) and 'Semiotic counter-strategies: retrospect 1982', collected in *Readings and Writings*, London, Verso, 1982.

Peter Wollen, 'The avant-gardes: Europe and America', *Framework* no. 14, 1981.

THIRD WORLD AND POSTCOLONIAL CINEMA

Culturally rich, formally innovative, and politically provocative, Third World and postcolonial cinema forms a vital current within world cinema. Taken in a broad sense, 'Third World Cinema', far from being a marginal appendage to First World cinema – Hollywood's 'poor relative' – actually produces most of the world's feature films. If one excludes films made for television, India is the leading producer of fiction films in the world, producing up to 1,000 feature films a year. Asian countries, taken together, produce over half of the yearly world production. Nor is this a recent development. In the 1920s India was already producing more films than Great Britain. Countries like the Philippines were producing over 50 films a year by the 1930s, Hong Kong over 200 by the 1950s. But although the cinematic traditions of many countries later recognised as belonging to the Third World go back to the first decades of this century – Brazil's cinematic *bela epoca* occurred between 1908 and 1911 – it was in the 1960s that Third World cinema as a self-aware movement emerged on the First World film scene by winning prizes and garnering critical praise.

THIRD CINEMA: QUESTIONS OF TERMINOLOGY

The term 'Third World' refers to the colonised, neo-colonised or decolonised nations and 'minorities' whose structural disadvantages have been shaped by the colonial process and the unequal division of international labour. The term itself challenges the colonising vocabulary which posited these nations as 'backward' and 'underdeveloped'. As a political coalition, the 'Third World' broadly coalesced around the enthusiasm generated by anti-colonial struggles in Vietnam and Algeria, and specifically emerged from the 1955 Bandung Conference of 'non-aligned' African and Asian nations. Coined by French demographer Alfred Sauvy in the 1950s by analogy to the revolutionary 'third estate' of France – i.e. the commoners in contrast with first estate (the nobility) and the second (the clergy) – the term posited three worlds: the capitalist first world of Europe, the US, Australia and Japan; the 'second world' of the socialist bloc (China's place in the schema was the object of much debate); and the third world proper.

The fundamental definition of the 'third world' has little to do with crude economic ('the poor'), developmental categories (the 'non-industrialised'), racial ('the non-white'), cultural ('the backward'), or geographical ('The East', 'The South') categories. These are all imprecise because the third world is neither necessarily poor in resources (Mexico, Venezuela and Iraq are rich in oil), nor simply non-white (Argentina, and Ireland, are predominantly white) nor is it non-industrialised (Brazil, Argentina, India all have heavy industries), nor culturally 'backward'. Instead 'Third World' signifies an international experience of protracted structural domination.

In relation to cinema, the term 'Third World' refers to the collectively vast cinematic productions of Asia, Africa and Latin America, and the minoritarian cinema in the first world. Some, such as Roy Armes (1982/1987), define Third World Cinema broadly as the ensemble of films produced by Third World countries (including films produced before the very idea of 'Third World' was current). Others, such as Paul Willemen, prefer to speak of 'Third Cinema', which they see as an ideological project, that is as a body of films adhering to a certain political and aesthetic programme, whether or not they are produced by Third World peoples themselves (see Pines and Willemen, 1989). Originally emerging from the Cuban revolution, from Peronism and Peron's 'third way' in Argentina, and from such film movements as *Cinema Novo* in Brazil, the term 'third cinema' was launched as a rallying cry in the late 1960s by Fernando Solanas and Octavio Getino. They defined third cinema as:

> the cinema that recognizes in [the anti-imperialist struggle in the Third World and its equivalents within the imperialist countries] ... the most gigantic cultural, scientific, and artistic manifestation of our time ... in a word, the decolonization of culture. (Solanas and Getino, 1969/1976)

As long as they are taken not as 'essential' pre-constituted entities, but rather as collective projects to be forged, both 'Third World Cinema' and 'Third Cinema' retain important tactical and polemical uses for a politically inflected cultural practice.

In purely classificatory terms, one can posit overlapping circles of denotation. First, a core circle of 'Third Worldist' films produced by and for Third World people (no matter where those people happen to be) and adhering to the principles of Third Cinema. Second, a wider circle of the cinematic productions of Third World peoples (retroactively defined as such), whether or not the films adhere to the principles of Third Cinema and irrespective of the period of their making. Third, another circle consisting of films made by First or Second World people in support of Third World peoples and adhering to the principles of Third Cinema. And fourth, a final circle, somewhat anomalous in status, at once 'inside' and 'outside', comprising post-1970s diasporic hybrid films, for example those of Mona Hatoum, Isaac Julien, Gurinder Chadha, Hanif Kureishi, which both build on and interrogate the conventions of Third Cinema, and are therefore often referred to as 'post-Third Worldist' or 'postcolonial' (see Postcolonial cinema, p. 124). By far the largest category would be the second, the cinematic productions of countries designated as 'Third World'. This category would include the major traditional film industries of countries like India, Egypt, Mexico, Brazil, Argentina and China, as well as the more recent post-independence or post-revolution industries of countries like Cuba, Algeria, Senegal, Indonesia, and scores of others.

THE ORIGINS OF THIRD WORLD CINEMA

The Third World's cinematic counter-telling basically began with the postwar collapse of the European empires and the emergence of independent Third World nation-states (although there were, of course, implicitly anti-colonial films prior to this period of collapse). In the late 1960s and early 1970s, in the wake of the Vietnamese victory over the French, the Cuban revolution, and Algerian Independence, Third-Worldist film ideology was crystallised in a wave of militant manifesto essays – Glauber Rocha's

Vidas Secas – 'hungry cinema?'

'Aesthetic of Hunger' (1965), Fernando Solanas and Octavio Getino's 'Towards a Third Cinema' (1969) and Julio Garcia Espinosa's 'For an Imperfect Cinema' (1969) – and in declarations and manifestoes from Third World Film Festivals calling for a tri-continental revolution in politics and an aesthetic and narrative revolution in film form. Rocha called for a 'hungry' cinema of 'sad, ugly films', Solanas–Getino for militant guerrilla documentaries, and Espinosa for an 'imperfect' cinema energised by the 'low' forms of popular culture.

Although on one level the 1960s 'new cinemas' within the Third World came in the wake of the European 'new' movements – neo-realism, the French new wave – their politics were far to the left of their European counterparts (see Italian neo-realism, p. 76; The French *nouvelle vague*, p. 80). The manifestoes of the 1960s and 1970s valorised an alternative, independent, anti-imperialist cinema more concerned with provocation and militancy than with *auteurist* expression or consumer satisfaction. The manifestoes contrasted the new cinema not only with Hollywood but also with their own countries' commercial traditions, now viewed as 'bourgeois', 'alienated', and 'colonised'. Just as the French new wave film-makers raged against *le cinéma de papa*, so Brazil's *Cinema Novo* directors, rejected the entertainment-oriented *chanchadas* and the European-style costume epics of film studios like Vera Cruz, much as young Egyptian film-makers rejected the 'Hollywood on the Nile' tradition. And the 'new cinema' directors from India, for example Satyajit Ray, rejected both Hollywood and the commercial tradition of the Bombay musical, preferring the model

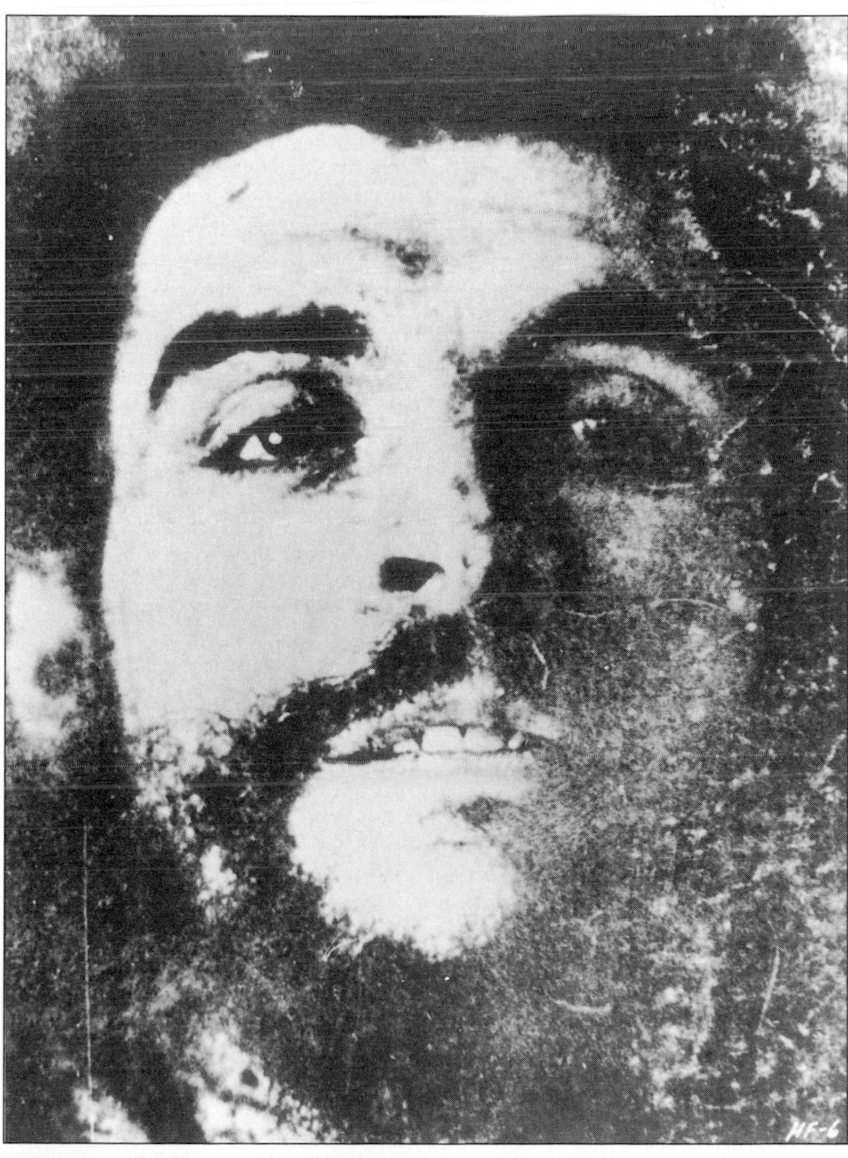

Provocation and militancy – *Hour of the Furnaces*

Not Hollywood on the Nile – *The Sparrow*

of the European art film (see Hindi cinema, p. 127).

In retrospect, the Third World 'new waves' seem to have been overly binaristic in their rejection of antecedent commercial film traditions. The tendency in subsequent years has been to emphasise indigenous precursors and films (see for example Kamal Selim's *Al Azima/The Determination*, 1939, in Egypt, and Dhiren Ganguly's *Bilat Ferat/England Returned*, 1921, in India) and at times to recuperate, if only through parody, consecrated popular traditions. (Buñuel's critical recuperations of popular genres such as the melodrama and the *comedia ranchera*, in his Mexican films of the 1950s, for example, opened a path later followed by directors like Arnaldo Jabor and Raul Ruiz.) After the first, 'euphoric', period of Third World Cinema then, the early manifestoes were critiqued, positions were modified and updated, and cinematic praxis evolved in a whole range of directions.

REWRITING THE PAST

According to Frantz Fanon colonialism is 'not satisfied merely with holding a people in its grip . . . By a kind of perverted logic, it turns to the past of the people, and distorts, disfigures and destroys it' (1964, p. 210). In the face of Eurocentric historicising, Third World and minoritarian film-makers have rewritten their own histories, taken control over their own images, spoken in their own voices. It is not that their films substitute a pristine 'truth' for European 'lies', but that they propose counter truths and counter narratives informed by an anti-colonialist perspective, reclaiming and reaccentuating the events of the past in a vast project of remapping and renaming.

This rewriting has operated within a double time frame: the reinscription of the past inevitably also rewrites the present. While revisionist historical films such as Luis Alberto Lamata's *Jericó* (1991) and Carlos Diegues's *Quilombo* (1984) challenged Eurocentric accounts of the early years of European conquest and slavery, respectively, other films have rewritten more recent events. Med Hondo's *Sarraounia* (*Queen Sarraounia*, 1986) for example, tells of an African woman at the end of the nineteenth century who outwitted the French and saved her people from colonialism. Filipino filmmaker Eddie Romero's *Ganito Kami Noon, Papano Kayo Ngayon* (*This is the Way We Were Then: How are You Now?*, 1976) treats the nationalist coming to consciousness of a Filipino just before the war against Spain in the 1890s. And Jorge Sanjinés's *El Coraje del Pueblo* (*Courage of the People*, 1971) dramatically restages a 1967 massacre of Bolivian tin miners, using miners as actors.

A number of films were made during the anti-colonial struggles themselves, from NLF films in Algeria (in the late 1950s), through Fidelista films during the anti-Battista campaign in the same period, to FRELIMO films in Mozambique and the work of the Radio Venceremos Film and Video Collective and the El Salvador Film Institute in El Salvador, in the 1970s.

But many more films were made with the luxury of historical hindsight, after the consolidation of independence. In the wake of the revolution of 1948, the Chinese film industry celebrated the victory against the Kuomintang in films like Chang Chun-hsiang's *Red Banner on Green Rock* (1951) and Leonid Varlamov's *Victory of the Chinese People* (1950). Ousmane Sembène's *Emitai* (1972), meanwhile, reached back into the relatively recent past of Senegalese resistance to French colonialism during the Second World War, and specifically the refusal of Diola women to supply French soldiers with rice. The same director's *Camp de Thiaroye* (*The camp at Thiaroy*, 1988) treats a similar rebellion of Senegalese soldiers who refuse to accept unequal pay in the French army, a refusal for which they are unceremoniously massacred. Lakhdar-Hamina's *Assifat al-Aouraz* (*Wind from the Aures*, 1965) tells a fictional story about Algerian popular struggle against the French. His *Chronicle of the Years of Embers* (1975) offers an epic account of the century of struggle that culminated in the Algerian revolution. Omar Khleifi's *Al-Fajr* (*The Dawn*, 1966) and *Fallaga* (*The Fellaheen*, 1970) deal with the Tunisian liberation struggle, Sarah Maldoror's *Sambizanga* (1972) with the liberation struggle in Mozambique, Ahmed Rachedi's compilation film *L'Aube des Damnés* (*Dawn of the Damned*, 1965) with anti-colonial struggles throughout Africa.

Many of the Third World films concerned with rewriting the past conduct a struggle on two fronts, at once political and aesthetic, synthesising revisionist historiography with formal innovation. Humberto Solás's *Lucia* (1969) rejects the conventional single fiction in favour of a complex tripartite structure. Each part is set in a different historical period (colonial 1895, bourgeois revolutionary 1933, the post-revolutionary 1960), each revolves around a woman named Lucia (creole aristocrat, middle-class urban, rural worker class), each is filmed in a distinct genre style (Viscontian tragic melodrama, Bertolucci-style new wave political and existential drama, Brechtian farce) and each has its own visual features (dark, hazy, brightly lit). The result is to suggest that historical interpretation is inseparable from stylistic mediation. Med Hondo's *Soleil O* (1970), which mixes documentary and fiction, dream and dance in a poetic exorcism of colonialism has a similar effect. The same director's *West Indies* (1979) sets a cinematic opera on a slave ship, calling attention to both oppression and resistance during five centuries of colonial domination and revolt. A large number of films mingle documentary and fiction, in a politicised variation on a stylistic trademark of the *nouvelle vague*. Manuel Octavio Gomez's *First Charge of the Machete* (1969), for example, reconstructs a 1868 battle against the Spanish in Cuba in the manner of a contemporary documentary, using high contrast film, hand-held camera, direct-to-camera interviews, ambient light, and so forth.

ALLEGORICAL INTERPRETATIONS

Fredric Jameson has argued that all Third World 'texts' are 'necessarily allegorical'. Even those texts invested with an apparently private or libidinal dynamic 'project a political dimension in the form of national allegory: the story of the private individual destiny is always an allegory of the embattled situation of the public third-world culture and society' (Jameson, 1986, p. 69; for an excellent critique see Aijaz Ahmad, 1986).

Although it is difficult to endorse Jameson's somewhat hasty totalisation of all Third World texts as allegorical – because it is impossible to posit any single artistic strategy as uniquely appropriate to the cultural productions of an entity as heterogeneous as the Third World, and allegory is in any case relevant to cultural productions elsewhere, including those of the First World – the concept of allegory is nonetheless a useful one. If understood in a broad sense, as any kind of oblique or synecdochic utterance soliciting hermeneutic completion or deciphering, 'allegory' is a productive category for dealing with many Third World films.

In the 1930s and 1940s in India, the female star 'fearless Nadia' rescued oppressed peoples from foreign tyrants, in ways which were read at the time as anti-British allegories (see Behroze Gandhy and Rosie Thomas, 1991). In the more recent history of Third World Cinema we find at least two major strands of allegory. First, there are the teleological Marxist-inflected nationalist allegories of the early period, where history is revealed as the progressive unfolding of an immanent historical design. Glauber Rocha's *Deus e o Diabo na Terra do Sol* (*Black God, White Devil*, 1964), for example, allegorises the people's coming to political consciousness through a stylised tale about a cowherd who moves from religious millenarianism through outlaw banditry and finally to revolution. Second, we have the modernist self-deconstructing allegories of the later period, where the focus shifts from the 'figural' signification of the onward march of history to the fragmentary nature of the discourse itself. Here, allegory is deployed as a privileged instance of language-consciousness in the context of the felt loss of larger historical purpose. Rogerio Sganzerla's *Bandido as Luz Vermelha* (*Red Light Bandit*, 1969), for instance, posits a homology, as Ismail Xavier points out, between a red-light district in a Third World country as a realm of 'garbage' and the film itself as a collection of film and mass-media refuse, and thus refuses the redemptive narrative of an earlier period (Xavier, 1982, pp. 124–63). A third variant, neither teleological nor modernist, might be found in those films where allegory serves as a form of protective camouflage against censorious regimes – where, for instance, the film uses the past to speak of the present, as in de Andrade's *Os Inconfidentes* (The Conspirators, 1971), or subversively adapts a classic, as in dos Santos's adaptation of Machado de Assis' *O Alienista* (*The Psychiatrist*, 1970).

THE DECLINE OF THE THIRD WORLDIST PARADIGM

During the 1980s and 1990s, Third Worldist euphoria has slowly been ebbing away in the light of the collapse of communism, the frustration of the hoped-for 'tricontinental revolution' (with Ho Chi Minh, Fanon, and Che Guevara as talismanic figures), the realisation that the 'wretched of the earth' are not unanimously revolutionary (nor necessarily allies to one another), the appearance of an array of Third World despots, and the recognition that international geopolitics and the global economic system have obliged even socialist regimes to make a sort of peace with transnational capitalism.

The same period also witnessed a terminological crisis in relation to the term 'Third World' itself, which was increasingly seen as an inconvenient relic of a more militant period. Arguing from a Marxist perspective, Aijaz Ahmad argues that Third World theory is an 'open-ended ideological interpellation' that papers over class oppression in all three worlds, while limiting socialism to the now non-existent 'second world' (see Ahmad, 1986, and Burton, 1985). As Geoffrey Reeves puts it, the Third World concept homogenises

> markedly different national histories, experiences of European colonialism and extent of incorporation into capitalist production and exchange relations, levels and diversity of industrialization and economic development and ethnic, racial, linguistic, religious, and class differences. (Reeves, 1993, p. 10)

The decline of 'Third Worldist euphoria' brought with it a rethinking of political, cultural and aesthetic possibilities. As the rhetoric of revolution began to be greeted with a certain scepticism, cultural and political critique began to develop in alternative ways. Such developments were 'post-Third Worldist' in that, while assuming the fundamental legitimacy of the anti-colonialist movement, they attempted to explore the social and ideological fissures within the Third World nations (see Shohat and Stam, 1994).

As a result both of external pressures and internal self-questioning, the cinema was itself subject to transformation. The anti-colonial thrust of earlier films gradually gave way to more diversified themes and aesthetic models as film-makers partially discarded the didactic model predominant in the 1960s in favour of a postmodern 'politics of pleasure', incorporating music, humour and sexuality. (This diversification is evident in the trajectories of individual film-makers – see the difference between dos Santos *Vidas Secas*, from 1963, and his *Na Estrada da Vida* (*Road of Life*) of 1980, or Solanas's *La Hora de los Hornos* (*Hour of the Furnaces*) of 1969 and his *Tangos: Exilios de Gardel* of 1983.)

Another development in this transformation was to do with an increased awareness of feminism. Largely produced by men, Third Worldist films were not generally concerned with a feminist critique of nationalist discourse. They often favoured the generic (and gendered) space of heroic confrontations, whether set in the streets, the casbah, the mountains, the jungle. The minimal feminine presence corresponded, more or less, to the place assigned women both in the anti-colonialist revolutions and within Third Worldist discourse. Women occasionally carried the bombs, as in *Battle of Algiers*, but only in the name of the nation. More often women were made to carry the 'burden' of national allegory (the woman dancing with the flag in *Battle of Algiers*, the prostitute whose image is underscored by the national anthem in *La Hora de los Hornos*) or scapegoated as personifications of imperialism (the allegorical 'whore of Babylon' figure in Rocha's films). Gender contradictions were subordinated to anti-colonial struggle: women were expected to 'wait their turn'. The minoritarian or post Third Worldist films of the 1980s and 1990s, by contrast, while not so much rejecting the nation as interrogating its repressions and limits, suggest that a purely nationalist discourse is gravely limited. Such discourse cannot apprehend the layered, dissonant identities of diasporic or postcolonial subjectivity and focuses too much on the public sphere. So, films like Mona Hatoum's *Measures of Distance* (1988), Tracey Moffatt's *Nice Coloured Girls* (1987), and Gurinder Chadha's *Bhaji on the Beach* (1993), use the camera less as revolutionary weapon than as monitor of the gendered and sexualised realms of the personal and the domestic, seen as integral but repressed aspects of collective history.

Displaying a growing scepticism with regard to meta-narratives of liberation, these post-Third Worldist films, do not, however, necessarily abandon the notion that emancipation is worth fighting for. But rather than flee from contradiction, they install doubt and crisis at the very core of the films. Rather than enunciating a grand anti-colonial meta-narrative, they favour heteroglossic proliferations of difference within polygeneric narratives, seen not as embodiments of a single truth but rather as energising political and aesthetic forms of communitarian self-construction.

A number of post-Third Worldist diasporic film and video works explicitly link issues of postcolonial identity to issues of aesthetics. The Sankofa production *The Passion of Remembrance* (1986) thematises

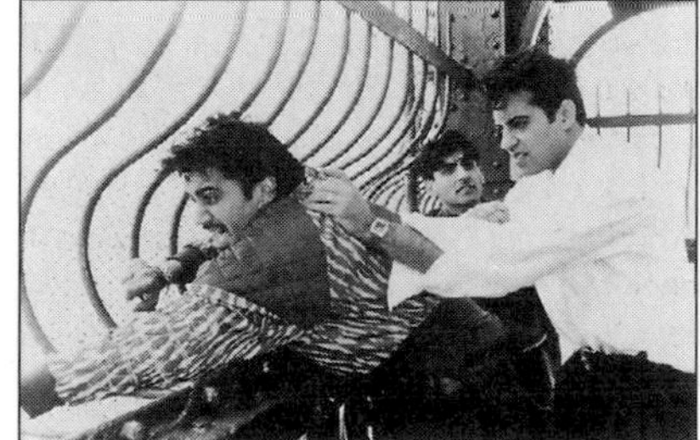

Cinemas of diaspora and hybridity: *Bhaji on the Beach*

post-Third Worldist discourses and the fractured identities (in this case black British identity) by staging a 'polylogue' between the slightly puritanical 1960s black radical voice of nationalist militancy, and the 'new,' more playful voices of gays and lesbian women, all within a profoundly anti-illusionist aesthetic. And works such as Assia Djebbar's *La Nouba des Femmes du Mont Chenoua* (*The Nouba of the Women of Mount Chenoua*, 1979), Elia Suleiman's *Homage by Assassination* (1991), and Tracey Moffatt's *Night Cries* (1990) break away from earlier macro-narratives of national liberation, reimagining the nation as a heteroglossic multiplicity. While remaining anti-colonialist, these experimental films call attention to the diversity of experiences within and across nations. Colonialism had simultaneously aggregated communities fissured by glaring cultural differences and separated communities marked by equally glaring commonalities, and these films suggest that many Third-World nation-states were highly artificial and contradictory entities. The films produced by Third World 'postcolonials' residing in the First World (the forced or voluntary exile of Third World film-makers has led to a kind of diasporic Third World cinema within the First World), in particular, raise questions about dislocated identities in a world increasingly marked by the mobility of goods, ideas, and peoples that follows on from the 'multinationalisation' of the global economy.

FOURTH WORLD AND INDIGENOUS MEDIA

The concept of the 'Third World' also obscures the presence of a 'Fourth World' existing within all of the other worlds, the world of those peoples variously called 'indigenous', 'tribal', or 'first nations', the descendants of the original inhabitants of territories subsequently subject to alien conquest or settlement. (As many as 3,000 native nations, representing some 250 million people, according to some estimates, function within the 200 states that assert sovereignty over them.)

First World people first became 'sensitised' to the situation of Fourth World peoples when the diverse campaigns mobilised around the global ecological crisis in the 1980s and 1990s insisted that indigenous peoples have often been the best custodians of natural resources. Film-makers translated this awareness, for better or worse, in such ecologically minded films as John Boorman's *The Emerald Forest* (1985), Ruy Guerra's *Quarup* (1989), Hector Babenco's *At Play in the Fields of the Lord* (1991), and even Menahem Golan's *The Forbidden Dance* (1990).

The role of Fourth World people in First World documentaries (for example, *When the Mountains Tremble*, an account of Rigoberta Menchu and the indigenous peoples of Guatemala) and in Third World films is not, of course, just a recent phenomenon. In the 1950s and 1960s, for example, the Cuzco School, in Peru, made mixed-mode documentary fictions such as *Kukuli* (1961) and *Jarawu* (1966) in the Quechua language. In Bolivia, Jorge Sanjinés made feature films in Quechua such as *Yawar Mallku* (*Blood of the Condor*, 1969), which speaks of popular indigenous revolts against US-supported policies of sterilisation, and in Aymara, *Ukamau* (1966), with the collaboration of the indigenous people themselves.

Fourth World peoples more usually appear in 'ethnographic films', which of late have attempted to divest themselves of vestigial colonialist attitudes. While in the old ethnographic films, self-confident 'scientific' voice-overs purported to deliver the 'truth' about subject peoples unable to answer back (while sometimes prodding the 'natives' to perform practices long abandoned), the new ethnographic films strive for 'shared film-making', 'participatory film-making', 'dialogical anthropology', 'reflexive distance', and 'interactive film-making' (see, for example, David McDougall, 1995). This new humility on the part of film-makers is evidenced in a number of documentary and experimental films which discard the implicit elitism of the pedagogical or ethnographic model in favour of a model which emphasises instead the relative, the plural, and the contingent. Film-makers have experienced a salutary self-doubt about their capacity to speak 'for' the other. In Sérgio Bianchi's *Mato Eles?* (*Should I Kill Them?*, 1983), a venerable Indian asks the director exactly how much money he made on the film. It is the kind of inconvenient question which would normally make its way to the editing-room trashcan. But Bianchi leaves the question in and thus voluntarily exposes his work to some of the risks of a real dialogue, and to the potential challenge offered by interlocutors. It is no longer a matter of how one party represents the other, but rather how one collaborates with the other. The goal, rarely achieved as yet becomes to guarantee the effective participation of the 'other' in all phases of production.

POSTCOLONIAL CINEMA

The issue of media appropriations of the Fourth World throws into sharp focus some of the theoretical ambiguities of a term that became important in the late 1980s: 'postcoloniality'. While Fourth World peoples often invest a great deal in a discourse of territorial claims, symbiotic links to nature, and active resistance to colonial incursions, postcolonial thought stresses deterritorialisation, the artificial, the constructed nature of nationalism and national borders, and the obsolescence of anti-colonialist discourse.

The wide adoption, since the late 1980s, of the term 'postcolonial' to designate work thematising issues emerging from colonial relations and their aftermath, clearly coincided with the eclipse of the older Third World paradigm.

Since the 'post' in 'postcolonial' suggests, on one level, a stage 'after' the demise of colonialism, it is imbued with an ambiguous spatio-temporality. 'Postcolonial' tends to be associated with 'Third World' countries that gained independence after the Second World War, yet it also refers to the 'Third World' diasporic presence within 'First World' conurbations. The term 'postcolonial', as Ella Shohat suggests, blurs the assignment of perspectives (Shohat, 1992). So: given that the colonial experience is shared, albeit asymmetrically, by (ex)coloniser and (ex)colonised, does the 'post' indicate the perspective of the ex-colonised (Algerian, for example), the ex-coloniser (in this case, French), the ex-colonial settler (*pied noir*), or the displaced hybrid in the metropole (Algerian in Paris)? Since most of the world is now living 'after' colonialism, the 'post' might seem to have the effect of neutralising significant differences between, say, France and Algeria, Britain and Iraq, the US and Brazil. Furthermore, by implying that colonialism is over, the term 'postcolonial' risks obscuring the debilitating and enduring residues of colonialism.

Postcolonial theory is one of many theories to become prominent in the 1980s and 1990s that is concerned with complex, multi-layered identities and subjectivities. Terms having to do with various forms of cultural mixing, e.g. religious mixing (syncretism), botanical mixing (hybridity), linguistic (creolisation), and human–genetic mixing (*mestizaje*), have proliferated as a result of this concern.

The emphasis on various forms of 'mixedness' in postcolonial writing calls attention to the multiple identities, already present under colonialism, but further complicated by the geographical displacements characteristic of the post-independence era. Presupposing a theoretical framework that is influenced by anti-essentialist poststructuralism and refuses to police identity along purist either/or lines – thus reacting both against the colonialist phobias and the fetish of racial purity – 'hybridity theory' also situates itself in opposition to the overly rigid lines of identity drawn by Third Worldist discourse. In the historical moment of the post-independence displacements which generated dually or even multiply-hyphenated identities (Franco-Algerian, Indo-Canadian, Palestinian-Lebanese-British, Indo-Ugandan-American, Egyptian-Lebanese-Brazilian) it is clear that such lines can no longer be drawn with any confidence.

Post-independence identities, as the product of a conflictual merging, feature a more stressful hyphen, as it were, than those multiple identities deriving from a simple move from one country to another.

Diasporic identities, moreover, cannot be seen as homogeneous. Displacements are often piled onto other displacements. A number of films – among them Stephen Frears's *Sammy and Rosie Get Laid* (1987), Gurinder Chadha's *Bhaji on the Beach* and Isaac Julien's *Young Soul Rebels* (1991) – bear witness to the tense hybridity of former colonials growing up in what was once the 'motherland'. In the multicultural neighbourhood of *Sammy and Rosie Get Laid*, the inhabitants have 'lines out', as it were, to the formerly colonised parts of the globe. Other films focus on diaspora communities living in countries which, if not a former imperial master, at least form part of a powerful First World. This is the case for example of the Indian diaspora in Canada in Srinivas Krishna's *Masala* (1991) or the US (*Mississippi Masala*, 1991), or the Iranian diaspora in New York in Parviz Sayyad's *The Mission* (1983). Indeed, one might speak of a genre of postcolonial hybrid films. This would also include such films as John Akomfrah's *Testament* (1988, about a Ghanaian in England), Tefvik Baser's *Abschied vom Falschen Paradies* (*Farewell to False Paradise*, 1989, Turks in Germany), Barry Alexander Brown's *Lonely in America* (1990, Indians in the US), Jocelyn Saab's *The Razor's Edge* (1985, Lebanese in Paris), Ghasem Ebrahimian's *The Suitors* (1988, Iranians in the US), Mehdi Charef's *Le Thé au Harem d'Archimède* (*Tea in the Harem*, 1984, Algerians in France) and Stanley Kwan's *Full Moon in New York* (1990, Chinese in the US).

Postcolonial theory deals very effectively with the cultural contradictions and syncretisms generated by the global circulation of peoples and cultural goods in a mediated and interconnected world. What is at stake is a kind of commodified or mass-mediated syncretism. One finds proleptic expression of this kind of syncretism in the Indian film *Shree 420* (Mr 420, 1955), directed by Raj Kapoor, in which the Chaplinesque tramp figure (Kapoor) sings '*Mera joota hai Japani* ... My shoes are Japanese/My trousers are English/My red cap is Russian/But my heart is Indian'. (The song is cited in *Mississippi Masala*.) Here the protagonist insists that his syncretism is merely sartorial, since while his clothes are foreign, his heart is still Indian.

The culinary metaphors typical of multicultural discourse often imply a fondness for this kind of mélange. Significantly, Indian film-makers speak of blending the *masalas* – literally, Hindi for 'spices', but metaphorically, an expression for 'creating something new out of old ingredients' – as a key to their recipe for making films (see Rosie Thomas, 1985). Indeed, as we've seen, the word *masala* forms part of the titles of two Indian diasporic films, *Masala* and *Mississippi Masala*. In the former film, the god Krishna, portrayed as a gross hedonist, appears to a nostalgic Indian grandmother thanks to an interactive VCR. While mocking the official multiculturalism of Canada, the filmic style of this serves up a kind of *masala*, where the language of the Hindu 'mythological' mingles with the language of MTV and the mass media.

The fact that racists tropes have been reversed and purist notions of identity rethought in postcolonial writing and cinema should not obscure the vexing question of the agency involved in 'postcolonial hybridity'. A celebration of syncretism and hybridity *per se*, if it is not articulated with questions of hegemony, risks sanctifying the *fait accompli* of colonial violence. As a descriptive catch-all term, 'hybridity' fails to discriminate between the diverse modalities of hybridity, such as: obligatory assimilation, political cooptation, cultural mimicry, and so forth. Syncretism, in other words, is power laden and asymmetrical. (Africans in the New World were virtually forced to syncretise as a way of concealing and thus retaining their own religious practices behind a Euro-Christian façade.) Nevertheless, however problematic the notion of hybridity or syncretism may be, as an aesthetic strategy, as we will see, it has been very important.

ALTERNATIVE AESTHETIC STRATEGIES

Post-Third Worldist, minoritarian, and postcolonial cinemas have explored a wide spectrum of alternative aesthetics. This spectrum includes films (and videos) that bypass the formal conventions of dramatic realism in favour of such modes and strategies as the carnivalesque (Arthur Omar's *Triste Tropico*, 1977), the anthropophagous (dos Santos's *Como Era Gostoso Meu Frances* (*How Tasty was My Frenchman*, 1971)), the magical realist (Ruy Guerra's *Erendira*, 1983), the reflexive modernist (Chahine's *Alexandria Why?*, 1979) and the resistant postmodernist (Isaac Julien's *Young Soul Rebels*, 1991). These alternative aesthetics are often rooted in non-realist, often non-western or para-western cultural traditions featuring other historical rhythms, other narrative structures, other views of the body, sexuality, spirituality, and the collective life. Ideologically post-Third Worldist, they interrogate nationalist discourse through the grids of class, gender, diasporic and sexual identities. Many incorporate para-modern traditions into clearly modernising or postmodernising aesthetics, and thus problematise facile dichotomies such as traditional and modern, realist and modernist, modernist and postmodernist.

One often encounters the view that Third World art or cultural practices are untouched by avant-gardist modernism or mass-mediated postmodernism. This view is often subliminally imbricated with the description of the Third World as 'underdeveloped', or 'developing', as if it lived in another time zone apart from the global system of the capitalist world. Like the sociology of 'modernisation' and the economics of 'development', the aesthetics of modernism (and of postmodernism) often covertly assumes a telos toward which Third World cultural practices are presumed to be evolving. The Third World, in this view, is condemned to a perpetual game of catch-up in which it can only repeat in a contorted way the history of the 'advanced' world. (A more adequate formulation would, perhaps see time as scrambled and palimpsestic in all the worlds, with the pre-modern, the modern, the postmodern and the para-modern coexisting globally, although the 'dominant' might vary from region to region.)

The Third World, however, has known many modernist and para-modernist movements. Quite apart from the confluence of Brechtian modernism and Marxist modernisation in the 'new cinemas' of Cuba (Alea), Brazil (Guerra), Senegal (Sembene), and India (Sen) in the 1960s and 1970s, there have been many modernist and avant-garde films in the Third World, going all the way back to films like *Rex Lustig* and Adalberto Kemeny's *Sao Paulo: Sinfonia de uma Metropolis* (Sao Paulo: *Symphony of a Metropoli*, 1928) and Mario Peixoto's *Limite* (1930), both from Brazil, and forward through the Senegalese director Djibril Diop Mambety's narratively digressive *Touki Bouki* (1973) and, from Mauritania, Med Hondo's stylised *Soleil O* (1970) and *West Indies* (1975) to the underground movements of Argentina and Brazil, through Kidlat Tahimik's ironic anti-colonialist experiments in the Philippines.

One cannot assume, then, that 'avant-garde' always means white and European, or that Third World art is always realist or pre-modern. On the contrary, vast regions of the world, and long periods of artistic history, have shown little allegiance to or even interest in realism. Much African art, for example, has cultivated what Robert Farris Thompson calls 'mid-point mimesis', i.e. a style that avoids both illusionistic realism and hyperabstraction (Thompson, 1973). And in India, a two-thousand year tradition of theatre circles back to the classical Sanskrit drama, which tells the myths of Hindu culture through an aesthetic based less on coherent character and linear plot than on the subtle modulations of mood and feeling (*rasa*).

Syncretism

Syncretism becomes particularly appropriate to Indian cinema with reference to cinema language. The popular Hindi films of the 1950s, for example, as Ravi Vasudevan points out, mingled plots drawn from Hindu mythology and from Hollywood, with aesthetic styles ranging from a relatively realist mode to anti-illusionistic tableaux effects rooted in folk painting. Many of these films were condemned by critics for what, in retrospect, appears to be their aesthetic strength – their mixing of cultural and cinematic mode.

Syncretism and hybridity have also been crucial thematic and aesthetic resources in Caribbean and Latin American Cinema. The region is, in any case, rich in neologisms which evoke ideas of mixture: *mestizaje, diversalite, creolite, Antillanite, raza cosmica*.

Mexican film-makers like Emilio Fernandez ('El Indio'), working with Gabriel Figueroa, carried on the tradition of the Mexican painters (Riveira, Siqueiro Orozco) by forging a syncretistic mélange of Hollywood aesthetics with Mexican muralism. Paul Leduc picks up the same tradition at a later point, first in his *Frida* (1985), where he creates a cinematic analogue to the style of Frida Kahlo's paintings and later in his *Barroco* (1989), a free adaptation of Alejo Carpentier's *Concierto Barroco* (1974), where the themes of *mestizaje*, artistic syncretism and colonialism all come into play. Like the novel, the film has us make the same journey as Columbus and the conquistadores, but in reverse, with Mexico as the starting point. The novel's two central characters, the Mexican mestizo Amo and the Afro-Caribbean Filomenio personify the racially synthetic character of Latin American culture. With scenes set in Mexico, Cuba, Spain and Italy, the film offers us a tour of the syncretic cultures of the Americas (during which we encounter indigenous fertility rituals, Afro-carnivals, Christian Holy Week processions) along with a compendium of musical styles: mairachi, Andalusian songs, salsa, bolero, flamenco, Yoruba ceremonial music, Catholic liturgical chants, in a baroque concert of musical tensions and affinities. Thus *Barroco* roots its images and sounds in a culture at once indigenous, African, Moorish–Spanish, Sephardi–Jewish and European–Christian.

Mexico is not the only South American country producing such syncretic films. In Brazil, dos Santos's *O Amuleto de Ogum* (*Ogum's Amulet*, 1975) celebrates umbanda, the Brazilian religion which combines Afro-Brazilian elements – the *orixas*, a central belief in spirit possession – with Catholicism, Kabala, and the spiritism of Alain Kardec. *O Amuleto* simply assumes *umbandista* values without explaining or justifying them to the uninitiated. The audience is presumed to recognise the ceremony which 'closes' the protagonist's body, and to recognise his protection by Ogum – the warrior god of metal and the symbol, in Brazil, of the struggle for justice. At the same time, the film does not idealise *umbanda*: one priest in the film works for popular liberation; the other is a greedy charlatan.

Ava y Gabriel (1990), by the Caribbean (Curaçao) film-maker Felix de Rooy, meanwhile, finds artistic equivalents for the theme of hybridity in evidence elsewhere. The story revolves around a black painter in Dutch-dominated Curaçao in 1948 who wants to paint a black Madonna. Syncretism in *Ava y Gabriel* is to be found both in its painterliness and its use of language: the film is spoken in a number of languages – Dutch, English, French, and Papiamento, the last itself already a mixture of Dutch, Spanish and African languages. Raul Ruiz, finally, although he does not explicitly thematise syncretism or *mestizaje* can be seen as a syncretic diasporic artist, in that he takes all of the world's myths and forms and fictions as his province in a dazzling *combinatoire* with multicultural overtones but without a multicultural agenda. In films like *Troi couronnes du matelot* (*Three Crowns of the Sailor*, 1983), Ruiz practises an 'aesthetic of digression', multiplying stories but always returning to a central theme or situation. Far from an austere 'aesthetic of hunger', Ruiz practises a gluttonous absorption and proliferation of styles. Within Ruiz's narratological syncretism, the entire world becomes a story or image bank on which to draw.

Archaic sources and para-modern aesthetics

As was said before, (post-) Third World artists have often drawn on the most traditional elements of their cultures, elements less 'pre-modern' than 'para-modern'. (In the arts, the distinction archaic/modernist is often non-pertinent, in that both share a refusal of the conventions of mimetic realism. It is thus less a question of juxtaposing the archaic and the modern than deploying the putatively archaic (carnival, Afro-diasporic religion, magic) in order, paradoxically, to modernise, in a dissonant temporality which combines an imaginary past communitas with an equally imaginary future utopia. In their attempts to forge a liberatory language, alternative film traditions draw on para-modern phenomena such as popular religion and ritual magic. Here again we encounter syncretism and hybridity. In some recent African films such as Souleymane Cisse's *Yeelen* (1987), *Jitt* (1992), and *Kasarmu Ce* (*This Land is Ours*, 1991), magical spirits become an aesthetic resource, a means for breaking away, often in comical ways, from the linear, cause-and-effect conventions of dominant cinema.

The values of African religious culture have come to inform a good deal of Afro-diasporic cinema: for example, Brazilian films like Rocha's *Barravento* (1962), Cavalcanti's *A Forca de Xango* (*The Force of Xango*, 1977), Cuban films like *Patakin* (Gomez, 1983)and *Ogum*, and African-American films like Julie Dash's *Daughters of the Dust* (1991), all of which inscribe African (usually Yoruba) religious symbolism and practice. Indeed, the preference for Yoruba religious symbolism is itself significant, since the performing arts – music, dance, costume, narrative, poetry – are absolutely integral to the religion itself, unlike other religions where the performing arts are subordinated to theology and sacred texts.

Another element of 'archaic' culture is orality: oral stories themselves and oral methods of storytelling. Many films present 'bottom up' history conveyed through popular memory, legitimising oral history by 'inscribing' it on the screen. History, these films suggest, can also take the oral form of stories, myths, and songs passed on from generation to generation.

The fecundating power of oral tradition is especially apparent in African and Afro-diasporic cinema. *Yeelen*, for example, stages one of the oral epics, a kind of quest or initiation story, of the Bambara people. In Africa, the reinscription of the oral has often served a practical purpose: Sembène, for example, turned from novelist to film-maker in order to reach non-literate audiences. He wanted to become the 'mouth and ears' of society, the one who 'reflects and synthesizes the problems, the struggles, and the hopes of his people' (Sembène, quoted in Pfaff, 1984, p. 29).

Here the cinema inherits the social function (but not the conservative ideology) of the *griot*, the oral archivist of the tribe, the praise singer who tells of births, deaths, victories and defeats. (The communal expression of the *griot* paradigm might be contrasted with the more individualist '*caméra stylo*' of the French new wave, rooted in the romantic notion of the heroically individual *auteur*.) Although *griots per se* are increasingly marginal to contemporary African life (indeed, Momar Thiam's *Sa Dagga*, 1982 charts the arc of their decline) their style of oral narration, deployed as a formal resource, informs a number of African and Afro-diasporic films (see Bachy, 1989). In Babacar Samb-Makharam's *Jom ou L'Histoire d'un Peuple* (*Jom, or History of a People*, 1981), for example, a *griot*-narrator narrates the themes of the film, often direct to camera. Writing about the use of narrative in Gaston Kaboré's *Wend Kunni* (1982), Manthia Diawara delineates some of the mediations which intervene between the oral traditions themselves and their filmic re-elaboration. More important than the more superficial traces of oral literature in film (presence of the *griot*, heroes and heroines borrowed from the oral tradition), he argues, are the deep structural transformations the cinema effects in the narrative points of view. Rather than merely being 'faithful' to the oral tradition, in other words, films can transform that tradition. *Wend Kunni*, for example, 'incorporates an oral rendering of the tale which it also subverts'. If the *griot*'s narrative implies a restoration of the traditional order, the film points to the hope of a new order. The film thus practises the 'subversive deployment of orality', deterritorialising the story and transforming its meaning (Diawara, 1989).

But oral-inflected narratives are hardly limited to African films, nor are *griots* the only agents of oral storytelling. Felix de Rooy's *Almacita di Desolato* (1986) weaves legends from Curaçao, Aruba and Bonnaire to narrate a symbolic battle between creative and destructive forces in a turn-of-the-century Afro-community in Curaçao. In both Gerima's *Ashes and Embers* and Dash's *Daughters of the Dust*, the voiced tales of elderly women relate repressed histories of resistance passed down across the generations (see Taylor, 1986).

The question of orality, then, illustrates in a striking way the folly of imposing a linear narrative of cultural 'progress' in the manner of 'development' theory, which sees people in traditional societies as mired in an inert pre-literate past, incapable of change and agency. In the arts, the aesthetic reinvoicing of tradition can shore up collective agency in the present – favouring collective engagement over consumerist entertainment, and participation over passivity (see Gabriel, 1989).

Selected Reading

Aijaz Ahmad, 'Jameson's rhetoric of otherness and the "national allegory"', *Social Text* no. 15, autumn 1986.

Manuel Alvarado, John King and Ana Lopez (eds), *Meditating Two Worlds*, London, BFI, 1993.

Teshome Gabriel, 'Towards a critical theory of Third World films', in Pines and Willemen, *Third Cinema*.

Fredric Jameson, 'Third World literature in the era of multinational capitalism', *Social Text* no. 15, autumn 1986.

Jim Pines and Paul Willemen (eds), *Questions of Third Cinema*, London, BFI, 1989.

Ella Shohat, 'Notes on the postcolonial', *Social Text* nos 31/32, 1991.

Ella Shohat and Robert Stam, *Unthinking Eurocentrism: Multiculturalism and the Media*, London, Routledge, 1994.

Fernando Solanas and Octavio Getino, 'Towards a Third cinema', 1969; in Fusco, 1987

Rosie Thomas, 'Indian cinema: pleasures and popularity', *Screen* 26(3–4), 1985.

Vidas secas (Barren Lives) (Brazil 1963 *p.c* – Producoes Cinematograficas L.C. Barreto et al.; *d* – Nelson Pereira dos Santos; sd)

Apart from low budgets, import duties on materials, and 'under the line' production costs many times higher than in the west, Third World film-makers also confront limited, less affluent markets than those of the First World. Furthermore, they must compete with glossy, high-budget foreign films.

'Hunger' characterises not only the subject and aesthetic of *Vidas secas*, but also its production methods. The total production cost of the film was $25,000, while John Ford's *The Grapes of Wrath*, made twenty-three years earlier and on a similar theme, cost thirty times as much. Based like *The Grapes of Wrath* on a naturalist novel, the film tells the story of migrants driven by drought from the Brazilian northeast. The trajectory of one peasant family comes to encapsulate the destiny of thousands of oppressed migrants. *Vidas secas* cinematises the novel's third-person 'indirect free style' into a more or less direct, but still third-person, presentation of a character's thoughts and feelings. The material is articulated through the points of view of the characters, within a hierarchy of power that passes from Fabiano to his wife Vitoria down to the two boys and even the dog. We are given a kind of democratic distribution of subjectivity, deploying diverse cinematic registers: point-of-view editing, subjectivised camera movement: exposure (a blanched, overexposed shot of the sun blinds that dizzies both character and spectator); camera angle (the camera inclines with the movement of the boy's head); and focus (Baleia's vision goes out of focus as Fabiano stalks him, as if the dog were bewildered by his master's behaviour). The cinematography of *Vidas secas* is dry and harsh, like the landscape. The film's director of photography, Luiz Carlos Barreto, unable to afford the expensive 20,000-watt lights conventionally used for filling in shadowy areas in high contrast daylight locations, turned necessity into cinematic virtue, for example by sacrificing full exposure in favour of silhouetted human figures against sun-drenched backdrops, light flaring into the camera lens, backlit vultures perched on skeletal trees.

The mimetic incorporation of the lived tempo of peasant life forms part of the film's meaning: the spectator's experience will be symbolically dry like that of the characters. Rather than sensationalise its subject matter, only the most quotidian of events are portrayed in a world where very little 'happens'.

La Hora de los hornos (Hour of the Furnaces) (Argentina 1968 *p.c* – Solanas Productions; *d* – Fernando Solanas and Octavio Gettino; sd)

Avant-garde militant documentaries like *La Hora de los hornos* fuse political radicalism with artistic innovation. The film orchestrates a multiplicity of styles and strategies, along with revolutionary homages to tricontinental culture heroes (Che Guevara, Frantz Fanon, Ho Chi Minh, and more problematically, Peron). The film raises a number of important critical issues: the convergence in the film of the 'two avant-gardes' (the political and the aesthetic), the relation between the film's open process of production and the text itself, the various strategies deployed to turn passive film consumers into active accomplices; the authors' failure to analyse the contradictions of Peronist populism; the problematic mixture of anti-authoritarian language and demagogic manipulation. A cinematic summa, with strategies ranging from straightforward didacticism to operate stylisation, the film borrows freely from avant-garde and mainstream, fiction and documentary, *cinéma-vérité* and advertising. It inherits and extends the work of Eisenstein, Vertov, Ivens, Rocha, Birri, Resnais, Buñuel and Godard. Much of *La Hora*'s persuasive power derives from its ability to give abstract concepts clear accessible form. The sociological abstraction 'Oligarchy', for example, is concretised by shots of the 'fifty families' that monopolise much of Argentina's wealth. 'Class society' becomes the image ('quoted' from Birri's film *Tire Die*) of desperate child beggars running alongside trains in hope of a few pennies tossed by blasé middle-class passengers. Thus *La Hora* engraves its ideas on the spectator's mind.

Parody and satire also form part of the strategic arsenal of the film. Satiric vignettes pinpoint the retrograde nostalgia of the Argentine ruling class. One example is the annual cattle show in Buenos Aires, which interweaves shots of the crowned heads of the prize bulls with the faces of the aristocracy. An iconoclastic sequence titled 'Models' invokes Fanon's exhortation in *The Wretched of the Earth* to 'pay no tribute to Europe by creating states, institutions and societies in its mould'. As the commentary derides Europe's 'racist humanism', the image track parades the most highly prized artefacts of European high culture: the Parthenon, *Déjeuner sur l'herbe*, Roman frescoes, portraits of Byron and Voltaire. In an attack on the ideological hierarchies of the spectator, hallowed art works are lap-dissolved into meaningless metonymy. The most cherished monuments of western culture are equated with the commercialised fetishes of consumer society. Classical portraiture, abstract painting, and Crest toothpaste are levelled as merely diverse brands of imperial export.

Battle of Chile (Chile 1973–6 *p.c* – Equipo Tercer Ano; *d* – Patricio Guzmán and the Equipe Tercer Ano; sd)

Battle of Chile provides an illuminating comparison case with *La Hora de los hornos* in terms of slightly different political positions (left Peronism versus ecumenical leftism), production methods (collaborative in both cases), and cinematic strategies (montage and voice-over commentary in *La Hora*, spare commentary and respect for actual space and time in *Battle of Chile*). Shot during the period of the Allende government in Chile, but completed in exile later, the film was collectively authored in the heat of militancy, at considerable danger to the film-makers themselves. But while *La Hora* develops a quasi-religious cult of self-sacrifice, *Battle of Chile* recognises the possibility of death soberly and without mystification. Like *La Hora*, *Battle of Chile* is a film of epic length (4.5 hours) divided into three parts. The differences begin with genre: if *La Hora* is agitprop, *Battle of Chile* is an analytic documentary. Eschewing a number of classical documentary modes (strict chronology, thematic compilation footage, a day-in-the-life approach) the film-makers synthesised these methods in a dialectical style that combined their advantages, emphasising nodal points in the struggle between left (led by Allende) and right (the military, the right-wing parties). The film focuses on key battlegrounds – the parliament, the economy, the universities, the media. Within this topical approach, the film-makers combine political analysis (made before, during, and after the filming) and on-the-spot film-making performed in the heat of the political and ideological battle. The major difference in strategy between *La Hora* and *Battle of Chile* has to do with the positioning of the spectator. Where *La Hora* strives constantly for rhetorical effect, *The Battle of Chile* eschews rhetoric in favour of recording history in the making. Where most films lead us to identify with individual characters, here the identification is with a community of aspiration. *Battle of Chile* generates the excitement we normally associate with a fiction film, but its drama is built into the events themselves.

The editing of *Chile* favours single-shot sequences, a kind of politicised Bazinianism that respects not only the spatio-temporal integrity of the materials, but also the integrity of the people who speak, including those with whom the film-makers do not agree. Yet the overall structure conveys a subtle class inflection, conveyed not in contrastive parallel editing but rather in the film's undergirding social architectonics. Class differences inform everything we see: the élite address the film-makers as 'Sir', common people say 'companero', the élite drive cars, the common people go to demonstrations on foot or in trucks, and so forth. One remarkable sequence was filmed by an Argentinian during an attempted *coup*. He films a soldier firing directly at him and killing him: the camera blurs as the cameraman falls to the ground. Since the shot is directed at the camera, in cinematic terms at ourselves as spectators, the sequence has a remarkable impact, analogous in some ways to the direct-to-camera/spectator effects of certain Hitchcock films, yet here it conveys what the commentary itself calls 'the very face of Fascism'.

Xala (Senegal 1975 *p.c* – Filmi Domireew/Société Nationale Cinématographique: *d* – Ousmane Sembene; sd col.)

Xala gives satiric voice to Fanon's insights concerning 'the pitfalls on national consciousness', especially the process by which the African élite comes to occupy positions formerly occupied by the colonisers. The film revolves around a fable of impotence, in which the protagonist's *xala*, a divinely sanctioned curse of impotence, comes to symbolise the neo-colonial servitude of the black élite in countries like Senegal. (The novel and film of *Xala* were of course key references in Jameson's landmark essay on 'Third World allegory'.) The protagonist, El Hadji, is a polygamous Senegalese businessman who becomes afflicted with 'xala' on the occasion of taking his third wife. In search of a cure, he visits various medicine men, who fail to cure him. At the same time, he suffers reverses in business, is accused of embezzlement and ejected from the Chamber of Commerce. In the end, he discovers that the 'xala' resulted from a curse sent by a Dakar beggar whose land El Hadji had expropriated. He finally recovers by submitting to the beggars' demands that he strip and be spat upon; the film ends with a freeze-frame of his spittle-covered body.

In the world of *Xala*, the patriarchal structures of colonialism have given way to indigenous African class and gender oppression, precluding the utopia of liberation promised by nationalist discourse. Impotence thus betokens post-independence patriarchy as failed revolution. Here, the traditional ritual of marriage provides a structuring device for a political story. News of the protagonist's wedding-night impotence quickly spreads through the community, provoking the most diverse speculations about its origins. As Françoise Pfaff points out, each of the protagonist's wives plays an allegorical role, representing the Senegalese people at different stages and in different relations to colonisation and to tradition: the dignified, patient traditional wife Awa, the trendy westernised Oumi, and the object of sexual consumerism N'gone (see Pfaff, 1982). Laura Mulvey sees *Xala* as a reflection on the various discourses on the fetish as 'something in which someone invests a meaning and a value beyond its actual meaning or value'. Fetishism is itself allegorical, she points out, in that it calls 'attention to a nodal point of vulnerability, whether within the psychic structure of an individual or the cultural structure of a social group' (Mulvey, 1991). As a symptom, the fetish requires, like allegory, an act of decipherment. The Sembene film articulates the psychosexual with the socio-economic, turning the protagonist's impotence into a symptom of something else: the neo-colonial dependency of the black African élite.

De cierta manera (One Way or Another) (Cuba 1977 *p.c* – Instituto Cubano del Artes e Industria Cinematogra; *d* – Sara Gomez)

One Way or Another deals with the question of *machismo*, and in this sense resembles other Cuban films such as Humberto Solas's *Lucia* (1968), Pastor Vega's *Retrato de Teresa* (*Portrait of Teresa*, 1977) and Tomas Gutierrez Alea's *Hasta cierto punto* (*Up to a Certain Point*, 1983). Although *One Way or Another* focuses on the problem of social marginality, the question of *machismo* comes in through the story of the evolving relationship between Mario, a worker from a poor district, and Yolanda, a middle-class teacher drafted to teach in the poor neighbourhood. The film deploys the metaphor of slum clearance and construction in a film which operates a certain 'deconstruction' both of conventional gender roles and of conventional generic formulae. Gomez weaves fictional and non-fictional segments, professional and non-professional performers, in a multi-levelled reflection on the relations between the sexes, between classes, between generations and among workers.

Iskandariya Leh? (Alexandria Why?) (Egypt 1979 *p.c* – Nisr International Films; *d* – Youssef Chahine; sd)

This semi-autobiographical film about an aspiring film-maker haunted by Hollywood dreams offers an Egyptian perspective on colonising film culture. Chahine's protagonist begins as a Victoria College student who adores Shakespeare's plays and Hollywood movies. The film is set in the 1940s, a critical period for the protagonist, and for Egypt, when Allied troops were stationed in the country and Axis forces threatened to invade Alexandria. *Alexandria Why?* weaves diverse materials (newsreels, clips from Hollywood films, staged reconstructions, Chahine's own youthful amateur films) into an ironic collage. The opening credit sequence mingles black-and-white 1940s travelogue footage of Alexandria beaches with newsreel footage of Europe at war, implementing a 'peripheral' Egyptian perspective on Europe. In the following sequence we watch a series of newsreels and Hollywood musicals along with the spectators in Alexandria. An anthology of musical clips featuring stars like Helen Powell, and songs such as 'I'll Build a Stairway to Paradise' are inserted into a reception context redolent of First World/Third World power relations as well as of the worldwide hegemonisation of the American Dream. The 'Three Cheers for the Red, White and Blue' number, for example, at once charming and intimidating in its climactic image of cannons firing at the camera (here the Egyptian spectator), celebrates American power and renders explicit the nationalist subtext of First World 'entertainment'.

Alexandria Why? interweaves documentary and staged theatrical fiction in innovative ways. Impossibly fluid movement matches, for example, take us from newsreel material to staged footage to theatrical play. Second World War actuality footage is manipulated to incorporate the film's characters, and whether these materials are diegetic or non-diegetic is deliberately blurred. The final sequence mocks the power that replaced European colonial power in Egypt after the Second World War: the US, deriding the chimera of Americanisation that enthralls the protagonist, and allegorically middle-class Egyptians generally. On arriving in the musical's national homeland, the protagonist is greeted by the Statue of Liberty transformed into a laughing, toothless prostitute.

History in the present. The postcolonial irony of *Nice Coloured Girls*

Nice Coloured Girls (Australia 1987 *p.c* – Tracey Moffatt; *d* – Tracey Moffatt; sd)

While Third World and First World minoritarian women have experienced different histories and sexual regimes, they have also shared a common status as colonial exotics. Escaping these paradigms, *Nice Coloured Girls* interweaves tales about contemporary urban Australian Aboriginal women and their 'captains' (sugar daddies) with stories of Aboriginal women and white men over 200 years before. In sharp contrast to the colonial construction of the Aboriginal female body seen as a metaphorical extension of an exoticised land, *Nice Coloured Girls* places dynamic, irreverent, resourceful Aboriginal women at the centre of the narrative, offering a multi-temporal perspective on their 'nasty' actions – mild forms of prostitution and conning white Australian men into spending money. By shuttling between present-day Australia and past texts, voices and images, the film contextualises their behaviour in relation to the asymmetrical exchanges typical of colonial encounters. While from the vantage point of Eurocentric decorum the Aboriginal women are amoral schemers, the historical context of settler colonialism and its sexualised relations to both land and women switches the ethical and emotional valence. Whereas images of the past are set inside a ship, or in daylight on the shore, images from the present are set in the night-time city, pointing to the historical 'neonisation', as it were, of Aboriginal space. The film can thus be seen as a 'revenge' narrative in which Aboriginal women trick Euro-Australian men into fantasising a 'fair' exchange of sex and goods, then take their money and run.

The title of *Nice Coloured Girls* is itself ironic; it subverts the 'positive' image of 'nice' coloured girls as the objects of colonial exoticisation, valorising instead the 'negative' image of 'nastiness'. By reflexively foregrounding the artifice of its production through stylised sets, excessive performance style, and ironic subtitles, the film undermines any expectation of sociologically 'authentic' or ethically 'positive' representations. The constant changes of discursive register – *vérité*-style hand-held camera, voice-over ethnographic texts, subtitled oral narratives – undermine any univocal mode of historical narration. Rather than reverse the dichotomy of sexualised Third World women and virginal European women by proposing an equally virginal image of Aboriginal women, the film rejects the binaristic mode altogether by showing 'nastiness' as an understandable response to a specific economic and historical conjuncture, and finding the kernel of contemporary power relations in the colonial past.

Sankofa (USA 1993 *p.c* – Ngod Gward Productions; *d* – Haile Gerima; sd)

Sankofa synthesises the modern and the traditional through an Afro-magical *egungun* aesthetic, i.e. an aesthetic that invokes the spirits of the ancestors as embodiments of a deep sense of personal and collective history. Named after an Akan word for 'recuperating what's lost', the film begins with a drummed invocation exhorting the ancestral spirits to 'rise up, step out, and tell your story'. An urgent whispered voice-over says: 'Spirit of the dead, rise up and possess your bird of passage, come out, you stolen Africans, spirits of the dead, you raped, castrated, lobotomized.' This device of a collective call by a presiding spirit, turned into a structural refrain, authorises a transgenerational approach that mingles the present (a bewigged black fashion model posing against the backdrop of the Mina slave fort) and the past (the fort's former historical atrocities). In a kind of psychic and historical time machine, the fashion model becomes possessed by Shola, a nineteenth-century house slave, and is made to experience the cruelties of slavery, the rapes and

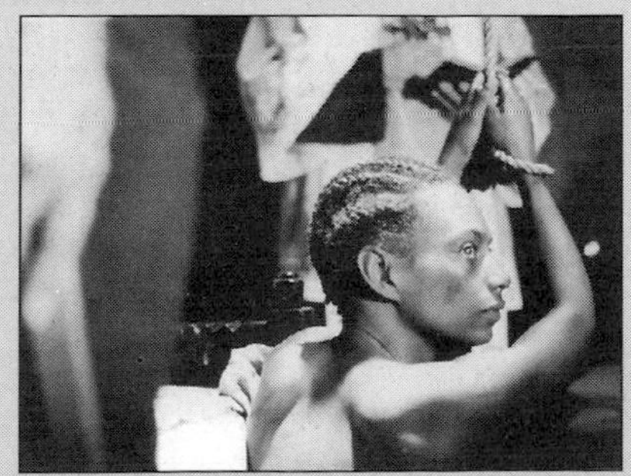

Personal and collective history – *Sankofa*

the brandings, and to acknowledge her own kinship with her enslaved ancestors. Gerima repeatedly pans over friezes of black faces, evoking an ocular chorus, bypassing an individualising point-of-view structure to evoke a community of the gaze. The narrative forms a multifocal, communitarian *Bildungsroman*: the fashion model confronts the sources of her own alienation; the 'headman' who beats slaves becomes a double agent working for liberation. The cultural facets of African life (communal child care, herbal remedies, the primordial role of music and stories) are constantly stressed. Orality exists both as a diegetic presence – characters literally tell stories/histories of Africa, of the middle passage – and as a meta-cinematic device structuring the entire film as a collective narration, where disembodied voices exhort, prophesy, exorcise, criticise, all in a 'polyrhythmic' style where avant-garde inflected moments of aesthetic contemplation alternate with dramatic moments of decisive action.

HINDI CINEMA

India is the world's largest national film industry. It amalgamates five major 'regional' film industries based in Bombay (the Hindi and Marathi cinemas), Madras (Tamil, Telugu and Malayalam cinemas), Hyderabad (mainly Telugu), Calcutta (Bengali, Assamese and Oriya cinemas) and Bangalore (Kannada cinema). The Indian Censor Board has recorded films made in 51 languages, including Arabic, German, Persian and several Indian dialects, that is to say, languages not considered to be official by the Indian Constitution. The major industries are concentrated in eight languages. According to Censor Board figures, these were distributed in 1993 as follows: 183 Hindi, 168 Tamil, 148 Telugu, 78 Kannada, 71 Malayalam, 57 Bengali, 35 Marathi and 20 Oriya films.

The massive scale of the Indian film industry – which overtook Japan in 1971 to become the biggest in the world – its linguistic and cultural variety, geographical spread, complex aesthetic histories, combined with the relative paucity of scholarly works able to provide an understanding of this industrial–cultural sector can mean that the subject is intimidating. For the better part of its history, the Indian film industry has survived without state support (unlike Hollywood, which benefited considerably from the US government's readiness to use strong-arm tactics, for instance, to help Hollywood achieve or maintain market domination in various regions of the globe). The Indian industry grew under colonial rule, was implicated in the independence struggle and maintained an ambivalent stance towards the government over censorship and tax legislation (the latter amounting to, on average, half the price of every ticket). The industry developed its own capital resources, at times 'unaccounted' for, that is to say, drawn from an illegal 'parallel economy', which the cinema is seen sometimes to represent. Indian cinema is thus located, economically and therefore aesthetically (although the nature of the relationship between economics and aesthetics remains, to be analysed adequately), in between two realms, each with its own values: an official realm, with its economic and cultural values, and the more covert realm of the film economy with its 'parallel' though overlapping values. In this respect, Indian cinema is simultaneously a contentious, suspect domain and arguably a key sector that, by bridging the two economies, holds the nation together while providing the main cultural forcefield within which the stresses and strains affecting India are manifested and contested.

Until the mid-1980s, most debates on Indian film concentrated on and deployed varieties of populist ideologies – positive or negative arguments, that is, formed around notions of mass culture versus élite culture and the cinema's seminal role in the creation of an indigenous audience in the context of pre-independence nationalisms. (After independence, cinema and the print media's populist ideologies helped form a consumption sector extending beyond the metropolitan areas.)

These mass-culture debates were and are in turn framed by a larger set of arguments and positions involving, on the one hand, the critique or defence of the Indian state as policymaker, legitimator of an 'official' Indian mass culture and arbitrator of 'authenticity' and, on the other hand, an exploration of the commercial industries and the various state-sponsored art-house initiatives in the context of their claim to represent the 'reality of' Indian experiences. (These arguments, in contrast with comparable discussions in Europe and America, have only recently come to include television in their frame of reference.)

Indian cinema's relative independence from foreign investment has marked and inflected the conceptualisations of its histories. However, since relatively few film prints from its history have survived (from the 1,400 or so silent films produced, less than a dozen appear to be still extant) and other kinds of archival records are equally scarce, very little serious research has been done into the history of Indian cinema.

Instead, there has been extensive discussion of the somewhat exceptional case of a colonised nation already possessing, when independence was achieved, a well-entrenched entertainment industry. These discussions have focused largely on the regulatory role of the state in this sector of production. State-sponsored intitiatives in the film industry, as in other public sector economic areas, had to reconcile several contradictory responsibilities. The state had a monopoly over, for instance, the manufacture and distribution of raw stock and other materials as well as over the 'channelling' of the distribution of foreign films. But its role was relatively minor in attempts to diversify the culture of film through agencies such as the National Film Development Corporation, which sought to provide alternatives to mainstream cinema's market domination.

Consequently, it is quite possible to see both the history of Indian cinema, and the debates surrounding and accompanying it as paralleling the history of India's private sector economy in general: determined by several initiatives seeking to foster cultural and political indigenism before independence, the industry was implicated in the promotion of a kind of 'Indianness', in bolstering the Nehruite programmes for a 'socialist form of society' as well as a mixed economy. More recently, the industry has been affected by 'economic liberalisation', a process whose impact is readily evident in the rapid changes in television caused by the entry of foreign cable networks into the country.

SOME HISTORICAL PROBLEMS

It is possible to distinguish four main periods in Indian cinema.

The first one is the silent film era, dominated by the culture of *swadeshi* ('own country', a term which refers to the Indian National Congress's call to boycott all imported material and cultural goods). This phase is represented by the name of the man widely revered as the founder of the Indian film industry, Dhundiraj Govind (Dadasaheb) Phalke. As well as elsewhere in the world, this period of Indian cinema coincides with the early stages of the industrialisation of culture, a process that accelerated significantly in the latter part of the nineteenth century. In India, this generated a specific set of cultural and aesthetic problems resulting from the encounter between traditional non-perspectival representational practices and the emergent lens-based media with their inbuilt notions of perspective and space. The issues relating to this encounter are debated by Indian art and film historians (see Geeta Kapur, 1987, 1993; Ashish Rajadhyaksha, 1987, 1993) in terms of 'frontality' of pictorial composition (lack of oblique angles and problematic connections between one space and another). These aesthetic issues parallel the more directly political and historical issue of the need to imagine a unified spatio-temporal Indian dimension suitable for independence struggles.

The second period extends from the late silent era into the 1930s, that of the studios and production houses modelled to some extent on their Hollywood counterparts. This phase ended with the onset of the Second World War and was marked by experimentation with styles which combined, in spite of the Hollywood organisational model, aspects of British and especially German cinemas with Indian modes of storytelling, models that characteristically do not adhere to western-style distinctions between the realms of fantasy and reality. The imperative to construct spatial coherence within multi-shot sequences and to establish an editing style seeking to convey continuity of gesture and physical movement from one shot to the next, was not generally accepted or applied, as can be seen in the few surviving silent action films as well as in many 1930s works.

The third phase saw the rise of an independent industry partly funded by the tremendous, often illegal, wealth generated during the war, and consequently viewed with suspicion by the state. It is also at this stage that new, extended consumer sectors began to be addressed more directly. Aesthetically, this period is associated with the gradual consolidation of a 'classic' type of melodrama (in the literal sense of musical drama) with its own rules of narration, often derived from late nineteenth-century popular novels which were characterised by the 'serial imbrication' of multiple storylines within one narrative stream. As well as being indebted to popular fiction, mainstream Indian cinema developed its own notions of 'character', involving exemplary figures, in whom various social pressures coalesce, surrounded by social or familial groups. Western conventions of psychological verisimilitude which transform social–historical issues into personal, internal neuroses, occasionally form part of the Indian narrative canvas but do not define its notion of character, at least not at this stage (the work of Satyajit Ray represents a shift in this respect). The Indian melodrama proved to be particularly suited for exploring the tensions involved in the modernisation and secularisation of society. Melodrama interrogated the relationship between public and private, urban and rural, industrial and agricultural, capitalist and pre-capitalist modes of production and social organisation. It also dramatised in the context of patriarchy mutating issues concerning the control of women's sexuality as an older type of patriarchy mutates into a more modern one, and so on into a recognisably modern form.

The fourth period is marked by the fruition of several state initiatives sponsoring a 'new', or 'parallel' cinema movement in the 1960s and 1970s, often in regions that had not yet established local industrial infrastructure. This development made its impact on the development of India's state-owned television, Doordarshan, and on institutions such as the Directorate of Film Festivals, the National Film Archive of India, the Film Insitute, the National Film Development Corporation and so on. This most recent phase is marked by a greater diversity of narrative styles and aesthetic conventions in the context of the emergence of, broadly speaking, three main streams of cinema: the state-sponsored cinema which sought to develop the pioneering work of Satyajit Ray (the Indian film-maker closest to western notions of the director as *auteur*) in a variety of directions; the commercial cinema which refined its own melodramatic narrative orchestrations and sought to achieve greater visceral impact; and the 'middle cinema' which sought to combine elements of both of the previous tendencies (as in the work of Shyam Benegal). A fourth, numerically marginal but aesthetically tone-setting current evolved from the work of Ritwik Ghatak (1925–76) and aspires to an 'epic' mode of storytelling drawing on a variety of Indian and western representational traditions in order to elaborate a new idiom adequate to the representation of the cultural and historical complexities which are constellated in 1990s Indian society.

SOME INDUSTRIAL ISSUES

Phalke Films

Contrary to most accounts, Dadasaheb Phalke (1870–1944) was not India's first film director. Production in India had begun shortly after the first Lumière screenings in Bombay in 1896, mainly under the auspices of, on the one hand, multinational distributors of film equipment who hired cameras and crews to make what later came to be described as documentaries, and, on the other hand, independent film-maker exhibitors, notably Harishchandra Bhatavdekar. In the first two decades of the twentieth century, cinema grew alongside, but as a poor cousin of, the thriving Gujarati, Urdu and Hindi stage industries. However, Phalke was influential, in, first, setting up his own, domestically based, production concern (Phalke Films, founded in 1912) and, second, in aligning his enterprise with the polical economy of *swadeshi.*

Already a noted figure in the printing industry, Phalke saw his first film in 1910 (*The Life of Christ*) and was, in his own words 'gripped by a strange spell . . . Could we, the sons of India, ever be able to see Indian images on the screen?' He went on to make mythologicals using popular legends from the *Hindu Puranas* which led to his reputation as the inventor of the staple genre of India's pre-Second World War cinema: the Hindu mythological (a notable early example of which was Phalke's *Kaliya Mardan*, 1919).

Phalke Films was characteristic of the small, cottage-type companies that proliferated in Indian cinema prior to the establishment of the first professional studio, Kohinoor (founded in 1918 and closed in 1932). Kohinoor was set up by D. N. Sampat, one of the most famous producers in Indian cinema whose productions (by directors such as Kanjibhai Rathod and Homi Master) were among the first successfully to address a pan-Indian audience and to boast movie stars (Raja Sandow, the Bilimoria brothers, Zubeida, Sulochana, and others). Other companies followed suit: in Bombay there were the Imperial Film Company, the Ranjit, Krishna and Sharda studios, in Calcutta the Aurora Film Company and Indian Kinema, all established in the late 1920s, all attempting a variety of genres including stage adaptations, adaptations from novels and variations of American genres. Generally speaking, the most successful ones were those which most aptly indigenised their sources and approaches, usually within a broadly defined *swadeshi* context. For instance, Sharda's stunt and action movies starring Master Vithal adapted historical legends from India's middle ages, and there were also adventure sagas derived from Parsee Theatre's main source, Firdausi's *Shahnama*, and, of course, episodes from the *Mahabharata* and *Ramayana*. These adaptations helped to define an indigenous audience within specific distribution circuits patterened on those created by Madan Theatres, Pathé, Globe and Empire which specialised in showing American and European films, rarely overlapping with the 'native' product.

Phalke's arguments for a *swadeshi* cinema ('My films are *swadeshi* in the sense that the ownership, employees and stories are *swadeshi*') achieved virtually policy status through the work of the first major Cinematograph Committee set up in 1927. This Committee strongly endorsed the Rajput historical fantasy *Janjirne Jankare* (*At the Clang of Fetters*) and the Rabindranath Tagore adaptation *Balidan* (*The Sacrifice*), both released in 1927 and hailed as Indian cinema's coming of age, proving that Indian cinema could make films that were on a par with those made in the west. These films overcame what the Committee's report described as Indian cinema's three main limitations: an inability to tell stories, technical inadequacy and excessive length.

Prabhat Studios

Sound cinema emerged in 1931 with the

release of the Parsee Theatre adaptation *Alam Ara*, telling of the rivalry between two queens at the court of Kumarpur. Subsequently, most of the silent film studios closed down or were transformed into new companies, among the most famous of which are Prabhat, New Theatres and Bombay Talkies. This phase, between 1931 and the onset of the Second World War, witnessed the first of two so-called golden ages in Indian cinema (the second one consisting of the famous melodramas of the 1950s). These two periods monopolise almost all critical and historical discussion on Indian film history, generating the country's first *auteurs* and film 'classics'.

The Prabhat studio, especially after it moved to Pune in 1933, became India's élite production house, with V. Shantaram as its star director–producer. Shantaram had emerged from the Gandharva Natak Mandali, a Marathi theatre company, and worked as actor, editor and director at Baburao Painter's Maharashtra Film Company. He then made sound versions of Baburao Painter's twenty historicals and mythologicals, later deploying a German-derived version of Expressionism for his celebrated socials (for example *Kunku Duniya Na Mane/The Unexpected,* 1937; *Manoos/Admi/Life is for the Living*, 1939; *Shejari/Padosi/The Neighbour*, 1941) which have been the focus for discussions of pre-1950s melodrama. Another Prabhat film, the Saint film *Sant Tukaram* by V. Damle and S. Fattelal (1936), has become the focus for seminal arguments regarding the differences between notions of 'the popular' in pre-independence India as opposed to the populist ideologies promulgated by post-independence producers (see, for instance, K. Shahani, 1986; G. Kapur, 1993 and M. Gopal Singh, 1995).

The social dimension of genre film-making (see A. Rajadhyaksha and P. Willemen, 1994) owes much to literary adaptations produced by Prabhat and New Theatres (in Calcutta) in the 1930s, especially adaptations from the novels of Bankimchandra Chattopadhyay, Rabindranath Tagore and, later, Saratchandra Chattopadhyay in Bengal as well as Govardhanram Tripathi (Gujarati), Hari Narayan Apte (Marathi), O. Chandu Menon (Malayalam) and others. These novels emerged from the late nineteenth-century reform movements which often addressed social stress and strains brought about by modernisation pressures as such pressures manifested themselves in relation to changes in the status of women and the condition of the peasantry. Saratchandra especially, as perhaps twentieth-century India's most influential writer, set the terms for several stereotypes (rural India, the widow, and so on) which were to recur in film melodramas which were also indebted to his convoluted narrative structures.

New Theatres

Filming Saratchandra's stories was the way the film studio New Theatres (founded in 1931) sought to establish a 'respectable' cinema. (That a notion of quality should automatically imply literariness is a controversial aspect of Indian cinema in that it betrays the depth to which English ideologies penetrated 'indigenous' cultural priorities and frameworks.) The founder of New Theatres, B. N. Sircar stated: [T]he first film I made was Saratchandra's *Dena Paona* (1931). The first director ... was Premankur Atorthy, the famed littérateur. The film was not a success. Yet I could perceive that following the path of literature would lead to the discovery of the right path ...' This approach resulted in the studio's most famous film, and one of the best-known films of pre-independence India, P. C. Barua's *Devdas* (1935), discussed extensively by Ashis Nandy (1995), for example. The eponymous character, Devdas, became a popular stereotype deployed on numerous occasions (including remakes) throughout Indian cinema: the lovesick, weak, narcissistic hero defeated by life.

New Theatres was also the studio where a host of India's best-known directors emerged: Debaki and Nitin Bose, Dhiren Ganguly, the cameraman/director Bimal Roy, the latter in his turn, after moving to Mombay and making Hindi film, creating the conditions for the assimilation of major Bengali musicians and directors into the 'all-India' cinema.

The third major studio of the period was Bombay Talkies (founded in 1934) which had antecedents in the orientalist Indo-German and Indo-British co-productions of Himansu Rai in the 1920s (often directed by the Austro-German Franz Osten, whose career in India came to an end when he was imprisoned as a Nazi at the start of the Second World War). The Bombay Talkies movies, especially Osten's work, fed a long-running debate about notions of Indianness and 'the oriental' extending into the work of Ismail Merchant and James Ivory. Initially, Osten's films were intended to break into the European market and took their aesthetic cues from Ufa in Germany. This was also the first time that private sector capital (mainly from insurance companies) was mobilised for an idustrial enterprise promising regular dividends to investors. With the hit *Achhut Kanya* (*The Untouchable Girl*, 1936), starring Ashok Kumar and Devika Rani, the studio formulated the enduring screen image of 'village India', with its stock characters (the landowner, the peasant, the innocent hero, social evils and medieval corruption) and most importantly, a kind of simplified Hindustani which had by then become the 'national' language. Personnel involved in Bombay Talkies went on to found the even more influential studio Filmistan, founded in 1942 but effectively launched by the Bombay Talkies hit *Kismet* (*Fate,* 1943). The Filmistan period, which lasted for sixteen years, marks the bridge between pre-war and post-independence commerical Indian cinema (the so-called Massala cinema), introducing a raft of stars (Dev Anand, Dilip Kumar, Shammi Kapoor and others) and establishing the formula of the song–dance–action fantasy films which have come to be seen as typical of Indian cinema in general.

Art, industry and the state

This transition was first chronicled by independent India's first Film Enquiry Committee Report which used strong language to comment on the shift from the pre-war studio system to the postwar rise of speculators:

> Within three years of the end of the War, the leadership of the industry had changed hands from established producers to a variety of successors. Leading 'stars', exacting 'financiers' and calculating distributors and exhibitors forged ahead ... Film production ... became in substantial measure the recourse of deluded aspirants to easy riches ... (Report of the Film Enquiry Committee, 1951)

To a great extent this critical attitude towards the development of an utterly market-oriented mass entertainment industry bypassing the state's requirements and preferred directions of development, must be seen in context of the international and the Indian élite's acclaim for the début of Satyajit Ray with *Pather Panchali* (*Song of the Road,* 1955). Ray's work drew on the Bengali novel and to some extent built on the New Theatres' attempt to bring literary respectability to the cinema. However, Ray pursued this project with far greater ambition and control than before. The epic story of the boy Apu's growth to adulthood in the Apu Trilogy (*Pather Panchali, Aparajito/The Unvanquished,* 1956, *Apur Sansar/The World of Apu,* 1959) clearly provided Indian cinema with its first internationally significant works of art. Joined in the late 1950s by contemporaries Mrinal Sen, later known for his Calcutta trilogy (*Interview,* 1970, *Calcutta '71*, 1972 and *Padatik/The Guerrilla Fighter,* 1973), and by Ritwik Ghatak, Ray introduced a new dimension to notions of authenticity, substantially influencing what the Indian state would come to define in the 1960s and 1970s as an official aesthetic of 'good' or 'art' cinema.

On the other hand, it is also possible, and indeed necessary, to contextualise Ray's work by seeing it in relation to the tradition of the Hindi melodramas of the 1950s, the genre which has become the focus of most of the significant theoretical work on Indian cinema since the 1980s. For instance, Ravi Vasudevan's analysis of those melodramas, substantiated by the critical work of Kobita Sarkar and Chidananda Das Gupta, demonstrates how Ray inaugurated a formal opposition between melodramatic, externalised modes of representation and a more internalised, character-oriented kind of narration coming closer to the middle class's notion of what 'good' cinema should be like (see Vasudevan, 1993). Vasudevan discusses many of the classic melodramas of the fifties, such as Gyan Mukherjee's *Kismet* (1943), Mehboob's *Andaz* (1949), Raj Kapoor's *Awara* (*The Tramp,* 1951), and Guru Dutt's *Pyaasa* (1957) in order to analyse the narrative codes, iconic characterisations and social caste and gender identities of the characters in the films in which Ray negotiates India's transition to modernity, examining the various forms modernity can take, and assessing its limits as well as its productive capacities. The firn industry's representatives tended to explain the difference between the industrial cinema and Ray's cinema in economic terms, invoking the role of state support and the attempted creation of an élite audience in contrast to the mass entertainment approach which tended to assume the underdevelopment of both the industry and its audiences, seeing questions of modernity either as threats to 'tradition' or as questions of the size, scale and technical infrastructure of the productions.

In the 1960s, the crucial effort to redefine the perceived splits within Indian cinema came from Chidananda Das Gupta who introduced the phrase 'All-India film' to describe the mainstream Hindi entertainment cinema and its equivalents in other Indian languages. Das Gupta argued that this kind of cinema had taken on the role of cultural leadership, reinforcing the unifying tendencies in India's social and economic changes and providing an inferior alternative to a leadership that might have emerged had it not been for the rift between the intelligentsia, to which the leaders belonged, and 'the masses' (see Das Gupta, 1968/1981).

Das Gupta's argument strengthened the tendency to define the mainstream Indian cinema as playing a kind of default role, making Hindi the national film language and creating, by way of the melodramas, a nationally integrative cultural domain. In the 1970s, the New Indian Cinema, sponsored by the Film Finance Corporation, intervened to redefine the terms of the debate. The New Indian Cinema itself, as a movement, is usually dated back to Mrinal Sen's satire *Bhuvan Shome* (1969) and Mani Kaul's formal experiment *Uski Roti* (*A Day's Bread,* 1969). The theoretical underpinning of this movement was presented by one of its most important directors, Kumar Shahani.

Kumar Shahani's films (*Maya Darpan/Mirror of Illusion,* 1972, *Tarang/Wages and Profit,* 1984, *Khayal Gatha/Khayal Saga* 1988, *Kasba/Ravine,* 1990) and his extensive writings proclaim a radically new vanguard practice Indian cinema underpinned by an analysis of its history. In his key essays 'Notes Towards an Aesthetic of Cinema Sound' (1984) and 'Film as a Contemporary Art' (1990), Shahani approaches the cinematograph in terms of its ability to deploy a sound–image dialectic, rather than in terms of an aspiration towards a technical 'realism' in camera–sound recording combinations. Shahani, detouring through Brecht, sought to recover Indian narrative traditions and art forms which would allow him to develop a new kind of 'epic' cinema. Shahani drew on Indian classical music and other performing arts to reconceptualise the very notions of narrative and sequentiality while demonstrating how these older Indian art forms in fact continued to be active within so-called lower art forms such as film and contemporary kinds of 'popular' performances. In so doing, Shahani suggests alternatives to the sterile varieties of lyrical or dramatic realisms which beset both the industrial cinema and the construction of 'Indianness' in allegedly ethnographically realist representations.

In 1975, two major box-office successes of the Hindi cinema, *Sholay* (*Embers*) with its many stars and an early hit song for the

Kaliya Mardan (India 1919 *p.c* – Hindustan Cinema Films; *d* – Dadasaheb Phalke; st b/w)

Dadasaheb Phalke is regarded by many as the founder of the Indian film industry. *Kaliya Mardan* is the one film of Phalke's to survive which approximates something close to its original length (which was 6,000 feet). The story tells the Pauranic tale of the child Krishna, showing his antics as he steals butter with his young friends, causing mayhem in the village while also demonstrating his godly powers. In the important final scene, young Krishna defeats the demon snake Kaliya in a fierce underwater battle, rising triumphantly to the surface as everyone mourns his assumed death. One of the most remarkable sequences is the opening in which Phalke introduces his daughter Mandakini, who plays Krishna, through a series of close-ups showing her preparing for the role in the tradition of Indian folk theatre.

Kaliya Mardan demonstrates many of the stylistic traits that the director was famous for. A crucial convention, practised in Indian cinema ever since, is the use of frontal address, with Krishna/the hero as an icon that is 'recognised' by the audience (the audience, represented by the villagers, is included within the frame at times) and defines several conventions of *mise-en-scène* and even a particular notion of screen realism. Phalke indicates this realism with scenes shot on location and by images showing rustic life in Maharashtra.

Pather Panchali (India 1955 *p.c* – Govt of West Bengal; *d* – Satyajit Ray; sd (Bengali) b/w)

Pather Panchali marked Satyajit Ray's debut and was the internationally acclaimed first film of his Apu Trilogy. Set in the early years of twentieth-century Bengal, the story is told mainly through the eyes of the child protagonist, Apu. The film chronicles the entry of modernity into the rural landscape. At the end of the film, Apu's family leave their broken hut and move to Benares. The subsequent films in the trilogy show Apu growing up in Benares and Calcutta, get-

The internationally acclaimed *Pather Pachali*

ting married and facing the death of his young wife.

The making of the film, the technological innovations of shooting on location and assimilating the style of the Italian neo-realists (notably De Sica) including their naturalistic acting style, are issues that have been widely discussed (see Das Gupta, 1980; Andrew Robinson, 1989, which also includes an extensive bibliography). The trilogy's realism in its portrayal of rural India clearly meant a lot to the newly independent Indian intelligentsia, and can in themselves be placed within what is now understood as a specifically Nehruite project of modernisation.

Pyaasa (India 1957 *p.c* – Guru Dutt Films; *d* – Guru Dutt; sd Hindi b/w)

Guru Dutt's famous melodrama about the travails of a young poet in India, played by the director himself, was the first of three films on the theme of exile and nationhood which established Dutt as one of the great exponents of melodrama in film.

Pyaasa tells the story of Vijay, an Urdu poet in Calcutta, and his love story with a prostitute, Gulab. Vijay descends into squalor; rejected by his publisher, denied his rights by the husband of his former lover Meena, eventually he is believed dead. In the most astonishing sequence in the film, Vijay 'travels' through a sick, hungry and depraved India, ending up at a place where his former tormentors – who have become rich with the 'posthumous' publishing of his work – have organised a public meeting to commemorate his death. He denounces them and the hypocrisy of the state, and is overrun in the ensuing stampede. Eventually he and Gulab leave in order to invent their own utopia elsewhere.

Exile, nationhood, music and melodrama – Guru Dutt's *Pyaasa*

The film is seen as being the pinnacle of the tradition of Indian melodrama, notably in its use of music (by S. B. Burman), its elevation of the hero into an iconic presence, and its upgrading of the literary tradition and the 'socials' of 1930s film into a valid, properly cinematic idiom. Although the story claims to be original, comparisons can be made to Saratchandra Chatterjee's well-known novel, *Srikanta*. Dutt's masterly camerawork, especially in the long crane shots and in the use of light and shadow, contributes to the tragic feel of the story.

Sholay (India 1975 *p.c* – Sippy Films; *d* – Ramesh Sippy; sd Hindi col. scope)

This big-budget hit introduced a new era of Hindi commercial cinema in the 1970s. The story is concerned with the rivalry between an ex-policeman, Thakur Baldev Singh, and a bandit, Gabbar Singh. Its style references the spaghetti western, as well as adapting scenes from the films of such directors as John Ford, Burt Kennedy, Charlie Chaplin and Sam Peckinpah. This creates an effect which Paul Willemen describes as like 'a skilfully designed shopping mall with the viewer being propelled past successive window displays, each exhibiting an eye-catching presentation of some aspect of the popular cinema's history'. The film broke new ground in India in its marketing strategies, with the LP of the soundtrack, and notably Gabbar's dialogues, almost outselling the music. It also introduced the new 1980s style of lumpen heroism associated with the film's writers Salim Khan and Javed Akhtar, who claim to have authored the screen persona of Amitabh Bachchan.

superstar of the 1980s, Amitabh Bachchan, and the low-budget mythological *Jai Santoshi Maa*, introduced a new era in which the Hindi cinema was to spearhead a major technological and cultural change via the medium of television. Earlier, in 1971, the Motion Picture Export Association of America had announced a boycott of the Indian market on account of Indian economic and cultural 'protectionism'. In 1975, as a culmination of Indira Gandhi 'nation in danger' rhetoric shoring up protectionist economic measures, a state of national emergency was declared, the same year in which television introduced several satellite experiments preparing the government's major expansion of broadcasting and media industries in the early 1980s. *Sholay* and *Jai Santoshi Maa*, each in their own way, signalled a technological and an aesthetic readiness on the part of the Indian film industry to assimilate and propagate the upgrading of the media industry. This development had already been announced in Bachchan's earlier hit melodramas, *Zanjeer* (*The Chain*, 1973) and *Deewar* (*The Wall*, 1975), in which the feudal laws of kinship and the tragic vigilante hero are proposed as substitutes for the ineffectual laws and role of the Indian state. Veena Das's reading of *Jai Santoshi Maa* tries to account for the unexpected impact achieved by a film which presents an entirely invented legend of kinship relations, bypassing the established pantheon, and launches a mother goddess who became a popular icon, especially among working-class women.

The relevance of the work of filmmakers and critics such as Shahani is that they attempt to understand the basic dynamics which structure Indian film culture as a changing forcefield rather than trying to fetishise some of its component factions or trends. This approach has become startlingly relevant in the current, late 1990s situation in which cinema has to face the massive, largely unforeseen, invasion of cable and satellite television. This latest development has received, as yet, little theoretical attention in India (or elsewhere, for that matter), even though it threatens not only cinema, but the very edifice of what has structured both the pre- and post-independence debates on Indian cinema: the Indian state as a disciplinary and regulatory authority.

SELECTED READING

Chidananda Das Gupta, 'The cultural basis of Indian cinema', 1968, in *Talking About Films*, New Delhi, Orient Longman, 1981.

Tejaswini Niranjana *et al.* (eds), *Interrogating Modernity: Culture and Colonialism in India*, Calcutta, Seagull Books, 1993.

Ashish Rajadhyaksha and Paul Willemen, *Encyclopaedia of Indian Cinema*, London and Delhi, BFI/Oxford University Press, 2nd edn, 1999, 1st edn, 1994.

Kumar Shahani, 'Film as a contemporary art', *Social Scientist* 18(3), March 1990.

PART 5

GENRE

Frankenstein (1931)

HISTORY OF GENRE CRITICISM

INTRODUCTION

While literary genre criticism has a long history, it was introduced into anglophone film criticism comparatively recently, in the mid-1960s and early 1970s (Buscombe, 1970; Pye, 1975). In cinema itself, generic forms were one of the earliest means used by the industry to organise the production and marketing of films, and by reviewers and the popular audience to guide their viewing. In this respect, genres – like stars a decade later – emerged from the studio system's dual need for standardisation and product differentiation. The genres, each with its recognisable repertoire of conventions running across visual imagery, plot, character, setting, modes of narrative development, music and stars, enabled the industry to predict audience expectation. Differences between genres meant different audiences could be identified and catered to. All this made it easier to standardise and stabilise production (see The studios, p. 11).

These industrial associations account for the late entry of generic categories into film criticism, which, in its attempt to divest itself of its literary or sociological heritage, sought to demonstrate the presence of individual artists (*auteurs*) despite rather than in relation to industrial conditions. Genre conventions in Hollywood cinema had, of course, been remarked upon by film criticism before genre itself became a theoretical issue. But here the term 'convention' was used pejoratively, referring to the second-hand meanings and stereotypes associated with mass production which militated both against the personal expression of the artist and the authentic portrayal of reality. When *auteur* criticism took on the cause of Hollywood cinema it was committed to reproducing the author as 'artist' in what was largely genre product. In Colin McArthur's view (1972) this meant sifting the 'irrelevancies brought to particular works' by studio personnel and genre conventions in order to lay bare the core of thematic and stylistic motifs peculiar to the film-maker (see Nicholas Ray, p. 257).

The relationship of genre and *auteur* criticism will be pursued later. Important to note here is that cinematic genre criticism grew out of the growing dissatisfaction with *auteur* analysis of Hollywood product which, Tom Ryall (1978) argues, 'tended to treat popular art as if it were "high culture"' (see *Auteur* theory and British cinema, p. 264). Seminal to this work of reassessment were essays written in different contexts in the 1950s by André Bazin on the western ('The Western, or the American Film par Excellence', and 'The Evolution of the Western', 1971), focusing on two genres which were central to early genre criticism's concern with popular art (see The western, p. 147; André Bazin, p. 148; The gangster film, p. 173).

In the 1960s Laurence Alloway wrote an influential piece in *Movie* ('Iconography of the Movies', 1963) and mounted and wrote an introductory booklet to an important season at the Museum of Modern Art in New York, *Violent America: The Movies 1946–64* (1971). His approach was rigorously uncompromising in its insistence on formulae and ephemera as the basis of the popular Hollywood cinema claimed as the product of great 'artists' by the *auteurists*. In the early 1970s several articles on genre appeared in the British journal *Screen*, and three books were produced concentrating on the two genres central to the debate – *Horizons West* (Kitses, 1969), *Underworld USA* (McArthur, 1972) and *The Six-Gun Mystique* (Cawelti, 1971) – and here for a while the theoretical debates around genre stopped. As *auteur* theory was challenged by the emphasis of cine-semiotics on the text itself as the site of production of meaning and author and spectator positions so the specificities of genre were lost in the general concern with narrative and processes of signification.

Meanwhile, in the 1970s interest shifted from the western and gangster genres which had dominated the 1960s, to exploration of *film noir*. This was a generic category used by film criticism rather than the industry. It demarcated a body of films which could be explored in the new terms being introduced into Anglo-Saxon criticism from the French journal *Cahiers du Cinéma*. Under the influence of a revival of interest in Marxist aesthetics, *Cahiers du Cinéma* was detaching itself from its championship of Hollywood *auteurs*; it suggested a system of categorisation that would discriminate between those films whose formal organisation reinforced their manifest ideological themes, and those which through a process of fracture and disjuncture exposed ideological contradictions. Under this rubric a whole range of Hollywood films, which *auteurism* had virtually been unable to place, could be reappropriated for critical validation. In the late 1970s in response to the assimilation of psychoanalysis and feminism by film theory, melodramas were seen to provide excellent material for the investigation of these interests. As in the case of *film noir*, a neglected, if not despised, area of Hollywood production was brought into critical view (and feminist film theory has since taken up the even lower-rated women's picture as an adjunct to work on melodrama), but little in these investigations took the issues of genre theory itself much further. Exceptional in this respect was an American study by Will Wright, *Sixguns and Society* (1975), which attempted a structuralist analysis of the western (see Will Wright, p. 151). In the preliminaries to his analysis of the western itself Wright attempts to adapt Lévi-Strauss's concept of myth to an explanation of how genre conventions represent problems and shifts in social meanings – in how a society communicates with itself. However, the book's concentration on an individual genre begs the question of how genre itself operates in cinema and what the questions are that are posed by a genre approach to cinema.

In the late 1970s two studies attempted in different ways to revitalise work on the question of genre. Tom Ryall's *Teachers' Study Guide* (1978) on the gangster film set out to analyse the work and debates of the 1960s and 1970s, clarifying the main issues, and to relocate these in relation to structuralist and post-structuralist questions about ideology and signification. In so doing he attempted to indicate how genre criticism can be useful to the student of film. Stephen Neale's monograph, *Genre* (1980), rather than historicising such debates (a task taken on by Paul Willemen in his short introduction), attempted to recast them, conceptualising genre in terms of linguistic and psychoanalytic theory. Before looking more closely at these ideas, however, it is necessary to ask precisely what are the questions posed by a genre approach to cinema.

WHAT IS GENRE CRITICISM?

Tom Ryall (1978) distinguishes genre criticism from the two approaches dominant at the time of its development: *auteurism*, and an earlier tradition which saw films as providing social documents. He sees as a central concern of genre criticism the relationship between the art product, its source and its audience. Both *auteur* and 'social document' approaches use a linear model of this relationship, privileging artist or social reality as the originating source of the art product, which, representing their expression, is then consumed by its audience. In contrast, Ryall suggests, the model offered by genre criticism is triangular, with art product, artist and audience as three equally constituting moments in the production of the text – a view which posits a dynamic and mutually determining relationship between them. The basis of this equality lies in the way the conventions of genre operate. They provide a framework of structuring rules, in the shape of patterns/forms/styles/structures, which act as a form of 'supervision' over the work of production of film-makers and the work of reading by an audience. As a critical enterprise, genre analysis, which looks for repetitions and variations between films rather than originality or individuality, was developed as a more appropriate tool for understanding popular cinema than authorship theories. Following the structuralist intervention and revival of Marxist aesthetics, genre analysis enables film criticism to take account of conditions of production and consumption of films and their relationship to ideology. Thus Ryall places his original triangle – film/artist/audience – in two concentric circles, the first representing the studio, or particular production institution – the film's immediate industrial context – and the second representing the social formation – here American society, western capitalism – of which the film industry and cinematic signification are a part. Whereas the triangular model displaces the notion of a single originating source, the concentric circles displace an earlier Marxist linear model used to account for historical and social determination – in which the base is seen as unproblematically reflected in the superstructure. In this reconceptualisation art and society are not opposed to each other as two abstract and discrete entities; rather art is understood as one of the social practices in which society exists. Ryall's model, then, attempts to grasp the range of determinants – historical, economic, social, cinematic, aesthetic, ideological – involved in the production of meaning in the cinema, without foreclosing on the question of which element dominates in any given instance.

Ryall's conceptual models enable us to establish the general ground of genre criticism. When we move from this overall project to the particularities of how it works, however, we confront many of the problems which have dogged genre criticism in the cinema. While the existence of the major genres is in some ways a self-evident fact, the business of definition and demarcation is less clear-cut. Description gets tangled up with evaluation, both of which snag on the problem of historical change – new films often deny accepted definitions and appear to the genre critic to mark a decline from 'classic' examples. The problem of evaluation reappears in the need for genre criticism to sort out its relation to *auteurism* and the relative weight it gives to the play of conventions compared to the work of the author in the production of particular genre films. The understanding of genre formulae and conventions as a form of cultural tradition poses the problem of how to conceptualise the relation between cultural and other social practices and the ideological roles of the different genres; and this involves consideration of the studio system as part of this relationship. Finally, given that film theory went on to focus on the production of meaning across all texts, and through all cinematic strategies, we have to ask what pertinence genre criticism can have to this project.

GENRES: PROBLEMS OF DEFINITION

Work on individual genres sooner or later comes up against the problem of where one genre stops and another begins. Much early genre criticism concentrated on producing accounts of defining characteristics for particular genres. To do this the critic must start out with at least a provisional notion of what constitutes the genre. Andrew Tudor points succinctly to the problem in this:

> To take a genre such as the 'western', analyse it, and list its principal characteristics, is to beg the question that we must first isolate the body of films which are 'westerns'. But they can only be isolated on the basis of the 'principal characteristics' which can only be discovered from the films themselves after they have been isolated. (Tudor, 1974, p. 135)

The danger here is that the 'provisional notion' crystallises around certain films or a certain period of genre production as a prescriptive 'essence'. Earlier developments then become an 'evolution' towards a 'classic' moment and later deviations constitute decline or decadence. This is very clearly indicated in the work of the two founding critics of genre study of film, André Bazin and Robert Warshow: both wrote seminal pieces about the western, but both picked on different films from different periods as classic examples of the essence of the genre (see The western, p. 147). At issue here is the place of differentiation within the type in genre analysis. Looking to historically discarded literary genres such as Elizabethan revenge tragedy or Restoration comedy as models, Robert Warshow saw repetition rather than differentiation as providing the aesthetic force of a genre:

> For a type to be successful means that its conventions have imposed themselves upon the general consciousness and become the accepted vehicles of a particular set of attitudes and a particular aesthetic effect. One goes to any individual example of the type with very definite expectations, and originality is to be welcomed only in the degree that it intensifies the expected experience without fundamentally altering it. (Warshow, 1970, pp. 129–30)

The Searchers – 'the western ... the American film *par excellence*'

Laurence Alloway (1971), on the other hand, writing in the context of late 1960s developments in genre theory, resists the temptation to establish 'classic' timeless dimensions in popular forms. He insists on the transitional and ephemeral character of any particular period of genre production. Rather than attempting definitive accounts of particular genres or genre films he talks about 'cycles, runs or sets', so drawing attention to the shifts and differences which constitute 'internal successive modifications of forms'. Colin McArthur's study of the gangster film (1972) extends this view of differentiation within particular forms to the problems of demarcating one form from another. He argues that one must talk about the gangster/thriller, because the limits of each form are fluid, constituting a spectrum with an infinite number of gradations. He describes the forty-year development of this sprawling genre as 'a constantly growing amoeba, assimilating stages of its own development' (McArthur, 1972, p. 8). Anthony Easthope (1980) has suggested the usefulness of Tzvetan Todorov's argument that a specific genre should be understood as an abstract, theoretical and provisional structure, incarnated in specific examples, but itself transformed by each new production so 'any instance of a genre will be necessarily different' (Easthope, 1980, p. 40). Stephen Neale's work similarly argues against attempts to define genres as discrete, strictly differentiated and fixed systems in which the critic searches across the range of cinematic codes for relationships of repetition representing rigid rules of inclusion and exclusion. Neale's position, discussed more fully below, emphasises the role of 'difference' in generic production (see also Vernet, 1978).

However, even with a flexible model, empirical assumptions will enter any discussion of specific genres. If these are to be rigorously founded the critic must decide which of the cinematic codes are pertinent to the definition of a particular genre. In his survey of the early development of British genre criticism, Tom Ryall identifies three broad sets of terms used to net the constituents of individual genres: socio-historical actuality, thematic/ideological constructions deriving from history and iconography or visual imagery.

Iconography

The notion of iconography was perhaps particularly influential in the work of the 1960s and early 1970s on genre because it offered a parallel course to the one already laid out by

The Big Sleep – gangster/crime film with contract star Bogart

the *auteur* validation of Hollywood films. If to literary minds their plots were corny and the dialogue banal this was because the literary critic had no language to cope with cinema as a visual medium. *Auteurism* developed the notion of *mise-en-scène* to fill this gap; genre critics turned to iconography. Edward Buscombe (1970), for instance, argued forcibly that it was in terms of iconography – rather than, for example, narrative structure or rhythm that the dynamic of particular genres should be specified: 'Since we are dealing with a visual medium we ought surely to look for our defining criteria at what we actually see on the screen . . .' (Buscombe, 1970, p. 36). Whereas *mise-en-scène* provided the means of materialising the author's personal vision, the notion of iconography gave life to the conventions of generic production, investing them with historical and cultural 'resonances' which, put to work in new combinations and contexts, could produce new articulations of meaning. By iconography Buscombe meant recurrent images, including the physical attributes and dress of the actors, the settings, the tools of the trade (horses, cars, guns, etc.). Colin McArthur (1972) makes a similar categorisation for the gangster/thriller, attributing to these icons a degree of formal organisation – a 'continuity over several decades of *patterns* of visual imagery' (McArthur, 1972, p. 24, our emphasis). Although iconography was undeniably 'visual', McArthur in a later unpublished BFI seminar paper, 'Iconography and Iconology' (1973), located it in the 'profilmic arrangements of sign-events'. In other words it was not produced by specifically filmic codes but was taken up and transformed by cinema from cultural codes already in circulation, a point returned to below.

Crucial to the functioning of such iconic conventions is the cumulative knowledge and expectation of the audience:

> In *Little Caesar* (1930) a police lieutenant and two of his men visit a nightclub run by gangsters. All three wear large hats and heavy coats, are grim and sardonic and stand in triangular formation, the lieutenant at the front, his two men flanking him in the rear. The audience knows immediately what to expect of them by their physical attributes, their dress and deportment. It knows, too, by the disposition of the figures, which is dominant, which is subordinate. (McArthur, 1972, p. 23)

This knowledge provides the ground on which the 'popular' in the commercial cinema attains its dynamic, the means by which significance, art, is produced sometimes without the artist; for accretions of the cinematic past in generic convention generate a set of expectations in audiences and these provide, as Bourget has suggested, opportunities for their disruption, postponement or displacement; disturbances not necessarily attributable to individual film-makers (Bourget, 1977).

Buscombe has given a celebrated example of iconography at work in his account of the opening of *Guns in the Afternoon*:

> Knowing the period and location, we expect at the beginning to find a familiar western town. In fact, the first few minutes of the film brilliantly disturb expectations. As the camera moves around the town, we discover a policeman in uniform, a car, a camel, and Randolph Scott dressed up as Buffalo Bill. Each of these images performs a function. The figure of the policeman conveys that the law has become institutionalised; the rough and ready frontier days are over. The car suggests, as in *The Wild Bunch*, that the west is no longer isolated from modern technology and its implications. Significantly, the camel is racing against a horse; such a grotesque juxtaposition is painful. A horse in a western is not just an animal but a symbol of dignity, grace and power. These qualities are mocked by it competing with a camel; and to add insult to injury, the camel wins. (Buscombe, in Grant, 1977, p. 44)

Of course, it could be argued that while the genre allows for the introduction of the car into a western under pressure from the industry to mine relatively unworked aspects of its relation to the historical west – in this case the closing of the frontier – only the touch of the baroque sensibilities of a Sam Peckinpah could have dreamed up the camel. However, it is the accumulated tradition of the western that allows a camel to produce so forceful a shock and sense of estrangement.

It can be seen from these examples that while iconography is manifested in visual terms it contains considerably more than simple visual imagery – dress connotes character, the three gangsters formation will initiate certain movements in plot, and so on. Moreover, in particular visual motifs iconography focuses a wide range of social, cultural and political themes which are part of the currency of the society for which it works. The art criticism of Erwin Panofsky was often cited by critics looking for a visual rather than literary heritage to illuminate cinematic conventions. Colin McArthur (1973) argues that the iconography of the western or ganster films carries cultural meanings which are 'read' by contemporary western audiences in much the same way that an ordinary Frenchman of the thirteenth century could 'read' Chartres Cathedral and that a seventeenth-century Venetian could 'read' Francesco Maffei's painting of Judith of Bethulia. This aspect of iconography provided the source of some debate with *auteur* critics, and the ground on which the genre critics attempted to argue a more subtle relation between socio-historical actuality and particular genres (see Genre: history and ideology, below).

Iconography dominated genre study as long as the western and gangster genres remained the focus of empirical interest – perhaps because of its capacity to mediate between historical traditions and particular cinematic forms. However, despite its basis in visual imagery, iconography fails to take account of the finer detail of visual style – camera movement, lighting, editing, for example. Nor does it deal with patterns of narrative structure. And while it enabled the critic to infer action and character attributes in a film's play of meaning, the shift of interest into new generic areas – *film noir*, or melodrama for instance – found the 'iconographical programmes' which seemed appropriate to the western or gangster film restricting, so that the notion of genre was often displaced in favour of visual style or dramatic modality (see Place, and Harvey, in Kaplan, 1978). A further problem was the tendency of the focus on iconography to produce taxonomies which, while they provided the underlying structure of individual genres and were an extremely useful empirical tool for collating the range of cultural knowledge such genres assumed, could offer little illumination of any particular example beyond its membership of a particular genre (see Ryall, 1978, pp. 13 and 24–6). Thus genre criticism would often turn back to authorship to account for individual films, and both Jim Kitses and Colin McArthur provide authorship case studies, though qualified ones, to follow on their seminal accounts of the western and gangster/thriller genres respectively (see Genre and authorship, p. 142).

The problems of an iconographical approach to genre were displaced by the British appropriation of semiotics and structuralism in the 1970s, which seemed to offer a totalising account of the production of meaning in the cinema. However, semiotics and structuralism tend to work at an abstract, formal level, and while they may explain how iconography functions, the iconographical programmes worked out by the earlier genre critics provide an empirical base for locating particular genres and a means of tracing the historical and cultural traditions which give them their social dimension. Later writing on melodrama, for instance – a genre with very fluid boundaries, many sub-generic offshoots and a complex relation to other forms and traditions – has, arguably, suffered from the absence of such empirical groundwork in its frequent lack of precision.

HISTORY AND IDEOLOGY

The foregoing discussion of iconography has already broached the question of the relation of cinematic genres to historical traditions and cultural conventions. This dimension was important to the evaluation of Hollywood genre films in terms of popular rather than high art. In the case of the western and gangster film these connections could be traced to historical actuality itself:

> the western and the gangster film have a special relationship with American society. Both deal with critical phases of American history. It could be said that they represent America talking to itself about, in the case of the western, its agrarian past, and in the case of the gangster film/thriller its urban technological present. (McArthur, 1972, p. 18)

While it is evident that for these genres at least history provides basic subject matter and many aspects of form, the question that confronts genre study is how the relation of history to fiction is to be understood. McArthur's notion of a society 'talking to itself' suggests less a search for historical reconstruction or, in the case of the gangster film, reflection, than what Tom Ryall calls the 'social perception of historical actuality'. This shifts the focus from historical 'fact' to ideology; here, as Tom Ryall (1978) suggests, the historical raw material of a genre is perceived in terms of a network of thematic constructions – for instance, Jim Kitses's (1969) analysis of the history of the west in American consciousness as a conflict between the themes of garden versus wilderness (see The western, p. 150).

At issue here is the relation of socio-historical reality and cultural and aesthetic convention. On the one hand, as Colin McArthur (1972) points out, our ideas about the American west or Prohibition are as likely to be gleaned from the cinema as from history books. On the other, Robert Warshow has argued that once historical reality is taken up in an aesthetic process, aesthetic determinations take over: genre films refer not to historical reality but to other genre films and they evolve according to the rules of generic production:

> Moreover, the relationship between the conventions which go to make up such a type and the real experience of its audience or the real facts of whatever situation it pretends to describe is only of secondary importance and does not determine its aesthetic force. It is only in an ultimate sense that the type appeals to its audience's experience of reality; much more immediately, it appeals to previous experience of the type itself: it creates its own field of reference. (Warshow, 1970, pp. 129–30)

Neither of these positions confront the problem of determining what meanings are being circulated. However, together they raise interesting questions about the interplay between ideologies and aesthetic conventions in the construction of 'social perceptions of history'. Judith Hess (in Grant, 1977) starts from the position that generic convention, as a product of formulaic repetition for a capitalist-financed studio system, can only produce meanings in support of the status quo. Genre films drew audiences and were financially successful 'because they temporarily relieved the fears aroused by a recognition of social and political conflicts' (Hess in Grant, 1977, p. 54). They did this by encouraging 'simplistic solutions – the adherence to a well-defined, unchanging code, the advocacy of methods of problem solving based on tradition' (Hess in Grant, 1977, p. 55). Clearly behind such a view of the working of convention in the cinema is the assumption that films address the problems of the real world directly, and provide solutions on a realisable level. Genre films are indictable because they construct reality according to outworn, reactionary conventions. An opposite view, in relation to the gangster film, is put by Robert Warshow, who argues that the popularity of this genre rests not in its official solution to a social problem – 'crime does not pay' – but its ability to provide at an imaginative level a quite different response to American society:

> the importance of the gangster film, and the nature and intensity of its emotional and aesthetic impact, cannot be measured in terms of the place of the gangster himself or the importance of the problem of crime in American life ... What matters is that the experience of the gangster as an experience of art is universal to Americans.
>
> ... the gangster speaks for us, expressing that part of the American psyche which rejects the qualities and demands of modern life, which rejects 'Americanism' itself ... the gangster is the 'no' to that great American 'yes' which is stamped so big over our official culture and yet has so little to do with the way we really feel about our lives. (Warshow, 1970, pp. 130, 136)

For Warshow, generic convention is distinct from the social reality on which it feeds, thus allowing the possibility of ideological criticism. The aesthetic compulsion of generic repetition then suggests, as it were, a neuralgic point – 'there is something more here than meets the eye'.

The emergence in the late 1960s of a concern with the workings of ideology in cinematic forms found a progressive potential for genre in the requirement for differentiation at the commercial as well as aesthetic level – the difference being precisely what draws the audience back into the cinema for the pleasure of repetition, and what makes 'the same' perceptible (see The studios, p. 11). Jean-Loup Bourget (1977) argues that 'wherever an art form is highly conventional, the opportunity for subtle irony or distanciation presents itself all the more readily' (Bourget, 1977, p. 62).

The concept of radical reading – suggesting that generic conventions allow meanings to be constructed against a film's ideological grain – introduces a further problem in the task of relating genres to socio-historical reality: the question of whether the meanings we construct for a genre are those understood by the audience who went to see the films when they first appeared, or those which belong to a contemporary perception of both socio-historical and cinematic actuality. This means respecting the historical conditions of production and consumption (see Ryall, 1978, pp. 11–12) and drawing on the understanding given us by semiotics of the potentially multiple meanings of any signification and our dependency on particular cultural contexts for specific readings.

Genre and industry

So far discussion has focused on how authorial concerns and socio-historical reality have been seen as caught up in the interplay between aesthetic structures and their audiences – arguably producing something far removed from either social actuality or a director's intentions. It remains to consider the place of this activity in the film industry and the wider institution of cinema. While history has often been posed as a source of a genre's subject matter, and social or psychic reasons credited with maintaining an audience's interest in a particular genre, the economic organisation of the film industry along the lines of commodity production is cited as the reason for the existence of genres themselves. As the market for entertainment is notoriously difficult to predict and control, profit is dependent on the successful identification and capture of particular audiences. Generic production grew out of the attempt to repeat and build on initial successes. The studio system developed to facilitate such production: 'each genre had its regular scriptwriters, sometimes on a yearly contract, its directors, its craftsmen, its studios' (Metz, 1974, p. 122). Tom Ryall (1978) describes how 'the standardisation of product obliged by the economic necessities of large scale industrial production led to particular studios concentrating on particular genres' (Ryall, 1978, p. 4). And Edward Buscombe (1974), argued that at Warner Bros. 'stars and genre were ... mutually reinforcing' (Buscombe, 1974, p. 59) – the presence of Cagney and Bogart on contract there favoured production of gangster films and vice versa (see Warner Bros., pp. 19–22). Moreover, if a studio spent a lot of money acquiring a star or another sort of 'generic asset' – e.g. an elaborate western townscape or nightclub set – the cost could be spread over extended periods of production and returns maximised against capital outlay.

It was not only production that was organised along generic lines. Distribution and exhibition sought to market films and attract audiences by mobilising a set of expectations through advertising and promotional gimmicks, while film journalism and critical reviewing perpetuated generic divisions by working within generic expectations and assumptions.

In this context it has been argued that any study of Hollywood or the studio system must be a study of genre. The problem, however, is not to identify the economic rationale for genres, but to know what such knowledge tells us about this particular aspect of cultural production. Tom Ryall argues that it indicates one set of constraints

Shane – the western 'talking about America's agrarian past' . . .

. . . and the gangster film – 'its urban technological present' – *Machine Gun Kelly*

in the production context of film-making which must be taken into account but not accorded sole determination over the end products. This context, particularly in an entertainment industry, is not and cannot function monolithically. Not only is product differentiation an economic necessity, but:

> the production personnel of a film will include a number of people whose practices fall under the general rubric of 'the creative', e.g. directors, scriptwriters, actors, actresses, designers and so on. A corpus of individuals whose ideology of film will inevitably differ from that of those whose primary allegiance is to a Wall Street finance house. Any description of the Hollywood system will have to take account of the many different often contradictory, tendencies which jostle with each other during the production of a film. (Ryall, 1978, p. 32)

More recently Stephen Neale (1980) has tried to extend the purchase of industrial consideration on genre by utilising the concept of cinematic institution or machine developed by Christian Metz and Stephen Heath amongst others, and taking a cue from Ryall's references to generic marketing and reviewing practices. From this perspective the industry is seen not so much as an economic or manufacturing system, but rather as a social institution constituted in a number of discursive practices which include both production and consumption. Genres are not simply the outcome of a certain kind of studio organisation but involve the consolidation in the spectator of a set of viewing orientations, expectations, positions. Behind this lies an attempt to provide a more dialectical model of the relation between industry, text and audience and to conceptualise it as a process rather than a series of reflections between a number of discrete, fixed and static positions. This reconceptualisation of the film industry as cinematic institution prepares the ground for Neale's interest in locating genre within a general, psychoanalytic theory of narrative.

Genre and authorship

Having outlined the different ways in which genre criticism was established it remains to consider how its relation to authorship was conceived after its initial challenge to this tradition. Only Laurence Alloway appeared to accept the total displacement of the author by generic convention, arguing that collective authorship and diffusion of responsibility are the actual working conditions of Hollywood and that authorship is therefore much less appropriate than genre theory in analysis of the American cinema:

> The rhetoric of art discussion tends to require . . . personal authorship and a high level of permanence, criteria not easily satisfied in the popular cinema . . . reflex homage to personal originality too often makes us dismiss as aesthetically formulaic a negligible film that may be an interesting, valid, even original development within the convention. (Alloway, 1971, p. 60)

At the other extreme is the view that while indubitably genre conventions exist, their productivity is dependent on the animating power of an author:

> if genre exists as a distinct quantity it is in terms of a repertoire of stock situations, selected from the events of the American frontier, that are themselves unspecific, ambiguous and intrinsically without meaning . . . neither a structure of archetypal patterns and myths nor of history is sufficiently precise to constitute a genre, nor do recurrent locations, clothes and props do more than signal a temporal and geographical context for a film. (Collins, 1970, pp. 74–5)

Thus history and myth are mediated through the obsessions of the author to animate the conventions of the western with a power attributed by Buscombe and others to the genre itself.

Most genre criticism, however, avoids the extremes of either of these positions, positing a relation between genre convention and authorial concerns which in different ways could be beneficial to the latter. In one view there can be a coincidence between genre and author which enables the director to use its conventions as a kind of shorthand, enabling him or her to go straight to the heart of his/her concerns and express them at a formal level through the interplay of genre convention and motif – a common view, for instance, of the relation between John Ford and the western. In another view the author works in tension with the conventions; attempting to inflect them, so as to express his or her own vision in the differences set up between the expected playing out of the convention and the new twists he or she develops – a vision expressed in counterpoint (see McArthur, 1972, p. 17; see The *auteur* theory, p. 143). A third view posits genre as a beneficial constraint which provides a formal ordering and control over the drive to personal expression, preventing its dissolution in an excess of individualism and incomprehensibility, but at the same time capable of containing a certain non-naturalistic dimension – the theatricality or Expressionism of a baroque sensibility. Colin McArthur argues such a position in relation to Jules Dassin, whose work within the apparent greater freedom of European cinema he sees as inferior to his earlier Hollywood productions.

Finally it remains to note that authorship was often the only recourse for genre critics who wanted to move from discussing the constituents and functioning of the genre itself to discussing their operation in particular films. If genre films could not be evaluated against some presupposed definitive model, then their particularity had to be netted by overlaying another grid, and authorship was the obvious one to hand. Both the major book studies of genres that culminated the first phase of genre study, *Horizons West* and *Underworld USA*, devoted their second halves to looking at individual genre films categorised by author. Thus the question of the place of the author did not disappear. Moreover the difference in *Underworld USA* between the chapters on John Huston and Nicholas Ray suggest that genre and author codes do have different weight in different cases and that these distinctions may parallel those between *auteur* and *metteur-en-scène* (see The *politique des auteurs*, p. 246).

GENRE: REDIRECTIONS IN THE 1980s

Both Tom Ryall (1978) and Stephen Neale (1980) imply in their respective assessments of the first 'wave' of genre criticism the need to place genre within a more 'totalising' theory of cinema. Tom Ryall draws on the concepts of 'cultural production' and 'reading' as a means of shifting genre criticism from the circular and taxonomic tendencies of its earlier phase. The notion of cultural production places film-making as one more practice in a 'network of social practices which constitute a social formation' (Ryall, 1978, p. 24). It therefore stands in dynamic relationship to these practices, overlapping with them, mediating them, participating in a shared body of cultural knowledge or group of discourses, while at the same time operating within its own history and productivity. From this perspective film-making is in the business of producing or reproducing and circulating varieties of pleasure and cultural meaning. Access to cultural meaning is through the activity of reading, understood as the mobilisation of a particular set of conventions and audience expectations. Genre study for Ryall, then, becomes the 'elaboration of perceived meaning where the individual film is tied to its generic roots on the basis of the reading process' (Ryall, 1978, p. 26). The point is not to allocate particular films to their respective genres, but to investigate the implications of our being able to do this at all. Such an examination of how and why the perceived meanings of a film are produced in particular contexts is not tied to the specific text, but can pull back to look at the social motivations and expectations that governed its production, marketing and consumption.

For Stephen Neale, Ryall's approach, although giving valuable insight into the way genre can be reconceptualised, is not totalising enough. Film-makers and audience, history, industry, and society still retain a degree of discreteness and autonomy, confronting each other as a series of dichotomies rather than in a dialectic process. For Neale, any aspect of film must be understood in terms of the social process of cinema as a whole. Working within a psychoanalytic framework, this must in turn be understood in terms of the role of signification in producing and regulating subjectivity. Here subjectivity is understood not as a discrete and fixed identity. Three basic propositions are important in this respect. First, that the subject is driven by the desire to repeat a past pleasure that can never be attained because something can only be perceived as the same through a gap of difference. Second, that identity is always conferred from the position of another – a 'you' is essential to the meaning of 'I'. (All signification repeats this basic pattern, constructing interpersonal subject positions which speaker and addressee must fill in order for signification to take place.) Third, that in consequence of one and two, an autonomous and stable identity can never be attained; rather subjectivity is a process, in which individuals move in and out of positions constructed for them in the various discourses which constitute society.

By virtue of these propositions, genres have to be seen as specific modes of the narrative system, which function to exploit and contain the diversity of mainstream cinema. As components of the cinematic machine they represent 'systems of orientations, expectations and conventions that circulate between industry, text and subject' (Neale, 1980, p. 19). Above all, genres work on the terrain of repetition and difference which it is the work of narrative to regulate. Neale is at pains here to stress repetition and difference as a relation rather than as distinct elements. There can be no difference except in so far as it emerges from repetition and, vice versa, it is only the element of difference that allows repetition to become visible.

Genres, then, are not discrete systems, consisting of a fixed number of listable items and separated out from the rest of cinema, but 'constitute specific variations of the interplay of codes, discursive structures and drives involved in the whole of mainstream cinema' (Neale, 1980, p. 48). In order to locate the 'specific variation' of a particular genre we have to know how narrative organises the codes and discourses which are its material. Narrative is 'a process of transformation of the balance of elements that constitute its pretext; the interruption of an initial equilibrium and tracing of the dispersal and refiguration of its elements' (Neale, 1980, p. 20). Generic specification starts therefore with a consideration of the way in which equilibrium and disruption are articulated. Difference between genres occurs in the particular discourses invoked, the particularity of emphasis on and combinations of elements that are shared with other genres – for instance the relative placing and relations between the discourses of law and heterosexual love are what differentiate the melodrama from the *film noir*, not the exclusivity of one kind of discourse to one genre. Such different emphases and relations between different discourses produce different positionings of the subject. Genre specification can therefore be traced in the different functionings of subjectivity each produces, and in their different modes of addressing the spectator.

Neale's intervention into genre criticism represents an attempt to reorientate the task of genre specification in order to achieve a greater flexibility in demarcation – for instance the emphasis on the relation of repetition and difference allows for the textual productivity of overlaps and contradictions – and a greater sense of how genre may draw on other forms of cinematic signification. As it stands, his account operates at a highly abstract level, the specification of discourses appearing no easier than the categorisation of icons, and often relying on an already established iconographic base as clues to their presence.

GENRE THEORY SINCE THE EARLY 1980s

While studies, theories and histories of individual genres have appeared in great numbers since the early 1980s, studies, theories and histories of genre as such have been few and far between. Within film, media and cultural studies, general theorising, in particular, has tended to focus on issues of narrative, representation, race and ethnicity, sexual difference, identity, and spectatorship, and to explore the merits and limits of postmodernism, post-structuralism, semiotics, psychoanalysis, cognitive psychology, and formalism. Nevertheless, some general theories – and some general questions – have been both advanced and debated.

In two books published in the early 1980s, *Hollywood Genres: Formulas, Film-making, and the Studio System* (1981), and *Old Hollywood/New Hollywood, Ritual, Art, and Industry* (1983), Thomas Schatz puts forward a number of general ideas about the cultural function and significance of Hollywood's genres, about the nature of Hollywood's genre system, and in the second book in particular, about the changes wrought to both by the demise of the studio system and the rise of what he and others have called 'the New Hollywood'(see p. 98). Starting from the premiss that Hollywood's genres have their basis in the economic impulse to repeat or to build upon commercially successful formulas, that this basis was further underpinned on the one hand by the routines and practices of studio production and on the other by the reciprocal links between producer and consumer, artist, industry and audience he sees as integral to the way genres and the industry as a whole tend to work, Schatz argues that these formulas are not only socially and culturally meaningful, but that they perform what he calls a 'ritual' function for the audience and hence for American society as a whole. Borrowing the term, and the idea, from Henry Nash Smith's book, *The Virgin Land* (1950), and acknowledging the limits and qualifications necessitated by some of the commercial and technological aspects of the cinema, Schatz nevertheless sees genres and genre film-making, as Smith sees pulp fiction and pulp writing, 'as a form of collective cultural expression' (Schatz, 1981, p. 13), and hence as a vehicle for the exploration of ideas, ideals, cultural values and ideological dilemmas central to American society. Each genre possesses its own 'generic community' and tends to deal with its own set of dramatic and ideological conflicts and problems. Thus,

> What emerges as a social problem (or dramatic conflict) in one genre is not necessarily a problem in another. Law and order is a problem in the gangster and detective genres, but not in the musical. Conversely, courtship and marriage are problems in the musical but not in the gangster and detective genres. Individualism is celebrated in the detective genre (through the hero's occupation and world view) and in the gangster film (through the hero's career and eventual death), while the principal characters in the musical compromise their individuality in their eventual romantic embrace and thus demonstrate their willingness to be integrated into the social community. (Schatz, 1981, p. 25)

In this way, genres possess their own individual identity and significance, but also belong to a larger generic and cultural system. This system is in turn divisible into genres of two basic kinds or types: genres of 'determinate space' on the one hand, and genres of 'indeterminate space' on the other:

> In a genre of determinate space (Western, gangster, detective, *et al.*), we have a symbolic arena of action. It represents a cultural realm in which fundamental values are in a state of sustained conflict. In these genres, then, the contest itself and its necessary arena are 'determinate' – a specific social conflict is violently enacted within a familar locale according to a prescribed system of rules and behavioral codes. (Schatz, 1981, p. 27)

In addition, and in part because conflict in the genres of determinate space centres on the nature and control of the space, the setting, itself: this setting, its props, its inhabitants and their dress, tend to figure significantly in a developed and highly coded visual iconography. (Hence the extent to which the concept of generic iconography was developed in relation to genres of this kind.) By contrast:

> genres of indeterminate space generally involve a doubled . . . hero in the guise of a romantic couple who inhabit a 'civilized' setting, as in the musical, screwball comedy, and social melodrama. The physical and ideological 'contest' which determines the arena of action in the Western, gangster, and detective genres is not an issue here. Instead, genres of indeterminate space incorporate a civilized, ideologically stable milieu, which depends less upon a heavily coded place than on a highly conventionalized value system. Here conflicts derive not from a struggle for control of the environment, but rather from the struggle of the principal characters to bring their own views in line either with one another's or, more often, in line with that of the larger community.
>
> Unlike genres of determinate space, these genres rely on a progression from romantic antagonism to eventual embrace. The kiss, or embrace signals the integration of the couple into the larger cultural community. In addition, these genres use inconographic conventions to establish a social setting – the proscenium or theater stage with its familiar performers in some musicals, for example, or the repressive small-town community and the family home in the melodrama. But because the generic conflicts arise from attitudinal, (generally male–female) oppositions rather than from a physical conflict, the coding in these films tends to be less visual and more ideological and abstract (Schatz, 1981, pp. 27–9).

In *Old Hollywood/New Hollywood*, Schatz puts forward similar ideas. However, he also argues that since the decline of the studio system, the genre system and its ritual function have broken down. A 'radical', 'experimental' or 'modernist' group of film-makers made genre films which self-consciously 'examined the very nature of the genres themselves and their ongoing cultural appeal' (Schatz, 1983, p. 27): 'Gangster films like *Bonnie and Clyde* and *Mean Streets*, detective films like *The Long Goodbye* and *The Conversation*, musicals like *New York, New York* and *All That Jazz*, Westerns like *Ulzana's Raid* and *McCabe and Mrs Miller*, war films like *The Deer Hunter* and *Apocalypse Now*, romantic comedies like *Annie Hall* and *Smile* – these and other films were designed for widespread distribution and are genre films, but they finally do more to challenge and reflect upon their generic heritage than to mindlessly sustain it' (Schatz, 1983, pp. 27–8).

Generic blockbusters like *Love Story* (1970), *The Poseidon Adventure* (1972), *The Sting* (1973), *Jaws* (1975) and *Star Wars* (1977) did attract 'the closest thing to a "mass audience" in the New Hollywood', 'but often this was due as much if not more to the hype of the marketing campaigns than the quality of the films themselves'. (Schatz, 1983, p. 20). In short, 'without the steady production and audience feedback of the old integrated system, the ongoing discourse – the process of cultural exchange – between audience and industry has ended' (Schatz, 1983, p. 26). Ended too, therefore, is genre's ritual function.

Schatz's work is mentioned in passing by Rick Altman in his book on *The American Film Musical* (1987). Altman notes that while Schatz and other champions of the ritual approach to genre like John Cawelti (1971 and 1976), Leo Braudy (1976), Frank McConnell (1975), Michael Wood (1973) and Will Wright (1975) were all ultimately 'attributing ultimate authorship to the audience, with the studios simply serving, for a price, the national will', 'a parallel ideological approach was demonstrating how audiences are manipulated by the business and political interests of Hollywood' (Altman, 1987, p. 94). Citing *Cahiers du Cinéma*, *Jump Cut* and *Screen* as vehicles of the latter (a trend to which Neale (1980) also clearly belongs), Altman is at pains to stress the irreconcilable differences between the two approaches: 'Whereas the ritual approach sees Hollywood as responding to societal pressure and thus expressing audience desires, the ideological approach claims that Hollywood takes advantage of spectator energy and psychic investment in order to lure the audience into Hollywood's own positions. The two are irreducibly opposed' (Altman, 1987, p. 94).

Altman is here content to note that these two approaches 'continue to represent the most interesting and well defended of recent approaches to Hollywood genre film' (Altman, 1989, p. 94). He himself goes on to argue that the ritual and ideological functions or dimensions of genre are, in fact, negotiable, variable, unpredictable, a position which is later echoed by Neale (1990), who argues that the ritual approach tends to ignore 'the role of institutional determinations and decisions, by-passing the industry and the sphere of production in an equation between market availability, consumer choice, consumer preference, and broader social and cultural beliefs' (Neale, 1990, p. 64), and that the ideological approach is open to charges of 'reductivism, economism, and cultural pessimism' (Neale, 1990, p. 65). He instead proposes 'context-specific analysis' (Neale, 1990, p. 65).

Altman's discussion of the ritual and ideological approaches to genre occurs during the course of a broader discussion of genre and genre theory. During the course of this broader discussion, he offers both a model – or conceptual grid – for the analysis of individual genres, and a framework or procedure – for the analysis of genre as such. First, following Fredric Jameson (1975), he argues that one can distinguish between 'semantic' and 'syntactic' approaches to genre and genres:

> While there is anything but general agreement on the exact frontier separating semantic from syntactic views, we can as a whole distinguish between generic definitions which depend on a list of common traits, attitudes, characters, shots, locations, sets, and the like – thus stressing the semantic elements which make up the genre – and definitions which play up instead certain constitutive relationships between undesignated placeholders – relationships which might be called the genre's fundamental syntax. The semantic approach thus stresses the genre's building blocks, while the syntactic view privileges the structures into which they are arranged. (Altman, 1987, p. 95)

He then goes on to argue that these two approaches are complementary, not mutually exclusive, to propose that every genre possesses semantic traits and syntactic characteristics, and to argue in addition that

> When genres are redefined in terms of their semantic and syntactic dimensions, new life is breathed into the notion of genre history. Instead of simply enumerating the minor variations developed by various studios or directors within a general, fundamentally stable generic framework, genre history based on a semantic/syntactic hypothesis would take as its object three interrelated concerns: 1) the introduction and disappearance of basic semantic elements (e.g., the musical's deployment of a succession of styles – from operetta and chansonnier crooning and opera to swing and folk to rock and nostalgia); 2) the development and abandoning of specific syntactic solutions (e.g., the move from the early sound period identification of music with sadness, usually in three-person plots assuring a sad, solitary odd-man-out, to the post-1933 emphasis on music as celebration of a joyous union of opposites, in the culture as well as the couple); 3) the ever-changing relationship between the semantic and syntactic aspects of the genre (e.g., the way in which diegetic music, the musical's semantic element par excellence, is transformed from a flashy but unintegrated element of spectacle into a signifier of success and a device for reversal of the traditional image over-sound hierarchy). (Altman, 1987, pp. 97–8)

Like Schatz's distinction between genres of determinate and indeterminate space, Altman's distinction between generic semantics and generic syntax remains unexplored and untested by others. It is attractive in its economy, and in the methodological purchase it appears to offer genre theorists and genre historians. However, as Altman himself points out, questions – particularly questions of definition and clarification – remain. To what extent, for instance, can a musical style (like operetta, folk or swing) be considered a semantic element, a building-block, to use Altman's term, of the musical considered as a genre? To be sure, different musical styles convey different meanings. They therefore perform a semantic function. But surely the building blocks of the musical are not musical styles, but, simply, songs and passages of music? (And not all of them are diegetic: passages of dance in numerous musicals are accompanied not by diegetic but by non-diegetic music; what matters, both in songs and in passages of dance, is that, as Altman himself points out, the hierarchy of image over sound is reversed, and the body and its activities on the one hand and the means and devices of cinematic enunciation on the other are organised around, and subordinated to, sound, music, and the soundtrack.) Moreover, in so far as the style of music used in a musical acquires a generically specific semantic dimension, surely that dimension is syntactically governed? These particular questions relate to the two more general questions Altman raises himself: 'Just where ... do we locate the border between the semantic and the syntactic? And how are these two categories related?' (Altman, 1987, p. 99). These questions, and others, remain unexplored.

Altman's propositions about the semantic and syntactic dimensions of genre arise in the context of a more general concern with the aims and procedures of genre analysis. The aims include the identification and explanation of the attributes of a genre, an explanatory account of the genre's history, and an account of 'the way in which the genre is moulded by, functions within, and in turn informs the society of which it is a part' (Altman, 1987, pp. 14–15). Central to these aims is the establishment of a generic corpus, a group of films which can clearly be considered as musicals or westerns, horror films, gangster films and so on. Within this context, Altman considers the role of industrial and journalistic discourse and its terms. It is a role he considers crucial in establishing the possible presence or existence of genres, but of limited value in nearly all other respects. Even here,

> The fact that a genre has been posited, defined, and delimited by Hollywood is taken only as prime facie evidence that generic levels of meaning are operative within or across a group of texts roughly designated by the Hollywood term and its usage. The industrial/journalistic term thus founds a hypothesis about the presence of meaningful activity, but does not necessarily contribute a definition or delimitation of the genre in question. (Altman, 1987, p. 13)

For Altman, the location of an industrial term, and of the group of films to which that term has been applied, is merely the first step in a multi-stage process. Having established a preliminary corpus in this way, the role of 'the genre critic' is to subject the corpus to analysis and to locate a method for defining and describing the structures, functions and systems specific to as many of the films within it as is possible. The next step is to redefine the corpus in the light of the critic's analysis:

> Texts which correspond to a particular understanding of the genre, that is which provide ample material for a given method of analysis, will be retained within the generic corpus. Those which are not illuminated by the method ... will simply be excluded from the final corpus. In terms of the musical, this would mean admitting that there are some films which include a significant amount of diegetic music, and yet which we will refuse to identify as musicals in the strong sense which the final corpus implies. (Altman, 1987, p. 14)

Having thus established a final corpus, the critic is then in a position to produce a history of the genre, and an account of its social significance.

Altman's own analysis of the musical, and his own redefinition of its corpus, is itself impressively comprehensive and inclusive in scope. However, despite the many merits of his analytical definition, he finds himself excluding from a redefined corpus films like *Dumbo* (1941) and *Bambi* (1942), and able only to include films like *The Wizard of Oz* (1939), Fox's Shirley Temple films, and Universal's Deanna Durbin vehicles by means of a particularly tortured and circuitous argument. And it is with this stage of Altman's procedure, and the limited role it assigns industrial and journalistic discourse, that Stephen Neale takes issue in 'Questions of Genre' (1990).

Neale disagrees with the proposition that the aim of generic analysis is the redefinition or rearrangement of a corpus of films: 'Such an aim is in the end no different, in effect if not in intention, from ... the worst, pigeonholing inheritances of neo-classical literary theory. We can easily end up identifying the purpose of generic analysis with the rather fruitless attempt to decide which films fit, and therefore properly belong to, which genres. We can also end up constructing or perpetuating canons of films, privileging some and emoting or excluding others' (Neale, 1990, p. 31). In addition, an aim such as this is in danger of curtailing the very cultural and historical analysis upon which Altman rightly insists as an additional theoretical aim. The danger lies not only in the devaluation of industrial/journalistic discourses, but in the separation of genre analysis from a number of the features which define its public circulation. These features include the fact that genres always exist in excess of a corpus of films; the fact that genres comprise expectations and audience knowledge as well as films; and the fact that these expectations and the knowledge they entail are public in status (Neale, 1990, p. 31).

Neale continues, quoting Todorov (1976, p. 102), and moving on to place industrial and journalistic discourse, and the discourses of promotion and publicity that surround the films themselves, at the heart of genre study. Borrowing Gregory Lukow and Steve Ricci's term 'inter-textual relay' to refer to these discourses (Lukow and Ricci, 1984, p. 29), he writes:

> As Todorov has argued (while himself tending to equate genres solely with works): One can always find a property common to two texts, and therefore put them together in one class. But is there any point in calling the result of such a union a 'genre'? I think it would be in accord with the current usage of the word and at the same time provide a convenient and operant notion if we agreed to call 'genres' only those classes of texts that have been perceived as such in the course of history. The accounts of this perception are found most often in the discourse on genres (the metadiscursive discourse) and, in a sporadic fashion, in the texts themselves.
>
> As far as the cinema is concerned (Todorov here is writing about literature – and High Literature at that), this metadiscursive discourse is to be found in its inter-textual relay. Clearly, generic expectations and knowledges do not emanate solely from the industry and its ancillary institutions; and clearly, individual spectators may have their own expectations, classifications, labels and terms. But these individualized, idiosyncratic classifications play little part, if any, in the public formation and circulation of genres and generic images. In the public sphere, the institutional discourses are of central importance. Testimony to the existence of genres, and evidence of their properties, is to be found primarily there. (Neale, 1990, pp. 51–2).

Neale goes on to argue that industrial and journalistic labels and terms constitute key evidence of and for the history and the historicity of genres: 'they ... offer virtually the only available evidence for an historical study of the array of genres in circulation, or of the ways in which individual films have been generically perceived at any point in time' (Neale, 1990, p. 52). This is important because 'both the array and the perceptions have changed' (Neale, 1990, p. 52), and Neale goes on to give two examples. He points out on the one hand that 'the western', as an established term of generic description, only came into existence in or around 1910. It is therefore unlikely that the term was applied to *The Great Train Robbery* (1903), which has often been classified since as an important early western. He in addition quotes Charles Musser (1984), who argues that *The Great Train Robbery* is best understood, and was understood at the time, not as a western, but as a crime film that drew also on the paradigms and conventions of melodrama, 'the chase film', and the 'railway genre'. On the other hand, Neale points out that the terminology used in the catalogues of film companies in the early part of the century indicates considerable differences between the generic regimes characteristic of early cinema and the more familiar regimes of the studio and post-studio era. He quotes both from the Kleine catalogue of Moving Picture Machines, Stereoptikons, Slides, Films (1905, p. 5) and from the Biograph Bulletins, 1896–1908 (1971, pp. 59–73).

Thus instead of the westerns, horror films and war films of later years, the Kleine Optical Company's catalogue for 1905 lists films in the following groupings:

1. Story
    a. historical
    b. dramatic
    c. narrative
2. Comic
3. Mysterious
4. Scenic
5. Personalities

Meanwhile, Biograph's 'Advance Partial List' of films for sale in 1902 lists its 'subjects' under the following titles and headings: Comedy Views, Sports and Pastime Views, Military Views, Railroad Views, Scenic Views, Views of Notable Personages, Miscellaneous Views, Trick Pictures, Marine Views, Children's Pictures, Fire and Patrol Views, Pan-American Exposition Views, Vaudeville Views, and Parade Pictures (p. 55).

This kind of work is pursued in Neale's article 'Melo talk: on the meaning and use of the term "Melodrama" in the American Trade Press' (1993) (which is discussed in the section on melodrama below), and also in *Genre and Hollywood*. The latter in addition takes up a number of questions raised by Alan Williams (1984) in a review of Schatz (1981) and Neale (1980), and attempts to set forth a number of new ideas and new definitions.

Williams's questions are fundamental: perhaps the biggest problem with genre theory or genre criticism is the term genre. Borrowed, as a critical tool, from literary studies ... the applicability of 'genre' as a concept in film studies raises some fairly tough questions. Sample genres are held to be Westerns, Science Fiction Films, more recently Disaster Films, and so on. What do these loose groupings of works – that seem to come and go, for the most part, in ten- and twenty-year cycles – have to do with familiar literary genres such as tragedy, comedy, romance, or (to mix up the pot a bit) the epistolary novel or the prose poem' (Williams, 1984, p. 121).

He continues,

> For the phrase 'genre films', referring to a general category, we can frequently, though not always, substitute 'film narrative.' Perhaps that is the real genre. Certainly there is much more difference between *Prelude to Dog Star Man* and *Star Wars* than there is between the latter and *Body Heat*. It's mainly a question of terminology, of course, but I wonder if we ought to consider the principal genres ... as being narrative film, experimental/avant-garde film, and documentary. Surely these are the categories in film studies that have among themselves the sorts of significant differences that one can find between, say, epic and lyric poetry. (Williams, 1984, p. 121)

Responding to this, Neale first points out that the genres and genre categories characteristic of literature are by no means always as systematically coherent or long-lived as

Williams appears to suggest. Comedy, romance and tragedy are all long-lived as terms, but the criteria that define them and the types of work the terms encompass have in each case shifted radically over time. (See Beer, 1970, on romance, and Koelb, 1975, on tragedy.) In addition, the western and science fiction are literary genres as well as being genres in the cinema. Even the disaster film has its analogue in a series of novels written in the late 1960s and early 1970s. (Novels like *Airport* by Arthur Hailey and *The Poseidon Adventure* by Paul Gallico.)

This leads on to a second point. Western novels, science fiction novels (even disaster novels) are frequently thought of, precisely, as genre fiction, a term which marks a division between this kind of fiction and 'literary fiction' or simply 'literature' proper. The latter is usually considered the province of 'genuine' literary art and 'authentic' authorial expression. The former, by contrast, is usually considered formulaic, artistically anonymous, and therefore artistically worthless. However, as Kress and Threadgold (1988) and Threadgold (1989) have shown, there is a distinct history to these kinds of attitudes and to the ways in which genre and conceptions of genre have figured within them. An almost symmetrical inversion has occurred since the end of the eighteenth century. Prior to the advent of Romanticism, industrialisation, urbanisation, mass literacy, and the regular production of fiction of all kinds for the mass market, genre, and the kind of order and decorum it implied, was valued and promoted as a mark of high culture, and as in contrast to the anarchy, the lack of order – the lack of genre – seen as characteristic of low culture (political pamphlets, ballads, chapbooks and the like).

Genre, then, has always been a value-laden term and has always been used to mark divisions between (as well as within) fields of artistic production. Ideology rather than logic has always governed or overshadowed definitions of genre. Thus in support of Williams's argument, there is no logical reason whatsoever why avant-garde films and documentaries should not be considered as genres, particularly as they both possess their own infrastructures of production, distribution, exhibition, promotion and critical discussion – their own intertextual relays and their own terms of description – in addition to their own conventions and textual features. There is no logical reason either why 'the narrative film' should not be treated as a genre. However, Neale's third point is that there is equally no reason for the categories 'narrative film' and 'Western' (or 'Science-Fiction' or 'Disaster Film') to be treated as mutually exclusive. Most texts, and most films, are multiply generic: *Star Wars* and *Body Heat*, to use two of Williams's examples are, simultaneously, 'films', 'fiction films', 'Hollywood films' and 'narrative feature films'; the former is also 'science-fiction', 'space opera' and/or 'action–adventure', and the latter a 'thriller' (and possibly also 'neo-*noir*').

This point stems, finally, from a discussion, a discussion of definitions and debates about genre within speech–act theory, pragmatics and philosophy. Both speech–act theory and pragmatics are branches of linguistics. They are concerned with language in use, and in particular with the rules and conventions governing the production, reception and comprehension of specific kinds of linguistic utterance in specific kinds of context. (See Blakemore, 1992; Davis, 1991; Enkvist, 1991; Leech, 1983; Levinson, 1983; Lyons, 1981; pp. 171–219; and Mey, 1993.) Issues of genre are central to pragmatics and speech–act theory because generic expectations and conventions characterise all forms and instances of utterance, not just those conventionally thought of as aesthetic. As Mary Louise Pratt points out, 'Genre is not solely a literary matter. The concept of genres applies to all verbal behavior, in all realms of discourse. Genre conventions are in play in any speech situation, and any discourse belongs to a genre, unless it is a discourse explicity designed to flaunt the genre system' (Pratt, 1981, p. 176)

Jacques Derrida (1992) has criticised aspects of speech–act orientated genre theory on the grounds that texts can always exceed or evade specific expectations, labels and contexts. He would therefore contest the notion that texts 'belong' to genres. He would also deny, though, that any utterance, text or discourse could ever escape being generic. A particular utterance, text or discourse might well be able to 'flaunt' a particular 'genre system'. But it could never entirely evade what he calls 'the law of genre', for the simple reason that all utterances, whenever they are actually encountered, are always encountered in a context of one kind or another, and are therefore always confronted with expectations, with systems of comprehension, and in all probability with labels and names.

From this perspective, all films, like all linguistic utterances, 'participate' (to use Derrida's term) in genres of one kind or another – and usually in several at once. The laws of genre – and the laws of genres – are thus exclusive neither to Hollywood nor to the commercial cinema in general. They pervade the cinema, films, and the viewing of films as a whole.

Selected Reading

Rick Altman, *The American Film Musical*, Bloomington, Indiana University Press, 1987.

André Bazin, 'The western, or the American film *par excellence*' and 'The evolution of the western', in Hugh Gray (ed. and trans.), *What is Cinema?* Vol. 2, Berkeley, University of California Press, 1971.

Jim Kitses, *Horizons West*, London, Secker & Warburg/BFI, 1969.

Colin McArthur, *Underworld USA*, London, Secker & Warburg/BFI, 1972.

Stephen Neale, *Genre*, London, BFI, 1980.

Steve Neale, 'Questions of genre', *Screen* 31(1), 1990.

Steve Neale, 'Melo talk: on the meaning and use of the term "melodrama" in the American Trade Press', *The Velvet Light Trap* no. 32, 1993.

Tom Ryall, *Teacher's Study Guide No. 2: The Gangster Film*, London, BFI Education, 1978.

Thomas Schatz, *Hollywood Genres: Formulas, Film-making, and the Studio System*, New York, Random House, 1981.

THE WESTERN

INTRODUCTION

Arguably the western represented the starting point of genre criticism in Britain, contributing to the popular culture debate evidence of the capacity of Hollywood formula films to produce works of significance and value. In the 1960s, discussions of genre mostly used the western as their chief example, and were less interested in the critical problems of the notion of genre itself than they were in demonstrating the value of western films.

Alan Lovell characterised the critical context of this debate in the following way:

> For Anglo-Saxon critics, the western is typical of most of the vices of the mass media. It is endlessly repetitive, utterly simple in form and expresses naive attitudes. For French critics, the western contains nearly all the things they most admire in the American cinema, its directness, its intelligence, its energy, its formal concerns. (Lovell, 1967, p. 93)

This work of reclamation reflected its British context in the struggle to deflect, sometimes by incorporating, a Leavisite literary tradition, and in its concern to argue via the western for the place of Hollywood films in education. Two main concerns can be traced: the first, the status of the western as popular art and the capacity of such forms to handle questions of value and morality; and the second, the contribution of convention to great films or the work of great directors (see Hall and Whannel, 1964, Ch. 4).

THE WESTERN AND HISTORY

A key notion in the validation of the Hollywood western has been its relation to history and to national cultural motifs. As we are repeatedly told, the material of the western is drawn from a brief period in the winning and settling of the American frontier:

The building of railways and crossing of frontiers in *Iron Horse*

> Hollywood's West has typically been from about 1865 to 1890 or so ... within its brief span we can count a number of frontiers in the sudden rush of mining camps, the building of railways, the Indian wars, the cattle drives, the coming of the farmer. Together with the last days of the Civil War and the exploits of the badmen, here is the raw material of the western. (Kitses, 1969, p. 8)

Although a widespread anti-mass media view of the western was that it travestied the west, only a few serious approaches to the genre attempted to found their arguments on its historical truth. The French critic, Jean-Louis Rieupeyrout, argued enthusiastically that the pleasures of the western derive from its reconstruction of the adventures of the frontier. He had spent much time researching the sources of individual western films and considered that proof of authenticity should change condescending attitudes to the form. However the potential naïvety of his notion of historical reflection is mitigated by his accepting as historical sources secondary elaborations in oral folklore, and newspaper journalism, so that an imaginative response to frontier tales becomes part of the fabric of history (Rieupeyrout, 1952). The majority of commentators, however, have been concerned with either the contribution of history to the thematic structure and narrative functioning of the western, or with the transformations performed by successive fictionalisations of the West.

The problem of relating history and the western has been posed in different ways. One form of the question is to ask why this particular brief stretch of history is capable of sustaining such a wide range of cultural elaboration over so long a period. Two answers emerge. One, from the perspective of cultural history, argues that the conditions of existence in the west put into particularly sharp focus and provided imagery for a deep-seated ideological tension in America's view of itself and of progress – a tension axed around the conflicting ideals of unfettered individualism and community values represented in opposing views of the west as desert or garden. The second, looking for greater socio-economic precision, argues that within these narrow geographic and temporal boundaries assembled an exemplary cross-section of social types, representing a range of economic and social interests in struggle and caught in a variety of activities eminently susceptible to the kind of narrativisation that can illuminate the underlying play of historical forces.

From such approaches arises a second way of posing the history/western question, i.e. the relation of fictionalised history not simply to the past it represents, but to the contemporary audiences for whom it is constructed. While some critics see the genre as crucially linked to the American problem of national identity (see Kitses, 1969) and imply the enduring viability of a set of representations produced out of a particular historical experience for succeeding generations, others argue for greater historical determinism, attempting to link different phases of western production to changes in economic and ideological conditions (Wagner, 1961; Wright, 1975), or even to particular political leaders in power (French, 1973).

For critics in the first category, a crucial factor is the precise moment in the conquering of the west that the western takes up – a moment critical in the formation of America as a nation, balanced between the past and the future, 'when options are still open' (Kitses, 1969, p. 12). Most critics agree that the fact that this moment of choice is past intensifies its possibility for ideological elaboration. Options closed off by history and a developing social order can safely be reopened, nostalgically indulged, judged and closed off again (see Pye, 1977/78; Warshow, 1970).

The implication that the western is specific to American culture and history raises the question of the genre's almost universal appeal and its production in different cultural contexts, e.g. the Italian westerns made between 1965 and 1975. Rieupeyrout (1952) deals with this problem by assuming a universal fascination with enacted history. Bazin (1971) sidesteps it by asserting a mythic dimension through which the western finds in frontier history sympathetic material for reworking older and more universal themes. Other critics assert the importance of the movement westward and of America itself for older European nations, the 'idea of the West' having dominated western civilisation since classical times (Kitses, 1969, pp. 8–9).

FOUNDING FATHERS

Most influential in Anglo-Saxon criticism of the western were André Bazin's two essays, 'The western, or the American film *par excellence*', and 'The evolution of the western' (1971), and Robert Warshow's 'Movie chronicle: the westerner' (1970), all written in the 1950s. Both writers were concerned with defining the essence of the western film in order to locate its cinematic and cultural significance. They examine the development of the genre and attempt to determine its outer boundaries, so that they can distinguish acceptable transformations from violations. At the centre of their investigations stands a 'classic example' against which they evaluate earlier and later developments. Writing, however, from different perspectives and in different cultural contexts both their choice of example and their estimation of the value of the western differ.

André Bazin

As a celebrated proponent of cinematic realism (see Bazin, p. 337) Bazin's account of the genre's realism is surprisingly oblique as he steers round the obvious pitfalls of a naïve view of the relationship between the western and history:

> the relations between the facts of history and the western are not immediate and direct, but dialectic. Tom Mix is the opposite of Abraham Lincoln, but after his own fashion he perpetuates Lincoln's cult and memory. (Bazin, 'The western, or the American film *par excellence*', 1971, p. 143)

Between history and cinema a process of mythologising has taken place.

> Those formal attributes by which one normally recognises the western are simply signs or symbols of its profound reality, namely the myth. The western was born of an encounter between a mythology and a means of expression ... (Bazin, 'The western', 1971, p. 142)

For Bazin myth is an idealisation of historical reality; the historical and sociological conditions of the west permit imaginative elaborations dealing with fundamental realities that exceed the particular moment, replaying in contemporary form metaphysical and moral dramas that recur throughout the history of cultural expression. The particular myth that Bazin elaborates is 'the great epic Manicheism which sets the forces of evil over against the knights of the true cause' (Bazin, 'The western', 1971, p. 145), at the centre of which is the woman posed as representative of the good. This myth is demanded by the actual sociological conditions of the west and the role of women in the conquering and civilising of the frontier, but it both points back to earlier cultural forms, for instance the courtly romance, and also works through problems of the ambiguous relation of law and social justice, or morality and individual conscience, endemic to civilisation itself.

For Bazin the ideal example of this mythologising of history is *Stagecoach* (Ford, 1939) made in a brief period (1937–40) in which the western arrived at its classic peak, that 'ideal balance between

Stagecoach – Bazin's classic western mythologising history

social myth, historical reconstruction, psychological truth, and the traditional theme of the western *mise-en-scène*' (Bazin, 'The evolution of the western', 1971, p. 149). Against this classic achievement Bazin poses the postwar emergence of the 'superwestern' which, under pressure to deal with serious themes appropriate to the times, and self-conscious of its own history, effectively treated the western as 'a form in need of a content', stepping outside the parameters of its own concerns to bring in 'aesthetic, social, moral, psychological, political or erotic interest, in short some quality extrinsic to the genre and which is supposed to enrich it' (Bazin, 'The evolution of the western, 1971, p. 151). *High Noon* (1952) and *Shane* (1952) are examples of this tendency. However, Bazin argues, the traditional western did not die, but continued to be nourished at its popular base, in the B-westerns churned out in great numbers during the 1950s, e.g. *The Gunfighter* (Henry King, 1950); or by older directors whose experience in western traditions was not to be deflected by new trends, e.g. *The Big Sky* (Howard Hawks, 1952). The 1950s also produced a group of newer directors who managed to make a class of western which, while developing a more contemporary flavour, did not break with the spirit of the true western, a class which Bazin termed 'novelistic', and characterised by their lyricism and their sincere rather than patronising approach to the form, e.g. *Johnny Guitar* (Nicholas Ray, 1954), *Bend of the River* and *The Far Country* (Anthony Mann, 1952 and 1954).

Robert Warshow

Like Bazin, Warshow, writing in 1954, sets out to define the essence of the western and like Bazin he sees its value in its capacity to handle moral ambiguity in traditionally epic terms. However, while Bazin writes from a Catholic/existentialist perspective and locates the struggle between good and evil as informing history itself, Warshow is concerned with the aesthetic realisation of ideological conflicts attendant on the development of twentieth-century American capitalism. His concern, as for many writers on the western since, is the relation of the individual to society, the westerner rather than the western. Warshow defines the western hero in relation to the same problematic which, he argues, produced the gangster as tragic hero. The latter's acquisitive urge and inevitable defeat represents 'the "no" to that great American "yes" which is stamped so big over our official culture and yet has so little to do with the way we really feel about our lives' (Warshow, 1970, p. 136). However, while the gangster's desperate need to prove himself drives him from one bout of activity to another, the westerner is self-contained, knows his worth, and needs only to be able to live by his code. In this respect he represents a type of hero, of individualism, not realisable in twentieth-century society. In these terms the historical west is important only in as much as it is past – 'Where the westerner lives it is always about 1870 – not the real 1870, either, or the real West . . .' (Warshow, 1970, p. 141) – and in so far as the material it offers the cinema, 'the land and the horses', provide a 'moral openness'. In the western, guns are carried openly rather than secretly as in the gangster film, forcing the hero into moral self-responsibility. The other crucial aspect of this hero for Warshow is his relation to violence. Unlike the opportunism of the gangster, the westerner's violence is a statement of his being, and he waits for the quintessential moment in which to express this (Warshow, 1970, p. 140).

For Warshow then, the central problem of the western is individual masculine identity and the violence necessary to its expression. His conception of the place of women in the western is the antithesis of

Bazin's, for whom woman is the object of a metaphyiscal struggle between good and evil. In Warshow's account the role of women is associated with the establishment of community and the necessary qualifications of individualism and violence brought by the civilising of the frontier. Prior to this moment 'the West, lacking the graces of civilisation, is the place "where men are men": in western movies, men have the deeper wisdom and women are children' (Warshow, 1970, p. 138).

The western's move from primitivism to full maturity Warshow cautiously attributes to a deeper realism – more in terms of philosophical outlook and the ageing of the stars than in terms of historical truth. The western grows up when it foregoes its innocent Romanticism and recognises the tragic limitations of the frontier ethos, as for instance in Henry King's *The Gunfighter* (1950). However, when the impulse to realism breaks totally with this ethos and the code of the westerner for the sake of a ' "reinterpretation" of the West as a developed society' we arrive at a different genre, social drama for which the western setting is irrelevant except as a backdrop. *High Noon* (1952) provides an example of this kind of breakdown. Warshow also identifies an opposite tendency away from realism towards an aesthetic embalming of western conventions in response to their mythological and cinematic potential. Here Bazin's exemplum, *Stagecoach* (1939) and Ford's later *My Darling Clementine* (1946) stand accused.

Alan Lovell: the western's formal history

Both Bazin and Warshow define the essence of the western and choose their classic examples with scant reference to the historical development of the genre, basing their judgements on their own respective metaphysical and ideological concerns. Alan Lovell (1967) sought a more objective way of establishing the parameters of the genre by examining its formal history. Such an attempt, he argues, must take account of the themes and forms introduced into the western through its source materials and of how it combined, displaced or transformed these in its movement towards establishing a coherent and stable structure. Lovell defines four principal elements which contributed to the formation of the western genre:

> 1. a structure drawn from nineteenth-century popular melodramatic literature, involving a virtuous hero and wicked villain who menaces a virginal heroine;
> 2. an action story, composed of violence, chases and crimes appropriate to a place like the American West in the nineteenth century;
> 3. the introduction of the history of the migration westwards and the opening of the frontier signalled in such films as *The Covered Wagon* (1924) and *The Iron Horse* (1924); and
> 4. the revenge structure, which was present by the time of *Billy the Kid* in 1930.
>
> (Lovell, 1967, p. 97)

For Lovell, the history of the western over the next twenty years can be understood in terms of the working of these elements into a coherent formal structure. From this perspective *My Darling Clementine* (1946) becomes the classic centre of the genre. In this film the narrative is structured by the revenge theme, which is itself integrated into the historical theme of civilising the west, as the hero's quest for personal revenge is translated into the establishment of law and order for the nascent township of Tombstone, under the influence of the heroine schoolteacher from the East (see John Ford, p. 300).

Although not all these elements necessarily recur in every western since *My Darling Clementine*, the structural balance identified in that film, Lovell argues, is determining in the genre's subsequent development. Against frequent assertions that 1950s westerns broke with their primitive past to become more adult, sophisticated and individualised, Lovell argues for the continuity between pre- and postwar westerns, positing a tradition that runs from *My Darling Clementine* (1946) through *The Gunfighter* (1950) to *Guns in the Afternoon* (1962), and citing the shared characteristics of *The Left-Handed Gun* (1958), often seen as one of the 'more modern' westerns, and *My Darling Clementine*. From this perspective, shifts in emphasis in the genre become interesting not in terms of breaks with a classic past but rather in terms of significant differences produced in relation to a maintained continuity. Thus *The Oxbow Incident* (1943), maligned by Warshow for its illegitimate concern with problems of social organisation in the West, becomes interesting for its recasting of familiar elements in a darker, more pessimistic tone.

From this position Lovell goes on to argue against the assumed naïvety of the pre-war westerns, and against the attribution of a precocious progressivism to the so-called adult westerns of the 1950s – sympathetic treatment of the American Indian for instance may be less a contemporary concern with racial questions than an exploration of ambiguous attitudes to the coming of civilisation to the west which are contained in the structure of the genre. However, Lovell does not deny that 1950s westerns also bear the marks of the prevailing climate of ideas or of the influx of a postwar generation of new and more cinematically conscious directors. But rather than a transformation of the genre, this represents 'the imposition of a new sensibility on the old forms', and Lovell argues that 'part of the fascination of the western in the 1950s results from the confusions caused when this ... comes into contact with the traditional forms of the genre' (Lovell, 1967, p. 101). It is then arguable that some of these films are simply confused, but that others such as *Guns in the Afternoon* (1962) or *The Tall T* (1957) demonstrate the productive power of genre confronted with 'new sensibility'.

Jim Kitses: *Horizons West*

Jim Kitses's book (1969) on the western and western directors represents an attempt to deepen knowledge of the genre by consciously confronting, in its influential first chapter, many of the problems of generic criticism exhibited in earlier writings on the subject, namely prescriptiveness, the task of relating the western to history and the problem of understanding it as myth. Whereas Alan Lovell tackles the problem of arbitrary prescriptiveness by describing the history of a central tradition, Kitses attempts a synchronic and structural account of the genre's basic elements. Thus he takes account of the genre's complex historical and socio-cultural inheritance in order to propose, rather than a central model, 'a loose, shifting and variegated genre with many roots and branches' (Kitses, 1969, p. 17), which can account for films made at any period. History, in his account, is not the record of the genre's development but what has made the genre so fruitful.

Kitses sees history as contributing to the western in two ways. First, it provides the national cultural tradition in which the western is rooted and to which it speaks, and second, in a narrower sense, it offers as 'raw material' that brief historical span which covers the opening of the American frontier, 1865–90.

For a definition of the particular cultural tradition underlying the western, Kitses turns to Henry Nash Smith's seminal study, *Virgin Land*. Citing a range of political and cultural output, Nash Smith identifies as central to America's national consciousness an ambiguous attitude to the west, torn between the symbols of garden and desert. Several commentators have seen this ambiguity as providing much of the thematic preoccupations of the western (see Lovell, 1967; McArthur, 1969). Under the master opposition, wilderness/civilisation, Kitses elaborates a series of antinomies which together represent a 'philosophical dialectic, an ambiguous cluster of meanings and attitudes that provide the traditional/thematic structure of the genre' (Kitses, 1969, p. 11). The shift in meanings from the top to the bottom of each set of oppositions – the wilderness starting with the individual and freedom and ending with tradition and the past, while civilisation starts with the community and restriction and ends with change and the future – demonstrates both the flexibility of the structure and the ideological tension which it embodies. While the structure animates many forms of cultural activity, the use of frontier history in the western brought it into particularly acute focus, for the period was placed 'at exactly that moment when options are still open, the dream of a primitivistic individualism, the ambivalence of at once beneficient and threatening horizons still tenable' (Kitses, 1969, p. 12). A third factor in the genre's appropriation of frontier history was that it had already been reworked in folkloric and mythic terms. Kitses attempts to differentiate the varieties of meaning attendant on the concept of myth, and to distinguish between a mythic dimension frequently attributed to twentieth-century popular culture, and the tales of gods and heroes handed down through oral traditions from classical and medieval times. While the western does not represent myth in the latter sense, it 'incorporates elements of displaced (or corrupted) myth on a scale that can render them considerably more prominent than in most art' (Kitses, 1969, p. 14). Such incorporation takes place through the western's particularly varied inheritance from the popular literary forms in which frontier history was first reworked. Following Northrop Frye's definition of archetypes, Kitses argues that different literary modes are characterised by types of hero and patterns of heroic action. Central to the western was the mode of romance 'which insisted on the idealisation of characters who wielded near-magical powers' (Kitses, 1969, p. 15), and provided 'the movement of a god-like figure into the demonic wasteland, the death and resurrection, the return to a paradisal garden' (Kitses, 1969, p. 20).

However, the incursion of morality play, melodrama, revenge tragedy into the tradition together with the input from wild-west shows and cracker-barrel humour meant that the western could develop within different modes and draw on a rich and complex profusion of mythic and archetypal elements. Finally the cultural resources of the western are enriched cinematically by the repertoire of visual iconography most frequently commented on in generic studies (e.g. Buscombe, 1970; Collins, 1970).

Thus Kitses provides an account of the western as a four-part structure:

1 frontier history;
2 the thematic antinomies of wilderness/civilisation;
3 archetype;
4 iconography.

Contrary to the argument that a non-prescriptive genre criticism must be limited to description (see Ryall, 1970), Kitses sees in the conceptual richness of the western genre a potential source of value, capable of realisation in the hands of 'the artist of vision in rapport with the genre' (Kitses, 1969, p. 20). The peak of authorial westerns, however, is dependent on the structure produced by a particular social, cultural and formal history, a structure, moreover which includes the existence of the large popular audience who supported the development of the 'mass production at the base' which in turn 'allows refinement and reinvigoration' at the peak (Kitses, 1969, p. 21). Thus, 'the western is not just the men who have worked within it . . . an empty vessel breathed into by the film-maker' (Kitses, 1969, p. 26) but represents a vital structure 'saturated with conceptual significance' (Kitses, 1969, p. 21).

Will Wright

Will Wright's much debated intervention (1975) in discussion of the western (see Frayling, 1981) sought to shift the looseness of its validation in terms of general moral or archetypal themes, cultural or psychological conflicts. He insists first that the significance of the western must be located in its appeal to contemporary popular audiences, which are subject to historical change, and second that it must be treated as an aspect of communication, subject to the rules that govern the production of symbolic meaning. He calls on the structural linguistics of Saussure and Jakobson and the structural anthropology of Lévi-Strauss to support his argument that all human endeavour is an effort to communicate meaning. In Wright's view the work of myth or mass culture is not to achieve emotional expression of problems arising elsewhere, in the psyche or cultural climate, but itself contributes to them through the forms of knowledge it produces. Thus in the cinema the western myth 'has become part of the cultural language by which America understands itself' (Wright, 1975, p. 12). What interests Wright in structuralism is its promise of a methodology for understanding scientifically how social communication works. Where he differs from the structuralists is in his retention of a sociological concern to analyse what meanings are produced in particular societies in given historical periods. What he is attempting then is to make content analysis more rigorous (Wright, 1975, p. 10).

In approaching the western from this standpoint Wright starts out from a number of basic premisses. First, integrating Lévi-Strauss's view of primitive myth with Kenneth Burke's narrative theory, Wright contends that modern societies, despite the apparent authority of science, history and literature, still have recourse to myth as a means of producing knowledge of and order in the world. Second, he argues that westerns represent industrially produced stories made from mythic material already in social circulation which are amenable to the same, if liberalised, kind of analysis that Propp used on the Russian oral folk-tale or Lévi-Strauss on the myths of tribal peoples (Lévi-Strauss, p. 328). Third, he asserts that because analysis of the western as myth stresses the social and historical (rather than formal, authorial or industrial) production of meaning, its mythic significance can only be found in what the mass of people went to see. The 'classic' westerns are those most popular in the period in which the genre achieves clear definition and contours, not examples chosen in terms of a schema already constructed in the critic's mind, whether generic, cultural or authorial. Box-office popularity is in its turn an indicator of the 'meanings viewers demand of the myth' (Wright, 1975, p. 12). Wright therefore confines his structural analysis to those westerns which grossed $4 million dollars or more. From these films he seeks to derive the 'communicative structure of the western' (Wright, 1975, p. 12), and from shifts in the structure over the decades to reveal a pattern of change and development 'corresponding to changes in the structure of dominant institutions' (Wright, 1975, p. 14).

Wright's final premiss is that the history of the American west supplies the western with appropriate material for the production of myth. This it does in two main ways. First it furnished a dramatic concatenation of social types and actions productive of the kinds of oppositions from which, in Lévi-Straussian terms, myth is made; and second, these character types and actions were capable of carrying the meanings and shifts in meaning which could make sense of the social conflicts dominant in American society at any one time (Wright, 1975, p. 6).

The meaning of the myths circulated by the western is located in two basic structures: one of binary oppositions in which its characters are placed; and another, the organisation of these characters' functions into narrative sequences. Here Wright uses the Proppian notion of 'character function' – which he interprets as a single action or attribute referring to roles performed in the plot – as a link between Lévi-Straussian oppositions and an argument mounted by the philosopher, Arthur Danto, that any narrative sequence, in so far as it describes a change in an initial state of affairs, also includes an explanation of it. In the explanatory function of narrative, combined with the representative function of the characters, Wright finds the power of the western myth to provide 'a conceptual response to the requirements of human action in a social situation' (Wright, 1975, p. 17). On this basis Wright proceeds to categorise the plots of westerns in terms of their constituent 'character functions' and the way character functions are organised into narrative sequences and narrative sequences into plots.

Wright's final task is to provide 'an independent analysis of the social institutions of America and demonstrate the correlation between the structure of the western and the structure of those institutions' (Wright,

1975, p. 130). This is not a relation of direct causation. Wright argues, however, for institutional determination on the way individuals live their lives, a determination which may be in conflict with the cultural traditions and values of a society, because institutional requirements tend to change more rapidly. This then produces 'a conceptual dilemma . . . for the people of the society' to which a myth such as the western speaks. Drawing on social analysts such as Kenneth Galbraith, Jürgen Habermas, and C. B. MacPherson (a somewhat heterogeneous grouping of authorities), he argues that 'the classical western plot corresponds to the individualistic conception of society underlying a market economy', that 'the vengeance plot is a variation that begins to reflect changes in the market economy', and that 'the professional plot reveals a new conception of society corresponding to the values and attitudes inherent in a planned, corporate economy' (Wright, 1975, p. 15).

The language of reflection here indicates the weak link in Wright's conception of the social function of myth: cultural production and social institutions confront each other as discrete entities, the influence of box-office returns providing the only explanation as to why film-makers should provide audiences with the cultural models of social action necessary for their survival as institutions change. Moreover, the predominance of 'myth' in his analysis necessitates excluding many aspects of the film-making and reading process that intervene between the institutional needs of society and the finished film. This leads to a view of genre cinema as essentially conservative. For Wright assumes that, in its reliance on a structure of binary oppositions, 'myth depends on simple and recognisable meanings which reinforce rather than challenge social understandings' (Wright, 1975, p. 23). Works by individual artists, however, construct more complex, realistic and unique characters, which are not amenable to analysis by binary opposition. Thus the 'social action' proposed by any particular phase of a genre is seen as adapting to institutional demands rather than resisting them or exploring their contradictions.

The Gunfighter – the tragic western hero (male) outside of social values and civilised society (female)

GENDER AND SEXUALITY IN THE WESTERN

Disagreement may arise over the place of woman in the western, but most commentators assume its address to a male problematic and a male audience. For instance, John Cawelti in *The Six-Gun Mystique* (1971) argues that the western speaks to adolescent or working-class males about 'the conflict between the adolescent's desire to be an adult and his fear and hesitation about the nature of adulthood' and 'the tension between a strong need for aggression and a sense of ambiguity and guilt about violence' which the working-class male feels in relation to the authority of corporate America (Cawelti, 1971, p. 82 and p. 14).

In very different terms, Raymond Bellour has argued (1979) that the western depends upon 'a whole organised circuit of feminine representations (the young heroine, the mother, the saloon girl, the wife, etc.) without which the film cannot function' (Bellour, 1979, p. 88). For Bellour the western is a variation of the classic Hollywood narrative text (see The classic narrative system, p. 40) which, in line with the nineteenth-century novel, centres on the symbolic figure of the woman as source of the disruption that sets going a narrative trajectory of male desire and its ultimate resolution in heterosexual couple formation.

Feminist response to the dominance in the western of a male-defined problematic has taken two forms. Jacqueline Levitin (1982) has attacked the western for the circumscribed roles it gives women. She analyses their function in catalysing the choices that face the hero, and the narrative contortions undergone by those exceptional westerns which attempt to support a female hero – for instance *Johnny Guitar*. She also suggests that the historical west offered opportunities for greater freedom and social power for women, as well as potential female hero figures, which are transformed and traduced in the process of producing patriarchal fiction. In this respect she argues that the history of the west provides material which could be colonised by feminism. The problem in her account is the assumption that all that is required is greater historical accuracy; she seems to ignore the work of fantasy and fiction at play in the childhood memories she cites of identification with the male hero, and the problems of finding forms that will fulfil this task for women.

The question of the female audience and the western is taken up by Laura Mulvey in a consideration of how women deal with the male system of spectatorship she had analysed (1975) (Laura Mulvey on visual pleasure, p. 336). Mulvey draws on Freud for an argument both about how the western relates to the male Oedipal scenario and about the transsexual identification of women with male heroes described by Levitin. In both cases what she sees at work is a fictional indulgence of the fantasy of omnipotence belonging to the pre-Oedipal phase, experienced by both boys and girls, before the socially required gender positions are taken up. This phase is characterised by narcissism, allowing for object choices and identifications based on similarity rather than difference, so that boys and girls are able to take up one another's positions. This forms the basis of transsexual identification. Despite its hypothetical freedom from social categorisation, Mulvey notes that the pre-Oedipal phase is nevertheless conceived in traditionally 'masculine' terms – as active, phallic. For the boy the Oedipal passage into 'manhood' requires forsaking the fantasy of omnipotence, submission to sexual difference ('masculinity') through the castration scenario, and the channelling of his desire towards the woman positioned within the couple, marriage. For the girl, passage through the Oedipal phase requires not merely channelling active desire towards the correct goal, but forsaking it altogether by taking up the feminine position traditionally conceived as 'passive'. However because of the relative weakness of the castration scenario for women, the 'active' fantasies of the non-gender specific pre-Oedipal phase are never entirely repressed.

The western serves the pre-Oedipal fantasies of the gendered audience in two distinct and gender-specific ways. If, as Bellour suggests, the Oedipal resolution of 'couple formation' is the implicit goal of every western, the 'not marriage' choice, Mulvey argues, is also central to its agenda. The indulgence of this male fantasy, involving a disavowal of the feminine sphere, frequently leads in the western to a splitting of the hero:

> Here two functions emerge, one celebrating integration into society through marriage, the other celebrating resistance to social demands and responsibilities, above all those of marriage and family, the sphere represented by woman. (Mulvey, 1981, p. 14)

In the first option 'the fiction "marriage" sublimates the erotic into a final closing social ritual'. In the second the male spectator is offered 'a nostalgic celebration of phallic, narcissistic omnipotence … difficult to integrate exactly into the oedipal drama' (Mulvey, 1981, p. 14) – the hero rejects the woman and rides alone into the sunset.

However the dominance of the male hero, and role of woman as a signifier in a male scenario in this as in most genres does not, Mulvey argues, mean the films do not address the female spectator. They do so through the mechanism of transsex identification in which pre-Oedipal 'active' and narcissistic fantasising, never finally repressed in women, is given cultural outlet and reinforcement by the logic of narrative grammar, which 'places the reader, listener or spectator with the hero' (Mulvey, 1981, p. 13).

> In this sense Hollywood genre films, structured around masculine pleasure offering an identification with the active point of view, allow a woman spectator to rediscover that lost aspect of her sexual identity, the never fully repressed bed-rock of feminine neurosis. (Mulvey, 1981, p. 13)

From this perspective it could be argued that in the western, female pleasure may be derived from its offering to women identification with a male figure asserting desire in pre-Oedipal terms, the male fantasy of self-sufficiency serving women's own ambivalence towards the 'correct' feminine position.

Male spectators and the western

In his book *Genre* (1980) Stephen Neale touches briefly on the question of spectatorship and the western from the masculine perspective. Laura Mulvey had argued in 'Visual Pleasure and Narrative Cinema' (1975) that the role of the male hero for the male spectator is that of an ideal ego, through whose gaze the spectator gains symbolic possession of the female body placed as the central spectacle in the fiction. Neale is interested in Paul Willemen's qualification of this argument (1976) in which he points out that in the Freudian scenario the scopophilic instinct (the drive to look) is in the first instance 'auto-erotic', taking as its object the subject's own body. If the cinema can be seen as pleasuring such formative desires, then the male body can be 'a substantial source of gratification for a male viewer' (Willemen, 1976, p. 43). Mulvey had suggested that the narrative function of the hero acts in part as a deflection of such desires in so far as they threaten the social taboo against homosexuality. Neale takes this further, arguing that the spectator's gaze at the male hero is legitimated, 'rendered "innocent"', because in following his actions eroticism is deflected into the hero's pursuit of the woman, who constitutes an ideologically acceptable sexual object. What interests Neale here is the way the western plays on this ambiguous production of male hero as an object for the spectator's gaze. He argues that many of the structural antimonies of the western, described by Kitses, can be set in opposition around the way the hero's body is represented, 'opening a space for … the male as privileged object of the look' (Neale, 1980, p. 58). Thus the opposition law/outside law can be set up in the way the body of the hero, 'through the codes of dress, comportment, movement, adornment' (Neale, 1980, p. 58), relates to those of American Indian, outlaw, townspeople, farmers, elaborated through similar codes; or in the dynamic oscillation between natural landscape and township, realised in the play of 'light, texture, colour' over the male figure, and in the pace and rhythm of his movements. For Neale, the drama of the western revolves around its exploration of various modes of the inscription of law on the human body. Since it is the hero who engages with the law, the father/son relationship dominates the scenario, and the western can be said to be 'about' the male half of the Oedipus trauma (Neale, 1980, p. 59).

Italian westerns

Finally the representation of sexuality and gender identity in the western received a revealing inflection in the decade of Italian production of what became known as the 'spaghetti western' – 1965–75 – a period associated most strongly with the names of directors Sergio Leone and Sergio Corbucci, and the American star Clint Eastwood, whose fame was made by the Dollars Trilogy. Little serious work has been done on how the popularity of this sub-genre affects the demarcation of the western *per se*, although Christopher Frayling (1981) has attempted a pioneering work of archival research on this phenomenon in which he mounts an argument that Leone's films, at least, represent a critique of Hollywood's reconstruction of the west and its meanings. The films clearly mark a challenge to the dominance of Hollywood over genre production, complicating the question of the relation of genre motifs to the culture which produced them, and demonstrating the work of translation and transformation that goes on between cultures, especially in the cinema. Anglophone critics of the period were appalled at what they saw as a travesty of the traditional western and its time-honoured values. Behind the outrage at what was considered gratuitous violence and sexual sadomasochism can be sensed an unease about the production of a more rampant, less romanticised expression of masculine identity. On the whole it is the Eastwood/Leone Dollars Trilogy through which this period of production has entered film studies, and the films are liable to be discussed as much in terms of the Eastwood image and how it speaks to a post-1960, 'post-feminist' crisis in male identity as in terms of its contribution to and development of western traditions.

Westerns in the 1980s and 1990s

In the 1970s and early 1980s Hollywood appeared to have given up on the western. The genre lacked appeal to the youth market which now constituted the dominant part of the audience. Other genres such as horror and science fiction offered more immediate sensations. But the end of the 1980s saw a cautious revival, led by *Young Guns* (1988), a version of the Billy the Kid story which attempted to retool the genre for contemporary film-goers by casting bratpack actors such as Emilio Estevez, Kiefer Sutherland and Charlie Sheen.

In the 1990s there was a concerted effort to counter criticism of the western's ideological shortcomings with a series of politically correct films. Kevin Costner's *Dances with Wolves* (1990) was a pro-American Indian story, though still told from a white man's point of view. Black westerns (*Posse*) and 'feminist' westerns (*Bad Girls*, *The Quick and the Dead*) attempted to contest the centrality of the white male to the narrative structure. But instead of trying to subvert the very idea of masculinity upon which the western had traditionally relied, their strategy was simply to show that blacks and women could be just as tough as men. Only *The Ballad of Little Joe*, with its story of a woman who passes as a man and who falls in love with a feminised Chinese man, tried to work against the stereotypes. *Unforgiven* (1992) is not a radical work, but its story of a reluctant gunfighter (played by Clint Eastwood) dragged out of retirement to avenge a wronged woman manages some subtle digs against racism, sexism – and ageism too, considering that Eastwood was over sixty when he made the film.

The Indie-Western? *Dead Man*

The so-called New Western History developed by professional historians has amply demonstrated that western films have barely scratched the surface when it comes to dramatising the role of women, blacks, American Indians, Hispanics and other ethnic minorities in the American west (Cronon, Miles and Gitlin, 1992; Nelson Limerick, 1987; Nelson Limerick, Milner II and Rankin, 1991). History is a rich source of material for those who would offer narratives other than those dominated by the macho white male. A few films such as US 'independent' director Jim Jarmusch's *Dead Man* encroach on this territory. But Hollywood seems reluctant to take the plunge. While it no longer has confidence in the certainties of the traditional western, it lacks the ability to imagine what would take their place. It may be that only when women and minorities are better represented in the film industry will the western genre undergo some genuinely radical mutations. But that position seems a long way off.

Selected Reading

André Bazin, 'The western, or the American film *par excellence*' and 'The evolution of the western', in Gray (ed. and trans.), *What is Cinema?* Vol. 2, Berkeley, University of California Press, 1971.

Ian Cameron and Douglas Pye (eds), *The Movie Book of the Western*, London, Studio Vista, 1996.

William Cronon, George Miles and Jay Gitlin (eds), *Under an Open Sky: Rethinking America's Western Past*, New York, W.W. Norton, 1992.

Jim Kitses, *Horizons West*, London, Secker & Warburg/BFI, 1969.

Alan Lovell, 'The western', *Screen Education* no. 41, September/October 1967.

Colin McArthur, 'The roots of the western', *Cinema* (UK) no. 4, October 1969.

Laura Mulvey, 'Afterthoughts on "Visual pleasure and narrative cinema" inspired by *Duel in the Sun*', *Framework* nos 15/16/17, summer 1981.

Douglas Pye, 'Genre and history: *Fort Apache and Liberty Valance*', *Movie* no. 25, winter 1977/78.

Jane Tompkins, *West of Everything: The Inner Life of Westerns*, New York, Oxford University Press, 1992.

Robert Warshow, 'Movie chronicle: the westerner', in *The Immediate Experience*, New York, Atheneum Books, 1970.

Will Wright, *Sixguns and Society: A Structural Study of the Western*, Berkeley, University of California Press, 1975.

My Darling Clementine (USA 1946 *p.c* – 20th Century–Fox; *d* – John Ford; sd b/w)

At the centre of this romantic western (typifying Bazin's 'classical' form and period of the genre) is the figure of Wyatt Earp. Thematically, this hero, cattleman-cum-town marshal, represents the rugged individualism of the frontier consciousness, assured in male company and as an agent of legal justice, but uneasy as a member of the burgeoning white community and especially in the company of women.

Structurally, the figure is an agent of eastern expansion into the west, pacifying American Indian and destroying outlaw. The positive qualities of the west are expressed in conditions of early settlement through community life, crackerbarrel wit, dance and music, all characteristic qualities of John Ford's authorship (see John Ford, p. 300).

In the same way that the west is seen in its negative and positive aspects, so too is the east. The schoolteacher, Clementine, provides positive elements such as education and stability, seen as necessary to the utopian promise of western settlement, elements which are celebrated in the scene at the dance in the shell of the new church under the sign of the Stars and Stripes. The negative elements – vice and decadence – are embodied in the figure of the consumptive Doc Holliday.

As an agent in the transformation of positive eastern values into the west, and the ejection of all negative values from the west, Earp's centrality is clear. Interestingly, despite the essential nature of that agency to the narrative and ideological project of the film, the figure's unease is evident. This phenomenon can be viewed as presaging generic shifts in the role of the gunfighter, authorial developments in Ford's view of America as well as exemplifying the characteristic laconic liberalism of the star persona of Henry Fonda.

Johnny Guitar (USA 1954 *p.c* – Republic; *d* – Nicholas Ray; sd col.)

Johnny Guitar is an example of the 1950s baroque western (see *Rancho Notorious*) which deviated in significant ways from the conventions of the earlier romantic form: for example, in its representation of a stylised landscape and décor contrasting with the ornate interior of Vienna's place (hanging chandelier, grand piano, red-suffused lighting) and the dark, windswept, barren exteriors. An impulse toward myth and melodrama is also revealed in the central conflict between the two female adversaries.

The mythic dimension can be seen in the frenzied performance of Mercedes McCambridge as Emma, whose black widow's weeds lead the mob of settlers and townspeople. Elements of melodrama emerge from the treatment of Vienna as a central agent in the fortunes of the partly criminalised all-male group. Her isolation from both these groups can be identified in the action (the quietness as she lights the lamps and sits at the piano) and in the organisation of spatial relations during the scene of the search, during which the contrast of her white dress with the predominant blacks and reds around her is notable. It is here, too, that the coded social and sexual antagonisms between the two monumental female adversaries can be located.

The film also demonstrates the significant displacements affecting the conventions of the western when the protagonists are female. The most revealing displacement is the marginalisation of male action as the dramas of gunfighters/outlaws and settlers/ranchers alike are subordinated to the central female conflict (see Nicholas Ray, p. 257).

Cowboy (USA 1957 *p.c* – Phoenix; *d* – Delmer Daves; sd col.)

This is a romantic western replete with recurrent plot strategies and familiar iconic references. The film traces the initiation of an eastern greenhorn (Harris) into the culture of the west, specifically the cattle trail and the life of cowboy. In the film, the rhythm of working life, with its daily routines rooted in the passing of the sun and the seasons, and the cameraderie of the male team are celebrated. Harris's initiation is represented both comically (false starts at bronco-busting, treating saddle sores with whisky, eating haunches of American Indians, for example) and tragically (the death at the campfire). The play between the comic and the dramatic modes is paralleled in the character relationship between the initiate and the 'man of the west' (Reece). The tension in their relationship derives from Reece having taken Harris on the trail unwittingly, in return for a loan; this is expressed, for example, in scenes in which Reece's apparently harsh treatment of the novice Harris is played off against shots which indicate his respect for Harris's resilience. The film's sanction of Reece's authority – and, thereby, the celebration of the west over the comic refinement of the east – is shown in scenes depicting Reece's humanity, from which Harris's absence (e.g. during Doc Bender's tired gunfighter/marshal testimony) or marginalisation(e.g. during Reece's speech about enclosures) is marked. This procedure serves to validate a romantic view of western expansion, accommodating rather than contrasting the harshness and dangers of life on the trail. It also accounts for the merely vestigial references to pacified American Indians, sexually available women and the constraints of urban living, none of which can have an authorised place in the all-male itinerant, working group which represents the ideal western lifestyle.

The Wonderful Country (USA 1959 *p.c* – DRM; *d* – Robert Parrish; sd col.)

In westerns set in frontier townships, a common structure (following Kitses's model of antinomies) is the 'taming of the wilderness' through the imposition of eastern law and the agency of the marshal/lawman (see *Destry Rides Again*, *My Darling Clementine* and *Rio Bravo*).

In contrast, westerns centring on the figure of the gunfighter/outlaw typically form a journey–structure in which the hero drifts or is chased from town to town (see *Butch Cassidy and the Sundance Kid*, *The Gunfighter* and *The James Brothers*). In one strand of such westerns, the figure of the gunfighter takes on a more ambivalent role as an agent of western expansion.

Representative of this strand, *The Wonderful Country* features Brady (Robert Mitchum) as the unsettled protagonist forced to travel between two cultures, American and Mexican. Exceptionally, the film plays explicitly with ideas of national culture and identity. The title is both an ironic commentary on, and, finally, affirmation of, a national identity as the hero seeks a role in either culture before reluctantly 'choosing' America.

During the party scene, for example, the ambivalence of the hero is connoted ironically by a use of costume, confusing the two national cultures, which also underlines the spatial separation of Brady from the military party and its elaborate rituals. The display of cultural acceptance is interrupted twice by Brady, once in attempting to refuse a liaison offered by Ellen and again in an act of spontaneous violence resulting in a gunfight killing. Brady's actions put him beyond the pale of the authorised social order; it is notable that his ejection results from individual action and expression of sexuality.

The woman's role exceeds western conventions, since Ellen's sexuality is both a threat to the hero's tenuous security in America and a critical comment on the hypocrisy of the nation's authorised culture. In this respect, Ellen resembles the *femme fatales* of *film noir*.

The party scene's visual style also demonstrates the connections between the two cultures in parallel night-time scenes of eating and leisure, contrasting the veiled power structure of the American scenes with the explicitly brutalised power relations of the Mexican scenes.

Ride the High Country (USA 1962 *p.c* – MGM; *d* – Sam Peckinpah; sd col. scope; UK title: **Guns in the Afternoon**)

In the opening sequence Joel McCrea as Stephen Judd rides into a little town in the Californian Sierras. Judd, a former sheriff, is down on his luck and needs a job. As he rides slowly up the main street he sees crowds waving and cheering. Bemused, he acknowledges the applause, but a uniformed policeman makes it clear the cheering is not for him, shouting at him to get out of the way as a motor car rushes past, scaring his horse. Then down the street come a horse and a camel, racing to the finishing line.

The incongruity of the camel and the anachronism of the car are a shock to the viewer expecting a traditional western. Change is everywhere – and decay too. Judd is feeling his age. 'I expected a younger man', says the banker to whom he applies for a job. 'I used to be', Judd replies ironically. At the funfair he discovers his old partner Gil Westrum (Randolph Scott), kitted out in a fake Buffalo Bill wig and buckskins, posing as the Oregon Kid and running a crooked shooting gallery. The old west has been reduced to a threadbare parody.

These opening scenes introduce the theme which Peckinpah was to develop in the rest of the film, and in much of his subsequent work: that of the ending of the west. The question he poses is, how can the traditional code of the western survive into an era when the certainties that underpin it have eroded? Individual morality has been replaced by corporatism, greed and cynicism; even Hudd's partner betrays him, though he is redeemed in a final act of heroism.

In Peckinpah's films the white male hero is subjected to a series of ordeals, moral and physical, which test to the full his ability to retain his integrity and sense of self. Typically, Peckinpah's heroes cannot adjust to a world that has overtaken them. There is no community which they can relate to, only, if they are lucky, a few kindred souls, doomed like them to assert their defiance in acts of heroic resistance. *The Wild Bunch* (1969), Peckinpah's masterspiece, is his most extreme demonstration of the tragedy of heroes in a world which has no use for them.

Ulzana's Raid (USA 1972 *p.c* – Universal; *d* – Robert Aldrich; sd b/w)

This is an example of a cavalry western with a characteristic chase structure, challenges to authority as the all-male group is gradually depleted in running battles, and a final victory over the savage enemy.

Ulzana's Raid is distinctive in three ways. First, the enemy raid is pointedly motivated by reaction to white injustice on the American Indian reservation, and the resulting excessive brutality of the raid is grounded in a materialistic analysis of American Indian culture after white subjugation. This strand is represented in the figure of Ke-Ni-Tay/Luke, an American Indian scout and brother-in-law to the offending Ulzana. Ke-Ni-Tay straddles two cultures, informed by one but committed by contract ('I signed the paper') to another. It is Ke-Ni-Tay who provides the explanation for the otherwise unfathomable consequences of the American Indian attack on the galloper and the settler mother and son, and the subsequent torture of the settler father, Rukeyser. This component therefore remains rooted in the representation of the American Indian as savage, but substantially qualifies and accounts for the conditions that produce the savagery. In this sense, the film offers a corrective to the previous cycle of pro-American Indian liberal films (e.g. *Little Big Man* and *Soldier Blue*).

Second, the scenes of attack and the product of torture are uncharacteristically represented graphically, deploying codes of suspense and surprise in a form appropriated from the gothic horror film. The film is therefore representative of both the increased stylisation of the western film of the period (c.f. spaghetti westerns) and the mutation of the western genre into horror and sci-fi during the 1970s.

Third, the film is a supreme example of play with an audience's generic expectations, notably in the attack on the wagon when the galloper's shooting of Mrs Rukeyser, his suicide and the abandonment of the boy offend all expectations of masculine heroism in the western and confound audience expectations of the American Indians' actions. Similarly, Rukeyser's tragic underestimation of the American Indians' capacity ('No drunk Indian's gonna take my farm from me!') is brutally punished through the trick of the bugle call, a reflexive, almost parodic, comment on audience familiarity with western conventions. The pleasure of such moments registers the exemplary role of *Ulzana's Raid* as an economic, non-nostalgic example of the final commercial days of the western genre.

The reluctant gunfighter – Clint Eastwood in *Unforgiven*

Unforgiven (USA 1992 *p.c* – Warner Bros.; *d* – Clint Eastwood; sd col.)

William Munny and his companion, the Kid, have finally accomplished their mission and killed the man responsible for mutilating a young prostitute. Waiting outside town for a rendezvous with those who hired them, the two men discuss their deed. Munny, a veteran gunfighter reluctantly brought out of retirement for this job, is reflective and undemonstrative. The Kid, who up till now has been full of youthful bravado, is in shock, giving way to alternate outbursts of boasting and remorse. Deep down, as Munny senses, he is aghast at what he has done. In a scene remarkable for facing up to the act of violence at the heart of the western genre, Munny articulates what it has taken him a lifetime to learn:

'It's a hell of a thing, killing a man – you take away all he's got and all he's ever gonna have.'

'Yeah, well,' says the Kid, 'I guess he had it coming to him.'

'We all have it coming, Kid,' says Munny.

Unforgiven is not a feminist film, but it takes seriously the issue of violence against women. It is not an anti-racist film, but Morgan Freeman's role as Munny's companion is one of the best a black man has had in a western. Ultimately William Munny behaves in a typical western hero manner – he goes out and shoots the bad man. But the film does not shy away from the consequences of what it means to kill another human being. *Unforgiven* is a film made in full knowledge of everything that has been said against the western – its racism, sexism, its obsession with violence. It negotiates in a subtle and cunning way an accommodation with the critics of the western, yet manages to preserve the fundamentals of the genre all but intact.

MELODRAMA

INTRODUCTION: PROBLEMS OF DEFINITION

The study of melodrama as a cinematic genre is a recent development still in its early stages. It achieved public visibility in 1977, when the Society for Education in Film and Television commissioned papers for a study weekend, some of which were subsequently published in *Screen* and *Movie* in the UK and in *The Australian Journal of Screen Theory*. Around this time and since a spate of articles has appeared in British, French and American film journals and interest in the genre has been extended to work on television, particularly soap operas.

The British foundations of this work were laid in two very different contexts. In 1972 a small independent film journal, *Monogram*, opened a special issue on melodrama with a detailed and seminal account of the historical sources and aesthetics of the 'great Hollywood melodramas of the 50s', written by Thomas Elsaesser as part of a project of re-evaluating the American cinema. Then in 1974, *Spare Rib*, a general interest magazine for the Women's Movement, published a review by Laura Mulvey of Fassbinder's *Fear Eats the Soul* in which she used the film's acknowledged homage to Douglas Sirk's *All That Heaven Allows* to argue a case for feminist interest in the genre. Elsaesser's and Mulvey's contributions represented two very different approaches to melodrama, and dominant film theory and feminist work coexist uneasily on this terrain.

One major source of difficulty in the ensuing debate is the diversity of forms that are gathered under the heading of melodrama. Until the 1970s the term hardly existed in relation to the cinema except pejoratively to mean a 'melodramatic' and theatrical mode which manipulated the audience's emotions and failed aesthetically to justify the response summoned up. The film industry used the category to denote dramas involving the passions – hence crime melodrama, psychological melodrama, family melodrama. Closely related are two further categories, the women's film and romantic drama. To these, film critics have added the maternal melodrama and the argument that most American silent cinema should be considered as melodrama, with the work of D. W. Griffith constituting a virtual subset of its own. Ascription of literary and theatrical sources is equally diverse, running from Greek tragedy, through the bourgeois sentimental novel, Italian opera to Victorian stage melodrama. In the face of such confusion, arguments that melodrama constitutes a 'mode' or 'style' crossing a range of different periods and forms are persuasive. However this does not evade the problem of generic definition, for recent writers on melodrama are united in seeking to trace in it the convergence of capitalist and patriarchal structures, a project which requires historical, cultural and formal specificity. The categories set out above belong to particular phases of generic production and particular socio-historic circumstances – although with considerable overlapping and transformation of material between them.

Early film melodrama – Griffith's *Hearts of the World*

Lack of generic specificity may arise in part from the fact that interest in melodrama first entered film criticism via the channels of *mise-en-scène* and the *auteur*. Criticism from this standpoint (e.g. *Movie*) saw in the work of Ray, Minnelli, Ophuls and Preminger a transformation of banal and melodramatic scripts through the power of authorial vision expressed in *mise-en-scène*. Later, film criticism which re-evaluated Hollywood in terms of ideological textual analysis looked to *mise-en scène* for a formal play of distanciation and irony. The work of Douglas Sirk was discovered around 1971 and lined up alongside Ophuls and Minnelli, preparing the ground for the central place occupied by melodrama in debates on ideology and film aesthetics during the 1970s, and at the same time allowing more critical space to the role of generic convention (see Halliday, 1971; Willemen, 1971). These beginnings in *mise-en-scène* and ideological criticism account for the tendency of much writing on melodrama to focus on the 1950s family melodramas made by a small number of *auteurs*, Minnelli, Ophuls, Ray, Preminger, Sirk (e.g. Schatz, 1981). This contrasts with the constitution of *film noir* as a critical category which led to the greater visibility of a corpus of non-authorial works. On the other hand, more recent work on the women's film, which is not so predicated on preceding film critical traditions, has allowed a much wider range of titles to emerge.

Early feminist investigation of Hollywood had dismissed much of the work validated by *auteurism* as enshrining a male viewpoint on the world which was oppressive to women. However, Molly Haskell's (1979) influential chapter on the women's film of the 1930s and 1940s drew attention to a whole area of submerged and despised production, featuring domestic or romantic dramas centred on female protagonists played by stars valued by the women's movement. Critical work on melodrama has tended to elide the women's film with the family melodrama. Only feminists have drawn attention to the women's film as a category of production aimed at women, about women, drawing on other cultural forms produced for women often by women – e.g. women's magazine or paperback fiction – and to raise questions about the aesthetic and cultural significance of this gender specification.

Theorising family melodrama

While on the surface appearing far removed from the western and gangster, genres whose plots are often rooted in actual historical events, the family melodrama is nevertheless frequently defined as the dramatic mode for a historic project, namely the centrality of the bourgeois family to the ascendancy and continued dominance of that class. For example, Geoffrey Nowell-Smith (1977) argues that 'melodrama arises from the conjunction of a formal history proper (development of tragedy, realism, etc.), a set of social determinations, which have to do with the rise of the bourgeoisie, and a set of psychic determinations which take shape around the family' (Nowell-Smith, 1977, p. 113). This description places melodrama within a network of different concerns, the relationship between which is at issue according to the theoretical and political commitments of the writer.

One problem that emerges is the relation between the socio-historical conjuncture that gives rise to a particular form and its subsequent aesthetic development and history. Another set of problems are introduced in the meeting of Marxism and feminism, which offer competing notions of patriarchy, capitalism and bourgeois ideology, sex and class as key terms for the analysis of the family in melodrama. When Freudian psychoanalysis is brought to bear on melodrama interesting tensions are produced between the application of those ideas in film theory and in feminism. The feminist emphasis on the problem of the construction of femininity in patriarchal culture introduces questions of gender in relation to both the industrial and aesthetic constitution of a form: what, for instance, is the relation between specific audiences and the forms produced in their name? How is the male Oedipal scenario – so often cited as the bedrock of classic narrative cinema and frequently the explicit subject matter of 1950s melodramas – to be understood in forms which offer an unusual space to female protagonists and 'feminine' problems, and are specifically addressed to a female audience?

The question of gender is also a factor in the argument as to whether melodrama is better considered as an expressive code rather than a genre and as to whether it can be considered 'progressive' or not. The taxonomies that arise out of genre analysis bring into focus iconographic motifs, themes, and situations which have a material or structural force in feminist analysis of women's lives, but which in *mise-en-scène* analysis produce metaphorical significance on behalf of patriarchy. Similarly, ironic distanciation or disruption at the level of style may seem progressive in giving the spectator, both male and female, access to 'structures of feeling' normally closed off, but do little to shift the social relations between the sexes represented at the level of plot and character. Such shifts of emphasis characterise the complexities of the melodrama debate.

Thomas Elsaesser: melodrama as a problem of 'style and articulation'

Writing in 1972, Elsaesser's approach draws on the 1960s concern to validate Hollywood through *mise-en-scène* analysis and the post-1968 interest in irony, distanciation and ideological criticism, reworking both in the context of his own concerns with aesthetic affect ('Tales of sound and fury', 1972). Much of Elsaesser's article is concerned to counter the conventional relegation of the form for its blatant use of 'mechanisms of emotional solicitation' (Elsaesser, 1972, p. 8). He counteracts this view from two main directions. First, he seeks to show how the aesthetics of melodrama as a popular and commercial form give access to truths about human existence denied to more culturally respectable forms such as European art cinema. Second, he seeks to demonstrate how it is possible under certain social and production conditions for the melodrama to be ideologically subversive.

In common with other critics Elsaesser establishes melodrama as a form which belongs to the bourgeoisie. In its first manifestations – which Elsaesser cites as the eighteenth-century sentimental novel and post-Revolution romantic drama – it constituted an ideological weapon against a corrupt and feudal aristocracy. The bourgeois family's struggle to preserve the honour of the daughter from despotic and unprincipled aristocrats marked a contest over space for private conscience and individual rights. Elsaesser identifies certain features in early bourgeois melodrama as important to its later developments: the capacity of the eighteenth-century sentimental novel and romantic drama to make individual conflicts speak for a society which, he argues, lies in the popular cultural tradition it inherited, leading from the medieval morality play to music-hall drama, the most significant aspect of which was its 'non-psychological conception of the dramatis personae' (Elsaesser, 1972, p. 2); and formal devices such as ironic parallelism, parody, counterpoint and rhythm. Another significant feature is the siting of the struggles of individualism in the family. For Elsaesser the family is not, except in early forms of melodrama, important in itself as a political institution; rather, through the highly charged formal motifs of melodrama, it provided a means of delineating social crises in concretely personalised and emotional terms.

These constituents of the melodrama – its non-psychological conception of character and formally complex *mise-en-scène*, its containment of action within the family and consequent emphasis on private feeling and psychic levels of truth – enable Elsaesser to construct the family melodrama of the 1950s as the peak of Hollywood's achievement. According to Elsaesser's argument, by the time melodrama was taken up in the cinema it was already saturated with significance beyond the specific socio-historical conditions that gave rise to it. He therefore looks to cinematic history to illuminate how the strategies of melodrama are realised in film. He argues that in the beginning all silent cinema was forced into a melodramatic mode – not simply because of its temporal closeness to Victorian popular forms (see Fell, 1974, and Vardac, 1949), but because the requirements of expression outside verbal language fortuitously pushed the medium into modes which favoured a melodramatic world-view. While the coming of sound meant the dominance of the verbal register and a consequently different dramatic mode, the development of new technologies in the 1950s – colour, widescreen, deep-focus, crane and dolly – often in the hands of German directors with backgrounds in Expressionism, made a complex visual *mise-en-scène* again possible, in which the spoken word would be submerged as only one strand in a musical counterpoint.

Coincident with the development of the technology for such a dramaturgy was the popularisation of Freudian psychoanalysis in America in the 1940s and 1950s. The family reappears as a site of dramatic action, though in a far different ideological context from its heroic stance in the emergence of melodrama as a bourgeois form. The domestic melodrama provides not the exterior spaces of the western or urban gangster film to be conquered by a hero, who, in search of Oedipal identity can express himself in action, but a closed self-reflexive space in which characters are inward looking, unable to act in society (Elsaesser, 1972, p. 10).

Not only do the location and mores of the family reduce the scope for dramatic action, but the characters themselves, in line with the melodramatic tradition, are unaware of the forces that drive them. The intensity and the significance of the drama, then, are not carried in what the characters say, or in the articulation of inner struggle as in tragedy: rather it is the *mise-en-scène* of melodrama, providing an 'aesthetics of the domestic', that tells us what is at stake. The 'pressure generated by things crowding in on the characters ... by the claustrophobic atmosphere of the bourgeois home and/or small town setting' (Elsaesser, 1972, p. 13) is intensified through the demand of the 90-minute feature film for compression of what may be far more expansively expressed in its literary sources. There is, Elsaesser argues, a sense of 'hysteria bubbling all the time just below the surface' and a 'feeling that there is always more to tell than can be said' (Elsaesser, 1972, p. 7).

Elsaesser draws on Freudian concepts for the interpretation of *mise-en-scène*, arguing that the aesthetic strategies of 1950s melodrama function similarly to Freud's dream-work. Sometimes this is a matter of the stock characters' lack of self-awareness producing an explicit form of displacement at the level of the plot:

> the characters' behaviour is often pathetically at variance with the real objectives they want to achieve. A sequence of substitute actions creates a kind of vicious circle in which the close nexus of cause and effect is somehow broken and – in an often overtly Freudian sense – displaced. (Elsaesser, 1972, p. 10)

In other cases it functions:

> by what one might call an intensified symbolisation of everyday actions, the heightening of the ordinary gesture and a use of setting and décor so as to reflect the character's fetishist fixations. (Elsaesser, 1972, p. 10)

This account provides the basis of Elsaesser's argument that in the hands of gifted directors and at the right historical moment it can be used to critique the society it represents. Key terms here are pathos and irony. The externalisation of feelings and reactions into décor, gesture and events objectifies and distances emotions, producing pathos or irony 'through a "liberal" *mise-en-scène* which balances different points of view so that the spectator is in a position of seeing and evaluating contrasting attitudes within a given framework ... resulting from ... the total configuration and therefore inaccessible to the protagonists themselves' (Elsaesser, 1972, p. 15). Thus melodrama can suggest causes beyond individual responsibility, to be found on a 'social and existential level' (Elsaesser, 1972, p. 14).

The melodramatic aesthetic gains its social force in a circular movement of displacement: while capitalist society creates psychic problems which become acutely focused in family and sexual relations, so events within the family are displaced outwards into the *mise-en-scène* indicating forces that exceed specific family conditions. From this position Elsaesser suggests that the shift in 1950s Hollywood from the linear trajectory of the active hero conquering the spaces of the west or the city, to the impotent hero trapped within a domestic interior and confined by the codes of behaviour appropriate to the family, indicates a shift in the ideological conditions obtaining under postwar advanced capitalism. The melodramatic form had come full circle from its initial championing of individual human rights via the bourgeois family's struggle against a feudal aristocracy to a later critique of the ideology of individualism in which the bourgeois family becomes the site of the 'social and emotional alienation' consequent on a corrupt individualism and the failure of the drive to self-fulfilment (Elsaesser, 1972, p. 14).

The major distinction between Elsaesser's position and the work that followed later lay in his use of Freud and Marxism. While noting the rich potential of Freudian subject matter for Hollywood melodrama and assuming rather than analysing the Oedipal hero as dominating the form, it is on the formal mechanisms of a Freudian 'dream-work' that Elsaesser bases his argument for the rich and complex significance of the melodrama's *mise-en-scène*. And what he takes from Marxism is not so much a classical definition of class relations as a notion of alienation translated into existential terms. Consequently, his arguments do not analyse nor distinguish between class and gender relations in Hollywood melodrama, beyond the displacement of one into the other, 'the metaphysical interpretation of class conflict as sexual exploitation and rape' which, according to Elsaesser, dominates the form throughout its history (Elsaesser, 1972, p. 3). This means that the question of how a female protagonist may affect plot structures or the trajectory of the hero's Oedipal drama remains unexamined. Furthermore the emphasis on melodrama as 'form' and '*mise-en-scène*' neglects questions which generic specifications would have raised; for instance, the distinctions and relations between the women's film, romantic drama, family melodrama – questions important to an understanding of the place of women in melodrama. Issues of class and gender, but particularly of gender, were to figure in the next stage in the emerging debate about melodrama.

SEX AND CLASS IN MELODRAMA

Later work on melodrama was to prise Elsaesser's groundbreaking work away from its metaphorical and existential proclivity for *mise-en-scène* analysis. What followed was either a more sociological approach to its subject matter (see Kleinhans, 1978; French, 1978), which understood the family as a political institution and site of real oppression, particularly for women; or work influenced by the development of feminist film theory which produced accounts of the social or sexual positions made available in the narrative to protagonists and spectators. Here *mise-en-scène*, rather than being metaphorically resonant, was seen as symptomatic, indicating the 'return of the repressed', or insoluble contradictions.

Central to the debates that emerge in these reassessments of melodrama is the significance of the bourgeois family as a product of patriarchy and capitalism. At issue here is how the social relations of capitalist production – class – articulate with the social relations of capitalist/patriarchal reproduction – the family. Once the bourgeoisie stops rising it is no longer easy to see in it a direct symbolisation of class struggle – as is argued of the eighteenth-century sentimental novel or post-Revolution romantic drama, for instance. However, the family is felt to be related to class at an ideological level. On the one hand, it seems to operate as a trans-class institution; on the other, it reproduces individuals as class subjects. The family, however, does not simply secure class subjects; it also produces sexed individuals. Arguably the neuralgic point for debates around cinema melodrama is the interrelation of sex and class. In this respect Freud and Marx compete to provide the terms of analysis of the family; according to which authority is given more emphasis, the family is viewed as the site of sexual repression (Nowell-Smith, 1977; Mulvey, 1977/78) or of displaced socio-economic contradiction (Kleinhans, 1978). From Freud is taken the Oedipal drama, particularly the moment of castration and repression; from Marxism the concept of the division between productive and personal life, in which the contradictions inherent in the alienated labour of capitalist production are supposed to be compensated for within the family, where, however, they are merely displaced (see Kleinhans, 1978).

Geoffrey Nowell-Smith and the male Oedipal crisis

Geoffrey Nowell-Smith (1977) locates melodrama as a bourgeois form by distinguishing its address from that of classical tragedy. Whereas tragedy does not depict the class to which it is addressed, the social relations depicted in melodrama presume authority to be distributed 'democratically' among heads of families rather than vested in kings and princes. Thus 'the address is from one bourgeois to another bourgeois and the subject matter is the life of the bourgeoisie'. While this apparent egalitarianism avoids questions about the class exercise of power, the relation between social power and gender becomes potentially more visible – less a question of the symbolisation of one by the other (see Elsaesser, 1972) than of their articulation together. The paternal function becomes crucial in establishing both the right of the family to a place in the bourgeois social hierarchy and, through the mechanism of inheritance, the property relations which underpin this position. The problem for the family is the possible failure of the father to fulfil this function suitably, together with the risky business of raising the son into a patriarchal identity in order that he may take over his property and his place within the community. One root cause of such possible failure is the confinement of sexual relations within the family – evoking the Oedipal drama – and the problematic position of women there.

However while Nowell-Smith makes the relations of power, gender and sex more visible he still leans towards a masculine construction of melodrama. Like Elsaesser, he distinguishes melodrama from the western in the way it closes down on potential social action and turns inward for its drama. Although he does not make the home an existential space, it becomes simply the arena of the 'feminine' characterised by passivity and negativity. Feminist film theory had argued that representation of the 'feminine' as positive, rather than 'non-male', was impossible within the framework of classic Hollywood narrative. Nowell-Smith draws on such arguments to deal with the 'feminine' presence in melodrama. While acknowledging it frequently figures female protagonists he argues that 'masculinity' still constitutes the only knowable heroic norm, so that acute contradictions are involved in the production of active female characters. The space allowed female characters, while it cannot represent femininity, facilitates an exploration of problems of male identity.

From here Nowell-Smith goes on to give an account of melodrama as a patriarchal form, taking the Oedipal drama (more literally than does Elsaesser) as its subject matter. The Hollywood melodrama of the 1950s is structured in terms of conflict between the generations, in which the son has to accept his symbolic castration by the father before he can take up his place in the patriarchal and bourgeois order, proving himself, by becoming both an individual and like his father, capable of reconstituting the family unit for the next generation (Nowell-Smith, 1977, p. 116).

Like Elsaesser, Nowell-Smith draws on Freud for an understanding of the mechanisms of melodramatic narrative and *mise-en-scène*. However, rather than concepts elaborated in *The Interpretation of Dreams*, Nowell-Smith deploys Freud's account of a childhood fantasy, the 'family romance', and his theory of conversion hysteria. The family romance provides the means of understanding the melodrama as being both about the family, foregrounding female characters, and about patriarchal identity. In the family romance the child questions its parenthood, exploring through the question 'Whose child am I?', or 'would I like to be?', different family arrangements. Thus the structure allows differential and even taboo sexual relations to be explored, reorganised and eventually closed off in the final resolution of a reconstituted family to which melodrama is committed.

However, Nowell-Smith argues, such resolution is consequent on castration and therefore on repression; for fiction this means an initial laying out of the problems, entry into the fantasy, which, nevertheless cannot be articulated explicitly. This leads Nowell-Smith to the notion of *mise-en-scène* as 'excess' – a 'too much' of music, colour, movement which indicates not simply a heightening of emotion but a substitution for what cannot be admitted in plot or dialogue, a process for which Freud's theory of 'conversion hysteria' provides an analogy (Nowell-Smith, 1977, p. 117). From a perspective that views classic Hollywood in terms of the 'classic realist text' (see The classic realist text, p. 332), such 'hysterical moments' can be seen as a breakdown in realist conventions, where elements of the *mise-en-scène* lose their motivation and coherence is lost. Such moments of breakdown cannot be done away with by a 'happy end' but represent the 'ideological failure' of melodrama as a form, and so its 'progressive' potential.

Chuck Kleinhans: melodrama and real life

Chuck Kleinhans (1978) offers a different perspective. A Marxist–feminist sociology of the family, rather than Freudian theories of sexuality, provides the premiss of his arguments: 'Since bourgeois domestic melodrama emerges with the ascension of capitalism, and since it deals with the family, it makes sense to look at the family under capitalism to better understand melodrama' (Kleinhans, 1978, p. 41). He characterises the social relations of capitalist production in terms of a split between 'productive' work and personal life now confined to the home – the sphere of reproduction. The alienation of the labour process within capitalist forms of production is disguised and compensated for in the notions of personal identity and happiness supposed to be found in the family a bourgeois conception of 'people's needs' shaped by the ideology of individualism. At the same time women and children are marginalised outside production and confined to the home, while women become responsible for providing the fulfilment that capitalist relations of production cannot – a need whose source lies outside the family and therefore cannot be achieved. 'This basic contradiction forms the raw material of melodrama' (Kleinhans, 1978, p. 42).

Kleinhans argues that, in the piling on of domestic conflict and disaster, in its concentration on 'the personal sphere, home, family, and women's problems' (Kleinhans, 1978, p. 42) and its closeness to real life, melodrama deals more directly than many other genres with themes and situations close to its audience's experiences. In so doing its function is similar to that of the family itself, displacing social contradiction, working through the problems of keeping the family intact at the cost of repression and women's self-sacrifice. In these terms melodrama is a profoundly conservative form. Its penchant for ambiguity, far from providing an ironic critique of bourgeois society, disperses critical focus among a number of possible readings. In *All That Heaven Allows*, for instance, the unsuitability of Cary's second marriage to her gardener is equally and indifferently a problem of class, of age, of lifestyle – thus attenuating the film's purchase on its subject matter. For Kleinhans these films are symptomatic – indicating the strategies of bourgeois ideology for evading structural problems. They are not, however, instances of ideological breakdown or aesthetic radicalism and it is only analysis from quite a different position to that of the film which can reveal its project.

Laura Mulvey: the two voices of melodrama

Laura Mulvey's (1977/78) contribution shifts the emphasis away from melodrama as a 'progressive' genre by reinserting questions about the place of women both in the subject matter of melodrama and in its conditions of production and consumption. While sharing some of Kleinhans's concerns, her feminist perspective produces a very different intervention. Kleinhans sees the family as a product of capitalist social relations residing in the split between 'productive' and 'reproductive' life: patriarchy does not enter as a term in his analysis, and, as with Elsaesser, the question of gender specificity in melodrama disappears.

For Mulvey however, it is in patriarchy that the pertinent and irresolvable contradictions lie. For her the notion that melodrama exposes contradictions in bourgeois ideology by its failure to accommodate the 'excess' generated by its subject matter (see Nowell-Smith, 1977) fails to understand either the degree to which family and sexual relations are constituted as contradictory or the role of melodrama in providing a 'safety valve' for them. Drawing on Helen Foley's view (about Aeschylean tragedy) that 'overvaluation of virility under patriarchy causes social and ideological problems which the drama comments on' (Mulvey, 1977/78, p. 54), Mulvey argues that 'ideological contradiction is the overt mainspring and specific content of melodrama, not a hidden, unconscious threat' (Mulvey, 1977/78, p. 53). Consequently *mise-en-scène* can no longer be the means of privileged critical access to progressive interpretation, but rather, in 1950s Hollywood melodrama, represents the specific aesthetic mode which distinguishes it from tragedy, working overtime to carry what the limited stock figures of bourgeois melodrama cannot consciously be aware of, 'giving abstract emotion spectacular form' (Mulvey, 1977/78, p. 55). Thus Mulvey closes off the notion of a formal subversiveness being inherent in the melodramatic mode.

Instead, she looks to the production conditions of melodrama and its relation to its imputed female audience, whose material and cultural conditions of existence the form, despite the 'symbolic imbalance' of narrative structures, was forced to acknowledge: it is, after all, the patriarchal need for coexistence with women that produces the crisis melodrama seeks to alleviate. Because she insists on the real contradictions of patriarchal ideology for women, rather than their metaphorical significance for men, Mulvey begins to show how melodrama can both function for patriarchal ends, bringing about a narrative resolution of its contradictions, and at the same time perform a quite different function for women: offering the satisfaction of recognising those contradictions, usually suppressed (Mulvey, 1977/78, p. 53).

This view leads Mulvey to distinguish between those films which are 'coloured by a female protagonist's dominating point-of-view' and those which deal with male Oedipal problems by examining 'tensions in the family, and between sex and generations' (Mulvey, 1977/78, p. 54), constructing the hero as Elsaesser's and Nowell-Smith's victim of patriarchal society. Sirk, she argues, worked in both traditions, his independently produced *Tarnished Angels* and *Written on the Wind* conforming to the second pattern, his work for Ross Hunter at Universal, who specialised in women's pictures (see *All That Heaven Allows*), belonging to the first. Women's pictures, variously known in the trade as 'weepies', 'sudsers', 'four handkerchief pictures', etc., were tailored to the female matinée audience, generally deriving from women's magazine fiction or novelettes, and had a tangential relation, yet to be fully explored, to the family melodrama derived from the bourgeois novel. These films are characterised by an attempt to reproduce the woman's point of view as central to the narrative, and if there is subversive excess in melodrama, this is where Mulvey locates it. Whereas the patriarchal mode of melodrama is able to produce some form of readjustment of its values, some reconciliation between the sexes, the attempt to entertain the woman's point of view, to figure feminine desire, produces narrative problems of an order impossible to tie up, except in the fantasies of women's magazine fiction. In *All That Heaven Allows*, Cary, a widowed mother of two, past child-bearing age, is able to unite with her younger, employee lover only when a last-minute accident renders him bedridden and incapable. However, such a fantasy, while resolving certain of the narrative's contradictions, touches on 'recognisable, real and familiar traps, which for women brings it closer to daydream than fairy story' (Mulvey, 1977/78, p. 56).

PROGRESSING THE DEBATE: PATRIARCHY AND CAPITALISM

Two major and interlinked areas of debate emerged from Mulvey's and Nowell-Smith's interventions. The first concerns the 'obscured dialectic between class politics and sexual politics, bourgeois ideology and the patriarchal order' (Pollock, 1977, p. 106); the second the question of whether gender difference can be said to have aesthetic consequences in fictional structures.

Ron and Cary under the 'golden rain tree' in *All That Heaven Allows*

Griselda Pollock: the repressed feminine

Griselda Pollock (1977) takes up the first issue in a consideration of what precisely is repressed in the Oedipal moment. She notes a confusion in discussion of melodrama as to whether its representation of the family signifies an interrogation of bourgeois family relations, or the displacement of con tradictions found in bourgeois social relations, or both. Behind this lies an issue about the primacy of patriarchal or of capitalist relations – of sex or class determination. Pollock wants to argue the necessity of thinking of the family, and the place of women within it, as a product of both in dialectical articulation together. In this respect she sees both Nowell-Smith (1977) and Mulvey (1977/78) as in danger of 'reifying sexuality outside the social formation', arguing that 'the contradictions which *All That Heaven Allows* exposes are between different social positions, not just irreconcilable desires or the sexuality of women' (Pollock, 1977, p. 110). Taking issue with the view that femininity in patriarchal culture is unrepresentable because unknown and unknowable, Pollock argues that femininity can be produced only as specific social positions. In western society the social position of mother is crucial to the perpetuation both of capitalist social relations and patriarchal dominance, demanding the subjugation of female sexuality in social and cultural life. From Pollock's perspective the women's point-of-view movies and male Oedipal dramas have one thing in common: the relocation of the woman as mother, a position that, while fathers may disappear, be rendered silent or impotent, dominates the conclusion of these films.

However, such relocation faces the problem of 'the extraordinary and disruptive role played by the woman's uncontained, withheld or frustrated sexuality in the dynamic of the narrative' – which includes 'female sexuality outside familial roles' (Pollock, 1977, p. 111) and the continued sexuality of mothers. This leads Pollock to posit the 'repressed feminine' as the key to understanding melodrama. In her terms the 'feminine' represents a psycho-sexual position, hypothetically available to either sex, but foregone and repressed in the reproduction of sons in the patriarchal, masculine position and daughters as mothers. What is important here is that femininity is understood not simply as an empty, negative, passive space, but something positively 'lost' in the construction of the social and sexed subject positions necessary to patriarchal, bourgeois society. Although Pollock does not do so, the fantasy of the family romance could be invoked here to explain the patriarchal function of both women's film and male family melodrama. In one of its forms it allows the child to disown the father and fantasise the mother's independent sexuality with another man. This, for the male child in particular, allows both an exploration of incestuous desire and identification with the female position; for the female child, it allows a refusal of the repression required for the confinement of female sexuality to reproduction.

Taking up Mulvey's (1977/78) 'safety valve' theory of melodrama, Pollock goes on to suggest that many of the contradictions exposed in 'progressive' analysis of melodrama are in fact ones which patriarchal and bourgeois culture can contain. And this is as true of the women's picture tradition as of the male family melodrama; the woman's point of view in *All That Heaven Allows* is not in the last analysis what is disruptive. Cary in fact is offered as a passive spectator of her own fate, quite in line with patriarchal ideology, whereas in *Home from the Hill*, on the surface a male melodrama, the figure of the woman, totally robbed of point of view, holds nevertheless enormous control in the disposition of narrative events.

Pollock's intervention in the debate constitutes a useful appraisal of its theoretical assumptions. She attempts to construct terms in which the women's picture and family melodrama can be thought through together in terms of a problematic which embraces the dialectic of sex and class. However, attractive as Pollock's conception of the source of potential disruption in melodrama might be, the notion of the 'feminine position' outside of patriarchal and bourgeois social relations is highly abstract, and not much further forward in providing a sense of the articulation of sex and class which she demands.

Christian Viviani: class and sex in the maternal melodrama

Christian Viviani (1980) is concerned with 'woman' as an already culturally coded figure capable of mobilising audience response towards new conceptions of social organisation. He attempts an analysis of the ideologies reworked in a subset of Hollywood melodrama which appears to effect a passage between its Victorian forms, epitomised in the work of Griffith, and the women's film – a subset which Viviani dubs 'the maternal melodrama'. His analysis of this sub-genre in the 1930s deals with the transformation of European, Victorian themes under pressure from New Deal ideology. In this, the role of woman as mother is pivotal, suggesting something of the way issues around female sexuality and maternity can be dramatised as a displacement or resolution of class issues (see Elsaesser, 1972). Viviani's contention is that as a fictional mode, melodrama seeks to move its audience emotionally by an appeal to everyday feelings and experiences which are then magnified in intensity through a

Stella Dallas – 'maternal sacrifice … as means to upward mobility and social hope'

complexity of baroque incident and coincidence. The fallen mother is a figure who can readily summon up such feelings, particularly for the male audience for whom she carries a charge of Oedipal eroticism. At the same time, the sexual transgression of the mother is capable of evoking not only a moral but a class register, for the variations in moral attitude to her speak different class ideologies.

The dramaturgical structure on which this is based, and which was adopted by Hollywood from the European Victorian stage, involved

> a woman [who] … separated from her child, falls from her social class and founders in disgrace. The child grows up in respectability and enters established society where he [sic] stands for progress … The mother watches the social rise of her child from afar; she cannot risk jeopardising his fortunes by contamination with her own bad repute. Chance draws them together again and the partial or total rehabilitation of the mother is accomplished, often through a cathartic trial scene. (Viviani, 1980, p. 7)

This basic structure could be organised ideologically according to two different codes of judgement, one moral, the other social. For the European-influenced and smaller cycle, the woman's fall 'was traceable to her adultery, committed in a moment of frenzy and expiated in lifelong maternal suffering' (Viviani, 1980, p. 6). In Hollywood this vein represented a female equivalent to Warshow's 'gangster as tragic hero' (see Warshow: the gangster film as an experience of art, p. 174). Although still morally condemned, the heroine's descent into the 'more realistic, more tawdry or desperate ambiance of music halls and furnished rooms', marked an opposition to the permanence of the bourgeois household, a 'veritable ideal of this thematic, totally impregnated by Victorian morality' (Viviani, 1980, p. 8). Her fate of 'anonymity and silence' was the opposite of the tale favoured by Hollywood of success and rise to fame. However, though admitting its potentially critical slant on European aristocratic moral codes, Viviani argues that this cycle looked decidedly reactionary from the perspective of the New Deal:

> Heroines who are submissive, resigned, sickly, even naive defenceless, lacking in energy or decisiveness were hardly good examples for the movie-going public of 1932 and 1933 who needed to be mobilised to face the economic crisis. The direct lineage of Madame X was an uncomfortable reminder of an earlier state of mind which had led to the Wall Street crash. (Viviani, 1980, pp. 9–10)

As America became more isolationist and nationalistic the moral codes of the maternal melodrama shifted gear. The foundations of such a shift had been laid in the work of Griffith, who had performed the necessary transposition from a European aristocratic urban milieu to an American, petit-bourgeois and rural one, which both bore the brunt of an ideological criticism (as for instance in *Way Down East*, 1920), but was capable of regeneration. New Deal ideology, according to Viviani, 'is incarnated halfway between city and country' (Viviani, 1980, p. 12), and it is the figure of woman with her culturally given connection to nature, who can facilitate this incarnation, which both castigates 'the residue of an outworn morality' hung on to by the idle city rich and the rigidity of rural society in the name of the 'pantheistic philosophies of Thoreau and Whitman'. In the American maternal melodrama of the 1930s, epitomised by *Stella Dallas* (1937), the motif of maternal sacrifice is rearticulated in relation to themes closer to American society of that time: 'prejudice, education, female understanding, the "good marriage" of the children' (Viviani, 1980, p. 10). In this context moral sin is replaced by social error and a new kind of heroine can emerge whose sacrifice is less dumb acquiescence to an inevitable and remote fate than a struggle to survive in a society whose values need correcting:

> Integrated into the world of work, she unconsciously participates in the general effort to bring America out of the crisis; she is set up as an antagonist to a hoarding, speculating society, repository of false and outworn values. (Viviani, 1980, p. 12)

Her child becomes a stake in this regeneration, not taken away from the mother as in the European cycle, but given up 'to insure him an education, a moral training that only a well-placed family can give him' (Viviani, 1980, p. 13).

'These films recount the tale of a woman's loss due to a man's lack of conscience and show her reconquering her dignity while helping her child re-enter society thanks to her sacrifices. It is a clear metaphor for an attitude America could adopt in facing its national crisis' (Viviani, 1980, p. 14).

The figure of the mother could effect such ideological work because of the powerful emotions she calls on in the viewer, producing 'an illusion destined to mobilise the public in a certain direction, an illusion that transposed the anguish of an era, an illusion … knowingly grounded in eroticism' (Viviani, 1980, p. 16). By implication the power of such eroticism to effect displacement or resolution of class difference lies in the flexible class definition of the woman. On the one hand, this is dependent on familial and sexual placing, transgression of which produces the woman in the position of outcast. On the other, ideologies of maternity and femininity – e.g. the woman sacrifices self for child, or acts out of true love for a man – can be utilised to argue for an ideological shift in the moral balance of power between different class forces.

FEMINIST APPROACHES TO THE FEMALE PROTAGONIST

Laura Mulvey's essay 'Visual Pleasure and Narrative Cinema' has been seminal in suggesting the role the figure of woman plays in patriarchal fiction (see Laura Mulvey on visual pleasure, p. 336). Her concern there, as she has since explained it (see Mulvey, 1981), was to examine the masculinisation of spectator position and identification in classic Hollywood cinema. However, as she herself argued (1977/78), a female protagonist at the centre of the narrative disturbs this structure. This view has led to work by feminists on the possible aesthetic consequences of gender difference. Pam Cook (1978) argued that *Mildred Pierce* represented a mixed genre film in which the male voice of *film noir* combated the female voice of the women's film. Barbara Creed (1977) considered the narrative consequences of the generic necessity of the women's melodrama (in her terms any melodrama that supports a central heroine) to produce the figure of the woman as leading protagonist. She investigated the differences between the narrative structures developed to cope with a female protagonist and those which characterise most other genres. The problem the melodramatic structure faces is one of producing drama while conforming to social definitions of women in their domestic roles as wives and mothers (Creed, 1977, p. 28).

From a small group of women's pictures she derives a typical narrative structure capable of supporting a central feminine protagonist 'which involves a pattern of female role transgression; the entry of an exceptional male; marked change in the heroine's point of view; suffering and sacrifice; and, finally, her acceptance of a more socially desirable role' (Creed, 1977, p. 28). She goes on to show how in the three

Mildred Pierce – women's film and *film noir* in conflict

women's pictures she studied the discourse of the doctor is used to bring the transgressing woman's viewpoint into line with the accepted codes of feminine behaviour. For Creed, the displacement of the female protagonist's dilemma into *mise-en-scène* and into a range of other characters, far from combating an ideology of individualism, simply restates her problem in terms of other people's needs – reproducing a scenario in which the woman does not speak, but is spoken for (Creed, 1977, p. 29). Like Kleinhans, she sees melodrama as interesting for the questions which an analysis constructed elsewhere – by Marxism or feminism – can show it touching on but not able to ask. Whereas in Kleinhans's case there are questions of capitalist relations of production and class, Creed suggests that the unspoken question of women's melodramas is to do with the taboo subject of female sexuality.

Melodrama and the status quo

Most accounts of melodrama in literature and cinema, including those discussed above, agree on one thing: that in its post-revolutionary bourgeois forms the boundaries of the field in which it operates are those of the established social order as lived in everyday domestic terms. For instance, Stephen Neale (1980) argues that whereas in most other genres the establishment of law and order is the object of the narrative, melodrama focuses on problems of living within such order, suggesting not 'a crisis of that order, but a crisis within it, an "in-house" rearrangement' (Neale, 1980, p. 22).

Jean-Loup Bourget (1978) presents the same idea in ideological rather than moral terms: '… America after questioning the myth of progress, urbanisation and socialisation, is content with a rhetorical question and at the end of the story reinstates the same belief' (Bourget, 1978, p. 32). Elsaesser concretises these generalities in an acute description of the *mise-en-scène* of the domestic, arising from an account of *Hilda Crane*, which, he argues, 'brings out the characteristic attempt of the bourgeois household to make time stand still, immobilise life and fix forever domestic property relations as the model of social life and a bulwark against the more disturbing sides in human nature' (Elsaesser, 1972, p. 13). Thomas Schatz (1981) in a recent survey of 1950s melodramas notes the paradoxical narrative function of marriage and the family, which provides both dramatic conflict and resolution. Of *Young at Heart* he argues:

> We have seen the central characters as either victimised by or utterly hostile to the existing social–familial–marital system, but somehow romantic love and parenthood magically transform familial anxiety and despair into domestic bliss. (Schatz, 1981, p. 229)

The necessity for melodrama of producing dramatic action while staying in the same place gives it a characteristically circular thematic and narrative structure – many cinematic melodramas start out from a flashback so that their end literally lies in their beginning. And it gives melodrama a characteristically ambiguous modality and address, which has given rise to different interpretations. Bourget, writing about the romantic dramas of 1940s Hollywood, describes their hesitation between, on the one hand, a heavy-handed moralistic realism, operating in parable-like fashion in support of the bourgeois family, and on the other, the disbelief of whimsy, of escape offered by 'romance'. Stephen Neale, writing from a psychoanalytic perspective, describes this ambiguity of melodrama as a form of pathos to do with the narrativisation of desire, which, by its very nature, can never be fulfilled (Neale, 1980, p. 30).

While these accounts vary in the degree to which they see subversive potential within, or despite, such constraints, they are alike in concentrating on formal analysis of the genre. Only a feminist interest in the relation of the films to the lives of their audience has suggested that the formal ambiguity within which the genre works is neither simply a meretricious ploy to soak the drama for all the pathos it is worth without confronting serious issues, nor a mass-medium's attenuation of the tragic vision, but provides a structure that relates to the material conditions of women's lives.

What appears as the affect of form in one critical context, is given a material reality in another. This observation is not quite the same as noting the 'real life' occurrence of events that seem exaggerated or absurd in the films. Links between the form and the lives of the presumed female audience are commonly made by industry, establishment critics and feminists. The audience for women's films and melodramas is most often characterised as composed of frustrated housewives, oppressed by the duties of motherhood and marriage, by sexual frustration and lost fantasies of romantic love. In this view, the women's films and melodramas of the 1940s and 1950s gave cultural expression to these frustrations, offering in vicarious outlets escapist fantasy, rage, or sublimation. In the words of Molly Haskell (1979), the films represent 'soft-core emotional porn for the frustrated housewife'.

What the industry and Marxist feminism have in common is an implicit view of the housewife's life and the emotions it calls forth as being narrow, circumscribed, petty, boring, frustrated, etc. Critics, and many of the directors and writers involved in these films, regard them with contempt or mild patronage, looking for value in what can be made of the situations in terms of the 'human condition'. Hence the great interest in the notion of the form's power lying in its capacity to subvert its content. Recent work on melodrama, however, has ceased to look for textual progressiveness. This is partly due to the displacement of *mise-en-scène* by a psychoanalytically construed concept of narrative as the key to a film's ideological operation. In this view classic narrative functions precisely to engage with 'difference' – whether social, sexual, or unconscious – but always from the reassuring perspective of 'the same' to which everything is returned at the end. From quite a different approach, the notion of progressive reading has become suspect because of the formalism that constitutes meaning textually, without reference to the reading situation and practices of actual audiences. Further work on melodrama and the woman's film has been pursued predominantly by feminists, proceeding in two main directions: one a formal, narrative/discourse orientated approach; another, frequently focusing on TV soap opera, an audience orientated approach. The former is concerned to analyse the work performed by narrative structure and the process of enunciation when a female protagonist is posited as subject of desire and discourse rather than its object (see Lea Jacobs, 1991, and Mary Ann Doane, 1983). The latter traces a homology between the ambiguous modality of melodrama, its circular structure, and the contradictions within which women's lives are constructed. The woman's film and melodrama provide fictional structures and forms of pleasure which reproduce a 'female' subject, and at the level of the text some of the material conditions in which women live (see Modleski, 1979, and Brunsdon, 1981). In these terms the duplicitous complexity with which Kleinhans charges *All That Heaven Allows* – where the displacement of problems to do with class, age, sexuality into female problems of personal relations renders them simply confusing – is not so much a question of ideological poverty in the analysis of class, or age, etc., but of the difficulty of mapping the 'question of femininity', of women's issues, across other social definitions.

RECENT WORK ON MELODRAMA AND THE WOMAN'S FILM

In 1987, many of the articles discussed above were collected together and introduced by Christine Gledhill in *Home is Where the Heart Is: Studies in Melodrama and the Woman's Film*. Far from signalling the culmination of work in these areas, the publication of *Home Is Where the Heart Is* coincided with and further helped to promote and to focus a great deal of additional publication and research, including books by Robert Lang (1989), Jackie Byars (1991), Lea Jacobs (1991), Jeanine Basinger (1993), and Barbara Klinger (1994), and another collection of articles, *Melodrama: Stage, Picture, Screen* (1994), edited by Jacky Bratton, Jim Cook and Christine Gledhill and based on papers delivered at a major international conference on melodrama held in London in 1992. In addition, E. Ann Kaplan discusses melodrama and the woman's film at some length in her book, *Motherhood and Representation* (1992), and the directing and scripting of woman's films by women are discussed by Judith Mayne in *Directed by Dorothy Arzner* (1994) and by Lizzie Francke in *Script Girls, Women Screenwriters in Hollywood* (1994), respectively.

Each of these books and studies presents new insights and/or new research. Lang's book is the first systematic study of the 'family melodramas' directed by Griffith, Vidor, and Minnelli. It thus includes extensive discussion of *The Crowd* (1928), as well as *Stella Dallas* and *Ruby Gentry* (1942), and *Madame Bovary* (1949), as well as *Some Came Running* (1958) and *Home From The Hill* (1960), placing all these films within the context of familial, Oedipal and patriarchal issues and concerns.

Jackie Byars's book is a study of gender in the films of a particular period, the 1950s, and highlights the extent to which the films themselves drew on and interacted with wider social and cultural debates and representations. Focusing on men as well as on women, she extends the canon of films traditionally discussed by referring in detail to films like *Picnic* (1955), *From Here to Eternity* (1953) and *A Streetcar Named Desire* (1951) as well as to films like *All That Heaven Allows* and *Imitation of Life* (1959). She also addresses issues of class and of race, as well as issues of gender.

Barbara Klinger's book also focuses on the 1950s, and specifically on the films directed at this time by Douglas Sirk. Eschewing both traditional *auteurism* and conventional textual analysis, Klinger's concern is to trace the array of contemporary contexts within which Sirk's films, their devices, their stars and their style were understood. Her approach thus represents – and seeks to bring together – recent interest in historiography and in historiographical research, on the one hand, and recent interest in audiences, in audience research and in the multiplicity of readings audiences can and do make of films on the other.

Kaplan's book situates an array of films and of cycles of films from different periods in the cinema's history within and across changing – and unchanging – ideologies and representations of motherhood. Within this context she considers such topics as the maternal woman's film, such themes as maternal sacrifice, and such paradigms of motherhood as 'the Angel' and 'the Witch'.

Lea Jacobs considers in detail a particular cycle of films – the 'Fallen Woman' films of the late 1920s, the 1930s and the early 1940s – which in many ways represented and embodied a challenge to traditional ideologies of motherhood and femininity. Focusing on the issue of self-regulation and self-censorship, and using specific archival case files, Jacobs's study demonstates on the one hand how social ideologies and the practices of the film industry interacted at a specific point in time, and on the other how that process of interaction was always also a process of negotiation, a two-way or sometimes a three- or four-way process whose results – the films themselves – were often highly complex, highly ambiguous and highly contradictory.

These features and characteristics are also stressed in Mayne's book, the first book-length study of the work of Dorothy Arzner, and in Francke's book, the first book-length account of the work of several generations of female scriptwriters in Hollywood. They also form the basis of Basinger's account of the woman's film in her book, *A Woman's View*. For Basinger, as for many others,

> what emerges on close examination of hundreds of women's movies is how strange and ambivalent they really are. Stereotypes are presented, then undermined then reinforced. Contradictions abound, which at first sight seem to be merely the result of carelessness, the products of commercial nonsense. But they are more than plot confusion. They exist as an integral and even necessary aspect of what drives the movies and gives them their appeal. These movies were a way of recognizing the problems of women, of addressing their desire to have things be other than the way they were off-screen. (Basinger, 1993, p. 7)

Unlike others, though, she offers a 'working definition' of the woman's film that extends well beyond the traditional canon, the traditional label and the traditional confines of 'melodrama'. 'A woman's film', she writes 'is a movie that places at the center of its universe a female who is trying to deal with emotional, social, and psychological problems connected to the fact that she is a woman' (Basinger, 1993, p. 20). It thus includes – or should include – 'Rosalind Russell's career comedies, musical biographies of real-life women, combat films featuring brave nurses on *Bataan*, and westerns in which women drive cattle west and men over the brink' (Basinger, 1993, p. 7).

The point that Basinger makes here is clearly both polemical and logical. It is also a point that raises questions about generic labels and terms, and about the relative weight to be accorded institutional terms – the terms used by Hollywood, and by contemporary reviewers, critics and journalists – as opposed to those used and defined by subsequent theorists and subsequent historians. Similar questions have been raised by Ben Singer (1990) and by Steve Neale (1993), who have researched the deployment and definition of 'melodrama' as a term both inside and outside Hollywood, and its relationship to female-centred narratives on the one hand, and to the woman's film on the other. Both find significant differences between the understanding and use of the term in and around the film industry and other contemporary institutions of entertainment – the theatre, and in Neale's case television and radio – and the understanding and use of the term in and around film, media, and cultural sudies.

Broadly speaking, both Singer and Neale have found that 'melodrama' meant 'thriller', and hence was used principally to describe and to label crime films, adventure films, war films, westerns and horror films. Singer, who is concerned with the 1900s, the 1910s and the 1920s, quotes from a 1906 article entitled 'The Taint of Melodrama': 'Ask the next person you meet casually how he defines a melodramatic story, and he will probably tell you that it is a hodge-podge of extravagant adventures, full of blood and thunder, clashing swords and hair's breadth escapes' (Singer, 1990, p. 95). Neale, who is concerned with sound period through to the end of the 1950s as well, quotes from an issue of *Life* magazine (27 August 1925, p. 26): 'melodrama, on the screen, is identified almost entirely with fast physical action; cowboys or sheiks or cavalrymen riding madly across country, men hanging by their teeth from the ledges of skyscrapers, railroad wrecks, duels, heroines floating on cakes of ice toward waterfalls, and every known form of automobile chase.' He also quotes from numerous trade reviews, and notes that the only two films made by Hollywood with the word 'melodrama' in the title – *Manhattan Melodrama* (1934) and *Washington Melodrama* (1941) – were both thrillers or crime films.

As Singer and Neale both go on to point out, woman's films – and films marked generally by domestic settings, by romance and/or by pathos and sentiment – were called dramas, not melodramas, and Neale goes on to speculate that this use of the term may derive from theatrical genre, 'drama'. The only female-centred films regularly described as melodramas were, precisely, action films and thrillers of one kind or another, from the 'serial queen' adventure films that Singer discusses – *The Perils of Pauline* (1914), *The Exploits of Elaine* (1914–15), *The Hazards of Helen* (1915) and others – through such female-centred aviation films as *Tail Spin* (1939) and *Women in the Wind* (1939), to the numerous female-centred detective films and Gothic thrillers of the 1940s – *Murder Among Friends* (1941), *Second Chance* (1947), *Mary Ryan, Detective* (1949), and *Gaslight* (1944), *Shadow of a Doubt* (1948), *Undercurrent* (1946) and *Secret Beyond the Door* (1948).

(For further discussion of the aviation films, see Paris, 1995, pp. 114–16; for further discussion of the Gothic thriller, see Waldman, 1983; Walsh, 1984; Doane, 1987; and Barefoot, 1994.)

Neither Neale nor Singer deny a relationship between the woman's film, as traditionally defined, and nineteenth-century theatrical melodrama. But they both point to the heterogeneous – the multi-generic – nature of nineteenth-century melodrama. And they both point to the possibility that the meaning of melodrama as a term may have altered as melodrama itself altered and changed. Singer argues that there was a division between cheap, popular, sensational melodrama and high-brow and middle-class theatre at the turn of the century. Despite the fact that elements of nineteenth-century melodrama fed into the latter, the former became the site of an equation between 'melodrama' and thrills, spills and action, blood, thunder, villainy and vulgarity upon which commentators, critics, audiences and reviewers in film and in the theatre increasingly drew. Neale's argument is similar, though drawing on Rahill (1967), he places the division further back in time, arguing for a correspondence between the woman's film and what Rahill calls 'modified melodrama', a form of melodrama that emerged initially in the second half of the nineteenth century, and in which: 'The "heart" became the target of playwrights rather than the simple nervous system, and firearms and the representation of the convulsions of nature yielded the centre of the stage to high-voltage emotionalism, examination of soul-states, and the observation of manners ... The unhappy end became common' (Rahill, 1967, p. xv). Neale argues that it was this form of melodrama, an inheritor of *drame*, that became known simply as drama. The action-based forms fed first in the theatre and then in the cinema into action-based genres of various kinds and tended to retain the melodrama label. Some of these points were made some time ago by Michael Walker (1982), who sees nineteenth-century melodrama as a matrix both for action genres and what he calls 'melodramas of passion'.

Whichever account is accepted, it is clear that melodrama, the woman's film, and the precise nature of the relationship between them remain key areas of debate and research. It is equally clear, though, as Christine Gledhill points out above, and as Vardac (1949) and Fell (1974) both pointed out some time ago, that melodrama is related to other genres too, and that further research – and further debate – is urgently needed in these areas as well.

Selected Reading

Jeanine Basinger, *A Woman's View: How Hollywood Spoke to Women, 1930–1960*, London, Chatto & Windus, 1993.

Pam Cook, 'Duplicity in *Mildred Pierce*', in Kaplan (ed.), *Women in Film Noir*, London, BFI, 1978.

Barbara Creed, 'The position of women in Hollywood melodramas', *Australian Journal of Screen Theory* no. 4, 1977.

Thomas Elsaesser, 'Tales of sound and fury: observations on the family melodrama', *Monogram* no. 4, 1972.

Christine Gledhill (ed.), *Home is Where the Heart Is: Studies in Melodrama and the Woman's Film*, London, BFI, 1987.

E. Ann Kaplan, *Motherhood and Representation: The Mother in Popular Culture and Melodrama*, London, Routledge, 1992.

Chuck Kleinhans, 'Notes on melodrama and the family under capitalism', *Film Reader* 3, 1978.

Barbara Klinger, *Melodrama and Meaning, History, Culture, and the Films of Douglas Sirk*, Bloomington and Indianapolis, University of Indiana Press, 1994.

Laura Mulvey, 'Notes on Sirk and melodrama', *Movie* no. 25, 1977/78.

Laura Mulvey, 'Afterthoughts on "Visual pleasure and narrative cinema" inspired by *Duel in the Sun*', *Framework* nos 15/16/17, summer 1981.

Steve Neale, 'Melo talk: on the meaning and use of the term "melodrama" in the American Trade Press', *The Velvet Light Trap* no. 32, 1993.

Geoffrey Nowell-Smith, 'Minnelli and melodrama', *Screen* 18(2), summer 1977.

Griselda Pollock, 'Report on the weekend school', *Screen* 18(2), summer 1977.

Ben Singer, 'Female power in the serial-queen melodrama: the etiology of an anomaly', *Camera Obscura* no. 22, 1990.

Linda Williams, 'Something else besides a mother: *Stella Dallas* and the maternal melodrama', in Gledhill, *Home is Where the Heart Is*.

A Fool There Was (USA 1914 *p.c* – The Box-Office Attractions Company; *d* – Frank Powell; st b/w)

This film plays on a typical theme of nineteenth-century stage melodrama – the disaster that besets a respectable family when its head falls prey to a fashionable vamp (a stereotype instituted in Theda Bara's role here, and which made her a star). Examples of early film melodrama style can be found in the film's use of the static camera, the lack of close-ups and the reliance on natural light sources. Viewed from the perspective of 1950s family melodramas this can be seen as a lack of technological development; or it can be understood as the continuity, even fulfilment, of certain nineteenth-century theatrical traditions (see Vardac, 1949). Melodramatic effects, for instance, are produced by the crosscutting between pathetic scenes of the wife with her angelic daughter or in church, and the scenes of dissolution at the vamp's apartment or of despair in the husband's home, wrecked through his squandering time and money on his mistress and drink. The husband himself becomes the site of a struggle between two representations of women: the wife, who hearing of the vamp's desertion declares 'If he is as you say my place is with him', and the dark-haired sexual woman. Melodramatic expression is carried, as in the theatre, by furnishing and fittings – a *chaise-longue*, a card table, half-empty bottles and glasses, costume – the wife's squashed down hat, the furs and silky gowns of the vamp, and significant gesture – the vamp's stare which drives the wife from her husband's arms. The scene utilising the staircase was to become a standard feature of a cinematic rhetoric in the expression of melodramatic confrontation (see *Rebel Without a Cause*, *The Little Foxes*, *The Magnificent Ambersons*, *Written on the Wind*). Here, the husband is tempted to return to wife and daughter until the vamp appears in her nightdress at the top of the stairs to drive them away, causing the husband to collapse, his hand reaching through the banister in a gesture of helpless appeal. The necessary reliance on natural light is turned to theatrical affect by lighting schemes exploiting the dramatic conflict of darkened rooms pierced by shafts of light as curtains and blinds are drawn or closed. And a substitute for the play of light and shade is found in the wreaths of incense that swathe the vamp in her apartment, evoking an atmosphere of decadence and mystery.

Hearts of the World (USA 1918 *p.c* – Artcraft/D. W. Griffith Productions for the Allied Governments; *d* – D. W. Griffith; st b/w)

Nicolas Vardac (1949) and John Fell (1974) have argued that the cinema, rather than originating an entirely new art form, constituted a summation of long-developing trends in the nineteenth-century novel, theatre and painting, pointing to the increasing pictorialisation of the verbal arts, to the point that stage melodrama and spectacle sought to eliminate dialogue, concentrating on action, tableau-like *mise-en-scène*, crosscutting, lighting effects and the mandatory, spectacular 'sensation

Hearts of the World – Griffith's stress on pictorial values

scene'. Vardac in particular stresses the apparently contradictory combination of realism and romance in these trends, the effort being to achieve as realistic and spectacular a rendering of the romantic and melodramatic as possible. This accounts perhaps for Griffith's paradoxical status as the father both of cinematic melodrama and realism. His theatrical inheritance can be seen in the staging of spectacular battle scenes, crosscut with intimate domestic scenes; stress on pictorial values and the influence of Victorian genre painting are present in the use of circular iris for poignant scenes of tenderness and farewell (for instance when the boy parts from his young brother) or wavy, 'cinemascope' framing for the advancing enemy columns; the influence of stage melodrama appears in the archetypal, non-individualised roles (the girl, the boy), in the detail of domestic interiors and in the central, pathetic role of the young girl whose innocence and suffering provides a moral index of the actions of men. This reaches its climax in plot structure and pictorial *mise-en-scène* when the enemy's ultimatum falls on the girl's projected wedding day and, deranged by events, she wanders with her wedding dress in her arms over the smoke-filled battlefield, finally to spend her wedding night by the body of her dead fiancé. The search for realism can be seen in location shooting in France and in the development of continuity editing and the use of close-ups which allows for an intimate and naturalistic style of acting – for instance the changes of expression that play across Lillian Gish's face as she realises her mother is dead, passing from panic to a stony stare of derangement.

Broken Blossoms (USA 1919 *p.c* – UA/ D. W. Griffith; *d* – D. W. Griffith; st b/w)

The source of *Broken Blossoms* is 'The Chink and the Child', a short story from the collection *Limehouse Nights* (1916), written in the purplest of prose by Thomas Burke. Griffith preserved a great deal of the book's melodrama – the heightened tone of the intertitles, the crude stereotypes (brutal father who abuses his virginal daughter) and the occasional narrative coincidence which is used to propel the plot forward (for example, Burrow's friend happening to be in Cheng's shop at the moment when Lucy makes a noise upstairs, thereby allowing him to inform her father of her hideaway).

However, throughout production, and especially during release and promotion, Griffith saw the film as sitting more comfortably in another generic camp – the art film. The film is notable for its luminous, soft-focus, visual quality, for which special lenses had to be made by Hendrik Sartov. Moreover, the narrative leads inexorably towards a tragic end, with the death of all three central protagonists.

An extravagant first-run roadshow was designed to heighten expectations for the film by showing it in first-class theatres with high prices, before it went on general release. 'Griffith deliberately set out to "sell" a reading of *Broken Blossoms* as a work of high art' (Kepley, 1978); a transaction which also, significantly, involved promotion of himself as Hollywood's greatest film artist. To emphasise the film's artistry, a special prologue was written and acted out 'live' before the roadshow screenings. This short sequence was designed to frame the sentiments of the film itself, by describing a young girl, brutalised by a figure representing fate, eventually transcending her squalid life, albeit in death.

This elaborate commercial mechanism was also designed to deflect attention from the film's potential sensationalism. As with *The Birth of a Nation* (1915), *Broken Blossoms* laid itself open to accusations of racism. The subject matter of the film automatically tapped into the Yellow Peril fear in late nineteenth-/early twentieth-century American society; a fear which encompassed labour issues, sexual fears, and military threats during the First World War. Many films of this period, for example, *The Cheat* (1915) explicitly reflected this fear. To distance himself from this miscegenation, Griffith made conscious efforts to soften the character of the Chinaman from Burke's more sinister original; a movement aided by Richard Barthelmess's effeminate, unthreatening body language and melancholic acting.

'Despite the exoticism of the story and some of the oriental flavour, the film is also realistic ... The shabby room of Burrows, the grim tavern, the tenement streets, the threadbare shops – although studio sets – seem perfectly real' (Lennig, 1981, p. 7). Its dominant identity is, however, as a mood piece, concentrating on tone rather than non-stop events and actions (as the most famous of Griffith films are often credited with producing). This different agenda of *Broken Blossoms* results in a slower pacing, created by longer cutting rates (some shots last well over a minute – exceptionally long by Hollywood standards, even of this period). Schickel calls it 'the first memorable European film made by an American' (Schickel, 1996, p. 394).

Broken Blossoms was Griffith's favourite film, and it was also a respectable financial and critical success. For many, it marked a momentary detour from Griffith's usual product, although its low-key, melancholic-but-hopeful tone was recaptured in his 1924 film *Isn't Life Wonderful.*

Way Down East (USA 1920 *p.c* – D. W. Griffith; *d* – D. W. Griffith; st b/w with col. sequence)

Way Down East is based on a Victorian melodrama of the same name. Griffith bought the rights in 1920, a time when films were moving away from melodrama to become more naturalistically rooted in contemporary issues. Both play and film, as Kosloff, Lennig and Kaufman have all observed, drew on certain themes and specific events in Hardy's *Tess of the D'Urbervilles.*

The melodramatic origins of the film are made evident in the set of stereotypical characters (virginal heroine, clean-cut hero, idealised mother, stern father, shrewish busybody), as well as in the instances of narrative coincidence (for example, the heroine Anna Moore, having started a new life in another town, happens to be seen by her ex-landlady, who knows the secret about her dead illegitimate baby). The film also contains several inexplicable moments which seem to operate from what Peter Brook calls the 'occult realm'. Foremost among these are the scene showing David, who has yet to meet Anna, waking from a bad dream while she gets married to the film's villain, and the scene in which David 'senses' Anna's arrival at his farm while it is spatially impossible for him to see her.

But *Way Down East* is not just unadorned melodrama. According to Cardullo, '[f]ilming the whole of Anna's story, as opposed to solely the plot of the play, gave Griffith one large advantage; he could make it appear less melodramatic, or better, he could enhance the *realism* of the melodrama' (Cardullo, 1987, p. 17). Melodrama, although often forming the emotional core of Griffith's films, is always accompanied by a sense of the 'photographically realistic'; we are shown – we see – concrete realities, with locations and interiors 'made real' through meticulous detail. In narrative terms, Griffith usually chooses to show us events rather than allowing them to take place off-screen. For example, with the ice-flow rescue of Anna at the film's climax, '[i]n the play, we only hear of Anna's incredible rescue. In the film, her rescue becomes credible because *we see it happen* ...' The rescue off-stage allows Poetic Justice to claim at least a partial role; in the film, the rescue is all down to David's (and Bartelmess's) courage in actually braving the rapids. It becomes an almost strictly human act.

Significantly, whereas the play opens with Anna's arrival at the Bartlett farm, and only gradually reveals her secret, Griffith chooses to tell the story chronologically. In the play therefore, Anna's guilty secret is gradually revealed to both spectator and other characters at the same time. In the film, the spectator knows of the secret as it happens, well in advance of the recognition scene which finally reveals it to the other characters. The spectator, thereby, is positioned side by side with Anna throughout the film, intensifying the emotional effect of the melodramatic chain of events.

Sunrise (USA 1927 *p.c* – Fox Film Corporation; *d* – F. W. Murnau; st b/w)

The plot of this film is typical of nineteenth-century domestic melodrama, involving the temptations held out to a young farmer, living happily with his wife and child, by a city vamp, who consumes his small financial resources, and finally suggests murdering his wife. Much of the iconography of the domestic melodrama is there: the oil lamps, soup bowls, peasant bread and chequered tablecloth signifying domestic virtues; conflicting representations of femininity – the wife

Sunrise – 'silent cinema in melodramatic mode'

and mother with blonde hair pulled back flat in a bun, associated with traditional peasant country life, the sexual woman in silky garb, black bobbed hair, smoking, jitterbugging and associated with the modern city; the moon and mists over the marshes as the site for the young farmer's succumbing to the murder plot. This iconography contributes to the extreme moral polarities between which the man is pulled, and which are intensified by the non-individualisation of the characters, designated only as the man, the wife, the woman from the city, etc.

While much of the film's iconography, melodramatic structure and *mise-en-scène* looks back to nineteenth-century theatrical melodrama, it also looks forward in its style to the full development of cinematic melodrama. Most notable is, first, the influence of German Expressionism which Murnau brings to Hollywood, particularly in the distorted perspectives of the interior sets, the stereotyping of the woman from the city, the dramatisation of typography in the intertitles that spell out the murder plot, the split screen, superimpositions and dissolves that link the woman and the city; second, Murnau's development of the moving camera, which led Bazin to put him on the side of the realists. Arguably, however, the moving camera (for instance to bring the young farmer to the city woman on the marshes) and the long-take, deep-focus, tracking shot which allows us to travel with the young couple on the trolley from lakeside to city is part of the externalisation of emotion into cinematic *mise-en-scène* which Elsaesser (1972) describes as the hallmark of full-blown Hollywood melodrama in the 1940s and 1950s.

Finally, the film's use of sound marks its transitional status. For while it utilises a synchronous soundtrack, it fulfils the nineteenth-century melodramatic ideal of reducing dialogue in favour of music and pictorial *mise-en-scène*, adding only a few expressive sound effects.

Stella Dallas (USA 1938 *p.c* – Goldwyn Productions; *d* – King Vidor; sd b/w)

This is a classic and much debated woman's film, so designated because of its central woman protagonist, its 'feminine' subject matter and its address to a female audience. These features overlap with the melodramatic mode in so far as domestic subject matter, family relations, and the expression of 'feelings' are seen as both sources of the melodramatic and belonging to the feminine province. In this context, and given the cultural ghetto in which the women's film, until recently, existed, the melodramatic becomes a pejorative designation, associated with tear-jerking pathos and sentimentality, provided frequently by the presentation of women as victims of their circumstances or nobly self-sacrificing. Christian Viviani (1980) has described a shift in the articulation of the maternal self-sacrifice theme in 1930s Hollywood when, under pressure of New Deal ideology, the motif of the mother's fall and degradation gave way to her energetic attempts at recovery, providing a more upbeat ending. It is this spirit that motivates *Stella Dallas* where the motif of maternal sacrifice is called on to collaborate in the portrayal of the family as a means to upward mobility and social hope. Stella's 'failing' is not so much the utilisation of her charms to catch a rich man as a means of escaping her depression-oppressed family, but her refusal to tone her ambitions and lifestyle in with those of her upper-class husband or to suppress her sexuality once a mother, and then later allowing her bonding with her daughter to replace conjugal relations. Stella's punishment is the crushing realisation that her lack of financial and social capital will hinder the possibility of a 'happy', upwardly mobile marriage for her daughter. She therefore proves her superior motherhood by deliberately alienating her daughter to make such a marriage possible, and thereby loses for ever the relationship which motivates the sacrifice.

The debate about the film is how to understand the implications of the ending. Does it represent the punishment of the erring mother, or is it more contradictory? Arguments that this is the case point to the difference in the maternal sacrifice theme when played out in a woman's film. The scene in which Laurel turns down the offer of a fur coat is an interesting example of this, where Laurel is entranced with the 'good taste' and economic well-being of the Morrison household to the detriment of Stella's good-hearted vulgarity. The scene is played out through women's magazine iconography – the dressing-table, mirror, cold-cream and hair bleach – and the activities of the 'feminine' world. However this iconography does not simply dramatise the problem of female upward mobility; it also plays on the dependency of such mobility on the right appearance, a rightness that has little to do with the real underlying relations between mother and daughter.

This suggests a second twist to the maternal sacrifice theme offered by the women's film. E. Ann Kaplan has argued (in Gledhill, 1987) that the mother/daughter bond characteristic of the women's film is potentially threatening to patriarchal social and sexual relations. This, Kaplan argues, gives a special meaning to the film's ending when Stella is forced to accede to the sacrifice of the bond so that her daughter can enter heterosexual monogamy and contribute to social progress, while she herself is reduced to mere spectatorship, outside the scene of action. However, Linda Williams gives a different inflection to the ending by concentrating on its address to a female audience (in Gledhill, 1987). Williams argues that the multiple identification through which the 'feminine' is constructed in the film means that the female audience identifies with the contradictions of Stella's position itself. The only possible unifying point of identification is Stephen Dallas, who, however, is totally lacking in 'spectatorial empathy'. The audience stand-in at this point is Helen Morrison, the only person to recognise Stella's sacrifice, and who purposefully includes Stella into the scene patriarchy would exclude her from by leaving the wedding parlour curtains open. We *see* Stella's patriarchal placement, but *feel* the loss of mother and daughter to each other.

Gaslight (USA 1944 *p.c* – MGM; *d* – George Cukor; sd b/w; UK title: **The Murder in Thornton Square**)

The nineteenth-century theatrical roots of Hollywood melodrama are explicitly drawn upon – and transformed – in *Gaslight*. The film's stage origins, its Victorian setting, and its melodramatic

A female Gothic tradition? *Gaslight*

narrative led *Variety* to comment that the film verges 'on the type of drama that must be linked to the period on which the title was based,' but also to compliment it for 'lacking the ten-twent-thirt element that had been a factor in the stage play'. The reviewer's reference is to the ten, twenty and thirty cent admission charges levied at the beginning of the century by theatres specialising in low-brow melodrama (see Rahill, 1967, pp. 272–83). The production values of the MGM film clearly indicate more prestigious aspirations, but the Victorian furnishings displayed in *Gaslight* have the additional function of forming a decorous surface that conceals but at the same time accentuates the force of the film's melodramatic material. Thus the scene in which the married couple attend a musical recital lends itself to the display of production values characteristic of many period films, but also allows the melodrama to be acted out behind this ornate façade. Indeed, the decorum of the occasion partly serves to heighten the force of the disruption.

The fact that in *Gaslight* the husband and wife have a relationship tantamount to that of oppressor and oppressed has allowed the narrative to be interpreted as approaching a critique of patriarchy and the institution of marriage. Key issues here are the confirmation or denial of the woman's perception, and her ability to articulate her fears. Thomas Elsaesser (1972, p. 11) lists *Gaslight* as belonging to a cycle of 'Freudian feminist melodramas' – films 'playing on the ambiguity and suspense of whether the wife is merely imagining it or whether her husband really does have murderous designs on her'. Other writers have gone on to develop this theme, relating such a cycle to a 'female Gothic' tradition, given a particular inflection by the shifting demands made on women in wartime and postwar America (see, for instance, Waldman, 1983).

In *Gaslight* there is a confirmation of the woman's point of view. But if this signifies a validation of female experience it can be argued that it also ushers in a restoration of the patriarchal order. The detective who comes to the wife's rescue and confirms what she has seen and heard, provides a sympathetic male to counterbalance the figure of the tyrannical husband. The narrative closure also serves to locate the film within the codes of classic Hollywood cinema – the sensationalism of the melodrama is ultimately contained by the film's narrative resolution. The question here is to what extent can this resolution accommodate what has gone before?

Rebel Without a Cause (USA 1955 *p.c* – Warner Bros.; *d* – Nicholas Ray; sd col. scope)

Rebel Without a Cause – Jim (Dean) seeking masculine identity

This film takes up issues of concern to Eisenhower's America – the problem of youth, of middle-class suburban conformity, of definitions of masculinity (see Ehrenreich, 1983) – and plays them out within a melodramatic *mise-en-scène*. In this respect it stands between the social problem picture and family melodrama. In so far as it falls into the category of family melodrama we find a clear delineation of the bourgeois, Oedipal problem described by Geoffrey Nowell-Smith (1977) – the son's need to find his masculine identity, 'to be both himself and at home' – complicated by a failure of the 1950s father to provide the necessary patriarchal stature against which the son can test himself (see also *Written on the Wind*). For David Rodowick (1982) paternal inadequacy enacts the ideological 'failure' of melodrama as a form in the 1950s, when the necessary affirmative conclusion involves a return to a social and sexual order shown to be so palpably problematic in the body of the film. Peter Brooks's argument (1976) that melodramatic rhetoric forces language to reveal meaning in excess of what can be socially signified suggests how the *mise-en-scène* of this film invests a contemporary social problem with melodramatic demands and desires. This is clearly announced in the opening credits in which the music, colour, scope and Dean's self-dramatising play with the monkey and adoption of a foetal position draw from the problem of teenage delinquency its melodramatic potential, linking desire for meaning with Oedipal regression. The 'chicken-run' scene is only one of several set-piece 'action tableaux' in this film, which turn teenage ritual into melodramatic theatre, externalising the demand for meaning in dramatic action and expressive *mise-en-scène*. The apparent 'openness' of landscape in this scene, in which the teenagers construct the possibility of meaningful action, is belied by the rest of the film in which the only field of action is the home or the school, and the only source of satisfaction the construction of meaningful family relations. In this respect Nowell-Smith's (1977) invocation of the Freudian 'family romance' as the motivating fantasy of family melodrama is literalised in the film. Thus despite the gang heroics, the neuralgic centre of the chickie-run lies in moments such as Plato's fantasy of his long-standing friendship with Jim in which building on a chance question of Judy's he constructs his image as an ideal father figure. The narrow terrain of possible action is dramatised when Jim returns to his home to a family row with his father and mother about the right course of action following Buzz's death, enacted, classically, on the staircase, the narrowness of Jim's choices externalised in the construction of his figure by the dark brown verticals of banister, door-frame mouldings and curtain folds. Finally, melodramatic enactment is carried in the improvisatory, yet theatrical acting style used in the film, which in the case of James Dean is pushed to excess and retrospectively draws on his melodramatic star image.

All That Heaven Allows (USA 1955 *p.c* – Universal–International; *d* – Douglas Sirk; sd col.)

One of Sirk's woman's pictures, the film concerns a middle-American bourgeois family for whom the death of the father poses a problem in the now available sexuality of the mother. Her rejection of the suitably respectable, middle-aged Harvey for her young gardener not only threatens the lifestyle and values of her children, but the social identity of the family and of the bourgeois community. The film plays out the family crisis from the woman protagonist's point of view, focusing on her conflicting desires. The themes of romance and renunciation which produce the heroine's crisis and mark the film's ending similarly pull the film into the woman's picture category.

The opening sets the small-town, middle-American context and signals women's picture concerns with its pan from whitewood church spire to the arrival of Sarah returning crockery to Cary. Ron Kirby, the gardener, is introduced as the fantasy hero of women's fiction – tall, dark, self-contained, at work in the background but attentive, gentle, yet authoritative. He is romantic because 'different' – in his style of masculinity (his work with nature), in age, in social class, and above all in his appreciation of the codes of romantic women's fiction: the golden rain tree 'can only thrive where there is love'. Music supports the motif of romance, which the Sirkian *mise-en-scène* takes up and pits against family melodrama themes in the shot of Cary caught in her mirror, the golden rain-tree twig beside her and her children crowding in behind, the clash of harsh and warm colours signalling either the conflicting demands about to ensue, or operating an ironic critique of the genre, depending on one's critical perspective.

The ironic *mise-en-scène* of *Written on the Wind*

The heroine's conflict between her maternal role and personal and sexual desire is overlaid by class, for Ron offers an escape into the realm of the personal, truth to self, from the realm of class status, represented by her dead husband's world. The romantic hero offers the possibility of unifying the two divided sides of a woman's life, represented in signs and symbols drawn from women's magazines and fiction: the 'natural', personally converted barn with roaring log fire, the man who speaks firmly what the heroine wants yet is compelled to resist – 'home is where you are' – the shared concern over the restored Wedgwood teapot. The register is self-consciously melodramatic as Sirkian *mise-en-scène* foregrounds the symbolic dimension of the transaction, its setting and surrounding objects.

The critical question raised by the film is whether Sirkian *mise-en-scène* distances the audience, to ironise the smug, bourgeois world of Eisenhower's middle America (see Willemen, 1971) or whether, as in Chuck Kleinhans's (1978) argument, the film works with mystificatory ambiguity, providing a range of reasons for the failure of Cary and Ron's relationship, none of which are conclusive, or, as in Mulvey's (1977/78) view, the placing of a female character as main protagonist in a family melodrama distorts the genre's 'safety valve' function for patriarchy, raising, in a way very recognisable to female audiences, the problems and questions of women's desire. Feminist critics might want to ask if the desire that romance feeds on is ironised along with Eisenhower's America?

Written on the Wind (USA 1956 *p.c* – Universal–International; *d* – Douglas Sirk; sd col.)

This film was central to the rediscovery of melodrama in the early 1970s, when a revaluation of Douglas Sirk pointed to the ideological critique operated by his ironic *mise-en-scène* on 1950s middle-class America.

Its plot enacts a typical family melodrama in which the constriction of its range of action is reinforced by the circularity of its flashback structure and the hopeless, limited and incestuous channels for its protagonists' desires locked as they are within the bourgeois patriarchal family. Behind the son's impotence lies the father's failure as patriarch (see also *Rebel Without a Cause*), further manifested in the excessive, misdirected desire of his daughter, expressed here in the displacement of her desire for Mitch into her active pursuit of a lower-class petrol-pump attendant. In this respect the plot foregrounds the interconnection of class and sexuality which Elsaesser and others contend is central to melodrama, class struggle being enacted as a problem of desire, in which female sexuality plays an ambiguous but central role (see Pollock, 1977).

The play of class and sex is carried in the iconography of the film – all the signs of conspicuous bourgeois consumption of the Hadley mansion, the oil pumps working incessantly against the skyline, the contrasting colours and costume of the conflicting couples – particularly reds associated with Marylee (sports car, flowers, negligée) and the cool green twinsets of Lucy. Such use of décor, costume and consumer goods is typical of Hollywood family melodrama, as is also the use of the space of hallway and landings where characters cross paths, eavesdrop. exchange confidences, malicious innuendo or accusations (see *The Magnificent Ambersons, Rebel Without A Cause*). Climactic here is the staircase used as the site of final confrontation or denouncement. Overlaying 1950s melodramatic plot structure and iconography is the special injection of Sirkian irony into its excessive *mise-en-scène*; his play with cliché (the nodding mechanical horse and grinning child that confront Kyle at the moment he believes himself impotent); an obsessive play with mirrors (Mitch's entrance with a drunken Kyle over his shoulder is first caught in a hallway mirror), screens and windows (Marylee looking through her window panes to the policeman and the petrol-pump attendant), and above all an Expressionist use of colour, which breaks with realist conventions for the sake of wresting ironic contrasts from objects and faces (the harsh lighting and make-up on Lucy's and Mitch's faces as they attempt to soothe Kyle at the country club, where the palm court music is also in striking contrast to the extremities expressed by Kyle).

Sirkian *mise-en-scène* can also be read in terms of the repression so often said to provide melodrama with its outbreaks of expressive excess, which in turn draws its audience into the emotional drama rather than putting them at a critical distance. The breaking out of repression at the level of plot, florid *mise-en-scène* and crosscutting typical of melodramatic style are epitomised in the scene where the Hadley father falls to his death while Marylee dances wildly and erotically to blaring pop music in her bedroom. The scene also exemplifies the extension of 'musical counterpoint' so crucial to nineteenth-century theatrical melodrama into visual and aural *mise-en-scène* (see Elsaesser, 1972).

CONTEMPORARY CRIME

Criminals, crime, victims of crime, and official and unofficial agents of law, order and justice have featured in films since the turn of the century. The earliest American crime films include *A Career in Crime* (1900), *The Bold Bank Robbery*, *The Adventures of Sherlock Holmes* (1905) and *The Lonely Villa* (1909). They were followed in the early 1910s by films like *The Monogrammed Cigarette* (1910, *One of the Honor Squad* (1912), *Suspense* (1913) and *Detective Burton's Triumph* (1914). (For a comprehensive listing and description of early crime films, see Langman and Finn, 1994.)

The Monogrammed Cigarette shows how the daughter of a famous detective solves her first case. *The Bold Bank Robbery*, as its title suggests, depicts the robbery of a bank by a gang of thieves. And *The Lonely Villa* shows a woman and her children besieged in their home by burglars and their eventual last-minute by the woman's husband. Broadly speaking, the differences in focus and emphasis among and between these three films – the first with its focus on an agent of investigation and its emphasis on detection, the second with its focus on the perpetrators of crime and its emphasis on criminal activity, and the third with its focus on the victims of crime and its emphasis on their response – correspond to the differences in focus and emphasis characteristic of the three principal genres of crime as a whole: the detective film and the investigative thriller, the gangster film and the suspense thriller. As is often the case in the American cinema, these genres and their characteristics often overlap and cross-fertilise in individual cycles and films. *The Big Combo* (1995), for instance, can be seen as a hybrid gangster and detective film. And *Underworld USA* (1960), a gangster film, nevertheless involves a mystery, a process of investigation, and an (unofficial) agent of justice – elements normally characteristic of investigative thrillers. In addition, as Derry (1988), points out, the suspense thriller can focus on individual criminals as well as on victims, and can thus encompass films like *The Day of the Jackal* (1973). Nevertheless, all three genres remain distinct, at least as tendencies, and by and large can be charted with respect to three major figures, the criminal, the victim, and the agent of law and order, and two major aesthetic effects, suspense and surprise.

THE DETECTIVE FILM

Discussion of the detective film has been dominated by discussion and debate about *film noir*, and hence by discussion and debate about the hard-boiled detective and the hard-boiled tradition in general. Even those like Cawelti (1976) and Schatz (1981) who neither use nor debate *film noir* as term, tend to focus on the hard-boiled tradition and hence on films, like *The Maltese Falcon* (1941) and *Farewell, My Lovely* (1946), which are central to most versions of the *noir* canon. As a result, detective films made prior to the 1940s, and those which in general are considered neither as *noir* nor as hard-boiled, have often either been ignored or mentioned merely in passing as inauthentic counterpoints to *noir* and the hard-boiled tradition. And as a result, very little has been written about these films beyond the occasional enumeration of titles, cycles and dates. *Films noirs* and the hard-boiled tradition are discussed at some length in Part Three (see pp. 134–91). Here, attention will be paid to the presentation of ideas and findings relevant to all detective films and investigative thrillers, beginning with research into the origins of detective and investigative fiction and some of the theories put forward to explain its genesis, its socio-cultural role, and its popular appeal. Because of the preoccupation in film studies with *noir* and the hard-boiled tradition, many of these findings and ideas derive from research on detective fiction rather than from research on the detective film as such.

Most commentators cite the following as key to the development of detective and investigative fiction in the late eighteenth and nineteenth centuries: the Gothic mystery; William Godwin's novel, *The Adventures of Caleb Williams*; the memoirs of Vidoq and the memoirs, fictional and real, of other detectives and policemen; Edgar Allan Poe's Dupin stories; 'city mystery' fiction (books like Eugene Sue's *The Mysteries of Paris* and George Lippard's *The Quaker City*); Victorian sensation fiction (especially the novels of Charles Dickens, Wilkie Collins, Charles Reade and Mary Elizabeth Braddon) and its counterpart on the stage; the American dime novel; American pulp fiction; the novels of Emile Gobariau, and, of course, Sir Arthur Conan Doyle's Sherlock Holmes stories.

There are differences in emphasis among and between different commentators, depending on the extent to which stress is laid on the elements of enigma and investigation or on the figure of the detective. These differences, and the distinctions that underlie them, are important, both because the investigation of a criminal enigma need not necessarily be undertaken by professional detectives, witness many of Hitchcock's films, and because narratives centred on detectives – or the police – need not necessarily focus on a process of investigation, as witness *Detective Story* (1951), *The Offence* (1973) and *The Onion Field* (1979). Moreover even if, like *Serpico* (1973) and *Prince of the City* (1981), they do, they need neither stress nor entail a central enigma. Indeed, it is a basic tenet of those like Hamilton (1993), Hoppenstead (1982) and Panek (1987 and 1990), who have written specifically about the American tradition of crime fiction, that American detective stories, with their roots in the dime novel and pulp literature, have always been concerned as much with action and adventure as they have been with the solving of mysteries. And as Matthew Solomon (1995) has shown, dime novels, pulp fiction and the actin–adventure tradition were as much a source of early American (and European) detective films as the tradition that placed the emphasis on ratiocination.

Among the conditions of existence of modern investigative fiction and the figure of the fictional detective, commentators have cited the emergence in the nineteenth century of the professional detective, professional detective agencies and a professional police force; the secularisation of concepts of crime, sin and punishment (Cawelti, 1976, pp. 54–5; Knight, 1980, pp. 13–15); urbanisation, population growth, and the reconfiguration of class (Cawelti, 1976, pp. 101–5; Hutter, 1983, pp. 234–5; Kaemmel, 1983; Porter, 1981, pp. 151–4); concomitant shifts in attitudes towards criminals and the police (the heroisation of the latter and the demonisation of the former) (Mandel, 1984, pp. 1–11; Porter, 1981, pp. 147–56); and the introduction of scientific and bureaucratic procedures for tracking down and capturing criminals as part and parcel of what some, following Foucault (1979), have seen as a wholesale shift towards a mode of social control based – literally and figuratively – on a particular model of surveillance (Cawelti, 1976, pp. 57–8; Palmer, 1978, p. 200; Porter, 1981, pp. 123–5). The weight of some of these factors – together with the fact that in most detective stories the enigma is resolved, the criminals caught and punished, and order restored – have led many to see the genre as almost inevitably conservative. (See in particular, Kaemmel, 1983; Mandel, 1984; and Porter, 1981.)

Foucault himself wrote that the nineteenth century witnessed a fundamental change in the dominant 'episteme' of punishment and crime, a change in which 'we have moved from the exposition of the facts or the confession to the slow process of discovery; from the execution to the investigation' (Foucault, 1979, p. 69), and of which the detective story itself is both product and sign. One way of reading this change is in terms of the development of a post-romantic cult of mystery (Alewyn, 1983). Certainly, the generation of mystery and the provisional of (rational) solutions to it have played a central part in accounts of the pleasures and structures involved in investigative fiction. Caillois, for example, argues that 'At bottom, the unmasking of a criminal is less important than the reduction of the impossible to the possible, of the inexplicable to the explained, of the supernatural to the natural' (in Most and Stowe, 1983, p. 3), while psychoanalytic accounts stress the relationship between enigma and mystery, the desire to know and fantasies of the primal scene (Pederson-Krag, 1983; Neale, 1980, pp. 42–3; Porter, 1981, pp. 100–12).

The aesthetics of investigative fiction have been discussed in some detail, especially by those working within a structuralist, formalist, or neo-formalist framework. Drawing on remarks made by one of the characters in Michael Butor's novel, *Passing Time*, Todorov makes the point that most whodunnits contain not one story but two: the story of the crime and the story of the crime's investigation. Using this point as a basis, he goes on to distinguish between the whodunnit proper and the thriller. The latter, he argues, 'suppresses the first and vitalizes the second. We are no longer told about a crime anterior to the moment of the narrative; the narrative coincides with the action' (Todorov, 1977, p. 47). Instead of curiosity, the effect here is one of suspense, and it is worth noting that its characteristics dovetail with the action–adventure tradition mentioned above.

The formalist concept of retardation, meanwhile, is central to Porter's account of detective fiction. Here, emphasis is placed on the means by which the revelation of the first story – the story of the crime – is forestalled by various digressive means and devices. These include peripeteia, 'a discovery or event involving deflection or rebound from progress toward resolution. Examples of this are parallel intrigues, including rival investigations or love motifs that intermittently suspend the principal investigation, and false trials and false solutions' (Porter, 1981, p. 32). They also include 'the antidetective or criminal, who may remain passive and not impede the Great Detective's search or actively intervene in a variety of ways to prevent unmasking or capture. There are also other blocking figures, such as recalcitrant or confused witnesses, false detectives like Watson or Lestrade, who take time misrepresenting the evidence, and false criminals or suspects' (Porter, 1981, p. 32). In addition, they include the taciturnity of the detective, false clues, 'the episodes themselves, which, as in an adventure novel or odyssey, intervene in greater or lesser numbers between a given point of departure and a fixed destination' (Porter, 1981, p. 33), and passages of extended description and dialogue.

In *Narration in the Fiction Film* (1985), David Bordwell draws on a number of formalist concepts in his discussion of the detective film. He reworks the concepts of syuzhet and fabula to mean the narrative events and cues with which the viewer is actually presented, on the one hand, and the narrative as a whole, including those events and actions the viewer is left to infer, on the other. From this perspective, the fabula in the detective film is seen to consist both of the story of the crime, and also, depending on the nature of the film, of portions of the story of the investigation. The syuzhet is marked by the manipulation of information concerning the story of the crime, and by retardation in the story of the investigation.

For Bordwell, the crux of the detective film is knowledge, and in particular its suppression and restriction, and this accounts both for its modes, styles and tactics of narration, and for the 'emotional states' to which it often gives rise:

> The detective film justifies its gaps and retardations by controlling knowledge, self-consciousness, and communicativeness. The genre aims to create curiosity about past story events (e.g., who killed whom), suspense about upcoming events, and surprise with respect to unexpected disclosures about either story [fabula] or syuzhet. To promote all three emotional states, the narration must limit the viewer's knowledge. This can be motivated realistically by making us share the restricted knowledge possessed by the investigator; we learn what the detective learns, when she or he learns it. There can be brief marks of an unrestricted narration as well … but these function to enhance curiosity or suspense. By restricting the range of knowledge to that possessed by the detective, the narration can present information in a fairly unselfconscious way; we pick up fabula information by following the detective's enquiry. Again, the narration can signpost information more overtly, but this is occasional and codified. (Bordwell, 1985, p. 65)

In illustrating these points, Bordwell refers to *The Big Sleep* and *Farewell My Lovely*, both of them generally regarded, as already mentioned, as hard-boiled and *noir*. In her discussion of *Terror by Night* (1946), Kristin Thompson (1988) draws on a similar set of precepts and concerns but applies them instead to a Sherlock Holmes film, one in a series made at Universal in the 1940s. Thompson's aim here is neither to elucidate the workings of the investigative thriller, nor to validate *Terror by Night* as a genre film. It is rather to validate the use of formalist ideas as a means by which to illuminate the workings of what she calls 'the ordinary film'. Concentrating on the general issues of knowledge and retardation, she argues that the film is not a straightforward murder mystery, as might be expected, but rather a film that 'in its second half … becomes more oriented toward suspense; we wonder not, who is the murderer, but will the detective find out who he is in time?' (Thompson, 1988, p. 62). The film contains investigative material and an initial mystery, but these elements function as delaying mechanisms, as means by which to build up those forms of suspense associated with the thriller rather than the classic Holmes whodunnit as such.

The extent to which films like *Terror by Night* have been neglected is a function not only of the dominance of *noir* in academic writing on the detective film, but also of the dominance of neo-*noir* in Hollywood's output since the late 1960s. While detectives of a relatively traditional kind have appeared with regularity on TV, they have, unlike investigative thrillers, been almost completely absent from the cinema. Partly in consequence, contemporary critics, theorists and historians have rarely been prompted to examine traditional detective films in more detail.

Selected Reading

David Bordwell, *Narration in the Fiction Film*, London, Methuen, 1985.

Dennis Porter, *The Pursuit of Crime, Art and Ideology in Detective Fiction*, New Haven, Yale University Press, 1981.

Tzvetan Todorov, *The Poetics of Prose*, Ithaca, Cornell University Press, 1977.

THE GANGSTER FILM

Introduction

Until the emergence of genre criticism, writing on the gangster film was divided between censorship issues and journalistic accounts of the historical phases and thematic and iconographic features of the genre and its various sub-genres. Until the 1970s, Warshow's 'The Gangster as Tragic Hero' (1970) was almost the sole attempt to deal with the aesthetic and ideological significance of this enormously popular and endlessly proliferating genre, supported by a somewhat different, more generalised approach in Lawrence Alloway's *Violent America* (1971), which concentrated on the depiction of violence. It was not until the arrival of one of the founding texts of genre criticism, Colin McArthur's *Underworld USA* (1972), that we find in Tom Ryall's words, 'a systematic attempt to define the genre, and to indicate the achievement within it of a selection of notable *auteurs*' (see Ryall, 1979, p. 14).

Insight into the reasons for this early neglect can be gleaned from Andrew Tudor's (1974) account of the genre where he compares it unfavourably with the western, characterising the 'urban nightmare' so often attributed to the gangster film as a 'brutal universe … mechanistic, offering little in the way of social and emotional riches' (Tudor, 1974, p. 201). This says much about what the western contributed to establishing genre criticism as a way of talking seriously about popular culture:

> Unlike the western there is no code governing the violence, no set of rules for the regulation of this war of all against all. (Tudor, 1974, p. 201)

A feminist perspective might suggest that what is at stake here is the too naked expression of a certain form of male heroics. The gangster's 'self-interested individualism is totally unfettered ... It is the cowboy's world but without his integrity and without his sense of character' (Tudor, 1974, p. 202).

Clearly one problem that confronted early genre criticism in relation to the gangster film was its seemingly symbiotic relation to contemporary events as circulated in a sensational press rather than to an already mythologised history. As Andrew Tudor puts it:

> the construction of the genre was almost contemporaneous with the construction of the events themselves ... It was stimulated by the late 20s boom in publicity for gangster activities. The fame of Capone and the notorious St. Valentine's Day massacre of 1929 created a storm of publicity. Quick to see the possibilities, the studios reacted, and on the crest of this wave came Mervyn LeRoy's *Little Caesar*. (Tudor, 1974, pp. 196–7)

Another related problem confronted by film criticism was the extreme fragmentation of the genre, whose 'classic' period lasts, according to most accounts, only three years, but which was preceded by a flourishing and highly distinctive type of gangster film in the 1910s and the 1920s – one in which emphasis was placed on the gangster's repentance, self-sacrifice and moral regeneration – and which was followed by fragmentation under what Schatz summarises as 'threats of censorship, boycott, and federal regulation' (Schatz, 1981, p. 82).

This fragmentation can be enumerated in terms of various cycles, phases and subgenres: the G-Man cycle, *film noir*, crime melodramas and so on. The mythic coherence which could be attributed to the western and which supported claims that it connected with long-established traditions was difficult to establish for the gangster film with its seemingly opportunistic shifts and turns according to changes of the physiognomy of crime and law enforcement in America – Tudor cites, for instance, the lack of anything like the 'Garden–Desert thesis' for the gangster film (Tudor, 1974, p. 196). A succinct account of how changes in 'the reality of American crime' surface in generic change can be found in Colin McArthur (1972, pp. 64–5).

Little Caesar – a reaction to contemporaneous events in the 1930s

For early criticism the apparently close relation between generic change and contemporary reality encouraged notions of 'reflection'. This was made all the easier by the association of the classic gangster film with the Warner Bros. Studio, widely known for its 1930s 'social issue' movies, and with the development of sound by that studio, again popularly understood as an instrument of realism. This supposed realism contributed and still contributes to recurring 'moral panics' about the effects of the films' violence, glorification of the criminal and misogyny on young audiences, and consequently the history of the genre has been interlaced with censorship problems. Beyond this, early work on the genre was much concerned with tracing the appearance of different cycles and sub-genres in terms of social sources, subject matter and dominant conventions, much of which is taxed with problems to do with periodisation, cycle demarcation and definition and ultimate origins (see Whitehall, 1964; French, 1967/68).

Warshow: the gangster film as an experience of art

In this context Warshow's seminal 'The Gangster as Tragic Hero' (1970) attempted to break the grip of readings of gangster films as if they reflected or were accountable to historical or sociological renderings of American contemporary reality:

> the importance of the gangster film, and the nature and intensity of its emotional and aesthetic impact, cannot be measured in terms of the place of the gangster himself or the importance of the problem of crime in American life. Those European movie-goers who think there is a gangster on every corner in New York are certainly deceived, but defenders of the 'positive' side of American culture are equally deceived if they think it relevant to point out that most Americans have never seen a gangster. What matters is that the experience of the gangster as an experience of art is universal to Americans. (Warshow, 1970, p. 130)

In Warshow's view the data of social reality are reorganised to produce a reality of the imagination whose referential field is other gangster films rather than the 'real world'.

McArthur: the gangster/thriller as iconography

Writing on the gangster film produced as part of, or since, the emergence of genre studies, has generally taken Warshow's argument as its starting point. Most notable within the first category was Colin McArthur (1972), one chapter of which was concerned to lay out the basic unity of the genre's iconography, which he understands as 'the continuity over several decades of patterns of visual imagery, of recurrent objects and figures in dynamic relationship' (McArthur, 1972, p. 23). These stable iconographic elements can be divided into three categories (see Ryall, 1979):

1 The physical presence, attributes and dress of the actors and actresses and the characters they play;
2 The urban milieux in which the fiction is played out;
3 The technology at the character's disposal, principally guns and cars.

These elements recur consistently, in spite of shifts between different phases or subsets of the genre. As Ryall argues, McArthur's iconographical approach enables him to produce a flexible, dynamic account of the genre, whereas Warshow's attachment to the 'rise and fall' narrative freezes the genre at an early point in its development (Ryall, 1979, p. 18). Ryall outlines McArthur's categorisation of the following phases or cycles:

1930s
– the 'classic' gangster film (*Little Caesar, The Public Enemy, Scarface*)
– the FBI film (*G-Men, Bullets or Ballots*)
– the 'social background' film (*Angels with Dirty Faces, Dead End*)
1940s
– the *film noir* (*The Big Sleep, The Maltese Falcon*)
– the 'police documentary' (*The House on 92nd Street*)
– the morally orientated gangster film (*Force of Evil*)
1950s
– the syndicate film (*Murder Inc., New York Confidential*)
– the historical reconstructions (*Al Capone, Machine Gun Kelly*)
1960s
– the 'forties thriller' reprised (*Warning Shot, The Moving Target*).
To these we might now add:
Late 1960s/1970s
– the 'police movie' (*Dirty Harry, Magnum Force*)
– *film noir* reprised (*Chinatown, Marlowe, Klute*)
1980s
– the 'classic' gangster film reprised (*Scarface*)

The gangster film and ideology

McArthur's book constituted a groundbreaking exercise in making visible and delineating the genre. Two major problems remained: one, to offer a convincing analysis of the relationship of the genre to reality which would also account for generic change; the other, to extend the account of the aesthetic and imaginative reach of the genre beyond the limitations of the classic moment as in Warshow, or of a concentration on iconography at the expense of all the other elements in a film production, both cinematic and extra-cinematic. The debates about ideology and aesthetics which superseded generic criticism would seem to have ideal material in the gangster film, but on the whole recent studies of the genre have not chosen this route, preferring to elaborate the genre's formal development in terms of production histories – studios, censorship, technologies, etc. – or in terms of narrative and cinematic codes. Ideological readings tend to be sensitive to textual appraisals of what Warshow describes as the obverse of the American dream, the 'urban nightmare'. In this respect the gangster/thriller is most often poised between the western on the one hand and the horror film on the other.

Warshow (1970), having rescued the gangster from reductionist 'realist' readings, had to go on to define and defend the significance of this perverse 'creature of the imagination'. The loss of tragedy to American culture is the cornerstone of Warshow's argument. American capitalism claims to eliminate tragedy from human experience by making individual happiness the ostensible goal and rationale of all its social arrangements. This ethos in turn destroys the conditions for the production of tragic art, which depends on a social order which subordinates the fate of the individual to 'a fixed and supra-political ... moral order or fate' (Warshow, 1970, p. 127). However, if banished from 'official ideology', the 'tragic sense' does not disappear, because of fundamental contradiction between the ideals of equality and individualism, and the ambiguous nature of happiness when conceived in terms of 'success'. Happiness as success not only pitches the individual against others, inviting his or her downfall, but breeds its obverse, a 'sense of desperation and inevitable failure' (Warshow, 1970, p. 129). This, argues Warshow, is 'our intolerable dilemma: that failure is a kind of death, and success is evil and dangerous, is ultimately – impossible' (Warshow, 1970, p. 133). The gangster film enables this dilemma to be played out and resolved in a way that its message is both 'disguised' and involves the minimum of distortion:

> the gangster is the 'no' to that great American 'yes' which is stamped so big over our official culture and yet has so little to do with the way we really feel about our lives. (Warshow, 1970, p. 136)

Roaring Twenties – Cagney arrested in the warehouse raid

The notion that the gangster film represents 'the modern sense of tragedy' is frequently assumed and will be returned to later. Similarly the link between the gangster film and capitalist ideology has been elaborated by many critics. For some, the problems posed by the contradictions of capitalism open onto wider philosophical issues to do with appearance, reality, the individual and society, self assertion and death.

The formal history of the gangster film

Jack Shadoian (1977) has offered one of the more interesting developments of the Warshow thesis. In place of iconography he utilises the idea of 'structure' as the form's unifying principle. His deployment of this concept in relation to other cinematic codes such as narrative, *mise-en-scène*, lighting, etc., enables him to mount an interesting history of the way the necessities of generic and formal change produce shifting possibilities of pleasure and meaning. Less successful perhaps are his occasional attempts to link these shifts back to political and social realities of the time.

Shadoian's thesis is that the basic structure of the gangster/crime film is 'ready-made for certain kinds of concerns' (Shadoian, 1977, p. 3). Along with Warshow and several other commentators since who see the fictional gangster as 'a product of advanced urban civilisation', Shadoian argues that these concerns arise out of the contradictions of the 'American dream' in the context of industrialism and post-industrial corporate capitalism – for instance 'between America as a land of opportunity and the vision of a classless, democratic society' (Shadoian, 1977, p. 5) – contradictions which come to a head in the gangster film in the drive to success, 'the urge for it, the fear of it, the consequences that both having it and not having it entail' (Shadoian, 1977, p. 5).

The structure that emerged with the classic gangster film carried these contradictions with it. The legal and social status of the criminal produced a figure, the gangster, outside and opposed to society, who 'violates a system of rules that a group of people live under' (Shadoian, 1977, p. 3). The position of the hero as outside but related by conflict and violence to society produces a perspective from which that society must be viewed; in this way 'meanings emerge, whether deliberately or not, about the nature of society and the kind of individual it creates' (Shadoian, 1977, p. 3). In this respect the gangster differs from the western 'outlaw'; in the west society – civilisation – has yet to be constructed and fought for. The gangster/crime film speaks to the 'American Dream' at a different stage.

From his starting point in the formal and aesthetic working of the genre, Shadoian moves on to a flexible account of its ideology in which the personal, psychic and political intertwine. Central to his analysis is its construction of the contradictions of capitalism as the simultaneous summoning and restriction of desire. Above all the gangster/crime film deals with desire confronted by constraint. It pits 'basic human needs in opposition to a world that denies them' (Shadoian, 1977, p. 119). 'The gangster', says Shadoian, 'is a creature who wants, and although he shares this trait with characters in other genres, the degree of his compulsion is probably unique' (Shadoian, 1977, p. 14).

In Shadoian's analysis gangster/crime film develops towards inward and existential examination of human existence in modern American corporate society, accompanied by the increasing formalisation of the genre, and indeed of cinema itself. He discerns, for instance, a shift from the use of the gangster outside as a means of gaining a new perspective on society to a *film noir* concern, expressed in an increasing use of 'symbol, metaphor and allusion', with the nature of society itself, in which the distinction between gangster and society, and society and self becomes confused and a new 'flavour of guilt and atonement' replaces the 'amorality, cynicism and self-confident' behaviour of the classic gangster hero (Shadoian, 1977, p. 120).

The formal history of the genre illuminates this shift. The 'classic' gangster took off from a known public fascination with real criminals, already being processed by sensational journalism. The films quickly diverged from reality, while maintaining a realist address. They were, in Shadoian's terms, travelogues and documentaries into alien territory – the world of the gangster, whose otherness became increasingly marked by stylisation which prepared the ground for the genre's transformation when the combined forces of censorship, the passing of the Depression, the logic of generic renewal and sophistication, made the gangster's heroic rise and near tragic fall no longer a viable structure. *The Roaring Twenties* and *High Sierra* stand nostalgically poised between the world of the classic gangster offering 'resonant myths of defeat that echoed with heroic, positive reverberations' and the more pessimistic world of *film noir* where 'views of freedom and possibility narrow' (Shadoian, 1977, p. 59). In the 1950s the existential confusion of *film noir* shifts into a new organisation of the basic structure of gangster versus society. 'If *noir* scrambled the terms of the opposition, the 1950s inverts them' (Shadoian, 1977, p. 211). In the era of affluence crime and corporate capitalism are equated, an equation which not only inverts the 'classic' gangster's position as outsider, but also the struggle celebrated by the western, in which civilisation is attained by overcoming primitivism and savagery. In the 1950s gangster film, the evils of civilisation can only be purified by a reversion to instinctive actions and emotions. In this period, the gangster has gone the farthest in achieving control, reason, logic, and precision and has consequently lost contact with his real self more than others. Within the overall structure of the gangster film, then, 'when the gangster … becomes that which he used to oppose, the genre finds his substitute, one who can assume his former function' (Shadoian, 1977, p. 214). The hero who will combat society as crime in the name of the American dream is one who has to detach himself from society. If he is a policeman, since the force is incorporated into crime, he must 'act independently of the machinery'. This process of detachment involves the hero being 'restored to his fundamental drives, his basic instincts' (Shadoian, 1977, p. 212), and occurs only through the agency of violence, the reassertion of desire once embodied in the gangster.

With the end of the 1960s and entry to the 1970s, Shadoian argues that the genre, in line with the overall development of cinematic codes, reaches a point of sophistication and self-referentiality that makes the shift towards modernism inevitable. The unfeasibility of representational storytelling forces the genre into evasive strategies such as replaying stories from the past, or creating characters and heroes 'who can scarcely be defined as human' at all (Shadoian, 1977, p. 291). A further consequence of this shift is an increase in violence and the creation of 'highly aggressive fictions that have little regard for facts' (Shadoian, 1977, p. 291). Use of colour and the dominance of *auteurs* further heightens violence and anti-realism. Violence in this sense has to be understood aesthetically:

> The brutalisation of the audience, which took on systematic form in the 50s, has detached itself from urgent content and become an aesthetic factor with its own logic of communication. It has become the genre's core experience, and its ultimate statement. (Shadoian, 1977, p. 8)

Studio, technology and style

The emergence of the gangster film as a distinct genre in the 1930s, and its reputed realism and contemporaneousness, has often been associated with the consolidation of the Warner Bros. Studio, which produces many of the 'classic' titles. Nick Roddick (1983) explores the association of Warners in the 1930s with the 'social conscience' movie, arguing that there exists 'a certain similarity between American social history and the themes produced by Warners during the 1930s' (Roddick, 1983, p. 65) (see Warner Bros., p. 19).

The studio system was developed as a means of rationalising production in relation to the market; 'there was an identifiable audience need to be met, and the studio system was designed to meet it economically – and therefore as profitably – as possible' (Roddick, 1983, p. 10). The major studios set out to produce clear and differentiated identities to avoid duplication of effort, specialising in 'a particular kind or style of film' (Roddick, 1983, p. 8).

The development of sound, in which Warners played a large part and which contributed to its studio identity, shifted Hollywood production generally in the direction of realism and away from fantasy and the exotic. Warners followed the route of realism and contemporaneity with a heavy emphasis on what can be loosely designated 'social problem' pictures, although Roddick points out that only just under one-third of Warners output in the 1930s dealt with contemporary American society and 'the vast majority bear little or no immediate social message' (Roddick, 1983, p. 73). Nevertheless Warners did consciously identify themselves with the New Deal. The question is what such identification could mean ideologically or aesthetically. Warners, a more emphatically 'family' business than any of the other majors, was also 'the most tightly run, economical and streamlined of the big five during the 1930s' (Roddick, 1983, p. 22). Yet while Warners were geared to 'a mass-production system', what they were producing for consumption was, quite consciously, 'art'. The relationship of their films to the real world, Roddick argues,

> was not a direct one: it was an aesthetic one. What is more, the terms in which the films are discussed in the studio memos – structure, balance, impact, pacing, credibility – are terms which are basically concerned with the artistic, not the physical nature of the product. Even in cases where financial considerations are clearly the origin of the memo, the aim is always to get the best effect in the most economical way. The criterion remains, in the final instance, artistic. How else is 'the best effect' to be designated? (Roddick, 1983, p. 25)

With a liberal leaning towards contemporary issues, a pressure towards realism increased through a heavy investment both of capital and identity in sound, and an equal pressure towards maximising use of studio space and avoidance of costly location work, the implicit aesthetic problem for Warners was how to turn reality into drama and narrative. As Roddick points out a tradition already existed in the fiction of Balzac, Dickens and their derivatives for the association of social realism and crime, an association made vivid in the 1930s as gangsterism, and potential social breakdown consequent upon prohibition and the Depression, hit the

Angels with Dirty Faces – the 'social background film'

newspaper headlines. Crime movies, then, 'provided a potentially perfect formula for fulfilling Warners' early talkie policy of realistic and at the same time popular entertainment' (Roddick, 1983, p. 77). Not only did they give 'a dramatic focus to fairly ordinary problems or aspirations – poverty, unemployment, sexual inadequacy, alienation, ambition, greed – by making them criminal motives' (Roddick, 1983, p. 77), they also offered in the criminal 'a hero whose antisocial individualism could speak to the contradictions of capitalist ideology, be romanticised and identified with by the audiences of the small-town and neighbourhood theatres' (Roddick, 1983, p. 99) to which the gangster films were directed.

Roddick identifies two levels of production in Warners' output of contemporary pictures in the 1930s. While the more directly 'social problem' pictures ranged across genres, taking in crime thrillers, gangster films, newspaper films, and were, because of their importance to the studio's corporate image, 'allocated top writers, major stars and comparatively large budgets ... and were road-shown in the major theatres with strong promotional campaigns guaranteeing them longer than usual runs' (Roddick, 1983, p. 78), the consolidation of the 'classic' gangster film itself was a more tightly generic and economical affair. Such films,

> were relatively cheap to make, since they used contemporary dress, sets (seedy restaurants, backroom offices and hotel rooms) and exteriors that rarely if ever called for anything other than the standing sets of the backlot. Additionally, once the formula was perfected – as early, basically, as 1931 – the scripting and pre-production process was ideally suited to Warners' streamlined studio methods. (Roddick, 1983, p. 99)

They were also extremely popular, and clearly provided an economic and an aesthetic base to the more prestigious productions. Eventually, it would seem, the aesthetic force of generic convention displaced the foregrounding of social issues in Warners' crime movies, which came to be seen rather as 'mystery melodramas' (Roddick, 1983, p. 82).

In considering the ideological significance of studio policy, Roddick is concerned to dispel either a too radical, or too recuperative view of Warners' social realism. He cites Hans Magnus Enzensberger's comment on advertising – 'that it is not the creation of a false need, but the false meeting of a real need' (Roddick, 1983, p. 8) – in order to suggest the contradictions inherent in the consolidation of studio style and genre as a means of 'manipulating' the market. The liberal ideology of the studio bosses, the commitment of studio style to a 'hard-hitting' realism, meant in Roddick's view that inevitably, 'in tackling the symptoms, Warners should tackle some of the causes' for instance of the Depression or Fascism (Roddick, 1983, p. 74). The limitations of what could be done were set both by the contradictions of liberalism's attempts to make capitalism work and by the demands of fiction. Social responsibility, economic self-interest, and the demand for narrative resolution made it a sine qua non 'that a film which tackled a problem had to offer a solution, even if the real-life problem seemed likely to remain unsolved for some time to come' (Roddick, 1983, p. 66). Nevertheless 'the contradictions of American society in the 1930s were the material on which the studio drew, if not something it necessarily set out to highlight' (Roddick, 1983, p. 66). If the studio by its very nature and situation could not produce social change, its product was a medium through which indirectly a need for change could be registered.

Thomas Schatz's chapter on the gangster film in *Hollywood Genres* (1981) follows the general line pursued by Warshow, Shadoian and Roddick, and offers some interesting elaborations on the latter's concern to trace the interplay of studio, technology, aesthetics and ideology. Sound, he argues, not only effected a decisive shift towards realism, but was the catalyst for the consolidation of the crime film as a staple of the studio's output, contributing much to its aesthetic formalisation. Warners' experimental *The Lights of New York* (1928),

> demonstrated that sound effects and dialogue greatly heightened the impact of urban crime dramas. As later films would confirm, synchronous sound affected both the visual and editing strategies of gangster movies. The new audio effects (gunshots, screams, screeching tyres, etc.) encouraged film-makers to focus upon action and urban violence, and also to develop a fast-paced narrative and editing style ...
>
> Similarly the gangster persona itself – with his propensity for asserting his individual will through violent action and self-styled profiteering – offers an ideal figure for cinematic narrative elaboration. The fact that his assertiveness flaunts social order even heightens his individuality. (Schatz, 1981, pp. 85–6)

Like other writers, Schatz argues that the aesthetics of the genre organise a range of meaning around the gangster hero of far greater imaginative power than the attempts of censorship bodies to assert against him the values of the status quo (see Censorship, p. 7). One good reason for this perhaps is that the gangster speaks, if contradictorily, for the status quo, for its buried underside as well as its affirmative goals. As Schatz comments, 'the urban lone wolf's brutality and antisocial attitudes in Hollywood films are simply components of an essentially positive cultural model – that of the personable and aggressive but somewhat misguided self-made American man' (Schatz, 1986, p. 84). It is therefore perfectly possible, when the Hays Code intervenes, to shift the role of hero from gangster to cop and maintain the same expressive style: 'Cagney as gangster in *The Public Enemy* is basically indistinguishable from that of Cagney as government agent in *G-Men* ... He may be advocating a different value system in each role, but his self-assured swagger, caustic disposition, and violent demeanour are basic to each' (Schatz, 1986, p. 84). Clearly part of this continuity is to do with the star, and several commentators (e.g. McArthur, 1972) have noted the importance of the stars of these films – Cagney, Robinson, Bogart, Muni, etc. – to the consolidation of the genre's conventions.

Schatz sees the ideological significance of the classic gangster film as stemming from an interplay of such aesthetic factors with the conditions of production and consumption of genre, to which the studio had to submit. Once a business is mounted in the field of entertainment, promulgation of safe ideologies is complicated by the technical and aesthetic requirements of the 'product':

> Despite the film industry's avowed efforts to support the status quo ... film-makers and audiences were cooperating in refining genres that examined the more contradictory tenets of American ideology. (Schatz, 1986, p. 95)

For

> camerawork, editing, dialogue, characterisation, and even the star system work together to engage our sympathy for the criminal. So from a technical (as well as thematic) standpoint, the gangster–hero functions as an organising sensibility in these films, serving to offset the other characters' naive moralising and to control our perception of his corrupt, Kafkaesque milieu. (Schatz, 1986, p. 93)

In this respect the death of the hero is not a sop to the various pressure groups that concerned themselves with the morality of Hollywood. It is an aesthetic and ideological necessity, which recognises both sides of the contradiction that provides the dynamic of the genre. The appeal of the gangster is his ability to grasp those goals for which the status quo says we should strive despite the minimal options it offers. 'For a brief time, at least, the gangster is on top of his own pathetically limited world' (Schatz, 1986, p. 89). The strength of this appeal qualifies the apparent endorsement of social order of the genre's ending; paradoxically the gangster's 'very death is the consummate reaffirmation of his own identity' (Schatz, 1986, p. 90).

The necessity of this ending has the same formal force as 'the romantic embrace which resolves the musical comedy, or the gunfight which resolves the western' in maintaining 'a narrative balance between the hero's individuality and the need for social order' (Schatz, 1986, p. 90). But it is balance that is arrived at, not the elimination of one side of the contradiction in favour of the other. (This accounts perhaps for critical unease with more recent variants of the genre, with what is often seen as the proto-Fascist police movie exemplified in the Eastwood *Dirty Harry* series, in which the cathartic end in death is denied.)

The death of the gangster: tragedy or melodrama?

For most critics the moralistic intentions behind many of the gangster films' tacked-on endings of retribution are far outweighed by the imaginative necessity of the hero's death. It is this – the inevitability and mode of the gangster's death – which permits critics' frequent appeal to tragedy as a justification for taking the genre seriously (in much the same way as the western claims prestige as epic). As Steve Jenkins (1982, p. 44) suggests, the death of the gangster is qualitatively different from death in other genres. Death comes with an inevitability that precludes suspense, often arbitrarily, and always with finality. The gangster dies at the hand of fate, isolated, and yet a public spectacle. What makes this death appear tragic is variously defined. Jenkins, noting that the gangster's death generally ends the film, offers the suggestive comment that 'the genre concentrates on the progress of an individual male character ...' (Jenkins, 1982, p. 44). As we have seen, Warshow finds the ending tragic because its rise and fall structure contains within it the failure of a struggle for individual self-assertion with which we identify, but which we also know society cannot allow. Schatz pursues an indentification of the tragic in the gangster film by looking for the gangster's tragic flaw, which he isolates as 'his inability to channel his considerable individual energies in a viable direction' (Schatz, 1981, p. 88). However he immediately qualifies this by suggesting society is itself partly responsible, 'in that it denies individual expression and provides minimal options to the struggling, aggressive male from an inner-city, working-class background' (Schatz, 1981, p. 89). Shadoian in claiming that the gangster film offers a 'tradition of popular tragedy in film' cites the 'combination of hubris, social fate and moral reckoning' (Shadoian, 1977, p. 15) in the gangster's story, arguing that *Little Caesar* is to the gangster film what *Oedipus Rex* is to Greek tragedy. Crucial to his argument is the gangster's choice of his fate, and the awesomeness of his overthrow.

What is interesting here is the need to rediscover the tragic and the sense that it has to be redefined in 'modern' terms. It is also notable that the designation, tragedy, is applied almost exclusively to the 'classic' gangster films of the 1930s with their clear rise and fall structure. Shadoian goes so far as to suggest that the interaction of the needs provoked by the Depression with a cinema still in its 'age of innocence' was productive of a tragic catharsis in the classic gangster film denied to later phases of the genre. However, melodrama, closely related to tragedy, may provide a different understanding of the conflicts and violence which make the gangster's death seem tragic.

Robert Heilman (1968) and Peter Brooks (1976), have both discussed the relationship between tragedy and melodrama. Heilman's concern is to preserve the category of tragedy from its frequent, mystifying reduction to melodrama. Awesomeness of fate, even if chosen, does not by itself define the tragic hero. What is crucial is his internalisation of conflict, his coming to awareness of division within and of his own responsibility. Brooks seeks to historicise the distinction by suggesting that the two forms belong to different sets of historical socio-economic and cultural circumstances. Following a somewhat similar line to Warshow, Brooks argues that tragedy belongs to a social hierarchy, organised around the monarchy and church, which integrates individual lives to a transcendental, sacred order, embracing the forces of good and evil. Brooks, like Heilman, sees our identification with the hero's coming to self-awareness, his introspective contemplation of his internal divisions, as the source of tragedy's lesson. The downfall itself relates back to communal sacrificial rites, and is a mechanism for catharsis rather than insight.

However, with the destruction of traditional social hierarchies bringing to an end the transcendental sacred order, the problem arises of how to found a new ethical order; how to prove the existence of good and evil and find the means for their expression within a secular framework and in a way that would satisfy the ethical and psychic needs of the new bourgeois 'individual'. For Brooks, melodrama attempts to do this by finding a new moral order 'occulted' within individual lives lived in an everyday, ordinary world. Thus, melodramatic rhetoric seeks to 'infuse the banal and the ordinary with the excitement of grandiose conflict' (Brooks, 1976, p. 40). Good and evil can only be grasped as features of personal life; thus 'they are assigned to, they inhabit persons who indeed have no psychological complexity but who are strongly characterised' (Brooks, 1976, p. 16). What such rhetoric entails is a 'victory over repression', which is 'simultaneously social, psychological, historical and conventional' (Brooks, 1976, p. 41). Such victory means saying – asserting – what social and verbal constraints do not permit to be said; it means forcing language beyond its limitations as a symbolic system to yield fullness of meaning and identity to speakers and audience in moments of 'ringing identification' (Brooks, 1976, p. 42).

The gangster/crime film can be understood in terms of the ethical–psychic terms offered by Brooks. We have already noted Shadoian's 'the gangster is a creature who wants'. Schatz also suggests the primal nature of the gangster's self-assertion: 'destiny may kill him, but the intensity of the hero's commitment to his fate indicates that power and individuality are more important than a long life' (Schatz, 1981, p. 94). The gangster/crime film provides a context in which the desire for power and acquisition can be named and asserted against all the codes that would control and repress it.

Nevertheless such desire cannot overthrow the social order. As Brooks comments:

> The ritual of melodrama involves the confrontation of clearly identified antagonists and the expulsion of one of them. It can offer no terminal reconciliation, for there is no longer a clear transcendent value to be reconciled to. There is, rather, a social order to be purged, a set of ethical imperatives to be made clear. (Brooks, 1976, pp. 16–17)

This inability to move beyond the bourgeois world is found in the gangster/crime film. For instance Shadoian observes that,

> the genre offers no alternative to the American way of life. America's political, social and economic flaws are not hidden, but the system, in principle, is never seriously argued with. (Shadoian, 1977, p. 11)

The capacity of the genre to transmute the values of society and gangster allows a critique of society to emerge. However, 'upper-middle, middle-class, or prole heroes continue in the same system after convulsing it. In the end they act on behalf of its ideal nature' (Shadoian, 1977, p. 11).

In this context the function of the tableau-like endings of gangster films noted by Steve Jenkins can be set in a wider perspective:

> At the moment of the gangster's death these female characters are placed in opposition to the representatives of the law in a recurring tableau-like representation of the significance of that death ... By placing the dead gangster between the law (man) who stands over the body, and the woman, who often kneels by it or cradles the dead man's head, the distinction is clearly made between the official 'meaning' of the death (public enemy dealt with) and its resonance for the audience's emotional investment in the character, the spectator's interest in the gangster's human qualities, which is developed through the woman's romantic interest. (Jenkins, 1982, pp. 47–8)

Clearly from Brooks's account of the melodramatic, both sets of meanings carry weight. The distance of the genre from tragedy may be responsible for the poverty of the 'official' meaning: 'nor is there, as in tragedy, a reconciliation to a sacred order larger than man. The expulsion of evil entails no sacrifice ... There is rather confirmation and restoration' (Brooks, 1976, p. 32). Melodrama's fundamental Manichaeism discerned by Brooks may also account for the apparent division in the hero which leads some critics to label him a tragic figure. Schatz, for instance, argues that 'the ultimate conflict of the gangster film ... involves contradictory impulses within the gangster himself' (Schatz, 1981, p. 85). But his account of this conflict hardly suggests the introspection and coming-to-self-awareness of the tragic hero:

> This internal conflict – between individual accomplishment and the common good, between man's self-serving and communal instincts, between his savagery and his rational morality – is mirrored in society ... (Schatz, 1981, p. 85)

More appropriate perhaps is Brooks's contention that if the melodramatic protagonist be conceived as 'theatre for the interplay of manichaeistic forces, the meeting place of opposites, and his self-expressions as nominations of those forces at play within himself – himself their point of clash – the role of character as a purely dramaturgic centre and vehicle becomes evident' (Brooks, 1976, p. 101).

Charles Eckert (1973/74) has offered a different evaluation of the relation of melodrama and realism in the gangster film. The search for a 'moral occult' in his view is less a need to refind categories of good and evil than to impose a displacement of the origin of social conflict in class. Drawing on Lévi-Strauss's theory that,

> a dilemma (or contradiction) stands at the heart of every living myth ... The impulse to construct the myth arises from the desire to resolve the dilemma; but the impossibility of resolving it leads to a crystal-like growth of the myth through which the dilemma is repeated, or conceived in new terms, or inverted ... (Eckert, 1973/74, p. 18)

Eckert contends that the melodrama of the gangster film displaces the class conflict which is at the centre of much of its Depression/Prohibition originated material into a series of oppositions of ethics – the good life versus the wrong; of region – the rural small-town versus the city; and of lifestyle – the snobbish rich versus the true proletarian. While the 'realist' scenes of *Marked Women* dealing with the problems of the prostitute/witnesses 'attempt to conceptualise the dilemmas that the women face'

Marked Woman – Bette Davies takes the witness stand

(Eckert, 1973/74, p. 17), the crucial question, why the poor are poor, is displaced into the oppositions floated by the melodrama, which themselves achieve resolution in the figure of the gangster in whom melodrama discovers the villain, an exploiter characterised less by his role as capitalist than by his sadism. In Eckert's terms, then, ethical conflict framed as a 'moral occult' is the mystified means of reconciliation to the status quo. What are occulted are the 'real conditions of existence' – the social relations and forces of production.

THE SUSPENSE THRILLER

In part, perhaps, because it has been so associated with the work of one particular director, Alfred Hitchcock, the suspense thriller as a genre has received very little attention. There are books on thrillers, suspense, and suspense films (Davis, 1973; Gow, 1968; and Hammond, 1974, for instance). But most of them suffer from imprecision and/or from a tendency to focus on an array of generically disparate films. An exception here is Charles Derry (1988). While marked by Hitchcock's shadow, and while marred by a tendency to concentrate almost exclusively on films made since the late 1940s, Derry's book is rigorous, systematic and otherwise wide ranging in its choice of examples.

Derry notes that suspense thrillers focus either on victims of crime or on pursued and isolated criminals. One of their distinguishing features is therefore a lack of attention to official detectives or the police, and this is the basis of Derry's definition: 'The suspense thriller', he writes, is 'as a crime work which presents a generally murderous antagonism in which the protagonist becomes either an innocent victim or a nonprofessional criminal within a structure that is significantly unmediated by a traditional figure of detection' (Derry, 1988, p. 62.).

Given that this is a broad – though precise – definition, a definition that encompasses films as diverse as *North by Northwest* (1959), *The Manchurian Candidate* (1962), *Wait Until Dark* (1967) and *The Postman Always Rings Twice* (1946), Derry goes on to identify six major sub-types. The first is 'the thriller of murderous passions', which 'is organized around the triangular grouping of husband/wife/lover. The central scene is generally the murder of one member of the triangle by one or both of the other members. The emphasis is clearly on the criminal protagonist ... [and] ... The criminal motive is generally passion or greed' (Derry, 1988, p. 72). Examples include *Double Indemnity* (1944), *Blood Simple* (1984) and *Body Heat* (1981). The second is 'the political thriller', a category which includes *Seven Days in May* (1964), *All the Presidents Men* (1976), *The China Syndrome* (1979) and *Blow Out* (1981). Films like this 'are organized around a plot to assassinate a political figure or a revelation of the essential conspiratorial nature of governments and their crimes against the people. These films generally document and dramatize the acts of

The 'thriller of murderous passions' – *Body Heat*

The thriller of moral confrontation, *Body Double*

assassins, conspirators, or criminal governments, as well as the oppositional acts of victim–societies, countercultures, or martyrs' (Derry, 1988, p. 103).

The third type is 'the thriller of acquired identity', which is exemplified by films like *The Running Man* (1963) and *Dead Ringer* (1964). These films 'are organized around a protagonist's acquisition of an unaccustomed identity, his or her behavior in coming to terms with the metaphysical and physical consequences of this identity, and the relationship of this acquisition to a murderous plot' (Derry, 1988, p. 175).

Fourth and fifth are 'the psychotraumatic thriller' and 'the thriller of moral confrontation'. The psychotraumatic thriller is 'organized around the psychotic effects of a trauma on a protagonist's current involvement in a love affair and a crime or intrigue. The protagonist is always a victim – generally of some past trauma and often of real villains who take advantage of his or her masochistic guilt' (Derry, 1988, p. 194). Examples include *Spellbound* (1945), *Marnie* (1964), *Hush, Hush, Sweet Charlotte* (1964) and *Body Double* (1984). The thriller of moral confrontation is exemplified by films like *The Window* (1949), *Strangers on a Train* (1951), *Sudden Terror* (1970) and *Outrage* (1973). It is 'organized around an overt antithetical confrontation between a character representing good or innocence and a character representing evil. These films often are constructed in terms of elaborate dualities which emphasize the parallels between the victim and the criminal' (Derry, 1988, p. 217).

The sixth and final sub-type is 'the innocent-on-the-run thriller', which is 'organized around an innocent victim's coincidental entry into the midst of global intrigue' and in which 'the victim often finds himself running from both the villains as well as the police' (Derry, 1988, p. 270). Examples include *The Man Who Knew Too Much* (1955), *The Parallax View* (1974), *Three Days of the Condor* (1976) and *Into the Night* (1985).

In addition to constructing these categories, Derry also addresses the issues of thrills and suspense. In discussing thrills, he draws on the work of psychoanalyst Michael Balint (1959), and in particular on Balint's distinction between 'philobats' (lovers of thrills) and 'ocnophobes' (haters of thrills). He notes that thrillers tend to plunge ocnophobic protagonists into deadly – and thrilling – situations, situations in which familiar objects, spaces and activities are replaced by – or become – objects, spaces and activities which are unfamiliar and threatening. In discussing suspense, he distinguishes between the role of surprise and the role of curiosity. He argues that suspense is not necessarily related to the resolution of enigmas or to 'the vague question of what will happen next' (Derry, 1988, p. 31). It is dependent, instead, on 'the expectation that a specific action might take place': 'the creation of suspense demands that enough information be revealed to the spectator so that he or she can anticipate what might happen; suspense then remains operative until the spectator's expectations are foiled, fulfilled, or the narrative is frozen without any resolution at all' (Derry, 1988, pp. 31–2). In the interplay between expectation and narrative development, what becomes suspended in suspense is time: 'During those moments that suspense is operative, time seems to extend itself, and each second provides a kind of torture for a spectator who is anxious to have his or her anticipations foiled or fulfilled' (Derry, 1988, p. 32).

In insisting on the importance of specific information and knowledge, Derry's argument parallels the argument put forward by Dove (1989). For Dove, as for Derry, suspense 'is dependent to a greater degree upon what the reader has been told than upon what he wants to find out. The more the reader knows (without knowing everything), the more he wants to know' (Dove, 1989, p. 4). Dove, however, is less interested in sub-types than in broad generic variations on the structures that he sees as fundamental to all forms of suspense. These structures comprise four phases or states: "cumulation" (the phase that accommodates the development of promises, clues, questions, tensions which will determine later developments); "postponement" (the phase in which the promise of early resolution is deferred); "alternation" (the period of doubt, where the chances regarding the outcome are uncertain); and "potentiality" (the crisis, in which the chances appear to be favoring a given outcome)' (Dove, 1989, p. 50). These phases mark developments and shifts in the 'relational components of the story' (Dove, 1989, p. 51), and it is here that generically specific variations tend to occur.

These components include a 'mover', 'A', an 'object', 'B', the tensions involved in the confrontations between them, 'C', and the exclusion of possible solutions or directions which would resolve the story too quickly, 'D'. In the thriller, where the basic issue is 'What is going to happen?', the identity of 'A' and 'B' are obvious: 'no question who or what is the menace, or the victim. "C" is generated by the conflict of "A" vs "B." The "D" component is clearly defined, as are the phases or states' (Dove, 1989, p. 59). In the '"pure" or non-detectional mystery', the question is 'What is happening? "A" (the person, problem, menace) is not identified until late; "B" (the identity menaced) emerges somewhat earlier. "C" arises from the disturbance created by loss of security ... [and] "D" is the vulnerability/inadequacy of "B"' (Dove, 1989, p. 60). In the detective story, the question posed is 'What really did happen? In this story "A" is the detective, the element that makes the story move ... "B" is the problem, which would include the guilty person(s) ... "D" is . . . the obscured past, which hold[s] the story in bounds ... [And] "C" is the repeated revelation–frustration of the detective's pursuit' (Dove, 1989, p. 60). And in the 'tale of the Supernatural', the question is 'Is anything happening? "A" and "B" are customarily ambiguous, "A" often so until the end, and "B" may not emerge until late in the story ... "C" is frequently present before "A" or "B" ... [And] "D" is the irrationality–uncertainty–perversity–invulnerability of "A"' (Dove, 1989, p. 61).

Dove's book concentrates on written fiction and his terminology (alphabetical and otherwise) is occasionally eccentric and difficult to follow. However, his formulae work as well for films as they do for novels, and he allows throughout for hybrids and combinations. The extent to which his formulae extend beyond the traditional realms of crime to encompass the supernatural is (yet another) indication of the extent to which popular genres are rarely tidy and self-contained, even, perhaps especially, from a structural point of view. Further confirmation that this is the case can be found in historical surveys of crime films of the kind produced by Langman and Finn. As in Dove's – and Derry's – books, categories and sub-types tend to abound. Here, though, they are founded less on form than on content, less on structural characteristics than on cyclical features and variations. They include 'The courtroom film' (Langman and Finn, 1995a, pp. xii–xiii), 'The newspaper–crime film' (Langman and Finn, 1995a, p. xiii), 'The expose drama' (Langman and Finn, 1995b, pp. xviii–xix) and 'The social conscience drama'. While some of the films within these categories are marked by the structural features analysed by Dove and Derry, others are not. Whether regarded as genres or as sub-types, the point here is that they rarely feature in critical or theoretical discussions of the crime film as such.

Selected Reading

Charles Derry, *The Suspense Thriller, Films in the Shadow of Alfred Hitchcock*, Jefferson, McFarland Press, 1988.

George N. Dove, *Suspense in the Formula Story*, Bowling Green, Bowling Green University Press, 1989.

Charles Eckert, 'The anatomy of a proletarian film: Warners' *Marked Woman*', *Film Quarterly* 27(2), winter 1973/74.

Steve Jenkins, *The Death of a Gangster*, London, BFI Education, 1982.

Colin McArthur, *Underworld USA*, London, Secker & Warburg/BFI, 1972.

Nick Roddick, *A New Deal in Entertainment: Warner Bros. in the 1930s*, London, BFI, 1983.

Robert Warshow, 'The gangster as tragic hero', in *The Immediate Experience*, New York, Atheneum Books, 1970.

Scarface (USA 1932 *p.c* – Caddo Company; *d* – Howard Hawks; sd b/w)

Loosely based on the Capone story, *Scarface* along with *The Public Enemy* and *Little Caesar*, has contributed to the definition of the 'classic' gangster film, exhibiting a rise-and-fall structure and many of the iconographic and thematic elements later developed in the genre. The gangster hero in these films is depicted as a paradoxical figure, at once representing the worst in society and the best in his striving towards the goals of the American dream: wealth, individualism, success, power. All the iconographic elements of the genre are visible: cars, guns, hats and coats, backroom gangsters and brash front-men. The emphasis on consumerism, particularly clothes, indicates increasing wealth and status: for example, lapel flowers, smoking jackets, handkerchiefs, the array of shirts and the interior sprung mattress shown to Poppy. Poppy herself is part of Camonte's success, for in the gangster film accession to gang leadership is often worn by taking the leader's girlfriend.

Also demonstrated is the extravagant violence of these early films which provoked attacks from censorship bodies. Here it is exemplified in the total destruction of the restaurant (cf. *The St Valentine's Day Massacre*, 1967, where this incident is repeated), and by the introduction of the machine gun. Socio-economic explanation of the gangster is suggested in Camonte's gleeful wave at the Cook's sign, 'The World is Yours'.

If the film is more violent than its two 'classic' contemporaries, however, it is also more comic – and indeed, Robin Wood (1982) identifies *Scarface* as one of Hawks's comedies. For example, the antics of Angelo juggling between the telephone and a stream of hot water are used to counterpoint the destruction of the restaurant. In this context the figure of Scarface is offered as an innocent primitive and much of the comedy in the film comes from this – for example Camonte's reply to Poppy's suggestion that his flat is 'kind of gaudy': 'Isn't it though? Glad you like it'.

G-Men (USA 1935 *p.c* – Warner Bros.; *d* – William Keighley; sd b/w)

This film exemplifies a second phase in the development of the gangster genre in which the gangster hero is replaced by a new protagonist, the crime fighter. This development was at least partly determined by the revision of the Production Code in 1934 and its criticism of films glorifying gangsters; in 1930 films like *The Public Enemy* had been able to circumvent such criticisms by providing moral epilogues but by 1935 this was no longer adequate. Nevertheless, much of the genre's iconography is here indistinguishable from earlier gangster films like *Little Caesar*: for example, the hat-wearing card players, office and nightclub locations, the gunman and coffin, Cagney's persona and acting style, unchanged in the shift from gangster to cop, the bank robbery, the East Side milieu.

The Roaring Twenties (USA 1939 *p.c* – Warner Bros.; *d* – Raoul Walsh; sd b/w)

This film demonstrates a number of gangster film motifs: the documentary *March of Time* style; sociological explanation of the gangsters and their lifestyle, characteristic of Warners' 1930s gangster films (see *The Public Enemy*); the set-piece montage of gang warfare; the raid on a rival warehouse and narrow escape; the conflict between the gangster for whom crime is a matter of material survival, represented by Eddie, and the psychotic gangster, George; the heroine, whose classy femininity is the object of the gangster's sexual desire and social aspiration but who is unobtainable, in contrast to the gangster's faithful moll, Panama (see *Scarface, The Public enemy, Portrait of a Mobster*); the role of the lawyer, who for social reasons or personal weakness gets involved with the mob but ultimately crosses the gangster leader by virtue of his superior knowledge of how the system works; the gangster's lifelong and faithful friend who goes down with him in his fall (see *Portrait of a Mobster*).

On the other hand the film also signals the shift from the 'classic' gangster film and G-Men cycle towards *film noir*, in what Shadoian (1977) calls its 'ambiguously elegiac perspective' on the gangster motifs. In this respect the authorship of Walsh is significant in that his other crime melodramas for Warners, *They Drive by Night* and *High Sierra*, also exhibited a *noir* dimension. Here it is exhibited in the Expressionist architecture and lighting of the warehouse raid, and in the unsocially motivated cynicism, and psychotic violence of George (see Raoul Walsh, p. 292; Warner Bros., p. 19).

Underworld USA (USA 1960 *p.c* – Globe Enterprises; *d* – Samuel Fuller; sd b/w)

This film exemplifies both the syndicate cycle of gangster films which dominated the genre in the 1950s and the themes and preoccupations of Samuel Fuller. This intersection of *auteur* with genre was facilitated by Fuller's setting up his own 'independent' production company – Globe Enterprises (see Samuel Fuller, p. 287).

Features typical of the gangster film are the parallels drawn between the organisations of FBI and the underworld; the relationship between gangsterdom and big business which is fully developed in the syndicate movie; brutal realistic violence often performed in startling ways – for instance, Gus gives chewing gum to the Mencken child and then runs her down; the roles of the subsidiary characters, for example Gus, the emotionless gunman, and Cuddles, the moll, who sees through the values of both underworld and revenge motivation of the hero. Finally, while in plot terms the film belongs to the syndicate cycle, there are elements which also suggest the influence of *film noir*, and its transformation in the emergence of the police movie in the 1960s.

The emphasis on night-time shooting, with seedy, urban, shadow-infested locations, is reminiscent of *film noir*, while the isolation of the hero who belongs neither to police nor underworld but has an investigative primitive role, a revenge motif and an ambiguous if not callous attitude to women, looks back to the *noir* private eye and forward to the lone crusading cop, exemplified in the *Dirty Harry* series. The role of the family has also been transformed through the impact of *film noir*, from the incestuous clannishness of the classic gangster film to its unobtainability and delineation as object of victimisation or source of the hero's betrayal – a theme which continues into the 1960s police movies.

Consideration of the intersection of genre and *auteur* raises the question how far Tolly's inability to acquire a family is indicative of Fuller's growing pessimism about American society or how far it is due to the influence of the *noir* thriller. A similar issue is raised about the characterisation of Tolly, who is both sympathetic yet by virtue of his psychotic behaviour – e.g. his use of Cuddles's love-making to get information from her – distanced from us: is this *noir*-influenced characterisation, an element in Fuller's world-view, or a response by both genre and *auteur* to the 1950s 'crisis of American individualism'?

Dirty Harry (USA 1971 *p.c* – Warner Bros./Malpaso; *d* – Don Siegel; sd col.)

Dirty Harry is a big-budget 1970s police thriller using as its central protagonist the psychotic policeman in place of the psychotic gangster of earlier decades. It is both representative of the police movie sub-genre and of the work of its director, Don Siegel, who had also directed earlier psychotic gangster pictures – e.g. *Baby Face Nelson* (1957), *The Lineup* (1958). It also marks the collaboration between Clint Eastwood and Siegel and the inception of the Dirty Harry character. The film, then, marks an interesting interplay between genre, author and star (see Don Siegel, p. 000).

William Park (1978) has described the police movie as a union of psychological melodrama and observation of social conditions. The cop hero is both isolated and a representative American Everyman, positioned between black and hispanic minorities on the one hand and Wasps on the other. Having worked his way up through the force he despises middle-class liberalism and its conscience-ridden advocacy of civil liberties; on the other hand he works with a black or hispanic partner – here, Chico. He lives alone, has no private life and is up against a source of corruption which is unseen but penetrates even the precinct.

Gangster cinema with a documentary 'feel' – *Mean Streets*

The cop hero fights corruption on all sides motivated by an idealistic moral anger which justifies his breaking all laws, except the policeman's taboo against taking a bribe.

Siegel himself contributed to the development of this character in *Coogan's Bluff* (1968) and *Madigan* (1968), the former marking the effective transposition of Eastwood's 'Man With No Name' from its enormous popularity in spaghetti westerns to a contemporary American urban setting, in which the cynical policeman confronts an obstructive, short-sighted police bureaucracy. Here Harry is up against the liberalism of the mayor whose vote-seeking allegiance to civil rights means he cannot identify, let alone act against evil when it confronts him. Alan Lovell (1975) has noted the 'gothic' dimension to the construction of the villain, Scorpio, who is isolated, sadistic and sexually perverted. This element seems quite removed from the journalistic strand of the movie which deploys the hunt/chase structure to incorporate elements of social observation – e.g. signs of social tension in the use of blacks and symbols of protest movements (Scorpio's peace badge buckle).

The union of melodramatic structure and signifiers of political minority opposition has produced conflicting ideological assessments of the police movie sub-genre, the Dirty Harry character and this film. For instance Harry's confrontation with the black bank robber parallels Scorpio's sadistic games later in the film such as the burying of Anne Mary Deacon. Hero and villain are both isolated loners and Harry displays both sadism and voyeuristic tendencies. The issue is how far this parallel suggests a critique of Harry's attitudes and how far it exemplifies a cynicism on the part of the film in which there is small choice between Fascism and madness.

Mean Streets (USA 1973 – Taplin–Perry–Scorsese; *d* – Martin Scorsese; sd col.)

Mean Streets exemplifies the New Hollywood Cinema of the late 1960s–mid-1970s, discussion of which has noted its debt to art cinema: narrative fragmentation, introspective protagonists, generic self-consciousness, and detailed social realism.

Location shooting, long takes and intimate, shaky hand-held camerawork characteristic of *ciné-vérité* complements the naturalistic representation of a specific subculture to afford a 'documentary' picture of New York's Little Italy that convinces despite being shot largely in Los Angeles. However, this 'documentary' representation is also stylistically heightened by a battery of anti-realist devices that flags the new wave: jump-cuts, slow-motion, 'unmotivated' camera movement, and often intrusively annotative music.

In generic terms, the film's claustrophobic Expressionism bears out Scorsese's claim that *Mean Streets* 'became a very clear attempt at doing a *film noir* in colour' (*Pulp Fictions: The Film Noir Story*, NYCVH/BBC, tx. BBC 2, 4.8.95). Other suggestively *noir* elements include the film's mainly night-time, seedy urban setting, the representation of an oppressive, inescapable milieu, and a narrative concern with figures who exist within or on the fringes of the criminal underworld. Indeed, structurally *Mean Streets* recalls the gangster film. Caught between his ambitions as a scion of the local don and the demands of his Catholic conscience, between materialism and morality, Charlie's situation replicates a

Concern with social and ethnic identity marks *Homicide* as a film of the 1990s

familiar thematic/ideological opposition. Moreover, *Mean Streets* exhibits numerous gangster film motifs whether one considers iconography (eg. suits, cars, guns), character (Giovanni as godfather, Charlie as 'family' heir, Shorty as hitman), or incident (meetings, deals, threats, a car chase, shootings).

Even so, in *Mean Streets*, as in much New Hollywood Cinema, and again following the new wave, genre shifts from being predominantly a means of representation to being, in part, an object of representation. Through this, the film engages in a revision of generic conventions that implicitly confronts their underlying assumptions. Not only does *Mean Streets* invert the ideological emphasis of the classic gangster film by representing the mob not as a criminal 'other' but as the dominant patriarchal norm, but Charlie's Catholic conscience is unwontedly placed as transgressive, and the film ends with him effectively defeated by Little Italy's criminal mores.

Generic revision further intersects with the film's other formal qualities. The film's 'documentary' address functions as a critical defamiliarisation, stripping gangsterism of its generic glamour before a 'revelation' of its shabby actuality. Similarly, the reciprocity of the film's comparatively loose cause–effect chain and introspective protagonist switches narrative stress from gangster activity to a reflection upon, and questioning of, its connotations.

Homicide (USA 1991 *p.c* – Bison Films; *d* – David Mamet; sd col.)

Homicide was David Mamet's third film as a director, and while it displays Mamet's interests as both playwright and film-maker – the highly wrought and rhythmic use of vernacular language, a thematic focus on the entanglement of misdirection and (self)-deception – it is also a revealing instance of the development of the detective genre in the 1980s and 1990s. On one level, the film is a character study of Bobby Gold (Joe Mantegna), a Jewish police detective known by his colleagues as 'the orator' for his specialist skills in verbal negotiation. In the midst of a high-profile search for black 'cop-killer' Randolph, Gold is sidetracked by the murder of an old Jewish woman, Mrs Klein. Gold is gradually drawn into the case, initially as a result of official pressure exerted by the victim's wealthy family, but increasingly by his own sense of Jewish identity – or lack of it. Gold's mounting obsession with this case distracts him from the 'Randolph' case, which commands the energies of the tight-knit circle of detectives (his 'family', as his partner Sullivan (William H. Macy) puts it) among whom Gold finds his sense of identity. It is this explicit concern with social and ethnic identity that marks the film as a film of the early 1990s.

Gold's inability to understand and predict the forces he encounters in the Klein case ultimately leads to personal and professional disaster. In this respect, the film recalls other films and trends of the 'post-classic' era: like *After Dark, My Sweet* (1990) and *Red Rock West* (1994), *Homicide* might be regarded as an example of 'neo-*noir*', in that it recapitulates many of the motifs of *film noir*, including a *femme fatale* and a complex intrigue. In addition, *Homicide* echoes several films of the 1970s – *The Parallax View*, *The Conversation* (both 1974) – in its intimations of conspiracy: Gold finds evidence of both organised anti-Semitism and an underground Jewish 'resistance'. But Gold's investigative prowess ends there. Like Jake Gittes in *Chinatown* (1974) and Harry Caul in *The Conversation*, but unlike most of the detective heroes of the studio era, Gold is characterised by his ultimate impotence as a detective. Just as Gittes wears an undignified plaster over his nose for much of *Chinatown*, the stigmata of incompetence displayed by Gold include a bruise on the side of his head and the torn strap on his holster.

The film thus explicitly raises questions of identity and 'identification' – of Gold with his police colleagues and with the Jewish figures, and of the audience with Gold. Our ambivalent relationship with Gold is governed by the interlocking structures of *alignment* (information) and *allegiance* (morality and emotion) in the film. This is best seen in one of the film's major turning points, where Gold's scepticism and indifference towards the Klein case is transformed into a compulsive fascination. Impatient with what he sees as the presumptuous and paranoid behaviour of the Klein family, he is overheard – by Mrs Klein's granddaughter – uttering a stream of anti-Semitic abuse on the phone with Sullivan.

The granddaughter is revealed to the audience just before Gold becomes aware of her. This concealment of the granddaughter is characteristic of the alignment structure associated with the detective film: throughout, we know most of what the detective knows, and occasionally a little more than he knows, as we do at this point. The effect is to underline the scandalous and offensive nature of Gold's remarks. But any absolute condemnation of Gold is undercut by the subsequent action, in which Gold attempts to apologise for his behaviour – in seeking to atone, he does what is socially and morally desirable. Moreover, his humiliation is made more palpable than is the grieving of the family, who are depicted as severe and demanding (leading some critics to charge Mamet himself with an anti-Semitism parallel with Gold's). Our sense of allegiance with Gold is thus partially restored.

In the film's denouement, Gold misses a vital rendezvous in the Randolph case, and so precipitates a gun-battle between his colleagues and Randolph, in which Sullivan is killed. Of all the sources of identity evoked by the film, the relationship between partners is the only one that emerges unscathed. In this way, the film affirms one of the most traditional ideological norms of the detective film: that the most precious relationship a man can have is with the man with whom he works. The film ends with a knot of irony which compounds Gold's failure, loss and isolation. Gold's conspiracy theory of the Klein murder is deflated, rendering Sullivan's death meaningless; and yet, we *have* seen evidence of anti-Semitic activity. The film thus ends by underlining the gap between Gold's motives and the outcome, as well as the gap between the bathos of the particular case and the unresolved menace of anti-Semitism – the empty spaces into which Gold's sense of identity vanishes.

FILM NOIR

INTRODUCTION

'Whoever went to the movies with any regularity during 1946 was caught in the midst of Hollywood's profound postwar affection for morbid drama. From January through December deep shadows, clutching hands, exploding revolvers, sadistic villains and heroines tormented with deeply rooted diseases of the mind flashed across the screen in a panting display of psychoneuroses, unsublimated sex and murder most foul.'

This article from a 1947 *Life* magazine quoted in *Hollywood Genres* (Schatz, 1981, p. 111) is revealing not only for the way in which, at a time when the genre was still young, it manages to touch on many of what were later to be seen as the essential elements of *film noir*, but also for the high moral tone it adopts towards 'panting', 'morbid drama'. At a time when few popular American films were taken seriously, concern about the explicitness of the sexuality and, curiously in the light of later work, the 'realism' of the violence of *noir*, amounted to moral panic. Critics' dislike was compounded by economic snobbery: the low budgets and B-film status of many film *noirs* were seen as a priori proof that the films were 'trash'. Within this framework the *noir* films by émigrés whose earlier work was considered 'art' were seen as particularly lamentable. As documented in Stephen Jenkins's book (1981), it became an English and American critical truism to decry Fritz Lang's decline into the production of what Gavin Lambert, for instance, saw as mere 'workmanlike commerce' (Jenkins, 1981, p. 2).

The major period of *noir* production is usually taken to run from *The Maltese Falcon* in 1941 to *Touch of Evil* in 1958. Even after this time, however, British and American critics failed to take *film noir* seriously. As Paul Schrader comments, 'For a long time *film noir*, with its emphasis on corruption and despair, was considered an aberration of the American character. The western, with its moral primitivism, and the gangster film, with its Horatio Alger values, were considered more American than the *film noir*.' Schrader goes on to suggest that the fundamental reason for the neglect of *noir* was the importance of visual style to the form: 'American critics have been traditionally more interested in theme than style ... it was easier for the sociological critics to discuss the themes of the western and the gangster film apart from stylistic analysis than it was to do for the *film noir*' (Schrader, 1972, p. 13).

In France the situation was very different. Initially, interest focused on the links between *noir* films and the writing of the 'hard-boiled' novelists such as Chandler, Hammett, Woolrich, Cain and McCoy, who all either wrote screenplays or source novels for *noir* films. The phrase *film noir* itself derives from the *série noire* books – mainly translations of the above-named American writers. Interestingly, it seems that this examination of writers as one of the sources for *film noir* became, in Britain and America, a method of ascribing respectability – see, for example, Jenkins's comments on the overvaluation of the role of the literary Hammett in histories of *film noir* compared with the contribution of, for example, Woolrich (Jenkins, 1982, p. 276).

The fantasy woman comes to life in *Woman in the Window*

Equally relevant to the French context was the rise of authorship theories known historically as the *politique des auteurs* (see The *politique des auteurs*, p. 240). The re-evaluation of *noir* films by particular directors, especially Lang, Huston, Ray, Fuller and Aldrich, involved a new depth of investigation and, especially, a close examination of *mise-en-scène*. The basic aim of such studies was, however, the tracing of continuities across careers rather than the lateral investigation of work produced in particular periods and production contexts. The most interesting questions about *noir* do not concern the marks of directorial difference. Rather, the crucial issue, as phrased by Silver and Ward, is that of 'cohesiveness': the wide influence of *noir* across the work of different directors and genres. Silver and Ward take a random sample of seven *films noirs* and note that 'different directors and cinematographers, of great and small technical reputations, working at seven different studios, completed seven ostensibly unrelated motion pictures with one cohesive visual style' (Silver and Ward, 1981, p. 3).

Although it is generally accepted that crime and criminal acts provide the basis for the majority of *noir* films and the *noir* style (see Durgnat, 1974) the influence of *noir* spreads beyond the gangster/thriller genres influencing melodramas, horror films, detectives, even (although this would not be universally agreed) westerns and musicals. Indeed, Schrader has suggested that *noir* can be seen as touching 'most every dramatic Hollywood film from 1941 to 53' (Schrader, 1972, p. 9).

CATEGORIES AND DEFINITIONS

Given the potential expansiveness of the term, *noir* demanded both a theoretical system which could pin down what it was that made *noir noir*, and criticism which examined its generic marks and investigated the structural, thematic and visual systems integral to the whole series of films. Before work on defining the crucial elements of *noir* and an examination of their workings could begin, however, preliminary attempts were made to categorise those films which seemed central to *noir*.

The first book-length study of *noir* (Borde and Chaumeton, 1955) began this work by mapping out various recurrent themes within *noir* (violence, crime, psychological emphasis) and relating these to particular films. This in turn provided the basis for Durgnat's eccentric and amorphous (1974) article which listed nearly 300 films under headings such as 'psychopaths', 'gangsters', and 'middle-class murder'. The latter category was subdivided into lists including 'corruption of the not-so innocent male' (e.g. *Double Indemnity*, *The Postman Always Rings Twice*); 'woman as heroic victim' (e.g. *Rebecca*, *Gaslight*) and 'mirror images' (e.g. *Rebecca*, *The Woman in the Window*). Durgnat's article, written in 1970, was influential in mapping the territory but it pointed up the need for more rigorous and specific definition – for many, his inclusion of films like *2001* was mere provocation.

Paul Schrader touches on what he sees as some of the recurring visual marks of *noir* – the majority of the scenes lit for night, rain-drenched streets, doom-laden narration, compositional tension rather than action and a fondness for oblique lines and fractured light. Generally appreciative of Durgnat's categorisation, Schrader suggests that the family tree is structured around a halting of the upwardly mobile thrust of the 1930s. 'Frontierism has turned to paranoia and claustrophobia. The small-time gangster had made it big and sits in the mayor's chair. The private eye has quit the police force in disgust, and the young heroine, sick of going along for the ride is now taking others for a ride.' Writing more historically than Durgnat, Schrader identifies an intensification of this downward movement as the *noir* period continues and categorises *noir* temporally by subdividing it into three main periods. These are: wartime 1941–6 (characterised by 'the private eye and the lone wolf ... studio sets and more talk than action', e.g. *The Maltese Falcon*, *Gilda*, *Mildred Pierce*), postwar realistic 1945–9 ('crime in the streets, political corruption and police routine' and 'less romantic heroes', e.g. *The Killers*, *Brute Force*) and finally psychotic action and suicidal impulse 1949–53 ('the psychotic killer as active protagonist, despair and distintegration', e.g. *Gun Crazy*, *D.O.A.*, *Sunset Boulevard*) (Schrader, 1972, pp. 11–12).

Spider woman Norma Desmond traps her prey in *Sunset Boulevard*

Both Durgnat and Schrader state that they do not see *film noir* as a genre. Instead, Schrader suggests that it should be seen as a period or movement similar to German Expressionism or Italian neo realism. Critics of this use of the term claimed that unlike the quoted movements *noir* did not involve an overt, or even implicit, commitment to a political/aesthetic programme and that to imply that it did misrepresented the divergent attitudes of *noir* film-makers and *noir*'s precise industrial production context.

Janey Place (with Peterson, 1974; 1978) also uses the term 'movement' and justifies her use of it in some depth. She claims that 'unlike genres, defined by objects and subjects, but like other film movements, *film noir* is characterised by a remarkably homogeneous visual style with which it cuts across genres' (Place, 1978, p. 39). In the earlier article Place and Peterson attempt to identify the elements of this 'consistent thread'. They outline the difference between the dominant 'high-key lighting style' which eliminates 'unnatural' shadows on faces and gave 'what was considered to be an impression of reality' and *noir's* chiaroscuro 'low-key lighting' which eschews softening filters and gauzes and 'opposes light and darkness, hiding faces, rooms, urban landscapes – and by extension, motivations and true character – in shadow and darkness'. The night scenes integral to *film noir* would, in the *blanc* style, have been shot 'day for night' with special filters. A central element of the *noir* look, however, was the high contrast image and jet black (rather than *blanc* grey-black) skies given by 'night for night' shooting. Place and Peterson go on to describe *noir*'s *mise-en-scène* 'designed to unsettle, jar, and disorient the viewer in correlation with the disorientation felt by the *noir* heroes'. Typically, they argue, *noir* is distinguished by the use of 'claustrophobic framing devices' which separate characters from each other, unbalanced compositions with shutters or banisters casting oblique shadows or placing grids over faces and furniture, 'obtrusive and disturbing' close-ups juxtaposed with extreme high-angle shots which make the protagonist look like 'a rat in a trap'. Overall, the visual style of *noir* as described by Place and Peterson amounts to a disorientating anti-realism which exists in opposition to the harmonious *blanc* world of the realist film.

Place's insistence on the distinguishing character of the visual style of the *noir* is challenged in an article by James Damico (1978). Arguing against the view of *noir* as movement and for it as a genre, Damico claims that the visual style of *noir* is actually an iconography. He suggests that the common denominator of *noir* films is their narrative structure and proposes a model by which *films noirs* may be isolated, objectified and their examination facilitated.

> Either because he is fated to do so by chance, or because he has been hired for a job especially associated with her, a man whose experience of life has left him sanguine and often bitter meets a not-so-innocent woman of similar outlook to whom he is sexually and fatally attracted. Through this attraction, either because the woman induces him to it or because it is a natural result of their relationship, the man comes to cheat, attempt to murder, or actually murder a second man to whom the woman is unhappily or unwillingly attached (generally he is her husband or lover), an act which often leads to the woman's betrayal of the protagonist, but which in any event brings about the sometimes metaphoric, but usually literal destruction of the woman, the man to whom she is attached, and frequently the protagonist himself. (Damico, 1978, p. 54)

While Place's and Damico's respective use of the terms 'movement' and 'genre' is closely argued in relation to their individual stress on either visual style or narrative structure, other writers have used them differently, or have opted instead for 'series', 'cycle' or 'sub-genre'. Subsequent authors have not automatically accepted Damico's contention that his schema provides an alternative reading of *noir* which is in opposition to accounts stressing visual style. For example, Paul Kerr's article on the industrial context of the B-*film noir* unproblematically includes both Place and Damico in a general introduction to the genre's characteristics (Kerr, 1979/80, p. 49). Sylvia Harvey, meanwhile, offers a useful synthesis within a framework which accepts visual style as the most fundamental aspect of *noir*. The defining contour of genre, Harvey suggests, is dissonance: 'the sense of disorientation and unease' produced by 'that which is abnormal and dissonant' (Harvey, 1978, p. 32).

THE HISTORICAL SPECIFICITY OF *FILM NOIR*

Underlying all these different attempts at categorisation of *noir* lies the issue of its historical specificity. How did it become so dominant in Hollywood for more than twenty years, touching (one might almost say consuming) almost every genre while retaining a specific visual and narrative structure? What caused it to decline? And if, as this line of questioning suggests, there was a relationship between historical period and the stylistic and thematic elements of *noir*, how should this relationship be characterised?

Before dealing with how various theorists have answered these questions it is important to signal the debate about the delineation of the genre's historical period. Following Schrader, most critics have understood the major period of *noir* to fall between *The Maltese Falcon* in 1941 and *Touch of Evil* in 1958 (Schrader, 1972, p. 8), although the search for immediate precursors has been a popular academic occupation (e.g. Flinn, 1972, claims that the 65-minute B-movie *Stranger on the Third Floor* is the earliest *film noir*). This strictly time-bound view is, however, implicitly challenged by some listings. Durgnat's family tree lists several titles made outside of the 1942–58 period, including several more usually seen as precursors, such as Warner Bros. gangster films. A more complex challenge to Schrader's time limits comes from Silver and Ward (1981), whose book includes synopses of later films which were clearly influenced by *noir*, often to the point of intentional homage. The genesis of films like *Klute* (1971), *Hustle* (1975), *Body Heat*

(1981) and Schrader's own *American Gigolo* (1980) was provocatively prefigured by his comment that 'as the current political mood hardens, filmgoers and film-makers will find the *film noir* of the late 40s increasingly attractive' (Schrader, 1972, p. 8). These later films may be better described as 'film *après noir*', as suggested by Larry Gross (Gross, 1976), but this merely recasts, rather than eliminates, questions about the relationship between *noir* and its specific historical configuration.

Industry and aesthetics

Borde and Chaumeton comment briefly on the influence of German Expressionism, which they see as transmitted chiefly through the agency of *émigré* directors Lang and Siodmak, but then go on to say that *noir* is better understood as a 'synthesis' of 'the brutal and colourful gangster films' made by Warner Bros., the horror films associated with Universal and the 'detective fiction shared by Fox and MGM'. They also identify in the genre the 'inexhaustible sadism' of animation, the 'absurdity and casual cynicism' of American comedy and the influence of certain realist and/or social commentary films, notably LeRoy's *I Am a Fugitive From a Chain Gang* (1932) (Borde and Chaumeton, 1978, p. 63). Rather than helping to explain why a synthesis in the form of *noir* should have taken place during the 1940s and 1950s, the diversity of their sources tends to obscure the issue. They do make it clear, however, that *noir* grew from within the American as well as European industries.

Schrader's account stresses the historical time limits of genre, but does little to explain the industrial context for the 'halting of 30s optimism' except to speculate that the end of the war and Depression freed the industry from the task of 'keeping people's spirits up' (Schrader, 1972, p. 9). His combination of a listing of sources (to which others have added *Citizen Kane*) linked to a vague statement of postwar gloom can be seen as the most dominant paradigm for understanding the industrial/aesthetic context for *noir*.

Paul Kerr challenges the generality of such accounts, suggesting a re-examination of the conjuncture between 'a primarily economically determined mode of production known as "B" film-making' and what were primarily ideologically defined modes of 'difference' known as the *film noir* (Kerr, 1979/80, p. 65). More specifically, Kerr argues that some of the stylistic features of *noir* such as night for night shooting, disorientating lighting and camera angles and the generation of tension through editing and short bursts of extreme violence, were direct results of economic factors such as the desire to thwart union restrictions and use stock footage. Furthermore, production took place in the context of the need to demonstrate a clear difference from the realism of A-films, with which the B-*noirs* were paired in double bills. Kerr's account goes on to examine the decline of *noir*, which he relates to various technical developments, such as Technicolor, which were the products of an ideological pressure for increased verisimilitude, and changes in the economic structure of the industry, particularly the anti-monopoly Bill of Divorcement which contributed to the end of the double bill (Kerr, 1979/80, pp. 56–65).

Genre and social context

Kerr's article is explicitly written as a counter-attack on the series of books and articles which have dealt with the wider social/economic/political configurations of the *noir* period. Again, Borde and Chaumeton (1978) offer a fairly typical account. They suggest the influence of 'vulgarised' psychoanalysis in America and the publicity given to crime. While both of these form recurring elements in *noir* narratives, Borde and Chaumeton's comments lack historical specificity. A more detailed and influential account of *noir's* social context can be found in Colin McArthur (1972). McArthur notes that 'it is useless to try to align the wholly fictitious events of the thriller with actual events', but then goes on to speculate on the reasons for the emergence of the thriller as *film noir*. These 'speculations' include the aftermath of the Depression, the war and the cold war and the 'general mood of fear and insecurity' produced by an uncertain future. 'It seems reasonable to suggest', he continues, 'that this uncertainty is paralleled in the general mood of malaise, the loneliness and angst and the lack of clarity about the characters' motives in the thriller.' McArthur also cites the misogyny associated with 'the heightened desirability and concomitant suspicion of women back home experienced by men at war' and the horrors of Auschwitz and Hiroshima, which he sees echoed in a shift from 1930s gangsters overtly concerned with the social origins of crime to *noir* thrillers such as *Dark Corner* (1946), 'a cry of loneliness and despair in a sick world' (McArthur, 1972, pp. 66–7).

These speculations are suggestive, but McArthur offers few clear suggestions as to how they are actually articulated in the texts. Furthermore, there is a paradox in his positing a relationship between the social/psychological formations of a particular period and angst, a term which is a-historical. Given the point in the development of critical theory at which the study was undertaken, it is perhaps inevitable that McArthur falls back on *auteurist* notions to explain the connection between these events and the texts. It was, he suggests, the 'sour and pessimistic sensibilities' of directors such as Lang, Siodmak and Wilder, 'forged in the uncertainty of Weimar Germany and decaying Austria–Hungary', which provide the vital link between *film noir* and America in the 1940s and 1950s.

The connection between 'postwar gloom' and the 'meaninglessness', 'depression' and 'angst' of *noir* became almost *de rigeur* in critical analyses. Perhaps the most extreme examples linking an apparently angst-laden period and *noir* via the agency of *auteurs* comes in the articles about *noir* and existentialism. Robert G. Porfirio (1976), for example, attempts to connect French existentialist philosophy to *noir* through 'hard-boiled' writers, especially, and dubiously (see Jenkins, 1982) Hammett and Hemingway. Writing about the Flitcraft parable, for instance, included in the novel *The Maltese Falcon* was taken from but omitted from the film, Porfirio claims it reveals that 'Spade is by nature an existentialist, with a strong conception of the randomness of existence'. Porfirio's analysis implicitly depends upon making an unproblematic leap between the historical configurations within which existentialism developed in France and the 'world' that exists within the *noir* texts.

Women in *film noir*

A very different approach to the historical context of *noir* can be seen in the feminist writing collected in *Women in Film Noir* (Kaplan, 1978, rev. edn 1998). Making a decisive attempt to shift discussion away from angst, these writers concentrate on the structuring role of patriarchal ideology within the texts. Their interest in *noir* comes from an understanding of the period of its growth as one of social and economic transition following the disruption of the war years, producing problems for male power and control, and a concern to analyse the genre's treatment of women. Kaplan, for instance, notes that:

> The *film noir* world is one in which women are central to the intrigue of the films, and are furthermore usually not placed safely in … familiar roles … Defined by their sexuality, which is presented as desirable but dangerous, the women function as an obstacle to the male quest. The hero's success or not depends on the degree to which he can extricate himself from the women's manipulations. Although the man is sometimes simply destroyed because he cannot resist women's lures, often the world of the film is the attempted restoration of order through the exposure and then destruction of the sexual, manipulating woman. (Kaplan, 1978, pp. 2–3)

In contrast to the seamless, unproblematic assimilation of existentialism by the *noir* text assumed by Porfirio's article, these feminist analyses emphasise the text as a site of contradiction. Thus, rather than searching for symbolic truths residing statically within the text, many of the writers (e.g. Gledhill,

Johnston and Cook) are concerned to discern structural relationships which they then rework through conceptual frameworks provided by Marxist and psychoanalytically influenced feminism. Gledhill, for instance, says that to understand the significance of *film noir* for women

> It would be necessary to analyse the conjecture of specific aesthetic, cultural and economic forces; on the one hand the on-going production of the private eye/thriller ... on the other, the postwar drive to get women out of the workforce and return them to the domestic sphere; and finally the perennial myth of woman as threat to male control of the world and destroyer of male aspiration – forces, which in cinematic terms, interlock to form what we now think of as the aberrant style and world of *film noir*. (Gledhill, 'Klute 1', 1978, p. 19)

Gledhill's analysis of *film noir* is based on examination of a series of structural elements which open up contradictions around the ambiguously placed *noir* women. Her 'five features' of *noir* are: the investigative structure of the narrative which 'probes the secrets of female sexuality within patterns of submission and dominance' (Gledhill, 1978, p. 15); flashbacks and voice-overs which can sometimes open up a textual gap between a male narrator and the woman he is investigating, as in *Gilda*; a proliferation of points of view, with, typically, a struggle between men and women; unstable characterisation of the heroine, who is likely to be a treacherous *femme fatale*; and the sexualised filming of this heroine, who is also enmeshed in the contradictory visual style of *noir*.

This last point is expanded by Place (1978). Working from the basis provided by her earlier work with L. S. Peterson (1974), Place examines the visual motifs through which two archetypical women – the spider woman and the nurturing woman – are articulated. Writing about the spider woman, Place comments that 'the sexual woman's dangerous power is expressed visually' and details her inconography: long hair, cigarette smoke as a cue for immorality, a habitat of darkness and, perhaps most importantly, a domination of composition, camera movement and lighting which seems to pull 'the camera (and the hero's gaze with our own) irresistibly with them as they move' (Place, 1978, p. 45). Despite her apparent power, the *femme fatale* 'ultimately loses physical strength' and is actually or symbolically imprisoned (Place, 1978, p. 45). For Place, however, this visual and narrative containment is not what is retained from *noir*. Instead, it is the power of the *femme fatale* that we remember, 'their strong, dangerous and above all exciting sexuality' (Place, 1978, p. 37).

Klute – 'film *après noir*'

Place's analysis signals the importance in these analyses of the different emphases placed on the recuperative potential of *noir* – i.e. on the extent to which the text is able to contain and mask the social contradictions structured into its narrative and visual systems. Here is considerable divergence between theorists. Unlike Place, and Dyer (1978), who argues for Gilda/Rita Hayworth's 'resistance through charisma' to textual and ideological containment in *Gilda*, Pam Cook offers a reading of *Mildred Pierce* in which the film's textual organisation works to suppress the *noir* heroine's discourse 'in favour of that of the male', with Mildred finally designated guilty by the law and returned to a safe, subordinate domestic situation (Cook, 1978). Gledhill's examination of Klute, an example of what has been described as 'film *après noir*', discerns a similar final positioning for a different, but equally equivocal heroine – redefinition, yet again, as guilty (Gledhill, '*Klute* 2', 1978). These feminist analyses make a provocative intervention into critical debates about *film noir*, which have generally been characterised by a masculine perspective on the part of critics and a concentration on the existential dilemmas of the *noir* hero.

Noir and neo-*noir*: recent developments

Since the early 1980s, what Larry Gross initially identified as 'film *après noir*' has – usually now under the heading of 'neo-*noir*' – become a major contemporary phenomenon. In addition to obvious homages and remakes films like *The Postman Always Rings Twice* (1981), *Against All Odds* (1984) and *Night and the City* (1994) nearly every crime thriller made in Hollywood is now almost automatically labelled as *noir* or as neo-*noir* by reviewers and critics in the trade press, in newspapers and listings magazines, and in specialist film journals alike. In tandem with these developments, academic writing both on *noir* and on neo-*noir* has itself become a major phenomenon. With '*noir* classics' from the 1940s and 1950s now also regularly recycled as such on video and on television, '*film noir*' has, at least as a term, become firmly established.

Recent writing on neo-*noir* – a term perhaps first fully established in the 1992 edition of Silver and Ward (pp. 398–443) – has tended to distinguish between trends, modes and cycles within what tends to be viewed, nevertheless, as a single phenomenon. Leighton Grist (1993), for instance, carefully distinguishes between what he calls 'modern', 'modernist' and 'postmodern' instances of neo-*noir*. 'Modern' neo-*noir*, exemplified by films like *Harper* (1966) and *Farewell My Lovely* (1975), tends to introduce 'a number of signifiers of modernity', signifiers which can include 'an updated setting, the use of colour, greater sexual frankness, and the transmission of decidedly modern attitudes and mores' (Grist, 1993, p. 267). 'Modernist' neo-*noirs*, made more or less at the same time, include *Point Blank* (1967), *The Long Goodbye* (1973), *Chinatown* (1974) and *Taxi Driver* (1976), and are marked by a 'questioning of the conventions and discourses of *film noir* narrative'. 'Essentially challenging crucial ideological assumptions embedded in the genre, these films enact a process of formal and thematic demystification' (Grist, 1993, p. 267). In 'postmodern' neo-*noirs*, by contrast, *noir*'s 'generic conventions may be reprised, but rarely interrogated' (Grist, 1993, p. 274). Marked by what he sees as an uncritical deployment of allusion and pastiche, 'postmodern' neo-*noir* is above all a feature of the 1980s and 1990s, and is exemplified by films like *Body Heat* (1981), *Blade Runner* (1982), and *The Hot Spot* (1990).

Recent writing on *noir* itself is divisible into a number of distinct and different trends. First, there are a number of articles and books which tend to summarise, reorder or recycle the tenets of earlier accounts. Among these are Crowther (1988), Walker (1992), and Palmer (1994). Palmer's book contains an innovative chapter on 'The *Noir* Woman's Picture', and a concluding chapter on neo-*noir*. Walker's introductory summary is both succinct and thorough, usefully dividing the protagonists who enter or who are plunged into what he calls 'the *noir* world' into 'seeker heroes' (often detectives, policemen, or investigative figures of one kind or another) and 'victim heroes'. He also suggests that '*film noir* is not simply a certain type of crime movie, but also a generic field: a set of elements and features which may be found in a range of different film' (Walker, 1992, p. 8).

Maltby (1992), Neve (1992, pp. 145–70), Polan (1986, pp. 193–249), and Telotte (1989), all address themselves to the issues of *noir*'s original historical context and significance. Polan and Telotte see *noir* in terms of contemporary discursive structures and preoccupations. For Polan, *noir*'s conventions and devices, its differences and defamiliarisations, relate to various crises within America's social and symbolic order in the 1940s. For Telotte, *noir* was a privileged site for expressing and exploring the difficulties and problems of communication in a changed postwar world.

Maltby's and Neve's accounts are both more empirically based and more partial and specific in focus. Maltby is concerned with the contemporary significance of those films subsequently labelled as *noirs* for leftists and liberals working in Hollywood in the late 1940s or commentating on its output and its trends. Citing Siegfried Kracauer, John Houseman, Abraham Polonsky and others, he shows how, amongst other things, liberal worries about the contemporary mass media and about the future of purposeful social commitment and activity now that the war against Fascism was over found expression in a number of anxieties about contemporary crime films. John Houseman, for instance, complained about 'their absolute lack of moral energy' and 'their listless, fatalistic despair' (Maltby, 1992, p. 41). He went on to write:

> One wonders what impression people will get of contemporary life if *The Postman Always Rings Twice* is run in a projection room twenty years hence. They will deduce, I believe, that the United States of America in the year following the end of the Second World War was a land of enervated, frightened people with spasms of high vitality but of low moral sense – a hung-over people with confused objectives groping their way through a twilight of insecurity and corruption. (Maltby, 1992, p. 41)

These anxieties were exacerbated by the onset of the cold war and by the hearings at the HUAC, and Maltby himself goes on to argue that at this point the paranoid rhetoric of *noir* took a decidedly rightward turn.

Similar ground is covered by Neve. He himself, though, is concerned to demonstrate a strong left-wing and liberal current in *noir* throughout the 1940s and the early 1950s, citing writers, directors and producers like Edward Dmytryk, Robert Rossen, Adrian Scott, John Berry, Joseph Losey, Albert Maltz, Dore Schary and Orson Welles, and films like *Cornered* (1945), *The Stranger* (1946, *They Won't Believe Me* (1947), *Force of Evil* (1949), *Where Danger Lives* (1950), *The Narrow Margin* (1952) and *The Prowler* (1951).

Continuing but to some extent also reorientating earlier work on gender, women, and the figure of the *femme fatale*, a further trend in recent writing on *noir* has been an attention to issues of masculinity. For Frank Krutnik, 1991, and for Deborah Thomas, 1992, issues of masculinity are central to *film noir*, which they see as dramatising and exploring 'a particular crisis in male identity' (Thomas, 1992, p. 59). Both tend therefore to read *noir*'s female characters as functions of male dilemmas and male anxieties. For Thomas, the 'redemptive' or 'domesticating' woman is as threatening for the male protagonist as the *femme fatale*, while for Krutnik the *femme fatale* tends to 'represent conflicting elements within male identity' (Krutnik, 1991, p. 63). For Krutnik, though, the problems faced by *noir*'s male protagonists extend beyond their relations with women. Women are only one source or index of more general 'disturbances in or threats to the regimentation of masculine identity and social/cultural authority' in the 1940s (Krutnik, 1991, p. 164). Krutnik here echoes Dyer (1978), and also Florence Jacobowitz (1992), who argues that *noir* is a 'genre wherein compulsory masculinity is presented as a nightmare' (Jacobowitz, 1992, p. 153).

Elizabeth Cowie (1993), also addresses the issue of gender, but her argument is a different one – indeed, she is explicitly critical of those who stress the masculine orientation of *film noir*. She draws attention to the frequent role played by women as source novelists and as scriptwriters for *noirs*, to the absence of *femmes fatales* in numerous *noirs*, and to the extent to which *noirs* like *Raw Deal* (1948) and *Secret Beyond the Door* (1948) are 'women's stories'. She goes on to argue that while the issue of sexual difference in *noir* is always crucial, the gender of its originators and of its protagonists, together with the gender appeal of the films themselves, is much more variable than most commentators on *noir* have hitherto been willing or able to acknowledge.

Cowie is in general highly sceptical about *noir* as a category, and about the coherence of the phenomenon the term is usually used to identify. 'The term has succeeded', she writes,

> despite the lack of any straightforward unity in the set of films it attempts to designate. Unlike terms such as the 'western' or the 'gangster' film, which are relatively uncontroversial ... *film noir* has a more tenuous critical status, a devotion among *aficionados* that suggest a desire for the very category as such, a wish that it exist in order to 'have' a certain set of films all together. *Film Noir* is in a certain sense a fantasy. (Cowie, 1993, p.121)

Cowie's scepticism is tempered by her thesis that *noir* 'names a certain inflection or tendency which emerges in certain genres in the early 1940s' (Cowie, 1993, p. 129), one in which 'American cinema finds for the first time a form in which to represent desire as something that not only renders the desiring subject helpless, but also propels him or her to destruction' (Cowie, 1993, p. 148).

Vernet (1993) points on the one hand to historical contradictions and non-sequiturs in those accounts which link *noir* to hard-boiled fiction. *Noir* is argued to be a postwar or 1940s phenomenon. Yet hard-boiled fiction emerged in the 1920s and 1930s, and film versions were made in the 1930s themselves. On the other hand, he points to political and ideological factors predisposing the discovery (or invention) of *film noir* by intellectuals and *cinéastes* in postwar France. In addition, he argues that the Expressionist visual style and the chiaroscuro look reputedly specific to *noir* and hence to the 1940s and 1950s is in fact a longstanding tradition in American cinematography, one which not only pre-dates the 1940s, but also the 1920s, the period in which those associated with Expressionism in Germany first began to make Expressionist films.

Neale (forthcoming) mobilises these points and others in arguing that *noir* is as a critical category and as a canon of films both logically and chronologically incoherent. He points to inconsistencies in versions of the canon (some include films like *Suspicion* (1941) and *Secret Beyond the Door* (1948) while others do not), and to historical anomalies in arguments proposing that a category including films like *Stranger on the Third Floor* (1940), *The Maltese Falcon* (1941) and *This Gun for Hire* (1942) is a postwar phenomenon. He argues that the significance attributed to *noir* as an index of contemporary American society is disproportionate to the number of films involved and tends to ignore the nature and diversity of Hollywood's output as a whole. He argues in addition that a number of the features said to be characteristic of *noir* – the use of chiaroscuro, for instance, and the use of flashback and voice-over, scenarios of destructive and murderous passion, an emphasis on perverse forms of character motivation and behaviour and on the depiction of extreme mental states, and a stress on suspicion, distrust and deceit in the depiction of relations between male and female protagonists – can all be found in genres and cycles – such as the Gothic woman's film and Val Lewton's horror series at RKO – which proponents of *noir* tend to regard as either non-canonic or marginal. And he also argues, conversely, that a number of canonic *noirs* lack some or all of these features. All in all, he suggests, the notion of *noir*, and the attachment to it of film scholars, critics, theorists and historians, now functions to block rather than to facilitate historical research. Meanwhile, somewhat paradoxically, the widespread dissemination of what was once an esoteric critical term has, in tandem with the advent and ubiquity of neo-*noir*, ensured that '*film noir*' itself now has a generic status it never had in the 1940s and 1950s.

Selected Reading

Ian Cameron (ed.), *The Movie Book of Film Noir*, London, Studio Vista, 1992.

Elizabeth Cowie, '*Film Noir* and women', in

Joan Copjec (ed.), *Shades of Noir*, London, Verso, 1993.

Mary Ann Doane, *The Desire to Desire – The Woman's Film of the 1940s*, Indiana University Press, Bloomington, 1987.

Raymond Durgnat, 'The family tree of *film noir*', *Cinema* (UK), August 1970, reprinted in *Film Comment* 10(6), November/December 1974.

Steve Jenkins, *Fritz Lang*, London, BFI, 1981.

E. Ann Kaplan (ed.), *Women in Film Noir*, London, BFI, 1978; rev. edn, 1998.

Paul Kerr, 'Out of what past? Notes on the B-*film noir*', *Screen Education* nos 32/33, autumn/winter 1979/80.

Frank Krutnik, *In a Lonely Street: Film Noir, Genre, Masculinity*, London, Routledge, 1991.

R. Barton Palmer, *Hollywood's Dark Cinema: The American Film Noir*, New York, Twayne, 1994.

Dana Polan, *Power and Paranoia: History, Narrative, and the American Cinema, 1940–1950*, New York, Columbia University Press, 1986.

Paul Schrader, 'Notes on *film noir*', *Film Comment* 8(1), spring 1972.

Double Indemnity (USA 1944 *p.c* – Paramount; *d* – Billy Wilder; sd b/w)

Barbara Stanwyck's performance as Phyllis Dietrichson in *Double Indemnity* represents one of the most powerful and disturbing *noir* portraits of a *femme fatale* – the destructive, duplicitous woman who transgresses rule of female behaviour by luring men with the promise of possessing her sexually and then using them for her own, murderous, ends. Immensely successful despite early studio qualms about the 'appropriateness' of a thriller with such a dark heroine, the film had substantial effect on later *noirs*.

Corruption of the not-so-innocent male in *Double Indemnity*

One of the characteristics of *noir* films is their use of voice-over narration. In the scene following on from the renowned *double entendre*-filled first meeting between bored housewife Phyllis and insurance salesman Walter Neff, we hear Neff's voice-over delivering a classically hard-boiled, retrospective description of events. It is not until a little later that we see that he is in fact dictating it into an office machine for the benefit of Keys, Neff's father figure and in Johnston's analysis 'signifier of the patriarchal order' ('*Double Indemnity*', 1978). Discussing narration in her essay (1978) on *Klute*, Christine Gledhill comments that for the audience 'the temporal separation of the moment of telling and the event told lead to something of a dislocation between what they observe and the storyteller's account of it. This aspect is intensified in that the storyteller is often proved wrong by subsequent events and may even be lying' (Gledhill, 1978, p. 16). Neff's voice-over suggests that he despises Phyllis and wants to be rid of her while the audience knows that this is not the case. Later that evening, Phyllis arrives at his apartment. As Claire Johnston points out, yet again a gap is created, this time between image and voice-over. 'The voice-over suggests an appointment which the image denies: "it would be eight and she would be there"' (Johnston, 1978, p. 105).

During this meeting at his apartment, Phyllis is identified visually and through the voice-over with the darkness in the apartment and with the rain. During the whole scene he is softly lit, while at certain moments the chiaroscuro low-key lighting makes her appear jewel hard. Most crucially, the interaction between Phyllis and Neff is both sexual and violent. The real moment of sexual catharsis is not the first kiss, but the embrace which follows Neff's commitment to help her to kill her husband. The importance of the intention to do violence to Mr Dietrichson is outweighed by the sadistic eroticism between the two of them.

The death of the transgressive woman – in a narrative which closely adheres to Damico's (1978) ideal *noir* structure – does not end the film. With Phyllis's death, the gap between retrospective narration and image can be resolved into a present. The trajectory of *Double Indemnity* follows the shattering of the primal friendship between Keys and Neff and the imperilling of the smooth workings of the insurance system (and the patriarchal order it represents) by Neff's involvement with the world of women. In particular, Phyllis concretised Neff's unacknowledged desire to 'buck the system' by testing the fallibility of Keys and, in Johnston's analysis, the law he represents. The elimination of her and her challenge to the patriarchal order means that the film can finish with a brief re-establishment of the homo-erotic relationship between Keys and Neff, signified by their affectionate ritual with Neff's last cigarette.

Secret Beyond the Door (USA 1948 *p.c* – Diana Productions/Universal; *d* – Fritz Lang; sd b/w)

Secret Beyond the Door is the third in Lang's trilogy of films with Joan Bennett, but whereas the first two, *Woman in the Window* (1944) and *Scarlet Street* (1945), centre on a male protagonist, here the central protagonist is a woman. Moreover, as Stephen Jenkins points out, in this film it is the woman who investigates the man, inverting the structure of the earlier two films, and implying that the Bennett character, Celia, is in the narrative position previously taken by the Edward G. Robinson characters (Jenkins, 1981, p. 104). That position is not, however, one of dominance, for in the previous films, Robinson becomes a victim of his own desire and this brings him into conflict with the law. This situation produces a relationship between the male figure and the law which is mediated by the woman as object of desire. A similar narrative structure is played out in *Secret Beyond the Door*, and its reversal of gender

The chiaroscuro lighting effects of *The Secret Beyond the Door*

makes the film of considerable interest. At the same time, questions of generic reference arise. All three films have a related and marked visual style, with strong use of chiaroscuro lighting effects, and both *Woman in the Window* and *Secret Beyond the Door* invoke dream states.

The connection of desire with death is also central to both films, and to *film noir* as a whole. However, few writers place *Secret Beyond the Door* as a *film noir*. Instead it is associated with the 'woman's film' and the 'Gothic' (see Jensen, 1969; Waldman, 1983; Doane, 1987). Lang himself claimed that Hitchcock's *Rebecca* was a direct inspiration for this film and certainly an array of Gothic elements can be found in it. Celia throws caution to the wind and pursues her desire, marrying Mark Lamphere after a seventy-two hour acquaintance. Arriving at his gloomy ancestral home she learns of his former wife who died of an unnamed illness, and finds a son who hates his father and whom he believes has killed his mother, as well as a scheming woman employee lurking at a window.

There are, however, other elements in the film that contradict or disturb the genre expectations of the Gothic. Celia is not very young, and not at all inexperienced – she is sophisticated and self-possessed. As a result the Gothic elements in *Secret Beyond the Door* appear marked as such, foregrounding the genre expectations and thereby dismantling them. In Mark's 'hobby' of collecting rooms at Levender Falls Lang introduces another reference which is also part of the Gothic tradition: Bluebeard, his murdered wives, and the one forbidden locked room of his castle. So, too, the seventh of Mark's rooms is forbidden to his visitors, and to his new wife. It becomes necessary, then, for Celia to gain entry to the room, to discover its contents and thereby the contents locked away in Mark's mind and the reasons for his contradictory behaviour towards her. What she finds there is a replica of her own room, which had formerly belonged to Mark's late wife Eleanor, and therefore it must be anticipating her own death. Unlike most Gothic heroines however, Celia is not an innocent player in this *mise-en-scène* of murderous desire. She too is touched by the passion of death – indeed she and Mark meet and fall in love overlooking a scene of passion and death as two men fight over a woman in a Mexican square.

On the one hand, as both Reynold Humphries (1988) and Stephen Jenkins (1981) have argued, Celia's story is subordinated to and in the service of the man's. On the other hand, the woman rescues the man from his neurosis, itself caused by his feelings for a woman. The film abandons its Gothic narrative and resolves its characters' *noir* obsession with death; or almost, for it playfully concludes with another reference to *Rebecca* as the vengeful Miss Robey sets fire to the seventh room, and now it is Mark who rescues Celia.

Kiss Me Deadly (USA 1955 *p.c* – Parklane Pictures; *d* – Robert Aldrich; sd b/w)

Kiss Me Deadly was made comparatively late in the *noir* cycle and represents its most extreme and psychotic vision. Unlike some earlier films, the *noir* world of *Kiss Me Deadly* is not a substratum of society into which the protagonist gradually and inexorably slips. Mike Hammer, a seedy private detective who specialises in providing evidence in divorce cases, is already part of that world when the film begins, and the anti-realist *noir* style is therefore present from the very first frames in the night for night shooting of the road, with its white lines emphasised almost to the point of abstraction, while the half-naked body of

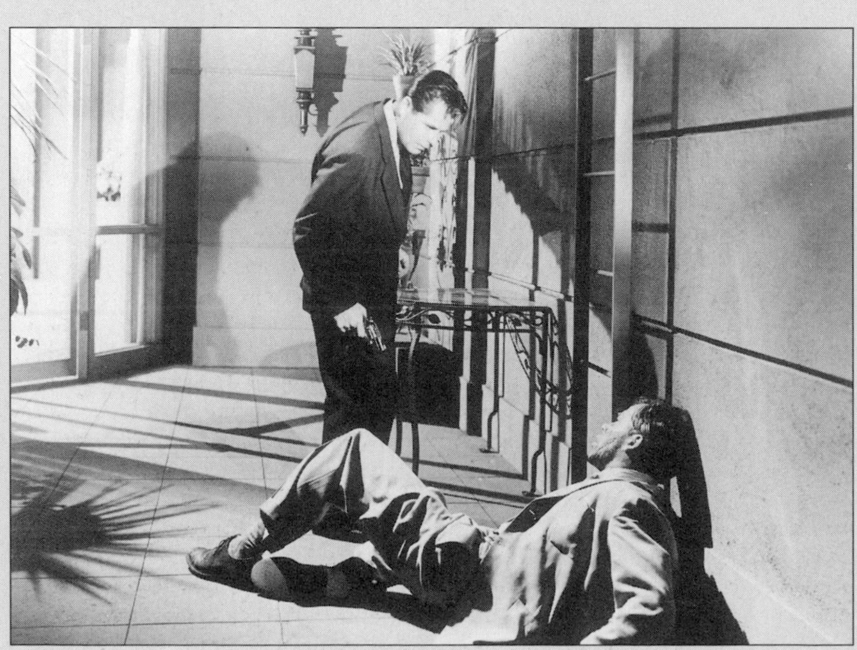

Night for night shooting and menacing shadows mark the *noir* style in *The Big Heat*

the hysterical, running woman is disturbingly segmented by the framing. This is accompanied on the soundtrack by the noise of her frenzied breathing and followed by the credits, which arrive, disconcertingly, in reverse.

Mike Hammer, unlike earlier *noir* heroes (e.g. Sam Spade), is an entirely unsympathetic character: morose, violent and stupid.

Narrative and *mise-en-scène* mark him as a man trapped by forces beyond his control. These elements, especially when linked to the extreme violence of the film, have allowed *Kiss Me Deadly* to be seen as a prime example of 'existential' *noir*. At the same time, the film is useful for discussion of the sexual dissonances of *noir*. Hammer's encounters with women, for example, are all marked by female sexual aggressiveness. Lily Carver (Gaby Rogers), who makes an explicit play for Hammer, causes world destruction at the end of the film through rampant 'female' acquisitiveness coupled with a desire to look at the forbidden. Velda (Maxine Cooper), meanwhile, is given a position of power from which she criticises both Hammer and the entire trajectory of the film (in her speech about his pursuit of 'the great whatsit' half way through the narrative). It could be argued that the occurrence of this speech criticising the male quest right at the centre of the film produces a radical disjuncture in a genre predicated upon such a quest.

Chinatown (USA 1974 *p.c* – Paramount; *d* – Roman Polanski; sd col.)

Made at a time when Hollywood's staple genres were undergoing intense revision, nostalgic evocation or comic parody (see New Hollywood, p. 98) *Chinatown* has been seen by all its major commentators as a film which alludes to – and critically reworks – the conventions, the ideology and the mythology of the traditional hard-boiled detective film in a number of recent critical assessments including Cawelti (1995), Eagle (1994), Gallafent (1992) and Grist (1992).

Evocation, allusion and critical revision are apparent from the start. The credit sequence, with its black-and-white Paramount logo, its art deco graphics, and its romantic – and nostalgic – trumpet theme, clearly serves to signal past styles and conventions. But the film's first images (explicit black-and-white photos of an adulterous affair) and the film's opening scenes (shot in Panavision and Technicolor, at times accompanied by a minimal, fragmentary and atonal score and containing Jake Gittes's declarations that he is a businessman, that his motive is money and that divorce work is his 'metier') serve to highlight a series of differences – and dissonances – between the traditional and the modern. And these in turn serve to foreground a process of revision rather than nostalgia.

Many of the film's revisions centre on the figure of the private eye. Not only is he unashamedly involved in divorce work (something which as Cawelti (1995) and others point out traditional private eye figures like Philip Marlowe explicitly eschew) he is also naïve (for all his surface cynicism), inept as a hard-boiled wit and generally out of his depth, especially when he adopts the role of moral crusader. As Grist (1992) points out, from the moment he is set up by the fake Mrs Mulwray, 'he finds himself in a situation beyond his control' (Grist, 1992, p. 270). His interventions make things worse, his deductions are nearly always wrong (catastrophically so in the case of Evelyn Mulwray and her daughter) and his overestimation of his own abilities ('I won't make the same mistake twice') eventually fatal. The enigmas of the plot involve forms of sexual and political corruption and power Gittes is totally unable to anticipate.

The figures of Noah Cross and Evelyn Mulwray are central. Cross has been seen by Eagle (1994) as a descendant of the corrupt and powerful father figures characteristic of numerous 1940s *noir* films. Evelyn Mulwray meanwhile is seen as a character who not only evokes but also undermines the figure of the *noir femme fatale*. While she is at times duplicitous, her duplicity is justified both by her knowledge, and by her motives; Gittes lack of trust in her is one of the factors that leads directly to the film's tragic denouement. On both counts, commentators have seen the film as mounting a critique of patriarchal ideology.

Cross's given name – Noah – interconnects with biblical and water motifs that pervade the film. One of the film's major clues, Mulwray's glasses, is found in the pool in his garden connecting the water motif with a third strand of imagery: eyes, spectacles, eye-like shapes and optical devices. It is the mark of the care with which this and other strands of imagery are thought through that the flaw in Evelyn's eye echoes the broken tail light on Hollis's car and is in turn echoes by the nature of the gun-shot wound that kills her. Thus it could be said that visual appearances always prove to be deceptive and that this strand of imagery can be read as a pun on the term 'private eye'.

SCIENCE FICTION AND HORROR

As has often been noted, it is sometimes very difficult to distinguish between horror and science fiction. Not only that, it can at times be difficult to distinguish between horror and the crime film, and science fiction, adventure and fantasy as well. Films like *Frankenstein* (1931), *Psycho* and *Wait Until Dark* (1967), and *Star Wars*, *E.T.* (1982), *The Thing* (1982) and *The Hound of the Baskervilles* (1939) all in their own ways testify to the propensity for multiplicity and overlap among and between these genres in Hollywood. It is therefore hardly surprising that water-tight definitions of science fiction and horror – or for that matter fantasy, adventure and crime – are hard to come by. Nor is it surprising that articles and books on science fiction and horror often discuss the same or similar films. However, if there are areas and instances of hybridity and overlap, there are also areas and instances of differentiation – few would describe *Dracula* (1931) as science fiction, just as few would describe *Silent Running* (1972) or *Logan's Run* (1976) as horror films. In consequence, horror and science fiction will be treated separately.

SCIENCE FICTION

There are numerous definitions of science fiction. Some are normative and exclusive, designed to distinguish between 'good' and 'bad' science fiction or to promote a particular form or trend. This is especially true of those who commentate on written science fiction, and of those concerned to distinguish between its 'pulp' and its 'literary' forms on the one hand, and its written and filmic forms on the other. Some, like Richard Hodgens's, are more descriptive and all embracing. 'Science fiction', he writes, 'involves extrapolated or fictitious science, or fictitious use of scientific possibilities, or it may be simply fiction that takes place in the future or introduces some radical assumption about the present or the past' (Hodgens, 1959, p. 30). (This passage is cited during the course of a chapter on definitions of science fiction by Sobchack, 1988, pp. 17–63. See also Hardy, 1986, pp. ix–xv and Kuhn, 1990b.) What this means, among other things, is that in science fiction, science, fictional or otherwise, always functions as motivation for the nature of the fictional world, its inhabitants, and the events that happen within it, whether or not science itself is a topic or theme.

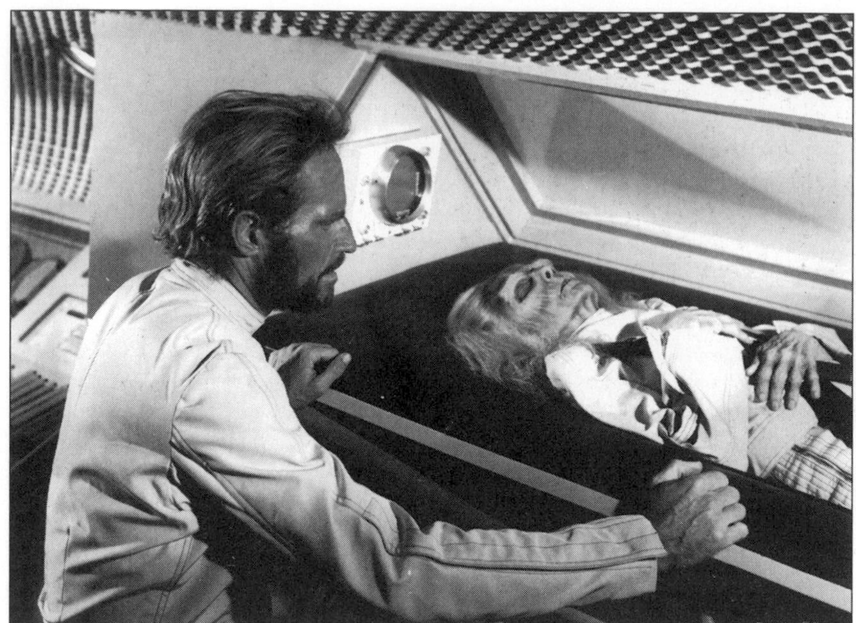

Allegorical science fiction – *Planet of the Apes*

As a term, 'science fiction' was first used in the nineteenth century, but only became fully established in the late 1920s in and around American pulp magazines like *Amazing Stories*, and in particular *Science Wonder Stories* (James, 1994, pp. 7–11). It thus largely postdated the vogue for 'invention stories', for 'tales of science', for 'tales of the future' and for the 'voyages imaginaires' which were associated in particular with Jules Verne, and which characterised the late nineteenth and early twentieth centuries (James, 1994, pp. 12–30). This vogue coincided both with a second industrial revolution, a new machine age, and a cult of and for scientific invention, and with an acceleration of the processes of colonial expansion and imperial rivalry that had already fuelled a tradition of exploration stories, adventure stories, and stories of territorial conquest. It also coincided with the invention of film, itself seen, of course, as a new scientific and technical marvel.

The earliest generic vehicles for this vogue were 'trick films' like *The X-Ray Mirror* (1899) and Méliès's *voyages imaginaires*, both of which helped to establish the bond between science fiction, special effects technology and set design that has remained a feature of the genre ever since (Barnouw, 1981; Brosnan, 1974; Hammond, 1974, pp. 114–25; Hutchison, 1987; Frazer, 1979). In 1910, the first filmed version of *Frankenstein* helped establish a link between science fiction and horror in the cinema, a link that was to be reforged in Gothic mode in the 1930s, in apocalyptic mode in the 1950s, and in body horror mode since the late 1960s. A little later, series and serials like *The Exploits of Elaine* (1914), *The Flaming Disc* (1920) and *Terror Island* (1920) helped to cement a similar link between science fiction, action and adventure. This link was maintained in the 1930s and 1940s by low-budget serials like *Flash Gordon* (1936), *Batman* (1943) and *Superman* (1948) and revived in the form of the upmarket blockbuster by George Lucas and others in the late 1970s. Finally, a tradition of large-scale speculations on the future of modern society – and allegories in science fictional form about its current condition – was established in Europe by films like *Metropolis* (1926), *La Fin du monde* (1930) and *Things to Come* (1936). It was revived in America, usually on a more modest industrial scale, during the course of the boom in science fiction in the 1950s, then again in the late 1960s and early 1970s with films like *The Day the Earth Stood Still* (1951), *On the Beach* (1959), *Planet of the Apes* (1968) and *Soylet Green* (1973). Since then it has tended to merge into the horror and action–adventure traditions, and to become ever more distopian in outlook. These are the principal forms of science fiction in the cinema. They thus incorporate most but not all of the categories of 'templates' into which science fiction as a whole is divided in Pringle, 1997, pp. 21–37. These templates are listed as 'space operas', 'planetary romances', 'future cities', 'disasters', 'alternative histories', 'prehistorical romances', 'time travels', 'alien intrusions', 'mental powers' and 'comic infernos'.

Although there exist several books which detail the history of these trends (notably Baxter, 1970; Hardy, 1986; and Brosnan, 1978), science fiction in the cinema has tended to lack a tradition of critical theory. There is a great deal of writing about individual films, periods and topics, but very little about science fiction as a genre. The major exceptions here are Sobchack's *Screening Space* (1988) (a reworking of her earlier book, *The Limits of Infinity*, 1980), the section on science fiction in Schatz (1983), and J. P. Telotte (1995).

Screening Space begins with a chapter on definitions, and moves on to consider iconography, and the genre's use of language and sound (Sobchack, 1988, pp. 64–145, 146–222). Sobchack concludes on the one hand that 'Although it lacks an informative iconography, encompasses the widest possible range of time and place, and constantly fluctuates in its visual representation of objects, the SF film still has a science fiction "look" and "feel" to its visual surfaces' (Sobchack, 1988, p. 87). This 'visual connection' between SF films

> lies in the consistent and repetitious use not of *specific* images, but of *types* of images which function in the same way from film to film to create an imaginatively realized world which is always removed from the world we know or know of. The visual surface of all SF film [sic] presents us with a confrontation between a mixture of those images to which we respond as 'alien' and those we know to be familiar. (Sobchack, 1988, p. 87; emphasis in original)

Thus 'The major visual impulse of all SF films is to pictorialize the unfamiliar, the nonexistant, the strange and totally alien – and to do so with a verisimilitude which is, at times, documentary in flavor and style' (Sobchack, 1988, p. 88).

This relationship between the strange and the familiar is, she argues, as pertinent to the soundtrack as it is to the image. Vocabulary and language are often highlighted as issues in science fiction. In *2001 – A Space Odyssey* (1968), for example, 'we are constantly made aware of how language – and, therefore, our emotions and thought patterns – have not kept up with either our technology or our experience' (Sobchack, 1988, p. 177). And sound itself, the sound of machinery, the sound of natural forces, and 'the sound of the alien' (Sobchack, 1988, p. 218), functions in films like *Five* (1951) and *The Thing* (1951) both as a generic marker, and as one of the points at which the strange and familiar meet.

Focusing almost exclusively on the 1950s, Schatz argues that 'The milieu of the science fiction is one of contested space, in which the generic oppositions are determined by certain aspects of the cultural community and by the contest itself' (Sobchack, 1988, p. 86). The contest here is the contest between 'the human community' and some kind of 'alien or monstrous force' (Sobchack, 1988, p. 86). The milieu, whose attributes are usually 'a direct extension of America's technological capabilities' may be a small town, a city, or even the world as a whole (Sobchack, 1988, p. 86). However, the distinction between the

The Thing – the strange and the familiar

human community and the alien force is by no means always straightforward. In films like *It Came from Outer Space* (1953) and *Invasion of the Body Snatchers* (1956), the distinction is blurred: 'the members of the community so utterly assimilate the group values that they are turned into automatons' (Sobchack, 1988, p. 87). It becomes hard to tell alien and human apart. In this way, within a constellation of generic concerns that includes nature, science, technology, social and communal organisation and that which is alien or other, the idea of the human, upon which the dramatisation of these concerns centrally depends, is broached as an issue.

For Telotte (1995) the issue of humanness lies at the heart of science fiction, and it is focused in particular by the figure of the robot and by its most recent avatar, the cyborg. He traces the function and the meaning of these figures in films from *Metropolis* on, placing them within both their cyclic and cultural contexts. He thus sees such 1930s films as *Mad Love* (1935), *The Bride of Frankenstein* (1935) and *Island of Lost Souls* (1933) as depicting in the then current horror mode 'violent efforts to redefine the human body as some sort of raw material' for scientific artifice and experiment (Telotte, 1995, p. 86), and hence as expressing contemporary concerns about the subjection of the human to the powers of technology and science. He sees the serials of the 1930s and 1940s as revealing 'a growing fascination with the technological and its potential for reshaping the human' (Telotte, 1995, p. 18) while at the same time drawing a line between the two through stories which 'repeatedly celebrate a human might and human feelings, particularly a human determination to stay something other than a subject, serialized thing' (Telotte, 1995, p. 100). He sees such 1950s films as *Forbidden Planet* (1956) as marking a 'newly recognized ability to duplicate anything, including the human body' (Telotte, 1995, p. 19), and such 1970s films as *Westworld* (1974), *Futureworld* (1976) and *Demon Seed* (1977) as expressing 'growing anxieties' both about 'our place' in a world in which that capacity has been enhanced by artificial intelligence (Telotte, 1995, p. 19) and about the ensuing loss of 'all distinction between the private and the private' (Telotte, 1995, p. 146). And finally, in the 1980s and 1990s, as 'science fiction ... returned to the level of popularity it enjoyed in the 1950s' (Telotte, 1995, p. 148), he sees films such as *Blade Runner* (1982), *Cherry 2000* (1986), *Total Recall* (1990) *Robocop* (1987) and *Terminator 2* (1991) repeatedly depicting the body 'as an image that is constantly being reconfigured and presented for display' (Telotte, 1995, p. 149), and repeatedly using the robotic to interrogate, to blur and often to reverse the polarities between the artificial and the human. While the trend in the 1980s was 'toward showing the human as ever more artificial', the trend in the 1990s has been 'toward rendering the artificial as ever more human' (Telotte, 1995, p. 22).

As Telotte is well aware, the boundaries of the human and the issues of difference they raise are rendered more complex by the fact that they necessarily include issues of sexuality, ethnicity and gender. Following Haraway (1985), such issues have been explored in a number of essays edited by Kuhn (1990) and by Penley *et al.* (1991). Nearly all these essays refer at least in passing to *Alien* (1979) and to *Blade Runner*, films which have become canonic touchstones not just for discussions of difference, but also for those engaged in debates about 'postmodernism' and the nature of 'postmodern' aesthetics and representation.

Aside from Bruno's (1990) essay on *Blade Runner*, an essay which touches on time, space, memory, history, pastiche, simulacra, and the definite absence of authenticity, the concluding chapter in Sobchack's book is probably the most sustained attempt to engage with some of these issues. Sobchack here argues that since the 1960s, science fiction in the US has undergone a number of fundamental changes. These changes

> go much further than a simple transformation of the nature and manner of the genre's special effects or of its representation of visible technology. Whether 'mainstream' and big-budget or 'marginal' and low-budget, the existential attitude of the contemporary SF films is different – even if its basic material remained the same. Cinematic space travel of the 1950s had an aggressive and three-dimensional thrust – whether it was narrativized as optimistic, colonial, and phallic penetration and conquest or as pessimistic and paranoid earthly and bodily invasion. Space in these films was semantically inscribed as 'deep' and time as accelerating and 'urgent'. In the SF films released between 1968 and 1977 ... space became semantically inscribed as inescapably domestic and crowded. Time lost its urgency – statically stretching forward toward an impoverished and unwelcome future worse than a bad present. (Sobchack, 1988, pp. 225–6)

With the release of *Star Wars* and *Close Encounters of the Third Kind* (both 1977), a further transformation occurred: 'technological wonder had become synonymous with domestic hope; space and time seemed to expand again' (Sobchack, 1988, p. 226). Finally, during the course of the 1980s, postmodern norms take hold:

> most of today's SF films (mainstream or marginal) construct a generic field in which space is semantically described as a surface for play and dispersal, a surface across which existence and objects kinetically dis-place and dis-play their materiality. As well, the urgent or hopeless temporality of the earlier films has given way to a new and erotic leisureliness – even in 'action-packed' films. Time has decelerated, but it is not represented as static. It is filled with curious things and dynamized by a series of concatenated events rather than linearly pressured to stream forward by the teleology of the plot. (Sobchack, 1988, pp. 227–8)

Sobchack cites films like *Liquid Sky* (1983), *Strange Invaders* (1983) and *Night of*

The dystopian world of *Blade Runner*

the Comet (1984) as examples of what she means. Whether her argument applies to films like *Aliens* and *Terminator 2* remains, perhaps, open to question.

Selected Reading

Donna Haraway, 'A manifesto for cyborgs: science, technology and socialist feminism in the 1980s', *Socialist Review* no. 80, 1985.

Annette Kuhn (ed.), *Alien Zone, Cultural Theory and Contemporary Science Fiction Cinema*, London, Verso, 1990.

Steve Neale, 'Issues of difference: *Alien* and *Blade Runner*', in James Donald (ed.), *Fantasy and Cinema*, London, BFI, 1989.

Constance Penley, Elisabeth Lyon, Lynn Spiegel and Janet Bergstrom (eds), *Close Encounters: Film Feminism, and Science Fiction*, Minneapolis, University of Minnesota Press, 1991.

Vivian Sobchack, *Screening Space: The American Science Fiction Film*, New York, Ungar, 1988.

J. P. Telotte, *Replications: A Robotic History of the Science Fiction Film*, Urbana, University of Illinois Press, 1995.

THE HORROR FILM

Introduction

Horror films had for some time comparatively little serious discussion, and only in the second half of the 1970s was the genre put on the agenda of film studies. From 1935 to the late 1940s accounts of local authority bannings of H-films and of reports on their harmful social effects, especially on children, proliferated in the British trade press. The 1950s witnessed renewed panic around the spectacular international success of a native development of the genre by the Hammer studio (see Hammer Productions, p. 84) and British film journals carried articles on the psychology of the genre. Quite distinct was the French response; during the 1950s and 1960s French journals located the genre within the category of the *fantastique* and made links with surrealism, as well as investigating the new British contribution largely ignored at home. Then in the late 1960s two books appeared by Carlos Clarens and Ivan Butler arguing for the horror film as art, pointing to the long literary tradition of 'the art of terror', and chronicling a history of the genre in the cinema. These groundbreaking contributions were followed in the early 1970s by a spate of books on both sides of the Atlantic devoted to the monsters and stars of the horror film, offering historical and psychological studies. Anglo-Saxon journals in the meantime devoted space to 'special effects' and returned again to the question of social/psychological significance of the 1970s boom in horror with violence, frequently against women. In the late 1970s/early 1980s feminists mounted public protest at the perpetuation of a widespread cultural misogyny by such films.

The titles of the 1970s horror film books reveal the emergence of a cultist knowledge stored up over the decades by the closet horror film addict. Robin Wood has commented on this characteristic:

> The horror film has consistently been one of the most popular and, at the same time, the most disreputable of Hollywood genres. The popularity itself has a peculiar characteristic that sets the horror film apart from other genres: it is restricted to aficionados and complemented by total rejection, people tending to go to horror films either obsessively or not at all. They are dismissed with contempt by the majority of reviewer–critics, or simply ignored. (Wood, 1979, p. 13)

This attribute of the horror film's popularity is further illustrated by the number of specialist journals devoted to its different aspects – *Midi–Minuit Fantastique*, *Twilight*, *Cinefantastique* (US), *The Horror Élite*, *L'Écran Fantastique*, *Vampyr*, *Little Shoppe of Horrors*, etc. All this attests to the special relationship of the horror film with its 'aficionados' which early on became the centre of critical attention and arguably inhibited theoretical elaboration of the genre. Frequently the form is identified by industry

Not inviting critical acclaim – *Creature from the Black Lagoon*

and critics alike as aimed at the 'youth market' or 'adolescents of whatever age' (see Evans, 1973; Kapsis, 1982; Wood, 1979).

However the relegation of the horror film was not solely a result of critical disdain for its supposed audience. Other factors arose from its mixed heritage and development in a wide range of different forms and cultures, which appear to defy coherent categorisation. Historical approaches demonstrate a heterogeneity of inputs and developments rather than the integrated evolution of generic tradition attributed to the western or gangster film – e.g. Universal's Gothic horror films of the 1930s; German Expressionism; 1950s science fiction monster movies; Hammer horror in the UK; Corman's Poe cycle; the onset of the psychological thriller with *Psycho* (1960), all cited in T. J. Ross's introduction to *Focus on the Horror Film* (1972). A tension remains between older European traditions and Hollywood, producing the problem of relating the forms which developed in the European art cinema in terms of the *fantastique* or supernatural (see Clarens, 1968) and the formation of a popular Hollywood genre. As with melodrama, the origins of the horror film looked back to European literary traditions – the Victorian Gothic novel for instance – and a central strand of the genre has retained its mythical European location, 'Transylvania'. This heterogeneity is increased by the input of two European movements, German Expressionism (see Eisner, 1969), and surrealism, the former often cited as indispensable to the 'horror style' of Hollywood, the latter arguably more influential on European developments in the work of, for instance, Franju or Dreyer, or 'Europeanised' directors in Hollywood such as Polanski. Some critics attempt to get round this impasse by defining the horror film in terms of its aesthetic effect – its intention to horrify. Andrew Tudor (1974) argues, for instance, that the heritage from German Expressionism was important because 'the style itself is capable of infecting almost any subject matter with its eerie tone … the sense of mystery, of lurkers in the shadows is the constant factor' (Tudor, 1974, p. 208). However, the mechanics of the horror movie did not provide the material for the elaboration of the existential/moral dramas central to early attempts to regain classic Hollywood for serious critical consideration. For example, both Andrew Tudor, who writes mainly about Gothic horror, and Brian Murphy, who deals with 1950s science fiction monster movies, agree that the genre offers a 'never-never land' governed by absolutely inflexible laws:

> men turn into werewolves only but always on nights of the full moon; vampires always dislike garlic, cast no reflection in mirrors, and can be destroyed only by having their hearts pierced with a wooden stake; and it is the nature of Frankenstein's monster that he can never be destroyed … horror's never-never land is bearable because it is so entirely rational.
> (Murphy, 1972, p. 34)

The Gothic mode in particular, with its self-referentiality, refused elaboration in more social terms. Thus several commentators have argued (Ross, 1972; Tudor, 1974) that of all the genres the horror film shows least connection with American history, thereby cutting it off from a major source of legitimation. This, added to the rigid simplicity of the horror film's conventions, deprives it of the resonances that inform and deepen, for example, the western or gangster film (Tudor, 1974). As a result, and compounding the problem, the directors and stars of the horror movie have generally been unable to escape the pejorative implications of cultism and failed to win acclaim as *auteurs* of the cinema.

The chief route to cultural legitimation,

therefore, has been through popular anthropological or Freudian/Jungian reference, which assumes 'inside us a constant, ever-present yearning for the fantastic, for the darkly mysterious, for the choked terror of the dark' (Clarens, 1968, p. 9). As the capacity of religion and its equivalents to fill this need receded with the advance of rationalism and technology in the nineteenth century, the simultaneous discovery of the unconscious and the cinema released a new source of imagery for 'rendering unto film ... the immanent fears of mankind: damnation, demonic possession, old age, death, in brief the nightside of life' (Clarens, 1968, p. 13; Butler, 1970, pp. 15–16). For Clarens this symbolic approach to the horror movie provides clear, normative boundaries. Thus *Psycho* and its imitators are rejected because, 'in Jungian fashion, I feel more compelled to single out and explore the visionary than the psychological' (Clarens, 1968, p. 13). Similarly he excludes much European work because it uses horror as a means rather than as an end in itself. This emphasis leads him to speculate that the horror movie declines in the late 1960s when horror ceases to be clothed in mythic forms. Other critics have turned to the notion of aesthetic affect as a source of evaluation. So, for example, distinctions are drawn between the horror produced by suggestion – the terror of the unimaginable – and the *guignol* effects of things seen. The former is often associated with the European tradition, or the New (and Europeanised) Hollywood of Polanski and others, while the latter is identified as the Hollywood Gothic or more recent 'splatter' movies:

> Sublime terror rests in the unseen – the Ultimate Horror. Things seen, fully described, explained, and laid to rest in the last reel or paragraph are mere horrors, the weakest of which are the merest revulsions over bloodshed and dismemberment ... (Rockett, 1982, p. 132).

Ivan Butler identifies the promise of 'too much' – the production of expectations that cannot possibly be rendered in visual terms – as a major aesthetic problem of the horror film, and dissociates his claims for the genre as art from any tendency towards 'beastliness for its own sake'. These attempts to establish both the boundaries of the genre and a basis for its evaluation have not gone unchallenged. David Pirie's book (1973), largely about the horror films produced in the 1950s and 1960s by the English production company Hammer, argues that the aesthetics of Gothic horror are based on the act of showing rather than on suggestion. And in a more recent study Charles Derry (1977) has charted not only the emergence of three distinct sub-genres in the decades following *Psycho* (1960), but has traced their historical predecessors in the 'classic' horror movie and other genres. From this preliminary investigation of critical approaches to the horror movie a broad distinction emerges between those seeking predominantly psycho-sociological explanation of the genre – what it represents for its audiences – and those attempting to analyse the aesthetic affects offered to the audience by the play of the genre's conventions.

... 'the normal aspect of nature that turns abnormal' ... *The Birds*

Psycho-sociological explanation

The problem facing all such accounts is to explain the meaning of the monster, or of the threat that produces the horror. 'Normality' is our everyday commonsense world – in more recent interpretations, the world of the dominant ideology, sanctioned by the established authorities. As suggested above, approaches to this problem via the notion of reflection have been thwarted by the horror film's lack of historical or social context, although where the genre borders on science fiction, political readings become possible. The outcropping of mutant monsters in the horror/science fiction films of the 1950s are frequently understood as reflecting a 'doom-centred, eschatological fear' provoked by cold-war politics and the nuclear deterrent, which yet relied on the scientist and 'co-operation with the military' for protection (see Murphy, 1972, pp. 38–9). Ernest Larsen (1977) argues in similar vein that those horror films which take up aspects of the disaster movie – for instance *Alien* (1979) and *Dawn of the Dead* (1978) – 'advance ... the notion that modern technology is so overwhelming that it tends to obliterate any possibility of its liberatory use ... science has, as the handmaiden of capitalism, created an uncontrolled monster' (Larsen, 1977, p. 30).

Such readings suggest that traditional sources of horror in the unknown or the supernatural are less potent to the post-Second World War western audience than the horrors that society has already perpetuated and seems in some scenarios likely to exceed – horrors often referred to as the 'American nightmare'. Such a premiss provides the basis for at least two of Charles Derry's (1977) sub-generic categories for the modern horror film, though, in his account, the forms they take derive from cinematic history. Thus he distinguishes first, 'the horror of personality', inaugurated by *Psycho*, where the horror, rather than projected in a monster and so distanced and externalised, is now seen to be 'man' himself. Such a source of horror requires not supernatural or pseudo-scientific but psychological explanation, and represents a response to the escalation of violence, mass killings and the Kennedy assassination of the early 1960s. The *Dr Jekyll and Mr Hyde* series, Hitchcock's 1940s psychological thrillers, and *film noir* have all contributed to the generic realisation of this popular obsession. The second sub-genre Derry labels 'the horror of Armageddon', which in continuity with the 1950s science fiction mutant monster cycle, and exemplified by *The Birds* (1963), deals with a 'normal aspect of nature that turns abnormal', resulting in 'a struggle that is obviously ultimate, mythical and soul-rending' (Derry, 1972, p. 50). Such films Derry sees as representing a 'modern, cataclysmic corner of our everyday fears' traceable to anxiety about the spread of totalitarian, automaton-like political regimes and the threat of nuclear warfare. Their narratives are articulated in three major themes, proliferation, besiegement and death, the first and the last of which serve to demarcate this cycle from another closely related one, the disaster movie. Derry's final category is 'the horror of the demonic', which reverts to the presence of evil forces as a time-honoured explanation of the horror of the world, thereby suggest-

Dawn of the Dead – 'science has . . . created an uncontrolled monster'

ing the possibility of a moral order in the wings. While Derry's cataloguing of the conventions and strategies of these sub-genres and his sensitivity to cinematic and generic traditions illuminate the development of the horror movie, his appeal to eruptions of violence in society to explain its existence tends to assume a relationship between films and society in which the former directly reflect the latter rather than mediating or representing it.

The notion of the 'nightmare' opens up a different and more common approach to understanding the horror film through popular Freudianism and anthropology. Concepts of the unconscious, of repression, of the cinema as an analogy for dreaming, displace the literalism of the 'reflection' thesis. With varying degrees of sophistication they are used to explain the monster as that which must be excluded, or repressed, so that the western drive towards technological progress and world domination can proceed. According to this view, the threat is neither external to society, nor to the cinema. Rather the horror movie represents a medium in which the underside of the 'normal' world makes its appearance in a play of fantasy and ritual. Notions of the primordial, the tribal, figure centrally in this scenario, and sexuality is a key component. Depending on the politics of the writer this perspective leads to a view of the horror film as adaptive (Evans, 1973), symptomatic (Kennedy, 1982; Snyder, 1982), or potentially progressive (Williams, 1980/81; Wood, 1979). Walter Evans, for example, works on the commonly attributed youth of the audience for horror to advance the view that the Gothic horror film's appeal is to 'those masses in American film and TV audiences who struggle with the most universal and horrible of personal trials: the sexual traumas of adolescence'. In a later account he argues that monster movies 'respond to a deep cultural need largely ignored in Western society . . . the need for rituals of initiation' (Evans, 1975, pp. 124–5).

Harlan Kennedy, on the other hand, uses the terminology of the 'unconscious' and 'id' to explain the recent resurgence of werewolf movies in terms of atavistic throwbacks manifested in political behaviour. Watergate and the facts and imagery of Vietnam which are now beginning to receive popular circulation, the guilty conflation of the Vietcong abroad and the American Indians at home, the 'wolf-like features of Richard Nixon', all point in the American cinema of the 1980s to an obsession with the horror of the split personality.

The impulse displayed here to explain the modern horror film in terms of a specifically American crisis of conscience is characteristic of many recent accounts of the genre. Rather than political traumas, many writers focus on the American 'way of life' as symptomatic of the distortions and repressions consequent on the development of American capitalism. Consumerism is identified as a prime symptom, behind which stands middle-class life, or the family and patriarchal social relations as sources of horror – for example *Night of the Living Dead* (1968), *The Hills Have Eyes* (1977), *Communion* (1976), *Martin* (1976). Stephen Snyder (1982), for example, argues in relation to *The Shining* (1980), *The Texas Chainsaw Massacre* (1974), *Burnt Offerings* (1976) and *Halloween* (1978) that 'the notion of . . . (middle-class) life as tantamount to the world of horror has been mushrooming'. This location of horror in the home is symptomatic of a 'network of anxieties . . . often realised in terms of the troubling insatiateness which underlies the structure of American family life' (Snyder, 1982, p. 4). Rather than a 'Watergate syndrome', Snyder identifies in the American 'collective psyche' a 'leisure culture syndrome' (Snyder, 1982, p. 5), in which 'traditional masculine values of conquest coupled to a mindless consumerism', threaten to unhinge 'our sanity' (Snyder, 1982, p. 4). Tony Williams (1980/81) takes this argument further, seeing the family as a key institution for the production of individuals in the social roles required for the perpetuation of the – patriarchal – state and therefore itself an instrument of repression and supported by other apparatuses of oppression, the church, the police, etc. The source of horror, then, is not so much in the family's economic role but in the monstrous reactions which inevitably erupt against its repressiveness when fantasy attempts to obliterate what cannot be changed by political means. In the terms of William's argument, the horrors of Vietnam are not perpetrated by werewolf-like authorities. Vietnam simply provides the opportunity for a re-enactment of the monstrous fantasies engendered within the heart of the repressive patriarchal family.

Robin Wood: the return of the repressed

The most sustained discussion of the horror film in such terms has been provided by Robin Wood in his introduction to a booklet, *American Nightmare* produced to

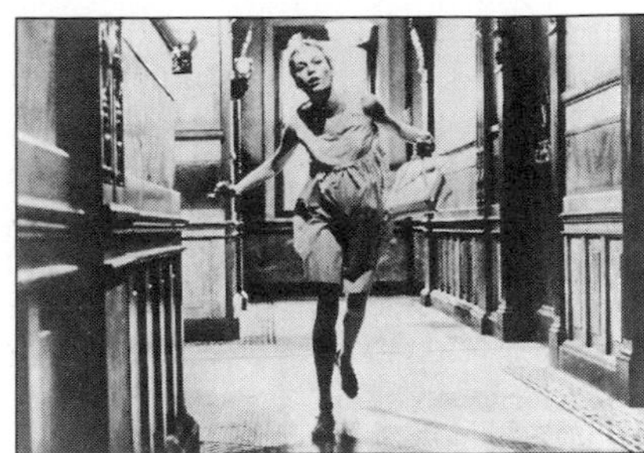

Pregnant with suspense and the supernatural – Polanski's *Rosemary's Baby*

accompany a season of horror films at the Toronto Festival of Festivals (1979). Wood attempts to provide a teleological account of the post-*Psycho* American horror film as the appropriation and reworking of European traditions in popular cultural forms relating to the American way of life. Wood's analytical apparatus, drawing on Marcusean Freud, combines the notion of ideology as a form of social conditioning with a view of the unconscious as the receptacle of energies repressed by the patriarchal family. Citing Gad Horowitz's distinction between basic and surplus repression, Wood argues that 'surplus repression' in western civilisation occurs in the production of individuals conditioned to be 'monogamous, heterosexual, bourgeois, patriarchal capitalists' (Wood, 1979, p. 8). What is repressed is sexuality, in its fullest, polymorphous sense, in the interests of producing narrowly defined gender roles, and the strictly functional deployment of the individual's creative energy. The tensions consequent on such repression and the threatened return of the repressed are siphoned off 'through the projection onto the Other of what is repressed within the Self, in order that it can be discredited, disowned, and if possible, annihilated' (Wood, 1979, p. 9). Exploiting the analogy of cinema and dream, and its degraded status as escapist entertainment, the horror movie is able to escape both inner and outer censor to explore in the figure of the monster – a stand-in for 'the Other' – the nature of the sexual energies repressed and denied:

> One might say that the true subject of the horror genre is the struggle for recognition of all that our civilisation represses and oppresses: its re-emergence dramatised, as our nightmares, as an object of horror, a matter for terror, the 'happy ending' (when it exists) typically signifying the restoration of repression. (Wood, 1979, p. 10)

Significant here is not escape from the real world, but what is escaped into. The distance from the 'reality' evoked by fantasy makes radical criticism of that world possible. In fact the centre of energy in the horror film, as most commentators point out, is the monster: 'the definition of normality in horror films is in general boringly constant'. It is rare for the monster not to be treated sympathetically, for, 'central to the effect and fascination of horror films is their fulfillment of our nightmare wish to smash the norms that oppress us' (Wood, 1979, p. 27). From this basis Wood goes on to deal with the American form's development. While normality has always, in the horror film, been represented by the 'heterosexual, monogamous couple, the family, and the social institutions (police, church, armed forces) that support them' (Wood, 1979, p. 26), and often defined in terms of dominant American stereotypes, even when the action takes place in Europe, the monster and its associates were, in the early period of Gothic horror, conceived as foreign. Wood argues that this represents for the early horror film a mechanism of 'disavowal' while at the same time allowing horror to be located in a 'country of the mind'. The various phases of the horror film – e.g. the Val Lewton cycle of the 1940s, the extra-terrestrial invaders or mutant monster of the 1950s – can, then, be seen as 'the process whereby horror becomes associated with its true milieu, the family ... reflected in its steady geographical progress towards America' (Wood, 1979, p. 29). In post-*Psycho* movies the *doppelgänger* is not a foreign phenomenon but integral to the psychic life of the American family.

Wood argues for the potential progressiveness of the horror film in the focus of its destructiveness and its ambivalence toward the 'monsters' who destroy.

> While by definition the monster is related to evil ... horror films ... are progressive precisely to the degree that they refuse to be satisfied with this simple designation – to the degree that, whether explicitly or implicitly, consciously or unconsciously, they modify, question, challenge, seek to invert it. (Wood, 1979, p. 23)

In Wood's view this ambivalence offers the possibility of a challenge to 'the highly specific world of patriarchal capitalism' (Wood, 1979, p. 23). The pleasures such films offer their makers and audiences is the release of repressed energies and the destruction of those social norms which demand the repression in the first place. Opposed to this progressive, or 'apocalyptic' strand in the horror films is the 'reactionary wing', defined in its designation of the monster as nothing but evil. This strand confuses repressed and aberrant sexuality with sexuality itself, its ideological project being the reinstatement of repression in the name of normality, supported by a Hollywood version of Christianity. Such films serve the dominant ideology by allowing some release of repressed energies only to rename them evil and cynically justify their further repression.

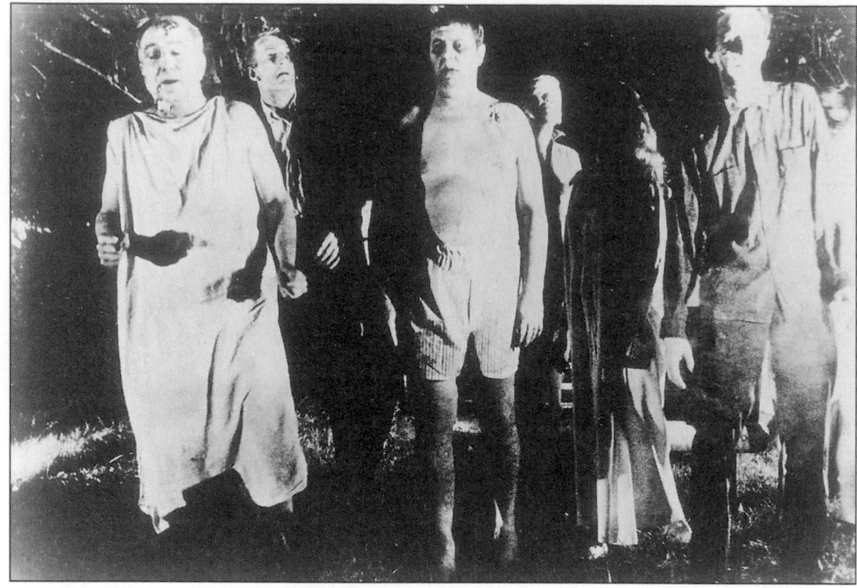

Night of the Living Dead – bringing it all back home

Horror as affect

The approaches discussed above share a belief in the possibility of understanding the horror film in terms of historically and culturally specific meanings already in circulation in the society which has produced them. Notions derived from anthropology and psychoanalysis such as the 'collective unconscious', 'repression', the 'id', the 'interpretation of dreams' support readings of the hermetic, self-referential fantasy world of the horror film as the working through in 'irrational' imagery of material lodged in the unconscious, material not to be found in the epics of history or social contemporary reality which provide the more intellectually acceptable explanations of the western or the gangster film. The advent of 'personal politics' in the 1970s, and the socio-historical critiques of the family and sexuality provide a theoretical, if controversial, grounding to claims for the social relevance of the horror film.

However, the horror film has also been approached in terms of what it does to the audience, rather than what it represents. The significance of the horror film is not so much in the content released through its symbolic imagery – primitive fears, repressed energies, etc. – but the way it plays on insecurities as to the basis and adequacy of rational explanation. The audience goes to horror films not only to see things to be feared, or that have been repressed, but to experience fear, to explore the outer limits of knowledge and of cinematic represention itself.

W. H. Rockett (1982) argues that the horror film has to manoeuvre delicately between the contradictory needs of the aesthetic territory it inhabits. In an epistemological and cultural universe dominated by an Aristotelian logic the overriding compulsion of representation is to produce order by demonstration, showing an action's origins, development and ultimate consequences. The horror film attains the dimensions of terror to the extent that it can resist the Aristotelian compulsion to 'open the door, and show what is behind it'.

'Terror relies on convincing the audience of the fallibility of the logic we assume governs the world. To achieve this the horror film makes the audience oscillate between terror (of uncertainty), horror and revulsion (both at things ultimately glimpsed or shown) and finally relief. It can achieve this through a play with off-screen space, or with space hidden in the frame, "to emphasise what we do not see", or by breaking not simply the "fixed laws of Nature" but one or more of the laws of the horror film ... which the "fixed laws" aficionados of the genre have come to believe in with a almost religious fervour' (Rockett, 1982, p. 133). Moreover, although the horror film may be compelled to open the door, to show the audience something of what is behind, the oscillation between the reassurance of suspended disbelief and the experience of terror is maintained by the door being closed again, to produce further uncertainty. Finally, Aristotelian closure may be denied if the monster's destruction is left in question. However Rockett's description of this fine balance rests on a judgement of value: those horror films which go for quick sensation and show all and more fall victim to the Aristotelian logic and fail to reach the sublimity of terror. Terror depends, however, on the existence of the ground rules which are to be questioned; implicitly it also depends on the Aristotelian gullibility or debased tastes of the audience that sustains them.

The post-structuralist approach

Stephen Neale in his monograph on genre (1980) attempts to elucidate the horror film's form and address in relation to its circulation in critical discourse – an attempt, in other words, to account for all the work described so far. A major distinction between his approach and those discussed above is the place he finds for so-called anti-realist, anti-Aristotelian or 'progressive' elements within the embrace of classic narrative cinema, where they play their part in the contradictory functioning of the dominant ideology. Neale's position derives from the link Lacanian psychoanalysis makes between the Oedipal scenario consequent on the child's confrontation with sexual difference and 'castration', and the functioning of language. This link knits together three dimensions of human experience. First, desire is haunted by lack, depends on it for its existence and continuation and in the Freudian/Lacanian scenario is primarily about repossessing the plenitude and unity experienced in infancy with the mother. Second, structural linguistics state that in language there are no positive terms; meaning arises in the gap, the difference, between terms. Third, while castration inaugurates desire and compels the child to separate from the mother and enter the symbolic order, achieving individual identity in language, language itself institutes in the subject a splitting of identity. 'I' achieves its meaning only in relation to an implied 'you'. The patriarchal subject then is one driven to construct an illusory identity, unity, coherence on a foundation of lack, difference, separation. In this context the unconscious is not so much a receptacle for repressed contents which in a liberated society would emerge comfortably into the light of day (see Wood, 1979, and Williams, 1980), but a consequence of the human subject's endeavour to construct meaning out of difference, for any attempt to possess the object of desire through coherent, full representation also calls into play its opposite, its founding lack.

According to this perspective the activity of representation is a fetishistic process, which seeks to disavow lack by instituting presence elsewhere (e.g. in the cinema the fetishisation of the star's hair or clothing, producing a perfection which obscures the 'castration' threat of female sexuality). However, as Neale argues, the fetishistic substitute implicitly acknowledges its instituting lack, involving a play on the motif of presence/absence and a 'splitting of belief' in the subject – 'I know very well this is so, and yet . . .' From the psychoanalytic perspective, then, the pleasures and fascinations of classic narrative cinema arise out of its capacity to play on these contradictions – especially as they centre on sexual difference – while at the same time it preserves the integrity of subjective identity outside the contradictions that found it. The fetishism of cinematic representation takes place on three interrelated levels. First, following Christian Metz, Neale argues that the fascination of the cinematic image itself derives from its play of presence and absence – we know that the events and figures we watch on the screen are not really there, yet we believe we grasp them as though in some way they were more real than life. Second, the function of classic narrative structure is to command 'the viewer's adherence to a coherent and homogeneous diegesis'. In other words the fetishism of fiction has to be supported by the production of the conditions in which the audience will accept the make-believe, will be willing to suspend disbelief, accept the fiction as a 'real world', and so support the reality–effect of classic Hollywood. Finally, further and specific 'regimes of credence' – conventions of verisimilitude – are produced by the different genres.

In this context Neale sees the horror film as bound up with fetishism in an overdetermined way. For a start, in the body of the monster it addresses directly the question of sexual difference and castration. But also, in relation to the foregoing discussion, its fetishistic fictionality is trebled in that it deals in areas predefined as pertaining to imagination, fantasy, subjectivity. Genres like the gangster, war film or western, focusing on questions of law/disorder, derive their regimes of credence from discourses and codes defined as 'non-fiction' e.g. newspaper reporting, sociology, historical documentation. The horror film, on the other hand, dramatises questions about the definition of the 'human' and the 'natural' against the concept of the 'unnatural/supernatural'. The order it refers to is metaphysical, its narrative disequilibrium produced in the disjunction between the 'real' world and the 'supernatural'. The narrative quest of the horror film then is to find that discourse capable of solving this disjunction, explaining events (Neale, 1980, p. 22). Given that the discourses mobilised by the horror film are 'characterised as representing not factual reality but poetic or psychological realities' the 'kinds of legitimating documents and references employed . . . will tend to be ancient texts, parapsychological treatises, myths, folklore, religion' (Neale, 1980, p. 37).

Clearly the maintenance of verisimilitude, the 'splitting of belief' in the audience, is harder for fantasy genres like the horror film, hence the requirement for 'rigorous conventionalisation' noted by some of its critics, and its cultural marginalisation as fodder for adolescents and children. At the same time the cinematic work involved in making credible an avowedly fictional world produces the particular brand of fetishistic fascination – with special effects and so on – exhibited by the cinephilia of the aficionados. Accepting that the neuralgic point of narrative in the horror film is sexual difference, and that its successful suspension of disbelief produces affects – horror, anxiety, fear – 'linked to the problematic of castration' (Neale, 1980, p. 39), the horror film, Neale argues, engages the spectator directly in the play of fetishism. This is taken further in the materialisation of the monster. While

The Texas Chainsaw Massacre – is the monster always male?

the fascination with the monster brings the spectator close to the source and terror of desire and close to the truth of his condition as a patriarchal subject, the fetishistic structure of cinematic narrative ensures that the monster also acts as a displacement of this lack:

> Hence the monster may represent the lack, but precisely by doing so it in fact functions to fill the lack with its own presence, thus coming to function as a fetish simultaneously representing and disavowing the problems of sexual difference at stake. (Neale, 1980, p. 44)

This happens in two ways. First, in the narrative search for the means of controlling the 'play of the monster's appearance/disappearance', in order to contain the lack in place of which the monster appears. Second, in the emphasis the horror film puts on the 'appearance' of the monster, the special effects used both to make the monster terrifying and convincing and to highlight the key moments of its first appearance or birth, and of its destruction. From this investment in the fetishistic moment Neale concludes, against the 'horror by suggestion' critics, that it is essential for the genre that the monster is physically materialised.

Neale elaborates further the significance of the monster in relation to sexual difference. The monster is defined as monstrous in relation to notions of masculinity and feminity. However these categories intersect with and are complicated by definitions of the 'monstrous' versus the 'human'. On the one hand, the notion of the 'human' does not recognise sexual difference, producing homogeneity in place of heterogeneity. On the other, the monster is rarely without human traits. Its heterogeneity, then, could be seen as a displaced instance of the sexual difference for which it acts as a fetish: the monster's consequently double heterogeneity 'functions to disturb the boundaries of sexual identity and difference' (Neale, 1980, p. 61). Nevertheless, Neale goes on to speculate, since the monster is frequently given male gender and woman is his victim, his desire for the woman – whether lustful or homicidal could be understood as representing the horror that female sexuality produces for the male subject in the castration scenario.

In Stephen Neale's account, then, the violence and sexual ambiguity of the monster, whether Gothic creature or deranged psychotic, the hovering of the horror film around the abnormal and taboo, far from representing a release of the repressed and a challenge to the patriarchal status quo, simply offers a fetishistic feast in acknowledgement and perpetuation of the perversity on which patriarchy is founded, the simultaneous fascination with and, disavowal of, female sexuality: 'The horror film is concerned ... not only with curiosity, knowledge and belief, but also, and crucially, with their transgressive and "forbidden" forms.' From this, he argues, arises the dominance of religious, or religio-scientific forms of explanation within the horror film, and of critical accounts of the genre 'rooted in mysticism and other forms of irrationalism' (Neale, 1980, p. 45).

Feminism and the horror film

Several commentators on the horror film have pointed out the role of woman as victim – a role treated with increasing viciousness as the sexual violence of recent cycles increases. Stephen Neale's account of the monster from a Lacanian psychoanalytic perspective suggests that its association with sexual difference and the castration scenario makes it a representation of female sexuality itself. However, the interpretative consequences of this argument have been challenged in Linda Williams' (1983) reintroduction of the question of the woman's 'look' into psychoanalytic accounts of the mechanisms of classic narrative structure. Accepting the notion of the voyeuristic nature of cinematic pleasure in which the woman's look is denied in order to secure the safe identification of a male audience with the male hero's gaze at the objectified female, and accepting also that the horror film makes a special play with the relations of looking, knowledge and desire, Linda Williams offers a different system of interpretation, submitting the Lacanian scenario to the empirical realities of female sexuality: women are not castrated, a fact that a symbolic system found on such a notion has to negotiate somehow.

The interest of the horror film for Linda Williams is that it provides an exception to the general denial of the woman's look in the cinema, for a central moment of these films is the gaze of the heroine at the monster. On one level, the woman is punished for daring to look; instead of the mastery that is conferred on the male gaze the act of her looking paralyses the woman and enables the monster to master the looker. However, Williams goes on to question the meaning of the woman's look, and of her relation to the monster, arguing that the power of the monster lies not in its castration, but in its sexual difference from the 'normal male':

> In this difference he is remarkably like the woman in the eyes of the traumatised male: a biological freak with impossible and threatening appetites that suggest a frightening potency precisely where the normal male would perceive a lack. (Williams, 1983, p. 87)

To ground this rereading of sexual difference, Williams interrogates the notion of woman as a 'castrated version of the man'. Drawing on Susan Lurie's 'Pornography and the Dread of Woman' (1980), she argues that the mother's traumatic representation of sexual difference to the male child lies in her not being castrated: she does not possess a penis, yet is not mutilated, thus suggesting a totally other, non-phallic potency. Similarly 'the monster is not so much lacking as he is powerful in a different way' – as is, for example, the vampire. This then leads Williams to argue that the woman's look at the monster

> is more than simply a punishment for looking, or a narcissistic fascination with the distortion of her own image in the mirror that patriarchy holds up to her; it is also a recognition of their similar status, as potent threats to a vulnerable male power. (Williams, 1983, p. 90)

This rereading of the castration scenario then enables Williams to account for several features of the classic horror film: the 'vindictive destruction of the monster', the frequent sympathy of the female characters for the plight of the monster, their similar constitution 'as an exhibitionist object by the desiring look of the male', the frequent weakness of the male heroes, and 'the extreme excitement and surplus danger when the monster and the woman get together' (Williams, 1993, p. 90).

This is clearly a reading against the grain of a dominant view of how female sexuality is represented, a reading made easier by the Gothic horror film's use of mythical figures. The coming of the psychological thriller in the 1960s, however, with its abandonment of mythic monsters and its self-conscious Freudianism, makes the possibilities of such subversive reading more problematic. *Peeping Tom* (1959) which along with *Psycho* (1960) inaugurated the cycle is, according to Williams, exceptional in that it offers 'a self-conscious meditation on the relations between a sadistic voyeur/subject and the exhibitionist objects he murders', for what the woman sees at the moment of confrontation is not the monster but her own reflection literally distorted in the concave mirror he holds up to her. The film marks a break in 'the history of the woman's look in the horror film' in that it constructs a heroine who refuses to recognise herself in the mirror: 'she sees it for the distortion it is and has the power to turn away, to reject the image of woman as terrified victim and monster proffered by the male artist' (Williams, 1993, p. 93). The cost of such a breakthrough, however, is a simultaneous refusal of 'the only way patriarchal cinema has of representing woman's desire': Helen can resist because she is without sexual desire herself. *Psycho*, and the cycle it inspired, including the controversial *Dressed to Kill* (1980), display no such self-consciousness about the structures they operate. These films reduce the gap between woman and monster, so eliminating that flash of sympathetic recognition which in Gothic horror suggests the 'possibility of a power located in her very difference from the male' (Williams, 1993, p. 96).

In the modern psychological thriller/horror film 'the monster who attacks, looks like and, in some sense, is a woman' and we are asked to believe 'that the woman is both victim and monster', for she is 'responsible for the horror that destroys her' (Williams, 1993, p. 93). For Williams the twenty years between *Psycho* and *Dressed to Kill* saw an intensification of this shift so that 'the identification between woman and monster becomes greater, the nature of the identification is more negatively charged and women are increasingly punished for the threatening nature of their sexuality', to the point that, in the recent spate of 'women-in-danger' exploitation films and 'video nasties', the psychopathic murderer is rarely seen: the body of the female victim is the only visible horror in the film. Subsequent approaches to the horror film may perhaps best be characterised, at least initially, with reference to a special issue of *Screen* that appeared in 1986, adorned with a graphic still from *The Evil Dead* and entitled 'Body Horror'. The articles included in the issue concentrate on the representations of bodily mutilation as these appeared in such works of the period as the zombie films of Romero, Cronenberg's *Shivers* (1976), *Rabid* (1977), and *The Brood* (1979), as well as *Last House on the Left* (1972) and *The Texas Chain Saw Massacre* (1973). The films in question are characterised by one of the contributors, Philip Brophy, in the following terms: 'The gratification of the contemporary Horror film is based upon tension, fear, anxiety, sadism and masochism – a disposition that is overall both tasteless and morbid. The pleasure of the text is, in fact, getting the shit scared out of you – and loving it; an exchange mediated by adrenalin' (Brophy, 1986, p. 5). Brophy goes on to describe American horror films of the 1970s in terms of what he calls 'horrality', a mode of textual manipulation whereby the spectator's feelings and expectations are self-consciously played upon by the film he or she is viewing. These are films that at once foreground themselves as constructions and terrorise their audiences by means of this very constructedness and self-conscious artifice. For Brophy, a film of this

Dressed to Kill – 'woman is responsible for the horror that destroys her'

kind '*knows* that you've seen it before; it *knows* that you know what is about to happen; and it knows that you know it knows you know' (Brophy, 1986, p. 5). Self-awareness and the horrific effect come together in the destruction of the body, a destruction that is shown explictly on screen. A prime example is the opening scene in *Scanners* (1981), where by the sheer power of thought a scanner blows the head of another scanner apart, a process we see in all its physical detail. In the last scene of the same film we see the transformation of Vale's body as his brother, Revok, scans him and gains power over him: 'Veins ripple up the arm, eyes turn white and pop out, hair stands on end, blood trickles from all facial cavities, heads swell and contract' (Brophy, 1986, p. 9).

For Brophy, body horror is taken to its logical limit by John Carpenter's *The Thing* (1982), the horror of which derives from the Thing's total disregard for, and ignorance of, the human body. This results in a violent and self-conscious melding of spectacular display and horror, exemplified in the transformation of a severed head into a spider-like entity, as legs extend themselves from it in real time, turning it upside down to become a mobile body of extraordinary monstrosity. As the crew watch it walk out of the room, one of them says: 'You've got to be fucking kidding!', a line that identifies the film's display as a horrific and comic transgression that affects those on-screen as it does us, the audience, and at the same time draws attention to it as a special effect, a spectacular violation of the limits of what it is to represent the human body. The humour of the scene, for Brophy a crucial characteristic of the modern horror film, has much in common with that of *The Evil Dead* (1982), being 'mostly perverse and/or tasteless' (Brophy, 1986, p. 12) and having its source in the EC comics of the 1950s. The result is a cinema of the moment, concerned neither with past nor future, existing only for immediate effect.

Brophy's article is descriptive, contenting itself with noting certain of the major features of modern horror. Barbara Creed's piece, published in the same issue, 'Horror and the Monstrous Feminine: An Imaginary Abjection', offers by contrast a theoretical reading of the horror film based on psycho analytic concepts deriving from the work of Julia Kristeva. Creed turns to Ridley Scott's film *Alien* in an attempt to clarify the issues this raises – issues of otherness and the monstrous-feminine. By 'monstrous-feminine' she refers to woman seen from the point of view of Freud's understanding of castration – as shocking, terrifying, horrific, as the site of abjection. The theoretical underpinnings for this project, to be found in Kristeva's *Powers of Horror* (1982), aim to establish the abject as a new theoretical entity beyond meaning, beyond the confines of the human (as understood within patriarchal society), but which nonetheless can be given significance within a psychoanalytic (Lacanian) understanding of the formation of the subject. Creed's purpose is to show the inescapable relevance of this to an analysis of dominant culture and the subordination of women within that culture.

Kristeva pictures the abject as a place where meaning collapses, where 'I', the sub ject, am not. The abject is thus to be identified with what threatens life, and it must, therefore, be radically excluded from the place of the living subject. The abject, in other words, is all that the subject excludes in order to be what it is, to have the identity that it does. The abject is, for Kristeva, what in Judaism is characterised as 'abomination': sexual perversion, murder, the corpse, incest and the feminine body. In effect, the abject concerns everything that figures in the archaic relation to the mother. Given this context, it is hardly surprising that Kristreva considers the ultimate in abjection to be the corpse. The body expels from itself wastes such as faeces and urine and by so doing continues to live. The corpse represents a condition in which waste has encroached upon everything; the body has become its own waste product, and the living subject is no longer the one who expels: in an ultimate reversal, it is itself the object of expulsion. Thus, the corpse – at least within the Old Testament tradition – is wholly abject. It constitutes a basic form of pollution, a body without a soul. It is this notion that Creed applies to horror films. Bodies without souls, such as vampires and zombies, and corpse-eaters such as ghouls, comprise the basic iconography of the horror film, an iconography of abjection. Creed carries this further when she argues that the major project of the horror film is the construction of the maternal figure as abject. She considers that, within our culture, central images of pollution are related to the mother, in particular, images of menstrual blood. These images of pollution are horrific, since images of this kind, of blood, pus, faeces, vomit, and so on, signify a split between two orders: the maternal authority and the law of the father. These images of waste threaten an integral and unified subject that is constructed as such within the symbolic, the world of meaning, of social order and paternal law, and, as a result, they induce loathing and disgust. At the same time, these images hark back to an archaic period when the child's relation to its mother was such that it did not experience embarrassment and shame at the emergence of its bodily wastes. Thus, images of filth and waste give rise not only to fear and loathing but also to pleasure, a perverse pleasure deriving from the archaic mother–child relation which was marked by untrammelled playing with the body and its wastes. The menstrual blood in *Carrie* is taken by Creed to give significant backing to this argument.

This approach allows Creed her fundamental point, that 'the central ideological project of the popular horror film' is 'purification of the abject' through what Kristeva calls 'a descent into the foundations of the symbolic construct' (Creed, 1986, p. 53). This means that the horror film brings about a confrontation with the abject such that the abject (the zombie, the vampire, etc.) is ejected and the boundaries of the symbolic, of the human world, are re-established. Horror films are a kind of modern defilement rite in which all that threatens the rule of order and meaning, all that is of the Other, is separated out and subordinated to the paternal law. This project is, for Creed, fundamentally reactionary, and she finds it in *Alien*, which represents 'the monstrous-feminine in terms of the maternal figure as perceived within a patriarchal ideology' (Creed, 1986, p. 56). The archaic mother, the monstrous-feminine, is present in the film as primordial abyss, manifest in the alien spacecraft, as well as in the images of blood and the all-devouring, toothed vagina. The same presence is also embodied in the monstrous figure of the alien born from the rupturing of Kane's chest, and in the *Nostromo*'s computer, Mother, whose children, born from the sleeper-pods of the spaceship at the beginning of the film, are devoured by the toothed alien during the course of the narrative. The archaic mother is not represented as such in these scenes, nor indeed does she appear at any point in the film's subsequent development. She is, however, present in the film's *mise-en-scène*, in the womb-like imagery of the alien craft, with its tunnels leading to the rows of hatching eggs, and in the body of the *Nostromo*, the mother ship. Present in the voice of the controlling computer, she is also present in the birth of the alien, who is her representative, and in its destruction of the *Nostromo*'s crew. For Creed, the archaic mother informs all things, though she is localised in none of them.

It is the underlying strategy of *Alien* to contain this pervasive alterity, this radically ungraspable and unrepresentable Other, within a structure that makes of the alien the mother's fetish. That the alien is the mother's phallus is made perfectly clear when it arises from Kane's body. However, the alien is more than a fetish:

> it is also coded as a toothed vagina, the monstrous-feminine as the cannibalistic mother. A large part of the ideological project of *Alien* is the representation of the maternal fetish object as an 'alien' or foreign shape. (Creed, 1986, p. 68)

The film finally signals the accomplishment of its phallocentric project in its presentation of Ripley's body as she undresses just before her final confrontation with the alien in the escape capsule. We have here a reassuring and pleasurable image of the 'normal' woman, the humanity of whose maternal feelings are expressed in her stroking the cat as if it were her baby. The final sequence not only disposes of the alien, but also represses 'the nightmare image of the monstrous-feminine' which has been constructed in the film 'as a sign of abjection' (Creed, 1986, p. 69). Thus, at the end of *Alien* the abject is literally expelled from the image in a restoration of the symbolic order.

The question of the body is again addressed in psychoanalytic terms by Carol Clover in her influential (1992) book. Her concern is predominantly with the slasher movies of the 1970s, such as *The Texas Chain Saw Massacre* (1974) and *Halloween* (1978), films that lead her to reconsider certain of the assumptions she sees as basic to much recent academic and theoretical writing about mainstream Hollywood. Her argument begins from Laura Mulvey's well-known contention that the cinematic gaze is structured by male or masculine perceptions, something that is made clear when the object of the gaze is a woman. For Clover, Mulvey's position amounts to saying that '[t]he cinematic apparatus ... has two ways of looking at a woman, both organised around defending against her "castration" and both of which, therefore, presuppose a male (or masculine) gazer: a sadistic–voyeuristic look, whereby the gazer salves his pleasure at female lack by seeing the woman punished, and a fetishistic–scopophilic look, whereby the gazer salves his unpleasure by fetishizing the female body in whole or in part' (Clover, 1992, p. 8). However, Mulvey's account by no means exhausts the pattern of identification and subject position put into play by slasher films. Brian De Palma's *Carrie* is a case in point: though the camera positioning invites us to take up the perspective of Carrie's tormentors, the overall development of the film is such that by the end the viewpoint that prevails is Carrie's own. Our involvement with her sufferings earlier in the film is essential to our coming to sympathise with, and to understand, her revenge on her school and her final destruction of her mother. Clover's project leads her to question one of film theory's 'conventional assumptions', namely, that 'the cinematic apparatus is organized around the experience of a mastering, voyeuristic gaze' (Clover, 1992, p. 9).

This means that Clover tends to concentrate on matters of point of view and identification. For the male viewer, seeking a male character with whom to identify, there is, in her view, little to hang on to. Of the good characters in slasher films, characters such as boyfriends or schoolmates of the girls, few are developed and even those who acquire some presence in the narrative soon die. Traditional authority figures, such as policemen, fathers and sheriffs, are usually risibly incompetent, and are themselves often killed, leaving the girl, the film's protagonist, to confront the killer on her own. As for the killer, he is usually invisible or scarcely seen during the first part of the film, as in *Halloween*, and what is revealed when finally we do get to see him is not something that is likely to evoke sympathy. He is often fat, deformed, or dressed as a woman, or more extremely, as in *The Texas Chain Saw Massacre*, wearing a mask of human skin. (A frame enlargement appears on the cover of Clover's book.) The killer may even be a woman. Any male viewer of *Friday the Thirteenth I* who thinks to identify with the killer is in for a rude awakening, when he discovers in the film's final sequences that the killer is not a man at all but a middle-aged mother. In any event, the killer is either himself killed or otherwise thrust out of the narrative. No male figure of any significance survives to tell the tale.

The main character of these films is the final girl, such as Laurie in *Halloween*, and hers is the main storyline. As Clover remarks, she is intelligent and watchful, being the first to recognise that something is wrong and the only one able to deduce the extent of the threat posed by the killer. Her perspective comes close to our own understanding of the situation:

> We register her horror as she stumbles on the corpses of her friends. Her momentary paralysis in the face of death duplicates those moments of the universal nightmare experience – in which she is the undisputed 'I' – on which horror frankly trades. (Clover, 1992, pp. 44–5)

She is the slasher film's hero, and by the end our attachment to her is almost complete. This shifting of perspective from the masculine to the feminine becomes, for Clover, the aesthetic base of the slasher genre, a feature she addresses in terms of what she calls 'the play of the pronoun function'. An example of this is the opening sequence of *Halloween*, in which we view the action in the 'first person' before it is revealed to us who that first person actually is. A continuous shot shows us a murder from the killer's point of view, a point of view that a reverse-shot reveals finally to be that of a six-year-old boy, Michael Myers. In *Friday the Thirteenth I*, 'we' stalk teenagers over the course of the film, and are invited to think of 'ourselves' as male, due to glimpses of 'our' booted and gloved body, items conventionally coded as masculine. By the end, however, 'we' are revealed as female. Similar uncertainties as to sexual position inform *Dressed to Kill* and *Psycho*. This unsettling of spectatorial position is embodied particularly in the final girl. In films like *Hell Night* (1981) and *Texas Chain Saw Massacre II* the active investigating look is that of the final girl, making the killer the object of the look and herself the spectator. Though it is through the killer's eyes that we see the final girl at the beginning of the films, it is through her eyes that we see the killer, often around the middle of the film and increasingly towards the end. The gaze therefore becomes female. This would seem to reverse the priorities associated with classic Hollywood cinema: 'the female exercise of scopic control results not in her annihilation, in the manner of classic cinema, but in her triumph; indeed, her triumph *depends* on her assumption of the gaze' (Clover, 1992, p. 60). What the slasher film offers, then, is a profound variation on the classic structure; in these films, the categories of masculine and feminine, which are traditionally correlated with male and female, are unified in one and the same character, who is anatomically female and whose point of view the spectator is encouraged to share. In the killer, we find a feminine male and in the hero a masculine female. This, however, is not the whole of the character of the final

Peeping Tom – the heroine rejects the terrified victim/monster image

girl. While she can be described as masculine, she also registers as feminine in her fears and doubts. Even in her final struggle with the killer, she shifts between strength and weakness, attack and flight, fear and anger, error and effectiveness. Like her name – Laurie, Terry, Will, Marti, Ripley, and so on – she is female and androgynous. She is 'not masculine but either/or, both, ambiguous' (Clover, 1992, p. 63).

The final girl, then, appears as a figure who, for Clover, embodies a dialectic or logic of representation underpinning the aesthetic effectiveness of the slasher film. It is this approach that informs her discussion of one of the most subtle and complex of modern films, Michael Powell's *Peeping Tom* (1960), whose protagonist, Mark Lewis, is male. Her argument is that Powell is interested in Mark the assaultive gazer, the one who kills with his camera, in as much as he is the outcome of Mark the assaulted gazer, assaulted, that is, by his father, whose investigation into the physiology and psychology of fear involved filming his son's childhood in unremitting and excruciating detail. It is in this context that Clover sees Mark's suicide as the act of a tragic figure. If the film opened with a scene of pure aggression, it closes on a scene of pure helplessness, a helplessness made evident by the sound of a recorded dialogue from his childhood. As Mark dies, we hear a voice we take to be his father's, saying 'Don't be a silly boy; there's nothing to be afraid of'. After the screen darkens, we hear the voice of a small boy: 'Good night, Daddy – hold my hand.' The film is thus structured around Mark's experience of fear and pain. His assaults on women, assaults carried out by his camera, are not simply sadistic; they are inseparable from and 'animated by his own historical pain' (Clover, 1992, p. 176). In other words, *Peeping Tom* is a film crucially concerned with male lack, a characteristic it shares with the slasher films of a later period. At the end of *Peeping Tom*, Mark's suicide is accomplished in an ecstatic act that unites him with the female subjects of his earlier killings. It is an act of castration that takes place on camera and that is effected by the camera, and it unites Mark's actual assumption of the feminine position with his recognition of it. The film's enactment of the sado-masochistic dialectic thus involves at the same time a self-conscious and self-reflexive articulation of the dialectic of film and spectator.

The psychoanalytic approach to horror cinema has been challenged by Andrew Tudor (1989). The book offers a cultural history of the horror movie, and it is from this context that Tudor's objections emerge. He finds psychoanalytic accounts to be 'inordinately reductive', in as much as they presuppose the credibility of a particular outlook to which the widest possible range of cultural phenomena are to be subordinated. The terms of the theory are also the terms in which the reading is constructed, the result being that the revealed meanings are presupposed by the method of uncovering them. There is a further, related problem: the readings produced are esoteric, and are excluded by definition from the conscious understanding of any audience. As against this, Tudor proposes to study narrative structures, his intention being to distinguish three main types of narrative, each of which he derives from the analysis of a set of paired oppositions. Thus, horror narratives routinely place a 'known' world under threat from an 'unknown' of some sort, with the narrative development involving a series of moves from order to disorder and back to order. The oppositions that he tabulates are of the following kind: in line with the basic contrast between known and unknown, he places the secular everyday against the supernatural; 'normal' sexuality against 'abnormal' sexuality; social order against social disorder; culture against nature; health against disease, and so on. On the side of the known stands 'Good', while 'Bad' is subsumed under the unknown. On the basis of how these contrasts interrelate, Tudor goes on to distinguish between three types of narrative: narratives of knowledge, invasion and metamorphosis.

The knowledge narrative, exemplified by the 1931 *Frankenstein*, is based on contrasts between life and death, and normal and abnormal physical matter. The narrative turns around the way Frankenstein's scientific knowledge and expertise mediate between these contrasted elements. As a result either of Frankenstein's intent or of his 'meddling' with what is best left alone, this knowledge gives rise to that which threatens the order and security of the known, familiar world. This in turn leads on to a period of disorder and rampage, brought about by the monster, during which time attempts are made to overcome the threat, attempts based on the very knowledge that induced the disruption in the first place. Eventually, the monster is subdued and order restored.

Invasion narratives, in which the unknown simply invades the known, are all rampage: the monster appears and goes on the rampage, until the customary blend of knowledge and expertise returns it to the unknown. Examples include *Jaws* (1975), *Alien* (1979), *The Fog* (1979), and the *Dracula* films.

The most complex and interesting narrative form is that of metamorphosis. It involves many of Tudor's basic oppositions, the most significant being the contrasts between the conscious and the unconscious self, normal and abnormal sexuality, sanity and insanity, social order and disorder, and health and disease. In modern films, the unconscious self becomes equated with abnormal sexuality, disorder, insanity and disease, engendering psychological patterns of considerable richness and subtlety. Metamorphosis narratives may also combine with the other two types, resulting in invasion narratives that become fused with stories of physical change and transmutation, as in *The Thing* (1982), or knowledge narratives involving extreme alterations in bodily states, as in 'body horror' films like Cronenberg's *The Fly* (1986). The metamorphoses may befall either individuals or groups, so that in Jekyll-and-Hyde stories, for example, we have knowledge precipating

Body horror – *The Fly*

a disorder embodied in the man of knowledge himself, as well as narratives including *Psycho*, where Norman's abnormal psychic state leads to a transformation of his whole being, *Peeping Tom*, *Halloween*, *The Exorcist* (1973), *A Nightmare on Elm Street* (1984) and *Videodrome* (1982). Group narratives include *The Crazies* (1973) and the zombie films of Romero, beginning with *Night of the Living Dead* (1969), as well as the earlier works of Cronenberg, such as *Rabid* (1976) and *Shivers* (1974).

Tudor does not lay down either necessary or sufficient conditions for defining 'horror'. A common criterion for the identification of horror, bodily mutilation, is not part of his typology. Furthermore, a comedy like *The Mask* (1994) can be located in accord with his criteria on the borderline between metamorphosis narratives of the individual and group types. The value of Tudor's analysis derives from the discrimination it encourages between what seem to be two historically distinct worlds of horror. At some point in the 1960s (perhaps the pertinent film is *Psycho*, which may be thought to enact just this shift from one world to another) a marked alteration in emphasis took place, with films prior to the period exhibiting a relative security in their values, and films after it inviting the label 'paranoid'. Earlier films presuppose a world in which disorder is ultimately subject to human intervention, while the authorities, such as the police and the army, and institutions, such as the law courts, educational bodies and hospitals, remain credible embodiments of social and cultural meaning. In films of the later, paranoid type, 'both the nature and the course of the threat are out of human control, and in extreme metamorphosis cases, disorder often emerges from *within* humans to potentially disrupt the whole ordered world' (Tudor, 1989, p. 103). The nature of the two conditions may be graphically exemplified by the contrast between Howard Hawks's *The Thing from Another World*, made in 1951, and John Carpenter's 1982 reworking, *The Thing*. In the world of 'secure' horror, the contrasts that hold sway, those between life and death, normal and abnormal, human and alien, and so on, are clearly marked as contrasts between what is human and what is external to the human, and thus what threatens the human is more easily defended against. In 'paranoid' horror, the principal oppositions are internal to the human condition as such: conscious/unconscious, health/disease, sanity/insanity, and so on, insinuate the unknown into the known in ways not found in earlier examples of the genre. Cronenberg's *The Fly* exemplifies the mode characteristic of the later kind of film, as do the slasher films discussed by Carol Clover, and the 'body horror' cinema addressed by psychoanalytic criticism. The world presupposed by these films is different from that of earlier horror. The earlier sense of a world whose moral and social order is worth defending has disappeared, as has the sense that institutions and authorities have a legitimate claim on the loyalties and cooperation of the protagonists. The new order is one that came to definitive birth with Romero's *Night of the Living Dead* (1968).

Jonathan Lake Crane continues and develops Tudor's historical approach in *Terror and Everyday Life* (1994). For Crane, *Night of the Living Dead* initiates a cinema of nihilism, in which 'Altruism, respect for others, and valiant acts will have the same nil effect on material circumstances as those actions that are motivated by baser desires and feelings' (Crane, 1994, p. 14). It is in this film that Crane finds the supreme expression of contemporary nihilism, which turns around the figure of the last survivor, the black male, Ben. Despite his extraordinarily heroic efforts in repelling the zombie attack on the farmhouse, in pulling the other defenders together and working out a plan of defence, he is mistaken for a zombie, and casually shot by a redneck member of the posse. We then see grainy still images of his body being dragged away on a meathook, being thrown on an unlit pyre, and then incinerated. As Crane puts it, 'Ben's strong presence vanishes instantly with his ridiculous and unncessary death' (Crane, 1994, p. 14). This line of argument does not encourage Crane to support the position on abjection that we have seen Creed take up; he is, on the contrary, opposed to psychoanalysis, like Tudor, because of what he sees as its excessively reductionist mode of explanation. Not only this, but Kristeva and others have gone wrong in arguing that terror, in whatever form it takes, is always a question of the 'I'. This is to make the matter of response to the horror film 'a private escapade, a lonely search for solitary satisfaction, a simple matter of individual psychological economy' (Crane, 1994, p. 38). It is to cut the films off from the times and culture of the people who made and understood them, and to confine the horror cinema within the constrictions of the 'I'. For Crane, on the other hand, new horror films do not entertain the unconscious, but instead offer 'meaningless death in response to the terrors of everyday life' (Crane, 1994, p. 39). Contemporary horror frees itself from the conventions of the past, conventions that, it would seem, include the subjectivity described by psychoanalysis, and turns its attention to terrorising the body in ways that mean nothing to any but contemporary audiences. Crane's position finds succinct expression in his account of John Carpenter's version of *The Thing*: 'When [the protagonists] perform superbly, they die. When they screw up, they die. Whatever happens, they die' (Crane, 1994, p. 137). Modern films regard efficacious knowledge as 'a quaint chimera', and 'they work, like deadly and incurable epistemological viruses, to destroy all we once took on faith' (Crane, 1994, p. 138). The value of Crane's work lies in the degree of clarity he introduces into how we think about horror films. His procedure, like Tudor's, is descriptive; in this it differs profoundly from earlier, more ambitious attempts to 'theorise' horror cinema as a whole.

Selected Reading

Philip Brophy, 'Horrality – the textuality of contemporary horror films', *Screen* 27(1), January–February 1986, pp. 2–13.

Noël Carroll, *The Philosophy of Horror*, New York and London, Routledge, 1990.

Carol J. Clover, *Men, Women and Chain Saws*, London, BFI, 1992.

Barbara Creed, 'Horror and the monstrous-feminine – an imaginary abjection', *Screen* 27(1), January–February 1986, pp. 44–70. Reprinted in *The Monstrous-Feminine*, London, Routledge, 1993.

Davie Pirie, *A Heritage of Horror: The English Gothic Cinema 1946–72*, London, Gordon Fraser, 1973.

Andrew Tudor, *Monsters and Mad Scientists*, Oxford, Basil Blackwell, 1989.

Linda Williams, 'When the woman looks', in Doane, Mellencamp and Williams (eds), *Revision: Essays in Feminist Film Criticism*, Frederick MD, AFI Monograph Series, University Publications of America AFI 1983.

Robin Wood, 'Introduction', in Britton, Lippe, Williams and Wood (eds), *American Nightmare: Essays on the Horror Film*, Toronto, Festival of Festivals, 1979.

Frankenstein (USA 1931 *p.c* – Universal; *d* – James Whale; sd b/w)

The creature of Whale's 1931 *Frankenstein* is both helpless and powerful, worthless and godlike, abject and sublime, a contrast that is central to the figure's aesthetic power.

The paradoxical nature of the monster is made particularly apparent in the creation scene, set in Frankenstein's laboratory. Out of the darkness of the storm comes the creative energy of lightning, a fusion of light and fire giving life to a creature of darkness and death. As T. R. Ellis (1985) has argued, the monster's fear of fire is tied, first, to his own violent origins and, second, to the Promethean overtones of the film. The monster seems to remember the shock of his birth and the place of fire in it. The monster's fear also arises from Henry's Promethean mythology who created man, and stole fire from heaven to ensure the survival of the being he had made. Henry also calls on fire to endow his creation with life, but 'the great ray' is natural not divine. The creature's extreme fear of fire derives, therefore, from his origin in the non-divine, the human. Whale uses the suffering and confusion induced by the monster's conflictual nature, and endured by him throughout the film, as an expression of the paradox inherent in his creation.

However, Henry is not simply a crazed version of a figure from ancient myth. *Frankenstein* also subverts themes and images from Christianity. If Frankenstein has created a new Adam, then, in Ellis's words, 'this "Adam" will never inhabit a garden of Eden, but a world of pain and fear' (Ellis, 1984, p. 48). At the moment when the creature's hand first moves, indicating that he is alive, there is dialogue which was censored before the release of the print as we now have it. Henry exults: 'now I know what it is to *be* God'. One of the paradoxes fundamental to the Christian conception of the Incarnation is manifest in the Crucifixion, where Christ, the Creator, dies at the hands of His creation. Henry's death at the windmill is an echo and parody of this, as he too dies at the hands of what he has created. The blasphemy of the idea is evident in the burning arms of the windmill outlined in a fiery cross against the blackened sky. However, the film not only plays on religious connotations from the Crucifixion, it also inverts the ultimate mystery, the Resurrection. The opening scene in the graveyard presents Henry and Fritz as 'Resurrection men', grave robbers, in a setting that makes extensive use of images of the cross, a statue of the crucified Christ and a statue of death. It is against this background of death that Whale cuts to a close-up of Henry holding on to the casket he and Fritz have raised out of the earth. In an echo of Christ at the tomb of Lazarus, he says: 'he's just resting, waiting for a new life to come.' Thus, the film begins with a pseudo-resurrection, and ends what is, despite the tacked-on ending, final and irrevocable death, a narrative progression that itself seems a parody of the Passion of Christ. Jonathan Lake Crane has argued that the monster is an outcast whose fate calls into question the assumptions and values of the 'normal' world, the estate of the Frankensteins and the village community that serves it (Crane, 1994). However, if we place the film against the romantic background of Mary Shelley's novel, we may think that the subversive perversity of its conception of the creative act, an act more like that of an artist than the scientist, goes further than Crane allows. In Henry Frankenstein, Whale has created a character whose will and ambition serve to undermine the very foundations of paternal heritage and identity.

Psycho (USA 1960 *p.c* – Paramount; *d* – Alfred Hitchcock; sd b/w)

For Robin Wood, the death of Marion Crane is 'probably the most horrible incident in any fiction film' (Wood, 1965, p. 109). The meaninglessness of it is what shocks him and, he would argue, the audience also. The murder seems completely irrational and useless: it ruptures the identification with Marion that the film has thus far been at pains to build up, overwhelming a fictional universe whose concerns had hitherto been merely neurotic with extremes of nightmare and psychosis. Marion's decision to steal Cassidy's $40,000 and her subsequent flight from Phoenix to Fairvale seem the result of neurotic compulsion, a compulsion we are induced, by music and techniques of identification, to sympathise with. Her confrontation with Norman thus becomes 'the core of the film'. The scene establishes a continuity between the normal and the abnormal, between Marion's neurotic compulsion and the psychotic behaviour of Norman, that survives the ensuing brutal disruption. With Marion's death we have no one except Norman with whom to identify. As a result, the techniques Hitchcock earlier employed for aligning us with Marion are now used to make us 'become' Norman, the remainder of the film being an ever-increasing descent into the depths of his 'psychological hell-state', his 'chaos-world' (Wood, 1965, p. 110). This means that the film's central protagonist, in whose psyche the major characters are united, is the spectator. Lila's exploration of the Bates's mansion is our exploration of Norman's psyche, and her confrontation with mother in the cellar is our confrontation with the well-springs of Norman's being.

Central to Wood's and to most accounts of *Psycho* is the shower scene. As the bloody water spirals in an anti-clockwise direction down the plughole, the camera cranes down after it into the blackness. As it tracks back from the dark pupil of Marion's dead eye, the camera takes on the anti-clockwise movement of the water. The lacuna between these two moments is the elision of death, the point at which the film represents a lack beyond representation. It is here that we may recognise the film's principle of organisation; the enactment of an intrusion or rupture, that the film both can and cannot show. It is evident in a pattern of repetitions that find expression in a number of ways, including the doubling of actions (the hotel in Phoenix echoes by the Bates's motel, Marion's narrative duplicated by Norman's, and so forth) and physical similarities between characters, such as Marion and Lila. Explained by their being sisters, their likeness is reflected in similarities between Sam Loomis and Norman Bates, a likeness that requires more elucidation, drawing on the confrontation between two types of sexuality, one seemingly 'normal', the other rotted from within. Similarly, one might cite Lila's sudden shock as she encounters her own reflection in a mirror in Mrs Bates's bedroom. This encounter between self and self is repeated and transformed later in the scene in the cellar, when Lila confronts Mrs Bates's dead body, animated by light from the bulb swinging from the ceiling, as simultaneously the 'living' body runs shrieking towards her from the opposite end of the cellar brandishing the knife that killed her sister.

Lila is confronted by one person in two bodies. The most striking coinherence of two persons in one body is the superimposition of mother's skull onto Norman's face, as Norman is finally possessed by her. The sequence is played out with Norman looking directly at the camera, and with no spectator, except the film's viewer, present. It may be in part this close engagement with Norman that reminds us here of Marion, whose dead eye stared directly into the camera, as she lay on the bathroom floor after her annihilation at mother's hands, the mother who is now heard saying 'They can see she wouldn't hurt a fly'. Mother's words are audible only to the film's audience, Norman's lips remaining fixed until the scene ends with his enigmatic smile. The final emergence of mother is therefore something that takes place only for us. It is an event that is grimly sardonic and humorous: in ascribing guilt to Norman, she is proclaiming her liberation from the confines of her son's inadequate psyche. She creates herself by annihilating her own creation. The superimposition, visible only to the viewer, of mother onto Norman is continued into the next and final shot of the film, the withdrawal of Marion's car from the swamp where Norman had concealed it. Here death emerges out of death: the self-conscious use of filmic devices effects the transcendence of death in the very images that celebrate its triumph of negativity. The end of the film is thus not simply ambivalent: it is poised between two very different ways of understanding the significance of death, and it commits itself to neither.

Star Wars (USA 1977 *p.c* – Lucasfilm/Fox; *d* – George Lucas; sd col.)

At the time of its initial release, *Star Wars* was the biggest box-office hit of all time, it served to reorientate late 1960s and 1970s science fiction away from 'the bittersweet questioning of tendencies within modern society [as exemplified by films like *Planet of the Apes* (1968), *Soylent Green* (1973 and *Rollerball* (1975)] to an unabashed celebration of escapism, gee-whizz heroics and innocence [as exemplified by *Close Encounters of the Third Kind* (1977), *Superman – The Movie* (1978) and *Star Trek – The Motion Picture* (1979)]' (Hardy, 1986, p. 290). Accompanied by a major merchandising campaign, *Star Wars* is an early instance of what Justin Wyatt has called 'high-concept' film-making, in which 'the style and look of the films ... function with the marketing and merchandising opportunities structured into the projects in order to maximise profits within a conglomerized, multi-media industrial environment' (Wyatt, 1994, p. 190). In spawning two further 'episodes', *The Empire Strikes Back* (1980) and *The Return of the Jedi* (1983), the film also became an instance of 'post-classic' (or post-studio period) sequel or series production. In addition, it helped to pioneer a new generation of special effects (in particular 'motion control', the computerised control of the camera movements used in filming models, especially model airships), and the use of Dolby stereo. As well as this, *Star Wars* is a relatively early and highly influential instance of the use of allusion and pastiche as dominant stylistic devices in post-1960s Hollywood films (see New Hollywood, p. 98).

There are allusions in *Star Wars* to a number of specific films: C-3PO is modelled on the robot Maria in *Metropolis* (1926); the bombing raids and serial dogfights have their origins in *Twelve O'Clock High* (1949), *The Dam Busters* (1955) and *633 Squadron* (1964); the victory celebration at the end is based on sequences in Leni Riefenstahl's *Triumph of the Will* (1936); and the return of Luke Skywalker (Mark Hamill) to his aunt and uncle's burnt-out homestead is modelled on a similar scene in John Ford's *The Searchers* (1965). However, although some of these allusions arguably help to cue or to reinforce some of the film's major generic points – notably science fiction, the western and the war film – they are neither foregrounded as such, nor used to develop the film's narrative or its characters and themes. By contrast, the science fiction adventure serials of the 1930s and 1940s, the genre 'memorialized' (to use Noel Carroll's term) in and through much of the film's pastiche, are more central in their effects, not just on the characterisation, storyline and setting, but also on its structure and style of narration (Carroll, 1982).

This is evident in a number of ways: from a storyline which ranges across the galaxy, and which pits a small group of heroes against an ostensibly more powerful set of villains in a mission to save it from total domination, to the adoption of the procedures of serial construction. The latter find articulation in the way the film cuts back and forth between locations and actions; a narrative built on and around 'cliffhanging' moments; and the cuts to, from and into ongoing conversations or actions as the film moves from scene to scene, often via such 'old-fashioned' devices as the horizontal or vertical wipe.

The principle of serial construction is established at the start – labelled 'Episode 4' – and is preceded by a set of rolling titles serving to summarise the story so far, and which then plunge straight into an ongoing action: the pursuit and capture of Princess Leia (Carrie Fisher) and her spaceship by Darth Vader (Derek Prowse) and the forces of the Empire. This sequence also highlights two of the principal formal and technological elements which serve to update and to modernise the film, its visual effects and its use of sound. While the first shot of the film displays the use of models (and motion control), it also shows off the possibilities of Dolby stereo and of modern multi-track recording – the roar of the spaceships, the whizz and the rattle of laser-fire, the squeaking first line – 'Hear that?' (see Sergi, 1995).

In using and updating a minor genre, *Star Wars* arguably illustrates the Russian formalist thesis that aesthetic innovation proceeds by means of the adoption of the principles of hitherto uncanonised art. (See Erlich, 1981, pp. 259–60.) The film's particular combination of naïvete and sophistication, innocence and knowingness, also helped to initiate what Robert Ray and others have seen as a major tendency not just within post-1960s Hollywood cinema, but within post-1960s mass culture as a whole (Ray, 1985).

Alien (USA 1979 *p.c* – Brandywine Productions/20th Century–Fox; *d* – Ridley Scott; sd col.)

To characterise something or someone as alien is to characterise them as Other. This at least is an assumption that seems appropriate to a film such as Ridley Scott's *Alien*, as Annette Kuhn makes clear (Kuhn, 1992). Drawing on nineteenth-century definitions of the alien and on law from the same period concerning immigrants, Kuhn shows how new ideas concerning the treatment and regulation of immigrants entered our culture at the turn of the century, a period coinciding with the origins of cinema. She sees a connection between these ideas and the treatment of extra-terrestrials in the science fiction of both literature and cinema. Aliens are seen as threatening, in so far as their numbers, visibility and 'difference' are such as to constitute the opposition: Them v. Us. Other aliens, like the lone voyagers in *The Day The Earth Stood Still* (1951) and *E.T. The Extraterrestrial* (1982), come as messiahs, to save us from the effects of our technology and arrogance. Aliens of this kind are not threatening. Kuhn argues that, in all these cases, the Us/Them divide can be mapped onto other divisions, such as culture v. nature, reason v. instinct and good v. evil. These boundaries are shifting and permeable, and nowhere more so than in *Alien*.

The alien of this film, and of the rest of the series, is one of the most threatening ever devised in the cinema, and the Us/Them divide maps unambiguously onto an opposition between the human and the non-human. However, as Kuhn points out, the non-human can be subdivided further: 'into the techno-products of corporate culture (Ash, the Company's android; Mother, the spaceship's duplicitous computer system) as against the rampantly fecund, visibly Other alien, a manifestation of monstrous Nature' (Kuhn, 1992, p. 13). Nonetheless, the narrative dynamic of the film is such that the overall movement of the film blurs these distinctions. The alien takes over the *Nostromo*, the crew's 'home', after penetrating Kane's body and then bursting out of it. In a manner reminiscent of John Carpenter's direction of *Halloween* (1978), Scott makes effective use of off-screen space, in order to suggest not only that the alien threat is everywhere, but that it menaces the very possibility of a human space. This sense of threat comes to a climax in the final sequence, when Ripley confronts the alien in the escape craft. After destroying the *Nostromo*, she places the cat in a sleeping pod, and settles back at the control console in relief. As she does so, she notices the shiny metallic shape of the alien coiled amongst the pipes and ducts of the craft's engine. She strips down and steps into a pressure suit, and eventually expels the creature by opening the inner world of the craft to the outer world of space: she defeats the alien by accepting the utterly alien universe of intergalactic vastness. We see the escape craft from the alien's point of view, as it is blasted into the void by the power of the engines, and we hear its cries of ultimate distress.

What is remarkable about *Alien* is the complexity of its presentation of what is alien. The alien eggs are discovered in an alien ship, belonging to a civilisation of which we learn nothing, except that its technology seems one in which the organic and inorganic have been intimately married. We see one long-dead member of the crew, the nature of whose death we come subsequently to understand. As for the alien itself, we learn little or nothing in this film of its origin, though it seems to have as its sole purpose annihilation and conquest. Furthermore, there is alienness of another kind at work, that of the company, represented by Ash and Mother. It is the a humanity of the company's concern with power and profit that forces the crew members into contact with the alien, and brings about their eventual destruction. This theme is developed in the two later films, *Aliens* (1986) and *Alien³* (1992), as is the theme of motherhood, which is complementary to it. By the time Ripley plunges to her death in *Alien³*, giving birth to the creature which is forcing its way out of her chest, the values of the company have been wholly repudiated. Ripley herself takes on the role of alien mother, and in doing so accepts her death. Her acceptance of death is an unequivocally human act, and yet paradoxically it requires that she accept the alien within her. The categories of human and alien thus become inextricably bound up with one another, and the opposition between Us and Them is finally undermined. This subversion of position is what constitutes the major critique of the values of the company and the culture of profit and exploitation it represents.

The Thing (USA 1982 *p.c* – Universal; *d* – John Carpenter; sd col.)

Noel Carroll has argued that monsters in horror films are both threatening and impure (Carroll, 1990, p. 43). They pose a psychological threat to individual identity (*The Exorcist*, 1973), a moral threat to the underlying order of society (*Rosemary's Baby*, 1968), or, as in the case of *The Thing*, a cosmic threat to the entire organic and human world. The idea of impurity involves the transgression of two or more fundamental cultural categories. This means that monsters are constructed out of various combinations of disparate elements. One such combination is fusion, a process involving the transgression of such categorical distinctions as inside/outside, living/dead, insect/human, machine/flesh. Examples include vampires, mummies, ghosts and zombies, creatures who are both living and dead. Elements from contradictory categories are fused or condensed together to form a single creature, with a unified identity. Fission is the other basic type, in which contradictory elements are distributed over different identities. Examples include doubles, alter egos and werewolves.

However, the entity in *The Thing* evades Carroll's system. It exhibits elements of both fission and fusion, and neither of these. As a fission monster, it is spatially split across the members of Science Station 4, and also temporally divided, in as much as it imitates first a dog (which carries it from the Norwegian to the American station) and subsequently various crew members. The blood tests reveal it to be an entity in some way composed of an infinite number of copies of itself. It also exemplifies fusion, as the dead specimen that Dr Copper and MacReady bring back from the Norwegian station makes clear. The conclusion Copper draws from his examination is that the chaotic mass of tissue appears to have died in the process of forming itself into a single entity out of many distorted and barely recognisable shapes. Towards the end of the film, after the Thing, in the form of Blair, has killed Garry, MacReady attempts to destroy it with dynamite. The Thing displays itself in spectacular fashion, seeming to recapitulate all the beings, human and otherwise, it has ever been. Here the entity appears as a fusion that only transgresses the ontological boundaries between human, animal and alien, as well as those between the living and the dead, but also the temporal boundaries that separate the past from the present. However, it differs from the fusion monsters described by Carroll in as much as it does not achieve any stable or homogeneous identity. The lack of identity derives from the fact that when the entity manifests itself it reveals itself as always elsewhere, as unlocatable. During the metamorphosis of the dog, or the extraordinary transformation of Norris's head into a spider-like creature with legs, the sheer exuberance of the exhibition suggests the excessive and ungraspable nature of what we are seeing. The Thing seems to exist, if it can be said to exist at all, as a process of metamorphosis rather than as an entity with identifiable properties and qualities. This lack of definitive form not only reinforces our sense that the mode of being of the Thing is undecidable, it also shapes the narrative. Thus, when MacReady and Childs face each other surrounded by the dying flames of the burning camp, the question as to who may or may not be the Thing is not merely left open but is in principle something that cannot be resolved. The lack of closure enacts the radical, primordial otherness of the monster. The narrative dynamic embodies in itself the nothingness or absence from which we are to imagine the Thing as still emerging.

Thus, what is crucial to the film is not so much the actions the station crew take in response to the Thing, but the Thing itself, or rather, the lack or absence that it embodies. This means that the film's spectacular special effects are the pivot around which the spectator's interest turns (see New technologies, p. 46). This point is made disparagingly by Steve Jenkins, in a highly adverse review: 'the special effects, in true "modernist" fashion, exist in and for themselves' (Jenkins, 1982, p. 159). However, the reason for this self-reflexive mode of the effects can be justified as a consequence of the entity's existence as a kind of neither/nor: the more palpably it makes itself present, the more evidently is it absent, somewhere else. In this sense, Jenkins is right: to display effects in this manner is highly 'modernist'. Present in its absence, absent in its presence, the modernist text is precisely one that makes these antinomies palpable. This is also to describe what for psychoanalysis is the fetish, and Carpenter's emphasis on effects can be linked with the evident fetishism of the special effects of other films contemporary with *The Thing*, such as *Alien* and *Star Wars*. Steve Neale has argued in relation to the effects of these films that they 'depend upon and intensify the fetishistic aspects of "fantasy" in particular and of the cinema and its signifier in general' (Neale, 1980, p. 105). If this is so, *The Thing* moves beyond the reification of its effects in order to engage its audience with the lack of representation as such. Its horror is not only that of the transgression of cultural categories but of what lies beyond categorisation, beyond the limits of the thinkable. It is to imagine the Thing as a sublime and impossible object.

This presentation of the film runs counter to Jonathan Lake Crane's account. For him, *The Thing* is centrally concerned to annihilate meaning. No matter how intelligent or well thought out the protagonists' actions, they have no effect. 'When they perform superbly, they die. When they screw up, they die. Whatever happens they die' (Crane, 1994, p. 137). The collapse of meaning, of all human significance, is inevitable and total. One response to this might be that Lake has confused the representation of negation with the negativity of representation. What *The Thing* dramatises is an inversion of the negation of being into the being of negation. Negation itself assumes a positive existence. Far from this resulting in a loss of meaning, it transforms an unsatisfied desire for meaning into a desire for unrealised meaning, a desire to keep meaning 'open'. By the end of *The Thing* desire has become a desire for desire itself. If we follow Slavoj Zizek in seeing this as the structure of hysteria (Zizek, 1991, p. 144), we may say that *The Thing* effects a psychic conversion from fetish to hysteria. Instead of signalling the collapse of human significance, it inaugurates its renewal.

Dead Ringers (Canada 1988 *p.c* – Mantle Clinic II/Morgan Creek; *d* – David Cronenberg; sd col.)

Dead Ringers seems to demand interpretation. Cronenberg himself provides a key: 'In *Dead Ringers* the truth, anticipated by Beverly's parents — or whoever named him – was that he was the female part of the yin/yang whole. Elliot and Beverly are a couple, not complete in themselves. Both characters have a femaleness in them' (Rodley, 1992, p. 147).

It is certainly the case that repression and female sexuality are central to an understanding of the horror film in general and to *Dead Ringers* in particular, as the work of Barbara Creed has demonstrated (Creed, 1989). Nonetheless, this kind of approach by no means exhausts the significance of the film. As Pam Cook has noted, one of the most striking features of *Dead Ringers* is how it avoids generic categorisation and interpretation: '[the film's] poeticism defies the rational explanation which would give the audience a spurious sense of mastery' (Cook, 1989, p. 4). At the centre of this is the complex handling of the notion of twins which is itself also inseparable from the concept of the double. This is a theme central to psychoanalysis, and it is explored in these terms by Otto Rank, for whom the double is intimately related to problems associated with narcissism. Rank shows how self-love of the kind exhibited by Oscar Wilde's Dorian Gray, the love of a subject for its image or double, which excludes love of another person, has two aspects: love, and hate or fear. This ambivalence within narcissism is a form of defence against narcissism, a defence necessary to allow the subject its own identity which is otherwise threatened by that of the other, the double, the self-image. *Dead Ringers* can be seen as an instance of this dialectic. As Beverly is drawn ever more deeply to Claire, participating in and even abetting her use of drugs, and abandoning himself to sexual passion, so his narcissism returns him to his twin: his double. And yet, according to Rank, the relation of younger to elder brother is always fraught with rivalry. The younger brother 'is, as it were, a reflection of his fraternal self that has come to life; and on this account he is also a rival in everything that the [elder] brother sees, feels, thinks' (Rank, 1979, p. 75). The ensuing complexities are manifest in the way Elliot gradually succumbs to Beverly's drug-taking and loss of control, a reversal of dominance similar to that explored by Cronenberg in *Scanners* (1980).

It is this dialectic of reversal that allows Cronenberg to transform and go

Doubling up – *Dead Ringers*

beyond much that is basic to the horror film, including the 'body horror' that had characterised some of his own earlier work, such as *Rabid* (1976), *Scanners* (1980) and *Videodrome* (1982). This further level of complication enters the film with the introduction of the theme of the Siamese twins, Chang and Eng. The force of this depends on the thematic emphasis on the split between mind and body: the Mantle twins are, in effect, one body split in half, while their minds seem joined (as Elliot puts it, he and Beverly share the same nervous system). It is in this context that Cronenberg is inclined to speak of the Mantle twins as monstrous, as creatures 'as exotic as *The Fly*' (Rodley, 1992, p. 144), a film which he describes as 'metaphysical horror' (Rodley, 1992, p. 134). By 'metaphysical' Cronenberg is invoking the 'metaphysical' poetry of the seventeenth century in which normally unharmonious elements are violently yoked together' (Rodley, 1992, p. 131). The result is a combination of dissimilar elements and the discovery of unforeseen resemblances in things apparently unlike. Throughout the film, we are presented with such resemblances in things apparently unlike, and the violent revelation of dissimilarity or difference in what seems similar.

THE MUSICAL

The Hollywood musical is a product of the advent of sound, of the industry's commitment to an ethos and to forms of entertainment represented, among other things, by the theatrical musical, by Broadway, and by Tin Pan Alley, of its stake in the music publishing, recording and radio industries (acquired during the conversion to sound in the late 1920s), and of developments in and on the musical stage in America and elsewhere during the previous eighty to ninety years. Film versions of stage musicals like *The Merry Widow* and *The Student Prince*, and of operas like *Carmen* and *La Bohème*, had been produced during the silent era. So, too, had filmed records of dancers and dances. As Collins points out, these and nearly all other films were usually accompanied by live music, and were often shown in contexts and venues which included musical performances of one kind or another (Collins, 1988, pp. 269–70). As he goes on to argue, it was the presence and popularity of these musical acts that helped prompt the first experiments with sound in the mid-1920s, and that helped function as a model for the preludes and shorts produced by Warners and others at this time. And as he goes on to suggest, the ensuing 'tension between live musical acts and film presentation', between 'the increasing technological sophistication of the medium ... and the sense of nostalgia for a direct relationship with the audience' has marked the musical ever since, providing the focus for such studies as those by Feuer (1993) and Altman (1987), and the motivation for his own concentration on the 'ever-shifting relationship between performance, spectacle, and audience.' (Collins, 1988, p. 270). In the meantime, as Wolfe (1990) has pointed out, the established nature and shape of the musical short helped govern the use of musical sequences in *The Jazz Singer* (1927), the film usually cited as the first feature-length musical. During the course of the next three years, over 200 musical films of one kind or another were made, and despite a decline in the number of musicals produced and released in the early 1930s, the musical had re-established itself a routine component in Hollywood's output by 1934 (Altman 1996, pp. 294–8, Balio, 1993, pp. 211–18, Barrios, 1995).

The musical has always been a mongrel genre. In varying measures and combinations, music, song and dance have been its only essential ingredients. In consequence its history, both on stage and on screen, has been marked by numerous traditions, forms and styles. These in turn have been marked by numerous terms – 'operetta', 'revue', 'musical comedy', 'musical drama', 'the backstage musical', 'the rock musical', 'the integrated musical', and so on. As we shall see,

The backstage musical – *42nd Street*

historians, critics and theorists of the musical sometimes disagree about the meaning of some of these terms. As we shall also see, some invent their own. Nevertheless, it is possible to provide some basic definitions, to indicate areas of debate and disagreement, and in the process to highlight the extent to which the musical has always been, despite its accessible and effortless image, multifaceted, hybrid, and complex (Collins, 1988, p. 269).

Revue, to begin with, is usually and uncontentiously defined as a series of comic and musical performances lacking a narrative framework (lacking what in the theatre is called a 'book'), and unified, if at all, only by a consistent style, design or theme, a common set of comic targets, or a single producer, director or venue (Bordman, 1985, Kislan, 1980, pp. 78–92). Pure revue in the cinema is rare, though there was a vogue for revue in the late 1920s and early 1930s when as Balio, citing Walker (Walker, 1979, p. 184), points out, it 'was used by producers to showcase stars and contract players and to offer "proof positive that everyone could now talk, sing and dance at least passably well"' (Balio, 1993, p. 211). And as Delameter points out, the influence of revue is evident in the backstage musical, where the show in preparation is usually a revue of one kid or another (Delameter, 1974, p. 122).

One of the distinguishing marks of operetta, by contrast, is the presence of a book. Important too, though, is the nature of the book, the nature of the setting, and the nature and importance of the music (*Variety* argues that 'In operetta the score is the primary consideration ... The book, dancing (if any), comedy (if any), production and acting (if any) are all secondary to the music and singing' ('This Is Operetta', 20 February 1946, p. 49)). To quote Rubin, 'operetta is characterized by its European origins, its elegance and sophistication of its tone, its use of melodic, waltz-time music, its picturesque and exotic settings, and its strongly integrative organization around a melodramatic, romance-oriented book' (Rubin, 1993, p. 18). In the cinema, operetta is usually exemplified by the films of Jeanette MacDonald and Nelson Eddy (*Sweethearts* (1938), *Rose Marie* (1936) and others, all based on stage hits by proponents of American operetta like Victor Herbert and Sigmund Romberg, and all produced as a series by Hunt Stromberg at MGM (Balio, 1993, pp. 223–4), by a cycle of stage adaptations made in the late 1920s and early 1930s (Balio, 1993, pp. 211–12), and, as an offshoot of this cycle, by a group of four Jeanette MacDonald and Maurice Chavalier films made at Paramount, *The Love Parade* (1929), *The Smiling Lieutenant* (1931), *One Hour with You* (1932), and *love Me Tonight* (1932), all highly acclaimed by critics for their risqué wit, and for their inventive use of editing, space and sound (Altman, 1987, pp. 150–1; Balio, 1993, pp. 212–14, Knight, 1985; Mast, 1987, pp. 123–4).

Operettas of a fairly traditional kind continued to be made in the 1940s and 1950s, some of them as vehicles for new musical stars like Kathryn Grayson and Howard Keel, and some of them also, like the remakes of *The Desert Song* (1953) and *Rose Marie* (1954), as contributions to a contemporary vogue for action, adventure and spectacle (always in colour, and often in CinemScope, Todd-AO or VistaVision too). However, the fact that so many of the 1950s film were remakes is significant. For most commentators argue that by then, traditional operetta as a form capable of generating new work was moribund or dead (Bordman, 1981, pp. 144–8; Kislan, 1980, pp. 104–5). However, some, like Bordman

(1981, pp. 149–69) and Traubner (1983, pp. 377–421), argue that it had already given rise to a new form, 'musical drama' (or 'the musical play').

Musical drama is usually exemplified by a tradition of Broadway musicals that begins with *Show Boat* in 1927, and runs through *Oklahoma!* (1943), *Carousel* (1945), *South Pacific* (1949), and other works by Rodgers and Hammerstein, *Brigadoon* (1947), *My Fair Lady* (1956), and other works by Lerner and Loewe, and shows like *West Side Story* (1957) and *Fiddler on the Roof* (1964), all of which have been made into films, and many of which were road show productions in the 1950s and 1960s, a period in which Hollywood increasingly turned to Broadway for pre-sold, prestige material (Collins, 1988, p. 277). along with a tendency to use what Delameter calls '"big" voices' (Delameter, 1974, p. 123), one of the hallmarks of musical drama – one of the elements it derives from operetta – is the importance of its storyline (one which could accommodate pathos, dramatic conflict, and even on occasion an unhappy ending), its attention to situation and character, and the 'sharply integrative' organisation of its music, its singing and its dancing. Integration of this kind became an ideal not only among those who wrote, directed and choreographed musical dramas, but also among critics, theorists and historians. It has tended to produce a canonic crest-line, a tradition of landmark films, shows and personnel. Although as Solomon points out 'there is no evident reason' for preferring integration (Solomon, 1988, p. 71), and although there are significant differences between Broadway's crest-line and Hollywood's, both have resulted on occasion in partial and distorted accounts of the musical's history.

The notion of integration and the idea of 'the integrated musical' appear at first sight to be quite straightforward. However, as Meuller (1984) has pointed out, things are not necessarily as simple as they seem. Focussing on the relationship between the musical numbers and the plot, he argues that there are at least six different possible permutations, from numbers which are 'completely irrelevant to the plot', to those 'which contribute to the spirit or theme' or 'which enrich the plot, but do not advance it', to those 'which advance the plot' (Meuller, 1984, pp. 28/29) either through their setting and narrative function – it is here that he tends to place the backstage musical – and/or through their lyrical content.

The precision Meuller seeks to bring to the concept of integration is unusual. Most uses of the term are rather vague. It can act as a synonym for almost any form of motivation, and sometimes even as a synonym for stylistic or aesthetic coherence. This is one reason why its history, both on stage and in the cinema, is also rather vague. There is no doubt that operetta and musical drama are important. But a number of the films and shows cited by Meuller and others are musical comedies. This is certainly true of the Astaire–Rogers film made at RKO in the 1930s, the principal focus of Mueller's article. It is also true of the Princess theatre shows written by Guy Bolton, Jerome Kern and P.G. Wodehouse in the late 1910s, often cited as early examples of integration by historians of the musical on stage (among them Bordman, 1982, 101–5; Kislan, 1980, pp. 113–16; Smith and Litton, 1981, pp. 122–3).

Issues of integration notwithstanding, musical comedy has always been much more heterogeneous than operetta or musical drama, as befits a genre – or sub-genre – whose origins lay as much in the minstrel show, vaudeville and other forms of variety entertainment as in turn-of-the-century farce (Bordman, 1982, pp. 3–77; Smith and Litton, 1981, pp. 2–87). What has remained constant has been a commitment to comedy and the comic, to popular and vernacular styles of music, song and dance, and a willingness to sacrifice coherence or integration for the sake of either or both. Most Hollywood musicals are musicals of this kind. Films like *College Holiday* (1936) and *The Road to Morocco* (1942) have always outnumbered films like *West Side Story* (1961), *Swing Time* (1936), and *Meet Me in St Louis* (1944).

Alongside formal and sub-generic categories such as these, the musical has often been discussed under the headings provided on the one hand by the names of its producers, directors, choreographers and performers, and on the other by the names of the studios responsible for its production. Once again, though, treatment of these topics has been somewhat uneven, governed more by critical taste and ideological preoccupation than by historical precision. During the studio era, for instance, most of the major and minor companies made musicals. But research into the production policies and output of these companies has been very uneven, and this is as true of the musical as it is of other genres. Thus while there is a whole book devoted to the output of the Freed unit of MGM (Fordin 1975), there are no book-length studies of the musicals produced by Fox, by RKO, by Warner Bros, or by Paramount, let along those produced by Columbia, Universal or Republic. Moreover, while scholars like Mordden (1988, p. 234) and Schatz (1988, p. 447) respectively document Warners' role in the revival of the musical in the early 1930s, and MGM's numerical dominance of the genre in the postwar period, they are not really able to account for either. The same is true of Collins's account of Paramount's propensity for operetta and of Warners' propensity for contemporary settings and backstage conventions in the 1930s, and of MGM's propensity for self-reflexivity in the 1940s and 1950s (Collins, 1988, pp. 271–3, 275–7). And the same is also true of Rubin's observation that Fox's musicals in the 1940s tended on the one hand to feature big hands and exotic settings and on the other to eschew 'integration, coherent narrativity, consistent characterization, or even simply logic' (Rubin, 1993, p. 159). In addition, aside from Fordin's book on Freed, there are no detailed studies of the work of unit producers like Charles Rogers, Hunt Stromberg, Joe Pasternak or Pandro S. Berman, though it should be noted that Schatz contains references to all these figures, and a particularly interesting account of the roles played by Rogers and Pasternak in the development of a formula for Deanna Durbin's musicals at Universal in the late 1930s (Schatz, 1988, pp. 237–42).

Pandro S. Berman is probably best known as unit producer on the Astaire–Rogers musicals at RKO in the 1930s. These films, and Astaire's role within them as choreographer and director of musical numbers as well as singer, dancer and star, have been subject to extensive analysis, not least as relatively early examples of integrated musicals on screen. Meuller's book-length study (1985) documents in detail the modes of integration in these and other Astaire films, Astaire's eclectic style as choreographer, the traditions of dance upon which he drew, and in particular his style as choreographer for the camera, filming and editing sequences of dance in such a way as to preserve the integrity of the body and the space within which it moves.

Along with the work of Ernst Lubitsch and Rouben Mamoulian at Paramount in the early 1930s, the Astaire–Rogers films are generally cited as important points of reference for the work of Vincente Minnelli, Gene Kelly, Stanley Donen, and others at MGM in the 1940s and 1950s. Minnelli's commitment to integration is well documented, not least in his interviews and autobiography (Minnelli, 1974 and Delameter, 1981, pp. 265–74). From this point of view, Elsaesser's account of Minnelli's films is exemplary (1981). As he points out, the central characters are engaged in a struggle to assert their identity, to articulate their vision of the world. In the musicals they succeed, and a key device in this respect is what Genne (1992) has termed 'the dance–drama', a lengthy sequences of dance in which the terms of the struggle are laid bare. Dance–dramas are also used by Donen and Kelly, who are both committed to integration too. Where they differ from Minnelli is in their preferences for stories involving strong male friendships, in their deployment of a sparser, brighter and more evenly lit *mise-en-scène*, and in their use of what Genne calls 'street dances' (like 'Singin' in the Rain') in preference to the 'festive' or 'party' scenes that tend to figure in Minnelli's films.

Minnelli, Donen, Kelly and Astaire all tend to contrast their work with that of

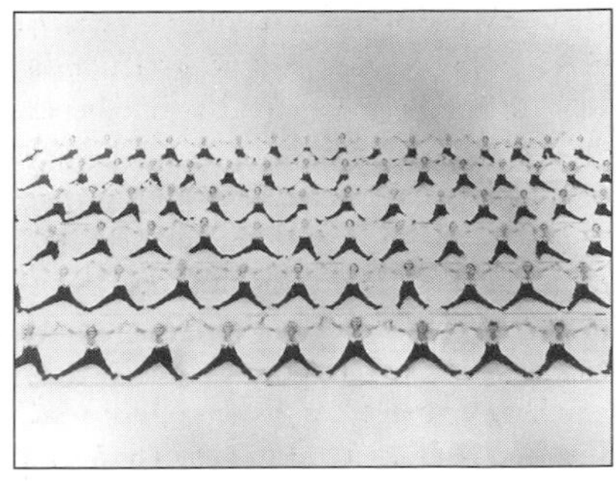

Dames – musical as 'spectacle organised around the female body'

Busby Berkeley, not least on the grounds of integration, motivation and display. However as Rubin has pointed out, Berkeley's work – both on screen and on stage – belongs to a tradition that includes the circus, nineteenth-century extravaganza, the Wild West Show, and the spectacular revue, a tradition that has always eschewed integration, and one whose persistence leads him to argue that 'the history of the musical ... [is] ... not so much a relentless, unidirectional drive toward effacing the last stubborn remnants of nonintegration, but a succession of different ways of articulating the tension and interplay between integrative (chiefly narrative) and nonintegrative (chiefly spectacle) elements' (Rubin, 1993, pp. 12–13). Rubin points out that in films like *The Gang's all Here* (1943), Berkeley sought 'to spectacularize the entire film' (Rubin, 1993, p. 161), to turn the conventional relationship between the narrative and the numbers inside out. Alain Masson (1981) makes a similar point about George Sidney's work, arguing both that Sidney systematically exploited the artifice and the disjunctive potential of the musical and that his critical reputation has tended to suffer as a result.

Berkeley's work has also been criticised for what Lucy Fischer (1981) has called its 'optical politics'. In an analysis of *Dames* (1934), Fischer points out that women literally become two-dimensional images, subordinated to a voyeuristic gaze whose instrument is the camera and whose source is resolutely male. In this context, it is worth nothing that Berkeley made a number of musicals with Esther Williams in the 1940s and 1950s, and that along with Sonja Henie and Eleanor Powell, Williams is one of a trio of female performers whose films have been analysed by Faller in terms of what he calls

The subversive power of Eleanor Powell in *Lady be Good*

their 'subversive power' (Faller, 1992, p. v). In each case, Faller sees the relationship between the narrative and the numbers as the site of a potential contradiction between the powers and performance skills demonstrated in and through the numbers and the ideological work of the plot. Thus Henie's solitary skills as a skater and Williams' solitary skills as a swimmer so dominate the numbers in their films that narratives which seek to pair them up with men 'fail to contain' them (Faller, 1992, p. 205). Meanwhile Powell's skills as a dancer result, almost uniquely, in narratives which centre as much on a successful career as on domesticity or romance.

The relationship between gender, narrative and spectacle in the musical has been explored in the case of male performers too. Cohan, for example, argues that Fred Astaire's 'male image' is grounded in 'the so-called "feminine" tropes of narcissism, exhibitionism, and masquerade' (Cohan, 1993, p. 48), while Rickard (1996) argues not only that the dance sequences in the Astaire–Rogers films serve to sexualise Astaire's masculinity, but also that this sexualisation is authorised for the audience by Rogers's gaze. More traditional analyses of star personae and musical performance skills can meanwhile be found in Babington and Evans (1985), who discuss Jeanette MacDonald, Maurice Chevalier, Fred Astaire, Ginger Rogers and Gene Kelly. As well as Kelly and Astaire, Delameter (1981) discusses Alice Faye, Betty Grable, Danny Kaye, Bill Robinson and others, though principally as dancers rather than as actors, singers or stars. Reflecting the tendency to focus on dance rather than music and song in the Hollywood musical, he also discusses such choreographers as Hermes Pan, Robert Alton, Jack Cole, Michael Kidd and Bob Fosse.

This account has so far focussed on the studio era. However, although the musical is often viewed as a quintessential studio form, and although the number of musicals produced has certainly declined since the 1960s, the genre has by no means disappeared entirely. Aside from the occasional 'revisionist' musical like *Nashville* (1975) and *All the Jazz* (1978) (viewed by Collins (1988, p. 277) as 'metafictional' extensions of the self-reflexive Freed unit films), and aside from the even more occasional revival of something akin to the traditional musical like *Evita* (1996), the numerically dominant form over the last thirty years has been the rock musical.

The rock musical was born in the 1950s with teenpics like *Jailhouse Rock* (1957) and *the Girl Can't Help It* (1956). Apart from research on the synergistic connections between the film and popular music industries and their effects on musical films, debate since then has tended to focus on the extent to which it has challenged or changed the values and conventions of the traditional

Beyond the traditional musical? *Saturday Night Fever*

Hollywood musical. For Grant, the anarchic rebelliousness and raw sexuality associated with rock 'n' roll in the 1950s were potentially disruptive of the genre's commitment to romance and community. He argues, however, that by 'the stressing of rock's potential for community, and the taming of rock's energy through a deliberate moulding of its stars ... rock 'n' roll changed much more than ... the musical film; (Grant, 1986, p. 199). For Telotte (1980), by contrast, the musical has changed fundamentally since the 1950s, not because of its music, but because of a shift in the balance between its 'real' and its 'ideal' components. On the one hand musicals like *Grease* (1978) and *The Wiz* (1978) 'tend to integrate the musical components at the expense of a realistic plot. As a result they seem to deny or denigate the reality of the world that has given birth to the music' (Telotte, 1980, p. 3). On the other, musicals like *Saturday Night Fever* (1977) and *The Buddy Holly Story* (1978) realistically motivate singing and dancing as diegetic action while setting them in counterpoint to a narrative world otherwise filled with difficulties, dangers and frustrations. In this way they address the limitations – as well as the potential – of music and dance as means of escaping, transcending or changing the everyday world.

The 'escapist' status of the musical has been addressed at length by Dyer, Feuer and Altman. For Dyer (1981), musicals offer aesthetically 'utopian' solutions to real social needs and contradictions. The same is true for Feuer, who stresses the extent to which its artificial, quasi-modernist devices serve the conservative ends of show-biz by seeking to bridge the gap between producer and consumer and create in its stead an illusion of community. In this way the Hollywood musical can be seen as a form of modern industrial mass entertainment which nevertheless 'aspires to the condition of folk art' (Feuer, 1982/1993, p. 3).

For Altman (1987), the resolution of contradictions and oppositions is not just a function of the musical, but also a method of analysis. Wishing to construct a rigorous critical definition of the musical, and a systematic history of its forms, its cultural functions, and its history, Altman constructs a corpus of films on the basis of perceived structural, stylistic and ideological characteristics, all of which entail opposition and mediation. Central to the corpus is a 'dual-focus' structure in which 'the text proceeds by alternation, confrontation, and parallelism between male and female leads (or groups)' (Altman, 1987, p. 107), and in which a romance plot and a couple (or couples) provide the basis for the construction and reconciliation not just of differences of gender, but also – depending on the film – of differences of class, age, wealth, personality and outlook and so on as well. What this means, among other things, is that traditional narrative values like causality and motivation, and the conventional opposition between the narrative and the numbers, are displaced by structures and devices of comparison and contrast whose role is to articulate the dualities with which any particular film is concerned. Among these devices are 'the audio dissolve' and the 'video dissolve'. Where the former 'superimposes sounds' (Altman, 1987, p. 63) in moving from one portion of the soundtrack to another (from conversation, for example, to music and song), the latter serves to connect 'two separate places, times, or levels of reality' (Altman, 1987, p. 74). Both devices thus serve both to mark and to bridge oppositions.

Altman also constructs a new typology of musical forms. Using the relationship between the musical's romance plot and its ideological oppositions as a basis, he suggests that there are three basic musical types: 'the fairly tale musical', in which 'restoring order to the couple accompanies and parallels ... restoration of order to an imaginary kingdom', 'the show musical', in which 'creating the couple is associated with the creation of a work of art (Broadway show, Hollywood film, fashion magazine, concert, etc.)', and 'the folk musical', in which 'integrating two disparate individuals into a single couple heralds the entire group's communion with each other' (Altman, 1987, p. 126).

Altman's book is to date the most sustained and detailed attempt to provide a theoretically rigorous account of the Hollywood musical. However, while it encompasses an impressive array of films and examples, and while its typology is convincing, it is not without its problems. Like Dyer and Feuer (1983/1992), Altman tends to argue that the musical always resolves the contradictions with which it is deals. This position is not uncommon among theories of genre, as we shall see. But it tends on the one hand to obviate the need for further research, since the answers to questions about ideology in particular are always known in advance. One the other, it tends to underestimate the extent to which musicals like *Brigadoon* (1954) and *Maytime* (1937) blatantly signal their resolutions as unreal, and the extent to which musicals like *West Side Story* and in particular *It's Always Fair Weather* (1955) (Babington and Evans: 166–86 and Wood, 1975: 146–64) lay the costs of their resolutions uncomfortably bare. Meanwhile Altman's insistence on the centrality of romance and a dual-focus structure is problematic, both because these elements characterise most romantic comedies as well as many musicals, and because some musicals lack either or both. Aside from *The Wizard of Oz* (1939), an example acknowledged by Altman himself (1987, p. 104), one might cite *Ziegfeld Follies* (1946), which as a revue lacks an overarching plot, *Hold That Co-Ed* (1938), in which the dual cultural values of skilful, hard work and entrepreneurial flair are embodied in the alliance between a football coach and a local politician rather than in the film's perfunctory romance, *Poor Little Rich Girl* (1936), a Shirley Temple film which lacks both a romance and a dual-focus structure, *Jupiter's Darling* (1955), which is triply rather than dually focussed, and *Meet Me in St Louis*, which contains two romances, neither of which is dual focus in nature, and neither of which embodies the film's central opposition between domestic and familial harmony and domestic and famial discord.

Responding to an earlier version of these ideas (Altman, 1981), Babington and Evans cite *Gold Diggers of 1933* (1933) and *Easter Parade* (1948) as exceptions as well (1985, p. 80). While less ambitious than Altman, their own discussions of these and other musicals tend to be more attentive to the genre's multifarious nature as well as to the films' specificities. To that extent, their book shares the virtues of those ideologically orientated analyses which, are rather more localised and context specific, rather more focussed on particular issues, aspects, periods, performers and films than a book like Altman's.

Selected Reading

Rick Altman (ed), *Genre: The Musical*, London, RKP, 1981.

Rick Altman, *The American Film Musical*, Bloomington, Indiana University Press, 1987.

Jim Collins, 'The Musical', in Wes D. Gehring (ed.), *Handbook of American Film Genres*, New York, Greenwood Press, 1988.

Jane Feuer, *The Hollywood Musical*, London, Macmillan, 1982 and 1993.

Martin Rubin, *Showstoppers: Busby Berkeley and the Tradition of Spectacle*, New York, Columbia University Press, 1993.

John Mueller, *Astaire Dancing: The Musical Films*, New York, Knopf, 1985.

Gold Diggers of 1933 (USA 1933 *p.c* – Warner Bros.; *d* – Mervyn LeRoy; sd b/w)

Discussion of the 1930s musical usually sets up Busby Berkeley and Fred Astaire as contrasting poles. In the simplistic teleological version of the genre's history it is Astaire's intimacy which is acclaimed as advancing the musical towards its later integrated and 'realistic' modes, while Berkeley becomes a dead end of baroque spectacle.

For Leo Braudy, Berkeley's 'attitude towards individuals is that of a silent film director, iconographic and symmetric'; Braudy also points up the crucial distinction between Berkeley's and Astaire's roles in their films – Berkeley the 'non-participating choreographer–director', Astaire the 'dancer–choreographer himself ... a participant' (Braudy, 1976, p. 142). To put it simply, Berkeley contributed a great deal to the use of movement in cinema, but almost nothing to dance (see Delameter, 1981).

Gold Diggers of 1933 (choreographed by Berkeley) is one of the musicals Richard Dyer singles out for analysis in 'Entertainment and utopia'. He sees the relationship between numbers and narrative as particularly problematic in this film, given its explicit narrative concern with the effects of the Depression: 'The thrust of the narrative is towards seeing the show as "solution" to the ... problems of the characters; yet the non-realist presentation of the numbers makes it very hard to take this solution seriously' (Dyer, 1977, p. 8).

This is clearly the case with the 'Shadow Waltz' – one of Berkeley's more fanciful set-pieces, yet interestingly atypical in its relative lack of overt sexual symbolism. While the female body is as usual the raw material for aesthetic composition and scopic concentration, the end result is, for Berkeley, a little tame, even prim. With the exception of one shot of reflected legs, the *mise en scène* is not directly voyeuristic. This is perhaps not unrelated to the number's slight straining after European high cultural values (it is, after all, a waltz).

Dyer's argument is less convincing in relation to 'Remember My Forgotten Man', although this number is a prime example of his categories of intensity and – all the more powerful because inflected negatively – community. It, too, is not typical Berkeley, nor even typical of the whole genre, in being direct social comment, worlds away from the same film's 'Petting in the Park' or any of the Astaire love ballads. It was certainly read as aberrant by some critics in the 1930s: 'I can take most war films cheerfully on the chin, but I want none of them in musical comedies, where they certainly do not belong. For downright offensiveness and bad taste, that last reel wins the Croix de Garbage' (quoted in Roth, 1981, p. 55).

Precisely why seriousness and social awareness were thought so incompatible with a musical rendering, even so early in the genre's history, is an intriguing question. Certainly 'My Forgotten Man' shows that the attempt could be brought off, indeed the number now strikes us among Berkeley's most impressive, demonstrating his undeniable mastery in the orchestration of space, spectacle and editing without the usual stress on fetishistic voyeurism.

Top Hat (USA 1935 *p.c* – RKO; *d* – Mark Sandrich; sd b/w)

Like all the Astaire–Rogers films, this can be profitably considered in terms of its sexual politics, the ideology of the perfect romance. *Top Hat* offers a particularly pure example of the way in which heterosexual desire in the musical 'occupies a central as opposed to a secondary or peripheral place in the discursive ensemble ... its presence is a necessity, not a variable option' (Neale, 1980, p. 23).

The two couple-dances, 'Isn't This a Lovely Day' and 'Cheek to Cheek' could, with appropriate caution, be analysed in

The 'mutual game' of dance – Astaire and Rogers perform in *Top Hat*

terms of signifactory potential of non-representational signs, for although, as Dyer says, the methodology for any such reading remains particularly undeveloped (Dyer, 1977, p. 4), a clear difference between these dances is perceptible.

Isn't This a Lovely Day' offers a rare pleasure in mainstream cinema – the couple as equals. It is the courtship dance which has the same structural function in all Astaire–Rogers films, as the antagonistic couple forget their personal animosity in the joy of shared dancing. The dance is in one respect Astaire's pursuit of Rogers, but it never becomes an oppressive celebration of male prowess. The star personas of the couple are a contributing factor – Astaire is not the conventional macho hero, Rogers is never the demure feminine heroine. In this dance their equality is further reinforced by Rogers's 'masculine' clothes (dress being one of the key non-representational signs). The dance becomes a mutual game, the couple's joy further multiplied by the realisation that each knows the rules of the other's game. Once again, this is a reading of non-representational signs, in this case gesture. The setting is 'rural' (in the park) as opposed to the glossy interiors that serve as the space for the later dances in each of their films, and they end by shaking hands rather than kissing. They remain equal in dance (whatever the relative skills of the performers) as long as signifiers of conventional romance are avoided.

The different complexion of the second couple-dance, 'Cheek to Cheek', indicates the importance of non-representational signs. Now the dancers are in evening dress, Rogers's dress a particularly elaborate 'feminine' creation. The setting is the nightclub, interior glamour as opposed to pastoral outdoors. The style of dancing has changed, traditional gender roles are as strongly reinforced here as they were unnecessary earlier; aspirations to the balletic have replaced the previous informality. The couple's steps are now organised around his dominance ('leading' is the appropriate dance term) where they had been identical or humorously competitive: If 'Cheek to Cheek' reinforces the terms of classical Hollywood romance, then 'Isn't This a Lovely Day' at least suggests an alternative, perhaps utopian view, of romance based on equality.

This shift from dislike to mutual discovery to conventional romance recurs not only throughout this and other Astaire–Rogers films, but throughout most musicals, comedies and romances in Hollywood production. The Astaire–Rogers relationship has assumed mythic status as an ideal of the ideology of romance, so that the responsibility of analysis lies with teasing apart the contradictions in that ideology. In their progression from side-by-side to cheek-to-cheek, these films clearly close down more egalitarian possibilities. However, the existence of the earlier dances of mutual discovery raises the question of whether subversive moments can escape eventual narrative recuperation.

Meet Me in St Louis (USA 1994 *p.c* – MGM; *d* – Vincente Minnelli; sd col)

Meet Me in St Louis is in part the product of an interest in and celebration of rural and provincial America at the time. It was also one of the first in a cycle of films to feature a nostalgic, turn-of-the-century setting, a theme which emerged in the mid-1940s and continued through into the early 1950s (other examples include *Mother Wore Tights*, 1947, and *Cheaper By the Dozen*, 1950). It is considered an exemplary example of the integrated musical produced by Vincente Minnelli, Gene Kelly and Stanley Donen at MGM.

The film is divided into four parts: spring, autumn, winter and summer. Each part begins with a framed sepia photograph of the Smith home in St Louis; these still images – which slowly transform into motion and colour – introduce one of the film's key thematic elements: the house. The opening musical number, 'Meet Me in St Louis', introduces the interior of the house, the Smith family members and their housekeeper, as the song is 'passed' from one to another and from room to room. The 'travelling song', as Beth Eliot Genne (1984) terms it, derives from the opening number of Rouben Mamoulian's *Love Me Tonight* (1932), and was a standard feature of the Minnelli/Donen/Kelly musicals at MGM; particularly of note is it synthesis of camera movement, décor, character movement, gesture and music.

Following the introduction of a secondary romance plot (between the older sister, Rose, and her beau, Warren), the film's principal romance is inaugurated (once again through song), when young Esther (Judy Garland) sees her new neighbour, John – when 'the girl next door' first encounters 'the boy next door' (characters derived, as Genne points out, from the backyard musicals in which Garland began her career). Importantly, neither romance is dual focus in nature, nor do they consistently embody the film's main thematic oppositions: John and Warren espouse the same values as Esther and Rose, and bring complication and conflict only in so far as at various points they are (mistakenly) perceived to be a threat to the Smith family, its unity, and its location in their house in St Louis. However, it is the father who is the main vehicle of thematic and dramatic opposition as it is his job move to New York which jeopardises the stability of the household.

Esther and John actually meet and fall in love during a party at the Smith house (and in particular during the virtually wordless 'gaslight' sequence, a kind of numberless number, and the 'Over the Banister' song that follows). The party is one of several 'festive sequences' in the film (and indeed in the work of Minnelli generally). These sequences serve, among other things, to mark the relationship between the Smith family and the wider local community in St Louis, and to articulate the integration of the one within the other. The autumn section contains the Halloween sequence, a variant which serves to articulate a countercurrent or underside, one in which a resident within the community is feared and attacked, and is marked as not belonging.

Central to this sequence is the youngest daughter, Tootie, who is a vehicle for the expression of an underside to the cosiness of familial and provincial life and values, often in and through images (verbal and visual) of hysteria, violence and death. For the most part these expressions are marked as comic. But they take on a seriousness and desperation when in the winter 'section' she destroys the snowmen she has built in the garden. Here, in a quintessential Minnelli sequence, the frustration of wishes and desires finds articulation in the destruction of a décor, and in the destruction, specifically, of the products of artistic and imaginative vision. Significantly, it is this act which leads to the father's change of heart (filmed amid a half-empty house, its contents packed away for the move to New York), allowing the desires of Tootie and Esther and of the other members of the family finally to prevail amid the carefully choreographed décor of the 1904 World's Fair.

Singin' in the Rain (USA 1952 *p.c* – MGM; *d* – Gene Kelly and Stanley Donen; sd col.)

Following *On the Town* (1949), *Singin' in the Rain* is the second film Gene Kelly and Stanley Donen made together at MGM (a third, *It's Always Fair Weather*, was released in 1955). It can be categorised in a number of ways: a musical comedy involving (mild) satire and parody; an integrated backstage musical; a 'show musical' (which is how it is categorised by Altman, 1987); a 'catalogue' musical (a vehicle for the numbers written by a particular composer, songwriter, or songwriting team – here the team of lyricist Arthur Freed and composer Herbert Nacio Brown); and also as a vehicle for Gene Kelly as singer, dancer and star, and for Kelly's (and Donen's) idea about dance and the presentation of dance in musical film.

However, one of the film's major features is the extent to which it escapes, mixes and modifies some of these categories. Its film-industry setting means that it becomes a 'backscreen' rather than a backstage musical as such. As Beth Eliot Genne has argued, the style pioneered by Donen and Kelly in *On the Town* – the use of bright, evenly lit primary colours, spare sets, and an accelerated pace – is here mixed with elements derived from the work of Minnelli – notably the extensive use of the boom camera in the filming of some of the numbers, the incorporation of a dance drama, and the occasional use of chiaroscuro (evident, for instance, in the title number) (Genne, 1984, p. 357). And as Peter Wollen has argued, the film is at one and the same time a show musical, a folk musical, and a fairy-tale musical – a combination of all three of Altman's categories (Wollen, 1992, p. 55).

In addition, while most of the film's musical numbers are motivated (and hence integrated) by their showbiz context, by diegetic performance, and/or by situation, character and plot, play is made with some of the devices used to motivate numbers and hence with the concept of integration. For example, 'Broadway Rhythm', itself a mix of dance drama and conventional backstage production number, is introduced as an idea for a production number for the film being made within a film. It so obviously fulfils this function for *Singin' in the Rain* itself, and hence exceeds its motivation as a mere idea, that the line which follows its conclusion – 'Well, what do you think R.F.?' –becomes a joke.

'You Were Meant For Me' is one of a series of courtship dances that occur in Kelly's films. The courtship dance was a feature of the Astaire–Rogers films, but Kelly's dance style and persona is very different. Whereas Astaire's style combines ballroom and tap, and is known for its detachment, poise and control, Kelly's technique is a combination of ballet, modern dance and tap, and is noted for its athleticism, energy and slapstick (explored in the 'Make 'Em Laugh' number that Kelly choreographed for Donald O'Connor). In addition, whereas Astaire is associated with 'high society', Kelly is considered more 'proletarian', more virile and masculine: 'For Kelly, obsessed with the validity of male dance, the presence of the body was all-important, a male body that is acceptably exhibitionist in its athleticism' (Wollen, 1992, p. 57). Partly for this reason, Kelly's films, while concerned with heterosexual romance, are always also concerned with male friendship (see Delameter, 1981, pp. 133–67 and 206–27, and Genne, 1984, pp. 176–423).

As Babington and Evans point out, Kelly's persona also contains an element of self-assured self-regard and fake charm. The characters he plays have consequently often to be chastened (and frequently are conmen or hams) (Babington and Evans, 1985, p. 183). In *Singin' in the Rain*, these elements are linked to Don's character prior to his encounter with Kathy. They are also linked to the themes of artifice and deception, authenticity and truth pervade the film, and, via the differences between Don's verbal account of his early career and the visual account which the film provides us, to the opposition or mismatch between sound and image that provides one of their principal vehicles. Peter Wollen goes so far as to argue that 'the core issue in the film is that of the relationship between sound and image. Things can only end happily when, so to speak, a properly "married print" is produced, in which voice and image naturally joined together' (Wollen, 1992, p. 55). He goes on to say that 'The underlying theme is that of nature as truth and unity, versus artifice as falsehood and separation' (1992, p. 55). However, things are a little more complex than this. As 'You Were Meant For Me' shows, artifice can be authentic; the real opposition is between honesty and dishonesty, truth and falsehood, whether in the realm of artifice, or in the realm of nature.

Gentlemen Prefer Blondes (USA 1953 *p.c* – 20th Century-Fox; *d* – Howard Hawks; sd col.)

Because of its director, there have been many attempts to accommodate this film within an auteurist framework (see Howard Hawks, p. 294). All have faced severe problems, with Andrew Sarris going so far as to omit the film completely from his entry on Hawks in *The American Cinema* (1968). Robin Wood relegates it to the 'Failures and Marginal Works' chapter of his book on Hawks, deeming it not 'meaningful', lacking in 'satisfactory unity', bereft of any 'firm positive centre' – all, taking into account Wood's critical framework at that time, and highly pejorative remarks (Wood, 1981, p. 171).

Equally, standard histories of the genre have found it something of a rogue text. Its sexual knowingness, brashness and indebtedness to vaudeville traditions make it difficult to set alongside the balletic pretensions of the 1950s Kelly or the aestheticised ideals of Minnelli. It quite literally clashes. Its use of Marilyn Monroe and Jane Russell, however, bring it into line with the increased use of sexual stereotyping that has often been seen as typical of Hollywood production later in the decade.

A third dominant approach has been to read it in terms of its particular inflection of the Monroe star persona, though this can raise just as many problems as attempting to manoeuvre it into the 'Hawksian canon'. Perhaps a new way into the text, more precisely into its sexual politics (signalled as important by the unusual absence of any even remotely attractive male characters) is through the critically neglected role of Jane Russell.

This film contains one of the most extraordinary numbers in any Hollywood musical. Russell self-parodically pouts 'Ain't There Anyone Here for Love?' against the heaving backdrop of the American Olympic team. These men, clad in fetching flesh-coloured shorts, perform what appear to be flamboyantly masculine exercises are in fact used as chorus-girl gyrations. The number can be taken as a striking example of the tensions of homoeroticism in Hawks' films, but it is also a generic parody – casting Russell as Dick Powell in an inverted Berkeley production number.

Quite how one reads the courtroom number is open to debate. A legitimate case could be made for mounting a critique of its fetishistic exploitation of Russell, or for enjoying her manipulation of the various legal, social and sexual codes and institutions ranged against her. As with the previous number, as indeed with so many musical texts, the choice of reading must be considered in terms of how on regards the interpretation of non-representational signs, and of how much weight one places on the potential escape of reputedly subversive energies before the recuperation of narrative closure. Russell is narratively subordinated into marriage, but the privileged images of the film, one could argue, are her capture of the courtroom and her cry of 'Doubles, anyone?' to the bulging narcissists of the Olympic team. Notions of authorial control, star persona, generic specificity and cultural context would all have to be considered in any such analysis.

Sweet Charity (USA 1968 *p.c* – Universal; *d* – Bob Fosse; sd col.)

By the late 1960s, the moment of production of this film, the musical was in most respects stranded by shifts in industrial practice and cultural sensibility. The traditional audiences of cinema were largely captured by television, and the mainstream musical could hardly be expected to redirect itself towards the new youth market since that market's preferred musical entertainment had little to do with Irving Berlin or Rodgers and Hammerstein. The Elvis Presley films were an attempt to combine the old cinematic practice with the new musical practice, but they functioned largely as objects for fan adoration. Hollywood was deceived by the great success of *The Sound of Music* into investing in other expensive musicals, such as *Sweet Charity*, which flopped.

Despite its commercial failure, however, *Sweet Charity* has been seized on by devotees of the musical, and, more importantly, Bob Fosse has been hailed as the new saviour–*auteur* of the genre. Recognised as a major choreographer in earlier films such as *The Pajama Game* (1957), Fosse directs dance in a distinctive and immediately recognisable way (see Delameter, 1981). 'Hey, Big Spender' has taken its place in the nostalgic repertory of Hollywood musical numbers. But to obtain a perspective on *Sweet Charity* beyond the authorial and adulatory, the film must be considered in terms of its historical moment.

'Hey, Big Spender' is memorable for reasons that go beyond talent – it is the most sexually direct musical number since the heyday of Berkeley. And it can be so because of relaxed censorship laws – moreover it *needs* to be so to receive the description 'adult' intended to attract a late 1960s audience. (Fosse was to capitalise on such social nuances again with *Cabaret* in 1972, Hollywood's first foray into decadent chic.) 'If They Could See Me Now', however, is of a different register. Editing trickery apart (and the film can be dated now by the self-congratulatory flashiness of the editing),

Reviving the musical? *Sweet Charity*

this number is a throwback to vaudeville. The film is trying to have it both ways – the so-daring sleaze of 'Big Spender' and the old-fashioned barnstorming of 'If They Could See Me Now'. The use of top hat and cane in the latter clearly marks it as an attempted tribute to earlier musical styles, but the effect is muddled.

Sweet Charity was also acclaimed for introducing a central star performance reminiscent of the genre's classic period (see Kobal, 1971). Shirley MacLaine does, indeed, perform a creditable impersonation of a musical star, but she is indulged by Fosse (especially in 'If They Could See Me Now') to an extent undreamed of in, say, the 1940s musical. The very notion of a old-style musical star functioning in the late 1960s seems anachronistic. MacLaine's one register is the relentless projection of being lovable – difficult to bring off in any text, and floundering in misplaced energy in *Sweet Charity*, where Fosse's determination to be modern is uppermost. The jagged, mannered stylisation of a number like 'The Aloof' cannot coexist with the gushing warmth of MacLaine without resulting in a seriously ruptured text.

On a Clear Day You Can See Forever (USA 1970 *p.c* – Paramount; *d* – Vincente Minnelli; sd col.)

With Minnelli's musicals (as that very phrase shows) issues of authorship occupy the centre of critical discussion. *On a Clear Day* could also be approached in terms of its place within a declining genre (like *Sweet Charity*) or consideration of Barbra Streisand's star persona, but its chief interest is as a Minnelli text (see Cook, 1977).

Thomas Elsaesser's classic account of Minnelli suggests that all the director's films, of whatever genre, 'aspire to the condition of the musical' and goes on to assert that:

> Minnelli's films are structured so as to give the greatest possible scope to the expansive nature of a certain vitality (call it 'will', or libido) – in short, to the confrontation of an inner, dynamic reality and an outward, static one ... What characterises the Minnelli musical is the total and magic victory of the impulse, the vision, over any reality whatsoever. (Elsaesser, 1981).

The confrontation referred to is of course best embodied in the numbers/narrative tension, with the numbers bearing the victorious magic. Minnelli films like *The Pirate* (1948), *Yolanda and the Thief* (1945), and *Brigadoon* (1954) are usually produced as evidence to clinch the case. What makes *On a Clear Day* so interesting, not only as a Minnellian text but also for the genre as a whole, is that there are no 'numbers' as such.

Questions of authorship – Minelli's late film *On A Clear Day You Can See Forever*

On a Clear Day, like most musicals, strives to attain an ideal, utopian world. This world is not, however, the ideal romance of *Top Hat*, the perfect show of *Gold Diggers of 1933*, the mythicised New York of *On The Town*, or even the dream village of *Brigadoon* – it is purely abstract, wholly internalised, a utopian state of mind. Thus *On a Clear Day* has a distinct, seductive appeal to certain theories of the genre, in that it can be posited as a transcendent soaring conclusion to the genre's striving after the ideal – and the film's narrative resolution can only aid such a reading. It comes at virtually the close of Minnelli's career, so it is perfectly suited to round off that particular authorial narrative. At this point, however, the theoretical pretence breaks down, and we are left with something resembling Prospero's-last-speech-is-Shakespeare's-farewell to the theatre criticism transposed from Stratford to Hollywood.

In such writing about Minnelli's musicals as with all dedicated auteurist criticism, the pleasure of the text is the central issue – but the text in question is the body of films that make up the authorial supertext. The individual film is valued according to how well it can be moulded to fit into that wider text. Thus in terms of the musical and Minnelli, certain films receive what might strike uninitiated viewers as undue attention. *The Pirate*, *Yolanda and the Thief* and *Brigadoon* were all commercial failures, none of them has an important place within popular and fan histories of the genre, but all three are indispensable to academic criticism of the musical.

On a Clear Day follows this pattern, perhaps even more strongly, since it is virtually incomprehensible to viewers not immersed in Minnelli certainly it is liable to strike them as miscast (a film posited on delicacy of touch and intellectual audacity of conception is seriously hampered by the presence of such an abrasive star as Streisand) and confused. For the Minnelli watcher, though, it is liable to prove deeply satisfying. If nothing else, the film shows how far the musical has come from its once unassailable position as socially central definer and dispenser of mass entertainment.

TEENPICS

A period in life between childhood and adulthood has been recognised and marked by most societies in most periods of history (Graff, 1995). However, during the course of the twentieth century in America and elsewhere in the industrialised west, this period has tended to increase, and alongside a series of social policies, practices and institutions which have increasingly treated those under twenty as both distinct and separate from adults, two key terms have emerged in America to mark it: 'adolescence' (a term first coined by psychologist G. Stanley Hall in 1904), and 'teenager' (a term first used in the popular press in the 1920s, and first fully established during the course of the Second World War) (Kett, 1977). According to Maltby, a '"self-conscious subculture" of the young developed during the 1920s and 1930s as a largely urban white middle-class response to the increasing leisure opportunities afforded by changing social attitudes' (Maltby, 1989, p. 140). But as he himself goes on to argue, the first fully commercialised, cross-class, transnational – though for the most part equally white – forms of teenage culture emerged in America in the 1950s, as significant numbers of young people with increasing amounts of disposable income and leisure time comprised for the first time in the west both an increasing proportion of the population as a whole and an expanding sector of the market for services and goods.

In parallel fashion, Hollywood has always made films about young people (Considine, 1981). It has also made films designed or presumed to cater for what it called 'the juve trade' – juvenile spectators. (There is a distinction between the two. Films about the young are not necessarily addressed to the young; films presumed to address the young do not necessarily focus on or feature young characters. The 'bad boy' films of the late 1890s and 1900s were presumed to appeal to nostalgic middle-class men (Kramer unpublished), while B-westerns and action serials, which featured adult characters and actors, were often presumed to appeal to young teenage boys, and animal films like *National Velvet* (1944) and *The Yearling* (1946) were aimed at an audience of families.) However, the teenpic itself is normally held to emerge, like modern teenage culture, during the course of the 1950s.

One of the conditions underlying its emergence was a growing awareness on Hollywood's part of the importance of the teenage audience. Flying in the face of the industry's presumption that 'Everyone who was not too young, too old, too sick, or living in the remotest backwoods' attended most movies most of the time (Quigley, 1957, p. 21), audience research conducted in

The social-problem film – *Blackboard Jungle*

the late 1940s indicated that 'age [was] the most important personal factor by which the movie audience is characterized' and that 'the decline of movie attendance with increasing age is very sharp' (Lazarsfield, 1947, pp. 162–3). Coming at a time when the industry faced unprecented challenges and changes in the form of divorcement and divestiture, competition from television and other leisure pursuits, suburbanisation, a shift in audience demographics, a precipitous decline in ticket sales and audience attendance, these findings reinforced the growing importance of the teenage market for films and of targetting this market by drawing on aspects of teenage culture and by catering for teenage interests, tastes and concerns (Doherty, 1988, pp. 20–5 and 45–66).

A reflection in part of the industry's uncertainties, the teenpic was at this point heterogeneous, multi-dimensional, and often contradictory in its forms, concerns and modes of address. A number of genres, traditions and production trends, some of them quite distinct, contributed to its initial development. Firstly, there were mainstream dramas and social problem films like *The Wild One* (1954), *The Blackboard Jungle* and *Rebel without a Cause* (both 1955), each of them produced by mainstream studios (Columbia, MGM and Warner Bros respectively), and each of them drawing on a tradition of films about juvenile delinquency, juvenile wildness and juvenile crime that stretched back as far as the 1920s and 1930s and that included films like *Flaming Youth*, *Youth Astray* (1928), *Dead End* (1937), and *Wild Boys of the Road* (1933). However, their immediate origins lay in two separate cycles of juvenile delinquency films made during and just after the Second World War and that included films like *Are these our Children?* (1943), *Where are my Children?* (1944) and *I Accuse my Parents* (1944) on the one hand, and *Gun Crazy* (1949), *City across the River* (1949) and *Knock on any Door* (1949) on the other. The idea and the image of the juvenile delinquent continued to colour films of all kinds made about teenagers in the 1950s and early 1960s, from sensationalised crime dramas and social problem films like *Teenage Crime Wave* (1955), *Girls in Prison* (1956), *Juvenile Jungle* (1958) to musicals like *Jailhouse Rock* (1957) and *West Side Story* (1961), though distinctions need to be made between those films which sought, at least ostensibly, to condemn juvenile delinquency, those which sought to understand it, and those which sought, either way, to use it to appeal either to a teenage or adult audience.

The cultural context within which delinquency emerged as an issue at this time has been explored by Gilbert (1986), the industrial context within which the films emerged by Doherty (1988, pp. 105–41) and Betrock (1986). Gilbert stresses the extent to which a realignment of the relations between the media, the market, the teenage consumer, teenage tastes and teenage behaviour threatened hitherto dominant patterns of cultural authority. Doherty and Betrock stress the heritage and the growing influence of independent production and 'exploitation'.

The term 'exploitation' originally referred both to the publicity techniques used to maximise a film's commercial potential and to the making of films which drew on topical, controversial or otherwise easily saleable subjects. During the studio era, both types of exploitation were common. But they were governed and controlled by the industry's organisations, notably the MPPDA (the Motion Picture Producers and Distributors of America) and its successor, the MPAA (the Motion Picture Association of America), and those films which exploited topics banned by the Production Code were refused a seal of approval and denied access to the theatres controlled by the majors (Schaefer, 1994). However, films which deliberately flouted the Code were produced by small-scale independents for independent distribution and exhibition, and many of these films – among them *The Burning Question* (a.k.a. *Assassin of Youth, Reefer Madness* and *Tell Your Children*) (1936), *High School girl* (1935), *The Road to Ruin* and *Girls of the Underworld* (1932) – used youthful deviance as a framework for dealing with exploitable 'adult' topics like drugs, prostitution, unmarried motherhood and venereal disease (Muller and Farris 1997, pp. 13–31). Following divorcement, the MPAA found it much more difficult to enforce the Code. Meanwhile, the decline in audiences and in the number of films produced by the majors meant that many exhibitors were crying out for films to show, preferably films with exploitable potential, and films which would appeal to those still going to the cinema on a regular basis and to those whose tastes were not catered for by television. As a result, a number of small independent producers and production companies like Samuel Arkoff, Allied Artists and American International Pictures (AIP), together with a handful of unit producers at mainstream studios, like Sam Katzman at Columbia and Albert Zugsmith at Universal, began to tailor their films to the teenage market and to 'marginal' (rather than mainstream) adult audiences, to adopt the techniques and the practices of exploitation, and in the process to defy or at least test the limits of the Production Code and the bounds of 'good taste' as established by the MPAA. Many of these films were about juvenile delinquency and juvenile crime, and the resulting mix of mainstream and independent productions, practices and genres, and of adult, marginal adult and teenage components and points of appeal, is just one index of the 'ambivalence' James Hay sees as fundamental not just to the teenpic, but to teenage culture in general (Hay, 1990, p. 336).

A similar ambivalence marks other 1950s and early 1960s trends and genres, not least 'weirdies' and rock 'n' roll and pop films and musicals, and not least because a similar mix is characteristic of them all. '"Weirdie" was inexact nomenclature for an offbeat science fiction, fantasy, monster, zombie and/or shock film, usually of marginal financing, fantastic content, and ridiculous title' (Doherty, 1986, p. 146). Developing alongside cycles of 'adult' science fiction and low-budget monster films made by the majors, produced both by the majors themselves and by independents like AIP, weirdies in particular sought to capitalise on the popularity of horror and science fiction with teenage spectators. Hence the appearance alongside *The Incredible Shrinking Man* (1957), *I Married a Monster From Outer Space* (1958) and *The Deadly Mantis* (1957) of films with titles like *I Was a Teenage Werewolf* (1957) and *Teenagers from Outer Space* (1959).

Films like this drew on and fed into a wider teenage culture that included horror and fantasy comics. Other films drew on pop and rock 'n' roll. Following the use of 'Rock Around the Clock' on the credits of *The Blackboard Jungle*, Sam Katzman produced the first rock 'n' roll musical, *Rock Around the Clock*, the following year. Unlike *The Blackboard Jungle*, an adult-orientated social problem film, *Rock Around the Clock* was, as Doherty points out, 'the first hugely successful film marketed to teenagers *to the pointed exclusion of their elders*' (Doherty, 1986, p. 74, emphasis in original). It was arguably, therefore, the first modern teenpic, as well as the progenitor of a cycle of rock 'n' roll films that included *Shake, Rattle, and Rock* (1956) and *Rock, Rock, Rock!* (1956), which were both produced by independents and *The Girl Can't Help It* and *Rock, Pretty Baby* (1956), which were both produced by the majors.

These cycles and genres were soon joined by hot-rod films like *Dragstrip Riot* (1958) and *Hot-Rod Girl* (1956), by calypso and beatnik films like *Calypso Joe* (1957) and *The Rebel set* (1959), and by what Doherty calls 'clean teenpics', musicals and light romances like *April Love* (1957) and *Gidget* (1959) which recall a tradition stemming back to the Deanna Durbin, Mickey Rooney and Judy Garland films of the late 1930s and early 1940s (Considine, 1981, pp. 124–6), which parallel what some have seen as the incorporation and neutralisation of rock 'n' roll by the white musical establishment (Martin and Segrave, 1993, pp. 103–8), and which Doherty himself argues addressed teenagers and teenage concerns within an unambiguously white, middle-class adult framework of values. 'In the clean teens baroque phase, AIP's Beach Party cycle (1963–65), parents were banished altogether,' he writes. 'As compensation, though, there was little in this portrait of teenage life that would disturb a worried father. Adults were usually absent, but their values were always present. Fulfilling the best hope of the older generation, the clean teenpics featured an aggressively normal, traditionally good-looking crew of fresh young faces, "good kids" who preferred dates to drugs and crushes to crime' (Doherty, 1986, p. 195).

Doherty's views are echoes by Morris (1994). However, there are a number of unspoken and perhaps rather glib assumptions at work here, not just about the relative merits of preferring dates to drugs and crushes to crime, but also about the relationship between teenage and adult values, about the ethnic politics of early rock 'n' roll, about rebellion and deviance as hallmarks of teenage authenticity, and, indeed, about the authenticity of teenage culture itself. As Graff points out, despite 'striking legacies, images, and myths to the contrary', there are numerous 'paths' to growing up, not just one (Graff, 1995, p. xiii). And as Lewis points out, 'When we are talking about youth we are talking about a fundamentally mediated culture, one that continues to re-present itself in terms of the products it buys, the art that defines it, and the art it defines as its own' (Lewis, 1992, p. 4). It is this 'dialectic of cultural autonomy and media appropriation' that lies at the heart of the teenpic, and that helps generate the ambivalence noted by Hay (1990), and the conflicts and contradictions to which that ambivalence gives rise.

Underlying the extent to which marginalised films, marginalised filmgoing practices, and marginalised venues like drive-ins 'contributed to the formation of teen spectators and a "teen culture" in the 1950s (Hay, 1990, p. 335), Hay points out that teen films often 'co-opted, parodied or resisted' the preferred genres and 'narrative practices of US film culture' (Hay, 1990, p. 336). However, he also points out that teen films and teen culture were never 'wholly autonomous' (Hay, 1990, p. 336). They too could be co-opted and resisted. The ensuing conflicts and contradictions often found articulation in 'rites of passage' narratives, in stories which placed their protagonists 'betwixt and between' (Hay, 1990, p. 336) and adulthood and childhood, and which explored issues of autonomy, identity, allegiance and difference in the context of the teenage peer group on the one hand and adult society the other, and in the ways in which – and the extent to which – hitherto dominant generic norms were inflected or reworked in the process:

> these films in some fashion involve narrative conflict both over finding one's place within a relatively autonomous society of youths and over defining, negotiating and resisting differences between youth and adulthood. In the sense that teenpics were given to modelling conflict in this manner and through generic conventions that also deterritorialized and reterritorialized the conventions of traditional Hollywood genres, they can be said to define doubly the relation of 'the minor' to a 'parent' culture. (Hay, 1990, p. 336)

The clean-teens films of the late 1950s and early 1960s are particularly exemplary of the problems and issues at stake here, especially in so far as they tend to centre on female characters, and especially in so far as they share a number of the features and concerns of contemporary woman's films like *Picnic* (1955) and *Peyton Place* (1957), as Hay points out. But subsequent teenpics are exemplary too, not least because, for demo-

Back to the Future. The product of *adult* consciousness

graphic reasons, teenagers have since then comprised 'the primary battleground for commercial motion picture patronage in America' (Doherty, 1986, p. 231), not least because 'Since 1960, teenpics have been an industry staple, if not the dominant production strategy for theatrical movies' (Doherty, 1986, p. 231), and therefore not least because the relationship between what is marginal and what is central, what is minor and what is mainstream, has shifted and changed.

There have been important variations in the nature and volume of teenpics since the early 1960s. In the late 1960s and early 1970s, 'youth movies' drew much more on an image of counter-cultural rebellion than on an image of irresponsible juvenile delinquency. And as 'the boundaries between counter (film) culture and mainstream (film) culture all but evaporated, (Doherty, 1986, p. 233), films like *The Graduate* (1967), *Bonnie and Clyde* (1967) and *Easy Rider* (1969) and *Five Easy Pieces* (1970) mounted serious critiques of the parent culture. Following a crisis wrought by overproduction in the late 1960s and early 1970s, and in the wake of a counter-culture in general decline, the industry resumed production of teenpics in regular numbers in the late 1970s and 1980s. Some, like *Halloween* (1978), *Night of the Comet* (1984) and *A Nightmare on Elm Street* (1984), were low-budget horror, sci-fi and slasher films. Some, like *Caddyshack* (1980) and *National Lampoon's Animal House* (1978), were 'gross-out' or 'animal' comedies. Some, like *Sixteen Candles* (1984), *Pretty in Pink* (1986) and *The Breakfast Club* (1985), were teen-centred dramas and romances. And some, like *Rumble Fish* (1983) and *River's Edge* (1986), were teen-centred art or social-problem films. They were joined by bratpack westerns like *Young Guns* (1988) and *Young Guns 2* (1990) and by musical biopics like *Great Balls of Fire!* (1989) and *La Bamba* (1987). (For an overview of teenpics since the late 1970s, seen Bernstein, 1997.)

Despite their generic diversity, these films can all be defined as teenpics because they all focus on teenage characters. However, issues of definition are complicated by the fact that since the early 1970s, Hollywood has been decisively 'juvenalized' (Doherty, 1986, p. 235): not only do most Hollywood films aim to cater for a teenage audience, but directors and producers like George Lucas and Steven Spielberg, who as Doherty points out were 'Reared on the teen-oriented fare of the 1950s' (Doherty, 1986, p. 235), have through films like *Star Wars* (1977) and *Raiders of the Lost Ark* (1981) helped established a teen-friendly trend toward big-budget action, adventure and fantasy films, and through films like *American Graffiti* (1973) and *Back to the Future* (1985) a trend toward the recycling of 1950s teenage culture. They are further complicated by the fact that Doherty and Lewis (1992) both detect what Doherty describes as a 'palpable desire for parental control and authority' in post-1960s teenpics (Doherty, 1986, p. 237), and by the fact that so many teenpics are marked by what he terms 'double vision':

> As teen-oriented movies have become the industry's representative product, the throwaway, unconscious artistry of the 1950s has been supplanted by a new kind of calculated and consciously reflexive teenpic ... Thus films aimed at teenagers are not only more carefully marketed and calculating [sic] created, they also function more explicitly on two levels. *Fast Times at Ridgemont High* (1982) and *Risky Business* (1983) are teenpic-like in their target audience and content, but their consciousness is emphatically adult. (Doherty, 1986, p. 236).

Points like these recall and refocus some of the questions raised by Hay (1990). When reference is made in *Clueless* (1995) to a 1970s tennis player, an early 1960s historical epic, and an eighteenth-century novel, who are these references aimed at? When in *Back to the Future* a rites-of-passage narrative is set in the 1950s, and focussed not on the young male protagonist but on his father, and when in *Stand by Me* (1986) a rites-of-passage narrative, set again in the 1950s, is narrated by an adult male in retrospect, whose fantasy is being enacted? To whom is that fantasy addressed? What process of negotiation and exchange, of deterritorialisation and reterritorialisation is taking place? Along with developments like the advent of black, teenage films, the trend toward pre-teens films in the early 1990s, and a recent decline in the proportion of teenagers in America's population, in the proportion of teenagers attending Hollywood's films, and therefore in the volume of teen-orientated films, questions like these testify to the complexity and interest of a genre which has for years been important to Hollywood, but rarely, it seems, to genre critics, theorists and historians.

Selected Reading

Thomas Doherty, *Teenagers and Teenpics: The Juvenalization of American Movies in the 1950s*, Boston, Unwin Hyman, 1988.

Jon Lewis, *The Road to Romance and Ruin: Teen Films and Youth Culture*, New York and London, Routledge, 1992.

Rebel without a Cause (USA 1955 *p.c* – Warner Bros; *d* – Nicholas Ray; sd col. scope)

Today, the name James Dean is often suffixed by the definition 'the first American teenager'. There were, of course, many cinematic teenagers before Dean, most significantly the delinquents of *The Blackboard Jungle* (1955) and Marlon Brando and his gang in *The Wild One* (1954). In fact, the famous exchange in that latter film between a local girl and Brando – 'What are you rebelling against?' 'What've you got?' – forms a kind of genetic code for the nameless anomie and disaffection that runs through so much of the rebel-teen dramas that were to follow. *Rebel* was released by Warner Bros. who, like so many of the other studios in the mid-1950s, were becoming increasingly aware of the advisability to tap the teen audience in the context of a shrinking overall audience.

Disaffected teen delinquents in films before *Rebel* were almost always from deprived backgrounds or just plain 'born bad'. *Rebel* significantly broke new ground by portraying middle-class alienated teens. In the context of the growing suburbanisation of the US in the 1950s and the consequent upward mobility of the times, it is easy to understand why *Rebel* and Dean's performance were so embraced by teenagers, most of them middle class themselves rather than the urban 'street rats' of earlier films.

Dean's status as an icon rests less on his originality than on the fact that his image collates a number of key teenage discourses: nameless angst; a frustrated longing for both peer and parental approval balanced against a certain freedom from social regulations; and, most importantly, eternal youth borne out of the fact that he died young in a car accident, encapsulating the live-fast-die-young philosophy. Out of the mere three films Dean made, Ray's melodrama is responsible far more than the period literary adaptation *East of Eden* (1955) or the generational saga *Giant* (1956) for founding this 'first teenager' reputation and elucidating these discourses. Here we find one of the most memorable (and oft-quoted) expressions of teen angst in Jim's cry "You're tearing me apart!", provoked by his parents' squabbling over him in the police station at the start of the film. To a certain extent, like the delinquent dramas before it, *Rebel* wants to account for teen angst as experiential, stemming from dysfunctional family life rather than from human essences. What makes *Rebel* such resonant text is that at once it is archetypal for a teenpic and at the same time atypical in its complex deployment of erotic subtexts.

The film is at pains to provide a cod-Freudian explanation of Jim's disaffection: his apron-wearing, henpecked father is 'castrated' in the parlance of the time, provoking a crisis in masculinity in his son. This crisis is displaced onto homoerotic strain that underlines Jim's friendship with Sal Mineo's effete Plato. The erotic charge between father and son, reinforced by the tilting camerawork and Dean's intense performance, in the scene where Jim begs his father to stand up to his mother, is echoed in the scene where Plato – having become the *ad hoc* son to Jim's father with Judy (Natalie Wood) as mother – upbraids Jim for leaving him to go off for a love scene with Judy. The reproach can be read superficially as Plato re-enacting the original abandonment by his absent father, but also as a lover's criticism. With hindsight, the repressed sexual tensions in the film are reinforced by our knowledge of Mineo's homosexuality and Dean's reputed bisexuality. Perhaps less remarked upon, though, is the hint of incest in Judy's anguished relations with her own father who we learn called her a 'dirty tramp' because of her lipstick at the beginning of the film, and who subsequently rejects his daughter's attempts to sit on his lap.

But beyond these domestic tensions, *Rebel* offers another explanation (again, typical of the 1950s) for Jim Stark's alienation: existential malaise. The film is sprinkled throughout with watered-down existential notions, or at least a kind of atheistic pessimism: Jim's problem stems as much from his abandonment in a lost, mechanistic and uncaring universe, devoid of meaning, as it does from faulty parenting and gender confusion. Our first sight of Jim is of him abjectly lying on the pavement playing with a mechanical monkey. This first introduces a theme concerning the animality of being, elaborated on later when Jim describes his home as a 'zoo' and imitates the sound of bull in the observatory.

The film also reprises the notion of the essential triviality of being, dwarfed by a larger cosmos and the forces of fate (which kill Buzz): "from the infinite reaches of space, the problems of man seem trivial and naïve and indeed," intones the astronomer in the observatory scene. The spectral sense of the inextricability of death that *Rebel* brings to the fore is yet one more reason why this film and James Dean helped to 'invent' the teenager.

Grease (USA 1978 *p.c* – Paramount; *d* – Randal Kleiser; sd col.)

After the release of *American Graffiti* in 1973, the 1970s and 1980s saw a number of films – including *Porky's* (1981), *American Hot Wax* (1977) and *La Bamba* (1986) – that were set in the 1950s and which addressed both a youth audience and older viewers who had grown up in those decades. US television series such as *Happy Days* (which was modelled loosely on *American Graffiti*) and its 'spin-off' *Laverne and Shirley* received top ratings. Although films and television series had always used historical settings before, this particularly virulent preoccupation with the 1950s was interpreted by some cultural commentators as evidence of a different order of nostalgia, one shaped by the forces of postmodernism. The film's incorporation of both 1950s iconography and allusions to films of the era can be read as forms of 'pastiche' which Fredric Jameson describes as one of the most significant features of postmodernism: 'Pastiches is, like parody, the imitation of a peculiar and unique style, the wearing of a stylistic mask, speech in a dead language: but it is a neutral practice of such mimicry, without parody's ulterior motive, without the satirical impulse' (Jameson, 1991).

Although one can find postmodern irony in *Grease*'s pastiche of the 1950s, making it slightly counter to Jameson's claim that pastiche is humourless, it is none the less far from satirical. (Compare it with John Waters's *Hairspray* (1988), a much more obviously satirical film.) *Grease*'s story – turning on whether or not lovers, clean-cut Sandy (Olivia Newton-John) and tough-guy Danny (John Travolta) will manage to find common ground – sticks fairly closely to its narrative frames of reference, the clean-teen pics of the late 1950s and early 1960s.

Grease lays in place an intertextual relay of allusions to reinforce its pastiche. In one song, Rizzo (Stockard Channing) makes fun of Sandy by imitating her and comparing her to Sandra Dee, one of the best-known wholesome actresses of the period. Annette Funicello, a teen pin-up of the 1950s due to her appearance in *The Mickey Mouse Show* and later a co-star of the *Beach Blanket* movies, is name-checked while her co-star, Frankie Avalon, appears as a guardian angel in the musical number 'Beauty School Drop-out'. With its white studio-set backdrop and elaborate costumes, this sequence, as does the 'Greased Lightning' number, imitates the fantasy sequence numbers of many films of the period (*An American in Paris* (1951), *Funny Face* (1956). Although the audience is invited to smile at the knowingness of these allusions, the film none the less also invites us to empathise with Sandy and Danny: when Sandy sings 'Hopelessly Devoted to You', no satirical notes are detectable, thus reinforcing *Grease*'s status as pastiche rather than parody or satire.

Jameson's analysis of postmodernism is inflected by his Marxist political position, and there is a sense in which he decries postmodernist texts plundering of other periods as a way of repackaging iconography for consumers as part of the late-capitalist economy. *Grease* was enormously successful at the box office on its release and certainly generated capital for its producers at a prodigious rate. In a manner that was increasingly common for blockbusters from the 1970s onwards, the film was promoted and 'exploited' (in the economic sense of the word) prodigiously through merchandising, with the soundtrack album and the singles from it achieving vast worldwide sales. Like *Saturday Night Fever* before it (which also starred John Travolta), the success of *Grease*'s soundtrack encouraged film-makers and producers to see how films, particularly ones aimed at the youth market, could function as part of a larger 'synergistic' franchise involving numerous products, including albums, tee-shirts, videos and games.

But perhaps the strangest postmodern irony about *Grease* is that while it was originally marketed at teenagers of the 1970s and their parents who grew up in the 1950s, for its re-release in 1998 it was marketed at those very same teens of the 1970s, now parents themselves, offering them a chance to revisit their own youth with their children. This re-release generated even more income than its first debut: *Grease* truly oils the wheels of capitalism.

Gummo (USA 1997, *p.c* – Independent Pictures/Fine Line Features; *d* – Harmony Korine; sd col.)

Understanding a film like Harmony Korine's *Gummo* in the context of the teen pic, requires a broader historical context. The US film industry in the 1980s and 1990s has seen the flowering of the 'indie' movie. Like its parallel term 'indie music', the 'independent' or 'indie' prefix originally referred to a film's financing. Historically, instead of being developed and produced by a major studio, the archetypal indie film was made by a production company and co-financed by an independent distributor (which in some cases might be one and the same thing). Miramax (co-producers of *Hardware* (1990) and *Smoke* (1995)), and New Line (co-producers of *Hairspray* (1988) and *My Own Private Idaho* (1991)) were two of the quintessential independent producers/distributors of the 1980s and 1990s. However, each was bought by Disney and Turner Broadcasting respectively in 1993, and like almost every other independent outfit, their 'independence' is now really a matter of style and marketing.

The discourse of the indie film overlaps with 'cult' and 'underground' films, all of which are marked by a high valuation of such notions as authenticity, subversiveness and estrangement from the mainstream. Just as a jangly guitar sound is the cornerstone of the indie music sound, today independence in film is more a matter of aesthetic and thematic tropes, such as grainy or deliberately unpolished cinematography, disjunctive or sparse soundtracks deliberately obfuscatory or fragmentary editing, little-known stars, and narratives which concern offbeat or unusual stories and often youthful, marginalised characters. For this youth-orientated audience, an indie film's value is measured partly by its distance *from* the polish, coherence and digestibility which are seen as defining mainstream cinema. The wider this distance, the richer the film is (in a phrase coined by Sarah Thornton adapted from Pierre Bourdieu) in 'subcultural capital'.

In cruder terms the more shocking to adult audiences, the better! *Gummo* emerges from this context.

The son of documentary film-maker, Korine began his film-making career at the age of 18 by writing Larry Clark's also controversial film *kids*, which featured an abundance of teenage sex. A crucial feature of the journalistic and publicity discourse around that film turned on the fact of Korine's youth, the way that Clark met him through a mutual interest in skateboarding and that Korine had 'lived the life' – all of which denote both his authenticity and that of the film. In interviews, Korine was keen to stress the improvised nature of *Gummo* and his personal familiarity with the people depicted in it. The film focuses on a number of characters living in a Midwestern town which some time before suffered a tornado. We meet few adults, and there is a suggestion that this catastrophe has wiped away the usual moral frameworks and, in a sense, prompted the fragmentary discontinuous style of the film. '[The tornado] killed the people left and right . . . a lot of people's fathers died . . . I saw a girl fly through the sky and I looked up her skirt. School was smashed', intones the voice-over. As Gavin Smith observes (*Sight and Sound*, April 1998, vol. 8 no. 4, p. 24), 'With all authority and social restraints swept away by an act of God, Korine's kids live in a world where all transgression seems permitted and unchallenged'. Two of the main characters, adolescents Tummler (Nick Sutton) and Solomon (Jacob Reynolds) spend their time looking for stray cats to kill, a plot point which sparked controversy on the film's release in both the US and the UK. With its violence and strenuous refusal to judge its characters or their actions, the film positions itself at the other end of the spectrum from the clean-cut traditions of teen pics.

In the UK, *Gummo*'s status as a 'cool' indie film was enhanced by its being championed in style magazines such as *Dazed and Confused* and the more marginal film magazines such as *Neon* and vilified by 'establishment' newspapers like *The Evening Standard*. This solidifies its status as a work both resolutely opposed to the recuperating strategies and generic conventions of many 'rites-of-passage' teen pics and yet very much belonging to its own indie youth-orientated tradition.

Not suitable for parents – *Gummo*

COMEDY

The publication in recent years of a number of books on comedy – among them Gehring (1994), Horton (1991a), Karnick and Jenkins (1995a), Neale and Krutnik (1990), Palmer (1987), Rowe (1995a), and Sikov 1989 and 1994) – is clearly indicative of a significant revival of interest on the part of film critics, theorists and historians. In its various guises, comedy has always been a significant staple in Hollywood's output. It has also, since the days of Chaplin, been a topic of critical debate, though generally within evaluative paradigms compatible with liberal humanist values, hence within frameworks of concern that have tended to focus on issues of aesthetic integrity, self-expression, and direct or indirect social and cultural worth. (See among others, Agree (1958), Mast (1976), McCaffrey (1968) and Robinson (1969), and to some extent also, Cavell (1981). Aesthetics, evaluation and socio-cultural issues are by no means absent from more recent books. But the agendas within which they are working are in general rather different from those governing earlier writing and research. They include feminism, gender and sexual politics; structuralism, semiotics, post-structuralism and psychoanalysis; cultural studies, race and ethnicity; and the 1980s turn toward archival and historical research.

The diversity of topics addressed and approaches adopted in these books is at least in part related to the diverse and multi-faceted nature of comedy itself. Encompassing a range of forms, sites and genres – from jokes to intricately plotted narratives, from slapstick to farce, from satire to parody, from shorts and cartoons to features – comedy can also entail an array of defining conventions – from the generation of laughter to the presence of happy endings to the representation of every life – and is able in addition to combine with or to parody virtually every other genre or form (Neale and Krutnik, 1990, pp. 10–25). It is therefore hardly surprising that discussions of comedy have drawn on a variety of disciplines – from philosophy to narrative theory, from anthropology to psychology, and psychoanalysis – and that most comprehensive overviews tend to combine a multi-disciplinary approach with a breaking down of the subject into a number of distinct topics, aspects and themes.

Most discussions of comedy begin by acknowledging a basic distinction between what might be called its comic units – gags, jokes, funny moments and the like – and the narrative and non-narrative contexts in which they occur. This distinction is important, both because it links to issues of film history, and because it raises questions about definition and hence about the criteria governing comedy as a genre. For many commentators, gags, jokes and funny moments are fundamental to all forms of comedy, and hence to definitions of comedy either as a single genre or as a diverse but related cluster of genres and forms. An initial distinction can then be drawn between those in which they occur outside, or are dominant over, narrative contexts and narrative concerns, and those in which they are not. Hence Horton's proposal that 'comedies are interlocking sequences of jokes and gags that place narrative in the foreground, in which case comedy leans in varying degrees toward some dimension of the noncomic (realism, romance, fantasy), or that use narrative as only a loose excuse for holding together moments of comic business (as in a Marx Brothers' film)' (Horton, 1991b, p. 7).

This proposal is made in response to Mast's (1976) emphasis on narrative, and in particular to his thesis that 'There are eight comic film plots' (Mast, 1976, p. 4). It echoes the proposals and critiques of Jerry Palmer, who argues that Mast's typology suffers from logical inconsistencies – it includes the 'parody of genres' and the 'sequence of gags' as plots – and avoids the issue of funniness by focussing on the 'maximum' units of comedy (like plots) rather than 'minimum' units like jokes and gags (Palmer, 1987, p. 28). To be fair to Mast, it is worth pointing out that he emphasises 'comic climate', the way in which what happens in a plot is signalled as comedy rather than drama (Mast, 1976, pp. 9–13), and that for some time in the west comedy was defined as a narrative with a happy ending, a definition which avoids the issue of gags, jokes and comic climate altogether (Neale and Krutnik, 1990, pp. 11–17). Nevertheless, Palmer's, Horton's and subsequent critiques – like those of Karnick and Jenkins (1995a, p. 72) – clearly point to the inadequacies of Mast's typology, and of any approach to comedy which ignores its minimum units.

Palmer himself is concerned to argue not only that gags, jokes and funny moments are fundamental to comedy, but also that they exhibit similar structural and logical features. These include a preparation stage and a culmination stage (often in the form of a verbal or visual punchline), an instance or moment of shock or surprise (a peripetia or reversal of fortune), and a system of logic – 'the logic of the absurd' – in which the plausible and the implausible always combine, but in unequal measure: while plausibility is always present, implausibility is always dominant, and it is this dominance that allows us to perceive the events, actions and utterances with which we are presented in comedy as comic (rather than poetic or tragic), and that thus endows them with what Palmer calls 'comic insulation'.

Palmer goes on to argue that these features mark comic plots and situations as well, thus that although comic units of all kinds have their own shapes and structures, they are susceptible to a degree, at least, of narrative integration. Elsewhere, Gunning (1995) and Crafton (1995) have debated the extent to which such integration is possible, the extent to which gags, jokes and other comic units necessarily undermine or diverge from the narrative contexts in which they may be found. For Crafton, gags and jokes are inherently digressive. If narrative can be defined 'as a system for providing the spectator with sufficient knowledge to make causal links between represented events ... the gag's status as an irreconcilable difference becomes clear. Rather than providing knowledge, slapstick misdirects the viewer's attention, and obfuscates the linearity of cause–effect relations' (Crafton, 1995, p. 119). For Gunning, some gags are susceptible to narrative integration and can themselves be perceived as possessing narrative features, especially if narrative is itself re conceived as a 'process of integration in which smaller units are absorbed into a larger overarching pattern and process of containment' (Gunning, 1995, p. 121). Neale and Krutnik, meanwhile, seek to identify degrees of integration, ranging from purely digressive gags and jokes to fully integrated 'comic events' (1990, pp. 43–61). They also draw on the work of Coursodon (1964) and of other French writers like Lebel (1967), Mars (1964), Pasquier (1973) and Simon and Percheron (1976) in drawing up a scale of structural complexity in gags, ranging from the simple 'comic effect' (a funny expression, a pratfall, a single, self-contained piece of comic actin) to the elaborate 'articulated gag,' which may involve a multi-stage chain of events and effects.

A great deal of attention has been paid to gags, jokes and other comic units. (In addition to those cited above, see Carroll (1991), Jenkins (1986), and Sweeney (1991)). Aside from their intrinsic interest, there are two fundamental reasons for this. The first is that they are points at which laughter is designed to occur, and can therefore act as a focus for ideas, theories and debates about laughter and humour. The second is that they are bound up with the early history of comedy in the cinema, and with a number of specialist producers, directors and performers, from Mack Sennett to Jerry Lewis, from Frank Tashlin to Woody Allen, from Laurel and Hardy to Hope and Crosby, and from Charlie Chaplin and Buster Keaton to Danny Kaye, Steve Martin, Jim Carrey and a number of others.

Laughter and humour have, of course, been discussed for hundreds of years. No single theory has dominated the study of these topics in the cinema. Mast occasionally draws on Bergson (1956) and Freud ([1905] 1976 and [1927] 1985). Eaton (1981), Neale (1981) and Neale and Krutnik (1990, pp. 71–82) all also draw on – and to some extent modify – Freud's ideas. Neale and Krutnik draw on the work of Olson (1968). And Palmer draws on the work of Douglas (1968). Douglas also features in Palmer's later book (1995), an overview of theories of laughter and humour. His central argument here is that laughter and humour are multi-dimensional, hence that most theories of humour are partial. He considers these theories under four main headings: 'occasion' (theories which stress the contexts and rules which permit, encourage or solicit humour and laughter); 'function' (theories which stress the social and psychological purposes of humour and laughter); 'structure' (in which work on the shape and the logic of gags and jokes comes into play); and what he calls 'limits' – the points, psychic and social, at which humour or laughter can simply fail or disappear. In his discussion of structure, he notes that most modern theories of humour involve notions of incongruity, and this is certainly true of most theories of jokes and gags in the cinema, including his own. However, he also notes that such notions and forms may be historically and culturally 'local,' specific to the west in the modern era, rather than universal (Palmer, 1995, p. 143).

Local or not, gags, jokes, and slapstick humour in general have formed the basis for a tradition in film comedy that is virtually as old as film itself. (Gunning, 1995 contains a lengthy discussion of what is perhaps the first example, the Lumière's *L'Arroseur arrosé* (1895)). Derived initially from existing forms of variety entertainment, notably vaudeville, and music hall, but also the circus, the comic strip, burlesque and revue, and fed by later forms like radio, television and nightclubs, this tradition has been treated as a site within which a whole series of comic performers, including most of those listed above, have been able not only to present their skills, but also to subvert or to question narrative values and conventions – and occasionally socio-cultural ones as well.

A particularly influential account of this tradition can be found in Seidman (1981). Under the heading of 'comedian comedy,' Seidman proposes an array of distinct – and eccentric – characteristics, themes and devices linking performers and films within this tradition and differentiating both from those found elsewhere in Hollywood comedy and in Hollywood cinema in general. Seidman starts from the premiss that nearly all the performers within this tradition began their careers, honed their skills and established their personae outside the cinema, in media and in forms of entertainment geared to live or quasi-live performance, and hence to the possibility – or the illusion – of direct interaction with an audience. He goes on to note the prevalence in their films of devices which draw on and foreground these contexts and characteristics, and which thereby conflict with, contradict or undermine the norms characteristic of most other Hollywood films and hence of most other Hollywood genres – asides and direct address to camera, allusions to the artificial nature of films and their devices, and allusions to the world of show business outside the fictional universe of any one particular film.

The comedians in comedian comedy are thus privileged figures, able to step outside and to play with the rules governing most narrative films and their genres. But they are also anomalies and misfits. In the films, they often portray eccentric or deviant characters, characters given to dreaming, to disguise, to regression and to bouts of madness. To that extent, the opposition between eccentricity and social conformity is to be found elsewhere in Hollywood comedy is here internalised as an aspect of the comedian's character, one which is inextricably linked to his or her performance skills, and one which is therefore irresolvable.

In recent years, the concept of comedian comedy has been refined, extended and modified (Krutnik, 1984 and 1995). It has also been criticised as a-historical (Jenkins, 1993; Karnick and Jenkins, 1995a). The male-centredness of comedian comedy has been noted. And the extent to which masculinism and masculinity are rehearsed, explored, endorsed or undermined has been looked at in detail (Bukatman, 1991, Krutnik, 1994 and 1995, Rowe, 1995a, pp. 102–6, Sanders, 1995, and Winokur, 1996, pp. 171–8). In response, several studies have recently appeared of Mae West (Curry, 1995; Hamilton, 1996; Rowe, 1995a, pp. 116–24). And in addition, given the 'low' – and popular – status of comedian comedy, and given the prevalence within it of Jewish performers and personnel, a number of studies have introduced (or reintroduced) issues of ethnicity and class (Jenkins, 1993; Musser, 1990b and 1991; and Winokur, 1996).

Meanwhile, a number of studies have appeared which either question any absolute distinction between comedian and narrative, situational, or 'polite' forms of comedy, or which seek to draw attention to the presence of the latter in early film and thus to question or modify the ways in which the early history of comedy in the cinema – and the careers of particular comic performers – have been written (Bowser, 1990, pp. 179–84; Gartenberg, 1988; Kramer, 1988, 1989 and 1995, Koszarski, 1990, pp. 174–80; Musser, 1990a; Neale and Krutnik, 1990, pp. 109–31; Riblet, 1995). This can be seen both as a reaction to the canonic dominance of slapstick comedy and slapstick performers in accounts of early cinema, and as a sign of the revival of interest in narrative and in situational traditions and forms.

Of these, romantic comedy has received the greatest attention in recent years, at least in part because of its revival by Hollywood in the mid-1980s under the guise of what Neale and Krutnik have termed 'the new romance' (Neale and Krutnik, 1990, pp. 171–3; Krutnik, 1990; Neale, 1992). Neale and Krutnik argue that the emergence of the new romance, as exemplified by films like *Blind Date* (1987), *Roxanne* (1987), *When Harry Met Sally* (1989) and *Only You* (1992), constituted the revival not just of an 'old-fashioned' genre, but also of an ideology of 'old-fashioned' heterosexual romance and hence of the rituals, signs and wishes that mark it. Its appearance followed a period in the 1970s and early 1980s during which significant challenges had been mounted to that ideology, and during which romantic comedy itself seemed either to have taken the form of Woody Allen-like 'nervous romances' (Neale and Krutnik, 1990, pp. 171–2; Krutnik, 1990), or else to have disappeared altogether (Henderson, 1978).

Recent work on new romances like *Moonstruck* (1987) by Rowe and others suggests that the new romance may not be as ideologically homogeneous as Neale and Krutnik have proposed (Rowe, 1995a, pp. 200–9 and 1995b; Evans and Deleyto, 1998). Meanwhile many of these debates echo debates about the 'screwball' films of the 1930s and 1940s, about films like *The Awful Truth* (1938) and *Bringing up Baby* (1938). The screwball cycle, which emerged in 1934 with *It Happened One Night* and *Twentieth Century*, has on the one hand been seen as one of the few 'genres of equality' to have emerged during the course of the studio era (Woodward, 1991). On the other, it has been seen as a cycle which, in and through its aesthetic characteristics – an energetic mix of slapstick, wise cracks, intricately plotted farce and the comedy of manners combined with vividly eccentric characterisation and a disavowable undercurrent of sexual innuendo – served to revivify the institution of marriage and traditional gender relations at a time when both were being bolstered by government policy following periods of intense turbulence, challenge and change during the Jazz Age and the early years of the Great Depression.

In contrast to the screwball films, very little has been written on the 'sex comedies' of the 1950s and 1960s – films like *Pillow Talk* (1959) and *Lover come Back* (1961) – aside from Neale and Krutnik (1990, pp. 169–71) and some of the writing on Doris Day contained in Clark, Merck and Simmonds (1981). There are signs of a revival of interest in the 'sophisticated' comedies of romance, sex, marriage and remarriage that preceded the screwball cycle in the late 1910s and the 1920s, especially those directed by Cecil B. DeMille (Higashi, 1994, pp. 142–66 and Musser, 1995). However, there are as yet no histories of romantic comedy in Hollywood which encompass all these trends. Neale (1992) proposes a number of basic conventions, including 'the meet cute', 'the wrong partner', the learning process the couple nearly always have to undergo, and the initial hostility it eventually dispels. And Babington and Evans (1989) discuss a number of individual romantic comedies from a number of distinct periods and cycles.

The existence of comedies of remarriage (the term derives from Cavell, 1981) suggests an area of overlap between romantic comedy and domestic comedy. However, like other forms of narrative comedy, and in curious contrast to the attention given to domestic and familial drama, domestic comedy remains largely unexplored. The same is true of parody and satire. Recent books by Hutcheon (1985) and by Rose (1993) are largely concerned with literature, or with art forms other than the cinema. Both note that parody and satire involve imitation, citation and reference. And both note that they are not always comic in intention or effect. Neale and Krutnik refer briefly to satire and parody in the cinema (1990, pp. 18–20). And Crafton (1995) discusses the role of caricature and parody in Warner Bros cartoons.

Satire – the debunking of prevalent social norms, institutions and mores – is clearly central to any theory or discussion of comedy's socio-cultural role and significance. Comedy has often been viewed as either actually or potentially subversive, or at least an inherently positive force for social renewal and social change. This view has long been influential in literary studies of comedy, and often finds an echo in the cult of slapstick, comedian and low forms of comedy in particular. It has been recently revived in and through the writings of Bakhtin (1968), and in and through the work of those, like Fischer (1991), Paul (1991 and 1994), Rowe (1995a and 1995b) and Winokur (1996), who have used or adopted Bakhtinian ideas, especially their stress on the upturning of the social world and its rules in all forms of carnival comedy.

Others, however, have offered a different view. Neale and Krutnik argue that deviations from the norm are conventional in comedy and hence that 'subversion' is a licensed and integral aspect of comedy's social and institutional existence (1990, pp. 83–94). And more recently, Purdie has explicitly attacked the views of Bakhtin and others, arguing that all forms of comedy involve a recognition of the norms whose transgression they entail, and hence a claim to social membership at the expense not only of those who are comedy's butts, but also of those who do not get its jokes (1993). Either way, it is likely that, as is the case with most genres, comedy's ideological significance and impact varies from film to film, cycle to cycle, and audience to audience, and is probably best assessed at specific and local levels rather than at the level of universal generalisations.

Selected Reading

Stanley Cavell, *Pursuits of Happiness: The Hollywood Comedy of Remarriage*, Cambridge, Mass., Harvard University Press, 1981.

Peter William Evans and Celestino Deleyto (eds), *Terms of Endearment: Gender and Sexuality in Hollywood Romantic Comedy of the Eighties and Nineties*, Edinburgh, Edinburgh University Press, 1998.

Sigmund Freud, 'Humour' (1927) in *Art and Literature*, Harmondsworth, Penguin, 1985.

Andrew S. Horton (ed.), *Comedy/Cinema/Theory*, Berkeley, University of California Press, 1991.

Henry Jenkins III, *What Made Pistachio Nuts? Early Sound Comedy and the Vaudeville Aesthetic*, New York, Columbia University Press, 1993.

Kristina Brunovska Karnick and Henry Jenkins III (eds), *Classical Hollywood Comedy*, London, Routledge, 1995.

Frank Krutnik, 'The faint aroma of performing seals: the "nervous" romance and the comedy of the sexes', *The Velvet Light Trap* no. 26, 1990.

Steve Neale, 'The *Big* romance or *Something Wild*?: romantic comedy today', *Screen* 33(3), 1992.

Jerry Palmer, *Taking Humour Seriously*, London, Routledge, 1995.

Kathleen Rowe, *The Unruly Woman, Gender and the Genres of Laughter*, Austin, University of Texas Press, 1995.

Steve Seidman, *Comedian Comedy: A Tradition in the Hollywood Film*, Ann Arbor, UMI Research Press, 1981.

Lover Come Back (USA 1961, *p.c* – Universal/Seven Pictures/Nob Hill/Arwin; *d* – Delbert Mann; sd col.)

Heading towards a marital solution – *Lover Come Back*

Lover Come Back was the second in a series of sophisticated sex comedies pairing Doris Day and Rock Hudson. It shares with its predecessor, *Pillow Talk* (1959) a *mise en scène* that flaunts a glossy high-consumer life-style (sumptuous fashions, lavish apartments, exclusive restaurants, fancy cars); and a narrative of sexual subterfuge which pits a wolfish playboy against a resistant career woman. What *Lover Come Back* adds to the earlier film's concoction is a satire of the values and strategies of America's industry of desire, the advertising business – Day and Hudson play account executives for rival Madison Avenue companies. Hudson's Jerry Webster is a semi-parodic take on the urban bachelor fantasy. The playboy, a recurring figure in the sex comedies of the 1950s and 1960s, is an idealised figure of male liberty who is opposed to the domesticated suburban husband. Webster not only embodies a fantasy of untrammelled, 'uncastrated' masculinity, but his approach to advertising reveals that he is also a master of seductive manipulation – he boasts that 'given a well-stacked dame in a bathing suit' he could sell after-shave lotion to beatniks. By contrast, Carol (Day) attempts to establish an ethical grounding for the business of selling. The opposed values system of the two are outlined when they compete for the Miller wax account: Carol's efforts are easily outstripped by Jerry's elaborate bribery – alcohol, showgirls – of the company's millionaire owner.

As a woman who resists seduction, both personally and professionally, Carol's discourse is mined continually to expose the sexuality she 'represses'. She is the butt of numerous sexual jokes: when she declares that the agency to win the account will be 'the one that shows Mr Miller the most attractive can', the film cuts immediately to a chorus-line of bunny-girls hired by Jerry to wiggle their backsides for Miller's entertainment. Equating the consumer object with the fetishised female body, this gag insinuates that, as a woman, Carol is wrong to assume she can find a place in the advertising industry's enterprise of seduction. The film develops the negative value of Carol's ambitions by doubling her with the showgirl Rebel Davies (Edie Adams), an alternative 'career woman' who subjects herself readily both to Jerry's seductions and to the system of commercial representation that will transform her body into an all-purpose signifier of consumerised desire.

The satire of advertising practice (Jerry creates an advertising campaign for a non-existent product – VIP; to capitalise on the success of the campaign he decides to invent a product to fit the sales pitch) overwhelms the amorous narrative in the first half of the film. When Carol meets Jerry she mistakenly assumes him to be the chemist hired to work on the mystery product. Seizing upon her misapprehension, Jerry continues to masquerade as 'Linus Tyler', so he can trick her into bed. The 'Tyler' that Jerry constructs is a male image tailored to the interpretation of Carol's desiring self, an image that reflects back her own qualities – dedication, honesty, sensitivity, sexual inexperience. At the same time, however, the identity masquerade throws up for examination conflicting figurations of masculinity: Webster is split into an aggressive 'masculine' persona and a more passive, 'feminised' persona. Even though, for contemporary viewers, Hudson's high-profile outing as a gay man brings into sharp relief the element of performance integral to his 1950s image as an idealised heterosexual male, the performative status of gender identity – especially male identity – is foregrounded in the comedies of the 1950s and 1960s.

The subterfuge plot provokes Carol's extended humiliation, as Jerry lays siege to her sexual defences – hence, as the film has it, to her professional identity. But as she is on the verge of surrendering herself, Carol learns of his duplicity, and exacts her revenge. The manipulation and hostility of Jerry's behaviour does not amount to a viable model for union, so the film engages in several frantic and convoluted narrative manoeuvres as a means of shifting the emphasis from the elaboration of seductive enterprise to a generically-conventional marital resolution. An advertising-council hearing degenerates into an orgy as they test the VIP product generated by Webster's chemist – candy that is super-saturated with alcohol. Jerry and Carol awaken the next morning in a Maryland motel room, with a marriage licence in tow. But while VIP allows Carol's sexual defences to be circumvented, Webster experiences a quite staggering role reversal. All of a sudden, he is desperate to embrace his own 'castration' by remaining wedded, while she wants nothing to do with him. After a lengthy separation, they remarry nine months later, as Carol is wheeled into a hospital delivery room to give birth. This cynically slick observance of Production Code morality makes clear the film's lack of commitment to the concept of romantic marital union. By making the route to the union so ridiculous, *Love Come Back* signals a termination of the indulgences of the 'good life' whilst stripping the renunciation of any force. The emphasis on Jerry's extreme change of character also excludes any portrayal of the radical adjustment Carol must make in sacrificing her career ambitions for the vocation of motherhood. The final image of Carol, prone and powerless on the hospital trolley, constitutes an overpowering vision of the 'taming' of the independently minded career woman.

The Patsy (USA 1964 *p.c* – Paramount/ Jerry Lewis; *d* – Jerry Lewis; sd col.)

Jerry Lewis was the last star comedian under long-term contract to a major film company of the Hollywood studio era – he was signed to Paramount Pictures, in 1948, with partner Dean Martin, and remained with the company until 1965. After the traumatic dissolution of his successful ten-year partnership with Martin in 1956, Lewis triumphantly re-established himself as a solo performer and continued as a top box-office attraction. His long-lasting success, and the protection accorded to him by Paramount, enabled him to make a series of eccentric, and controversial films in the 1960s, which he starred in, directed, co-wrote, and often co-produced. Together with eight comedies Lewis made with directorial mentor Frank Tashlin (from *Artist and Models* in 1955 to *The Disorderly Orderly* in 1964), these films were highly regarded by French *ciné*-critics – like Jean-Luc Godard, who proclaimed Lewis a 'genius' – but castigated by American reviewers, who read Lewis's ambitions as rampant egomania. Lewis's self-directed project reached its apogee in *The Patsy*, a highly idiosyncratic, personal art film masquerading as a comedian comedy. *The Patsy*, like *The Errand Boy* (1961), addresses the processes of stardom, comedy and the entertainment business, but it also more explicitly invokes Lewis's own public image an career.

The narrative of *The Patsy* concerns the making of an entertainment star. After the death of famous comedian, Wally Brandford, his staff decide they will train 'some nobody' – the painfully inept Lewisian bellboy Stanley Belt – to take his place. Stanley's body continually sabotages the professionalised showbiz routines he is taught, however, and fearing disaster the Brandford team abandon him as he is about to make his début on 'The Ed Sullivan Show'. Their desertion spurs Stanley to prove he is not at the mercy of the showbiz machine – he improvises a sketch, 'A Big Night in Hollywood', which propels him to stardom. The Sullivan appearance puts Stanley in a commanding position, where he can turn the tables on his ertswhile manipulators. But success has its costs: as he fires off instructions to his former puppet masters, the business-suited ex-bellboy acts with the polished self-assurance (and implicit self-regard) of callous swinger Buddy Love, the monstrous alter-ego of meek chemistry professor Julius Kelp in Lewis' *The Nutty Professor* (1963). As the danger of corruptive egomania is introduced as a possible consequence of stardom, Lewis drops the fictional mask of Stanley Belt, to reveal himself as 'Jerry Lewis', Hollywood director, the film ends with Lewis commanding the film crew of *The Patsy* to break for lunch. As this final scene implies, Lewis is hijacking the Hollywood comedian comedy, to transform it into a highly unconventional vehicle for a discourse of the self. Stanley's path to stardom is interlaced with knowing references to Lewis's own career: the record act he performs briefly during his stand-up début echoes Lewis's own first showbiz speciality; the bellboy costume evokes his first self-directed film, as well as his youthful stint as a bellhop in the Catskills; and the Ed Sullivan performance is adapted from a sketch on one of his own solo TV shows from 1957.

The Patsy is the most acutely self-mythologising of Lewis's films: it celebrates the ascendancy of the multi-faceted creative presence 'Jerry Lewis' over the familiar Lewisian misfit, Stanley Belt. This flamboyant *auteurist* agenda directly interferes with the way the film operates as a comedian-centred film. While American critics were outraged by the 'unfunniness' of Lewis' self-directed films, many French critics recognised that Lewis was no longer content to be 'simply funny'. From the start, his performance represented a very extreme form of 'low' physical comedy, through which he created a wild, at times discomforting spec-

Comedian comedy and personal art cinema. Jerry Lewis acts it up in *The Patsy*

tacle of deformation built upon verbal and bodily unruliness, sexual confusion, gender-role slippage, and a fragmented or uncentred sense of self. *The Patsy* reveals Lewis's performative hyperbole taken to even greater extreme – as is illustrated by the sustained spectacle of embarrassment created from Stanley's first appearance in the film, his body erupting in painful slow motion under the withering gaze of the Brandford retinue. At such moments, Lewis extends the spectacle of pain and embarrassment rather than forcing a quick, clean wrap-up – thus exposing the discomfort that precisioned gag-making can disavow. In the films he directed, Lewis frequently toys with the familiar techniques of visual comedy by diverting the gag from its signalled trajectory, or refusing a conventionally-ordered build-up. Rather than providing the expected mechanism of disruption and reordering, Lewis's gags play with the conventional forms, procedures and discursive registers of film comedy, initiating a process of deformation which denies a comfortable place to laugh from. The clearest example of such meta-nagging is *The Patsy*'s stand-up routine, where a conventional mode of comic performance is turned inside out.

The personal inflections woven into Stanley's journey to the top of the entertainment business suggests that the studied dislocation of comic conventions was motivated by Lewis's desire to assert and to validate his newly differentiated space within the Hollywood system. The 'Jerry Lewis' who orders the end of *The Patsy* is a totalising presence who exceeds both his familiar orbit as star–comedian and the machinery of professional showbiz. The film rejects the Oedipal paradigm dominant in comedian comedy since the mid-1930s, to find its ultimate grounding in the complex discursive regime that surround 'Jerry Lewis' – as comedian, as celebrity, as enunciator. The self-directed films often balance the dispersal, fragmentation, and excess of Lewis's filmic and performative style with a sentimental valorisation of the 'true self', and in *The Patsy*, Ellen Betts (Ina Balin), the sole woman in the Brandford team, is the one who can recognise Stanley's inner worth. However, the maternal/sexual bond she connotes is vaporised when 'Jerry Lewis' takes command, just after Stanley has proposed marriage. Heterosexual procreation is sidestepped – the 'Jerry Lewis' who rises from the ashes of Stanley Belt is not of woman born. Lewis' self-directed project necessitated an insistent reformulation of difference, and sexual divisions, along with more general distinctions between self and other, are subjugated to differences existing within the overarching 'creative presence'. Such are the perils of art.

Annie Hall (USA 1977 *p.c* – UA; *d* – Woody Allen; sd col.)

Marking an ambitious departure from his earlier comedies, Woody Allen's *Annie Hall* is an inventive hybrid of comedian comedy, romantic comedy and melodrama. The film fractures the familiar structure of romantic narrative, by jumping back and forth across the history of the relationship between Alvy Singer (Allen) and Annie Hall (Diane Keaton), and by using a range of absurdist devices – comic monologues, an animated sequence, spoof documentary scenes – to further interrupt the telling of the story. Although many of the scenes expected from a romantic comedy are included, their disordering within the film's discourse prevents them from functioning in a traditional manner. This unusual formal method contributes to *Annie Hall*'s effectiveness as a 'nervous romance' that explores the difficulty of sustaining attachments in a post-1960s world, where traditional conceptions of heterosexual intimacy have lost their powers of legitima-

Diane Keaton and Woody Allen explore their intimacy in the nervous romance *Annie Hall*

tion. 'Nervous' romances like *Annie Hall*, *Manhattan* (1979) and *Starting Over* (1979) introduce the concerns of male-centred melodrama into the province of romantic comedy, focusing on beleaguered men caught in the emotional flak of the post-feminist age. But *Annie Hall* differs from other 'nervous' romances of the 1970s in refusing simply to scapegoat the woman, making it clear that the problems with this particular relationship stem from the male protagonist himself.

Allen's film is obsessed with the consequences of the disintegration of a secure agenda and direction for heterosexual relations, suggesting that while the conventions that traditionally mapped intimate conduct were oppressive and restricting, they also served as guidelines from which individuals could wring their own variations. *Annie Hall* implies that the disarray of these conventions in the 1970s has resulted not in 'liberation' but in confusion and blockage. This situation is mined for comic effect, especially during the first hesitant encounter of Alvy and Annie, which culminates with subtitles that highlight the gap between their words and their thoughts. Alvy and Annie are most clearly at ease with one another when the formal regime of sexual language is circumvented through mutual play – in the brief scene where the lobster is let loose in the kitchen, which recalls both the screwball mode of films like *Bringing Up Baby* (1938) and the comic double act of Keaton and Allen in *Sleeper* (1973).

Other conventions of the romantic comedy film receive a similarly unconventional treatment. Where *Pillow Talk* (1959) uses split-screen framing to parallel the divided lovers, suggesting their ultimate compatibility, *Annie Hall* uses the device to show how little Alvy and Annie have in common: first, by revealing the incompatible worlds of the Hall and Singer families; second, by juxtaposing their respective visits to the psychiatrist, which expose a fundamental lack of agreement over the meaning of their sex life. Romantic comedy is founded on the promise that the differences between the man and the woman will ultimately be overcome, but Alvy (New York, Jewish, death- and sex-obsessed intellectual) and Annie (eccentric, Middle American airhead) cannot find common ground without a damaging loss of self. *Annie Hall* abandons dual-focused narrative that generally characterises romantic comedy, to centre Alvy as the narrator and focaliser. However, this account is profoundly self-critical and self-questioning. The fragmented structure of the film makes it appear as if Alvy is trying to order the chaotic jumble of his life, to come to terms with the pain and disillusion of his relationship with Annie and his long-term difficulty with women. Ultimately, he finds release through aesthetic sublimation, by writing a play based on his experiences with Annie (with the teasing implication that the film itself may play such a role for Allen's much publicised relationship with Keaton). But in art, unlike 'real life', the relationship does succeed; in the play, the man and the woman make up at the point where the relationship of Alvy and Annie ended.

The film places the relationship with Annie in the broader context of Alvy's life and character. In his self-obsessive anxiety, Alvy is a 'feminised' male who reveals a neurotic need for control and reassurance, and who over invests in sexual fantasy as a means of asserting his masculine competence. A major row erupts with Annie over her reliance upon smoking a joint to get herself in the mood for sex. Annie's use of artificial stimulation troubles his fragile sense of sexual security: comparing sex to his professional activity as a comedian, Alvy says that in both spheres he needs to believe that the response (orgasm, laughter) is authentic. But while he criticises Annie for using cannabis as an emotional crutch, that is precisely the status that sex has for him – a point made early in the film, when, at a party packed with New York's creative and intellectual elite, Alvy seeks to bed his high-flying first wife as a means of subjugating (her) mind to (his) body. Similarly, the film shows that Alvy's love for Annie is possessive and destructive, his inability to tolerate the autonomy of her desires exemplified by his hostile response to her wish for a singing career, where she can make her 'voice' heard.

ACTION–ADVENTURE

The term 'action–adventure' is nowadays used mainly to describe what was perceived in the 1980s and 1990s to be a new and dominant trend in Hollywood's output, a trend exemplified by the *Alien* films (1979, 1986, 1993), the *Indiana Jones* films (1981, 1984, 1993), the *Rambo* films (1988, 1990, 1995), the *Die Hard* films (1988, 1990, 1995) and the *Terminator* films (1984, 1991), as well as by films like *Total Recall* (1990), *Point Break* (1991), *The Last of the Mohicans* (1992) and *Braveheart* (1995).

This trend encompasses a range of films and genres – from swashbucklers to science fiction films, from thriller to westerns to war films – and is thus a clear instance of Hollywood's propensity for generic hybrid-

The popular spectacle of masculinity. Bruce Willis in *Die Hard*

ity and overlap. The term 'action–adventure' has been used, though, to pinpoint a number of obvious common to these genres and films: a propensity for spectacular physical action, a narrative structure involving fights, chases and explosions, and in addition to the deployment of state-of-the art special effects, an emphasis in performance on athletic feats and stunts. The hyperbolic nature of this emphasis has often been accompanied by an emphasis on the 'hyperbolic bodies' and physical skills of the stars involved: Arnold Schwarzenegger, Sylvester Stallone, Dolph Lundgren, Bruce Willis, Brigitte Nielsen, Linda Hamilton and others. It is thus not surprising that the two major books published to date on these films – by Susan Jeffords (1994) and by Yvonne Tasker (1993) – both focus on the ideological implications of this emphasis and both contain the word 'bodies' in their titles.

In the wake of her previous book, (1989), Jeffords's aim is 'on the one hand to argue for the centrality of the masculine body to popular culture and national identity while, on the other, to articulate how the polarizations of the body altered during the years of the Reagan and Bush presidencies' (Jeffords, 1994, p. 13). Her argument in essence is that

> whereas the Reagan years offered the image of a 'hard body' to contrast directly tot he 'soft body' of the Carter years, the late 1980s and early 1990s saw a reevaluation of that hard body, not for a return to the soft body but for a rearticulation of masculine strength and power through internal, personal, and family-oriented values. Both of these predominant models . . . are overlapping components of the Reagan Revolution, comprising on the one hand a strong militaristic foreign-policy position and on the other hand a domestic regime of an economy and a set of values dependent on the centrality of fatherhood. (Jeffords, 1994, p. 13)

In arguing her case, Jeffords, links a reading of the narrative structure of the films she discusses to the policy statements of Reagan, Bush and their spokespeople. However, she does not specify a mechanism through which the presidential ideologies she discusses find their way into the films. She is therefore forced to rely on analogy. This is a procedure – and a problem – common to numerous ideological analyses of genres and cycles, though it should be said that in this case Jeffords's analysis dovetails with arguments made about 1980s action films by Britton (1986), Kellner and Ryan (1988, pp. 217–43), Sartelle (1996), Traube (1992, pp. 28–66) and Wood (1986, pp. 162–88). However, others have taken a different view, both about the ideological significance and scope of 1980s action films, and about their aesthetic characteristics and values. Pfeil, for instance, argues that the category of 'white, heterosexual masculinity' that often underpins these analyses is not as monolithic as is often implied, that the films as a whole are often multivalent (combining appeals to the populist left as well as the right), and that distinctions need to be made among and between the films themselves, particularly between those produced by Joel Silver at Warners and Fox – the first two *Die Hard* films and the first two *Lethal Weapon* films – and others like *Batman* (1989) and *Total Recall* (1995, pp. 1–36). For Pfeil the former are sites in which 'fantasies of class and gender-based resistance to the advent of a post-feminist/post-Fordist world keep turning over, queasily, deliriously, into accommodations' (1995, p. 28), in which, within a 'very specifically white/male/hetero American capitalist dreamscape, inter- and/or multi-national at the top and multiracial at the bottom,' 'all the old lines of force and division between races, classes and genders are both transgressed and redrawn' (1995, p. 2). While 'the rhythms of excitation and satisfaction in these films' assert male violence, 'their own speeded-up processes of gratification undermine any claim to male authority' (1995, p. 8). The repeated spectacle of 'torn but still beautifully exposed slick-muscled bodies' raises rather than answers a number of questions: 'how do we distinguish between their (re)assertion of gendered difference and their submission to the camera . . . as objects of its gaze and our own? What, likewise, is the boundary line between the diehard assertion of rugged male individualism and its simultaneous feminization and spectacularization?' (1995, p. 29).

Terminator 2, a sci-fi variant of action adventure

Similar points are made by Willis (1997, pp. 27–59) and also by Tasker. Tasker points to the ambivalent populism of many of these action films, and to the fact that the muscular hero within them is often literally 'out of place': 'Increasingly . . . the powerful white hero is a figure who operates in the margins, while in many senses continuing to represent dominance. This is an important trait in many action pictures and is central to the pleasures of the text' (Tasker, 1993, p. 98). Equally central are style, spectacle, atmosphere and tone. Tasker is particularly interested in the knowing visual excess and the tongue-in-cheek humour characteristic of these films. She is therefore particularly insistent that ideological readings based solely on an analysis of their plots may be reductive, misleading, or both. As an example, she cites *Red Sonja* (1985), a sword-and-sorcery follow-up to Schwarzenegger's *Conan* films (1982 and 1984). Early on in *Red Sonja*, we learn that Sonja herself (Brigitte Nielsen) has rejected the sexual advances of queen Gedren. She becomes a swordswoman, and it is in this guise that she encounters Schwarzenegger as Kalidor: 'An analysis of the ideological terms at work in a film like *Red Sonja* is not difficult – the film follows Sonja's journey to a "normal" sexual identity, or at least the rejection of lesbian desire. After the initial "threat" of lesbianism, Sonja becomes a masculinised swordswoman who refuses Kalidor/Schwarzenegger until he can beat her in a "fair fight"' (Tasker, 1993, p. 30). However, the comedy and the excess perme-

Sylvester Stallone in *Rambo: First Blood Part II* – the 'hard body' of the Reagan years

Brigitte Nielsen as woman warrior – *Red Sonja*

ating the presentation of the fight and the 'texture' of the film as a whole 'call into question the very terms deployed – the "normal" sexual identity to which Sonja is led' (Tasker, 1993, p. 30).

Tasker continues, noting the extent to which exaggeration and parody are involved in the presentation of the body in these films. For her this means that the body and the terms of its gender can become the site of transgression and play, the focus of an attention that can make strange, as well as reinforce, norms of gender and sexual identity. Similar points are made by Holmlund in an article on *Lock Up* (1989) and *Tango and Cash* (1989), though while stressing the extent to which in these films heterosexual masculinity is presented as 'masquerade', she concludes by nothing that 'Masculinity may be only a fantasy, but as the success of Sylvester Stallone's films, including their invocation by right-wing politicians like Reagan and Bush, so amply demonstrates, masquerades of masculinity are eminently popular, and undeniably potent' (Holmlund, 1993, pp. 225–6). Her conclusion thus dovetails as much with Jeffords's position as it does with Tasker's.

Related issues and disagreements are raised by the 'women warrior' films discussed by Tasker, films like *Fatal Beauty* (1987), *China O'Brien* (1988) and the *Alien* trilogy, and by what Brown (1996) and Willis (1997, 98–128) see as an increasing trend towards 'hardbody heroines' and 'combative femininity' in action films in the 1990s. An additional complication here is the fact that *Fatal Beauty* centres on a black female star, Whoopi Goldberg, and thus constitutes an exception to what most commentators have perceived not just as an ethnic bias in action-adventure, but as a systematic project of marginalisation, demonisation and subordination *vis-à-vis* non-whites whose immediate roots lie in the racist and imperialist policies of Reagan and Bush. (In addition to Jeffords, Kellner and Ryan, and others cited above, see Marchetti, 1989).

One way to contextualise, if not necessarily to resolve, these issues and debates is to contextualise the films themselves by locating them within a tradition. 'Action–adventure' is not a new term. It was used by *The Film Daily* in 1927 to describe a Douglas Fairbanks film called *The Gaucho* (1927) (27 November 1927, p. 6). And it was used, among others, to categorise 'The New Season Product' in *The Motion Picture Herald* in 1939 (3 June 1939, p. 17). Used separately, the terms 'action' and 'adventure' have an even longer history, and films in the action–adventure tradition have been a staple in Hollywood's output since the 1910s.

With its immediate roots in nineteenth-century melodrama and in a principle strand of popular fiction, action–adventure has always encompassed an array of genres and sub-types: westerns, swashbucklers, war films, disaster films, space-operas, epics, safari films, jungle films and so on. As Sobchack points out, 'Although these groups of films may appear a disparate lot, their patterns of action and character relationships display characteristics which clearly link them together and distinguish them from other genres' (Sobchack, 1988, p. 9). 'In a sense,' he continues, echoing Cawelti (1976, pp. 39–41),

> all non-comic genre films are based on the structure of the romance of medieval literature: a protagonist either has or develops great and special skills and overcomes insurmountable obstacles in extraordinary situations to successfully achieve some desired goal, usually the restitution of order to the world invoked by the narrative. The protagonists confront the human, natural, or supernatural powers that have improperly assumed control over the world and eventually defeat them. (Sobchack, 1988, p. 9)

Set 'in the romantic past or in an inhospitable place in the present', the exotic milieux and the 'flamboyant actions of the characters' in the adventure film afford numerous opportunities for filmic spectacle (Sobchack, 1988. p. 10). Its basic narrative structure, meanwhile, gives rise to two characteristic variations. 'One focuses on the lone hero – the swashbuckler, the explorer who searches for the golden idol, the great hunter who leads the expedition, the lord of the jungle'. The other, the 'survival' form, most apparent in war films, prison films and disaster films, 'focuses on a hero interacting with a microcosmic group, the sergeant of a patrol, the leader of a squadron, the person who leads a group of castaways out of danger and back to civilization' (Sobchack, 1988, p. 12). As Marchetti points out, the plots in adventure films of all kinds are usually episodic, 'allowing for wide variations in tone, the inclusion of different locations and incidentally introduced characters, and moments of spectacle, generally involving fights, explosions, or other types of violence' (1989, p. 188). It might be noted that among the variations in tone to which Marchetti refers, tongue-in-cheek humour and tongue-in-cheek knowingess are as common in swashbucklers as they are in modern action–adventure films. And it might also be noted that even where locations are restricted, as they often are in prison and submarine films, space, the control of space, and the ability to move freely through space or from one space to another are always important.

In his discussion of the swashbuckler, Sobchack notes that the hero is 'defined as much by his physical expressiveness as by his good deeds' (Sobchack, 1988, p. 13). He also argues that in the survival genres, 'women play a decisive role in the success or failure of the group,' thus returning us to issues of gender and the body within the context of the adventure film as a whole. Displays of the male body and of hero's physical prowess are traditional in all kinds of adventure films, especially those of the lone-hero variety. Swashbucklers themselves tend to rely more on costumes and coiffeur rather than muscles (though as Richards (1977, pp. 15/40) points out, displays of the naked male torso – often in scenes of torture or violence – are regular feature of such films). But the reverse is the case in the Tarzan films and in epics like *Samson and Delilah* (1949). And just as modern performers like Schwarzenegger and Stallone are well known for their physique, so too were Victor Mature, Burt Lancaster (who trained as an acrobat) and Johnny Weismuller (who played Tarzan at MGM and Columbia, and who was once an Olympic swimmer).

These displays reach back beyond Elmo Lincoln's performances as Tarzan in late 1910s and early 1920s and Douglas Fairbanks's performances in films like *The Three Musketeers* (1921), *Robin Hood* (1922) and *The Thief of Baghdad* (1924). (On the Fairbanks films, see Richards, 1977, pp. 12–13, 25–6; Koszarski, 1990, pp. 270–1; and Taves, 1993, pp. 67–8). They include the performances of such muscular stars as House Peters, Richard Talmadge, Jack Tunney and Joe Boromo in the numerous adventure serials, 'railroad melodramas' and circus films that pervaded the 1920s, as well as those of Tom Mix, Ken Maynard and others, stunt-orientated westerns like *Riders of the Purple Sage* (1924), *The Arizona Wildcat* (1928) and *The Glorious Trail* (1928). They also include performances of various kinds in the stunt-based aviation films of the late 1920s and early 1930s, the Errol Flynn films made at Warners in the mid to late 1930s and early 1940s, the Tyrone Power films made at Fox in the late 1940s, the postwar cycle of adventure films featuring the likes of Robert Taylor, Burt Lancaster, Alan Ladd and Cornell Wilde, such subsequent postwar epics as *Spartacus* (1960), *Ben-Hur* (1959) and *El Cid* (1961), and the numerous adventure serials, Tarzan films and jungle melodramas that appeared throughout the 1930s, the 1940s and the 1950s.

Hence, as Tasker points out, 'the appearance of ... "muscular cinema" during the 1980s calls on a much longer tradition of representation' (Tasker, 1993, p. 1).

Selected Reading

Susan Jeffords, *The Remasculinization of America, Gender and the Vietnam War*, Bloomington and Indianapolis, Indiana University Press, 1989.

Susan Jeffords, *Hard Bodies: Hollywood Masculinity in the Reagan Era*, New Brunswick, Rutgers University Press, 1994.

Gina Marchetti, 'Action–Adventure as Ideology', Ian Angus and Sut Jhally (eds), *Cultural Politics in Contemporary America*, New York, Routledge, 1989.

Thomas Sobchack, 'The Adventure Film', in Wes D. Gehring (ed.), *Handbook of American Film Genres*, New York, Greenwood Press, 1988.

Yvonne Tasker, *Spectacular Bodies, Gender, Genre and the Action Cinema*, London, Routledge, 1993.

Brian Taves, *The Romance of Adventure, The Genre of Historical Adventure Movies*, Jackson, University of Press of Mississippi, 1993.

PART 6

AUTHORSHIP AND CINEMA

River of No Return (1954)

INTRODUCTION

Debates about authorship in the cinema have occupied a privileged position in film studies since the 1950s – when the French journal *Cahiers du Cinéma* formulated the *politique des auteurs* – until the early 1980s when film studies' focus was less concerned with authorship than with audience studies. Basically a polemical critical strategy aimed at the 'quality' French cinema and the critical writing that supported it, the *politique* proposed that, in spite of the industrial nature of film production, the director, like any other artist, was the sole author of the finished product. This proposition has been appropriated, attacked and reformulated in many different ways, and its long-lasting relevance to critical debates is some indication of the value of *Cahiers*' initial polemic.

Historical and political changes, particularly since the late 1960s, brought about a radical rethinking of the underlying assumptions of traditional *auteur* study of cinema, and an assault on the ideology of the artist as sole creator of the art work. Appropriating concepts from structural linguistics, semiology and psychoanalysis, film theory in the 1970s began to question the underlying assumptions of *auteur* theory such as 'coherence', 'self-expression' and 'creativity'. In spite of these assaults, *auteur* study was not destroyed, but rather transformed: from a way of accounting for the whole of cinema into a critical methodology which poses questions for film study, and for cultural practices in general. The history of this transformation is traced in this section.

The question of authorship and its application to the industrial context of cinema has often been presented and argued a-historically. Such was the case for example in the writings of the American film critic Andrew Sarris, who reformulated *Cahiers' politique* as the '*auteur* theory', transforming the original polemic for a new cinema of *auteurs* into a critical method for evaluating films (mostly Hollywood films, some European art cinema) and creating a pantheon of 'best directors' which is still effective in much film criticism today. It can be seen from many film courses (and from many cinema programmes) that the notion of the 'great director' is still important to the way cinema is learned and understood. Recognising the marks of 'greatness' can be a source of pleasure for some spectators watching the film, in the same way as recognising the elements of genre can be a source of pleasure as well as knowledge. These pleasures are used in the marketing of films to attract audiences by offering the possibility of using their specialist knowledge of cinema.

All too often the critical assault on authorship has refused to recognise the force of these pleasures, and the importance of taking them into account, finding itself in the impasse of a puritanical rejection. A historical approach helps us out of that impasse because it attempts to show how and why *auteur* theory emerged and was transformed, beginning the work of understanding different critical attitudes to cinema, the different pleasures we get from it, and how they change with history.

CINEMA AS ART OR COMMODITY?

Before the *politique des auteurs* emerged in France in the 1950s traditional film criticism (largely sociological) assumed that the industrial nature of film production prevented a single authorial voice making itself heard (or seen) in film. For some critics this meant that cinema could not be regarded as art: a commodity product at the service of the laws of the capitalist economy, it could do no more than reflect the ideology of the capitalist system. For others, cinema only achieved the status of art when a film or body of films could be seen as the expression of certain intentions carried out by an individual person, who was an artist by virtue of his or her struggle against the industrial system of production to attain control of that process of production in order to express his or her personal concerns. Few artists achieved this empirical control; Carl Dreyer is an example of a film director whose career can be seen to be defined by his uncompromising insistence on control of production: his status as one of the great artists of cinema resides as much in the intransigence of his position with regard to the film industry as in the aesthetic quality of the relatively small number of films he was able to make (see Nash, 1977). Moreover, the 'butchering' of many of these films by 'uncomprehending' (commercially motivated) distributors is seen as further evidence of the fundamental antagonism between art, or the interests of the artist, and the interests of commodity production. The artist is conceived of as a solitary isolated figure struggling for creative autonomy against the interference of outside bodies.

THE ARTIST AS CREATIVE SOURCE

The ideology which located the individual artist as the source of true creativity can be traced back to historical shifts which have radically changed the position of the artist in society. Before the Renaissance, the artist was seen as a craftsman producing useful objects: God was the locus of creativity rather than man. When creativity was extended to painters and poets the divine gift of inspiration and genius was relocated in the artist, who was directly dependent upon the patronage of the ruling class. A division emerged between craftsman, or artisan who produced for consumption, and artist whose innate genius presented a potential challenge to the assumptions of the prevailing social order. However, the artist's autonomy was limited by his or her dependence upon the patronage of the ruling class.

The emergence of the capitalist commodity economy changed the traditional relationship of the artist to society from direct dependence upon the patronage of a clearly defined group to indirect dependence on a large, anonymous group which was always expanding, i.e. the market. This shift produced a new conflict: on the one hand the artist was now 'free' to exploit the market to sell the results of his or her labour to the highest bidder; on the other hand the romantic notion of 'artistic genius' resisted the forces of the market in the interests of artistic autonomy in opposition to 'commercial, socially conformist art' (see Murdock, 1980).

In a capitalist economy, art is a commodity subject to the laws of the market: the division between mass-produced culture and art proper merges with the distinction between craftsman and artist to marginalise the artist from society. Since artistic activity cannot be totally rationalised according to the laws of profitability governing commodity production, if it is to survive at all it can only do so through state intervention in the form of subsidies, in which case the artist is guaranteed a minority prestige status, subsidised by a society of which only a tiny part represents his or her audience. The minority status of art can be seen to perform a double function: to guarantee critical approval for those who control it (the subsidising agencies), and to provide a safe, licensed space for artistic activity, necessarily marginalised. This marginalisation effectively neutralises the potentially critical voice of the artist in society.

The practice of attributing cultural products back to the name of an individual artist performs an important function in the process of commodity production, ensuring that a product is marketed in a particular way, as 'art' rather than 'mass production', and consumed by a particular knowledgeable audience. In practice, however, the distinction is far from clear-cut: art is constantly appropriated by popular culture, and vice versa. Thus it could be argued that the status of any cultural product as art (or otherwise) depends less on its intrinsic aesthetic value, or indeed on any intrinsic property, than on the way it is taken up and exploited by the laws of the market.

THE FUNCTION OF AUTHORSHIP IN CINEMA

The distinction between 'art' and 'commercial product' has its own history within the history of cinema, and can be seen to perform different functions at different moments (see Art cinema, p. 108). In the early days of Hollywood, for instance, the enormous commercial potential of cinema was recognised, and the rush to exploit that potential meant that innovation and experiment were held at a premium. The early Hollywood industry was in a relatively open state, and copyright laws were minimal, so much pirating took place. The practice of marking a film with the logo of its production company grew up as a way of protecting the rights of the company over the film, but the logo could also function as a mark of authorship, and hence as a guarantee of artistic value. The artistic experiments which emerged from Hollywood in this period were greatly admired by Russian and European avant-garde film-makers. In Hollywood itself, the films were marketed as exceptional cinematic events: their status as art was part of their commodity value, and the mark of the presence of the 'artist' (Griffith's logo, Chaplin's 'Tramp' persona) performed a function in the marketing process.

There is, however, a danger in reducing the concept of authorship to the status of a simple function (see Foucault, 1979). As the history of *auteur* study of cinema shows, the idea of authorship can be taken up in many different ways. It could be argued, for instance, that after the coming of sound the idea of film as art gave way in Hollywood to the idea of entertainment, although a place was reserved for prestige productions which were usually literary adaptations. In this case the creative source of the film was taken to be the writer of the original work rather than the director. As the strength of the major studios grew, producers and stars became more important in the marketing process than directors. At the time of the emergence of the *politique des auteurs*, then, the idea that a Hollywood film could be related back to the intentions of an individual director in the same way as it was in the case of films which fell into the category of art cinema, had an important polemical impetus. It attempted to break down the barrier between art cinema and commercial cinema by establishing the presence of artists in the apparently monolithic commodity production of Hollywood. Although the idea of the director as artist was prevalent in writing on art cinema, it was not important to writing on Hollywood at that time.

In the wake of *auteur* theory's polemic for popular cinema, and the anti-*auteurist* politics which followed May 1968, art cinema became unfashionable in film criticism. It also declined in economic importance, and its distribution and exhibition became on the whole restricted to a small art house and film society circuit. Yet it is possible to argue that at the same time its importance and influence in some form or other on cinema in general increased rather than waned. 'New Hollywood cinema', for instance (e.g. Altman, Penn, Coppola) owed much to the erstwhile enemy of Hollywood, art cinema (New Hollywood, p. 98). Also, and significantly, the director's name once again became important in marketing Hollywood cinema: hoardings advertising 'Samuel Fuller's *The Big Red One*' and 'John Carpenter's *Halloween*' alongside '*Don Giovanni*: a film by Joseph Losey' and '*Kagemusha*: an Akira Kurosawa film'. It could be argued then that art cinema suffered from critical neglect at a time when the division between art cinema and popular cinema was generally breaking down.

AUTHORS IN ART CINEMA

Tracing the history of the emergence of art cinema after the Second World War, David Bordwell gives a cogent account of the ways in which art cinema differs from classic narrative cinema (Bordwell, 1979). He sees the loose narrative structure of art cinema as motivated by a desire for realism, i.e. an attempt to represent 'real' problems in 'real' locations, using psychologically complex

A Hitchcock hoarding – important in marketing

characters to validate the drive towards verisimilitude: social, emotional and sexual problems are reflected in individual characters, and only become significant in so far as they impinge upon the sensitive individual.

This drive towards realism seems incompatible with the idea of a creative artist as source of meaning in art cinema: the artist's voice is intrusive and disrupts verisimilitude. Yet, Bordwell argues, art cinema specifically uses authorship to unify the film text, to organise it for the audience's comprehension in the absence of clearly identifiable stars and genres. Art cinema addresses its audience as one of knowledgeable cinemagoers who will recognise the characteristic stylistic touches of the author's *œuvre*. The art film is intended to be read as the work of an expressive individual, and a small industry is devoted to informing viewers of particular authorial marks: career retrospectives, press reviews and television programmes all contribute to introducing viewers to authorial codes.

In art cinema, then, the informed, educated audience looks for the marks of authorship to make sense of the film rather than to the rambling story of the characters, who are often aimless victims rather than controlling agents. Audience identification shifts from characters to author: the audience is often given privileged information over the characters (e.g. the device of the 'flash forward') which strengthens identification with the author. Although apparently at odds with the realist project of art cinema, this controlling authorial discourse provides the final guarantee of 'truth' for the audience: if the realism of locations and character psychology represents the world 'as it is', the authorial discourse can be said to confirm the essential truth of the individual's experience of that world. This textual organisation differs from that of the 'classic realist text' (see Classic realist text, p. 32). However, the dominance of authorial discourse is by no means secure in art cinema – Bordwell sees the art film in terms of a shifting, uneasy relationship between the discourses of narrative, character and author. In this way art cinema maintains hesitation and ambiguity rather than the resolution of problems: the essential ambiguity of life reflected in art.

If, as Bordwell argues, art cinema can be established as a distinct mode, different from classic Hollywood or the modernist avant-garde, there are nonetheless interesting areas of overlap. Some 'classic' films (e.g. those of Sirk, Ford or Lang) display affinities with art cinema, and it is possible to argue that Hitchcock's films emphasise the narrational process and authorial discourse and problems of point of view in much the same way as the art film does. On the other hand, some modernist film-making has taken up and extended art cinema strategies beyond its own limits (Dreyer, Resnais, Straub/Huillet) and in some cases has begun to question it (Godard). One interesting way of approaching art cinema might be in terms of its relationship to, or difference from, other modes of film-making. For instance, while it could be argued that New Hollywood cinema owes much to art cinema, conditions of production are different in Hollywood, so that Hollywood art films represent a complex transformation of the codes of art cinema (see Neale, 1976).

Ingmar Bergman

If, as Bordwell (1979) argues, one of the principles of art cinema that distinguishes it from classic narrative cinema is the marked presence of the author/artist as organising source of a film or group of films, so that the author becomes a kind of protagonist in the drama, a point of identification for the knowledgeable viewer, then it is possible to argue that traditional film criticism has responded to art cinema in its own terms, by supporting the relationship of complicity between artist/director and critic. The task of the critic is to be more knowledgeable than the ordinary, fairly knowledgeable viewer, to pass on their insights to this viewer on the assumption that they aspire to the privileged status of author and critic. This identity between author, critic and audience set up by traditional film criticism supports the circulation of art films as 'serious', 'intellectual' cinema, minority fare as opposed to mass entertainment.

It could be argued that the transformation of traditional *auteur* analysis of films has made it difficult to take the idea of the *auteur* seriously. However, the name of the director-as-author did not cease to be important in the marketing of film, and while theoretical film criticism abandoned straightforward *auteur* analysis, much of the criticism in 'quality' newspapers and film journals remained, and remains, devoted to the idea of the director as artist. Since it seems that the function of the author/artist at one time limited to art cinema has extended to popular commercial cinema too, and the name of the artist can perform the function of attracting a large, knowledgeable audience (rather than the minority audience of art cinema proper) for commercial cinema, then a study of art cinema in terms of authorship could offer useful information about the viewer's pleasure in recognising the marks of authorship in cinema in general. Art cinema could provide a means of critical entry into commercial cinema, not in terms of the confirmation of traditional *auteur* analysis, but in the interests of understanding the relationship between art cinema and commercial cinema in order to question the conventional division between 'art' and 'entertainment'.

In spite of the basic polemic of *auteur* theory in favour of popular cinema, Ingmar Bergman retained a place in the pantheons

Isolation of the artist/victim in Bergman's *Sawdust and Tinsel*

of *auteur* critics, and many of the critics writing for *Cahiers du Cinéma* in the 1950s and 1960s admired the formal strategies of art cinema. Its influence can be seen in the films of the French new wave, and the films of Jean-Luc Godard, for example, show a shift away from the desire to explore the formal possibilities offered by art cinema to an interest in using the strategy of montage to criticise it. In Britain, *Movie* magazine included critical (but supportive) accounts of art films as well as Hollywood movies during the 1960s (see Cameron, 1972). However, these approaches tended to remove films and directors from their historical context in the interests of defending films as art in their own right. A different approach is taken by Maria Bergom-Larsson (1978). She writes from a position informed by an analysis of the political and ideological function of cinema and film criticism, attempting to place Bergman historically in Swedish culture and ideology, and to read the films in terms of the director's preoccupation with the myths of his society. Although she retains the idea of the director as the organising source of his films, the emphasis on history and ideology enables her to break with the idea of the 'great artist' and to produce a convincing critique of Bergman's position which is illuminating for art cinema in general. She concentrates on ideological content rather than formal strategies, but her approach could usefully be combined with Bordwell's to discuss Bergman's films in the context of art cinema.

Maria Bergom-Larsson argues that the place of the artist in society has shifted radically from centre stage to the wings: serious critical art has lost its social function, artists cannot make a living from their work, and art is now increasingly subsidised by state intervention. Although taxes are paid by everyone, only a minority is in a position to enjoy art. The artist has two alternatives: to refuse the marginalised position allotted to artists and organise with other artists to make a political intervention into society; or to accept the futility of artistic production and continue to work entirely for his or her own sake, a retreat from politics into solipsism. By his own account, this last route is the one taken by Bergman, and many of his

INGMAR BERGMAN

Sawdust and Tinsel (Sweden 1953 *p.c* – Sandrew Productions; *d* – Ingmar Bergman: sd b/w)

Bergman has used the metaphor of the circus to characterise the position of the artist in society as one of risk: the artist puts his or her life on the line for the chance amusement of others. In this film the clown, Frost, represents the suffering artist–victim, treated with derision by the uncomprehending spectators. Failure of communication between artist and audience emphasises the former's tragic isolation.

The story of the clown, told in flashback, shows how Frost is unable to communicate this anguish to his wife Alma, or to the audiences of soldiers who are watching her bathe naked. Frost's humiliation has a sexual dimension: Alma's sexual antics for the benefit of the soldiers are depicted as a threat to his manhood. Not only is he unable to communicate his anguish, he is unable to control Alma or to rescue her from the humiliating situation. Only when he finally collapses in despair does Alma recognise his suffering and take up the position of anxious mother towards him. The depiction of woman as mother is a recurring image in Bergman's films and has been taken as a positive representation of woman by some critics.

In terms of art cinema, the flashback sets up an interesting relationship between cinema audiences and film. It is treated non-realistically, and the symbolic use of image and sound intensifies the tragedy of Frost's predicament, encouraging the cinema audience to identify with him rather than the uncomprehending audience of soldiers in the film: by responding to the 'expressive' use of film language in the flashback they are able, like the author of the film, to understand Frost's suffering. The flashback is introduced by the voice-over of one of the characters in the film, but it could be argued that Bergman's authorial 'voice' takes over the scene, marked in the 'expressive' *mise-en-scène*, and confirming identification between Frost, Bergman as artist, and the viewer.

The Seventh Seal (Sweden 1957 *p.c* – Svensk Filmindustri; *d* – Ingmar Bergman; sd b/w)

Bergman has commented that the increasing isolation of the artist in society was partly a result of the divorce of art from the church (see Bergom-Larsson, 1978). When the artist was part of a creative collective and all art was in the service of God the artist had no need to question the function of art or his own place in the world; truth was guaranteed. The modern artist, by contrast, has no guarantees, either of universal truth or of his own place in the world: his life has been put at risk.

In the film, the knight and his squire faced with a constant struggle with the figure of death represent the doubters and searchers who have lost the security of their faith in God, and are consequently condemned to a precarious existence in a world where meaning can no longer be taken for granted. The strolling players, on the other hand, do not experience life as hostile; indeed, the jester and his family perform in the service of God and so succeed in escaping both the suffering of life and the cruelty of death. The jester's vision of the Virgin Mary is a source of joy rather than a threat to him.

In terms of art cinema, the film illustrates the preoccupation with myth and symbols which can be found in the work of several directors (for example, Fellini and Antonioni). Symbols perform several functions in art cinema: they indicate that the self-enclosed world of art is separate from the 'real' world; they present an element of difficulty to the art cinema audience, which is encouraged to think, to recognise and decode signs, rather than follow the narrative; and they maintain a level of unresolved ambiguity in the film, the principal strategy employed by art cinema to indicate that art cannot provide any final truths.

Wild Strawberries (Sweden 1957 *p.c* – Svensk Filmindustri; *d* – Ingmar Bergman; sd b/w)

A consistent theme in Bergman's work is that of the family (see also *The Seventh Seal*, 1957, and *The Silence*, 1963, and later television work e.g. *Scenes from a Marriage*, 1974). The family is defined by Bergman as authoritarian and patriarchal, strictly dividing the roles of men and women so that men are confined to the public sphere of work, technology, intellect, etc., and women to the private sphere of family, pleasure, sexuality and emotion. Bergman sees this patriarchal family as dehumanising, particularly for men, and seems to offer a criticism of the family at one level (see Bergom-Larsson, 1978). He accepts, however, the place allotted to women and sees the values associated with femininity as more 'natural'. It is arguable that this leads him to idealise the role of woman as mother, seeing it as both refuge and salvation for men dehumanised by patriarchy. The link between women and reproduction is crucial to Bergman's world-view, so that he sees social change in the area of sexuality (e.g. abortion) which might free women from their place in the family as problematic for men (e.g. *Persona*, 1966). The image of woman in Bergman's films is, it could be argued, the locus of male problems with sexuality, although some critics have responded to that image as a positive or progressive representation.

This film examines the effect of the patriarchal family on a father who has become successful in social terms as an eminent doctor. His success is only a mask, however, and the film sets out to reveal that behind the distorted mask lies a 'real human being' (cf. *Sawdust and Tinsel*, 1953).

The use of flashback and dream to represent subjective states of mind is characteristic of art cinema. In this film they function as an interruption into 'everyday reality': Borg's car journey to collect his accolades is presented as less important than his journey into the inner recesses of his mind. Truth is seen to reside in this inner, emotional world rather than in the public world.

The Silence (Sweden 1963 *p.c* – Svensk Filmindustri; *d* – Ingmar Bergman; sd b/w)

Bergman's ambiguous response to the breakdown of the patriarchal family can be seen in this film. The two sisters Anna and Ester are obsessed with the death of their father, which has cast them adrift. They respond to this in different ways; Anna exploits her active sexual desires, while Ester turns her aggression against herself. Both are depicted as perverse and doomed, condemned to a sterile existence in the midst of a society in a state of collapse. It is arguable that the isolation of the protagonists is represented as both necessary and self-destructive: the audience is offered two positions from which to judge events, one of acceptance of necessity, or one of moral disgust (art cinema's 'ambiguity').

The film was made at a time when political debate among Swedish intellectuals about Sweden's internal affairs, and about the United States' involvement in Vietnam was growing. By 1963 Bergman occupied a top position within the Swedish cultural establishment and resisted as a 'political vogue' all criticism of that establishment (see Bergom-Larsson, 1978). His resistance to politics can be seen in *The Silence*: the two sisters remain remote from the political upheavals in the world outside as do most Bergman characters. On the other hand, the violence of the external world erupts in the inner world too, in the personal relationships and obsessions of the protagonists.

It has been argued that Bergman's representation of women changes in the films made after 1960. The woman-as-mother figure changes to an image of woman as anguished, tortured subject, taking over the role of the male protagonists in the earlier films. After 1960, Bergman begins to 'speak through' his female characters, offering them as a central point of identification for the audience, which has led some critics to see his later work as offering a progressive view of women as strong, and a shift from a male to a female perspective (see Steene, 1979).

films take the predicament of the artist as their central theme. The consequences of this decision to adopt a position of isolated individualism are that individuals can only be seen as victims of social forces: unable to play a positive role in society, they experience social change as traumatic, a threat to emotional and psychological security. Many of Bergman's characters are shown to be caught in the conflict between the inner emotional world and the menacing outer world of society, often depicted in a state of violent upheaval. One of the most important aspects of social change has been in the area of sexuality and the family: the changing status of women is also regarded as a problem by Bergman, and provides the third major theme of his films, one that has been widely discussed by feminist film critics (see Steene, 1979).

Federico Fellini

David Bordwell (1979) has identified the later Italian neo-realist films as early examples of international art cinema. From this perspective the career of Fellini is particularly interesting, since it moves from a short period of collaboration with neo-realist directors like Roberto Rossellini and Alberto Lattuada, through their acknowledged influence in Fellini's early films, to be a fully-fledged, personal art cinema in which the basic principles of neo-realism are reversed.

When Fellini began directing films in 1950, the social and economic conditions which produced Italian neo-realism had already changed considerably. Neo-realism had offered an 'objective' look at society at a time when anti-Fascist struggles were important in Italy (see Cannella, 1973/74). After the Second World War, with the break-up of the Fascist dictatorship and improving economic conditions the social criticism and analysis of neo-realism gave way to a personal art cinema in which subjective states of mind were more important than objective social conditions. If neo-realism saw its characters in the context of society, art cinema sees society mediated through its characters, who are represented as individuals rather than social types. If the neo-realist director tried to be as inconspicuous as possible, allowing the material to speak for itself, the art cinema director inserts his or her own discourse between the audience and the subject matter of the film (see Italian neo-realism, p. 76; Art cinema, p. 106).

Fellini is often compared with Ingmar Bergman (see Rosenthal, 1976). Although the two directors share common themes, their treatment of them differs radically. Fellini's 'personal' cinema contains a strong autobiographical element; although Bergman can be seen to 'speak through' his characters he is never directly autobiographical. Fellini's films often take up a non-intellectual, even anti-intellectual position, whereas Bergman is concerned with the problematic position of intellectuals in society. If Fellini identifies with 'wise fools', the outcasts of society as offering insight and truth, Bergman identifies with the alienated intellectual, another kind of social outcast.

SELECTED READING

David Bordwell, 'The art cinema as a mode of film practice', *Film Criticism* 4(1), 1979.

Michel Foucault, 'What is an author?' *Screen* 20(1), spring 1979.

Graham Murdock, 'Authorship and organisation', *Screen Education* 35, summer 1980.

FEDERICO FELLINI

La strada (The Road) (Italy 1954 *p.c* – Ponti-De Laurentiis; *d* – Federico Fellini; sd b/w)

An echo of neo-realism can be seen in the subject matter of this film: the destruction of childlike innocence by a brutal and uncomprehending world. However, Fellini treats the subject entirely in terms of human relationships, so that the film is a celebration of lost innocence rather than a criticism of social attitudes.

The character of Gelsomina is reminiscent of Charlie Chaplin's 'Tramp' persona: potentially subversive, or at least critical of conventional society, it is offered as a point of identification for the audience, although the essential ambiguity of art cinema is maintained since both characters are represented as 'essentially human', and the audience is simply asked to recognise 'the human condition'.

Gelsomina is an outcast, a childlike innocent whose view of the world is untouched by adult cynicism. In a later film, *Giulietta degli spiriti* (1965) (*Juliet of the Spirits*), Giulietta Masina plays a similar role as a naïve housewife whose personal vision of the world, expressed in fantasy, dominates the film and acts as a criticism of a corrupt and sterile society. The image of woman as a potential critical force in this film bears comparison with that in Ingmar Bergman's films.

In terms of art cinema, the protagonists of *La strada* are aimless: no one knows where 'the road' leads. This is illustrated by Gelsomina's apparently positive decision to leave Zampanò and go home. As soon as the small band appears, however, she arbitrarily decides to follow them.

Reminiscent of Chaplin's 'Tramp' persona – Gelsomina in Fellini's *La strada*

Otto e mezzo (Eight and a Half) (Italy 1962/63 *p.c* – Cineriz; *d* – Federico Fellini; sd b/w)

The film which marks Fellini's movement into an autobiographical cinema in which his own fantasies and childhood memories are explicitly worked through. The film is presented through the eyes of its central male character, Guido, a film director, who has been taken to represent Fellini himself. The film might be said to entirely express the point of view of its author, with whom the audience is asked to identify. It could be compared with *Giulietta degli spiriti*, in which, it has been argued (Bordwell, 1979), Fellini's authorial discourse is displaced by the fantasies of the central female protagonist.

Guido might also be taken to represent the 'artist–victim', a recurring figure in Ingmar Bergman's work also. Whereas he is entirely at the mercy of his subjective obsessions however, the artist–victim in Bergman's films suffers because of his relationship, albeit alienated, from society. Guido bears some resemblance to Isak Borg in *Wild Strawberries*: his success is a mask which hides his inner inadequacy.

Guido's inadequacy is manifested on one level in sexual impotence, and in his relationship to women in general. It is arguable that Fellini's use of surrealism and fantasy enables the audience to take a distance on Guido's obsessions and criticise them, and, by implication, the social forces that give rise to them (e.g. the Catholic family). A question would be whether these formal strategies, characteristic of art cinema, invite the audience to think about the films, or encourage it to accept their underlying preconceptions.

FOR A NEW FRENCH CINEMA: THE *POLITIQUE DES AUTEURS*

The *politique* was signalled by Alexandre Astruc's 1948 article 'The Birth of a New Avant-Garde: la Caméra-Stylo', calling for a new language of cinema in which the individual artist could express his or her thoughts, using the camera to write a world-view, a philosophy of life. Astruc was writing as a left-wing intellectual and film-maker in postwar France, where the extreme social fragmentation and isolation of the left after the war resulted in the need for reconstruction and stabilisation formulated in individual rather than political or collective terms. Furthermore, during the war the Americans had developed lightweight 16 mm cameras which made possible film-making in small groups as opposed to the methods of studio production in Hollywood or France and this, combined with the growth of television, made the possibility of wider access to the means of production seem real and immediate. Moreover, after the Second World War French intellectuals and film-makers were able to see those Hollywood films which were previously unavailable at the Cinémathèque in Paris. Against this background of contradictory historical circumstances, the European intellectual tradition which saw the artist as a voice of dissent in society took on a polemical force in film criticism (see Buscombe, 1973).

The film-makers and critics who subsequently wrote for *Cahiers du Cinéma* were committed to questions of form and *mise-en-scène* and to the necessity for a theoretical analysis of the relationship of the artist and the film product to society, rather than to the untheorised political commitment of other journals of film criticism in France at the time, notably *Positif* (see Benayoun, 1962). So the *politique des auteurs* emerged in opposition not only to established French film criticism with its support for a 'quality' cinema of serious social themes, but also to the untheorised committed political criticism of the left, which ignored the contribution of individuals to the process of film production (see Truffaut, 1954/1976).

ANDRÉ BAZIN

It is sometimes tempting to dismiss the *politique des auteurs* as a simple manifesto for individual personal expression, which is why it is important to understand the historical and political context (the upheaval of left-wing politics in the 1950s, the cold war, anti-Stalinism) from which it emerged. It was the status of personal feelings within left-wing cultural struggle that was at stake in the early formulations of the *politique* in the pages of *Cahiers* and in its relationship to the film-making practice of the *nouvelle vague*, and although this polemic was often lost in the process of appropriation, it remained relevant to arguments in film theory (see Hess, 1974).

There was considerable debate within *Cahiers* about the *politique*. The shift towards the film-maker/director as the organising source of meaning in the film was resisted by André Bazin, who believed that the film-maker should act as a passive recorder of the real world rather than manipulator of it – a contradictory position, given his admiration for Hollywood directors such as Orson Welles and Alfred Hitchcock. There were political implications in the disagreement: Bazin's notion of society as based on the interdependence of individuals and social forces was at odds with the idea of a society of conflict and opposition espoused by many of *Cahiers*' younger writers. At the same time Bazin criticised the notion that a body of work could be ascribed to an individual *auteur* as though the individual was not part of society and history, subject to social and historical constraints (see Bazin, 1957/1968). Bazin argued for a sociological approach to film which would take into account the historical moment of production. However, when it came to his own analysis of the work and directors he thought important, his position often led him into a critical impasse (see Bazin, p. 337).

Bazin's criticism of the *politique* was perceptive: the evaluation of films according to the criterion of the 'great director' who transcended history and ideology was the least productive aspect of the *politique des auteurs*, together with the importance given to the critic's personal taste that went with it.

AUTEURS VERSUS *METTEURS-EN-SCÈNE*

Closely linked to this discussion about the status of the individual artist in artistic production was the distinction the *auteur* critics made between an *auteur* and a *metteur-en-scène*. The idea of *mise-en-scène* (the staging of the real world for the camera) was central to the interest in form and cinematic language that many *Cahiers* critics shared, but their notion of the individual artist as primary source of meaning in film led them to make a distinction between those directors who simply directed (who had mastered the language of cinema) and those who were true *auteurs*, in the sense that they put forward a coherent world-view in their films and manifested a uniquely individual style. Again Bazin differed: a film's *mise-en-scène* should efface individual style to allow the inner meaning to shine through naturally so that the spectator could come to his or her own conclusions without being manipulated. Bazin's emphasis on the transparency of cinematic language was at odds with many *Cahiers* critics' interest in the possibility of manipulating the language of cinema to express the director's personal concerns. Bazin's argument comes close to eliminating human intervention in the process of production altogether (see Wollen, 1976).

This defence of formalism against notions of transparency (film as window on the world) and realism (film expressing the truth of reality) remained important to the *Cahiers* critics even through the reassessments that took place in that journal during the 1960s under the impact of structuralist theory. The structuralist attack on humanism and personal expression was to have major repercussions for the *politique* and for the centrality of the individual artist within it. Nonetheless, the basic argument that the director of a film should be considered an important source of meaning in that film remained relevant to debate in film studies, though the terms of the debates had changed.

STYLE AND THEME

Jean Renoir

Renoir's film-making career spanned more than 40 years; he worked in many different production situations and is now considered one of the great film artists, whose films display a consistency of cinematic style and thematic concerns which remain constant through the years. He was a major influence on new wave film-makers (e.g. François Truffaut) and a favourite *auteur* of André Bazin because of his subtle use of *mise-en-scène*, a style based on absence of montage, deep-focus photography and fluid camera movement, exemplifying the transparency of style which Bazin argued could most effectively reveal the essence of the real world for the spectator. Equally, Renoir's humanist view of the world expressed in the way he integrated actors with objects and space coincided with Bazin's interest in the way cinema could be used to express the relationship between individuals and society as one of mutual interdependence (see Bazin, 1971).

While these stylistic and thematic concerns can certainly be seen in Renoir's work, it is also evident that history (the 1930s Popular Front in *Le Crime de Monsieur Lange*, the impending Second World War in *La Grande Illusion*) and different production situations (the American Renoir) also had an impact on the films and, it could be argued, should be taken into account in any study of Renoir as an *auteur*. While *auteur* study sometimes allows us to understand films better by detecting the director's concerns over a body of work, it should not obscure questions of history and ideology as equally important determining factors, not only on the films but on the way we read them. Today's viewers, used to the static realism of television programmes, may find Renoir's *mise-en-scène* excessive, even melodramatic.

Renoir made over 35 films between 1924 and 1961. Any serious attempt to approach his work as an *auteur* would need to look carefully at as many of these films as possible. His work is used here to discuss one aspect of the *politique des auteurs*: the use of the name Jean Renoir as a means of classifying and evaluating films according to the assumed presence of a consistent personal vision or world-view. This *auteurist* approach could be questioned by a consideration of Renoir's work in the context of the 1930s Popular Front, which affected a whole generation of French filmworkers, and the different production conditions he met in America (see Fofi, 1972/73; Rivette and Truffaut, 1954).

Fritz Lang

It is possible, as in the case of Renoir, to see an author's work as a whole in terms of a linear development of themes and style (e.g. from early Renoir to mature Renoir, although critical opinion may differ on the relative merits of 'early' or 'late'). Thus Renoir falls into the category of the *auteur* as artist in critical writing about his work, a view which is supported to a great extent by the concerns of that work and his own pronouncements on it. From this perspective, the artist/*auteur* is the sole source of meaning, transcending history, both in terms of conditions of production and the conditions in which the film is seen by different audiences.

The career of Fritz Lang is similar to Renoir's in many ways: he worked as scriptwriter and director in the German film industry in the 1920s and early 1930s, leaving to go to Hollywood in the mid-1930s, where he had a prolific career except for a brief period of blacklisting in the 1950s (see Bogdanovich, 1968, p. 83). His work is generally divided by critics into 'early' and 'late', German and American, and critical opinion differs as to the relative merits of each.

In the context of the *politique des auteurs*, Lang's work is interesting because it demonstrates how authorship can be traced across apparently totally different sets of films, such as German and American Lang, to confer the status of art on commercial cinema. Lang's American films have been described as artistically inferior to those he made in Germany. But *Cahiers du Cinéma* (e.g. no. 99, 1959) was interested primarily in Lang's American work as part of their polemic for a reassessment of American cinema in general, and they were responsible for rescuing Lang's American films from the dismissive category of routine commercial production to which they had been relegated, tracing a consistent world-view through them, and a consistent use of Expressionist *mise-en-scène* which had its roots in the German films.

There are problems with locating a director's work so firmly within a particular artistic movement like German Expressionism. First, the use of a term borrowed from painting tends to locate the film as art rather than commodity production, endorsing the notion of self-expression and obscuring the numerous processes involved in producing a film (see Petley, 1978). Second, the term 'Expressionist' can be used to cover such a variety of formal practices of film-making that it becomes meaningless. However, the value of placing Lang's work historically within German Expressionism is that as an author he can be shown to be working within a specific historical and cultural moment (see Johnston, 1977). Also, Expressionism itself is generally regarded as a movement which arose quite directly out of social change in Europe at the turn of the century: Expressionist artists attempted to express this changing, fragmented world and the alienated place of the individual within it. In Germany, Lang used Expressionism to explore his interest in social criticism, an interest which can be directly related to an historical moment. However, the 'modernist' momentum behind the German Expressionist movement and the artistic experiments which flourished in the postwar boom of the early 1920s in Germany cannot be directly mapped onto Lang's work in Hollywood. Rather, his American films show the way in which a director's social and artistic concerns are transformed by different production contexts (German Expressionism, p. 67).

Selected Reading

André Bazin, 'La politique des auteurs', *Cahiers du Cinéma* no. 70, April 1957, trans. in Peter Graham (ed.), *The New Wave*, London, Secker & Warburg/BFI, 1968.

John Caughie (ed.), *Theories of Authorship: A Reader*, London, RKP/BFI, 1981.

JEAN RENOIR

Boudu sauvé des eaux (Boudu Saved from Drowning) (France 1932 *p.c* – Michel Simon/Jean Gehret; *d* – Jean Renoir; sd b/w)

Renoir's consistent interest in the idea of 'natural man' is manifest here in the person of Boudu, who flouts polite conventions and is restless and disruptive within the bourgeois milieu of the man who saves him from drowning. This concern with the positive antisocial values of the anarchic outsider can be traced as a theme throughout Renoir's work, but since this film was made in the 1930s during his involvement with left-wing politics, it is equally relevant to place this concern within the context of French cinema of the time and to take into account the collaboration between Renoir and Michel Simon (Boudu). Simon co-produced the film under the banner of his own production company, while Renoir wrote and directed. The character of Boudu, the anarchic renegade in opposition to *petit-bourgeois* values is in many ways a vehicle for Simon who was often associated with such roles (e.g. in Jean Vigo's *L'Atalante*, 1934).

In terms of Renoir's characteristic *mise-en-scène* the film uses deep-focus

'Natural man ... flouts polite conventions' in Renoir's *Boudu sauvé des eaux*

photography and moving camera to indicate a coherent space which the camera reveals, disclosing people and objects as if by accident. Bazin saw Renoir's use of camera movement to integrate actors and space as exemplary of a style which captures reality for the spectator, the camera acting as an 'invisible guest' at the scene to be filmed.

Le Crime de Monsieur Lange (The Crime of M. Lange) (France 1935 *p.c* – Oberon; *d* – Jean Renoir; sd b/w)

A film made directly out of Renoir's political commitment to the Popular Front and its ideas of the unity between white-collar and labouring workers against capitalist businessmen and employers. The idea of unity in a common cause, here represented by the workers' co-operative, is central to much of Renoir's work, whether that cause be war (*La Grande Illusion*, 1937), art (*French Can-Can*, 1955), or social change as in the case of this film. Contradictions arise and are resolved by group solidarity and mutual caring, but the continued existence of the problem boss Batala, can only be resolved by extreme and violent action. Lange must become a hero (like Arizona Jim) and kill the villain, placing himself outside the law for ever. It could be argued that a dark note of irony overshadows the 'happy ending'. Lange sacrifices himself (and Valentine) for the cooperative, and finally a group of workmen help them to escape. The cooperative survives at the expense of individual sacrifice.

In terms of *mise-en-scène*, Renoir characteristically creates a coherent and identifiable space, centred on the courtyard where all communal discussion and action take place. Individual workers move between the courtyard and their workplaces in the block, and the fluidity of movement of the actors between on-screen and off-screen space, combined with a naturalistic use of sound makes the interaction between individuals and group and the sense of solidarity especially convincing. However, the 'Arizona Jim' sub-plot, with its emphasis on fiction and fantasy, seems to work against the realism of Renoir's style, thus complicating the overall meaning of the film and its endorsement of Popular Front ideology.

La Grande Illusion (Grand Illusion) (France 1937 *p.c* – Réalisations d'Art Cinématographique; *d* – Jean Renoir; sd b/w)

The context of war is used to work through Renoir's concern with class and racial differences and human affinities. The aristocrat, the bourgeois, the intellectual and the 'common man' have different attitudes and manners. War is said to make them all equal, but the French aristocrat de Boeldieu has more in common with von Rauffenstein, his German enemy, than with his fellow Frenchmen. His solidarity with them is based on patriotism and a 'gentlemanly' sense of generosity which causes him to sacrifice himself so that they may escape successfully. Renoir's sympathy for the aristocrats and their doomed way of life is evident in his treatment of their relationship: a characteristic humanism. Yet it is arguable that this can appear contradictory, undermining humanism by putting blatantly Fascist remarks in the mouth of von Rauffenstein, and raising the question of how far sympathy for individual human beings can be maintained when the primary struggle is against Fascism. The idea of 'unity in a common cause' is more complex and contradictory here than in *Le Crime de Monsieur Lange*, manifested in the differences between characters and a greater fragmentation of space. However, Renoir's *mise-en-scène*, the use of deep-focus, long takes and sideways and panning shots, can be seen as realistic, depicting a world fragmented by war into which death, loss and fear are constantly erupting. This *mise-en-scène* seems to endorse the film's central pacifist theme, emerging from the policies of the Popular Front at the time.

La Grande Illusion – Renoir's concern with class differences

La Règle du jeu (The Rules of the Game) (France 1938 *p.c* – La Nouvelle Edition Française; *d* – Jean Renoir; sd b/w)

A further exploration of social differences, this time in the context of a house party where the love intrigues of high-society guests are mirrored by parallel activities among the servants. An extremely complex film in which contradictions are raised and left unresolved. Renoir uses the theatrical conventions of farce to explore the extent to which personal relationships, and by extension social structures, are based on pretence, accident and misunderstanding. The idea of 'social cohesion' is brought into question as it becomes clear that social unity is illusory, based on an acceptance of deceit.

If the stability of the status quo is based on illusion and deceit, who has the greatest vested interest in maintaining the illusion? The upper classes, evidently; but they cannot totally control events, much as they try. A servant's sexual jealousy can cause chaos in the system. The film reflects Renoir's growing concern with the opposition art (artifice) versus life (reality), and the overlapping of the two. In terms of his relationship with the Popular Front, he has returned to his bourgeois roots in the subject matter of his film, but his treatment of the theme is lucid and detached. The hunt which the house party guests partake in, is shown as a metaphor for the exploitative power of the upper classes. The apparent naturalism of the *mise-en-scène* is offset by the incident in which the Marquise sees her husband and his mistress through binoculars, and misreads what she sees. The audience knows what is happening, the Marquise misreads the scene because of her subjective position. This disjuncture between objectivity and subjectivity shows Renoir's awareness that appearances are deceptive. The question remains: does Renoir's humanism, his concern for each of his characters and their vested interests, obscure the serious social questions about class differences that the film raises?

Renoir's interest in theatrical conventions, and in acting, relevant to all his work, is particularly important in this film, where it becomes part of the thematic structure.

This Land is Mine (USA 1943 *p.c* – RKO Radio; *d* – Jean Renoir; sd b/w)

Made during Renoir's period in the US, he co-wrote, co-produced and directed this film under the auspices of RKO, who also provided the facilities for Welles and *Citizen Kane*. We can assume that Renoir had considerable artistic control, although it is interesting to see how the context of a Hollywood studio production and actors affected the film, which looks quite different from his earlier work.

Nevertheless the theme is familiar: a community divided by war, misunderstandings and deception. The demands of Hollywood narrative can be seen in the use of a central character through whose maturing consciousness the problems are resolved, and a touch of American Freudianism can be discerned in the relationship between Albert and his possessive mother. The studio sets look strangely constricting in relation to the characters compared with the real locations used in previous extracts. How then do these factors: the use of stars as central protagonists, the psychological realism of the Hollywood narrative, the conditions of studio production, combine to affect the place of this film within the Renoir *œuvre* constructed by *auteur* study? The theme of war, collaboration and resistance is characteristic, but the director's point of view may have been affected by different conditions of production. Renoir was criticised for his attempt to make a propaganda film about the Nazi occupation which gave a less blatantly heroic view of occupied France.

The Woman on the Beach (USA 1947, *p.c* – RKO Radio; *d* – Jean Renoir; sd b/w)

Another example of Renoir's American work, again for RKO. The film is almost entirely dominated by the requirements of the *film noir* genre as it developed in the post-war US. In contrast with earlier films, the narrative problems are here internalised in terms of individual psychology, projected against a dreamlike Expressionist set. The film seems most relevant to later Renoir, with its theme of solitude and formalised *mise-en-scène*.

> 'It was a story quite opposed to everything I had hitherto attempted. In all my previous films I had tried to depict the bonds uniting the individual to his background. The older I grew, the more I had proclaimed the consoling truth that the world is one; and now I was embarked on a study of persons whose sole idea was to close the door on the absolutely concrete phenomena which we call life. (Renoir, 1974)

How then was Renoir's perspective changed by the experience of working in postwar America? Certainly the expressive use of montage, and fragmentation of space would not have found approval from Bazin. When seen as a transition to later Renoir, as *auteur* study prescribes, it seems less strange. But despite Renoir's words above claiming his own point of view is expressed in the film, the conditions of Hollywood production, and the generic conventions of *film noir* could be said to have as much claim on the final product as Renoir's authorial 'voice'.

French Can-Can (France/Italy 1955, *p.c* – Franco London Film/Jolly Film; *d* – Jean Renoir; sd col.)

Made after his return to Europe, an example of mature Renoir in which the relationship between art (artifice) and reality (life) is developed and explored. Although the film pays homage to the Impressionist painters and the popular theatre of turn-of-century France in its use of colour photography, music and spectacle, it is pessimistic about the potential of art to change anything. Danglard's belief in the importance of the Can-Can as art has the quality of an obsession imposed as a repressive discipline on the girls he employs, whom he also exploits. Since he labours under such extreme financial difficulties and is always on the verge of bankruptcy and imprisonment, his involvement with the theatre seems perverse, and his final exhortation to Nini that the artist must dedicate himself *totally* to his or her art seems to be an argument for 'art for art's sake'. This cynical view of the relationship between art and life contrasts sharply with earlier films such as *Le Crime de Monsieur Lange*, and the use of a single central character (Danglard) as a focus for identification tends to obscure contradictions arising from the subject matter (such as that between the pleasurable aspects of the Can-Can as spectacle, and the repression/distortion/exploitation of the female body on which it depends).

Le Caporal épinglé (The Vanishing Corporal) (France 1961, *p.c* – Films du Cyclope; *d* – Jean Renoir; sd b/w)

Interesting to compare with *La Grande Illusion*. Thematically it has many of the same preoccupations. But whereas in *La Grande Illusion* the struggle against Fascism is given real importance, in this film the urge to escape, the concern with 'freedom', is seen as a human obsession, a perversity in the face of the obvious advantages in staying in prison, opting out of the struggle.

Human perversity is shown in one of the scenes at the end of the film: the sombre funeral procession which the French POW escapers join appears bizarre in the context of war which values life so cheaply, and in the train the over-friendliness of the drunken German to the Frenchmen makes a mockery of human relationships, and threatens their safety. The French corporal and his friend admire the trouble-free life of the peasant couple, yet they themselves are perversely driven to return to Paris and give up the comradeship that the war has provided, each going their separate ways. The comic emphasis and use of sentimentalised characters barely obscure the implications that human impulses exist in their own right, irrespective of social realities. The will to escape takes on the aspect of a childish game, and at the end of the film the question remains – what is there left to fight for? Considered in the context of Renoir's earlier films made with the Popular Front, the question takes on added poignancy.

FRITZ LANG

Der müde Tod (Destiny) (Germany 1921 *p.c* – Decla-Bioscop; *d* – Fritz Lang; st b/w)

Lang's first major film as a director, and an example of his use of Expressionist motifs, such as the obsession with allegory and myth as a framework for representing individuals overpowered and destroyed by the repressive forces of a hostile world. The film's Expressionist *mise-en-scène* creates an enclosed imaginary world in which human figures are overpowered by the huge sets (Petley, 1978). However, the film is not totally pessimistic about the fate of individuals. If human desire ultimately cannot prevail against destiny, here represented by death, it is nonetheless shown to be entirely motivated by the need to resist such a cruel and inevitable fate.

Dr Mabuse der Spieler: I – Der grosse Spieler/Ein Bild der Zeit (Dr Mabuse the Gambler) (Germany 1921 *p.c* – Ullstein–Uco Film/Decla–Bioscop/Ufa; *d* – Fritz Lang; st b/w)

Lang began his career by writing scripts for detective films and never lost his interest in this genre as a medium for expressing a critical view of society. Expressionist art is full of representations of evil, supernatural figures who attempt to control events but are ultimately controlled by them, and Mabuse is one of these. But the film does not entirely condemn him: the police are also subject to the movement of events, and while Mabuse and the policeman von Wenk struggle against each other they are both at the mercy of a hostile world. Thus it could be argued that Lang attempts to create a position for the spectator from which to criticise the social system which produces such manipulative monsters.

Dr Mabuse der Spieler: II – Inferno Ein Spiel von Menschen unserer Zeit (Germany 1921 *p.c* – Ullstein–Uco Film/Decla–Bioscop/ Ufa; *d* – Fritz Lang; st b/w)

Characteristically, the power-crazed Dr Mabuse tries to control the destiny of others, here by using disguise and hypnosis to lead his enemy Inspector von Wenk to his death. *Dr Mabuse* can be seen as an early example of a theme central to all Lang's work: the danger of trusting appearances. However, Mabuse's apparently supernatural powers do not make him omnipotent: his attempt to kill von Wenk is foiled, indicating that he is as much at the mercy of events as his victims. Mabuse's fantasies of himself as superman finally bring about his destruction.

Die Nibelungen: II – Kriemhilds Rache (Germany 1923–4 *p.c* – Decla–Bioscop/Ufa; *d* – Fritz Lang; st b/w)

Die Nibelungen is a film based on the original saga, which describes the destiny of the hero Siegfried. The form of the legend allows Lang to explore his concern with the individual pitted against fate, but in Part II the innocent Siegfried is replaced as protagonist by his revengeful widow Kriemhild, whose destructive obsession brings about chaos, manifested in the *mise-en-scène* by a tension between geometric composition and the fluid movement of actors within the frame. Kriemhild's unnatural rigidity and manic gaze emphasise her transformation into the manipulative monster who is ultimately defeated by her obsession. It is possible to see her as a forerunner of the American Lang's *femmes fatales*: women as destructive and violent erotic forces created by a violent male-dominated society.

Metropolis (Germany 1926 *p.c* – Ufa; *d* – Fritz Lang; st b/w)

Expressionism is usually seen as an artistic movement arising out of the economic reconstruction of Germany after the First World War. A so-called 'agrarian mysticism' was manifested in a revulsion against city life and the dehumanising exploitation of technology by capital. While it would be wrong to characterise this idealism as proto-Fascist, certainly the Expressionist emphasis on the irrational and the primitive could in some cases seem like a retreat into mysticism (see Petley, 1978). It is interesting here to compare Expressionism with futurism, which saw itself as a revolutionary modernist movement committed to the enormous potential for social change offered by technological advances. Somewhere between the humanism of Expressionism and the anti-humanism of futurism lies *Metropolis*: a criticism of the manipulative capitalist system which both oppresses the people and transforms them into a monstrous destructive power. The irrational resurgence of the masses is not entirely endorsed by the film however: rather they are seen as victims of a manipulative system, and the destruction of the machines by the workers does not bring about the destruction of that system itself (see Kracauer, 1947). The reintroduction of a formalised geometric *mise-en-scène*,

Expressionism in the geometric *mise-en-scène* of Lang's *Metropolis*

The 'Kammerspiel' film – a new psychological realism in Lang's *M*

broken up during the scenes of revolution, testifies to the re-establishment of order. Beneath this final resolution lies a question: 'But who now holds the power?' It is arguable that the abstract Expressionist *mise en-scène* allows this critical space to open up: it represents social structures topographically, so that each of the characters is seen to inhabit an ideological position rather than appear as a coherent psychological entity. The final resolution could be seen as ironic rather than positive, offering the audience the possibility of a critical perspective (see Johnston, 1977).

M (Germany 1931 *p.c* – Nero Films; *d* – Fritz Lang; sd b/w)

This film marks an aesthetic turning-point in Lang's work, which can be placed historically. The postwar boom in which Expressionism had flourished came to an end, and a new psychological realism emerged in the 'Kammerspiel' film, supported by the introduction of sound which made it possible for individual psychology to be represented through characters' speech. The fragmentation of society came to be reflected in the tormented individual psyche. M, like the protagonists of Lang's later American films, is a victim of the tension between his desires and a hostile, destructive environment.

The world is divided between two organisations: the police and the criminals. 'Normality' is the state of uneasy equilibrium between them which is disturbed by the irrationality of the murderer of children, and which must be restored at all costs. When M defends himself in a long speech which has little effect on criminals or police, we are made aware of the limitations of a so-called rational society which relies on repression to maintain normality. M's challenge to society takes the form of an individualistic struggle against his fate: in Lang's view such a struggle can reveal the mechanisms of the system, but it can never defeat it. It is the individual who is ultimately defeated, and the rational, hierarchical organisation which survives. Yet it is arguable that this makes clear that the underside of normality is a destructive drive which allows its victim no pity and will tolerate no questioning. In arousing the spectator's compassion for M, Lang also makes it possible to criticise the structures upon which normal society rests. Another argument suggests that Lang sees an alternative to the individual's self-defeating struggle in the organisation of the community into social action (see Lusted, 1979).

Rancho Notorious (USA 1952 *p.c* – Fidelity Pictures/RKO Radio; *d* – Fritz Lang; sd col.)

Lang's career in Hollywood began *c.* 1935 when he fled from an offer by Goebbels to become head of the German film industry. He seems to have had less freedom in the Hollywood studio system than in Germany, and suffered some interference in his projects. His Expressionist style and interest in the psychological thriller format were well suited to the studio system, and in general he collaborated on scripts and controlled the sets for his films. Nonetheless, his interest in social criticism and formal experiment (he was much influenced by Bertolt Brecht, with whom he collaborated on *Hangmen Also Die*, 1943) had to come to terms with the demands of genre, and although the political climate of America in the 1930s and early 1940s was reasonably sympathetic to these interests, in the 1950s Lang found himself blacklisted for a short period.

Rancho Notorious can be seen as an example of the intersection of these conflicting interests. The film was a reworking of the western revenge genre in terms of Brechtian strategies (i.e. fragmented episodic narrative, use of songs to break into the storyline) all intended to distance the audience from the spectacle. Completely recut by the studio, much of the film's self-reflexiveness became subservient to the demands of narrative and the psychology of the vengeful hero. Yet Lang's interests break through: the hero is a detective figure following a trail of clues; obsessed with revenge, he is transformed into a monster with a manic stare; Marlene Dietrich as *femme fatale* foregrounds the obsessional nature of the masculine desire that creates her as fetish–object; and the abstract, stylised *mise-en-scène* recalls Lang's Expressionist beginnings.

Rancho Notorious – in which Lang uses 'Brechtian' distancing strategies

The Big Heat (USA 1953 *p.c* – Columbia; *d* – Fritz Lang; sd b/w)

Made during a difficult period in Lang's American career, this film is primarily a genre piece: a police thriller. However, it is clear that Lang's interests coincided very well with the genre. Bannion is fighting the racketeers who control the city administration, he becomes obsessed with revenge after his wife's death, and becomes involved in the corrupt and destructive underworld with its deformed and distorted figures (the *femme fatale* is one of these products of a diseased world). As with all Lang's American films, the question remains whether his view of the individual's struggle with society is pessimistic, or whether he sees a way out of the impasse in organised community action (see Lusted, 1979).

Beyond a Reasonable Doubt (USA 1956 *p.c* – RKO Radio; *d* – Fritz Lang; sd b/w 15)

Lang's last film in America, sometimes thought to be the most definitive statement of his preoccupations. The hero, Tom Garrett, becomes caught between two opposing organisations: the opponents of capital punishment, and the law. He attempts to manipulate one on behalf of the other, becoming obsessively caught up in the masquerade and his wish to beat the system. The result is a schematic, abstract film in which, it can be argued, identification with the characters is impossible: instead the spectator comes to recognise the inhumanity of a system reflected in the increasing inhuman obsessions of the central protagonist. The abstraction of the geometric compositions, the minimal schematic narrative, all combine to produce a bleak criticism of a ruthless, hostile society which can be pushed to its limits but never overcome, except, perhaps, by organised community action. Interestingly again, the world of the burlesque and its exploitation of women's bodies provide one important aspect of Lang's social criticism.

AUTEURS AND *METTEURS-EN-SCÈNE*

The distinction between *auteur* and *metteur-en-scène* introduced by *Cahiers* critics was intended to support the idea of a cinema of personal vision, defined in terms of the presence of a true *auteur*. Like much of the polemic behind the *politique*, it drew attention to significant factors which had not been considered before, and raised questions which are still unresolved in film criticism.

The term *mise-en-scène* refers to the staging of events for the camera, but can also be used loosely to mean the formal organisation of the finished film, the 'style' in which film-makers express their personal concerns. Sometimes film-makers master the *mise-en-scène* competently, but the overall meaning expressed is not theirs, in which case they qualify as *metteurs-en-scène* rather than true *auteurs*. In *auteur* study these criteria provide one way of evaluating 'good' and 'bad' films, and 'good' and 'bad' directors.

The distinction *auteur/metteur-en-scène* led to some unfortunate evaluations by film critics, and to some critical pantheons originating in the critics' subjective taste (see The *auteur* theory, p. 256). It had its roots in the historical division between 'art' and 'entertainment' which had previously prevented cinema from being taken seriously. Part of the 'scandal' created by the *politique* was caused by its application of such criteria to popular American cinema, generally thought of as mass entertainment reproducing dominant ideology and incompatible with the interests of art.

Alfred Hitchcock

For the *Cahiers auteur* critics, Hitchcock was the classic *auteur*: a master of cinematic *mise-en-scène* who created an unmistakable and homogeneous world-view, controlling the audience so that they were completely at the mercy of his intentions. Hitchcock's habit of making a personal appearance in his films contributed further to the myth, but more than this his world-view is intimately bound up with the mechanisms of cinematic language and the relationship of spectator to film. Many of Hitchcock's films deal with the act of looking or spying, given a centrality which transcends the plot, so it can be argued that a narrative of human psychology emerges in which characters and cinema audience are involved in a play of exchange of looks. This drama of exchange opens up a scene of obsession, guilt, paranoia and phobia in which author, characters and audience are all implicated, but which Hitchcock as author ultimately controls (see Wollen, 1969).

It was this aspect of Hitchcock's work, interpreted as raising serious questions of morality, which intrigued and influenced many *Cahiers* critics and film-makers, especially Chabrol, Rohmer and Truffaut, whose films contain many direct references to Hitchcock (see Truffaut, 1968).

The *Cahiers* approach was echoed by Robin Wood in Britain, who argued that Hitchcock's work not only explored important moral dilemmas through its obsessional characters, but included the audience in the drama, forcing them to acknowledge previously unrecognised moral ambiguities in themselves. Later, Raymond Bellour, writing under the influence of French structuralist criticism, used Hitchcock's work to demonstrate the closed structure, in formal and ideological terms, of the classic Hollywood text (Bellour, 1977).

Many of Hitchcock's films use the detective or spy genre as a pretext for exploring the predatory aspects of human behaviour, be it in a sexual or a political context. Moreover, it has been argued, using psychoanalytical concepts which attempt to go beyond 'Hollywood Freud', that Hitchcock's work is exemplary of a cinema in which voyeurism and scopophilia (the drive to look) is manipulated in such a way that the male gaze (of author, characters and spectators) predominates, thus raising the question of the subordinate place of the figure of women in Hollywood cinema. Victim and predator may seem at some points to be interchangeable in Hitchcock's work but ultimately, the argument goes, the drama is resolved in favour of the male and at the expense of the female, confirming patriarchal ideology. Hitchcock's work is seen as drawing attention to that ideology, at the same time as representing its apotheosis (see Mulvey, 1975; see also Psychoanalysis and film, p. 335; Feminist film theory, p. 353). Hitchcock's interest in the drama of looking is not only reflected in his choice of the investigative thriller genre as a form of expression: he is considered a master of the classic point-of-view shot structure in which a shot of a character looking at something is followed by a shot of what they are looking at. This shot/reverse-shot structure has been identified as a basic element of continuity in Hollywood narrative cinema (Classic Hollywood narrative, p. 39) and Hitchcock uses it frequently to build up narrative suspense.

The *Cahiers auteur* critics who championed Hitchcock saw him as the major exponent of cinema at its purest. They liked the manipulation of the language of editing in Hitchcock's films because it corresponded to their own interests as film-makers, and because the world-view expressed was that of the isolated individual trapped in a hostile world not of his or her own making, an alienation manifested in Hitchcock's use of the fragmentation of montage editing. Later theoretical work, by Laura Mulvey for example, attempted to reassess Hitchcock's films in terms of ideology rather than the criteria of the 'purely cinematic', thus beginning to place the work of this grand *auteur* within history.

In order to establish Hitchcock as a true *auteur* the critic must be able to trace the development of a consistent theme, expressed in a style which is perfectly suited to that theme, across all his films. Those films which do not fit the critic's construction of Hitchcock's world-view are either ignored, or treated as minor or flawed works. These gaps and inconsistencies can provide the basis of a challenge to traditional *auteur* study by drawing attention to its partiality of approach, and to the need for a historical analysis to explain those films considered uncharacteristic.

John Huston

'It seems significant that attempts to trace a consistent pattern in Huston's work should lead one chiefly to an awareness of absences' (Wood, 1980).

Wood, until then a confirmed *auteurist*, is expressing a dissatisfaction with Huston's work which is shared by many *auteur* critics. While a pattern can be traced through his films, such a pattern reveals no marked development nor any complexity of relationship between films. His personal concerns are heterogeneous rather than consistent, although Wood sees his preoccupation with a central, isolated male protagonist as a continuing pessimistic theme. Huston's *mise-en-scène*, however, fails to express this theme as an *auteur*'s should: it is a decorative flourish rather than a coherent artistic statement. Huston is merely a *metteur-en-scène*.

Wood's argument echoes that of the *Cahiers auteur* critics, to whom the *metteur-en-scène* was inferior to the *auteur* because his or her work lacked the inspiration, the personal expression, to create a world-view proper. Although they could discern a consistent thematic in the films of John Huston, there was no consistency of style, even though he often produced, wrote and directed his films. Arguably, it is precisely this lack of a coherent personal vision which makes the *metteur-en-scène* more interesting in some respects than the *auteur*: by removing the author from the centre of the work a number of other factors can be discovered to be at work in the film, and the critic would need to look further than the presence of authorial intentions to analyse the source of meaning, to history, for example, or to production conditions (The studios, p. 11). The very unevenness of Huston's work invites another form of analysis than *auteur* study. By making the distinction *auteur/metteur-en-scène* the *Cahiers* critics highlighted one of the problems of the *auteur* approach: the attribution of a film's meaning to the intentions of an individual director who transcended history.

Selected Reading

André Bazin, 'Hitchcock versus Hitchcock', in Albert J. LaValley (ed.), *Focus on Hitchcock*, Englewood Cliffs, NJ, Prentice-Hall, 1972.

Laura Mulvey, 'Visual Pleasure and Narrative Cinema', *Screen* 16(3), autumn 1975.

Robin Wood, 'John Huston', in Richard Roud (ed.), *Cinema: A Critical Dictionary*, vol. 1, London, Secker & Warburg, 1980.

Robin Wood, *Hitchcock's Films Revisited*, New York, Columbia University Press, 1989.

ALFRED HITCHCOCK

Blackmail (UK 1929 *p.c* – John Maxwell; *d* – Alfred Hitchcock; st & sd b/w)

Hitchcock worked in Britain until 1940, and his films of this period are important in many ways, not least for their relationship with other British films (see Smith, 1972). Influenced by his period in Germany where he encountered German Expressionism, they show a desire to experiment with the possibilities of cinematic language. He began directing films at a time of technological change (the transition to sound) when the opportunities for experiment within the film industry were still open, and in contrast to much of the British cinema made at this time, his films can be seen to work against the conventional notions of realism which have dominated mainstream British cinema.

The film shows an experimental use of montage editing (cutting shots of the dead man's arm against shots of the heroine's legs as she walks home after the murder, building to the climax of the landlady's scream when she discovers the body) and of the zoom-in for dramatic effect. This device both depicts Alice's subjective state of mind and engages the spectator's emotions, a strategy found in much of Hitchcock's work. Hitchcock's symbolic use of the 'act of looking' can be seen in the use of pictures which return the looks of the guilty protagonists: the jester looks mockingly at Frank, and the policeman looks sternly at Alice.

Alice can be seen as one of Hitchcock's earliest guilty aberrant females (cf. *Under Capricorn* (1949), *Psycho* (1960), *The Birds* (1963), *Marnie* (1964)) and sound is used expressively to stress her guilt. The emphasis on the word 'knife' could be compared with the montage stabbing sequence in the shower in *Psycho*, to show a similar concern with the obsessional state of mind of the murderer.

Foreign Correspondent (UK 1940 *p.c* – Walter Wanger Productions; *d* – Alfred Hitchcock; sd b/w)

Between 1935 and 1938 Hitchcock made a cycle of thriller films which established him as England's 'great director'. He moved to the US in 1939 and this was his second film made there. Not generally regarded as a major Hitchcock film it nevertheless provides an example of transition between his English and American work, particularly in the use of comedy and parodied English stereotype characters, which both crosses and interrupts the forward drive of the narrative characteristic of the thriller genre. Looking forward to later work, note the use of apparently innocent objects to suggest threat or problem (e.g. the mass of umbrellas shot from above as the assassin escapes; the windmills which become a significant feature in the plot; the errant derby belonging to the comic Englishman which leads to a vital clue). Thus the author and the spectator share a joke initiated by the former, at the expense of, and for the pleasure of the latter. It could be argued that this play with the spectator is central to all Hitchcock's films.

Blackmail – Hitchcock working against conventional notions of realism

Mr and Mrs Smith (USA 1941 *p.c* – RKO Radio; *d* – Alfred Hitchcock; sd b/w)

Hitchcock's interest in the relationship between couples, which he portrays as perverse, can be found in most of his films. Often the couple is yoked together unwillingly, or under difficult circumstances, united by a sexual desire which is bound to be frustrated. The film shows the workings of male desire in its worst light: in order to reconcile himself with his wife, the hero must spy on and pursue her, disrupt her plans to marry another man, causing everyone concerned acute embarrassment. Beneath the comedy lies the darker side of personal relationships: the sado-masochism of the male/female relationship, the overturning of social and moral codes under the impact of sexual desire, and the consequent prevalence of paranoia, which seems to be totally justified in Hitchcock's world view.

Shadow of a Doubt (USA 1943 *p.c* – Universal; *d* – Alfred Hitchcock; sd b/w)

One of Hitchcock's themes in which *Cahiers* critics (including Bazin) were particularly interested was the 'double' relationship between characters in which guilt was transferred from one to the other (see Bazin, 1972). One character takes on the features of another so that the question of a fixed identity attributable to one person becomes problematic: examples from Hitchcock's films would be *Strangers on a Train*, *Psycho*, and *Vertigo*, although the theme appears in some form in all of his work. The concept is particularly disturbing when the relationship is between members of the same family, as in *Psycho*, where the identities of mother and son are fused and in conflict. It is rarely explicitly recognised, however, that this doubling of identities introduces a perverse sexual element into the narrative, and it is often this very perversity which motivates events.

In this film, Hitchcock uses two different genres to underline the splitting of the characters' identities: the thriller/*film noir*, to which the psychopathic killer belongs, and the small-town melodrama, locus of the 'nice' family into which he intrudes. Hitchcock was particularly fond of the thriller genre because of its potential for dramatising the splitting of identity theme, and he has objected to the fact that Hollywood produced so many 'woman's pictures', the category into which the small-town melodrama conventionally falls. Thus the trouble in the superficially nice family, trouble represented by young Charlie and her fantasies of excitement is given another disturbing dimension by the introduction into the scene of her 'double' and namesake, uncle Charlie, visitor from another world.

Under Capricorn (USA 1949 *p.c* – Transatlantic Pictures; *d* – Alfred Hitchcock; sd col.)

By this time Hitchcock's international reputation was well established. He co-produced many of his films of this period, and arguably had sufficient control in Hollywood to do as he wished. In 1948 he experimented with long takes in *Rope* (1948), only cutting when the film itself ran out and had to be replaced. This produced 10-minute-long takes which were unusual in Hitchcock's *mise-en-scène*, since the long take generally excludes the shot/reverse-shot point-of-view technique for which he is well known, and which forms the basis of his narrative suspense. *Under Capricorn* is also a deviation from the usual Hitchcock method, employing long takes and moving camera usually associated with realism, and very little shot/reverse-shot, in a totally unrealistic manner. It could be argued that Hitchcock uses the moving camera in such a way as to draw attention to it *as a camera*, reminding the spectator that she or he is not actually present on the scene in the same way as the director. An example would be the long pan around the room from table to door, a gratuitous camera movement. The scene in which Henrietta comes down the staircase dressed for the ball, watched by the two men, demonstrates an interesting use of the movement of a tracking shot into a close-up of the ruby necklace held behind Sam's back, which, we see, he hurriedly hides. This shot replaces the conventional 'reaction shot' which would show his feelings from the expression on his face. It might be interesting to discuss how this substitution of shots affects the meaning of the scene, if at all, and what sort of position is created for the spectator in relation to the characters. It is, of course, characteristic of Hitchcock to emphasise small gestures in this way to create a sense of unease which cannot be easily explained, and the acute social embarrassment caused by Sam's intrusion in the ball sequence, and Henrietta's flight is also typical.

Psycho (USA 1960 *p.c* – Shamley; *d* – Alfred Hitchcock; sd b/w)

It has been noted that in Hitchcock's films the spectator is often held in a state of anxiety which may or may not be resolved by the narrative (in *The Birds* for instance it is arguable that it is not). This '*mise-en-scène* of anxiety' is played out on many levels in the film not least in the sexual relationships between characters. It has been argued (see Mulvey, 1975) that Hitchcock's films organise the play of looks between characters and cinema audience in terms of the dominance of the male (heterosexual) gaze, i.e. that the relationship between male and female characters is a struggle based on dominance and subordination in which the former finally dominates the latter, thus neatly resolving the narrative in favour of patriarchal ideology. This account is very useful in discussion of the ideological implications of Hitchcock's films, especially in *Psycho*, where fear and guilt is induced in the female protagonist by the investigatory looks of male characters, and her inability to escape these looks places her in a subordinate and vulnerable position. The notorious attack in the shower could also be seen in terms of an attempt to link the 'look' of the camera and of the audience with the aggression of the stabbing, thus reducing the female protagonist to the status of object rather than subject: the female transgressor is not, as she thought, in command of her own destiny, the power of the 'look' is taken from her (the image of Marion's dead, unseeing eye is significant in this respect) and she is fixed as an object.

Hitchcock directs the famous shower scene in *Psycho*

However, it could also be argued that the question of sexuality is complicated in *Psycho* by the fact that both Marion and Norman have male *and* female characteristics. Like many of Hitchcock's heroines (see *Blackmail*, *Marnie*, *The Birds*) Marion, a woman, attempts to cross conventional sexual divisions by becoming active rather than passive, by becoming a thief in order to get what she wants. Similarly, although Norman Bates, voyeur, is male, and his 'look' at Marion could be assumed to be male, as a killer he is bisexual (part mother/part son), and this sexual ambiguity (we never know which part is dominant) is unresolved at the end, even though it is 'explained' by the psychiatrist. What kind of fantasy/pleasure is evoked for the spectator when the edges of 'male' and 'female' sexual categories are blurred?

The Birds (USA 1963 *p.c* – Alfred Hitchcock/ Universal; *d* – Alfred Hitchcock; sd col.)

Melanie Daniels, like many Hitchcock heroines, takes destiny into her own hands and pursues Mitch Brenner, reversing the conventional male/female roles. In doing so she brings the bird attack onto the Bodega Bay community, culminating in her own symbolic 'rape' by the birds. The film compares with *Psycho* in that it shows the independently curious woman, an active subject, as the object of violent aggression and punishment. The theme of aggression is manifested on the level of *mise-en-scène* in the use of montage, low-angled shots, and a composition of characters within the frame based on disequilibrium.

There is a classic Hitchcockian use of point of view as Melanie moves towards the stairs and the attic door, which could be seen to serve a double function: to build suspense from the rhythm of shot/reverse-shot, and to emphasise Melanie's subjectivity through point of view before she is reduced to an object in the attic. After the bird rape when Melanie regains consciousness, she looks straight into the camera and defends herself against its 'look', equating it with an act of aggression.

Hitchcock's interest in mixing genres can be seen, as the romantic melodrama becomes a science fiction horror story in which the untroubled surface of a community and a family is radically disturbed.

Marnie (USA 1964 *p.c* – Geoffrey Stanley Inc/Universal; *d* – Alfred Hitchcock; sd col.)

Marnie, like Marion in *Psycho* (and other Hitchcock heroines) threatens the social order: not only is she a compulsive thief who steals large sums of money from her employers but she is a mistress of disguise, changing her identity at will to avoid being caught. This double problematic (aggression and masquerade) it could be argued is particularly threatening to a society in which men control the exchange of money and the place of women. Characteristically, Hitchcock develops the explicitly sexual aspect of this problem through the relationship of dominance and subordination between Marnie and Mark Rutland: Marnie is an object of desire for Mark *because* she is a threat. Mark's compulsive desire to master the problem provides the central drive of the narrative, and as usual in Hitchcock's films the characters are shown to be the victims of their own desires so that the narrative resolution (Mark brings about Marnie's 'cure') is profoundly ambiguous. Both protagonists are in the grip of their compulsions, but Mark's go unexamined. The 'problem' is displaced on to the female character: she is the problem to be solved through the narrative. It has been argued that Hitchcock's films epitomise the construction of the place of woman in patriarchal society as the locus of male problems and fears (Mulvey, 1975).

The opening scenes provide an illustration of this argument: the camera tracks the figure of the woman in such a way as to mark her as an object of curiosity: we see what she does but we are denied her face. We watch as she substitutes one identity for another, washing black dye from her hair. Curiosity and suspense build up until the shot in which she lifts her head and looks straight into the camera. The moment is explicitly erotic and marked as transgression: the rule, 'Don't look at the camera' is broken since Marnie exchanges looks with the audience. Arguably, her subjective desire is explicitly marked as a threat.

Topaz (USA 1969 *p.c* – Universal; *d* – Alfred Hitchcock; sd col.)

An example of later Hitchcock, a political thriller. The male protagonist finds himself drawn into a world which is dangerous and difficult to make sense of. In the film, suspense is built up by the spectator's identification with Devereux, who watches events from a distance, is involved but unable to control them. It could be argued that the 'look' of Dubois's camera at secret documents echoes Hitchcock's constant preoccupation with the forbidden gaze and the desire to see and that the whole drama is built around 'getting a look' at something forbidden. This is reflected in the *mise-en-scène* by the obsessional play of looks around the briefcase which is fetishised by the repeated shots which focus on it as an object of desire, endowing it with excess meaning. The 'play of looks' seems to have become almost abstract, a formalist game, in spite of the political context of the film. Politics is another MacGuffin, a red-herring, a hollow pretext for Hitchcock's preoccupations (see Truffaut, 1968).

Frenzy (UK 1972 *p.c* – Universal; *d* – Alfred Hitchcock; sd col.)

The film shows the behaviour of another guilty Hitchcock protagonist under threat of discovery, this time given a 'black' twist characteristic of the later work. The psychopathic killer goes to enormous lengths to protect himself from being found out: perhaps a metaphor for Hitchcock's view of the place of the spectator as secret voyeur in the cinema? Certainly suspense is built around this central problem of discovery. Characteristically, the woman's body, now fixed with rigor mortis, is the problem for the psychopath, and it could be argued that the fragmentation of the *mise-en-scène* draws attention to the underlying fantasy of the cutting up of the woman's body (cf. *Psycho*). One question is how far the *mise-en-scène* sets up spectator identification with the guilty protagonist and his fear of being found out.

JOHN HUSTON

The Maltese Falcon (USA 1942 *p.c.* – Warner Bros.; *d* – John Huston; sd b/w)

Although Huston both directed and wrote this film, it could be argued that its interest lies less in his authorship than in other elements which contribute to its meaning. It was adapted from a Dashiell Hammett novel and is in the *film noir* genre; the production company was Warner Bros., whose relative economic independence as a studio enabled them to engage in some radical projects in the 1930s and 1940s (Buscombe, 1974). Humphrey Bogart worked with Huston on many films in which the less favourable aspects of his image were represented (as Dobbs in *The Treasure of the Sierra Madre* (1947), as Allnut in *The African Queen* (1951), for instance); the film also pushes the complexities of its narrative to extremes. In a sense it could be said to be *about* all these elements: narrative, *mise-en-scène*, genre, stars, character, studio production, rather than any single coherent authorial theme, although the general debunking of heroism and the placing of men and women at the mercy of their fate rather than in control of it might be said to be typical of Huston's work.

The Treasure of the Sierra Madre (USA 1947 *p.c* – Warner Bros.; *d* – John Huston; sd b/w)
An example of Huston's use of Humphrey Bogart as a character actor. Dobbs can be seen to represent a corruptible version of the 'Huston hero': the non-conforming individualist. Huston's interest in corrupt, imperfect men has been noted by Robin Wood as

The train transformed into coffin in the fantasy sequence in *Freud*

his central theme, and the pessimism identified by Wood is illustrated in the scenes at the end of the film (Wood, 1980).

Moulin Rouge (UK 1952 *p.c* – Romulus; *d* – John Huston; sd col.)

Huston directed, produced and co-wrote the film, which nevertheless, like *The Maltese Falcon*, shows more concern with the formal properties of *mise-en-scène* than with creating a world-view. Indeed the film tries rather to recreate *a world*, specifically in the use of colour, composition and spectacle to reconstruct the Toulouse Lautrec prints. On the level of theme, the banal drama of the disfigured artist seems sentimental and moralistic: the human drama takes second place to the dramatic spectacle of the *mise-en-scène*. V. F. Perkins (1972) has argued that this lack of coherence between style and theme is a serious flaw, leading to a pretentiousness of style.

Freud (Freud – The Secret Passion) (USA 1962 *p.c* – Universal–International; *d* – John Huston; sd b/w)

Much admired by Huston supporters for its depiction of its central male protagonist, Freud, as a flawed imperfect character, a victim of his obsessional urges. Freud's search for the truth from his patient leads to her final hostile rejection of him: a characteristically pessimistic touch from Huston. The director's interest in a highly formalised *mise-en-scène* is demonstrated in the hypnosis-induced fantasy sequence.

AUTEURS AND STUDIO

William Wyler

André Bazin, in his assessment of William Wyler as 'the Jansenist of *mise-en-scène*' argues for the value of a *mise-en-scène* 'defined by its own absence', a 'style without style' which allows the spectator to perceive the world presented by the film as directly as possible, without human intervention (Bazin, 1980). Wyler was probably the best director to use in support of Bazin's argument for the transparency of film, i.e. the ability of cinema to reproduce a place for the spectator as close as possible to his or her relationship to 'reality'. For Bazin, this 'reality' consisted of the harmonious integration of objects in time and space; this was the way, according to him, that the human eye perceived the real world: as a unity. Deep-focus photography made it possible for film to reproduce this relationship (Part 7, p. 337).

There is a tendency among critics of Bazin to reduce his philosophy to that of a naïve realism which sees film as a 'window on the world'. Despite the fact that his arguments have been perceived to be contradictory at points, they remain useful in raising questions for *auteur* analysis of film. In relation to his assessment of Wyler's work, for instance, what are the implications of an *auterist* analysis (i.e. one that returns to the director as source of meaning) which depends upon the critic establishing a 'lack of style'? How can the *auteur* be identified as present by an argument which depends precisely on his absence? This raises a crucial question for *auteurism* itself (one which will be raised again): how precisely do we identify the marks of authorship in a film or body of films?

In view of this contradiction in Bazin's position it could be argued that Wyler's work is most interesting as a product of the Hollywood studio set-up in the 1930s and 1940s. Unlike Welles, for instance, Wyler seems to have been quite at home in the context of studio production, and his films exhibit a range of production values and genres, and a range of contributions from stars, writers, technicians and others, which combine to make a 'studio product' rather than works of 'artistic genius'. This provides a different basis for approaching Wyler's films since it can be argued that it is this multiplicity of contributions which makes up the 'style' that Bazin's analysis suppresses.

It is also, incidentally, this *auteurist* approach which leads some critics to dismiss Wyler's films outright as 'atrophied' and 'studio-bound', and, significantly, too bound to the melodrama genre, conventionally associated with the 'woman's film', a much maligned phenomenon (see Petley, 1978). For these critics, Wyler is simply a cog in the studio machine, reproducing the respectable middle-class ideology of the studio heads (in particular Samuel Goldwyn) (see MGM, p. 16). A closer examination of the melodramas in terms of the contradictions they work through might encourage a reassessment of Wyler's films (see Melodrama, p. 146).

Orson Welles

The myths surrounding Welles's 'larger-than-life' personality, his turbulent relationship with the film industry and his struggles for artistic control have contributed to a general critical consensus which ascribes all meaning in the films to Welles himself. The fact that Welles not only directed, but wrote and acted in most of them, has contributed to this view, and Welles himself has supported it:

> Theatre is a collective experience, but cinema is the work of a single man, the director ...
>
> ... You've got to have all your helpers, all the necessary collaborators; it's a collective endeavour, but in essence a very personal outcome, much more than the theatre to my mind, because film is something dead, a band of celluloid like the blank sheet on which you write a poem. A film is what you write on the screen. (Welles, quoted in Wollen, 1977, p. 26)

In the context of 1940s Hollywood studio production, this view perpetuates the myth of the lone individual struggling against the dictates of a monolithic commercial organisation, the industry, which is interested in profit rather than 'art'. The idea that cinema is produced in the same mode as writing (which also occurs in Astruc's argument for the *caméra-stylo*, p. 240) is hardly tenable in the context of Hollywood studio production, where precisely 'writing' (the script) is a separate area of work, generally placed lower in the hierarchy than that of the director.

Nevertheless, because of Welles's persistent struggle against the interference of the industry his films are an interesting example (compared with Wyler's, for instance) of cinema authorship at a time when the studio system in Hollywood was still very strong, and studio control over the process of production was such that the contribution of the director was often effaced altogether. However, as Welles himself was aware, that contribution was dependent on other factors than the presence of 'genius' and 'personal vision': 'If I were producer–director, if I had a financial interest in the production, it would all be different. But my services are hired and on salary alone I was at the mercy of my bosses' (Welles, quoted in Wollen, 1977, p. 26).

The legend of Orson Welles (his dazzling artistic virtuosity which could not survive in the philistine world of Hollywood, condemning him to wander from country to country, working when and where he could) has by and large determined the way in which his work has been approached by critics. Even when it has provoked bitter controversy (see Kael, 1971), that work is seen in terms of authorship, rather than in historical terms for its place in the development of studio technology, for instance, or as an indication of the politics of 1930s and 1940s Hollywood. Welles came to the film industry from radical theatre and radio, a political and aesthetic background which clashed rather than merged with the prevailing ideology of the studio system. His films were markedly different from other studio products of the time in that they combined the techniques of deep-focus photography, wide-angled lenses, upward-tilting shots, lighting from below, long tracking shots and sets with ceilings in a new way which went against the grain of the prevalent realist aesthetic.

This difference was not noted by Bazin, who admired the films of Orson Welles, if anything, more than those of Wyler – surprisingly, since those films depend above all on the techniques of 'expressive montage' that Bazin was arguing against, and Welles's style can hardly be called 'self-effacing' (see Bazin, 1978). All his films have a distinctive *mise-en-scène*, which represents a recognisable world-view (see the interview in Wollen, 1977). It is difficult to see how Welles's films correspond to Bazin's ideas about the 'democratic' realism offered by the development of deep-focus photography at this point in cinema history. For this reason they can be useful in testing Bazin's argument (Bazin, p. 337) and to test the assumptions of *auteur* theory by looking at Welles's work in terms of its tension with the studio system and the industry of 1940s Hollywood.

Selected Reading

André Bazin, 'William Wyler or the Jansenist of *mise-en-scène*', in Christopher Williams (ed.), *Realism and the Cinema*, London, RKP/BFI, 1980, pp. 36–52.

Laura Mulvey, *Citizen Kane*, London, BFI, 1992.

WILLIAM WYLER

The Little Foxes (USA 1940–1 *p.c* – RKO–Goldwyn; *d* – William Wyler; sd b/w)

Bazin praises the fact that the cinematic adaptation of the Lillian Hellman play is faithful to the original text; paradoxically it is also 'one of the most purely cinematic works there is' (Bazin, 1980).

The crux of Bazin's argument is that Wyler has retained the theatrical setting of the play ('the dramatic architecture'), using the elements of cinematic *mise-en-scène* (static camera, depth of field, the minimum of cuts, and reframing) to construct extra meaning. Each of these cinematic elements emphasises the dramatic tension inherent in the scene: the criminal immobility of Regina (Bette Davis) in the face of her husband's imminent death.

The film can be seen to be a studio production, manifested in the carefully constructed sets, costume, and the use of a repertory of actors. Samuel Goldwyn was an independent producer who had a respectable critical reputation as a producer of 'quality' films with serious overtones. Many of his films were adaptations of literary or theatrical works, and *The Little Foxes* is an adaptation of a play by a writer (Lillian Hellman) with a serious intellectual reputation. There is a level on which the Regina character acts as a criticism of the bourgeois values which the other protagonists exemplify. At the same time she is represented as repressed and 'unnatural', and the criticism gives way to the liberal humanist values represented by the dying husband, played by Herbert Marshall, the focus for audience identification. However, the tragic overtones surrounding Bette Davis as Regina ensures that contradictions are not finally closed off. On one level the film is a family melodrama, a 'woman's picture' (written by a woman, centred on a female protagonist, addressed to a female audience). It is arguable that the values supported by *The Little Foxes* are those of humanism and self-sacrifice, asserted at the expense of the 'independent woman', a conflict of values typical of the family melodrama (see Melodrama, p. 157)

The Best Years of Our Lives (USA 1946 *p.c.* – Goldwyn; *d* William Wyler; sd b/w)

It has been argued that the techniques of deep-focus, long takes and reframing as deployed in this film are particularly suited to social realism, revealing the events staged for the camera as though they were in 'real space', encouraging a position of tolerant understanding in the spectator, who is confronted with a series of 'serious social problems': the crippling effects of war on body, mind and spirit which threaten to disturb the normal social order (see Bazin, 1980).

The film has been much praised, as Wyler's best work with Goldwyn, as an exemplary piece of social realism, and for its 'classic' technique, courtesy of photographer Gregg Toland. It is rarely discussed in terms of ideology, however, as a 'post-war reconstruction' film exemplifying the need for individual courage, perseverance and self-sacrifice in peace time as well as war. Something of a departure for Goldwyn, it is less concerned with the aspirations of the middle class, and more with class itself as a problem, giving the film an edge of social criticism.

According to Bazin, the *mise-en-scène* of *The Best Years of Our Lives* corresponds to the 'geometry of normal vision', allowing the spectator to 'see everything' and to 'choose to his liking'. It is questionable whether the film actually does allow for this democratic participation, or whether viewers today would see its stark geometric *mise-en-scène* as realistic.

The Little Foxes – sympathy for Regina alienated by deep-focus

ORSON WELLES

Citizen Kane (USA 1940 *p.c* – Mercury Productions/RKO; *d* – Orson Welles; sd b/w)

Citizen Kane is regarded by many as an example of Welles's artistic genius; he produced, co-wrote, acted in and directed the film – an apparently classic case of cinema authorship. In spite of the fact that Welles has acknowledged the importance of photographer Gregg Toland's contribution, and others have insisted that scriptwriter H. J. Mankiewicz is the real author of the film (see Kael, 1971), *Citizen Kane* retains its reputation as the first Wellesian masterpiece, a stylistic *tour de force*.

Stylistic virtuosity is indeed one of the primary pleasures the film offers, not least for the way it plays with the conventions of

Citizen Kane – the first Wellesian masterpiece

Hollywood cinema (the personal biography genre, the *March of Time* newsreels) to produce something which looks quite different from other films of the period. Bazin hailed *Citizen Kane* as inaugurating a new period in cinema: a break with the 'expressive montage' of Russian cinema, and the shot/reverse-shot editing of American narrative films in the 1930s, in favour of the democratic realism of deep-focus photography (Bazin, 1978). Welles employed a variety of cinematic techniques for symbolic rather than realistic effects: deep-focus photography, low-angled shots and the constructed ceilings made necessary by depth-of-field, wide-angle shots, overlapping dialogue and whip-pans in the marriage sequence. Deep-focus photography combines with an experimental use of shot/reverse-shot, sound and lighting to symbolise the increasing distance and alienation between Kane and his wife Susan.

Kane himself is the kind of hero/villain who recurs in Welles's films. Welles's politics, emerging from the Popular Front of the time, ensure that the film is on one level critical of Kane, his will to power and inevitable moral decline (Wollen, 1969). However, the film's basis in melodrama gives its theme a tragic dimension: Kane is a villain almost in spite of himself, a tragic hero caught in contradictions he cannot control. Kane was loosely based on William Randolph Hearst, a newspaper tycoon with massive interests in the film industry. The legal action taken by Hearst failed to prove the connection, but it delayed the release of the film and made it difficult for RKO to find bookings, so they never allowed Welles such artistic control again (The studios, p. 30).

Citizen Kane is interesting from a number of perspectives: as part of the Welles *œuvre*; for its technical virtuosity, made possible by the studio technology of the time; in relation to the power politics of the Hollywood industry; and for its enduring place in critical pantheons, in spite of its box-office failure.

The Magnificent Ambersons (USA 1942 *p.c* – Mercury Productions/RKO; *d* – Orson Welles; sd b/w)

Citizen Kane was something of a critical success, but it was not commercially successful. Welles had a similar production set-up for *The Magnificent Ambersons* at RKO (i.e. his own company of actors and the superb technical resources of the studio) but the studio took a much greater part in supervising the film to make sure that this time it recouped their investment (RKO Radio pictures, p. 30).

The film's central figure is once again an egocentric male protagonist whose arrogance finally causes his downfall. The story concerns the disintegration of an aristocratic American family under pressure of social change, but the social dimension was submerged by the studio's insistence on emphasising the melodramatic elements of the film, and cutting it accordingly.

Welles's style, which consists of a combination (or rather, conflict) of opposing strategies, such as moving camera versus static camera, close-up versus long takes, light versus dark, whispering versus shouting, gives the world created in the film a sense of turmoil and upheaval. Again it is fragmentation and contradiction that dominate rather than unity; however, this fragmentation, manifested in the behaviour of the protagonists and the disintegration of the family and its traditions, is not only characteristic of Welles's 'world-view': it is prevalent in Hollywood cinema of the 1940s, particularly in the *films noirs* (*Film noir*, p. 184).

Touch of Evil (USA 1958 *p.c* – Universal –International; *d* – Orson Welles; sd b/w)

It is arguable that Welles's best films were made in Hollywood, where he had the resources of the studios at his disposal. Other arguments, suggested above, indicate that his relationship with the studios was turbulent, and that the films reflect this relationship. His output of films is small and he has many uncompleted projects, a symptom of the mutual distrust with which director and studio regarded one another. In the context of Hollywood production values, the demands of narrative, genre, the star system, the need to produce commercially viable products (commodities), the baroque world and flamboyant style of Welles's films may seem monstrously self-indulgent, asserting the value of 'art' against 'commerce'. Yet, it can be argued, it is this *excess* of style which pushes against the limits of Hollywood studio production, threatening to overturn them and therefore revealing them as limits (see Heath, 1975).

Touch of Evil was directed by Welles after an absence from Hollywood lasting ten years. The film ran into problems with its production company Universal–International, who gave Welles *carte blanche* throughout the shooting, then prevented him from completing the cutting, and cut some of it themselves.

Welles's excessive style is manifested in extreme camera angles and violent fragmentation of shots, light/dark contrasts typical of Expressionist *mise-en-scène*. Excess is also marked in the extensive use of tracking camera which underlines the obsessional 'tracking' of Quinlan (Welles) by Vargas (Charlton Heston). The sense of a perverse, nightmarish world is emphasised by the *mise-en-scène*, and by the way Vargas is shown struggling to follow and eavesdrop on Quinlan, a struggle with which the spectator is encouraged to identify, but which, because of its marked perversity, brings the relationship between the two men into question. Although Quinlan is depicted as evil and must be exposed by Vargas, it could be argued that Welles pushes at the limits of the conventions to question the narrative resolution, implicating the spectator in questions of moral ambiguity.

Welles's stylistic and thematic concerns were fairly consistent, especially in those films he made in Hollywood. It might be productive therefore, to compare the Hollywood films with films he made outside of the Hollywood production system to test the notion that 'artistic freedom' is only possible outside the 'constraints' of commodity film production.

THE FRENCH NEW WAVE

The new wave covers a brief period in French cinema history from 1959 to around 1964, when certain historical, technological and economic factors combined to enable some young film-makers to influence French cinema temporarily in very diverse ways (The French *nouvelle vague*, p. 80). The cinema industry in France in the 1950s was economically shaky: when Roger Vadim's film *Et Dieu ... créa la femme* (1956) (*And Woman was Created*) was a commercial success in spite of being made on a low budget, the industry opened its doors, temporarily, to low-budget production. Technological developments contributed to keeping costs low and enabled film-makers to experiment with lightweight, cheaper equipment and stock. Many young film-makers started out as critics, concerned with attacking the 'quality' films of Clément, Delannoy, Clouzot and others which made up the established French art cinema, hence the polemical emphasis in *Cahiers* on popular American cinema and its *auteurs*.

At this point in time, then, it suddenly became possible for a group of young French film-makers to experiment with expressing their personal concerns on film, to become *auteurs* in their own right. They admired the technical skill and the personal vision of the great Hollywood directors: much of their work is in homage to them. At the same time they wanted to experiment with new cinematic forms in opposition to the established genres and stereotypes. They borrowed widely from the rich traditions offered by the great moments of cinema, giving them a new immediacy made possible by technological and economic developments. The new wave took cinema out of the studio and into the streets, celebrating its new-found possibilities (see Bordwell and Thompson, 1979, p. 318).

As might be expected, this cinema of experiment and change could not continue to be commercially successful, and by 1964 the backers had seen enough failures to make them more cautious. The experimental flowering died for the most part. Some film-makers were absorbed into the industry; a few survived, to continue to make films which have influenced world cinema and whose directors have, like their Hollywood mentors, achieved the status of *auteur* in the eyes of the critical establishment (see Kinder and Houston, 1972, p. 181).

The economic and ideological context in which the French new wave emerged is discussed elsewhere (see The French *nouvelle vague*, p. 80). Between 1959 and 1965 the work of the new wave directors was particularly interesting in relation to the *politique des auteurs* and its defence of popular American cinema.

Jean-Luc Godard

Godard has continued to be the most radically experimental and the most politically aware of the new wave directors, constantly raising new problems which are both formal, to do with cinematic and other kinds of language, and political, to do with transforming existing social structures (see Williams, 1971/72).

As one of the *Cahiers* critics who argued polemically for the artistic value of popular cinema, Godard made films which not only reflected those concerns, but had far reaching implications for film-making as well as theoretical film criticism. His films constantly refer outside themselves to other films, other traditions, using this method of extra-textual reference and quotation to bring together apparently incompatible ideas and forms to contradict and conflict with each other. Arguably, it is this process of questioning and transformation that makes Godard such an important 'modern' director. During the events of 1968, Godard, like many intellectuals, became politicised and his film-making practice changed. The pre-1968 films are discussed here in the historical context of the French new wave and its relationship to the *politique des auteurs* (see Auteur theory and British cinema, p. 258); Authorship and counter-cinema, p. 305).

François Truffaut

Truffaut's critical writing for *Cahiers du Cinéma* in the 1950s was passionate and flamboyant, denouncing established French cinema in favour of the technical expertise, inventiveness and 'personal vision' of certain Hollywood films (Hawks, Walsh, Fuller, Ford and above all Hitchcock) and of 1930s French cinema (Renoir in particular). Truffaut's polemical article 'A Certain Tendency of the French Cinema' (1954) was important in marking the critical shift towards the *politique des auteurs* by the *Cahiers* critics. Yet Truffaut's importance as a polemical critic does not seem to be carried over into his films. Unlike Godard, who has constantly tested and developed his critical and theoretical ideas with an intellectual toughness which has allowed him to grow and change, Truffaut (one of the new wave directors who survived to found his own production company) seems to have remained locked within a conservative romantic ideology (which is indeed one strand within the *auteurist* position) and his work – influenced as it is by the French cinema of the 1930s, the films of Alfred Hitchcock, and the American B-picture – has remained within the conventions of narrative cinema. Don Allen says:

> The word 'revolutionary' might be applied to Truffaut in two senses only. First because he was committed to the violent destruction by spectacular critical attacks of what he judged bad; secondly, and more literally, because 'revolution' for him has implied turning the wheel back to his cinematic golden age, the 30s. The cinema which Truffaut advocates is firmly based on the best characteristics of this period, and in particular on the total authorship and consequent directional freedom of such lyrical film creators as Jean Renoir and Jean Vigo. (Allen, 1974, p. 13)

Selected Reading

François Truffaut, 'A certain tendency of the French cinema', *Cahiers du Cinéma* no. 31, January 1954, trans. in Bill Nichols (ed.), *Movies and Methods*, Berkeley, University of California Press, 1976.

JEAN-LUC GODARD

À bout de souffle (Breathless) (France 1959 *p.c* – SNC; *d* – Jean-Luc Godard; sd b/w)

One of the first new wave films to be financially successful. It was Godard's first feature: he scripted, directed and edited, but there was collaboration with Chabrol and Truffaut, and with cameraman Raoul Coutard. New wave film-makers often worked together, although they each had very different positions and developed in different directions. The film can be seen as a homage to Hollywood, but it is arguable that the mixing of Hollywood conventions with those from other cinemas allows space for critical distance as well as the pleasures of recognition.

The plot is based on the conventions of the American gangster movie, and the 'hero' Michel (played by Jean-Paul Belmondo) models himself on Humphrey Bogart, whose image on movie posters appears throughout this film. The references to other films, and to other popular forms like comics or newspapers, is a strategy employed by Godard to show that film is a multiple system, that it is made up of influences from other arts. It is not simply a question of filling the film with 'in-jokes', although this is certainly part of the pleasure in watching it, but of bringing diverse elements into conflict.

The *Cahiers* critics also admired Italian neo-realism, and it could be argued that the documentary style of the film conflicts with the Hollywood stereotypes to reveal the conventional nature of both: neither can be seen as embodiments of 'truth'. However, the hand-held moving camera appears to support the romantic ideology of 'individual freedom' which underpins many new wave films, and the philosophy of the *politique des auteurs.*

Michel is a nihilistic anti-hero whose fascination with 'things American' – not only cinema but his independent American girlfriend – leads to his betrayal and death. He is also characteristic of the aimless protagonists of European art cinema (Authors in art cinema, p. 236).

The low-budget, experimental quality of the film (natural lighting, natural sound and fast-moving hand-held 35 mm camera) combined with use of real locations, acts as a critical juxtaposition with Hollywood studio production. At this stage Godard tries to encourage a critical reaction from the audience without losing the pleasurable fantasies that cinema offers.

Bande à part (**The Outsiders**) (France 1964 *p.c* – Anouchka Films/Orsay Films; *d* – Jean-Luc Godard; sd b/w)

The title refers to a group of renegade outsiders, thieves who prey on bourgeois society, but are doomed, of course, to failure. Based on a popular American thriller, the plot has been stripped down to its basic elements as part of Godard's strategy of 'denaturalising' narrative structures for the audience, arguably preventing direct involvement or identification.

Nevertheless the spontaneity (almost childlike innocence) of the protagonists is extremely seductive, and is celebrated on one level by the film. Again, the self-conscious mixing of genre conventions has the effect of denaturalising them. For example, the romantic isolation of the characters is set against their dance, which is an explicit reference to the American musical. Arguably, Godard allows the spectator to celebrate, enjoy *and* criticise traditional pleasures offered by cinema.

Godard reduces the conventions of the thriller genre to their most schematic elements: in this case a climactic 'shoot-out' from which all tension is removed. The narrative conventions appear banal because of Godard's ironic treatment of them: they are revealed *as* conventions. By showing that conventions are not eternal or universal Godard poses the possibility of changing the combinations to produce new meanings. It could be argued that this is the value of his work on film language itself, which is more highly developed in later films.

Une Femme mariée (**A Married Woman**) (France 1964 *p.c* – Anouchka Films/Orsay Films, *d* – Jean-Luc Godard; sd b/w)

Godard uses a banal plot (this time a melodrama of the affair between a bourgeois mother/housewife and her actor–lover) to raise questions about cinematic language and social conditions.

The film plays with sound and image disjunctures, visual and verbal signs, subjective monologues and documentary-style images, positive and negative photographic images to reveal the interrelationship of different language systems, and the way they come together to make up cinema. He takes the different systems apart and recombines them to create new meanings, for example, through the use of visual/verbal puns, not just an intellectual exercise but a productive activity similar to that of modern poets.

The 'heroine's' fragmented interior monologues are also a kind of poetry which reflect her status as woman/housewife/consumer rather than try to present her as a psychologically coherent character. The sequence of lovers in bed is important not only as an explicit reference to another new wave film, *Hiroshima, Mon Amour* (1959), but also in its use of the fade-out to fragment narrative. The representation of female sexuality in the film raises questions about the place of women in Godard's work.

Pierrot le fou (France/Italy 1965 *p.c* – Rome–Paris Films; *d* – Jean-Luc Godard; sd col. scope)

Another adaptation from a popular novel, in which Godard fragments the narrative fiction in order to raise questions which throw the romantic aspirations of the protagonists into perspective. The debt to Hollywood is evident in the use of the gangster film convention of the couple in retreat from a hostile society, but the film uses various formal strategies to question that notion. Its protagonists are doomed, by the conflict between their inner desires and the violence and corruption of society, to destruction. Godard uses CinemaScope and colour to emphasise the seductive nature of their dream of an idyllic paradise. Social reality constantly interrupts the idyll, however, and the protagonists are driven back into society, which finally kills them. In spite of Godard's evident ambiguity towards politics at this stage, the film looks forward to the explicitly political concerns of later work.

The film's central theme is that of the escape of the young couple away from civi-

Godard's reference to the American musical in *Bande à part*

lisation. The film also illustrates Godard's strategy of fragmenting the narrative, juxtaposing written texts with film image. Godard has often been accused of a puritanical distrust of the seductive potential of the cinematic image: here, Scope and colour emphasise the lush beauty of the fantasy island, while written texts constantly intrude to 'jog' the spectator out of the fiction in the direction of politics.

The film's basic romanticism is conservative in many respects: for example, in the representations of Marianne as instinctual and Ferdinand as 'the thinker', and in the anarchism of Ferdinand's final gesture of self-destruction: the only alternative, it would seem, to utopianism.

Masculin–Féminin (France/Sweden 1966 *p.c* – Anouchka Films/Argos Films (Paris), Svensk Filmindustri/Sandrews (Stockholm); *d* – Jean-Luc Godard; sd b/w)

Masculin–Féminin looks forward to later Godard in which political questions are raised more directly. The problem presented here is the relationship between the 'personal' and the 'political'. The hesitant, tentative relationship between two young people (a young man involved in Communist Party politics and a woman involved in herself and pop music) is used as the basis for an enquiry into sexual relationships and the representation of sexuality.

The narrative is divided into sections, or 'acts', indicating Godard's growing interest in Brecht's theories of 'epic' theatre and the use of tableaux to break up narrative fiction to allow the spectator to stand back critically from time to time. Note the use of the 'interview' sequence to break down identification with characters.

The film is interesting in terms of Godard's development towards a rigorous theoretical style in which camera movement, long takes and editing are used in an abstract manner to foreground and question the language of cinema, and the use of this strategy of abstraction to attempt to place the spectator in a critical position *vis-à-vis* the film (and its protagonists), breaking down identification and therefore raising the question of pleasure, a question to which Godard was constantly to return as a political priority (as it was indeed for Brecht also).

In the context of the new wave, Godard's use of Jean-Pierre Léaud could be compared with the different use of that actor by François Truffaut (see below). In the 'interview' sequence Paul answers that *la tendresse* is the most important thing in his life: a reference to Truffaut, who had become associated with this expression, and to Léaud's appearance in Truffaut's films. This 'extra-textual' reference, a form of quotation, has the effect of emphasising the fact that Léaud is an actor, that an actor is a 'sign' whose meaning can change according to different contexts, and that Godard is using Léaud as sign in a different way from Truffaut. The difference is significant, since Godard's project is, increasingly, to criticise notions of human spontaneity and freedom, whereas Truffaut is often concerned to celebrate them, and mourn their loss.

FRANÇOIS TRUFFAUT

Les Quatre cents coups (The 400 Blows) (France 1959 *p.c* – Les Films du Carosse, SEDIF; *d* – François Truffaut; sd b/w)

The series of films Truffaut made with Jean-Pierre Léaud playing Antoine Doinel (as a boy, then growing up into an increasingly conformist young man) are thought to be based loosely on his own life. Truffaut himself endorses this view, and of course he also acts in some of his films.

There are contradictions within this (auto)biographical mode which could be explored. Jean-Pierre Léaud/Antoine Doinel may 'stand for' François Truffaut, but other factors intrude to complicate any simple idea of self-expression. *Les Quatre cents coups*, for instance, owes much to Jean Vigo's film *Zéro de conduite*, and the use of camera movement to capture 'real space' is reminiscent of 1930s Renoir films. In the late 1950s and early 1960s films about young people were prevalent; in fact several of the new wave film-makers were working in this genre. It could be argued that Léaud/Doinel 'represents', therefore, much more than 'Truffaut'.

Truffaut's interest in the theme of individual freedom and spontaneity is manifested in the opposition between scenes on location in Paris, where the camera is constantly moving, tracking and panning, and closed interior scenes where the camera is predominantly static. Motion is used to represent freedom (Antoine and René are constantly running) and stasis to represent confinement, a structural polarisation which runs through the film. Arguably, the presence of structure questions the idea of absolute freedom, since it is only in opposition to confinement that freedom exists (see Kinder and Houston, 1972). This is the question that underlies the final shot of the film: a freeze-frame in which Antoine, free at last from reform school, is left totally alone: the *reductio ad absurdum* of romantic/anarchistic positions.

Jules et Jim (France 1965 *p.c* – Films du Carosse, SEDIF; *d* – François Truffaut; sd b/w scope)

Truffaut's concern with exploring the complexities of the idea of individual freedom is worked through in *Jules et Jim*. The representative of spontaneity here is a woman, and the effects of her behaviour are reflected in the triangular relationship between herself and the two men rather than in any resistance to social institutions, as in *Les Quatre cents coups*.

Catherine, played by Jeanne Moreau, represents the primitive forces which are both the source of creative activity (art) and the impulse behind mindless, nihilistic destruction. The social background is that of the bohemian intellectual spirit in Paris before the First World War, fragmented and shattered by the war and the rise of Fascism. Jules and Jim have a peaceful and productive rapport which is transformed when Catherine enters their lives, never to be regained. She represents the freedom they desire, which ultimately destroys them and their relationship.

The disruptive force of Catherine's wild and instinctual impulses is manifested in her unease in her marriage to Jules, reflected in the use of a restless, wandering camera and the constant motion of the protagonists. The effects of displacing the contradictions inherent in the idea of individual freedom on to a female character is, it could be argued, to create her as a monster who constantly threatens the apparent stability of the male world. Jules and Jim are the victims of their own self-destructive fantasies, but the film does not explore the extent to which Catherine is also the victim of those fantasies.

La Peau douce (Silken Skin) (France 1964 *p.c* – Films du Carosse, SEDIF; *d* – François Truffaut; sd b/w)

One of Truffaut's preoccupations (shared by other new wave film-makers) was with the institution of marriage and the problem it presents for men, a theme central to many Hollywood films also. *La Peau douce* owes much to Hitchcock (e.g. *Vertigo*) in its portrayal of a man trapped and destroyed by his desires. Like most Truffaut heroes, Pierre Lachenay looks for freedom, which is conceived entirely in terms of the options offered by bourgeois society, in this case an obsession with a young and beautiful mistress as a way out of a sterile marriage.

The film can be seen in terms of Truffaut's debt to American cinema, especially the work of Hitchcock, and of his view of male sexuality as constantly under threat, manifested in the use of a weak obsessive hero destroyed by his own fantasies. In this respect the film could be usefully compared with Claude Chabrol's *La Femme infidèle* (1968) to show contrasting treatment of the same theme, and with Agnès Varda's *Le Bonheur* (1965) – a view of male fantasies from a woman's perspective (the only woman director in the French new wave).

Catherine . . . the destructive force in the *Jules et Jim* relationship

THE *AUTEUR* THEORY

ANDREW SARRIS AND AMERICAN FILM CRITICISM

Andrew Sarris was writing film criticism in the late 1950s when America was emerging from a period of cold-war politics, which partly explains why he took up the *Cahiers politique*'s argument against social realism. The argument was, inevitably, transformed by being transplanted into American culture, but was in many ways similar to that of the original *politique des auteurs*, directed against established criteria of film criticism (see Murray, 1975).

Postwar American film criticism (typified perhaps by the writing of James Agee) had been primarily sociological, asserting the value of social realism. The best films, it was argued, were those 'quality' productions which dealt with serious social issues: this was how the 'art' of film was described. Yet at the same time, the 1940s and 1950s in Hollywood had produced a vast number of popular entertainment films in general dismissed by critics because of their blatant commercialism, which was considered incompatible with artistry and seriousness. The critical mood changed when in the 1950s Hollywood began to sell old movies to television, making it possible for many people to review and reassess the earlier work of those directors considered to be at their peak in the 1950s.

In the late 1950s and early 1960s Andrew Sarris wrote film criticism for small magazines like *The Village Voice* and *Film Culture*, the locus of much debate and polemic. Ironically, at the same time as he began arguing for the *auteur* theory and popular American cinema, that cinema and its 'mass audience' was beginning to decline and many of his friends were involved in actively opposing it through their film-making practice (in 1961 the New American Cinema Group published in *Film Culture* a 'revolutionary manifesto' for a new independent cinema in opposition to Hollywood). After the repressive cold-war period of the 1950s, a general cultural shift in American society in the 1960s towards greater intellectual freedom established a climate in which polemical writing could flourish. Sarris's critical polemic was directed against social realism in favour of formal concerns, against 'serious art' in favour of the 'art of popular cinema'. It had a double impetus: towards bringing forward Hollywood films as worthy of critical consideration, and towards using the director as a criterion of value (as opposed to the star, the screenwriter or the producer). It could be argued that this emphasis on the role of director and on formal concerns was linked with the decline of the Hollywood studio system and the growth of small-scale production facilities which allowed greater individual access to facilities for production: many artists in America had begun experimenting with 16mm film after the war for instance. Thus some of the social conditions which gave rise to the French *politique des auteurs* also contributed to the emergence of the *auteur* theory in America. Although Sarris was not a film-maker he came into contact with the French new wave at the Cannes Film Festival in 1961 and spent a year in Paris in 1962 watching old Hollywood films at the Cinémathèque. He was the editor of the English-language version of *Cahiers du Cinéma* published in London and New York, and was certainly responsible for introducing the *politique des auteurs*, translated as the *auteur* theory and elaborated into a system of evaluating and classifying Hollywood cinema. In *The American Cinema* (1968) Sarris was to establish a critical pantheon which graded directors according to the extent to which their personal vision transcended the hierarchical system within which they worked. Earlier, in 'Notes on the *Auteur* Theory in 1962', he clarified his version of the *auteur* theory, which, he emphasised, was not prescriptive. It was a means of evaluating films *a posteriori* according to the director's technical competence, the presence of a distinct visual style, and an interior meaning which arose precisely from the tension between directors and the conditions of production with which they worked. At this stage *auteurs* were not limited to American cinema, but later (in *The American Cinema*, 1968) Sarris elaborated his 'theory' (which might better be called a rationalisation) in terms of Hollywood cinema in particular, and some other great directors who were said to have influenced those working in Hollywood. Sarris never denied the importance of recognising both social conditions and the contributions of other workers besides the director in the production process, but he claimed that in the case of great directors, they had been lucky enough to find 'the proper conditions and collaborators for the full expansion of their talent'. Nevertheless, he rarely, if ever, mentions 'collaborators' and manages to summarise the career of Orson Welles without mentioning Gregg Toland, Herman J. Mankiewicz or production conditions at all. One of Sarris's most vocal opponents, Pauline Kael, devoted *The Citizen Kane Book* (1971) to the refutation of his theory that the director alone was the *auteur* of a film.

The basis of Sarris's argument in 1962 was the conviction that although it was impossible to deny the importance of history (the social conditions of production) in understanding any work of art, it was equally important not to reduce the work to its conditions of production. Recognition of the contribution of individual personal concerns was important therefore as part of the argument against a sociological criticism which saw film as a direct reflection of 'reality', without human mediation. To this extent he took issue with André Bazin (see p. 337) as well as with contemporary American film criticism.

Another important strand of his argument was the polemic for the recognition of the artistic achievements of popular Hollywood cinema:

> After years of tortured revaluation, I am now prepared to stake my critical reputation, such as it is, on the proposition that Alfred Hitchcock is artistically superior to Robert Bresson by every criterion of excellence, and, further, that, film for film, director for director, the American cinema has been consistently superior to that of the rest of the world from 1915 through 1962. Consequently, I now regard the *auteur* theory primarily as a critical device for recording the history of the American cinema, the only cinema in the world worth exploring in depth beneath the frosting of a few great directors at the top. (Sarris, 1962/63, p. 130)

In his introduction to *The American Cinema* (1968) Sarris develops this polemic on behalf of popular cinema even further, classifying Hollywood in terms of its directors, and in terms of a hierarchy, running from 'pantheon directors' (the best) down to 'miscellaneous' (the least distinguished). Like any pantheon, Sarris's classifications are questionable, subject to differences of personal taste and historical change. Nonetheless, it can be argued that the assumptions underlying the polemic (that there are 'good' and 'bad' directors, 'good' and 'bad' films, and that these evaluations can be accounted for simply in terms of the *auteur* theory) are an important element in the way that we look at films. Part of the pleasure in criticising films is to be able to discern what is 'good' and what is 'bad', and it is easy to forget that these judgements are both subjective and culturally specific. The *auteur* theory, in so far as it privileges one area of cinema over others, and the director over other determining factors in the process of production, encourages the acceptance of these ideological assumptions as natural rather than open to question. Rather than accepting Sarris's categories then (and it is surprising how far they have continued to hold good for most *auteur* criticism in film studies) they can be used to provoke questions. For example: what is the value of assessing the quality of a film according to the consistency of its 'world-view'? Does it matter which world-view is being presented?

'Pantheon directors': D.W. Griffith

Sarris argued that the history of American cinema could be written in terms of its great directors:

> Very early in his career, Griffith mastered most of the technical vocabulary of the cinema, and then proceeded to

> simplify his vocabulary for the sake of greater psychological penetration of the dramatic issues that concerned him … The debt that all film-makers owe to D. W. Griffith defies calculation. Even before *The Birth of a Nation*, he had managed to synthesize the dramatic and documentary elements of the modern feature film. (Sarris, 1968, p. 51)

According to this argument, history could be explained through the actions of a few 'great men', and indeed, this is the way Griffith is usually regarded. His film career spanned the history of the industry from its beginnings to the introduction of sound, and in that time he had struggled with an increasingly monolithic studio system for the right to artistic control over his films. He was credited with developing a specifically cinematic language, which was to become the basis of American narrative film through skilful editing together of panning shots, extreme long shots, full-screen close-ups and judicious use of split screen, dissolves, iris and other masking devices. This cinematic vocabulary was, of course, available to other film-makers working at that time, but Griffith's worldwide reputation among critics and film-makers as a pioneering artist of the cinema arose from the way in which he combined these elements to produce profoundly moving epic statements about history and the men and women who were caught up in it despite themselves. He was not afraid to embark on extravagant experiments and broke away from the studios in 1914 when his extravagance apparently became too much for them, and he began to produce, write and direct his own films (Petley, 1978, pp. 81–5).

His skill in editing and his experimental flair, although closely tied to narrative, were influential on film-makers all over the world. The montage tempo of *Intolerance* (1916), for instance, was admired by the cinematic avant-gardes in France and Russia for the way it managed to convey abstract ideas and feelings, taking the language of cinema much further than the one or two-reeler comedies and dramas produced within the studios (see Bordwell and Thompson, 1979, pp. 293–8). Griffith's films were also different for the way they dealt with the great epic themes of history and civilisation, investing cinema with a prestige generally denied it in relation to the other arts; at the same time he tried to reach the widest possible audience by using popular forms such as melodrama to convey the 'humanity' of his characters. This combination of the epic and the personal, of history and melodrama, became the basis of classic Hollywood narrative cinema (see Early cinema, p. 93).

While there is no doubt that the exploitation of cinema's potential for spectacle and emotional involvement in Griffith's films was instrumental in establishing the artistic reputation of silent American cinema throughout the world, it is doubtful whether this great step forward can be entirely put down to Griffith himself, as Sarris's argument (and others) would suggest. Griffith's work was made possible by a combination of historical, economic and ideological factors which a traditional *auteur* analysis such as Sarris's ignores.

'The far side of paradise': Nicholas Ray

Sarris introduces Section II of *The American Cinema* thus:

> These are the directors who fall short of the pantheon either because of fragmentation of their personal vision or because of disruptive career problems. (Sarris, 1968, p. 83)

It could be argued that this second section is potentially more interesting than that of the 'Pantheon Directors' because it raises the question of how far the idea of 'personal vision' can be maintained in the context of Hollywood studio production. For many *auteur* critics Ray was the supreme example of the artist whose vision transcended conditions of production; for others he was the opposite, a Hollywood hack.

The extremes of critical positions in the debate surrounding Ray's films match the extreme differences between those films, and the inconsistencies within many of them. It could be said that the violence of their themes reverberates on the level of form so that they test the limits of the Hollywood system of representation. This, together with the myths surrounding Ray's dramatic conflicts with the Hollywood studio hierarchy at times in his career, combines to produce an image of Ray as the archetypal romantic artist, in a continual state of crisis *vis-à-vis* the world (see Orson Welles, p. 250).

The overall sense of crisis and fragmentation which characterises Ray's work, its 'unevenness', paradoxically has made it possible for *auteur* critics to construct it as an *œuvre*, seeing in its moments of perception and insight a unified personal vision (see Perkins, 1972). Thus such radically different films as *They Live by Night* (1948), *Rebel Without a Cause* (1955) and *Johnny Guitar* (1954) can all be seen as manifestations of a theme of almost mythic dimensions:

> Moral crisis and salvation, a thirst for liberty, the clash of the individual and society, and the beauty of those ideals which men and women will pursue past all discretion to the point of their own annihilation. (Wilmington, 1973, p. 46)

Sarris's call for a sense of proportion in relation to Ray's work, and his hint that it might be productive to look at the films from the point of view of Ray's relationship to the industry (Sarris, 1968, p. 107) is perceptive. The fragmentation of the director's world-view can be seen as the result of contradictory elements which emphasise the difference between each film rather then their similarity, differences which can be attributed to their place in history.

Ray's film career can be roughly divided into four phases: the years at RKO Studio (1948–52); an independent phase between 1954 and 1958; an 'epic' period (1961–3) and a final phase in which he rejected Hollywood completely, working in Europe and latterly in New York on underground, experimental projects. His 'best' films are generally thought to belong to the first two phases, although there are several 'bad' films there too; placing the films in their production context enables those evaluations made according to the criteria of the *auteur* theory to be reassessed.

'Expressive esoterica': Donald Siegel

In 1968 Sarris categorised Siegel as one of the unsung directors with difficult styles or unfashionable genres or both (Sarris, 1968, p. 123) and described his *œuvre* thus:

> Siegel's style does not encompass the demonic distortions of Fuller's, Aldrich's, Losey's, and, to a lesser extent, Karlson's. Siegel declines to implicate the world at large in the anarchic causes of his heroes. Nor does he adjust his compositions to their psychological quirks. The moral architecture of his universe is never undermined by the editing, however frenzied. (Sarris, 1968, p. 137)

The implication is that while Siegel's films manifest a consistent theme (the anarchic individual at odds with the social order) the structural austerity of his style represents containment rather than disruption or formal excess. The aforesaid theme is frequently found in Hollywood narrative cinema, and a comparison between Siegel's films and those of Nicholas Ray (see above) raises the question of the role of *mise-en-scène* in producing different interpretations of basic ideological material. While Ray's *mise-en-scène* manifests turmoil and upheaval in the structural organisation of the film itself, Siegel's direction, by contrast, uses montage to emphasise containment and order with schematic economy. This stylistic economy often makes it difficult for the critic to separate out Siegel's personal concerns from the generic concerns of the low-budget action film with which he worked for much of his career, and on which his reputation rests. For instance, the theme of the psychotic outlaw hero compelled to transgress social norms is present in much Hollywood cinema of the 1940s, 1950s and 1960s, particularly in thriller and western genres (cf. Fritz Lang, Nicholas Ray). While other directors can be seen to use these genre elements in the interests of social criticism, Siegel uses them to construct a view of society in which 'good' is indistinguishable from 'evil', justifying the individualism which motivates the violent actions of its protagonists. The spectacle of violence is an essential component of the action film, both as a source of pleasure for the audience and as a problem to be resolved by the narrative. Often violence triggers off a chain of events which can only be resolved through violence, and it could be argued that Siegel sees violence and its repression as inseparable elements in the maintenance of social stability, rather than as symptoms of a diseased social order.

Writing about Siegel's work in 1975, and with the benefit of hindsight, Alan Lovell offers a different perspective on the director from Andrew Sarris. Lovell criticises his own earlier attachment in the first version of his book (1968) to the combination of *auteur* theory and structural anthropology which was thought to offer a way out of the subjectivism of traditional *auteur* study. This auto-critique is used as the basis for a historical analysis of the changes that affected film theory, and Hollywood cinema itself, in the intervening years. Changes which, in Lovell's view, necessitate a complete rethinking of the analytic methods brought to bear on film study. Lovell's historical, descriptive approach is in sharp contrast to his, and Sarris's, 1968 evaluation of Siegel's work. From a post-structuralist perspective he calls for a critical position on authorship which will take note of the social nature of all artistic production:

> The production process of particular films has to be related to the general production situation, available artistic forms, ideological meanings, intended audiences. The director works within this situation and he can do little to change it. (Lovell, 1975, p. 12)

In arguing for a consideration of the ideological meanings at work in particular films in terms of the conjunction of a variety of different determining elements, Lovell comes close to positing as a critical method the 'conjunctural analysis' proposed by work on British cinema discussed below (see Ealing studios, p. 82).

Lovell divides Siegel's work into three phases: apprentice years (1946–53); development of distinctive themes and style (1954–9); and extension and changes in theme and style (1959) as he gained artistic control. But he goes on to emphasise that the reconstruction of the Siegel *œuvre* is complicated by forces outside the director's control: changes in the American film industry which transformed Hollywood cinema from a highly profitable economic enterprise into a declining form of popular entertainment (Lovell, 1975, p. 30). Lovell's analysis rings particularly true in the context of the rapid decline of the traditional system of production, distribution and exhibition of films under the impact of new technology.

Film as commodity product: Roger Corman

Sarris places Corman in his 'Oddities, One-Shots, and Newcomers' category, although he lists as many as twenty-five films directed by Corman between 1955 and 1967, many of which represent a consistent contribution to a genre (for instance, the Poe cycle of horror films and the gangster films). Apart from its value as a polemical 'scandalisation' category, this section – which includes Charles Laughton, Howard Hughes and Ida Lupino – perhaps best demonstrates the contradictions inherent in an *auteur* theory which depends upon a conception of an individual personal vision transcending conditions of production and material. Behind Sarris's summary dismissal of Corman's work seems to lie the implication that he fails to produce 'high art' from popular culture, and so falls short of being a true *auteur*.

There have been many attempts to reclaim the status of *auteur* for Corman (e.g. Will and Willemen, 1970; Wheeler Dixon, 1976). It is possible to argue, in spite of these attempts, that Corman's resistance to the criteria imposed by Sarris's *auteur* theory (such as 'art' and 'good' films) makes it possible to question the basic premisses of those criteria.

'Meaningful Coherence'

Auteur theory enables the critic to impose unity in retrospect on a body of films produced in a variety of production set-ups. This unity is attributed to the presence of the director as the essential source of meaning, across different genres, studios, etc. The director as *auteur* is therefore opposed to Hollywood production conditions, and it is from this *relationship of opposition* that true authorship arises, distinguishing 'art' from 'mass entertainment'.

Corman's films cannot be fitted into this formation, since they remain firmly linked to the production set-up of low-budget 'exploitation' films in Hollywood in the 1950s, and rather than displaying any tension or opposition, seem to revel in their own 'trashiness'. Meaning seems to emerge directly from *conditions of production* rather than the director's personal vision. The profit motive, the need to make 'a quick buck' is so dominant that the *auteur*'s intentions seem to recede in the face of this assertion of film as commodity product, and coherence seems to reside rather in genre conventions and production values.

Popular Cinema as Art

Auteur theory demands that popular entertainment cinema be taken seriously: to take the work of a Hollywood director seriously is to take seriously the materials and conventions with which they work, to put popular cinema on a level with art.

The 'exploitation' material with which Corman works depends upon ripping off, and often parodying, more up-market expensive productions. Since it does not take Hollywood seriously itself, and overtly displays this lack of seriousness, it is difficult to reconcile with the demands of the *auteur* theory to evaluate films as 'good' or 'bad'. Bad acting, bad direction are the hall-marks of exploitation films, and, it has been argued, their strength. They cannot be considered 'classic' works; indeed, they refuse the notion of classicism.

The Critic's Role

Sarris stresses that authorship is discerned retrospectively by the critic, who looks closely at a film or a body of films to abstract the essence of the *auteur*. The role of the critic is one of contemplation and reassessment, and in this context authorship theory attempts to break with the ideology of mass production of films for immediate consumption by a paying audience. Exploitation films are precisely produced for immediate consumption (the drive-in circuit in America) and their value is assumed to be exhausted when they cease to make money. The disposable ideology of 'trash' exploitation films seems to be incompatible with the notion of the discerning critic analysing and evaluating films according to their status as classic works (see Nowell-Smith, 1976).

It is arguable that Sarris's *auteur theory* reached an impasse with Corman's work. By virtue of its own criteria of value it excluded discussion of film as commodity product, and it was precisely this discussion which was brought to bear against traditional *auteurism* in later, post-structuralist film theory.

Selected Reading

Wheeler Dixon, 'In defense of Roger Corman', *The Velvet Light Trap* no. 16, autumn 1976.

Andrew Sarris, *The American Cinema: Directors and Directions 1929–1968*, New York, Dutton, 1968.

D. W. GRIFFITH

The Birth of a Nation (USA 1915 *p.c* – Epoch Producing Corp; *d* – D. W. Griffith; st b/w)

Griffith's first major independent production after several smaller-scale experiments with narrative and montage. Large-scale epic production was not confined to Griffith: it was a feature of both the contemporary American and Italian cinema (Petley, 1978, p. 81). Nonetheless, the scale of the production envisaged by Griffith, his reputation for being intractable, and the controversial subject matter, discouraged investment from traditional sources, so that Griffith had to finance and distribute the film independently.

The Birth of a Nation is not only important in relation to the development of Hollywood narrative cinema, but also in terms of its ideological implications, which can be seen to be linked with its narrative structure. The combination of epic historical spectacle and family melodrama forms the basis here (as in other films) of a humanist ideology dedicated to individual freedom and the resolution of all contradictions of class, race and sex in terms of an ideal unity. The racist Ku Klux Klan can be seen to represent unity (i.e. unity of whites against the emancipated blacks) which gives an ideological perspective on the value placed on family unity, and on the unity of the couple, in this film and other Griffith films. *The Birth of a Nation* was based on a racist novel, *The Clansman*, and its racist content has been the subject of much controversy.

Griffith's development of cinematic narrative and spectacle, his use of the combination of the two genres, historical epic and melodrama, demonstrate a particular use of narrative fiction films as powerful, moving political propaganda. When compared with contemporary Russian cinema (Eisenstein and Pudovkin, for example), in spite of cross-fertilisation ideological differences emerge. If the epic quality of *The Birth of a Nation* encourages us to forget the way it elides and suppresses contradictions because of its spectacular dimension, it can be argued that the Russians exploited cinematic strategies in order to *produce* contradiction and criticism: a very different view of the function of art, and the artist, in society.

Intolerance (USA 1916 *p.c* – Wark Producing Corp; *d* – D. W. Griffith; st b/w)

Intolerance is considered to be a virtuoso work: those cinematic strategies which Griffith had been developing in earlier films come together here to form a complex combination of technique and spectacle.

The narrative structure is based on the intercutting of four different stories illustrating social intolerance and its effects at different historical periods. Apart from the

Intolerance – Griffith's historical tableau

difficulty the spectator may have in following four separate plots, the variety of technical devices contributes to the overall effect of complexity which gives the film the quality of a historical tableau, or tapestry, in which detail is ultimately less important than the movement of history itself. How far can this effect be attributed to the intentions of Griffith himself? The translation of traditional material (the Modern Story is borrowed directly from popular melodrama, for instance) into a sophisticated, innovative cinematic language can be seen as a high point in Griffith's development of the multiple plot narrative, or as a breakthrough in the silent cinema of this period. It was a time of technical innovation generally, in Hollywood and the rest of the world, and this film influenced film-makers in France and Russia. The Russians in particular admired its use of montage editing to bring together different stories and themes, and to manipulate the spectator's emotions, although it is unlikely that they would have subscribed to the theme of democracy based on individual freedom (see Bordwell and Thompson, 1979, pp. 159, 307–8).

Hearts of the World (USA 1918 *p.c* – Griffith Inc; *d* – D. W. Griffith; st b/w)

A combination of documentary and melodrama, this film's theme is the destructive effect of war on family and personal relationships. The scenes of war are spectacular, as usual in Griffith's films, but in general the film underwrites the necessity of defending democracy and individual freedom by dwelling on the drama of personal suffering.

Some documentary footage was used, and the war provides the background to the drama, so that the film works as powerful humanist propaganda. Scenes of love, caring and happiness in the family and between the boy and girl are dwelt upon: this innocence is shattered by the war, and the girl in particular (played by Lillian Gish) is forced to come to maturity through personal suffering and unhappiness, a characteristic which became part of her star persona. The suffering imposed on the family and the couple by the mobilisation order and the devastation of war is taken to almost grotesque lengths when the girl, distraught after the destruction of her village, finds the boy unconscious on the battlefield and lies down beside him.

NICHOLAS RAY

They Live by Night (USA 1948 *p.c* – RKO Radio; *d* – Nicholas Ray; sd b/w)

Ray's first film for RKO, which at that time was in the 'progressive' hands of Dore Schary. Ray came from radical community theatre into postwar Hollywood; this is probably the only project he was able to film as he wished. The film, which belongs loosely in the sub-*film noir* category 'gangster couple on the run', is a sympathetic portrayal of the illusion of freedom cherished by the two young protagonists, forced to live outside the law and trying to realise their own desires from their position as outsiders. This attempt brings them into conflict with the system from which they are seeking to escape and which ultimately destroys them. The romanticism of the couple cannot be denied: their innocence and playful naïveté might seem absurd, were it not for the fact that it is opposed to a hostile and threatening social system which allows no room for romantic fantasy. Meaning resides in this play of oppositions: from the point of view of the lovers, normality appears grotesque, yet their innocence is also unreal, and we know that they are doomed (cf. *You Only Live Once* (1967), *Bonnie and Clyde* (1967), *Pierrot le fou* (1965)). Ray returned to the theme of rootless young persons again (in *Rebel Without a Cause* (1955), *Knock on any Door* (1949)) often depicting them at odds with social institutions such as the family or the legal system. The extent to which this theme in itself can be regarded as critical of American society provides an interesting area for debate: what is the role of genre, or narrative, for instance, in articulating such criticism? How far is social criticism possible within the Hollywood system of representation?

They Live by Night – a theme critical of American society?

On Dangerous Ground (USA 1951 – *p.c* RKO Radio; *d* – Nicholas Ray; sd b/w)

They Live by Night spent two years in the vaults of RKO Studios before being released. Howard Hughes arrived at the studios, demanding personal approval on everything in the production process: consequently, Ray often found himself with uncongenial projects (*A Woman's Secret* (1949), *Born to be Bad* (1950) – two of Ray's 'bad' films from this period).

At the end of the 1940s Ray was reunited with his sympathetic producer John Houseman and regained some of the control he had lost. He worked on the script of *On Dangerous Ground*, which can be seen as a development of preoccupations in *They Live by Night*, looking forward to later films.

The protagonists of this film are victims of a destructive society, mirrored in their own violence. *Mise-en-scène* and editing (Sarris has called Ray's style 'kinetic') emphasise conflict and fragmentation, which is not seen as exclusive to city life, but has spread to the country too: the brutality of the cop Jim Wilson is seen as the effect of a social system built on repression of human desires. Characteristically, Ray depicts social repression as one of the root causes of psychological disturbance, but the psychologically disturbed hero was a common feature in Hollywood of the 1950s across many genres, as was the film's theme in which the hero policeman makes a journey from the urban landscape of the police thriller/*film noir* to the pastoral haven of the American countryside (cf. *The Asphalt Jungle* (1950)). In this film the haven or sanctuary is fraught with danger, perversion and a sense of loss.

The Lusty Men (USA 1952 *p.c* – Wald/Krasna Productions; *d* – Nicholas Ray; sd b/w)

This film, his last in black-and-white, was made at the end of Ray's 'apprenticeship' with RKO, and as Mike Wilmington points out, he was surrounded by so many excellent collaborators that it is not easy to single out his contribution (Wilmington, 1973/74, p. 35).

All these RKO films might be regarded as 'work in progress': they are stylistically very different, even when a consistent Ray thematic can be detected in them. Yet all of Ray's *œuvre* displays this stylistic inconsistency, manifesting a willingness to experiment and explore the limits of cinematic language. Victor Perkins (1972) constructs a coherent unified *auteur* from this experimental principle. Another argument might construct the Ray *œuvre* as the site of multiple contributions, constantly shifting, in which the contribution of Nicholas Ray is sometimes dominant, sometimes not, according to the specific historical moment in which each film was produced, and the different contexts in which it is received, which might produce different 'readings'.

In terms of Ray's treatment of genre, the thematic opposition between disorder (rootlessness) and normality (stability) is here transposed on to the rural setting of the rodeo film, a sub-genre of the western. An opposition is drawn between 'rodeo' (male: rootlessness/isolation) and 'home' (female: stability/family), both terms seen as incompatible. Typically, the obsessions of the characters in the fiction, their inability to control their impulses, drive the narrative forward, and ultimately the problem is resolved through death.

In comparison with other Ray films, the muted (almost realistic) *mise-en-scène* gives this film a rigour and certainty of style which differs from the 'experimental' excess which characterises Ray's *œuvre* overall. Nonetheless, it can be argued that it occupies a pivotal place in that *œuvre*, looking back to the concerns of earlier films and forward to *Johnny Guitar* (1954). The strength of Susan Hayward's portrayal of Louise Merrit is interesting in this respect. She seems to be the first of Ray's 'strong' heroines, to be developed in splendid ambiguity in *Johnny Guitar* (see Haskell, 1974), a film considered by some to be Ray's personal statement against the McCarthy witch-hunts (see Kreidl, 1977).

Johnny Guitar (USA 1954 *p.c* – Republic; *d* – Nicholas Ray; sd col.)

Kreidl (1977) describes *Johnny Guitar* as a political western with a female hero, an anti-McCarthy parable made during self-imposed exile in Spain. In fact, the film was shot in Arizona; but certainly its theme of a disenchanted outsider who returns home to find a land ravaged by hatred, distrust and revenge which he must find the strength to resist is both characteristic of Ray's work and appropriate to cold-war America.

Kreidl argues that Ray is more clearly the sole author of *Johnny Guitar* than of *Rebel Without a Cause*, which was a collaborative effort. It seems Ray had a high degree of control over the production: the film was made away from the scrutiny of Hollywood executives, and Ray was an investing co-producer. His 'signature' can be seen in the symbolic use of colour to code the different characters, the exploitation of the widescreen through horizontal composition, and the expressive use of sets and décor.

V. F. Perkins (1972) also emphasises the importance of décor and *mise-en-scène* as an expression of Ray's recurring preoccupations. He points to the division in *Johnny Guitar* between 'upstairs', Vienna's private, feminine retreat, and 'downstairs', the public, masculine, violent world where she must shed her femininity to survive.

Indeed, the political themes of the film are partly worked through in terms of the characters' sexuality: in order to resolve the unhappy situation Johnny Guitar must become stronger, more masculine, which in turn allows Vienna's 'true' femininity to emerge. Vienna's oscillation between masculinity and femininity has been seen by feminist critics as both offering the possibility of a positive role for women in the western (e.g. Haskell, 1974), and more negatively as a symptom of the way the genre activates women's predisposition to transsexual identification only to finally replace them, albeit uneasily, in the feminine position (Gender and sexuality in the western, p. 152).

Rebel Without a Cause (USA 1955 *p.c* – Warner Bros.; *d* – Nicholas Ray; sd col. scope)

The box-office success of *Johnny Guitar* led to Ray's return to America and the offer from Warner Bros. to direct a film in the new 'youth movie' genre. Kreidl (1977) traces the different conditions and contributions which

Johnny Guitar – positive roles for women in the western

affected the final product, in his view a collaborative venture representing the way in which Ray preferred to work. Nonetheless, Kreidl considers this Ray's finest work, and finds it ironic that its international success rests largely on the presence of James Dean, whose performance as Jim Stark is exemplary of Hollywood 1950s Method acting.

Kreidl argues that the film breaks with the classic Hollywood narrative tradition, and points to Ray's characteristically dislocated *mise-en-scène* combined with horizontal composition to exploit the potential of CinemaScope. He sees the upside-down shot and the tilted camera used in the family confrontation scene as code breaking in the context of Hollywood emerging from the cold war.

V. F. Perkins (1972), however, sees these strategies in classical terms as the perfect representation of Ray's ideas, projecting the world as he and his angry, alienated characters experience it. For Perkins the Chicken Run represents Ray's world-view in microcosm: life as a meaningless, chaotic journey towards death, unless one stops to question it, as Jim Stark does, in order to find an alternative.

The James Brothers (The True Story of Jesse James) (USA 1956 *p.c* – 20th Century-Fox; *d* – Nicholas Ray; sd col.)

In 1955 *Rebel Without a Cause* was a huge commercial success, enabling Ray to work in Hollywood at a time when CinemaScope and colour (the film industry's answers to television) were increasingly important. These developments in CinemaScope and colour in the 1950s contributed to the emergence of a new kind of super-western, (spectacular in style, and dealing with psychological themes) of which *The James Brothers* is one.

Like many of Ray's films, *The James Brothers* is regarded both as a hackwork and a masterpiece. The genre components are strong, but Ray's concern might be seen in the treatment of the outlaw band as both alienated from and trapped by the society it opposes. The violence within the gang is matched by the violence which society uses against the threat that the outlaws represent to capitalism (in the form of the railroad and the banks).

While Ray's sympathies can be seen to lie with the renegade outlaws, his use of *mise-en-scène* to depict the violent confrontations between them and the established social order suggests an interest in social conflict itself, an interest which can be traced throughout his work. Ray's '*mise-en-scène* of violence' could be compared with other westerns of this period to discuss different treatments of these common themes of violence and social unrest.

DON SIEGEL

Baby Face Nelson (USA 1957 *p.c* – Fryman-ZS for United Artists; *d* – Don Siegel; sd b/w)

Siegel's films of this period show a consistency of style and thematic concern which it is possible to link with later films, in spite of the fact that they were made for different production companies. It is, however, difficult, to establish whether this consistency derives from genre conventions, authorship concerns, or both. *Baby Face Nelson* is one of the series of reconstructions of 1930s gangster movies characteristic of the genre in the late 1950s (compare, for instance, Corman's *Machine Gun Kelly* (1958) for different authorial concerns in the same genre). The psychotic, anarchistic protagonist who is a threat not only to normal society but also to organised crime is an essential element of the genre. Equally, the narrative can be seen to depend upon a central character who is the locus of contradictions, and whose function in the narrative is to cause problems which threaten the stability of social institutions, so that the resolution of the problem must be his elimination. A comparison with other films of this period in the same genre might point to the presence of different authorial concerns. Some of Siegel's own variations on the conventions might be identified as: the connection made between the gangsters and children (note the playground setting, and the hero's name 'Baby Face') and the use of prohibitive roadsigns to indicate imminent transgression of the law. Both of these motifs occur in other films directed by Siegel: however, they might also be identified as intrinsic to the gangster genre (see The gangster film, p. 173).

The Lineup (USA 1958 *p.c* – Columbia; *d* – Don Siegel; sd b/w)

This film shows similar preoccupations to *Baby Face Nelson*. The psychotic protagonist, Dancer, is seen in apparently tranquil surroundings at the ice-rink. In the context of normal activities of play and leisure, the process of scrutiny whereby Dancer and The Man recognise each other takes on additional menacing force; the ordinary people around them are oblivious to the potential violence in their midst. When Dancer does lose control, killing The Man by exploiting the fact that he is crippled, escaping in a violent car chase, attempting to use a child as a cover for his escape, turning on his mentor (Julian) and killing him, his psychosis appears as the other side of normal human behaviour, a threat which must be eliminated if society is to continue.

The relationship between Julian and Dancer, the former more rational, mature, and the latter irrational, anarchic, echoes that between Sue and Nelson in *Baby Face Nelson* and that between Charlie and Lee in *The Killers* (1964). Relationships such as this in which one member of a couple contains and/or restrains the potential violence of another, less stable member, is common to this (and other) genres within the action film category (e.g. the western). An interesting area for investigation might be the function of episodes of excessive and spectacular violence in relation to the implied perversity of these couples, and its development in the more recent 'buddy movies'. In Siegel's films the violence which unites these couples seems to function as a displacement for the 'perverse' desires which mark his protagonists off from 'normal' society, represented by the heterosexual family unit.

The Killers (USA 1964 *p.c* – Universal; *d* – Don Siegel; sd col.)

Many of the preoccupations outlined above are developed in this film, made at a time when Siegel's reputation was well established and he was moving into bigger productions and different projects. At the same time, as Alan Lovell points out, Hollywood film production was shrinking, particularly in the area of modestly budgeted productions, and Siegel's film work was interspersed with television work. *The Killers* was made for television, but considered too violent to be shown, and manifests the economy of construction typical of Siegel's style. However, critics have pointed out moments of obscurity and incoherence in the narrative (motivations left unexplained) which they consider make this film less impressive than, for example, *The Lineup* (see Lovell, 1975). In this context, a comparison with the Hemingway story, and the earlier film the killers (1946) directed by Robert Siodmak, might be useful. The shift in emphasis in the Siegel film away from the victim towards the killers themselves and their relationship (again one of mentor and pupil) has interesting consequences: it is the intellectual curiosity about the motivations of their victim which initiates the narrative, and finally destroys the killers. The fact that motivations remain unclear and the narrative enigma is unresolved on one level means that in this film the problem of 'the irrational' is not solved in the way that it is in earlier films. We are left with the nihilistic image of the killer Charlie in the throes of a violent death as the money scatters over the street.

The treatment of the killer couple in this film parallels that in *The Lineup*: again the concept of childhood is used to contrast the psychotic infantilism of gangsters (note Lee's obsessional playing with objects) with the vulnerability of 'normal' children (in the Blind School). Here the psychotic protagonists have a superficial veneer of normality (they are dressed like business executives) but violence constantly threatens to erupt

The Killers – Siegel's preoccupation with psychotic protagonists and extreme violence

(note the gratuitously violent attack on the blind woman). As in other Siegel films, the psychotic protagonists stand in opposition to 'normal', caring society, and to the organised criminal gang, from a position of extreme individualism. While Siegel himself stresses his lack of sympathy with such characters his continuing interest in them raises the question of his own position, or world-view.

The Killers seems to occupy an interesting place in Siegel's *œuvre*, indicating the beginnings of a fragmentation on the levels of form and content under the impact of changing conditions of production in the film industry, and changing social mores in America in the 1960s.

Madigan (USA 1968 *p.c* – Universal; *d* – Don Siegel; sd col. scope)

In *Madigan* the changes in production values indicated above can be seen quite clearly. A police film in the 'action' category, it demonstrates the ways in which the genre was developed partly to attract audiences away from television. Cinema censorship was relaxed so that more extravagant violence and more explicit sex were introduced. Detective Dan Madigan's sexual problems with his wife draw a parallel between psychotic killer and detective which runs through the film (the criminal Benesch uses Madigan's gun to kill) and which is opposed to the liberal humanism represented by the police commissioner.

Siegel's preoccupations (in so far as they can be separated out from the conventions of the genre) have also developed. The existence of the perverse psychotic Benesch, who represents the breakdown of moral and social order, is seen as a justification for the extreme individualism of Madigan's behaviour, as is the inadequacy of correct police procedure to cope with this social breakdown. Madigan is a victim of society in the process of disintegration, and the failure of liberalism to come to terms with it, two sides of the same coin.

The opposition drawn between an obsessional cop and the assumed alliance between perverse morality and liberalism is further developed in the films featuring Siegel's collaboration with star Clint Eastwood, resulting in a cynical justification of those obsessional qualities in the service of the law which could be seen as a departure from the earlier films.

Coogan's Bluff (USA 1969 *p.c* – Universal; *d* – Don Siegel; sd col.)

The beginning of the Siegel/Eastwood collaboration, in which the 'macho' elements of Eastwood's star persona came together with Siegel's interest in the 'maverick' cop as antidote to a disintegrating liberal society, to produce a self-reflective film full of ironic references to its own premisses.

The fact that Coogan himself comes from Arizona and represents certain 'unfashionable' virtues associated with the western, such as stoicism, individualism, courage, is a constant source of reference in the film, which is set in the degenerate urban society of New York (degenerate = alternative drug culture). This is also a reference to Eastwood's rise to stardom in westerns, apparently a parodic reference, but the Eastwood image is eventually validated in opposition to society's decadence and liberalism. 'Alternative' society is also apparently parodied (note the disco scene) but the homicidal violence which underlies it, and the assumption that it has its roots in corruption and psychosis (Linny Raven and Ringerman) establishes it as a threat to society against which the confused liberalism of Julie, the probation officer, is inadequate.

Coogan's methods are not totally validated by the narrative; in many ways he is the mirror reflection of the decadence he is fighting. However, the power of Eastwood's star presence in validating the conservative values represented by Coogan must be taken into account, particularly since they are opposed to 'inferior', 'feminine' values, represented by Julie, Linny Raven and Ringerman. It could be argued that the film reflects upon the process of posing schematic oppositions in this way, looking for some middle ground in its constant play with the notion of 'pity', associated with the colour red, and Julie. Julie's compassion is questioned for its naïve liberalism, but it is also seen as an antidote to Coogan's 'hard', masculine values and his resistance to social change.

The film is useful in demonstrating the ways in which certain aspects of Eastwood's star persona mesh with Siegel's developing concern with the maverick loner, the development of the police film in relation to the permissive culture of America in the 1960s, and Siegel's ambivalent response to these changes.

The Beguiled (USA 1971 *p.c* – Universal; *d* – Don Siegel; sd col.)

> *The Beguiled* is the best film I have done, and possibly the best I will ever do. One reason that I wanted to do the picture is that it is a woman's picture, not a picture for women, but about them. Women are capable of deceit, larceny, murder, anything. Behind that

> mask of innocence lurks just as much evil as you'll ever find in members of the Mafia. Any young girl, who looks perfectly harmless is capable of murder. There is a careful unity about the film, starting with the first frame. We begin with black-and-white and end with black-and-white; we start with Clint and the mushrooms, and end with them; we start with Clint practically dead and end with him dead. The film is rounded, intentionally turned in on itself. (Siegel, quoted in Lovell, 1975, p. 59)

As an 'art' film, *The Beguiled* can be seen as exceptional in the context of Siegel's work as a whole; it is nonetheless, like all of his films, the product of a number of contradictory elements. Some of these are: the incorporation of the 'art' movie into Hollywood film production in the 1970s, together with the notion of the director as artist (partly in response to the *auteur* theory); the collaboration between Siegel and Eastwood which led to the foregrounding of the most misogynist fantasies of both (cf. Eastwood's *Play Misty for Me* (1971)) and explicitly raises the question of the representation of male and female sexuality in Siegel's work in general, and in the action film in particular; the unstable conditions of production in Hollywood at this time which made it possible to make an a-typical, formally adventurous film, albeit strictly on a one-off basis. Formally adventurous though it may be, it can be argued that the fantasy it represents is central to Siegel's work and Eastwood's star persona; a paranoid fantasy of sexual relationships in which perversity and psychosis are placed within an all-female society which is destructive and threatening.

Dirty Harry (USA 1971 *p.c* – Warner Bros.; *d* – Don Siegel; sd col.)

As an example of a big-budget 1970s police thriller with a psychotic villain and a potentially psychotic hero, *Dirty Harry* brings together many of the strands in Siegel's work discussed above, looking back to earlier films (*Baby Face Nelson*, *The Lineup*, *Madigan*, *Coogan's Bluff*) in its treatment of genre, but displaying a more coherent grasp of the contradictions inherent in the society against which the hero sets himself.

The familiar opposition and parallels between the outsider cop, the psychotic killer and the liberal politicians remain, but they are complicated by the inclusion in this film of a social awareness which takes into account contradictory questions of race, sex and class which makes simple oppositions impossible. Harry is seen to recognise this when, at the end of the film, having finally killed the villain after obsessively hunting him down, he acknowledges his own futile isolation by throwing away his police badge.

The film shows Siegel's development into big-budget production, one element of which is the presence of Eastwood playing Harry. It also demonstrates historical changes in the gangster police film. Notable in the context of Siegel's works is the process of scrutiny (cf. *The Lineup*) employed alternately by the killer and by Harry; the confrontation between Harry as a renegade cop and the mayor as liberal politician; the confrontation between Harry as lone 'enforcer' (complete with magnum gun) and the black bank robber with whom he plays a sadistic and violent game, reflecting his cynical and nihilistic position. However, it could also be argued that the film carries the individualistic, 'macho' elements of the Eastwood persona to almost extreme limits, arguably allowing for criticism of the conservative ideology it represents by verging on parody.

ROGER CORMAN

Machine Gun Kelly (USA 1958 *p.c* – AIP; *d* – Roger Corman; sd b/w)

Before directing this film, Corman had made at least seventeen films for the exploitation market with the production company AIP (American International Pictures), all cheaply made using 'sensational' material and saturation booking to exploit all the potential markets. In the case of this film, the company was cashing in on the 1950s cycle of gangster movies (often remakes of 1930s films: cf. Siegel's *Baby Face Nelson*) popular with young people on the drive-in circuits.

Low-budget production values can be discerned in the use of black-and-white CinemaScope, unknown actors and cheap sets. David Will argues that the film resembles a comic strip (Will and Willemen, 1970, p. 73) but goes on to say that, like pop artist Lichtenstein, Corman redefines the 'validity of the lowest forms of commercial cinema' (Will and Willemen, 1970, p. 74). However, the production conditions in which Corman works are very different from those of a painter. His collaboration with a team of writers, technicians and actors can be seen from a glance at his filmography. Before attributing to him the status of artist therefore, the contributions of R. Wright Campbell (script) and Floyd Crosby (photography) in particular would have to be considered. One reason why Corman's work does not fit easily into Sarris's *auteur* theory is that the process of commodity production militates against the attribution of authorship to a single source. In this context the reconstruction of a body of films under the name 'Corman' privileges one element of the production process at the expense of others which may equally contribute to meaning in films.

Black-and-white CinemaScope, unknown actors and cheap sets characterise *Machine Gun Kelly*

An *auterist* construction of this film as a Corman work finds his personal concerns in the treatment of its gangster protagonist. Kelly is a pathological hero. In Corman's world 'heroism' is by definition a pathological state (cf. *The St Valentine's Day Massacre* (1967)) which precludes any 'normal' relationships. However, the pathological hero is also a feature of the gangster genre: the 'Corman variation' on the genre can be seen in the bleak pessimism of this film, which implies that the only possible resolution is the complete destruction of society as it exists in order to rebuild from scratch.

The Haunted Palace (USA 1963 *p.c* – Alta Vista; *d* – Roger Corman; sd col. scope)

By 1960 both Corman and AIP had become well established. Corman himself became a major international director whose films opened international film festivals and were the subject of articles in European critical journals. The series of horror films known as the Poe Cycle reflect this change in their more expensive production values, slicker style, and use of more respectable literary source material. *The Haunted Palace* comes towards the end of the cycle, which finished with *The Tomb of Ligeia* (1964).

Critical renown and respectability do not, however, affect the basically commercial nature of the films, which continue to revel in their own conventions. Typical elements of the horror genre include the theme of black magic which undermines and is opposed by the community; the rational man of science who believes himself able to explain everything; the 'good' woman as victim; and the themes of psychic possession and physical deformity. The 'Corman variation' on the conventions can be seen in the atmosphere of decadence and social decay; the opposition between civilised manners and aggressive primitive desires in one pathological individual; an obsession with death and the past; and an all-pervasive sense of doom and despair. In

Themes of psychic possession and physical deformity in Corman's *The Haunted Palace*

terms of *mise-en-scène* the contributions of art director Daniel Haller and cameraman Floyd Crosby, both regular collaborators with Corman, are important. Haller is noted for his ability to make cheap sets look expensively mounted, and Floyd Crosby for his fluid camerawork. The importance of actor Vincent Price to this horror cycle should also be stressed.

The Tomb of Ligeia (USA 1964 *p.c* – Alta Vista; *d* – Roger Corman; sd col.)

The basic elements of the genre are present in the form of the decaying aristocratic society; the possession of a person by supernatural forces; and the inclusion of a dream sequence to indicate the preoccupation with primitive desires repressed by society.

Auteur critics have seen Corman's interests in the concern with the past, the return of the repressed, the divided pathological hero tortured by the past and death, and with female sexuality as a potential force for the destruction of existing society. In this film the 'hero', Fell, is destroyed in Ligeia's arms in the final apocalyptic blaze which concludes the narrative.

The treatment of female sexuality in this film could be seen in relation to Corman's general interest in strong, destructive female figures, and is interesting as a precedent for many of the films later produced by Corman for his own production–distribution company, New World Pictures, which has built up a reputation for producing films with a 'feminist' bent in exploitation packaging (see Morris, 1974 and 1975).

In the context of Corman's work the use of popular Freudian psychology should also be noted. In one sense it is 'camped up' as part of the commodity film package but it is also powerfully and seriously used in the scene in which Rowena is hypnotised, and in her dream. It could be argued that the audience is made aware of the process of manipulation, and then invited to participate in that process.

The St Valentine's Day Massacre (USA 1967 *p.c* – Los Altos/20th Century-Fox; *d* – Roger Corman; sd col.)

An example of Corman's move into big-budget production. An interesting comparison could be made with the low-budget *Machine Gun Kelly* (1958), to discuss different production values, and with other historical reconstruction gangster films such as *Portrait of a Mobster* (1961), *Bloody Mama* (1970), *Bonnie and Clyde* (1967).

The film has a semi-documentary framework: the opening legend states that 'every character and event herein is based on real characters and events and the film's voice-over commentary gives biographical facts about each character as he appears. It is arguable that this device works to produce an epic sense of the inevitability of fate, which has often been seen as fundamental to the gangster genre. Will argues, however, that this film is different in that violent action is employed by Corman to reveal the rules and rituals of the gangster's world, rather than as a defining characteristic of that world (Will and Willemen, 1970, p. 75). Corman's own interest in, and respect for, the conventions of the genre have been seen in the use of colour and Scope (i.e. the plush red velvet of Capone's 'boardroom', suggesting his power and the extent of his aspirations; the use of Scope to suggest domination of space and territory). Capone himself is a monstrous, distorted psychopathic figure in the tradition of the genre, and of Cormanesque heroes. The extreme violence portrayed in the flashback (shot with red filter) elevates violence to the level of ritualistic exchange between the gangs, drawing a parallel between the gangsters and American big business.

AUTEUR THEORY AND BRITISH CINEMA

THE BRITISH CRITICAL CONTEXT: *MOVIE*

The British authorship debate, as it emerged in the magazine *Movie*, was formulated rather differently because of historical factors specific to British culture. British critical tradition had its roots in an art criticism which stressed the importance of the critic's personal taste in assessment of works of art; a literary criticism which stressed the social and moral function of art, and the importance of the author's unified world-view as a criterion of value; a general cultural resistance to industrial modes of production geared to entertainment rather than art; and a Marxist social criticism which regarded mass media as essentially manipulative and dangerous, to be counteracted by the insights of a critical élite. This tradition was challenged by the 'popular culture debate' in the 1950s and 1960s, in which film criticism played an active part (see Lovell, 1975; Rohdie, 1972/73).

These conflicting strands came together in the film criticism of the magazines *Sequence* and *Sight and Sound* with their dismissal of much Hollywood cinema as unworthy of serious critical attention and emphasis on European art cinema as a cinema of personal vision and integrity. Some of the critics who wrote for these magazines were also film-makers unable to find work in the contracting British film industry and forced to work as independents (Lovell, 1969).

At the time the new wave was developing in France (see The French *nouvelle vague*, p. 80) the British film-making tendency which came to be known as the Free Cinema movement appeared, committed to the idea of 'personal vision' which was at the root of the *politique des auteurs*, but without its emphasis on popular American cinema. Later, many of the Free Cinema film-makers became established in the British industry (e.g. Lindsay Anderson, Karel Reisz) carrying this commitment with them (see British social realism 1959–63, p. 88).

At this stage in British film criticism authorship in cinema had been stressed in opposition to the industrialised mass production of Hollywood entertainment films: this argument assumed that art cinema produced mostly 'good' films, and Hollywood

Look Back in Anger – criticised for its lack of feeling for cinema

produced mostly 'bad' films because it was controlled by capital, whose interests it reproduced. In this context the magazine *Movie* appeared in 1962 with an energetic attack on these defensive critical positions and on British cinema itself for its lack of style and imagination (see Perkins, 1972). *Movie* writers compared the mediocrity of British cinema with the technical expertise of Hollywood and put the former down to a cultural context which precluded the possibility of British directors achieving any artistic control. They pointed to the climate of critical opinion which ignored questions of form and demanded 'quality' pictures with serious social themes, and to the lack of British *auteurs* with their own personal style. They argued that *how* a film put over its theme was indistinguishable from *what* it attempted to say, emphasising detailed analysis of *mise-en-scène* as the primary critical approach, because it was in the formal organisation of film that meaning was to be found, not in any relation it might have to society. This emphasis on formal analysis was the link between *Cahiers' politique des auteurs* and *Movie*'s *auteur* theory, but *Movie* critics lacked the film-making context of the new wave which gave *Cahiers* its polemical force. They also lacked the strong national cinema, Hollywood, which lent strength to Andrew Sarris's arguments; but it was to Hollywood that the *Movie* critics turned as part of their attack on British cinema.

Movie's attack on British cinema for its lack of inventiveness, based as it was on an *auteurist* position which saw only that style and personal vision were absent, failed to analyse the economic, social and ideological factors underlying the British production context and, by looking towards Hollywood as a model, paradoxically supported the domination of British film production by the American industry. The concentration on the formal organisation of the film text itself at the expense of other forms of analysis led to a reinforcement of some of the least productive aspects of the *auteur* theory: the 'good' film as the coherent, non-contradictory expression of the director's personal vision and the task of evaluation given to the perceptive critic whose insights mark them off from the ordinary viewer. However, *Movie*'s championing of the *auteur* theory and popular Hollywood cinema at this point had far-reaching effects on British film criticism, initiating debates which still continue. Its contribution to film education has been considerable; many *Movie* writers were teachers engaged in debate about the status of film studies in schools and universities, concerned to establish film as a serious object of study on a level with other arts such as literature and music. Their support of Hollywood as a cinema of *auteurs* was important to this struggle.

FREE CINEMA AND BRITISH SOCIAL REALISM

The critical tradition against which *Movie* directed its attack (i.e. *Sequence* and *Sight and Sound* critics and the film-makers who emerged from Free Cinema) had also defined itself in opposition to current values in British cinema. Critics such as Lindsay Anderson and Karel Reisz argued in the pages of *Sequence*, and later in *Sight and Sound*, for a 'new' cinema which would discard outmoded artifice in favour of the simplicity and freshness of personal observation of everyday reality. In 1947 Anderson criticised Rossellini's *Paisà* for its lack of personal statement and in 1955 condemned *On the Waterfront* for its flashy excesses of style, for masking its right-wing ideology with a display of technical tricks. In this article Anderson described his view of the artist:

> The directors whom Tony Richardson would be more justified in castigating are surely those false creators with professional talent beyond the ordinary, with heavyweight pretensions, but without equivalent honesty, insight or sensibility who undertake significant subjects only to betray them. It is less a question of 'dominating' one's material than of being truthful about it. (Anderson, 1955, p. 130)

Although as socialists these writers were interested in popular cinema as a means of reaching a large audience, they positioned themselves against the artificiality and stereotypes of Hollywood, which they saw as conformist, in favour of a personal poetic observation of reality, an affectionate look which respected its material enough to avoid distortion. In this approach meaning was an essence which pre-existed the film, brought to life by the director with the minimum of interference. The *Movie* critics argued against this that meaning was inseparable from form (*mise-en-scène*) and that only through close attention to the cinematic language specific to each film could meaning be deduced, constructed after the event.

As co-founders of Free Cinema, Lindsay Anderson, Karel Reisz and Tony Richardson made 'personal' documentaries on 16mm (e.g. *O Dreamland*, Anderson, 1953; *Momma Don't Allow*, Reisz/Richardson, 1955) during the 1950s until the industry opened up to the production of the social realist films of the 1960s. For a brief period they were able to resist the monopoly of large-scale production set-ups in order to maintain artistic autonomy (see Hill, 1979). The Woodfall Group, formed by John Osborne and Tony Richardson in 1958 to make a film of the successful stage play by Osborne, *Look Back in Anger*, was criticised in *Movie* for its commitment to a social realism which put lofty themes before a feeling for cinema (see Perkins, 1972).

As Alan Lovell points out, the Free Cinema/*Sequence* current emerged out of specific social and historical factors and disappeared for similar reasons:

> The impact was not a sustained one. Under the pressure of a situation that neither its aesthetic nor its economic and social analysis of the cinema could properly cope with, the Free Cinema/*Sequence* position was modified into one simplified diagram of the cinema, a mixture of Marxist and liberal attitudes – art is personal expression, personal expression is extremely difficult with a capitalist economic system, the artist's position is a very difficult one in our society. (Lovell, 1972, p. 158)

When the Free Cinema/*Sequence* film-makers moved into the feature-film industry in the 1960s they took with them this combination of 'personal expression' and the need for a sense of social responsibility. Their unwillingness to compromise may account for the small number of films they actually made and the fact that those films now seem to belong to a particular moment in British film culture. It could be argued that *Movie*'s attack on British social realist films of the 1960s and on British film culture in general for its lack of style and *auteurs* fails to analyse its historical context. The very absence that *Movie* deplored has opened the way to critical investigation of British film history which reconstructs it in other terms than those which demand the presence of *auteurs* as a criterion of value (see British cinema: *auteur* and studio, p. 276).

Lindsay Anderson

Although Lindsay Anderson is acknowledged to be one of the most active and influential of British film directors he has directed few feature films since the late 1960s which makes it difficult to establish him as a cinema *auteur*. Anderson's *œuvre* covers his critical writings for *Sequence* and *Sight and Sound*, sponsored promotional films, work in the theatre as producer, director and actor, television commercials and films made with the Free Cinema movement, besides his feature films (see Lovell and Hillier, 1972). Conventionally, *auteur* theory would look for a consistent world-view across all this work and indeed it would be possible to detect a continuity of thematic and stylistic concerns (i.e. a committed left-wing view of British society and an interest in questions of artistic forms). However, those concerns have made it difficult for Anderson to work consistently within the British film industry, which has only periodically been open to aesthetic innovation, and those feature films he has made often seem confused and contradictory rather than homogeneous. Lovell argues that in the context of an entrenched bias towards realism in British cinema the production of non-naturalistic films within the British feature film industry constitutes a major achievement and this is perhaps the most productive way to understand the significance of Anderson's work (see Lovell, 1975/76).

As one of the most active members of the Free Cinema movement, Anderson argued for the freedom of the film-maker to make personal statements through his or her films, that those statements should act as a commentary on contemporary society and should reflect the commitment of the film-maker to certain basic values for which he or she should be prepared to fight. Anderson's 'basic values' might be described as a kind of militant liberal humanism which saw the weaknesses of liberalism in its lack of commitment rather than in its theoretical or political position.

The aesthetics of Free Cinema were basically those of documentary reportage; however, it is arguable that they were never simply documentary. The use of sound–image disjunctions in Anderson's *O Dreamland* (1953) is an example of the way that the documentary mode was often transformed into personal commentary. Although the documentary strand of Free Cinema seems to feed directly into British social realism, the 'freedom of personal expression' strand did not and many of the Free Cinema directors, including Anderson, who moved into the industry found themselves at odds with it. Anderson's interest in surrealism and in broadly Brechtian ideas taken from British theatre can be seen in all

Public school life in *If . . .*

The Entertainer – 'promotion for home-grown British produce'

his feature films and could be said to differentiate them from 'mainstream' British social realism. Those interests are perhaps most clearly identifiable in *If* . . . (1968) and *O Lucky Man!* (1973), albeit in a sometimes confused and contradictory way.

Tony Richardson

A co-founder of the Free Cinema movement, Richardson was active in radical theatre, especially as a producer, and worked with John Osborne to produce *Look Back in Anger*, *The Entertainer* and *Luther*. When the British film industry opened up temporarily in the late 1950s his theatrical experience and film-making experience in Free Cinema made it possible for him to move into feature-film production in 1958 under his own production banner – Woodfall Films (see British social realism 1959–63, p. 00).

In their polemic for recognition of the great *auteurs* of Hollywood cinema *Movie* critics attacked what they called 'the Woodfall answer' to the stalemate situation in the British film industry for its lack of cinematic flair and imagination (Perkins, 1972). Indeed, at first glance the films produced by Woodfall do seem constricted by their origins in the contemporary British theatre and novel, and by an over-earnest commitment to social realist themes. However, in the context of the project of Free Cinema they display significant differences from the rest of the British social realist films of the period. It is debatable whether Richardson manages to produce a personal statement through his films in the way that Anderson and Reisz have, but his films are interesting for the way they indicate the interrelationship between film and the other arts in Britain at this period.

Karel Reisz

Reisz co-directed *Momma Don't Allow* (1955) with Tony Richardson and made *We Are the Lambeth Boys* (1959) both as part of the Free Cinema project; and the concerns expressed in these films can be detected in his first feature film *Saturday Night and Sunday Morning* (1960) although somewhat transformed by the context of British social realism.

In an interview published in *Cinéma International* in 1967, Reisz described his style:

Rebelling against bourgeois society – *Morgan, a Suitable Case for Treatment*

> The style in which you make a film reflects faithfully what you have to say; there are no two ways of saying the same thing. The way you hold the camera reveals exactly what you have chosen to reveal. In my case, it's a question of filming based much more on observation than on abstraction. This implies a tendency to use the camera in the most simple way; I want the people in front of the camera to feel very free in their movements, instead of having to change places for the camera, that is in terms of the camera. (p. 690)

This formulation echoes the polemical writing of Lindsay Anderson and the commitment of the Free Cinema film-makers to personal observation, social commitment and sincerity of style. In terms of theme,

LINDSAY ANDERSON

If . . . (UK 1968 *p.c* – Memorial Enterprises; *d* – Lindsay Anderson; sd b/w and col.)

Co-produced and directed by Anderson, the film is interesting both in the context of Anderson's work as an explicit, if not entirely coherent, expression of his personal concerns and as a break with the naturalism of British social realism.

The film combines fantasy and social satire in a critique of public school life and mores and was explicitly influenced by Jean Vigo's *Zéro de conduite*. Anderson admired Vigo, Humphrey Jennings and John Ford as personal film-makers who combined their own concerns with a sincerity and honesty of style.

The film was made in colour and black-and-white and although this was primarily due to economic pressures it works to add greater stylisation to the film, which is concerned with the power of the imagination and its place in political action. It could be argued that the effect of this stylisation is to give the spectator a critical distance on the events in the film, denying the pleasure of identification in favour of a more intellectual perception. The influence of surrealism on the film, represents Anderson's interest in repressed desires and their return in the form of destructive fantasies, and in the role of fantasy in political action.

TONY RICHARDSON

The Entertainer (UK 1960 *p.c* – Woodfall/Hollis; *d* – Tony Richardson; sd b/w)

The presence of John Osborne as scriptwriter and Laurence Olivier heading the cast in this film adaptation of Osborne's stage success is an indication of the cross-fertilisation process between theatre and cinema which was prevalent in many British films of this period. This process, plus the social–realist project of taking social questions seriously, added prestige to film production and caused it to be seen as art in contrast to television and popular American cinema. Indeed, the films could be seen as promotion for home-grown British produce as opposed to Hollywood fare as well as a polemic for the necessary social commitment of the artist.

The theme of the film, carried over from John Osborne's play, evokes the moral decay of Britain against the background of the deterioration of the popular art of music hall, and asks where social criticism might come from in the future. It is not simply an adaptation of the play, however, but tries to raise questions about the critical function of art in the context of cinema too.

In terms of the *auteur* theory it stands as an example of the British films *Movie* critics were arguing against (i.e. a 'quality cinema' of serious social themes lacking true *auteurs*).

A Taste of Honey (UK 1961 *p.c* – Woodfall; *d* – Tony Richardson; sd b/w)

Again an adaptation (of Shelagh Delaney's stage play), produced, directed and co-scripted by Richardson for his own company Woodfall Films, this film is an interesting contrast to *The Entertainer* because it was shot entirely on location and therefore looks less theatrical.

In the context of British social realism the film seems to fall into the category (or genre) 'youth movie' and is interesting for its use of a female protagonist as the youthful alienated heroine and its concern with the problems of female and homosexual sexuality in the context of the family. In terms of Richardson's roots in Free Cinema the film approaches the freer sexual mores of the 1960s through its working-class protagonists, who are mostly depicted as comic–grotesque, except perhaps for the heroine and her black boyfriend. Free Cinema was concerned with reconstructing the working-class 'ethnographically'; however, this was from the point of view of the middle-class intellectual film-maker whose personal statement and social commitment were embodied in the film. In this film the element of personal statement is less easily identifiable with the result that social criticism is subordinated to the realist project of confirming for the audience what it already knows to be true.

KAREL REISZ

Saturday Night and Sunday Morning (UK 1960 *p.c* – Woodfall; *d* – Karel Reisz; sd b/w)

Adapted from the novel by Alan Sillitoe and scripted by him, this film marks an important moment in Reisz's career, since it was an unprecedented box-office success. Reisz respected the principles of Free Cinema in attempting to reconstruct with maximum authenticity and minimum distortion the daily life of a young working-class man in conflict with his provincial background. However, the film departed from Free Cinema in its use of the strategies of narrative fiction to 'get inside' the psychology of its central protagonist.

'In *We are the Lambeth Boys* I had tried to analyse only the relationship of some adolescents to society. The documentary form imposed limits on me and it was difficult to show the personal ties binding a boy to his mother, to his fiancée, to his friends. By contrast, the fiction film allowed me to do this and, through the characters in Alan Sillitoe's book, I discovered what might have been the private life of these "Lambeth Boys" ' (quoted in Lefèvre and Lacourbe, 1976, p. 279).

As an example of British social realism this film belongs to the 'youth problem' genre prevalent in the 1950s and 1960s; Albert Finney's portrayal of a rebel anti-hero, engaged at times with his society yet alienated from it, has often been taken to account for the success of the film (see British social realism 1959–63, p. 88).

Reisz's concerns can be seen in the treatment of Arthur's critical view of his society. The working-class male protagonist, whose problems are represented in sexual as much as class terms, is set against a provincial industrial background which he seeks to escape because of its narrow restrictive moral codes, recalling Free Cinema's middle-class view of working-class life: Arthur's virility is closely linked to his desire to change the conditions of his existence.

Morgan, a Suitable Case for Treatment
(UK 1966 *p.c* – Quintra; *d* – Karel Reisz; sd b/w)

This film began as a TV play: another example of the close relationship between film and other media in British cinema at this time. Although Reisz has moved away from his background in Free Cinema an element of social criticism remains: Morgan's 'madness' enables him to see what is wrong with the world.

The film illustrates the kind of dramatic situation that John Osborne's *Look Back in Anger* introduced into English drama – the young male protagonist whose rebellion against bourgeois society pushes him towards madness. In terms of Reisz's work, there is a development away from the social–realist format of *Saturday Night and Sunday Morning* towards fantasy and surrealism. The sexuality of the hero is a continuing theme; however, his sexual competence is in question here. Morgan's impotence is in sharp contrast to the virility of Arthur, the working-class rebel hero of *Saturday Night and Sunday Morning*, though ultimately they are both depicted as victims of their society.

Reisz's later films, such as *Morgan, a Suitable Case for Treatment* (1966) and *Isadora* (1968), show a preoccupation with unconventional individuals, often artists or intellectuals, at odds with a restricted and unsympathetic society. It is difficult to see a direct connection with Free Cinema here. Although Reisz shared the basic principles of Free Cinema, it is arguable that his personal concerns moved away from those principles in a way that Anderson's, for instance, did not.

Selected Reading

Alan Lovell, *The British Cinema: The Unknown Cinema*, London, BFI Education Dept Seminar Paper, 1969.

Robert Murphy (ed.), *The British Cinema Book*, London, BFI, 1997.

Sam Rohdie, 'Review: *Movie Reader, Film as Film*', *Screen* 13(4), winter 1972/73.

MOVIE AND *MISE-EN-SCÈNE* ANALYSIS

Although each *Movie* critic writes about film from a different perspective (see Perkins, 1972/73) they share an approach to film criticism which can be traced back to a British tradition of literary criticism, best exemplified perhaps by the journal *Scrutiny*, especially contributors such as F. R. Leavis, L. C. Knights and Denys Thompson, and the debate about the value of mass culture in which it was engaged (see Filmer, 1969). The 'popular culture debate' hinged upon an opposition between traditional high art and popular mass culture. For some critics, the former was capable of providing moral insights for the perceptive reader, while the latter, because it was mass produced for the entertainment of a passive popular audience, could do no more than reproduce the status quo. Cinema, as part of the mass media, was thought to preclude the possibility of individual statements because of its industrial mode of production and was placed in the category of popular culture (see Collins, 1981). During the early 1960s left-wing critics began to question the inferior status given to the mass media, arguing that it was not a monolithic phenomenon and that it offered the possibility of reaching a mass audience in a way that high art, which was only available to a privileged minority, did not. As a result of this debate, Hollywood, the mass cinema *par excellence*, began to be reassessed. The *auteur* theory, which insisted that statements from individual directors were possible even in the Hollywood system of commodity production, performed an important function at this point in the attempt to break down resistance to mass art. At the same time, methods of film analysis were carried over from the literary criticism tradition. This tradition emphasised the 'organic' relationship of form to content and close analysis of the text as a means of discovering the themes and values embedded in it.

Movie's approach, based on detailed attention to form, merged quite well with that strand of the *Cahiers' politique* which saw analysis of *mise-en-scène* as a way of discovering an author's themes or moral values. Some confusion exists about the term *mise-en-scène* in film criticism, partly because it is imported from theatre and partly because of its collapse into *auteur* theory, where it came to mean 'style' or 'formal conventions'. Strictly speaking, *mise-en-scène* refers to the practice of stage direction in the theatre in which things are 'put into the scene', i.e. arranged on the stage (see Bordwell and Thompson, 1979, p. 75). When applied to film, it refers to whatever appears in the film frame, including those aspects that overlap with the art of the theatre: setting, lighting, costume and the behaviour of the figures. By this definition the term does not include specifically cinematographic qualities such as photographic elements, framing and length of shot, camera position, and movement, or editing. In formal analysis of film, then, *mise-en-scène* analysis is only one important area demanding attention. By extension from theatre to cinema, the term has come to mean the director's control over what appears in the frame, the way the director stages the event for the camera. *Cahiers du Cinéma* took this a stage further by making an evaluative distinction between *auteur* and *metteur-en-scène* in which the latter would be concerned simply with the craft of staging events for the camera rather than with organising the whole film according to a personal vision (see The *auteur* theory, p. 240).

While *Movie* critics subscribed to the *auteur* theory as an evaluative method, their concept of *mise-en-scène* was broader than *Cahiers*' and referred to the overall formal organisation of films, their 'style'. *Movie*'s brand of *mise-en-scène* analysis is based on a deductive method whereby detailed description of films is seen to be the basis for criticism, a method which sees film criticism as a practical activity rather than as a theoretical project. *Movie*'s attachment to this form of *mise-en-scène* analysis and *auteur* theory at the expense of other approaches seems to have led it into a critical impasse. By virtue of its own criteria of value (i.e. criteria of classicism, such as the 'organic unity' of a given film or body of films) it was forced to resist the impact of historical change, whether this was manifested in new film-making practices which did not embody classical unity and coherence or in new critical theories, e.g. Godard, or Soviet cinema (see the exchange of views between the *Movie* critics in Cameron, 1972, p. 19, and in 'The return of movie', *Movie* no. 20, spring 1975, p. 1). Indeed, it could be argued that the combination of a deductive empirical method and *auteur* analysis cut many *Movie* writers off from engaging with more general political and ideological questions.

One of the oldest debates in film criticism is between the advocates of the art of *mise-en-scène* (see Bazin, p. 337) and the advocates of the art of editing (e.g. Eisenstein, p. 319) a debate which has tended to polarise issues rather than open up discussion of the inter-relationship between the two methods of

JOSEPH LOSEY

The Criminal (UK 1960 *p.c* – Merton Park Studios; *d* – Joseph Losey; sd b/w)

Losey's career began in American radical theatre in the 1930s. His work as a theatre director was influenced by Russian theatre and by the theory and practice of Piscator and of Brecht with the Berliner Ensemble, about which he wrote several articles. He collaborated closely with Brecht on a theatre production of *Galileo Galilei* just before directing his first feature film *The Boy With Green Hair* in 1947 and has acknowledged the Brechtian influence not only on this film but on his work in general.

Losey's cinema is primarily intellectual. In an interview in *Image et Son* no. 202 he described his wish to stimulate thought in the audience (p. 21) through the use of an abstract *mise-en-scène* which encourages critical distance rather than emotional involvement and identification with characters (p. 25). In the context of Brecht's ideas, the 'cerebral' quality that Charles Barr objects to in *King and Country* can be seen to form the basis of Losey's work. Barr's resistance to the 'alienation effect' is perceptive and perhaps symptomatic of a critical approach which distrusts any signs of formal excess which might disturb the balance of form and content.

Because of his left-wing views Losey was blacklisted by the House Un-American Activities Committee and came to England in 1951, where he had some difficulty at first in finding work because of restrictions on the number of foreign directors allowed to work in Britain (see Roud, 1979). After completing several low-budget productions in between directing commercials for television, he had a success with *Blind Date* (1959) which led to a larger budget for *The Criminal* (1960), a story about prison life and organised crime which attracted Losey because he saw a parallel between the rigid criminal code and the organisation of big business. The film was not a success in Britain, but when it opened in Paris in 1961 French critics acclaimed the film as a masterpiece and Losey as a great director. It was largely due to the support of the French critics that Losey's reputation as an international *auteur* was established, making it possible for him to gain a measure of artistic control over his projects.

The Damned (UK 1961 *p.c* – Hammer/ Swallow; *d* – Joseph Losey; sd b/w scope)

The expatriate Losey worked for Hammer Studios on this science fiction film: an

Losey links a rigid criminal code with big business in *The Criminal*

unlikely partnership which resulted in one of the most pessimistic of all Hammer's postwar science fiction films, revolving around an insane government plot to preserve contaminated children from the outside world and a woman-hating teenage gang leader who stumbles on the results.

The Damned is staple Hammer diet: sensational science fiction full of violence, but it also manifests Losey's characteristic use of *mise-en-scène* and his political concerns. Some of Losey's preoccupations can be seen in the parallel drawn between the obsessional government scientist, Bernard, and the mindless violence of gang leader, King, and in the opposition drawn between Bernard the scientist, preoccupied with death, and Freya the artist, dedicated to life. The use of the innocent but deadly children to represent the contradictions between absolute purity (non-contamination) and the corruption of the system which has brought them into being is reminiscent of Losey's first film *The Boy With Green Hair* (1948).

Eva (Eve) (France/Italy 1962 *p.c* – Paris Film/Interopa Film; *d* – Joseph Losey; sd b/w)

The critical success of *The Criminal* in France established Losey's artistic reputation and caused Jeanne Moreau to suggest his name as a director of *Eva*. The production laboured under constant difficulties: disagreements between Losey and the producers over the script, Moreau and Losey both ill, the producers pushing Losey to complete the film. The music Losey wanted (Miles Davis and Billie Holliday) was unobtainable and the producers forced him to cut the film drastically to keep costs low, finally making further cuts without his consent (see Rissient, 1966, pp. 129–30).

In spite of these difficulties, the film is considered to be one of Losey's most important, both in its conception and its theme. Carefully structured in a prologue, three acts and an epilogue, it deals with an impossible relationship between a strong independent woman and a puritanical working-class Welshman who assumes his right to dominate her and is finally destroyed by his obsession. The film contrasts two characters from different societies to point up contradictions in the notion of sexual liberation. The portrayal of Eva by Jeanne Moreau is cold and detached and her 'independence' is established simply by her ability to control her own sexuality and to humiliate Tyrian through it. The interaction of class and sexual struggle in the film is interesting in relation to British films of this period which also attempt to deal with the subject of changing social values.

Accident (UK 1967 *p.c* – Royal Avenue, Chelsea; *d* – Joseph Losey; sd col.)

Losey collaborated with Harold Pinter on the scenario of *The Servant* in 1963, which again took up the themes of sexuality, class and relationships of domination and subordination in the confrontation between master and servant. Pinter's concern with using the suggestive possibilities of language to make apparently normal situations seem strange and full of hidden menace meshed well with Losey's precisely structured *mise-en-scène* to create a nightmarish world of corruption in which the characters are turned in on themselves, obsessed with their own destruction.

Accident, their second collaboration, also deals with a closed world: an academic community, compulsively claustrophobic, in which class and sexual tensions erupt, disturbing the narrative continuity of the film. Discontinuities of time and place in the construction of the film contribute to a 'strangeness' which is intended to alienate the spectator, much as the central protagonists of all Losey's films feel themselves to be alienated, displaced in a world which imposes its rules upon them, destroying their individuality.

The studied formalism of this film, combined with the highly mannered performances from the actors, is typical of Losey's later work. The themes of the closed community with its stifling moral code and of class and sex struggles as destructive and self-defeating recur in all his films. The role of the mysterious Anna as a catalyst, or agent of destruction, takes up the recurring theme of the dangerous, sexually emancipated woman in Losey's work (e.g. Jeanne Moreau in *Eva*, 1962, Monica Vitti in *Modesty Blaise*, 1966, Melina Mercouri in *The Gypsy and the Gentleman*, 1957, Micheline Presle in *Blind Date*, 1959).

construction (see Henderson, 1976). Without collapsing the different positions of the *Movie* critics into the Bazinian world-view, it is possible to trace in some of their arguments a preference for a cinema of *mise-en-scène* untroubled by obtrusive editing or camera movements and a predilection for a classic cinema which eschews blatant formal effects in favour of a style which is adequate or equivalent to content. *Movie*'s pantheon (see Cameron, 1972) is headed by the great classic Hollywood directors, Alfred Hitchcock and Howard Hawks, closely followed by a range of directors whose styles, the overall composition of their films, are seen by *Movie* to be entirely compatible with their themes or values. By this criterion they are judged to be true *auteurs*.

Movie can be credited with initiating a critical debate in Britain about the artistic value of popular cinema; it is however debatable whether its basic critical preconceptions were very different from those of *Sight and Sound* against which it argued; it simply applied these values to a different body of films – Hollywood rather than art cinema. After 1975, however, it attempted to come to terms with the different questions raised for British film criticism by structuralism and semiology and with the contradictions raised for its own critical position by the New Hollywood cinema (New Hollywood, p. 98).

Joseph Losey

Two articles on the films of Joseph Losey in *Movie Reader*, edited by Ian Cameron, 1972, provide different examples of *Movie*'s critical method based on *mise-en-scène* analysis and *auteur* theory.

Paul Mayersberg writing on *The Damned* (1961) starts with a close analysis of the opening sequence of the film, from which he proceeds to deduce Losey's symbolism (themes or values). He supports the analysis by reference to other Losey films in which he traces similar values, then returning to close analysis of *The Damned* to find other themes which in turn he relates to other Losey films, in a constant movement from the particular to the general. Mayersberg points to the importance of *mise-en-scène* as a conveyor of meaning in Losey's work.

> In his use of décor as an element in the construction of his movies Losey has no equal in the cinema. He and [Richard] Macdonald devise a setting that will characterise the person associated with it: the white simplicity of the psychiatrist's room in *The Sleeping Tiger*, the angrily contrasted surface textures of Stanford's flat in *Time Without Pity* conveying the moody violence of the man, the nudes in Bannion's flat [in *The Criminal*] which give the appearances of luxury, but are in reality no more than a grandiose extension of the pin-ups on the walls of the prison cells. (Mayersberg, 'Contamination', 1972, p. 74)

Charles Barr's article ('*King and Country*', 1972, p. 75) also uses close analysis of the film to indicate his dissatisfaction with its 'cerebral' quality, nevertheless acknowledging that its schematic formal beauty articulates with logical precision the hopelessness of its theme. Barr makes reference not only to other Losey films but to other Hollywood films, and to Shakespeare's *King Lear*, to show how *King and Country* differs both from standard British films and from other anti-war films.

Both these approaches move from the specific (the film text) to the general (other film texts), constructing the *auteur*'s personal values from analysis of single films and tending to ignore historical factors like conditions of production, or even the director's known interests and ideas. In the late 1960s some British Marxist structuralist film critics took *Movie* to task for its resistance to general theoretical and political questions and for the emphasis placed on the critic's interpretation of the films rather than on more 'objective' criteria. It could be argued that Mayersberg and Barr evaluate Losey according to their own personal taste and that a more objective approach would have been to place Losey in his historical context. However, it should be remembered that *Movie*'s attempt to validate Losey as a cinema *auteur* was part of their attack on British cinema for its lack of style. Losey had difficulty finding work in Britain after he was blacklisted in America, a fact which *Movie* saw as symptomatic of the stalemate situation in the British film industry at that time.

Otto Preminger

The *Movie* critics' approach to *auteur* analysis generally, but not always, depended upon a form of deductive criticism which *a posteriori* reconstructed the *auteur* by abstracting personal themes and style from the films themselves. This reconstructed *auteur*, in so far as it consisted of meanings inscribed only in the director's *œuvre* and not elsewhere (e.g. in biographies or interviews) bore no necessary resemblance to the actual person who directed the films, although of course it always shared the same name. It was a construction built by the critic and in this sense *Movie*'s *auteur* analysis was different from a more romantic *auterist* approach which celebrates the presence of a visionary artist at the centre of the work. However, the disadvantage of this approach is that it places primary importance on the film itself and the relationship of the critic to it: the film is removed from its historical context and the critic's interpretation is privileged. This interpretation can be challenged by others but in general the subjectivity of the critic remains unquestioned: his or her task is to pass on insights and interpretations to the reader. One way of demonstrating the difference between *Movie*'s critical approach and the approaches the *Movie* critics rejected is to look at examples of these approaches and how they each construct an *auteur*. In the case of Otto Preminger for instance, there are clearly defined differences between the popular myth of the man himself (temperamental, intolerant autocrat – see Crawley, 1980), Preminger's own account of his relationship to the Hollywood film industry (see Pratley, 1971) and *Movie*'s *auteur* analyses of some of his films (see Perkins, 'Why Preminger?', 1972). Each of these accounts represents not only a different way of describing Otto Preminger, but also a different idea of where the truth of the matter (the 'essential' Otto Preminger) is to be found.

An interview article in *Films Illustrated* (January 1980) begins by laying out the myth of Preminger as a tyrant, a myth which it sees perpetuated by the popular press (and Billy Wilder!). In the course of the interview the interviewer comes to know Preminger and his career better, so that by the end he has discovered the 'real' Otto Preminger: a liberal human being quite different from the popular myth. The investigator goes behind the image to find the truth.

The Cinema of Otto Preminger (1971) by Gerald Pratley is also based on interviews. However, its project is one of serious academic criticism, an attempt to evaluate Preminger as a great artist. In this account, Preminger's struggle for independence from the major Hollywood studios is seen as the struggle of the artist for freedom of expression, a freedom which is impossible within the hierarchical organisation of the studio system. Preminger's films are seen as reflections of this struggle for self-expression: because he asserts complete control over every aspect of the film-making process, including distribution, the films remain indisputably his, true reflections of what he wants to express.

The *Movie* critics' approach is different in that they start from the films themselves; nevertheless they reconstruct a 'Preminger' which has something in common with both the above and they are also concerned with finding the 'truth of the matter'. Preminger is a key *Movie auteur* because of his formal restraint, his lucidity, and because his visual style displays an equivalence between form and content characteristic of classic Hollywood cinema. This balance, or harmony between form and content is basic to the detached, liberal world-view which *Movie* ascribes to Preminger.

One of the advantages of looking at different ways of constructing an *auteur* is that it enables us to see that the *auteur* is, precisely, a construction, and that different constructions (different readings) are possible, no one construction bearing the truth in preference to another. While one account taken on its own may tell us quite a lot about a body of films, several accounts used comparatively could tell us more about the films *and* throw light upon the critical preconceptions of the *auteur* theory. Another advantage is that popular forms of critical writing generally considered to be too journalistic for serious academic study can be seen to be equally, if not more, influential on our thinking about films as the academic critical writing with which we are more familiar in studying films.

As with many *auteurs*, Preminger's work is generally divided into two periods: a first period between 1931 and 1952, which covers the single film he directed in Vienna and the stormy years spent as a contract director and producer for 20th Century–Fox, and a second period from 1953 to 1979 which covers his work as an independent producer–director following the consent decree of 1951 (the antitrust laws). In this second period, the mid-1960s saw a decline in Preminger's reputation, only temporarily relieved by *Such Good Friends* (1971). In spite of this unevenness, however, *auteur* analysis looks for consistency in Preminger's *œuvre*, whether this can be defined heroically in terms of a constant and dedicated struggle by Preminger the man against all forms of censorship, or in terms of a consistent moral attitude discernible in the films themselves.

Elia Kazan

Movie 19 (winter 1971/72) is devoted to a study of Kazan's career and provides an interesting introduction to his work which consists of a lengthy interview and extensive bio-filmography as well as detailed critical analysis of several films.

One reason why this detailed knowledge of the man, his background and ideas should be seen to be important in this case could be the assertively personal quality of Kazan's films and the extent to which they seem to manifest the changing concerns and attitudes of a man clearly caught up in, and acutely aware of changing historical circumstances. There is a strong autobiographical thread in Kazan's work: unlike Preminger, he cannot be said to have a 'detached' view of the world; like Losey, he is aware of the need to formulate a political position and engage the audience in critical activity. He differs from both of them in that he inscribes himself, as a human being rather than as an artist, across his work. This aggressive self-display has caused some English critics to distrust his films, seeing in its 'flashy excesses of style' (see Anderson, 1955), an overemphasis on the individual's role in history, or a vulgarity of expression (Robin Wood) which betrays the function of the 'true' artist: to educate with restraint, without rhetoric (Wood, 'The Kazan problem', 1971/72).

A different argument might be that it is precisely the unevenness, the emotional excess which characterises Kazan's work which makes it interesting, raising questions about the relationship of art and the artist to society and to politics, and of the individual to history.

Because of his roots in the left-wing radical theatre of 1930s in America, where questions of form and content, of style and politics, of art and society were constantly debated, the influence of social realism, naturalism and agitprop can be seen throughout his films, providing a sometimes uneasy mixture with classic Hollywood narrative cinema; an uneasiness

OTTO PREMINGER

Laura (USA 1944 *p.c* – 20th Century–Fox; *d* – Otto Preminger; sd b/w)

In an interesting article 'From *Laura* to *Angel Face*' Paul Mayersberg (1972, p. 44) argues that Preminger's early films show a preoccupation with certain types of women which can be seen to recur throughout his work. Choosing ten out of the sixteen American films of this period he attempts to show that this preoccupation manifests a continuity which is all the more surprising in that Preminger was not in a position to choose his scripts. What emerges from Mayersberg's investigation of women in Preminger's work is the discovery of a basic moral problem: the status, or value of truth and knowledge in the abstract. His protagonists, believing themselves to be rational and in control of themselves, find that they are in fact at the mercy of events and their own desires. The realisation enables them to change, or, when it does not, the results are often tragic.

This problem is certainly central to *Laura.* Laura herself is an enigmatic figure whose image changes according to the shifting point of view of other characters. The detective, Mark, previously a rational man, finds himself seduced by the enigma and in danger of losing his detached perspective: this almost leads to his death.

Mark is played by Dana Andrews who subsequently often played the role of the apparently detached, rational observer whose world-view is threatened (see *Beyond a Reasonable Doubt*, 1956, *Night of the Demon*, 1957). The representation of woman as enigma in *Laura* is, it could be argued, more central to *film noir* than to

Woman as enigma in Preminger's *Laura*

Preminger's work in general (see *Film noir*, p. 184).

Angel Face (USA 1952 *p.c* – RKO Radio; *d* – Otto Preminger; sd b/w)

Preminger's last film before going independent. He was borrowed from 20th Century–Fox by RKO and, according to him, given considerable freedom by Howard Hughes to do as he wanted on this film.

A good companion piece to *Laura* because of the central relationship between the sceptical male protagonist (Robert Mitchum) and the beautiful but dangerous young woman (Jean Simmons) by whom he is seduced. This type of female character is prevalent in much Hollywood cinema (in thriller, detective and *film noir* genres especially): the duplicitous woman, beautiful on the surface but basically evil and dangerously seductive precisely because of this double-edged quality (see Kaplan, 1978). In the context of Preminger's work, the duplicitous woman threatens to make the male lose his rational perspective. (See, however, *Such Good Friends*, 1971, in which this relationship is reversed.)

River of No Return (USA 1954 *p.c* – 20th Century–Fox; *d* – Otto Preminger; sd col.)

The move to independent production gave Preminger control over the entire production process.

> Being an independent producer indicates a change which I am convinced will go much further than it has so far, which developed during the last few years, the change from mass production by major studios to individual productions. Today, independent producers (like myself, Kazan, Wallis, Kramer) produce a picture like we produce plays on Broadway, which means selecting a subject, having a screenplay written, casting it, being autonomous; it is the individual's authority and his responsibility. He stands and falls with the success of this one picture. There is no supervision from any front office, there are no alibis that we used to have. (Preminger, 1956, quoted in Pratley, 1971, p. 97)

However, *River of No Return* was made for 20th Century–Fox, to whom Preminger owed several films under his contract. It provided him with the opportunity to use the new CinemaScope lenses and the widescreen format adapted well to his preference for a *mise en-scène* which employed long takes rather than abrupt cuts. For Preminger, CinemaScope and long takes allowed the audience to contemplate the scene, whereas cutting disturbed them. This view of the potential of CinemaScope is to some extent shared and developed by V. F. Perkins (1972) and Charles Barr (1974) and is relevant to the kinds of *mise-en-scène* analysis employed by *Movie* critics.

Preminger's 'objectivity' might be seen in the opposition between two different ways of life, represented in the struggle between Robert Mitchum and Marilyn Monroe (uncompromising moral rectitude versus moral pragmatism). This struggle is resolved in favour of Robert Mitchum, raising the question of how far 'objectivity' is possible in classic narrative cinema, where the narrative ending works to resolve opposing views.

Carmen Jones (USA 1954 *p.c* – 20th Century–Fox; *d* – Otto Preminger; sd col. scope)

As an independent producer Preminger developed a reputation for dealing with 'controversial' subjects: sexuality (e.g. *Bonjour Tristesse*, 1957), race (e.g. *Carmen Jones, Porgy and Bess*, 1959) and drugs (*The Man with the Golden Arm*, 1955) some of which led to battles with the censorship bodies of the American film industry. *Carmen Jones*, however, although it figures an all-black cast, is not in itself about race. It belongs to an interesting and little-investigated American genre: the black musical (cf. *Cabin in the Sky*, 1943).

As Paul Mayersberg points out ('Carmen and Bess', 1972) the film is primarily concerned with the theme of freedom, one of Preminger's preoccupations, exemplified by the tension between anarchic freedom and military rigidity. The musical film is particularly adept at articulating 'utopian' themes of freedom and self-expression, and Preminger says of this film:

> This was really a fantasy, as was *Porgy and Bess*.The all-black world shown in these films doesn't exist, at least not in the United States. We used the musical–fantasy quality to convey something of the needs and aspirations of coloured people. Later, I moved into objective reality with *Hurry Sundown*. (quoted in Pratley, 1971, p. 11)

Anatomy of a Murder (USA 1959 *p.c* – Columbia; *d* – Otto Preminger; sd b/w)

In the context of Preminger's *oeuvre*, this film is interesting for its return to the theme of *Laura*: the central protagonist, a lawyer (James Stewart), finds himself involved in a situation in which the 'truth' is very hard to establish and is in this film called into question by the narrative resolution. The jury finds Lieutenant Mannion (Ben Gazzara) not guilty, but the truth of the matter remains undecided, and the lawyer finds himself 'hoist by his own petard' when his clients disappear without paying his fee.

The film is interesting in the context of Preminger's work because the enigma revolves around the female protagonist (Lee Remick) and the question of whether or not she was raped. Her guilt or innocence is central to the narrative and remains undecided (cf. *Laura*).

The credits for the film are also interesting because they are designed by Saul Bass, one of the most famous of Hollywood's graphic designers, who collaborated with Preminger on many of his independent productions. The contribution of credit sequences is usually overlooked in film analysis, although they can play a large part in 'setting the scene' for the audience.

ELIA KAZAN

A Streetcar Named Desire (USA 1951 *p.c* – Group Productions; *d* – Elia Kazan; sd b/w)

An example of Kazan's collaboration with Tennessee Williams: he directed two movies from Williams's plays (*A Streetcar Named Desire* and *Baby Doll*) and directed several for the stage throughout the 1950s. It was independently produced, and manifests Kazan's roots in radical theatre. The ideas about acting which emerged from the Actors' Studio, co-founded by Kazan in 1948, can be seen in Brando's performance as Stanley, which is given value because of its directness and immediacy in relation to the mannered, 'dishonest' acting style of Vivien Leigh (Blanche). A conflict, or tension is set up between 'honesty' (realism) and 'hypocrisy' (artifice), a tension which can be seen throughout Kazan's work. In this particular case Kazan's populist politics can be identified in the value placed upon Stanley's virile working-class persona: his violence seems to be justified in the face of Blanche's social pretensions. The extreme 'femininity' of Vivien Leigh's performance has the effect of feminising, and (in this film) devaluing the middle class. One way of approaching the film is in terms of the way that race, class and sexuality interact to reinforce certain class positions and identifications for the audience, and the contribution of acting, gesture and *mise en-scène* to this process. How, for instance, does the power of Brando's performance affect the way the audience views the sadism and brutality of the Stanley Kowalski character and mitigate our response to Blanche as his victim? Is it conceivable that the sexual and racial roles could be reversed? The problem of Kazan's 'excessive' style raised by some *Movie* critics could be discussed in terms of the director's intentions to disturb, or move his audience.

The revolutionary figure with whom Kazan identified – *Viva Zapata!*

Viva Zapata! (USA 1952 *p.c* – 20th Century–Fox; *d* – Elia Kazan; sd b/w)

In 1951–2 Kazan became directly involved in the proceedings of the House Un-American Activities Committee by giving testimony to the Committee against some of his colleagues, and critics have seen a direct relationship between these events and the films Kazan went on to make in the 1950s. Certainly Kazan has characterised his own position as antagonistic to any party line and in favour of intellectual freedom, while still retaining his left-wing sympathies, and insists that the films he made during and after his testimony were more explicitly left-wing.

Kazan worked closely with John Steinbeck on the script; they were both interested in the revolutionary figure of Zapata, and Kazan seems to have identified with him directly:

> the figure of Zapata was particularly attractive to me, because after he got all

> the power that comes with triumph, he didn't know what to do with it or where to put it or where to exert it. He felt about things as I was beginning to feel about my own situation. So all these three things – the fact that he was extremely colourful and interesting, the fact that he represented a left position that was anti-authoritarian, and the fact that in some way he related to my life story, at that point in my life – were reasons why I became so interested in the subject. (quoted in Ciment, 1974, p. 89)

Of note is the way Kazan uses the crosscutting editing technique basic to Hollywood narrative cinema, combined with music, to create intense excitement, involving the spectator in a process of identification with Zapata and his peasant supporters. Comparison with *A Streetcar Named Desire* raises the question of Kazan's manipulation of audience response through editing and *mise-en-scène.*

On the Waterfront (USA 1954 *p.c* – Horizon/Columbia; *d* – Elia Kazan; sd b/w)

After Darryl F. Zanuck cut *Man on a Tightrope* (1953) without his permission, Kazan insisted on cutting rights on this film and following its success he became an independent producer with absolute rights on all his projects.

The central theme of individual conscience and social responsibility has been seen as an attempt by Kazan to re-establish his political integrity after giving evidence to the House Un-American Activities Committee: Kazan characterises all his films of this period as emerging from a desire to question himself and the world around him. Indeed, the narrative of *On the Waterfront* arguably revolves around the idea of the difficulty of taking up political positions. Lindsay Anderson (1955) is one critic who sees the ending of the film as validating right-wing individualist politics, a view which perhaps fails to take the whole film into account. Nevertheless, a problem remains with the use of narrative and a central heroic figure to raise political questions: a problem which runs through much of Kazan's work. Terry Malloy is the central charismatic character with whom the audience is intended to identify, rejecting with him the other available positions offered by the other characters (or, indeed, any which might not be offered). The extent to which Brando's performance strengthens this identification, overcoming any questions we may have about the film's political stance, is an interesting point for discussion. In relation to *A Streetcar Named Desire*, for instance, there are important differences between Stanley Kowalski, characterised as essentially masculine and embodying a virile immigrant strength which arguably represents the New America, and Terry Malloy, a character who exists precisely in order to question those values, but finds himself unable to discard them completely, since he must 'become a man'.

The relationship between Terry and Edie Doyle (Eva Marie Saint) represents the problem posed in sexual terms: the softness and passivity embodied in Edie (her 'feminine' virtues) are also to be found in Terry (he is a sexually ambivalent character in this respect). These 'feminine' qualities of caring and tenderness are to some extent validated by the film, as is illustrated by the meeting between Terry and Edie in the bar. However, they are qualities associated with passivity, and Edie rejects them in Terry because the political struggle against the union bosses requires 'masculine' toughness. To a certain extent she also rejects her own traditionally 'feminine' role by becoming more politically active after the death of her brother. Terry is required to 'become a man' in the struggle for freedom, and the extent to which political struggle is identified with 'masculine' qualities, particularly in this film, but also in Kazan's work in general, is an interesting issue.

Baby Doll (USA 1956 *p.c* – Newtown Productions; *d* – Elia Kazan; sd b/w)

This is Kazan's other filmed version of a Tennessee Williams play and is interesting as an early example of a more explicit expression of sexuality on the screen which emerged in America during the late 1950s and the 1960s. In spite of pressure from the Catholic Legion of Decency, Kazan refused to make any changes and persuaded Warner Bros. that the notoriety would help to sell the picture. The gigantic sign which advertised the film, showing Carroll Baker in a crib sucking her thumb, is now legendary (Censorship, p. 7).

Kazan shared Williams's obsession with the crumbling way of life in the South and with the idea of the virile immigrant–outsider who acts as a force for change and rejuvenation. Kazan wanted Brando to play this role, but he refused. Characteristically, the political questions are represented in terms of sexual problems: Archie Lee's inability to fulfil his side of the marriage agreement in material terms is explicitly linked with his sexual frustration and Baby Doll's arrested development.

Baby Doll is the first of Kazan's films in which blacks from time to time act as a chorus, commenting on the whites' behaviour (see also *A Face in the Crowd*, 1957, *Wild River*, 1960). However, Kazan has said that he intended to portray the bigoted white Southerners sympathetically (if comically) in this film and sees it as the beginnings of a more liberal position in his work.

In terms of *mise-en-scène*, the opposition white–black is striking and was intended to represent symbolically the death of the old South in the face of new blood: the immigrants and the blacks. White is associated with femininity and weakness, black with masculinity and strength (see interview with Kazan, *Movie* no. 19, p. 9).

The use of the opposition between blonde woman and dark man can be compared with its use in other Kazan films (Eva Marie Saint versus Marlon Brando in *On the Waterfront*, Lee Remick versus Montgomery Clift in *Wild River*). Kazan's complex version of the dumb-blonde stereotype is embodied in the performance of Carroll Baker as *Baby Doll*: arrested sexual development combined with material acquisitiveness. At the same time she has much in common with other Kazan heroes, in particular those represented by Marlon Brando and James Dean, a continuity underlined by the similarity of their acting styles emerging from the Method acting developed by the Actors' Studio.

A Face in the Crowd (USA 1957 *p.c* – Newtown Productions; *d* – Elia Kazan; sd b/w)

Kazan worked closely with writer Budd Schulberg on the script which was adapted from a Schulberg short story. The film is a mixture of authentic realism (in the location scenes, the choice of some Nashville natives as actors and in the journalistic format) and psychological fantasy in its portrayal of Lonesome Rhodes's tragic downfall.

In the context of Kazan's work, the film illustrates the portrayal of the left-wing intellectual (played by Walter Matthau) as basically impotent, the relationship between personal relationships and political beliefs (i.e. the perverse attraction between Marcia and Lonesome Rhodes) and the distinction drawn between surface appearances and underlying reality, here played out in the tension between what the public sees and what goes on behind the scenes. The theatrical metaphor is apt, given Kazan's background in the theatre and his interest in Method acting as a style most suitable for directly and truthfully expressing the character's innermost feelings.

Wild River (USA 1960 *p.c* – 20th Century–Fox; *d* – Elia Kazan; sd col.)

The film which perhaps shows most clearly Kazan's debt to John Ford in its humanising of political questions, its nostalgia for those values inevitably threatened by progress and its lyrical approach to its subject.

Kazan had been fascinated by Roosevelt's New Deal policies, particularly

Kazan humanising political questions – *Wild River*

in the context of the Tennessee Valley Authority, where he spent a lot of time when he was a Communist in the 1930s: he describes the film as the story of his love affair with the people of Tennessee and New Deal policies (see Ciment, 1974).

The basic conflicts in the film are between city and country, intellectual and uneducated, bureaucracy and traditional values, manifested in the relationship between the southern Garth family and the Tennessee Valley Authority Agent (Montgomery Clift) who tries to move them off their island, becoming deeply involved with them in the process.

The central relationship between Carol (Lee Remick) and Chuck (Montgomery Clift) evolves around the river, and the film raises issues about the use of the woman to represent 'the natural', the qualities which the intellectual bureaucrat feels he is lacking, to which he is attracted, but of which he is also afraid, because he must prove himself as a man (cf. *On the Waterfront*). The *mise-en-scène* depends on widescreen and long takes, which seems to support the validation of 'natural qualities' projected by the film, although Kazan has suggested that the absence of montage editing was forced on him by the aesthetics of the CinemaScope shape and that the style of the film was not intentional (Ciment, 1974, p. 122).

which it might be productive to explore rather than to dismiss. Similarly, Kazan's growing interest in psychoanalysis and sexuality is often represented as a disturbing force intruding with some violence into a social order which retains its balance precariously. This mixture of politics and sexuality in Kazan's work attracted French critics, as did the acknowledged influence of John Ford (see Tailleur, 1971; Ciment, 1974). The response of English critics, as noted above, has been more ambiguous. Interestingly, the contributors to *Movie 19* are split between those who find his work uneven, lacking balance and restraint (Robin Wood, V. F. Perkins) and those who find this unevenness the symbolic expression of Kazan's world-view (Jim Hillier, Michael Walker).

Selected Reading

Michel Ciment, *Kazan on Kazan*, London, Secker & Warburg/BFI, 1974.

Jim Hillier, '*East of Eden*', *Movie* no. 19, winter 1971/72.

AUTEURS IN BRITISH CINEMA

Carol Reed

The film career of Carol Reed is interesting because it spans thirty-five years of the British film industry, years in which his status as a British *auteur* seemed assured, until his artistic decline in the 1960s. The distinction between *auteur* and *metteur-en-scène* is often invoked in relation to his work, which could be used in comparison with that of Michael Powell, for instance, to open up discussion of authorship in British cinema. Reed's reputation as a distinguished *metteur-en-scène* seems to rest on the evidence of a few films from his total production (Reed directed more than thirty films in many different genres) and a few privileged moments in some films which can be seen to epitomise the 'essence' of his style: the concern with employing cinematic *mise-en-scène* to emphasise social and psychological conflict.

Reed's uncertain status in the history of British cinema might be attributed to specific historical factors rather than to a lack of 'personal vision'. He had close working relationships with writers such as Edgar Wallace and Graham Greene, both of whom profoundly influenced his career and whose contributions are arguably more important than Reed's to some films (e.g. *Our Man in Havana*, 1959, an adaptation of Greene's novel).

Michael Powell

> Let us not be afraid to use the words; for us, no doubt remains: the name of Michael Powell deserves a very high place among the greatest directors in the history of cinema. Among the most misunderstood also; for who, today, can cite a reasonable number of films made by the man who dared to sign *Peeping Tom*? And what a prestigious filmography! From the magnificent *The Thief of Bagdad* to the subtle *Black Narcissus*, from the celebrated *The Red Shoes* to the fabulous *The Tales of Hoffmann*, from the spellbinding *Gone to Earth* to the surprising *A Matter of Life and Death*, all works capable of delighting the most fastidious of cinephiles! Twenty-five films mark out this exemplary career given over entirely to the service of an art; twenty-five works, spread out over thirty years, through which Michael Powell proves himself beyond any possible argument as an authentic *auteur*, creator of a personal universe with clearly defined boundaries, always open to artistic innovations as to the most unconventional subjects, capable of making with the same good grace (and the same pleasure) a tale from *A Thousand and One Nights* or a simple propaganda piece commissioned by the British government! (Lefèvre and Lacourbe, 1976, pp. 274–5)

These are the words of two French critics who have championed the cause of Michael Powell: their tone of hyperbolic excess is perhaps a symptom of the need to counteract the general hostility with which Powell's work had until then been received (particularly by British critics). It also points to the limitations of traditional *auteur* theory itself in so far as it fails to account for the fact that the power of these films lies as much in their 'strangeness' in the context of British cinema as in their inherent aesthetic value or in the possibility of attributing them to the personal vision of one man.

British cinema: realism and the 'quality film'

In his article 'Art, Culture and Quality: Terms for a Cinema in the Forties and Seventies' John Ellis traces, through the (often contradictory) discourses of British film critics during the 1940s, the concern to build a national cinema based on the concept of the 'quality' film:

> The quality film has purpose, form, and morality. It is linked to a strong humanist perspective, stressing the importance of international understanding between the various cultures of mankind. Film has a particularly important role in promoting this understanding, through the fiction film of quality. This is a unified construction, harnessing technique to produce a flowing visual narrative which refuses to indulge in overstated emotionality. It is imperative that this film has a close and deep relation to reality, not only reproducing its surface, but touching the very spirit of the real. (Ellis, 1978, p. 34)

Ellis's analysis reveals that while some Powell films were seen by critics to correspond to this definition, others were seen to resist it (see *The Red Shoes*, 1948) while still others were reviled because they engage in a criticism of the basic tenets of the definition (see *A Canterbury Tale*, 1944). The idea of the 'quality' film is found to depend upon the notion of the artist (be it scriptwriter, director or producer) as a central unifying force, dominating the multiple elements at work in the production process to produce a unified construction. If the film fails to conform to this definition, it is judged a 'bad' film, and the artist has failed in his task as defined by the critic.

The ideological function of criticism

A historical analysis of critical writing about the cinema can be used to show how defi-

CAROL REED

The Stars Look Down (UK 1939 *p.c* – Grafton; *d* – Carol Reed; sd b/w)

Carol Reed's cinema career began at a time when the British film industry was gaining strength in the 1930s. He directed for Ealing Studios and for Gainsborough, but also worked independently and later produced and directed his own projects.

The Stars Look Down – pre-war propaganda for nationalisation of the coal industry

In terms of the influences on Reed's work: the 1930s saw the birth of Grierson's documentary cinema, which had some influence on the feature films produced at the time. This film, an adaptation of an A. J. Cronin novel, invites comparison with Griersonian documentary in its representation of class struggle in a small mining community. Graham Greene in a contemporary review compared the film favourably with Pabst's *Kameradschaft* (1931).

In the context of British cinema the film is interesting as pre-war propaganda for the nationalisation of the coal industry and against the dangers of private ownership. The conflict between the two male protagonists, Joe and David, both originally working class, is one of ideas. It is the position of David, who becomes a left-wing intellectual dedicated to the true interests of the miners, which is validated against that of the opportunistic, entrepreneurial Joe (cf. Ealing's *The Proud Valley*, 1939).

The character of Joe (opportunistic working-class man out for himself), is a stereotype which figures strongly in British cinema, calling to mind anti-heroes of the late 1950s and 1960s such as Joe Lampton (*Room at the Top*), Arthur Seaton (*Saturday Night and Sunday Morning*), and Vic Brown (*A Kind of Loving*).

Our Man in Havana (UK 1959 *p.c* – Kingsmead; *d* – Carol Reed; sd b/w scope)

Reed was at the peak of his stylistic achievement with *Odd Man Out* (1947) and went on to make three more films for which he is probably best remembered and which form the basis of his artistic reputation (*The Fallen Idol*, 1948, *The Third Man*, 1949, *Outcast of the Islands*, 1951). This was the period of his fruitful collaboration with novelist Graham Greene and producer Alexander Korda. On the basis of this reputation he was able to move into bigger productions and made *Trapeze* in the US in 1956, for instance, although it is generally recognised that the films he made after 1953 are not 'good' films, that is to say, they lack the mark of a 'true *auteur*'.

The reasons for this 'decline' may lie less with Reed the artist than with changes taking place in the British film industry in the 1950s. The shrinkage of the industry itself under the impact of television led to a small (and temporary) explosion of independent and experimental production whose interests merged with the new cinema of social realism heralded by *Room at the Top* in 1958 and *Look Back in Anger* in 1959 (British social realism 1959–63, p. 88).

Our Man in Havana is interesting in that it was made at this point of historical change in the industry and, in terms of Reed's *œuvre*, marked a return to collaboration with Graham Greene which, together

nitions of authorship and concomitant evaluation of films as 'good' and 'bad', change in relation to different historical contexts. When value judgements are placed in their historical contexts they lose their appearance of truth or finality: instead they can be seen to perform a specific ideological function in relation to the cinema audience at a particular historical moment, defining what is 'good' and what is 'bad' for them. Traditional *auteur* criticism can be seen to perform a similar function (see Lefèvre and Lacourbe above). Michael Powell's films have been met with a variety of contradictory critical responses, from outright condemnation (the case of *Peeping Tom*, 1960, in Britain) to extravagant praise. When these films are seen in conjunction with critical writing about them, their changing status according to historical contexts becomes clear.

A traditional *auteur* analysis of Powell's work is complicated by the fact that many of the films were produced in collaboration with Emeric Pressburger, whom Powell met and worked with at London Films in 1938 and with whom he formed the independent production company, The Archers, in 1942 under the auspices of Rank. An *auteur* study of the work of Michael Powell should distinguish between the Powell–Pressburger films and the others (e.g. the 'Quota Quickies' on which Powell served his apprenticeship), which would raise historical questions about the changing structure of the British film industry, and its effect on the 'Powell *œuvre*'. In this way Michael Powell's work can be used to test some of the basic assumptions of the *auteur* theory: for example, that the *auteur* is the director of the film; or that meaning lies within the film itself, waiting to be found by the discerning critic.

Selected Reading

Ian Christie, *Arrows of Desire*, rev. edn, London, Faber & Faber, 1994.

John Ellis, 'Art, culture and quality: terms for a cinema in the forties and seventies', *Screen* 19(3), autumn 1978; rev. 1996.

BRITISH CINEMA: *AUTEUR* AND STUDIO

Ealing Studios

In his introduction to *Powell, Pressburger and Others*, Ian Christie points out that *auteur* theory has had little to say about British cinema.

> During the last twenty years, there has been a certain symmetry between, on the one hand, the advance of *auteur* analysis as applied to American cinema, with a corresponding lack of attention to the industrial 'base' of Hollywood; and on the other hand, an almost exclusively 'industrial' conception of British cinema in terms of monopoly control, government subsidy and the like, with comparatively little attention paid to *auteurs*. Leaving aside the continued presence of a recognisably Griersonian discourse in British film criticism, the British cinema is constituted as a cinema of producers and production finance. If this seems too sweeping, consider that the only major studies of British cinema to be published within the last five years are two on Ealing Studios, one centring on Hammer and a biography of Alexander Korda. (Christie, 1978, p. 2)

This argument raises some interesting questions. Does *auteur* analysis automatically exclude analysis of the industrial 'base'? Certainly, traditional *auteur* study tends to concentrate on the director as source of meaning at the expense of conditions of production. Conversely, analyses of conditions of production often fail to account for the director's contribution altogether. In the two studies on Ealing Studios mentioned by Christie, Charles Barr's (1977) and John Ellis's (1975), both authors attempt to relate conditions of production to ideological readings of the films, with important consequences for *auteur* analysis. John Ellis traces in detail the nexus of working relationships and methods within the apparently homogeneous group known as 'Ealing', showing how the group's reputation for working together as a team, or 'family' was based on a hierarchical division of labour between 'creative workers' and technicians, with producer Michael Balcon retaining final control. Within

with his own masterly use of CinemaScope, might have proved his salvation had the time and place been different.

MICHAEL POWELL

Peeping Tom (UK 1960 *p.c* – Michael Powell (Theatre); *d* – Michael Powell; sd col.)

Peeping Tom marked the end of Powell's career as a major British film director: significantly, perhaps, it was made at the moment of inauguration of the new wave of social realism in the British cinema of the 1960s (see British social realism 1959–63, p. 88). Powell's work is distinguished by a persistent *anti-realism*, which, at certain historical moments, it has been argued, stood in opposition to the prevailing aesthetic of realism in British film culture, an aesthetic founded on ideological notions of 'quality', 'sensitivity', 'seriousness' and 'good taste' (Ellis, 1978). Powell's films, more often than not, have been seen by critics as violating (by implication criticising) all their most hallowed canons. In the case of *Peeping Tom* they were unanimous as never before: the film went beyond the pale.

Ian Christie has traced the outraged response of contemporary reviewers to the film, arguing that in their blanket rejection of it they accurately pinpointed its transgression, which was to draw attention to those basic mechanisms of cinema which it is the project of realism to efface. Some of these basic mechanisms are: the projection of the home movie to a spectator in a darkened room; the manipulation of the spectator; the disturbing implications of voyeurism implicit in the situation (Christie, 'The scandal of *Peeping Tom*', 1978).

Another useful approach would be to place scenes from the film in conjunction with a range of critical responses which construct the film in different ways, to show historical and ideological shifts in *auteur* analysis.

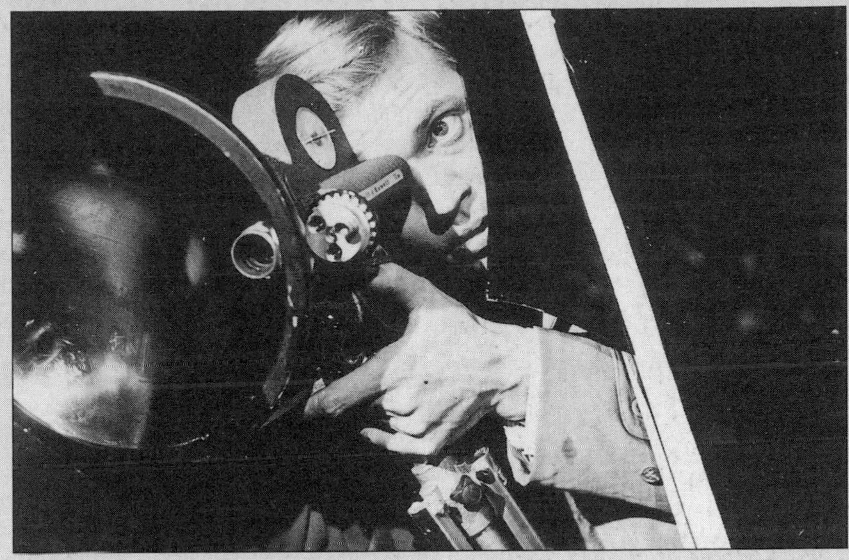

Peeping Tom – the film that went beyond the pale

this framework, members of the 'creative élite' consisting of producers, directors and scriptwriters collaborated in the early stages of pre-production, but Balcon's decisions were final. Robert Hamer, for instance, constantly found his projects vetoed because his concerns were significantly different from those of the studio. At production stage, too, requirements of time, space and money dictated certain shooting methods which produced a particular style of film: short takes and static shots. Some directors (Hamer again, and Mackendrick) who wanted to work differently found this very difficult. Rushes were viewed by the editor in consultation with Balcon rather than with the director, but final editing was done in collaboration with the director, a situation which could lead to conflict, as it did on *Kind Hearts and Coronets* (Ellis, 1975, p. 103).

This historical analysis of the institutional framework within which the film-makers worked reveals the contradictions underlying the prevailing view of the studio as a liberal and democratic working team; by showing how the concerns of some directors were in conflict with the studio's attempt to perpetuate an 'Ealing product' it begins to differentiate between films, arguing that the product cannot be seen as homogeneous. This approach suggests that the organisational structure of Ealing militated against the emergence of *auteurs*, though directors like Hamer and Mackendrick have been given that status in retrospect by critics.

In a later article (1978) John Ellis shows how the formulation by critics of the relationship of 'artist' to film at a particular historical moment (Britain in the 1940s) was both hesitant and contradictory, caught between the project of creating a national 'quality' film in which the director is a central unifying force, and a concept of the director as an individual personality controlling the medium by the force of his or her preoccupations. This hesitancy about the relationship of artist to society, about the extent to which they should be held accountable or should be free to follow their own concerns, can be seen to run through British film culture (as in the cases, for example, of Grierson's documentary movement and Free Cinema). The critics' response to those film-makers who have achieved artistic autonomy through independent production companies (Cineguild and Archers in the 1940s for instance) has been divided between admiration and outrage. Some Powell–Pressburger films positively offended critics because they deliberately opposed the accepted definition of British cinema as 'quality' cinema, founded on notions of realism and good taste.

'Made in Ealing' describes how the hierarchial organisation and system of controls in operation at Ealing Studios under Michael Balcon both supported the project of producing a particular kind of 'quality' film and effectively prevented other, different projects from being realised. Ellis shows that the personal concerns and methods of working of some directors (notably Robert Hamer, but also to a certain extent Alexander Mackendrick and Thorold Dickinson) were generally at variance with the interests of the studio. Charles Barr (1977) argues along similar lines that there is a 'mainstream' Ealing (nonetheless important and interesting for being so) manifested mainly in the films of Basil Dearden and T. E. B. Clarke, and an 'oppositional' Ealing (the films of Robert Hamer and Alexander Mackendrick) which not only shows different concerns from the 'mainstream' but reflects critically upon it. Barr's reading of Hamer and Mackendrick places them in their historical context, showing how they contradict and undermine the Ealing project in general while working within its different genres and stereotypes and how they indirectly reflect upon the frustrations experienced by those film-makers whose interests conflicted with those of the studio. *Auteur* analysis here has the advantage of differentiating between a body of films in such a way as to bring out contradictions, thus challenging dismissive critical accounts which stress the homogeneity of the films produced by Ealing. Barr combines several different forms of reading: ideological, historical and *auteurist*, to build up a complex and fascinating account of the work of Ealing Studios which leads to a reassessment of those films in which *auteur* study plays an important part. Both Ellis and Barr concentrate on the conflicts between directors and studio head Michael Balcon, seeing the 'oppositional' films as a result of that conflict. However, there are other potentially critical voices in the film-making process – that of the writer, for instance. It should be possible to read some Ealing films in terms of multiple conflicting contributions, so that the director is not always seen as the major critical voice.

Robert Hamer

Ellis describes the relationship between Hamer and Ealing studios in terms of Hamer's antipathy to certain of the studio's fundamental values, which made his career there somewhat uneasy:

> His attitude to the studio was one of profound ambivalence: he left after *Kind Hearts and Coronets* to make *The Spider and the Fly* for Rank (edited by Ealing's Seth Holt), but then returned for several years. He existed at the extreme edge of, but still within, the community of ideas and assumptions which the studio held. (Ellis, 1975, p. 95)

The extent to which Hamer was part of the community of ideas and assumptions which the studio supported is open to debate. In a detailed analysis of *Kind Hearts and Coronets* Charles Barr attempts to show the ways in which the film's complex and multi-layered structure works against the form of realism prevalent in the Ealing 'mainstream' to produce meanings which undermine its commonsense humanism and, more than this, inscribe a scenario of frustrated desire which comments both on British society itself and on Ealing's depiction of it. The dispute between Hamer and Balcon over the editing of the trial sequence is usually described in terms of different interests: Balcon wanted to emphasise the class aspects of the scene, Hamer was interested in the sexual aspects. This illustrates another point of conflict between Hamer and Ealing: the studio's attitude towards sexuality is generally recognised to have been repressive, linked to ideas of 'good taste' and 'quality' as hallmarks of British cinema, and to notions of sexuality which place women safely within the family and men in the public, cultural sphere (Ellis, 1975). Hamer is known to have been interested in sexual and psychological themes and Charles Barr makes a good case for his films as forming part of the 'underground current' in British cinema: the cinema of sex and violence which surfaces in the Gainsborough productions of the 1940s and in the films of Powell/Pressburger, burgeoning forth in Hammer productions a decade later.

Alexander Mackendrick

The status of *auteur* conferred upon Hamer and Mackendrick is justified in terms of readings of their films which reveal the tensions they display with all that Ealing represents. However, Ealing itself did not remain the same and the differences of inflection between the films of Hamer and Mackendrick are as much the result of the changing historical situation as of different personal concerns.

Mackendrick was active in Ealing from 1949 onwards; by the early 1950s the self-effacement of the individual in the Ealing community was consolidated and sexuality was more or less excluded from the films. The established order was now to be learned from, rather than questioned (see Barr, 1977). It is against this background that Mackendrick co-wrote and directed *The Man in the White Suit*.

Hammer Productions

The approaches to Ealing Studios outlined above exemplify a form of analysis which attempts to locate films historically in terms of the multiple, often contradictory, elements which contribute to their meanings and so provides one way out of the impasse of traditional *auteur* study, which attributes meaning simply to the assumed intentions of the director. This kind of *conjunctural analysis* acknowledges the director's contribution, although it is not necessarily always the most important or the most helpful in understanding particular films. The conjunctural analyses of Ealing Studios above attempted to show how *auteurs* such as Hamer and Mackendrick emerged from specific conditions of production. The apparent similarities between Ealing and Hammer (see Hammer Productions, p. 85) and the fact that Hammer was born as Ealing died, apparently giving life to that side of British cinema which Ealing 'suppressed' (concerned with psychology, sexuality and violence) suggest that a conjunctural analysis might also be useful in differentiating between the films produced by Hammer.

However, one of the most impressive critical accounts of Hammer, David Pirie (1973), takes a traditional *auteur* approach in which Terence Fisher emerges as the Hammer director *par excellence*, creating his own world-view from basic studio material. Pirie argues that Fisher's romantic vision (which he traces back to pre-Hammer productions) transforms even the most banal low-budget project (e.g. *The Devil Rides Out*, 1967) into a work of 'classic' distinction, making a qualitative difference between Fisher and other directors in much the same way as the *Cahiers* critics, and others, differentiated between *auteurs* and *metteurs-en-scène*.

By all accounts, Hammer directors seem to have had very little personal control over their films. They were employed on a freelance basis, had little to say about casting and scripts, and had to work strictly within the constraints of time, money and space imposed by low-budget commercial production. Under such conditions, the contributions of production workers other than the directors (such as the set designers, for instance) were important, especially in making cheap horror films look expensive. With this in mind, one might ask whether a traditional *auteur* approach is adequate to understanding Hammer's films.

Terence Fisher

One of the functions of the *auteur* theory is to bestow the status of art on apparently trivial material by showing how a director's *œuvre* displays a consistency of style, theme and structure which differentiates it from other work in the same genre, thus allowing us to look at it in a new way. *Auteur* study can be useful in critical reassessment of areas of cinema history previously neglected or dismissed, such as British cinema for instance, opening up questions of pleasure which might otherwise be lost and which are not the same as those offered by genre study or study of production conditions.

The sensational, 'exploitation' projects with which Hammer studios made its name provide a good example of overtly popular, commercial material which outraged critics when it first appeared. One way to begin the work of reassessment would be to examine the historical reasons for the (temporary) unacceptability of this material to 'serious' British film criticism. Another way would be to give new value to the material by viewing it, as Pirie does, in the context of the literary tradition of Romantic poetry and Gothic writing in British culture. This perspective, combined with *auteur* analysis, allows Pirie to argue convincingly that Hammer produced a 'revolutionary kind of popular art' so that it becomes possible to view the Hammer films as 'good' rather than 'bad', giving them the status of 'quality' films in retrospect. If Fisher's films remain within the bounds of the 'quality film', however, other Hammer films do not (e.g. *Taste the Blood of Dracula*, 1969), which suggests that Pirie's approach might not be applicable to the entire Hammer output.

Pirie takes the work of Terence Fisher as a test case: by establishing Fisher's status as an *auteur* he demonstrates that Hammer films are worthy of the serious critical attention so often denied to them. Significantly, he sees Fisher's art as that of a nineteenth-century storyteller, comparable to that of the best Gothic novelists, tracing in his films a coherent world-view based on a strict dualism, an ambiguity towards sexual excess and the body and a strong belief in the power of rational thought to overcome evil and corruption. It is interesting to speculate to what extent Fisher's work can be identified with the 'mainstream' Hammer product and how far his style and thematic concerns meshed with the interests of the studio. By all accounts Fisher and Hammer were in complete harmony, which was not the case with all their directors (see *Little Shoppe of Horrors* no. 4, April 1978).

John Gilling

Gilling's career as director with Hammer was short and somewhat problematic: it seems that he had differences with the producers, especially with Anthony Hinds, who wrote many of the scripts for Hammer Productions under the name of John Elder (see *Little Shoppe of Horrors* no. 4, 1978). Gilling was himself a scriptwriter with an enormous number of films to his credit for British International Pictures, some of which he had also directed.

His first directorial venture into horror was *The Flesh and the Fiends* (1959) which prompted Hammer to invite him to direct for them for the first time (he had previously scripted a couple of their films). *The Shadow of the Cat* (1960) has been described as Gilling's masterpiece, and as David Pirie (1973) points out it was significantly different from Hammer's 'normal' style (epitomised by Terence Fisher), formally adventurous and evocative of Edgar Allan Poe.

Gilling's reputation as an important director of horror films derives from the two films he made for Hammer about Cornwall: *The Plague of the Zombies* (1966) and *The Reptile* (1966). In contrast to Fisher's work, they are among the most deeply pessimistic films that Hammer ever made. *The Plague of the Zombies* raises questions about 'mainstream' Hammer (exemplified by the work of Terence Fisher) and a different kind of Hammer product in which the formal and thematic concerns of the director can be seen to be different from, and perhaps at odds with, the overall concerns of the studio.

Peter Sasdy

Sasdy, a Hungarian director who had worked for television, seems to have been interested in the potential for social criticism in the sado-masochistic themes of sexuality and violence on which the Dracula legend was based. In *Taste the Blood of Dracula* this potential was used to attack the hypocritical façade of the bourgeois Victorian family, in particular its hierarchical structure in which the word of the father was law. The family is split open as, under the spell of Dracula, the children become actively destructive of the old patriarchal order. Finally, the families decimated and the fathers dead at the hands of their children, Dracula himself must be destroyed if any form of new society is to emerge. But, in contrast to the treatment of Dracula in other Hammer films, his destruction is profoundly ambiguous in the light of this representation of him as a positive agent of liberation, and his return perhaps to be welcomed rather than feared.

Selected Reading

Charles Barr, *Ealing Studios*, London, Cameron & Tayleur/Newton Abbott, David & Charles, 1977; rev. edn, 1993.

Ian Conrich, 'Traditions of the British horror film', in *The British Cinema Book*, Robert Murphy (ed.), London, BFI, 1997.

John Ellis, 'Made in Ealing', *Screen* 16(1), spring 1975.

John Ellis, 'Art, culture and quality: terms for a cinema in the forties and seventies', *Screen* 19(3), autumn 1978, rev. 1996.

Philip Kemp, *Lethal Innocence: The Cinema of Alexander MacKendrick*, London, Methuen, 1991.

David Pirie, *A Heritage of Horror: The English Gothic Cinema* 1946–1972, London, Gordon & Fraser, 1973.

Dead of Night – Ealing's last venture into the dark 'other world' of horror

ROBERT HAMER

Dead of Night (UK 1945 *p.c* – Ealing Studios; *d* – Robert Hamer (*The Haunted Mirror*); sd b/w)

John Ellis argues that the basic strategies of Ealing's realist cinema were closely linked to those of classic narrative cinema. Formal innovations were contained within a realist project which carried with it 'a certain mode of watching', encouraging the audience to recognise (or rather misrecognise) itself in the representation of full and finished characters, coherent entities living at the centre of society (Ellis, 1975, p. 107).

Ellis emphasises that this process of identification is complex and that Ealing managed to pose some real social problems in this mode. It is tempting to see Hamer's section of *Dead of Night, The Haunted Mirror*, as a metaphor for the process of recognition/misrecognition and as a criticism of it. The complacent middle-class hero finds the coherence of his own identity

Egyptian culture versus British imperialism in Fisher's *The Mummy*

and then the ordered pattern of his life split and fractured by violent images from some mysterious past projected by the mirror, images which gradually take him over and transform him into a madman, violently possessed by sexual jealously. The Ealing image of the 'ideal hero', represented by Ralph Michael, could be said to be radically questioned by this film, distancing the spectator from the process of identification. The place of the woman in restoring the status quo could be discussed in relation to Ealing's representation of women. In a sense, Joan controls the narrative: she gives Peter the mirror, and her presence seems to dispel the 'other world'. Finally she defeats it by smashing the mirror.

The film can also be seen as a link with later developments in the British horror film, where a complacent social order is frequently disrupted by repressed forces. After *Dead of Night* Ealing did not open the gate to the dark 'other world' again. Instead it accepted the terms of constraint on sexuality and violence which *The Haunted Mirror* implicitly criticises.

ALEXANDER MACKENDRICK

The Man in the White Suit (UK 1951 *p.c* – Ealing Studios; *d* – Alexander Mackendrick; sd b/w)

Charles Barr sees the film as a critical statement about England 'governed by consensus' and about the relationship of opposition between the old and the new, between father and son (Barr, 1977, p. 134).

John Ellis (1975) provides a reading of the film which places it more centrally (less critically) with Ealing's output drawing on a description of the studio's 'creative élite' as a group of middle-class intellectuals who conceived of 'the people' in a certain way, as petty bourgeois shopkeepers and clerks rather than factory workers.

In the 1975 article Ellis criticises *The Man in the White Suit* for concentrating on individuals 'at the point of exchange' rather than workers 'at the point of production'. However, it could be argued that it is through this emphasis on 'the point of exchange' that the film is able to criticise the social relationships which 'mainstream' Ealing takes for granted: relationships between workers and bosses, between father and daughter, between men and women, as organised by capitalism – not necessarily a conscious criticism, however, since Mackendrick himself sees the film in psychological terms:

> I'd like to make another 'hysterical comedy' like *The Man in the White Suit* which is my favourite film. A man lives in a social group. This group seems normal and he abnormal. Little by little you realise that it is he who is full of good sense. In a psychotic world, neurotics sometimes seem normal. (*Positif* no. 92, 1968)

Charles Barr analyses a scene from the film in which the heroine Daphne is asked to use her sexuality to get Sidney to change his mind, and responds by making a point of putting a price on her services, a scene which is a good example of Mackendrick's use of comedy to make a critical statement about social relationships.

> Behind the mask of Ealing comedy, this seems to me to express a vision of the logic of capitalism as extreme as anything in Buñuel or Godard. For the metaphor of prostitution, compare Godard's *Two or Three Things I Know about Her*. In its seriousness and ruthlessness, in what it does with its comedy 'licence', it is, in case a reminder is needed, light years away from anything in the work of T. E. B. Clarke. (Barr, 1977, p. 142)

One might add about *The Man in the White Suit*: for the metaphor of the role of the intellectual in society, compare Godard's *Tout va bien* (1972).

It could be argued that Daphne (Joan Greenwood) is a significantly different type of heroine from the ideal of femininity represented in 'mainstream' Ealing, although she necessarily remains within the terms of the stereotype. The character of Daphne tests the limits of the stereotype, much as *The Man in the White Suit* itself can be seen to rest the limits of the genre 'Ealing comedy'.

One way of exploring some of these questions about Mackendrick's relationship to Ealing might be to compare those films he made in Ealing with those he made after he left. It is arguable that the later films, while superficially different, show the same underlying structural and thematic concerns and the same critical intelligence: towards Hollywood and America in *Don't Make Waves* (1967) and towards the adult world in *A High Wind in Jamaica* (1965) and *Sammy Going South* (1963) (see Simpson, 1977).

TERENCE FISHER

Dracula (UK 1957 *p.c* – Hammer; *d* – Terence Fisher; sd col.)

Fisher inaugurated Hammer's horror cycle with *The Curse of Frankenstein*, which was greeted with critical outrage when it appeared in 1957, but became a huge box-office success. Hammer was quick to capitalise on this success, and *Dracula* went into production about a year later. Pirie's detailed analysis of the film relates it specifically to Bram Stoker's novel, stressing its essentially British version of the legend and describing how Fisher's allusive style apparently meshed perfectly with the studio's concern to convey visually Dracula's sensuality and its effect on women (Pirie, 1973, p. 86).

The Mummy (UK 1959 *p.c* – Hammer; *d* – Terence Fisher; sd col.)

Pirie attributes the *mise-en-scène* entirely to Fisher, although some of its 'pictorial sensuality' must be due to the work of designers (Pirie, 1973, pp. 57–8).

The violation of an Egyptian princess's tomb is the pretext for a revenge curse on a family of British archaeologists. A primary opposition set up in the film is a political one between British imperialism and Egyptian culture and the 'return of the repressed' theme centres here on the struggle between a 'primitive' culture and so-called civilisation. Compare this with similar struggles between primitive forces and scientific reason in the *Dracula* and *Frankenstein* films directed by Fisher for Hammer. It might be argued that the dualism attributed to Fisher's world-view by Pirie is, rather, a requirement of the genre (see The horror film, p. 194).

The Hound of the Baskervilles (UK 1959 *p.c* – Hammer; *d* – Terence Fisher; sd col.)

Fisher's work is often admired for the precision with which he unfolds a narrative: he has been described as a master storyteller.

> Some of the most completely successful of Fisher's films are those in which the lines are drawn with absolute clarity. This is amply demonstrated by a film like *The Hound of the Baskervilles*, where he uses Conan Doyle's plot to establish a stylish dialectic between Holmes's nominally rational Victorian milieu and the dark fabulous cruelty behind the Baskerville legend. The opposition is expressed within the first ten minutes of the film when he moves from the 'legend' with its strong connotations of the Hellfire Club and Francis Dashwood (the demonic noblemen torment a young girl) to the rational eccentricities of Baker Street. (Pirie, 1973, pp. 56–7)

This opening sequence provides an interesting contrast with John Gilling's *The Plague of the Zombies* in which the hero–doctor is, unlike the 'Renaissance Man' Sherlock Holmes, as susceptible to the threat represented by repressed evil as the other characters in the film.

The Brides of Dracula (UK 1960 *p.c* – Hammer; *d* – Terence Fisher; sd col.)

In agreeing to direct this film for Hammer, Fisher laboured under the difficulties imposed by the absence of Christopher Lee as Count Dracula. *Dracula* (1957) had been an enormous success and in order to cash in on this, Hammer were forced to find a way to make a sequel without Count Dracula himself. In spite of these production constraints, Pirie identifies some characteristic Fisher touches, particularly in the film's finale.

> The spirited climax sees Van Helsing in danger of succumbing after being bitten until, in a moment of puritanical strength, he purges the wound with a red hot iron and then uses the blades of an old windmill to make a moonlight cross which destroys the vampire. Sadly, this was the last appearance of Van Helsing in Hammer's repertoire for some time, but the figure of the scholar/scientist/poet/ priest whose weapons are books and ritual formulae is never absent from Fisher's work for very long (next appearing as Professor Meister in *The Gorgon*) and owes much to Stoker's Dutch hero. (Pirie, 1973, pp. 88–9)

Also of note in this film is the implied lesbian sexuality; although only an oblique reference here, it was to reappear in more explicit form in later Hammer products, which became increasingly sensational.

Plague of the Zombies – shock effects and dream imagery disturb the surface of the film

Dracula, Prince of Darkness (UK 1965 *p.c* – Hammer; *d* – Terence Fisher; sd col. scope)

Pirie places Fisher's 'artistry' in this film on a par with European art cinema, evoking a comparison with Ingmar Bergman – 'The detailed portrayal of Dracula's re-birth in *Dracula, Prince of Darkness* is a precise observation of a *religious* (or anti-religious) ritual and on this basis it might easily be compared on a stylistic/thematic level with, say, the mass in Bergman's *Winter Light*' – and regretting that Hammer proceeded to hand over the Dracula series to a succession of directors. According to Pirie, none of the subsequent films can quite compare with Fisher's (Pirie, 1973, pp. 89–93).

A different, perhaps more critical treatment of the myth is offered by Sasdy's *Taste the Blood of Dracula* (1969) – see below.

The Devil Rides Out (UK 1967 *p.c* Hammer; *d* – Terence Fisher; sd col.).

Pirie evaluates this film as one of Fisher's best, and places it in a specifically English tradition of horror. According to Pirie, Dennis Wheatley's unremarkable novel is transformed by Fisher and scriptwriter Richard Matheson. Referring in particular to the scene in which Mocata, the head of the coven, visits the Eaton household in search of the young couple who have been taken from his clutches, and the film's climax in which the four agents of good spend a night within the pentacle assailed by the forces of evil, he argues that the subtle script combined with Fisher's allusive and restrained *mise-en-scène* produce a new and powerful aesthetic masterpiece consistent with Fisher's dualistic world-view (Pirie, 1973, pp. 60–4).

JOHN GILLING

The Plague of the Zombies (UK 1966 *p.c* – Hammer; *d* – John Gilling; sd col.)

As indicated above, Fisher's directorial style is basically within a realist narrative tradition: he is often described as a great storyteller, with an economic style which relies upon the setting up of tensions between schematic oppositions (such as 'good' and 'evil') and which resolves those tensions in favour of 'good', which means reason and science will prevail.

Gilling's style and concerns in *The Plague of the Zombies* can be seen to be significantly different from Fisher's: the film is overtly surrealistic in form, using shock effects, camera angles and dream imagery to disturb the surface of the film itself, producing a feeling of disequilibrium which is never there in Fisher's more cerebral treatments of the genre. It could be argued that it is an excess of form in Gilling's films which is troubling and which makes them peculiarly 'un-British' (in the sense that David Pirie would describe the 'British' manifestation of the Gothic horror film).

The characters in Gilling's film do not represent schematic oppositions: certainly the scientist figure (played by André Morell) is not the obsessional, rational, 'objective' character personified by Peter Cushing, who uses knowledge as a defence against 'evil'. Instead he is an agnostic, experimental scientist who admits that there are areas of thought and experience which defy the tyranny of reason. For this kind of character it is necessary to become actively involved in these areas, risking his rational objectivity.

PETER SASDY

Taste the Blood of Dracula (UK 1969 *p.c* – Hammer; *d* – Peter Sasdy; sd col.)

In contrast to Fisher's schematic treatment of the Dracula legend, Sasdy's version is based on a more complex conception of the implicitly destructive relationship of Count Dracula to 'normal' society. Sasdy is concerned with psychological and social rather than metaphysical themes and he bases them firmly on physical eroticism rather than spiritual values.

The film dwells on the implications of oral sexuality which underly the myth, making much of the blood-tasting rituals and the physicality of the process of vampirisation, and it presents these rituals as transgression of the bourgeois moral codes. The regression of the children to forbidden oral sexuality seems to be associated particularly with female sexuality and is seen as a positive force, since it is a source of energy which can be turned against the corrupt fathers and their decadent inversion of Catholic religious ritual (cf. Sasdy's next film *Countess Dracula*, 1970).

Sasdy's *mise-en-scène* is restrainedly surreal, stressing the fantasy aspect of eroticism and the destructive drives which underlie it. The bourgeois façade of Victorian society is seen to be cracking open at the seams under the impact of all that it represses. *Taste the Blood of Dracula* goes far beyond the bounds of the standards of 'restraint' and 'good taste' set by Fisher's work and indicates some of the changes Hammer introduced into its products to maintain its audience (Hammer Productions, pp. 85 and 185).

STRUCTURALISM AND *AUTEUR* STUDY

FRENCH INTELLECTUAL CONTEXT

The 'structuralist controversy' (as it has come to be known) emerged from the fierce debates raging among left-wing intellectuals in the universities of Paris during the mid-1960s. These debates caused reverberations in British intellectual life which were still felt in the 1980s.

The year in which *Movie* first appeared (1962) was also the year of publication in Paris of anthropologist Claude Lévi-Strauss's *La Pensée sauvage* which included a critique of Jean-Paul Sartre's 'developmental' view of history and was to bring forward debates with far-reaching effects in many disciplines: linguistics, literature, anthropology, history, sociology, art, music, psychoanalysis and, not least, philosophy and politics. In contrast to the existentialists, Lévi-Strauss argued that history does not reveal the present as the necessary culmination of events in the past: rather, history offers us images of past societies which are structural transformations of those we know today, neither better nor worse. In this sense, modern 'man' is not so much a superior development of his antecedents as a complex amalgam of different historical levels which can be shown to coexist in our modern minds (Leach, 1970). This view of 'man' as the result of the interaction of historical forces rather than occupying a position of superiority in relation to the past set in motion an intellectual shift which was to recast the problems posed by nineteenth-century thought and demand that they be looked at in a new way.

Structuralism, by drawing attention to the underlying sets of relationships both within and between cultural objects (or events), claimed that it was these relationships that should occupy the attention of the analyst rather than the search for some pre-existing essential meaning hidden behind the mask of language. Structuralism and the allied discipline semiology were a radical challenge to those empirical methods which took for granted as pre-given the objects of its analysis. However, as its critics were later to point out, structuralism itself fell into some of the ideological traps it was so anxious to avoid: the search for 'underlying structural relationships' often involved a reduction of those relationships to a fixed, static underlying structure, waiting to be revealed; and structures themselves were often seen as existing outside of time and place, outside of history. Nonetheless, the fundamental challenge of structuralist thought remained, and in the intellectual climate of Paris took on a social and political dimension.

Political implications of structuralism

The Marxist philosopher Louis Althusser, one of the most influential writers to advocate the importance of structuralist theory for political philosophy and criticism (though he denied that he was a 'structuralist'), made an attempt to define the historical moment or 'conjuncture' which made possible the development of this theoretical work in France (Althusser, 1969).

Althusser's ideas about ideology and representation were profoundly influential on British cultural theory, particularly the film theory of the journal *Screen*. He attempted to establish the 'relative autonomy' of ideology from the economic base of society, taking issue with the orthodox Marxist view that cultural artefacts were directly determined by economic factors on the grounds that such a view ignored the way in which the different elements of the social formation interact to affect one another at any given moment (see Spectatorship and audience research, p. 366).

Althusser's ideas formed part of a historical movement in which traditional disciplines such as philosophy, linguistics and literary criticism became increasingly politicised and in which theory was given an active role in determining political strategy and practice. Broadly speaking, the 'structuralist method' took issue with the notion that human beings could be conceived of as 'free' individuals in control of society. It argued, on the contrary, that while individuals ('man') might experience themselves as the origin and source of all meaning, action and history, and the world as an independent constituted domain of objects, in fact both individuals and objects were caught up in a system of structural relationships and it was this system that made the construction of a world of individuals and things, the construction of meaning, possible (Belsey, 1980).

The focus of attention for structuralist critics was language, but language as an activity of construction rather than as a mask for inner meaning which the critic could conjure up at will. Literary texts had certain reading practices built into them, some of which contributed to the process of reproducing capitalist relations of production, while others challenged or resisted that process. Classic realist fiction, the dominant literary form of the nineteenth century, addressed the reader as the central point from which the meaning of the text would emerge: the reader matched the author as the controlling source of the coherence and intelligibility of the text. Some twentieth-century modernist literary practices, on the other hand, were structured to produce contradiction rather than harmony and coherence, and these avant-garde texts challenged the central place given to author and reader in classic realism. Instead of a search for immanent meanings, intentions or causes, such texts demanded the abandonment of attempts to master and control meaning in favour of an activity of reading which can never exhaust the meaning of the text, but is rather a process of reading and writing in which texts are constantly transformed. The structuralist impulse to displace universal categories such as 'man' and 'human nature' from their 'natural' place at the centre of the world and history has political implications, since an understanding of individuals and society as formed contradictorily rather than essentially or finally fixed provides the basis for theories of radical social transformation. However, the 'de-centred self' proposed by structuralism also posed problems for political action.

Ideology and the subject

It has been argued that structuralism was concerned from the beginning with the dissolution of the notion of 'man' as a full and original presence, the source of all meaning. Stephen Heath, for instance, one of the first British critics to write about structuralism in relation to literary criticism, argued that 'structure' should be understood as a process, or network of processes, whereby individuals are put in place in society and that language played an important part in 'calling up' individuals, thereby transforming them into 'subjects' in society (Heath, 1972, pp. 35–6).

This account of 'the subject', developed from Althusser (1971), implies that while individuals may experience themselves as possessing a consciousness which enables them to freely form the ideas in which they believe, in fact this experience is an *imaginary* or *ideological* one, based on misrecognition. The ideological construction of subjects as individuals free to exchange their labour is seen to be important to capitalist relations of production, which therefore seek to perpetuate it, using language as their means. Broadly speaking, then, ideology cannot be thought of as a set of ideas or thoughts which individuals can take up and discard at will. Rather, it consists in the material practices and representations within which the subject is inscribed and is largely unconsciously acquired. Returning to questions of authorship, while traditional criticism envisages the work of art as the expression of the intentions of the individual artist containing an identity which can be directly recovered by the critic, structuralism proposes that the 'author', far from controlling the meaning of the work, is an *effect* of the interaction of different texts, or discourses, which have their own autonomy.

Language as convention

Many critics of structuralism thought that it tended to rely on a rather mechanistic concept of the subject as a fixed structure, totally at the mercy of language. Later, when structuralism was displaced by semiotic analysis, Julia Kristeva and writers from the theoretical journal *Tel Quel*, principally concerned with modernist practices of writing which attempt to disturb the ideological construction of the subject as unified and coherent, drew on psychoanalytic and linguistic theory to develop the concept that the subject itself is no more than the marks left by the process of intersection of different and conflicting texts. The 'I' which we use to designate our presence as individuals was seen as a convention, or code which was the result of the interaction of a number of codes, rather than a unified expression of the individuality of the person using the code. Moreover, this emphasis on the conventional nature of language enabled the semioticians to give language a material base in society and history, independently of individual language users, who inherited a set of institutional conventions without which they would not be able to communicate. These conventions pre-dated the writer and continued to be readable in his or her absence (Culler, 1975). By evacuating the coherent, intentional subject from language in this way, semiotics hoped to bring into play new, revolutionary practices of writing which would mobilise unconscious desires as a force for social change.

The end of the author

Structuralist and semiological criticism insisted that language functions independently of the author: does the individual author then disappear? While the theoretical interventions of structuralism may have called into question some of the fundamental premises of traditional critical approaches, the influence of these ideas has been uneven, especially in Britain and the United States. Moreover, the sway of the author remains powerful as a social institution and it would be utopian to assume that structuralism or new practices of writing could have achieved its annihilation. In France the structuralist intervention paved the way for radical changes in cultural practices, particularly in cinema after the political upheavals of May 1968, when the attribution of individual authorship to films was attacked as part of an assault on traditional methods of production, distribution and exhibition. In Britain during the 1970s, the French ideas were influential in producing new theories and practices of cinema. Sylvia Harvey has argued that the importation of these ideas into British and American criticism occurred at the expense of the theoretical and political context which engendered them in France:

> Those ideas which, in France, were the product of a momentary but radical displacement, a critical calling into question of all the levels of the social formation, have become in Britain and the United States little more than a hiccup in the superstructures, a slight grinding of gears in that social machine whose fundamental mode of operating has not changed. (Harvey, 1978, pp. 1–2)

This argument tends to underestimate the extent to which cultural practices in Britain were affected by French theory and politics (the development of independent oppositional cinema during the 1970s, for instance). The French debates are marked by a consciousness of their social, political and historical background which adds vigour and relevance to their arguments, a process of self-reflection which at its best takes nothing for granted. Their insertion into anglophone culture transformed these arguments.

STRUCTURALISM AND BRITISH FILM CRITICISM

It is perhaps significant that the first indications of the intervention of structuralist ideas into British film criticism should circulate around the work of Jean-Luc Godard, a French critic and film-maker whose ideas were profoundly affected by French structuralist thought and by the political upheavals in France (see Jean-Luc Godard, p. 253). It is also significant that this discussion first appeared in the pages of *New Left Review*, since it is largely through the writings of a small but influential group of left-wing intellectuals that structuralism emerged in Britain. This emergence, in contrast to the French situation, has been slow and painful, symptomatic perhaps of an intellectual tradition which is firmly entrenched in empiricism and distrusts theoretical enquiry.

The beginnings of 'English cine-structuralism'

The debate between Robin Wood and Peter Wollen about Jean-Luc Godard in *New Left Review* no. 39, 1966, offers an opportunity to see a confrontation between one kind of critical approach developed in the pages of *Movie* (see above p. 258), and a Marxist criticism influenced by structuralism which was to be developed in the journal *Screen* in the 1970s. It also offers an opportunity to see an early example of the way in which structuralist ideas 'seeped into' British film criticism, producing problems and contradictions. As Peter Wollen (pseud. Lee Russell) points out in his article, there is no simple opposition between his approach and that of Robin Wood, but there are important differences of emphasis which produce conflicting views of Godard's work and of the function of the artist in society.

A sense of tradition: Robin Wood

Wood isolates a single central theme in Godard's *œuvre* around which all the other themes cohere: 'the sense of tradition'. Through detailed analysis of one scene in *Bande à part* (1964) he argues that Godard's view of contemporary society is a pessimistic one: seeing it as fragmented, lacking cultural tradition, the film-maker looks back nostalgically to a time when a relatively stable society enabled the great classic tradition (defined by Wood in terms of 'harmony') of art to appear. For Wood, Godard is a modern artist who constantly tries to resolve the problem of the lack of stable cultural tradition by fabricating his own tradition, essentially personal rather than social. Even Godard's 'most savage statement of discontinuity' in *Les Carabiniers* is seen as bitter self-parody: his position is characterised as a tragic one. In Wood's view the relationship of form to content is perfectly equivalent; the style and structure of the films express Godard's tragic statement that the loss of tradition leads to the loss of personal identity and relationships.

It is possible to trace in Wood's approach to Godard's work a clear statement of the critic's own humanist concerns and it was this approach with which British Marxist film critics took issue. Nevertheless, the differences between Wood's and Wollen's approaches are not always clear-cut: the articles mark a historical point of transition rather than a break.

Unresolved contradictions: Peter Wollen

Lee Russell/Peter Wollen agrees that the issue of tradition is a 'key' one in studying Godard (rather than 'the essential one') but points to a difference of approach in his article which is more than a difference of opinion: it is 'a clash of world-views'.

Wollen begins, not with an inner theme, but with French society and politics: the social and historical context for Godard's work. He traces a set of structural oppositions running through the films: action versus destiny, culture versus society, art versus tradition. These oppositions form unresolved contradictions in the films, they do not cohere to form an ideal unity. Indeed, the artist, in Wollen's view, far from being a

Les Carabiniers – Godard's bitter self-parody?

central unifying force in society, is generally marginal to it, sometimes antagonistic, often simply indifferent. Wollen goes on to criticise Godard's romantic individualistic position and the absence of politics in the films, an absence of which the film-maker is aware and which he regrets. According to Wollen, Godard's way forward from his despairing view of society should be in the direction of politics, which is 'the principle of change in history'. A very different view of the artist and of art in society can be seen at work here. Far from transcending society with a unique and unifying personal vision, the artist is placed firmly within history: no longer the romantic 'outsider', his or her task is to contribute to social change through the critical activity of political film-making.'

However, like Wood, Wollen retains a central place for Godard as *auteur* in this article and still subscribes to the critical method which depends upon bringing forward meanings hidden behind language. Nevertheless, it is possible to see the beginnings of a shift away from the notion of the *auteur* as originating source of the work towards the idea of the work as a set of contradictory relationships between structural elements which interact to *produce* the author's world-view rather than express it. Wollen is working towards a 'world-view' which is less that of a coherent totality, the expression of a pre-given set of ideas, than a collage of different positions transformed in the process of history. Underlying Wollen's arguments is a criticism of the relativism of subjective criticism and a desire to move towards a more rigorous objective method. At the same time, Wollen is careful to point out that he is writing from a particular position, which he elaborates in the course of the article. The subjectivity of the critic is not denied, but it is beginning to be called into question.

Wollen was to revise his position on Godard in the light of his post-1968 films, developing his argument about thematic oppositions in Godard's work into a political strategy of film-making which would counter, or oppose, Hollywood cinema, and assessing his contribution as a political film-maker. (see Authorship and counter-cinema, p. 305). The dualism of Wollen's structural criticism (elaborated in *Signs and Meaning in the Cinema*, 1969, 1972, 1998) came under attack with later developments in anglophone film theory, as did his attempt to make an alliance between structuralism and *auteur* theory (see *Auteur* structuralism under attack, p. 293). But the problems in Wollen's arguments do not detract from the contribution they make to shifting the ground of British film criticism away from empiricism towards a different problematic: the relationship of science and theory to artistic practice and to politics.

Against interpretation: Alan Lovell

The methodological differences arising from the Wood–Wollen debate were elaborated in a later discussion between Robin Wood and Alan Lovell in *Screen* (March/April 1969 and May/June 1969). Lovell criticises Wood's selective approach: classification of an *auteur*'s films according to thematic resemblances, the choice of which, Lovell argues, is based on the critic's subjective system of values. The result is that certain films achieve the status of 'great art' entirely according to Wood's personal dispensation, his approval of certain moral values which he claims all great artists will express, irrespective of social, historical and cultural context. In order to break through this critical impasse, this subjective dogmatism in which the critic's values are validated by recourse to an absolute, transcendental system, Alan Lovell suggests that criticism needs to become more objective by developing an analytic apparatus, part of which would be 'the *auteur* principle conceived as a search for the basic structure of an artist's work through examination of its recurrent features . . .' (Lovell, 1969, p. 54).

It should be descriptive rather than evaluative in intent, and collaborative in order to avoid the solipsism of individual critics being accountable only to themselves. It should be provisional in nature, rather than assertive or evaluative.

Lovell argues for a descriptive, analytic approach against subjective interpretation, but in doing so he avoids a basic problem: the critic searching for basic structures is not simply an objective scientist; critics are still engaged in the activity of reading and producing meanings and the question of subjectivity remains. Lovell's suggestion that criticism should be a social rather than a private activity does not come to terms with the troubling question of what the relationship of the 'private' and 'personal' to the social might be, a question which dogged most early structuralist writing.

In the revised edition of his booklet on Don Siegel (1975), Alan Lovell reformulated his position in the light of historical and theoretical changes which led him to believe that structuralism had failed in its original radical task of displacing the author as creator from the centre of the work, and called for more attention to the production conditions within which directors worked. The shift in Lovell's argument away from formalism toward social and ideological analysis of films is an indication of the general shift that took place in French and English structuralist criticism in the early 1970s. The shift defined itself against 'mechanistic' structuralism and posited a theoretical advance, a re-reading of structuralist method which attempted to articulate a new relation between history, ideology and the author. The *Cahiers du Cinéma* collective text on John Ford's *Young Mr Lincoln* (see p. 301) is perhaps the best example of the process of self-criticism involved in this intellectual shift, which profoundly influenced the path of British film theory, particularly in the journal *Screen*.

Young Mr Lincoln – proffered a rich text for the structuralist debate

Auteur structuralism: Geoffrey Nowell-Smith

The 'English cine-structuralists' as they came to be called, after Eckert and Henderson (see *Auteur* structuralism under attack, p. 293), were not a homogeneous group. Though they shared a concern with developing materialist methods of analysis the use of structuralism differed from critic to critic. Indeed, the Marxist framework within which each critic worked was also very different and often contradictory. One of those approaches is represented by Geoffrey Nowell-Smith in his book on Visconti (1967) who states his intention of retrieving Visconti's work from the place assigned to it by traditional criticism:

> This does not mean exalting the later work at the expense of the earlier, but making it one's primary concern to consider the work as a whole, as the product of a single intelligence, and to seek out the connections between each film at whatever level they are to be found. In Visconti's case the connections are multifarious and can be traced in his choice of actors, his use of decors, his concern with certain historical questions and so on. The development of each film out of the problems posed by the last can also be easily demonstrated. But there are further links within his work which exists at a deeper level, less easily discernible and which are perhaps even more important. (Nowell-Smith, 1967, p. 9)

Nowell-Smith emphasises that he is not using *auteur* structuralism to support the idea that every detail of a film is the sole responsibility of its author, the director, or as a mode of evaluating films as 'good' or 'bad'; rather it is a 'principle of method' around which the critic organises his or her work. 'The purpose of criticism becomes therefore to uncover behind the superficial contrasts of subject and treatment a structural hard core of basic and often recondite motifs' (Nowell-Smith, 1967, p. 10).

However, as Nowell-Smith demonstrates, *auteur* structuralism is not so much an answer to the early excesses of the *auteur* theory as a problem in itself. In narrowing the field of enquiry to the internal formal and thematic analysis of the work it tends to ignore the possibility of historical changes affecting the basic structure, and the importance of non-thematic elements and *mise-en-scène*. Moreover, certain directors, of whom Visconti is one, cannot be discussed simply in structuralist terms because external factors of history and production are so important to their work. Nowell-Smith begins with a defence of *auteur* structuralism which is radically questioned by the critical method he then chooses to adopt: discussion of Visconti's work not only in terms of its internal relationships, but also in its social and historical context.

To characterise these early *auteur*-structuralist writings as theoretical failures would be to misunderstand the nature of theoretical enquiry which proceeds from problem to problem rather than looking for 'correctness' or immediate solutions. It would also be to underestimate the value of polemic in critical debate. Most of the *auteur* structuralists reformulated their original positions, although the project of a materialist enquiry remained.

Selected Reading

Alan Lovell, 'Robin Wood – a dissenting view', *Screen* 10(2), March/April 1969.

Lee Russell/Peter Wollen, 'Jean-Luc Godard', *New Left Review* no. 38, September/October 1966.

Peter Wollen, *Signs and Meaning in the Cinema*, London, Secker & Warburg/BFI, 1969; rev. edn, 1972, exped 1998.

Robin Wood, 'Ghostly paradigm and HCF: an answer to Alan Lovell', *Screen* 10(3), May/June 1969.

EARLY STRUCTURALIST FILM ANALYSIS

A good example of the difficulties posed by structuralist analysis occurs in the juxtaposition of two different approaches to the films of Frank Capra in *Cinema* (no. 5, 1970) by Jeffrey Richards, which considers Capra's work historically in the context of its relationship to American populism, and by Sam Rohdie, which attempts to separate out basic structural oppositions and to see how

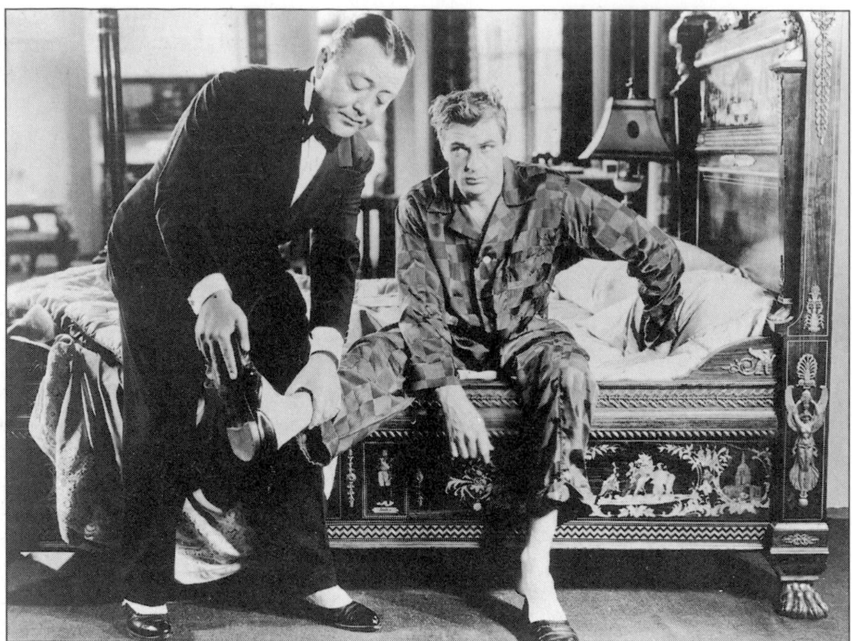

Mr Deeds Goes to Town – the first and most famous of Capra's populist heroes

they interrelate with narrative structure and cinematic language to produce meaning. Richards's argument is that Capra brought his own Italian-immigrant vision to the 'fundamental principles which underlay American life from the Revolution to the New Deal'. Its analysis of populist ideology and history provides background information which offers a valuable filter through which to view Capra's films and to understand them better. However, Richards pays no attention to form or to differences between films which might show that there were contradictions in populism, or in Capra's version of it. Instead he assumes a transparent relationship in which a set of pre-given ideas are unproblematically reflected in the films, where they can be directly perceived by the viewer.

Structuralist or semiological criticism, on the other hand, argued for the importance of formal relationships and of the mediating function of language to an understanding of the way in which ideology works. According to this argument, ideology does not exist as a pre-given entity, but is deeply bound up with form, in effect, *produced* in and through language; thus there is no 'ideology' in the abstract, only systems of representation which work to produce ideology in specific and contradictory forms.

Sam Rohdie's article attempts to come to terms with a particular articulation of populist myth in Capra's *Mr Deeds Goes to Town* (1936) using an approach based on textual analysis. He isolates the way in which the structural oppositions he identifies at work in the film (which are in fact identifiable in most American cinema) are reversed in this case to produce a resolution of the conflicts opened up at the beginning of the narrative. The thematic structures of opposition are shifted in the course of the narrative to produce the dissolution of oppositions. The cinematic language employed also displays an oppositional structure which produces meaning (e.g. close-up versus medium shot, soft focus versus sharp definition). Rohdie does not go much further than 'decoding' the oppositional structures, questioning the value of structuralism as a theoretical tool because it cannot deal with the powerful impact of the film, or the contributions of authorship, genre and the language of cinema itself to that impact. Indeed, it seems to provide a rather banal and reductive account of the way the film works.

The *Cahiers du Cinéma* analysis of *Young Mr Lincoln* (1939) (see below, p. 301) provides an interesting example of the extension of structuralist method to questions of authorship and genre. The analysis attempts to separate out precisely what is specific to Ford, to cinematic language and to ideology in the film. A comparison with *Mr Deeds Goes to Town* seems productive because both films draw on American populist myth, but from different perspectives.

Selected Reading

Jeffrey Richards, 'Frank Capra and the cinema of populism', *Cinema* (UK) no. 5, February 1970.

Sam Rohdie, 'A structural analysis of *Mr Deeds Goes to Town*', *Cinema* (UK) no. 5, February 1970.

STRUCTURALISM, INDIVIDUALISM AND *AUTEUR* THEORY

Structuralism, from its beginnings, posed itself against those forms of criticism which regarded the work of art as a closed, self-sufficient system in which the intentions of the author were to be found. In *La Penseé sauvage* (1962) anthropologist Claude Lévi-Strauss attacked Sartre's existentialist concept of the ego as consciousness, fully present to itself and freely able to create its own values. According to Lévi-Strauss, the final goal of the human sciences is not to constitute 'man' but to dissolve him. In a well-known remark about the language of myth he refuted the idea that 'man' could be conceived of as a 'language user', existing outside structures and therefore able to master and use them at will: 'We are not therefore claiming to show how men think in myths but rather how the myths think themselves out in men and without men's knowledge' (quoted in Leach, 1970, p. 51) (see *Auteur* structuralism under attack, p. 293).

Lévi-Strauss introduces the Freudian concept of the unconscious to explain the way in which (as he sees it) the human mind assimilates the deep structures which are seen to underpin all social organisation and forms of communication. In his attack on the notion of the individual self, Lévi-Strauss collapses individuality into a formulation of the human mind as a kind of 'collective unconscious' which assumes the universality of the structures he identifies. Individual myths, indeed all individual 'utterances' are different versions of these universal structures: emphasis is put upon the structures rather than on the utterances. This approach tends to be ahistorical, denying the particularity of different kinds of utterance, and returns constantly to the presence of a structure hidden in the myth. It has been pointed out that, like the critical tradition it is supposed to reject, it assumes the presence of an intention, whether this intention is shifted over to the side of the myth itself, or back to the 'human mind', conscious or unconscious.

In a radical re-reading of Freud, French psychoanalyst Jacques Lacan has also offered a challenge to the self-sufficiency of the individual subject, redefining the unconscious not as a deep well or reservoir of repressed thoughts or feelings, but as 'structured', indeed as 'structured like a language'. Far from being a place, Lacan argues, the unconscious is in fact a network of deep structural patterns in which our conscious thinking and discourse are intimately caught up, in the same way as the act of speech is transformed by the underlying linguistic structures (see Benoist, 1970). Freudian psychoanalysis does not attempt to recover the intention hidden behind each utterance, or to seek out the underlying structures, but by paying close attention to the relationship between the conscious discourse and what is absent from it (an absence marked by jokes, slips of the tongue, etc.) it attempts to throw light upon the structural activity which produced the discourse. According to Lacan (1977) the individual self is not, as traditional ego-psychology would have it, a unified ego, but is constantly produced and transformed by the activity of the unconscious, a 'self' divided between the unconscious id and the conscious ego, which can never be captured or reconstituted as a coherent presence which transcends language and society (see Psychoanalysis, p. 346).

The Marxist philosopher Louis Althusser drew on Lacan's theories when he attempted to reformulate Marx's concepts of identity and alienation into a 'theory of the subject': the unconscious network of structures which simultaneously holds people in place and produces the illusion of 'free men' (Althusser, 1971).

How does this sustained attack on 'individuality', 'presence' and 'intention', the attempted dissolution of 'man' relate to the principles of *auteur* study, which precisely depends upon the presence of an authorial (authoritative) voice as the prime source of meaning in the work? If the author/subject is constituted only in language, and language is by definition social and independent of any particular individuality, then why does the author return, as it does in some structuralist accounts of film? The early work of Christian Metz, for instance, depends upon a literal application to cinema of the linguistic distinction between *langue* and *parole*, defining cinema as a language without a *langue*, or underlying system of rules, a realm of pure performance or expression, which seems to confirm the idea of authorship in its conventional sense. In the absence of a general *langue* there is only the singular usage, and the language user (the author) is free to express his or her intentions directly. Significantly, this notion of language as direct expression also appears in Astruc (1948), one of the earliest defences of the *politique des auteurs* (see *Politique des auteurs*, p. 240). It is hardly surprising, then, that *auteur* structuralism was also caught in this dilemma: the attempt to redefine the *auteur* as a structure, an 'effect' rather than a punctual source of meaning in the film(s) nonetheless retained the notion of the underlying intention present in the basic structures, and therefore failed to displace conventional *auteur* theory (see Nowell-Smith, 1970).

The divided author: Samuel Fuller

Because of his anti-communism, Fuller has often been dismissed as a 'Fascist' or an 'imperialist' film director. The value of an *auteur* study of his work is to show that his position is more ambiguous and contradictory than it appears. By looking at the way in which the basic thematic structures of his work shift from film to film it is possible to argue that the importance of Fuller's films lies in the questions that they raise for politics and for cinema.

The attraction of Fuller's work for structuralist critics seemed to lie in the contradictions it produces: its 'pro-Americanism' rests on an ambiguity towards American society and ideology; its 'pro-individualism' rests on a notion of the individual as profoundly divided and alienated from society. In this play of oppositions, the original unity of the work of art, and of the individual *auteur*, are displaced. Thus *auteur* structuralism seemed to offer an alternative to the traditional *auteur* theory which celebrated the personal vision of the artist and to the unqualified support it gave to popular American cinema, whose values were increasingly coming under attack, particularly in France after the political events of May 1968 when many intellectuals became politicised. The works of those directors like Fuller whose films offered a criticism of traditional American values became important for polemical reasons. It is no accident that Fuller's name is closely linked with that of Jean-Luc Godard and that Brecht and Eisenstein are invoked in critical accounts of his work.

> Fuller's world is essentially dualistic: both war and marriage depend on a pair of partners, the self and other. Fuller explores his themes by breaking down the polarity of the two sides in war and by superimposing hate and love on the same pair. Thus the two basic situations for Fuller are those of the double agent and of the racially mixed marriage. In the first situation the protagonist is not clearly defined as being on one side or the other; he must live a complex dialectic of allegiance and treachery. In the second situation, relations of racial hatred and personal love are antagonistically combined within the same pair. This kind of thematic structure enables Fuller to explore the nature of American identity, *vis-à-vis* both the external enemy – Communism – and the internal divisions and hatreds which divide the country – especially race hatred.
> (Wollen, 'Introduction', 1969, p. 10)

Other accounts of Fuller's work also stress conflict and contradiction (e.g. Perkins, 1969, and Garnham, 1971, both characterise Fuller's themes as based on opposition) but see the *thematic* content expressed in *style*, which together reflect Fuller's moral values, or world-view. In contrast to these approaches, Peter Wollen is less interested in drawing out Fuller's moral values than in identifying the basic structures which make his work possible: the structures provide the basic raw material with which the director works to produce meaning, which is not necessarily attributable to the director's manifest intentions.

However, Peter Wollen still assumes an intention, conscious or unconscious, on Fuller's part, a set of 'personal concerns' which organise the basic structures and give them meaning. Indeed, it is difficult to imagine how the idea of intention might be totally dispensed with, without ignoring entirely the contribution of individuals to the process of constructing meaning. What becomes clearer when comparing Wollen's approach with others is that the author's world-view is a critical construction which changes depending on the point of view adopted by the critic.

Selected Reading

Nicholas Garnham, *Samuel Fuller*, London, Secker & Warburg/BFI, 1971.

CULTURAL POLITICS

Cahiers' category 'e'

The events of May 1968 heralded radical changes in French film criticism which were to have a profound effect on British criticism too. Dissatisfied with its early *auteurist* work, the French journal *Cahiers du Cinéma* began a series of articles on cinema, ideology and politics which drew on the development of French structuralist thought in politics, psychoanalysis and literary criticism within the framework of an explicitly Marxist approach. The project of this politicised film criticism was to develop a new theory and practice of the cinema and the fierce debates which followed (principally between *Cahiers du Cinéma* and *Cinéthique*) were taken up in Britain in the pages of the journal *Screen*, which allied itself to this programme of political and theoretical struggle when it emerged in a new form in 1971.

The following years also saw the proliferation of radical film making groups dedicated to making political cinema and to mounting an attack on the existing structures of the film industry. Technological and economic developments made small-scale film production more viable and an increasing political awareness among film-makers and film critics meant that the ideological function of Hollywood cinema came under scrutiny. Hollywood was seen as the principal agency of cultural imperialism in its domination of world cinema; for many people the task of revolutionary cultural struggle was to dismantle its hold on the popular imagination, to produce new, politically aware audiences. To this end, attention was turned towards the question of how to find new structures, new forms to express new revolutionary content: the debates of the Russian formalists, the ideas of Brecht became the models for film-makers and critics (see Harvey, 1978).

The refusal of dominant cinema also involved an attack on hierarchical production systems in favour of collective working methods and rejection of the idea that any individual should be enshrined as the author of a film. *Auteur* criticism, which focused on the director as central controlling presence, was seen as supporting the hierarchical division of labour and the individualist ideology of the dominant system. However, there was disagreement about how that system should be conceptualised. Critics were divided between those who argued for the necessity of building alternative structures 'outside' the dominant mode of production and those who argued for a theoretical concept of the dominant mode which would allow for intervention within it.

The journal *Cahiers du Cinéma* did not subscribe to the notion of Hollywood as an ideological monolith and struggled to produce a theoretical conception of the commercial industrial system, and of the place of the director within it, which allowed more space for contradiction. In an influential editorial which appeared in *Cahiers du Cinéma* in the autumn of 1969 the editors proposed dividing films into seven categories 'a'–'g' according to whether they allowed ideology a free passage, or whether they attempted to turn ideology back upon itself to reveal the contradictions which it was the nature of ideology to efface. The fifth category 'e' was defined as those films which seem at first sight to belong firmly within the ideology, but which reveal on closer inspection that:

> An internal criticism is taking place which cracks the film apart at the seams. If one reads the film obliquely, looking for symptoms, if one looks beyond its apparent formal coherence, one can see that it is riddled with cracks: it is splitting under an internal tension which is simply not there in an ideologically innocuous film. This is the case in many Hollywood films, for example, which while being completely integrated in the system and the ideology end up by partially dismantling the system from within. (Comolli and Narboni, 1969, quoted in Harvey, 1978, p. 35)

Cahiers cited the films of John Ford, Carl Dreyer, and Roberto Rossellini as examples of this category and their subsequent analysis of Ford's *Young Mr Lincoln* (1939) demonstrated the importance of the authorial sub-code in that film to the process of internal criticism. Thus films which appeared to be basically 'reactionary' (i.e. instruments of the dominant ideology) could, on rereading, prove to be 'progressive' in so far as they produced a criticism of that ideology. *Cahiers du Cinéma* followed up its definitions of classes of films with analyses of individual texts (*Young Mr Lincoln*, *Sylvia Scarlett* (1936), *Morocco* (1930)) to demonstrate how they each challenged dominant ideology in specific ways. *Cahiers*' approach allowed for the possibility of progressive texts to be found in Hollywood cinema and it was this position which had most effect on the theoretical work of *Screen*. *Auteur* criticism in Britain began to look at the films of certain Hollywood directors in terms of the way they resisted dominant ideology, laying bare its operations. Those directors whose work seemed to offer a radical criticism of the system through manipulation, conscious or unconscious, of its language were the most important; their work was evaluated according to the extent to which it could be read as breaking with the traditional pleasures offered by mainstream cinema, which attempted to seduce the audience into losing itself in a self-contained fictional world, putting its doubts and questions aside (see The classic realist text, p. 332).

The 'progressive' *auteur*: Douglas Sirk

One of the basic premisses of the critical ambivalence towards Hollywood in the early 1970s was that the project of mainstream cinema is illusionist; that is, that it attempts to create an illusion of reality on the screen in such a way that the spectator becomes totally absorbed in the spectacle and is prepared to accept the illusion as 'truth', at least for the time spent viewing the film. Any critical resistance is overcome and the ideology of mainstream cinema is accepted as 'natural'. This argument depends upon the idea that while all ideology is actually inconsistent, bourgeois ideology struggles to overcome its own inconsistencies. 'Progressive' cinema, then, can be defined as anti-illusionist, or anti-realist, in the sense that it works to produce those contradictions which bourgeois ideology attempts to efface. In order to do this it must work on the illusionist strategies of mainstream cinema to disturb the 'illusion of reality', to remind the spectator that the illusion is ideological rather than natural, that it can therefore be questioned. Not all non-realist films can be seen as progressive however: many Hollywood films are blatantly unrealistic, while still preserving the illusion of a coherent self-contained world which becomes imaginatively real for the period of watching. To qualify as progressive, a Hollywood film would have to be perceived as producing a criticism, at some level, of its manifest ideological project. A subtext would be discernible which works against the grain of that project, denaturalising it.

The films of Douglas Sirk provide an opportunity to examine the influence of these ideas on British film theory. Sirk was a European left-wing intellectual with a background in art history and the German theatre of the 1920s and early 1930s. He was not only familiar with the debates about art and politics in the Soviet Union and Germany during that period: he had lived through the advent of the Third Reich and the consequent campaign against left-wing artists and intellectuals which signalled the demise of one of the most thriving periods in German theatrical history, a theatre of criticism and social commitment (see Elsaesser, 1971). Sirk's theatrical productions owed much (formally at least) to the Expressionist emphasis on *mise-en-scène*, on the supremacy of gesture, light, colour and sound over the spoken word, which drew attention to the symbolic aspect of the stage–spectacle rather than its realism. At the same time he was interested in the controversial political dramas of Brecht and Bronnen, which were designed to shock the conventional, primarily middle-class German theatre audience. As the Nazi authorities interfered more and more with the running of the theatre, Sirk turned to the cinema, becoming a director for Ufa, since there was still considerable freedom for directors within the German film industry at that time (1934) (see Halliday, 1971, p. 35). His success was established with the melodrama *Schlussakkord* (1936), and continued with *Zu neuen Ufern* (1937), which shows explicitly Sirk's interest in the ideas of Brecht and Weill and in film as social criticism. Thus, before he moved to America in 1937, Sirk's theatrical productions and German films reveal the extent to which he was able to transform the materials at his disposal in his own interests.

Sirk's first experience of Hollywood (between 1939 and 1949) was rather bleak (in common with that of many European *émigré* directors). Working as a contract scriptwriter for Columbia, he was consistently denied work as a director, in spite of successes with films made by independent producers. After a year spent in Germany in 1949, where he found the film industry more or less destroyed, he returned to America where he signed up as a director with Universal. After a few years he began to impose his own style and personal concerns on the material handed to him by producer Ross Hunter and others, in the form of sometimes 'impossible' scripts. He gradually gained more control over his projects and with the help of a sympathetic studio (Universal) and collaborators (photographer Russell Metty, scriptwriter George Zuckerman, producer Albert Zugsmith) a group of melodramas emerged which have been identified as characteristically Sirkian, showing the same interest in form and politics as his German theatre and film work, albeit less explicitly (see Halliday, 1971; Mulvey and Halliday, 1972).

The argument for Sirk as a 'progressive' *auteur* rests on the assumption that he was working as a director in uncongenial circumstances (Nazi Germany in the 1930s, America in the 1950s). His own political beliefs and interests as a left-wing intellectual were under attack, he was working in a hierarchical industrial situation and therefore did not have complete control over his projects, yet he managed to produce work which can be read as critical of the prevailing ideology at one level, not necessarily the most obvious one (see Willemen, 1971). One problem with this argument is that the films chosen by critics to illustrate it (*Schlussakkord*, *Zu neuen Ufern* and *La Habanera* from the 1930s, the Universal melodramas from the 1950s) were all produced at a time when Sirk had considerable control over his projects (see Halliday, 1971, p. 35; Mulvey and Halliday, 1972, p. 109).

Moreover, it is well known that he had several sympathetic collaborators within Universal studios, which makes it difficult to argue that Sirk was totally responsible for the 1950s melodramas associated with his name. It has also been argued that it is the overt project of melodrama as a genre to act as a safety valve, siphoning off ideological contradictions and deliberately leaving them unresolved (see Melodrama, p. 164). From this perspective, Sirk would appear to have been less in tension with his material, producing a hidden, underlying criticism, than at one with it; any criticism of the prevailing ideology to be found in his work could therefore be seen as overt and, moreover, sanctioned by that ideology.

The argument for the 'progressivity' of Sirk's films raises important questions about the relationship of authorship to genre, of directors to the conditions in which they work and of how ideology is produced in films.

The 'deconstructive' *auteur*: Frank Tashlin

> Tashlin's modernity, then, rests not so much with his subject matter but with his radical break with the notion of an author communicating his personal 'vision' or 'truth' about his 'world-view'. In Tashlin's films reality is deconstructed, reactivated and re-produced. (Johnston and Willemen, 'Introduction', 1973, p. 6)

The Edinburgh Film Festival Book (Johnston and Willemen, 1973) on Frank Tashlin introduces the concepts of film as text and author as producer into the British authorship debates. A text is defined as an open structure: while it has its own set of internal relationships it also relates outwards to other texts: this relationship is the one of *intertextuality* by which all texts form part of a network of other texts. Thus no film is a self-contained, organic whole, but many films, particularly those which conform to the model of the 'classic realist text' disguise their intertextuality and present themselves as closed and unified (see The classic realist text, p. 332). Willemen ('Tashlin's method') argues that Tashlin's 'modernity' resides in the way that he 'breaks' with the classic realist text and uses intertextuality as an active, structuring principle in his work. His films refer to other Tashlin films, either directly or indirectly: he quotes from other Hollywood films and genres and refers to the film production process itself; he brings together different types of visual discourse, like television programmes, comic books, animated films. The end result is a 'demystification' of the process of film production by drawing attention to its multiple, collective nature. But the true value of Tashlin's work lies in the way that all these elements are combined to form new structures: the method of *combination* is basic to Tashlin's comedy, which rests on the type of combination used, i.e. illogical, incongruous, breaking the laws of verisimilitude, therefore *deconstructive*.

The activity of combination is described as *bricolage* (after Lévi-Strauss), a process of assembly and dismantling in which the *bricoleur*, given a number of codes to play with, proceeds to combine them into original constructions; every *auteur* ends up with a construction not quite like anybody else's. Tashlin's difference from other directors lies in the fact that he draws an analogy between the way in which he constructs his films and the way in which the social reality of American consumer ideology is constructed. So Tashlin's work does not so much satirise 1950s American consumer-orientated society, as has often been thought, as draw attention to its basic process of construction.

This account of Tashlin's method differs from conventional *auteur* study in several ways: the director is seen, not as a great artist, but as a producer of meaning, working within an economic system employing a particular language; moreover, that language is not a personal, private ideolect, it is social, a set of codes available to anyone in a society at a given time. The director cannot transcend those codes, only rework them to produce new meaning. As an attempt to identify the basic mechanisms of Tashlin's comedy this account goes some way towards providing the means for understanding the 'deconstructive' or subversive quality of his work and the pleasure it affords. However, the textual analysis which would demonstrate *how* the director is implicated in the film texts is missing; it is taken for granted that Tashlin's intentions coincide with those of the critic giving a 'deconstructive reading' of his work.

FRANK CAPRA

Mr Deeds Goes to Town (USA 1936 *p.c* – Columbia; *d* – Frank Capra; sd b/w)

Jeffrey Richards (1970) has argued that Mr Deeds was the first and most famous of the Capra populist heroes, played by Gary Cooper, a popular archetype of the good American who fits the Lincoln prototype physically: tall, lean, slow talking, while evoking for the audience the values of his other film roles in westerns. *Mr Deeds Goes to Town* epitomises the confrontation between the populist hero and the intellectual: 'in no other (Capra) film is there such an onslaught on intellectuals'. This 'onslaught on intellectuals' can be seen in the sequence in which Mr Deeds conducts his own defence, refuting the evidence of the experts who pronounce him insane. As a populist hero, he wins his case by virtue of common sense and knowledge of the people, as opposed to the abstract ideas of the experts.

The key role of the Capra heroine in restoring the hero's shattered confidence in human nature can be seen in Mary's passionate speech defending Deeds. Her declaration of love enables him to help himself, self-help being an important factor in populist mythology. According to Richards, the populist theme of 'good neighbourliness' is basic to Capra's work, asserting the values of the small community, co-operative enterprise and human friendship. It is these values which Mary defends in her speech and in her admission of love (a reversal of her previous cynicism) and on which Deeds draws in his questioning of the witnesses from Mandrake Falls (his home town). They share a common language which is quite different from the language of the big city (as in the play with the word 'pixillated' on which Mr Deeds' fate rests). Richards reads this validation of populism directly from the film, equating it with Capra's authorial concerns.

Sam Rohdie argues that the narrative opens by posing the opposition between town/country, sophisticated/naïve, then proceeds to reverse these oppositions, producing a situation where 'country', 'naïve' appear as good, honest, right minded, indeed, sophisticated, until all the characters (except the lawyer) are united in the populist values of rural America; a utopian resolution, representing ideal unity.

The play of structural oppositions can be seen in the values assigned to different characters, who are given the status of stereotypes. Names are important in identifying those values, e.g. Longfellow Deeds (good deeds), Cedar (the 'oily' lawyer), Babe (the soft, sweet baby). The courtroom scene demonstrates the structural importance of the shifting of these oppositions. In order for the narrative resolution to take place, both Mary and Deeds must reverse positions: she must validate his values, reversing her own, and he must subscribe to her values (words and sophisticated argument) in order to save himself. Rohdie argues that the comedy of the film rests on the unmasking of the *town* and all it stands for in fakery, cynicism and inhumanity, by the *country*. Rohdie's structural analysis, despite his disclaimers, raises important questions for the kind of approach taken by Richards, which assumes the transparency of ideology and authorial intentions.

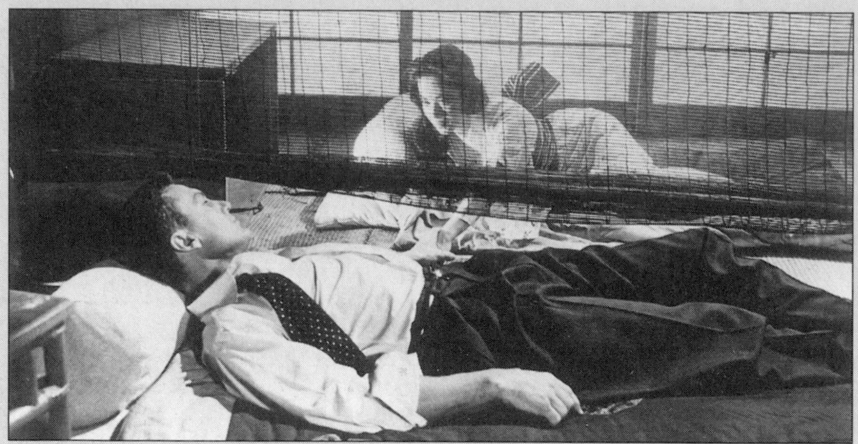

Racial and sexual tension in Fuller's *House of Bamboo*

SAMUEL FULLER

House of Bamboo (USA 1955 *p.c* – 20th Century–Fox; *d* – Samuel Fuller; sd col.)

Fuller began his career in movies as a story and scriptwirter, directing his first film in 1948 (*I Shot Jesse James*). His early films were nearly all made for 20th Century–Fox, in general quick cheap B-features. Nicholas Garnham points to the fact that in spite of the conditions under which the films were made, Fuller manages to achieve an extraordinary consistency of style and theme. For example, the preponderance of long-takes in his films is unusual in low-budget film-making, since economy dictates the use of cutting and static shots rather than risky, therefore expensive, camera movements (Garnham, 1971, p. 28).

At the same time, Fuller's style is often described as having the directness of poster art, a propagandistic quality which is primitive and direct rather than realistic, producing alienating shock effects, hence the constant evocation of Brecht in relation to his work and the acknowledged influence of Fuller's films on the work of Jean-Luc Godard. This didactic quality attracted the Marxist structuralist critics, who were interested in the ways in which cinematic language could be put to political use.

Sam Rohdie (1969) points to a central problem in the film as being one of identification. The male protagonist, Eddie (Robert Stack), is a double agent and most of the other characters in the film pretend to be what they are not. Thus the audience's assumptions are constantly unsettled. The problem of identification is worked out in terms of racial and sexual tension: between Eddie and the Japanese Mariko and between this couple and the male gang. For an American public, these tensions pose problems of allegiance and national identity (Rohdie, 1969, p. 29).

Fuller's films are often described as the most violent in American cinema, a violence translated into images rather than appearing directly on the screen, the violence of intellectual shock rather than shocking exhibition of violence. Rohdie argues that Fuller's 'assault on the audience' is reinforced by 'a violence of editing, colouring and the staging of shots' (Rohdie, 1969, p. 40).

House of Bamboo is the last film Fuller made for Fox before founding his own production company, Globe Enterprises, in 1956.

Verboten! (USA 1958 *p.c* – Globe Enterprises for RKO; *d* – Samuel Fuller; sd b/w)

Fuller had always wanted to make a film of his war experiences and returned to Europe to seek out people he met during the war so as to get accurate reconstruction. However, this film was never realised, and *Verboten*! is only partly a war film: it deals, like *Run of the Arrow* (1957) with the aftermath of war.

Peter Wollen traces the paradoxical themes in *Verboten!* – the tension between Fuller's anti-war attitudes and the increasing postwar involvement of America in launching and waging wars of conquest; an interest in the children of war, orphaned and therefore in need of 'foster parents' who will give them the right guidance (cf. *China Gate*, 1957); the need for union between violently opposed factions in order to produce social stability (cf. *House of Bamboo*, 1955, and *Run of the Arrow*, 1957) (Wollen, '*Verboten!*', 1969).

Verboten! is very close to *House of Bamboo* in its symmetrical structure of infiltration and betrayal. Bruno has infiltrated the American HQ and Franz betrays the Werewolf (neo-Nazi) organisation to the Americans from the inside. The hero's fiancée, Helga, is (like Mariko) at the centre of the structure: her friends and her brother are members of the Werewolf organisation, her fiancé is an American official. Arguably, it is from this almost schematic play of oppositions that ideological contradictions emerge.

It is arguable that Fuller's pro-Americanism is necessarily ambiguous, and that this ambiguity is crystallised in the figure of David, who speaks the words of American democracy which are also the words of imperialism. David's relationship to his wife and unborn child is also imperialist. We can ask here how Fuller makes the audience aware of this ambiguity.

Underworld USA (USA 1960 *p.c* – Globe Enterprises; *d* – Samuel Fuller; sd b/w)

Described by Fuller as a 'quickie', the original project was to make a film about contemporary America showing that crime does indeed pay. However, the censor objected and Fuller was unable to be as explicit about the subject as he wanted.

As with many Fuller films, there is a central tension between the 'hero' and society, conceived as hostile, a battleground. Fuller's view of his hero (Tolly Devlin) is profoundly pessimistic: he is a psychopath, the offspring of a corrupt and brutal society. Also pessimistic is the view of American society as a totalitarian system controlled by organised crime, against which democratic action has little or no effect. Tolly Devlin's motive for fighting the syndicate is the individualistic one of revenge and he never grasps the social meaning of his actions, a theme common to many Fuller films. In spite of this, it is on social outcasts such as Tolly, Sandy and Cuddles that the democratic future of America depends and Tolly's perverse obsession with violent revenge is a bizarre reflection of American values of family loyalty and national identity. Similarly, the vulnerability of the family and personal relationships in the gangster/*film noir* genre (see Harvey, 1980) gives the opportunity to introduce the recurrent Fuller theme of concern for 'children without parents', i.e. the future of America. Tolly himself is an orphan and is unable to acquire a 'family' in the course of the film.

Victor Perkins points to the political impulse behind Fuller's extreme individualism:

> The film ends on a zoom into a close-up of Tolly's clenched fist. (This has been a visual motif throughout the film.) The propaganda purpose of Fuller's pictures is to instil into a democracy the vigour of his hero. The ideal would be a compromise between Tolly's individualism and the needs of society. But Fuller is not concerned with ideals. Instead the tension of equal and opposite forces, each dangerous and each salutary, maintains his world in its spectacularly perilous equilibrium. (Perkins, 1969, p. 74)

By posing Tolly's psychotic individualism against the corrupt and brutal society which produced him, it can be argued that Fuller produced a devastating critique of his own society.

Zu neuen Ufern – the trial of Gloria Vane

Arguably also Fuller's style, which is often described as 'propagandistic' or 'journalistic' (demonstrated in his use of the rhetoric of newspaper photographs, both literally in the headline announcing the Mencken child's death – or as a principle of construction – in the shock cuts), is instrumental in producing this critique.

DOUGLAS SIRK

Zu neuen Ufern (To New Shores)
(Germany 1937 *p.c* – Ufa; *d* – Detlef Sierck (Douglas Sirk); sd b/w)

After the enormous success of *Schlussakkord* (1936), Sirk's first full-blown melodrama, he went on to direct this film, which he describes as incorporating his interest in melodrama as a vehicle for encouraging social criticism in the audience and in characters who are uncertain about their aims in life and so find themselves going in circles – the 'tragic rondo' (see Halliday, 1971, pp. 47–8). Jon Halliday describes the film as a tough social criticism of the British ruling class and colonialism in nineteenth-century Australia (Halliday, 'Notes on Sirk's German films', 1971). The tragic, vacillating figure in this case is Sir Albert Finsbury, a weak British officer.

The trial scene usefully demonstrates Sirk's interest in adapting Brecht–Weill for cinema. The trial of Gloria Vane (Zarah Leander) is introduced by an old woman singing a song about Paramatta (the women's prison in Australia to which Gloria is about to be consigned by a class-prejudiced court) outside the courtroom; she has a large placard with a number of pictures on it: the camera passes from her to the courtroom where Gloria is sentenced, back out to the placard, whereupon a picture of Paramatta dissolves to Paramatta itself. This explicitly Brechtian strategy has the effect of drawing attention to the formal construction of the film and, some would argue, introducing a critical distance for the audience.

This scene also shows Sirk's interest, influenced by German Expressionism, in using *mise-en-scène* to create an independent, dreamlike world on the screen entirely divorced from 'reality'. Sharp contrasts of light and dark combined with stylised acting and sets are an extension of the theatrical conventions of melodrama.

All That Heaven Allows (USA 1955 *p.c* – Universal International; *d* – Douglas Sirk; sd col.)

One of Sirk's woman's pictures (Melodrama, p. 170), this film has been praised both as a critique of American bourgeois values (Halliday, *All That Heaven Allows*, 1972) and as a poignant working through of the contradictions faced by women in patriarchal society (Mulvey, 1977).

The film presents events through the point of view of its central female protagonist, using the visual code of *mise-en-scène* to indicate her state of mind. This ironic use of *mise-en-scène* can either be read as an attempt by the director to comment on the conservative values supposedly adhered to in the melodrama's subject matter, or as part of the melodramatic convention in which stylised *mise-en-scène* is used to offer the audience privileged information over the characters (Elsaesser, 1972).

In the family melodrama, it has been argued, dramatic conflict is engendered by working through the contradictions, par

Written on the Wind – a criticism of the patriarchal American family

ticularly for women, of heterosexual monogamy and motherhood. *All That Heaven Allows* centres these problems in the point of view of its heroine, arguably producing problems for the classic Hollywood narrative which are out of the director's control. From this perspective, the film is less a 'progressive text' than a safety valve for painful ideological contradictions (see Mulvey, 1977).

Written on the Wind (USA 1956 *p.c* – Universal International; *d* – Douglas Sirk; sd col.)

Sirk's theatrical background can be seen in the organisation of the *mise-en-scène*: strong primary colours, contrasts of dark and light, exaggerated acting and gestures combine to produce a world dominated by physical and psychological violence, marked by an emotional excess which threatens to overturn the stability of the established order. This film is a tragic melodrama, concentrating on male oedipal problems with the patriarchal order (see Mulvey, 1977).

Kyle Hadley (Robert Stack) is an example of one of Sirk's vacillating characters (cf. Cary in *All That Heaven Allows*, Sir Albert Finsbury in *Zu neuen Ufern*), but his hysterical response to his supposed sterility has also been identified as one of the basic motifs of tragic melodrama. The 'negative' destructive impulses of Kyle and his sister Marylee (Dorothy Malone) are played off against the 'positive' qualities of the 'good' couple, Mitch (Rock Hudson) and Lucy (Lauren Bacall) to produce a criticism of the patriarchal American family and the ideals of masculinity and femininity on which it depends. Marylee's orgiastic 'dance of death' explicitly draws a parallel between excessive female sexuality and the overthrow of the patriarchal order, a view of female sexuality as threat which is common in American cinema and which is arguably mobilised here in the interests of social criticism.

The symbolic use of colour in the *mise-en-scène* to refer to the values held by different characters is typical of melodramatic conventions, but could also be seen as a particular use of ironic commentary by the director in order to distance the audience from their emotional response and induce a critical awareness (i.e. a 'Brechtian' strategy which can undermine the pathos and catharsis characteristic of tragedy as a form).

FRANK TASHLIN

Will Success Spoil Rock Hunter? (Oh! For a Man!) (USA 1957 *p.c* – 20th Century–Fox; *d* – Frank Tashlin; sd col. scope)

> The construction of an attractive female form is an elaborate process, and proceeds along the same principles which underlie Tashlin's films. (Willemen, 'Tashlin's method', 1973, p. 129)

So, apparently, does the construction of an attractive male form. Film star Rita (Jayne Mansfield–archetypal constructed female form) attempts to build the diminutive Rock (Tony Randall) into an approximation to her 'better half', Bobo (Mickey Hargitay). But it is not only difficult and painful for 'real' people to live up to the ideal that society constructs for them, it can also destroy them. Tashlin's comedy produces a gap between the 'real' and the constructed ideal which provides both theatre of the absurd and a brilliant deconstruction of American society's view of what it takes to be a man or a woman. Spot the quotes, references and in-jokes. Does Tashlin's comic method, and the playing off of the 'real' against the 'ideal' work to provide a criticism of American ideology?

Love Happy (USA 1949 *p.c* – Lester Cowan Productions; *d* – David Miller; sd b/w)

Before becoming a director, Tashlin worked in Hollywood as an animator (for Disney, also on *Bugs Bunny*, etc.) and as a gagman and comedy scriptwriter. In 1948 he collaborated with Ben Hecht on the script of this Marx Brothers comedy.

The film would never be included in an *auteur* study of the Tashlin *œuvre*; but in some ways it exhibits precisely those qualities of 'intertextuality' and concern with collaborative production which, it has been argued, were developed by Tashlin as a director.

Love Happy provides an example of the screwball comedy which influenced Tashlin's later work; also an example of his contribution as scriptwriter (arguably most evident in the cartoonist's sensibility observable in the rooftop chase). Perhaps most important, it demonstrates the collaborative process which makes up a Hollywood film. Although Tashlin's contribution is important, so is that of the Marx Brothers, the director David Miller, and the art director Gabriel Scognamillo.

Will Success Spoil Rock Hunter? – the construction of an attractive male form

The evacuation of the author: Raoul Walsh

Structuralist criticism leads the critic away from conventional *auteur* criticism towards a consideration of other areas of cinema in an attempt to displace the *auteur* from the centre of the work. However, in the process, the specificity of a particular director can be lost altogether (see Nowell-Smith, 1970). Structuralism at its best aims to understand the interaction of multiple structures in and between texts, seeing the *auteur* structure as one among many in any given film: it may or may not be dominant. Rather than dissolve the author altogether, a structuralist approach to film could determine the specific relationship of different authors to each film.

It is arguable that in the Edinburgh Film Festival book on Raoul Walsh (Hardy, 1974) which takes as its subject the *auteur* theory itself as much as the *auteur* Walsh (see MacCabe, 1975), Walsh is made to disappear (almost) completely. Apart from the first article by Peter Lloyd, which treats the director in terms of conventional *auteur* theory, the other writers find him either enmeshed in the structures of the studio (Buscombe), or in the structures of the text (Willemen), or in the structures of patriarchal ideology (Cook and Johnston).

Ed Buscombe (1974) argues that the films directed by Walsh for Warner Bros. between 1939 and 1951 are typical of the known general policy of the studio at that time, to such an extent that one must call into question the simple notion of Walsh as an *auteur* who dictated the style and content of his pictures. On the contrary, Walsh was obliged to make use of the stars and genres available at Warners to produce films which conformed to the studio product. Similarly, he was working with a group of left-wing producers and writers whose contributions must be taken into account. Buscombe surmises that these conditions of production must have been congenial for Walsh because he stayed with Warners until 1951; thus they were not so much 'constraints' as conditions which provided possibilities for good work in certain directions rather than others. The problematic absence in Buscombe's account is Walsh himself. Without analysis of film texts it is impossible to say what the director's contribution might have been. Did he simply reproduce the studio product as Buscombe seems to suggest? The presence of left-wing personnel on the studio production team could not guarantee a left-wing product and 'studio style', if it is to mean anything at all, must be composed of many contradictory elements since the studio itself presumably consists of shifting power relationships which change with history (see Warner Bros. p. 19).

RAOUL WALSH

The Roaring Twenties (USA 1939 *p.c* – Warner Bros.; *d* – Raoul Walsh; sd b/w)

Peter Lloyd argues that Walsh's relationship with Warner Bros. was ambiguous, in that his concern with individual personal action went against the grain of the studio's commitment to a 'socially conscious' cinema (Lloyd, 1974, p. 18).

Buscombe takes a different view. Having characterised Warners' studio product during the 1930s as the manifestation of the 'vaguely and uncertainly radical yearnings which the studio shared with the New Deal', he claims that Walsh's first three pictures for Warners fit squarely into this mould and that *The Roaring Twenties* makes a connection between social deprivation and crime which perfectly expresses New Deal ideology (Buscombe, 1974, p. 56). (See Warner Bros., p. 19.)

These different readings of Walsh's Warner Bros.' films raise the question of the relationship between director, studio and genre, and of how 'studio style', as opposed to the director's style can be distinguished.

They Drive by Night (USA 1940 *p.c* – Warner Bros.; *d* – Raoul Walsh; sd b/w)

Buscombe argues that this film 'exemplifed perfectly both the strengths and limitations of Warners' radicalism' (Buscombe, 1974, p. 57). The desperation of the truck drivers is specifically linked to an economic insecurity deriving from mass unemployment in society at large, but the solution to this social problem is presented entirely in individual terms: 'George Raft eventually becomes the owner of his own haulage company and so insulates himself from the pressures which affect the mass below him' (Buscombe, 1974, p. 57).

It is interesting to speculate whether the 'individualism' noted by Buscombe can be seen as an indication of Walsh's contribution rather than the studio's. If the film can be described as 'ideologically radical', at least in terms of the New Deal, how does the figure of the independent woman (played by Ida Lupino), who acts on her desires and is ultimately destroyed by them, and who presents a serious problem to the hero of the film (George Raft) attaining his own desires, fit into this description? It could be argued that in this respect, this film fits less with the studio product than with Walsh's work in general (cf. *The Revolt of Mamie Stover*, see below).

High Sierra (USA 1941 *p.c* – Warner Bros.; *d* – Raoul Walsh; sd b/w)

> The whole film in fact deals with people who are in various ways outcasts from society, and while Bogart's own alienation has a metaphysical dimension, the attempt to relate crime to social causes is a real one. There is every difference between this and the gangster films of the 40s and 50s, which tend to see crime as a manifestation of some purely psychological disturbance. (Buscombe, 1974, p. 57)

The 'metaphysical' dimensions of Bogart's alienation may have been contributed by John Huston, who co-scripted this film but was not a regular member of the team of writers with whom Walsh worked.

The film has a strong melodramatic element. The family Roy Earle (Bogart) meets, represents an ideal for him: when the crippled daughter Velma is 'corrupted' he is shattered, left with a grotesque parody of a family in the moll, Marie (Ida Lupino) and a stray dog, in the tradition of the 'absent family' of the thriller/*film noir* genre (see Harvey, 1980).

In terms of Walsh's *œuvre*, the rejection of Velma by Roy occurs when it is clear to him that he has lost control of her. Although Velma is portrayed unsympathetically and it is Roy Earle's point of view that is offered for identification, the gangster's bitterness and isolation could be read as an indictment of his patriarchal attitude to women and of the very ideas he cherishes. It is characteristic of the genre that the stoicism, honesty and compassion of the gangster's moll, Marie, provide a primary focus of identification for the audience.

The Revolt of Mamie Stover (USA 1956 *p.c* – 20th Century–Fox; *d* – Raoul Walsh; sd col. scope)

Cook and Johnston's (1972) argument about this film raises questions of the representation of female sexuality in Walsh's work in general and of how this representation cuts across the distinctions made by critics between, for example, Walsh's Warner Bros. films and the others.

The opening of the film – in which we see Mamie getting out of a police car at a dockside – depicts the ways in which Mamie/Jane Russell is established as a threat (her 'look' directly into camera, etc.); central sections of the narrative in which her 'image' is seen as part of a system of exchange controlled by men, and then as it threatens to slip out of the grasp of Jimmy/Richard Egan (that is, as Mamie is about to be totally economically independent and in control of the system of exchange); the resolution of the narrative in which Mamie is 'put in place' by Jimmy, a totally symbolic resolution because she is actually in a position economically to control most of the island. She gives up all her money and returns to home and family.

The question of the 'distancing' devices used in the film is of interest, e.g. the way in which Mamie's 'image' is seen to be controlled by men, apparently drawing attention to the workings of patriarchal ideology. The symbolic, arbitrary structure of the narrative resolution, by appearing totally unrealistic, could be said to raise the question of the problem of male control of women, and the 'fetishised' image of Jane Russell seems to emphasise her function in the film as a sign of 'phallic displacement', thus drawing attention to the 'positive woman' figure as a projection of male sexual anxieties.

Paul Willemen (1974) examines the film *Pursued* (1947) closely, analysing its textual operation in terms of a network of shifting relationships between the formal signifiers in which the place of the subject of the discourse (the director) and of the audience (the reader of the text) is never fixed. Willemen displaces the linear form of communication which is generally assumed to exist between the subject of an utterance (the 'addresser') and the receiver of that utterance (the 'addressee') in favour of a concept of the film text constructed like a fantasy in which both 'subject' and 'reader' are dispersed across the network of overlaps and substitutions among the different characters. The effect is to deny the possibility of the full presence of the director/*auteur* as organising source; only the traces of his presence remain and this only in the interstices (i.e. gaps) of the text. Thus the author is to be found in the marks of interruption and incoherence; the subject, by definition, is always fading away.

If this argument seems somewhat reductive, taking Lacanian psychoanalytic theory to an extreme in order to demonstrate a primary truth, it nevertheless has the advantage of showing that conventional *auteur* theory, by unifying *auteur*, text and critic and constructing them in terms of intention and presence, is an ideological operation dedicated to smoothing over contradictions. In Willemen's construction, Walsh's specificity is dissolved into the specificity of the textual operation of the film: or rather, according to this argument, it precisely depends upon the specific *reading* given to any text(s) at any given moment.

Pam Cook and Claire Johnston (1974) argue that conventional *auteur* theory avoids coming to terms with the organisation of the film text and the way it mediates ideology; if ideology is described in analysis of film it is usually seen as an expression of the director's world-view rather than in terms of the structure of the film itself. They propose looking at Walsh as a 'subject within ideology, and, ultimately, the laws of the human order' and, specifically, at the film text in terms of the way it articulates the ideology of patriarchy, since it is this ideology which defines a par-

The Revolt of Mamie Stover – Mamie (Jane Russell) threatening to take control

ticular social place for women. The authors argue that the Hollywood system is of interest to feminist critics because the image of 'woman' that it presents is fetishistic, i.e. it endows this image with masculine attributes of power which efface woman's sexual difference, fixing her as the locus of male castration anxiety. In this system, woman is 'spoken' as a sign, as an object to be exchanged by men rather than the subject of desire (see Cowie, 1978). However, because women are, in social reality, more than objects of exchange, the process of fixing 'woman' in place is problematic for the patriarchal order, which must constantly work to overcome the contradictions within itself. So the fetishistic system is seen to be relatively unstable: its contradictions can either be effaced, or exploited to draw attention to the system itself. The authors argue that Walsh's *œuvre* can be read in this way as drawing attention to the patriarchal ideology within which it is placed: its interest lies precisely in the way it *presents* that ideology to the spectator rather than effacing it.

The text Cook and Johnston choose to analyse, *The Revolt of Mamie Stover* (1956), revolves around the problem of the exchange and circulation of money at a time of economic crisis: the Second World War. It is vital that women support the economy when men are absent, yet the very absence of men means that women threaten to take over the system of exchange rather than support it. In *The Revolt of Mamie Stover*, women, in this case prostitutes, exemplified by the central character Mamie (played by Jane Russell) are exchanged like money, in the same way that Mamie's highly fetishised image is exchanged. The ideological problem that the narrative tries to resolve is that it is precisely the objects men need to exchange (money, women, images) which threaten to escape and take control of the system controlling their circulation. The function of the positive, independent woman image exemplified by Mamie/Jane Russell is to trigger the process of 'putting into place' by which the narrative contains this threat. The character's strength and independence is thus apparent rather than real, since she is a sign with a specific function in the narrative system. The 'symbolic order' of the narrative is seen to correspond to the symbolic order of patriarchy itself, in that both work to override contradiction by attempting to fix women in place, in the case of film by means of the codes of cinematic language. Because Walsh's films seem to present this problem quite explicitly in terms of the power relationships between men and women and in terms of the struggle by men to keep control of the system of exchange and therefore of women, patriarchal ideology seeps through the very structure of the films, in the organisation of images and narrative, and rises to the surface.

In this account, Walsh the *auteur* is again displaced from centre stage to make way, this time, for ideology. Again, the problem of the specificity of the director's contribution is sidestepped in favour of more generalised concepts such as *narrative structure* and *patriarchal ideology*. Text, and director, are treated a-historically (see also Gledhill, 1978).

These three articles succeed in evacuating Walsh as *auteur*, as originating source of meaning of his films, from his work. At the same time they fail to deal with the question of precisely what Walsh's contribution to the production of meaning might be as director of a body of films.

Selected Reading

Edward Buscombe, 'Walsh and Warner Bros.', in Hardy (ed.), *Raoul Walsh*, Edinburgh Film Festival, 1974.

Pam Cook and Claire Johnston, 'The place of woman in the cinema of Raoul Walsh', in Hardy (ed.), *Raoul Walsh*, Edinburgh Film Festival, 1974.

Jon Halliday, *Sirk on Sirk*, London, Secker & Warburg/BFI, 1971.

Claire Johnston and Paul Willemen, 'Introduction', in Johnston and Willemen (eds), *Frank Tashlin*, Edinburgh Film Festival/SEFT, 1973.

Laura Mulvey, 'Sirk and melodrama', *Movie* no. 25, 1977.

AUTEUR STRUCTURALISM UNDER ATTACK

Signs and Meaning in the Cinema

Peter Wollen's defence of *auteur* structuralism in *Signs and Meaning in the Cinema* (1969, 1972) is perhaps the most cogent argument for the retention of the *auteur* theory in some form or other. The problem of authorship and cinema is not satisfactorily resolved by the attempts on the part of proponents of some of the more reductionist and formalist developments of structuralist method to dissolve the *auteur* altogether into the generalities of other structures. The theoretical problems inherent in British *auteur* structuralism have often been pointed out (Eckert, 1973; Henderson, 1973). Henderson's careful reading of Wollen's chapter on the *auteur* theory reveals the lack of theoretical foundation in *auteur* structuralism and the empiricism underlying many of Wollen's rhetorical strategies. It also points to the fundamental incompatibility of the two critical approaches, which produces contradictions in the arguments which must finally destroy *auteur* structuralism itself: that is, while *auteur* theory as it stands (and as it is retained by Wollen) rests on the principle that the subject is the producer of a unique or distinctive meaning, the structuralism of Lévi-Strauss and others is founded upon the interchangeability of subjects in the production of meaning. Henderson's impressive demolition of *auteur* structuralism is the prelude to a criticism of structuralism itself in the light of theoretical developments emerging from the French *Tel Quel* group and others which called for a new theory of textual operation and of the place of the subject in the process of production of meaning (Henderson, 1973, p. 33). Nonetheless, as Henderson himself points out, it is only in the destruction of *auteur* structuralism itself that the new question can be liberated. The value of *auteur* structuralism resides in the problems it poses and the questions it provokes.

Wollen argues that *auteur* structuralism provides a critical approach which can retain the impetus of the original *politique des auteurs* (i.e. to decipher the presence of authors in Hollywood film production as opposed to European art cinema) while avoiding its excesses by providing the more objective criteria of basic structures rather than subjective ones of personal taste. Structuralism allows the critic to define a core of repeated motifs in the director's *œuvre*: however, it must also analyse the system of differences and oppositions which marks one film off from the others in the *œuvre*, and which produces meaning in each film. It is not enough to reduce films to basic oppositional structures: the critic must also pay attention to the whole series of shifting variations within and between films. Different levels of complexity of combination mark the work of some directors as 'richer' than others. For Wollen, Ford's work is richer than Hawks's because Hawks's films can be summed up in terms of schematic sets of oppositions, whereas Ford's work manifests many different and shifting levels of variation. It is interesting that Wollen retains the categories of 'good' and 'bad' films which structuralist method could, in theory at least, have dispensed with. In the first edition of his book Wollen discounts the importance of other contributions (such as those of the star or the studio) to the production of meaning in film: the *auteur* structure, for him, is the primary or dominant one. Strangely, it is at this point of greatest tension between *auteur* theory and Lévi-Strauss's structuralism that Wollen calls on Lévi-Strauss and equates film with myth (Wollen, 1972, p. 105). For meaning in myth is indeed collectively produced: there is no place in myth for the individual language user.

An important part of Wollen's polemic is his reformulation of *auteur* theory in terms of the *auteur* as unconscious catalyst rather than intentional presence, an argument he elaborates in the Postscript to the 1972 revised edition:

> *Auteur* analysis does not consist of retracing a film to its creative source. It consists of tracing a structure (not a message) within the work, which can then *post factum* be assigned to an individual, the director, on empirical grounds. It is wrong, in the name of a denial of the traditional idea of creative subjectivity, to deny any status to individuals at all. But Fuller, or Hawks or Hitchcock, the directors, are quite separate from 'Fuller' or 'Hawks' or 'Hitchcock', the structures named after them, and should not be methodologically confused. There can be no doubt that the presence of a structure in the text can often be connected with the presence of a director on the set, but the situation in cinema, where the director's primary task is often one of coordination and rationalisation, is very different from that in the other arts, where there is a much more direct relationship between artist and work. It is in this sense that it is possible to speak of a film *auteur* as an unconscious catalyst. (Wollen, 1972, p. 168)

While there is clearly a tension at work here between the traditional notion of structure as present in the work (noted by Henderson) and a new formulation of the *auteur* as a 'fiction' in the text rather than as intentional subject, this new formulation precisely looks forward to the theory of meaning production that Henderson argues for. The *auteur* as catalyst can be read as one element in the play of assemblage of different elements which makes up the film text(s).

The *auteur* as structure: Howard Hawks

A comparison of the different critical approaches to the work of Howard Hawks taken by Robin Wood (1968, 1981) and Peter Wollen (1969, 1972) demonstrates basic differences in conceptualising the *auteur* theory and Hawks's place within it which illuminate the historical context for British *auteur*-structuralist criticism.

Both writers are concerned with the status of film as an art and its relationship to the other, established arts. Both use the *auteur* theory to support the contention that film does indeed deserve the status of 'art' rather than (or as well as) 'entertainment' by demonstrating that Hawks's work is on a par with the great classical tradition (which in Wood's case means Shakespeare, Bach, Mozart). While Wood supports this tradition in opposition to modernism, however, Wollen is primarily concerned, especially in the Postscript to the revised edition of *Signs and Meaning in the Cinema*, with a defence of modernism which attacks the roots of Wood's critical assumptions.

An Intuitive Artist

Wood argues that art is defined by the extent of the artist's personal involvement with his material and not by the common distinction between 'art' and 'entertainment', which is virtually meaningless when applied to the classical tradition. The classical tradition is opposed to the modern tradition in that in the former the artist develops an already existing language rather than developing a new one. Hawks belongs in the classical tradition because he is totally unselfconscious; he does not draw attention to the forms he uses, therefore his work is ultimately unanalysable: the critic responds intuitively and spontaneously to the intuitive and spontaneous work that is the film. Although Hawks worked within many of the Hollywood genres, his personal vision transforms those genres; therefore he should be classified not according to genre, but according to his way of looking at the world. For Wood, Hawks's only limitation as an artist is his refusal to think of himself as such and his commitment to film as commercial entertainment. Hawks's masterpieces were produced in those moments when he was 'suddenly completely engaged by his material', when his 'intuitive consciousness' is fully alerted.

A Structure of Reversal

Wollen (1969, 1972, 1998, p. 53 in 1998 edn) uses Hawks as a test case for *auteur* theory. Hawks is a director who is generally judged on the basis of his adventure dramas and found wanting. It is only by looking at the whole of his work, at the crazy comedies as well as the dramas, that a core of repeated motifs emerges which give added dimension to the films and makes it possible for the critic to decipher a Hawks's world-view through the play of oppositions and reversals between the dramas and the comedies. Wollen is critical of that world-view and supports his criticisms by differentiating between Hawks's work and that of Ford and Boetticher: they are all concerned with similar problems of heroism and masculinity, but the problem is articulated quite differently by each one. For Wollen, the strength of Hawks lies not in his spontaneous, intuitive artistry but in the systematic organisation of structural reversals throughout his work as a whole. Wollen does not subscribe to Hawks's values, as Wood appears to, but this does not prevent him from attempting to establish Hawks's status as an *auteur* on the basis of criteria which go beyond his personal taste as a critic.

Hawks Versus Ford

Both writers compare Hawks with Ford, arriving at totally different conclusions. Wollen sees Ford as going beyond the question of the value of individual action to society and to American history: Ford does not simply validate American individualistic values, he begins to question the historical basis of these values. Hawks, on the other hand, finds the solution to individual isolation in the camaraderie of the self-sufficient all-male group, cut off from society, history, and women, who are a threat to this male world.

For Wood, the comparison between Hawks and Ford reveals Hawks to be the more modern of the two artists because the idea of a stable social tradition is absent from his work. While Ford looks back nostalgically to lost values, Hawks deals with the problem of modern society by rejecting it, by creating his own world of personal loyalties in which an ideal society would be one in which the individual had maximum possible freedom from social constraints. 'Within the group, one feels an absence of *civilised* sensibility, but the strong presence of the uncultivated, instinctive sensibility that must underlie any valid civilisation: intuitive–sympathetic contact, a sturdily positive, generous spirit' (Wood, 1968, p. 92).

A Feminist View

One might wish to question the value of any view of society in which the 'sturdily positive, generous spirit' does not extend beyond the male group to the other half of society: women. Women exist at the periphery of Hawks's male group, at the point at which it threatens to break down. It is this representation of 'woman' as a point of tension or anxiety in male society – in effect a troublesome question which refuses to go away – which has attracted the attention of feminist film critics to Hawks's work. Hawks's films appear to epitomise the workings of patriarchal ideology in the way that they represent the 'otherness' of women as a threat which can only be resolved (uneasily) by the

HOWARD HAWKS

Scarface (USA 1932 *p.c* – Hughes Productions; *d* – Howard Hawks; sd b/w)

This film clearly belongs in the so-called 'classic' cycle of the gangster film in which the gangster hero is depicted as a paradoxical and schizophrenic figure, representing the worst in society and the best, in so far as he is striving towards the goals of the American Dream (i.e. wealth, individualism, success and power). In the context of Hawks's work, however, Robin Wood has identified *Scarface* as one of his comedies. Camonte is presented as an innocent primitive with whom we should sympathise rather than pass moral judgement. Much of the comedy resides in the way that the male characters are ridiculed (as in the comic violence involving Angelo and Camonte's innocent enjoyment of his own bad taste). Wood pays close attention to Hawks's *mise-en-scène* to demonstrate how the audience is both drawn in to enjoy the gangsters' sense of complete freedom through violence, and yet distanced by the horror of it (Wood, 1968, p. 64). The combination of farce and horror makes the film truly disturbing, and it could be argued that Hawks here presents a complete reversal (and possible criticism) of the values he seems to justify in the dramas.

Wollen sees this opposition between the comedies and the dramas as vital. In the comedies the retrograde, Spartan heroism of the dramas is exposed to reveal their underlying tensions: the regression to infantilism and savagery and the sexual humiliation of the male (Wollen, 1972, p. 91). If in the dramas man is master of his world, in the comedies he is its victim. It is in this opposition that Hawks's value as an *auteur* is to be found, because it lends complexity to the representation of sexuality in his work as a whole.

Bringing up Baby (USA 1938 *p.c* – RKO Radio; *d* – Howard Hawks; sd b/w)

Wood characterises Hawks's comedy thus:

> There is the extremeness of it, in the context of the light comedy genre: we are almost in the world of the Marx Brothers. There is the sexual reversal, the humiliation of the male, his loss of mastery, which makes the comedies an inversion of the adventure films. Finally, there is the *resilience* of the male, his ability to live through extremes of humiliation retaining an innate dignity. (Wood, 1968, p. 68)

He sees this film as based on the opposition between duty and nature, order and chaos, superego and id, the oppositions manifested in the struggle between the man and the woman in the progress from order to chaos and back to order again. The safety of David's world is shattered by Susan's anarchistic behaviour and can only be precariously rebuilt, leaving the spectator with an uneasy feeling that the male–female couple relationship will never be ideal. Wood points to the representation of the woman in this film as an anarchic, destructive natural force, dominating the weak and foolish male intellectual.

Wollen agrees that the comedies are the reversal of the dramas in that the hero becomes victim and that Hawks's comedy often centres around sex and role reversal (i.e. domineering women and timid, pliable men). The association of women with nature, and therefore with danger and disruption, is common to Hawks's films in general – although *Scarface* presents an interesting variation on this theme in that these primitive forces are represented by a male hero. Hawks generally keeps the male and female worlds strictly apart: when they are combined in one character (e.g. Tony Camonte) they lead to self-destruction.

The comedy in this film is again farcical, sadistic and destructive. It could be argued that Hawks undermines the ideology of male heroism only at the expense of putting forward a view of women which mirrors the fears and anxieties of men. Another argument might be that the use of structural oppositions and reversals in this work allows the ideology to be presented in a schematic form, thus inviting the audience to criticise it.

His Girl Friday (USA 1939 *p.c* – Columbia; *d* – Howard Hawks; sd b/w)

His Girl Friday is one of Hawks's mature comedies which works out the sets of oppositions outlined above in an extremely complex structural network using all the elements described by Wood and Wollen as specific to the comedies, but reversing many of them. A structural study of Hawks's work is useful for revealing the varied and shifting combinations of basic structures that are possible. Wollen argues that the greater the complexity of combinations the richer the work becomes.

The male world is again opposed to the female world, but this time amorality and irresponsibility lie with the former and the latter is associated with a desire for stability, home and family. Both worlds are controlled by men: the frenetic newspaper office by the unscrupulous Walter Burns (Cary Grant) and the home and marriage scene by the stolid, safe insurance salesman Bruce (Ralph Bellamy). Hildy (Rosalind Russell) is torn between the two: her 'feminine' qualities enable her to be critical of the moral chaos of the newspaper world but in the end, in an extraordinary reversal, she rejects marriage and respectability and takes her 'natural' place in that world as a 'newspaperman'.

Hildy is an example of Hollywood's 'positive heroines' and of the use of this stereotype by Hawks. She holds her own in an exclusively male world and is critical of it. However, it is arguable that the 'positive heroine' only succeeds in Hawks's male world because she behaves like a man: her 'femininity' is negated. This sexual reversal is illustrated in terms of verbal language: at first Walter dominates Hildy and Bruce by his command of words, but later the situation is reversed when Hildy tells Walter off. Her verbal diatribe is the mirror image of his; similarly, her rugby tackle which brings down the Sheriff is 'heroic' in a masculine sense and heralds her final capitulation to Walter Burns's demands that she rejoin the male world of the newspaper. Nevertheless, Hildy's struggle to retain her own identity and the impossibility of that struggle produce an ironic commentary on the problems of sexual difference which is characteristic of Hawks's work.

Sergeant York (USA 1941 *p.c* – Warner Bros.; *d* – Howard Hawks; sd b/w)

Apparently atypical of Hawks's work, this film nonetheless represents a validation of the virtues of individual heroism. Alvin York (Gary Cooper) is an ordinary man forced by circumstances (America's involvement in the First World War) to become a reluctant hero. While violence and heroism are against his principles, he sacrifices those principles for the sake of his country and discovers that he is, in fact, a 'natural' hero. This structure is similar to that of *His Girl Friday* and the values attached to home life and community, while initially opposed to those attached to war, are eventually shown to be interchangeable with them. It could be argued that the reversal of oppositions in this film works to validate the ideology of individual heroism and patriotism.

To Have and Have Not (USA 1944 *p.c* – Warner Bros.; *d* – Howard Hawks; sd b/w)

Harry Morgan (Humphrey Bogart) refuses to commit himself to help the French patriots escape until he finds himself directly and personally involved, and even then political action against Fascism is justified in personal terms, so that the film appears less an anti-Fascist statement than a validation of individual action against corrupt authoritarian forces. The first meeting between Slim (Lauren Bacall) and Harry is interesting because of the woman's self-assurance and insistence on meeting the man on equal

Bringing up Baby – anarchic woman and foolish male intellectual?

terms. However, this is immediately undermined in the sequence in which Harry forces Slim to return the wallet she has stolen, thus asserting his mastery and control of her.

The uneasy relationship between Slim and Harry is characteristic of Hawks's work. Peter Wollen has pointed to the ritualistic quality of Hawks's male groups: one of the ways in which women enter the group is by learning the rituals, by acting like men. Slim's 'feminine', 'caring' qualities are rejected by Harry because they threaten his self-sufficiency. The only way she can help him is by subscribing to his code, in effect, by becoming 'masculinised'.

Robin Wood takes this film as a test-case for his view of the *auteur* theory. One of the arguments which critics of *auteur* study of films put forward is the collaborative nature of film production in Hollywood: the director's contribution is only one among many, and not necessarily the most important one. *To Have and Have Not* would seem to support this view: it is a genre movie (i.e. 'adventures

Sergeant York – Alvin York (Gary Cooper) as 'natural' hero

in exotic location') conceived by the studio (Warner Bros.) as a starring vehicle for Bogart, adapted from a novel by Hemingway, scripted by William Faulkner and Jules Furthman and specifically indebted to at least two other films (*Morocco*, 1930, and *Casablanca*, 1942). Starting with his conception of Hawks's world-view, Wood looks carefully and in detail at all these possible contributions in order to establish that the film is in fact 'quintessentially Hawksian' (Wood, 1976).

The Big Sky (USA 1952 *p.c* – Winchester Pictures; *d* – Howard Hawks; sd b/w)

The idea of love between men recurs in Hawks's films and has been explicitly acknowledged by him. It appears most clearly in the westerns and it could be argued that it is fundamental to this genre.

Robin Wood does not see the male relationships in Hawks's films as homosexual since they coexist with, and often finally yield to, heterosexual love. For Wood, the love between men is an immature relationship which gives way in the progress of the hero to maturity and responsibility (i.e. heterosexuality and marriage).

Wollen, however, refers to 'the undercurrent of homosexuality' in Hawks's films which he sees as closely linked to the director's idealisation of the all-male group and rejection of women. Men are equals, whereas women are closely identified with nature and the animal world (cf. *Bringing up Baby*, *Gentlemen Prefer Blondes*, 1953). Marriage, and the heterosexual relationship, is a threat to the integrity of the élite male group.

Narrative plays an important role in resolving the complex network of 'perverse' relationships running through the film: the relationships between the two men, between the American Indian woman and two white men (one sadistic, the other tender) and between the white men and American Indian woman are resolved ambiguously and, it could be argued, in a somewhat arbitrary fashion. It could seem that Hawks's view of these relationships is at odds with the demands of narrative resolution. Hawks's particular inflection of the 'male love' theme seems to pose it in opposition to heterosexual love, as an ideal in contrast to the problems inherent in homosexuality, thus raising sexual difference itself as a problem.

Gentlemen Prefer Blondes (USA 1953 *p.c* – 20th Century–Fox; *d* – Howard Hawks; sd col.)

This film is one of Hawks's comedies in which sexual role-reversal is predominant. Wollen points to the scenes of male humiliation (e.g. Jane Russell's song number in which the Olympic athletic team are reduced to passive objects) as an example of Hawks's comic strategy of reversals.

Wood sees this film as one of Hawks's failures: while all the essential elements are there, they do not fuse into a satisfactory coherent whole. However, Richard Dyer (1979) has argued that this lack of coherence is one of the most interesting aspects of the film: the 'lack of fit' between the different elements, in particular, what Dyer sees as the miscasting of Marilyn Monroe in the part of Lorelei, works to undermine the consistency of Hawks's world-view.

Of all the genres within which Hawks worked the musical seems the most unlikely: indeed *Gentlemen Prefer Blondes* is his only musical and is generally referred to as one of his comedies. While viewing the film as a comedy is revealing in the context of his other work, it is interesting to speculate on his use of the musical numbers here to point up moments of extreme tension between the male world and the threat to it represented by the female. The 'excessive' nature of the musical numbers has been pointed out by Robin Wood, who finds them vulgar and crude. If, as Wood argues, *Gentlemen Prefer Blondes* represents a break in Hawks's work with his usual 'classical' style, it could be seen as one of the points at which the ideology of his world-view begins to fall apart at the seams, making it particularly useful for an ideological reading.

Rio Bravo (USA 1959 *p.c* – Armada; *d* – Howard Hawks; sd col.)

Robin Wood argues that this film lies firmly within the tradition of the western, at the same time representing the most complete statement of Hawks's position that exists. Genre and director fuse perfectly.

> The action of *Rio Bravo* is played out against a background hard and bare, with nothing to distract the individual from working out his essential relationship to life. The virtual removal of a social framework – the relegating of society to the function of a *pretext* – throws all the emphasis on the characters' sense of *self*: on their need to find a sense of purpose and meaning not through allegiance to any developing order, but within themselves, in their own instinctual needs. (Wood, 1968, p. 39)

Wood points to the positive qualities of the male group in *Rio Bravo*, seeing in the relationships between the men a moral vision which confirms Hawks's 'spirit of generosity' (Wood, 1968, p. 48). Peter Wollen sees it slightly differently: the self-sufficient all-male group represents an exclusive élite, imposing severe tests of ability and courage on its members (Wollen, 1972, p. 82).

Wollen's shift of emphasis makes Hawks's treatment of the male group seem oppressive rather than positive, particularly in relation to women, who never really become full members of the group however hard they try to prove themselves worthy (Wollen, 1972, p. 86).

Some feminist critics (e.g. Molly Haskell, 1974) have defended Hawks's 'positive heroines' as strong female figures. However, it is arguable that Feathers (Angie Dickinson) is first recognised as a problem for the male hero, Chance (John Wayne), when she takes the initiative, and then recuperated as a threat when the hero conquers her, precisely confirming Hawks's view of the necessity for strong male heroes. In this context, the threat of male humiliation is expressed through the use of screwball comedy in the scene between Feathers and Chance at the end of the film. On the level of *mise-en-scène*, the exoticism of Feathers' room, the sharp contrasts between red and black, seem to reinforce her function as a sign of threat to the stability of Hawks's male world. It could be argued that Hawks takes John Wayne's star persona to an extreme point of stylisation, so that it almost becomes self-parody, undercutting the masculine values of stoicism and self-sufficiency normally associated with the western hero.

initiation of this 'other' into the codes of male society: in effect by recognising and then recuperating the 'otherness', the difference of women.

Selected Reading

Jim Hillier and Peter Wollen (eds), *Howard Hawks: American Artist*, London, BFI, 1996.

Peter Wollen, *Signs and Meaning in the Cinema*, London, Secker & Warburg/BFI, 1969; 1972; 1998.

Robin Wood, *Howard Hawks*, London, Secker & Warburg/BFI, 1968; rev. edn, BFI, 1981.

AUTEUR STUDY AFTER STRUCTURALISM

THE PASSING OF *AUTEUR* STRUCTURALISM

British *auteur* structuralism had attempted to bring together two apparently incompatible theories to resolve the problems inherent in both. On the one hand, it tried to preserve a place for the individual in artistic production, generally retaining the notion found in the *politique des auteurs* of the artist as a potentially critical voice in society. On the other, it saw the individual as enmeshed in linguistic, social and institutional structures which affected the organisation of meaning: the individual was not a free human being in control of the work, whose conscious intentions could be simply retrieved or decoded by the critic. What could be decoded was an authorial system, not to be confused with a real author, which was only one code among many others and not always dominant (see Wollen, 1972). Nevertheless, *auteur* structuralism, as a method of 'reading', still posited the *auteur* code as dominant, since it rarely attempted to account for any other codes. So, while claiming to dissolve the *auteur* into a generality of codes, it continued to provide a partial analysis which maintained a place for the author, still seen as the director, at the centre of their work.

The contradictions inherent in *auteur* structuralism created the need for new theoretical enquiry to deal with them. At the same time, the historical context in which *auteur* structuralism first emerged had changed. In France after 1968 a new emphasis on art as political practice brought the idea of individual authorship into question. Also in question was the structuralist 'method' itself, in so far as it was used to decode an abstract, static code or system outside history and society. What was needed, it was argued, was a more dynamic concept of the text which took account of the processes within which it was constantly transformed.

The modernist answer: Peter Wollen

British film criticism produced diverse answers to the theoretical problems generated by *auteur* structuralism. Peter Wollen argued for a bringing together of modernist art practice which draws attention to the text as a system of signs, and a theory of language (semiology) which would break with the functionalist approach which saw the work as the expression of thought or intention (Wollen, 1972). The work, he argued, generated meanings through an internal conflict of codes, independently of author or critic; it was a kind of 'factory where thought was at work': author and reader collaborated to produce different and conflicting meanings or interpretations, an activity which would always be 'work in progress' and could never provide a comprehensive, final or 'correct' meaning.

The pluralist answer: Ed Buscombe

Ed Buscombe suggested three possible ways out of the impasse of *auteurism*, all of which would displace the traditional notion of the *auteur*: a sociology which would attempt to understand how society makes sense of cinema; a theory which would examine the effects of ideology, economics and technology on the cinema; a history which would look at the language of cinema and the effects of films on other films (Buscombe, 1973).

The psychoanalytic answer: Stephen Heath

Stephen Heath argued that it was precisely this shift, or displacement of the idea of the individual *auteur* at the centre of the work that was in need of theorisation (Heath, 1973). Close textual analysis, and the employment of psychoanalysis as a tool of analysis, would reveal not the presence of the author, but the play of the unconscious across a body of films and the ways in which the system of each particular film constructed a set of positions for the spectator which determined his or her relationship to the film.

The social answer: Alan Lovell

Alan Lovell insisted that film production was, like all artistic production, primarily social (Lovell, 1975). A film was the result of the interaction of all the elements in the production situation and available artistic forms, ideological meanings and intended audiences. The director had little control over these factors, therefore his or her intentions were less important than the effect of this interaction of multiple elements in the films, which was responsible for producing their ideological meanings.

These arguments seemed to signal the end, at least in theoretical film study, of *auteur* study as it had been known. The shift of emphasis towards the text as the place where meaning was produced, and towards analysis of ideology militated against the classification of films under the name of an author/director. Some textual analysis continued to draw on the idea of an 'authorial code' which could be detected in individual films: this code was not important in itself however, except as part of the textual system. The question raised for film study by the death of *auteur* structuralism (a death, it could be argued, implicit in its formation) was an awkward one: why study 'authorship' at all?

The answers outlined above were not without their own problems. Wollen's idea of the partial autonomy of textual operations and the collective process of reading did not entirely dispense with the problem of intentionality: at the same time it did not attempt to deal with the problem. On the other hand, Buscombe's pluralist approach which argued for attention to other methods of analysis besides that of *auteur* study, if it was formulated simply in terms of the adding together of different methods, seemed to avoid the problem of the author altogether since it did not come to grips with the organisation of all these different elements into a system of meaning. Moreover, recasting authorship in terms of its production by the 'textual system' rather than the other way about, as suggested by Heath, seemed to place too much emphasis on the text itself as a self-contained object outside the system of production and exchange in which films were marketed as commodity products. Geoffrey Nowell-Smith argued that the process of assemblage by which a film is put together to be marketed, militated against the attribution of a single meaning to one intentional source. From this perspective authors and critics could not be seen simply as 'effects', dispersed across the textual system. It was precisely the authorial sub-code, or the fragmented marks of authorship, which enabled the critic to reconstruct a coherent *auteur*. There was no *necessary* fit between the process of commodity production and that of consumption, but neither should be seen as somehow escaping its place in the social formation (Nowell-Smith, 1976).

If the author code can be seen, then, as one of the organising principles of coherence in the film which enables us to grasp meaning, to read it, the problem still remains of what methods to use to identify the marks of the author as distinct from the other elements. So, paradoxically, the post-structuralist debates about authorship and cinema, far from evacuating the problems, had the effect of drawing attention to questions of different methods of 'reading' films, and to the social function of criticism itself.

Historicising *auteur* study

The question raised by structuralism for film theory was 'why study authorship?', the answer to which can partly be found in the multiple problems *auteur* analysis raises for film criticism in general; the history of *auteur* criticism can be seen as the history of different methods of reading films, and of the shifting and complex relationship between spectator/critic and film. Different critical approaches to the work of an *auteur* can be brought together to demonstrate the historical specificity of 'authorship' as a category and the way in which different readings depend upon and produce different relationships between author, film and spectator. In the study of Hollywood cinema in particular, *auteur* analysis can be posed against other approaches to the text (e.g. through genre, or industry) as a principle of opposition which goes against the grain of the industrial system. The difference between the critics' construction of the *auteur* and the real director's own assessment of his or her films helps to show that the *auteur* is indeed a construction, which cannot necessarily be related back to the intentions of a real person. This more complex, historical approach to authorship demonstrates the partiality of different methods of studying cinema, rather than posing one method as more adequate than others.

John Ford

John Ellis (1981) has outlined the principles of a historical approach to studying authorship. Ellis's approach is limited to a consideration of a director working within the Hollywood system over a long period whose status as an *auteur* in film criticism changes with history. Furthermore, the best kind of director for the purpose would be one whose own account of his work was decidedly not theoretical: interview material could then be used to point up differences between critics' and director's statements. The approach is based on the study of a wide range of critical texts and a large number of films all of which should show as many differences as possible: the more 'unevenness' there is between texts and between films the easier it is to demonstrate that *auteur* study is an ideological project which attempts to unify and systematise. There are very few directors who would fulfil these requirements. John Ford is an obvious choice because of his veteran status in the Hollywood industry, his critical reputation as a monumental artist of the cinema and the ability of his films to engage the audience on many complex levels. Ford's relationship to the industry and to critical taste is complicated: his film-making career covers artistic experiments, genre films, studio product and independent productions; his critical reception has varied from Oscars to complete disdain. Moreover, many of his films take as their subject matter questions of imperialism, racism and sexism in American society and history: some of them (e.g. *Young Mr Lincoln* (1939), *The Wings of Eagles*, 1957) seem to undermine their ostensible ideological message through their textual operations, raising the question of the viability of relating them back to the director's intention (or to any other intentional source).

This approach has the advantage of illuminating the notion of authorship as well as the work of the chosen *auteur* and, because of the emphasis on the process of reading, is able to confront questions of ideology, personal taste and politics in relation to film study. Since it is structured specifically around John Ford and his relationship to the Hollywood industry, however, and it seems as though Ford is the only director whose work could be utilised in this way, the problem remains of how to approach authorship with different directors and in other production situations. For example, the concept of authorship retained by Ellis is the one of *opposition* to the institutional structures of Hollywood (genre, industry): one question would be whether other institutional structures (e.g. New German Cinema, art cinema, independent cinema) bring into play different principles of authorship.

As Ellis points out, the attention given to different critical texts in his approach is not just a way of establishing relative differences between them: a marked distinction emerges between those accounts which assume the relationship between the director and his films is one of continuity of self-expression (e.g. Andrew Sarris, see p. 256), and those which distinguish between the man Ford and the *auteur* construction 'Ford' (e.g. Peter Wollen, see p. 284). In the first case, these readings, combined with interview material, can be seen to perform a particular function in the construction of a persona which will contribute to the process of marketing the Ford commodity. The second kind of readings work against this by positing a 'Fordian system' which is the result of the critical activity of reading rather than the discovery of an expressive essence. In these terms, authorship study is posed as an operation of reading and criticism rather than the straightforward consumption of the Ford commodity.

The difficulty of systematisation, the extent to which any attempt to construct a Fordian system falls short of the complete

Ford *œuvre*, can be shown by examining the ways in which Ford films contradict one another, undermining the possibility of attributing a set of positive values to Ford or 'Ford'. The use of star John Wayne, for instance, in many different and often contradictory roles, works against the idea of a Fordian world-view outside of history and change (and indeed, against the idea of a Wayne persona outside of history and change).

A comparison of films from the 1930s indicates the extent of the differences and contradictions. *The Informer* and *Grapes of Wrath* appear as 'quality' films with serious intent: they seem more worthy of critical attention/approval than genre films such as *Steamboat Round the Bend* or even *Stagecoach*, partly because 'Fordian concerns' can be discerned more easily in them. Such a comparison raises quite directly questions of authorship, genre, industry and critical taste (i.e. what one expects from a 'good' movie). One of the positive aspects of *auteur* study employed to decode an underlying authorial system is, it could be argued, the way in which it takes issue with critical notions of some films as more 'culturally respectable' than others. However, close analysis of film texts can point to the contradictions within them which seem to fragment or undermine any unifying discourse (e.g. *The Wings of Eagles*, *Young Mr Lincoln*).

In this way, Ellis argues, *auteur* study can be seen to raise a multitude of questions both for itself and for other critical methods. At the same time it can be revealed as a partial approach which ignores questions of the industry, except as a set of constraints or limitations on expressivity, or questions of production of meaning in film texts, except as the expression of the author's intentions. Looking at authorship as an activity of reading can raise the general question of criticism and its role in relation to film, for instance, by highlighting the way in which textual operations always tend to exceed or escape attempts to delimit their meanings by critical writing.

Selected Reading

Lindsay Anderson, '*The Searchers*', *Sight and Sound* 26(2), autumn 1956, reprinted in Caughie (ed.), *Theories of Authorship*, London, RKP/BFI, 1981.

Edward Buscombe, 'Ideas of authorship', *Screen* 14(3), autumn 1973.

John Caughie, 'Teaching through authorship', *Screen Education* no. 17, autumn 1975.

John Ellis, 'Teaching authorship: Ford or fraud?', in Gledhill (ed.), *Film and Media Studies in Higher Education*, London, BFI Education, 1981.

Geoffrey Nowell-Smith, 'Six authors in pursuit of *The Searchers*', *Screen* 17(1), spring 1976.

Peter Wollen, *Signs and Meanings in the Cinema*, London, Secker & Warburg/BFI, 1972; rev. edn, 1998.

AUTHORSHIP AS 'DISCURSIVE ACTIVITY'

Auteur structuralism had insisted that the author should no longer be thought of as a 'real' person existing independently of the films, the intentional source of meaning, and that a new formulation was required which located him or her as producer of meanings within the films themselves. One such formulation defined the authorial 'voice' as a code, or sub-code (e.g. Wollen, 1972), one of many codes which made up the films and which could be objectively defined by reference to the films in question. However, there still remained the problem of the status of the *auteur* code; why should it be privileged over others, such as those of genre, or studio? Moreover, the emphasis on the film text as a set of objectively definable codes tended to stultify it, fixing meaning in a somewhat mechanical way. What was needed, it was argued (e.g. Heath, 1973; Nowell-Smith, 1976) was a theory of meaning production which understood the particular way in which each text worked to produce meaning: objective knowledge of the codes required to decipher meanings was not enough – a 'reading' of the text implied attention to the process of interaction of codes in producing a particular message. This notion of the text as the intersection of various codes stressed the multiplicity of codes at work in any utterance and hence the importance of recognising the effects of different texts upon one another (their 'intertextuality'). The author was not simply an objectively definable sub-code, but rather a 'discursive subject' identifiable as a 'speaker' in the text through the network of different discourses by which it is made up. This discursive subject did not reside in a single point of view or authorial position: it was produced in the interaction of discourses, and itself contributed to the production of meaning. It was the particular historical manifestation of a general set, or system of codes, of specific modes of writing (*écriture*) in circulation at any given moment in a given society. This concept of the 'discursive subject' had the advantage of constituting the subject as productive at the same time as determined by forces of history and language, thus avoiding more mechanical structuralist formulations of the 'subject structured by language'.

The idea of the author as discursive subject, produced by the film text defined as a network of discourses, offered a more flexible account of the relationship between text and reader in which the latter, while clearly now seen as equally responsible with the author (if not more so) for constructing meanings, was also caught in history and society. Thus different readings would produce different, historically specific meanings, and the text was no longer seen as a finished, complete object: it was transformed by, and accumulated meanings in, the historical process of reading. The reader's codes intersected the codes in the text, of which the authorial code was one, to produce meaning (see Brewster, 1973).

Cahiers du Cinéma's 'John Ford'

This idea of 'text' as constituted by the interaction of different historically specific codes provides the context for the collective text by the editors of the French film journal *Cahiers du Cinéma*: 'John Ford's *Young Mr Lincoln*' (1972). After 1968, *Cahiers* reformulated its position on authorship and cinema, producing a programme of work which would approach cinema as an ideological system and a table which classified films according to the relationship each film held with the dominant ideology. The fifth category in the table referred to those films which seemed at first sight to be caught within the dominant ideology, but on closer inspection were revealed to be cracking apart under the tension of internal contradictions (see *Cahiers*' category 'e', p. 207). A 'symptomatic' reading would reveal the contradictions and demonstrate the extent to which the film dismantled the ideology from within.

Cahiers' symptomatic reading of *Young Mr Lincoln* attempted to uncover cracks in the system of the film, disjunctures between the different codes which made up the text, specifically between the generic framework of the film (the 'early life of the great man' genre), its fictional sub-codes (the 'detective story' plot superimposed on the genre) and the Fordian authorial sub-code. According to *Cahiers*' argument, while the generic code allowed the film to present Lincoln (against historical evidence) as the great reconciler, in accordance with the ideological product of the film to promote a Republican victory in the American Presidential election of 1940, this code was contradicted by others at work in the film: the detective-story plot which made Lincoln ambiguously both the 'bringer of the truth' and the involuntary puppet of the truth, and the Fordian sub-code (working in parallel to the detective story) which identified Lincoln with his dead mother and dead ideal wife (vehicle of the truth of the community) at the same time as presenting him as implementer of the truth of the community. These two codes work against the depiction of Lincoln as the 'great reconciler', turning him into a kind of monster. In order to implement their symptomatic reading, *Cahiers* employed a code of psychoanalytic decipherment which also worked, in parallel with the detective-story code and the Fordian sub-code, against the 'early life of the hero' generic code to subvert the manifest ideological project of the film.

There are several problems inherent in this analysis: for instance, *Cahiers* do not establish the 'ideological project' of *Young Mr Lincoln* except by reference to the intentions of Darryl F. Zanuck – head of production at 20th Century–Fox – largely ignoring the role played by political and economic factors. Moreover, their use of psychoanalysis as a tool of decipherment tends to remove the film from its historical and political background: thus their reading of the generic code and its ideological motivation in this film can be seen to give it too much importance, leading to an underestimation of the importance of the Fordian system in the film. These problems point to an interesting contradiction: while attempting to displace the author (Ford) as intentional source of the film, the *Cahiers* analysis ends up by confirming the importance of the Fordian authorial system to *Young Mr Lincoln* and by implication the continuing relevance of *auteur* analysis in the study of American cinema.

Stephen Heath's *'Touch of Evil'*

In his (1975) analysis of *Touch of Evil* (1958), Stephen Heath also, like *Cahiers du Cinéma*, approaches the film as a textual system, as a narrative product which opens up problems and contradictions in order to resolve them, to re-establish stability in the final resolution of tensions. Heath is primarily concerned with the way in which different codes, different 'orders of discourse' cross the text in an activity which 'constructs the ideological subject'. The work of the narrative is seen as the 'setting in place' of this subject which is both author and reader of the text. One of the analytical tools used is, again, psychoanalysis, employed here to unravel the unconscious workings of language and ideology which cut across and resist the systematic coding of the narrative. Heath's close analysis of the textual system of *Touch of Evil* (influenced by Roland Barthes's *S/Z*: see p. 331) does not refuse other, more traditional kinds of reading, but attempts to displace them and so bring them into question. He recognises the historical and institutional factors which have contributed to producing 'Orson Welles' as the author of the film, immediately recognisable in its distinctive style. His analysis, however, is interested in the author as 'an effect of the text', in so far as that effect is significant in the production of the filmic system of *Touch of Evil*. Heath disperses Welles-as-author across the system of the film: 'Welles' is produced as a kind of fiction in the text, one fiction among others. Heath's choice of a film directed by Orson Welles seems to confirm his notion of the author as a fiction: Welles appears as an actor in this film as he does in most of the films he directed; thus he is, self-evidently, part of the fiction. Yet Heath does not quite deal with the power and significance of Welles's presence as author/actor. Quinlan/Welles's first appearance in the film is marked as the colossal entry of a great 'star' into the narrative (supported by the

JOHN FORD

The Informer (USA 1935 *p.c* – RKO Radio; *d* – John Ford; sd b/w)

This film was acclaimed by critics as a masterpiece when it first appeared because of its formal concerns (Expressionism, a return to the imagery of silent cinema) and incorporation of serious social themes of hunger and unemployment in Ireland in the 1920s. Later it was to be condemned by the same criteria: as formally pretentious and approaching its theme with an over-serious sentimentality (see Anderson, 1981).

In terms of the Fordian system, Victor McLaglen is one of Ford's repertory of actors and the comic–grotesque quality of his performance, his weakness set beside his basic humanity, can be found in his performances in other Ford films. The IRA is described by Sarris as 'the ultra-Fordian community' (Sarris, 1976): comparison of its treatment here with Fordian communities in other films (e.g. the families in *My Darling Clementine,* 1946, the army in *She Wore a Yellow Ribbon*, 1949 and *Sergeant Rutledge*, 1960) might illuminate the influence of Irish Catholicism on his work. Peter Wollen (1972) sees a development in Ford's career in terms of a shift in structural oppositions: from an identity between 'civilised versus savage' and 'European versus Indian' to their separation and final reversal so that in *Cheyenne Autumn* (1964) it is the Europeans who are savage, the victims who are heroes. How does *The Informer* fit into this pattern of shifting antinomies? Does Wollen's structural model apply to the whole of Ford's work, or only to the westerns?

Ford made this film for RKO – the 'studio of his conscience ... of his moral commitment to his material' (Sarris, 1976) as opposed to Fox, 'his bread and butter base' – and a comparison could be drawn with *The Grapes of Wrath* (Fox) to discuss how far differences might be attributable to studio policies (see The studios, p. 27). The prestige production of *The Informer* might be attributable to Ford's concern with taking on projects at this stage in his career which would further his reputation and give him more control: hence the collaboration with Dudley Nichols and the adaptation of a serious novel.

Stagecoach (USA 1939 *p.c* – Walter Wanger Productions; *d* – John Ford; sd b/w)

Critical opinion has generally been united over this film, hailing it as a 'classic', in spite of the fact that it is blatantly a genre piece with no 'artistic' pretensions: in fact, the western-genre conventions completely submerge the origins of the film in a novel by Guy de Maupassant (turned into a western story by Ernest Haycox).

Wollen's structural antinomies (civilised versus Savage, European versus American Indian) are worked out in terms of the opposition between the savage Apache and the beleaguered stagecoach 'community'. The community is riven with contradictions of class and sexuality between the various characters, but these contradictions are transcended by the primary opposition between American Indian savage/American civilised values, allowing the extermination of the American Indian to be validated and celebrated. It has been argued that this view of American history is reversed and questioned in other Ford films (Wollen, 1972).

The beleaguered stagecoach community in Ford's classic – *Stagecoach*

The landscape of Monument Valley has become a kind of stylistic signature in Ford's westerns, raising the question of how to identify the marks of authorship in relation to genre conventions.

Stagecoach has often been held up as an example of the classical art of narrative based on montage editing prevalent in Hollywood cinema of the 1930s (see Bazin, 1967). The film thus provides an opportunity to look closely at the organisation of shots and the relationship between image and sound which provides the basis of this narrative system.

Although the film is clearly a genre piece, and also an example of 'classical' narrative cinema, it could be argued that it nonetheless deals with 'serious' questions (e.g. class, sexuality, race) as much as *The Informer* or *The Grapes of Wrath* (1940), in spite of the fact that critics do not generally give it the status of a 'quality' film.

How Green Was My Valley – Ford's film mourning the loss of family unity

The Grapes of Wrath (USA 1940 *p.c* – 20th Century–Fox; *d* – John Ford; sd b/w)

The film which established Ford's reputation as the great poet of American cinema, but one which it is, paradoxically, difficult to identify as belonging only to Ford without ignoring the contributions to the final product of, for example, Nunnally Johnson's adaptation of Steinbeck's novel, Gregg Toland's photography, not to mention producer Darryl F. Zanuck, as the partial approach of *auteur* study tends to.

In terms of the Fordian system, Ford's reputed populism could be detected in the depiction of the family as a community and the role of the mother in unifying the family. Arguably, however, this populism emerges as much from Steinbeck's concerns, or from New Deal ideology as from a Fordian system. Comparison with other Ford films (e.g. *Young Mr Lincoln*, p. 301) and with other Hollywood populist films (e.g. Frank Capra's *Mr Deeds Goes to Town*, p. 289) could illuminate this question. Sarris argues that Steinbeck's criticism of American society is undermined by New Deal homilies (Sarris, 1976).

The structural opposition between wilderness (or desert) and garden identified by Wollen (1972) as the master antinomy in Ford's films is worked out here in terms of the opposition between the Arizona desert and the luxuriant promised land of California, which proves to be less than ideal. The journey, or quest of the Joad family has been identified as part of Ford's thematic system: the search for the promised land involves a movement between desert and garden which changes in emphasis, and therefore in meaning, from film to film.

It is arguable that the film's aesthetically beautiful images, attributable to Ford and Toland, are in contradiction to the angry, critical words of Steinbeck and Johnson, a contradiction produced perhaps by Ford's desire to enhance his directorial career at this time with prestige productions (Sarris, 1976).

How Green Was My Valley (USA 1941 *p.c* – 20th Century–Fox; *d* – John Ford; sd b/w)

A lavish, prestige production which Ford took over from William Wyler in the early stages of preparation and which won six Academy Awards. The film draws attention to its literary origins in a novel by using the device of voice-over narration through which a central character (the boy Huw Morgan) remembers the past (Sarris, 1976, relates this strategy to the many writers-turned-director in the industry in the 1940s).

The film centres on family and community, a thematic element in many Ford films, but here providing the entire motivation for the film. The combination of nostalgia for past values and the representation of the community as the location of positive values such as loyalty, discipline and gallantry has been identified by Robin Wood as Ford's major preoccupation (Wood, 1968). Whereas the fragmentation of the family in *The Grapes of Wrath* provides the basis for a criticism of social conditions, *How Green Was My Valley* seems to look back to the Depression as a time when social conditions destroyed family unity, the project of the film being to mourn its loss.

In terms of genre, the film belongs to a certain type of family melodrama prevalent in Hollywood in the 1940s (see Higham and Greenberg, 1968). Ford's films often use melodrama to move the audience and this film is one of the all-time great weepies, yet it also combines 'serious' political questions with a genre not usually valued highly for its seriousness.

My Darling Clementine (USA 1946 *p.c* – 20th Century–Fox; *d* – John Ford; sd b/w)

After the Second World War Ford's reputation fell into something of a critical decline (see Sarris, 1976). This film was his second western in twenty years and did little to restore that reputation.

It is arguable that the traditional conventions of the genre (action sequences, gun fights) are displaced or transformed by the emphasis placed in this film on domestic activity; that is, on day-to-day activities of personal hygiene, dressing up, courting, going to church, etc., which represent the civilising forces which take over the desert/wilderness, transforming it into a cultivated garden.

Wollen (1972) sees the progress of Wyatt Earp (Henry Fonda) from 'nature' to 'culture' as relatively unproblematic compared with other Fordian heroes (e.g. Ethan Edwards in *The Searchers*, 1956). The scene in the barbershop is seen by Wollen as symbolic of this progress: the barber 'civilises' the unkempt Earp, splashing him with

My Darling Clementine – and Chihuahua – the taming of the West

honeysuckle scent, an artificial rather than a natural perfume, thus marking his transition from nomad to settled, civilised man, administrator of the law. However, it could also be argued that Earp's progress can only be measured against the decline of Doc Holliday (Victor Mature), which is seen in terms of the loss of an anarchic spirit which is the basis of poetry and subversive sexual energy. Moreover, Earp's bearing during his transformation remains stiff and unwieldy, even in the communal dance sequence. The transition from nature to culture is heavily marked as comic, and could be seen as more problematic than Wollen allows. Furthermore, the highly stylised *mise-en-scène* (extreme perspectives, predominance of long shots, and 'Expressionist' lighting, i.e. dark/light contrasts) might offer the audience a critical distance both on the genre conventions and the narrative events.

The opposition between the two women, Clementine and Chihuahua, is also interesting in terms of the transition from nature to culture discussed by Wollen in relation to the central male character. This taming of energy is often depicted in Ford's films as necessary but regrettable, so that the films seem to question the 'progress' of history.

Fort Apache (USA 1948 *p.c* – Argosy Pictures; *d* – John Ford; sd b/w)

Sarris (1976) argues that the last two decades of Ford's career were the most vigorous in that 'he became fully his own man'. Contemporary critics, however, did not agree, and saw the late Ford as self-indulgent, relegating him to the status of an honoured has-been, now engaged in reworking tired old themes with the same stock company.

Peter Wollen's (1972) structural approach can be seen as an attempt to redress the critical balance. By looking for underlying patterns of shifting oppositions he was able to argue that the shifting pattern became more complex as Ford's work developed. *Movie*, following *Cahiers du Cinéma*, had declared its preference for Sam Fuller over Ford; in the mid-1960s *Cahiers* re-evaluated Ford, but only in terms of 'key' *auteur* films.

Wollen's approach provided the possibility of looking again at the whole of Ford's work, and not necessarily in terms of 'good' and 'bad' films, rather in terms of an underlying 'Fordian system'. Although this approach attempted to come to terms with the unevenness of Ford's work, with its differences and contradictions, Wollen himself deals mainly with westerns, which seem most amenable to analysis according to structural oppositions. The question still remains of how the more 'aberrant' works fit into the schema. Ford's work seems to resist schematic systematisation, which is what makes it so useful for a critical approach to *auteur* study.

This film was the first in a series of cavalry westerns which demonstrated a changing attitude towards the American Indians in Ford's work (see *Stagecoach*, p. 302). However, it could be argued that this liberalised attitude in the films was less a political shift (on the part of Ford or anyone else) than a way of dramatising the conflict of values within the cavalry community. Wollen may be right in pointing to a reversal between the oppositions savage (American Indian) and civilised (European) in Ford's later work, but it is not a simple reversal in which the American Indians take the place of the Europeans at the centre of the drama.

This film also marks the shift from Henry Fonda to John Wayne as the hero of Ford's films. The confrontation between Captain York (Wayne) and Lieutenant Colonel Thursday (Fonda) is useful for discussing the iconographical differences between the two stars as deployed in the Fordian system.

Ford's late westerns appear significantly different from other examples of the genre in 1950s and 1960s Hollywood, retaining Fordian set-pieces and a stylised *mise-en-scène* in the face of technological developments such as CinemaScope.

She Wore a Yellow Ribbon (USA 1949 *p.c* – Argosy Pictures; *d* – John Ford; sd col.)

Wood (1968) identifies this film as one in which Fordian values are clearly marked. The cavalry is seen to represent the ideal community built on traditions of loyalty, discipline, and allegiance to an established code of behaviour. Women and men alike must submit to this code.

Olivia Dandridge, who accompanies Captain Brittles on his last mission, can be seen as a potential threat to the cavalry traditions, mostly because of her exuberant sexuality. The ageing Captain Brittles (John Wayne) and the high-spirited Olivia are both excluded from the military in spite of the fact that they both represent some of its highest values. It could be argued that the film questions on one level the rigidity of the military order (cf. *Fort Apache*).

The film portrays the American Indians as brutal savages in contrast to the 'civilised' values of the cavalry (see also *Stagecoach*, p. 302) and shows John Wayne in a role of 'father figure' which is significantly different from his persona in other Ford films (see *Stagecoach*; *Fort Apache*).

It could also be argued that Ford's cavalry westerns are marked by an opposition between panoramic views of the western landscape and the closed, tight compositions of the more intimate sequences involving the cavalry. If so, how does this work to affect the meanings produced by the films?

The Searchers (USA 1956 *p.c* – C. V. Whitney Pictures Inc; *d* – John Ford; sd col.)

As John Ellis (1981) argues, Ford's work can be used to raise a wide range of questions about the ways in which films are produced and consumed and the critical methods employed to analyse cinema. *The Searchers* is a paradigmatic case: it has achieved the status of a key text in film studies for the possibilities it offers as the site of different, often conflicting, analytical methods which work productively with and against one another (see *Screen Education* no. 17).

The film's perceived usefulness in different contexts can be partly ascribed to its problematic place in the Fordian *œuvre*, which makes it necessary to look outside the film itself for an explanation of its 'lack of fit'. Critics are deeply divided in their evaluations. Anderson (1956), for example, denies that the film has any place in the humanistic world-view he defines as Ford's, while Wollen (1972) sees the film as perhaps Ford's most complex working through of the opposition wilderness/garden which forms the basis of his work. For Wollen the complexity lies in the overlapping of these oppositions within and between characters, particularly between Ethan Edwards (John Wayne), a tragic hero torn apart by the divisions American Indian/European, savage/civilised, nomad/settler, his 'opposite', Scar, the American Indian chief with whom he shares many characteristics, his companion in the quest to find Debbie, part-Cherokee Martin Pawley, and the European family of homesteaders who represent the eventual transformation of wilderness into garden. This structural complexity enables the film to complicate, perhaps undermine, any simple progress from wilderness to garden, savage to civilised, which may be seen as its manifest ideological project.

For Wollen, then, Ford's particular inflection of material basic to the mythology of the western forms a sub-text or code which contradicts the genre's ideological bias, an analysis which can be used to challenge allegations that the film is racist. However, as John Caughie points out (1975), even if it could be proved that a critique of racism was 'intended', the narrative resolution in which Debbie is returned to the white community and the 'natural order' restored at the very least removes the sting from the critique. Caughie also argues that the wilderness/garden opposition is supported by a sexual division in which men are active participants in the struggle towards civilisation and women passively represent the values for which they are fighting. It would seem, then, that the complexity noted by Wollen is not present at the level of sexist ideology.

Sergeant Rutledge (USA 1960 *p.c* – John Ford/Warner Bros.; *d* – John Ford; sd col.)

Wollen (1972) identifies a transition in Ford's work which equates 'non-Americans' (Irish, American Indians, Polynesians, blacks) with the traditional values of the American Dream which America itself has lost. It could be argued that this appropriation of other races in the service of 'American' values is imperialistic, to say the least. While the representation of the black Rutledge is often seen (see Ellis, 1981) to be a more liberalised view of the blacks than in Ford's earlier work (e.g. *Judge Priest*, 1934, *Steamboat Round the Bend*, 1935, *The Sun Shines Bright*, 1954), this 'liberalisation' seems to involve divesting Rutledge of both his blackness and sexuality, superimposing the values of courage and nobility associated with the American cavalry and so producing Rutledge as a 'noble savage' figure who transcends racism. The position of the black soldier is never raised in terms of his relation to the American Indians, the white man's ideology is accepted and the Apache are unquestionably regarded as the enemy, the destruction of whom will enable the black soldiers to become free Americans.

John Ellis (1981) argues that the film produces a commentary on racism by taking the myth of black supersexuality as its central problem, displacing the myth in favour of the proposition that blacks are asexual; Rutledge becomes a human being only in so far as he forswears his sexuality. This forswearing of sexuality in a higher cause can be traced in other Ford films (e.g. *My Darling Clementine*, *She Wore a Yellow Ribbon*, *Rio Grande*). According to Ellis, the film is only able to raise the problem of race and sexuality in this way because of its tightly coded narrative structure: the trial device enables commentary to be carried out at all points of ambiguity in the story, with returns from flashbacks to the cross-examination of witnesses. Thus multiple meanings are limited and controlled, and the film articulates its position against a certain kind of racism based on the myth of black supersexuality. Ellis's account focuses on the way in which narrative structure contributes to the construction of meaning in the film, independently of the intentions of the author.

ORSON WELLES

Touch of Evil (USA 1958 *p.c* – Universal International; *d* – Orson Welles; sd b/w)

Conventional *auteur* analysis has seen the heavily-marked style of Welles's films as a sign of the presence of a great artist and has pointed to the existence of Wellesian themes beneath the 'superficial' detective-story framework of *Touch of Evil* (e.g. Bazin, 1978). Welles himself understands the film as an expression of his hatred of police abuse of power, and identifies himself with the point of view of Vargas, who destroys the evil Quinlan. Heath (1973), however, argues for an understanding of the way the textual system works to produce 'Welles as Author–artist', seeing this production as part of the ideological project of the text. The end of the film provides a focus for these different approaches to authorship. It demonstrates Welles's distinctive style (in the play with image and sound, in the use of moving camera and 'strange' camera angles) and his presence as actor–star (in the form of Quinlan). It also provides a useful metaphor which might illuminate the kind of reading Heath is proposing: it shows Vargas tracking Quinlan in order to destroy him. The destruction of the crooked cop Quinlan is a prerequisite of the resolution of the narrative, but also, by implication, the destruction of the 'authorial voice' must be achieved if textual stability is to be restored, since it was the friction of this discourse with the narrative system that (according to Heath) opened up problems and contradictions in the text. The tracking-down and pinning down in death of Quinlan/Welles could be seen as a metaphor for the resolution of the excesses of the authorial discourse and a victory for 'classic' narrative. If this (rather fanciful) interpretation holds, then the ending of *Touch of Evil* produces Welles the artist as a tragic figure, pilloried and destroyed by the Hollywood system, thus supporting the myth to which Welles and his admirers have traditionally subscribed.

effects of Welles's distinctive cinematic style). This marking of the 'star presence' exceeds the fiction of the film, referring outwards to other films, other acting roles, i.e. to the industry itself. It does not just signify in the system of *Touch of Evil*, it seems to disturb that system, to unbalance the organisation of the narrative codes. It is this disturbance of, or opposition to the narrative system of 'classical' cinema which, in much traditional *auteur* criticism, indicates the presence of the authorial voice. By demonstrating that this 'voice' is produced by the film's textual system Heath avoids constructing Welles as an external, intentional source of meaning; however, by presenting the authorial discourse as 'an effect of the text' his reading implies that there is no general Wellesian system (verifiable by reference to other Welles films), only a Wellesian discourse produced by this film, *Touch of Evil*. The production of this discourse, moreover, is seen primarily in terms of formal strategies which do not include extra-textual references to history, politics or economic factors which might play some part in determining those textual strategies. Thus, Heath's construction of Welles as discursive subject in some ways confirms romantic notions of the artist's 'freedom of expression'.

Selected Reading

Ben Brewster, 'Notes on the text "*Young Mr Lincoln*" by the editors of *Cahiers du Cinéma*', *Screen* 14(3), autumn 1973.

Edward Buscombe, *Stagecoach*, London, BFI, 1996.

Editors of *Cahiers du Cinéma*, 'John Ford's *Young Mr Lincoln*', *Screen* 13(3), autumn 1972.

Stephen Heath, 'Comment on "The idea of authorship"', *Screen* 14(3), autumn 1973.

Geoffrey Nowell-Smith, 'Six authors in pursuit of *The Searchers*', *Screen* 17(1), spring 1976.

AUTHORSHIP AND COUNTER-CINEMA

Cahiers' category 'e' (see p. 287) was influential on British *auteur* criticism, which began to look at the work of certain Hollywood directors for the way in which it 'dismantled' or criticised prevailing ideology. But to many in post-1968 France these 'radical readings' of Hollywood texts appeared formalist; what was needed was not simply a deconstruction of ideology, but a fundamental restructuring of the industrial system of production, distribution and exhibition from which a new, revolutionary cinema could emerge, not only political in content, but *made politically* (see 'The Estates General of the French Cinema', 1972/73). This refusal of industrial, hierarchical methods of working was accompanied by a rejection of individual authorship. Many newly politicised film-makers formed small independent groups dedicated to collective working methods, skill-sharing and to producing films for a small and specific political audience. Jean-Luc Godard joined with other young Maoists to form the Dziga–Vertov Group during this period; Vertov's name was mobilised less as an authorial inspiration than for his practice, his battle to produce a cinematic language adequate to express the 'truth' of class struggle.

This emphasis on the need for a totally new *practice* of cinema was to be influential on the growth of independent film-making in Britain during the 1970s. But initially it emerged as a discussion of what *forms* this new cinema should adopt and was expressed, perhaps surprisingly, in quite conventional *auteurist* terms.

This formalist emphasis had a polemical force as a theoretical intervention into the prevailing assumptions of British independent political cinema, which was primarily documentary and realist. Jean-Luc Godard's work was taken up by Peter Wollen as exemplary of what a materialist oppositional cinema, a 'counter-cinema', might be (see *Avant-garde* and counter-cinema, p. 113).

Jean-Luc Godard

In his Postscript to the second edition of *Signs and Meaning in the Cinema* (1972) Wollen argued that since Hollywood provided the dominant codes with which films are read, it was only in confrontation with Hollywood that anything new could be produced and that it was in the work of Jean-Luc Godard that this kind of confrontation, interrogation and criticism could be found. In 'Counter-Cinema: *Vent d'est*' (1972) he took this argument a stage further by elaborating on those values of 'orthodox' cinema with which Godard's 'counter-cinema' took issue and evaluating his work up to 1972 in terms of its increasing opposition to, or break with, Hollywood cinema. Wollen argues that Godard's method of *negation*, or contrast, enables him to produce a revolutionary materialist cinema which takes account of 'Hollywood–Mosfilm' (Godard's term for 'bourgeois capitalist cinema') while working to criticise it. For Wollen, the value of this method is that it creates questions and disagreements in Godard's films, setting up a different relationship between spectator and films from that of traditional cinema, which he characterises in terms of *narrative coherence* and *identification*, the generation of pleasures which aim to satisfy the spectator rather than to change him or her. However, Wollen criticises Godard's rather puritanical rejection of the fantasy pleasures offered by mainstream cinema and argues that a 'revolutionary' cinema must address itself to the specific relationship between pleasure, entertainment, fantasy, ideology and science produced in film (see *Avant-garde* and counter-cinema, p. 113).

The article illustrates some of the advantages and disadvantages of *auteur* structuralism as a critical method. It reduces all Godard's films to a set of formal strategies of opposition and suggests that those strategies are always present in Godard's work, increasingly since 1968, evaluating films according to the presence (or not) of these strategies. While Wollen's account illuminates Godard's films belonging to a certain period between 1968 and 1972 and evaluates their importance as political cinema, it does not take account of the influence of history on those films; instead it holds them up as an ideal practice of materialist film-making. Moreover, in his attempt to establish Godard as an exemplary counter-cinema *auteur*, Wollen ignores the fact that *Vent d'est* was made by the Maoist Dziga–Vertov collective of which Godard was only one member.

This approach seems even more limited when Godard's pre-1968 and post-1972 work is taken into account. It could be argued that the value of Godard's work lies precisely in its evident sensitivity to historical and political change. While similar concerns can be traced through all his films and later video work, the ways in which those concerns shift and change bear testimony to the fact that the film-maker is caught up in history and changing conditions of production which can be seen to affect his work. Wollen's account deals with a period in which the ideas of structuralism, semiology and psychoanalysis, combined with a cultural politics emerging from the events of May 1968, explicitly informed Godard's work. It is questionable whether the strategies identified by Wollen could be effective outside that particular context. His argument about Godard is linked to a polemic for the necessity of developing a new, oppositional film-making practice and was influential on subsequent debates about independent political cinema in Britain.

Godard and history

Godard himself has insisted that the political upheavals in France represented for him not so much a break with the past as the possibility of developing the ideas he was already formulating (see MacCabe, 1980). He had already collaborated with Maoist militants on some films when in the immediate aftermath of 1968 it became possible for him as a film-maker to commit himself to engaging in totally new methods of work. Although his Maoism waned with the disintegration of French Maoism in 1972, the commitment to alternative methods of work has remained. However, in Godard's case those alternative methods have not remained the same. There are evident differences between the films emerging from his collaboration with Gorin and others in the Dziga–Vertov Group in 1969–70 and after the dissolution of the group in 1972. In 1974 he set up his own production company away from Paris in the French Alps with Anne-Marie Miéville: the films and television programmes they produced show a further shift of concern towards the investigation of the relationship between the personal and the political. In the 1980s Godard returned to using fictional forms and stars in his film projects – *Sauve qui peut – la vie* (1980) (*Every Man for Himself*), *Je vous salue, Marie* (1984) (*Hail Mary*) and others – while at the same time pursuing his fascination with history in 'documentaries' about cinema – e.g. *Histoires du cinéma*, 1993.

In the light of history, Godard's work can be seen to show a continuing preoccupation with theory and politics, with the language of cinema and the circulation of images in society, and with formulating new languages to express revolutionary questions, although the form of those preoccupations constantly changes, sometimes quite radically. One of the lessons of the political upheavals in the late 1960s which seems to have remained with Godard has been the idea of cinema as *social practice*: that is, a political commitment to bringing cinema into relationship with people's everyday lives, a different relationship from that of 'normal' cinema-going, which depends for its continuing commercial success on the fact that it is divorced from (an escape from) day-to-day existence. Such a commitment involves changing the traditional ways in which films are produced, distributed, exhibited and consumed. A productive way of looking at Godard's films would be in terms of this idea of social practice, in terms of their political, historical and social context and the way they pose problems for certain kinds of critical analysis, such as traditional *auteur* study. Godard's work is exciting because it is capable of raising a multitude of questions about cinema and politics. The particular combination of theory and practice in the films, the fact that they manifest the extent to which the film-maker is caught up in history rather than being consciously in control of his work, makes it difficult to apply traditional critical criteria to that work, although this has been done (see Perkins, 1972; Harcourt, 1974). The aggressive 'intertextuality' of Godard's films, that is, the way in which they break with classical unity of forms to assert their critical, dialectical relationship with other films, other texts, other ideas and historical situations, makes them a vital part of discussion about strategies for cultural politics (see Jean-Luc Godard, p. 253).

Selected Reading

Raymond Bellour and Mary Lea Bardy (eds), *Jean-Luc Godard: Sound & Image*, New York, Museum of Modern Art, 1992.

Colin MacCabe, *Godard: Images, Sound, Politics*, London, Macmillan/BFI, 1980.

Peter Wollen, 'Counter-cinema: *Vent d'est*', *Afterimage* no. 4, autumn 1972.

COUNTER-CINEMA AND FEMINISM

Another important strand of the counter-cinema movement was that of feminism. In this respect Agnès Varda presents an interesting comparison with Godard as an *auteur*.

Agnès Varda

Agnès Varda began her directorial career in the context of the French New Wave (The *politique des auteur*, p. 253). Her husband, Jacques Demy, was a New Wave film director whose primary interest was in re-working the conventions of the Hollywood Musical to point up its 'utopian' qualities. It may be suggested that his interest in utopian fantasies informed Varda's first film *Le Bonheur*, where it takes on a specifically feminist inflection.

Besides its interest in Hollywood, the French New Wave owed a considerable amount to the European tradition of art cinema. Although film-makers such as Godard, Truffaut and Chabrol looked first to Hollywood for inspiration, others, such as Alain Resnais looked towards art cinema and women film-makers like Marguerite Duras and Chantal Akerman can also be seen to emerge from this tradition. Little critical work exists so far on art cinema and its transformation by the New Wave directors, which has allowed unsympathetic critics to dismiss it rather too easily.

Varda's films seem to lean more towards the art cinema strand of the New Wave than the Hollywood strand. However, just as it would be simplistic to think of the films of Godard, Truffaut and Chabrol as dependent upon the Hollywood codes rather than critical of them, Varda's films cannot be seen as lying unproblematically within the art cinema tradition. It could be argued that she is interested in investigating the basic processes by which cinematic images captivate the audience, which would place her in the avant-garde tradition within art cinema rather than in the counter-cinema tradition of Godard (see Wollen, 'The two *avant-gardes*', 1976).

Sally Potter and Yvonne Rainer (See Feminist counter-cinema p. 118 and p. 355) represent other later examples where the feminist and counter-cinema impulses can be fruitfully discussed in the context of *auteurism*. Recent developments in independent cinema (See Feminist film theory pp. 364–5) also suggest that much work there also remains to be done. However the impact of the feminist engagement with auteurist theory was felt with especial force in the study of *auteurism* within the Hollywood studio system.

FEMINISM, *AUTEURISM* AND HOLLYWOOD

Claire Johnston (1973), argued for a new women's cinema which would confront the ideology of mainstream cinema by developing the means to challenge its depiction of reality. By interrogating the conventions of Hollywood, the iconography and stereotypes whereby it attempted to fix myths of women as natural and universal, a dislocation could be brought about between sexist ideology and the language used to perpetuate it which would provide the basis for strategies of subversion (see Avant-garde and counter-cinema, p. 114; Feminist film theory, p. 353).

This argument drew on *Cahiers*' Category 'e' (see p. 287) and on post-structuralist versions of *auteur* theory which challenged the idea of the director as intentional source of meaning, redefining it in terms of the unconscious preoccupations which could be decoded in the formal play of film texts and which were often outside the control of the director concerned. Johnston took issue with the idea that mainstream cinema was monolithically closed to intervention by women film-makers, arguing that the work of these few women directors who had managed to build up a consistent body of work in the Hollywood system was of interest to feminists precisely because of the ways in which their unconscious preoccupations could be seen to turn sexist ideology on its head, manipulating the codes of mainstream cinema in order to criticise it. Johnston used Dorothy Arzner (and Ida Lupino) as examples of women directors whose work manifested an internal criticism of mainstream ideology.

JEAN-LUC GODARD

À bout de souffle (Breathless) (France 1959 *p.c* – SNC; *d* – Jean-Luc Godard; sd b/w)

This is Godard's first feature film and the one he likes least. Made in the context of the early French new wave, it was based on an idea by François Truffaut and it is possible to see in the film's celebration of an individual freedom which transcends social relations a theme which is central to Truffaut's work rather than Godard's. In later films Godard was to question this idea of the criminal/outsider as 'free'.

At this stage, Godard's films remained within the Hollywood narrative conventions, resisting any political analysis of that cinema. The verbal and visual references to Hollywood seem to act more as an *hommage* than a criticism, although it could be argued that the strategy of 'quotation' and 'punning' has the effect of drawing attention to the Hollywood codes, offering the audience an added pleasure of recognition.

The character of Patricia is a play on the *femme fatale* of Hollywood's *film noir*, a representation of the figure of the woman as enigmatic and deceptive which recurs throughout Godard's work and seems to be part of his distrust of the deceptive quality of images in general. 'Woman' and 'image' are often conflated as the site of the problem of representation: however, the problem is posed differently in later films, which attempt to question the construction and circulation of the image of woman in society.

Masculin–Féminin (France/Sweden 1966 *p.c* – Anouchka Films/Argos Films (Paris) Svensk Filmindustri/Sandrews (Stockholm); *d* – Jean-Luc Godard; sd b/w)

Godard accepts the conventional divisions between men and women in *Masculin–Féminin*

Peter Wollen has noted and criticised the ambiguity towards politics in Godard's early films, but it is also possible to see those films as an unsatisfactory search for a cinematic form in which to discuss politics, a search which became acute in the mid-1960s when the political pressures became intense and opposition to the Vietnam war was a key political issue. In *Masculin–Féminin* the problem of politics and representation is seen in terms of the male protagonist's dilemma: Paul (Jean-Pierre Léaud) is caught between the 'masculine' world of party politics and the 'feminine' world of pop culture and consumerism. Both are inadequate in themselves: the politics of the French Communist Party are depicted as repressive and unable to come to terms with questions of art or sexuality, while the pop culture world depends for its appeal on a stultifying relationship between producer and consumer. Paul's attempt to unite the positive virtues of both fails and he ends up alone, alienated from both.

The division represented between the male and female worlds has recurred in different forms throughout Godard's work. He seems to accept the conventional social division which places women on the side of nature, instinct and consumption and men on the side of culture and production (and, by implication, politics). Although he is able to draw attention to the way in which consumer society uses images of women, he does not seem to question radically the social construction of these images.

Weekend – disillusionment with bourgeois French society

Weekend (France/Italy 1967 *p.c* – Comacico/Copernic/Lira Films; *d* – Jean-Luc Godard; sd col)

The year 1966 seems to have been one of despair for Godard in his search for politics and form – in *Made in USA* he rejected the forms of Hollywood cinema as inadequate to the task of raising political questions directly because its fictional forms represented politics as fantasy, 'out there' on the screen rather than as part of the spectators' lives. In *Deux ou trois choses que je sais d'elle* (*Two or Three Things I Know about Her*) he had investigated the possibilities of documentary style and a fragmented, episodic structure, referring explicitly to Brecht and his theory of 'distanciation' or 'alienation'. In 1967 he began to collaborate with Maoist militants and became interested in *cinéma-vérité*. The films made in this period show an intense desire to resolve the problem of representation and politics by casting about for many different solutions, none of which are found to be adequate. *Weekend* is perhaps the most desperate of all of them in its total disillusionment with French society, which is conceived of as monolithically bourgeois, brutalised by its own consumer ideology. In the face of the total insensitivity of this society, violence and brutality are seen to be the only solution. Godard uses surrealist images and montage to call into question the violence of bourgeois society and the bland images of art cinema by which it represents itself. The justification of violence and instinctive action which appears in this film recurs throughout Godard's work. Although with hindsight it seems politically regressive (revolutionaries eat the bourgeoisie!), in the context of French left-wing politics just prior to 1968, where the demand for guerrilla action in response to imperialist wars and the violence of bourgeois society was increasing, its political nihilism is perhaps more understandable.

Characteristically, Godard foregrounds the problems of finding a political language. The use of direct address to the camera/spectator in the extended quotations from Frantz Fanon suggests the desire to communicate directly with an audience which shares the political frame of reference of the speakers, unlike Corinne and Raymond, who represent the bourgeois audience, bored and uncomprehending. It was this 'uncomprehending bourgeois audience' that Godard was to leave behind in the aftermath of 1968 when he abandoned 'normal' cinema. He also left behind any critical acclaim his new wave films had accrued.

Godard's increasing politicisation did not prevent him from continuing to question the means of representing politics: arguably, the mixture of fiction, direct address to the camera, use of stars, extended quotation and theatre of the absurd allow the spectator to criticise the political discourse (provided that the spectator shares the political frame of reference of the film).

AGNÈS VARDA

Le Bonheur (France 1965 *p.c* – Parc Films/ Mag Bodard; *d* – Agnès Varda: sd col)

Varda was the only woman director to work within the New Wave and this film could be interestingly compared with early films of Godard and Truffaut for the way it questions the romantic point-of-view of its main protagonist, who conceives of "freedom" in bourgeois terms. The theme of freedom and the impossibility of attaining it is central to many early New Wave films, but the problem is usually presented entirely from the male protagonist's viewpoint, which is validated (e.g. Michel in *À bout de souffle* p. 253; Jules and Jim in *Jules et Jim* p. 255). It is arguable that Varda undermines that viewpoint by showing that it rests on an image, or myth of woman that is oppressive.

Although the film presents a romantic fantasy of love and marriage, it places that fantasy as male and shows how it controls the production of images for women to identify with. This is illustrated in the film by the treatment of the wedding preparations, the taking of photographs after the ceremony and the images of motherhood at the reception, all of which are seen to be caught up in a process of image-making at the same time as they present an ideal image of happiness. As Francois, the husband, makes love to his mistress, shots of his wife shopping with the children provide an ironic commentary on his idea of happiness. It could be argued that Varda attempts to take a distance on the male point-of-view and open it up to criticism.

WOMEN DIRECTORS IN HOLLYWOOD

One of the first tasks undertaken by feminist film criticism was that of rewriting the history of cinema to include the contribution of women film-makers, notably missing from traditional *auteur* pantheons. This new history quickly revealed the virtual absence of successful women directors within the Hollywood industry and, perhaps more surprisingly, the relatively small number of women who had worked independently in documentary and avant-garde cinema. Although the development of lightweight equipment and cheap film stock after the Second World War seemed to promise wider access to the means of production, the absence of women from the independent sector too seemed to suggest that ideological and economic factors played a greater part than technology in determining the place of women in cinema's history. In the case of Hollywood, feminist film criticism found that although women had worked as editors and scriptwriters, and of course as stars, very few ever made it to positions of power as directors or producers. One of the major contributions of feminist film history has been to draw attention to the hierarchical conditions of production and the ideological bias which have militated against the possibility of women having any significant control over the meanings produced by the industry (see also Benton, 1975). Sometimes this discovery has led to an overvaluation of the work of those women directors who managed to survive and a tendency to construct their films as positive feminist statements, or as feminist 'art', as in the case of Dorothy Arzner (e.g. Peary, 1974).

A different approach, developed from the counter-cinema argument, insisted that the writing of a history of the cinema to include the contribution of women directors would have to recognise that a simple chronology which 'redressed the balance' in favour of female *auteurs* would not be enough: what was required was a theoretical understanding of the complex relationship between ideological, technological and institutional factors which precisely made it impossible for positive feminist statements to emerge from the Hollywood system of production (see Johnston, 'Dorothy Arzner: critical strategies', 1975). A history of women's cinema did not simply already exist to be unearthed.

Dorothy Arzner

In order to understand how Dorothy Arzner's films can be seen as working in opposition to the ideology of classic Hollywood cinema it is important to ask first of all how that cinema has traditionally constructed the place of woman. One answer produced by feminist film theory (see Feminist film theory, p. 353) is that woman has been constructed as spectacle, as an object of male fantasy and as 'spoken by' that cinema rather than speaking in it (see *The Revolt of Mamie Stover*, p. 295). While this particular construction, it is argued, attempts to fix the place of woman as controlled and contained by the dominant male discourse, it produces an image of woman which is paradoxically characterised in terms of excess and transgression: 'woman', it seems, constantly threatens to escape suppression, the subordinate place assigned to her. This contradiction within patriarchal ideology produces momentary gaps in representation into which the woman's discourse can insert itself, 're-writing' the dominant discourse, making it appear 'strange' (see Johnston, 1975), thus calling it into question so that it no longer reigns supreme: the woman's critical discourse takes over as the structuring principle of the film(s). In the process, the conventions of classic Hollywood cinema (genre, narrative, iconography) are 'de-naturalised' or disturbed to reveal and question the way they construct a place for woman (see Cook, 1975). Through feminist rereadings of this sort the traditional relationship of imaginary fascination between mainstream cinema and its audience can be transformed in the interests of critical analysis. The problems with this kind of 'radical reading' of Hollywood films have been pointed out elsewhere (see *Cahiers du Cinéma*'s 'John Ford', p. 301). Clearly an approach based on textual analysis does not tell us much about the actual conditions of production and reception of Arzner's films in the 1930s and 1940s: in that sense it attempts to construct these films as contradictory texts without recourse to a traditional historiography. However, by focusing on the activity of 're-reading' and 're-writing' (see Roland Barthes, p. 330), it does raise important questions about the nature of dominant ideology and the possibility of feminist intervention within it by asking 'how might a "feminist discourse", as opposed to an

DOROTHY ARZNER

Dance, Girl, Dance (USA 1940 *p.c* – RKO; *d* – Dorothy Arzner; sd b/w)

Dance, Girl, Dance was the personal project of Erich Pommer, the former head of Germany's Ufa Studio, then in exile in Hollywood: he had conceived, cast, and started shooting the film and called in Dorothy Arzner to replace another RKO director. She reworked the script and sharply defined the central conflict as a clash between the artistic inspirations of Judy (Maureen O'Hara) and the commercial, gold-digging Bubbles (Lucille Ball). It is a mixed-genre film combining the conventions of the chorus/working-girl film (backstage musical) and the sophisticated romantic comedy. It is arguable that this combination produces a particularly acute contradiction in the film between, on the one hand, an image of woman as spectacle, and on the other, as the subject of her own desires, both of which are seen to be ultimately controlled by men. The film has been seen as playing with the generic conventions to point up this contradiction, using irony and parody to bring ideology to the surface of the film in its *mise-en-scène* (see Johnston 1975, and Cook, 1975). For instance, it has been argued that genre conventions are reworked to displace the male discourse and focus on the woman's point of view; the scene in which Judy turns on and interrogates the burlesque audience is particularly striking in this context. The film uses class stereotypes to point up differences in Judy's and Bubbles' aspirations: however, these class differences seem to be transcended by the similarities between the two women's problems within patriarchal society.

The same argument sees the 'happy ending' of this film as ironic, pointing up the power structures within which male–female relationships exist under patriarchy. Rather than attribute this irony entirely to Arzner, the film might be discussed in the context of the ironic endings characteristic of the woman's picture (see Melodrama, p. 156).

The woman's point of view? Dorothy Arzner

autonomous "women's art" be conceived?' Dorothy Arzner disclaimed any feminist intention on her part: a rereading of her work can show that meaning is not necessarily fixed according to the author's intentions, and that a film text can accumulate meanings through different readings at different historical moments. Thus films with no immanent political content can be used to raise political questions in a different context.

Dorothy Arzner began her career typing scripts in Hollywood in the 1920s. After the First World War the film industry was fairly open and she soon became an editor and scriptwriter. She was given her first directorial assignment by Paramount in 1927 and went on to direct several comedies and dramas in the category of the woman's picture. Although many women worked as editors and writers in Hollywood few became directors: however, to understand the nature of Arzner's extraordinary achievement it would be necessary to look at the structure of the industry at that time and the way it affected her work. She claims to have had considerable freedom on her projects (see Peary and Kay, 1975); at the same time she was publicised as a woman director and was limited to the woman's picture, a fact which raises important questions about the status of women in the Hollywood industry during the 1920s and 1930s. There are significant differences between the films she directed before the coming of sound and those she made afterwards, and again between the films she directed for different studios. The unevenness of her work, and the difficulty of assimilating it to a coherent *œuvre* as *auteur* study prescribes, seems to confirm the proposition put forward by a theoretical analysis of her films: that any challenge to the prevailing ideology they may offer presents itself in the form of symptoms rather than as a direct statement (see Cook, 1975).

Stephanie Rothman

The context for feminist discussion of Rothman's work is slightly different, though still emerging from the counter-cinema arguments. Rothman is a contemporary film-maker, a film school graduate and a feminist, working in 1970s Hollywood. The break-up of the classic Hollywood system of production and its mass audience after the Second World War led to the growth of independent production and distribution companies, one of which was Roger Corman's New World Pictures, founded in 1970. Through this company, which was initially geared to fast, low-budget production, Corman offered many young film-makers, including Rothman, the chance to direct within the Hollywood industry (see Roger Corman, p. 258). New World Pictures developed a reputation for dealing with serious political themes within the format of 'exploitation' film production (i.e. cheap remakes of more up-market productions in order to make a quick profit), acquiring a name as something of a feminist studio because of its promotion of the 'positive heroine' stereotype (see Hillier and Lipstadt, 1981). However, in spite of the apparent potential of this situation for a declared feminist like Rothman, it is arguable that the exploitation film depends for its success upon the image of woman as spectacle, as the object of male fantasy, just as much as classic Hollywood. A feminist statement emerging from exploitation cinema could not therefore simply appear naturally, it would have to be constructed through the manipulation (conscious or unconscious) of the exploitation codes in order to create new meanings which counter the myths of the male fantasies. Rothman often parodies the codes of exploitation genres to expose their roots in male fantasies and it is this use of formal play to criticise male myths of women which has interested many feminists and which, it has been argued, places Rothman's work in the tradition of women's counter-cinema (see Cook, 1976). Rothman is also of interest to feminists because for a short period she owned her own company (with husband Charles Swartz), Dimension Films, thus achieving an unusual level of control within the Hollywood industry. The company was dissolved in 1974 and Rothman has since gone back to writing scripts (see Terry Curtis Fox, 1976).

Selected Reading

Pam Cook, 'Approaching the work of Dorothy Arzner', in Johnston (ed.), *Dorothy Arzner: Towards a Feminist Cinema*, London, BFI, 1975.

Claire Johnston, 'Women's cinema as counter-cinema', in Johnston (ed.), *Notes on Women's Cinema*, London, SEFT, 1973.

Judith Mayne, *Directed by Dorothy Arzner*, Bloomington, Indiana University Press, 1995.

STEPHANIE ROTHMAN

Student Nurses (USA 1970 *p.c* – New World Pictures; *d* – Stephanie Rothman; sd col)

The first of Rothman's major films for Corman's New World studio, made in the "student nurse" genre that Corman is said to have invented. Working in the sexploitation, soft-porn genre produced mainly for male audiences, Rothman introduces several jarring notes which seem to be incompatible with the generic project. Her use of strategies such as parody and mixed styles could be seen to work to criticise the underlying preconceptions of sexploitation material, bringing them to the surface and exposing their sexism.

On another level, like many New World films, the film deals explicitly with social issues such as abortion, here presented from the perspective of the women characters and questioning masculine attitudes to female sexuality in a manner which would seem to be incompatible with the demands of sexploitation films. However, it might also be argued that abortion is just one more sensational element in a genre which depends for its existence on the exploitation of women's bodies as objects of erotic contemplation.

Knucklemen (Terminal Island) (USA 1973 *p.c* – Dimension Films; *d* – Stephanie Rothman; sd col)

This is an example of a film made by Rothman for her own production company, Dimension Films, continuing in the tradition of exploitation films. It can be argued that Rothman works on the action-sexploitation genre to challenge the pleasures it usually offers its audience, and so create new meanings out of basically uncongenial material. The question then is, how far is it possible to undermine such material, or does the use of it inevitably support the status quo? Comparison with other exploitation films could indicate how far the film's potential commercial audiences might be expected to perceive the feminist criticism of exploitation genre conventions.

The first part of the extract shows the two opposing camps – the one hierarchical and patriarchal, the other exploring the feasibility of a new social order in which notions of sharing and community, group discussion and responsibility are proposed. It also establishes the conventions of the action-sexploitation genre.

In particular, the bee-stinging sequence exemplifies a sadistic reversal of conventions which parodies male fantasies. Joy's exit from the pool, for example, is a parodic reversal of normal strip-tease procedure. Another generic reversal can be seen in the fact that it is the women's knowledge and ingenuity in turning the island's resources to their own use which eventually brings about the take-over by the radical group of the enemy camp. Many exploitation films employ the positive heroine stereotype as a mirror of the male (i.e. as physically aggressive) and one would expect the action genre in particular to validate this stereotype. In this film, the new social order is based on a division of labour which gives men and women equal but different roles, arguably questioning the patriarchal system in which women are seen as mirror images of the male.

AUTEURISM IN THE 1990s

> the various types of image don't already exist, they have to be created. A flat image or, conversely, depth of field, always has to be created or re-created – signs, if you like, always imply a signature. So an analysis of images and signs has to include monographs on major *auteurs*. (Gilles Deleuze)

> you have to have monographs on *auteurs*, but then these have to be grafted onto differentiations, specific determinations, and reorganisations of concepts that force you to reconsider cinema as a whole. (Gilles Deleuze)

In the afterword to the 1998 extended edition of *Signs and Meaning in the Cinema*, Peter Wollen says, 'I am still an *auteurist*.' It is tempting to see the coincidence of *auteurism* and millennialism contained in the notion, '*auteurism* in the nineties' as meaning 'the author is back'. Something of this attitude is suggested by Dudley Andrew's remark, 'After a dozen years of clandestine whispering we are permitted to mention, even to discuss, the *auteur* again' and by the fact that in 1995 both *Film Criticism* and *Film History* ran special issues on *auteurism*. The editorial of *Film Criticism* said its theme of 'The New *Auteurism*' had emerged organically, by sifting through 'our favourites' among submitted manuscripts. This was heralded as a landmark moment spontaneously offering a new wave of *auteur* criticism complete with the 'necessary corrective' of a more contextual and cautious perspective purged of the 'adulatory enthusiasms' of earlier versions. It was now possible to recognise the director as 'always a human function' in the collaborative process of film-making.

If these comments suggest that a long period of looking elsewhere in film theory has been rolled back to permit the re-emergence of *auteurists*, in practice, *auteurism* continued unabated after its initial adoption into Anglo-American film criticism in the 1960s. The different trajectories of structuralist *auteurism* (see Structuralism and *auteur* study, p. 282) and thereafter the emergence of an increasingly pluralistic critical environment, certainly had an impact on what articles were carried in what journals. But rather than constituting a surpassing of *auteurism* this was more a bypassing, and sometimes, in the case of queer theory, (see Feminist film theory, p. 362) a refocusing.

'... just a film' – *Eraserhead*

Auteur theory seemed to survive *incognito* for a while, waiting for the paradigms that had displaced it to grow tired or themselves seem old fashioned. Yet perhaps it was more a matter of waiting for different domains of work to connect and reconnect. Although Roland Barthes and Michel Foucault routinely are cited as providing two death-knells to *auteurism*, in each case the alleged killing now appears to have constituted a much more modest project of redirecting forms of critical attention. Barthes's celebrated declaration of the 'death of the author' was a strategic way of permitting two births: that of textuality, conceived as 'a tissue of quotations drawn from the innumerable centres of culture' (Barthes, 1977, p. 146) and that of the reader/viewer, conceived as 'the space on which all the quotations that make up writing are inscribed' (Barthes, 1977, p. 148). Barthes's voice can be heard in Stephen Heath's conception of the author as part of a mutually constituting activity of writing–reading/viewing. In this understanding the author is a rhetorical figure or trope, part of a, 'fan of elements ... of a certain pleasure which begins to turn the film' and thereby ensnare the viewer. And the legacy of privileging reader power is apparent in David Thomson's 1997 reconsideration of *The Searchers* (1956) where he imagines a different conclusion, one which sees Ethan 'riding on with Debbie, being utterly with her, not uncle but lover'. This speculation is justified because, 'We are beyond *auteurism* now; the films that last endure because of things no maker owns' (Thompson, 1997, p. 31). Similarly, when Michel Chion describes the initial circulation of Lynch's *Eraserhead* (1976) he seems close to Barthes's perspective: 'In the beginning there was not an author, just a film ... the film was perfect; it still belonged completely to its public, and the shadow of the author had not yet fallen on the screen'. After saying 'the author always represents to some extent the work's downfall', Chion provides suggestive reconfigurings of *auteurism* in such formulations as, 'there is nothing more common nowadays than an *auteur*. *Auteur* films (which create their *auteur*) are rarer stuff' (Chion, 1995, p. 3).

In this way there are many things we can say about a text before we say 'who writes it' or as Chion might argue before we are conditioned to look for all the idiosyncratic moments that constitute for some, what a David Lynch film *is*.

1970s TO 1990s: THE *AUTEUR* IN THE INDUSTRY

Michel Foucault's insistence that authors are constituted through discourses and institutions drew attention to the protocols of reading needing to be in place in order to 'find' an author. His suggestion that authorship *names* a particular way of handling texts is confirmed in two 1990s descriptions of the way the cultural category of *auteurism* has entered film production and distribution practices. Timothy Corrigan's account of 'the commerce of *auteurism*' and Justin Wyatt's studies of Francis Coppola and the New Hollywood, and of Robert Altman show how, since the mid-1970s, film-critical *auteurism* has become a crucial part of film publicity, marketing and film journalism.

Corrigan says the author 'has rematerialized in the eighties and nineties as a commercial performance of the business of being an *auteur*' (Corrigan, 1991, p. 104), and refers to 'the survival – and, in fact, increasing importance – of the *auteur* as a commercial strategy for organizing audience reception, as a critical concept bound to distribution and marketing aims that identify and address the potential cult status of an *auteur*' (Corrigan, 1991, p. 103). Since 'institutional and commercial agencies define *auteurism* almost exclusively as publicity and advertisement' it has become possible 'to already know ... the meaning of the film in a totalizing image that precedes the movie in the public images of its creator' (Corrigan, 1991, p. 106). Certain directors enjoy a celebrity which 'produces and promotes texts that invariably exceed the movie itself, both before and after its release' (Corrigan, 1991, p. 107).

Corrigan's examples are Coppola, Kluge and Ruiz, but his point is also demonstrated by noting the difference between the lengthy 'crawl' of credits at the end of films – a carefully attained and finely-monitored union achievement identifying personnel whose work appears on-screen – and those occasions when films are presented to us as, 'A Steven Spielberg Film' or 'Martin Scorsese Presents' even though these men are not directing. Their marquee value is a promotional device as well as the result of a whole package of 'deals' struck between personal and studio publicists.

Justin Wyatt's work on Coppola supports Corrigan's views by arguing that Hollywood studios, as economic–entrepreneurial entities, were happy to adopt *auteurism*, seeing it as simply the most recent (mid-1970s) description of established film-industry practices of contracting talent and marketing product (Wyatt, 1996, p. 19). So Paramount financed the short-lived Director's Company as a way of bringing together three hot directors of the moment – Coppola, Friedkin and Bogdanovich. Only three films were produced – Coppola's *The Conversation* (1974) and Bogdanovich's *Paper Moon* (1973) and *Daisy Miller* (1974). According to Wyatt, this initiative from Frank Yablans, Paramount's Chief Executive, only seems 'to accept the *auteur* theory when the real plan was for a "recontextualisation of *auteurism* within the studio structure"' (Wyatt, 1996, p. 16).

Thus the 1970s constitutes a historical moment of overlap between film-critical *auteurism* and an *auteurism* incorporated into studio film-making practice: the studios' 'ready acceptance of American *auteur* cinema in the 1970s was the result of characteristic industry-wide cautiousness' (Wyatt, 1996, p. 2) and if a film failed, studio executives could 'avoid culpability' by pointing to the *auteur*. The mid-1970s also saw a number of 'university-educated *auteurs*' and others working at the fringes or outside the formal education system, such as Spielberg, prepared to 'subtly update the safe studio genre package' (Wyatt, 1996, p. 45), resulting in 'big-budget auteur films' (Wyatt, 1996, p. 22) like *The Godfather* (1971), *Jaws* (1975) and *Star Wars* (1977). This 'ongoing redefinition of *auteurism* in the new Hollywood' (Wyatt, 1996, p. 148) generated the paradoxical situation whereby 'the dazzling box-office success of expensive *auteurist* movies ... led to an industry wide focus on blockbuster box office revenues' (Wyatt, 1996, p. 22). The result: directors dependent on studios to finance and distribute 'big' personal films.

In a later piece, Wyatt sees 'the industrial and institutional factors impacting (Robert) Altman's career over the past twenty-five years' as revealing 'the complexity of the "author–name" as a means to account for the economic aspects of authorship' (Wyatt, 1998, p. 64). He traces the way 'economic constraints and opportunities in the film marketplace' used *auteurism* to promote Altman at various times across thirty years of film-making. Altman's 'third' career phase, aligned with the independents in the 1990s, shows how 'media constructions – around advertising, subject matter, and the *auteur* – are crucial to the major independent's careers as a form of marketing'.

Fine Line promoted *The Player* (1992) by stressing 'Altman's alienation from the studio system,' repositioning him 'as a famous director returning to artistic form' (Wyatt, 1996, p. 62), a '"rejuvenated" *auteur*' (Wyatt, 1996, p. 64). The same *auteurist* plug was used with *Short Cuts* (1993), Altman's film derived from some Raymond Carver short stories: 'From two American masters comes a movie like no other'. No doubt too that some irony or cynical marketing is evident in the fact that Altman could make a film such as *The Player* whose message contains a 'romantic *auteurist*' denunciation of the impossibility of an *auteurist* director's cinema in contemporary Hollywood only to have that film marketed as an exemplary instance of a director's vision.

AUTEUR CRITICISM IN THE 1990S

While *auteurism* as a critical description of distinctive thematic–stylistic cinematic achievements was being absorbed into the promotional and publicity domains of film-making, it was also continuing as an energetic film-critical paradigm. In 1984 *Wide Angle* had a special issue on film authorship and the 1990s produced some of the best discussions of this critical orientation: James Naremore on 'Authorship and the cultural politics of film criticism'; Dudley Andrew on a revitalised *auteurism*; Timothy Corrigan (already cited) on 'The commerce of *auteurism*'; Alexander Doty's rethinking of *auteurism* by way of queer theory; and other new work on John Huston and Rainer Werner Fassbinder, are all products of this time. As was ever the case, *auteurism* continues to be practised in different ways with different consequences. James Naremore said that first-wave *auteurism* (if that is what we can call 1950s/1960s *auteurism*) 'took on different political meanings at different conjunctures'. While mounting 'an invigorating attack on convention' it also 'formed canons and fixed the names of people we should study' (Naremore, 1990, p. 21). That remains an accurate description of such 1990s *auteur* criticism as Bernard Eisenschitz's biography of Nicholas Ray – where an 'old' *auteurism* is supplemented by additional empirical information on the studio context – and Jay Boyer's study of Bob Rafelson for Twayne's 'Film-makers' series. The title of Boyer's book, *Bob Rafelson: Hollywood Maverick*, announces its link to the 1950s–1960s France, UK and US mode of *auteurism* which required a few artist–*auteurs*–maudits–mavericks to be destroyed or at least rejected/marginalised by 'the system' in order to be consecrated as *auteurs*. A revealing moment of heroic *auteurism* comes when Boyer is placing *Man Trouble* (1992) within Rafelson's *œuvre*: 'Things that do not make much sense in the film often fall right into line when you consider the film is Rafelson's' (Boyer, 1996, p. 120).

On other occasions critics try to practise *auteurism* differently. So in his reconsideration of Peckinpah's *Pat Garrett and Billy the Kid*, Jim Kitses (whose *Horizons West* was a landmark Anglo-American rendering of first-wave author–genre criticism) distances himself from those perpectives which seek to lionise Peckinpah as an artistic victim of philistine studio front-office intervention.

> the truth is that the director was frequently unable to sustain the collaborative relationships essential to the quasi-industrial system of mainstream feature film-making. Peckinpah's early break-through successes coincided with the broad diffusion within the film community of *auteur* theory, ... and insofar as the premise of the director as author was seen as a theory of production rather than a critical method, its impact may well have been unfortunate within Hollywood.
> (Kitses, 1998, p. 230)

Auteurism is also practised differently in some mid-1990s studies of Rainer Werner Fassbinder which in their care to distance themselves from earlier unhesitatingly *auteurist* studies of the director encapsulate many of the various directions of *auteur* criticism as interpretative tool in the 1980s and 1990s. In 1992, on the tenth anniversary of his death, several reassessments of Fassbinder's 43 films, 14 plays, 4 radio plays and many essays came forward. A special issue of *New German Critique* placed Fassbinder's work in a changed German social–political climate, the Museum of Modern Art issued a publication to accompany the first complete retrospective of Fassbinder's work shown in the United States (made possible by the Rainer Werner Fassbinder Foundation) and Thomas Elsaesser published his long-awaited book on Fassbinder. Elsaesser said Fassbinder was an 'undisputed *auteur*' whose films had been overwhelmed by the details of a pathological and sensational life, and admitted his project might seem an old fashioned, 'not to say a "retrograde" one, seemingly wishing to reinstate the "author" as the locus (and the work as the material manifestation) of an intentional plenitude, whose stages and intricacies it is the task of the critic to reconstruct' (Elsaesser, p. 9) To forestall this possibility, Elsaesser's book uses Fassbinder's work as a prism permitting a scrutiny of a 'politics of "self" and "identity"' which works to 'define differently what it means to be representative' and which also helps redefine 'the cinema and its representations of history' (Elsaesser, 1996, p. 43).

Drawing on retrospectives and conferences held in Berlin, Munich and at Dartmouth College, *New German Critique* justified its re-examination of the 'controversial legacy and . . . relevance for the present' of Fassbinder's cultural work by saying they hoped to prevent the twin traps of oblivion or mummification within the film-cultural museum.

> Historicizing Fassbinder from today's standpoint means engaging his work in current debates about film-making, *auteurism*, and personal cinema; about the writing and rewriting of German film history; about questions of genre; about questions of gender and homosexuality; but it also means engaging his work with problems the current political situation is presenting. Here Fassbinder's films could be made to speak about questions of identity and nationality, marginality, foreigners, and representing a troubled past to an audience who knows these troubles only through other representations – all issues which are setting the political agenda of the 1990s for a unified Germany.

Here the historicising distance means that current critical discussions of Fassbinder are far less likely to participate in gossipy biographical *auteurism* which raids both films and life to posit some explanatory revelation; and is also less likely to be overwhelmed by the aesthetic–charismatic notion of Fassbinder constituting a crossover emblematic figure for New German Cinema, carrying it single-handedly to an enthusiastic critical reception.

Gaylyn Studlar and David Desser's 1993 collection of articles on John Huston makes a move similar to the ones which justify the re-embrace of Fassbinder's work. When Studlar says the project is not driven by 'some nostalgic wish to elevate the director to a pantheon of directors from which he was formerly excluded' ('Introduction,' p. 4), this refers to Andrew Sarris's late 1960s book, *The American Cinema*, where Huston provides the opening entry for a section ('V: Less than Meets the Eye') devoted to directors 'with reputations in excess of inspirations. In retrospect it always seems that the personal signatures were written in invisible ink' (Sarris, 1968, p. 155). Sarris's revised (1980) assessment of Huston is included in the collection which claims as its principal aim the demonstration that 'a director-centered anthology, while "*auteurist*" in some sense of the word, need not perpetuate some idealistic notion of personalized cinematic authorship transcending the boundaries of either institutional or ideological constraints.' Instead the collection seeks to show how 'mutiple determinants' structure films directed by Huston, showing 'the ways in which Huston could be used to explore issues of authorship and sexual identity – and vice-versa'.

These different varieties of *auteurism* show that different modes of activating an *auteurist* critical gaze will achieve different results. For example, Paul Willemen adapts Yuri Lotman (author as structure to be constructed) and Stephen Heath (author as fan of elements) to generate his distinctive account of the author (Amos Gitai) as a crossroad where discursive chains meet and are held in a constellation by the text in context. This is quite different from the strand of relatively unproblematic 1990s *auteurism* which has repeated the 1950s version on such things as pop-music videos and the work of Quentin Tarantino. It is as if a romantic, literary notion of the author has been succeeded by a designer notion of the author: the author is now depicted as an irrepressible individuality appreciated and paid for by his or her ability to contribute to product differentiation, a process whose results are then redescribed by the film publicity–marketing system in terms of the conventional romantic notions of the author. This is convenient for business and promotional purposes (cf. Spielberg–Scorsese) as the author shifts between two statuses: exemplary individual and brand-name/corporate logo.

Since *auteurism* is not a unified critical practice, it is not surprising that the writing which seeks to establish the vision and sensibility of the author (equating film-makers with writers of world literature, a stockmarket version of the canon) is not the same discourse as Willemen's author-as-crossroads concept. Still, when Elsaesser says that any single-author study 'continues to have a powerful attraction for readers' (Elsaesser, 1996, p. 9), his point seems abundantly proved by such ventures as Faber's widely available 'Projections' and 'x on x' series (e.g., *Malle on Malle*), which began in 1989 with *Scorsese on Scorsese*, and Twayne's 'Film-makers' series. Each testifies to a continuing public interest in what film-makers have to say about the films they make.

But even within an overarching *auteurist* publishing project, individual studies might treat *auteurism* differently. For example, Susan Hayward's study of *Luc Besson* – whose cinema is part of French debates on the political–aesthetic status of a so-called postmodern 'cinema du look' which can be positively ('neo-baroque') or negatively ('post-card aesthetics') valorised – appears in MUP's series on French directors. Hayward claims Besson deliberately departs from the *nouvelle vague* generation of cinephilia and romantic *auteurism*. Although he writes, produces and directs his films, Besson describes himself as a *metteur-en-scène*, and is always keen to acknowledge the contribution of his crew, technicians and actors. According to Hayward, this is a calculated break with the narcissistic aesthetic of 1950s *auteurism*, which had 'glossed over the real complexities of the means of production (production practices)'.

AUTEURS AND ALTERITY

Today, when some radical political writing seeks to promote the work of those marginalised from cinema by virtue of their sex or race (Dyer, 1997, pp. 14, 16), a form of authorship can emerge which denies individual vision and requires of directors that they be legitimate representatives of minorities or tangentially of entire national cinemas (e.g. Tracey Moffat or Isaac Julien). An example is the white media's obsession with Spike Lee, who is regularly regarded as a sage on the inner city – his films are not evidence, but 'he' is. (Discussion of the problem of Italian-American gangsterism does not see Martin Scorsese called upon to represent 'his' people).

Another consideration of the issue of otherness and cinema comes in some writing from Judith Mayne and Alexander Doty, each concerned to theorise sexual preference and film authorship. At the outset of her piece on 'lesbian authorship' Mayne claims there is a potential contradiction in any critical enterprise which seeks to bring 'authorship into a discussion of lesbian representation' (Mayne, 1991, p. 177), arising from the (alleged) fact that 'within the context of cinema studies, the very notion of authorship is far more evocative of traditional, patriarchal film criticism than even is the case in literary studies' (Mayne, 1991, p. 177). Mayne explores this self-produced dilemma via a reading of Midi Onodera's short film, *Ten Cents a Dance* (Parallax) (1985), and its controversial reception, and eventually decides that 'the lesbian author is defined as both complicit in and resistant to the sexual fictions of patriarchal culture' (Mayne, 1991, p. 183).

In the course of the encounter between queer theory and *auteurism* conveyed in a discussion of George Cukor and Dorothy

Arzner, Alexander Doty says that queer *auteurs* can emerge by the practising in today's context of Andrew Sarris's late 1960s *auteurism* and/or could emerge if a critic adopted the category 'e' dimension of *Cahiers du Cinéma*'s 1969 reworking of *auteurism* (see p. 287). In this case the earlier *auteurism* attains a contemporary radicalism by being recruited to a 'hidden from film history' project. At the same time, Doty also argues for a notion of queer authorship as 'a use of *auteurism* which considers that meanings are constructed within and across film texts through the interplay of creators, cultures, and audiences. As a result, queer *auteurs* could either be "born" or "made" ' (Doty, 1993, p. 46) by way of the interplay of 'queer people on all sides of the camera – before it, behind it, and in the audience' (Doty, 1993, p. 48). A case could be made for a director, star, writer 'as queer on the basis of their being queer . . . or on the evidence that many of their films hold, or have held, a particularly meaningful place within queer cultural history, with or without knowledge of the director's sexuality' (Doty, 1993, p. 46). In addition, queer *auteurs* would be formed 'when the films of non-queer identified directors become interesting to queerly-positioned spectators for their (sub)texts'. By this stage the *auteurism* on offer seems closer to the Roland Barthes and Michel Chion formulations cited earlier.

AUTEURISM NOW

Making films is such an obviously collective and artisanal (producers, stars, scriptwriters, cinematographers, editors, costume and set designers, music composers) activity in its 'division of labour, disparate skills and shared responsibilities' (Coward, 1987, p. 79) that speaking in terms of individual authorship becomes increasingly problematic the more film scholarship uncovers the detail of these other contributions. Is it feasible to consider popular film as great art expressive of an individual vision without accounting for Ken Adam's art direction, in the Bond cycle, Saul Bass's titles in Hitchcock's films, or Edith Head's classical Hollywood fashion design? Alternatively, the example of ethnographic cinema offers a complex amalgam of authorship. Anthropologist and film-maker frequently form a two-person crew, with the former recording sound and explaining language and other phenomena and the latter shooting (Asch, 1990). Who is the author here?

The identification of directors as *auteurs* is a move critics make based on a retrospective account of a body of work. And that is why we should position *auteur* criticism inside the wider sweep of film history and its conditions for authorial discourses, rather than subordinating social and industrial forces to an individual expressive totality. As Edward Buscombe said a quarter of a century ago, before we rank individuals as a priority for film theory, we should go looking for the social impact of and on the cinema and the intertextual and industrial interconnections of films upon one another. And Dudley Andrew reminds us that André Bazin wanted *auteurism* practised in tandem with discussions of 'a genre or a national trend or a social movement' (Andrew, 1993, p. 78), and that Wollen's desire in *Signs and Meaning in the Cinema* was to isolate 'the *auteur*'s signal within the noise of the text' (Wollen, 1998, p. 79).

Sometimes that 'noise' will come from the recognition and description of those other artisanal contributions, as indicated above. At other times the 'noise' will indicate the changed global circumstances of film production, circulation and exhibition. As more and more countries try to compete with Hollywood in a suddenly deregulated world TV market, one in which blockbusters and associated promotional costs wipe out other genres and nations, the issue of how to measure the creativity of a film arises in a new way – how many creative principals should come from a given country or region in order for the film to qualify for public support? This leads to a focus on producers, distributors, exhibitors, scriptwriters, actors, and directors, which problematises existing notions of authorship across the cultural field.

There is now a certain tendency to examine how particular sites and practices produce the author, a concentration on how films circulate, the contexts in which they are apprehended and the rules which govern their interpretation. This approach contends that authorship is produced through such cultural apparatuses and technologies as: interview, criticism, publicity and curriculum, and also makes the important point that one should try to take account of the different conditions of possibility for creative claims. For example, despite the publicity contained in such things as *Premiere*'s special 1997 issue focusing on 'Women in Hollywood', the history of women scriptwriters in Hollywood is one of extreme dominance prior to the advent of the mature studio system, with great capacity to move into directing and producing; virtual exile throughout the studio system's heyday; but the contemporary paradox of the emergence of female studio heads and producers overseeing diminished earnings potential with no improvement in the capacity to crossover to become producers and directors and hence influence the conduct of production (Biebly and Biebly, 1996), the notable exception being Kathlyn Bigelow (Cook, 1998) an example where women writers have carved out some generic licence to write and direct action adventure. Large increases in the number of white women producers and studio executives have not seen salaries or power commensurate with those of men (Ryan, 1995).

It would be wrong to suggest that authorship as a category has ended or is irretrievably problematised. But whatever variety of it is practised in our contemporary context should attend to Jonathan Rosenbaum when he says that, now more than ever, film criticism must detach itself from the seductions of film publicity. Here, Rosenbaum claims that film critics do not raise sufficiently often 'the question of how often aesthetic agendas are determined by business agendas. When it comes to the role of business interests in shaping certain aspects of cinephilia, criticism is often simply in denial.' Rosenbaum is discussing the category of 'cult' films and the question of exactly how 'independent' independent cinema is in the late 1990s, in a context where the Sundance Festival (its premier showcase) is part sponsored by *Entertainment Weekly* and the *New York Times*. The 'independence' of the *auteur* and their 'vision' – as an element distinct from the rest of the cinema business – therefore remains a major issue for industry and criticism alike.

SELECTED READING

Dudley Andrew, 'The unauthorised *auteur* today', in Jim Collins *et al.* (eds), *Film Theory Goes to the Movies*, London, Routledge, 1993, pp. 77–85.

Michel Chion, *David Lynch*, trans. Robert Julian, London, BFI, 1995.

Alexander Doty, 'Whose text is it anyway?: queer cultures, queer *auteurs*, and queer authorship', *Quarterly Review of Film and Video* 15(1), pp. 41–54.

Peter Wollen, *Signs and Meaning in the Cinema*, expanded edition, London, BFI, 1998.

Justin Wyatt, 'Economic constraints/economic opportunities: Robert Altman as *auteur*', *The Velvet Light Trap* no. 38, autumn, 1996, pp. 51–67.

A personal vision? *Picnic at Hanging Rock*

PETER WEIR

The Truman Show (1998) directed by Peter Weir is an interesting Hollywood film which combines elements of Franz Kafka, media self-hatred, and a story and visuality borrowed from the 1960s English TV series *The Prisoner* (1967–8). Its star, Jim Carrey, dominated most of the world promotion for the picture. But for the purposes of an Australian-themed edition of *Variety*, the film was renationed to fit a notion of *auteurism* which held that Weir's direction 'made' the film and that this also 'made' the film Australian; suddenly a person's individual signature was coextensive with the place of his birth. After devoting a paragraph to extolling the authorial continuities in the work of New Zealand scriptwriter Andrew Niccol (Maslin, 1998, E1) the *New York Times*' review referred to *The Truman Show* as 'Peter Weir's film'. The simultaneous rerelease of *Picnic at Hanging Rock* (1975) provided Weir with the opportunity to recut 'his' early film and have it ranged alongside his latest work as part of an artistic trajectory exploring his belief: 'Your reality may not be my reality' (quoted in Gell, 1998). Although *auteur* work on Weir persistently encounters his request that the entire category be 'put . . . aside', one continues to hear that he has a personal vision which involves transcending the mundane and the immoral through idiosyncracy. This vision can be understood by way of Weir's personal biography, which in turn generates the preconditions for films appearing under his name (Shiach, 1993, pp. 1–2; Maslin, 1998, E18).

JANE CAMPION

After having directed a feature film, a mini-series, and a handful of shorts, Australian-based New Zealand film-maker Jane Campion was said, with *Sweetie* (1989), to possess a distinct connotative stamp, a set of concerns about power in the everyday and the underside of life, the abject, that which is best evaded and ignored. Other enduring themes might be cited as nature as an environmental force beyond control and sexuality's capacity to cut through cultural norms, and the ability of the 'other' to destablise the 'same' (Sweetie in *Sweetie* and Baines in *The Piano* (1993)). The smallest units of audiovisual style were taken as signs and symptoms of this vision: framing, tilts, cut-aways, visual jokes and music.

Where some aspects fail to fit this model, as in her TV drama, straightforward social realism is turned into the quirky counter-realism that is said to be the director's signature (Bloustein, 1992). But what happens to these *auteurist* certainties when we turn to the figure of Gerard Lee, who wrote and co-directed the 'Campion' short, *Passionless Moments* (1984) and who co-wrote the screenplay of *Sweetie*, based on personal experience? Or when we turn to Sally Bongers, the director of photography for *Sweetie* who has a distinctive style of lighting and framing that puts energy into set-ups rather than camera movements? It is an enduring problem for *auteurism* to distinguish between these industrial and personal identities and their responsibility for texts.

Looking for the signature of the director . . . *The Piano*

PART 7

THEORETICAL FRAMEWORKS

Three Colours: White (1994)

LOOKING AT FILM

The options currently available to the film critic provide a wide and varied spectrum of approaches that may seem both daunting and cumbersome to the novice film student. However, as this section shows, most modes of analysis share many common concerns, and the ultimate benefit is that formal patterns, thematic systems, and cultural insights enliven the interpretation and enjoyment of film. Every aesthetic discipline can be enriched by purposeful analysis, and study of the cinema has worked very hard to parallel older and more established forms of art in developing a rigour of interpretation that goes beyond mere subjective reactions. 'Looking at film' requires productive inquiry into aspects *specific* to the cinema and film practice. Thus this section surveys quite briefly the major avenues for investigating how films function, how they organise their illusory time and space, how they tell their stories and finally how they are watched and understood.

FILM AS REPRESENTATION

One option in approaching the specificity of the cinema is to confront its essential traits. The very definition of the cinema is rooted in the ability of its basic technology to present a series of representational images (and perhaps sounds) that create the illusion of movement where of course there is nothing but still images flashing at a prescribed speed. Once we think about it, cinema is all 'special effects'. Interest in the cinema must therefore begin with its materiality, with that which makes it a distinct medium even before it is an art form. Many of the founding critics and theorists of the cinema were interested in defining and even cataloguing pertinent traits and techniques in order to account for the cinema's specificity so that they could judge which films used those parameters more fully, 'more cinematically' than others. In order to evaluate a film (discuss its aesthetics) it is therefore necessary to account for its essence (ontology). A logical beginning for most scholars, and for film studies itself historically, has been to analyse film's ability to present an impression of reality.

The image, its presentation of an illusory time and space via shot composition, and the preservation or manipulation of that time and space in the form of editing, are in one way or another at the root of most critical and theoretical models of film analysis. Testing the extent to which these formal strategies can create an impression of real time and space, or by contrast, challenge any 'real' time and space, falls within the practice of evaluating film's methods of representation.

Interest in film as a representational medium can help to explain recurring themes and concerns in film criticism (e.g. in terms of the question, 'What are the fundamental cinematic devices?') but also helps to clarify the canonical privileging of certain films. For example, the persistent celebration of films like *La Règle du jeu* (Renoir, 1939), *Citizen Kane* (Welles, 1941), or *À bout de souffle* (Godard, 1959) is partly due to their use of formal, even essential, techniques of representation. 'Looking at films' closely therefore requires that we first learn to discern basic techniques and strategies of filmic discourse (the techniques cinema uses to display the world) including shot duration, camera mobility, deep-space staging, manipulation of the elements of *mise-en-scène* (such as lighting, acting style, costume, setting), sound strategies, and editing. Film criticism and interpretation therefore begin with understanding the basic strategies available to the film-maker, and then turn to evaluating individual films for how they make use of those devices. A good introduction to film as representation is to consider how the *mise-en-scène*, camera work, and editing of one film (say *La Règle du jeu*, 1939) differ from another of the same year but different mode of production (for instance John Ford's *Stagecoach*, 1939). What sort of time and space does each create and how? Cinema creates impressions of reality via the artifice of concrete representational ploys and the study of the cinema begins with an apprenticeship in noting them and evaluating their function.

In narrative cinema, the apparatus takes real movement, breaks it down to 24 frames per second and reanimates it via 2-dimensional images. For some critics, animation is cinema at its purest, since animation creates movement where there was never any 'real' motion at the pre-filmic stage. Bugs Bunny, unlike Jean-Paul Belmondo, never existed as a referential being to be photographed. Animation proves therefore the ultimate power of the cinema – to animate, or 'bring to life', rather than simply to recreate, but even within the realm of animation there is a wide range of representational styles and options. The dominant mode of Disney animation is based on editing rhythms and representational cues borrowed wholesale from live action. Disney employs selective focus, depth in composition, and complex shifts in colour to evoke an impression of 'real' space. Other Hollywood animators, like Warner Bros, ignored the plausible spatial cues so important to Disney Studios and dealt with a more graphic, flat, and artificial cartoon space. But the most 'cinematic' of all animation may be the so-called 'camera-less' animation, pioneered by Len Lye (see *Colour Box*, 1936, and *Colour Flight*, 1937) and Norman McLaren (*Dots*, 1940, and *Blinkity Blank*, 1954), whose images and occasionally even soundtracks are drawn directly onto the filmstock. Such animation makes the fullest use of the medium as it foregrounds the entire process of making, projecting, and finally perceiving movement where none ever existed.

EDITING

One of the most fundamental contradictions inherent to the cinema is its ability on the one hand to record the world visually as continuous time and space, and on the other to manipulate that reality by editing. Editing at its most basic definition is the selection and ordering of film images and may be said to 'liberate' the cinema from static long takes. Editing thereby becomes a strong narrative device since it allows the narrator to deliver information in bits and pieces. Strangely enough, such a simple concept has historically divided film-makers and aestheticians of the cinema. Film studies has long centred many of its aesthetic assumptions and conflicts on the opposition between two nearly mythical camps of thinking about editing: those represented by Soviet director and theorist Sergei Eisenstein and those following French critic André Bazin.

Eisenstein is a representative of the most extreme faith in the ability of editing to produce aesthetic shocks and conflicts. Montage editing in its strictest definition is a reliance on the power of rapid cutting to create meaning. Rather than depending upon 'real' time and space to deliver information, Eisenstein privileged montage editing to create dialectical materialist works: thesis (shot no. 1) and antithesis (shot no. 2) create a synthesis (something greater than either shot independently). Such an approach revels in the discursive function of cinema and its potential to reorganise reality. For instance, during the famous 'Odessa steps' sequence in *Battleship Potemkin* (1925), the temporal and spatial relations are purely fictitious: at one moment it seems that a mother's child has fallen behind her, but a subsequent shot reveals he is now below her, and just when it seems that all the fleeing people have made it to the bottom of the steps, it seems to begin all over again. Real time and space cues are secondary to the manipulative functions of montage (see Soviet cinema, p. 73).

On the other end of the spectrum is André Bazin, for whom excessive dependence upon montage editing violates the essence of the cinema and its aesthetic development. Bazin encouraged film-makers to preserve the illusion of real time and space by relying less upon the 'trickery' of manipulative editing and more on staging in long takes, in deep space or planes of action. He favoured continuity devices (eyeline matches, 180° rule) only when editing was necessary. For Bazin, unlike Eisenstein, cinema's 'evolution' is a continuous progression towards providing more convincing representations that mirror the complexity of our real experience of the world, which to him was complex, ambiguous and dense.

Most film-makers work in between these extreme positions, moving to one end of the spectrum or the other when there is a formal or narrative justification. Classic Hollywood cinema (see Classic Hollywood narrative, p. 39), for instance, stands as a compromise between these two ideologies of montage, following continuity editing regularly to make the editing unobtrusive when possible, but resorting to rapid montages for violent scenes (the shower scene in Hitchcock's *Psycho*, 1960) or the quick passing of time (the 'whirlwind romance' in *The Awful Truth*, McCarey, 1937).

FILM LANGUAGE

Critical consideration of 'film language' has matured during the twentieth century, paralleling and absorbing developments in the arts and linguistics, structuralism, and semiotics. For instance, early textbooks defined and discussed 'film grammar' (usually by listing various film devices) complete with 'good' and 'bad' examples. Raymond J. Spottiswoode (1935) set out to clarify 'the language and grammar which the film, as a prospective art form, has to acquire'. Many production manuals, like Karel Reisz and Gavin Millar's (1953) are underpinned by a similar approach as they recount for instance the best way to stage,

Battleship Potemkin (USSR 1925 *p.c* – Goskino; *d* – Sergei Eisenstein; st b/w)

One of the most famous scenes in *Battleship Potemkin*, the 'Odessa steps sequence', provides a striking example of Eisenstein's dialectical editing style in which montage functions to create conflict on many levels at once, motivating intricate and multiple reactions from the audience. The immediate function certainly is to prove the brutality of the Tsar's soldiers who appear as an inhuman line of boots, rifles, and shadows as they massacre hundreds of civilians. This theme is reinforced by tiny dramas (a war veteran with no legs hops acrobatically down the steps, a small group appeals for mercy and is gunned down, a doctor tries to help fallen victims amid the gunfire and chaos). But one of the larger responses engineered by Eisenstein is that the Tsar's soldiers win because they are more disciplined than the civilians who outnumber the soldiers but have no unity or guns. The mutineers on the ship, by contrast, are unified and armed, thus allowing them to respond with their big guns at the end of this scene.

The sequence builds tension by the use of these visual elements, but even more so by its unconventional editing. The Odessa steps become an impossible narrative space since establishing shots are not used consistently with the cut-ins, and time and space are distorted rather than clarified. For instance, the first half of the sequence includes montages of townspeople celebrating the triumph of the mutineers on the Potemkin in the harbour. But then, as David Bordwell writes, ' "Suddenly": one of the most famous titles in world cinema introduces four percussive shots of a woman's body jerking spasmodically. Barely comprehensible in projection, the jump-cut series of shots functions, Eisenstein

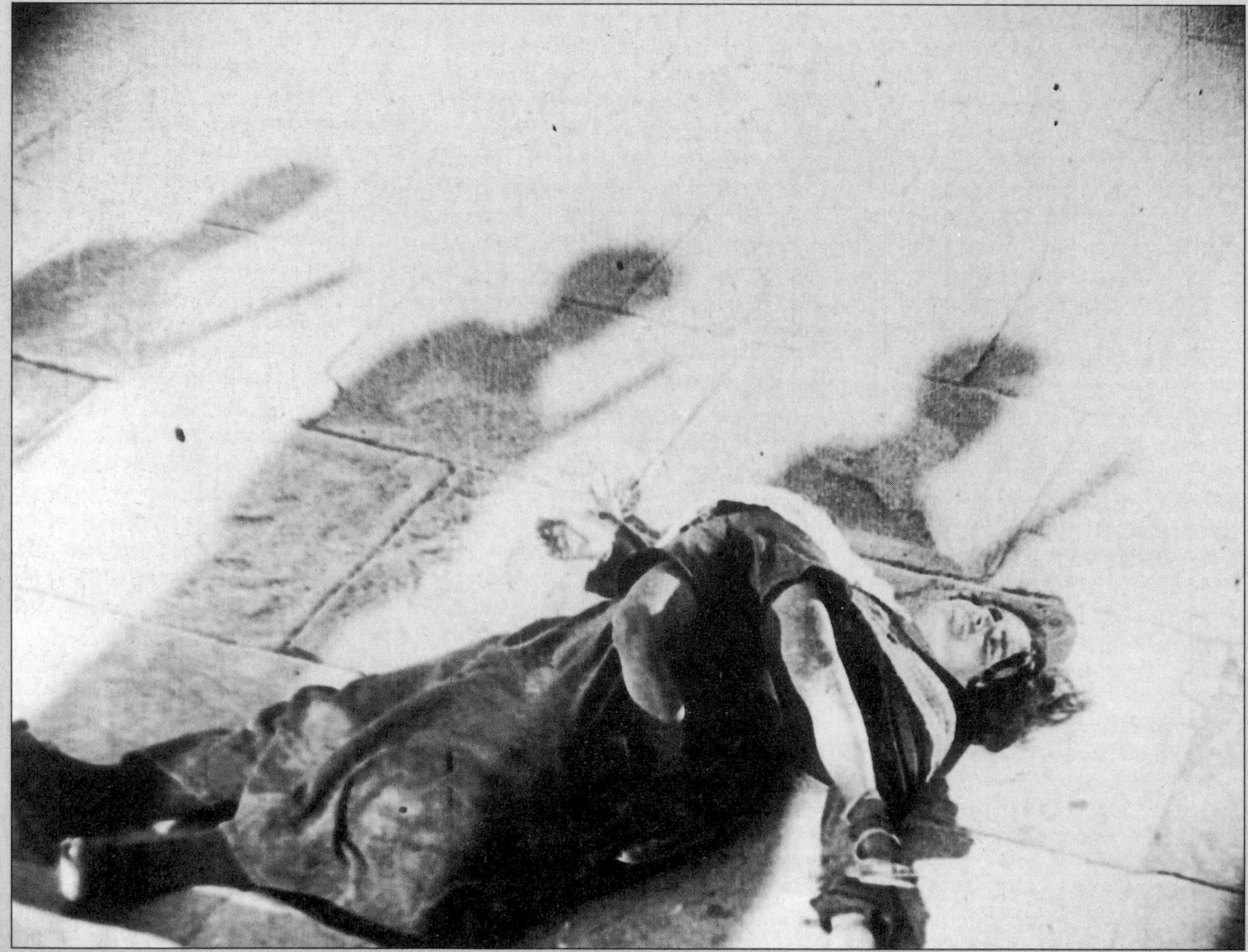

The functions of montage – *Battleship Potemkin*

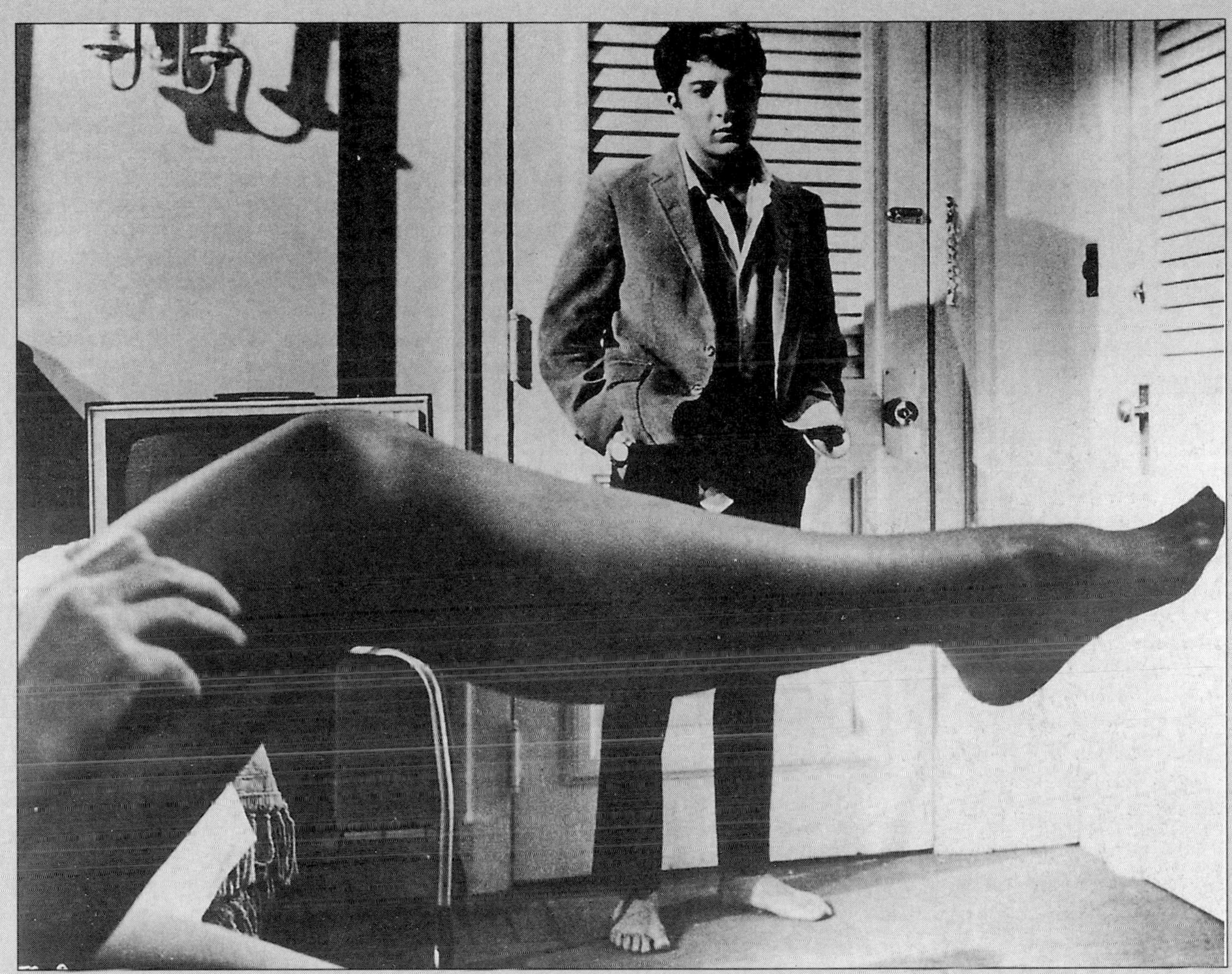

Framing the situation – scene construction allied to story in *The Graduate*

remarks, as the detonator in an explosion' (Bordwell, 1993, p. 74). The actual frame lengths for these four disorienting shots are seven, five, eight and ten!

The entire sequence layers discontinuous shots onto one another according to precise rhythmic and graphic conflicts, until time and space become subjective and discursive rather than representational. By the middle of the massacre, when it seems everyone should be dead or have reached the bottom of the steps, the entire cycle of running and dying seems to begin anew. This is when the longest single action of the scene – a young mother is shot and her baby's carriage rolls down the steps – is fragmented into 35 shots, which are intercut with 25 further shots which do not include the mother or the carriage (such as the shot of the rifles, the older woman looking, and people scurrying in different directions). Eisenstein's intricate dialectical approach to film form here constructs its most emotional and intellectual effects.

The Graduate (USA 1967 *p.c* – Joseph E. Levine/Embassy Pictures; *d* – Mike Nichols; sd col. scope)

Mike Nichols's *The Graduate* proves a particularly lively text as it allows the analyst to test for and locate a wide variety of narrative strategies. There are radical examples of montage: for example, in one scene a naked Mrs Robinson (Anne Bancroft) runs into a bedroom to startle the naïve Ben (Dustin Hoffman) – he turns his head three times, as if on Eisenstein's Odessa steps, and his perception of her body is delivered via incredibly short takes (3 to 5 frames). But there are also elegant long takes that allow the spectator to leisurely scan the widescreen image. The scene where Ben, who is now having an affair with Mrs Robinson, asks whether they cannot at least 'liven it up with a little conversation first this time', demonstrates both the value of long takes and the cleverness of creative widescreen framing.

This pivotal scene can be contrasted with the preceding scene in which Ben's mother tries in vain to get him to talk to her. The scene between Ben and his mother lasts only 73 seconds and is composed of eight shots (A.S.L. 9 seconds). The scene between Ben and Mrs Robinson lasts 9 minutes and 15 seconds, and it too is composed of eight shots (A.S.L. 70 seconds). Ben's attempt at conversation leads first comically then dramatically to information about the Robinson household, including the revelation that Mrs Robinson was pregnant with Elaine when the Robinsons married. The most jarring and shortest shots (5 and 6) happen at the point when Elaine becomes an issue.

During this scene, we see Ben rebel against Mrs Robinson's control, first by turning the lights on when she wants them off, but finally by crouching over her on the bed as she cowers in the corner of the frame in shadows. The moment when she stretches her leg across the screen as he tries to decide whether to leave clinches the argument, and Ben stays. This is not only exemplary scene construction but a fascinating combination of story information and film style.

Nichols employs the widescreen framing and depth to isolate multiple zones of action for the characters to move into and to punctuate the dialogue during the unusually long takes. But he also manipulates the lighting and lack of colour (their flesh provides the only real colour in the scene), and shifts the camera level to reinforce the powerful performances and make the narration intricately cinematic. *The Graduate*, certainly a parody of conventional romantic comedies, collides classic Hollywood style with self-conscious devices of the modern European art cinema. André Bazin and Sergei Eisenstein would both be intrigued.

Three Colours: White (Trois couleurs: blanc) (France/Switzerland/Poland 1994 *p.c* – Marin Karmitz; *d* – Kryzsztof Kieslowski; sd col.)

Three Colours: White, the second film in Kieslowski's trilogy (the other two are *Trois couleurs: bleu* and *Trois couleurs: rouge*), employs many of the director's recurring narrative strategies, especially his cross-cutting of several actions to suggest connections between characters and places before those relations are clarified by the story's time and space. *White*, in particular, relies on a challenging plot structure and the use of techniques not normally found in classic texts, such as flashforwards and subjective depth of information whose source cannot readily be assigned to a character.

White opens with a shot of a tattered suitcase on a conveyor belt. Next the narrator reveals a somewhat hesitant and uncomfortable young man outside the Palais de Justice in Paris. This sets up in the spectator's mind a connection between the suitcase and the young man. As the man enters the building, the film cuts several more times to the slowly moving suitcase to reinforce the abstract connection. Once inside, we learn that the man, Karol Karol, is Polish and is being divorced by his French wife, Dominique. Viewers looking for immediate significance in the editing logic will perhaps make the connection that Karol, who speaks very little French, is being manhandled and discarded by the judicial system much like the suitcase. But the film's narrative strategy will soon reveal how the narrative is based partly on pieces of a puzzle that may not fit together until much later, if at all.

During the trial – a scene built mostly on straight alternating shots of Karol on one side, Dominique on the other – Karol protests that he wants time to prove their love is not yet dead. There is a cut from Karol's concerned face to a travelling shot following Dominique, in her wedding dress, down a church aisle and out into blinding white light. This shot, however, is not followed by one of Karol again (which would cue us in conventional fashion that he was thinking about their wedding day). Instead, Dominique sits up as if coming out of a daydream and asks 'I beg your pardon?' of the judge. During the 21-second shot in the church, the judge apparently has asked Dominique a question which she, and the audience, did not hear.

Thus Kieslowski embeds what may be a subjective memory or flashback in the middle of a scene but does not clarify whose vision it is. Such tactics, coupled with the suitcase inserts, establish a pattern of revelation from different temporal or spatial points in the diegetic world without firmly anchoring them. Finally, this opening scene ends without clarifying these shot relations, but rather complicates them further: the fleeing Dominique pulls Karol's suitcase – the same one from the earlier shots on the conveyor belt – out of her car in front of the Palais de Justice and drives away. The problem for the attentive audience member is that the suitcase is not as tattered here as in the earlier shots. Only later will the film reveal that the beginning shots of the suitcase were flashforwards to a time when a desperate Karol will punch airholes in his suitcase and climb inside to be shipped home to Poland. Thus, *White*, provides an exemplary test case for analysing audience hypothesis making (expectation and retrospection), editing that breaks unity of time and space and the creative use of specifically filmic narrative devices.

shoot and edit someone falling down for comic or tragic effects. By the 1960s, however, stricter attempts to define where meaning is created in the cinema were tied closely and explicitly to theories of language, notably the theories of linguists Ferdinand de Saussure and Louis Hjelmslev. By adapting linguistic models of signification and carefully defining the specificity of film codes, theorists such as Christian Metz began to analyse rigorously film's marks of punctuation (for instance fades on the one hand and wipes on the other) and various systems of signification (see The early work of Christian Metz, p. 324).

The result of such analysis is to understand the wide range of options or codes open to film-makers and to test the spectator's ability to decode, or 'read', various film techniques. In this analysis, film is conceived of as a 'text' of multiple signifying or discursive structures (editing codes, sound codes, narrative formulae and so on). 'Textual analysis' is really the activity of testing a film or group of films for specific, pertinent language-system codes, some of which, like the shot/reverse-shot, may be specific to the cinema, while others, like low-key lighting, are shared with other visual media (photography, painting, theatre). In the end, textual analysis is the cautious semiotic labour of explaining just how a film makes meaning and how its functional codes change from one era to another, one national cinema to another, and even one director to another.

NARRATION

While one can analyse the cinema from many perspectives, for most of us, movies are primarily interesting because they tell stories. Narrative in any medium is a double process of what is told, the represented story, and how it is told, or the narration. Narratology is the study of stories (involving characters, actions, dialogue) and, in the case of cinema, the filmic presentation and elaboration of stories. Most film criticism derives in part from narratological methods and adopts vocabulary from outside film studies proper – Russian formalism, semiotics, psychoanalysis, post-structuralism – which is modified in the light of the specificities of filmic experience and cinematic vocabulary.

Narrative study typically begins with defining a film's story structures and themes. Story is understood as a series of interrelated events, characters, and actions out of which the audience creates a diegesis, or larger fictional world. Since most stories come to us with gaps and information narrated out of order, one of the spectator's primary tasks is to reconstruct the tale in terms of its fictional time and space, but also to clarify the cause–effect relations between elements. Film studies often speaks therefore of the story not as a passive object, but rather as a dynamic text, full of cues, repetitions, false paths, parallels, and contrasts that are only available to the viewer in bits and pieces which must be sorted through, extrapolated and reorganised to be fully understood. For this reason, narrative study of the cinema usually draws up narrative categories by distinguishing group styles from individual styles, or classic Hollywood cinema, with its predictably generic stories from the diversity of European art cinema (Art cinema, p. 106).

The second aspect of fiction film analysis is the study of narration. A fiction film's narration involves the discursive process of telling the story via various narrating systems such as the selection and ordering of story elements, the narrative voice and point of view, musical interventions, *mise-en-scène*, sound to image relations, and editing strategies. The textual analysis of any individual film or group of stories involves precisely the investigation of which narration devices are at work for which effects. For instance, discussion of something as general as 'suspense' in an Alfred Hitchcock film depends as much on Hitchcock's narration (manipulative camera positions, melodramatic music, continuity editing patterns, low-key lighting, etc.) as on what the characters actually do or say. Such study tends then to create a critically constructed narrator or narrative voice behind any story. For some, this narrator is simply synonymous with the director or *auteur*, but much film criticism since the 1980s depends more on a narrator who is constructed from the textual cues and labelled a 'narrative instance' rather than a 'real' person, operating everything single-handedly behind the scenes. Thus, a narrator functions as an abstract force and is understood via the marks of narration within the fiction film text.

FILM AND THE SPECTATOR

One of the liveliest areas of inquiry in cinema studies involves investigating and defining models of spectatorship. Even posing a simple question like: 'If films create meaning, what is the spectator's role in that process?' leads to surprisingly diverse approaches since film-going is not a simple, singular 'process' at all. Researchers have considered the viewer from a wide variety of perspectives that relate to the social, economic, physical, and psychological conditions of spectatorship (see Spectatorship and audience research, p. 366). The issue of spectatorship is particulary pertinent and problematic for discussions of the cinema and its apparatus since motion pictures depend upon so many more technological, industrial and perceptual factors than does the novel. Reading a book depends upon very complex linguistic and psychological operations, but seeing and hearing a movie involves additional, specific operations. Consequently most literary definitions of readers do not automatically fit the cinematic spectator and the processes of perception and meaning construction which constitute film spectatorship. The battle lines in film theory have long been drawn over which questions should even be asked concerning film viewing, much less which vocabulary should be employed, and while the debates parallel those in literary criticism, they are not identical.

The ultimate issue at stake in defining or explaining the film spectator concerns the problem of isolating how or where meaning is finally produced in the individual viewer (or in a group, society or mass audience for cultural critics). While competing models of spectatorship, like psychoanalytical and cognitive theories, may never agree on shared methodology or conclusions, the important thing for the film student is to acknowledge that a workable model for film viewing must incorporate a basic understanding of the series of operations that are continuously at work in our perception and comprehension of the sights and sounds we put together during the 'cinematic experience'. The most useful initial conception of a viewer therefore will be one that can account for how humans process the cinematic elements (shot/reverse-shots, dissolves, voice-over, three-point lighting and so on) into an understanding of a story, but then also how spectators relate those techniques to more general meaning construction.

The spectator must, therefore, be considered as actively perceiving images and sounds which can be related to each other within this specific film (as in the recognition of repeated low, canted camera angles on various characters across the course of say Spike Lee's *Do the Right Thing*, 1989) and from other textual or intertextual experiences (Expressionism has taught us historically to interpret tilted cameras as signifiers of psychological imbalance). Thus viewers perceive, identify, interpret, make hypotheses, sense emotions, fill in gaps and build fictional cause–effect relations as films unfold. Rather than becoming a static, ideologically determined subject, the spectator works actively on many levels simultaneously, consciously and unconsciously processing visual and audio cues (see Psychoanalysis, p. 346). Various modes of production and competing filmic traditions will obviously expect and/or demand different sorts of specific variations on these operations from their spectators – the labour of sorting out story time in *Stagecoach* (1939) will be much different than for Alain Resnais's *Hiroshima mon amour* (1959), for instance.

A spectating model based on the forward progression of hypothesis making, memory and textual and intertextual comparisons, is not unlike the semiotic model of diagramming syntagmatic and paradigmatic ordering. We look for scene-to-scene connections and consider options as we (and the text) advance. The viewing situation, with the ongoing series of sounds and images, requires the audience to proceed via expectation ('The soldier mentioned in passing that Geronimo is on the warpath, therefore I wouldn't be surprised if there will be a fight later on') and retrospection ('I wondered why that banker seemed so nervous, now I realise the narrator was cueing me not to believe everything he said; he is in fact a thief'.). The stronger the spectator's background in watching various modes of film-making (classic Hollywood films, art films, films by the same director, genre, film movement or national cinema), the easier it will be for the viewer to pick up on the codified cues. Purely ideological or psychoanalytic models of viewing too often side-step the actual operations and procedures of the cinematic experience. Most narrative-theory models work more systematically to prove how processes of narration control the audience's perception and comprehension, and try to demonstrate how the viewer makes sense of and interprets film texts.

To conclude then, while there is no such thing as any one theory of the cinema nor any one critical approach to the cinema, any study of film in its aesthetic or social dimensions, must as systematically as possible, confront the essence of film as an apparatus, a signifying practice and a narrative instance. The cinema's power, artistry and specific pleasure calls for close analysis of all the traits it shares with other media but also of all that makes the cinema unique. Film analysis has a long and diverse history, but what unifies all important theories and critical approaches is their fascination with defining and assessing the relations between the very functioning of the cinematic illusion, the filmic options open to film-makers across time, and the narrative patterns and traditions that allow meaning to accrue to those two-dimensional images that keep flashing at a set rate upon a white rectangular screen.

SELECTED READING

David Bordwell and Kristin Thompson, *Film Art*, New York, McGraw-Hill, 4th edn, 1993.

STRUCTURALISM AND ITS AFTERMATHS

An important strand of film theory could be said to have turned 'structuralist' in the 1970s. But what does 'structuralist' mean? The first thing to be clear about is that the structures involved are the structures of language. Structuralism derives from structural linguistics which is first and foremost a method for dealing with phonemes (minimal sound units), morphemes (minimal meaning units) and sentences.

While obviously there is a 'lot of language around' in the cinema, even in the silent cinema, no one showed much interest in applying the insights of structural linguistics to the sentences on the soundtrack. Instead, the 'structuralist enterprise' is best thought of as the exploration, more or less systematic, of a series of analogies: what is *language like* about phenomenon x? For a period in the 1950s and 1960s in France, a number of leading intellectuals made brilliant use of that analogy to restructure their disciplines. In part, the influence of structuralism on anglophone film theory can be seen as fuelled by a kind of intellectual fandom: the French structuralist intellectuals were exciting writers, and it seemed natural to wish to bring that excitement across the Channel to reinvigorate writing on film.

However, the francophone thinkers who made a difference within film theory were not numerous. There was the grandfather figure of structuralism, Ferdinand de Saussure, whose posthumously published *Course in General Linguistics* initiated the structuralist 'mind-set'; then there were Roman Jakobson in linguistics; Claude Lévi-Strauss in anthropology; Jacques Lacan in psychoanalysis; Louis Althusser in Marxist philosophy; Roland Barthes in literary criticism; and Christian Metz in film studies proper. Someone frequently associated with structuralism, but who vigorously repudiated the association, was intellectual historian Michel Foucault; and philosopher Jacques Derrida, in subjecting the thought of Saussure, Lévi-Strauss and Lacan to vigorous 'deconstruction', opened up a line of thought sometimes referred to as 'post-structuralist'.

But was 'structuralism' not always 'post-structuralism'? No doubt there was a certain 'scientistic' rhetoric about the structuralist enterprise at times. (Just as structural linguistics has allowed linguistics to turn itself into a science, so with structuralist anthropology, structuralist psychoanalysis, and so forth.) But in fact each of the great structuralist thinkers deployed the language analogy idiosyncratically, and each was perfectly willing to abandon the analogy whenever it began to get in the way of their work.

It should also be said that it was often not the most 'structuralist' side of these thinkers that attracted film theorists to them. A plausible way of characterising *Screen* theory of the 1970s is that it envisaged a four-way synthesis of linguistics, psychoanalysis, Marxism ('historical materialism') and a renewed literary criticism. (This once led David Bordwell, rather unflatteringly, to coin the phrase SLAB theory: Saussure, Lacan, Althusser, Barthes.) But it was not Lacan's formulation 'the unconscious is structured like a language' that was at the heart of his utilisation by film theory; and Althusser's intricate constructions around questions of ideology may in the end owe more to Nietzsche than to Saussure.

STRUCTURAL LINGUISTICS: FERDINAND DE SAUSSURE

Saussure started his scholarly life as a brilliant student of historical linguistics, the study of language change. But, by the time that he was delivering the lecture course in Geneva that became his major work, he had formulated a very different picture of what was needed if theoretical linguistics were to move forward.

Four key oppositions structure Sau-ssure's thought. (The preceding sentence, by the way, is a good example of 'structuralese': as we are about to see, the notion of opposition is central to the enterprise.) First, there is the opposition between the *diachronic* study of language and the *synchronic* study of language. At first Saussure had specialised in the diachronic – in the study of how language changes across (*dia*) time (*chronic*). Subsequently, however, he was looking for a way of studying language as it existed at a particular point in time: how does one bit of the system 'go with' (*syn*) the other bits, at the present time or at some particular time in the past? A filmic example: the 'language' of current cinema is clearly different from the 'language' of early silent cinema – which is why the latter strikes us as somehow foreign to us, until we watch enough silent films to 'learn the language'.

The notion of a 'system' of language relates to the second of Saussure's oppositions: that between *langue* and *parole*. In French the former means roughly 'language', the latter 'speech', but Saussure bends ordinary usage a bit to make them fit his thought. *Parole* is an actual bit of utterance: the sound of conversation in a pub is the sound of *parole*, just as any particular bit of film would be, by analogy. But *langue* is a more abstract, more puzzling thing. It is the system, a synchronic totality, which is somehow shared by speakers of a language and which allows for comprehension. If I am sitting in a pub in Poland, I will hear as many *paroles* as if I am sitting in a pub in Paddington; but I will not be able to understand many of them, because I lack the *langue* that is Polish.

How is *langue* structured? According to Saussure, both at the level of the sounds of language (phonemes) and of the meanings of language (morphemes), the key idea is that structures are sets of oppositions. In English, it is just the difference between 'p' and 'b' that allows us to distinguish between 'pin', a sharp sewing tool, and 'bin', a receptacle for trash. And there is no possibility for grounding meaning, where language is concerned, in something else – in a 'natural' relationship between sound and meaning, for instance. The fact that other languages have completely different words for 'pin' and 'bin' shows this. Saussure expressed this fact by way of his third key opposition, that between *signifier* and *signified*. The signifier is, roughly, the sound-shape, while the signified is the meaning. Thus, a single signifier can, in the *langue* that is English, be brought into systematic relation with two signifieds (as 'bank' means both the boundary of a river and the place where one deposits money); or, in the case of nearly exact synonyms, a single meaning, or signified, can be expressed by two different signifiers. Saussure used the term 'sign' to express the unity of a signifier with a signified. Again, in the Polish pub, I come into contact with a stream of signifiers, but, lacking the *langue*, I cannot process these as full signs, as signifier–signified units.

The fourth of Saussure's oppositions, *syntagmatic* versus *paradigmatic* (Saussure's own term for the latter was 'associative', but Jakobson's usage has prevailed), proposes a two-dimensional schema for locating the operations of difference within the stream of signs. The syntagmatic dimension of an utterance is the utterance itself, as made meaningful by 'one difference after another'. (In either Poland or Paddington, overindulgence in alcohol may lead to slurred speech, which is difficult to comprehend precisely because the normal differentials are lost.) More abstract is the paradigmatic dimension of an utterance. Here one must imagine, 'behind' each element of the utterance, the other possible elements that could fill that slot – or that could not. It is a fact about English that the substitution of 'p' for 't' in an '-in' context produces a viable English word, while the substitution of 'h' does not. A school of lingustics influential in the UK, Australia and Canada, systemic grammar, proposed a more direct terminology for this distinction: chain versus choice. Applied to film, 'chain' (the syntagmatic) would be the film itself as it unfolds, while 'choice' (the paradigmatic) would draw attention to what is 'there on screen' as meaningful through its contrast with what might have been there. (We see a close-up of a character, as part of the chain of the film; but part of the weight of the shot derives from our consciousness that other shot lengths would have been possible: how about a long shot? what difference would that difference make?)

Stepping back from the Saussurean oppositions in detail, we can see that they all bear on the reconstruction, in theory, of a shared 'something' which, at a given moment in time, allows there to be communication between a speaker and a hearer, or more generally an addresser and an addressee. Call that something '*langue*', or 'code', or (with linguist Noam Chomsky from the 1950s onwards) 'competence': the classic structuralist enterprise was to set out the rule system necessarily shared among members of the communicational community if its signs are to make interpersonal sense.

THE EARLY WORK OF CHRISTIAN METZ: APPLYING SAUSSURE

Christian Metz, whose academic formation was as a linguist, was in an excellent position to pioneer the exploration of the cinema-as-language analogy. He did so consciously as part of a reaction against the then dominant theoretical position of *Cahiers du Cinéma*'s founder, André Bazin, to which we will return (see Bazin, p. 337).

Metz believed that the cinema should be regarded not as an automatic, 'objective' process of registration (the Bazinian position), but as a language: a means of communication which organises and encodes its raw material in accordance with a set of cultural conventions. He hoped to discover the rules that governed film language and to lay the groundwork for a semiotics of the cinema: a theory and taxonomy of film as a sign system. In doing so, he addressed two problems: that of determining where the artifice which renders cinema a language can be found; and that of isolating those features common to all films on which a systematic classification might be based.

The cinema: *langue* or *langage*?

This question, which forms the title of one of Metz's longest early essays (Metz, 1974), distinguishes between two French words; although both can be translated into English as 'language', they designate slightly different concepts. *Langue* is spoken and written language in the restricted linguistic sense. *Langage* is a broader, generic term meaning any system of signs used for communication, including systems that may lack either the rigour (such as the Victorian 'language of flowers') or the subtlety (such as the language of computers, at least in the 1970s) of *langue* proper. To see cinema as *langage* is relatively uncontroversial and even commonplace: Bazin, for example, had no doubt that cinema was *langage*. To assimilate cinema to *langue* is more problematic – while being, of course, just what classic structuralism would be bound to attempt to do.

In addressing the question of whether cinema could be held to possess attributes analogous to verbal language, Metz applied criteria drawn from the work of the structural linguist André Martinet. According to Martinet, *langue* is distinguished from less systematic communicative modes by what he called its 'double articulation'. Any linguistic utterance can be analysed first into smaller individually meaningful components, known as *morphemes* or *monemes*, and second into the distinctive but not in themselves meaningful *phonemes* which each moneme or morpheme contains. Thus the utterance 'I like Ike' contains three monemes, and these monemes, as it happens, between them require the use of only three phonemes ('i', 'l', 'k'). The number of phonemes in a language is strictly limited (most natural languages have about 30 to 40), but because of the way language is articulated they can be used to generate an infinite number of possible utterances.

What makes the second articulation both possible and necessary is the arbitrary nature of the linguistic sign, the absence of a natural or analogical relationship between an object and the sign that stands for it. The cinema, however, is founded on the photographic resemblance between image and object. Whereas a new sentence in language is simply a new combination of a finite number of elements, each new film image is, strictly speaking, unique. It is also the case, Metz observed, that the cinema cannot be broken down into units smaller than the shot, and each shot is at least equivalent, in semantic content, to a whole sentence in language (not just a morpheme).

Metz concluded that there was no equivalent in the cinema of Martinet's second articulation (that between moneme and phoneme) and that even the first articulation (that between the sentence as a whole and its successive components) existed only at the level of the relations between large signifying units. Cinema therefore did not qualify as a *langue*, but it was a *langage*; more precisely it was a *langage d'art*, an expressive mode adapted to the communication of one-way messages. This did not mean that there was no scope for semiological analysis on the linguistic model, but it did imply that any such analysis could best be conducted not at the level of the shot but at the level of what he called the *grande syntagmatique*, the articulation of successions of shots into meaningful sequences.

Rio Bravo – popular structuralist fodder

The '*grande syntagmatique*'

It was in the elabouration of the notion of the *grande syntagmatique* that Metz found a reply to his first question about the artifice which qualifies the cinema as a language: the organisation of images into a narrative structure. Reality itself 'does not tell stories' – film can thus be considered as *langage* to the extent that it imposes a narrative logic upon the events it portrays.

The *grande syntagmatique* aimed to present a filmic syntax, to identify and classify the segments of narrative – the autonomous shot and seven kinds of longer sequences called 'syntagmas' – which, articulated together, produce the sequence of changing spaces over time which 'tells the story' of the film. Metz classified the segments according to a simple taxonomy of binary oppositions which, he hoped, would be exhaustive (see Metz, 1974, pp. 119–46). He believed that by charting the frequency of the various syntagmas in different films, it would be possible to describe their style with greater precision than before and to pinpoint changes in film language diachronically, over an historical period.

In spite of the many difficulties that Metz's proposed scheme quickly ran into, it remains an important landmark in the history of film theory. Devised (in 1966–7) at a moment when a need was felt for an alternative to *auteurism*, it initiated a series of attempts to find a rigorous methodology for dissecting films. Whatever its defects, it was the first and arguably to date the only major classification of narrative designed specifically for the cinema, whereas other structuralist and formalist analyses were conceived originally for other narrative media (myths, folktales, novels). The general question it addresses – how is it possible that we so easily view as continuous, and continuously-narrating, the succession of shots in classic narrative cinema – remains a valid one.

Metz himself moved on from the position taken up in his early essays. His desire to revise the *grande syntagmatique* was already evident in the copious errata and addenda sprinkled throughout the article when it was republished in *Essais sur la signification au cinéma* in 1968. Like many of his contemporaries, he regarded his research as work in progress rather than as a closed-off, definitive system. And his developing interest in psychoanalysis left him less interested in pursuing analogies between cinema and linguistic syntax than in exploring the cinema and dreamwork analogy –where, to be sure, still in a semi structuralist idiom, 'dream syntax' and 'dream semantics', via the mechanisms of metaphor and metonymy, had their place (Metz, 1974). It may still be the case, however, that it was contingent rather than inevitable that neither Metz himself nor any other theorist at the time settled down to the task of 'debugging' the *grande syntagmatique*.

Criticisms of Metz

The *grande syntagmatique* was attacked from the start on a number of counts. Attacks took two forms: criticism of detail, and criticism of the project more generally.

Where detail was concerned, it turned out – and this was itself not an uninteresting finding – that applying Metz to the syntax of a particular film was harder and more problematic than should have been the case. Although the syntagmas appear to be clearly defined, in practice they are difficult to identify. The analyst is often confronted with a segment that either could fall into more than one of Metz's categories or does not seem to belong to any of them. Jack Daniel (1976) argues that a comparison of the successive versions of the system reveals it to be based on 'current observations' and that the

Adieu Philippine (France/Italy 1960–1 *p.c* – United France/Alpha-Productions/ Rome–Paris Films/Euro-International Films; *d* – Jacques Rozier; sd b/w)

The first attempts to develop a cinema semiotics operated at a general, theoretical level and seemed to exclude the detailed examination of individual texts. For this reason, the only example in Metz's first book of the structural analysis of a specific film occupies a unique place both within the evolution of his thought and within the history of cinema semiotics as a whole. Though aware that this work was then (1967) still very much in its infancy, Metz believed that the part of his programme concerned with narrative was 'sufficiently far advanced to be applied to the image track of an entire film' and that it was possible to make a '*complete* inventory' (Metz's emphasis) using the eight basic categories outlined in the *grande syntagmatique* (Metz, 1974, p. 177).

For the early Metz, narrative realism was the essence of the cinema, and even the apparent innovations of the French new wave were for him no exception, despite some self-acknowledged difficulties with Godard's *Pierrot le fou* (Metz, 1974, pp. 217–19). *Adieu Philippine*, chosen, it seems, largely for reasons of personal taste and the availability of a shooting script and print, is described as a 'realist' film which presents few problems to a syntagmatic analysis. However, closer inspection reveals a number of points of resistance at which the film strains against the categories imposed on it by the *grande syntagmatique*. For example, the first syntagma is demarcated from the second by nothing more than Metz's imperial definition of the 'real action' of the film as 'individualised characters pursuing a definite goal' (Metz, 1974, p. 150) – a definition which is by no means self-evident. Similarly, the autonomous shot (syntagma 4) of Michel sitting idle in the television studio is identified as a directorial comment on the action ('this interpolative status . . . is "real" and not subjective') and thus defined as a 'displaced diegetic insert' (Metz, 1974, p. 153). But the shot *could* be a subjective insert, representing the thoughts of either Michel (a three-quarter profile shot of him precedes it) or the two girls (a shot of them succeeds it).

Apparently a minor quibble, this illustrates a significant feature of Metz's analysis: the way in which he endows a sequence with a meaning which is deliberately held in abeyance by the film itself. The *grande syntagmatique* attempts to assimilate *Adieu Philippine* to the realist narrative tradition at the expense of contradictions which can be found in Rozier's film and also, perhaps, in even the most 'classic' conventional text.

Metz saw the film as primarily a documentary on modern youth. But Rozier's initial idea was to trace the history of a young man conscripted to fight in Algeria (1960–2 was, of course, the period of the Franco-Algerian war) and to show the 'disturbed side of his character'. Public pressures against such reference to the Algerian question (witness the banning of Godard's 1960 film *Le petit soldat* by the French censor board and the minister of information), dictated that the serious theme be masked by employing the structure of a musical comedy romance (see Zand, 1963). A reading of *Adieu Philippine* which aims to pull out this political strand would need to point to the fact that Michel's departure for Algeria overarches the narrative (he discloses at the airfield that he is to be called up in a couple of months, and the film ends as he leaves for the army), as well as to the characters' growing malaise (is it only due to romantic rivalry?) and the eloquent silences: note (in the airfield sequence) Michel's poignantly unanswered questions to the girls reading his palm about where his imminent 'long journey' will take him ('où ça?', not translated in the subtitles) and what his life-line reveals. Metz's analysis, in contrast, collapses this scene together with the two preceding episodes, 'for alone they are treated too allusively for them to acquire any autonomy', under the general rubric of 'Sunday outing' (Metz, 1974, p. 153). The effect is to privilege an account of the film as a documentary about 'youth and its flirtations' at the expense of the other meanings (for instance, the shadow of Algeria) which are struggling to emerge and are just as crucial as the things which are overtly said.

The point here is not to impose a 'more correct' reading, but to show that Metz's apparently objective, unimpeachable analysis and the conclusions he draws from it about the work's thematic concerns are the result of a series of *choices* which remain unacknowledged (probably even unconscious), laying early structural analyses such as this open to charges of presenting ideologically loaded readings in the guise of impartial science. Rather than passively discerning and describing *the* immanent and 'true' meaning, it is objected, critical inquiry actively produces *a* meaning in a process of interaction with the artistic text, and should therefore openly discuss, reflect upon and, if necessary, even call into question its own operations.

impressive-looking diagram of 'successive dichotomies' is an unsuccessful attempt to impose a rigorous theoretical structure upon a random list of categories. The would-be analyst trying to apply Metz is also quickly confronted, as so often in cinema theory, by its visual bias: as suggested by the title '*grande syntagmatique* of the image track', the breakdown into syntagmas is dictated by the visual component of film. Difficulties arise where there is asynchronous or overlapping sound which does not match the division of images. The analysis of *Citizen Kane* in *Film Reader I* (1975) found this to be a major drawback.

These are the sorts of difficulties that the collaborative work of researchers in an area of study might well have been able to overcome. That no general will manifested itself along 'let's fix this!' lines is to be accounted for by the fact that a nervousness about the perceived reductive nature of the early Metzian project overall was very quickly felt. 'Do we want to be doing (only) this?' and 'Doesn't this restrict us to considering (only) a restricted group of films?' were questions quickly, perhaps too quickly, posed.

Metz had demarcated his study in a way which confined it to *denotative* rather than *connotative* meaning, as those terms were used by the linguist Louis Hjelmslev and in the semiotics of the early Roland Barthes (see Barthes, p. 330). Denotation, in the cinema, is the literal meaning of the spectacle; connotation encompasses all its allusive, symbolic meanings (Metz, 1974, p. 96). The artistic status of the cinema arguably resides in its connotative qualities, but it is, Metz argued, through the procedures of denotation that the cinema is *langage*. He hoped that eventually the semiotic model could be refined sufficiently to analyse both these strata and their interplay in producing meaning. (Indeed, the eventual Metzian 'psychoanalytic turn' could be seen as a move towards the analysis of connotation.) Meanwhile however it should confine itself in the first instance to the denotative level.

His critics found this proposal restrictive because of how it confined narrative to what it is perceived to be by a rather literalist audience. His model deliberately remains on the overt level at which the film 'tells its story', excluding visual subtleties such as 'framing, camera movements and light "effects"' which he saw as belonging to the realm of connotation. The classical *mise-en-scène* analysis, which examines whether and how the story is underlined or (on occasions) undermined by connotative visual strategies, is absent from the Metzian system, banished by the decision to concentrate on relationships between shots rather than shot

Tout va bien – a challenge to structural analysis

Tout va bien (France/Italy 1972 *p.c* – Anouchka Films/Vicco Films (Paris)/Empire Films (Rome); *d* – Jean-Luc Godard/Jean-Pierre Gorin; sd col.)

Tout va bien represents an attempt by Godard/Gorin to develop an alternative strategy of political film-making that would be more accessible than the resolutely anti-narrative Maoist 'Dziga–Vertov' films such as *Vent d'est* (1970). The decision to appropriate elements of 'mainstream' cinema such as international stars (Jane Fonda, Yves Montand) and a clearly defined story (preferably with love interest) was in some respects a major compromise dictated by the dissolution of a militant audience in the aftermath of May 1968 (see MacCabe, 1980, pp. 66–7). The film's ironic opening and closing sequences lay out the concessions enforced by the need to make the film commercially attractive, and the movie concludes with a caption 'a tale for the foolish one who still needs it', which seems to question the indispensability of narrative.

Tout va bien is on one level a film about the conditions of political film-making and aims to problematise the sections in which the narrative is centred on the intellectual, middle-class couple. But Andrew Britton (1976) succeeds, by downplaying the importance of the framing sequences, in producing a reading that runs directly counter to the director's intentions. Britton sees the main concerns of the film as played out in the confrontation between Susan/Fonda and Jacques/Montand, which focuses on the psychological development of 'two human individuals', the crisis in their personal relationship and their progress towards greater political consciousness (see also MacCabe, 1980, pp. 70–3).

This is where the value of a syntagmatic analysis comes in. The discipline of analysis foregrounds the fact that the central sections dealing with Susan, Jacques and the strike cannot be detached, as in Britton's account, from the overall structure of the film. Meanwhile, the difficulty of demarcating and defining syntagmas brings out the extent to which the film deviates from the conventions of classic narrative (see Thompson, 1976). More particularly it demonstrates the way in which the film disrupts the traditional alignments of sound and image, appearance and reality alignments which are assumed by Metz's *grande syntagmatique*. Note, for example, the indeterminate status of the 'radical song' sung by the workers, which could be classed as non-diegetic, but is allowed equal status with the framing interview sequences by Thompson, who sees the two stances taken up by the worker (submission and defiance) as two 'alternatives cut in together', neither of which is privileged as 'reality'.

Analysis of the film using Metz's categories can, therefore, be used to open up two sets of questions: first, to debate whether the use of narrative compromises the film or whether the text successfully resists being absorbed into the realist narrative tradition; and second, to reflect upon the usefulness of the *grande syntagmatique* itself.

form. The system also excludes the possibility of multiple levels of narrative signification, where the deceptively calm surface of the film may conceal all kinds of undercurrents of repressed meanings. Finally, it excludes a theory of the interaction between film and viewer. It is the viewer, according to 'Notes Towards a Phenomenology of Narrative' (1974), who perceives, recognises, defines narrative; on the contrary, argues more recent theory, it is the narrative which in part defines the viewer.

Another source of animus against Metz was his lack of interest in 'alternative cinemas'. The *grande syntagmatique* is designed for a specific type of film which could be broadly described as realist. Since each syntagma is defined by its logical, temporal and/or spatial relationship to the preceding and following ones, Metz's system presupposes that the film creates a consistent, self-enclosed fictional world. There is no provision for anti-realist juxtapositions of contradictory points of view (e.g. Godard's *Tout va bien*, 1972) or surrealist disruptions of traditional causality (e.g. Buñuel's *Un Chien andalou*, 1928).

This bias was no accident. In Metz's view, the evolution of film language went hand in hand with the rise to ascendancy of the realist narrative film. 'It so happens that these (specifically cinematographic) procedures were perfected in the wake of the narrative endeavour … It was in a single movement that the cinema became narrative and took over some of the attributes of language' (Metz, 1974, pp. 95–6). Thus Metz found a solution for his second initial problem. The feature common to all films and on which an exhaustive classification of syntagmas could be based is, he posited, narrative – indeed, narrative and cinema are identified as one and the same. In his essay on 'The Modern Cinema and Narrativity' (1966) he maintained that even the apparently anti-narrative films of the French new wave could be assimilated into the narrative tradition. The 'other avant-garde' which, rather than experimenting with new modes of representation, works towards an abstract, non-representational aesthetic, was given short shrift by Metz, who deplored its 'gratuitous and anarchic images' and 'heterogeneous percussions' (Metz, 1974, p. 225).

A system which purports to be comprehensive but which can only account for a certain type of film is, on the face of it, in trouble. Moreover, later debates within British film criticism on the 'classic realist text' questioned the endorsement implicit in Metz's early work of the direction in which the cinema has developed (see The classic realist text, p. 332). How far, it has been asked, was the development of the narrative film as we now have it really inevitable? Should an analytic method which presents itself as neutral and descriptive, rather than prescriptive, support the domination of a single aesthetic? Especially one which has been claimed in the course of these debates to have a regressive, repressive ideological function?

Still later, it is possible to feel that the 1970s reaction against the early, structuralist Metz involved accusing him of not doing everything, in a context in which the hope that everything could be done by a single (albeit complex) theory was still alive. Later, the move from structuralism to formalism was to involve a greater pluralism, a willingness to accept that one bit of the text, or one kind of text, may yield their secrets to an approach that other bits or genres resist. Questioning Metz's classic narrative bias was salutary, precisely because his analytical breakdown of classic narrative film syntax clarified what might be involved in the fight for other syntaxes. Equally, someone who wanted to pursue *mise-en-scène* analysis would hardly find the *grande syntagmatique* a barrier to so doing: different 'compartments of the text' are involved. And the same goes for someone who wanted to pursue ideological analysis.

Why read early Metz in the late 1990s? At the very least, it seems productive to approach the *Essais sur la signification au cinéma* as a heuristic device, an aid to learning. Applying the *grande syntagmatique* to individual films can both bring out how they work in mainstream cinema language terms and, on occasion, focus attention on their irregularities, ambiguities and unusual features. The possibility of a 'debugged' theory has recently been raised in France and Germany. But the fate of Metz's initiative bears witness to how difficult, if not impossible, it is to carry a 'cinema as language' position through with any sort of rigour.

While the work of Metz was taken up as a demonstration of structuralism within an explicitly film studies context, even more intellectual exhilaration was felt by 1970s film scholars when they grappled with the powerful theoreticians whose own work made no reference to film at all (Lévi-Strauss) or only marginal reference to film (Barthes).

THE STRUCTURAL STUDY OF MYTH: LÉVI-STRAUSS

Claude Lévi-Strauss writes as an anthropologist. The project of much of his work is to discover a hidden logic behind aspects of the life of traditional (so-called 'primitive' or 'savage') societies. His early work was devoted to demonstrating the elaborate logic of the rules governing marriage and kinship relationships; later he turned to the study of myth, using as his corpus the tales of the American Indian cultures of South America, and it is this work that proved influential within film theory, either directly or (because he 'aroused excitement among many different brands of intellectual'; Leach, 1974, pp. 8–9) indirectly through other disciplines (notably, the particular version of psychoanalysis which has become entrenched in film studies drawing on the work of Jacques Lacan which derives from Lévi-Strauss in certain key respects).

At first sight the myths studied by Lévi-Strauss appear rambling and arbitrary, and their surface themes seem to have little in common with the subject matter of contemporary western narratives. Yet, he believed, they can be shown to be driven by an internal dynamic of formidable formal power, while, at this deeper level, their concerns are not dissimilar to those of our own culture.

Mythological systems, for Lévi-Strauss, have crucial similarities to language systems. They operate according to a set of codes and conventions: as in Saussure's model of language, each individual utterance (*parole*), in this case each single version of a myth, conforms to the overall symbolic system (*langue*), the language or group of myths and all the rules that govern its permutations. Just as the language of a community binds its members together, so does myth; just as learning the language of its community represents for the child, moving from infancy (from the Latin *infans*, speechless) into speech, a process of integration into the social group, so are 'the novices of the society who hear the myths for the first time ... being indoctrinated by the bearers of tradition' (Leach, 1974, p. 59). In order to understand these myths, it is necessary to learn the grammar of their language. By comparing a number of different versions, the mythographer finds an underlying system governing the differences. This system can then be related to the society in which the myths are functional: the bizarre dramatis personae of myths, which may bring together plants, animals, gods, and/or human figures, function as symbols of the tribal sub-groups and the power relations between them; similarly, the narrative events illustrate tribal beliefs and taboos.

Lévi-Strauss took what was in the end, after the wonderful ingenuity of his formal analyses, a functionalist view of myth: myths 'express unconscious wishes which are somehow inconsistent with conscious experience ... The hidden message is concerned with the resolution of unwelcome contradictions' (Leach, 1974, pp. 57–8). The embellishments, digressions and repetitions of the narrative all help to disguise these. This sense of a disguised logic of myth rendered Lévi-Strauss's approach appealing to intellectuals of the left interested in the analysis of contemporary ideology: the aim of a structural analysis, it might seem, would be a 'demythologising', stripping away the camouflage and laying the contradictions bare. There was also an appeal to those persuaded by the psychoanalytic account of symptomatic repetition–compulsion: if we assume that the purpose of a myth is to embody contradictions while repressing them from its surface, it is only by attending to their compulsive recurrence (via the juxtaposing of as many variants as possible) that we force it to yield up its meaning.

Lévi-Strauss and film culture

Lévi-Strauss's name was initially linked with the moment in British film theory known as *auteur* structuralism, a phrase first used by the late Charles Eckert (1973). The attempt to connect Lévi-Strauss with an *auteurist* approach might seem curious given that a central premiss of his work is that myths have no single creative source: this indeed is what allows him to consider myth as a collective cultural phenomenon. He claims, in a celebrated and much-quoted passage, to demonstrate:

> not how men think in myths, but how myths operate [*se pensent* – literally, 'think themselves'] in men's minds without their being aware of the fact. And ... it would perhaps be better to go further and, disregarding the thinking subject completely, proceed as if the thinking process were taking place in the myths, in their reflection upon themselves and their interrelation. (Lévi-Strauss, 1970, p. 12)

Here we see the usual strategic question that is always raised when a theory about x is applied to y: is it more productive to insist on the specificity of realm x, to see realm x and realm y as crucially similar, or to use the partial similarity of the realms as a tool with which to explore their differences? There are obvious differences between the orally transmitted narratives of primitive tribes and the cultural products of an advanced industrial society, and Lévi-Strauss's own project was precisely to illuminate those differences with an animus – some would say a nostalgia – in favour of the former. The myths he analyses are very much not products of a capitalist culture industry, and there is a poignancy about their only-too-likely vanishing once the television sets arrive. On the other hand, the formal tools used to treat one myth as a transformation of another might perfectly well lend themselves to the treatment of one film as a transformation of another, and thus feed either an *auteurist* focus on how a 'strong director' develops his own 'mythology' (clearly a tempting strategy when considering figures such as Ford, Hawks, Lang or Hitchcock) or a more institutional focus on the groupings of films which emerge when one takes the industrial and collective nature of their production fully seriously. Thus, an *auteur* structuralist in the early 1970s such as Peter Wollen could take from Lévi-Strauss the emphasis on recurrences within an *œuvre* operating without the author's awareness of the fact (seeing the director as an 'unconscious catalyst', synthesising contradictory elements into an 'unintended meaning'; Wollen, 1972, pp. 167–8) while still differing from the anthropologist in identifying a kind of dominant voice, or 'voice beneath the voice', as that of an individual *auteur*. On the other hand, Charles Eckert, taking from Lévi-Strauss the emphasis on the collective, communal nature of myth, could propose as a suitable object of a structuralist analysis not a group of films sharing the same *auteur* signature, but 'communal blocks' selected on the basis of studio, production unit, movement or genre (Eckert, 1973, p. 49). And a sceptic like Brian Henderson could retort that such a 'non-*auteurist* structuralism' (Henderson, 1973, p. 32) still blurred the question of whether films could properly be considered as myths, whatever their organising principle.

Will Wright's book on the western, *Sixguns and Society* (1975), remains the one full-length study of the cinema to take Lévi-Strauss's work as its main 'idea and inspiration' (Wright, 1975, p. 16). For Wright, there is no doubt that 'the western, though located in a modern industrial society, is as much a myth as the tribal myths of the anthropologist' (Wright, 1975, p. 187). He sees it as performing a mythic function: disseminating 'simple and recognisable meanings which reinforce rather than challenge social understanding'. Wright claims that 'the structure of myth corresponds to the conceptual needs of social and self-understanding required by the dominant social institutions of that period', tracing a direct link between economic changes over some four decades of American history and transformations in the narrative structure of westerns (see The western, p. 151). Various criticisms of Wright's methodology have been

Kiss Me Deadly (USA 1955 *p.c* – Parklane Pictures; *d* – Robert Aldrich; sd b/w)

In his Proppian analysis of this film, Fell (1977) claims that, like its source, a novel of the same name by Mickey Spillane, it is a crude, routinely conventional text. Other critics, however, have been struck by its formalistic visual style, and Claude Chabrol's review for *Cahiers du Cinéma* (1956) puts forward an *auteurist* reading of the movie as a silk purse brilliantly created by the director (Robert Aldrich) out of 'the worst, most lamentable ... the most nauseous product of the genre fallen into putrefaction'. Stylised *film noir* conventions are much in evidence (see Alain Silver, 1975) as, for example, in the fragmented montage of the pre-credit sequence, extreme camera angles and the breaks of the 180° rule. Fell argues that the use of the devices remains strictly within the bounds of standardised formulae, while for other critics, it veers towards an excess that, in the view of one of them, turns *Kiss Me Deadly* into a 'purely formal film ... (of) terrible beauty' (Raymond Durgnat, 1962).

Fell's moralistic condemnation of the hero (or anti-hero) as 'sadistic, manipulative, brutishly suspicious and loutishly vulgar' is also open to debate. In Proppian terms, Mike Hammer might more suitably be considered as a character-function in the 'hard-boiled' detective genre. Durgnat describes Aldrich's women as androgynous, forceful, threatening, and Hammer as 'passive, sardonic and frigidly resistant'. This sexual ambiguity is interesting in relation to Fell's suggestion that Propp's schema assumes stereotypical role-playing (sexual or otherwise) and breaks down where this is not present.

The first eight minutes of the film are useful in discussion of Propp's opening functions. The customary 'initial situation' of his tales, the state of equilibrium whose disruption and restoration propel the Proppian narrative, appears to be missing. How right is Fell in seeing the first function as 'the hero leaves home'? Is Propp's schema, centred as it is on the home and the family, inappropriate to deal with the 'absent family of *film noir*'? (see Sylvia Harvey, 1978).

Fell argues that the thriller/detective genre, with its theme of the quest and 'energetic, visibly active plots' is particularly suitable for a morphological analysis. In the light of the above comments, it could be considered whether the *noir* thriller lacks the requisite stability and containment. More generally, how correct are 'Proppian' critics such as Fell (1977) and Erens (1977) in pointing to the potential of his method as a means of inter- and trans-generic comparisons? Are there certain genres which strain against his categories?

To Have and Have Not (USA 1944 *p.c* – Warner Bros.; *d* – Howard Hawks; sd b/w)

Hawks's films, which in Robin Wood's view exhibit 'a continual tendency ... to move towards myth' and whose figures are, he argues, elaborations on basic archetypes (Wood, 1968, pp. 26 ff.), could be used to illuminate Propp's approach to characterisation.

Frenchy is clearly a would-be dispatcher and 'approaches the hero with a request' three or four times. Harry Morgan is, for Wood (1968, p. 27) the vessel of 'a certain heroic ideal'; here, however, his 'heroic attributes', in particular his extreme individualism, are posed as a problem. Acting purely for oneself, in the style of the fairy-tale prince, is no longer self-evidently heroic, and becomes redefined by the historical context (it is worth noting that some critics see Morgan's hesitation as a metaphor for America's isolationism in the first years of the Second World War).

The villains are soon unmasked: Johnson, the minor villain, 'causes harm or injury' (the attempt to cheat Morgan) on a purely private level, and his displacement early in the film by the main villain in the bulky personage of Captain Renard signals the progressive compounding of personal conflicts by political ones.

The princess is harder to identify. Molly Haskell (1974) argues that Slim is not simply a 'sought-for' person but also a helper ('the peer comrade') quoting Hawks's intention to make her 'a little more insolent' than Morgan/Bogart. Interestingly, her 'sought-for' status is shared, on another level, with the Free French. Hélène de Bursac's resemblance to Slim in physique and dress is a kind of doubling. Robin Wood (1973, p. 34) suggests that the splitting of the female lead enables Hawks to hold apart the two narrative strands of love interest and the need for political commitment. In structural terms it could be argued that it is only the presence of Hélène that releases Slim from a straightforward (and more passive) 'princess' role. This could perhaps be an opportunity to examine the 'spheres of action' open to women in the classical narrative cinema. How many of Propp's seven basic roles are gender specific?

Though Propp anticipated that a single figure could occupy several spheres of action, or conversely, that several figures might share the same one (Propp, 1968, pp. 80–1), Fell complains that the splintering of functions in Hawks's films resists Proppian analysis: 'when personae commit human mitosis and divide into separate personalities, they muddle the conventional formulae by developing relationships with each other' (Fell, 1977, p. 27). He also tends to focus on details such as spittoons or the location of hotel rooms, which seems to miss Propp's point that such features are surface variables peripheral to the basic narrative structure. This suggests that certain self-styled 'structuralist' criticism takes over only the superficial trappings (terminology; impressive-looking diagrams) of the methodology it claims to employ.

Rio Bravo (USA 1959 *p.c* – Armada; *d* – Howard Hawks; sd b/w)

For Robin Wood, this film is remarkable for

the way in which it simultaneously draws on and transcends western genre conventions and in particular for Hawks's use of stock characters. Wood's list of these seven major western types (Wood, 1968, p. 36) could be compared to Propp's seven dramatis personae for correspondences or mutations: the overlap would seem to suggest an at least superficial compatibility between Propp's model and this particular genre, perhaps because of its roots in tradition, history and myth (in contrast to a *film noir* like *Kiss Me Deadly*). *Rio Bravo* evidences a number of significant variations on the basic categories which Wood attributes to Hawks's personal genius, whereas Will Wright suggests that such variant features as the emphasis on teamwork and the attenuated evil of the villains are due to historically determined changes in the narrative structure of the genre as a whole (see Wright, 1975, especially Ch. 3 and the section on the 'Professional Plot').

It would be productive to examine more closely the nature of these changes as they affect the characters of *Rio Bravo*. Fell (1977), following Wright (1975), sees the fight between heroes and villains as a contest of professional skills rather than as a moral struggle between good and evil; this could be compared to Wood's reading (1968), which affirms the conflict as an ethical one, though, for him, it is largely internalised as the search for self-awareness and respect. In either case, the importance of the villains is greatly diminished; it also means that the hero becomes more complex and problematic. The difficulties of assessing Chance, the ostensible hero-figure, could be discussed: are his heroic qualities (his sense of superiority, his stoicism) exaggerated in order to deride or to revalidate them? Could a case be made for Dude as victim–hero? Fell (1977) notes that he displays heroic features (he overcomes a misfortune, i.e. his alcoholism and traumatic past) and Wood (1968) accords him almost equal status with Chance. The partial doubling of the hero-role is significant. Dude is able to win his fight to rehabilitate himself only because he can forget his unhappy romance, a pattern which Chance, in starting an affair with Feathers, could conceivably be seen as set to repeat.

The portrayal of Feathers would appear to discount this possibility. However, as in *To Have and Have Not*, the two narrative strands of love interest and conquest of villainy are held almost entirely separate, with the result that, instead of linking heroic deeds to the winning of the princess in the manner of a Proppian fairytale, the film could be interpreted as suggesting that Chance's romantic liaison is a direct threat to his activities as law enforcer and leader of the male group. Is the penultimate scene in Feather's room simply a coda to the main action, or could it be read as signalling a new, but undeveloped narrative departure? These issues have of course been raised without recourse to Propp's schema, but it is arguably a helpful aid to isolating the film's troubling (i.e. deviant) features.

Hawks's work is useful in comparing different critical approaches (e.g. Fell (1977), Wright (1975), Wollen (1972) and Wood (1968) (see Howard Hawks, p. 294). The interest of structuralist critics in his films is noteworthy, and possible reasons (the popularity of Hawk's films; his heavy use of genre forms, etc.) could be explored. Fell and Wood (see 1976) both object that structuralist analyses are too insensitive and inflexible to account adequately for the colour and detail of individual films: this conclusion could be tested against Wollen's account of Hawks's work and Wright's interpretation of *Rio Bravo*, bearing in mind the modesty of Propp's original aim to provide a method of classification rather than a total theory.

offered, but at least for some readers the problem with his work is precisely the straightforwardness with which he proposes to match changes in myth structure with changes in social structure: in Lévi-Strauss, and in structuralism generally, the structures of language and of other language-like systems are granted considerably more autonomy than that. A general argument can be offered here: if changes in the western match changes in American history, and the latter is, after all, a single 'thing', then changes in all other Hollywood genres should equally be able to be shown to match the historical changes – a strong, and on the face of it an implausible – claim.

The ongoing influence of Lévi-Strauss on film studies lies less in the possibility of making wholesale application of his mythographic method to a corpus of films (however that corpus is established) than in drawing some lessons from his structuralist habit of thought. Lévi-Strauss takes his myths apart, so to speak, by looking at their thematic material as involving sets of oppositions, just as the sound system of language does. A key opposition in the first volume of *Mythologiques*, for instance, turns out to be that between raw food and cooked food. By the same token, a key opposition within the western genre has long been recognised to be that between 'the wilderness' (wild space) and 'the garden' (domestic space). The deployment of this opposition and a few more (masculine/feminine, illiterate/literate, lawlessness/legislation) can make the material of such a western as John Ford's *The Man Who Shot Liberty Valance* (1962) yield many unsuspected riches.

ROLAND BARTHES: THE ANALYSIS OF NARRATIVE

Roland Barthes' *S/Z*, first published in France in 1970 and translated into English in 1974, was to prove to be of the greatest importance not only in its home field of literary studies but as a model for film theory's engagement with textual analysis and with questions of the relationship between reader and text.

The narrative dissected by Barthes in *S/Z* – a novella, *Sarrasine*, written in 1830 by Honoré de Balzac – is proposed as an example of a realist text. Traditionally identified with the creation of a plausible and familiar world, realism is defined by Barthes in rather broader terms. Realist texts, in his view, make up the greater part of western literature, and *Sarrasine* is a realist text, even if its unholy cast of degenerate aristocrats and *demi-mondaines* and its improbably melodramatic narrative hardly seem straightforwardly the stuff of realism.

The commonsense equation of realism with plausibility is discounted in *S/Z*. Rather than assessing the credibility of Balzac's world-view, Barthes traces from a post-structuralist perspective a gradual and cumulative *structuring process*. The 'texture' of the realist text is, for him, created by the interweaving of different *codes*, each less important in itself than for the way in which they are combined. His 'slow-motion' reading of *Sarrasine* aims to show how the narrative is put together.

Clearly, this relationship between realism and narrative is quite different from that conceived by André Bazin, who saw film as a neutral medium for recording phenomena, and viewed with suspicion any attempt to organise and interpret what was for him a fundamentally ambiguous world. *S/Z* takes the opposite view: that highly organised narrative is an ingredient essential to the impression of realism. For Barthes, reality itself is not something passively revealed or reflected in art, but an impression constructed with care and artifice.

The point of reference of the realist text is not some independently existing 'real world'. Instead, the realist text is seen as involving the convergence of two sets of relations. On the one hand, the work is subject to its own tight *internal logic*, its *intratextual economy*. Characters act consistently; the narrative 'obeys a principle of non-contradiction' even if temporary snares may be set for the reader (*S/Z*, p. 156); actions follow predictable consequences so that, for instance, the disclosure that a character is asleep presupposes that at some future state she will wake up (cf. the *code of actions*, or *proairetic code*, *S/Z*, p. 18); and in general, 'everything holds together' (*S/Z*, pp. 181–2), that is, every detail, every action will play some – preferably more than one – functional role in the unfolding of the narrative, though ideally this functionality should not be too obvious (*S/Z*, pp. 22–3). Crucially, all the main enigmas posed in the course of the story must be resolved by the end.

On the other hand, the work depends on a set of *external relationships*, its position within a grid of other cultural texts: its *intertextuality*. Realism, Barthes argues, 'consists not in copying the real, but in copying a depicted copy of the real' (*S/Z*, pp. 54–6). In *Sarrasine*, for example, Marianina's marvellous beauty can only be defined in terms, not of some unmediated ultimate beauty, but of another cultural representation of it – 'the fabled imagination of the Eastern poets' (*S/Z*, pp. 32–4). The text convinces by being in harmony with, drawing on the credit of, other texts.

This definition of realism in terms of a work's formal operations rather than its subject matter leads Barthes into a distinction between the realist and the modernist text. The *writerly* (*scriptible*) text is modernist, non-representational, bereft of 'a narrative structure, a grammar or a logic', refusing definitive interpretation, opening up endless possibilities of meaning. The *readerly* (*lisible*) text is the other pole of the opposition: realist, representational, pre-eminently narrative, offering up only one, unequivocal meaning (*S/Z*, pp. 3–7). The 'writerly' and the 'readerly' should be seen as the notional extremes of a spectrum with real texts somewhere between the extremes. *Sarrasine* would at first seem to fall near the readerly end of the spectrum, but, given the breakdown of meaning at important moments in the story, and Balzac's 'excessive' use of intertextuality, it does not succeed in suppressing the artifice deployed in its own production. It can be celebrated as an imperfectly realist text, writerly enough to make a lazy and passive reading of itself difficult.

Reader/viewer and text

Part of the project of *S/Z* was to argue for the emancipation of readers from the role of passive consumers currently assigned them by the 'culture industry'. This, Barthes believed, had not always been the reader's fate: it is the product of a division of labour and commodification of art peculiar to the development of capitalism. This division of labour is not thereby inevitable. Barthes recalled in retrospect that 'what I tried to begin in *S/Z* was a kind of identification of the notions of writing and reading: I wanted to squash the two together' (Heath, 1971, p. 47). Rather than humbly, scrupulously attending to the text in order to discern its 'singular, theological meaning' (theology being historically the field in which 'getting right' the one true meaning of the sacred text has been most assiduously, at times murderously, pursued), the reader/ viewer should take up a less reverent attitude, seeking to *change* it by contributing to the process in which new meanings are generated: 'a form of work ... a labour of language' (*S/Z*, pp. 10–11). Which is not to say that this active reader is 'free' to change the text at will: the relationship between reader and text is a dialectical one. Not only does the reader act upon, 'produce' the text, but equally it acts upon, 'produces' her. In the same way that the text is not a pre-given, self-sufficient entity but an unstable, multiply determined and ever-developing process, so too, the argument runs, is the person who reads or views it.

This is an attractive picture, since it affords the text an important but not oppressive role in the lives of its reader/ viewer. One of the types of semiotic object which contributes to the formation of the human psyche is the artistic text. Each time we read a novel or view a film, we are perhaps, if only in a tiny way, reinforced (or, as the case may be, challenged) in our secure feeling of personal identity and all the preconceptions and prejudices that go with it. And each time *we* encounter the text, it cannot help but be *ours*.

Questions of method

S/Z is a work of system which at the same time is self-confidently and programmatically unsystematic. The minimal units into which it segments the text are determined as 'a matter of convenience' (*S/Z*, pp. 13–14; compare, for instance, the lengthy deliberations of Metz on precisely how to establish the minimal unit in a film). It claims to provide neither an exhaustive reading of *Sarrasine* nor a universal narrative structure. Its strategies are in sharp contrast to initial attempts by structuralist critics to anatomise the operations of narrative and other social sign systems. Their aim had been to develop exhaustive and immutable schemas. Such attempts to found a scientific poetics may have been, necessary in order to break with traditional criticism; by 1970, however, the problems with this approach were becoming apparent. (Metz's *grande syntagmatique* and its difficulties provide an example of this.) The notion that culturally determined sign systems could be explained by an Olympian observer in a neutral metalanguage, supposedly immune from those very determinants, collapsed.

In his 1966 'Introduction to the Structural Analysis of Narratives', Barthes had attempted to fashion 'a single descriptive tool', a hypothetical model which could be applied to 'different narrative species' in 'their historical, geographical and cultural diversity' (Barthes, 1966, pp. 80–1). Analysis should concentrate on the ways in which individual narratives conform to and depart from this universal model. In the opening pages of *S/Z*, however, he distances himself from such an attempt 'to see all the world's stories ... within a single structure', now holding it to be 'a task as exhausting ... as it is ultimately undesirable'. The reason given for this change of heart is that by forcing a text into 'a great narrative structure', it 'thereby loses its difference' (*S/Z*, p. 3).

Barthes was using the term *difference* in a manner inflected by the influence of his younger contemporary, the philosopher Jacques Derrida. In a post-Saussurean sense, Derrida argued that signifying practices in general, on the model of language, depend on the network of differences amongst signs. Each work of literature *differs*, obviously, from other works; equally, however, it *defers* to them, i.e. relies on them for its distinctive meaning (Derrida, 1967). This formulation can still be seen as breaking with traditional notions of 'uniqueness' or 'individuality' as hermetic, essential qualities. Meaning cannot be established by considering a text in isolation, only by locating it within a network of differences and similarities. And because difference is determined within a cultural matrix which expands and changes shape through history, it is therefore itself also subject to historical change.

A work of art should not be seen as a closed system, a completed, inert object which will always remain the same, but dynamically, as an endless process of rereading and rewriting. The uncovering of fresh information, the advent of later works may place a text in a new light. This model of the text proposes that it acquires its meaning(s) not primarily at the moment of production but at the various moments of reception.

How far does this imply the demoting of the author as originating source of meaning? Barthes offers an epigram: 'the birth of the reader must be at the cost of the death of the Author' (*Image – Music – Text*, 1977, p. 148). But *S/Z* itself is a flamboyantly 'authorial' text. The prose style is dense, allusive and peppered with neologisms, colourful images and surprising comparisons. Barthes felt that 'the fact that *S/Z* may be subject to certain values of style in the traditional sense is important, for ... to accept style is to refuse language as pure instrument' (*Signs of the Times*, 1971, p. 46). This is to refuse the scientism of early structuralism. At the same time, may not the reader herself wish at least sometimes to put into play, precisely, authorially-based models of textual meaning?

S/Z and film theory

In assessing the influence of *S/Z*, it is necessary to recall that it too, like *Sarrasine*, is subject to the principle of intertextuality. It was only one product of the intense theoretical speculation being generated in France at that time. *S/Z* appeared in 1970, the same year as the equally influential *Cahiers*' collective text on Ford's *Young Mr Lincoln*. As the ideas formulated in such analyses became assimilated by Anglo-American film culture, diffusion rather than 'application' in any strict sense turned out to be the order of the day. Less attention has been devoted to the specific features of *S/Z*'s breakdown of narrative (e.g. its proposed five codes) than to its more general propositions on the one hand and its exemplary status as a *tour de force* of attention to textual complexity on the other.

In fact, *S/Z* turned out to be a hard act to follow. Stephen Heath's analysis of *Touch of Evil* in *Screen* was probably the closest anyone came in English to providing an analysis with equal ambitions, with the work of Raymond Bellour and Marie-Claire Ropars in France needing acknowledgment too. But on the whole the enterprise of 'ultra-close reading' of films has been marginalised, with the sceptical side of *S/Z* playing no small part in this process: in dramatising its own method as a kind of fiction, Barthes's text opened the way for less methodical, more modest and/or more focused 'probes' of film texts for particular purposes. It should also be said that the development of 'queer theory' for the cinema in the 1980s and 1990s, to which *S/Z* can be seen in content terms as making a strong, distinctive contribution, has tended to eschew the very pleasurable but undeniably rather élitist mandarin qualities of Barthes's critical procedures.

NARRATIVE AND AUDIENCE

An important shift in emphasis occurred in the course of 'working through structuralism'. The first wave of structuralism analysed texts as autonomous, self-contained entities. But what if meaning is not immanent and pre-existing, but is created anew in every encounter between reader/viewer and text? Attention would have to be directed to what happens in the course of this encounter. The change of focus is described succinctly in the Introduction to the 1976 *Edinburgh Film Festival Magazine*: 'The main problem of film criticism can no longer be restricted to the object cinema, as opposed to the operation cinema (a specific signifying practice which places the spectator)' (Hardy *et al.*, 1976, p. 4).

Just as Barthes moved from structuralist scientism to a concern with the actual experience of reading and the pleasures (cerebral, visceral, and sometimes even erotic) which it provides, Metz moved from a concentration on 'film language' to the essays collected in *Psychoanalysis and Cinema* (1977) concerned with problems such as the effect produced upon us, the audience, by 'the operation cinema' and (a deceptively simple question) why we enjoy watching movies.

While an interest in developing a psychoanalytically-informed account of the cinema was one impetus behind this move away from free-standing textual analysis, it was the political commitment of *Screen* in the 1970s that most influenced the way in which theory was developed and consolidated. Under the pressure of the political events of May 1968 and its aftermath and the international economic crisis of the 1970s (and, it must be remembered, well before 'Thatcherism' was even glimpsable as the political future for the UK), it was increasingly felt that the kind of theory that was needed was one which would provide some insight not just into the mechanical nuts-and-bolts structure of narrative, but also into its ideological effects. Political commitment very much informed the way in which approaches to narrative theory and analysis pioneered in France were mediated into British film culture. *Screen*, the main platform for these debates, had a consciously 'interventionalist' policy. Its aim was not only to describe but also to change its object of study (see for instance Stephen Heath's remarks on the desirable 'emphases and options' for *Screen*, summer 1974, p. 126). Primary concerns for theoretical writing became: first, to work towards a greater understanding of the relationship between viewer and film; second, to assess the ideological implications of this process; and third, to do so not so much in the interests of scientific accuracy or high scholarly endeavour but rather with the political aim to develop 'a new social practice of the cinema' (Hardy *et al.*, 1976).

The classic realist text

One of the most accessible routes into this terrain proved to be Colin MacCabe's influential concept of 'the classic realist text' (MacCabe, 'Realism and the cinema: notes on some Brechtian theses', 1974). MacCabe summarised this concept in the form of two theses: (1) 'The classic realist text cannot deal with the real as contradictory'; (2) 'In a reciprocal movement the classic realist text ensures the position of the subject in a relation of dominant specularity' (MacCabe, 1974, p. 12).

In the first of these theses, MacCabe addressed himself to the formal organisation of the text, its internal consistency and cohesion – characteristics which had been identified by Barthes as hallmarks of the 'readerly' work. The classic realist text might seem able to accommodate contradiction in the form of different discourses of viewpoints vying for supremacy, usually assigned to various characters in the narrative. But this apparent pluralism is actually, he argued, illusory: irreconcilable contradiction would threaten the inner stability of the text. This threat is neutralised by according the warring discourses unequal status, and arranging them in a hierarchy. The one at the top, the dominant discourse, acts as the voice of truth, overruling and interpreting all the others.

The second thesis, on specularity, was developed along the following lines. Whereas in the nineteenth-century novel, a form which has often been seen as the direct historical predecessor of mainstream cinema, MacCabe suggested that the voice of truth is the 'narrative prose', the impersonal 'metalanguage' which constantly comments on and subsumes the 'object languages' of individual figures within the world of the fiction, in film the position of knowledge is taken over by the narration of events through images. Thus 'the camera shows us what happens – it tells the truth against which we can measure the other discourses' (MacCabe, 1974, p. 10). In support of this view he referred to scenes in *Klute* (Alan J. Pakula, 1971) and in *Days of Hope* (Ken Loach, 1975), where the 'erroneous' information purveyed on the soundtrack is played off against the 'truth' of what is seen (MacCabe, '*Days of Hope* – a response to Colin McArthur', 1976). The commonsense assumption that we can 'trust the evidence of our own eyes' indicates how potent our confidence in the visual can be.

This approach was at the time seen as constituting a break with the tradition within cinema aesthetics which conceives of the photographic image as an authentic record of the 'real world', a view found for instance in certain of Bazin's writings (see Bazin, p. 337). MacCabe was read as insisting that the realist narrative film bears no relation whatever to any 'essential reality', though it aims to give this impression. In fact, MacCabe's respect for Bazin was always considerable. It is precisely because of the strength of Bazinian intuitions about photography's relationship to the real that it becomes necessary to note how a voice-of-truth effect takes place. (The whole thrust of Bazin's interest in arguing for photographic techniques capable of sustaining ambiguity was, correspondingly, to work towards a cinema which would disperse or dialogise the singular voice of truth.) The problem is that the particular image comes to function as a guarantor of truth too simply and monolithically, that it is taken as truth as such by the viewer. Their position is one of an overseer, of 'dominant specularity', which is however illusory: a 'pseudo-dominance'. The hierarchy of discourses within the film favours a singular meaning, and the viewer, offered apparently unimpeded access to knowledge is discouraged from working to create their own reading. The viewer remains passive, placed 'outside the realm of contradiction and action – outside of production'. This 'petrification' of the viewer sustains the opposition between work production and leisure consumption which is an integral feature of capitalism.

The Althusserian background to MacCabe's position needs mentioning, though it is clearer looking back than in the 1970s that what was being asserted hardly stands or falls with 'Althusserianism'. The desolatingly tragic events of Louis Althusser's later life and the eclipse of the kind of possibility for the future felt to be represented in the 1970s (rather amazingly, it has to be said in retrospect) by the likes of the French Communist Party or forces to its left do not allow us to ignore the genuine interest and productivity of Althusserian thought. Althusser recast the classical Marxist model of economic base/ideological superstructure so as to propose for the latter a far more active role in society than had hitherto been allowed in the Marxist tradition. This gave the student of cultural forms a more important, even crucial, role in the political struggle than heretofore.

Ideology takes the form of systems of representation which can have a political effectivity of their own. The political order is secured, in most societies, not so much by coercion as by consent. The main agencies for organising and holding in place this consent are what Althusser calls the ideological state apparatuses. Of these the most important are institutions such as the education system, church and family. Art, too, is seen as comprised within the apparatuses which contribute to the unconscious formation of individuals by 'interpellating' them in various ways, summoning them to take up their role in society (Althusser, 1971). It is not a question here of the indoctrination of one class/sub-class by another (as some vulgar Marxist theories have it), since interpellation takes place at an unconscious level and in all men and women, but rather of a process of socialisation, an essential condition of communal existence within any economic order. In short, Althusser proposes that individuals are placed as social subjects in subtle and largely imperceptible ways – ways which simultaneously promote in them the impression of being consistent, rational and free human agents.

MacCabe's account of 'classic realism' sees the realist text as one more device for 'placing' or positioning individuals as social subjects, via the (interpellating) voice of truth and the authoritative 'speech' of the photographic image. The metaphor of the textually 'positioned subject' was indeed to become central to much 1970s theory: the effect of the operations of the realist text is to 'place' the *subject* in a fixed position of knowledge towards the text. At first sight this seems a curious assertion. Surely sharp disagreement is perfectly possible between individuals even about what might seem the most unambiguously classic of realist texts; how then can one speak in such general terms of a single 'subject position'? Naturally enough, the objection was raised that the 'viewing subject' is a meaningless abstraction, with little bearing on 'real' audiences in their social and historical diversity. Such criticism was in the first instance countered by introducing a conceptual distinction. On the one hand, there is the empirical spectator whose interpretation of film will be determined by all manner of extraneous factors like personal biography, class origins, previous viewing experience, the variables of conditions of reception, etc. On the other hand, there is the abstract notion of a 'subject-position', which could be defined as the way in which a film solicits, demands even, a certain closely circumscribed reading from a viewer by means of its own formal operations (Ellis, 1978). This distinction seemed fruitful to the degree that it allowed us to accept that different individuals can interpret a text in different ways, while insisting that the text itself imposes definite limits on their room to manœuvre. In other words, it promised a method which would avoid the two extremes of an infinite pluralism which posits as many possible readings as there are readers, each equally legitimate, and an essentialism which asserts a single 'true' meaning (see Spectatorship and audience research, p. 366).

The 'positioning' model or picture was elaborated along other lines as well. A whole approach to space in the cinema was mobilised in this cause. The development of single perspective in painting, which took place at a particular historical moment (the early years of the fifteenth century in Italy, the period known as the Quattrocento) and which is absent from many non-western art traditions, seemed analogous to MacCabe's sense of a single voice of truth or position of truth; and it was noted that, despite the possibilities offered by distorting lenses, the cinema depicts space in a manner very similar to Renaissance art. In fact the mechanical aid devised by Quattrocento painters to correct perspective errors, the *camera obscura* or darkened chamber, was the forerunner of the modern camera used for still and motion photography (see Bordwell and Thompson, 1979, pp. 144–5). This might seem to challenge the widespread notion that film technology has, thanks to scientific progress (the advent of sound, deep-focus cinematography and colour), moved steadily towards the ever more efficient and accurate reproduction of 'reality'; rather, the end in view is the embodiment of specifically humanist values and beliefs (see Ogle, and Williams's response, *Screen Reader 1*, 1977; Technology, p. 51). Following this line of argument led some writers to argue that cinema is already suffused with ideological assumptions at the level of the individual shot, that is, before the construction of narrative, by the very nature of its own machinery (see Baudry, 'Ideological effects of the basic cinematographic apparatus', 1974/75 and Bailblé, 'Programming the look', 1979/80). The organisation of components within the picture is not only informed by a particular world-view; it also demands of the spectator a certain complicity in these operations if they are to decipher its meaning.

More psychoanalytically orientated, but equally suitable for utilisation by the 'positioners' was the concept of 'suture'. Originally used by surgeons to denote the stitching which joins the edges of a wound, the term 'suture' was borrowed in the 1960s by Lacanian psychoanalysis as a means of understanding the relationship between the conscious and unconscious forces which produces the human subject. This relationship is seen in terms of an uneasy alliance between the two forms of psychic organisation called by Lacan the 'Imaginary' and the 'Symbolic'. The former, which is characterised by the unity it confers upon subject and object, bears a privileged relationship to vision: in early infancy, the child discovers its reflection in a mirror, its first apprehension of the body as unified (see Lacan, p. 346). This moment (which Lacan calls the 'mirror stage') is central to the operation of the human psyche, providing the basis of our narcissistic relationship to the rest of the world, in which others are seen as versions of ourselves and we each experience ourselves as unified beings at the centre of the world (see MacCabe, 1976, p. 13).

However, the fact that the mind does not develop and function in a vacuum casts doubt on our assumption of total individual autonomy. Just as Saussure insisted on the trans-individual, systemic nature of language, Lacanians argue that humanist accounts of the 'human individual' fail to recognise that from birth onwards this individual must define its identity (and be defined) within and against systems of pre-existing cultural relations. Successful social interaction requires individuals to engage in a complex network of rules and conventions (described by Lacanians as 'entry into the Symbolic'). This process begins from earliest childhood, decisive stages being the learning of language, and the aquisition of a fixed (hetero)sexual identity, preparing ('positioning') the child for cultural 'normality'.

This argument (which, it should be noted in passing, is rather more a construct of the first wave of anglophone importation of Lacan than a definitively Lacanian one, though not necessarily the less interesting for that) suggests that the chief constraints at work in the evolution of the subject lie beyond our conscious control. Thus while manipulating the elementary codes essential to everyday activities like holding a conversation, or watching and understanding a film, we 'forget' the intricate symbolic structures which are necessary to any meaningful social activity. Our psychic life is a perpetual flux and reflux between the favoured realm of the imaginary, which functions not as a temporary phase on the road to maturity, but as a recurrent desire of the individual to seek and foster the wholeness of a unified ideal ego; and that, less congenial to us, of the symbolic, which forces our acknowledgement of the morass of determinations at work in the construction of the psyche. It is here that the concept of 'suture' comes into play, understood as the constant striving of the ego to fill in these gaps, and to impose unity on the conflicting forces of the unconscious. Within film theory, suture was used to name the imposition of unity across not only these general 'symbolic' codes but across disunifying formal features specific to film, notably the diversity of shots and of gazes. Bluntly, 'suture' is a psychoanalytically underpinned name for continuity editing. And continuity editing, once again, was seen as positioning the subject and imposing upon him or her a single voice of truth.

Criticism of classic realism

Once proposed, MacCabe's concept of the classic realist text, and the whole family of closely related theories which might be grouped together under the rubric of 'positioned subject theory', seemed both to advance and to constrict the field. Is it, or 'suture', or 'apparatus theory' (Baudry), not too ambitious in attempting to provide a prototype applicable to all realist narrative? Might not the model of classic realism become a grid within which each text is inserted a little too smoothly as yet another revamping of the same old pattern? To unmask a text as formally realist (whether it be classic or progressive in its content) is in a sense to denounce it as acting on the viewer in a repressive way. So some of this work on realism was seen as tending to dismiss the mainstream narrative film wholesale as an ideological monolith, a purely manipulative 'ideological state apparatus' for 'the reproduction of labour power'. What possible productive engagement with popular cinema could survive this line? MacCabe's category of classic realism avoids a charge of intellectual snobbery by spanning the high-art/mass-culture divide, 'lumping together *The Grapes of Wrath* and *The Sound of Music*' (MacCabe, 1974, p. 12 – a formulation which in turn just may have inspired Richard Dyer to mount an influential and spirited defence of *The Sound of Music*), but it can sound uncomfortably close to implying a blanket condemnation ('lumping together' indeed!).

Twenty years on, a rather different problem seems to be the key one. It is not so much 'unfairness to the text', more polysemous and dialogic than the voice-of-truth account proposes, that the theory stands accused of (indeed, the endless defence of individual films by showing them to be complex and ambiguous can itself become monotonous and politically rather naïve, as Paul Willemen has pointed out (1994)), but 'unfairness to the viewer'. The split between the empirical viewer and a sort of 'ideal viewer' is not the real issue: it is hard to imagine any theory of reception which does not make some such move. The trouble is that any sense of agency on the part of the theorised viewer is minimised. The positioned subject is thus a very subjected subject.

This arises in part from the structuralist roots of the account. Language really is a good example of a system to which we are subjected, in a strong sense, even though the creativity of the speaker/hearer, as Noam Chomsky would put it, is precisely made possible by this subjection. But as the 1980s unfolded it became clear, if not always very palatable, that the privileged social science providing the model underpinning more local models had shifted from linguistics to (classic) economics; and, while the activities of rational economic people are no less abstract than those of Saussurean *langue*-speaking people, they do involve such elements as agency and choice. The notion that agency and choice are somehow humanist or bourgeois illusions seems itself a rather strange illusion, born perhaps out of the sense of blocked dreams of the left that characterised the cold-war era.

North by Northwest – a visual representation of reality?

One is indeed 'constrained' to understand a text, but one chooses, both whether to consume the text in the first place and what judgement to make of it once consumed. (Or perhaps we should say that, empirically, people have more or less choice – there are always constraints and limitations, and there is such a thing as addiction – but that any account of the media audience has to build choice into the model: this then makes particular cases of absence of choice interesting, and perhaps addressable.)

This way forward from 'positioned spectator' theories was anticipated by two lines of investigation arising out of textual–analytic observation. The first of these was stimulated by the practice, in non-'classic' cinema, of the long take. If film is unlike painting or still photography in one major respect, namely in providing not a single image but a series of images from ceaselessly shifting positions, so that the spectator is continually displaced within the fictional scene, this norm (no doubt 'domesticated' by continuity editing) is itself challengeable by the long, static take. These, as in, for instance, some of Chantal Akerman's films, far from providing a reassuringly secure viewing position, appear to disrupt the illusion of reality (see Johnston, 1976, and Heath, 1977/78). Certainly there is an impatience/discomfort commonly felt by audiences when a shot is held a little 'too long'. But should the long take not be more positioning/reassuring for an audience rather than less? The key to this puzzle could be seen as lying in the peculiar nature of film as narrative, which, in contrast to the single image, depends heavily on duration and performance, the holding of the viewer over an extended period of time. This feat requires a delicate balancing act, the playing out of a tension between 'process (with its threat of incoherence or loss of mastery) and position (with its threat of stasis, fixity or of compulsive repetition, which is the same thing in another form)' (Neale, 1980, p. 26). Stability alone would soon lead to impatience and boredom, and what is needed is a perpetual oscillation between delicious instants of risk and repeated temporary returns to equilibrium. Some writers believe that the pleasurability of the cinema resides in precisely this process of limited risk (see Heath, 1977). Such a model of the spectator's response might seem to contrast sharply with MacCabe's more static formulation of 'dominant specularity'; but what is even more important is to note that the spectator can choose to explore the 'held image' productively rather than be repulsed by it. No doubt this 'choice' may require training, 'cultural capital' and so forth, but these too are 'choosable', developable. The implacable Bazinian practice of the film-makers Straub/Huillet is one which is unintelligible save in terms of an imagined viewer capable of exercising agency and cognitively exploring the image actively; and if such a viewer is imaginable for these texts, why not imagine him or her for the texts of the 'delicate balancing act' too?

The second line of investigation focused on point of view (pov), one of the medium's major rhetorical figures. In a pov shot, the camera assumes the spatial position of one of the characters within the narrative in order to show us what she or he sees (see Branigan, 1975). Most directors use this device to varying extents, one of its acknowledged masters being Hitchcock (see Bellour, 1972). The MacCabe framework allows some very interesting questions to be raised about pov. If the use of pov shots is linked to the discourses of different characters, are these subsumed, in the mainstream cinema, by an impersonal, dominant discourse comparable to the 'omniscient narrator' of realist prose (see Heath on *Touch of Evil*, 1975), can it be argued that certain texts resist or undermine this voice of authority, the case sometimes made for the modernism of film makers such as Dreyer or Bresson (see Nash, 1976)? But, in a classic and unusually definitive argument, Nick Browne (1975/76) demonstrated something very striking about pov through a close analysis of a sequence from *Stagecoach* (1989). This sequence is dominated by pov shots, but these are ascribed to a 'good woman' character whose prejudices *vis-à-vis* a prostitute character we are clearly not invited to share: indeed, the meaning of the passage, in a strong sense, is: 'these prejudices are cruel'. This is a striking case because, on the one hand, it is as good a demonstration as any of, precisely, a MacCabe-like voice-of truth effect coming through the text as an overall dominant discourse. (It is interesting to speculate about what an empirical audience member who did feel that sitting down to eat at the same table as a prostitute was something to be avoided would make of the sequence: scriptwriter and director certainly go to some trouble to make such a viewer uncomfortable!) Yet, on the other hand, in so far as the MacCabe model might have predicted that the figure of pov would 'position' a viewer definitively ('I look through these eyes so I must take this position'), the sequence demonstrates how undetermining of judgement a particular bit of 'film form' is. And this opens up the 'likelihood', once again, that the viewer is a chooser of positions and an agent in terms of their uptake on what is there on the screen and on the soundtrack.

PSYCHOANALYSIS AND FILM

However, another line of thought in the 1970s was to prove to be powerful, reinforcing the anti-agency bias of the theory of the time while opening up an exciting new range of phenomena to view. This was psychoanalysis, but especially psychoanalysis at the service (far from historically always the case!) of feminism (on psychoanalysis, see further p. 341; Feminist film theory, p. 353).

Psychoanalysis is of its very nature a scheme of concepts designed to deal with the layer of our experience where we find ourselves not very agent like, or in the grip of some sort of 'agency' which is both ourself and foreign to our thought of ourself, an agency acting 'behind our backs'. In a clinical context, the patient seeks the psychoanalyst precisely because over a significant range of his or her life he or she seems strangely incapable of acting rationally and economically. And even where what is at issue is not a matter of pathology, the layer of experience where we become aware of something 'below' or 'beyond' our agency in what we do and what we make has seemed suited to exploration using the psychoanalytic armory.

Film has from its outset felt 'uncanny' enough to trigger psychoanalytic approaches. One of the most enduring problems facing film theory and criticism is the elusive quality of their own object. Images have a tangible existence on celluloid, yet this materiality is constantly belied by the conditions under which we receive them. On one level, there are the practical difficulties of access to facilities for studying actual films – still with us in the video age, but hugely greater earlier. But also, more fundamentally, the very nature of film seems to reside in a relentless flow of images, the pleasures and fascinations it offers stemming from a fleeting ephemerality which defies attempts to arrest and contain it. Empirical audience research accordingly seems inadequate if what is envisaged is accounting fully for the viewing experience, and for the relation between film narrative and spectator. The more or less vague, but cohesive and reasoned memory we retain from a visit to the cinema has little in common with the complex and subtle, barely perceptible processes that move us while we are actually watching a film. The sociological approach therefore appeared to need, at the least, complementing by work on an altogether different plane.

The tools and methods of psychoanalysis offered film theorists a means of understanding the operations at a micro-level of the 'mental machinery' activated by the passage of images on screen. The idea of suture, introduced above (see page 334), seemed a useful way of defining the minute shifts and revisions that take place in our state of mind throughout the viewing of a film: a constant movement of the spectator between the dual domains of the imaginary and the symbolic, a movement which 'holds us in place' (positioning theory again!) as we watch and enjoy the film. To elaborate further this difficult concept (see Miller *et al.*, 'Dossier on Suture', *Screen*, winter 1977/78), the process has been described as something like this. At the

Woman as image, man as bearer of the look – *Lusty Men* and *Under Capricorn*

beginning of each shot, the spectator enjoys a secure imaginary relationship to the film, a feeling bound up with the illusion of privileged control over and unmediated access to its fictional world. A moment later, though, this illusion is dispelled as the spectator gradually becomes conscious of the image frame, and hence of the fact that the fictional space is after all narrowly circumscribed. This realisation stimulates the desire to see and find out more, and the former illusion of the image as offering a 'window on the world' yields to an unpleasant perception of the film as artefact, a system of signs and codes that lie outside the spectator's control. However, this recognition is soon overcome by the advent of the next shot, which apparently restores the previous condition of the spectator's imaginary unity with the images and starts the cycle off again (Oudart, 'Cinema and Suture', in 'Dossier on Suture', 1977/78).

Such an account of the satisfaction afforded by 'invisible' continuity editing emphasises usefully the shot/reverse-shot pattern of narrative cinema and the involvement of the viewer in an intricate network of 'looks'. The point-of-view shot unattached to a particular character draws the spectator into the text by positing him or her as the privileged observer of the image, in the place of an imagined character occupying the position of the camera (see Dayan, 'The Tutor-code of Classical Cinema', 1974). In the following reverse-angle shot the point of origin of that look is assigned to a character within the fiction, thereby assuring that the viewer is not addressed directly by the film but remains safely outside it. In this way, the viewer is, in topographical terms, right inside the fictional space, yet never actually part of the action. No doubt the shot/reverse-shot figure is only one part of the total repertoire of film language, but it does afford a particularly clear model of the more general relationship, dubbed by Heath 'separation in identification' ('Lessons from Brecht', 1974), of spectator to the events taking place on the screen.

The concept of 'separation in identification' was echoed in contemporaneous theories of 'the look' or 'the gaze'. These also saw film narrative as a process generated primarily out of an interplay of looks: not only those exchanged between the characters of screen, epitomised by the point-of-view pattern, but also the look of the viewer, sitting in the cinema, at this fictional world, a look which the suturing process attempts to efface.

Metz was among those fascinated by the voyeuristic aspect of film viewing. In an essay first published in French in 1975 ('History/Discourse', 1976), he argued through this idea by comparing a visit to the cinema with a visit to the theatre. The performance of a play deliberately sets out to be a collective experience, an event which acknowledges the gathered populace implicitly or indeed sometimes even explicitly, as in direct asides to the audience. Thus 'actor and spectator are present to each other ... [in] a ceremony which has a certain civic quality, engaging more than the private man'. Film, by contrast, 'is exhibitionistic and it is not'; it 'knows that it is being looked at and does not know ... All the viewer requires – but he requires it absolutely – is that the actor should behave as though he is not being seen, and so cannot see him, the voyeur'.

The peculiar nature of film as a not-quite performing art is reflected both in its conditions of production (the fact that, unlike the theatre, actors and audience are never physically present in the same place), and of its reception (the individual's immobility and sense of isolation from other spectators, the total darkness, the self-contained nature of the event, lack of interval to break up the narrative flow, etc). In a striking image, Metz compared the cinema audience to fish gathered round the side of an aquarium, 'looking out' onto the fictional world, 'absorbing everything through their eyes and nothing through their bodies'; the activity of looking becomes disproportionately important to the film-goer compared to the more integrated physical experience of theatre-going. Suggestively, he linked this difference to the much later historical origins of the cinema, which 'was born at a period when social life was strongly marked by the concept of the individual' and which 'belongs to the private man' (Metz, 'History/Discourse', 1976).

In retrospect, this is an interesting anticipation of the 'decline of the public sphere' argument associated with the name of Jürgen Habermas, destined to be so influential in the 1980s and 1990s; it also in some ways paints a *curiously* individualistic picture, since from other perspectives it is precisely the highly social nature of the mass cinema audience of the first half of the twentieth century that gets eroded by the domestic practice of television viewing. However, the chief destiny of this emphasis on the voyeuristic nature of cinema was to feed into a full-bloodedly social account of gendered spectatorship.

Laura Mulvey on visual pleasure

If psychoanalysis is a conceptual system whose main purchase is on the layer of human experience where accounts stressing rationality, agency and autonomy are at their weakest, then the emergence of feminist theory in the 1970s and beyond, with its irresistable demonstration of the irrationality and at the same time the ongoing grievousness of gender hierarchy, involved making good use of what psychoanalysis has to say about the origins and maintenance of gender distinction. It fell to Laura Mulvey to propose, in an article destined to be more influential than any other single contribution to 1970s theory (Mulvey, 1975), an account of how the voyeuristic aspect of cinema spectatorship both arises from and perpetuates patriarchy.

Mulvey returns to the question of 'the look' from a feminist standpoint. She presents a picture of spectatorship familiar from suture-based accounts, with an uneasy and labile relationship between the forward drive of narrative and the potential of the static image to resist it, but adds to this a key factor: in the classic Hollywood film these two functions were almost always gender specific, reflecting and perpetuating the values of 'a world ordered by sexual imbalance'. In other words, the active, narrative role of making things happen and controlling events usually fell to a male character, while the female star, often virtually peripheral to functional events, remained more passively decorative. She functioned as the locus of masculine erotic desire, a spectacle to be looked at by both male characters and spectators, the latter, whatever their actual gender, being assumed to be and addressed as male by the operations of the film.

The Sternberg/Dietrich cycle has been seen as an extreme example of this tendency – Sternberg's celebrated remark that his films could well be projected upside down was cited by Mulvey as evidence that for him spectacle tends to take priority over narrative. Hitchcock was used as the contrasting example: here, the figure of the woman, representing a 'trouble' within the classic narrative, needs *punishing* by it to atone for the threat of narrative disruption, however voyeuristically pleasurable that spectacle has been. (The spectacle, threatening the stalling of the fictional flow, is treated as triggering the viewers' unpleasant awareness of themselves as looking which the mechanisms of cinema are usually concerned to repress.) Various compromises between spectacle and narrative are imaginable; a striking generic case is that of the backstage musical, which overtly employs the convention of the woman as showgirl, her spectacular performance of a song and/or dance anticipating this problem by 'matching' the look of the audience with that of male characters within the film, thus momentarily reconciling the tension between narrative and spectacle.

But *why* should the (sexually charged) image of the woman work so differently from that of the man? In 'demonstrating the way the unconscious of patriarchal society has structured film form', Mulvey drew on Freudo-Lacanian theories of child development. The key moments here are those involved with the discovery of sexual difference, notably the moment at which the male child sees (or realises, or ...) that his mother lacks a phallus, that she is 'castrated', and fears for the first time that he might suffer such a dire fate. A conservative tendency within classic psychoanalysis saw this as a moment universally necessary as part of the entry of the growing child into the symbolic order (with the little girl's 'acceptance' of 'castration' equally necessary), feminist theorists were concerned to call this inevitability into question, reformulating the process as a specific cultural phenomenon. Indeed, it is precisely the bizarreness, from any rational-agency perspective, of a gender-related ascription of more rationality and agency to the male than to the female that suggests that a psychoanalytic 'take' on the phenomenon might be appropriate. If the phallus becomes a privileged source of meaning, a 'positive term', despite its patent functioning only in terms of the diacritical functioning, *à la* Saussure, of gender difference, then this is a symptom of *social* pathology on a grand scale. The most miserable upshot of the weird overvaluation of the phallus is the devaluation it imposes on women. Instead of being defined by her own sexual attributes, her 'difference', 'woman' is perceived only negatively, as a lack: 'representation of the female form ... speaks castration and nothing else.'

Mulvey saw the main project of the classic Hollywood narrative cinema as the generation of pleasures for the male viewer which depended on deploying the body of the female star as a defence against the threat of castration she evokes. Her article drew attention to the ideological implications of the interdependence of deep-seated psychic processes and the operations of narrative cinema, each feeding on and reinforcing the other. The trenchancy of its writing is one of its most notable features.

> It is said that analysing pleasure, or beauty destroys it. That is the intention of this article... Not in favour ... of intellectualised unpleasure, but to make way for a total negation of the ease and plenitude of the narrative fiction film ... in order to conceive a new language of desire. (Mulvey, 1975)

Written 'compactly' to the point of presenting the reader with a real challenge, and refusing all the 'and yet ...' clauses that would get one's favourite movies off the hook, the article made its impact because, of all the work considered so far, it most redescribes so as to make visible features of mainstream cinema which had not been visible before, and which patently deserved to be challenged. It has generated a huge amount of further work, with much invested through the 1980s and 1990s in 'domesticating' it, so to speak, by advancing a fairer or more tolerant or more nuanced 'larger view'; but it is the clear and uncompromising nature of Mulvey's original formulations that has made the article such a continuing classic (see further on Psychoanalysis, p. 342; Feminist film theory, p. 353).

AFTERMATHS: THE STRUCTURALIST CONTROVERSY FADES

So much was acquired in the 1970s in film theory – and, necessarily, some acquisitions look in better shape than others. This is not the place to attempt to cover everything that happened to film theory once the very specific 'conjuncture' that produced the theoretical writing discussed above had become 'deconjoined'. But three topics may give a flavour of the way discussion has moved on: the fate of a pre-structuralist thinker, André Bazin; the fate of a post-structuralist thinker, Gilles Deleuze; and the prospects for formalism now.

Bazin

Any theorist proposing some sort of 'naïve realism', some sort of 'window on the world' theory of cinema would have been expected to draw heavy fire in the 1970s. André Bazin, however, was not just 'any theorist'. It was recognised at the time that his reputation rested upon an impressively substantial body of film theory and criticism, upon the editorial conducting of a journal, *Cahiers du Cinéma*, which was a model of the 'magazine that matters', and upon his direct influence on the directors of the French new wave. Still, his unabashed commitment to the importance of some kind of 'access to the real', available distinctively via photography, made his thought very hard to assimilate at a point where what seemed most important was to insist on cinema as language, language as arbitrary/diacritical, and ideology as omnipresent within cultural texts.

What was one to make of a crucial essay ('The Evolution of the Language of Cinema') which both rehabilitated certain products of the American cinema (crucially for later authorship debates), moved discussion on from a simple 'talkies are reactionary' line which blocked critical appreciation of what was actually happening in the cinema post-sound, gently debunked the widespread critical tendency to fetishise the accomplishments of a certain moment of the Soviet cinema at the expense of other styles and practices – but also proposed a dichotomy between 'directors who believe in the image and directors who believe in reality'? Reality?

Citizen Kane (USA 1940 *p.c* – Mercury Productions/RKO; *d* – Orson Welles; sd b/w)

In his book on Orson Welles and the essay on the evolution of the language of cinema, Bazin cites this film as exemplary of the tendency towards the long take and staging in depth, techniques which, he believed, allowed the viewer to perceive the inner unity of events.

However, *Citizen Kane* manifests an abundance of the trick effects which are roundly condemned by Bazin in his article 'The Virtues and Limitations of Montage'. Bazin acknowledges the presence of these elements in the film, but accounts for them as a counterpointing device to set off the sequences which employ long takes and deep-focus. Equally, however, it could be objected that in view of the profusion of other modes of representation, the long take could not be accurately described as the dominant feature of Welles's style.

Second, Bazin's opposition of the long take versus montage accounts for only one aspect of the film, suppressing the other myriad factors at work in producing meaning. For instance, although the scenes at the office of the *Inquirer* and in Xanadu are both in deep-focus, other elements such as, in the former case, specially constructed ceilings and low camera angles, convey an

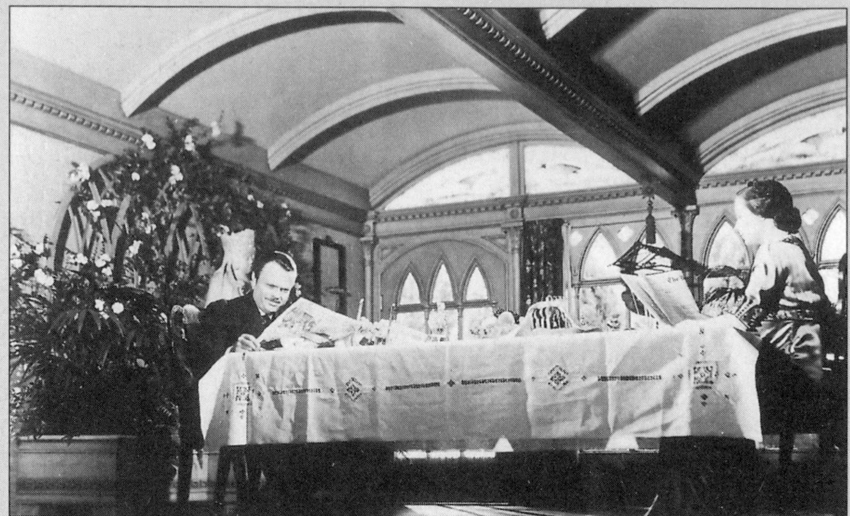

Expressionistic devices and low camera angles in *Citizen Kane* – some of the trick effects condemned by Bazin

impression of cramped and old-fashioned accommodation and, together with the characterisation of the staff, a blinkered and traditionalist editorial policy. In the latter scene, vast rooms, high ceilings (often not visible), the towering statuary and mantelpiece which dwarf Kane and his wife, combined with the use of lighting and sound all build up an atmosphere of bleakness and solitude. Elements such as sound and music are usually ignored by Bazin, who concentrates on visual components.

Bazin's proposition that *Citizen Kane* gives viewers a sense of the ambiguity of reality, allowing them to perform their own interpretative activity, is also questionable. Whether ambiguity is an automatic function of staging in depth is in itself open to debate, but even if this premiss is accepted, the lavish deployment of Expressionistic devices creates a mood of portent rather than of openness and ambivalence. For example, lighting and camera positioning, privilege Leland instead of Kane in the scene where the latter composes his 'declaration of principles'. Similarly, although staging in depth is used in the party scene, the cuts to Leland and placing in the foreground of his conversation with Bernstein amid the general revelry and euphoria again support his assertion that Kane will inevitably allow himself to be compromised. The weight given to Leland's scepticism of these moments betrays a fatality often seen by critics as characteristic of Welles's work – an element noted by Bazin who does not, however, find any incompatibility between this overwhelming sense of doom and what he describes as a liberal uncommitted *mise-en-scène*.

The Magnificent Ambersons (USA 1942 *p.c* – Mercury Productions/RKO; *d* – Orson Welles; sd b/w)

In discussing this film in terms of its 'luminous heterogeneous space', 'dramatic unity', and 'continuity of dramatic space', Bazin suppresses the dominant theme of fragmentation and hostility. Certainly, much use is made of deep-focus (note, however, the crosscutting in the dinner-party sequence to show the disintegration of the family gathering); but it creates not so much a 'heterogeneous space' as a battlefield where territories are demarcated, occupied, invaded and defended. A probing camera movement depicts George's incursion into Mrs Johnson's home; Eugene Morgan is shut out behind a transparent glass door; the argument between George and Fanny, who prevents him from another intrusion, takes place on the staircase, a traditional locus in cinema of struggles for power and ascendancy.

What emerges is not Bazin's philanthropic vision of harmony but a critical portrait of social class and its patrician values of private ownership (cf. George's possessive attitude towards his mother) and property rights. It could therefore be argued that the meaning of a film should not be inferred from any one of its formal aspects considered in isolation (e.g. deep-focus), but is generated by the combination and organisation of a whole range of other signifying factors.

The Little Foxes (USA 1940–1 *p.c* – RKO/ Goldwyn; *d* – William Wyler; sd b/w)

Bazin's article on Wyler describes him, curiously, as the 'Jansenist of *mise-en-scène*' probably referring to the virtues of self-discipline and asceticism advocated by this sect in opposition to the baroque indulgences of Jesuit doctrine and art. The title therefore appears to indicate a feature of Wyler's style but also contains an implicit value judgement since Jansenism is associated with two of France's greatest men of letters, Jean Racine and Blaise Pascal.

This double-edged significance is reflected in the argument itself; Wyler's is an 'intentionally self-effacing style' which aims at 'perfect neutrality and transparency', but he is, Bazin insisted, simultaneously an artist of the first order who, to achieve his purpose, makes masterly use of a number of stylistic devices: the juxtaposition of two pieces of dramatic action which forces spectators to divide their attention between them; the employment of long focal-length lenses (which Bazin contrasted with Welles's preference for distorting wide-angle lenses in *Citizen Kane*); the importance of the actors' looks as an index of the concealed undercurrents crossing the screen; and a *mise-en-scène* that centres on the human figures and places them in tightly constructed geometrical formations to signify the tensions between them.

Obviously, this notion of a 'style without a style' seems incompatible with the presence of a distinctive touch in Wyler's work. However, Bazin was careful to stress that realism does not 'come naturally' but can only be created by careful planning and the deliberate adoption of aesthetic strategies that may cause considerable technical difficulties – for example, the high lighting levels required by long focal-length lenses. Moreover, these aesthetic strategies have not remained constant. Though, he believed, the striving for realism has existed in the cinema since its invention, each era developed its own methods and criteria of usage from Lumière's single-shot/fixed-camera technique through the invisible editing of the pre-war classics to Welles's and Wyler's sophisticated use of deep-focus.

Wyler's genius lay in his success in inventing a highly crafted style which nonetheless gave the impression of being 'style-less'.

How, if at all, can the notion of realism as an aesthetic *choice* be reconciled with Bazin's belief in neutrality? The effect, for instance, of the portrayal of Horace's death requires a very idiosyncratic *mise-en-scène*. Deep space is used, but *not* deep-focus: thus Horace remains an indistinct blur as he dies in the far background of the image. The staging serves, as Bazin noted, to *conceal* the most significant event more properly than to reveal it. This casts doubt on his proposition that Wyler's is a transparent 'liberal and democratic' style which allows viewers to study the scene at their leisure, and could be used to argue that this is a distancing moment in the film since it causes a 'feeling of disquiet and almost the desire to push the immobile Bette Davis aside to see more clearly'. Another result is to confer upon Regina 'a privileged position of power in the dramatic geometry of space', to define her as the focus of interest (and perhaps sympathy?) at this point. Wyler uses immobile camera and severe *découpage* symbolically to reflect his theme of stasis and unnatural repression.

The Best Years of Our Lives (USA 1946 *p.c* – Goldwyn; *d* – William Wyler, sd b/w)

In 'The Long Take' Brian Henderson objects to what he sees as Bazin's false polarisation between the long take and montage styles. Only a very few film-makers work more or less exclusively with the sequence shot (a whole scene shot in a single take). Most 'long take' directors include some cuts within a scene and, because they are sparsely used, these cuts derive an exceptional significance, often marking a shift of balance in the dramatic relations at stake.

This can be seen in the bar scene in which Al and Fred meet up and discuss Fred's relationship with Al's daughter, Peggy. The two cuts to Al in the scene (whose irruption into the long take Bazin tries to justify as a 'safety measure' in case the viewer forgets about Fred's phone call to Peggy) could be seen as important punctuation marks, imposing tension and narrative development on an otherwise descriptive scene. This scene also illustrates the argument that Bazin's theory hinges solely on the visual properties of film and ignores the function of sound: the crux of the sequence lies precisely in the fact that we can see but not hear the decisive conversation. Arguably, the use of sound plays at least an equally instrumental role in creating tension as the composition of the image (see Technology, p. 52).

Directors with 'faith in the image' had historically tended to favour montage as a technique which allowed them to impose an interpretation on the events they portrayed. The effect, according to Bazin, was to create a 'meaning not objectively present in the images but derived purely from their juxtaposition'. This style was typified by the work of D. W. Griffith, Sergei Eisenstein and Alfred Hitchcock. The other kind of director, in contrast, would prefer long takes that preserved as far as possible the unity of time and space. Examples given by Bazin of practitioners of this approach included Erich von Stroheim, Jean Renoir and Orson Welles. Bazin made it clear that his sympathies lay with the latter method. The film image should, in his view, be evaluated 'according not to what it adds to reality but to what it reveals of it'.

These ideas followed on from those put forward in the 1945 essay 'The Ontology of the Photographic Image', where Bazin propounded the scandalous thesis that there is a sense in which, looking at a photograph, we are looking directly at the object photographed, and where, correspondingly, photography is praised as a 'process of mechanical reproduction from which man is excluded ... All the other arts are based on the presence of man; only in photography do we take pleasure in his absence' (Bazin, vol.1, 1958, p. 15).

It was inevitable that Bazin's belief that the film image should ideally be the transparent mediator of a putative 'reality' with minimal human intervention should have been attacked by structuralism-influenced critics. Bazin was held to have denied that film is a culturally determined language system. For him, the relationship between signifier and signified in cinema was not arbitrary but intimate and existential. This hypothesis is evidenced in Bazin's celebrated analogies between the photograph and the death mask or fingerprint; and indeed it would have been interesting to see what alternative theorisations of death-mask or finger-print signs would have been offered by the anti-Bazinian camp, had they deigned to.

The richness of Bazin's legacy was never invisible in the 1970s, and indeed, in so far as the period was a time of 'importing from France', his unmistakable influence on such 'accepted' figures as Metz could hardly be denied. Careful readers of his work grasped how, as an exceptionally perceptive critic as well as a theorist and aesthetician, he constantly stressed the actuality rather than the ideal. Perfect transparency was, he realised, precluded by the current limitations of film technology and might indeed never be possible. Even the 'Ontology' essay, after developing the carefully elaborated argument that photography is an impartial, automatic process of registration, ends with the rider: 'On the other hand, of course, cinema is also a language'. This ambivalence is again found in one of Bazin's favourite images for the relation between film and reality: an asymptote, a curve which gradually approaches a straight line but which meets it only at infinity.

Indeed, in his essay on Italian neo-realism, Bazin went as far as to claim that the need to enlist artifice to give the illusion of transparency generated a creative tension which was crucial to the work of art; true mimesis would result only in a flat and unheightened naturalism.

> We must beware of setting aesthetic refinement against a kind of crudeness, a kind of instant effectiveness of a realism satisfied just to show reality. Not the least of the merits of the Italian cinema will be, in my view, to have recalled once again that there is no 'realism' in art which is not first and foremost profoundly 'aesthetic'... Realism in art can only be achieved in one way – through artifice. (Bazin, vol. 4, 1962, pp. 20–1)

Bazin's notion of realism was certainly rather more complex than is sometimes admitted. Ideally, he wanted the cinematographic image to have the status of an objective record; in actuality, though, he saw this as neither possible nor, in the last analysis, desirable. Positing that 'there is not one but several realisms' (Bazin, vol. 1, 1958, p. 156), he set out to identify the very diverse methods by which these can be constructed. Most crucially, he always spoke for the creative energies of the historical moment in which he was writing: he was, instinctively and on principle, the least 'retro' or grumpy of theorists imaginable. Regrettably, the real accomplishment of the missed dialogue between Bazin and structuralism, now that both are in that past the redemption or preservation of which so preyed on Bazin's mind, still lies in the future.

Deleuze

Any attempt here at a proper exposition of Gilles Deleuze's two magisterial, difficult, idiosyncratic, rewarding volumes on the cinema would be inappropriate. But a brief orientational note on where these volumes stand in relation to 'structuralist controversy' writing may be useful.

Some strange destiny seems to have determined that the cinema is written about in France with superior perceptiveness and intelligence than elsewhere. André Bazin is a centrally important figure in this, but he himself was the beneficiary of a richer cultural context of moving-image awareness than prevailed elsewhere. This undoubtedly was a factor orientating the key figures in 1970s theory towards France. At the same time, it turned out, France was producing 'the thing called structuralism', and indeed something rather larger (recalling how many of the key 'structuralist' names hated that sobriquet). Need we rehearse the key names again? The point is that an orientation towards serious thought about cinema opened interest into serious French thought generally in a way which, for better or worse, put *Screen* a year or two in advance of broader 'theory' importation elsewhere, in literary studies for instance (the exception here is the political journal *New Left Review*).

However, none of the key names wrote directly about cinema, with the exception of a very few marginal pieces. The enterprise of 'using structuralism' was generally one of extrapolation: if we grasp Lacan, say, what can we do with that in so far as we are committed to understanding, and changing, the cinema? Metz is a great example of the extrapolator, because he essayed it twice, first bringing across to cinema the linguistics he knew, then bringing across to cinema the psychoanalysis he knew. But the tantalising prospect remains: what would it be like if we had had a Lacan seminar devoted to Welles rather than to Hamlet or Antigone, or Lévi-Strauss rather than Will Wright working through a serious corpus of westerns, or Foucault addressing the paradoxes of control via a study of the Hayes code (and its 'permissive' challenges) in detail?

Gilles Deleuze is unquestionably one of the 'key names' in postwar French thought. A philosopher whose readings of writers ranging from Hume to Nietzsche have been nothing if not radical, he collaborated with the psychiatrist and theorist Félix Guattari (himself Lacanian in formation – and the book is kinder to Lacan than to the rest of the psychoanalytic tradition) on a sprawling, witty, keenly intelligent book, *Anti-Oedipus* (1972), which, as the title suggests, took the Freudian bull by the horns. (It must be said that those continuing to espouse the Freudian side of 1970s film theory have seemingly felt immune from any need to counter-argue in the face of not only 'vulgar empiricist' challenges to Freud – not all quickly dismissable – but of the more theoretically congenial kind of challenge to that conceptual framework posed by Deleuze/Guattari). In a friction-free world, French-orientated film theory would have engaged with a major 1972 publication in French relevant to its concerns by, shall we say, 1974; but we do not live in such a world.

Then, stepping back from the Guattari collaboration, Deleuze produced a two-volume treatise on the cinema on his own. *Cinéma 1: L'Image-mouvement* appeared in 1983, followed by *Cinéma 2: L'Image-temps* in 1985; both volumes were in English by 1989. At last, one of the leading thinkers of postwar France had produced, for film theory, a work *of* film theory – or, more precisely, a work of philosophy but one which uses film integrally as its theme. Might one have expected that the 'theory' community would drop everything, so to speak, to absorb, respond to and work with what was offered?

Any such expectation would, it turned out, have been misplaced. Only in the 1990s, and with considerable tentativeness, is the invitation to thought offered by Deleuze being accepted. Why should this have been? It is as if one of the legacies of the structuralist controversy was a positive reluctance to read Deleuze productively.

No doubt one reason for this is that the Deleuze cinema books make extensive use of a philosopher, Henri Bergson, whose turn-of-the-century views on, in particular, time have been deeply unfashionable for many years. Further, Deleuze's Bergsonianism requires serious work on the part of the reader, and by the 1980s one can sense a certain 'theory fatigue' setting in within film studies: had we not had enough experience of 'hard thought' in the course of the structuralist adventure, had we not paid our dues in that respect? This is a factor in the second reason for reserve, Deleuze's extensive use of the semiotic categories of the American philosopher Charles Sanders Peirce. Peirceian semiotics, as an alternative to the language-analogy-based semiology drawn from Saussure, had been brought into the film theory world by Peter Wollen in *Signs and Meaning in the Cinema* but only in a cut-down way; a full engagement with Peirce probably requires a relinquishment of Saussure which inspires reluctance in the theory community.

But the third block to the reading of Deleuze, which is the least creditable, may have been the strongest. Deleuze writes in the most unabashedly, flagrantly '*auteurist*' style imaginable: his pages are crammed with the names of the great directors, treated precisely as such. It is probably no exaggeration to say that the following sentences from the Preface to Deleuze's first volume sealed its inital fate for many readers formed by the structuralist controversy:

> The great directors of the cinema may be compared, in our view, not merely with painters, architects and musicians, but also with thinkers. They think with movement-images and time-images instead of concepts. One cannot object by pointing to the vast proportion of rubbish in cinematographic production – it is no worse than anywhere else, although it does have unparalleled economic and industrial consequences. The great cinema directors are hence merely more vulnerable – it is infinitely easier to prevent them from doing their work. The history of the cinema is a long martyrology. (Deleuze, 1986)

How could one be expected to engage with the concepts being forged by Deleuze, and in particular with his arguments for a shift from movement image to time image as the crucial event in cinematic history, if he was going to go on about great directors!

In fact, the Deleuzian enterprise is anything but an exercise in canon-building, connoisseurship or hero-worship. Deleuze presents 'the great directors' as great because their work testifies to an intrinsic, ongoing crisis in the cinema, unfolding from its outset in a mappable variety of forms, which is intimately linked to the ongoing crisis of our culture more generally. The various styles of cinema, from earliest days to now, are related by Deleuze to the great philosophical themes of vision, truth, thought and time. Crucially, Deleuze finds a way of establishing a difference between, roughly, what others would call 'classic Hollywood cinema' and 'art-house cinema' which bypasses the by-now-usual refusal within film studies to privilege 'art' (see Art cinema, p. 106). He distinguishes between the cinema of the *movement image* and that of the *time image*. The former of these is the cinema of exhilaration, of narrative drive and suspense (with Hitchcock as its apogee), because it can count on a robust faith in 'action cinema', in a linkage of movement to other 'making sense' relations producing the seamlessly-edited popular film. But, after the Second World War, the major energies of the cinema, Deleuze feels, go into enterprises where this robustness is denied. The cinema of the ambiguous, as promoted by Bazin, develops a very different image (sometimes, as the Gene Hackman character in Arthur Penn's 1975 *Night Moves* puts it, watching such an image would be 'like watching paint dry'): something emerges which acts 'to prevent perception being extended into action in order to put it in contact with thought' (Deleuze, 1989, p. 1). Or:

> precisely what brings [the] cinema of action into question after the war is the very break-up of the sensory-motor schema: the rise of situations to which one can no longer react, of environments with which there are now only chance relations, of empty or disconnected any-space-whatevers replacing qualified extended space. (Deleuze, 1989, p. 272)

This is the cinema of our (post)modernity, the cinema of nations and persons not at one with themselves.

As with Bazin, the very conceptual acquisitions from the structuralist controversy have delayed engagement with work which could, in the first instance, seem to have been made 'old fashioned' by them, but which actually confront the syllabus, as it has settled down, with a great deal of unfinished business. No doubt the manner in which Deleuze brandishes his *auteurs* is provocative, but it does us no harm to be reminded of the considerable laziness with which the Barthes/Foucault phrase 'the death of the author' has been accepted as post-structuralist gospel. And it is of considerable importance now that, with the triumph of 'popular culture' arguments effectively secured, a non-nostalgic case for a cinema of greater demands should be on the table as well.

Formalism

In the wake of the structuralist debates, it is hard not to feel that the study of film has moved out of an activist phase into, for now, something more simply scholarly or appreciation based. Serious film history has gained much ground (see Early Cinema, p. 93), and as a manner of approaching film textuality the approach to analysis known as 'neo-formalism' and associated in particular with David Bordwell and Kristin Thompson, authors of the immensely influential text *Film Art*, has acquired a certain dominance. Again, this is not the place to offer a summary of the Bordwell and Thompson enterprise, but a final remark may be helpful in situating it with regard to the concerns of this chapter.

Kristin Thompson, in particular, has situated her work very explicitly in the tradition of aesthetic thought known as 'Russian formalism', a legacy from the pre-Stalinist Soviet Union. Probably the theorist from this period made most use of within 1970s theory was Vladimir Propp, whose *Morphology of the Folktale* turned out to be capable of partnering Lévi-Straussian analysis very productively when applied to film narrative. Yet, from today's perspective, the appropriation of Propp looks distinctly hasty – for the good reason that the development of theory was being conducted with immediately interventionist motives; and this can be said of that theory's relationship to Russian formalism more generally. If one attraction of the Russian formalists was that they wrote, from the left, in their own highly politicised times, a worry about their legacy was always that it might amount to 'just' formalism, that it might lead one not to be political enough.

A very different sense of time reigns in Kristin Thompson's most sustained presentation of the case for neo-formalism, *Breaking the Glass Armor* (1988). Under the slogan 'One approach, many methods', she challenges the 'imposed-method' aspect of 1970s film analysis.

> The critic begins with an analytical method, often derived from approaches in literary studies, psychoanalysis, linguistics, or philosophy; she or he then selects a film that seems suited to displaying that method.
> When I first began doing film analysis in the early 1970s, this kind of impetus for film criticism seemed almost self-evidently the way to go about things. (Thompson, 1988, p. 5)

Such an approach to analysis certainly makes up for the downplaying of agency on the part of both artist and audience which characterised much 1970s theory. 'Neoformalism assumes that artists are rational agents, making choices they judge appropriate to an end they have in view. Artists have intentions, even if the results they achieve are often unintentional' (Thompson, 1988, p. 35). And David Bordwell has argued for using contemporary cognitive psychology, with its emphasis on the individual's active part in grasping meaning through schemata, as the basis for conceptualising the film spectator. And so, film by film, the distinctive patterns of the film's form and of the audience's grasp of that form can patiently be revealed. After 1989, in a world of 'markets and regulation' securely globalised and lacking any visible challenge to the broad logic of its system (the world of 'development', Lyotard would say), we have all the time in the world.

SELECTED READING

Dudley Andrew, *André Bazin*, New York, Oxford University Press, 1978.

Roland Barthes, *Camera Lucida: Reflections on Photography*, trans. Richard Howard, London, Cape, 1982.

Roland Barthes, 'Introduction to the structural analysis of narratives', *Communications* no. 8, 1966, in *Image–Music–Text*, London, Fontana, 1977; trans. Stephen Heath.

André Bazin, *Qu'est-ce que le cinéma?* vols 1 and 4, Paris, Éditions du Cerf, 1958 and 1962 (some of these articles trans. by Hugh Gray, *What is Cinema?*, vols 1 and 2, Berkeley, University of California Press, 1971; 'William Wyler or the Jansenist of *mise-en-scène*', trans. in Christopher Williams (ed.), *Realism and the Cinema*, London, RKP/BFI, 1980, pp. 36–52).

David Bordwell, *Making Meaning: Inference and Rhetoric in the Interpretation of Cinema*, Cambridge, Mass., Harvard University Press, 1989.

David Bordwell and Kristin Thompson, *Film Art*, New York, McGraw-Hill, 4th edn, 1993.

Gilles Deleuze, *Cinema 1: L'Image-mouvement*, 1983, trans. by Hugh Tomlinson and Barbara Habbermas as *Cinema 1: The Movement–Image*, London, Athlone Press, 1986.

Gilles Deleuze, *Cinema 2: L'Image-temps*, 1985, trans. by Hugh Tomlinson and Robert Galeta as *Cinema 2: The Time–Image*, London, Athlone Press, 1989.

Stephen Heath, 'Notes on suture', *Screen* 18(4), winter 1977/78.

Colin MacCabe, 'Realism and the cinema: notes on some Brechtian theses', *Screen* 15(2), summer 1974.

Christian Metz, *Psychoanalysis & Cinema: The Imaginary Signifier*, London, Macmillan, 1977/1982.

PSYCHOANALYSIS

The meeting of psychoanalysis and film studies should be seen as historically paradoxical. It is interesting to note, for example, that in what is a very rare reference to the cinema, in the *Introductory Lectures on Psychoanalysis* (1916–17), Freud wrote as if the cinema were a cultural form directly antithetical to psychoanalysis: '[t]he uninstructed relatives of our patients, who are only impressed by visible and tangible things – preferably by actions of the sort that are to be witnessed at the cinema – never fail to express their doubts whether "anything can be done about the illness by mere talking" ' (Freud, 1991a, p. 41).

In the 1970s psychoanalysis was brought to the study of film only as a secondary, auxiliary theory. And yet the psychoanalytically influenced theories of cinema which emerged from this period have tended more easily to prompt new and valuable work than those theories on which they were initially dependent (Althusserian accounts of ideology, for example). What is more, film theorists have remained interested in psychoanalysis despite the widely acknowledged fact that the first manifestations of psychoanalytically oriented film theory led to an intellectual impasse (see Donald, 1989; Willemen, 1994, pp. 223–5). It can be argued that psychoanalysis has a crucial part to play in the future development of the study of cinema; but the conceptual significance of psychoanalysis can usefully be approached in terms of how it came to be used in film theory.

INSTITUTIONAL AND INTELLECTUAL CONTEXTS

Screen

Psychoanalysis emerged in anglophone debates about film in the early 1970s as part of the intellectual and polemical project of *Screen*, the journal of the Society for Education in Film and Television (SEFT), which was affiliated to, and part funded by, the British Film Institute (see Mulvey, 1996, pp. 24–5; MacCabe, 1993, pp. 15–17; McArthur, 1992, pp. 36–49; Alvarado *et al.*, 1993, pp. 1–6). *Screen*'s publishing project included articles which attempted to apply psychoanalysis to the study of film, either by examining the formal and narrative devices of particular films in terms of the play of desire and inhibition, meaning and its distortion which Freud (and Jacques Lacan after him) asserted to structure mental functioning, or by proposing a potentially exhaustive account of the 'metapsychology' of the cinematic 'apparatus' – that is, a theory which attempted to describe in general and all-embracing terms the psychological processes provoked and exploited in the experience of film-going.

The extent to which psychoanalysis, and more particularly the theories of Lacan, subsequently permeated into the wider British and North American academic culture is due in some measure to the way in which *Screen* assimilated, elaborated and developed European thought. In the 1970s, *Screen* was one of the most important conduits for the transfer of ideas between Europe, Britain and the United States. It is worth emphasising this point since anglophone film theory, no less than anglophone film-making (especially in Hollywood), was and is dependent on the international migration of ideas and artistic practices.

Screen in the 1970s was a dissident voice which occupied a more or less secure, if restricted, position within the British intellectual and educational establishment. Whereas, in France, radical thought had initiated far-reaching changes to the national education system in the aftermath of the events of 1968, in Britain such thinking emerged out of established educational values and procedures. The works of Louis Althusser, Lacan and Christian Metz were introduced to English-speaking audiences in a journal principally devoted to the teaching of film and television according to conventional norms. Psychoanalytic film theory was explored at a time when the momentum of theoretical innovation and an educational imperative were tightly interwoven but often antagonistic to one another. For *Screen* became, initially under the editorship of Sam Rohdie, both radical and subversive within its educational remit: members of its editorial board were committed both to a revolutionary politics and to a 'dialectical' pedagogy (see Brewster *et al.*, 1976, pp. 115–66).

Several concerns were apparent in the pages of *Screen*, as they were in comparable publications (especially the collections of essays published in the 1970s in conjunction with the Edinburgh Film Festival). Four of these concerns deserve to be singled out. First, there was a declared intention to participate in the formation of a systematic, perhaps even 'scientific', theory of cinematic discourse, an overarching understanding of cinema. (When Metz's psychoanalytically orientated essays were first translated and published in *Screen*, they were welcomed for their contribution to this project rather than for their attention to psychoanalysis as such.) Second, there was a revolutionary project, a commitment to ideological analysis and enlightenment, consisting in the effort to expose 'classic' narrative cinema as both capable of 'ideological effects' (a phrase derived from Althusser; see Baudry, 1992) and complicit in the commodification of pleasure and the repressive regime of capital. This project anticipated, and purported to make way for, the arrival of an intellectual cinema of solidarity and social change, a counter-cinema (see Avant-garde and counter-cinema, p. 113). Third, and complementarily, there was a feminist polemic against the strictures of patriarchy which found a critical incentive in analysing the way in which the image of woman is both celebrated and degraded in cinema for the benefit of a prurient and notionally male spectator. Fourth (rather problematically, given the other concerns), there was a love of American cinema (Walsh, Ford, Hawks, Ray, Aldrich, Fuller) and its European transmutations (Lang, Tourneur, Siodmak, Sirk, the *nouvelle vague*; see Mulvey, 1996, pp. 21–8). These, then, were further contexts for the influence of psychoanalysis on film theory: in each case psychoanalysis was taken to offer possibilities of intellectual advance.

It is as if psychoanalysis tended to be a coded form of some other theoretical or critical interest. The way in which film theory had recourse to, yet tried to remain distant from, psychoanalysis was apparent in, for example, Laura Mulvey's groundbreaking 1975 feminist essay (discussed above, see p. 336) first published in *Screen*:

> There is no way in which we can produce an alternative [to 'the phallocentric order'] out of the blue, but we can begin to make a break by examining patriarchy with the tools it provides, of which psychoanalysis is not the only but an important one . . .
> Psychoanalytic theory as it now stands can at least advance our understanding of the status quo, of the patriarchal order in which we are caught. (Mulvey, 1989, p. 15)

This hesitancy was echoed some time later by E. Ann Kaplan:

> Psychoanalytic discourse may . . . have oppressed women, in the sense of bringing us to accept a positioning that is inherently antithetical to being a subject and to autonomy; but if that is the case, we need to know exactly *how* psychoanalysis has functioned to repress what we could potentially become; for this, we must master the terms of its discourse. (Kaplan, 1983, p. 24)

It was only after having made this qualification that Kaplan stated, 'psychoanalysis becomes a crucial tool for explaining the needs, desires, and male–female positionings that are reflected in film' (Kaplan, 1983, p. 24).

Psychoanalysis, in other words, was appropriated for feminist film theory – which, in this respect, is analogous to other strands of film theory – in the uneasy belief that its insights were both reactionary and potentially instrumental in the feminist project of refashioning society, culture and habitual modes of thought (see Johnston, 1992; Kuhn, 1994, pp. 193–206). It was therefore felt to be necessary to qualify the use of psychoanalytic concepts, to emphasise their merely utilitarian function. Just as the most radical theorising in the 1970s tended simultaneously to reveal fascination with, but also disparagement of, classic American cinema, so – in a similar gesture of ambivalence – feminism welcomed psychoanalysis while always being on the point of disclaiming it.

What does not seem to have been in question, however, was the critical purchase which could be achieved, at least in the short term, by studying film psychoanalytically. Even though there were other discourses and theoretical groundings for 1970s film theory apart from psychoanalysis – most notably post-Saussurean linguistics and the comparable structuralist or semiotic attempt to chart, map out and catalogue the bounds of subjectivity and the manner of its regulation – arguably none could be said to have had at once so significant yet so undermined a status as psychoanalysis.

Psychoanalysis as the cause of division

In an article, 'Psychoanalysis and Film' (1975–6), signed collectively by four members of *Screen*'s editorial board, the authors expressed three reservations about the adoption of psychoanalysis by film theorists: 'the unproblematic acceptance of psychoanalysis implicit in the way it has been presented in *Screen*; the intelligibility of the various expositions of it; the validity of the attempts made to apply it directly to the cinema' (Buscombe *et al.*, 1992, p. 35).

The authors' objections to psychoanalysis turned not on the problem of whether the attempt to describe, analyse and critique classic narrative cinema systematically was ultimately unproductive, but on whether psychoanalysis could furnish the proper concepts for this systematic project. The question of whether psychoanalysis qualifies as a 'scientific' method of interpretation now seems somewhat dated, but the authors' basic argument remains important. The following remarks are noteworthy:

> Ever since Freud first developed his ideas, psychoanalysis has been raided by other disciplines and some of its concepts appropriated. In the course of this appropriation, the concepts have usually become imprecise and devalued. We're concerned that the differing uses of psychoanalytic concepts in *Screen* may be a mark of this process occurring in film theory. (Buscombe *et al.*, 1992, p. 42)

According to the authors this imprecise, clumsy appropriation of psychoanalysis, along with the unintelligibility to which it allegedly gave rise, threatened *Screen*'s claim to be an educational resource, alienating readers, even implying a reactionary account of film-going as a '"nasty" or "perverted" activity' (Buscombe *et al.*, 1992, p. 43).

The authors of this article resigned from the board of *Screen* shortly after its publication, their brief statement announcing this decision prompting a more lengthy response from the remaining editors. In this 'Reply' (1976), the editors reasserted their commitment to a radical analysis of film as well as to the pedagogical value of this analysis. In doing this, the authors offered an account of the success of *Screen* up to that point: '"success" = an effective contribution to the development of film theory and analysis and to maintaining the urgency of political questions within that development' (Brewster *et al.*, 1976, p. 111). The article continued:

> We see our tasks as that of analysing film and television in all their effects, that of understanding the operation of these effects in ideology and providing educational strategies in consequence, and that of using this analysis and understanding to bring into focus the difficulties and terms of political cinema ...
>
> Semiotics and psychoanalysis are important to us *in so far* as they can contribute to this multiple task, more by helping us to grasp the problems than by providing ready answers. (Brewster *et al.*, 1976, p. 112)

In other words, here again, psychoanalysis was asserted to be merely functional and contingently useful; its terms were marshalled as part of a larger, superior interpretative project and, in this context, they were used pragmatically without any fundamental questioning of their provenance, heuristic effectiveness or epistemological stability. The authors of 'Psychoanalysis and Film' did not in principle object to the enterprise of applying or appropriating concepts from psychoanalysis. What was at stake was the success of this enterprise, or lack of it, rather than the methodological principles underlying it. But the authors of the editorial 'Reply', in emphasising the secondary status of psychoanalysis, equally did not probe the question of what kinds of relationship might pertain between psychoanalysis and film theory other than the dependent one in which psychoanalytic concepts could serve as '"political weapon[s]"' (Brewster *et al.*, 1976, p. 112).

What stands out particularly, then, in the various contexts in which psychoanalysis became a part of film theory in the 1970s is the frequency of the association. Psychoanalysis had a role to play in the whole range of film theory's political and critical concerns in this period. However, although psychoanalysis was everywhere, and although psychoanalysis become a focal issue in the development of *Screen*'s project, it nevertheless was constantly referred to as being subordinate and ancillary to supposedly more pressing initiatives. Psychoanalysis had, therefore, a paradoxical status in 1970s film theory: at once dominant in terms of being perhaps the most important common factor in different theoretical projects, and marginalised or downplayed in each of these projects. This status allows for a provisional conclusion to be drawn as to the significance of psychoanalysis for the study of cinema: psychoanalysis has been, and continues to be, capable of becoming a theoretical faultline in film studies not because it yields particularly definitive propositions about subjectivity and social life which may be definitive and capable of generalisation and application. On the contrary, perhaps psychoanalysis becomes so significant and controversial precisely because it yields easily to being grafted onto other forms of analysis (Marxism, feminism, cinephilia), serving diverse intellectual needs, and because – ultimately – it is (or should be) unusually tolerant of paradoxes and unstable hypotheses.

THEORETICAL FOUNDATIONS

Paradoxes of the 'decentred' mind

The particular, if enduringly controversial, prestige which psychoanalysis enjoys in western culture is due in great measure to its proposition that mental functioning is fundamentally paradoxical. Psychoanalysis

Hollywood's fascination with psychoanalysis – Siodmak's *The Dark Mirror*

The Dark Mirror (USA 1946 *p.c* Universal–International *d* – Robert Siodmak; sd b/w)

The File on Thelma Jordon (USA 1950 *p.c* Paramount *d* – Robert Siodmak; sd b/w)

Hollywood, in a fashion typical of American culture at large, took to psychoanalysis with abandon long before psychoanalysis was found to be at the disposal of film theory. The thematic of the mind dangerously at odds with itself and more or less accurately psychoanalytic accounts of this state provided Hollywood film-making with narrative conceits and the occasion for opportunistic moral commentary. So, in *The Dark Mirror* (1946) a psychiatrist/psychoanalyst played by Lew Ayres assists the police in ascertaining whether one of two identical twins (played by Olivia de Havilland) is responsible for a murder – and if so, which one. He uses ink-blot tests, free association and the sisters' attraction to him to distinguish the malevolent murderer from her docile, inoffensive sister with whom, predictably enough, he falls in love.

To depict twins in this way has certain interesting sociological and philosophical implications. Underneath the conventional morality of the *film noir* lies a psychosexual drama concerning the disturbance of identity in the face of social regulation. Siodmak, as it were, literalises the idea – essentially psychoanalytic at least in origin – of a 'split personality' dangerously unintegrated into society. *The Dark Mirror* is exploring the same territory as Siodmak's later, finer *noir*,

The File on Thelma Jordon (1950), whose *femme fatale* protagonist, played by Barbara Stanwyck, is heard to utter on her deathbed: 'all my life I've been struggling: the good and the bad . . . you don't suppose they could just let half of me die'. What is at stake, therefore, is a rather self-aware, if vulgar, dramatisation of Freud's distinction between the concupiscent unconscious and the socially obedient conscious mind. The dramatisation reflects both a period of social reorganisation in American society and the socially structured dynamics of male fantasy and anxiety in which women are imagined as equally and wilfully capable of a murderous sensuality and a placid servility. *The Dark Mirror*, by presenting us with a 'good' and a 'bad' twin, simplifies and clarifies the components of this spectrum of fantasy and anxiety.

Blue Velvet (USA 1986 *p.c* De Laurentiis Entertainment *d* – David Lynch; sd col.)

The many variants and displacements of sexual behaviour (including, for example, fetishism or the reverberations of sexuality present in film-going) are posited by psychoanalysis as bound up with ways of acquiring, consolidating and dealing with knowledge. Sexuality impinges upon childhood, according to Freud, only in an indirect and perplexing way. However a child may fend off the encounter with adult sexuality, his or her own mature sexual disposition will be determined by the reshaping, recuperation, or theorisation of, the outlines of childhood experience. For Freud, adult sexuality is always to some degree a kind of remembering or rewriting of accidental events in childhood. Sexuality as such is thus intimately bound up with forms of knowledge and thinking. *Fantasy* is the order of mental life which negotiates between the conscious intellect and the wholly unfettered, animalistic desires of the unconscious. Human fantasy, according to psychoanalysis, is testament to the complex history of individual sexual behaviour, a history in which basic impulses are refashioned by memory, intuition and emotion.

Blue Velvet is a parade of dangerous or prohibited sexual behaviours: it depicts sado-masochism and rape as well as suggesting incest and homosexuality. In addition, however, it explores what could be called the hermeneutics of sexuality: the ways in which sexuality involves a variety of forms of knowledge and perception. So, on the one hand, the film details various psychosexual scenarios: Dorothy (Isabella Rosselini) demanding, initially at knifepoint, that Jeffrey (MacLachlan) hit and abuse her; Frank (Dennis Hopper) seeming to inhale through a breathing apparatus (apparently connected to nothing) while simulating mock-incestuous sex with Dorothy ('Daddy wants to fuck'); Frank announcing a completely indiscriminate, psychotic sexual urge ('I'll fuck anything that moves'). But it also insists on the manner in which these scenarios inevitably involve – and are meaningless without – different kinds of sensory information: Frank's olfactory stimulus (the breathing apparatus); his aversion to being looked at; a sensual listening and singing involving Frank and Ben (Dean Stockwell); a heightened, sexualised concentration on touch (the blue velvet connecting the mouths of Frank and Dorothy). The emphasis on the sensations accompanying, and allowing for, the protagonists' sexual behaviour means that the film's audience cannot simply observe the sexual spectacle on the screen; or rather, in watching this spectacle, the audience is invited to consider how multifarious are the ways in which sexuality depends on various sensory stimuli. (Voyeurism, in other words, will only partially explain the pathologies being opened up to the audience.) Furthermore, the film seems to demand that its spectators recognise that the sexual scenarios being staged would have to imply a complex history of experience, desire and trauma. When Frank shouts out, 'Come to Daddy!', he is being besieged by memory, by something traumatically half-remembered. And in one of the film's most powerful scenes, when Frank is all but overcome by Roy Orbison's 'Candy-Coloured Clown', he is again dragged back to a terrible past the only escape from which appears to be violent psychosis (he immediately attacks Jeffrey).

As well as this, the staging of the film encourages us to think twice about the significance of voyeurism as a dominant kind of second-order sexual pleasure. In the central scene, when Jeffrey 'observes' the twisted coupling of Frank and Dorothy, it seems as if the spectator is necessarily being forced to take Jeffrey's part as voyeur. But is Jeffrey a voyeur? Michel Chion, in a brilliant book on Lynch, suggests something else in respect of the scene in which Jeffrey observes Frank and Dorothy from a cupboard in Dorothy's apartment:

> the scene seems to arise from an archaic acoustic impression which endows it with the kind of troubling vagueness that can inspire bizarre theories. A child who overhears the sexual intercourse of adults might imagine, for instance, that the man's voice is muffled not because he is speaking against the woman's mouth or body, but because he has stuffed a piece of cloth into his mouth. This is the kind of fantasy on display in *Blue Velvet*, reviving the surrealistic sexual theories of children. Moreover, an additional unsettling element is the scene's sense of being outside time. The sentences which Frank repeats, often word for word, at short intervals: 'Don't you fucking look at me', reverberate as happens in the memory. There is no difference between the continuous scene at which Jeffrey is present and the

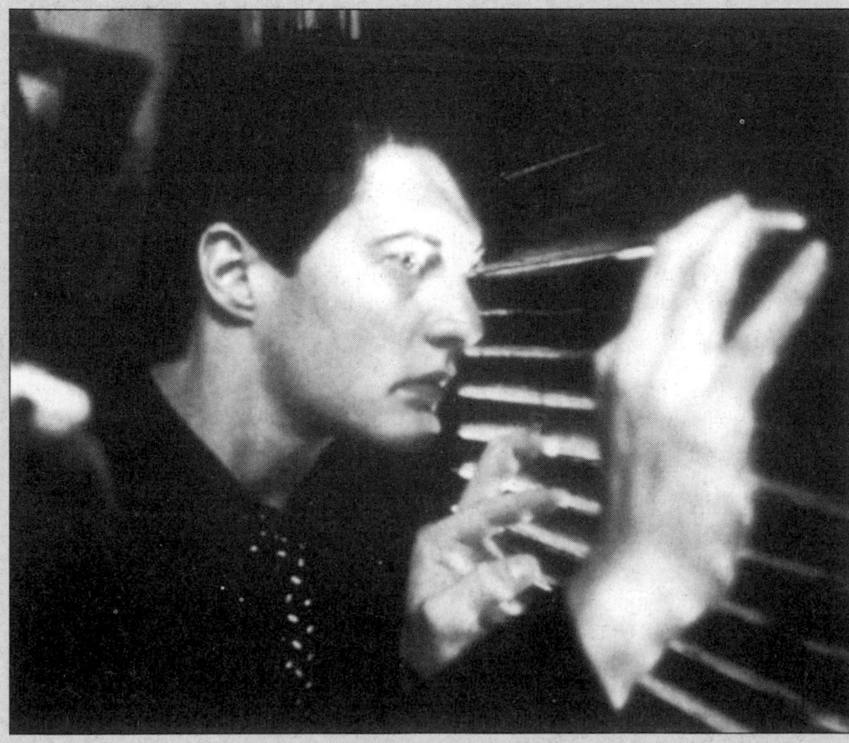

The play of voyeurism and fantasy – Lynch's *Blue Velvet*

> shots in which he remembers it. The scene is the very act of remembering, the unfolding of something which has already been inscribed. (Chion, 1995, p. 94)

For Chion, *Blue Velvet* is at one remove from fantasy – it creates tableaux of fantasies rather than simply recreating the fantasies as if they were being directly experienced. What we see on screen is not, according to Chion, the simple real-time event of Jeffrey watching Frank and Dorothy. Rather we see what a child might have visualised as happening between two adults having sex, if that child had no clear view of the adults but had only the evidence of his ears to go by.

This is not to say that Chion's reading is definitive. But it gets at some of the strangeness of *Blue Velvet* through an account of the film which explores the various ways in which sensory data mediates desire and knowledge. What is at stake in film-going is not just the limited experience of sadistic, identificatory voyeurism, but also the complex merging of the spectator's own, very specific experiences and sensitivity to the different kinds of sensory information provided by cinema. As with Jeffrey, what the film-goer sees is only a part of what he or she thinks, remembers, hears and feels.

Manhunter (USA 1986 *p.c* De Laurentiis Entertainment *d* – Michael Mann; sd col.)

Psychoanalysis theorises sexuality as involving both desire for a particular object (an 'object' being, say, a person of the opposite or the same sex, of a particular age or appearance or even an inanimate object – which may, as in fetishism, 'memorialise' a wholly different object) and a series of complex processes whereby the object is selected, wanted, perceived, framed, known, sought after, understood. Therefore alongside the psychoanalytic question concerning *what* is desired are the questions, *how* and *why* is this object desired. So Freud discusses the fetishist both in terms of the unexpected focus of his desire and in terms of the way in which the fetishist's sexual prop or device hides a history of an encounter with sexual difference, a repudiation of this difference and an ongoing (if concealed) intellectual or theoretical effort to disclaim or disavow this encounter. And Laura Mulvey theorises the 'male' spectator both in terms of a particular object (the woman as star) and in terms of the mechanics of desire attached to this object (involving an alleged interleaving of aggressive fantasy and paranoid anxiety licensed by the darkness of the cinema and the techniques of projection and editing). Any psychoanalytic theory of the cinema must be able to give an account both of cinema as object and of cinema as the instigator of various psychological states. In the cinema, it is not just a matter of the depiction of an erotically charged object (conventionally, the female star); it is also a matter of the processes by which this object comes, if it does, to have erotic, emotional or cognitive significance for viewers.

Object analysis – William Peterson's watching brief in *Manhunter*

This distinction between object and process, between wanting and knowing, is crucial to *Manhunter*. The film's protagonist, Will Graham (William Peterson), is renowned for his ability to feel his way into the minds of murderers, to identify with killers. Traumatised by this experience, contaminated by the ease with which he appears to be able to think and feel as one with murderers, he only reluctantly agrees to return to police work to investigate a series of brutal murders of young families. Watching the families' home movies, Graham tries to find in them clues to what the families have in common, believing that they are killed because of some particular trait they share (appearance, age, family size, affluence, etc.). In the decisive scene of the film, however, he realises that what the families have in common is that they appear in home movies: he has been looking too closely at what the movies depict rather than the fact that they exist as documents. The killer has chosen his victims because he has been able to watch the home movies and thus learn about the habits and environment of the families (it turns out that his occupation is to develop home movies) not because there is anything particularly compelling in the movies. Graham's mistake, thus, is to have confused the object of the movies with the process by which the object is represented and, in turn, perceived.

Manhunter, then, can be said to be exploring several issues of importance to psychoanalysis and film theory: the way in which looking can substitute for or augment more direct forms of sexual behaviour; the conflict between identification and theoretical insight; and the ways in which psychology and sexuality involve more than simply the isolation and recognition of an object. Moreover, *Manhunter* has at its centre the hypothesis that – to be understood – a film (in this case, the home movies) cannot simply be watched: it must also be reflected upon, theorised. Like Will Graham, the spectator is faced with an injunction to see more than just a series of images.

Blade Runner (USA 1982 *p.c* Blade Runner Partnership *d* – Ridley Scott; sd col.)

Total Recall (USA 1990 *p.c* De Laurentiis Entertainment *d* – Paul Verhoeven; sd col.)

Both adapted from the work of seminal science fiction writer Philip K. Dick, the title of the source for *Total Recall* is significant: *We Can Remember It for You Wholesale*. What is being suggested in both book and film is that memories can be a kind of commodity, circulating freely between minds, not indisputably 'owned' by a single individual. In *Blade Runner*, fugitive androids – replicants – are subjected to psychological testing which aims to establish whether what they appear to remember is 'real', actually experienced or artificially implanted. There is a daunting hypothesis here: perhaps the memories that seem to assure the individual of his or her authentic identity are capable of belonging, so to speak, to somebody else – perhaps they are capable of being conveyed from person (or replicant) to person. The enduring enigma of *Blade Runner* involves the question of whether the film's protagonist Deckard (Harrison Ford), who hunts down the replicants, is himself an android.

Slavoj Žižek has compared *Blade Runner* to classical *film noir*:

> Classical *noirs* ... abound with cases of amnesia in which the hero does not know who he is or what he did during his blackout. Yet amnesia is here a deficiency measured by the standard of integration into the field of intersubjectivity, of symbolic community: a successful recollection means that, by way of organizing his life-experience into a consistent narrative, the hero exorcizes the dark demons of the past. But in the universe of *Blade Runner* ... recollection

An authentic identity? Harrison Ford in *Blade Runner*

designates something incomparably more radical: the total loss of the hero's symbolic identity. He is forced to assume that he is not what he thought himself to be, but somebody–something else. (Žižek, 1993, pp. 11–12)

Blade Runner becomes in this way a drama of psychological catastrophe in which the foundations of the personality – memory, emotion, a secure sense of identity – are shaken. As such it lends itself to psychoanalytic readings of various kinds, propounding what amounts to a theory of memory close to the more radical suggestions about personality put forward by Freud and Lacan (for whom memory was never fully commensurate with experience, was always separated in some way from the authentic data of experience).

In *Total Recall* Doug Quaid (Arnold Schwarzenegger) is seen breaking free from a machine used to implant artificially 'memories' of a trip to Mars. Later in the film, now on Mars on the scent of an inter-planetary conspiracy, a doctor tells him that he is existing within the artificial 'reality' of this fabricated trip – he is still on earth, delirious, on the verge of insanity, tied down to the memory-machine. *Total Recall*, apart from being an extremely accomplished entertainment, filled with curiosity about the past and the future, is – as a whole – like a philosophical puzzle. When – if ever – was the memory of the Schwarzenegger character reprogrammed, mixed up with manufactured fictions? Is the entire film a fabricated, recreational remembering? *Total Recall*'s audience is put in the position of *Blade Runner*'s Deckard – who cannot finally be sure of himself – interrogating the film for signs of authentic subjectivity.

began with an apprehension of the human mind at odds with itself, constantly subject to conflicts of meaning, to contrary intentions and contradictory desires. Instead of assuming that the mind is coherently organised and self-identical in such a way that consciousness is absolutely autonomous, Freud insisted on the mind being, in various ways, split, disorganised and uncohesive. By asserting that consciousness is only a superficial and partial quality of mental functioning, Freud attempted to discredit a venerable philosophical tradition which posited judgement, conscious moral choice and intellectually informed belief as virtually the sum of the mind's operations (see Freud, 1991b, pp. 167–73). The hypothesis of the unconscious (and later the superego) called for subjectivity to be reimagined as being always dynamic, internally interactive, habitually duplicitous, caught between sober maturity and impulsive childishness, self-deluding and essentially irreducible to any conscious reflection or self-knowledge.

According to Freud, the human individual is perpetually caught up in a struggle between the recklessness of unconscious drives urgently seeking pleasure, and a rational, socially conditioned capacity for moderation which tends to relinquish the overriding objective of attaining pleasure in favour of a self-preserving pragmatism. So, for example, Freud understood dreams to be products of the interplay between desire and 'censorship' or repression, between socially impermissible sexual ambitions and the learned renunciation of these ambitions. A dream is initiated by a latent wish which, in conditions when conscious restraint is relaxed by sleep, attempts to find fulfilment only to meet with a residual objection from the agency of repression. The outcome of this conflict is the fleeting, confused but potentially revealing images experienced in dreaming. Dreams, a form of internal mental negotiation in the face of conflict, are compromises, half-achieved measures, neither an utter revelation of unconscious desires nor corroboration of the exclusive autonomy of the conscious judgement whose function is to discipline the unconscious. Contrary to some popular misconceptions, psychoanalysis does not portray the individual either as principally possessed by ferocious, irrational sexual appetites or as pre-eminently capable of a constant and disciplined self-awareness; rather, psychoanalysis depicts the human subject as always caught between an excessive, self-destructive preoccupation with pleasure and a practical, realistic knowledge of the potential consequences of pleasure if the quest for it is unrestrained.

Psychoanalysis, consequently, is known as having contributed in some decisive way to what is called the 'decentring of the subject' (see Žižek, p. 351) associated with modernism in European literature and with twentieth-century Continental philosophy. In one important respect, however, it can be said that this characterisation is misleading: there is often no apparent question of any 'decentring' of the psychoanalyst whose business it is to follow the erratic movements of the decentred subject. This is the central paradox of psychoanalysis as a set of explanatory strategies potentially capable of application, a paradox which is very marked in psychoanalytic film theory – which has often appeared not to be threatened by the crises of knowledge and certainty which it habitually attributes to its objects of study.

There are any number of ways of introducing psychoanalytic film theory through the discussion of psychoanalytic concepts as they are used in their original contexts. For the present task, however, discussions of two crucial terms are helpful: Lacan's idea of 'the mirror stage' and Freud's theory of 'fetishism'.

Jacques Lacan: the mirror stage

Lacan's theory of the mirror stage (developed in the 1930s) Lacan, although little acknowledged by psychoanalysts outside France, has been very influential on a wide variety of other disciplines. The premiss of the theory has a great simplicity, in that it deals with a particular moment in which, according to Lacan, subjectivity begins to find a form which is never altogether lost. Between the ages of six and eighteen months, Lacan claims in the essay 'The mirror stage as formative of the function of the I' (1937), the infant catches sight of itself in a reflecting surface, recognises its likeness and is jubilant in the spectacle of its own image. The infant perceives an image (or *Gestalt*, to use Lacan's term) which appears gratifyingly whole and which the infant, entirely incapable either of speech or of controlled movement, can call back to sight or to mind by a mere fixing of the gaze, by staring forward at its reflection.

This experience is, for Lacan, the individual's first 'identification', the first moments in which the individual becomes aware of his or her status as a self-recognising, thinking subject. In identifying with an image, the individual at once notices and acknowledges himself or herself, and covets the apparent unity of the image: identifying (in the sense of noticing) the image and, ambitiously and longingly, identifying *with* the image.

Lacan insisted on the element of delusion which structures the act of self-recognition: for the image is only an image, external to the perceiving subject even if it is a replica of the subject. The image appears to be the individual, but is in fact only a representation of the individual. It is useful here to distinguish between the effectively ungendered, pre-subjective 'infant' ('it') and the 'individual' or 'subject' ('he or she'). For Lacan 'this jubilant assumption of ... [a] specular image by the child' (Lacan, 1993, p. 38) is what constitutes the ego, what allows for the fabrication of the individual mind. Lacan wrote in his essay of 'the *méconnaissances* [misrecognitions] that constitute the ego, the illusion of autonomy to which it entrusts itself' (Lacan, 1993, p. 38). The ego, that is to say, is formed in a specious performance of mastery, in which the individual gets a sense of autonomy only by contemplating an external image and – narcissistically, out of a primal self-love – denying that it is external.

Thus, for Lacan, subjective 'identity' is always confounded by an original experience of misrecognition; the sense of 'identity' gained in front of the mirror occurs only in terms of an 'other' (the reflected image, which will be the prototype for other love-objects). To use Lacan's words: '[i]t is this moment that decisively tips the whole of human knowledge into mediatization through the desire of the other, constitutes its objects in an abstract equivalence by the co-operation of others' (Lacan, in Easthope, 1993, p. 37).

Lacan's writings are difficult and demanding, and this should not be downplayed. Althusser, for one, praised Lacan for the elaborate, contorted quality of his prose, sensing in it a revolutionary tenor. And, indeed, the appeal of Lacanianism for anglophone intellectuals in the 1970s (and afterwards) no doubt stemmed to some extent from the allure of its dense, involved argumentation. Lacan's texts offer both the characteristically psychoanalytic promise of a masterful insight into the delusions of human behaviour as well as a daunting rhetorical surface which appears to require a gratifying endeavour of intellectual initiation.

The short summary presented above is relatively restricted; two points, however, are crucial for film theory. First, of course, Lacan's emphasis on a thrilling visual experience, a relationship to an image appearing on a reflective surface is something which lends itself to accounts of the visual dimension of film-going. Second, the emphasis on *knowledge* is important – or rather, in this case, the emphasis on the self-defeating, illusory foundations of subjective knowledge. In front of the mirror, the individual is at once comforted in a sense of egoistic autonomy and visual mastery *and* duped, mocked by the doubling, splitting or distancing which is required if an image is to kindle in the individual the first fantasies of a knowing, intelligent self-recognition. Film theorists have been, and continue to be, interested in pointing out that narrative cinema offers a gratifyingly cogent kind of knowledge (in, for instance, its ordered plotting) but only by distracting attention from the extent to which this cogency is made up of disjoined images (whose fragmentary origins are disguised by camera viewpoints and editing techniques). Lacan's theory is exemplary of two crucial features of psychoanalytic thinking widely relevant to film theory: the conception of the simultaneous coexistence of activity and passivity, of mastery and powerlessness, of autonomy and doubling; and the insistence that conscious knowledge is related in an indissociable way to imaginary, fictitious scenarios and emotional longings. Lacan writes that 'the agency of the ego' is situated by the mirror image 'in a fictional direction' such that the 'I' is in 'discordance ... with reality' (Lacan, in Easthope, 1993, p. 34).

Sigmund Freud: fetishism and male sexual anxiety

This same thematic of a misguided knowledge structuring subjectivity can also be found in Freud's 1927 essay on 'Fetishism' – although it should be noted that Freud was more confident than Lacan about the extent to which the individual is able to make good the deluded intuitions of childhood. For Freud, fetishism is both a kind of sexual behaviour and a form of thinking, a way of ordering knowledge. The sexual behaviour referred to is the substitution by an adult male of an object or particular part of the body for the female genitals as the focus of sexual desire: the fetishist seeks to create scenarios of sexual pleasure in which the object of his desire is, for example, the nose or foot, or a certain fabric or article of clothing. In doing this, the fetishist succeeds in participating in the format of heterosexual, reproductive sexual activity through a kind of inventive mimicry or parody; the fetishist succeeds, according to Freud, in 'fend[ing] ... off' homosexuality (Freud, 1993, p. 29).

Instead of rejecting 'femininity' (that is, the woman's body) altogether, the fetishist 'over-values' and exploits aspects of, or adjuncts to, the female body in the pursuit of sexual pleasure. As such, according to Freud, the fetishist has a difficult and problematic relationship with women. He picks and chooses those aspects of 'femininity' which excite him, in a peculiarly selfish, narcissistic variant of sexuality. Freud explained this by describing the notional causes of a fetishistic object-choice, causes which he located in a young boy's seeing of a woman's (initially, according to Freud, his mother's) genitals. This sight is a traumatic experience for the boy, in that it intimates 'castration': the woman's lack of a penis is taken by the boy to denote a threat of castration. In the face of this, the future fetishist

> refused to take cognizance of the fact that a woman does not possess a penis. No, that could not be true: for if a woman had been castrated, then his own possession of a penis was in danger; and against that there rose in rebellion the portion of his narcissism which Nature has, as a precaution, attached to that particular organ. (Freud, 1993, p. 28)

The boy whom Freud described deals with this apparent threat by ignoring it in the very process of being traumatised by it. The intellectual act of disavowal of the reality of sexual difference which this involves is enabled by the creation of a fetish. For Freud, a fetish is simply a substitute for the penis which the woman lacks: the fetish is a symbolic, artificial or prosthetic genital organ. The boy understands the reality of sexual difference in an intuitive way but, unable to reconcile this difference with his narcissistic sense of danger, achieves a kind of compromise between intuition and anxiety in the form of a fetish-object which will later allow him at once to recognise and to ignore sexual difference:

> Yes, in his mind the woman *has* got a penis, in spite of everything; but this penis is no longer the same as it was before. Something else has taken its place, has been appointed its substitute, as it were, and now inherits the interest which was formerly directed to its predecessor. But this interest suffers an extraordinary increase as well, because the horror of castration has set up a memorial to itself in the creation of this substitute. Furthermore, an aversion, which is never absent in any fetishist, to the real female genitals remains a *stigma indelebile* [an indelible sign] of the repression that has taken place. We can see now what the fetish achieves and what it is that maintains it. It remains a token of tri-

> umph over the threat of castration and a protection against it. It also saves the fetishist from becoming a homosexual, by endowing women with the characteristic which makes them tolerable as sexual objects. (Freud, 1993, p. 29)

Freud's short account of fetishism weaves together several major psychoanalytic concerns and, as such, readers will be able to make an estimate of the value and interest of psychoanalysis on the basis of it. What is perhaps most fundamental about it is the way in which it shows both how intellectual processes are complicated by sexuality and, conversely, how sexual behaviour involves certain kinds of knowledge. What Freud called 'infantile sexual research' (and he means generally, but not exclusively, a boy's investigations into sexual characteristics) is the activity in which the individual's future sexual behaviour is formed, but also in which the individual's habits of thinking and understanding begin to be learned. The intellectual, cognitive aspect of fetishism (involving an inventive defence against a sexual shock) is, to a certain extent, exemplary of thinking as psychoanalysis conceives of it. Thinking is, according to Freud, bound up with sexuality, and more especially with sexual anxiety in the face of sexual difference and 'the threat of castration' (the themes of anxiety and the fear of dismemberment connect Freud's essay directly with Lacan's on the mirror stage). But, according to a similar logic, the transition from childhood sexual research to mature sexual behaviour cannot be separated off from the kinds of knowledge and understanding acquired and experienced in this process of transition. The fetishist deals, in however idiosyncratic a way, with the conflict between a knowledge of sexual difference and a narcissistic refusal of the fact of sexual difference. The fetishist is peculiar in his particular solution to this conflict, but psychoanalysis suggests that fetishism is not so different from other behaviours or states of mind in its negotiation between desire and anxiety, on the one hand, and knowledge and habits of understanding, on the other.

Sexuality and knowledge

If knowledge is understood to be inseparable from sexuality then it becomes necessary not only to interrogate the sexual overtones of particular forms of knowledge but also to maintain the question of knowledge – of theory, we might say – as being fundamental to sexual behaviour in its overt, but also in its decontextualised, manifestations (such as the notional manifestation of desire and anxiety in film-going). In film theory, there has been a tendency to emphasise sexuality and its roots in infantile vulnerability at the expense of the problem of the acquisition and complicated ordering of knowledge, and particularly to emphasise the regression to infantile forms of sexuality which is allegedly apparent, as we shall see in the next section, in film spectatorship. The feminist assault on narrative cinema in the 1970s was importantly linked to the proposition that film-going involves not, as it were, an innocent aesthetic experience or a simple involvement with narrative plotting but a re-enactment of, a reminder of, male sexual anxiety – that the understanding called for by narrative cinema involves a fear of women, disguised fetishistically as a controlled celebration of the female star, that narrative cinema invokes and then compensates for fears of castration (see Feminist film theory, p. 354).

This emphasis was, no doubt, faithful to the psychoanalytic project, whose formulation depended on the 'discovery' of infantile sexuality. However, despite the fact that the concern with the theme of sexual difference which emerged in film studies in the 1970s as a result of the alliance of feminism and psychoanalysis can be said to have consolidated film theory as a distinct and important intellectual discipline, the enthusiasm with which male sexual pathologies were claimed necessarily to dominate the formal and experiential qualities of narrative film remains problematic and finally unproductive.

APPLICATIONS

During the emergence of psychoanalytic film theory, a large number of writers were concerned to justify two propositions. On the one hand there was a concern to argue that the experience of cinema involves a regression to an infantile state of immobility and powerlessness – in the dark, sitting down, the spectator is trapped in a certain way, unable (like an infant) to influence the events being played out on the screen. On the other hand, however, was an argument that this position of powerlessness and restricted movement implies an energetic, sadistic act of watching which – in all but effect – suggests sexually motivated violence and a fantasy of the exercise of power.

Apparatus theory: Christian Metz and Jean-Louis Baudry

According to theorists like Metz and Baudry, then, to watch a film in a cinema is to be seduced, encouraged to regress furtively to a childhood state where fantasy is permitted free rein. Some quotations will give a flavour of this argument. Metz is drawn, in 'Story/discourse notes on two kinds of voyeurism', to use an unexpected if not entirely appropriate image in order to describe the cinematically induced infantile state. The film actor, according to Metz, 'lives in a kind of aquarium' (Metz, 1985, p. 547). And, Metz's essay continued,

> There are fish on the other side as well, their faces pressed to the glass, like the poor of Balbec watching the guests of the grand hotel having their meals. The feast, once again, is not shared – it is a furtive feast and not a festive feast. Spectator-fish, taking in everything with their eyes, nothing with their bodies: the institution of the cinema requires a silent, motionless spectator, a *vacant* spectator, constantly in sub-motor and hyper-perceptive state, a spectator at once alienated and happy, acrobatically hooked up to himself by the invisible thread of sight, a spectator who only catches up with himself at the last minute, by a paradoxical identification with his own self, a self filtered out into pure vision. We are not referring here to the spectator's identification with the characters of the film (which is secondary), but to his preliminary identification with the (invisible) seeing agency of the film itself as discourse, as the agency which *puts forward* the story and shows it to us. Insofar as it abolishes all traces of the subject of the enunciation [i.e. the camera, camera-operator or projectionist], the traditional film succeeds in giving the spectator the impression that he is himself that subject. (Metz, 1985, p. 548)

For Metz, any pragmatic awareness in the film-goer of his or her extraneous role with regard to the cinematic spectacle and its narrative progress is suspended in favour of an immersion in the free-play of fantasy. As the spectator settles into immobility, as if once again harnessed like an infant, he or she, steadily oblivious to this immobility, allows any conscious check on fantasy to slip away. This lull in attention occurs because the cinematic spectacle begins to appear aligned almost exclusively to the individual spectator's viewpoint; the spectator, ignoring the actual situation of film-going (being part of a group in an auditorium) as well as the artificiality of cinema's narrative techniques (camera movement, editing, lighting, *mise-en-scène*, etc.) succumbs to a lascivious, covetous, 'furtive' belief in his or her principal role in observing, and by extension in controlling or directing, the narrative progression of the film. A primordial fantasy of omnipotence is claimed, then, to overtake the motionless spectator. The 'vacant' spectator – emptied of critical, conscious knowledge – yields, in Metz's view, to an indulgent fantasy-state in which the conscious self has all but disintegrated ('filtered out into pure vision'), allowing the unconscious (the 'id') utter control of the spectating personality.

Metz went on, indeed, to compare this condition of 'pure vision' to the mirror stage, pointing out however – and quite rightly – that the spectator is not confronted with 'his' own image:

> The primary identification is no longer constructed around a subject-object, but around a pure, all-seeing and invisible subject, the vanishing-point of the monocular perspective which cinema has taken over from painting . . . All that remains is the brute fact of seeing: the seeing of an outlaw, of an *Id* unrelated to any *Ego*. (Metz, 1985, p. 548)

Recalling the emphasis made earlier on the intimacy of sexuality and knowledge, it can be noted here that if the id, the unconscious, is the 'reservoir' (to use a term of Freud's) of libidinal energy out of which arise the sexual drives, then the ego is, among other things, the place of conscious knowledge, the mental agency which intellectually inhibits the excessive overflowing of fantasy and sexual ambition. Metz's essay was typical of an early mode of writing about film influenced by psychoanalysis in that it insists on the absolute priority in film spectatorship of the unconscious. The cinema becomes in this account intrinsically licentious, sanctioning the resurgence of desire over conscious awareness and understanding.

What Metz's account lacked was any attention not only to notionally mature modes of film-going but also to any variability in the kinds of mental state provoked by film (see Cowie, 1984). Although the theories of Freud and Lacan are acutely attentive to the psychological vestiges of infantilism and the mind's readiness to give way to illicit opportunities of pleasure, it must be emphasised again that these theories are also attentive to the insistence with which the adult mind resists giving way to such opportunities. It is worth concentrating very briefly on Metz's choice of words in the passage quoted above. For there was another privileged viewpoint in his essay, along with the film-goer's 'pure vision': there was, that is to say, the critical viewpoint of the theorist. While refusing to the spectator a critical purchase on the cinematic spectacle, Metz the theorist claimed a kind of ultimate diagnostic knowledge which was, quite explicitly, imagined as being judgemental or juridical. In this essay the theorist employing psychoanalysis in order to denounce the surreptitious pleasures of the film-goer set himself up in a privileged position to point out and denounce the 'outlaw' – as if some kind of legal authority or officially sanctioned knowledge were at his disposal.

Baudry, in another pivotal essay, 'Ideological Effects of the Basic Cinematographic Apparatus' (1970), also invoked the mirror stage (although somewhat more indiscriminately than Metz), and was equally prone to florid language which revealed the critical blind spot of the film theorist identified as if with the authority of the psychoanalyst or law-enforcer:

> No doubt the darkened room and the screen bordered with black like a letter of condolence already present privileged conditions of effectiveness [for the performance of 'ideological effects'] – no exchange, no circulation, no communication with any outside. Projection and reflection take place in a closed space, and those who remain there, whether they know it or not (*but they do not*), find themselves *chained, captured, or captivated*. (Baudry, 1992, p. 309, emphases added)

In order to argue that the film spectator regresses to the world of childhood where fantasies of omnipotence compensate for an actual powerlessness, Metz and Baudry needed to claim that the faculty of conscious criticism and intuitive interpretation are disabled as part of the workings of the cinematic 'apparatus', while nonetheless employing just this critical faculty to come to this conclusion.

Laura Mulvey

The use of terms and concepts derived from psychoanalysis in the attempt to theorise the experience of spectatorship received an important fillip with the intervention of feminist theorists in debates about the unconscious components of film-going and the element of 'visual pleasure' in the experience of classic narrative cinema (see Feminist film theory, p. 353). The key text in this intervention is Laura Mulvey's 'Visual Pleasure and Narrative Cinema') which, apart from being a model of lucidity and theoretical economy, has remained the most referred to anglophone text in film studies (see discussion above). Drawing on the Freudian theory of fetishism (but with the circumspection about psychoanalysis mentioned earlier), Mulvey invoked certain distinctions to be found in Freud's work – between, notably, the 'active' pleasure of observing another human form ('scopophilia') and the less interactive pleasure of narcissistic self-regard (involving a gratifying reinforcement of the ego) – in order to describe film-going as involving not only 'temporary loss of ego' but also an (illusory) shoring up of the ego in the seemingly autonomous contemplation of an image (involving once more an identification with the camera or projector).

Whereas Metz's account tended to the bodiless abstraction of 'pure vision', Mulvey's feminist concerns allowed her to inflect the theme of the different orders of regressive fantasy notionally at stake in film-going with a specific observation concerning the way in which women are placed in the narrative and filmic (or 'pro-filmic') structure of classic narrative film (Budd Boetticher is quoted in this respect in Mulvey's essay, to telling effect). For Mulvey, the powerful look of the camera with which the spectator identifies jubilantly is directed at the figure of a woman who, in narrative terms also, is thus given a place only as what is observed and controlled. Mulvey coins the term, 'to-be-looked-at-ness' (Mulvey, 1989, p. 19); the woman is observed and controlled by the camera, the spectator, and the film's male protagonists.

Taking the feminist concern with patriarchy's subjugation and objectification of women to the context of the pleasures in looking which apparatus theory had posited as informing film spectatorship, Mulvey was able to extrapolate a theory of film spectatorship based on Freud's account of the development of the male child, and particularly on the threat posed to this development by the fact of sexual difference. So, for Mulvey, the cinema constantly re-enacts the crisis of castration anxiety provoked in the male child by the sight of the female genitals but, rather than facilitating the overcoming of this crisis in the acceptance and understanding of sexual difference, narrative cinema replays and redeploys it, unresolved, by instigating in the spectator the disordered knowledge of the fetishist, who adores the sexual object which he rejects as anything other than an opportunity for displaced sexual satisfaction. Thus, for Mulvey, determining the psychological 'acrobatics' of film-going (to modify Metz's term) is the historical fact of patriarchy which informs, and is reinforced by, narrative cinema.

Mulvey summarised her argument in the following way:

> The scopophilic instinct (pleasure in looking at another person as an erotic object), and, in contradistinction, ego libido (forming identification processes) act as formations, mechanisms, which this cinema ['traditional narrative film'] has played on. The image of woman as (passive) raw material for the (active) gaze of man takes the argument a step further into the structure of representation, adding a further layer demanded by the ideology of the patriarchal order as it is worked out in its favourite cinematic form – illusionistic narrative film. The argument returns again to the psychoanalytic background in that woman as representation signifies castration, inducing voyeuristic and fetishistic mechanisms to circumvent her threat. None of these interacting layers is intrinsic to film, but it is only in the film form that they can reach a perfect and beautiful contradiction, thanks to the possibility in the cinema of shifting the emphasis of the look. It is the place of the look that defines cinema, the possibility of varying it and exposing it. This is what makes cinema quite different in its voyeuristic potential

> from, say, strip-tease, theatre, shows, etc. Going far beyond highlighting a woman's to-be-looked-at-ness, cinema builds the way she is to be looked at into the spectacle itself. Playing on the tension between film as controlling the dimension of time (editing, narrative) and film as controlling the dimension of space (changes in distance, editing), cinematic codes create a gaze, a world, and an object, thereby producing an illusion cut to the measure of desire. It is these cinematic codes and their relationship to formative external structures that must be broken down before mainstream film and the pleasure it provides can be challenged. (Mulvey, 1989, p. 25)

Mulvey's intervention consolidated the psychoanalytic initiatives of theorists like Baudry, Metz and others by raising the questions of gender and sexual difference as these questions were articulated in feminist thinking. The great advantage of her approach was to provide a theoretical account which was not entirely abstract but which referred to social conditions as well as (and perhaps more importantly) to particular film texts. But, even though Mulvey was more sensitive to the detail of psychoanalytic theory than either Metz or Baudry, and more rigorous in pointing out that psychoanalytic descriptions involve paradoxical accounts of subjective experience (both voyeuristic 'activity' and narcissism, in this case), her account nevertheless claimed film-going to imply necessarily a 'subject-positioning' at once pruriently male (a woman film-goer was equally bound, according to this theory, to assume a 'male' viewpoint as man; see Mulvey, 1989, pp. 29–38) and, because of the regression claimed to be involved, divested of critical intelligence. Mulvey, it should be noted, was quite frank about her opinion that narrative cinema had to be overthrown as part of the feminist project – since this cinema did not allow for an emancipated, intellectual look; or if it did, this look was restricted to the film theorist.

One of the near contemporary objections to Mulvey's account of film-going was that it left little room for a (feminist, or even feminine) practice of enlightened, critically emancipated spectatorship to be thought of as part of the quotidian experience of narrative cinema (see Feminist film theory, p. 355). Mulvey's account, that is to say, has been regarded as inflexible, sceptical of the variability and idiosyncrasies of the experience of watching films and of the possibility that spectators derive mature, non-aggressive pleasure from this experience. Mulvey has responded to this objection with characteristic critical rigour, and in later work has elaborated her earlier theories in a rich blend of psychoanalysis, Marxism and narrative analysis, which does not abandon the initial goal of feminist film criticism: to understand how the signifying mechanisms in narrative cinema are capable, through their manipulation of mental states, of complicity in the historical perpetuation of social imbalance and, with this understanding, 'to discover a distance from ["the Hollywood screen"] ... that then brought its own rewards of intellectual curiosity and pleasure' (1996, p. 27). The question does remain, however, whether these rewards are more commonplace, more integral to film-going, than some film theory allows.

The delirious theoretical machine

The charge levelled at apparatus theory of being excessively mechanistic has been cogently expressed by Joan Copjec in a short essay, 'The Delirium of Clinical Perfection' (1986), in which she remarked: '[d]oesn't this theory of the cinematic institution provide an imprisonment rather than a release?' (Copjec, 1986, p. 61). Copjec's essay, which consisted principally in a commentary on the citation by feminist writers of Michel Foucault's theories, is not primarily concerned with any particular psychoanalytic paradigm (although Lacan is discussed). However, the questions it posed pertain directly to the relation between psychoanalysis and theories of cinema:

> My question is not whether or not the gaze is male, for I know that it certainly is. While it is clearly important to remark on a certain social ordering which rakishly tilts the axis of seeing so that privilege piles up on the side of the male, it is a slip, and enormously problematic to posit something like a gaze, an idealized point from which the film can be looked at. Defined in this way ... such a gaze can only be male. My question is prior to this other; I would ask, instead, if there is a gaze. (Copjec, 1986, p. 61)

What is crucial to this argument, or rather to these questions, is the suggestion that it is the particular *theory* in question which causes narrative cinema to be understood as allowing for only one, essentially fixed position from which to spectate. If theory is used mechanistically (as a 'tool' or a 'weapon') it may be that it necessarily generates images of itself in its accounts of aesthetic experience – that mechanisms, apparatuses, machines and divinely impersonal gazes begin to appear everywhere.

This suggestion is absolutely decisive for the development of psychoanalytically preoccupied film theory; it amounts to a paradigm shift in which film studies, in aiming for a more flexible and unpredetermined relation between theory, critical insight and aesthetic experience, becomes – for better or worse – disillusioned with the 1970s ambition to understand the formal and experiential elements in cinematic discourse and film-going systematically and absolutely. The way in which the relationship between film studies and psychoanalysis has been reconfigured, and the reasons for this reconfiguration, have been very well expressed by Mary Anne Doane in 'Remembering Women: Psychical and Historical Constructions in Film Theory':

> What is it that theory hopes to accomplish? What is its function? And, more specifically, what is the role of theory and the relation to its object in psychoanalysis? Apparatus theory rests on the assumption that what psychoanalysis lends to film theory is a kind of map, or even a cognitive machine. Psychoanalysis is the science of the unconscious; the cinema clearly appeals to the unconscious; therefore, psychoanalysis must be able to give us the laws of its discursive formation. The map can simply be laid over the new terrain. The desire of the analyst, which would require the replacement of the notion of the cognitive machine by that of the encounter, is rarely taken into account. Yet, psychoanalysis itself proposes the fragility of any theoretical construct, its affinity with paranoia and delirium, and hence the problematic status of knowledge and of he who purports to know. In other words, psychoanalysis must be contaminated by its own theorized but simultaneously untheorizable object – the unconscious. (Doane, 1990, p. 55)

The force of this argument lies in its questioning of what film theory involves as a kind of understanding and in its suggestion that film theory has its own predilections – and, even, its own repository of furtive and disguised pleasures. In one sense, this questioning is preliminary to the writing of theoretical accounts of film-going; but, historically, it has been possible only in the wake of the unself-questioning theories of the 1970s. By positing a necessary relationship between the way in which psychoanalysis is used in film theory (a methodological point) and the description of spectatorship which results, Doane called for a reflection on methodology which promises not only a substantial inquiry into the nature of psychoanalysis as a form of explanation of mental functioning but also – and as a consequence – a theory of the cinema which foregrounds the issue of reflection (that is, the issue of critical intelligence, rather than of spectacle) as potentially a crucial part of film spectatorship.

Doane's argument undermined the autonomy and purity of psychoanalytic film theory by suggesting that the act or effort of theorisation is not set apart from the mental dynamics which it attempts to describe. Even if film theory is taken to be something which occurs after and away from the experience of actually watching films, if it occurs in calmer, less emotionally involved circumstances, it is nevertheless a procedure of thought – specific, improvised, speculative, tied into particular fixtures of knowledge and individual experience – which, like all thought as far as psychoanalysis is concerned, cannot be detached from the turbulent and conflicting currents of mental life. If, arguably, there is no such thing as the utterly 'vacant' spectator or the spectator fully regressed to the childhood combination of powerlessness, sexual anxiety and aggressive fantasies of omnipotence, nor is there a state of theorisation which is not 'contaminated by its own theorized but simultaneously untheorizable object – the unconscious', to use Doane's apt formulation. Film theory and film spectatorship involve altogether more variable and complicated states of mind, more intricate intersections of desire and understanding than has often been allowed.

These arguments should be taken to apply at once to the experience of film-going and to the endeavour of theorising film. Or, rather, what is necessary is to consider how spectatorship and theory are, at certain moments, radically inseparable. It would be consonant with psychoanalytic insight to make two parallel assertions concerning the states of mind involved in the exposure to cinema. On the one hand, it can be said that film-going is not so much a surreptitious but uninhibited and decadent carnival of repressed, socially impermissible desires as a tense internal drama of forms of knowing and ways of feeling in which intellect, experience, memory and indications of sexual behaviour alternatively unravel and become reconfigured. On the other hand, film theory is not a clinical, aloof, quasi-juridical activity of diagnosis and reproach, so much as an interpretative process mixed up with pleasure and ambition which is never quite loosened from the film-goer's heightened experience of the interlocking of emotion and intellect. To put these assertions another way, it can be suggested that as the film-goer is, to a greater or lesser degree, an experienced theorist, so the film-theorist is, to a greater or lesser degree, a covert pleasure-seeker.

RETURNING TO FREUD

Alternative methodologies, new dangers

If the psychoanalytically informed work of Baudry, Metz, Mulvey and others in the 1970s led to an impasse, it nevertheless framed the agenda of film studies in a fundamental way, establishing complex modes of theorising as integral to the interpretation of cinema, introducing the problems of pathology and of the psychical investment in narrative into an area of study which would be the poorer without attention to them.

But if the impasse to which the first instances of psychoanalytic film theory led was in part a question of a restricted conception of mental functioning in the face of a complex cultural form, this is not therefore to suggest that the elision of psychoanalysis and film theory was or is misguided. Rather, it has become a matter of altering the methodological basis of psychoanalytic film theory from an interpretative practice which presupposed psychoanalytic concepts as critical 'tools' or political 'weapons' to an interpretative practice which interrogates the concepts which it employs. Instead of using psychoanalysis to understand film, film and psychoanalysis are, in subsequent work, used to explain and question one another simultaneously. This quizzical orientation in psychoanalytic film theory has proved to be singularly productive and has led to different accounts of cinema based on theories of subjectivity derived from a less unquestioning appropriation of psychoanalysis, including work based on psychoanalytic theories other than those of Freud and Lacan (see Creed, 1993; Donald, 1989; Studlar, 1992).

While this orientation suggests a vigorous and productive reappraisal of the relationship between psychoanalytic theory and film criticism which promises significant rewards, a note of caution should be sounded: early psychoanalytic film studies coincided with a moment of cogent political argument which sustained, for example, *Screen*'s theoretical polemic at a time when film studies had no real place within educational institutions. Whatever may be said against 1970s film theory, its influence was extraordinarily widespread and compulsive as a result of its combination in equal measure of intense theoretical and political engagement. Now that film studies has real institutional presence internationally (to the extent of risking being too widespread, heterogeneous and dispersed), there is a danger that, less easily tied into a political rationale, theoretical initiatives will increasingly lack urgency and energy. Film studies must retain an enthusiasm for serious and advanced theoretical projects and remain confident in the importance of cinema as a cultural form heavy with meaning. The danger is that the loss of the rousing context of 1970s political idealism in the face of the disastrous (in Britain, at least) social and educational changes of the 1980s and 1990s may have created conditions favourable to intellectual mediocrity.

Slavoj Žižek: inside the subject

The best of more contemporary psychoanalytically informed film theory and criticism involves at once an inquiry into the conceptual complexity of psychoanalytic texts, the exegesis of a very wide range of films (from Hollywood genre films to works of Third Cinema to early silent film), and a consequent revision of the terms of debate in film theory. One of the most notable exponents of this new kind of work is the Slovenian thinker Slavoj Žižek, whose ongoing project is apparent from the title of a collection of essays he has edited: *Everything You Always Wanted to Know about Lacan (But Were Afraid to Ask Hitchcock)* (1992).

Žižek's habitual way of theorising is to attempt to explain concepts from Lacan and Freud (as well as earlier European thinkers) in terms of moments in well-known Hollywood films and other works of popular culture. As a consequence of this practice, Žižek argues for the strangeness and sophistication of narrative film (even its unexpected theoretical complexity), while proposing a revisionary account of psychoanalysis and its interpretation of subjectivity. His work, which emerges from a Slovenian intellectual milieu which has been to some extent independent of the most conspicuous trends in European and North American film studies, involves an enticing rearrangement of the priorities of film theory in an academic climate in which the analysis of film is increasingly integral to a variety of older disciplines. (Žižek's interests extend to postmodernism, theories of ideology and political systems, to the study of which he also brings film.)

In the early days of psychoanalytic film studies the view that psychoanalytic concepts could be appropriated wholesale and then subordinated to different political and critical projects meant that the resulting theories were schematic and mechanistic both in their methodology and in their accounts of subjectivity. But the development of the collaboration between psychoanalysis and the study of cinema has meant that critical methods have evolved so that the study of cultural forms is less a matter of straightforward application of theory to text within a polemical context and more a question of the simultaneous negotiation between texts and theories: the result is a more nuanced account of the relationships between culture, history, social change and subjective experience which exhibits the accrued benefits of reinterpreting psychoanalysis through the study of cinema. When psychoanalytic texts are returned to and inspected often, they turn out to be stranger, more unstable and sophisticated than one might suppose from the condensations of psychoanalysis which are serviceable as critical 'tools'.

So, Žižek, questioning certain received characterisations of Lacanian theory (comparable to Metz's version of Lacanianism) at the end of his remarkable 1991 book, *Looking Awry: An Introduction to Jacques Lacan through Polpular Culture*, gives the following account of the psychoanalytic theory of subjectivity which at once reinterprets psychoanalysis and offers alternatives to received paradigms in film studies:

> The point of Freud's 'Copernican turn' is *not* to demonstrate that the subject is ultimately a puppet in the hands of unknown forces that escape his grasp (unconscious drives, etc.). It does not improve things to exchange this naive,

Hollywood does Freud, in Fritz Lang's *Woman in the Window* (1944)

> naturalist notion of the unconscious for a more sophisticated notion of the unconscious as 'discourse of the great Other' that makes the subject the place where language itself speaks, i.e., an agency subjected to decentered signifying mechanisms [for example, the cinematic apparatus or institution]. Despite some Lacanian propositions that echo this structuralist notion, this sort of 'decentering' does not capture the objective of Lacan's 'return to Freud.' According to Lacan, Freud is far from proposing an image of man as victim of 'irrational' drives . . . [H]e assumes without restraint the fundamental gesture of the Enlightenment: a refusal of the external authority of tradition and a reduction of the subject to an empty, formal point of negative self-relation. The problem is that, by 'circulating around itself', as its own sun, this autonomous subject encounters in itself something 'more than itself', a strange body in its very center. . . . The subject is perhaps nothing but a name for this circular movement, for this distance toward the Thing which is 'too hot' to be approached closely. It is because of this Thing that the subject resists universalization, that it cannot be reduced to a place – even if it is an empty place – in the symbolic order. (Žižek, 1991, p. 169)

If the question which continues to be addressed by psychoanalytically informed film theory and criticism concerns the psychological processes which contribute to the experience of cinema, Žižek's work suggests some responses which deserve further exploration. If the subject is thought of as 'circulating around itself' rather than always on the point of being overcome by the unconscious in such a way that conscious knowledge is disarmed, this might suggest a description of film spectatorship involving a subtle subjective movement, made up of ambivalent pleasures and identifications, of disturbing anxieties, but also of important compensatory kinds of knowledge and insight.

Žižek's remarks about subjectivity are akin to, but irreducible to, the theories of subjectivity which underpinned some of the earlier psychoanalytic interpretations of cinema discussed in this essay. By imagining subjectivity in terms of an unapproachable impediment, something obtrusive 'inside' the self, Žižek invites us to think of the elaborate interiority of subjectivity, of the mind's intricate spaces where passion and insight, despair and resolution, adult understanding and infantile abandon meet, conflict and interact. Instead of describing subjectivity as prone to the sudden, trance-like, overwhelming rule of unconscious impulses, Žižek (via Lacan) recollects the premisses of Freud's work. And when these premisses are conscientiously revisited it is possible both to see the limitations of the psychoanalytic paradigms which film theory once adopted and to sense how these paradigms can be developed.

For example, it is fruitful to consider the problem of memory and the history of personal experience as they pertain to filmgoing and film theory. Film could be said to reach into the resources of memory, to touch the residues of experience, in a way particularly acute for art. In watching and thinking about films, we become subject to indications of the past and to depictions of personalities which are often intelligible only if we have some conception of how general processes of mental functioning and formation are always interfered with by unique occurrences, sensations and experiences. Because of this, the cinema can be traumatic, it can come 'too close to home'; but equally it can be inspiring or revelatory. Even if a film is simply banal, uninteresting or entertaining, it is capable of generating profoundly complicated psychological responses. And this complexity can be theorised, at least in an initial way, in terms not of the captivity in which the cinematic apparatus holds the spectator but of the inner idiosyncrasies of spectatorial states of mind.

Historically, film theory has overemphasised a restricted account of fantasy and sexuality. By adding the problem of knowledge to the analysis of sexuality which is in place in film studies, the field can be opened up to new insights and a new vocabulary which carries theoretical weight as well as psychoanalytic integrity: alongside voyeurism, identification, fetishism, the sadistic gaze, the mirror stage (not to mention the spectator fish) are other intellectual and emotional phenomena which come into play in the experience of cinema: intuition, understanding, remembering, personal histories of pleasure and so on. And these additional phenomena are proper topics for further theorising.

Summarising, then, psychoanalysis has played, and continues to play, a crucial role in the study of film. Psychoanalysis allowed film theory to attain a polemical and theoretical distinctiveness and continues to be bound up with the development of film studies. By considering psychoanalysis in this context, it is possible to gain an important insight into the history of film theory as well as to evaluate its methodological and conceptual foundations. But the future of psychoanalytic film studies consists in travelling backwards and forwards between theoretical and cinematic texts so that film and psychoanalysis, two of the most distinctively twentieth-century discourses (and arguably the two most significant), are opened up to each other in a continual movement of mutual questioning, reinterpretation and theorisation.

Selected Reading

Elizabeth Cowie, *Representing the Woman: Cinema and Psychoanalysis*, London, Macmillan, 1997.

Anthony Easthope (ed.), *Contemporary Film Theory*, Harrow, Longman, 1993. This collection reprints key articles by Freud, Lacan and Laura Mulvey.

Stepthen Heath, *Questions of Cinema*, London, Macmillan, 1981.

E. Ann Kaplan (ed.), *Psychoanalysis and Cinema*, London, Routledge, 1990.

Vicky Lebeau, *Lost Angels: Psychoanalysis and Cinema*, London, Routledge, 1995.

Christian Metz, *The Imaginary Signifier: Psychoanalysis and Cinema*, trans. by Celia Britton, Annwyl Williams, Ben Brewster and Alford Guzzetti, London, Macmillan, 1982.

Laura Mulvey, *Visual and Other Pleasures*, London, Macmillan, 1989.

Slavoj Žižek, *Looking Awry: An Introduction to Jacques Lacan through Popular Culture*, London, MIT Press, 1992.

The 'guilt' of the woman – *Marnie*

FEMINIST FILM THEORY

Feminism is a social movement which has had an enormous impact on film theory and criticism. Cinema is taken by feminists to be a cultural practice representing myths about women and femininity, as well as about men and masculinity. Issues of representation and spectatorship are central to feminist film theory and criticism. Early feminist criticism was directed at stereotypes of women, mostly in Hollywood films (Haskell, 1973/1987; Rosen, 1973). Such fixed and endlessly repeated images of women were considered to be objectionable distortions which would have a negative impact on the female spectator. Hence, the call for positive images of women in cinema. Soon, however, the insight dawned that positive images were not enough to change underlying structures in film. Feminist critics tried to understand the all-pervasive power of patriarchal imagery with the help of structuralist theoretical frameworks such as semiotics and psychoanalysis. These theoretical discourses have proved very productive in analysing the ways in which sexual difference is encoded in classical narrative. For over a decade, psychoanalysis was to be the dominant paradigm in feminist film theory. More recently there has been a move away from a binary understanding of sexual difference to multiple perspectives, identities and possible spectatorships. This opening up has resulted in an increasing concern with questions of ethnicity, masculinity and hybrid sexualities.

CLASSIC FILM NARRATIVE

Claire Johnston was among the first feminist critics to offer a sustained critique of stereotypes from a semiotic point of view (1973/1991). She put forward a view of how classic cinema constructs the ideological image of woman. Drawing on Roland Barthes's notion of 'myth', Johnston investigated the myth of 'Woman' in classic cinema. The sign 'woman' can be analysed as a structure, a code or convention. It represents the ideological meaning that 'woman' has for men. In relation to herself she means no-thing (Johnston, 1991, p. 25): women are negatively represented as 'not-man'. The 'woman-as woman' is absent from the text of the film (Johnston, 1991, p. 26).

The important theoretical shift here is from an understanding of cinema as *reflecting* reality, to a view of cinema as *constructing* a particular, ideological, view of reality. Classic cinema never shows its means of production and is hence characterised by veiling over its ideological construction. Thus, classic film narrative can present the constructed images of 'woman' as natural, realistic and attractive. This is the illusionism of classic cinema.

In her groundbreaking article 'Visual Pleasure and Narrative Cinema' (1975/1989) (see Psychoanalysis, p. 349; for earlier discussion of Mulvey's work, see also p. 336) Laura Mulvey uses psychoanalysis to understand the fascination of Hollywood cinema. This fascination can be explained through the notion of scopophilia (the desire to see) which is a fundamental drive according to Freud. Sexual in origin, like all drives, *der Schautrieb* is what keeps the spectator glued to the silver screen. Classic cinema, adds Mulvey, stimulates the desire to look by integrating structures of voyeurism and narcissism into the story and the image. Voyeuristic visual pleasure is produced by looking at another (character, figure, situation) as our object, whereas narcissistic visual pleasure can be derived from self-identification with the (figure in the) image.

Mulvey has analysed scopophilia in classic cinema as a structure that functions on the axis of activity and passivity. This binary opposition is gendered. The narrative structure of traditional cinema establishes the male character as active and powerful: he is the agent around whom the dramatic action unfolds and the look gets organised. The female character is passive and powerless: she is the object of desire for the male character(s). In this respect, cinema has perfected a visual machinery suitable for male desire such as already structured and canonised in the tradition of western art and aesthetics.

Mulvey has disentangled the ways in which narrative and visual techniques in *cinema* make voyeurism into an exclusively male prerogative. Within the narrative of the film, male characters direct their gaze towards female characters. The spectator in the theatre is made to identify with the male look, because the camera films from the optical, as well as libidinal, point of view of the male character. There are thus three levels of the cinematic gaze (camera, character and spectator) that objectify the female character and make her into a spectacle. In classic cinema, voyeurism connotes women as *'to-be-looked-at-ness'* (Mulvey, 1989, p. 19).

Mulvey tackles narcissistic visual pleasure with Lacan's concepts of ego formation and the mirror stage. The way in which the child derives pleasure from the identification with a perfect mirror image and forms its ego ideal on the basis of this idealised image, is analogous to the way in which the film spectator derives narcissistic pleasure from identifying with the perfected image of a human figure on the screen (see above discussion, Lacan, p. 346). In both cases, however, during the mirror stage and in cinema, identifications are not a lucid form of self-knowledge or awareness. They are rather based on what Lacan calls '*méconnaissance*' (a 'mis-recognition'), that is to say they are blinded by the very narcissistic forces that structure them in the first place. Ego formation is structurally characterised by imaginary functions. And so is cinema. At about the same time as Christian Metz worked on this analogy in his essays on psychoanalysis and cinema, Mulvey argued that cinematic identifications were structured along the lines of sexual difference. Representation of 'the more perfect, more complete, more powerful ideal ego' (Mulvey, 1989, p. 20) of the male hero stands in stark opposition to the distorted image of the passive and powerless female character. Hence the spectator is actively made to identify with the male rather than with the female character in film.

There are then two aspects to visual pleasure which are negotiated through sexual difference: the voyeuristic–scopophilic gaze and narcissistic identification. Both these formative structures depend for their meaning upon the controlling power of the male character as well as on the objectified representation of the female character. Moreover, according to Mulvey, in psychoanalytic terms, the image of 'woman' is fundamentally ambiguous in that it combines attraction and seduction with an evocation of castration anxiety. Because her appearance also reminds the male subject of the lack of a penis, the female character is a source of much deeper fears. Classic cinema solves the threat of castration in one of two ways: in the narrative structure or through fetishism. To allay the threat of castration on the level of narrative, the female character has to be found guilty. The films of Alfred Hitchcock are a good example of this kind of narrative plot (see Modleski, 1988). The woman's 'guilt' will be sealed by either punishment or salvation and the film story is then resolved through the two traditional endings which are made available to women: she must either die (as in e.g. *Psycho*, 1960) or marry (as in e.g. *Marnie*, 1964). In this respect, Mulvey provocatively says that a story demands sadism.

In the case of fetishism, classic cinema reinstates and displaces the lacking penis in the form of a fetish, that is, a hyper-polished object. Mulvey refers here to Josef Sternberg's fetishisation of Marlene Dietrich. Marilyn Monroe is another example of a fetishised female star. Fetishising the woman deflects attention from female 'lack' and changes her from a dangerous figure into a reassuring object of flawless beauty. Fetishism in cinema confirms the reification of the female figure and thus fails to represent 'Woman' outside the phallic norm.

The notion of 'the male gaze' has become a shorthand term for the analysis of complex mechanisms in cinema that involve structures like voyeurism, narcissism and fetishism. These concepts help to understand how Hollywood cinema is tailor-made for male desire. Because the structures of Hollywood cinema are analysed as fundamentally patriarchal, early feminists declared that a woman's film should shun traditional narrative and cinematic techniques and engage in experimental practice: thus, women's cinema should be a counter-cinema.

A FEMINIST COUNTER-CINEMA

What should a feminist counter-cinema look like? For Mulvey, feminist cinema was to be an avant-garde film practice which would 'free the look of the camera into its materiality in time and space and the look of the audience into dialectics and passionate detachment' (Mulvey, 1989, p. 26). That such a counter-cinema would destroy the visual pleasure of the spectator was no problem for women; according to Mulvey they would view the decline of classic film narrative with nothing more than 'sentimental regret' (Mulvey, 1989, p. 26).

Feminist counter-cinema took its inspiration from the avant-garde in cinema and

Feminism and the avant-garde. Mulvey and Wollen's *Riddles of the Sphinx*

theatre, such as the montage techniques of Sergei Eisenstein, the notion of *Verfremdung* (distantiation) of Bertolt Brecht and the modernist aesthetic of Jean-Luc Godard. As such it was very much part of the 1970s political film-making. The privileged examples of feminist counter-cinema are Chantal Akerman's *Jeanne Dielman, 23 Quai du Commerce, 1080 Bruxelles* (Belgium 1975), Laura Mulvey and Peter Wollen's *Riddles of the Sphinx* (UK 1977) and Sally Potter's *Thriller* (UK 1979). It is interesting to note that the radical films of Marguerite Duras have drawn much less attention from anglophone feminist film critics. Important American experimental films are Yvonne Rainer's *Lives of Performers* and *Film About a Woman Who ...* (USA 1972 and 1974) and *Sigmund Freud's Dora* (made by Tyndall, McCall, Pajaczkowska and Weinstock, USA 1979). (See Feminist counter cinema, p. 188.)

How does feminist counter-cinema avoid the conventions of classic cinema and how does it accommodate a female point of view? In the short experimental film *Thriller*, for example, this is achieved by deconstructing a classic melodrama, Puccini's opera *La Bohème* (1895). The film splits the female character into two: Mimi I, who is placed outside of the narrative in which she is the heroine, Mimi II. The first Mimi investigates how she is constructed as an object in the melodramatic narrative. According to Ann Kaplan (1983), the investigation is both psychoanalytic and Marxist–materialist. On the psychoanalytic level, Mimi I learns how the female subject is excluded from male language and classic narrative. The only position she can occupy is that of asking questions. 'Did I die? Was I murdered? What does it mean?' On the Marxist–materialist level, Mimi I learns to investigate Mimi II's role as a seamstress and as a mother. As in Potter's second film, *The Golddiggers* (UK 1980) it is a woman of colour with a deep French-accented English voice (Colette Lafont), who does the critical questioning of the patriarchal image of white womanhood. Thus, in both films it is the 'foreign' female voice that speaks the discourse of theory and criticism.

Thriller communicates these theoretical discourses both visually and acoustically. The soundtrack includes the dominant female voice, as well as a repeated laugh, a repeated shriek and the sound of a heartbeat. These are typical components of the classical thriller and horror genres, while the film narrative does not give rise to any such suspense. Instead, it refocuses the attention of the spectator on the enigmas surrounding the female subject in classical discourse. *Thriller* deliberately violates conventional realist codes. The melodramatic story is partly told in shots which are pictures of photographs of a stage performance, and partly in reconstructed scenes in which the actors move in highly stylised movements. Another visual device is the use of mirrors. For Kaplan, the play with repeated and jarring mirror shots illustrates the mental processes that Lacan's mirror phase involves psychoanalytically. For example, when Mimi I recognises herself as object her shadow is thrown up on the screen. Mimi I is then shown with her back to the mirror, facing the camera. This image is repeated in a series of mirrors behind her (instead of 'correctly' reflecting the back of her head). For Kaplan, this complex shot signals Mimi I's recognition of her split subjectivity. The investigation leads the women to understand they are not split in themselves, nor should they be split narratively. The film ends symbolically with both Mimi's embracing.

Feminist counter-cinema did not only pertain to fictional film, but also to documentary. The problems of finding an appropriate form and style were perhaps even more acute for documentary film, because traditional documentary uses illusionism and realism to capture 'truth' or 'reality'. For many feminist film-makers in the 1970s, this idealism was unacceptable. It could not include self-reflexivity, one of the starting points of feminist film practice. Feminist documentary should manufacture and construct the 'truth' of women's oppression, not merely reflect it (Johnston, 1973). However, other voices were also heard. Because many stylistically traditional documentaries have been important historical documents for the women's movement, this kind of feminist formalism was questioned. Alex Juhasz criticised this kind of orthodoxy, which proscribed anti-illusionist techniques undermining identification. She points to the paradox that the unified subject which was represented in early feminist documentaries, presented the feminist viewer in fact with a 'radical, new and politicized reinterpretation of that female subjectivity, one which mobilized vast numbers of women into action for the first time' (Juhasz, 1994, p. 174).

We witness a theoretical contradiction of feminism here: while feminists need to deconstruct the patriarchal images and representations of 'Woman', they historically need to establish their female subjectivity at the same time. That is to say, they have to find out and redefine what it means to be a woman. A relentless formalism may be too much of a one-sided approach to the complex enterprise of (re)constructing the female subject.

Counter-cinema represents only a small fraction of the many films produced by women since the mid-1970s. Yet, these experimental films have been overpraised for their subversive powers while realist women's films were overcriticised for their illusionism (see Kuhn, 1982 and Kaplan, 1983). The suspicion of collusion cast on realist or narrative film has resulted in either a concentration of critical efforts on classic Hollywood cinema or in a largely unjustified acclaim of experimental women's cinema among the elected few who get to see it. This has resulted in a paradoxical neglect of contemporary popular films made by women for a wider audience; a lack of academic attention which continued long into the 1980s and even 1990s (see for a reappraisal of narrative feminist cinema: Humm, 1997; Smelik, 1998). Teresa de Lauretis (1984, 1987) was among the first to claim that feminist cinema should not destroy narrative and visual pleasure, but rather should be 'narrative and Oedipal with a vengeance' (de Lauretis, 1987, p. 108). According to her, feminist cinema in the 1980s should define 'all points of identification (with character, image, camera) as female, feminine, or feminist' (de Lauretis, 1987, p. 133).

THE FEMALE SPECTATOR

The account of 'the male gaze' as a structuring logic in western visual culture became controversial in the early 1980s, as it made no room for the female spectator nor for a female gaze. Yet, women did and do go to the movies. Mulvey was much criticised for omitting the question of female spectatorship. In a later essay (1981/1989), she addressed the vicissitudes of female spectatorship in her analysis of the western *Duel in the Sun* (King Vidor, 1946). Mulvey suggests that the female spectator may not only identify with the slot of passive femininity which has been programmed for her, but is also likely to enjoy adopting the masculine point of view. Mulvey elabourates on the notion of transsexual identification and spectatorship by pointing to the pre-Oedipal and phallic fantasy of omnipotence which for girls is equally active as for boys, and hence, from a Freudian perspective, essentially 'masculine'. In order to acquire 'proper' femininity, women will have to shed that active aspect of their early sexuality. Mulvey speculates that female spectators may negotiate the masculinisation of the spectatorial position in Hollywood cinema, because it signifies for them a pleasurable rediscovery of a lost aspect of their sexual identity. Even so, the female spectator remains 'restless in [her] transvestite clothes' (Mulvey, 1989, p. 37).

It was not until the end of the 1980s that female spectatorship was theorised outside the dichotomous categories of psychoanalytic theory. An account of female spectatorship in all its cultural contexts and multiple differences was then undertaken in a special issue of *Camera Obscura*, entitled 'The Spectatrix' (1989, nos 20–1). The editors Janet Bergstrom and Mary Ann Doane chose to give a comprehensive survey of international research on and theories of the female spectator in film and television studies.

THE FEMALE MASQUERADE

It has become a general assumption of feminist film theory that female spectators are more fluid in their capacity to identify with the other gender. For example, in her study of the fan phenomenon, Miriam Hansen (1991) has used the idea of spectatorial flexibility to explain why women in the 1920s

Space for the female gaze? *Duel in the Sun*

were drawn to the feminine positioning of Rudolph Valentino.

This spectatorial transvestism of the woman viewer points to a female masquerade. The concept of masquerade was first introduced into feminist film theory by Johnston (1975). The notion of masquerade was inspired by the role of the female character who cross-dressed as a male pirate. For Johnston, the female masquerade signified not only a masking but also an 'unmasking' in the deconstructionist sense of exposing and criticising.

Mary Ann Doane (1982/1991) explored the notion of masquerade further to understand woman's relation to the image on the screen. Drawing on the psychoanalytic work of Joan Rivière, Doane understands the masquerade, not as cross-dressing, but on the contrary as a mask of femininity. Rivière had noticed in her clinical observations that women who find themselves in a male position of authority put on a mask of femininity that functions as compensation for their masculine position.

How does this concept of the masquerade relate to issues of identification and spectatorship? As we have seen, the male gaze involves voyeurism. Voyeurism presupposes distance. Doane argues that the female spectator lacks this necessary distance because she *is* the image. Femininity is constructed as closeness, as 'an overwhelming presence-to-itself of the female body' (Doane, 1991, p. 22). The female spectator can adopt 'the masochism of over-identification' or 'the narcissism entailed in becoming one's own object of desire' (Doane, 1991, pp. 31–2). Doane argues that the female spectator is consumed by the image rather than consuming it. This position can be avoided not only through a transsexual identification, but also through the masquerade. The masquerade is effective in that it manufactures a distance from the image. By wearing femininity as a mask, the female spectator can create the necessary difference between herself and the represented femininity on the screen.

In a study of the woman's film of the 1940s, Doane (1987) returns to the rather negative ways in which Hollywood constructs female identification and subjectivity. For Doane, the female spectator of those melodramas is involved in emotional processes like masochism, paranoia, narcissism and hysteria. The woman's film, in spite of its focus on a female main character, perpetuates these processes and thus confirms stereotypes about the female psyche. The emotional investments of the viewer lead to overidentification, destroying the distance to the object of desire and turning the active desire of both the female character and the female spectator into the passive desire to be the desired object. Mere 'desire to desire' seems to be, then, the only option for women.

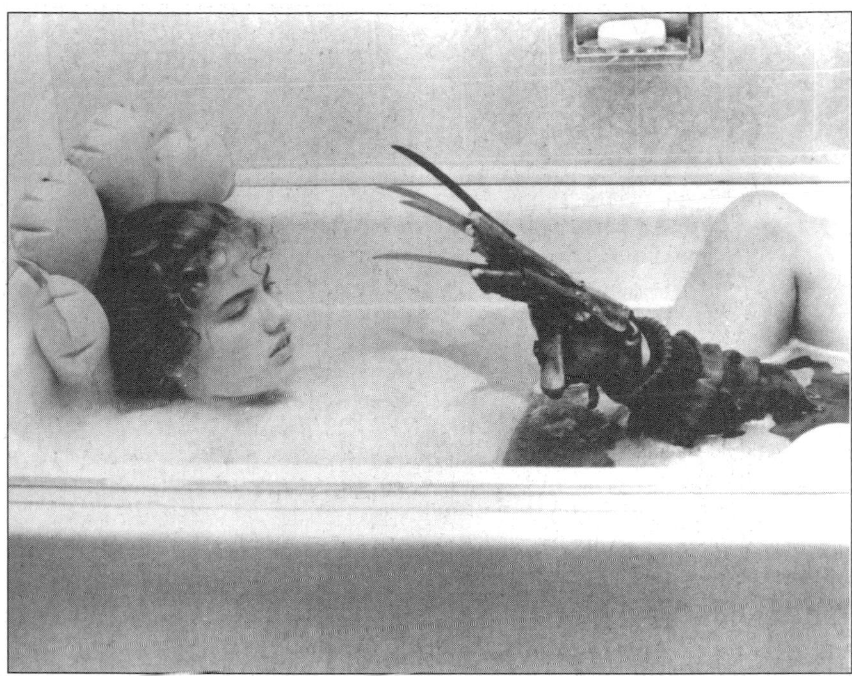

Nightmare on Elm Street – feminising the audience?

THE FEMALE LOOK

Do these rather dire interpretations of female spectatorship imply that the female look is impossible and that the look or gaze is necessarily male? In the early 1980s this seemed the case in feminist theory. In her analysis of Hollywood woman's films of the 1970s and 1980s, Ann Kaplan (1983) argues that female characters can possess the look and even make the male character the object of her gaze, but, being a woman, her desire has no power. The neo-feminist Hollywood movies involve a mere reversal of roles in which the underlying structures of dominance and submission are still intact. The gaze is not essentially male, 'but to own and activate the gaze, given our language and the structure of the unconscious, is to be in the "masculine" position' (Kaplan, 1983, p. 30).

The difficulties of theorising the female spectator made Jackie Stacey (1987) exclaim that feminist film critics have written the darkest scenario possible for the female look as being male, masochist or marginal. There have been some different voices, however. Gertrud Koch (1980) is one of the few feminists who early on recognised that women could also enjoy the image of female beauty on the screen. Especially the vamp, an image exported from Europe and integrated into Hollywood cinema, provides the female spectator with a positive image of autonomous femininity. Koch argues that the image of the vamp revives for the female spectator the pleasurable experience of the mother as the love object in early childhood. Moreover, the sexual ambivalence of the vamp, of for example Greta Garbo and Marlene Dietrich, allows for a female homoerotic pleasure which is not exclusively negotiated through the eyes of men. In Koch's view the vamp is a phallic woman rather than a fetishised woman, as she offers contradictory images of femininity which go beyond the reifying gaze. The vamp's ambiguity can be a source of visual pleasure for the female spectator. The disappearance of the vamp in cinema, therefore, means a great loss of possible identifications and visual pleasure for the female audience.

A similar focus on the pre-Oedipal phase and on the mother as love object and potential source of visual pleasure has been developed by Gaylyn Studlar (1988), though from a very different angle. Analysing films made by Josef von Sternberg starring Marlene Dietrich, she investigates the Deleuzian notion of masochism. Deleuze views masochism as the desire of the male to merge with the mother and subvert the father's phallic law. Its violence is contractual and consensual, in a way that sadism is not. Sadism negates difference of the mother and exults in the power of the father. Studlar argues that visual pleasure in cinema resembles more the psychic processes of masochism than of sadism. Cinema evokes the desire of the spectator to return to the pre-Oedipal phase of unity with the mother, and of bisexuality. The female spectator can thus identify with and draw pleasure from the powerful *femme fatale* in cinema. This is a sort of re-enactment of the symbiosis through which the spectator wishes to subject herself or himself to the powerful mother image. The condition of this active masochistic desire is that it be suspended, which is achieved by means of performance and masquerade on the part of the female character. These ritualisations of fantasy keep desire under control. For Studlar, the masquerade serves as a defensive strategy for women, by which they deflect and confuse the male gaze. She thus creates a place for the pleasure and desire of the female subject–spectator, albeit the pleasurable pain of desire.

Bisexual identification has also submerged in studies of very different film genres. In her study of the modern horror film, Carol Clover (1992) argues that both female and male spectators identify bisexually. She rests her case on the narrative role of the 'Final Girl': the one girl in the film who fights, resists and survives the killer–monster. The final girl acquires the gaze, and dominates the action, and is thus masculinised. The slasher film, like *Halloween* (1978), *Friday the Thirteenth* (1980) and *Nightmare on Elm Street* (1984) (and their sequels), openly plays on a difference between appearance (sex) and behaviour (gender). Clover argues that it is this 'theatricalization of gender' which feminises the audience. Whereas in classic horror (e.g. films by Hitchcock and De Palma) the feminisation of the audience is intermittent and ceases when the final girl becomes the designated victim (Marion in *Psycho*), in the modern horror film the final girl becomes her own saviour (see The horror film, p. 194). Her self-rescue turns her into the hero and it is at that moment that the male viewer 'gives up the last pretence of male identification'. For Clover, the willingness of the male spectator to throw in his emotional lot with a woman in fear and pain, points to masochism. Although Clover is aware of the misogyny of the genre of the slasher film, she claims a subversive edge in that it adjusts gender representations and identifications.

FEMALE SUBJECTIVITY

The question of female spectatorship and the female look circle around the issue of subjectivity. Female subjectivity has been explored not only in relation to spectatorship, but also with respect to the narrative structure of film. One of the key figures in this field is Teresa de Lauretis, who examined the structural representations of 'woman' in cinema (1984, 1987).

De Lauretis (1984) emphasises that subjectivity is not a fixed entity but a constant process of self-production. Narration is one of the ways of reproducing subjectivity; each story derives its structure from the subject's desire and from its inscription in social and cultural codes. Narrative structures are defined by Oedipal desire, which should be understood as both a socio-political economy dominated by men's control of women and as a way of emphasising the sexual origin of subjectivity. Sexual desire is bound up with the desire for knowledge, that is, the quest for truth. The desire to solve riddles is a male desire *par excellence*, because the female subject is herself the mystery. 'Woman' *is* the question and can hence not ask the question nor make her desire intelligible. In Hitchcock's *Vertigo* (1958), for example, Scottie's desire for the enigmatic Judy/Madeleine structures the narrative of the film.

Narrative is not oedipal in content but in structure, by distributing roles and differences, and thus power and positions. One of the functions of narrative, de Lauretis argues, is to 'seduce' women into femininity with or without their consent. The female subject is made to desire femininity. This is a cruel and often coercive form of seduction. Here de Lauretis turns Mulvey's famous phrase around: not only does a story demand sadism; sadism demands a story. She refers to the ways in which the female characters in *Vertigo*, but also in a 'woman's film' like *Rebecca* (also by Hitchcock, 1940), are made to conform to the ideal image that the man has of them. The function of portraits of female ancestors in both films is highly significant in this respect: they represent the dead mother, the ideal that the male hero desires to have and forces upon the female heroine. For de Lauretis, the desire of the female character is impossible and the narrative tension is resolved by the destruction (Judy/Madeleine) or territorialisation of women (the new Mrs de Winter). Desire in narrative is intimately bound up with violence against women and the techniques of cinematic narration both reflect and sustain social forms of oppression of women.

De Lauretis is hardly more optimistic than Mulvey about the female spectator. Not that she assumes identification to be single or simple; femininity and masculinity are identifications that the subject takes up in a changing relation to desire. De Lauretis distinguishes two different processes of identification in cinema. The first set is an oscillating either/or identification. It consists of a masculine, active identification with the gaze (Scottie) and a passive, feminine identification with the image (Judy/Madeleine). The second set is a simultaneous both/and identification. It consists of the double identification with the figure of narrative movement (the protagonist, the new Mrs de Winter in *Rebecca*) and with the figure of narrative image (here the image of Rebecca). This set of figural identifications enables the female spectator to take up both the active and passive positions of desire: 'Desire for the other, and desire to be desired by the other' (de Lauretis, 1984, p. 143). This double identification may yield a surplus of pleasure, but it is also the very operation by which a narrative solicits the spectators' consent and seduces women into femininity.

The notion of the female subject, then, seems to be a contradiction in terms, so much so that de Lauretis sometimes refers to the female subject as a 'non-subject' (de Lauretis, 1987, p. 36). 'Woman' is fundamentally unrepresentable as subject of desire; she can only be represented as representation (de Lauretis, 1987, p. 20). Feminist theory is built on the very paradox of the unrepresentability of woman as subject of desire, and historical women who know themselves to be subjects. For de Lauretis, the self-conscious experience of being both 'woman' and 'women' is the productive contradiction of feminism. Women's films like *Les Rendez-vous d'Anna* or *Jeanne Dielman* by Chantal Akerman, *Thriller* by Sally Potter, or *Sigmund Freud's Dora* by Tyndall, McCall, Pajaczkowska and Weinstock, are her privileged examples of films which explore and explode that very contradiction.

FEMALE DESIRE

A feminist critic who has also approached the question of female desire within psychoanalytic discourse is Kaja Silverman (1988). Drawing on Lacanian psychoanalysis, Silverman argues that each subject is structured by lack or symbolic castration. In western culture it is, however, the female subject who is made to bear the burden of that lack in order to provide the male subject with the illusion of wholeness and unity. Silverman suggests that in cinema this displacement is enacted not only through the gaze and the image but also through the auditory register. Contrary to the more frequent disembodiment of the male voice in cinema, the female voice is restricted to the realm of the body. This amounts to keeping it outside discourse. The female voice can hardly reach a signifying position in language, meaning or power and is hence all too easily reduced to screams, babble or silence in dominant cinema.

Silverman discusses the cultural fantasy of the maternal voice that surrounds the infant like an acoustic blanket. This fantasy for the maternal enclosure negatively signifies the fear of being swallowed up by the mother, whereas it positively signifies a regression to the state of harmony and abundance when mother and child are still one. Silverman argues that both these fantasies equate the maternal voice to pure sound and deny the mother any cultural role as a discursive agent. In her rereading of psychoanalysis Silverman attempts to make room for the mother and for female desire *within* discourse and the symbolic order.

Reinterpreting Freud's account of the psychological development of the little girl, Silverman puts great emphasis on the signifying role of the mother in early childhood. The entry into language means the end of the unity between mother and child as well as of an unmediated access to reality. The loss and separation entailed by the acquisition of language lead the child to desire the mother. The girl redirects her desire to the mother in what is called the negative Oedipus complex. This can only happen *after* the pre-Oedipal stage, because distance from the mother is necessary for her to be constructed as an erotic object for the daughter. Silverman thus recuperates female desire for the mother as fully Oedipal, that is to say within the symbolic order, within language and signification.

It is after the event of the castration crisis, the dramatic onset of sexual difference, that the girl leaves the negative Oedipus complex and enters the positive Oedipal phase, learning to redirect her desire to the father. For the rest of her life the female subject remains split between the desire for the mother and for the father. The two desires are the site of a constitutive contradiction and are consequently irreconcilable. For Silverman, the daughter's erotic investment in the mother can be a subversive force for a 'libidinal politics' because it is a form of desire which is opposed to the normative desire for the father. Silverman emphasises the negativity of the female negative Oedipus complex as a political potential. She argues that it is paramount for feminism to draw on the libidinal resources of the 'homosexual-maternal fantasmatic' (Silverman, 1988, p. 125).

Silverman also revises the traditional view on the divergence of identification and desire. In her view these two psychic paradigms are not always mutually exclusive and can actually coalesce. In the negative Oedipus complex the girl both identifies with and desires the mother, while the father figures neither as an object of desire nor of identification: for the girl he is merely 'a troublesome rival' (Freud quoted in Silverman, 1988, p. 153). In this stage of development the girl forms her identity through the incorporation of the mother's imago; she both wishes to possess and to be the mother. There is then a conjunction of identification and eroticism, which Silverman believes to have a vital relation to female narcissism. For her, feminism's libidinal struggle against the phallus lies in the intersection of desire for and identification with the mother.

In Silverman's reading, a fantasy for the maternal enclosure is the organising principle of *Riddles of the Sphinx* (Laura Mulvey and Peter Wollen, 1977). In this experimental film, the figure of the Sphinx occupies the position of an 'imaginary narrator', a distinctly fictionalised voice-over. This disembodied voice speaks a wide variety of discourses about motherhood, from psychoanalysis to feminist politics, thus firmly establishing the maternal voice within the symbolic order. The film is centred upon the female desire to recover the Oedipal or symbolic mother, represented by the Sphinx. *Riddles* springs off from the mother daughter relationship, of Louise and her child Anna. The maternal fantasy can be found not only in the pre-Oedipal dyad, but also in the homosexual–maternal *ménage à trois* of mother, grandmother and child. The film opens this maternal enclosure up to a feminist community of women, including Louise's friend Maxine, and the voice and work of artist Mary Kelly. This female collectivity, like female subjectivity is based upon the passionate desire for the mother.

SEXUAL DIFFERENCES AND ITS DISCONTENTS

Although feminists have not always agreed about the usefulness of pyschoanalysis, there has been general agreement about the limitations of an exclusive focus on sexual difference. One such limitation is the reproduction of a dichotomy, male–female, that needs to be deconstructed. The fear was that this binary opposition would somehow tie questions of pleasure and identification to anatomical difference. Especially within American feminism, the term sexual difference was therefore replaced by a renewed interest in the sex–gender distinction that Gayle Rubin had introduced in 1975. The term gender generally seemed to indicate a clearer distinction between anatomy (sex) and social construction (gender), and equally between sexual practice and gender identity. Another limitation of the exclusive focus on sexual difference within psychoanalytic film theory is its failure to focus on other differences such as class, race, age and sexual preference.

Lesbian feminists were among the first to raise objections to the heterosexual bias of psychoanalytic feminist film theory. Indeed, feminist film theory – not unlike the Hollywood cinema it criticised so fiercely – seemed unable to conceive of representation outside heterosexuality. The journal *Jump Cut* wrote in its special issue on Lesbians and Film (1981, no. 24/25): 'It sometimes seems to us that lesbianism is the hole in the heart of feminist film criticism' (p. 17). Apparently, almost ten years later matters had improved very little, as Judith Mayne (1990, 1994) complains that the denial of the lesbian identity of Hollywood director Dorothy Arzner points to a curious gap in feminist film theory, indeed to the 'structuring absence' of lesbianism (Mayne, 1994, p. 107). As Patricia White (1991) observes, the 'ghostly presence of lesbianism' does not only haunt Hollywood Gothics but also feminist film theory.

Desiring the other: *Desperately Seeking Susan*

In spite of the increasing focus on female spectatorship in feminist scholarship (see Feminist interventions, p. 368), the homosexual pleasures of the female spectator were indeed largely ignored. Yet, it is interesting to know what happens for the female spectator when a classic narrative features two female characters. This question arose as early as Julia Lesage's (1980) pioneering analysis of the improvisational interplay of the two female characters in Jacques Rivette's *Céline and Julie Go Boating* (1974). She shows that the abandonment of the classic story based on male–female distinctions produces new and previously unimaginable narrative permutations.

Stacey (1987) argues that in Hollywood films with two female protagonists, like *All About Eve* (1950) or *Desperately Seeking Susan* (1984), an active desire is produced by the difference between the two women. These stories are about women wanting to become the idealised other. An interplay of difference and otherness prevents the collapse of that desire into identification, prompting Stacey to argue that the rigid psychoanalytic distinction between desire and identification fails to address different constructions of desire. She suggests that a more flexible model of cinematic spectatorship is needed so as to avoid a facile binarism that maps homosexuality onto an opposition of masculinity and femininity.

De Lauretis (1988) has drawn attention to the difficulties of imagining lesbian desire within a psychoanalytic discourse that predicates sexual difference on sexual *in*difference. She here follows Luce Irigaray's notion of the symbolic law representing only one and not two sexes: patriarchy is deeply '*hommo-sexual*' as it erects the masculine as the one and only norm. Discussing the same problematic in a later essay, de Lauretis (1991) observes that the institution of heterosexuality defines all sexuality to such an extent that is difficult to represent homosexual–lesbian desire. She criticises both Stacey and Silverman for conceiving of desire between women as woman-identified female bonding and failing to see it as sexual. Here, and more extensively in her later book *The Practice of Love* (1994), de Lauretis returns to Freudian theory to account for the specificity of lesbian desire in terms of fetishism.

In answer to de Lauretis's criticism, Stacey (1994) argues in her study of female spectatorship that she is not concerned with a specifically lesbian audience but with a possible homo-eroticism for all women in the audience. Her point is not to de-eroticise desire, but to look for ways in which a film may eroticise identification. The female spectator is quite likely to encompass erotic components in her desiring look, while at the same time identifying with the woman-as-spectacle. The homo-erotic appeal of female Hollywood stars has indeed been widely recognised. Weiss (1992), for example, discusses the attraction of Hollywood stars for lesbian spectators in the thirties. Especially the androgynous appearances of Marlene Dietrich in *Morocco* (1930), Greta Garbo in *Queen Christina* (1933) and Katherine Hepburn in *Sylvia Scarlett* (1935) were embraced as an image of a gender-in-between and of sexual ambiguity. The star image of sexual androgyny served as point of identification outside conventional gender positions.

While these discussions of lesbian spectatorship are part of a wider movement in film studies to include the heterogeneity of the spectatorial situation, most discussions of spectatorship have been about white audiences. De Lauretis was criticised for not taking into account racial dynamics in the lesbian film *She Must Be Seeing Things* (1987) (see the discussion following de Lauretis's 1991 article). The issue of black lesbian spectatorship has so far hardly been raised. The collection *Queer Looks* (Gever *et al.*, 1993) addresses the combination of racial difference and homosexuality, but it focuses more on gay and lesbian film-making than on spectatorship as such.

GAY AND LESBIAN CRITICISM

The shift away from the restrictive dichotomies of psychoanalytic feminist film theory, has resulted in a more historical and cultural criticism of cinema by gay and lesbian critics. This involved rereadings of Hollywood cinema, for example of the implicit lesbianism of the female buddy film. In order to avoid that 'danger' Hollywood films often include explicit scenes of denying any lesbian intent. In *Julia* (1977) Jane Fonda slaps a man in the face who suggests that her friendship with Julia (Vanessa Redgrave) was sexual. Other films put a 'real' lesbian in the story as a way of showing that the female friendship of the two heroines is not 'that way' (*Girlfriends*, 1978). In some films the female buddies, however, become lovers, as in *Lianna* (1982) and *Personal Best* (1982). Several critics have pointed out that the lesbian subject matter of these films is acceptable to all kinds of audiences, because its eroticism feeds into traditional male voyeurism (Williams, 1986; Merck, 1993). Ellsworth (1990) investigated lesbian responses to the film and found that many lesbian spectators actively rewrote the film by imagining a different ending. Her research shows that lesbian spectators use interpretative strategies to challenge the dominant reading of a film.

The theme of lesbianism still runs strong in more recent female buddy films. *Fried Green Tomatoes* (1991) is one of those films about female friendship in which lesbianism remains unspoken, although it is a source of strength and inspiration. In *Thelma and Louise* (1991) the lesbian attraction between the women can only be expressed in a kiss on the mouth just before the leap to their death into the Grand Canyon. *Basic Instinct* (1991) features lesbian and bisexual characters as pathological killers, harping back on the time-old association in Hollywood films of lesbianism with death and pathology. What else is new? Angela Galvin (1994) suggests that the novelty may well lie in the heroine's absence of a mustache. The controversy over *Thelma and Louise* and *Basic Instinct* shows some of the various responses of feminist and lesbian criticism. While the films have been criticised for their reactionary representation of strong women and for their exploitation of voyeuristic themes, some spectators have appropriated them as 'lesbian films', enjoying images of empowered women who escape the Law (Tasker, 1993; Graham, 1995).

Alongside rereadings of Hollywood films, gay and lesbian criticism turned to films made by lesbians and gay men. Early films of European art cinema were rediscovered, such as *Mädchen in Uniform* (*Girls in Uniform*, 1931). Rich (1984) argues that the anti-Fascist politics of *Mädchen in Uniform* is interconnected with its lesbian theme and its struggle against authoritarian structures and sexual repression. Rich places the film in the historical context of Weimar with its vibrant lesbian subculture, especially in Berlin.

Mädchen in Uniform does not stand alone but is part of a tradition of gay and lesbian film-making within early cinema (see Dyer, 1990; Weiss, 1992). Other films were made by gay or lesbian film-makers, like the surrealist shorts of Germaine Dulac. Her films have been read as critiques of heterosexuality (Flitterman-Lewis, 1990). Fantasy plays an important role in these experimental films. In *La Souriante Madame Beudet* (*The Smiling Mme Beudet*, 1923) a woman fantasises murdering her bully of a husband and escaping from her bourgeois marriage, and *La Coquille et le Clergyman* (*The Seashell and the Clergyman*, 1927) exposes Oedipal male fantasies about the mystery of 'woman'.

Jean Genet's prison film *Un Chant d'Amour* (*A Song of Love*, France 1950) is a classic which has become enormously popular with gay audiences to the present day and which also has influenced gay film-makers. Dyer (1990) discusses the film's eroticism in terms of the tension between politics and pleasure. While some gay critics have reprimanded the film for its 'oppression' of gay men or were disturbed by its 'homophobic' representation of erotic pleasures, others took a more permissive or even celebratory attitude to the sado-masochism of the film. Dyer argues that the renewed political interest in perverse sexualities opened a Foucauldian reading of the film's eroticism in terms of the social and historical relation between sexuality and power.

The play of power and desire has become the theme of some gay and lesbian films in the 1980s, which Dyer calls a 'Genetesque' tradition. A ritualisation of power and desire can for example be found in the sadean theatre of *Verführung: die grausame Frau* (*Seduction: the Cruel Woman*, 1985) by Elfi Mikesch and Monika Treut. This highly formalised and aestheticised exploration of sado-masochism was one of the first films to bring female desire and lesbian sexuality within the domain of power and violence. Another film-maker that must be mentioned in this context is Ulrike Ottinger, whose fantasmatic films from *Madame X – eine absolute Herrscherin* (*Madame X – an Absolute Ruler*, 1977) to *Johanna D'Arc of Mongolia* (1989) humorously deconstruct traditional femininity and perversely celebrate nomadic lesbian subjectivities (Longfellow, 1993).

These films are very different from the lesbian romance, *Desert Hearts* (1985), which remains to date the only lesbian independent feature which made use of Hollywood conventions and was a box-office success. As Jackie Stacey (1995) points out, the film, quite surprisingly, was not followed by other successful lesbian romances nor did it receive much academic attention. She suggests that this may have to do with the popular lesbian romance film being 'a virtual contradiction in terms' (Stacey, 1995, p. 112). The film has, however, remained popular with lesbian audiences.

FEMINIST THEORY AND RACE

Persistent critique of psychoanalytic film theory has also come from black feminists, who criticised its exclusive focus on sexual differences and its failure to deal with racial difference. Jane Gaines (1988) is one of the first feminist critics to point to the erasure of race in film theories that are based on the psychoanalytic concept of sexual differences. She pleads for an inclusion of black feminist theory and of a historical approach into feminist film theory in order to understand how in cinema gender intersects with race and class.

White film critics have universalised their theories of representations of women, while black women have been excluded from those very forms of representation. The signification of the black female as non-human makes black female sexuality the great unknown in white patriarchy, that which is 'unfathomed and uncodified' and yet 'worked over again and again in mainstream culture because of its apparent elusiveness' (Gaines, 1988, p. 26). The eruptive point of resistance presents black women's sexuality as an even greater threat to the male unconscious than the fear of white female sexuality.

The category of race also problematises the paradigm of the male gaze possessing the female image. The male gaze is not a universal given but it is rather negotiated via whiteness: the black man's sexual gaze is socially prohibited. Racial hierarchies in ways of looking have created visual taboos, the neglect of which reflects back on film theory, which fails to account for the ways in which some social groups have the licence to look openly, while others can only 'look' illicitly. The racial structures of looking also have repercussions for structures of narrative. Gaines discusses the construction of the black man as rapist, while in times of slavery and long after, it was the white man who raped black women. The historical scenario of interracial rape explains much of the penalty of sexual looking by the black man, who was actually (rather than symbolically) castrated or lynched by white men. For Gaines this scenario of sexual violence, repression and displacements rivals the Oedipal myth.

Interventions such as Gaines's show that

the category of race reveals the untenability of many one-sided beliefs within feminist film theory, and points to the necessity of contextualising and historicising sexual difference. Thus, Lola Young (1996) examines the representation of black female sexuality by situating British films in their historical and social context. Intersecting theories of sexual difference with those of differences of race and sexual preference, along with ethnicity and class, will eventually make other forms of representation thinkable, although Young argues convincingly that white and black film-makers find it hard to challenge stereotypical images of black women.

Almost simultaneously with Young's book a special issue of *Camera Obscura* (no. 36) was published, the focus of which was: 'Black women, spectatorship, and visual culture'. In her reading of Neil Jordan's films *Mona Lisa* and *The Crying Game* Joy James comes to a very similar critique as Young: these films fail to fulfil the promise of transgressive relation ships and ultimately reproduce stereotypes of black female sexuality. Deborah Grayson examines the iconic representation of black women's hair in visual culture. Looking at diverse media and popular practices (e.g. dolls), she identifies the racialised signification of hair within American health and beauty culture. In a similar vein, Marla Shelton analyses the cross-over stardom of Whitney Houston. While Shelton celebrates Houston's successful construction of her own image and formation of different audiences, she points to the inherent conflicts that converge around this 'rainbow icon'. For example, Houston has found it hard to escape negative interpretations of her sexuality and of her role as a wife and mother. And while she has always had enormous cross-over appeal, according to Shelton, in more recent years Houston had to embrace and express her blackness in order to maintain a large audience.

Generally, little research has been available about black audiences (see Ethnographic research, p. 372). One of the exceptions is the work of Jacqueline Bobo (1995) on Steven Spielberg's *The Color Purple* (1985). The film was attacked in the black press for its racism. Yet, this critical view is mixed with reports of black spectators who found the film empowering. Bobo set out to research this apparent contradiction and interviewed a group of black women. The black female spectators were quite unanimously impressed by the film – 'Finally, somebody says something about us' – and felt strengthened by the triumph of the female protagonist Celie. They thought the criticism of the film (and also of Alice Walker's novel), particularly on the part of black men, quite unjustified. The women do recognise that the film continues the tradition of racist representations of blacks; Spielberg's interpretation of Sofia and Harpo is not considered to be successful. However, Bobo argues that, as black spectators, the women are by sheer necessity used to filtering out offensive racist images from what they see in cinema. The women negotiated their appreciation of the film through their personal history and past viewing experience. Moreover, Bobo found that certain technical aspects of the film contributed to spectatorial pleasure: *The Color Purple* introduced an innovative way of photographing black people so that they stood out against the background. This photographic technique made black people appear more distinctly on the screen than in the cinematic tradition of Hollywood.

The influential feminist critic, bell hooks (1992) confirms that black viewers have always critically responded to Hollywood. Black female spectators do not necessarily identify with either the male gaze or with white womanhood as lack. Rather, they 'construct a theory of looking relations where cinematic visual delight is the pleasure of interrogation' (1992, p. 126). For hooks this is a radical departure from the 'totalizing agenda' of feminist film criticism, and the beginning of an oppositional spectatorship for black women.

A search for an oppositional subjectivity can also be found in the practice of filmmaking. Ngozi Onwurah's film *The Body Beautiful* (1991), for example, inscribes new subject positions for the diasporan daughter of a British mother and a Nigerian father. Combining documentary with fictional elements, this hybrid film centres on the relation between the body of the mother and that of her daughter by foregrounding questions of authenticity and authority. In a rewriting of the Freudian primal scene – the daughter watching the lovemaking of her mature white mother with a young black man – the film takes on the ethnographic gaze at the 'Other', radically subverting traditional psychoanalytic discourse.

Richard Dyer (1988/1993) is one of the few film critics who has written about whiteness in cinema. He argues that it is difficult to think about whiteness, because it is often revealed as emptiness and absence. Because whiteness is constructed as the norm, it is unmarked. Yet, or rather, as such, it can represent everything. This eerie property of whitenes, to be nothing and everything at the same time, is the source of its representational power. In his reading of *Jezebel* (1938), Dyer points to the narrative technique of Hollywood colonial movies, where the white, sexually repressed heroine lives her emotions through the black servant. Such films conventionally oppose the chastity and virginity of white womanhood to the vitality and sexuality of the black woman, usually the white woman's servant. Its closure is the acquired ideal of white womanhood, although much of the pleasure of the film lies in the transgression of Jezebel (Bette Davis), exposing that ideal to be quite an ordeal.

ON MASCULINITY

While feminists have convincingly exposed western culture as male-dominated, this has not automatically produced a feminist theory of male subjectivity and sexuality. Pam Cook's (1982) essay in a special issue of *Screen* opened up a new area of investigation: the riddled question of masculinity in the age of feminism. Much as the dominant paradigm of feminist film theory raised questions about the male look and the female spectacle, it also raised questions about the eroticisation of the male body as erotic object. What if the male body is the object of the female gaze or of another male gaze; and how exactly does the male body become the signifier of the phallus? (*Screen*, 1992).

In the discussion of masculinity in cinema the issue of homosexual desire was raised (Dyer, 1982; Neale, 1983). Most critics agree that the spectatorial look in mainstream cinema is implicitly male. While for Dyer this means that images of men do not automatically 'work' for women, according to Neale the erotic element in looking at the male body has to be repressed and disavowed so as to avoid any implications of male homosexuality. Yet, male homosexuality is always present as an undercurrent; it is Hollywood's symptom. The denial of the homo-eroticism of looking at images of men constantly involves sado-masochistic themes, scenes and fantasies. Hence, the highly ritualised scenes of male struggle which deflect the look away from the male body to the scene of the spectacular fight.

The image of the male body as object of a look is fraught with ambivalences, repressions and denials. Like the masquerade, the notion of spectacle has such strong feminine connotations that for a male performer to be put on display or to don a mask threatens his very masculinity. Because the phallus is a symbol and a signifier, no man can fully symbolise it. Although the patriarchal male subject has a privileged relation to the phallus, he will always fall short of the phallic ideal. Lacan notices this effect in his essay on the meaning of the phallus 'the curious consequence of making virile display in the human being itself seem feminine' (Lacan, 1977, p. 291). Male spectacle, then, entails to be put in a feminine position. The immanent feminisation of male spectacle brings about two possible dangers for the posing or performing male: functioning as an object of desire he can easily become the object of ridicule, and within a heterosexist culture accusations of homosexuality can be launched against him (Neale, 1983; Tasker, 1993).

Masculinity studies became established in feminist film theory in the 1990s. In a special issue, on 'Male trouble' of *Camera Obscura* (1988) the editors Constance Penley and Sharon Willis argue that the great variety of images of contemporary masculinity are organised around hysteria and masochism. As they point out, these two symptomatic formations are a telling displacement of voyeurism and fetishism, the terms that have so far been used in feminist film theory to describe male subjectivity and spectatorship. Lynne Kirby, for example, describes male hysteria in early cinema. She argues that the disturbing shock effects of early cinema (the roller-coaster ride, the speeding train shots) construct a hystericised spectator. Hysteria was seen as a quintessential female condition, but with modern technology men were equally subjected to shock and trauma and hence, responded with hysteria. Male hysteria and masochism are further explored in books on male subjectivity by Tania Modleski (1991) and Kaja Silverman (1992).

Most studies of masculinity point to the crisis in which the white male heterosexual subject finds himself, a crisis in which his masculinity is fragmented and denaturalised (Easthope, 1986; Kirkham and Thumin, 1993; Tasker, 1993; Jeffords, 1994). The signifiers of 'man' and 'manly' seem to have lost all of their meaning, which makes Hollywood desperate to find a 'few good white men', in the words of Susan Jeffords. Yet, the crisis in masculinity is welcomed by gay critics as a liberatory moment. In his book on male impersonators Mark Simpson (1994) takes great pleasure in celebrating the deconstruction of masculinity as authentic, natural, coherent and dominant.

QUEER THEORY

Gay studies of masculinity often border on camp readings of the male spectacle (Medhurst, 1991b; Simpson, 1994). Camp can be seen as an oppositional reading of popular culture which offers identifications and pleasures that dominant culture denies to homosexuals. As an oppositional reading, camp can be subversive for bringing out the cultural ambiguities and contradictions that usually remain sealed over by dominant ideology.

This characteristic brings camp into the realm of postmodernism which also celebrates ambivalence and heterogeneity. Subcultural camp and postmodern theory share a penchant for irony, play and parody, for artificiality and performance, as well as for transgressing conventional meanings of gender. This queer alliance between camp and postmodernism has often been noted. Medhurst even provokingly states that 'postmodernism is only heterosexuals catching up with camp' (Medhurst, 1991a, p. 206). It is indeed an easy leap from Babuscio's understanding of camp as signifying performance rather than existence, to Judith Butler's notion of gender signifying performance rather than identity. Just as Babuscio claims that the emphasis on style, surface and the spectacle results in incongruities between 'what a thing or person *is* to what it *looks* like' (Babuscio, 1984, p. 44), Butler (1990) asserts that the stress on performativity allows us to see gender as enacting a set of discontinuous if not parodic performances. Thus, it also became an available notion for lesbians (see Graham, 1995). Both camp and postmodernism denaturalise femininity and masculinity.

It is significant that in the 1990s the notion of 'camp' is often replaced by the term 'queer'. Camp is historically more associated with the closeted homosexuality of the 1950s and only came to the surface in the 1960s and 1970s. Postmodernism of the 1980s and 1990s brought campy strategies into the mainstream. Now, lesbians and gay men identify their oppositional-reading strategies as 'queer'. Away from the notions of oppression and liberation of earlier gay and lesbian criticism, queerness is associated with the playful self-definition of a homosexuality in non-essentialist terms. Not unlike camp, but more self-assertive, queer readings are fully inflected with irony, transgressive gender parody and deconstructed subjectivities.

CONCLUSION

The diversity of contemporary feminist film theory reflects the variegated production of women's cinema of the 1990s. Women film-makers have increasingly conquered Hollywood. Several of them have been able to maintain a consistent production in diverse genres: comedy (Penny Marshall), romantic drama (Nora Ephron), and action movies (Kathryn Bigelow), to name just a few. This has also been the case for several women film-makers in Europe, such as Margarethe von Trotta (Germany), Diane Kurys (France), Claire Denis (France), and Marion Hänsel (Belgium). In a more non-commercial pocket of the market, there has been a significant increase in films made by lesbian, black and postcolonial directors: film-makers as diverse as Monika Treut and Patricia Rozema, Julie Dash and Ngozi Onwurah, Ann Hui and Clara Law. This decade has witnessed the popular success of feminist art films, like *Orlando* by Sally Potter (1992) and the Oscar-winning films *The Piano*, a costume drama by Jane Campion (1994) and *Antonia's Line*, a matriarchal epic by Marleen Gorris (1995). Dropping a few names and titles in no way does justice to the scale of women's cinema of this decade. It merely indicates a prolific diversity which resonates with film audiences in this decade of hybridity. The polyphony of voices, multiple points of view, and cinematic styles and genres, signify women's successful struggle for self-representation on the silver screen.

SELECTED READING

Jacqueline Bobo, *Black Women as Cultural Readers*, New York, Columbia University Press, 1995.

Diane Carson, Linda Dittmar and Janice R. Welsch (eds), *Multiple Voices in Feminist Film Criticism*, London and Minneapolis, University of Minnesota Press, 1994.

Mary Ann Doane, *The Desire to Desire: The Woman's Film of the 1940s*, Bloomington, Indiana University Press, 1987.

Patricia Erens (ed.), *Issues in Feminist Film Criticism*, Bloomington, Indiana University Press, 1990.

Jane Gaines, 'White privilege and looking relations: race and gender in feminist film theory', in *Screen* 29 (4), 1988, pp. 12–27.

bell hooks, *Black Looks: Race and Representation*, Boston, South End Press, 1992.

Clare Johnston, 'Women's cinema as counter-cinema', in *Notes on Women's Cinema*, London, SEFT, 1973; Glasgow, *Screen* reprint, 1991, pp. 24–31.

E. Ann Kaplan, *Women and Film: Both Sides of the Camera*, New York and London, Methuen, 1983.

Annette Kuhn, *Women's Pictures: Feminism and Cinema*, London, RKP, 1982; rev. edn, 1994.

Teresa de Lauretis, *Alice Doesn't: Feminism, Semiotics, Cinema*, Bloomington, Indiana University Press, 1984.

Teresa de Lauretis, *The Practice of Love: Lesbian Sexuality and Perverse Desire*, Bloomington, Indiana University Press, 1994.

Judith Mayne, *The Woman at the Keyhole: Feminism and Women's Cinema*, Bloomington, Indiana University Press, 1990.

Judith Mayne, *Directed by Dorothy Arzner*, Bloomington, Indiana University Press, 1994.

Tania Modleski, *The Women Who Knew Too Much: Hitchcock and Feminist Theory*, New York and London, Methuen, 1988.

Laura Mulvey, 'Visual Pleasure and Narrative Cinema', 1975, in *Visual And Other Pleasures*, London, Macmillan, 1989, pp. 14–26.

Laura Mulvey, 'Afterthoughts on "Visual Pleasure and Narrative Cinema", inspired by King Vidor's *Duel in the Sun*', 1981, in *Visual and Other Pleasures*, London, Macmillan, 1989, pp. 29–37.

Steve Neale, 'Masculinity as spectacle', *Screen* 24 (6), 1983, pp. 12–16.

Constance Penley (ed.), *Feminism and Film Theory*, London, BFI/Routledge, 1988.

Kaja Silverman, *Male Subjectivity at the Margins*, New York and London, Routledge, 1992.

Anneke Smelik, *And the Mirror Cracked: Feminist Cinema and Film Theory*, London, Macmillan, 1998.

Gaylyn Studlar, *In the Realm of Pleasure: Von Sternberg, Dietrich, and the Masochistic Aesthetic*, New York, Columbia University Press, 1988.

Matriarchal epic and feminist art film – Marleen Gorris's *Antonia's Line*

Morocco (USA 1930 *p.c* – Paramount; *d* – Josef von Sternberg; sd b/w)

For many feminist film critics Josef von Sternberg's star vehicle (see Stars, p. 36) for Marlene Dietrich has been the privileged example of the fetish image of woman in classic cinema. *Morocco* features Dietrich as the cabaret singer Amy Jolly, stranded in Morocco. In her first American movie, and in the many that would follow, the plot illustrates a repeated pattern in which the Dietrich character is caught between the desire of two men. Here, she must choose between wealthy European aristocrat La Bessière (Adolphe Menjou) and foreign legionnaire, Tom Brown (Gary Cooper). Dietrich is the image of glamorous eroticism and perfectly chiselled beauty. Claire Johnston reads the fetishised image of Amy Jolly as an illustration of the absence of woman *as woman* in classic cinema. Woman is a sign, a spectacle, a fetish. For Johnston the image of woman as a semiotic sign denies the opposition man–woman; the real opposition is male–non-male. This is illustrated by Dietrich's famous cross-dressing in the beginning of the film. The masquerade signals the absence of man; the fetishised image merely indicates the exclusion and repression of women (Johnston, 1973/1991, p. 26).

For Laura Mulvey (1975/1989) too, Dietrich is the ultimate (Freudian) fetish in the cycle of Sternberg's films. In order to disavow the castration anxiety that the female figure evokes, she is turned into a fetish; a perfected object of beauty which is satisfying rather than threatening. In this respect, it is significant that Sternberg produces the perfect fetish by playing down the illusion of screen depth; the image of the fetishised woman and the screen space coalesce. In this kind of 'fetishistic scopophilia' the flawless icon of female beauty stops the flow of action and breaks down the controlling look of the male protagonist. The fetish object is displayed for the immediate gaze and enjoyment of the male spectator without mediation of the male screen character. For example, at the end of *Morocco*, Tom Brown has already disappeared into the desert when Amy Jolly kicks off her gold sandals and walks after him into the Sahara. The erotic image of the fetishised woman is established in direct rapport with the spectator. The male hero, says Mulvey, does not know or see (Mulvey, 1989, pp. 22–3).

It is in this possible subversion of the male gaze that the female star can manipulate her image. Kaplan (1983) argues that Dietrich deliberately uses her body as spectacle. Her awareness of Sternberg's fascination with her image accounts for a displayed self-consciousness in her performance before the camera. According to Kaplan, this creates a tension in the image which together with Dietrich's slightly ironic stance, makes the (female) spectator aware of her construction as fetish (Kaplan, 1983, p. 51). For Mary Ann Doane (1982/1991, p. 26) this use of the woman's own body as a disguise points to the masquerade; the self-conscious hyperbolisation of femininity. This excess of femininity is typical of the *femme fatale*. For Doane, too, the masquerade subverts the masculine structure of the look, in defamiliarising female iconography.

For Gaylyn Studlar (1988) the film expresses a masochistic mode of desire. In Sternberg's films the masochistic subject is represented by a male character. Amy Jolly's repeated rejection and public humiliation of La Bessière points to his masochistic self-abnegation. Masochistic desire thrives on pain and La Bessière is indeed shown to relish the public moments of humiliation. The pleasurable humiliation is increased by the entry of the rival and it is no surprise that he helps Amy to find the man she loves, legionnaire Brown. Studlar reads the exquisite torture of the older, richer and higher-class man by the *femme fatale* (either a prostitute or a promiscuous

The fetish object *par excellence* – Marlene Dietrich in *Morocco*

woman), as a sustained attack on the symbolic father and phallic sexuality. At the end of the film La Bessière is reduced to the position of a helpless and abandoned child.

Studlar argues that in the masochistic scenarios of Sternberg's films, sex roles and gender identities are confused. La Bessière is the top-hatted, tuxedoed suitor to Amy. While Amy undermines his symbolic masculinity and social status, she in turn becomes the top-hatted, tuxedoed suitor to Brown. Dietrich's cross-dressing is counterpointed by the effeminised masculine beauty of Tom Brown. The feminisation of the *femme fatale*'s object of desire is further emphasised by the active female gaze. It is Dietrich who singles Brown out in the nightclub where she sings and who looks him over with an appraising gaze. She throws him a flower, which he wears behind his ear. Studlar argues that Dietrich's active look undermines the notion that the male gaze is always one of control.

Marlene Dietrich's tantalising masculinisation added to her androgynous appeal. Andrea Weiss (1992) argues that her sexual ambiguity was embraced as a liberating image by lesbian spectators. Rumour and gossip had already been shared in the gay subculture as early as in the 1930s. Dietrich's rumoured lesbianism has even been exploited by Paramounts' publicity slogan for the release of *Morocco*: 'Dietrich – the woman all women want to see'. In the cross-dressing scene, Amy Jolly performs a French song in a nightclub. She walks down into the audience looking at a woman at a table. She looks over her entire body, turns away and hesitates before looking at the woman again. Then she kisses the woman on her lips, takes her flower and gives it to Tom Brown in the audience. Amy Jolly inverts the heterosexual order of seducer and seduced, while her lesbian flirtation and her butch image make the scene even more subversive. However fleeting and transitory such moments may be in classic cinema, Dietrich's star persona allows the lesbian spectator a glimpse of homo-erotic enjoyment.

Reassemblage (USA 1982 *d* – Trinh T. Minh-ha; sd/col.)

Reassemblage is the first film by Vietnamese-American film-maker Trinh Minh-ha. On the surface it is a documentary about Senegalese women. However, it can also be seen as a poetic impression of the daily life of women living and working in a village in Senegal. Or as a self-reflexive study of the position of the documentary film-maker. The film is definitely an exercise in finding a new language to film the 'other'.

Trinh Minh-ha's work challenges First World feminism. Her focal point is the postcolonial female subject. Both in her writing and films she explores questions of identity, authenticity and difference. The focus of feminist film theory on a psychoanalytic understanding of difference as sexual difference has produced a dichotomy that does not allow for any understanding of the complexities of the many differences in which women live. Within a racialised context, difference means essentially division, dismission or even worse, elimination. Trinh Minh-ha dedicates her words and images to understanding difference, so as to be able to 'live fearlessly with and within difference(s)' (Trinh Minh-ha, 1989, p. 84). She also relies on post-structuralist philosophies of difference, notably Deleuze's nomadology, in order to explore the possibility of positive representations of difference; as something else than merely 'different-from'. She thus combines creative experimentation with theoretical sophistication. (See Alternative aesthetic strategies, p. 125.)

Reassemblage is a film that is fully aware of the anthropological tradition in filming difference and its appropriate gaze of the radical other. It is this kind of cinema that the film defies. It provides the spectator with images of village life, singling out the women for close-up attention and concentrating on the rhythms of their daily activities – shucking corn, grinding grain, washing babies. Repetition of certain shots adds to the rhythm of the montage: the albino child clinging to his black mother, the rotting carcasses of animals.

Trinh Minh-ha breaks with tradition by experimenting with sound. Originally an ethno-musicologist (and still a composer), she has used music to create a contest between the image and the sound. The sound is a-synchronous with the images, abruptly shifting from music, to voice-over, to silence in the same scene. Moreover, the voice-over is not 'the voice of God' of traditional documentary. Trinh Minh-ha herself speaks the commentary and critically reflects on her position as film-maker and on the anthropological recording method. She challenges the objectivity of the camera ('The best way to be neutral and objective is to copy reality in detail, giving different views from different angles'), flatly contradicting her ironical commentary in the images that are shown on the screen. In *Reassemblage* Trinh Minh-ha struggles to find a way of approaching the subject, the African other. She refuses to speak for the other women, rather, she wants to speak nearby the Senegalese. Her self-reflexively critical voice unsettles not only the subject filmed, but also the filming subject.

Reassemblage can be seen as an example of the counter-cinema that Claire Johnston and Laura Mulvey advocated (see p. 354). The film challenges the illusionism and the conventions that deliver the impression of reality. However, the film deconstructs mainstream documentary rather than classic Hollywood, and therefore it deals with issues of the gaze in an altogether different context. The gaze here is not the male gaze that objectifies the woman, but the western gaze that tries to objectify the racial other. This gaze bestows difference upon the other. The issues are thus not centred on visual pleasure and voyeurism, but on conventions of seeing the other. Trinh Minh-ha suggests that one can never really 'see' the other. There is no direct translation possible that makes the radical other accessible or available. The images, which are often strangely framed, or jarringly edited, also suggest that there is no immediate gaze to the other. Difference is fundamentally incommensurable and that is the source of its strength and fascination.

Antonia's Line (Netherlands/Belgium/UK 1995 *p.c* – Guild/Antonia's Line/Bergen/Prime Time Bard/NPS; *d* – Marleen Gorris; sd col.)

Marleen Gorris was the first woman director to win an Oscar for a feature film: the Academy Award for the best foreign film for *Antonia's Line* in 1996. This is all the more remarkable because she is known as an outspoken feminist film-maker. Her first film, *A Question of Silence* (1982) won many prizes at festivals and became a classic feminist hit. The reception was, however, mixed, and many male critics condemned it for its radical feminism, as was the case with her second film, *Broken Mirrors* (1984).

Antonia's Line breaks away from the focus on women's oppression and male violence of Gorris's earlier films. It features the almost utopian history of a matriarchal family within a European country village. Yet, Gorris's particular style can still be recognised in many of her 'authorial signatures'. Humm (1997) therefore argues that Gorris should be viewed as a feminist *auteur*. Her authorship can be situated for example in the genre subversion, the camera direction, the representation of silence as woman's voice, the importance of female friendships, subtle lesbian inflections in the story and biblical references.

Antonia's Line is a film which reflects de Lauretis's call for a feminist cinema that is 'narrative and Oedipal with a vengeance'. It is narrative, but without a male hero, and hence without the voyeurist pleasures of the male gaze. It is Oedipal in the sense that it is about a family, but instead of featuring the triangle of father, mother and child, the film establishes a line of mothers and daughters. The film opens with the old Antonia telling her great-granddaughter Sarah that today she will die. In its exploration of the epic genre, the film tells the story of Antonia's line. Upon her mother's death after the war, Antonia returns with her daughter Danielle to the village where she was born to take over the family farm. When Danielle expresses her wish for a child without a husband, Antonia takes her to town and mother and daughter choose a good-looking stud for impregnation. Danielle gives birth to daughter Therèse, who turns out to be a prodigy and a genius. Therèse, in her turn, becomes mother of the red-haired Sarah.

The establishment of a female genealogy without fathers (or sons, for that matter) is remarkable enough. In that sense, Antonia's family is truly matriarchal. The film's politics lie furthermore in the representation of what Silverman would call the homosexual–maternal fantasmatic. It is within the embrace of mutual love between mothers and daughters that the women can ruthlessly pursue their own desires. As their desires are at odds with patriarchy, they have to fight the bigotry of the village people and especially of the church. It is Antonia's wilful strength that enables women's autonomy for generations to come.

Female desire is represented in all of its diverse manifestations: Antonia's wish for independence, Danielle's quest for artistic creativity, Therèse's pursuit of knowledge, and Sarah's curiosity about life in general. The life of the mind – mathematics, music, philosophy – is eroticised in the film. This is matched by different kinds of female desires, like their friend Letta who wishes to procreate and produces thirteen children. The most moving moments of the film are, however, the scenes in which the women explore sexual desire. When Danielle meets the love of her life, Therèse's female teacher Lara, she sees the object of her desire in her mind's eye as the Venus of Botticelli. When Antonia is already a respected grandmother she tells the farmer Bas that she will not give him her hand, but that she is willing to give him her body; on her conditions. After their first sexual encounter, the film cuts to branches of cherry blossom blowing in the wind. The film thus creates an unexpected link between an older woman's sexuality and the fertility of spring.

Antonia's Line certainly idealises the productive and reproductive power of the homosexual maternal community. It is an inclusive community of family and friends that transcends class, age and religion, where the lesbian, the mentally handicapped, the unmarried mother, the lonely and the weak, and even men, can find refuge. However, this idealisation does not mean that the women are immune to the violence of the world outside. They are confronted with sadistic incest and brutal rape. But together they find the strength to survive and to punish the culpable men.

One of the distinctive features of the film is the use of a disembodied female voice, that is revealed in the last scene as Sarah's. It is a poetic voice that recounts the passing of time and the cycle of life and death. The voice-over brings once more the female fantasmatic firmly within language and history; that is, within the symbolic.

SPECTATORSHIP AND AUDIENCE RESEARCH

The often fraught and contested concept of the film spectator has been central to film theory since the 1970s. Different notions of spectatorship are deployed to determine the ideological effects of the cinema, spectatorial pleasure in the cinema, and how spectators can possibly resist the ideological positioning of the cinema. As Judith Mayne states,

> Spectatorship is not only the act of watching a film, but also the ways one takes pleasure in the experience, or not; the means by which watching movies becomes a passion, or a leisure-time activity like any other. Spectatorship refers to how film-going and the consumption of movies and their myths are symbolic activities, culturally significant events. (Mayne, 1993, p. 1)

Broadly, theorists distinguish between, on the one hand, the concept of the film spectator as a correlate institution of the cinema and a hypothetical point of address by filmic discourse, and, on the other hand, individual empirical viewers, as members of plural, socio-historical audiences. Miriam Hansen identifies the two central questions facing film theorists in a consideration of these two different notions of spectatorship: 'When, how, and to what effect does the cinema conceive of the spectator as a textual term, as the hypothetical point of address of filmic discourse? And once such strategies have been codified, what happens to the viewer as a member of a plural, social audience?' (Hansen, 1991, p. 2). This section focuses primarily on the latter question, the ways in which researchers in film theory and history have attempted to define and analyse the viewer, through historiographic approaches, audience research, investigations of fans, and viewer ethnographies. But while the distinction between the hypothetical spectator and the viewer is important, much of the work on viewers, audiences, and fans still overlaps with and responds to work on the film spectator. In order to comprehend the agenda and importance of viewer-based research, therefore, it is necessary to understand the concept of the spectator conceived as a hypothetical construct. As much of this material has been covered in the sections on structuralism, psychoanalysis and feminism, it will, therefore, be only briefly summarised here.

THE CINEMATIC APPARATUS AND TEXTUAL SYSTEMS

The concept of the film spectator can be traced back to 1970s semiotic and psychoanalytic theories of spectatorship. The spectator was conceptualised under the post-structuralist category of the subject, as understood through the writings of the psychoanalyst Jacques Lacan, and corresponding notions of ideology, especially as elaborated by the Marxist philosopher Louis Althusser.

Lacan appropriates the model of structural linguistics from Saussure and argues that our unconscious is a sign system that functions like a language. According to Lacan, the individual self is not a unified ego, but is consistently produced and transformed by the activity of the unconscious, which is itself produced through the language and perceptions of others. Althusser draws on Lacan's theories to reformulate Marx's concepts of alienation and identity into a theory of the subject. Althusser recasts the classic Marxist model of economic base/superstructure. He views ideology as 'relatively autonomous' of the economic base and determined by it only 'in the last instance'. Ideology takes the form of systems of representation which can have a political effectivity of their own. Althusser distinguishes between repressive state apparatuses (RSAs) (e.g. the police or army) which establish political order through force, and institutional state apparatuses (ISAs) (e.g. the Church, schools, the family, art) which establish order through consent. ISAs contribute to the unconscious formation of individuals by 'hailing' or 'interpellating' them as certain kinds of subjects, summoning them to take up their 'appropriate' role in society. In short, Althusser proposes that individuals are interpellated as social subjects in subtle and largely imperceptible ways – ways which promote in them the illusion that they are consistent, rational, and free human agents.

Arguing from psychoanalytic and Marxist perspectives, film theorists have analysed how the cinema, and especially the classic Hollywood cinema, works to interpellate the film spectator, binding his or her desire with dominant ideological positions, and, above all, how it conceals this ideological process by providing the spectator with the comforting assurance that they are a unified, transcendent, meaning-making subject. Methodologically, the contributions of 1970s film theory to theories of spectatorship can be defined along two separate but related trajectories (for examples of both trajectories, see Rosen, 1986).

First, works influenced by and identified with Metz and Baudry centre on the concept of the cinematic apparatus, the cinema understood as an institutional and ideological machine (see Apparatus theory, p. 348). The apparatus refers to the general conditions and relations of cinematic spectatorship, and apparatus theory considers the subject effects specific to cinema, to the kind of machine it is, to the kind of viewing situation it generally involves. Due to the specific ways the cinema is arranged spatially, perceptually and socially (the darkness of the cinema, the spectator's seeming isolation, the placement of the projector behind the spectator's head, and the framing and structure of the film image), the cinematic apparatus is theorised in terms of Plato's prison cave, the mirror stage (Lacan), principles of Renaissance perspective, and idealist philosophy. Through these arrangements, as well as through the 'realist effect' of the cinema, the spectator, according to apparatus theory, is positioned as the transcendent vanishing point of filmic address. Returned to a regressive state of imaginary wholeness, the spectator imagines himself or herself as a transcendent meaning-making subject (mobile rather than immobile, active rather than passive, creating rather than absorbing meaning). The cinema, according to apparatus theory, works to acculturate and interpellate viewers to structures of fantasy, dream and pleasure that are aligned with dominant ideology.

The second axis of 1970s film theory, while overlapping with apparatus theory in many ways, emphasises the specifically textual operations of the cinematic institution. Rather than the spatial, perceptual, and social arrangements of the apparatus, theorists like Raymond Bellour, Thierry Kuntzel and Stephen Heath provided extremely detailed analyses of individual classic Hollywood films which were seen to represent the cinematic institution. Relying on the linguistic concept of enunciation (taken from Emile Beneviste) as well as psychoanalysis and semiotics, these text-based theories of spectatorship analyse how the textual system of particular films solicit and interpellate the spectator's understanding and subjectivity – organising knowledge, authority, pleasure and identification through systematic processes of vision and narration. The subject of textual analysis seems superficially to be more active than the subject of the cinematic apparatus, in so far as the subject of textual analysis is asked to take part in a hypothetical reading. Yet, both apparatus theory and analyses of textual systems imply that the spectator's imaginary participation in the filmic event depends upon the false illusion that they are the enunciating author of filmic fiction.

In both apparatus theory and text-based systemic analyses, the spectator represents a term of discourse, an effect of signifying structures, and not an empirical movie-goer. The emphasis in these theories is on the way in which the cinematic institution inscribes certain viewing positions which the social viewer is asked to take up, a process of identification and desire that predetermines the viewer's subject position. Both apparatus theory and analyses of textual systems have been criticised for positing too monolithic and globalising a view of the film spectator. Critics have argued, first, that such abstract and generalisable conceptions of film spectatorship fail to account for how subjects are constituted differently by sexual, gendered,

Queen Christina (USA 1933 *p.c* – MGM; *d* – Rouben Mamoulian; sd b/w)

In her analysis of lesbian spectatorships, Andrea Weiss foreground the important role that rumour and gossip have played in gay subcultures and the ways in which gossip about stars affected viewers' responses to their films. Weiss claims that because dominant ideology seeks to make homosexuality invisible, gay history has been necessarily located in rumour, innuendo, and coded language. She describes how Hollywood marketed the suggestion of lesbianism in such stars as Dietrich, Hepburn and Garbo, to address straight male voyeuristic interest in lesbianism, but argues that this innuendo enabled female viewers to 'explore their own erotic gaze without giving it a name, and in the safety of their private fantasy in a darkened theatre' (Weiss, 1991, p. 286). These fantasies were supported by gossip about the presumed 'real life' lesbianism of the actresses, especially Dietrich and Garbo.

In *Queen Christina*, Weiss claims that Garbo gives her portrayal sufficient sexual ambiguity so that her actions and manner become coded for lesbian viewers. In addition to the scene where Garbo's Christina kisses Countess Ebba on the lips, Weiss identifies other coded lesbian elements. These include Garbo's androgyny, Christina's dressing in men's clothes, Christina's choice of desire over duty, the interaction between women in the film, and the film's complicated attitude toward marriage. For instance, Christina, who opts to die a 'bachelor' and not an 'old maid', tells a story about Molière, who said that marriage is shocking, which reverses the sentiment that the queen's refusal to marry is shocking. She includes his comment about enduring the idea of sleeping with a man in the room. For viewers privy to the gossip about Garbo's affair with scriptwriter Salka Viertal, this comment offers an inside lesbian joke.

In Weiss's reading then, gossip and rumour serve as means for lesbian spectators to define and empower themselves against dominant heterosexual ideology. Spectatorship is thus seen as an oppositional act of appropriation. But, as Weiss suggests, Hollywood texts like *Queen Christina* are already inflected with queer and camp codes, albeit intended to appeal to heterosexual men. Thus, queer readings redefine the dominant even as they appropriate from it. In Alexander Doty's terms, they make the notion that mass culture is 'straight' a 'highly questionable given' (Doty, 1993, p. 104).

Gone With the Wind (USA 1939 *p.c* – MGM/Selznick International; *d* – Victor Fleming; sd Technicolor)

Helen Taylor's ethnographic analysis of female viewers of *Gone With the Wind* takes a viewer-orientated approach to spectatorship that contradicts many of the assumptions of text-based analyses of the film. Taylor placed an ad in a wide range of British publications asking readers who were fans of *Gone With the Wind* to write to her about their memories, experiences and views of both the book and the film. She received a total of 427 letters and amassed 355 questionnaires, mostly from women (25 men responded). The respondents represented a cross-section of women of all ages, from different backgrounds, including a handful of black women and a few dozen Americans.

Taylor's analysis points to the importance of the social situation of viewing, as

Camp codes and sexual ambiguity – *Queen Christina*?

Read through the prism of personal histories – *Gone With the Wind*

many women recalled seeing the film with other women as part of a friendship ritual. It also underlines the importance of the book as a context for understanding the film. Text-based analyses of films rarely take into account the structure of expectations created by a novel when it is adapted. Taylor's respondents tended, on the whole, to have read the novel and seen the film several times; they viewed their experiences of these texts as separable but not isolated events. This tendency toward multiple, even obsessive, viewing and reading suggests that women's pleasure in the text exceeds plot and focuses instead on the affective dimension of the narrative and on an identification with and interest in Scarlett as a character.

Taylor also indicates how changes in the women's lives and consciousness affected their reading of the film. For many women, *Gone With the Wind* evoked a rich source of nostalgia, tied to the film's evocation of a past that is both real and mythic, and as a treasured part of many women's personal histories. At the same time, viewers' attitudes toward the film, and especially its racism, have altered over time, so that many viewers reported their increasing embarrassment and horror at the film's support of the Ku Klux Klan and in its racial stereotyping. Also, young viewers more frequently criticised the book's racism than older viewers. Attitudes towards the film's racism were also affected by respondents race. Many white women distinguished between Mammy and Prissy, viewing the former as a figure of nobility and dignity and the latter as a more irritating and offensive stereotype. Black viewers, by contrast, tended to see both characters as offensive stereotypes.

In addition to providing a larger social and historical context for understanding the film, Taylor's approach also challenges one of the most basic tenets of classic film theory. Text-based theorists emphasise the importance of closure and resolution in classic narrative. *Gone With the Wind*, however, has a famously unresolved ending, one that raises new enigmas rather than solving the old, and one that resists the clear happy ending of romance. Respondents seemed to prefer the unresolved ending to what they perceived as the unbelievable option of a 'Hollywood' one. This related both to their knowledge of the book and desire to have the film be true to Margaret Mitchell's intentions and to their pleasure in constructing their own fantasy endings. Unlike a definite ending, which could close off viewer participation, the ambiguous ending demanded a creative response from viewers who were free to choose different versions of what would happen 'tomorrow'.

and racial differences. And, second, critics claim that the attention to domination and control and the enforcement of assigned ideological positions seem to offer too little room to imagine models of resistance to the dominant ideology and ways to change the signifying systems.

FEMINIST INTERVENTIONS

Feminist film theory offered the first important critique of these models. The earliest feminist psychoanalytic interventions into spectator theory were articulated by Stephen Heath and Julia Lesage, but crystallised in Laura Mulvey's famous

1975 'Visual Pleasure' essay. Mulvey's essay critiques both the apparatus model and the text-based model of spectatorship theory for not taking into account the importance of the representation of the female form in the cinema's symbolic order and she points out that classic spectatorship is fundamentally gendered as masculine, which makes dominant routes of identification problematic for the female spectator (see Mulvey, p. 353).

Since the 1970s, feminist film theorists have grappled with Mulvey's provocative claims about the 'male gaze', often in contention with her bleak assessment of the female spectatorial position (cf. Bergstrom and Doane, 1989; Doane, 1991; Pribram, 1988; Gamman and Marshment, 1989; Hansen, 1986). Initially, feminist film theorists criticised Mulvey for duplicating the problem she identifies because in 'Visual pleasure' she leaves the female spectator out of her analysis. Addressing this problem, in her 'Afterthoughts on "Visual Pleasure and Narrative Cinema"', Mulvey envisions the female spectator's activity as an either/or hopscotch between positions of identification; she pictures the female spectator shifting unconsciously between an active masculine and a passive feminine identity.

Mary Ann Doane has argued that in opposition to transvestitism, the concept of female masquerade offers a more radical concept of spectatorship. Joan Rivière's 1929 essay, has been taken up in feminist theory as a divining rod pointing to the 'performative status' and 'imitative structure' of the feminine. Doane suggests that 'a woman might flaunt her femininity, produce herself as an excess of femininity, in other words, foreground the masquerade' in order to 'manufacture a lack in the form of a certain distance between oneself and one's image' (Doane, 1991, pp. 25–6). Doane uses the example of *Stella Dallas*'s self-parody as an instance of 'double mimesis' or self-conscious masquerade. When Stella effectively parodies herself, pretending to be an even more exaggeratedly embarrassing mother than she is in the rest of the narrative, she demonstrates her recognition of herself as a stereotype (a pose, a trope) while making the excessiveness of her role visible and strange, depriving the initial mimesis of its currency. Although Doane locates distanciation primarily in the text, rather than reception, she underlines the masquerade's potential usefulness for understanding the spectator's activity as well as the performer's: 'What might it mean to masquerade as a spectator? To assume the mask in order to see in a different way?' (Doane, 1991, p. 26). The trope of the masquerade, then, helps to describe a process of negotiation between textual address and the viewer. The concept of negotiation implies an ongoing process of give and take. It suggests that a range of positions of identification may exist within any text; and that, rather than having their response wholly determined by the text, audiences may shift subject positions as they interact with the text.

An interest in determining the specific mechanisms of female spectatorship has led many feminists to consider how specific genres and films address a female spectator. They have investigated certain films and genres which were specifically and historically aimed at a female audience, such as Rudolph Valentino films (Hansen, 1986) or the women's film (Gledhill, 1987; Doane, 1987). These studies are interested in the ways that a specific address to woman complicates a Mulveyian model which assumes an address to the male spectator. They suggest that in these moments the cinematic institution foregrounds its market orientation to a female consumer and thus opens up a potential gap or contradiction (albeit fleeting) between patriarchal ideology, on one side, and the recognition of female experience, desires and fantasies, on the other.

Theories of the gaze

Feminist film theory has provided a crucial forum for discussing, and models for understanding, modes of spectatorship for other empirical viewers who share the female spectator's alienation from the dominant gays and lesbians, and racial or ethnic minorities. One avenue of research in feminist film theory and theories of spectatorship has been what, for purposes of abbreviation, can be called 'gaze theory'. 'Gaze' theory tries to ascertain whether there are alternative gazes operating in the cinema, such as a 'female gaze' (Gamman and Marshment), a 'gay', 'lesbian' or 'queer gaze' (Doty, 1993; Evans and Gamman, 1995; Gever *et al.*, 1993; Hamer and Budge, 1994), a 'black gaze' (Roach and Felix, 1989) and so on.

Conceptualising alternative gazes to Mulvey's 'male gaze' offers ways to reconsider the film text as less monolithic in its address and tends to focus on contradictions and gaps in the cinematic institution's dominant ideology and, therefore, on ways the cinema might be seen as less controlling and more flexible in its constitution of the subject (see The female look, p. 357).

For instance, by considering a 'queer gaze', theorists have suggested ways we might reinterpret the fetishistic spectacle of masses of female bodies in Busby Berkeley musical numbers. Rather than predicate their assessment of Berkeley's sexual politics on the assumption that Berkeley's numbers are unequivocally addressed to a masculine spectator and that they wholeheartedly support the patriarchal ideology which they, undoubtedly, portray, queer theory focuses on how lesbian spectators might locate a lesbian erotic in the numbers (Doty, 1993, pp. 13–14). A number like the title song of Ray Enright's 1934 *Dames* (which features images of women two by two in bed, exercising in sexy pyjamas, and bathing together before turning into black-and-white abstractions) seems equally available to be read as lesbian imagery as well as in terms of the girl–girl eroticism favoured in straight male pornography. Even assuming a masculine address, then, different notions of the gaze help to understand these and other potentially oppositional ways in which viewers might be able to negotiate their experience of these texts.

The application of gaze theory to alternative models of spectatorship has been critiqued, however, for producing overly rigid models of social relationships and for sticking too closely to the terms of the monolithic apparatus and text-based models of spectatorship (Evans and Gamman, 1995; Williams, 1995). The single, unitary spectator of gaze theory has gradually been challenged by theories and histories of diverse viewing positions.

The questions feminist film theorists have raised about female spectatorship and the methods and models they offer have thus served as a springboard for a reconsideration of spectatorship models as determined by the semiotic–psychoanalytic framework. Theorists of female spectatorship and spectatorship among other minority groups have increasingly begun to analyse the social and historical factors that shape film spectatorship. Increasingly, film theorists, influenced by the Frankfurt School and British cultural studies, attempt to give the concept of the spectator historical specificity and/or ethnographic precision to account for different kinds of readings and possible forms of subcultural resistance. Some of the most important areas for a reconsideration of spectatorship and empirical viewers have taken place through revisionist histories of the cinematic institution and its audience, reception, research on fans and ethnographic research.

PRECLASSIC SPECTATORSHIP

In the 1970s, film theory and film history were largely separate areas of inquiry. In the 1980s, however, film theorists have increasingly turned to 'the contradictions posed by film history' (Hansen, 1991, p. 5) to challenge the theoretical model of the spectator as passive subject, pure absorber of dominant ideology, as well as the model of a singular dominating male voyeur. Concentrating on preclassic and postclassic moments in film history, film theorists and historians have questioned 'the orthodoxies of a classical spectatorship without abandoning the fundamental insight that there is something to be learned from the moving picture and its apparatus about the spectators who gaze at it, look at it, glance at it, or avert their eyes from it' (Williams, 1995, p. 4).

Many of the most important challenges to the classic model of spectatorship have taken place in revisionist histories of early cinema practices. These histories oppose the technological determinism of apparatus theory, which suggests that once the technological apparatus was invented, classic cinema, and its codes of realism, followed. Revisionist histories and theories suggest, instead, that more than technology was involved in the invention of classic cinema and that early cinema offered alternative models of spectatorship (see Early cinema, p. 93).

Perhaps the most influential among the-orists of early cinema practice is Tom Gunning, whose term 'the cinema of attractions' and, to a lesser degree, 'aesthetics of astonishment' (Gunning, 1990, 1995) now vie with Mulvey's 'male gaze' as the most frequently cited formulations in the field. Gunning plays on Eisenstein's sense of attraction as well as the term's more colloquial use in the context of fairgrounds, amusements and other commercial entertainment venues. He discusses how early cinema adopted a display aesthetic similar to these commercial attractions, an aesthetic which was defined by the goal of astonishing viewers with sensational displays and direct address, as opposed to suturing them into a classic narrative. Gunning points out that 'early cinema was not dominated by the narrative impulse that later asserted its sway over the medium' but was instead an exhibitionist cinema, 'a cinema that displays its visibility, willing to rupture a self-enclosed fictional world for a chance to solicit the attention of the spectator' (Gunning, 1990, pp. 56–7). Gunning sees an affinity between early cinema and late avant-garde cinema, both of which can be described as cinemas of 'attractions'.

In addition to providing a better understanding of film spectatorship in early and avant-garde cinema, Gunning's theories of attractions and astonishment point to aspects of spectatorship that have been ignored and undervalued in apparatus theory and under gaze paradigms. Rather than see these spectatorial relations to cinema as exclusive to early cinema, theorists have adopted Gunning's terms to account for pleasures in all forms of cinema that are irreducible to more technologically determined modes of ideological absorption and the voyeuristic look. The notion of 'attractions,' especially, has opened up theories of film spectatorship to consider the power of diverse spectacles in cinema to undermine and challenge narrative's realist grip.

Miriam Hansen has also re-evaluated early-cinema practices and reception to challenge the seeming inevitability of classic spectatorship and to consider how the cinema provided the conditions for an alternative public sphere. She views the cinema itself as a public sphere 'defined by particular relations of representation and reception' and dependent upon 'processes specific to the institution of cinema, that is, the uneven development of modes of production, distribution, and exhibition' (Hansen, 1991, p. 7). Hansen considers the relationship between the cinema and other aspects of public life to determine 'how the public, as a collective and intersubjective horizon, is constituted and constitutes itself under particular conditions and circumstances' (Hansen, 1991, p. 8). During a crucial phase of the cinema's development, Hansen claims, it depended on peripheral social groups (immigrants, women, members of the newly urbanised working class) and thus necessarily catered to people with specific needs, anxieties, and fantasies. She views the elaboration of classic modes of narration and spectator positioning as a response to the problem of making the cinema available to these diverse, unruly, and sexually mixed audiences. Instead of a teleology of classic cinema, however, Hansen sees early cinema as a composite public sphere which allowed a margin of improvisation, interpretation and unpredictability that made cinema a public event open to reappropriation by film viewers of diverse backgrounds and interests.

Audience composition

Historians have also been interested in the social make-up of early cinema audiences and have addressed issues of ethnicity, class and urban geography to provide a crucial counter-argument to more monolithic notions of spectatorship by focusing on the specific social make-up of audiences (Allen, 1979; Gomery, 1982; Jowett, 1974; Merritt, 1985). These histories often focus on Manhattan's nickelodeon boom which has functioned as a shorthand for the birth of the movies in general. Often historians concentrate on identifying changes in the class composition of nickelodeon and picture-palace audiences, frequently focusing on European immigrants as audiences or exhibition in ethnic white neighbourhoods. Counter to traditional histories of the cinema which framed early cinema as a lower-class amusement, revisionist historians starting in the 1970s emphasised the degree to which middle-class audiences altered the cinema, managing to appropriate and 'uplift' the cinema to suit their tastes and objectives (much as they had uplifted vaudeville). Robert C. Allen's (1979) text is key in this revisionist impulse. Allen examines the location of nickelodeons and claims that the majority of nickelodeons were not in immigrant neighbourhoods but in putatatively middle-class neighbourhoods or traditional entertainment districts that served a variety of social types.

In her emphasis on how classic cinema responds to early immigrant and working-class audiences, and not exclusively to middle-class interests, Hansen's work can be seen as a crucial modification of this view. Ben Singer's work (1995) on nickelodeons also calls the revisionist argument into question. Supplementing Allen's data, remapping the nickelodeons' placement in the city, and reviewing urban geography of the period, Singer finds that the immigrant and working-class foundations of cinema in traditional histories may not have been myth but a fairly accurate characterisation of early audiences.

Historical audience research has also focused on minority groups who, until recently, were marginalised by film theory and history. For instance, still working within American social history, Mary Carbine has examined African–American spectatorship in Chicago to challenge the emphasis on European immigration in histories of the nickelodeons. She notes that the nickelodeon boom also coincided with the 'Great Migration' of Southern blacks to northern cities in America. Examining the 'culturally specific' ways black spectators used early cinema, Carbine claims that the 'dynamic of reception was inflected with the dynamic of black performance', and especially the live performance of African-American blues and jazz (Carbine, 1990, p. 23). Carbine thus challenges notions of the seemingly isolated and passive spectator and points to the ways in which different audiences can transform the cinematic institution according to their own cultural needs and fantasies.

In a different vein, Richard deCordova has analysed the children's audience and the rise of matinees. He analyses reformist audience studies of the 1920s and 1930s and suggests that 'an investigation of the practices through which researchers attempted to understand the child audience may tell us something about audience research today and the various power relations that subtend it' (deCordova, 1990, p. 92). He points out the oddity of the child's neglect in film history, since the image of the child has functioned as a precondition of audience research generally (in its paternalistic reformist mode – and, we might add, in psychoanalytic theory as well). Rather than simply fill a gap in audience research, deCordova's research, along with Carbine's, suggests the degree to which traditional concepts of spectatorship are constructed according to exclusionary and ahistorical models.

RECEPTION THEORY

Overlapping with the new historiographic impulse in studies of spectatorship, but approaching the question from a somewhat different angle, is a burgeoning interest, since the mid-1980s, in reception. Rather than focusing on production or the cinematic text, reception studies take into account a broad range of extra-cinematic materials – including, as above, social history and audience composition, as well as reviews, commentary, fan discourse, star images or texts, commodity tie-ins, scandal, and other discourses and

events that produce the conditions of reading and reception for the film text.

Janet Staiger, for instance, takes what she describes as a historical materialist approach to reception studies of individual films. She considers how films become encrusted with meaning over time and analyses how the discourses surrounding individual films become part of their meaning and help to determine their reception in different periods. Her analysis includes not only contemporary reviews and discourses around films, but also later transformations of a film's reception and various discourses surrounding films, including academic readings. In her analysis of Griffith's *The Birth of a Nation*, for example, Staiger considers the initial controversy surrounding the film's release in 1915, related to questions of racism, and how racist attitudes intersect with other tacit assumptions – about 'what constitutes acceptable historiography; whether a film should be judged on the content or effects of its subject matter, narrational procedures, or some combination of them; and whether censorship of certain representations is more important than free speech' (Staiger, 1992, p. 146). She then shows how debates in the 1930s transformed the reception of *The Birth of a Nation*, as the film was appropriated by progressive radicals as a symptom of Fascist and monopoly capitalist ideologies and to demonstrate the links between racism and class exploitation.

BRITISH CULTURAL STUDIES

In addition to a renewed interest in historiography, film studies and theories of spectatorship have been profoundly influenced by cultural studies. The Birmingham Centre for Contemporary Cultural Studies, especially under the leadership of Stuart Hall, can justifiably lay claim to being the key institution in the widely expanding field of cultural studies. The Centre's Marxism was aligned with the work of Antonio Gramsci, and especially his notion of hegemony. Gramsci's theory of hegemony holds that cultural domination, or, more precisely, cultural leadership, is not achieved through force or coercion, but secured through the consent of those it will ultimately subordinate. The subordinated groups consent to the dominant because they accept as 'common sense' the view of the world offered to them by the dominant group. The concept of hegemony differs from Althusser's ISAs (institutional state apparatuses) in viewing cultural domination as not inevitably produced through language or ISAs but as the product of complex negotiations and alignments of interest. The achievement of hegemony is sustained only through the ongoing process of winning consent. In emphasising consent and 'common sense', Gramsci's concept of hegemony also provides a point of entry into imagining resistance. As opposed to 'top–down' theories of ideology, which reduce the subject into a passive dupe of the culture industry, Gramsci's concept of hegemony appealed to cultural studies because it offered a 'bottom–up' theory which attributes power to the subject and to subcultural groups to intervene in the signifying and political systems and to produce change. Gramsci envisions a class of organic intellectuals who can produce counter-hegemonic ideas, resistant world-views which can alter dominant ideology and effect change.

Considering how viewers might be seen as resisting dominant ideology has led researchers influenced by cultural studies to consider the active role of the viewer in interpreting texts. Stuart Hall's (1980) essay, 'Encoding/Decoding' has been particularly influential for rethinking how viewer's interpret texts. Hall argues against those who explain the processes of communication as a direct line from sender to receiver. As Graeme Turner explains, Hall points out that 'just because a message has been sent, this is no guarantee that it will arrive; every moment in the process of communication, from the original composition of the message (encoding) to the points at which it is read and understood (decoding) has its own determinants' (Turner, 1992, p. 89). While some viewers accept the dominant as encoded, and others adopt an opposing position, most viewers engage in negotiated decoding practices which acknowledge the dominant definitions of the world but may still lay claim to exceptions in local or specific cases as determined by geography, ethnicity, class, gender and so on.

This attention to the positions viewers bring to texts can be seen in subcultural studies. Emphasising the minority, rather than the majority, the subordinate rather than the dominant, subcultural studies examined the strategies subcultures used to negotiate or oppose the dominant to make their own meanings by actively appropriating and transforming the dominant through manipulating its codes (Hebdige, 1979).

Influenced by cultural studies, later film theory has been marked by a developing interest in viewers, to see how they resist ideological positioning through decoding practices and 'fail' to take up dominant positions. This relates to many of the above-mentioned challenges to the model of passive spectatorship, such as 'gaze theory', concepts of negotiated readings, and the interest in gaps and contradictions at the textual level – in fact, to any analysis of ideology which does not simply posit a top–down theory of passively absorbent spectatorship. What distinguishes cultural studies research most clearly in its analysis of reception is the introduction of pleasure as a category separate from ideology. Within earlier formations, pleasure was seen as part of the deceptive apparatus and was interrogated for the politics it concealed. A competing perspective, however, has viewed pleasure as a dimension of cultural decoding that is in some way resistant to dominant ideologies.

STARS AND FANS

Star studies have proved an especially fruitful area of investigation for theorists interested in the joint process of encoding and decoding (see Gledhill, 1991; Dyer, 1979 and 1989; also Stars, p. 33). The star text consists of cinematic and extracinematic elements (fan discourse, song sheets, publicity stills, interviews, etc.). From the perspective of ideological encoding, star studies emphasise the contradictions and gaps in star texts. Stars, as Richard Dyer argues, represent a 'structured polysemy, that is, the finite multiplicity of meanings and affects they embody and the attempt to structure them so that some meanings and affects are foregrounded and others are masked or displaced' (Dyer, 1979, p. 3). Rather than a simplistic relation between a given star text and a single ideology, Dyer claims that stars exist 'within and between ideologies' so that they may either manage and resolve contradictions, expose contradictions, 'or embody an alternative or oppositional ideological position (itself usually contradictory) to dominant ideology' (Dyer, 1979, p. 38). From the perspective of decoding, star studies emphasise the ways in which members of different classes, genders, races, ethnicities and sexualities appropriate or read the star text and how their readings manage, expose or resolve those contradictions. Dyer's analysis of Paul Robeson's star text, for instance, investigates the contradiction between the emphasis on blackness in Robeson's image – 'musically, in his primary association with Negro folk music, especially spirituals; in the theatre and films, in the recurrence of Africa as a motif; and in general in the way his image is so bound up with notions of racial character, the nature of black folks, the Negro essence, and so on' (Dyer, 1986, p. 67) and his status as a crossover star who appealed to white and black audiences alike. Dyer's analysis of the discourses surrounding Robeson in relation to his films shows that the discourse of blackness in Robeson's star image was managed differently by white and black audiences. Where Robeson represented a positive view of atavistic folk blackness as a radical alternative to white western culture, he could be seen simultaneously as fitting into white stereotypes of 'Sambo', Uncle Tom and the black brute.

Concomitant with an interest in stars, cultural studies has also opened the way for researchers to consider fans as active users of popular culture. Theorists have analysed fandom as an extreme case of viewer activity, a stigmatised activity marked by deviance and pathology; as a marker of cultural taste; and as a sensibility that helps construct coherent identities (see Lewis, 1992). Theorists have also analysed fans to determine the nature of spectatorial pleasure in texts and stars, and how fans read against the grain to construct oppositional meanings. Much of this research is still text based and focuses on fan discourse in popular magazines, reviews, box-office sales, interviews, publicity materials and star's performances in particular films to ascertain what elements of a star's persona fans respond to (Gaines, 1986; Roberts, 1993; Robertson, 1996). As with other areas of research, investigations of fans tends to focus on the way in which gender, race, ethnicity, class and sexuality shape fan responses. Shari Roberts, for instance, notes that while Carmen Miranda's star text 'offers various negative images of Latin Americans and of women, her persona also reveals these images as stereotypes, allowing for negotiated readings by fans' (Roberts, 1993, p. 4). Roberts notes that some fans were able to understand Miranda's stereotypical image as a kind of masquerade and 'were, thereby, through interpretation and fantasy, able to identify with her as one way to negotiate or cope with their own minority status in society' (Roberts, 1993, p. 18).

Empowerment and identification – *The Color Purple*

ETHNOGRAPHIC RESEARCH

To determine how 'real' viewers and fans actually decode texts, many theorists since the mid-1980s have turned to ethnographic analysis of viewers. The ethnographic approach has been more visible in television studies than in cinema (see Ang, 1985; Brunsdon, 1981; Hobson, 1982; Jenkins, 1992; Morley, 1980; Penley, 1991; Seiter, 1991). This is partly because television watching is the most representative and common spectating activity in contemporary industrial societies, but also relates to film studies' suspicion of sociological approaches in analysing media. In his article on ethnographic research into children's audiences, Richard deCordova reminds us that current interest in audience and ethnography represents a return to a set of interests and methods that characterised the earliest researches on film. But, as he suggests, this return to the repressed has arisen largely as a means of complicating psychoanalytic and semiotic models of spectatorship. Where early sociological studies viewed cinema as a threat to presumably vulnerable audiences like women and children, more recent ethnographic research has arisen as a response to the passive model of spectatorship in 1970s film theory – it has as its avowed aim the empowerment of spectators and an interest in how viewers actively interpret texts and take pleasure in them.

Using the encoding/decoding model, Jacqueline Bobo interviewed African-American female viewers of Spielberg's *The Color Purple* (1985) to 'examine the way in which a specific audience creates meaning from a mainstream text and uses the reconstructed meaning to empower themselves and their social group' (Bobo, 1988, p. 93). Against the largely negative reception of the film among both black and white reviewers, Bobo finds that African-American female viewers discovered something progressive and useful in the film. As sophisticated oppositional viewers of black representation in Hollywood, the African-American women Bobo interviewed were able to filter out the negative stereotypes, and they engaged with the film as part of a broader movement among African-American women to construct and consume more works orientated to African-American women's experiences and their history.

Other analysts have tried to reconstruct viewer's responses historically by asking viewers to send letters and fill out questionnaires about their memories of certain films and stars. Using this approach, Richard Dyer has analysed gay men's subcultural camp response to Judy Garland; Helen Taylor has investigated the lasting appeal of Fleming's *Gone With the Wind* (1939) among female fans; and Jackie Stacey has analysed the meanings and affects of 1940s female stars for British women. More than simply telling us about why certain people like certain film and stars, these ethnographic studies help us to understand the social dimensions of film viewing, and especially to consider the social and historical dimensions of identification. Dyer, for instance, notes the socio-historical dimension of gay men's attendance at Garland concerts which 'constituted a kind of going public or coming out before the emergence of gay liberationist politics' (Dyer, 1979, p. 145). Taylor counters the notion of singular spectator positioning by pointing to 'the varied and contradictory ways in which this one work has accumulated significance in their lives, making the notion of a single *Gone With the Wind* impossible' (Taylor, 1989, p. 232). And Stacey underlines the importance of extra-cinematic practices, such as copying stars style and clothing, or imitating their mannerisms, as important dimensions of cinematic identification (Stacey, 1994).

Ethnographic research has posed some methodological and ideological problems for film theorists. First, theorists have raised questions about the degree to which the subjects' statements can be taken at face value or need to be interpreted, an issue which raises the related problem of the researcher's position *vis-à-vis* their subjects, the degree to which they will read into their statements what they want to hear. A second problem is that since much interest in film spectatorship takes classic Hollywood films and stars as its subject, ethnographic research interested in viewers' initial responses to films must be reconstructed from viewers' memories and are thus potentially modified by nostalgia, changed perspectives or other shifts in their attitudes toward the films and stars they discuss. While these problems are still being debated, ethnographic research has, nonetheless, enriched spectator studies.

CONCLUSION

This overview of spectatorship and audience research has been necessarily schematic in tracing out the trends in approaches to spectators and viewers. Trends can, however, be trendy. Since the late 1980s, there has been a tendency to categorise spectatorship too schematically as an either/or proposition, particularly in relation to pleasure, an impulse 'to categorise texts and readings/responses as either conservative or radical, as celebratory of the dominant order or critical of it' (Mayne, 1993, p. 93). The 'dominant' model, which focuses on the hypothetical spectator, argues that the cinematic apparatus and texts interpellate viewers into essentialist positions of subjecthood and so believes that the ties to those texts must be broken. These models tend to view pleasure as a form of cultural domination, passively imbibed, which renders us all cultural dupes. The 'dominant' model rightfully points out the problem with unexamined pleasure, its complicity with an oppressive sexual regime. Still, these models do not provide a means to name the pleasures viewers do take.

On the other side of the debate, however, the 'resistance' model's assumption that the activity of making meaning resides solely with viewers, falls into a similar determinism. Cultural studies, in particular, has been identified with the resistance model, which valorises pleasure as redemptive. Meaghan Morris sums up the typical mode of argument in this 'banal' 'vox pop style': 'People in modern mediatised societies are complex and contradictory, mass cultural texts are complex and contradictory, therefore people using them produce complex and contradictory culture' (Morris, 1990, p. 30). In ascribing unqualified power to viewer response, this model suggests that, rather than interpellating viewers, the text produces a multiplicity of meanings from which the viewer can choose his or her point of identification. If the conservative model reifies pleasure in seeing texts as 'dominant' and audiences as dupes, the viewer-orientated model similarly reifies pleasure in ignoring the force of dominant ideology in favour of a free-for-all textual and cultural ambiguity. In ascribing an unqualified power to viewers' pleasure, this model often fails to account for the ways in which pleasure can merely affirm the dominant order.

Researchers have been trying increasingly to negotiate between these two extremes. The historiographic models discussed above provide a crucial intervention into this debate and help to mediate between these two positions. This process of negotiating between these models must continue if we are to understand the genuinely contradictory mechanisms at play in film spectatorship, the ideological effects of the cinema and spectatorial pleasure.

SELECTED READING

Robert C. Allen, 'From exhibition to reception: reflections on the audience in film history', *Screen* 31(4), 1990.

Jacqueline Bobo, '*The Color Purple*: black women as cultural readers', in *Female Spectators: Looking at Film and Television*, Pribram (ed.), London, Verso, 1988.

Mary Carbine, '"The finest outside the loop": motion picture exhibition in Chicago's black metropolis', *Camera Obscura* 23, May 1990.

Richard deCordova, 'Ethnography and exhibition: the child audience, the Hays Office and Saturday matinées', *Camera Obscura* 23, May 1990.

Mary Anne Doane, 'Film and the masquerade: theorizing the female spectator' and 'Masquerade reconsidered: further thoughts on the female spectator', in *Femmes Fatales: Feminism, film Theory, Psychoanalysis*, New York, Routledge, 1991.

Alexander Doty, *Making Things Perfectly Queer: Interpreting Mass Culture,* Minneapolis, University of Minnesota Press, 1993.

Richard Dyer, *Heavenly Bodies: Film Stars and Society*, New York, St. Martin's Press, 1986.

Tom Gunning, 'The cinema of attractions: early film, its spectator and the avant-garde', in *Early Cinema: Space, Frame, Narrative*, Thomas Elsaesser (ed.), London, BFI, 1990.

Miriam Hansen, *Babel and Babylon: Spectatorship in American Silent Film*, London, Harvard University Press, 1991.

Judith Mayne, *Cinema and Spectatorship*, London, Routledge, 1993.

Pamela Robertson, *Guilty Pleasures: Feminist Camp From Mae West to Madonna*, Durham, Duke University Press, 1996.

Jackie Stacey, *Star Gazing: Hollywood Cinema and Female Spectatorship*, London, Routledge, 1994.

Janet Staiger, *Interpreting Films: Studies in the Historical Reception of American Cinema*, Princeton, Princeton University Press, 1992.

Melvyn Stokes and Richard Maltby (eds), *American Movie Audiences: from the turn of the century to the early sound era*, London, BFI, 1999.

Helen Taylor, *Scarlett's Women: Gone With The Wind and Its Female Fans*, London, Virago, 1989.

Andrea Weiss, '"A queer feeling when I look at you": Hollywood stars and lesbian spectatorship in the 1930s', in *Stardom: Industry of Desire*, Gledhill (ed.), London, Routledge, 1991.

BIBLIOGRAPHY

PART 1: CLASSIC HOLLYWOOD CINEMA

Richard Abel, *The Ciné Goes to Town: French Cinema, 1896–1914*, Berkeley, University of California Press, 1994.

Robert C. Allen, 'William Fox presents *Sunrise*', *Quarterly Review of Film Studies* 2(3), August 1977.

Tino Balio (ed.), *The American Film Industry*, Madison, University of Wisconsin Press, 1976; new edn, 1985.

Gregory Black, *Hollywood Censored: Morality Codes, Catholics and the Movies*, New York, Cambridge University Press, 1994.

Ephraim Katz, *The International Film Encyclopaedia*, London, Macmillan Press, 1980; 3rd edn, 1998.

Geoffrey Nowell-Smith (ed.), 'Silent Cinema 1895–1930' Part 1 of *The Oxford History of World Cinema*, Oxford, Oxford University Press, 1996.

Anthony Slide, *The Big V: a history of the Vitagraph company*, Metuchen NJ, Scarecrow Press, 1976.

Robert Stanley, *The Celluloid Empire: a history of the American movie industry*, New York, Hastings House, 1978.

THE STUDIOS

John Belton, *American Cinema/American Culture*, New York, McGraw-Hill, 1994.

Tino Balio (ed.), *The American Film Industry*, Madison, University of Wisconsin Press, 1976; new edn, 1985.

Tino Balio (ed.), *Hollywood in the Age of Television*, London and Boston, Unwin Hyman, 1990.

David Bordwell, Janet Staiger and Kristin Thompson, *The Classical Hollywood Cinema: Film Style and Mode of Production to 1960*, New York, Columbia University Press/London, RKP, 1985.

Harry Braverman, *Labor and Monopoly Capital*, New York, Monthly Review Press, 1974.

Douglas Gomery, *The Hollywood Studio System*, New York, St Martins Press, 1986.

Mae D. Huettig, 'The motion picture industry today', in Balio, *American Film Industry*.

Paul Kerr (ed.), *The Hollywood Film Industry*, London, Routledge, 1986.

Gorham Kindem (ed.), *The American Movie Industry: The Business of Motion Pictures*, Carbondale, University of Illinois Press, 1982.

Thomas Schatz, *The Genius of the System: Hollywood Film-making in the Studio Era*, New York, Pantheon, 1988.

Robert Stanley, *The Celluloid Empire: a History of the American Movie Industry*, New York, Hastings House, 1978.

Janet Wasko, *Hollywood in the Information Age: Beyond the Silver Screen*, Oxford, Polity Press, 1994.

Paramount Pictures

Tino Balio (ed.), *The American Film Industry*, rev. edn, Madison, University of Wisconsin Press, 1976; new edn, 1985.

Kevin Brownlow, *Hollywood: The Pioneers*, New York, Knopf, 1979.

I. G. Edmonds and Reiko Mimura, *Paramount Pictures and the People Who Made Them*, New York, A. S. Barnes, 1980.

Joel W. Finler, *The Hollywood Story*, New York, Crown Publishers, 1988.

Douglas Gomery, *The Hollywood Studio System*, New York, St. Martin's Press, 1986.

Leslie Halliwell, *Mountain of Dreams: The Golden Years at Paramount*, New York, Stonehill, 1976.

Thomas Schatz, *The Genius of the System: Hollywood Film-making in the Studio Era*, New York, Pantheon, 1988.

Metro-Goldwyn-Mayer

Tina Balio (ed.), *The American Film Industry*, rev. edn, Madison, University of Wisconsin Press, 1985. 'Metro-Goldwyn-Mayer' (December 1932) and 'Loew's Inc.' (August 1939).

Bosley Crowther, *The Lion's Share: The Story of an Entertainment Empire*, New York, E. P. Dutton, 1957.

John Douglas Eames, *The MGM Story*, New York, Crown Publishers, 1975.

Joel W. Finler, *The Hollywood Story*, New York, Crown Publishers, 1988.

Hugh Fordin, *The World of Entertainment*, Garden City, NY, Doubleday, 1975.

Douglas Gomery, *The Hollywood Studio System*, New York, St. Martin's Press, 1986.

Thomas Schatz, *The Genius of the System: Hollywood Film-making in the Studio Era*, New York, Pantheon, 1988.

Warner Bros

Edward Buscombe, 'Walsh and Warner Bros', in Phil Hardy (ed.), *Raoul Walsh*.

Russell Campbell, 'Warner Bros in the 30s: some tentative notes', *The Velvet Light Trap* no. 1, June 1971.

Russell Campbell, 'Warners, the Depression and FDR', *The Velvet Light Trap* no. 4, spring 1972.

John Davis, 'Notes on Warner Bros' foreign policy 1918–1948', *The Velvet Light Trap* no. 4, spring 1972.

Nick Roddick, *A New Deal in Entertainment: Warner Brothers in the 1930s*, London, BFI, 1983.

James R. Silke, *Here's Looking at You, Kid; 50 Years of Fighting, Working and Dreaming at Warner Bros*, Boston, Little, Brown and Co., 1976.

Robin Wood, 'To have (written) and have not (directed)', *Film Comment* 9(3), May/June 1973.

Columbia Pictures

Tino Balio (ed.), *The American Film Industry*, Madison, University of Wisconsin Press, 1976; new edn, 1985

Edward Buscombe, 'Notes on Columbia Pictures Corporation, 1926–41', *Screen* 16(3), autumn 1975.

John Cogley, 'The mass hearings', in Balio, *American Film Industry*.

Michael Conant, 'The impact of the Paramount Decrees', in Balio, *American Film Industry*.

Tom Flinn, 'Letter', *The Velvet Light Trap* no. 11, winter 1974, p. 62.

Phil Hardy (ed.), *Raoul Walsh*, Edinburgh, Edinburgh Film Festival, 1974.

John Kobal, *Rita Hayworth: the Time, the Place and the Woman*, London, W. H. Allen, 1977.

Rochelle Larkin, *Hail Columbia*, New Rochelle, NY, Arlington House, 1975.

Robert H. Stanley, *The Celluloid Empire: a history of the American movie industry*, New York, Hastings House, 1978.

20th Century–Fox

Robert C. Allen, 'William Fox presents Sunrise', *Quarterly Review of Film Studies* 2(3), August 1977.

Cahiers du Cinéma, editors of, 'Collective text on John Ford's *Young Mr Lincoln*', *Screen* 13(3), autumn 1972.

Charles Eckert, 'Shirley Temple and the House of Rockefeller', *Jump Cut* no. 2, July/August 1974.

Steven N. Lipkin, '*Sunrise*: a film meets its public', *Quarterly Review of Film Studies* 2(3), August 1977.

Roy Pickard, *The Hollywood Studios*, London, Frederick Muller, 1978.

Rebecca Pulliam, 'The Grapes of Wrath', *The Velvet Light Trap* no. 2, August 1971.

John Howard Reid, 'The best second fiddle', *Films and Filming* 9(2), November 1962.

Tony Thomas and Aubrey Solomon, *The Films of 20th Century-Fox: a Pictorial History*, Secaucus NJ, Citadel Press, 1979.

RKO Radio Pictures

John Davis, 'RKO: a studio chronology', *The Velvet Light Trap* no. 10, autumn 1973.

Ron Haver, 'The mighty show machine', *American Film* 3(2), November 1977.

Pauline Kael, *The Citizen Kane Book*, London, Secker & Warburg, 1971.

Paul Kerr, 'Out of what past? Notes on the "B" *film noir*', *Screen Education* 32/33, autumn/winter 1979/80.

Russell Merritt, 'RKO Radio: the little studio that couldn't', *Marquee Theatre*, University of Wisconsin, Madison, Extension Television Centre, 1973.

Tim Onosko, 'RKO Radio: an overview', *The Velvet Light Trap* no. 10, autumn 1973.

Gerald Peary, 'A speculation: the historicity of *King Kong*' *Jump Cut* no. 4, November–December 1974.

Joel Siegel, *Val Lewton: the Reality of Terror*, London, Secker & Warburg/BFI, 1972.

Universal

Tino Balio, 'A mature oligopoly: 1930–1948', in Balio (ed.), *The American Film Industry*, Madison, University of Wisconsin Press, 1976, new edn, 1985.

Allen Eyles, 'Universal and International', *Focus on Film* 30, June 1978.

Michael G. Fitzgerald, *Universal Pictures: a Panoramic History in Words, Pictures and Filmographies*, New Rochelle, NY, Arlington House, 1977.

Charles Higham, *The Films of Orson Welles*, Berkeley, University of California Press, 1970.

Joseph McBride, *Orson Welles*, London, Secker & Warburg/BFI, 1972.

James Naremore, *The Magic World of Orson Welles*, New York, Oxford University Press, 1978.

Stephen Pendo, 'Universal's golden age of horror', *Films in Review* 26(3), March 1975.

Robert Stanley, *The Celluloid Empire: a History of the American Movie Industry*, New York, Hastings House, 1978.

STARS

Tino Balio, *United Artists: the Company Built by the Stars*, Madison, University of Wisconsin Press, 1976.

Tino Balio (ed.), *The American Film Industry*, Madison, University of Wisconsin Press, 1976; new edn, 1985.

Simone de Beauvoir, *Brigitte Bardot and the Lolita Syndrome*, London, André Deutsch/Weidenfeld & Nicolson, 1960.

Jane Clarke, Mandy Merck and Diana Simmonds, BFI Dossier no. 4: *Move Over Misconceptions: Doris Day reappraised*, London, BFI Publishing, 1981.

Jane Clarke, Mandy Merck and Diana Simmonds, 'Doris Day case study', in Gledhill, *Star Signs*.

Commission on Educational and Cultural Films, *The Film in National Life*, London, 1932.

Pam Cook, 'Star signs', *Screen* 20(3/4), winter 1979/80.

Pam Cook, 'Stars and politics', in Gledhill, *Star Signs*.

Richard deCordova, 'The emergence of the star system and the bourgeoisification of the American cinema', in Gledhill, *Star Signs*.

Philip Davies and Brian Neve (eds), *Cinema, Politics and Society in America*, Manchester, Manchester University Press, 1982.

Richard Dyer, *Teachers' Study Guide I: The Stars*, London, BFI Education Advisory Service, 1979.

Richard Dyer, *Stars*, 2nd edn London, BFI, 1998.

Richard Dyer, 'A Star Is Born and the construction of authenticity', in Gledhill, *Star Signs*.

John Ellis, 'Star/industry/image', in Gledhill, *Star Signs*.

Anne Friedberg, 'Identification and the Star: a refusal of difference', in Gledhill, *Star Signs*.

Christine Gledhill (ed.), *Star Signs: Papers from a Weekend Workshop*, London, BFI Education, 1982.

Christine Gledhill (ed.), *Stardom – Industry of Desire*, London, Routledge, 1991.

Stuart Halsey and Co., 'The motion picture industry as a basis for bond financing', in Balio, *American Film Industry*.

Molly Haskell, *From Reverence to Rape*, New York, Holt Rinehart and Winston, 1974.

Norman Mailer, *Marilyn*, London, Hodder & Stoughton, 1973.

Richard Maltby, 'The political economy of Hollywood: the studio system', in Davies and Neve, *Cinema, Politics and Society*.

Robert Mazzocco, 'The supply-side star', *New York Review of Books*, 1 April 1982.

Patrick McGilligan, *Cagney: the Actor as Auteur*, South Brunswick/London, A. S. Barnes/Tantivy, 1975.

Joan Mellen, *Big Bad Wolves: Masculinity in the American Film*, London, Elm Tree Books, 1978.

Edgar Morin, *The Stars*, New York, Grove Press, 1960.

Laura Mulvey, 'Visual pleasure and narrative cinema', *Screen* 16(3), autumn 1975.

Geoffrey Nowell-Smith, 'On the writing of the history of cinema: some problems', *Edinburgh Magazine* no. 2, Edinburgh Film Festival, 1977.

David Pirie, 'The deal', in Pirie (ed.), *Anatomy of the Movies*, London, Windward, 1981.

Murray Ross, *Stars and Strikes*, New York, Columbia University Press, 1941.

James F. Scott, *Film – the Medium and the Maker*, New York, Holt, Rinehart and Winston, 1975.

Jackie Stacey, *Star Gazing: Hollywood Cinema and Female Spectatorship*, London, Routledge, 1993.

Janet Staiger, 'Seeing stars', *The Velvet Light Trap* no. 20, summer 1983.

John O. Thompson, 'Screen acting and the commutation test', *Screen* 19(2), summer 1978.

CLASSIC HOLLYWOOD NARRATIVE

Charles Barr, 'CinemaScope: before and after', in Mast and Cohen, *Film Theory*.

Roland Barthes, *The Pleasure of the Text*, trans. Richard Miller, New York, Hill and Wang, 1975.

Roland Barthes, 'Introduction to the structural analysis of narratives', trans. Stephen Heath, in *Image–Music–Text*, London, Fontana, 1977.

David Bordwell and Kristin Thompson, *Film Art: An Introduction*, Reading, Mass., Addison-Wesley, 1979; 4th edn, New York, McGraw-Hill, 1993.

Nick Browne, 'The spectator-in-the-text: the rhetoric of *Stagecoach*', *Film Quarterly* 29(2), 1975–6.

Noël Burch, *Theory of Film Practice*, London, Secker & Warburg, 1973.

Thomas Elsaesser (ed.), *Early Cinema: Space, Frame, Narrative*, London, BFI, 1990.

Tom Gunning, 'The cinema of attractions', Wide Angle, 3(4): 63–70, 1986.

Alfred Guzzetti, 'Narrative and the film image', *New Literary History* 6(2), 1975.

G. Mast and M. Cohen (eds), *Film Theory and Criticism*, New York, Oxford University Press, 1974.

Laura Mulvey, 'Visual pleasure and narrative cinema', *Screen* 16(3), autumn 1975.

Steve Neale, 'New Hollywood cinema', *Screen* 17(2), summer 1976.

PART 2: TECHNOLOGY

INTRODUCTION

Rick Altman, 'The evolution of sound technology' in John Belton and Elizabeth Weis, *Film Sound: Theory and Practice*, New York, Columbia University Press, 1985.

Rick Altman, *Sound Theory, Sound Practice*, New York, Routledge, 1992.

Tino Balio (ed.), *The American Film Industry*, Madison University of Wisconsin Press, 1985.

Charles Barr, 'CinemaScope: before and after', in Mast and Cohen, *Film Theory*.

John Belton, *Widescreen Cinema*, Cambridge, Mass. and London, Harvard University Press, 1992.

Edward Buscombe, 'Sound and color', *Jump Cut*, no. 17, April 1978.

James Cameron, 'Technology and magic', *CineFex 51*, August 1992.

Charles Eidsvik, 'Machines of the invisible: changes in film technology in the age of video', *Film Quarterly*, 42(2), winter 1988–9.

A. R. Fulton, in Balio, *American Film Industry*.

Philip Hayward and Tana Wollen (eds), *Future Visions: New Technologies of the Screen*, London, BFI, 1993.

Stephen Heath, and Teresa de Lauretis (eds), *The Cinematic Apparatus*, London: Macmillan Press, 1980.

Gerald Mast and Marshall Cohen, (eds), *Film Theory and Criticism*, New York: Oxford University Press, 1974.

Frank Rickett, 'Multimedia', in Hayward and Wollen, *Future Visions*, 1993.

Paul Virilio, *Guerre et cinéma 1: logistique de la perception*, Paris: Cahiers du Cinéma, 1984; trans., *War and Cinema*, London, Verso, 1989.

Brian Winston, *Technologies of Seeing*, London: BFI, 1996.

Peter Wollen, 'Cinema and technology: an historical overview', in Heath and de Lauretis, *Cinematic Apparatus*, 1980.

SOUND

Rick Altman, *Sound Theory, Sound Practice*, New York, Routledge, 1992.

Tim Amyes, *The Technology of Audio Post-production in Video and Film*, Oxford, Focal Press, 1990.

Tino Balio (ed.), *The American Film Industry*, Madison, University of Wisconsin Press, 1976; new edn, 1985.

Evan William Cameron (ed.), *Sound and the Cinema*, New York, Redgrave Publishing Co., 1980.

Michel Chion, *L'Audio-Vision*, Paris: Éditions Nathan, 1990; trans., *Audio-vision*, New York, Columbia University Press, 1994.

Dougla Gomery, 'The coming of the talkies: invention, innovation and diffusion', in Balio, *American Film Industry*.

Stephen Jones, 'A sense of space: virtual reality, authenticity and the aural', *Critical Studies in Mass Communication* 10(3), 1993.

Patrick L. Ogle, 'Development of sound systems: the commercial era', *Film Reader 2*, January 1977.

COLOUR

Gorham Kindem, 'Hollywood's conversion to color: the technological, economic and aesthetic factors', *Journal of the University Film Association* 31(2), spring 1979.

DEEP FOCUS

Charles Harpole, 'Ideological and Technological Determinism in Deep-Space Cinema Images', *Film Quarterly* 33, Spring 1980.

Patrick L. Ogle, 'Technological and aesthetic influences upon the development of deep-focus cinematography in the United States', *Screen Reader 1*, London, SEFT, 1977.

Gavin Smith, 'A man of excess: Paul Schrader on Jean Renoir' in *Sight and Sound* 5(1), January 1995.

George E. Turner, 'Gregg Toland, ASC', *American Cinematographer* 63(11), November 1982.

Christopher Williams, 'The deep-focus question: some comments on Patrick Ogle's article', in *Screen* 13(1), 1977.

LIGHTING

Peter Baxter, 'On the history and ideology of film lighting' in *Screen* 16(3), autumn, 1975.

T. Earle-Knight, 'Studio lighting 1930–1980', *The BKSTS Journal*, January 1981.

Charles W. Handley, 'History of motion picture studio lighting', *Journal of the SMPTE* vol. 63, October 1954.

WIDESCREEN

Charles Barr, 'CinemaScope: before and after', in Mast and Cohen, *Film Theory*.

John Belton, *Widescreen Cinema*, Cambridge Mass. and London, Harvard University Press, 1992.

David Bordwell, 'Widescreen Aesthetics and *mise-en-scène* criticism', *Velvet Light Trap* no. 21, summer 1985.

David Bordwell, Janet Staiger, and Kristin Thompson, *The Classical Hollywood Cinema*, New York, Columbia University Press/London, RKP, 1985.

Philip Hayward and Tana Wollen (eds), *Future Visions: New Technology of the Screen*, London, BFI Publishers, 1993.

Stephen Huntley, 'Sponable's CinemaScope: an intimate chronology of the invention of the cinemascope optical system', *Film History* 5(3), September 1993.

Gerald Mast and Marshall Cohen (eds), *Film Theory and Criticism*, New York, Oxford University Press, 1974.

Velvet Light Trap, no. 21, summer 1985, special issue on widescreen, including articles by André Bazin and David Bordwell.

Victor Perkins, '*River of No Return*', *Movie* no. 2, September 1962.

Fred Waller, 'The archeology of cinerama', *Film History* 5(3), September 1993.

Tana Wollen, 'The bigger the better: from cinemascope to imax', in Hayward and Wollen (eds), *Future Visions*, 1993.

CAMERAS

David Samuelson, 'Cine equipment over fifty years', *The BKSTS Journal*, January 1981.

Brian Winston *Technologies of Seeing*, London, BFI, 1996.

ALTERNATIVE PRODUCTION FORMATS: 16 MM, 8 MM AND VIDEO

Hugh Baddeley, '"Sub-standard"': the development of 16mm in *BKSTS Journal* 63(1), January 1981.

Lili Berko, 'Surveying the surveilled: video, space and subjectivity', *Quarterly Review of Film and Video* 14(1–2), 1992.

Laura Hudson, 'Promiscuous 8', *Coil* no. 2, November 1995.

Stuart Marshall, 'Video: from art to independence: a short history of a new technology', *Screen* 26(2), March–April 1985.

Rodger J. Ross, 'The development of professional Super 8', *American Cinematographer* 56(11), November 1975.

Patricia R. Zimmerman, 'Trading down: amateur film technology in fifties America', *Screen* 29(2), spring 1988.

EDITING

Les Paul Robley, 'Digital offline video editing: expanding creative horizons', *American Cinematographer* 74(4–7), April–July 1993.

Janet Wasko, *Hollywood in the Information Age*, Cambridge, Polity Press, 1994.

THE NEW TECHNOLOGIES INTERACTIVE ENTERTAINMENTS

Robin Baker, 'Computer-technology and special effects in contemporary cinema' in Hayward and Wollen (eds), *Future Visions*, 1993.

Frank Beacham, 'Movies for the future: Storytelling with computers', *American Cinematographer* 76(4), April 1995.

Frank Biocca and Mark R. Levy, *Communication in the Age of Virtual Reality*, Hove and New Jersey, Lawrence Erlbaum Associates, 1995.

Andrew Cameron, 'Dissimulations: the illusion of interactivity', in *Millennium Film Journal* no. 28, spring, 1995.

Bob Cotton, Bob and Richard Oliver, *Understanding Hypermedia: From Multimedia to Virtual Reality*, London, Phai- don, 1993.

Charles Eidsvik, 'Machines of the invisible: changes in film technology in the age of video', *Film Quarterly* 42(2), winter 1988–9.

Bob Fisher, 'Dawning of the digital age', *American Cinematographer* 73(4), April 1992.

Philip Hayward and Tana Wollen (eds), *Future Visions: New Technologies of the Screen*, London: BFI, 1993.

Malcolm Le Grice, 'Kismet, protagony and the zap splat factor: some theoretical concepts for an interactive avant-garde cinema', *Millennium Film Journal* no. 28, spring 1995.

Nicholas Negroponte, *Being Digital*, London: Hodder & Stoughton, 1995

Joan Pennefather, 'From cinema to virtual reality', *Intermedia* 22(5), October–November 1994.

Jannine Pourroy, 'Through the proscenium arch', *Cinefex* no. 46, May 1991.

Gregory Solman, 'The illusion of a future', *Film Comment 2* 28(2), March–April 1992.

David Tafler, 'Beyond narrative: notes towards a theory of interactive cinema', *Millennium Film Journal*, autumn–winter 1988–9.

McKenzie Wark, 'The multimedia thing', *Metro* no. 103, 1995.

John Watkinson, *An Introduction to Digital Video*, Oxford, Focal Press, 1994.

Grahame Weinbren, 'In the ocean of streams of story', *Millennium Film Journal* no. 28, spring 1995.

VIRTUAL REALITY

Frank Biocca and Mark R. Levy, *Communication in the Age of Virtual Reality*, Hove and New Jersey, Lawrence Erlbaum Associates, 1995.

Karen Carr, Karen and Rupert England, *Simulated and Virtual Realities: Elements of Perception*, London, Taylor & Francis Ltd, 1995.

Terence Guthridge, 'Dr StrangeGlove, or how I learned to stop worrying and love virtual reality', *Metro* no. 101, 1995.

Ron Magid, 'ILM magic is organised mayhem', *American Cinematographer* 75(12), December 1994.

Nicholas Negroponte, *Being Digital*, London, Hodder & Stoughton, 1995.

Howard Rheingold, *Virtual Reality*, London, Secker & Warburg, 1991.

Barrie Sherman and Phil Judkins, *Glimpses of Heaven, Visions of Hell*, London, Hodder & Stoughton, 1992.

PART 3: NATIONAL CINEMAS AND FILM MOVEMENTS

GERMAN EXPRESSIONISM AND NEW GERMAN CINEMA

Timothy Corrigan, *New German Film: The Displaced Image*, Bloomington and Indianapolis, Indiana University Press, rev. edn, 1994.

Thomas Elsaesser, *New German Cinema: A History*, Basingstoke, MacMillan/BFI, 1989.

James Franklin, *New German Cinema: From Oberhausen to Hamburg*, Boston, Twayne, 1983.

Sandra Frieden *et al.* (eds), *Gender and German Cinema, vols* 1 and 2, Providence/Oxford, Berg, 1993.

Anton Kaes, *From 'Hitler' to 'Heimat': the Return of History as Film*, Cambridge, Mass., Harvard University Press, 1989.

Julia Knight, *Women and the New German Cinema*, London and New York, Verso, 1992.

Siegfried Kracauer, *From Caligari to Hitler: a Psychological History of the German Film*, Princeton, NJ, Princeton University Press, 1974.

Richard W. McCormick, *Politics of the Self: Feminism and the Postmodern in West German Literature and Film*, Princeton, NJ, Princeton University Press, 1991.

October No. 46, autumn 1988, special issue on Alexander Kluge.

Frederick Ott, *The Films of Fritz Lang*, Secaucus NJ, Citadel Press, 1979.

Julian Petley, *Capital and Culture: German Cinema* 1933–45, London, BFI, 1979.

Hans Günther Pflaum and Hans Helmut Prinzler, *Cinema in the Federal Republic of Germany*, Bonn, Inter Nationes, 1993.

Klaus Phillips (ed.), *New German Filmmakers*, New York, Frederick Ungar, 1984.

Eric Rentschler, *West German Film in the Course of Time*, Bedford Hills, Redgrave, 1984.

John Sandford, *The New German Cinema*, London, Eyre Methuen, 1980.

SOVIET CINEMA

David Bordwell, *The Cinema of Eisenstein*, Cambridge, Mass., Harvard University Press, 1993.

David Bordwell and Kristin Thompson, *Film Art*, Reading, Mass., Addison-Wesley, 1979, pp. 306–9, 5th edn, New York, McGraw-Hill, 1996.

Ephraim Katz, *The International Film Encyclopaedia*, Basingstoke, Macmillan, 1980, pp. 1074–79; 3rd edn, 1998.

Peter Kenez, *Cinema and Soviet Society 1917–1953*. Cambridge, Mass., Cambridge University Press, 1992.

Jay Leyda, *Kino: a History of the Russian and Soviet Film*, London, George Allen and Unwin, 1973.

Richard Taylor and Ian Christie (eds), *The Film Factory: Russian and Soviet Cinema in Documents 1896–1939*, London, RKP, 1988.

Denise Youngblood, *Soviet Cinema in the Silent Era, 1918–1935*, Ann Arbor, UMI Research Press, 1985; new edn, Austin, University of Texas Press, 1991.

ITALIAN NEO-REALISM

André Bazin, *Qu'est-ce que le cinéma?* vol. IV, Paris, editions du Cerf, 1962; also in Gray, ed. and trans., *What is Cinema?* vol. II, Berkeley, University of California Press, 1971, p. 99.

Peter Brunette, *Roberto Rossellini*, New York, Oxford University Press, 1987.

Morando Morandini, 'Italy from Facism to neo-realism' in Nowell-Smith, *Oxford History of World Cinema*, 1996.

Geoffrey Nowell-Smith, *Visconti*, London, Secker & Warburg/BFI, 1967; rev. edn, 1973.

Geoffrey Nowell-Smith (ed.), *The Oxford History of World Cinema*, Oxford, Oxford University Press, 1996.

Geoffrey Nowell-Smith with James Hay and Gianni Volpi, *The Companion to Italian Cinema*, London, Cassell/BFI, 1996.

Sam Rohdie, 'A note on Italian cinema during Fascism', *Screen* 22(4), 1981.

Christopher Wagstaff and Christopher Duggan, *Italy and the Cold War: Politics, Culture and Society*, Oxford, Berg, 1995.

THE FRENCH NEW WAVE

Roy Armes, *French Cinema since 1946*, vol. 2, London, A. Zwemmer Ltd., 1970.

Royal S. Brown (ed.), *Focus on Godard*, Englewood Cliffs NJ, Prentice-Hall, 1972.

Raymond Durgnat, *Nouvelle Vague: the First Decade*, Loughton, Essex, Motion Publications 1963.

Peter Graham (ed.), *The New Wave: Critical Landmarks*, London, Secker & Warburg/ BFI, 1968.

Susan Hayward, *French National Cinema*, London, Routledge, 1993.

Terry Lovell, 'Sociology of aesthetic structures and contextualism', in McQuail, *Sociology*.

Denis McQuail (ed.), *Sociology of Mass Communication*, Harmondsworth, Middlesex, Penguin, 1972.

James Monaco, *The New Wave*, New York, Oxford University Pres, 1976.

Jacques Siclier, 'New wave and French cinema', *Sight and Sound* 30(3), summer 1961.

Ginette Vincendeau (ed.), *The Companion to French Cinema*, London, Cassell/BFI, 1996.

THE BRITISH FILM INDUSTRY

Ealing Studios

Charles Barr, *Ealing Studios*, London, Cameron and Tayler/Newton Abbot, David and Charles, 1977; revised edn, London, Studio Vista, 1993.

John Ellis, 'Made in Ealing', *Screen* 16(1), spring 1975.

Robert Murphy (ed.), *The British Cinema Book*, London, BFI, 1997.

Tim Pulleine 'A song and dance at the local: thoughts on Ealing' in, Murphy, *British Cinema*.

Hammer Productions

Allen Eyles *et al.* (eds), *The House of Horror: the Complete Story of Hammer Films*, London, Lorrimer, 1973.

Peter Hutchings, *Hammer and Beyond*, Manchester, Manchester University Press, 1993.

James L. Limbacher, *The Influence of J. Arthur Rank on the History of the British Film*, Dearborn, Michigan, Henry Ford Centennial Library, n.d.

Little Shoppe of Horrors no. 4, April 1978.

Kim Newman (ed.), *The BFI Companion to Horror*, London, Cassell/BFI, 1996.

George Perry, *The Great British Picture Show*, London, Hart-Davis MacGibbon, 1974.

David Pirie, *A Heritage of Horror: the English Gothic Cinema 1946–1972*, London, Gordon Fraser, 1973.

David Pirie, *Hammer: A Cinema Case Study*, London, BFI Education, 1980.

British social realism 1959–63

Sue Aspinall and Robert Murphy (eds), *BFI Dossier 18: Gainsborough Melodrama*, London, BFI, 1983.

Michael Balcon, interview in 'In the picture', *Sight and Sound* 28(3–4): 133, summer–autumn 1959.

Geoff Brown 'Paradise found and lost: the course of British realism', in Murphy, *The British Cinema Book*, 1997.

Raymond Durgnat, *A Mirror for England: British movies from Austerity to Affluence*, London, Faber & Faber, 1970.

John Hill, 'Ideology, economy and the British cinema', in Barrett, Corrigan, Kuhn and Wolff (eds), *Ideology and Cultural Production*, London, Croom Helm, 1979.

John Hill, *Sex Class and Realism: British Cinema 1956–1963*, London, BFI, 1986.

Alan Lovell, *The British Cinema: the Unknown Cinema*, London, BFI Education Dept Seminar Paper, 1969.

Robert Murphy, *Sixties British Cinema*, London, BFI, 1992.

Robert Murphy, *The British Cinema Book*, London, BFI, 1997.

George Perry, *The Great British Picture Show*, London, Hart-Davis, MacGibbon, 1974.

Alexander Walker, *Hollywood, England: the British Film Industry in the 60s*, London, Michael Joseph, 1974.

Peter Wollen, *Signs and Meaning in the Cinema*, London, Secker & Warburg/BFI, 1969; rev. edn 1972; expanded edn, London, BFI, 1998.

PART 4: ALTERNATIVES TO CLASSIC HOLLYWOOD

EARLY CINEMA, AFTER BRIGHTON

Richard Abel, *The Ciné Goes to Town: French Cinema, 1896–1914*, Berkeley, University of California Press, 1994.

Richard Abel (ed.), *Silent Film*, New Brunswick, Rutgers University Press, 1995.

David Bordwell, Janet Staiger, and Kristin Thompson, *The Classical Hollywood Cinema: Film Style and Mode of Production to 1960*, London, RKP, 1985.

Ben Brewster, 'Deep staging in French films 1900–1914 in Elaesser, *Early Cinema*.

Ben Brewster, 'A Scene at the Movies' in Elaeser, *Early Cinema*.

Ben Brewster and Lea Jacobs, *From Theatre to Cinema: Stage Pictorialism and the Early Feature Film*, Oxford, Oxford University Press, 1997.

Eileen Bowser, *The Transformation of Cinema, 1907–1915*, New York, Scribner's, 1991.

Noël Burch, 'Primitivism and the avant-Gardes: a dialectical approach', in Rosen, *Narrative, Apparatus*.

Noël Burch, *Life to those Shadows*, Berkeley, University of California Press, 1990.

Leo Charney and Vanessa Schwartz (eds), *Cinema and the Invention of Modern Life*, Berkeley, University of California Press, 1995.

Paolo Cherchi Usai, *Una passione infiammabile – Guido alla studio del cinema muto*, UTET Libreria, 1991; trans. *Burning Passions: An Introduction to the Study of Silent Cinema*, London: British Film Institute, 1994.

Karel Dibbits and Bert Hogenkamp (eds), *Film and the First World War* (Amsterdam: Amsterdam University Press, 1995), pp. 86–96.

Thomas Elsaesser (ed.), *Early Cinema: Space, Frame, Narrative*, London, BFI, 1990.

Thomas Elsaesser, 'Comparative style analyses for European films, 1910–1918', lecture at the 'Deuxième colloque international de Domitor', Lausanne, July 1992.

John Fell (ed.), *Film before Griffith*, Berkeley, University of California Press, 1984, pp. 311–30.

John Fullerton, 'Contextualizing the innovation of deep staging in Swedish film', in Dibbits and Hogenkamp, *Film*.

André Gaudreault, 'Temporality and narrative in early cinima, 1895–1908', in Fell, *Griffith*.

Tom Gunning, 'The cinema of attractions': early cinema, its spectator and the avant-garde', *Wide Angle* 8(3–4): 63–70, 1986.

Tom Gunning, *D. W. Griffith and the Origins of American Narrative Film*, Urbana, University of Illinois Press, 1991.

Tom Gunning, 'Now you see it, now you don't: the temporality of the cinema of attractions', *The Velvet Light Trap* no. 32, 1993, pp. 3–12.

Miriam Hansen, *Babel & Babylon: Spectatorship in American Silent Film*, Cambridge, Harvard University Press, 1991.

Miriam Hansen, 'Early cinema, late cinema: transformations of public sphere', *Screen* 34(3): 197–210, autumn, 1993.

Lewis Jacobs, *The Rise of the American film: a critical history*, New York, Harcourt, Brace, 1939.

Jean Mitry, *Histoire du cinéma: art et industrie*, vol 1, Paris: editions Universitaires, 1968.

Charles Musser, *The Emergence of Cinema: The American Screen to 1907*, New York, Scribner's, 1991a.

Charles Musser, *Before the Nickleodeon: Edwin S. Porter and the Edison Manufacturing Company*, Berkeley: University of California Press, 1991b.

Kathy Peiss, *Cheap Amusements: Working Women and Leisure in Turn-of-the-Century New York*, Philadelphia, Temple University Press, 1986.

Terry Ramsaye, *A Million and One Nights: A History of the Motion Picture through 1925*, New York, Simon and Schuster, 1926; reprint 1964.

Philip Rosen (ed.), *Narrative, Apparatus, Ideology: A Film Theory Reader* (New York: Columbia University Press, 1986).

Barry Salt, *Film Style and Technology: History and Analysis*, 1st edn 1983; rev. edn London, Starword, 1992.

Kristin Thompson, 'From primitive to classical', in Bordwell *et al.*, *Classical Hollywood*.

Kristin Thompson, 'The international exploration of cinematic expressivity', in Dibbits and Hogenkamp, *Film*.

Yuri Tsivian, 'Bauer and Hofer: on two conceptions of space in European film culture', Celebrating 1895: An International Conference on Film Before 1929, Bradford, 19 June 1995.

William Uricchio and Roberta Pearson, *Reframing Culture: The Case of Vitagraph Quality Films*, Princeton, Princeton University Press, 1993.

NEW HOLLYWOOD

'Anti-Heroes', a series of articles on *Five Easy Pieces* by Jacob Brackman, Harold Clurman and John Simon, in *Film 70/71: An Anthology by the National Society of Film Critics*, ed. David Denby, New York, Simon and Schuster, 1971; pp. 33–43.

Raymond Bellour, 'To analyse, to segment', *Quarterly Review of Film Studies*, 1(3): 331–43, 1976.

John Belton, *American Cinema/American Culture*, New York, McGraw-Hill, 1994.

James Bernardoni, *The New Hollywood: What the Movies Did with the New Freedom of the Seventies* Jefferson, NC, McFarland and Co., 1991.

David Bordwell, *Making Meaning: Inference and Rhetoric in the Interpretation of Cinema*, Cambridge, Mass., Harvard University Press, 1989.

David Bordwell and Janet Staiger, 'Since 1960: the persistence of a mode of film practice', in Bordwell *et al.*, *Classical Hollywood*, pp. 367–77.

David Bordwell, K. Thompson and Janet Staiger, *Classical Hollywood Cinema: Film Style and Mode of Production*, London, RKP, 1985.

Stuart Bryon, '*The Searchers*: cult movie of the New Hollywood', *New York Magazine*, 5 March 1979, pp. 45–8.

Noel Carroll, 'The future of allusion: Hollywood in the seventies (and beyond)', *October* no. 20, 1982, pp. 51–78.

David Colker and Jack Virrel, 'The *New* New Hollywood', *Take One* 6(10): 19–23, September 1978.

Jim Collins, Hilary Radner and Ava Preacher Collines (eds) *Film Theory Goes to the Movies*, New York, Routledge, 1993.

Timothy Corrigan, *A Cinema Without Walls: Movies and Culture After Vietnam*, London, Routledge, 1991.

David Denby, 'Can the movies be saved?', *New York Magazine* 19(28): 23–35, 1986.

Thomas Elsaesser, 'The American cinema 2: why Hollywood', *Monogram* no. 6, 1971.

Thomas Elsaesser, 'The pathos of failure: notes on the unmotivated hero', *Monogram* no. 6, 1975, pp. 13–19.

Stephen Farber, 'Easy pieces', *Sight and Sound*, 40(3): 128–131, 1971.

Jean-Luc Godard and Pauline Kael, 'The economics of film criticism: a debate', *Camera Obscura* 8–10, 1982, pp. 163–84.

Douglas Gomery, 'The American film industry in the seventies', *Wide Angle* 5(4): 52–9, 1983.

GQ, October 1995, special issue on the New Hollywood.

Tom Gunning, 'The cinema of attractions': early cinema, its spectator and the avant-garde', *Wide Angle* 8(3–4): 63–70, 1986.

Jim Hillier, *The New Hollywood*, London, Studio Vista, 1992.

J. Hoberman, 'Ten years that shook the world', *American Film* 10(8): 38–39, 42–49, 52–59, 1985.

Keven Jackson (ed.), *Schrader on Schrader & Other Writings*, London, Faber & Faber, 1990.

Diane Jacobs, *Hollywood Renaissance: the New Generation of Filmmakers and Their Works*, New York: Delta, 1977/1980.

Pauline Kael, 'Why are the movies so bad?: Or, the numbers', in Kael, *Taking it All In*, New York: Holt, Rinehart and Winston, 1984, pp. 8–20.

Lucy Kaylin, 'Independents' day', *GQ*, October 1995, p. 180.

Jon Lewis, *Whom God Wishes to Destroy: Francis Coppola and the New Hollywood*, Durham and London: Duke University Press, 1995.

Kimball Lockhart, 'Blockage and passage in *The Passenger*', *Diacritics* 15(1): 74–84, 1985.

Axel Madsen, *The New Hollywood: American Movies in the 70s*, New York, Thomas Y. Crowell Co., 1975.

Steven Marcus, 'Introduction', to Dashiell Hammett, *The Continental Op*, New York, Random House, 1974, pp. ix–xxix.

Eileen R. Meehan, 'Holy commodity fetish, Batman!': the political economy of a commercial intertext', in *The Many Lives of Batman: Critical Approaches to a Superhero and his Media*, Roberta E. Pearson and William Uricchio, (eds), New York: BFI/ Routledge, 1991.

James Monaco, *American Film Now: The People, The Power, The Money, The Movies*, New York, Oxford University Press, 1979.

Steve Neale and Murray Smiths (eds), *Contemporary American Cirema*, London, Routledge, 1998.

Steve Neale, 'Hollywood corner', *Framework* 19, 1982, pp. 37–9.

Patricia Patterson and Manny Farber, 'The power and the gory', *Film Comment* 12(3), 1976.

William Paul, 'The K-mart audience at the mall movies', *Film History* 6(4): 487–501, 1994.

William Paul, 'Hollywood Harakiri', *Film Comment* 13(2): 40–3, 56–61, 1977.

Michael Pye and Lynda Myles, *The Movie Brats: How the Film Generation Took Over Hollywood*, New York; Holt, Rinehart and Winston, 1979.

Robert B. Ray, *A Certain Tendency of the Hollywood Cinema 1930–1980*, Princeton, NJ, Princeton University Press, 1985.

Brooks Riley, 'BBS Productions' in Richard Roud (ed.), *Cinema: A Critical Dictionary* vol. 1, London, Secker & Warburg, 1980, pp. 104–6.

Jonathan Rosenbaum, 'Rocky Horry playtime vs shopping mall home', in his *Moving Places: A Life at the Movies*, New York, Harper and Row, 1980, pp. 202–12.

Andrew Sarris, 'After *The Graduate*', *American Film* 3(9): 32–7, 1978.

Thomas Schatz, *Old Hollywood/New Hollywood*, UMI Research Press, 1983.

Thomas Schatz, 'The New Hollywood', in Collins *et al.*, *Film Theory*, pp. 8–36.

Thomas Schatz, The Genius of the System: *Hollywood Filmmaking in the Studio Era* (New York: Pantheon, 1988).

Eben Shapiro and Thomas King, 'Production costs put a tarnish on Tinseltown', a *Wall Street Journal* article reprinted in the *Sydney Morning Herald*, January 1996.

David Thomson, *Overexposures: the Crisis in American Filmmaking*, New York, William Morrow & Co, 1981.

David Thomson, 'The decade when movies mattered', *Movieline*, August 1993, pp. 43–7, 90.

Anne Thompson, 'Little giants', *Film Comment* 31(2): 56, 58–60, 63, 1995.

Mim Udovich, 'Tarantino and Juliette', *Details*, February, 1996, pp. 112–17.

Maggie Valentine, *The Show Starts on the Sidewalk: An Architectural History of the Movie Theatre, Starring S. Charles Lee*, New Haven and London, Yale University Press, 1994.

Wide-Angle 5(4), 1983 is a special issue on 'The New Hollywood.'

Justin Wyatt, *High Concept: Movies and Marketing in Hollywood*, Austin, University of Texas Press, 1994.

ART CINEMA

Alexandre Astruc, 'The birth of a new avant-garde: *la caméra-stylo*', 1948, originally in Écran Français, No. 144, 1948. Translated in Peter Graham (ed.) The New Wave, Condor, Secker & Warburg/ BFI 1968.

André Bazin, 'Qu'est-ce que le cinéma moderne?' in *Cinéma* no. 62, January 1962.

'Arguments for independence', *Views: the Magazine of the Independent Film and Video Makers' Association*, summer 1984.

David Bordwell, 'The art cinema as a mode of film practice' in *Film Criticism* 4(1), 1979, expanded in *Narration in the Fiction Film*, London, Methuen 1985.

David Bordwell and Kristin Thompson, *Film Art: An Introduction*, McGraw-Hill, 1993.

Edward Branigan, *Point of View in the Cinema: a Theory of Narration and Subjectivity in Classical Film*, The Hague, Mouton 1984.

John Ellis, 'Art, culture and quality: terms for a cinema in the forties and seventies', *Screen* 19(3), autumn 1978; revised in *Dissolving Views*: *Key Writings on British Cinema*, Andrew Higson (ed.), London, Cassells, 1996.

Christian Metz, *Film Language: A Semiotics of the Cinema*, New York, Oxford University Press, 1974.

Steve Neale, 'Art cinema as institution', *Screen* 22(1), 1981.

Geoffrey Nowell-Smith, 'Radio on', *Screen* 20(3–4), winter 1979–80.

Geoffrey Nowell-Smith, 'Art cinema' in G. Nowell-Smith *The Oxford History of World Cinema* pp. 567–75, Oxford, Oxford University Press, 1996.

Alain Robbe-Grillet, *Last Year at Marianbad*, John Calder, London, 1962.

Tom Ryall, 'Art house, smart house', *The Movie* no. 90, 1981.

EAST ASIAN CINEMA

Joseph L. Anderson and Loren Hoekzema, 'The spaces between: American criticism of Japanese film', *Wide Angle* 1(4): 2–6, 1977.

Joseph L. Anderson and Donald Richie, *The Japanese Film: Art and Industry*, Tokyo, Tuttle Company, 1959; expanded edn, Princeton, Princeton University Press, 1982.

Chris Berry (ed.), *Perspectives on Chinese Cinema*, London, BFI, 1991.

Chris Berry and Mary Ann Farquhar, 'Postsocialist strategies: an analysis of yellow earth and black cannon incident', in Ehrlich and Desser, *Cinematic Landscapes.*

David Bordwell, *Ozu and the Poetics of Cinema*, Princeton, Princeton University Press, 1988.

David Bordwell, 'Visual style in Japanese cinema, 1925–1945', *Film History* 7(1): 5–31, spring 1995.

Nick Browne, Paul G. Pickowicz, Vivian Sobchak, and Esther Yau (eds), *New Chinese Cinemas: Forms, Identities, Politics*, Cambridge, Cambridge University Press, 1994.

Noël Burch, *To the Distant Observer: Form and Meaning in the Japanese Cinema*, Berkeley, University of California Press, 1979.

David Desser, *Eros Plus Massacre: An Introduction to the Japanese New Wave Cinema*, Bloomington, Indiana University Press, 1988.

Linda Ehrlich and David Desser (eds), *Cinematic Landscapes: Observations on the Visual Arts and Cinema of China and Japan*, Austin, University of Texas Press, 1994.

Kathe Geist, 'Playing with space: Ozu and two-dimensional design in Japan', in Ehrlich and Desser, *Cinematic Landscapes.*

Kyoko Hirano, *Mr Smith Goes to Tokyo: Japanese Cinema under the Occupation, 1945–1952*, Washington, DC, Smithsonian Institution Press, 1992.

Hiroshi Komatsu, 'Some characteristics of Japanese cinema before World War I', in Nolletti and Desser, *Japanese Cinema.*

John Lent, *The Asian Film Industry*, Austin, Texas, University of Texas Press, 1990.

Keiko McDonald, *Japanese Classical Theater in Films*, Rutherford, NJ, Fairleigh Dickinson University Press, 1994.

Keiko McDonald, *Mizoguchi*, Boston, Twayne Publishing, 1984.

Arthur Nolletti and David Desser (eds), *Refraining Japanese Cinema: Authorship, Genre, History*, Bloomington, Indiana University Press, 1992.

Donald Richie, *Ozu: His Life and Films*, Berkeley, University of California Press, 1974.

Donald Richie, *The Films of Akira Kurosawa*, Berkeley, University of California Press, 1984.

Stephen Teo, *Hong Kong Cinema: The Extra Dimensions*, London, BFI Publishing, 1997.

Kristin Thompson, 'Notes on the spatial system of Ozu's early films', *Wide Angle* 1(4): 8–17, 1977.

AVANT-GARDE AND COUNTER-CINEMA

Arts Council of Great Britain, *Film as Film*, London: Arts Council of Great Britain, 1979.

Janet Bergstrom, '*Jeanne Dielman* by Chantal Akerman', *Camera Obscura* no. 2, 1977.

Andrew Britton, 'Living Historically', *Framework* no. 3, 1976.

Pam Cook, '*The Gold Diggers*: interview with Sally Potter', *Framework* no. 24, 1984.

Ian Christie, 'French avant-garde film in the twenties: from "specificity" to surrealism', in Arts Council of Great Britain.

David Curtis, *Experimental Cinema*, London, Studio Vista, 1971.

Teresa De Lauretis, *Technologies of Gender*, Bloomington and Indianapolis, Indiana University Press, 1987.

Teresa De Lauretis, 'Geurrillas in the midst: women's cinema in the 80s', *Screen* 31(1), spring 1990.

Phillip Drummond, 'Textual space in *Un Chien Andalou*', *Screen* 18(3), autumn 1977.

Phillip Drummond, 'Notions of avant-garde cinema', in Arts Council of Great Britain.

Deke Dusinberre, 'The ascetic task: Peter Gidal's *Room Film 1973*', in Gidal, *Structural Film*.

Peter Gidal (ed.), *Structural Film Anthology*, London, BFI, 1978.

Birgit Hein, 'The futurist film', in Arts Council of Great Britain, *Film as Film*.

David E. James, *Allegories of Cinema*, Princeton, NJ, Princeton University Press, 1989.

Claire Johnston (ed.), *Notes on Women's Cinema*, London, SEFT, 1974.

Claire Johnston, 'Women's cinema as counter-cinema', in Johnston, *Notes on Women's Cinema*, 1974.

E. Ann Kaplan, *Looking for the Other: Feminism, Film and the Imperial Gaze*, New York and London, Routledge, 1997.

Rudolf E. Kuenzli (ed.), *Dada and Surrealist Film*, New York, Willis Locker and Owen, 1987.

Standish D. Lawder, *The Cubist Cinema*, New York, New York University Press, 1975.

Scott MacDonald, *A Critical Cinema 2: Interviews with Independent Filmmakers*, Berkeley and Los Angeles, University of California Press, 1992.

Patricia Mellencamp, *A Fine Romance: Five Ages of Film Feminism*, Philadelphia, Temple University Press, 1995.

Annette Michelson, 'Paul Sharits and the critique of illusionism: an introduction', in *Projected Images*, Minneapolis, Walker Art Centre, 1974.

Laura Mulvey, 'Visual pleasure and narrative cinema', *Screen* 16(3), autumn 1975.

Laura Mulvey, 'Feminism, film and the avant-garde', *Framework* no. 19, 1979.

Constance Penley and Janet Bergstrom, 'The avant-garde – histories and theories', *Screen* 19(3), autumn 1978.

Yvonne Rainer, 'Yvonne Rainer: interview', *Camera Obscura* no. 1, 1976.

Yvonne Rainer, 'More kicking and screaming from the narrative front/backwater', *Wide Angle* 7(1–2), 1985.

A. L. Rees *A History of Experimental Film and Video*, London, BFI Publishing, 1999.

Sheldon Renan, *The Underground Film*, London, Studio Vista, 1968.

Robert Russett and Cecile Starr, *Experimental Animation*, New York, Da Capo, 1988.

Paul Sandro, *Diversions of Pleasure: Luis Buñuel and the Crises of Desire*, Columbus, Ohio, Ohio State University Press, 1987.

P. Adams Sitney, *Visionry Film*, Oxford, Oxford University Press, 1974; 2nd edn, 1979.

Michelle Wallace, 'Multiculturalism and oppositionality, *Afterimage* (USA) 19(3), October 1991.

Paul Willemen, *Looks and Frictions: Essays in Cultural Studies and Film Theory*, London/Bloomington, BFI and Indiana University Press, 1994.

Linda Williams, *Figures of Desire: A Theory and Analysis of Surrealist Film*, Urbana, Ill., University of Illinois Press, 1981.

Peter Wollen, 'Godard and counter-cinema: *Vent d'est*' (1972); 'The two avant-gardes' (1975), '"ontology" and "materialism" in film' (1976); 'Semiotic counter-strategies: retrospect 1982', collected in *Readings and Writings*, London, Verso, 1982.

Peter Wollen, 'The avant-gardes: Europe and America', *Framework* no. 14, 1981.

THIRD WORLD AND POSTCOLONIAL CINEMA

Barbara Abrash and Catherine Egan (eds), *Mediating History: The MAP Guide to Independent Video*, New York, New York University Press, 1992.

Aijaz Ahmand, 'Jameson's rhetoric of otherness and the "national allegory"', *Social Text* no. 15, autumn 1986.

Manuel Alvarado, John King and Ana Lopez (eds), *Mediating Two Worlds: Cinematic Encounters in the Americas*, London, BFI, 1993.

Benedict Anderson, *Imagined Communities: Reflections on the Origin and Spread of Nationalism*. London, Verso, 1983.

Roy Armes, *Third World Filmmaking and the West*, Berkeley, University of California Press, 1987.

Victor Bachy, *Tradition orale et nouveaux médias*, Brussels, OCIC, 1989.

Erik Barnouw and S. Krishnaswamy, *Indian Film*, New York, Columbia University Press, 1963; rev. edn, New York, Oxford University Press, 1980.

Charles Ramirez Berg, *Cinema of Solitude: A Critical of Mexican Film, 1967–1983*, Austin, University of Texas Press, 1992.

Chris Berry (ed.), *Perspectives on Chinese Cinema*, London, BFI, 1991.

'Black British cinema', ICA documents 7, London, ICA, 1988.

Julianne Burton, 'Marginal cinemas', *Screen*, 1985.

Julianne Burton (ed.), *Cinema and Social Change*. Austin: University of Texas, 1986.

Julianne Burton (ed.), *The Social Documentary in Latin America*, Pittsburgh, University of Pittsburgh Press, 1990.

Sumita Chakravarty, *National Identity in Indian Popular Cinema*, Austin, University of Texas Press, 1993.

Mbye B. Cham, and Claire Andrade-Watkins (eds), *Blackframes: Critical Perspectives on Black Independent Cinema*, Cambridge, MIT Press, 1988.

Mbye B. Cham, *Ex-Iles: Caribbean Cinema*, Trenton, NJ, Africa World Press, 1991.

Michael Chanan, *Chilean Cinema*, London, BFI, 1976.

Michael Chanan, *Santiago Alvarez*, London, BFI, 1980.

Michael Chanan (ed.), *Twenty-five Years of the New Latin American Cinema*, London, BFI/Channel Four Television, 1983.

Michael Chanan, *The Cuban Image*, London, BFI, 1985.

Helen W. Cyr, *A Filmography of the Third World*, Metuchen, NJ, Scarecrow Press, 1986.

Manthia Diawara, 'Oral literature and African film: narratology in *Wend Kunni*', in Pines and Willemen, *Questions*.

Manthia Diawara, *African Cinema*, Bloomington, Indiana University Press, 1992.

Manthia Diawara, *Black American Cinema*, London, Routledge, 1993.

John D. H. Downing (ed.), *Film and Politics in the Third World*, New York, Autonomedia, 1987.

Fritz Fanon, *The Wretched of the Earth*, New York, Grove Press, 1964.

Rosa Linda Fregoso, *The Bronze Screen: Chicana and Chicano Film Culture*, Minneapolis, University of Minnesota Press, 1993.

Coco Fusco, *Reviewing Histories: Selections from New Latin American Cinema*, Buffalo, Hallwalls, 1987.

Coco Fusco, *Young, British and Black*, Buffalo, Hallwalls, 1988.

Teshome Gabriel, 'Towards a critical theory of Third World films', in Pines and Willemen, *Questions*.

Behroze Ghandy and Rosie Thomas, 'Three Indian film stars', in Gledhill, *Stardom*.

Christine Gledhill (ed.), *Stardom: Industry of Desire*, London, Routledge, 1991.

Beverly G. Hawk (ed.), *Africa's Media Image*, Westport, CT, Greenwood Publishing Group, 1993.

Paul Hockings (ed.), *Principles of Visual Anthropology*, The Hague, Mouton, 1995.

Fredric Jameson, 'Third World literature in the era of multinational capitalism', *Social Text* no. 15, autumn 1986.

Fredric Jameson, *The Geopolitical Aesthetic: Cinema and Space in the World System*, Bloomington and London, Indiana and BFI, 1992.

Randal Johnson, *Cinema Novo X 5: Masters of Contemporary Brazilian Film*, Austin, University of Texas Press, 1984.

Randal Johnson and Robert Stam (eds), *Brazilian Cinema*, Rutherford, NJ, Fairleigh Dickinson University Press, 1982.

'The last "special issue" on race?' *Screen* 29(4), autumn, 1988.

'Latin American dossier,' parts 1, 2, *Framework* no. 10, spring 1979, pp. 11–38 and no. 11, autumn 1979, pp. 18–27.

John A. Lent, *The Asian Film Industry*, Austin, University of Texas Press, 1990.

Jay Leyda, *Dianying: Electric Shadows – An Account of Films and Film Audience in China*, Cambridge, Mass., MIT Press, 1972.

Lizbeth Malkmus and Roy Armes, *Arab and African Filmmaking*, London, Zed Press, 1991.

Angela Martin (ed.), *African Films: The Context of Production*, BFI Dossier no. 6, BFI, 1982.

Richard A. Maynard, *Africa On Film: Myth and Reality*, Rochelle Park, NJ, The Hayden Book Co., 1974.

David McDougall, 'Beyond observational cinema', in Hockings, *Visual Anthropology*.

Carl J. Mora, *Mexican Cinema: reflections of a Society 1896–1988*, Berkeley: University of California, 1988.

Laura Mulvey, 'Ousmane Sembène 1976: the carapace that failed', in *Third Text* nos. 16–17, autumn–winter 1991.

Hamid Naficy, *The Making of Exile Cultures: Iranian Television in Los Angeles*, Minneapolis, University of Minnesota Press, 1993.

Hamid Naficy and Teshome H. Gabriel (eds), *Otherness and the Media: The Ethnography of the Imagined and the Image*, Langhorne, PA, Harood, 1993.

Chon Noriega (ed.), *Chicanos and Film: Essays on Chicano Representation and Resistance*, New York, Garland Publishing, 1982. Reprinted University of Minnesota Press, 1991.

'Other cinemas, other criticisms', special issue, *Screen* 26(3–4), 1985.

Françoise Pfaff, 'Three faces of Africa: women in *Xala*', in *Jump Cut* no. 27, 1982.

Françoise Pfaff, *The Cinema of Ousmane Sembène*, Westport, CT, Greenwood, 1984.

Zuzana M. Pick (ed.), *Latin American Filmmakers and the Third Cinema*, Ottawa, Carleton University Press, 1978.

Zuzana M. Pick, *The New Latin American Cinema: A Continental Project*, Austin; University of Texas, 1993.

Jim Pines, *Blacks in Films: A Survey of Racial Themes and Images in the American Film*, London, Studio Vista, 1975.

Jim Pines and Paul Willemen (eds), *Questions of Third Cinema*, London, BFI, 1989.

'Racism, colonialism, and cinema', special issue, *Screen* 24(2), 1983.

Geoffrey Reeves, *Communications and the 'Third World'*, London, Routledge, 1993.

Mark A. Reid, *Redefining Black Film*, Berkeley, University of California Press, 1992.

Edward W. Said, *Orientalism*, London, RKP, 1978.

Edward W. Said, *Culture and Imperialism*, New York, Knopf, 1993.

Hala Salmane *et al.*, *Algerian Cinema*, London, BFI, 1976.

Jorge A. Schnitman, *Film Industries in Latin America: Dependency and Development* Norwood, NJ: Ablex, 1984.

Ella Shohat, *Israeli Cinema: East/West and the Politics of Representation*, Austin, University of Texas Press, 1989.

Ella Shohat, 'Notes on the postcolonial', in *Social Text* nos. 31/32, 1992.

Ella Shohat and Robert Stam, *Unthinking Eurocentrism: Multiculturalism and the Media*, London, Routledge, 1994.

Fernando Solanas and Octavio Getino, 'Towards a Third cinema', 1969; in Fusco, 1987.

Peter Stevens (ed.), *Jump Cut: Hollywood, Politics and Counter-Cinema*, Toronto, Between the Lines, 1986.

Clyde Taylor, 'Decolonizing the image', in Stevens, *Jump Cut*.

Rosie Thomas, 'Indian cinema: pleasures and popularity', in *Screen* 26(3–4), 1985.

Robert Farris Thompson, *African Art in Motion: Icon and Act*, Berkeley, University of California Press, 1973.

Trinh T. Minh-ha, *Woman, Native, Other*, Bloomington, Indiana University Press, 1989.

Trinh T. Minh-ha, *When the Moon Waxes Red*, New York, Routledge, 1991.

Trinh T. Minh-ha, *Framer Framed*, London, Routldege, 1992.

Gaizka S. de Usabel, *The High Noon of American Films in Latin America*, Ann Arbor, MI, UMI Research Press, 1982.

Allen I. Woll, *The Latin Image in American Film*, UCLA, Latin American Center Publications, 1980.

Allen I. Woll and Randall M. Miller, *Ethnic and Racial Images in American Film and Television*, New York, Garland, 1987.

Ismail Xavier, *Allegories of Underdevelopment: Aesthetics and Politics in Modern Brazilian Cinema*, Minneapolis, University of Minnesota Press, 1997.

HINDI CINEMA

Eric Barnouw and S. Krishnaswamy, *Indian Film*, New York, Columbia University Press, 1963; rev. edn New Delhi, Oxford University Press, 1980.

Veena Das, 'The mythological film and its framework of meaning: an analysis of *Jai Santoshi Maa*', *India International Centre Quarterly* 8(1), March 1980.

Chidananda Das Gupta, *The Cinema of Satyajit Ray*, New Delhi, Vikas, 1980.

Chidananda Das Gupta, 'The cultural basis of Indian cinema', 1968, in *Talking about Films*, New Delhi, Orient Longman, 1981.

Bagishwar Jha (ed.), *B. N. Sircar*, Calcutta, NFAI/Seagull Books, 1990.

Geet Kapur, 'Revelation and doubt: *Sant Tukaram* and Devi', 1987, reprinted in Niranjana *et al.*, *Modernity*.

Tejaswini Niranjana *et al.* (eds), *Interrogating Modernity: Culture and Colonialism in India*, Calcutta, Seagull Books, 1993.

Ashish Rajadhyaksha and Paul Willemen, *Encyclopaedia of Indian Cinema* 2nd edn, London and Delhi, BFI/Oxford University Press, 1999, 1st edn, 1994.

Ashish Rajadhyaksha, 'The Phalke era: conflict of traditional form and modern technology' (1987), reprinted in Niranjana *et al.*, *Modernity*.

Report of the Film Enquiry Committee (S. K. Patil, Chairman), New Delhi, Government of India Press, 1951.

Report of the Indian Cinematograph Committee 1927–28 (T. Rangachariar, Chairman), Calcutta, Government of India Central Publications Branch, 1928.

Andrew Robinson, *Satyajit Ray: The Inner Eye*, London, André Deutsch, 1989.

Kobita Sarkar, *Indian Cinema Today*, New Delhi, Sterling, 1975. Kobita Sarkar, 'Influences on the Indian Film', in *Indian Film Quarterly* January–March 1957.

Kobita Sarkar, 'Black and white', *Indian Film Review* December 1958.

Kumar Shahani, 'The saint poets of Prabhat', *Filmworld* Annual January 1980.

Kumar Shahani, 'Notes towards an aesthetic of cinema sound', *Journal of Arts & Ideas* no. 5, 1985.

Kumar Shahani, 'Film as a contemporary art', *Social Scientist* 18(3), March 1990.

Kumar Shahani 'Violence and Responsibility' in 'Dossier on Kumar Shahami', *Framework* 30–1, 1986.

Madan Gopal Singh, 'The space of encounter: a re-reading of *Sant Tukaram*', in Vasudev, *Frames*.

Aruna Vasudev (ed.), *Frames of Mind: Reflections on Indian Cinema*, New Delhi, UBS Publishers' Distributors, 1995.

Ravi Vasudevan, 'The melodramatic mode and the commercial Hindi cinema: notes on film history, narrative and performance in the 1950s', *Screen* 30(3), 1989.

Ravi Vasudevan, 'Shifting codes, dissolving identities: the Hindi social film of the 1950s as Popular Culture', *Journal of Arts & Ideas* nos. 23–24, 1993.

PART 5: GENRE

HISTORY OF GENRE CRITICISM

Lawrence Alloway, *Violent America: the movies 1946–64*, New York, Museum of Modern Art, 1971.

Rick Altman, *The American Film Musical*, Bloomington, Indiana University Press, 1987.

André Bazin, 'The western, or the American film *par excellence*' and 'The evolution of the western' in Hugh Gray (ed. and trans.), *What is Cinema*? Vol. 2, Berkeley, University of California Press, 1971.

Gillian Beer, *The Romance*, London, Methuen, 1970.

Biograph Bulletins, 1896–1908, compiled by Kemp R. Niver, Los Angeles, Locaire Research Group, 1971.

Diane Blakemore, *Understanding Utterances: An Introduction to Pragmatics*, Oxford, Blackwell, 1992.

Jean-Loup Bourget, 'Social implications in Hollywood genres', in Grant, *Film Genre*.

Leo Braudy, *The World in a Frame*, Garden City, Anchor Doubleday, 1976.

Edward Buscombe, 'The idea of genre in the American cinema', *Screen* 2(2), March/April 1970.

Edward Buscombe, 'Walsh and Warner Bros', in Hardy, *Raoul Walsh*.

John Cawelti, *The Six-Gun Mystique*, Bowling Green, Ohio, Bowling Green University Popular Press, 1971.

Richard Collins, 'Genre: a reply to Ed Buscombe', *Screen* 2(4/5), July/October 1970.

Steven Davis (ed.), *Pragmatics: A Reader*, Oxford, Oxford University Press, 1991.

Jacques Derrida, *Acts of Literature*, New York and London, Routledge, 1992.

Anthony Easthope, 'Notes on genre', *Screen Education* no. 32/33, winter/spring 1979/80.

Nils Erik Enkvist, 'On the interpretability of texts in general and of literary texts in particular', in Sells, *Pragmatics*.

Barry Grant (ed.), *Film Genre: Theory and Criticism*, Metuchen, NJ, Scarecrow Press, 1977.

Phil Hardy (ed.), *Raoul Walsh*, Edinburgh, Edinburgh Film Festival, 1974.

Judith Hess, 'Genre film and the status quo', in Grant, *Film Genre*.

Frederic Jameson, 'Magical narratives: romance as genre', *New Literary History* 7, 1975.

E. Ann Kaplan (ed.), *Women in Film Noir*, London, BFI, 1978; rev. edn, 1998.

Jim Kitses, *Horizons West*, London, Secker & Warburg/BFI, 1969.

Kleine Optical Company, Complete Illustrated Catalog of Moving Picture Machines, Stereoptikons, Slides, Films, Chicago, Kleine Optical Company, 1905.

Clayton Koelb, 'The problem of tragedy as a genre', *Genre*, 8(3), 1975.

Gunther Kress and Terry Threadgold, 'Towards a social theory of genre', *Southern Review* 21(3), 1988.

Geoffrey Leech, *The Principles of Pragmatics*, London, Longman, 1983.

Stephen C. Levinson, *Pragmatics*, Cambridge, Cambridge University Press, 1983.

Gregory Lukow and Steve Ricci, 'The audience goes public: inter-textuality, genre, and the responsibilities of film literacy', *On Film* no. 12, 1984.

John Lyons, *Language, Meaning and Context*, London, Longman, 1981.

Colin McArthur, *Underworld USA*, London, Secker & Warburg/BFI, 1972.

Colin McArthur, 'Iconography and iconology', London, BFI Education seminar paper, 1973.

Frank McConnell, *The Spoken Seen: Films and the Romantic Imagination*, Baltimore, Johns Hopkins, 1975.

Christian Metz, *Language and Cinema*, The Hague, Mouton, 1974.

Jacob L. Mey, *Pragmatics, An Introduction*, Oxford, Blackwell, 1993.

Charles Musser, 'The travel genre in 1903–04: moving toward fictional narratives', *Iris* 2(1), 1984.

Stephen Neale, *Genre*, London, BFI, 1980.

Steve Neale, 'Questions of genre', *Screen* 31(1), 1990.

Steve Neale, 'Melo talk: on the meaning and use of the term "melodrama" in the American Trade Press', *The Velvet Light Trap* no. 32, 1993.

Steve Neale, *Genre and Hollywood*, London, Routledge, forthcoming.

Mary Louise Pratt, 'The short story: the long and the short of it', *Poetics* vol. 10, 1981.

Douglas Pye, 'Genre and movies', *Movie* no. 20, 1975.

Tom Ryall, *Teachers Study Guide No. 2: The Gangster Film*, London, BFI Education, 1978.

Thomas Schatz, *Hollywood Genres: Formulas, Filmmaking, and the Studio System*, New York, Random House, 1981.

Thomas Schatz, *Old Hollywood/New Hollywood, Ritual, Art, and Industry*, Ann Arbor, UMI Research Press, 1983.

Roger D. Sells (ed.), *Literary Pragmatics*, London, Routledge, 1991.

Henry Nash Smith, *The Virgin Land*, Cambridge, Harvard University Press, 1950.

Terry Threadgold, 'Talking about genre: ideologies and incompatible discourses', *Cultural Studies*, 3(1), 1989.

Tzvetan Todorov, 'The origin of genres', *New Literary History* 8(1), 1976.

Andrew Tudor, *Theories of Film*, London, Secker & Warburg/BFI, 1974.

Marc Vernet, 'Genre', in *Film Reader* 3, 1978.

Robert Warshow, 'The gangster as tragic hero', and 'Movie chronicle: the westerner', in *The Immediate Experience*, New York, Atheneum Books, 1970.

Alan Williams, 'Is a radical genre criticism possible?', *Quarterly Review of Film Studies*, 9(2), 1984.

Michael Wood, *America in the Movies, or Santa Maria, It Had Slipped My Mind*, New York, Delta, 1975.

Will Wright, *Six Guns and Society: A Structural Study of the Western*, Berkeley, University of California Press, 1975.

THE WESTERN

André Bazin, 'The western, or the American film *par excellence*', and 'The evolution of the western', in Gray (ed. and trans.) *What is Cinema*? vol. 2, Berkeley, University of California Press, 1971.

Raymond Bellour, 'Alternation, segmentation, hypnosis: interview with Raymond Bellour', in *Camera Obscura* no. 3/4, 1979.

Edward Buscombe, 'The idea of genre in the American cinema', *Screen* 11(2), March/April 1970.

Edward Buscombe (ed.), *The BFI Companion to the Western*, London, André Deutsch, 1988; New York, Atheneum, 1988.

Edward Buscombe and Roberta Pearson (eds), *Back in the Saddle Again: New Essays on the Western*, London, BFI Publishing, 1998.

Ian Cameron and Douglas Pye (eds), *The Movie Book of the Western*, London, Studio Vista, 1996.

John Cawelti, *The Six Gun Mystique*, Bowling Green, Ohio, Bowling Green University Popular Press, 1971.

Richard Collins, 'Genre: a reply to Ed Buscombe', *Screen* 11(4/5), July–October 1970; reprinted in Nichols (ed.), *Movies and Methods*, Berkeley, University of California Press, 1976.

William Cronon, George Miles and Jay Gitlin (eds), *Under an Open Sky: Rethinking America's Western Past*, New York, W. W. Norton, 1992.

Christopher Frayling, 'The American western and American society', in Davies and Neve (eds), *Cinema, Politics and Society in America*, Manchester, Manchester University Press, 1981a.

Christopher Frayling, *Spaghetti Westerns: cowboys and Europeans from Karl May to Sergio Leone*, London, RKP, 1981b.

Philip French, *Westerns*, London, Secker & Warburg/BFI, 1973.

Stuart Hall and Paddy Whannel, *The Popular Arts*, London, Hutchinson Educational, 1964.

Jim Kitses, *Horizons West*, London, Secker & Warburg/BFI, 1969.

Jacqueline Levitin, 'The western: any good roles for feminists?', *Film Reader* no. 5, 1982.

Alan Lovell, 'The western', *Screen Education* no. 41, September/October 1967.

Colin McArthur, 'The roots of the western', *Cinema* no. 4, October 1969.

Laura Mulvey, 'Afterthoughts on "Visual pleasure and narrative cinema" inspired by *Duel in the Sun*', *Framework* nos. 15/16/17, summer 1981.

Stephen Neale, *Genre*, London, BFI Publishing, 1980.

Patricia Nelson Limerick, *The Legacy of Conquest: The Unbroken Past of the American West*, New York, W. W. Norton, 1987.

Patricia Nelson Limerick, Clyde A. Milner II and Charles E. Rankin (eds), *Trails: Towards a New Western History*, Lawrence: University Press of Kansas, 1991.

Douglas Pye, 'Genre and history: *Fort Apache and Liberty Valance*', Movie no. 25, winter 1977/78.

Jean-Louis Rieupeyrout, 'The western: a historical genre', *Quarterly of Film, Radio and Television* vol. 3, winter 1952.

Tom Ryall, 'The notion of genre', *Screen* 11(2), March/April 1970.

Richard Slotkin, *Gunfighter Nation: the Myth of the Frontier in twentieth-century America*, New York, Atheneum, 1992.

Jane Tompkins, *West of Everything: The Inner Life of Westerns*, New York, Oxford University Press, 1992.

Jean Wagner, 'The western, history and actuality', in Henri Agel (ed.), *Le Western*, Paris, Lettres Modernes, 1961.

Robert Warshow, 'Movie chronicle: the westerner', in *The Immediate Experience*, New York, Atheneum Books, 1970.

Paul Willemen, 'Voyeurism, the look and Dwoskin,' *Afterimage* no. 6, 1976.

Will Wright, *Six Guns and Society: A Structural Study of the Western*, Berkeley, University of California Press, 1975.

MELODRAMA

Guy Barefoot, 'Hollywood, melodrama and twentieth-century notions of the Victorian' in Bratton *et al.*, *Melodrama*.

Jeanine Basinger, *A Woman's View, How Hollywood Spoke to Women, 1930–1960*, London, Catto & Windus, 1993.

Jean-Loup Bourget, 'Faces of the American melodrama: Joan Crawford', *Film Reader* 3, 1978.

Jacky Bratton, Jim Cook and Christine Gledhill (eds), *Melodrama: Stage, Picture, Screen*, London, BFI, 1994.

Peter Brooks, *The Melodramatic Imagination*, New Haven, Yale University Press, 1976.

Charlotte Brunsdon, '*Crossroads*: notes on soap opera', *Screen* 22(4), 1981.

Jackie Byars, *All That Hollywood Allows, Re-Reading Gender in 1950s Melodrama*, London, Routledge, 1991.

Bert Cardullo, '*Way Down East*: play and film' in *Indelible Images*, USA: University Press of America, 1987.

Pam Cook, 'Duplicity in *Mildred Pierce*', in Kaplan, *Women in Film Noir*.

Barbara Creed, 'The position of women in Hollywood melodramas', *Australian Journal of Screen Theory* no. 4, 1977.

Mary Ann Doane, 'The "woman's film": possession and address', in Doane, Mellencamp and Williams (eds), *Re-Vision: Essays in Feminist Film Criticism*, Frederick MD, AFI Monograph Series, University Publications of America/AFI, 1983.

Mary Ann Doane, *The Desire to Desire, The Woman's Film of the 1940s*, Bloomington and Indianapolis, Indiana University Press, 1987.

Barbara Ehrenreich, *The Hearts of Men*, London, Pluto Press, 1983.

Lotte Eisner, *Murnau*, London, Secker & Warburg, 1973.

Thomas Elsaesser, 'Tales of sound and fury: observations on the family melodrama', *Monogram* no. 4, 1972.

John Fell, *Film and the Narrative Tradition*, Norman, OK, University of Oklahoma Press, 1974.

Lizzie Francke, *Script Girls, Women Screenwriters in Hollywood*, London, BFI, 1994.

Brandon French, *On the Verge of Revolt*, New York, Ungar, 1978.

Christine Gledhill (ed), *Home is Where the Heart Is: Studies in Melodrama and the Woman's Film*, London, BFI, 1987.

Jon Halliday, *Sirk on Sirk*, London, Secker & Warburg/BFI, 1971.

Molly Haskell, *From Reverence to Rape*, Harmondsworth, Penguin, 1979.

Lea Jacobs, 'Censorship and the Fallen Woman Cycle', in Gledhill, *Home is Where the Heart Is*.

Lea Jacobs, *The Wages of Sin, Censorship and the Fallen Woman Film, 1928–1942*, Madison, University of Wisconsin Press, 1991.

E. Ann Kaplan (ed.), *Women in Film Noir*, London, BFI, 1978; rev. edn, 1998.

E. Ann Kaplan, 'Mothering, Feminism and Representation: the Maternal in Melodrama and the Woman's Film from 1910 to 1940', in Gledhill, *Home is Where the Heart Is*.

E. Ann Kaplan, *Motherhood and Representation: The Mother in Popular Culture and Melodrama*, London, Routledge, 1992.

Stanley Kaufman, 'D. W. Griffith's *Way Down East*', *Horizon*, spring 1972.

Vance Kepley, '*Broken Blossoms* and the problem of historical specificity', *Quarterly Review of Film Studies*, winter 1978.

Chuck Kleinhans, 'Notes on melodrama and the family under capitalism', *Film Reader* 3, 1978.

Barbara Klinger, *Melodrama and Meaning, History, Culture, and the Films of Douglas Sirk*, Bloomington and Indianapolis, University of Indiana Press, 1994.

Sarah Kozloff, 'Griffith's *Way Down East* & Hardy's *Tess of the D'Ubervilles*', *Film/Literature Quarterly*, 13(1), 1985.

Robert Lang, *American Film Melodrama, Griffith, Vidor, Minnelli*, Princeton, Princeton University Press, 1989.

Arthur Lennig, 'D. W. Griffith and making of an unconventional masterpiece', *The Film Journal* 1(3/4).

Arthur Lennig, 'The birth of *Way Down East*', *Quarterly Review of Film Studies*, winter 1981.

Burns Mantle, Review of *Way Down East*, *Photoplay* 19(1), December 1920.

Judith Mayne, *Directed by Dorothy Arzner*, Bloomington and Indianapolis, University of Indiana Press, 1994.

Tania Modleski, 'The search for tomorrow in today's soap operas', *Film Quarterly* 33(1), 1979.

Laura Mulvey, 'Fear eats the soul', *Spare Rib* no. 30, 1974.

Laura Mulvey, 'Notes on Sirk and melodrama', *Movie* no. 25, 1977/78.

Laura Mulvey, 'Afterthoughts on "Visual pleasure and narrative cinema" inspired by *Duel in the Sun*', *Framework*, nos. 15/16/17, summer 1981.

Stephen Neale, *Genre*, London, BFI, 1980.

Steve Neale, 'Melo talk: on the meaning and use of the term "melodrama" in the American Trade Press', *The Velvet Light Trap* no. 32, 1993.

Geoffrey Nowell-Smith, 'Minnelli and melodrama', *Screen* 18(2), summer 1977.

Michael Paris, *From the Wright Brothers to Top Gun, Aviation, Nationalism and Popular Cinema*, Manchester and New York, Manchester University Press, 1995.

Griselda Pollock, 'Report on the weekend school', *Screen* 18(2), summer 1977.

Frank Rahill, *The World of Melodrama*, Philadelphia, Pennsylvania State University Press, 1967.

D. N. Rodowick, 'Madness, authority and ideology in the domestic melodrama of the 1950s', *The Velvet Light Trap* no. 19, 1982.

Thomas Schatz, *Hollywood Genres: Formulas, Filmmaking and the Studio System*, New York, Random House, 1981.

Richard Schickel, *D. W. Griffith*, New York, Limelight Editions, 1996.

Ben Singer, 'Female power in the serial-queen melodrama: the etiology of an anomaly', *Camera Obscura* no. 22, 1990.

Nicholas Vardac, *From Stage to Screen: Theatrical Method from Garick to Griffith*, Boston, Harvard University Press, 1949.

Christian Viviani, 'Who is without sin? The maternal melodrama in American film 1930–39', *Wide Angle* 4(2), 1980.

Diane Waldman, '"At last I can tell it to someone!" Feminine point of view and subjectivity in the Gothic romance film of the 1940s', *Cinema Journal* 23(2), 1983.

Michael Walker, 'Melodrama and the cinema', *Movie* nos. 29/30, summer 1982.

Andrea S. Walsh, *Women's Film and Female Experience, 1940–1950*, New York, Praeger, 1984.

Paul Willemen, 'Distanciation and Douglas Sirk', *Screen* 12(2), summer 1971.

Linda Williams, 'Something else besides a mother: *Stella Dallas* and the maternal melodrama', in Gledhill, *Melodrama*.

CONTEMPORARY CRIME

The detective film

Richard Alewyn, 'The origin of the detective novel'.

Tino Balio, *Grand Design: Hollywood as a Modern Business Enterprise, 1930–1939*, New York, Scribners, 1993.

David Bordwell, *Narration in the Fiction Film*, London, Methuen, 1985.

Eileen Bowser, *The Transformation of Cinema, 1907–1915*, New York, Scribners, 1993.

Roger Caillois, 'The detective novel as game' in Most and Stowe, *The Poetics of Murder*.

Ian Cameron (ed.), *The Movie Book of Film Noir*, London, Studio Vista, 1992.

John G. Cawelti, *Adventure, Mystery, and Romance, Formula Stories as Art and Popular Culture*, Chicago, Chicago University Press, 1976.

John Cawelti, '*Chinatown* and generic transformation in recent Hollywood films' in Grant, *Film Genre*.

Charles Derry, *The Suspense Thriller, Films in the Shadow of Alfred Hitchcock*, Jefferson, McFarland, 1988.

Thomas Elsaesser, 'The pathos of failure: American film in the 1970s – notes on the unmotivated hero', *Monogram* 69, 1975, pp. 13–19.

Michel Foucault, *Discipline and Punish*, New York, Vintage Books, 1979.

Edward Gallafent, 'Echo Park: *film noir* in the seventies' in Cameron, *Film Noir*.

Daniel J. Gerould (ed.), *Five Filmmakers: Tarkovsky, Forman, Polanski, Szabo, Makavejev*, Bloomington, Indiana University Press, 1994.

Mick Gidley (ed), *Modern American Culture, An Introduction*, London, Longham, 1993.

Barry Keith Grant (ed), *Film Genre Reader* II, Austin, University of Texas Press, 1995 (1979).

Leighton Grist, 'Moving targets and black widows: film noir in modern Hollywood', in Cameron, *Film Noir*.

Cynthia Hamilton, 'American genre fiction', in Gidley, *Modern American Culture*.

Mary Beth Haralovich, 'Sherlock Holmes: genre and industrial practice', *Journal of the University Film Association* 31(2), spring 1979.

Gary Hoppenstand (ed.), *The Dime Novel Detective*, Bowling Green, Bowling Green University Press, 1982.

Albert D. Hutter, 'Dreams, transformations, and literature: the implications of detective fiction', in Most and Stowe, *Poetics*.

Ernst Kaemmel, 'Literature under the table: the detective novel and its social mission', in Most and Stowe, *Poetics*, 1983.

Stephen Knight, *Form and Ideology in Crime Fiction*, Bloomington, Indiana University Press, 1980.

Richard Koszarski, *An Evening's Entertainment, The Age of the Silent Feature Picture, 1915–1928*, New York, Scribner, 1990.

Larry Langman and Daniel Finn, *A Guide to American Silent Crime Films*, Westport, Greenwood Press, 1994.

Ernes Mandel, *Delightful Murder, A Social History of the Crime Story*, London, Pluto Press, 1984.

Glenn W. Most and William W. Stowe (eds), *The Poetics of Murder: Detective Fiction and Literary Theory*, San Diego, Harcourt Brace Janovich, 1983.

Stephen Neale, *Genre*, London, BFI, 1980.

Ian Ousby, *Bloodhounds of Heaven: The Detective in English fiction form Godwin to Doyle*, Cambridge, Harvard University Press, 1976.

Jerry Palmer, *Thrillers: Genesis and Structure of a Popular Genre*, London, Edward Arnold, 1978.

Leroy Lad Panek, *An Introduction to the Detective Story*, Bowling Green, Bowling Green State University Press, 1987.

Leroy Lad Panek, *Probable Cause, Crime Fiction in America*, Bowling Green, Bowling Green State University Press, 1990.

Geraldine Pederson-Krag, 'Detective stories and the primal scene', in Most and Stowe, *Poetics*.

Dennis Porter, *The Pursuit of Crime, Art and Ideology in Detective Fiction*, New Haven, Yale University Press, 1981.

Murray Smith, *Engaging Characters: Fiction, Emotion and the Cinema*, Oxford, Clarendon Press, 1995.

Matthew Solomon, 'Dime novels and early cinema as the nickelodeon period begins: outlaw and detective stories', unpublished conference paper, 1995.

R. F. Stewart, ... *And Always a Detective, Chapters on the History of Detective Fiction*, Newton Abbott, David and Charles, 1980.

Julian Symons, *Bloody Murder: From the Detective Story to the Crime Novel; A history*, London, Pan Books, 1992 edn.

Kristin Thompson, *Breaking the Glass Armor, Neoformalist Film Analysis*, Princeton, Princeton University Press, 1988.

Tzvetan Todorov, *The Poetics of Prose*, Ithaca, Cornell University Press, 1977.

The gangster film

Lawrence Alloway, *Violent America: the Movies 1946–64*, New York, Museum of Modern Art, 1971.

Peter Brooks, *The Melodramatic Imagination*, New Haven and London, Yale University Press, 1976.

Charles Eckert, 'The anatomy of a proletarian film: Warners' *Marked Woman*', *Quarterly Review* 27(2), winter 1973/74.

Philip French, 'Incitement against violence', *Sight and Sound* 37(1), winter 1967/68.

Robert B. Heilman, *Tragedy and Melodrama*, Seattle, University of Washington Press, 1968.

Steve Jenkins, *The Death of a Gangster*, London, BFI Education, 1982.

Alan Lovell, *Don Siegel: American Cinema*, London, BFI, 1975.

Colin McArthur, *Underworld USA*, London, Secker & Warburg/BFI, 1972.

William Park, 'The police state', *Journal of Popular Film* 6(3), 1978.

Nick Roddick, *A New Deal in Entertainment: Warner Bros in the 1930s*, London, BFI, 1983.

Tom Ryall, *Teachers' Study Guide 2: The Gangster Film*, London BFI Education, 1978.

Jack Shadoian, *Dreams and Dead Ends*, Cambridge, Mass., MIT Press, 1977.

Thomas Schatz, *Hollywood Genres: Formulas, Filmmaking and the Studio System*, New York, Random House, 1981.

Andrew Tudor, *Image and Influence*, London, Allen and Unwin, 1974.

Robert Warshow, 'The Gangster as Tragic Hero', in *The Immediate Experience*, New York, Atheneum Books, 1970.

Richard Whitehall, 'Crime Inc', *Films and Filming*, 10(4–6), January/February/March 1964.

Suspense Thriller

Michael Balint, *Thrills and Regressions*, London, The Hogarth Press, 1959.

Brian Davis, *The Thriller: The Suspense Film from 1946*, London, Studio Vista, 1973.

Charles Derry, *The Suspense Thriller: Films in the Shadow of Alfred Hitchcock*, Jefferson McFarland Press, 1988.

George N. Dove, *Suspense in the Formula Story*, Bowling Green, Bowling Green State University Popular Press, 1989.

Gordon Gow, *Suspense in the Cinema*, New York, Castle, 1968.

Lawrence Hammond, *Thriller Movies: Classic Films of Suspense and Mystery*, London, Octopus, 1974.

Larry Langman and Daniel Finn, *A Guide to American Crime Films of the Thirties*, Westport, Greenwood Press, 1995a.

Larry Langman and Daniel Finn, *A Guide to American Crime Films of the Forties and Fifties*, Westport, Greenwood Press, 1995b.

François Truffaut (with Helen G. Scott), *Hitchcock*, New York, Simon and Schuster, 1967.

FILM NOIR

Raymond Borde and Étienne Chaumeton, *Panorame du Film Noir Americain*, Paris, Les Éditions de Minuit, 1955, reprinted in part as 'Sources of *film noir*', *Film Reader* 3, 1978.

Ian Cameron (ed.), *The Movie Book of Film Noir*, London, Studio Vista, 1992.

John Cawelti, *Chinatown* and Generic Transformation in Recent Hollywood Films' in Barry Keith Grant (ed.), *Film Genre Reader* II (Austin, University of Texas Press, 1995 (1979).

Pam Cook, 'Duplicity in *Mildred Pierce*', in Kaplan, *Women in Film Noir*.

Joan Copjec, *Shades of Noir*, London, Verso, 1993.

Elizabeth Cowie, '*Film Noir* and Women' in Copjec, *Shades of Noir*.

Bruce Crowther, *Film Noir, Reflections in a Dark Mirror*, London, Virgin Books, 1988.

James Damico, 'Film noir: a modest proposal', *Film Reader* 3, 1978.

Mary Ann Doane, *The Desire to Desire – The Woman's Film of the 1940s* (Indiana University Press, Bloomington, 1987).

Richard Dyer, 'Resistance through Charisma: Rita Hayworth and *Gilda*' in Kaplan, *Women in Film Noir*.

Raymond Durgnat, 'The family tree of film noir', *Cinema*, August 1970, reprinted in *Film Comment* 10(6), November/December 1974.

Herbert Eagle, 'Polanski' in Daniel J. Gerould (ed.), *Five Filmmakers: Tarkovsky, Forman, Polanski, Szabo, Makavejev*, Bloomington, Indiana University Press, 1994.

Tom Flinn, 'Three faces of film noir', *The Velvet Light Trap* no. 5, summer 1972.

Edward Gallafent, 'Echo Park: *film noir* in the seventies' in Cameron, *Film Noir*.

Christine Gledhill, '*Klute* 1: a contemporary film noir and feminist criticism', and '*Klute* 2: feminism and *Klute*', in Kaplan, *Film Noir*.

Leighton Grist, 'Moving Targets and Black Widows, Film Noir in Modern Hollywood' in Cameron, *Film Noir*.

Larry Gross, 'Film *après* noir', *Film Comment* vol. 12 no. 4, July/August 1976.

Sylvia Harvey, 'Woman's place: the absent family of film noir', in Kaplan, *Film Noir*.

Reynold Humphries, *Fritz Lang – Genre and Representation in his American Films*, Baltimore, John Hopkins Press, 1988.

Florence Jakobowitz, 'The man's melodrama, *The Woman in the Window* and *Scarlet Street*' in Cameron, *Film Noir*.

Stephen Jenkins, *Fritz Lang: The Image and the Look*, London, BFI, 1981.

Stephen Jenkins, 'Dashiell Hammett and *film noir*', *Monthly Film Bulletin* 49(586), November 1982.

Paul M. Jensen, *The Cinema of Fritz Lang*, London, Zwemmer, 1969.

Claire Johnston, '*Double Indemnity*', in Kaplan, *Film Noir*.

E. Ann Kaplan (ed.), 'Introduction', in *Women in Film Noir*, London, BFI, 1978; rev. edn. 1998.

Paul Kerr, 'Out of what past? Notes on the B-*film noir*', *Screen Education* no. 32/33, autumn/winter 1979/80.

Frank Krutnik, *In a Lonely Street: Film Noir, Genre, Masculinity*, London, Routledge, 1991.

Richard Maltby, '*Film noir*: the politics of the maladjusted text' in Cameron, *Film Noir*.

Colin McArthur, *Underworld USA*, London, BFI/Secker & Warburg, 1972.

Steve Neale, *Genre and Hollywood*, London, Routledge, forthcoming.

Brian Neve, *Film and Politics in America, A Social Tradition*, London, Routledge, 1992.

R. Barton Palmer, *Hollywood's Dark Cinema, The American Film Noir*, New York, Twayne, 1994.

J. A. Place, 'Women in *film noir*', in Kaplan, *Women in Film Noir*.

J. A. Place and L. S. Peterson, 'Some visual motifs of *film noir*', *Film Comment* 10(1), January/February 1974.

Dana Polan, *Power and Paranoia, History, Narrative, and the American Cinema, 1940–1950*, New York, Columbia University Press, 1986.

Robert Porfirio, 'No way out', *Sight and Sound* 45(4), autumn 1976.

Thomas Schatz, *Hollywood Genres: Formulas, Filmmaking and the Studio System*, New York, Random House, 1981.

Paul Schrader, 'Notes on film noir', *Film Comment* 8(1), spring 1972.

Alan Silver and Elizabeth Ward (eds), *Film Noir*, London, Secker & Warburg, 1981.

Alain Silver and Elizabeth Ward, *Film Noir: An Encyclopedia Reference to the American Style*, Woodstock, The Overlook Press, 1992 edition.

J. P. Telotte, *Voices in the Dark, The Narrative Patterns of Film Noir*, Urbana, Illinois University Press, 1989.

Deborah Thomas, 'Hollywood deals with the deviant male' in Cameron, *Film Noir*.

Marc Vernet, '*Film Noir* on the edge of doom' in Copjec, *Shades of Noir*.

Diane Waldman, 'At last I can tell it to someone!: feminine point of view and subjectivity in the Gothic romance film of the 1940s' in *Cinema Journal* 23(2), winter 1983.

Michael Walker, '*Film noir*: introduction' in Cameron, *Film Noir*.

SCIENCE FICTION AND HORROR

Science fiction

Erik Barnouw, *The Magician and Cinema*, New York, Oxford University Press, 1981.

John Brosnan, *Future Tense: The Cinema of Science Fiction*, New York, St. Martin's Press, 1978.

John Baxter, *Science Fiction in the Cinema*, London, Zwemmer, 1970.

John Brosnan, *Movie Magic: The Story of Special Effects in the Cinema*, London, MacDonald Press, 1974.

Giuliana Bruno, 'Ramble City: Postmodernism and *Blade Runner*' in Kuhn, *Alien Zone*, 1990.

James Donald (ed.), *Fantasy and Cinema*, London, BFI Publishing, 1989.

John Frazer, *Artificially Arranged Scenes: The Films of George Méliès*, Boston, G. K. Hall, 1979.

Paul Hammond, *Marvelous Méliès*, New York, St Martin's, 1974.

Donna Haraway, 'A manifesto for cyborgs: science, technology and socialist feminism in the 1980s', *Socialist Review*, no. 10, 1985.

Phil Hardy, *The Encyclopaedia of Science Fiction Movies*, London, Octopus Books, 1986.

Richard Hodgens, A brief tragical history of the science fiction film', *Film Quarterly* 13, 1959.

David Hutchison, *Film Magic. The Art and Science of Special Effects*, New York, Prentice-Hall, 1987.

Edward James, *Science Fiction in the Twentieth Century*, Oxford University Press, 1994.

Judith B. Kerman, *Retrofitting Blade Runner, Issues in Ridley Scott's Blade Runner and Philip K. Dick's Do Androids Dream of Electric Sheep?*, Bowling Green, Bowling Green State University Popular Press, 1991.

Annette Kuhn (ed.), *Alien Zone: Cultural Theory and Contemporary Science Fiction Cinema*, London, Verso, 1990.

Steve Neale, 'Hollywood strikes back – special effects in recent Hollywood movies', *Screen* 21(3), 1980.

Steve Neale, 'Issues of difference: *Alien* and *Blade Runner*' in Donald, *Fantasy and Cinema*.

Constance Penley, Elisabeth Lyon, Lynn Spiegel and Janet Bergstrom (eds), *Close Encounters: Film, Feminism and Science Fiction*, Minneapolis, University of Minnesota Press, 1991.

David Pringle (ed.), *The Ultimate Encyclopedia of Science Fiction*, London, Carlton, 1996.

Michael Pye and Lynda Myles, *The Movie Brats: How the Film Generation took over Hollywood*, New York, Holt, Rinehart and Winston, 1979.

Thomas Schatz, *Old Hollywood/New Hollywood, Ritual, Art, and Industry*, Ann Arbour, UMI Research Press, 1983.

Vivian Sobchack, *The Limits of Infinity: The American Science Fiction Film 1950–1975*, New York, Ungar, 1980.

Vivian Sobchack, *Screening Space: The American Science Fiction Film*, New York, Ungar, 1988.

Jean-François Tarnowski, 'Approche un definition du fantastique et de la science-fiction cinématographique (1)', *Positif* 195/6, 1977, 57–65.

J. P. Telotte, *Replications: A Robotic History of the Science Fiction Film*, Urbana, University of Illinois Press, 1995.

The horror film

Andrew Britton *et al.*, (eds), *American Nightmare: Essays on the Horror Film*, Toronto, Festival of Festivals, 1979.

Philip Brophy, 'Horrality – the textually of contemporary of horror films', *Screen* 27(1): 2–13, January–February 1986.

Ivan Butler, *Horror in the Cinema*, London, A. Zwemmer, 1970.

Noel Carroll, 'Nightmare and the horror film', *Film Quarterly XXXIV*, spring 1981, pp. 16–25. Carroll's later treatment of the nightmare theme is in *Philosophy of Horror*, London, Routledge, 1990, pp. 168–78.

Noel Carroll, 'The future of allusion: Hollywood in the seventies (and beyond)', *October* no. 20 spring 1982.

Noel Carroll, *The Philosophy of Horror*, Routledge: New York and London, 1990.

Carlos Clarens, *Horror Movies: an illustrated survey*, London, Secker & Warburg, 1968.

Carol J. Clover, *Men, Women and Chain Saws*, Princeton, NJ and London, BFI, 1992.

Pam Cook, review, *Monthly Film Bulletin* 66(660): 3–4, January 1989.

Jonathan Lake Crane, *Terror and Everyday Life*, Thousand Oaks, London, New Delhi, Sage, 1994.

Barbara Creed, 'Phallic panic: male hysteria and *Dead Ringers*', *Screen* 31(2): 125–146, summer 1990.

Barbara Creed, 'Horror and the monstrous-feminine – an imaginary abjection', *Screen* 27(1) 44–70, January–February 1986.

Charles Derry, *Dark Dreams: A Psychological History of the Modern Horror Film*, London, Thomas Yoseloff, 1977.

Mary Ann Doane, *et al.* (eds), *Revision: Essays in Feminist Film Criticism*, Frederick MD, AFI Monograph Series, University Publications of America AFI 1983.

Lotte Eisner, *The Haunted Screen: Expressionism in the German Cinema and the Influence of Max Reinhardt*, London, Thames & Hudson, 1969.

T. R. Ellis, *A Journey into Darkness; The Art of James Whale's Horror Films*, Ann Arbor, University Microfilms, 1985.

Victor Elrich, *Russian Formalism: History–Doctrine*, New Haven, Yale University Press, 1981.

Walter Evans, 'Monster movies: a sexual theory', *Journal of Popular Film* 2(4), autumn 1973.

Walter Evans, 'Monster movies and rites of initiation', *Journal of Popular Film* 4(2), autumn 1975.

Roy Huss and T. J. Ross (eds), *Focus on the Horror Film*, Englewood Cliffs, NJ, Prentice-Hall Inc., 1972.

Steve Jenkins, review, *Monthly Film Bulletin* 49(583): 158–160, August 1982.

Robert E. Kapsis, '*Dressed to Kill*', *American Film* no. 5, March 1982.

Harlan Kennedy, 'Things that go howl in the id', *Film Comment* 18(2), March/April 1982.

Annette Kuhn, 'Border crossing', *Sight and Sound* 2(3): 13 (NS), July 1992.

Ernest Larsen, 'Hi-tech horror', *Jump Cut* no. 22, November 1977.

Laura Lederer (ed.), *Take Back the Night*, New York, William Morrow and Co., 1980.

Susan Lurie, 'Pornography and the dread of woman', in Lederer, *Night*.

Brian Murphy, 'Monster movies: they came from beneath the 50s', *Journal of Popular Film* 1(1), winter 1972.

Stephen Neale, *Genre*, London, BFI, 1980.

Steve Neale, 'Hollywood strikes back – special effects in recent American cinema', *Screen* 21(3): 101–5, 1980.

Davie Pirie, *A Heritage of Horror: The English Gothic Cinema* 1946–72, London, Gordon Fraser, 1973.

Michael Pye and Lynda Myles, *The Movie Brats: How the Film Generation Took Over Hollywood*, New York, Holt, Rinehart and Winston, 1979.

Otto Rank, *The Double*, trans. Harry Tucker jun., Signet: New York, 1979.

Robert B. Ray, *A Certain Tendency of the Hollywood Cinema, 1930–1980*, Princeton, Princeton University Press, 1985.

W. H. Rockett, 'Perspectives', *Journal of Popular Film and Television* 10(3), autumn 1982.

Chris Rodley, (ed.), *Cronenberg on Cronenberg*, Faber & Faber, London, 1992.

T. J. Ross, 'Introduction', in Huss and Ross, *Horror Film*.

Gianluca Sergi, 'A cry in the dark: the role of post-classical Hollywood film sound', in Neale and Smith (eds), *Contemporary Hollywood Cirema*, London, Routledge, 1998.

Stephen Snyder, 'Family life and leisure culture in *The Shining*', *Film Criticism* 6(1), autumn 1982.

Andrew Tudor, *Image and Influence: Studies in the Sociology of Film*, London, Allen and Unwin, 1974.

Andrew Tudor, *Monsters and Mad Scientists*, Oxford, Basil Blackwell, 1989.

Linda Williams, 'When the woman looks', in Doane *et al.*, *Revision*.

Tony Williams, 'American cinema in the 70s: family horror', *Movie* no. 27/28, winter 1980/spring 1981.

Robin Wood, *Hitchcock's Films*, New York, A. S. Barnes, 1965, pp. 106–14.

Robin Wood, 'Introduction', in Britton, Lippe, Williams, Woods (eds), *American Nightmare: essays on the horror film*, Toronto, Festival of Festivals, 1979.

Justin Wyatt, *High Concept, Movies and Marketing in Hollywood*, Austin, University of Texas Press, 1994.

Slavoj Žižek, *For They Know What They Do*, Verso, London, 1991.

THE MUSICAL

Rick Altman, *The American Film Musical*, Bloomington, Indiana University Press, 1987.

Rick Altman (ed.), *Genre: The Musical*, London, RKP, 1981.

Rick Altman, 'The Musical' in Geoffrey Nowell-Smith (ed.), *The Oxford History of World Cinema*, Oxford, OUP, 1996.

Bruce Babington and Peter William Evans, *Blue Skies and Silver Linings, Aspects of the Hollywood Musical*, Manchester, Manchester University Press, 1985.

Tino Balio, *Grand Design, Hollywood as a Modern Business Enterprise, 1930–1939* (*History of the American Cinema*, vol. 5), New York, Scribner's, 1993.

Richard Barrios, *A Song in the Dark: The Birth of the Musical Film*, New York, Oxford University Press, 1995.

Gerald Bordman, *American Operetta: From HMS Pinafore to Sweeney Todd*, Oxford, Oxford University Press, 1981.

Gerald Bordman, *American Musical Comedy: From Adonis to Dreamgirls*, Oxford, Oxford University Press, 1982.

Gerald Bordman, *American Musical Revue: From the Passing Show in Sugar Babies*, Oxford, Oxford University Press, 1985.

Leo Braudy, *The World in a Frame: What We See in Films*, New York, Anchor, 1976.

Steven Cohan, 'Feminizing the song-and-dance man. Fred Astaire and the spectacle of mas culinity in the Hollywood musical', in Cohan and Mark, *Screening the Male*.

Steven Cohan and Ina Rae Hark (eds), *Screening the Male. Exploring Masculinities in Hollywood Cinema*, London, Routledge, 1993.

Jim Collins, 'The Musical' in Wes D. Gehring (ed.), *Handbook of American Film Genres*, New York, Greenwood Press, 1988.

Jerome Delameter, 'Performing arts: the musical', in Kaminsky, *American Film*.

Jerome Delameter, *Dance in the Hollywood Musical*, Ann Arbor, UMI Research Press, 1981.

Richard Dyer, 'The Sound of Music', *Movie* no. 23, 1976/77.

Richard Dyer, 'Entertainment and utopia', *Movie* no. 24, 1977; and Altman, *Genre: The Musical*.

Richard Dyer, '*A Star is Born* and the construction of authenticity', in Gledhill (ed.), *Star Signs*, London, BFI Education, 1982.

Thomas Elsaesser, 'Vincente Minnelli', in Altman, *Genre: The Musical*.

Greg S. Faller, *The Function of Star-Image and Performance in the Hollywood Musical: Sonja Henie, Esther Williams, and Eleanor Powell*, Ph.D. thesis, Northwestern University, 1987, Ann Arbor, UMI Dissertation Information Service, 1992.

Jane Feuer, *The Hollywood Musical*, London, Macmillan, 1982 and 1993.

Lucy Fischer, 'The image of woman as image: the optical politics of *Dames*', in Altman (ed.), *Genre*.

Hugh Fordin, *The Movies' Greatest Musicals: Produced in Hollywood USA by the Freed Unit*, New York, Ungar, 1975.

Beth Eliot Genne, *The Film Musicals of Vincente Minnelli and the Team of Gene Kelly and Stanley Donen, 1944–1958*, (Ph.D. thesis, University of Michigan, 1984), Ann Arbor, UMI Dissertation Information Service, 1992.

Barry K. Grant, 'The classic Hollywood musical and the "problem" of rock 'n' roll', *Journal of Popular Film and Television* 13(4), winter 1986.

Stuart Kaminsky, *American Film Genres*, Dayton, Pflaum, 1974.

Richard Kislan, *The Musical: A Look at the American Musical Theater*, Englewood Cliffs, Prentice-Hall, 1980.

John Kobal, *Gotta Sing, Gotta Dance: a pictorial history of film musicals*, London, Hamlyn, 1971.

Arthur Knight, 'The movies learn to talk: Ernst Lubitsch, René Clair, and Rouben Mamoulian', in Weis and Belton, *Film Sound*.

Alain Masson, 'George Sidney: artificial brilliance/the brilliance of artifice', in Altman, *Genre*.

Gerald Mast, *Can't help singin'. The American musical on stage and screen*, Woodstock, Overlook Press, 1987.

John Mueller, 'Fred Astaire and the integrated musical', *Cinema Journal* 24(1), autumn 1984.

John Mueller, *Astaire Dancing: The Musical Films*, New York, Wings Books, 1985.

Vincente Minnelli, with Herbert Acre, *I Remember It Well*, Garden City, Doubleday, 1974.

Ethan Mordden, *The Hollywood Studios: House Style in the Golden Age of the Movies*, New York, Knopf, 1988.

James Naremore, *The Films of Vincente Minnelli*, Cambridge, Cambridge University Press, 1993.

Stephen Neale, *Genre*, London, BFI, 1980.

Sue Rickard, 'Movies in Disguise: Negotiating Censorship and Patriarchy Through the Dances of Fred Astaire and Ginger Rogers' in R. Lawson-Peebles (ed.), *Approaches to the American Film Musical*, Exeter, Exeter University Press, 1996.

Nick Roddick, *A New Deal in Entertainment, Warner Brothers in the 1930s*, London, BFI, 1983.

Mark Roth, 'Some Warners musicals and the spirit of the New Deal', in Altman (ed.) *Genre: The Musical*.

Martin Rubin, *Showstoppers, Busby Berkeley and the Tradition of Spectacle*, New York, Columbia University Press, 1993.

Thomas Schatz, *The Genius of the System, Hollywood Filmmaking in the Studio Era*, New York, Pantheon Books, 1988.

Cecil Smith and Glenn Litton, *Musical Comedy in America*, New York, Theatre Arts Books, 1981.

Aubrey Solomon, *Twentieth Century-Fox: A Corporate and Financial History*, Metuchen, Scarecrow Press, 1988.

Joseph P. Swain, *The Broadway Musical, A Critical and Musical Survey*, Oxford, Oxford University Press, 1990.

J. P. Telotte, 'A sober celebration: song and dance in the "new" musical', *Journal of Popular Film and Television* 8(1), spring 1980.

Richard Traubner, *Operetta: A Theatrical History*, Oxford, Oxford University Press, 1983.

Alexander Walker, *The Shattered Silents: How the Talkies Came to Stay*, New York, William Murrow, 1979.

Alec Wilder, *American Popular Song: The Great Innovators, 1900–1950*, Oxford, Oxford University Press, 1972.

Elizabeth Weis and John Belton (eds), *Film Sound: Theory and Practice*, New York, Columbia University Press, 1985.

Charles Wolfe, 'Vitaphone Shorts and *The Jazz Singer*', *Wide Angle* 12(3), 1990.

Peter Wollen, *Singing in the Rain*, London, BFI Publishing, 1992.

Michael Wood, *America in the Movies*, London, Secker and Warburg, 1975.

Robin Wood, 'Art and ideology: notes on *Silk Stockings*', in Altman (ed.), *Genre: The Musical*.

Robin Wood, *Howard Hawks*, London, BFI, rev. ed., 1981.

TEENPICS

Bruce A. Austin (ed.), *Current Research in Film: Audiences, Economics and Law*, vol. 2, Norwood, Ablex, 1986.

Theodore W. Adorno, *Prisms*, London, Neville Spearman, 1967.

Theodore W. Adorno, 'Culture industry reconsidered', *New German Critique* vol. 6, autumn 1975.

Theodore W. Adorno, 'On popular music', in Firth and Goodwin, *On Record*.

Alan Betrock, *The I Was A Teenager Juvenile Delinquent Rock 'N' Roll Horror Beach Party Book: A Complete Guide to the Teen Exploitation Film, 1954–1969*, London, Plexus, 1986.

David Considine, 'The Cinema of Adolescence', *Journal of Popular Film and Television* 9(3), 1981.

Thomas Doherty, 'Teenagers and teenpics, 1955–1957: a study of exploitation filmmaking', in Austin, *Current Research*.

Thomas Doherty, *Teenagers and Teenpics, The Juvenalization of American Movies in the 1950s*, Boston, Unwin Hyman, 1988.

Simon Frith and Andrew Goodwin (eds), *On Record: Rock, Pop and the Written Word*, New York, Pantheon, 1990.

Frederic Jameson, *Postmodern: On the Cultural Logic of Late Capitalism*, Durham, NC/London, Duke University Press/Verso, 1991.

James Gilbert, *A Cycle of Outrage, America's Reaction to the Juvenile Delinquent in the 1950s*, New York, Oxford University Press, 1986.

Harvey J. Graff, *Conflicting Paths: Growing Up in America*, Cambridge, Mass., Harvard University Press, 1995.

James Hay, '"You're tearing me apart!": the primal scene of teen films', *Cultural Studies* 4(3), 1990.

Dick Hebdige, *Subculture: The Meaning of Style*, London, Methuen, 1979.

Joseph F. Kett, *Rites of Passage: Adolescence in America, 1790 to the Present*, New York, Basic Books, 1977.

Peter Kramer, 'Bad Boy: Notes on a Popular Figure in American Cinema, Culture and Society, 1895–1905', unpublished paper.

Paul Lazarus, 'Audience Research in the Movie Field', *Annals of the American Academy of Political and Social Science* 254, 1947.

Jon Lewis, *The Road to Romance and Ruin, Teen Films and Youth Culture*, New York and London, Routledge, 1992.

Richard Maltby (ed.), *Dreams for Sale: Popular Culture in the 20th Century*, London, Harrap, 1989.

Linda Martin and Kerry Segrave, *Anti-Rock: The Opposition to Rock 'n' Roll*, New York, Da Capo Press, 1993.

Gary Morris, 'Beyond the beach: social and formal aspects of AIP's beach party movies', *Journal of Popular Film and Television*, 21(1), 1994.

E. Muller and D. Farris, That's Sexploitation: The Forbidden World of 'Adults Only' Cinema, London, Titan Books, 1997.

Martin Quigley, 'Who Goes to the Movies and Who Doesn't', *Motion Picture Herald*, 10 August 1957.

Comedy

Joe Adamson, *Groucho, Harpo, and Chico and Sometimes Zeppo: A History of the Marx Brothers and a Satire on the Rest of the World*, New York, Simon and Schuster, 1973.

James Agee, *Agee on Film*, New York: Obolensky Inc., 1958.

James Agee, 'Comedy's greatest era (1949)' in Agee, *Agee on Film*.

Robert C. Allen, *Vaudeville and Film, 1895–1915: A Study in Media Interaction*, New York, Arno Press, 1980.

Bruce Babington and William Peter Evans, *Affairs to Remember: The Hollywood Comedy of the Sexes*, Manchester, Manchester University Press, 1989.

Mikhail Bakhtin, *Rabelais and His World*, Cambridge, Mass., MIT Press, 1968.

Tino Balio, *Grand Design: Hollywood as a Modern Business Enterprise, 1930–1939*, New York, Scribner's, 1993.

Charles Barr, *Laurel and Hardy*, London, Studio Vista, 1967.

John Belton, *American Cinema/American Culture*, New York, McGraw-Hill, 1994.

Henri Bergson, 'Laughter' (1900) in Sypher, *Comedy*.

Eileen Bowser, *The Transformation of Cinema, 1907–1915*, New York, Scribner's, 1990.

Andrew Britton, *Cary Grant: Comedy and Male Desire*, Newcastle-Upon-Tyne, Tyneside Cinema, 1983.

Andrew Britton, *Katherine Hepburn: The Thirties and After*, Newcastle-Upon-Tyne, Tyneside Cinema, 1984.

Scott Bukatman, 'Paralysis in motion: Jerry Lewis's life as a man' in Horton, *Comedy*.

Duane Paul Byrge, 'Screwball comedy', *East–West Film Journal*, 2(1), December 1987.

Noel Carroll, *An In-Depth Analysis of Buster Keaton's The General*, New York University Ph.D. thesis, 1976, Ann Arbor, UMI Dissertation Information Service, 1988.

Noel Carroll, 'Notes on the sight gag' in Horton, *Comedy*.

Stanley Cavell, *Pursuits of Happiness: The Hollywood Comedy of Remarriage*, Cambridge, Mass., Harvard University Press, 1981.

Jane Clark, Mandy Merck and Diane Simmonds (eds), *Move Over Misconceptions: Doris Day Reappraised*, London, BFI, 1981.

Jean-Pierre Coursodon, *Keaton et Cie*, Paris, Seghers, 1964.

Jean-Pierre Coursodon, 'Jerry Lewis', in Coursodon and Sauvage, *American Directors*.

Jean-Pierre Coursodon, *Buster Keaton*, Paris, Atlas L'Hermier, 1986.

Jean-Pierre Coursodon and Pierre Sauvage, *American Directors*, New York, McGraw-Hill, 1983.

Donald Crafton, 'Pie and chase: gags, spectacle and narrative in slapstick comedy' in Karnick and Jenkins (eds), *Classical Hollywood Comedy*.

Ramona Curry, '*Goin' To Town* and beyond: Mae West, film censorship and the comedy of unmarriage' in Karnick and Jenkins (eds), *Classical Hollywood Comedy*.

Tom Dardis, *Keaton: The Man Who Wouldn't Lie Down*, London, Andre Deutsch, 1979.

Tom Dardis, *Harold Lloyd: The Man on the Clock*, New York, Viking Press, 1983.

Mary Ann Doane, 'The Economy of Desire: the Commodity Form in/of Cinema', *Quarterly Review of Film and Video*: 11, 1989.

William Donnelly, 'A theory of the comedy of the Marx Brothers', *The Velvet Light Trap* no. 3, 1971/2.

Mary Douglas, 'The social control of cognition: some factors in joke reception', *Man* (new series) vol. 3, 1968.

Richard Dyer: 'Rock – the last guy you'd have figured', in Kirkham and Thurnim, *You Tarzan*.

Mick Eaton, 'Laughter in the dark', *Screen* 22(2), 1981.

Barbara Ehrenreich: *Hearts of Men: American Dreams and the Flight From Commitment*, Pluto Press, London (1983).

Andy Edmonds, *Fatty: The Untold Story of Roscoe Fatty Arbuckle*, London, McDonald, 1991.

Peter William Evans and Celestino Deleyto (eds), *Terms of Endearment: Gender and Sexuality in Hollywood Romantic Comedy of the Eighties and Nineties*, Edinburgh, Edinburgh University Press, 1998. *Film Comment*, special issue on animation 11(1), 1975.

Lucy Fischer, 'Sometimes I feel like a motherless child: comedy and matricide', in Horton, *Comedy*.

Sigmund Freud, *Jokes and their Relation to the Unconscious* (1905), Harmondsworth, Penguin, 1976.

Sigmund Freud, 'Humour' (1927) in *Art and Literature*, Harmondsworth, Penguin, 1985.

Northrop Frye, *Anatomy of Criticism, Four Essays*, Princeton, Princeton University Press, 1957.

Roger Garcia and Bernard Eisenschitz (eds), *Frank Tashlin*, Locarno, Éditions du Festival, 1994.

Jon Gartenberg, 'Vitagraph Comedy Production' in Eileen Bowser (ed.), *The Slapstick Symposium*, Brussels, Fédération Internationale des Archives du Film, 1988.

Wes D. Gehring, *Charlie Chaplin: A Bio-Bibliography*, Westport, Greenwood Press, 1983.

Wes D. Gehring, *W. C. Fields: A Bio-Bibliography*, Westport, Greenwood Press, 1984.

Wes D. Gehring, *Screwball Comedy: A Genre of Madcap Romance*, Westport, Greenwood Press, 1986.

Wes D. Gehring, *The Marx Brothers: A Bio-Biography*, Westport, Greenwood Press, 1987.

Wes D. Gehring, *Laurel and Hardy: A Bio-Bibliography*, Westport, Greenwood Press, 1990.

Wes, D. Gehring, *Groucho and W. C. Fields, Huckster Comedians*, Jackson, University Press of Mississippi, 1994.

Tom Gunning, 'Crazy machines in the garden of forking paths: mischief gags and the origins of film comedy' in Karnick and Jenkins, *Classical Hollywood Comedy*.

Marybeth Hamilton, *The Queen of Camp, Mae West, Sex and Popular Culture*, London, Pandora, 1996.

Brian Henderson, 'Romantic comedy today: *semi-tough* or impossible?, *Film Quarterly* 31(4), summer 1978.

Sumiko Higashi, *Cecil B. DeMille and American Culture: The Silent Era*, Berkeley, University of California Press, 1994.

Andrew S. Horton (ed.), *Comedy/Cinema/Theory*, Berkeley, University of California Press, 1991a.

Andrew S. Horton, 'Introduction' in Horton, *Comedy/Cinema/Theory*, 1991b.

Linda Hutcheon, *A Theory of Parody: The Teachings of Twentieth-Century Art Forms*, London, Methuen, 1985.

Henry Jenkins III, 'The amazing push-me/pull-you text: cognitive processing, narrational play, and the comic film', *Wide Angle* 8(3–4), 1986.

Henry Jenkins III, *What Made Pistachio Nuts? Early Sound Comedy and the Vaudeville Aesthetic*, New York, Columbia University Press, 1993.

Catherine Irene Johnson: *Contradiction in 1950s Comedy and Ideology*, UMI Research Press, Ann Arbor, 1981.

Claire Johnson and Paul Willemen (eds), *Frank Tashlin*, Edinburgh, Edinburgh Film Festival, 1973.

Dan Kamin, *Charlie Chaplin's One-Man Show*, Metcheun, Scarecrow Press, 1984.

Kristina Brunovska Karnick, 'Commitment and reaffirmation in Hollywood romantic comedy' in Karnick and Jenkins (eds), 1995.

Kristina Brunovska Karnick and Henry Jenkins III (eds), *Classical Hollywood Comedy*, London, Routledge, 1995.

Karyn Kay, '"Part-time work of a domestic slave," or putting the screws to screwball comedy', in Karyn Kay and Danny Peary (eds), *Women and the Cinema: A Critical Anthology*, New York, Dutton, 1977.

Pat Kirkham and Janet Thurnim (eds), *You Tarzan; Masculinity, Movies and Men*, Lawrence & Wishart, London (1993).

Norman M. Klein, *Seven Minutes, The Life and Death of the American Animated Cartoon*, London, Verso, 1993.

Richard Koszarski, *An Evening's Entertainment: The Age of the Silent Feature Picture, 1915–1928*, New York, Scribner, 1990.

Peter Kramer, 'Vitagraph, slapstick and early cinema', *Screen* 23(2), 1988.

Peter Kramer, 'Derailing the honeymoon express: comicality and narrative closure in Buster Keaton's *The Blacksmith*', *The Velvet Light Trap* no. 23, 1989.

Peter Kramer, 'The making of a comic star: Buster Keaton and *The Saphead*, in Karnick and Jenkins, *Classical Comedy*.

Frank Krutnik, 'The Clown-Prints of Comedy', *Screen* 25 (4–5), 1984.

Frank Krutnik, 'The faint aroma of performing seals: the "nervous" romance and the comedy of the sexes', *The Velvet Light Trap* no. 26, 1990.

Frank Krutnik, *Inventing Jerry Lewis*, Washington, Smithsonion Institution Press, 2000.

Frank Krutnik, 'Jerry Lewis and the deformation of the comic', *Film Quarterly* 48(4), 1994.

Frank Krutnik, 'A spanner in the works? Genre narrative and the Hollywood comedian' in Karnick and Jenkins, *Classical Comedy*.

Jean-Pierre Lebel, *Buster Keaton*, London, Zwemmer, 1967.

Tina Olsin Lent, 'Roman, love and friendship: the redefinition of gender relations in screwball comedy' in Karnick and Jenkins, *Classical Comedy*.

Leonard Maltin, *The Great Movie Comedians*, New York, Crown, 1982.

Leonard Maltin, *Of Mice and Magic: A History of American Animated Cartoons*, New York, Plume, 1987.

François Mars, *Le Gag*, Paris: Éditions du Cerf, 1964.

Gerald Mast, *The Comic Mind: Comedy and the Movies*, New York, Random House, 1976.

Donald McCaffrey, *Four Great Comedians*, New York, Barnes, 1968.

Donald McCaffrey, *Three Classic Silent Screen Comedies Starring Harold Lloyd*, London, Associated University Presses, 1976.

Albert F. McClean, *American Vaudeville as Ritual*, Lexington, University of Kentuck Press, 1965.

Charles Musser, *The Emergence of Cinema: The American Screen to 1907*, Scribner's, 1990a.

Charles Musser, 'Work, ideology and Chaplin's tramp' in Sklar and Musser, *Resisting Images*, 1990b.

Charles Musser, 'Ethnicity, role-playing and American film comedy: from *Chinese Laundry* to *Whoppee* (1894–1930)' in Lester D. Friedman (ed.), *Unspeakable Images, Ethnicity and the American Cinema*, Urbana, University of Illinois Press, 1991.

Charles Musser, 'Divorce, DeMille and the comedy of remarriage' in Karnick and Jenkins, *Classical Comedy*.

Steve Neale, 'Psychoanalysis and Comedy', *Screen* 22(2), 1981.

Steve Neale, 'The *Big* romance or *Something Wild*?: Romantic comedy today', *Screen* 33(3), 1992.

Steve Neale and Frank Krutnik, *Popular Film and Television Comedy*, London, Routledge, 1990.

Elder Olson, *The Theory of Comedy*, Bloomington, Indiana University Press, 1968.

Jerry Palmer, *The Logic of the Absurd*, London, BFI, 1987.

Jerry Palmer, *Taking Humour Seriously*, London, Routledge, 1995.

Sylvain du Pasquier, 'Buster Keaton's Gags', *Journal of Modern Literature* 13(2), 1973.

William Paul, *Ernst Lubitsch's American Comedy*, New York, Columbia University Press, 1983.

William Paul, 'Charles Chaplin and the annals of anality' in Horton, *Comedy*.

William Paul, *Laughing Screaming: Modern Hollywood Horror and Comedy*, New York, Columbia University Press, 1994.

Gerald Peary and Danny Peary (eds), *The American Animated Cartoon: A Critical Anthology*, New York, Dutton, 1980.

Susan Purdie, *Comedy, The Mastery of Discourse*, London, Harvester Wheatsheaf, 1993.

Joyce Rheuban, *Harry Langdon: The Comedian as Metteur-en-scène*, Rutherford, Farleigh Dickson University Press, 1983.

Doug Riblet, 'The Keystone Film Company and the historiography of early slapstick' in Karnick and Jenkins, *Classical Comedy*.

David Robinson, *The Great Funnies*, London, Studio Vista, 1969.

David Robinson, *Chaplin: His Life and Art*, London, Paladin, 1986.

Margaret A. Rose, *Parody: Ancient, Modern, and Postmodern*, Cambridge, Cambridge University Press, 1993.

Kathleen Rowe, *The Unruly Woman: Gender and the Genres of Laughter*, Austin University of Texas Press, 1995a.

Kathleen Rowe, 'Comedy, melodrama and gender: theorizing the genres of laughter' in Karnick and Jenkins, *Classical Hollywood Comedy*.

Jonathan Sanders, *Another Fine Dress: Role-Play in the Films of Laurel and Hardy*, London, Cassell, 1995.

Thomas Schatz, *Hollywood Genres: Formulas, Filmmaking, and the Studio System*, New York, Random House, 1981.

Steve Seidman, *Comedian Comedy: A Tradition in the Hollywood Film*, Ann Arbor, UMI Research Press, 1981.

David R. Shumway, 'Screwball comedies: constructing romance, mystifying marriage', *Cinema Journal* 30(4), 1991.

Ed Sikov, *Screwball: Hollywood's Madcap Comedies*, New York, Crown, 1989.

Ed Sikov, *Laughing Hysterically: American Screen Comedy of the 1950s*, New York, Columbia University Press, 1995.

Jean-Paul Simon and Daniel Percheron, 'Le Gag' in Jean Collet, Michael Marie, Daniel Percheron, Jean-Paul Simon and Marc Vernet, *Lectures du Film*, Paris, Albatross, 1979.

Robert Sklar and Charles Musser (eds), *Resisting Images: Essays on Cinema and History*, Philadelphia, Temple University Press, 1990.

Raoul Sobel and David Francis, *Chaplin: Genesis of a Clown*, London, Quarter, 1977.

Michael Stern, 'Jerry Lewis b. Joseph Levita, Newark, New Jersey, 1926 res. Hollywood', *Bright Lights* 1(3), 1975.

Kevin Sweeney, 'The dream of disruption: melodrama and gag structure in Keaton's *Sherlock Junior*', *Wide Angle* 13(1), 1991.

Wylie Sypher (ed.), *Comedy*, New York, Doubleday, 1956.

Robert C. Toll, *On With the Show: The First Century of Show Business in America*, New York, Oxford University Press, 1976.

Robert C. Toll, *The Entertainment Machine: American Show Business in the Twentieth Century*, New York, Oxford University Press, 1982.

Alexander Walker, *Sex in the Movies: the Celluloid Sacrifice*, Penguin Books: Harmondsworth, 1968.

Gerald Weales, *Canned Goods as Caviar: American Film Comedy of the 1930s*, Chicago, Chicago University Press, 1985.

Arthur Wertheim, *Radio Comedy*, New York, Oxford University Press, 1979.

Mark Winokur, *American Laughter, Immigrants, Ethnicity and 1930s American Film Comedy*, London, Macmillan, 1996.

Katherine Solomon Woodward, *The Comedy of Equality: Romantic Film Comedy in America, 1930–1950*, University of Maryland Ph.D. thesis, Ann Arbor, UMI Dissertation Information Service, 1991.

Action–Adventure

Andrew Britton, 'Blissing Out: The Politics of Reaganite Entertainment', *Movie*, 31(2), 1986.

Joseph A. Boone and Michael Cadden (eds), *Engendering Men: The Question of Male Feminist Criticism*, New York, Routledge, 1990.

J. A. Brown, 'Gender and the Action Heroine: Hardbodies and The Point of No Return', *Cinema Journal* 35(3), 1996.

John G. Cawelti, *Adventure, Mystery and Romance: Formula Stories as Art and Popular Culture*, Chicago, University of Chicago Press, 1976.

Steven Cohan and Ina Rae Hark, *Screening the Male: Exploring Masculinity in Hollywood Cinema*, London, Routledge, 1993.

Chris Holmlund, 'Masculinity as multiple masquerade: the "mature" Stallone and the Stallone clone' in Cohan and Hark, *Screening the Male*.

Susan Jeffords, *The Remasculinization of America: Gender and the Vietnam War*, Bloomington and Indianapolis, Indiana University Press, 1989.

Susan Jeffords, *Hard Bodies: Hollywood Masculinity in the Reagan Era*, New Brunswick, Rutgers University Press, 1994.

Douglas Kellner and Michael Ryan, *Camera Politica: The Politics and Ideology of Contemporary Hollywood Film*, Bloomington and Indianapolis, Indiana University Press, 1988.

Richard Koszarski, *An Evening's Entertainment: The Age of the Silent Feature Picture, 1915–1928*, New York, Scribner, 1990.

Gina Marchetti, 'Action-Adventure as Ideology' in I. Angus and S. Thally (eds), *Cultural Politics in Contemporary America*, New York, Routledge, 1989.

Fred Pfeil, *White Guys: Studies in Postmodern Domination and Difference*, London, Verso, 1995.

Jeffrey Richards, *Swordsmen of the Screen, from Douglas Fairbanks to Michael York*, London, Routledge and Kegan Paul, 1977.

Joseph Sartelle, 'Dreams and Nightmares in the Hollywood Blockbuster' in Geoffrey Nowell-Smith (ed.), *The Oxford History of World Cinema*, Oxford, Oxford University Press, 1996.

Thomas Sobchack, 'The Adventure Film' in Wes Gehring, *Handbook of American Film Genres*, Westport, Greenwood Press, 1988.

Yvonne Tasker, *Spectacular Bodies, Gender, Genre and the Action Cinema*, London, Routledge, 1993.

Brian Taves, *The Romance of Adventure: The Genre of Historical Adventure Movies*, Jackson, University of Press of Mississippi, 1993.

Elizabeth G. Traube, *Dreaming Identities: Class, Gender and Generation in 1980s Hollywood Movies*, Boulder, Westview Press, 1992.

Sharon Willis, *High Contrast: Race and Gender in Contemporary Hollywood Films*, Durham, N.C., Duke University Press, 1998.

Robin Wood, *Hollywood from Vietnam to Reagan*, New York, Columbia University Press, 1986.

PART 6: AUTHORSHIP AND CINEMA

INTRODUCTION

Maria Bergom-Larrson, *Ingmar Bergman and Society*, London, Tantivy/Swedish Film Institute, 1978.

David Bordwell, 'The art cinema as a mode of film practice', *Film Criticism* 4(1), 1979.

Ian Cameron, '*About These Women*', in *Movie Reader*, London, November Books, 1972, p. 100.

Mario Cannella, 'Ideology and aesthetic hypothesis in the criticism of neo-realism', *Screen* 14(4), winter 1973/74.

Michel Foucault, 'What is an author?' *Screen* 20(1), spring 1979.

Graham Murdock, 'Authorship and organisation', *Screen Education* 35, summer 1980.

Mark Nash, *Dreyer*, London, BFI, 1977.

Stephen Neale, 'New Hollywood cinema', *Screen* 17(2), summer 1976.

Stuart Rosenthal, *The Cinema of Federico Fellini*, London, Tantivy Press, 1976.

Birgitta Steene, 'Bergman's portrait of women: sexism or suggestive metaphor', in Erens (ed.), *Sexual Strategems: the world of women in films*, New York, Horizon Press, 1979.

FOR A NEW FRENCH CINEMA: THE '*POLITIQUE DES AUTEURS*'

Alexandre Astruc, 'The birth of a new avant-garde: *la caméra-stylo*', Écran Français no. 144, 1948, trans. in Peter Graham (ed.), *The New Wave*, London, Secker & Warburg/BFI, 1968.

André Bazin, 'La politique des auteurs', *Cahiers du Cinéma* no. 70, April 1957, trans. in Peter Graham (ed.), *The New Wave*, London, Secker & Warburg/BFI, 1968.

André Bazin, *Jean Renoir*, Paris, Éditions Champ Libre, 1971.

Robert Benayoun, 'Le roi est nu', *Positif* no. 46, June 1962.

Peter Bogdanovich, *Fritz Lang in America*, London, Studio Vista, 1968.

Edward Buscombe, 'Ideas of authorship', *Screen* 14(3), autumn 1973.

Cahiers du Cinéma no. 99, September 1959. Special issue on Fritz Lang.

Goffredo Fofi, 'The cinema of the Popular Front in France, 1934–38', *Screen* 13(4), winter 1972/73.

John Hess, 'World view as aesthetic', *Jump Cut* no. 1, May/June 1974; no. 2, July/August 1974.

Steve Jenkins (ed.), *Fritz Lang: The Image and the Look*, London, British Film Institute, 1981.

Claire Johnston, *Study Unit 10: Fritz Lang*, London, BFI Education Dept, January 1969, rev. edn, 1977.

Siegfied Kracauer, *From Caligari to Hitler: a Psychological History of the German Film*, Princeton: Princeton University Press, 1947.

David Lusted, *Study Notes for the Slide Set From 'The Big Heat'*, London, BFI Education Dept, June 1979.

Julian Petley, *British Film Institute Distribution Library Catalogue 1978*, London, BFI, 1978.

Jean Renoir, *My Life and My Films*, London, Collins, 1974; trans. Norman Denny.

Jacques Rivette and François Truffaut, 'Renoir in America', *Sight and Sound* 24(1), July/September 1954.

François Truffaut, 'A certain tendency of the French cinema', *Cahiers du Cinéma* no. 31, January 1954, trans. in Bill Nichols (ed.), *Movies and Methods*, Berkeley, University of California Press, 1976.

Peter Wollen, '"Ontology" and "Materialism" in film', *Screen* 17(1), spring 1976.

'Auteurs' and *'metteurs-en-scène'*

André Bazin, 'Hitchcock versus Hitchcock', in Albert J. LaValley (ed.), *Focus on Hitchcock*, Englewood Cliffs, NJ, Prentice-Hall, 1972.

Raymond Bellour, 'Hitchcock the enunciator', *Camera Obscura* no. 2, autumn 1977.

Edward Buscombe, 'Walsh and Warner Bros', in Phil Hardy (ed.), *Raoul Walsh*, Edinburgh Film Festival, 1974.

Laura Mulvey, 'Visual pleasure and narrative cinema', *Screen* 16(3), autumn 1975.

V. F. Perkins, *Film as Film: Understanding and Judging Movies*, London, Penguin, 1972.

John Smith, 'Conservative individualism: a selection of English Hitchcock', *Screen* 13(3), autumn 1972.

Gaylen Studlar and David Desser (eds), *Reflections in a Male Eye: John Huston and the American Experience*, Washington, DC, Smithsonian, 1993.

François Truffaut, *Hitchcock*, London, Secker & Warburg, 1968.

Peter Wollen, 'Hitchcock's vision', *Cinema* (UK), June 1969.

Robin Wood, *Hitchcock's Films Revisited*, New York, Columbia University Press, 1989.

Robin Wood, 'John Huston', in Richard Roud (ed.), *Cinema: A Critical Dictionary*, vol. 1, London, Secker & Warburg, 1980.

Auteurs and studio

André Bazin, 'William Wyler or the Jansenist of *mise-en-scène*', in Christopher Williams (ed.), *Realism and the Cinema*, London, RKP/BFI, 1980, pp. 36–52.

André Bazin, *Orson Welles: A Critical View*, London, Elm Tree Books, 1978; trans. Jonathan Rosenbaum.

Robert Carringer, *The Making of Citizen Kane*, Berkeley, University of California Press, 1995.

Stephen Heath, 'Film and System: Terms of Analysis', *Screen* 16(1), spring 1975; 16(2), summer 1975.

Pauline Kael, *The Citizen Kane Book*, London, Secker & Warburg, 1971.

Laura Mulvey, *Citizen Kane*, London, BFI Publishing, 1992.

Julian Petley, *British Film Institute Distribution Library Catalogue* 1978, London, BFI, 1978, pp. 119–22.

Peter Wollen, *Study Unit* no. 9: *Orson Welles*, London, BFI Education Dept, January 1969; reprinted October 1977.

The French new wave

Don Allen, *François Truffaut*, London, Secker & Warburg/BFI, 1974.

David Bordwell and Kristin Thompson, *Film Art: An Introduction*, Reading, Mass., Addison-Wesley, 1979; 4th edn, 1993.

Susan Hayward, *French National Cinema*, London, Routledge, 1993.

Marsha Kinder and Beverle Houston, *Close-up: A Critical Perspective on Film*, New York, Harcourt Brace Jovanovich, 1972.

François Truffaut, 'A certain tendency of the French cinema', *Cahiers du Cinéma* no. 31, January 1954, trans. in Bill Nichols (ed.), *Movies and Methods*, Berkeley, University of California Press, 1976.

Christopher Williams, 'Politics and production', *Screen* 12(4), winter 1971/72.

THE *AUTEUR* THEORY

James Agee, *Agee on Film: Reviews and Comments by James Agee*, London, Peter Owen Ltd., 1963.

David Bordwell and Kristin Thompson, *Film Art: an introduction*, Reading, Mass., Addison-Wesley, 1979; 4th edn, 1993.

Wheeler Dixon, 'In Defense of Roger Corman', *The Velvet Light Trap* no. 16, autumn 1976.

Bernard Eisensuhitz, *Nicholas Ray: An American Journey*, London, Faber & Faber, 1993.

Molly Haskell, *From Reverence to Rape*, New York, Holt, Rinehart and Winston, 1974.

Pauline Kael, *The Citizen Kane Book*, London, Secker & Warburg, 1971.

J. F. Kreidl, *Nicholas Ray*, Boston, Twayne Publishers, 1977.

Alan Lovell, *Don Siegel. American Cinema*, London: BFI, 1975.

Gary Morris, 'Introduction to New World Pictures', *Bright Lights* 1(1), autumn 1974.

Gary Morris, 'Interview with Roger Corman', *Bright Lights* 1(2), spring 1975.

Edward Murray, *Nine American Film Critics*, New York, Frederick Ungar, 1975.

The New American Cinema Group, 'The first statement of the group', *Film Culture* nos. 22/23, summer 1961.

Geoffrey Nowell-Smith, 'Six authors in pursuit of *The Searchers*', *Screen* 17(1), spring 1976.

V. F. Perkins, 'The cinema of Nicholas Ray', in Cameron (ed.), *Movie Reader*, London, November Books, 1972.

Julian Petley, *BFI Distribution Library Catalogue 1978*, London, BFI, 1978.

Andrew Sarris, 'Notes on the *auteur theory* in 1962', *Film Culture* no. 27, winter 1962/63.

Andrew Sarris, *The American Cinema: Directors and Directions 1929–1968*, New York, Dutton, 1968.

Andrew Sarris, *'You ain't heard nothing yet': the American talking film, history and memory, 1927–1949*, New York, Oxford University Press, 1998.

David Will and Paul Willemen, *Roger Corman: the Millennic Vision*, Edinburgh: Edinburgh Film Festival, 1970.

Mike Wilmington, 'Nicholas Ray: the years at RKO: Parts I and II', *The Velvet Light Trap* no. 10, autumn 1973; no. 11, winter 1973/74.

AUTEUR THEORY AND BRITISH CINEMA

Lindsay Anderson, '*Paisà*', *Sequence* no. 2, winter 1947.

Lindsay Anderson, 'The last sequence of *On the Waterfront*', *Sight and Sound* 24(3), January/March 1955.

Ian Cameron (ed.), *Movie Reader*, London, November Books, 1972.

Erik Hedling, *Lindsay Anderson: Maverick Filmmaker*, London, Cassell, 1998.

John Hill, 'Ideology, economy and the British cinema', in Barratt, Corrigan, Kuhn and Wolff (eds), *Ideology and Cultural Production*, London, Croom Helm, 1979.

Raymond Lefèvre and Roland Lacourbe, *Trente Ans de Cinèma Britannique*, Paris, Éditions Cinéma 76, 1976.

Alan Lovell, *The British Cinema: The Unknown Cinema*, London, BFI Education Dept Seminar Paper, 1969.

Alan Lovell, 'Free Cinema', in Lovell and Hillier, *Studies in Documentary*, London, Secker & Warburg/BFI, 1972.

Alan Lovell, *Don Siegel: American Cinema*, London, BFI, 1975.

Alan Lovell, 'Brecht in Britain: Lindsay Anderson', *Screen* vol. 16 no. 4, winter 1975/76.

Robert Murphy (ed.), *The British Cinema Book*, London, BFI, 1997.

Victor Perkins, 'The British cinema', in Cameron, *Movie Reader*.

Karel Reisz, Interview, *Cinéma International* no. 16, 1967.

Sam Rohdie, 'Review: *Movie Reader*, film as film, *Screen* 13(4), winter 1972/73.

Movie and *mise-en-scène* analysis

Lindsay Anderson, 'The last sequence of *On the Waterfront*', *Sun and Sound* 24(3), January/March 1955.

Charles Barr, '*King and Country*' in Cameron, *Movie Reader*.

Charles Barr, 'CinemaScope: before and after', in Mast and Cohen (eds), *Film Theory and Criticism*, New York, Oxford University Press, 1974.

David Bordwell and Kristin Thompson, *Film Art: An Introduction*, Reading, Mass., Addison-Wesley, 1979; 4th edn, 1993.

Ian Cameron (ed.), *Movie Reader*, London, November Books, 1972.

Michel Ciment, *Kazan on Kazan*, London, Secker & Warburg/BFI, 1974.

Richard Collins, 'Media/Film studies', in Gledhill, *Film and Media*.

Tony Crawley, 'Vot you mean, ogre?', *Films Illustrated* 9(101), January 1980.

Paul Filmer, 'Literary criticism and the mass media, with special reference to the cinema', in Wollen, *Working Papers*.

Christine Gledhill (ed.), *Film and Media Studies in Higher Education*, London, BFI Education, 1981.

Brian Henderson, 'The long take', in Nichols, *Movies and Methods*.

Jim Hillier, '*East of Eden*', *Movie* no. 19, winter 1971/72.

E. Ann Kaplan (ed.), *Women in Film Noir*, London, BFI, 1978; rev. edn, 1998.

Raymond Lefèvre, Interview with Joseph Losey, *Image et Son* no. 202, February 1967.

Paul Mayersberg, 'Carmen and Bess', in Cameron, *Movie Reader*.

Paul Mayersberg, 'Contamination', in Cameron, *Movie Reader*.

Paul Mayersberg, 'From *Laura* to *Angel Face*' in Cameron, *Movie Reader*.

Movie no. 19, winter 1971/72.

Bill Nichols (ed.), *Movies and Methods: An Anthology*, Berkeley, University of California Press, 1976.

V. F. Perkins, '*America, America*', *Movie* no. 19, winter 1971/72.

V. F. Perkins, *Film as Film: Understanding and Judging Movies*, London, Penguin Books, 1972.

V. F. Perkins, 'Why Preminger?', in Cameron, *Movie Reader*.

V. F. Perkins, 'A reply to Sam Rohdie', *Screen* 13(4), winter 1972/73.

Gerald Pratley, *The Cinema of Otto Preminger*, London/New York, A. Zwemmer/A. S. Barnes, 1971.

Pierre Rissient, *Losey*, Paris, Éditions du Cinéma, 1966.

Richard Roud, 'The reluctant exile', *Sight and Sound* 48(3), summer 1979.

Roger Tailleur, *Elia Kazan*, Paris, Éditions Seghers, 1971.

Michael Walker '*Splendor in the Grass*', *Movie* no. 19, winter 1971/72.

Robin Wood, 'The Kazan problem', *Movie* no. 19.

Peter Wollen (ed.), *Working Papers on the Cinema: Sociology and Semiology*, London, BFI Education Dept, 1969.

Auteurs in British cinema

Ian Christie (ed.), *Powell, Pressburger and Others*, London, BFI, 1978.

Ian Christie, 'The scandal of *Peeping Tom*', in Christie, *Powell*.

Ian Christie, *Arrows of Desire*, rev. edn, London, Faber & Faber, 1994.

Brendan Davies (ed.), *Carol Reed*, London, BFI, 1978.

John Ellis, 'Art, culture and quality: terms for a cinema in the forties and seventies', *Screen* 19(3), autumn 1978; revised in, *Dissolving Views: Key Writings on British Cinema*, Andrew Higson (ed.), London, Cassells, 1996.

Raymond Lefèvre and Roland Lacourbe, *Trente Ans de Cinéma Britannique*, Paris, Éditions Cinema 76, 1976.

British cinema: auteur and studio

Charles Barr, *Ealing Studios*, London/Newton Abbott, Cameron & Tayler/David & Charles, 1977; rev. edn, London, Studio Vista, 1993.

Ian Christie, 'Introduction', in Christie (ed.), *Powell, Pressburger and Others*, London, BFI, 1978.

Bernard Cohn, Interview with MacKendrick, *Positif* no. 92, February 1968.

Ian Conrich, 'Traditions of the British horror film' in *The British Cinema Book*, Robert Murphy (ed.), London, BFI Publishing, 1997.

John Ellis, 'Made in Ealing', *Screen* 16(1), spring 1975.

John Ellis, 'Art, culture and quality: terms for a cinema in the forties and seventies', *Screen* 19(3), autumn 1978; revised version in 'Dissolving Views'.

Philip Kemp, *Lethal innocence: the cinema of Alexander MacKendrick*, London, Croom Helm, 1991.

Little Shoppe of Horrors no. 4, April 1978, Special issue on Hammer.

David Pirie, *A Heritage of Horror: The English Gothic Cinema 1946–1972*, London, Gordon & Fraser, 1973.

Tim Pulleine 'A song and dance at the local: thoughts on Ealing' in Robert Murphy (ed.), *The British Book*, London, BFI Publishing.

Philip Simpson, 'Directions to Ealing', *Screen Education* no. 24, autumn 1977.

STRUCTURALISM AND *AUTEUR* STUDY

Louis Althusser, *For Marx*, trans. Ben Brewster, Harmondsworth, Middx, Penguin Books, 1969.

Louis Althusser, *Lenin and Philosophy and Other Essays*, trans. Ben Brewster, London, New Left Books, 1971.

Catherine Belsey, *Critical Practice*, London, Methuen, 1980.

Jonathan Culler, *Structuralist Poetics*, London, RKP, 1975.

Sylvia Harvey, *May '68 and Film Culture*, London, BFI, 1978.

Stephen Heath, *The Nouveau Roman: A Study in the Practice of Writing*, London, Elek Books, 1972.

Edmund Leach, *Lévi-Strauss*, London, Fontana, 1970.

Alan Lovell, 'Robin Wood – a dissenting view', *Screen* 10(2), March/April 1969.

Alan Lovell, *Don Siegel: American Cinema*, London, BFI, 1975.

Geoffrey Nowell-Smith, *Visconti*, London, Secker & Warburg/BFI, 1967; rev. edn, 1973.

Lee Russell/Peter Wollen, 'Jean-Luc Godard', *New Left Review* no. 38, September/October 1966.

Peter Wollen, *Signs and Meaning in the Cinema*, London, Secker & Warburg/BFI, 1969; rev. edn 1972; expanded edn, London, BFI, 1998.

Robin Wood, 'Jean-Luc Godard', *New Left Review* no. 38, September/October 1966.

Robin Wood, 'Ghostly paradigm and HCF: an answer to Alan Lovell', *Screen* 10(3), May/June 1969.

Early structuralist film analysis

Louis Althusser, *Lenin and Philosophy and Other Essays*, trans. Ben Brewster, London, New Left Books, 1971.

Alexander Astruc, 'The Birth of a New Avant-Garde: La Caméra-Stylo' (1948), in Peter Graham (ed.), *The New Wave: Critical Landmarks*, New York, Doubleday, 1968, pp. 17–23.

Jean-Marie Benoist, 'The end of structuralism', *20th Century Studies* no. 3, May 1970.

Nicholas Garnham, *Samuel Fuller*, London, Secker & Warburg/BFI, 1971.

Sylvia Harvey, 'Woman's place: the absent family of *film noir*', in E. Ann Kaplan (ed.), *Women in Film Noir*, London, BFI, 1978; rev. edn, 1998.

Jacques Lacan, 'The mirror stage as formative of the function of the I', in Jacques Lacan, *Écrits: a Selection*, trans. Alan Sheridan, London, Tavistock Publications, 1977.

Edmund Leach, *Lévi-Strauss*, London, Fontana, 1970.

Geoffrey Nowell-Smith, 'Cinema and structuralism', *20th Century Studies* no. 3, May 1970.

V. F. Perkins, '*Underworld USA*', in Will and Wollen, *Samuel Fuller*.

Jeffrey Richards, 'Frank Capra and the cinema of populism', *Cinema* (UK) no. 5, February 1970.

Sam Rohdie, 'A structural analysis of *Mr Deeds Goes to Town*', *Cinema* (UK) no. 5, February 1970.

Sam Rohdie, '*House of Bamboo*', in Will and Wollen, *Samuel Fuller*.

David Will and Peter Wollen, *Samuel Fuller*, Edinburgh Film Festival, 1969.

Peter Wollen, 'Introduction', in Will and Wollen, *Samuel Fuller*.

Peter Wollen, '*Verboten!*', in Will and Wollen, *Samuel Fuller*.

Cultural politics

Edward Buscombe, 'Walsh and Warner Bros', in Hardy, *Raoul Walsh*.

Pam Cook and Claire Johnston, 'The place of woman in the cinema of Raoul Walsh', in Hardy, *Raoul Walsh*.

Elizabeth Cowie, 'Woman as sign', *m/f* no. 1, 1978.

Thomas Elsaesser, 'Postscript', *Screen* 12(2), summer 1971.

Thomas Elsaesser, 'Tales of sound and fury', *Monogram* no. 4, 1972.

Christine Gledhill, 'Recent developments in feminist film criticism', *Quarterly Review of Film Studies* 3(4), autumn 1978.

Jon Halliday, *Sirk on Sirk*, London, Secker & Warburg/BFI, 1971.

Jon Halliday, 'Notes on Sirk's German films', *Screen* 12(2), summer 1971.

Jon Halliday, '*All That Heaven Allows*', in Mulvey and Halliday (eds), *Douglas Sirk*, Edinburgh Film Festival, 1972.

Phil Hardy (ed.), *Raoul Walsh*, Edinburgh Film Festival, 1974.

Sylvia Harvey, *May '68 and Film Culture*, London, BFI, 1978.

Sylvia Harvey, 'Woman's place: the absent family of *film noir*', in Kaplan, *Women in Film Noir*.

Claire Johnston and Paul Willemen, 'Introduction', in Johnston and Willemen (eds), *Frank Tashlin*, Edinburgh Film Festival/SEFT, 1973.

Peter Lloyd, 'Walsh, a preliminary demarcation', in Hardy, *Raoul Walsh*.

Colin MacCabe, 'Walsh an author?', *Screen* 6(1), spring 1975.

Laura Mulvey and Jon Halliday (eds), *Douglas Sirk*, Edinburgh Film Festival, 1972.

Laura Mulvey, 'Sirk and melodrama', *Movie* no. 25, 1977.

Geoffrey Nowell-Smith, 'Cinema and structuralism', *20th Century Studies* no. 3, May 1970.

Paul Willemen, 'Distanciation and Douglas Sirk', *Screen* 12(2), summer 1971.

Paul Willemen, 'Tashlin's method: an hypothesis', in Johnston and Willemen (eds), *Frank Tashlin*.

Paul Willemen, '*Pursued*: the fugitive subject', in Hardy, *Raoul Walsh*.

Auteur structuralism under attack

Richard Dyer, *Stars*, London, BFI, 1979; 2nd Edn, 1998.

Charles Eckert, 'The English cine-structuralists', *Film Comment* 9(3), May/June 1973.

Molly Haskell, *From Reverence to Rape*, New York, Holt, Rinehart and Winston, 1974.

Brian Henderson, 'Critique of cine-structuralism, Part I', *Film Quarterly* 27(1), autumn 1973; 'Part II', *Film Quarterly* 27(2), winter 1973.

Jim Hillier and Peter Wollen (eds), *Howard Hawks: American Artist*, London, BFI, 1996.

Peter Wollen, *Signs and Meaning in the Cinema*, London, Secker & Warburg/BFI, 1969; rev. edn 1972; expanded edn, London, BFI, 1998.

Robin Wood, *Howard Hawks*, London, Secker & Warburg/BFI, 1968; rev. edn, BFI Publishing, 1981.

Robin Wood, 'To have (written) and have not (directed)', in Nichols (ed.), *Movies and Methods*, Berkeley, University of California Press, 1976.

AUTEUR STUDY AFTER STRUCTURALISM

Lindsay Anderson, '*The Searchers*', *Sight and Sound* 26(2), autumn 1956, reprinted in Caughie (ed.), *Theories of Authorship*, London, RKP/BFI, 1981.

Lindsay Anderson, *About John Ford*, London, Plexus, 1981.

André Bazin, 'The evolution of the language of cinema', in Gray (ed. and trans.), *What Is Cinema?* vol. I, Berkeley, University of California Press, 1967.

André Bazin, *Orson Welles: A Critical View*, London, Elm Tree Books, 1978.

Edward Buscombe, 'Ideas of authorship', *Screen* 14(3), autumn 1973.

John Caughie, 'Teaching through authorship', *Screen Education* no. 17, autumn 1975.

John Ellis, 'Teaching authorship: Ford or fraud?', in Gledhill (ed.), *Film and Media Studies in Higher Education*, London, BFI Education, 1981.

Stephen Heath, 'Comment on "the idea of authorship"', *Screen* 14(3), autumn 1973.

Charles Higham and Joel Greenberg, *Hollywood in the 40s*, London, Tantivy Press, 1968.

Alan Lovell, *Don Siegel: American Cinema*, London, BFI, 1975.

Geoffrey Nowell-Smith, 'Six authors in pursuit of *The Searchers*', *Screen* 17(1), spring, 1976

Andrew Sarris, *The John Ford Movie Mystery*, London, Secker & Warburg/BFI, 1976.

Screen Education no. 17, autumn 1975. Special issue on *The Searchers*.

Peter Wollen, *Signs and Meaning in the Cinema*, London, Secker & Warburg/BFI, 1969; rev. edn 1972; expanded edn, London, BFI, 1998.

Robin Wood, *Howard Hawks*, London, Secker & Warburg/BFI, 1968; rev. edn, BFI Publishing, 1981.

Authorship as 'discursive activity'

Ben Brewster, 'Notes on the text "*Young Mr Lincoln*" by the editors of *Cahiers du Cinéma*', *Screen* 14(3), autumn 1973.

Cahiers du Cinéma, the editors of, 'John Ford's *Young Mr Lincoln*', *Screen* 13(3), autumn 1972.

Stephen Heath, 'Comment on "The idea of authorship"', *Screen* 14(3), autumn 1973.

Stephen Heath, 'Film and system: terms of analysis', *Screen* 16(1/2), spring/summer 1975.

Claire Johnston and Paul Willemen, 'Brecht in Britain: the independent political film', *Screen* 16(4), winter 1975/76.

Geoffrey Nowell-Smith, 'Six authors in pursuit of *The Searchers*', *Screen* 17(1), spring 1976.

Peter Wollen, *Signs and Meaning in the Cinema*, London, Secker & Warburg/BFI, 1969; rev. edn 1972; expanded edn, London, BFI, 1998.

Authorship and counter-cinema

Raymond Bellour and Mary Lea Bardy (eds), *Jean-Luc Godard: Sound & Image*, New York, Museum of Modern Art, 1992.

'The Estates General of the French cinema, May 1968', *Screen* 13(4), winter 1972/73.

Peter Harcourt, *Six European Directors*, Harmondsworth, Middx, Penguin, 1974.

Colin MacCabe, *Godard: Images, Sound, Politics*, London, Macmillan/BFI, 1980.

V. F. Perkins, *Film as Film: Understanding and Judging Movies*, Harmondsworth, Middx, Penguin, 1972.

Peter Wollen, *Signs and Meaning in the Cinema*, London, Secker & Warburg/BFI, 1969; rev. edn 1972; expanded edn, London, BFI, 1998.

Peter Wollen, 'Counter-cinema: *Vent d'est*, *Afterimage* no. 4, autumn, 1972.

Counter-cinema and feminism

Sarah Benton, *Patterns of Discrimination against Women in the Film and Television Industries*, London, Association of Cinematograph Television and Allied Technicians, 1975.

Pam Cook, 'Approaching the work of Dorothy Arzner', in Johnston (ed.), *Dorothy Arzner: Towards a Feminist Cinema*, London, BFI, 1975.

Pam Cook, '"Exploitation films" and feminism', *Screen* 17(2), summer 1976.

Anne Cottringer, 'Representation and feminist film practice', in Cowie (ed.), *Catalogue British Film Institute Productions 1977–1978*, London, BFI, 1978.

Terry Curtis Fox, 'Fully female', *Film Comment* 12(6), November/December 1976.

Sylvia Harvey, *May '68 and Film Culture*, London, BFI, 1978.

Jim Hillier and Aaron Lipstadt, *BFI Dossier no. 7: Roger Corman's New World*, London, BFI, 1981.

Claire Johnston, 'Women's cinema as counter-cinema', in Johnston (ed.), *Notes on Women's Cinema*, London, SEFT, 1973.

Claire Johnston, 'Dorothy Arzner: critical strategies', in Johnston (ed.), *Dorothy Arzner: Towards a Feminist Cinema*, London, BFI, 1975.

Terry Lovell, *Pictures of Reality*, London, BFI, 1980.

Barbara Martineau, 'Subjecting her Objectification', in Johnston (ed.), *Notes on Women's Cinema*, London, SEFT, 1973.

Judith Mayne, *Directed by Dorothy Arzner*, Bloomington, Indiana University Press, 1995.

Laura Mulvey, 'Feminism, film and the avant-garde', *Framework* no. 10, spring 1979.

Steve Neale, 'Art cinema as institution', *Screen* 22(1), 1981.

Gerald Peary, 'Dorothy Arzner', *Cinema* (USA) no. 34, autumn 1974.

Gerald Peary and Karyn Kay, 'Interview with Dorothy Arzner', in Johnston (ed.), *Dorothy Arzner: towards a feminist cinema*, London, BFI, 1975.

Peter Wollen, 'The two *avant-gardes*', in Hardy/Johnston/Willemen (eds), *Edinburgh '76 Magazine: Psychoanalysis/Cinema/Avante-Garde*, Edinburgh Film Festival, 1976

AUTEURISM IN THE 1990S

Dudley Andrew, 'The unauthorised auteur today', in Jim Collins *et al.* (eds), *Film Theory Goes to the Movies*, New York, Routledge, 1993, pp. 77–85.

Timothy Asch, 'Collaboration in ethnographic filmmaking: a personal view', *Anthropological Filmmaking*, Jack R. Rollwagen (ed.), Chur: Harwood Academic, 1990, pp. 1–29.

Roland Barthes, 'Death of the author', trans. Stephen Heath, in Barthes, *Image–Music–Text*, London, Glasgow, 1977; pp. 142–8.

André Bazin, 'La politique des auteurs', trans. Peter Graham, in Jim Hillier (ed), *Cahiers du Cinema: The 1950s: Neo-Realism, Hollywood, The New Wave*, Cambridge, Mass., Harvard University Press, 1985; pp. 248–59.

Denise D. Bielby and William T. Bielby, 'Women and men in film: gender inequality among writers in a culture industry', *Gender & Society* 10(3): 248–70, 1996.

Geraldine Bloustein, 'Jane Campion: memory, motif and music', *Continuum* 5(2): 29–39, 1992.

Jay Boyer, *Bob Rafelson: Hollywood Maverick*, New York, Twayne, 1996.

Edward Buscombe, 'Ideas of Authorship', in *Theories of Authorship*, John Caughie (ed.), London, RKP, 1981, pp. 22–34.

Michael Chion, *David Lynch*, trans. Robert Julian, London, BFI, 1995.

Jim Collins *et al.* (eds), *Film Theory Goes to the Movies*, New York, Routledge, 1993.

Timothy Corrigan, *A Cinema Without Walls: Movies and Culture After Vietnam*, New York, Routledge, 1991.

Rosalind Coward, 'Dennis Potter and the Question of the Television Author', *Critical Quarterly* 29 (4): 79–87, 1987.

Stuart Cunningham, *Featuring Australia: The Cinema of Charles Chauvel*, Sydney, Allen & Unwin, 1991.

Gilles Deleuze, *Negotiations 1972–1990*, trans. Martin Joughin, New York, Columbia University Press, 1995, pp. 46–61.

Alexander Doty, 'Whose text is it anyway?: queer cultures, queer *auteurs* and queer authorship', *Quarterly Review of Film and Video* 15(1): 41–54, 1993.

Richard Dyer, *White*, London, Routledge, 1997.

Bernard Eisenschitz, *Nicholas Ray: An American Journey*, trans. Tom Milne, London, Faber & Faber, 1993.

Thomas Elsaesser, *Fassbinder's Germany: History, Identity, Subject*, Amsterdam, Amsterdam University Press, 1996.

Film Criticism 19(3), 1995.

Film History 7(4), 1995, special issue on 'Auteurism Revisited.'

Elliot Forbes and David Pierce, 'Who owns the movies?' *Film Comment* 30(6): 43–50, 1994.

Michel Foucault, 'What is an author?', trans. Josué V. Harari, in *Modern Criticism and Theory: A Reader*, David Lodge (ed.), London, Longman, 1988, pp. 197–210.

Diana Fuss (ed.), *Inside/Out: Lesbian Theories, Gay Theories*, New York, Routledge, 1991.

Aaron Gell, 'Weir in the Money,' *Time Out*, New York 14–21 May 1998: 25.

Susan Hayward, *Luc Besson*, Manchester, MUP, 1998.

Jim Kitses, 'Pat Garrett and Billy the Kid', in Jim Kitses and Gregg Rickman (eds), *The Western Reader*, New York, Limelight, 1998, pp. 223–43.

Laurence Kardish with Juliane Lorenz, *Rainer Werner Fassbinder*, New York, Museum of Modern Art, 1997.

Annette Kuhn, *Queen of the 'B's: Ida Lupino Behind the Camera*, Westport, Connecticut, Praeger, 1995.

Janet Maslin, 'So, what's wrong with this picture?' *New York Times* 5 June 1998: E1, E18.

Judith Mayne, 'A parallax view of lesbian authorship', in Diana Fuss (ed.), *Inside/Out: Lesbian Theories, Gay Theories*, New York, Routledge, 1991, pp. 173–84.

L[loyd] M[ichaels], 'Editor's Note', *Film Criticism* 19(3): 1, 1995.

Anthony Mosawi, 'The control by novelists of film versions of their work', *European Law Review* 6(3): 83–87, 1995.

James Naremore, 'Authorship and the cultural politics of film criticism', *Film Quarterly* 44(1): 14–22, 1990.

New German Critique 63, autumn 1994. Special Fassbinder issue.

Jessie Algeron Rhines, *Black Film/White Money*, New Brunswick: Rutgers University Press, 1996.

James Ryan, 'And the producer of the movie is ... ' *New York Times* 24 September 1995.

Andrew Sarris, *The American Cinema: Directors and Directions 1929–1968*, New York, E. P. Dutton, 1968.

Jane Shattuc, *Television, Tabloids, and Tears: Fassbinder and Popular Culture*, Minneapolis: University of Minnesota Press, 1993.

Don Shiach, *The Films of Peter Weir: Visions of Alternative Realities*, London, Charles Letts, 1993.

Gaylyn Studlar and David Desser (eds), *Reflections in a Male Eye: John Huston and The American Experience*, Washington, DC, Smithsonian Institution Press, 1993.

Wide Angle 6(1), 1984 Special issue on authorship.

Peter Wollen, *Signs and Meaning in the Cinema*, London, BFI, rev. edn, 1998.

Justin Wyatt, 'Economic constraints/economic opportunities: Robert Altman as *auteur*', *The Velvet Light Trap* 38, autumn 1996, pp. 51–67.

PART 7: THEORETICAL FRAMEWORKS

LOOKING AT FILM

Jacques Aumont, Alain Bergala, Michel Marie and Marc Vernet, *Aesthetics of Film*, trans. and rev. by Richard Neupert, Austin, University of Texas Press, 1992.

David Bordwell and Kristin Thompson, *Film Art*, New York, McGraw-Hill, 4th edn, 1993.

Christian Metz, *Film Language: A Semiotics of the Cinema*, trans. by Michael Taylor, New York, Oxford University Press, 1978.

Richard Neupert, *The End: Narration and Closure in the Cinema*, Detroit, Wayne State University Press, 1995.

Karel Reisz and Gavin Millar, *The Techniques of Film Editing*, New York, Hastings House, 1953.

Raymond Spottiswoode, *A Grammar of the Film*, Berkeley, University of California Press, 1951.

STRUCTURALISM AND ITS AFTERMATHS

Andrew Britton, 'Living Historically', *Framework* 3, spring 1976.

Jack Daniel, 'Metz's grande syntagmatique: summary and critique', *Film Form* 1(1), spring 1976.

'Citizen Kane' (Collective test) in *Film Reader* 1, 1975.

Colin McCabe, Godard: *Images, Sounds, Politics*, BFI Cinema Series, London, Macmillan, 1980, p. 554.

Christian Metz, *Essais sur la signification au cinéma*, vols I & II, Paris, Éditions Klincksieck, 1968–72.

Christian Metz, *Film Language: A Semiotics of the Cinema*, trans. Michael Taylor, New York, Oxford University Press, 1974.

Christian Metz, 'The Modern Cinema and Narrativity' (1966) translated in *Film Language: A Semiotics of the Cinema*, trans. Michael Taylor, New York, Oxford University Press, 1974, pp. 185–227.

Kristin Thompson, 'Sawing through the bough', *Wide Angle* 1, 1976.

Nicole Zand, 'Le Dossier Phillipine', *Cahiers du Cinéma* 148, 1963.

LÉVI-STRAUSS: THE STRUCTURAL STUDY OF MYTH

Claude Chabrol, review of *Kiss me Deadly*, *Cahiers du Cinéma* 54, 1956.

Raymond Durgnat, 'The apotheosis of va-va-voom,' *Motion* 3, spring 1962.

Charles Eckert, 'The English cine-structuralists', *Film Comment* 9(3), May/June 1973.

Patricia Erens, '*Sunset Boulevard*: a morphological analysis', *Film Reader* 2, 1977.

John L. Fell, 'Vladimir Propp in Hollywood', *Film Quarterly* 30(3), spring 1977.

Sylvia Harvey, 'The absent family of *film noir*', in E. Ann Kaplan (ed.), Women in *Film Noir*, BFI, 1978, rev. edn 1998.

Molly Haskell, 'Howard Hawks – masculine feminine', *Film Comment* vol. 10 no. 2, March/ April 1974.

Brian Henderson, 'Critique of cine-structuralism', *Film Quarterly* 26(5), autumn 1973 and 27(2), winter 1973/74.

Edmund Leach, *Lévi-Strauss*, London, Fontana, 1974, chs 3 and 4.

Claude Lévi-Strauss, 'Overture' to The Raw and the Cooked, vol. I of *Mythologiques*, trans. John and Doreen Weightman, London, Jonathan Cape, 1970.

Christian Metz, 'Notes towards a Phenomenology of Narrative' (1966) translated in *Film Language: A Semiotics of the Cinema*, trans. Michael Taylor, New York, Oxford University Press, 1974, pp. 16–28.

Christian Metz, *Film Language: A Semiotics of the Cinema*, trans. Michael Taylor, New York, Oxford University Press, 1974.

Vladimir Propp, *Morphology of the Folktale*, trans. Laurence Scott, Austin and London, University of Texas Press, 1968.

Alan Silver, '*Kiss Me Deadly* – evidence of a film style', *Film Comment* vol 11 no. 2, March/ April 1975.

Peter Wollen, *Signs and Meaning in the Cinema*, London, Secker & Warburg/BFI 1969, 1972, rev. edn, London, BFI 1998.

Robin Wood, *Howard Hawks*, London, Secker & Warburg/BFI 1968, reprinted 1981.

Robin Wood, 'To Have (written) and Have Not (directed)', *Film Comment* 9(3), May/June 1973.

Robin Wood, 'Hawks de-Wollenised,' in *Personal Views*, London, G. Fraser, 1976.

Will Wright, *Sixguns and Society*, Berkeley, University of California Press, 1975.

ROLAND BARTHES: THE ANALYSIS OF NARRATIVE

Roland Barthes, *Image–Music–Text*, London, Fontana, 1977; selected and trans. by Stephen Heath.

Roland Barthes, 'Introduction to the structural analysis of narratives', in *Communications* no. 8, 1966, in *Image–Music–Text*, London, Fontana, 1977; trans. Stephen Heath.

Roland Barthes, *S/Z*, Paris, Éditions du Seuil, 1970, trans. Richard Miller, New York, Hill and Wang, 1974.

Jacques Derrida, *L'Ecriture et la différance*, Paris, Éditions du Seuil, 1967, (*Writing and Difference*, trans. A. Bass, London, RKP, 1979).

Stephen Heath, 'A conversation with Roland Barthes', in; *Signs of the Times*, Cambridge, 1971, pp. 41–51.

Narrative and audience

Louis Althusser, 'Ideology and Ideological State Apparatuses', in *Lenin and Philosophy and other Essays*, trans. Ben Brewster, London, New Left Books, 1971.

Claude Bailblé, 'Programming the look', *Screen Education* 32/33, autumn/winter 1979/80 (*Cahiers du Cinéma* 281, October 1977; 282, November 1977).

Jean-Louis Baudry, 'Ideological effects of the basic cinematographic apparatus' (1970), trans. by Alan Williams, in Gerald Mast, Marshall Cohen, Leo Braudy (eds), *Film Theory and Criticism: Introductory Readings*, 4th edn, Oxford, Oxford University Press, 1992.

André Bazin, *Orson Welles: a Critical View*, trans. Jonathan Rosenbaum, London, Elm Tree Books, 1978.

André Bazin, 'William Wyler or the Jansenist of *mise-en-scène*' in *Realism in the Cinema*, London, RKP/BFI, 1980, pp. 36–52.

Raymond Bellour, 'The Birds – Analysis of a sequence', London, BFI Education Dept, 1972 (reprinted 1981).

David Bordwell and Kristin Thompson, *Film Art*, New York, McGraw-Hill, 4th edn, 1993.

Edward Branigan, 'Formal permutations of the point-of-view shot', *Screen* 16(3), autumn 1975.

Nick Browne, 'The spectator-in-the-text: the rhetoric of *Stagecoach*', *Film Quarterly* 29(2), winter 1975/76.

John Ellis, 'Watching death at work – an analysis of A Matter of Life and Death', in Ian Christie (ed.), *Powell, Pressburger and Others*, London, BFI, 1978, esp. pp. 90 ff. *Film Reader* 4, 1979, 'Point-of-view/Metahistory of film'.

Phil Hardy, Claire Johnston, Paul Willemen (eds), *Edinburgh '76 Magazine: Psychoanalysis/Cinema/Avant-garde*, Edinburgh Film Festival, 1976.

Stephen Heath, 'Lessons from Brecht', *Screen* 15(2), summer 1974.

Stephen Heath, 'Notes on suture', *Screen* 18(4), winter 1977/78.

Stephen Heath, 'Film performance', *Cinetracts*, 1(2), 1977.

Stephen Heath, 'Film and system: terms of analysis', *Screen* 16(1/2), spring/summer 1975.

Brian Henderson, 'The Long Take', *Film Comment* 7(2), summer 1971.

Claire Johnston, 'Towards a feminist film practice' in Hardy *et al.*, *Edinburgh '76 Magazine*.

Colin MacCabe, 'Realism and the cinema: notes on some Brechtian theses', *Screen* 15(2), summer 1974.

Colin MacCabe, 'Days of Hope – a response to Colin McArthur', *Screen* 17(1), spring 1976a.

Colin MacCabe, 'Principles of realism and pleasure', *Screen* 17(3), autumn 1976b.

Christian Metz, *Psychoanalysis & Cinema: The Imaginary Signifier*, London, Macmillan, 1977/1982.

Mark Nash, 'Vampyr and the fantastic', *Screen* 17(3), autumn 1976.

Steve Neale, *Genre*, London, BFI, 1980.

Patrick Ogle, 'Technological and aesthetic influences upon the development of deep-focus cinematography in the United States', *Screen Reader 1*, London, Society for Education in Film and Television, 1977.

Paul Willemen, *Looks and Frictions: Essays in Cultural Studies and Film Theory*, London, BFI, 1994.

Christopher Williams, 'The deep-focus question: some comments on Patrick Ogle's article', in Ogle, *Screen Reader 1*.

Psychoanalysis and film

Daniel Dayan, 'The tutor-code of classical cinema', *Film Quarterly* 28(1), autumn 1974.

Stephen Heath, 'Lessons from Brecht', *Screen* 15(2), summer 1974.

Christian Metz, 'History/Discourse – a note on two voyeurisms' in Hardy *et al.*, *Edinburgh '76 Magazine*.

Jacques-Alain Miller, Jean-Pierre Oudart, Stephen Heath, 'Dossier on suture', *Screen* 18(4), winter 1977/78.

Laura Mulvey, 'Visual pleasure and narrative cinema', *Screen* 16(3), autumn 1975.

Aftermaths

Note: Quotations from Bazin in the text have been translated directly from.

André Bazin, *Qu'est-ce que le cinéma?*, vols 1 and 4, Paris, Éditions du Cerf, 1958 and 1962 (some of these articles have been translated in, *What is Cinema?*, vols 1 and 2, 1971; 'William Wyler or the Jansenist of *mise-en-scène*', translated in Christopher Williams (ed), *Realism and the Cinema*, London, RKP/BFI, 1980, pp. 36–52).

David Bordwell and Kristin Thompson, *Film Art*, 4th edn, New York, McGraw-Hill, 1993.

Gilles Deleuze, *Cinema 1: L'Image–mouvement*, 1983, trans. by Hugh Tomlinson and Barbara Habbermas, as *Cinema 1: The Movement– Image*, London, Athlone Press, 1986.

Gilles Deleuze, *Cinema 2: L'Image–temps*, (1985, trans. by Hugh Tomlinson and Robert Galeta as *Cinema 2: The Time–Image*, London, Athlone Press, 1989.

Gilles Deleuze and Felix Guattari, *Anti-Oedipus: Capitalism and Schizophrenia*, Minneapolis, University of Minnesota Press, 1983.

Paul Patton, Review of Gilles Deleuze, *Cinema 1 & 2*, *Screen* 32(2), 1991.

Vladimir Propp, *Morphology of the Folktale*, trans. Laurence Scott, Austin and London, University of Texas Press, 1968.

David N. Rodowick, *Gilles Deleuze's Time-Machine*, Durham, Duke UP, 1997.

Kristin Thompson, *Breaking the Glass Armor: Neoformalist Film Analysis*, Princeton, NJ, Princeton University Press, 1988.

Marie-Claire Ropars-Wuillemier, 'The Cinema, Reader of Gilles Deleuze', in C. V. Boundas and D. Olkowski (eds), *Gilles Deleuze and the Theatre of Philosophy*, Routledge, 1994.

PSYCHOANALYSIS

Manuel Alvarado, Edward Buscombe and Richard Collins, 'Introduction', *The Screen Education Reader*, London, Macmillan, 1993.

Jean-Louis Baudry, 'Ideological effects of the basic cinematographic apparatus' (1970), trans. by Alan Williams, in Gerald Mast, Marshall Cohen, Leo Braudy (eds), *Film Theory and Criticism: Introductory Readings*, 4th edn, Oxford, Oxford University Press, 1992.

Ben Brewster, Elizabeth Cowie, Jon Halliday, Kari Hanet, Stephen Heath, Colin MacCabe, Paul Willemen and Peter Wollen, 'Reply [to statement of resignation]', *Screen* 17(2): 110–16, summer 1976.

Edward Buscombe, Christine Gledhill, Alan Lovell and Christopher Williams, 'Psycho-analysis and film' (1975–6), in *The Sexual Subject: A Screen Reader in Sexuality*, London, Routledge, 1992.

Michel Chion, *David Lynch*, trans. Robert Julian, London, BFI, 1995.

Joan Copjec, 'The delirium of clinical perfection', *Oxford Literary Review*, 8(1–2): 57–65, 1986.

Elizabeth Cowie, 'Fantasia', *m/f* vol. 9 (1984), reprinted in Parveen Adams and Elizabeth Cowie (eds), *The Woman in Question*, London, Verso, 1990.

Barbara Creed, *The Monstrous-Feminine*, London, Routledge, 1993.

James Donald, 'Introduction', in James Donald (ed.), *Fantasy and the Cinema*, London, BFI, 1989.

Mary Ann Doane, 'Remembering Women: Psychical and Historical Constructions In Film Theory', in E. Ann Kaplan (ed.), *Psychoanalysis and Cinema*, London, Routledge, 1990.

Anthony Easthope (ed.), *Contemporary Film Theory*, Harrow, Longman, 1993.

Sigmund Freud (1993), 'The resistances to psychoanalysis' (1925 (1924)), in *The Penguin Freud Library*, Angela Richards and Albert Dickson (eds), trans. by James Strachey, vol. 15: *Historical and Expository Works*, Harmondsworth, Penguin, 1993.

Sigmund Freud, *The Penguin Freud Library*, vol. 1: *Introductory Lectures on Psychoanalysis*, Harmondsworth, Penguin, 1991a.

Sigmund Freud, 'The unconscious' (1915), in *The Penguin Freud Library*, vol. 11: *On Metapsychology*, Harmondsworth, Penguin, 1991b.

Sigmund Freud, 'Fetishism' (1927), in *The Penguin Freud Library*, vol. 7: *On Sexuality*, Harmondsworth, Penguin, 1991c; reprinted in Easthope, *Contemporary Film Theory*.

Claire Johnston, 'The subject of feminist film theory practice', in Buscombe *et al.*, *The Sexual Subject*, 1992.

E. Ann Kaplan, *Women and Film: Both Sides of the Camera*, London, Methuen, 1983.

Annette Kuhn, *Women's Pictures: Feminism and Cinema*, 2nd edn, London, Verso, 1994.

Jacques Lacan, 'The mirror stage as formative of the function of the I' (1937), in *Écrits: A Selection*, trans. by Alan Sheridan, London, Routledge, 1989; reprinted in Easthope, *Contemporary Film Theory*.

Colin McArthur, *The Big Heat* (London: BFI, 1992).

Colin MacCabe, *On the Eloquence of the Vulgar: A Justification of the Study of Film and Television*, London, BFI, 1993.

Christian Metz, 'Story discourse: notes on two kinds of voyeurism' (1974) in Bill Nichols (ed.), *Movies and Methods: An Anthology*, vol. 1, London, University of California Press, 1985.

Laura Mulvey, *Fetishism and Curiosity*, London, BFI and Indiana University Press, 1996.

Laura Mulvey, *Visual and Other Pleasures*, London, Macmillan, 1989.

Gaylyn Studlar, 'Masochism and the perverse pleasures of cinema' (1985), in Mast *et al.*, *Film Theory and Criticism*.

Paul Willemen, *Looks and Frictions*, London, BFI, 1994.

Slavoj Žižek (ed.), *Everything You Always Wanted to Know about Lacan (But Were Afraid to Ask Hitchcock)*, London, Verso, 1992.

Slavoj Žižek, *Looking Awry: An Introduction to Jacques Lacan through Popular Culture*, London, MIT Press, 1991.

Slavoj Žižek, *Tarrying with the Negative*, Durham, NC, Duke University Press, 1993.

FEMINIST FILM THEORY

Jack Babuscio, 'Camp and the gay sensibility' in Richard Dyer (ed.), *Gays & Film* 1977; rev. edn, New York, Zoetrope, 1984, pp. 40–57.

Janet Bergstrom and Mary Ann Doane (eds), *Camera Obscura: A Journal of Feminism and Film Theory*. Special issue 'The spectatrix', pp. 20–21, 1989.

Jacqueline Bobo, *Black Women as Cultural Readers*, New York, Columbia University Press, 1995.

Judith Butler, *Gender Trouble*, New York and London, Routledge, 1990.

R. Chapman and J. Rutherford (eds), *Male Order: Unwrapping Masculinity*, London, Lawrence and Wishart, 1988.

Carol Clover, *Men, Women and Chain Saws: Gender in the Modern Horror Film*, London, BFI, 1992.

Pam Cook, 'Masculinity in crisis' in *Screen* 23(3–4): 39–46, 1982.

Mary Ann Doane, 'Film and the masquerade: theorising the female spectator', (1982), reprinted in *Femmes Fatales: Feminism, Film Theory, Psychoanalysis*, New York and London, Routledge, 1991; pp. 17–32.

Mary Ann Doane, *The Desire to Desire: The Woman's Film of the 1940s*, Bloomington, Indiana University Press, 1987.

Richard Dyer, 'Don't look now: the male pin-up', in *Screen* 23(3–4): 61–73, 1982.

Richard Dyer, *Now You See It. Studies on Lesbian and Gay Film*, London, Routledge, 1990.

Richard Dyer, 'White', (1988) *The Matter of Images. Essays on Representations*, London and New York, Routledge, 1993, pp. 141–63.

Antony Easthope, *What A Man's Gotta Do: The Masculine Myth in Popular Culture*, London, Paladin, 1986.

Elizabeth Ellsworth, 'Feminist spectators and *Personal Best*', in Patricia Erens (ed.), *Issues in Feminist Film Criticism*, Bloomington, Indiana University Press, 1990, pp. 183–96.

Sandy Flitterman-Lewis, *To Desire Differently: Feminism and the French Cinema*, Urbana and Chicago, University of Illinois Press, 1990.

Jane Gaines, 'White privilege and looking relations: race and gender in feminist film theory', in *Screen* 29(4): 12–27, 1988.

Angela Galvin, '*Basic Instinct*: damning dykes', in Diane Hamer and Belinda Budge (eds), *The Good, the Bad and the Gorgeous: Popular Culture's Romance with Lesbianism*, London, Pandora, 1994, pp. 218–31.

M. Gever, J. Greyson and P. Parmar (eds), *Queer Looks: Perspectives on Lesbian and Gay Film and Video*, New York and London, Routledge, 1993.

Paula Graham, 'Girl's camp? The politics of parody', in Tamsin Wilton (ed.), *Immortal, Invisible. Lesbians and the Moving Image*, London and New York, Routledge, 1995, pp. 163–81.

Deborah Grayson, (ed), *Camera Obscura* 36, 1995, special issue, 'Black women, spectatorship and visual culture'.

Deborah Grayson, 'Is it fake? Black women's hair as spectacle and spec(tac)ular' in *Camera Obscura* 36: 13–30, 1995.

Miriam Hansen, *Babel and Babylon: Spectatorship in American Silent Film*, London, Harvard University Press, 1991.

Molly Haskell, *From Reverence to Rape: The Treatment of Women in the Movies*, Chicago and London, University of Chicago Press, 1973; rev. edn, 1987.

bell hooks, *Black Looks: Race and Representation*, Boston, South End Press, 1992.

Maggie Humm, *Feminism and Film*, Edinburgh, Edinburgh University Press, 1997.

Joy James, 'Black *femmes fatales* and sexual abuse in progressive white cinema' in *Camera Obscura* 36: 33–47, 1995.

Susan Jeffords, *Hard Bodies: Hollywood Masculinity in the Reagan Era*, New Brunswick, Rutgers University Press, 1994.

Claire Johnston, 'Femininity and the masquerade: *Anne of the Indies*, Edinburgh pamplet on Jacques Tourneur, 1975.

Claire Johnston, 'Women's cinema as counter-cinema', in *Notes on Women's Cinema*, (1973) SEFT, Glasgow, Screen Reprint, 1991, pp. 24–31.

Alexandra Juhasz, 'They said we were trying to show reality – all I want is to show my video': the politics of the realist, feminist documentary', in *Screen* 35(2): 171–90, 1994.

Jump Cut, special issue, 'Lesbians and film', 24/25, 1981.

E. Ann Kaplan, *Women and Film: Both Sides of the Camera*, New York and London, Methuen, 1983.

Lynn Kirby, 'Male hysteria and early cinema' in *Camera Obscura* 17, 1988, pp. 113–31.

P. Kirkham and J. Thumin (eds), *You Tarzan: Masculinity, Movies and Men*, London, Lawrence and Wishart, 1993.

Gertrude Koch, 'Warum Frauen ins Männerkino gehen', in G. Nabakowski, H. Sander and P. Gorsen (eds), in *Frauen in der Kunst. Band I.* Frankfurt am Main, Suhrkamp Verlag, 1980, pp. 15–29.

Annette Kuhn, *Women's Pictures: Feminism and Cinema*, London, RKP, 1982; rev. edn, 1994.

Teresa de Lauretis, *Alice Doesn't: Feminism, Semiotics, Cinema*, Bloomington, Indiana University Press, 1984.

Teresa de Lauretis, *Technologies of Gender: Essays on Theory, Film and Fiction*, Bloomington, Indiana University Press, 1987.

Teresa de Lauretis, 'Sexual indifference and lesbian representation', in *Theatre Journal* 40(2): 155–77, 1988.

Teresa de Lauretis, 'Film and the visible', in Bad Object-Choices (eds), *How Do I Look? Queer Film and Video*, Seattle, Bay Press, 1991, pp. 223–64.

Teresa de Lauretis, *The Practice of Love: Lesbian Sexuality and Perverse Desire*, Bloomington, Indiana University Press, 1994.

Julia Lesage, 'Subversive Fantasy in *Celine and Julie Go Boating*', *Jump Cut* 24/25, Winter 1980/81.

Brenda Longfellow, 'Lesbian Phantasy and the Other Women in Ottinger's Johanna d'Arc of Mongolia', *Screen* 34(2), 1993, pp. 124–36.

Judith Mayne, *The Woman at the Keyhole: Feminism and Women's Cinema*, Bloomington, Indiana University Press, 1990.

Judith Mayne, *Directed by Dorothy Arzner*, Bloomington, Indiana University Press, 1994.

Andy Medhurst, 'That special thrill: *Brief Encounter*, homosexuality and authorship' in *Screen* 32(2): 197–208, 1991a.

Andy Medhurst, 'Batman, deviance and camp', in Roberta E. Pearson and William Uricchio (eds), *The Many Lives of the Batman: Critical Approaches to a Superhero and his Media*, London, BFI Publishing, New York, Routledge, 1991b, pp. 149–63.

Mandy Merck, *Perversions: Deviant Readings*, London, Virago, 1993.

Tania Modleski, *The Women Who Knew Too Much: Hitchcock and Feminist Theory*, New York and London, Methuen, 1988.

Tania Modleski, *Feminism Without Women: Culture and Criticism in a 'Postfeminist' Age*, New York and London, Routledge, 1991.

Laura Mulvey, 'Visual pleasure and narrative cinema' (1975) in *Visual And Other Pleasures*, London, Macmillan, 1989, pp. 14–26.

Laura Mulvey, 'Afterthoughts on "Visual pleasure and narrative cinema", inspired by King Vidor's *Duel in the Sun*' (1981), *Visual And Other Pleasures*, London, Macmillan, 1989, pp. 29–37.

Constance Penley and Sharon Willis (eds), *Camera Obscura* 17, 1988, special issue, 'Male trouble'.

Steve Neale, 'Masculinity as spectacle', *Screen* 24(6): 2–16, 1983.

Ruby Rich, 'From repressive tolerance to erotic liberation: *Maedchen in Uniform*', (1981), reprinted in Mary Ann Doane *et al.*, *Revision: Essays in Feminist Film Criticism*, Los Angeles, American Film Institute and University Publications of America, 1984, pp. 100–30.

M. Rosen, *Popcorn Venus: Women, Movies and the American Dream*, New York, Avon, 1973.

Gayle Rubin, 'The traffic in women: notes on the "political economy" of sex', in R. R. Reiter (ed.), *Toward an Anthropology of Women*, New York, *Monthly Review Press*, 1975, pp. 157–10.

Maria Shelton, 'Whitney is every woman?: Cultural politics and the pop star', in *Camera Obscura* 36, 1995, pp. 135–53.

Kaja Silverman, *The Acoustic Mirror: The Female Voice in Psychoanalysis and Cinema*, Bloomington, Indiana University Press, 1988.

Kaja Silverman, *Male Subjectivity at the Margins*, New York and London, Routledge, 1992.

Mark Simpson, *Male Impersonators: Men Performing Masculinity*, London, Cassell, 1994.

Anneke Smelik, *And the Mirror Cracked: Feminist Cinema and Film Theory*, London, Macmillan, 1998.

Jackie Stacey, '*Desperately Seeking Difference*', in *Screen* 28(1): 48–61, 1987.

Jackie Stacey, *Star Gazing: Hollywood Cinema and Female Spectatorship*, London and New York, Routledge, 1994.

Jackie Stacey, ' "If you don't play you can't win" ': *Desert Hearts* and the lesbian romance film, in Tamsin Wilton (ed.), *Immortal, Invisible: Lesbians and the Moving Image*, London and New York, Routledge, 1995, pp. 92–114.

Gaylyn Studlar, *In the Realm of Pleasure: Von Sternberg, Dietrich and the Masochistic Aesthetic*, New York, Columbia University Press, 1988.

Yvonne Tasker, *Spectacular Bodies: Gender, Genre and the Action Cinema*, London, Routledge, 1993.

Trinh T. Min-ha, *Woman, Native, Other: Writing, Postcoloniality and Feminism*, Bloomington, Indiana University Press, 1989.

Andrea Weiss, *Vampires and Violets: Lesbians in the Cinema*, London, Jonathan Cape, 1992.

Patricia White, 'Female spectator, lesbian specter: *The Haunting*', in Diana Fuss (ed.), *Inside/Out: Lesbian Theories, Gay Theories*, New York and London, Routledge, 1991, pp. 142–72.

Linda Williams, '*Personal Best*: women in love' in Charlotte Brunsdon (ed.), *Films for Women*, London, BFI Publishing, 1986, pp. 146–54.

Lola Young, *Fear of the Dar 'Race': Gender and Sexuality in the Cinema*, London and New York, Routledge, 1996.

SPECTATORSHIP AND AUDIENCE RESEARCH

Robert C. Allen, 'Motion picture exhibition in Manhattan, 1906–1912: beyond the nickelodeon,' *Cinema Journal* 28(2), 1979.

Robert C. Allen, 'From exhibition to reception: reflections on the audience in film history,' *Screen* 31(4), 1990.

Louis Althusser, 'Ideology and ideological state apparatuses,' in *Lenin and Philosophy and Other Essays*, trans. Ben Brewster, London, New Left Books, 1971.

Ien Ang, *Watching 'Dallas': Soap Opera and the Melodramatic Imagination*, London, Methuen, 1985.

Ien Ang, *Desperately Seeking the Audience*, London, Routledge, 1991.

Bruce A. Austin, *The Film Audience: An International Bibliography of Research*, London, The Scarecrow Press, 1983.

Bruce A. Austin, *Immediate Seating: A Look at Movie Audiences*, California, Wadsworth, 1989.

Janet Bergstrom and Mary Ann Doane (ed.), 'The spectatrix,' *Camera Obscura* nos. 20–21, May–September 1989.

Jacqueline Bobo, '*The Color Purple*: black women as cultural readers,' in *Female Spectators: Looking at Film and Television*, ed. E. D. Pribram, London, Verso, 1988.

Charlotte Brunsdon, '*Crossroads*: notes on soap opera,' *Screen* 22(4), 1981.

Mary Carbine, ' "The finest outside the loop": motion picture exhibition in Chicago's black metropolis,' *Camera Obscura* 23, May 1990.

Richard deCordova, 'Ethnography and exhibition: the child audience, The Hays Office and Saturday matinées,' *Camera Obscura* 23, May 1990.

Philip Corrigan, 'Film entertainment as ideology and pleasure: a preliminary approach to a history of audiences,' in *British Cinema History*, Curran *et al.* (eds), London, Wiedenfeld & Nicolson, 1983.

Mary Ann Doane, *The Desire to Desire: The Woman's Film of the 1940s*, Bloomington, Indiana University Press, 1987.

Mary Anne Doane, 'Film and the masquerade: theorizing the female spectator' and 'Masquerade reconsidered: further thoughts on the female spectator', in *Femmes Fatales: Feminism, Film Theory, Psychoanalysis*, New York, Routledge, 1991.

Alexander Doty, *Making Things Perfectly Queer: Interpreting Mass Culture*, Minneapolis, University of Minnesota Press, 1993.

Richard Dyer, *Stars*, London, British Film Institute, 1979, revised edition 1998.

Richard Dyer, *Heavenly Bodies: Film Stars and Society*, New York, St. Martin's Press, 1986.

Caroline Evans and Lorraine Gamman, 'The gaze revisited, or reviewing queer viewing,' in *A Queer Romance: Lesbians, Gay Men and Popular Culture*, Paul Burston and Colin Richardson (eds), London, Routledge, 1995.

Anne Friedberg, *Window Shopping: Cinema and the Postmodern*, Berkeley, University of California Press, 1993.

Jane Gaines, 'War, women, and lipstick: fan mags in the forties,' *Heresies* 18, 1986.

Lorraine Gamman and Margaret Marshment (eds), *The Female Gaze: Women as Viewers of Popular Culture*, Seattle, The Real Comet Press, 1989.

Martha Gever, Pratibha Parmar and John Greyson (eds), *Queer Looks: Perspectives on Lesbian and Gay Film and Video*, London, Routledge, 1993.

Christine Gledhill (ed.), *Home is Where the Heart Is: Studies in Melodrama and The Women's Film*, London, BFI, 1987.

Christine Gledhill (ed.), *Stardom: Industry of Desire*, London, Routledge, 1991.

Douglas Gomery, 'The growth of movie monopolies: the case of Balaban and Katz,' *Wide Angle* 3(1), 1979.

Douglas Gomery, 'Movie audiences, urban geography, and the history of the American film,' *The Velvet Light Trap* 19, 1982.

Antonio Gramsci, *Selections from the Prison Notebooks*, trans. and ed. by Q. Hoare and G. N. Smith, London, Lawrence and Wishart, 1971.

Tom Gunning, 'The cinema of attractions: early film, its spectator and the avant-garde,' in *Early Cinema: Space, Frame, Narrative*, Thomas Elsaesser (ed.), London, BFI, 1990.

Tom Gunning, 'An aesthetic of astonishment: early film and the (in)credulous spectator,' in *Viewing Positions: Ways of Seeing Film*, Linda Williams (ed.), New Brunswick, Rutgers University Press, 1995.

Stuart Hall, 'Encoding/decoding,' in *Culture, Media, Language*, Hall *et al.*, eds, Birmingham, Centre for Contemporary Cultural Studies, 1980.

Diane Hamer and Belinda Budge (eds), *The Good, The Bad, and The Gorgeous: Popular Culture's Romance with Lesbianism*, London, Pandora, 1994.

Miriam Hansen, *Babel and Babylon: Spectatorship in American Silent Film*, London, Harvard University Press, 1991.

Miriam Hansen, 'Pleasure, ambivalence, identification: Valentino and female spectatorship,' *Cinema Journal* 25(4), 1986.

Dick Hebdige, *Subculture: The Meaning of Style*, London, Methuen, 1979.

Dorothy Hobson, *'Crossroads': The Drama of a Soap Opera*, London, Methuen, 1982.

Henry Jenkins, *Textual Poachers: Television Fans and Participatory Culture*, London, Routledge, 1992.

Garth Jowett, 'The first motion picture audiences,' *Journal of Popular Film* 3(1), 1974.

E. Ann Kaplan (ed.), *Women in Film Noir*, London, BFI, 1980; rev edn, 1998.

Lisa Lewis (ed.), *The Adoring Audience: Fan Culture and Popular Media*, London, Routledge, 1992.

Judith Mayne, 'Immigrants and spectators,' *Wide Angle* 2, 1982.

Judith Mayne, *Cinema and Spectatorship*, London, Routledge, 1993.

Russell Merritt, 'Nickelodeon theaters, 1905–1914: building an audience for the movies,' in *The American Film Industry*, Tino Balio (ed.), Madison, University of Wisconsin Press, 1985.

David Morley, *The 'Nationwide' Audience: Structure and Decoding*, London, BFI, 1980.

David Morley, *Family Television: Cultural Power and Domestic Leisure*, London, Comedia, 1986.

Meaghan Morris, 'Banality in cultural studies,' Patricia Mellencamp (ed.), in *Logics of Television: Essays in Cultural Criticism*, Bloomington, Indiana University Press, 1990.

Laura Mulvey, 'Visual pleasure and narrative cinema' and 'Afterthoughts on "Visual pleasure and narrative cinema", inspired by King Vidor's *Duel in the Sun* (1946)' in *Visual and Other Pleasures*, Bloomington, Indiana University Press, 1989.

Constance Penley, 'Brownian motion: women, tactics, and technology,' in *Technoculture*, Penley and Andrew Ross (eds), Minneapolis, University of Minnesota Press, 1991.

E. D. Pribram, *Female Spectators: Looking at Film and Television*, London, Verso, 1988.

Janice Radway, *Reading the Romance: Women, Patriarchy, and Popular Literature*, London, University of North Carolina Press, 1984.

Joan Rivière, 'Womanliness as masquerade,' in Victor Burgin James Donald and Cora Kaplan (eds), *Formations of Fantasy*, London, Methuen, 1986.

Jacqui Roach and Petal Felix, 'Black looks,' in Gamman and Marshment (eds), *The Female Gaze: Women as Viewers of Popular Culture*, Seattle, The Real Comet Press, 1989.

Shari Roberts, '"The lady in the tutti frutti hat": Carmen Miranda, a spectacle of ethnicity,' *Cinema Journal* 32(3), 1993.

Pamela Robertson, *Guilty Pleasures: Feminist Camp From Mae West to Madonna*, Durham, Duke University Press, 1996.

Philip Rosen (ed.), *Narrative/Apparatus/Ideology: A Film Theory Reader*, New York, Columbia University Press 1986.

Ellen Seiter, *et al.* (eds), *Remote Control: Television, Audiences, and Cultural Power*, London, Routledge, 1991.

Ben Singer, 'Manhattan nickelodeons: new data on audiences and exhibitors,' *Cinema Journal* 34(3), spring 1995.

Jackie Stacey, *Star Gazing: Hollywood Cinema and Female Spectatorship*, London, Routledge, 1994.

Janet Staiger, *Interpreting Films: Studies in the Historical Reception of American Cinema*, Princeton, Princeton University Press, 1992.

Helen Taylor, *Scarlett's Women: 'Gone With The Wind' and Its Female Fans*, London, Virago, 1989.

Graeme Turner, *Introduction to British Cultural Studies*, London, Routledge, 1992.

Andrea Weiss, ' "A queer feeling when I look at you": Hollywood stars and lesbian spectatorship in the 1930s' in Gledhill (ed.), *Stardom: Industry of Desire*, London, Routledge, 1991.

Linda Williams (ed.), *Viewing Positions: Ways of Seeing Film*, New Brunswick, NJ, Rutgers University Press, 1995.

INDEX

(Bold figures refer to material contained in Grey Boxes.)